Basic Standard Deduction Amounts

Filing Status	2015	2016
Single	$ 6,300	$ 6,300
Married, filing jointly	12,600	12,600
Surviving spouse	12,600	12,600
Head of household	9,250	9,300
Married, filing separately	6,300	6,300

Amount of Each Additional Standard Deduction

Filing Status	2015	2016
Single	$1,550	$1,550
Married, filing jointly	1,250	1,250
Surviving spouse	1,250	1,250
Head of household	1,550	1,550
Married, filing separately	1,250	1,250

Personal and Dependency Exemption

2015	2016
$4,000	$4,050

Income Tax Rates—Corporations

Taxable Income		The Tax Is:	Of the Amount
Over	But not Over		Over
$ 0	$ 50,000	15%	$ 0
50,000	75,000	$ 7,500 + 25%	50,000
75,000	100,000	13,750 + 34%	75,000
100,000	335,000	22,250 + 39%*	100,000
335,000	10,000,000	113,900 + 34%	335,000
10,000,000	15,000,000	3,400,000 + 35%	10,000,000
15,000,000	18,333,333	5,150,000 + 38%**	15,000,000
18,333,333	....	35%	0

* Five percentage points of this rate represents a phaseout of the benefits of the lower tax rates on the first $75,000 of taxable income.

**Three percentage points of this rate represents a phaseout of the benefits of the lower tax rate (34% rather than 35%) on the first $10 million of taxable income.

SOUTH-WESTERN
FEDERAL TAXATION

2017 EDITION
ESSENTIALS OF TAXATION: INDIVIDUALS AND BUSINESS ENTITIES

General Editors

William A. Raabe
Ph.D., CPA
Milton, Wisconsin

James C. Young
Ph.D., CPA
Northern Illinois University

David M. Maloney
Ph.D., CPA
University of Virginia

Annette Nellen
J.D., CPA, CGMA
San Jose State University

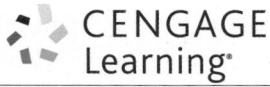

CENGAGE
Learning®

Australia • Brazil • Mexico • Singapore • United Kingdom • United States

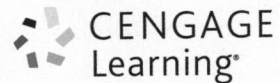

South-Western Federal Taxation:
Essentials of Taxation: Individuals and
Business Entities, 2017 Edition

**William A. Raabe, David M. Maloney,
James C. Young, Annette Nellen**

Vice President, General Manager, Science,
   Math, and Quantitative Business: Balraj Kalsi

Product Director: Mike Schenk

Sr. Content Developer: Kendra Brown

Product Assistant: Trisha Makley

Associate Marketing Manager: Charisse Darin

Content Project Manager: Nadia Saloom

Manufacturing Planner: Doug Wilke

Marketing Communications Manager: Sarah
   Greber

Production Service: Cenveo Publisher Services

Sr. Art Director: Linda May

Cover and Internal Designer: Red Hangar Design

Intellectual Property:
   Analyst: Brittani Morgan
   Project Manager: Nick Barrows

Cover Image: Getty Images/John Lund

Design Images:
   Concept Summary, Global Tax Issues,
   Tax in the News, Bridge Discipline:
   iStockphoto.com/Andrey
   Ethics & Equity: iStockphoto.com/LdF
   Comprehensive Tax Return Problems: peepo/
   iStockphoto
   Internet Activity: iStockphoto.com/Alex
   Slobodkin
   Financial Disclosure Insights: Vyaseleva
   Elena/Shutterstock.com
   Tax Plan Strategies: Sergey Nivens/
   Shutterstock.com
   Tax Fact: carroteater/Shutterstock.com
   Framework 1040: Concept Photo/
   Shutterstock.com
   Digging Deeper: tuulijumala/Shutterstock.com

For product information and technology assistance, contact us at
Cengage Learning Customer & Sales Support, 1-800-354-9706

For permission to use material from this text or product,
submit all requests online at **www.cengage.com/permissions**
Further permissions questions can be emailed to
permissionrequest@cengage.com

Unless otherwise noted, all items © Cengage Learning.

All tax forms within the text are: Source: Internal Revenue Service.

Student Edition ISBN: 978-1-305-87483-1
Student Edition with H&R Block and RIA Checkpoint ISBN: 978-1-305-87482-4

ISSN: 1544-3590
2017 Annual Edition

Cengage Learning
20 Channel Center Street
Boston, MA 02210
USA

Cengage Learning is a leading provider of customized learning solutions with
employees residing in nearly 40 different countries and sales in more than 125
countries around the world. Find your local representative at
www.cengage.com.

Cengage Learning products are represented in Canada by Nelson
Education, Ltd.

To learn more about Cengage Learning Solutions, visit **www.cengage.com**

Purchase any of our products at your local college store or at our preferred
online store **www.cengagebrain.com**

Printed in the United States of America
Print Number: 01   Print Year: 2016

Authors for the South-Western Federal Taxation Series

Greg Carnes
Ph.D., CPA
University of
North Alabama

Andrew Cuccia
Ph.D., CPA
The University of
Oklahoma

Steven L. Gill
Ph.D., CPA
San Diego State
University

Kristina Zvinakis
Ph.D.
The University of
Texas at Austin

Preface

COMMITTED TO EDUCATIONAL SUCCESS

South-Western Federal Taxation (SWFT) is the most trusted and best-selling series in college taxation. We are focused exclusively on providing the most useful, comprehensive, and up-to-date tax texts, online study aids, tax preparation tools, and research tools to help instructors and students succeed in their tax courses and beyond.

SWFT is a comprehensive package of teaching and learning materials, significantly enhanced with each edition to meet instructor and student needs and to add overall value to learning taxation.

Essentials of Taxation: Individuals and Business Entities, 2017 Edition provides a dynamic learning experience inside and outside of the classroom. Built with resources and tools that have been identified as the most important, our complete learning system provides options for students to achieve success.

Essentials of Taxation: Individuals and Business Entities, 2017 Edition provides accessible, comprehensive, and authoritative coverage of the relevant tax code and regulations as they pertain to the individual or business taxpayer, as well as coverage of all major developments in Federal Taxation.

In revising the 2017 Edition, we focused on:

- *Accessibility. Clarity. Substance.* The text authors and editors made this their mantra as they revised the 2017 edition. Coverage has been streamlined to make it more accessible to students, and difficult concepts have been clarified, all without losing the substance that makes up the *South-Western Federal Taxation* series.

- *CengageNOWv2 as a complete learning system.* Cengage Learning understands that digital learning solutions are central to the classroom. Through sustained research, we continually refine our learning solutions in CengageNOWv2 to meet evolving student and instructor needs. CengageNOWv2 fulfills learning and course management needs by offering a personalized study plan, video lectures, auto-graded homework, auto-graded tests, and a full eBook with features and advantages that address common challenges.

Learning Tools and Features to Help Students Make the Connection

FULL-COLOR DESIGN: We understand that students struggle with learning difficult tax code concepts and applying them to real-world scenarios. The 2017 edition uses color to bring the text to life, capture student attention, and present the tax code in a simple, yet logical format.

☐ Selected **content is streamlined** to guide students in focusing on the most important concepts for the CPA Exam while still providing in-depth coverage of topics.

☐ Examples are clearly labeled and directly follow concepts to assist with student application. An **average of over 40 examples in each chapter** use realistic situations to illustrate the complexities of the tax law and allow students to integrate chapter concepts with illustrations and examples.

COMPUTATIONAL EXERCISES: Students need lots of practice in areas such as computing tax return problems and adjusting rates. We have developed these exercises to give students practice in calculating the solutions they need to make business decisions.

☐ Found in end-of-chapter section of the textbook

☐ CengageNOWv2 provides algorithmic versions of these problems

Computational Exercises

1. **LO.3** Luciana, a nonshareholder, purchases a condominium from her employer for $85,000. The fair market value of the condominium is $120,000. What is Luciana's basis in the condominium and the amount of any income as a result of this purchase?

2. **LO.3** Sebastian purchases two pieces of equipment for $100,000. Appraisals of the equipment indicate that the fair market value of the first piece of equipment is $72,000 and that of the second piece of equipment is $108,000. What is Sebastian's basis in these two assets?

3. **LO.2, 4** Lisa sells business property with an adjusted basis of $130,000 to her son, Alfred, for its fair market value of $100,000.
   a. What is Lisa's realized and recognized gain or loss?
   b. What is Alfred's recognized gain or loss if he subsequently sells the property for $138,000? For $80,000?

4. **LO.4** Arianna's personal residence has an adjusted basis of $230,000 and a fair market value of $210,000. Arianna converts the personal residence to rental property. What is Arianna's gain basis? What is her loss basis?

ROGER CPA EXAM REVIEW QUESTIONS: While the SWFT series has always provided the most in-depth coverage of tax concepts, Roger CPA Exam Review Questions are included to further prepare students for success on the CPA Exam.

☐ Located in selected end-of-chapter sections

☐ Tagged by concept in CengageNOWv2

☐ Similar questions to what students would actually find on the CPA Exam

Roger CPA Review Questions

ROGER CPA Review

1. Kellye purchased her home in 2011 for $140,000. After living in it for five years, she sold it in 2016 for $170,000, its market value. What is the tax treatment of the sale of Kellye's home?
   a. A $30,000 gain is recognized, but not reported.
   b. A $30,000 gain is recognized and reported.
   c. A $30,000 gain is carried forward.
   d. The transaction is not reported.

2. Ike, a single taxpayer, is reassigned for his job and must move to a new state. While searching for a place to live, he encounters a person who is selling her home in order to move to Ike's current city. The two agree to trade their properties to each other without any further consideration. Ike's house has a fair market value of $200,000 and basis of $130,000. He has lived in the house for one year. The house he is acquiring in the trade has a fair market value of $300,000. What gain will Ike recognize for Federal tax purposes?
   a. $50,000   c. $0
   b. $100,000   d. $300,000

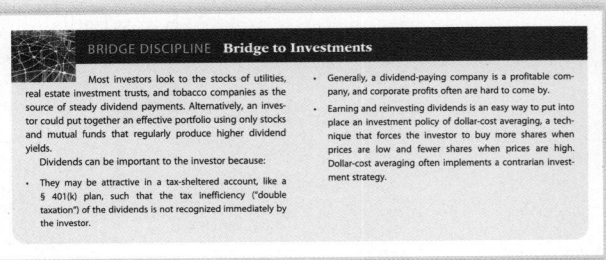

THE BIG PICTURE

CHOOSING A BUSINESS FORM AND OTHER INVESTMENTS

Bill and George are going to start a new business and have come to you for advice on the most appropriate organizational form for the business. They have narrowed the choice to a C corporation, an S corporation, or an LLC but would like you to advise them as to the primary advantages and disadvantages of the different forms. They have an adequate amount in savings to finance the business initially. Limited liability is a significant concern as is limiting the amount of taxes paid. Bill and George anticipate that the company will lose money in the first two years of operation. After that, however, they expect to earn $200,000 in before-tax profit and distribute any after-tax profit to the owners. Bill and George are both single, and both are subject to a 28 percent marginal tax rate.

George also is considering investing $10,000 in a limited partnership. As a way of leveraging the risks and rewards associated with his investments, Bill earlier had acquired a 30 percent interest in a boutique retail coffee franchise outlet. Bill now is considering selling this investment, which has experienced rapid appreciation. Because he is considering cashing out the gain, he needs to know the adjusted basis of his ownership interest.

Read the chapter and formulate your response.

THE BIG PICTURE: Tax Solutions for the Real World. Taxation comes alive at the start of each chapter as The Big Picture Examples give a glimpse into the lives, families, careers, and tax situations of typical individual or business filers. Students will follow the family, individual, or other taxpayer throughout the chapter showing students how the concept they are learning plays out in the real world.

Finally, to solidify student comprehension, each chapter concludes with a **Refocus on the Big Picture** summary and tax planning scenario. These scenarios apply the concepts and topics from the chapter in a reasonable and professional way.

BRIDGE DISCIPLINE BOXES AND END-OF-CHAPTER QUESTIONS:

Bridge Discipline boxes throughout the text present material and concepts from other disciplines such as economics, financial accounting, and finance. They help to bridge the gap between taxation issues and issues raised in other business courses. **Bridge Discipline questions**, in the end-of-chapter material, help test these concepts and give students the chance to apply concepts they've learned in the Bridge Discipline boxes.

BRIDGE DISCIPLINE **Bridge to Investments**

Most investors look to the stocks of utilities, real estate investment trusts, and tobacco companies as the source of steady dividend payments. Alternatively, an investor could put together an effective portfolio using only stocks and mutual funds that regularly produce higher dividend yields.

Dividends can be important to the investor because:

• They may be attractive in a tax-sheltered account, like a § 401(k) plan, such that the tax inefficiency ("double taxation") of the dividends is not recognized immediately by the investor.

• Generally, a dividend-paying company is a profitable company, and corporate profits often are hard to come by.

• Earning and reinvesting dividends is an easy way to put into place an investment policy of dollar-cost averaging, a technique that forces the investor to buy more shares when prices are low and fewer shares when prices are high. Dollar-cost averaging often implements a contrarian investment strategy.

FINANCIAL DISCLOSURE INSIGHTS   **Tax Losses and the Deferred Tax Asset**

Although a current-year net operating loss (NOL) represents a failure of an entity's business model to some, others see it as an immediate tax refund. But when an NOL hits the balance sheet as a deferred tax asset, the story is not over. The NOL creates or increases a deferred tax asset that may or may not be used in future financial accounting reporting periods. The key question for a financial analyst is whether the entity will generate enough net revenue in future years to create a positive tax liability that can be offset by the NOL carryover amount.

IFRS rules do not allow for a valuation allowance. Under IAS 12, a deferred tax asset is recorded only when it is "probable" (a higher standard than GAAP's "more likely than not") that the deferred tax amount will be realized, and then only to the extent of that probable amount. Thus, no offsetting valuation allowance is needed.

FINANCIAL DISCLOSURE INSIGHTS:

Tax professionals need to understand how taxes affect the income statement and balance sheet. **Financial Disclosure Insights**, appearing throughout the text, use current data about existing taxpayers to highlight book-tax reporting differences, effective tax rates, and trends in reporting conventions.

DIGGING DEEPER: Designed
to help students go further in their knowledge of certain topics, **Digging Deeper** links within the text provide more in-depth coverage that can be found on the book's website at **www.cengagebrain.com.**

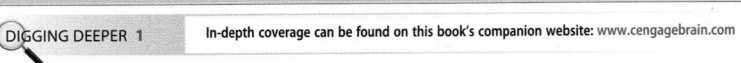

DIGGING DEEPER 1   In-depth coverage can be found on this book's companion website: www.cengagebrain.com

TAX PLANNING FRAMEWORK:

To demonstrate the relevance of tax planning for business and individual taxpayers, *Essentials of Taxation: Individuals and Business Entities* presents a unique **tax planning framework.** Introduced in Chapter 1, this framework extends to a series of **Tax Planning Strategies** incorporated throughout the remainder of the text. The inclusion of the tax planning framework, and the planning strategies in each chapter, makes it easier than ever to understand the impact careful tax planning has in today's world.

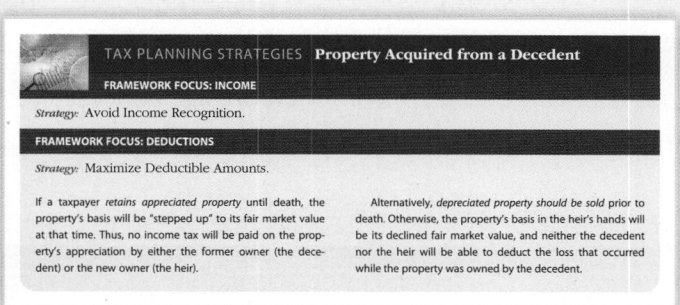

EXHIBIT 1.3	General Framework for Income Tax Planning	
Tax Formula	**Tax Planning Strategy**	**Tax Planning Examples**
Income and exclusions	➤ Avoid income recognition.	Compensate employees with nontaxable fringe benefits (see Example 19).
	➤ Postpone recognition of income to achieve tax deferral.	Postpone sale of assets (see Example 20).

TAX PLANNING STRATEGIES | **Property Acquired from a Decedent**

FRAMEWORK FOCUS: INCOME

Strategy: Avoid Income Recognition.

FRAMEWORK FOCUS: DEDUCTIONS

Strategy: Maximize Deductible Amounts.

If a taxpayer *retains appreciated property* until death, the property's basis will be "stepped up" to its fair market value at that time. Thus, no income tax will be paid on the property's appreciation by either the former owner (the decedent) or the new owner (the heir).

Alternatively, *depreciated property should be sold* prior to death. Otherwise, the property's basis in the heir's hands will be its declined fair market value, and neither the decedent nor the heir will be able to deduct the loss that occurred while the property was owned by the decedent.

TAX PLANNING STRATEGIES: The tax planning framework extends to subsequent chapters as **Tax Planning Strategies boxes** that are tied to the topical coverage of the chapters. Planning Strategies often contain examples to further illustrate the concept for students. Because some tax planning strategies do not fit neatly into the framework, the text also provides tax planning strategies called **Thinking Outside the Framework.**

GLOBAL TAX ISSUES: The **Global Tax Issues** feature gives insight into the ways in which taxation is affected by international concerns and illustrates the effects of various events on tax liabilities across the globe.

GLOBAL TAX ISSUES | **Choice of Organizational Form When Operating Overseas**

When the management of a corporation decides to expand its business by establishing a presence in a foreign market, the new business venture may take one of several organizational forms. As each form comes with its respective advantages and disadvantages, making the best choice can be difficult.

One common approach is to conduct the foreign activity as a *branch* operation of the U.S. corporation. The foreign branch is not a separate legal entity, but a division of the U.S. corporation established overseas. As a result, any gains and losses produced by the foreign unit are included in the corporation's overall financial results.

Another possibility is to organize the foreign operations as a *subsidiary* of the U.S. parent corporation. If this route is chosen, the subsidiary can be either a *domestic* subsidiary (i.e., organized in the United States) or a *foreign* subsidiary (organized under the laws of a foreign country).

One fundamental tax difference between these two approaches is that the gains and losses of a domestic subsidiary may be consolidated with the operations of the U.S. parent, while the operations of a foreign subsidiary cannot. Thus, the use of a domestic subsidiary to conduct foreign operations yields generally the same final result as the use of a branch. With both approaches, the financial statements of the U.S. parent reflect the results of its worldwide operations.

TAX IN THE NEWS | **Who Pays Corporate AMT?**

One of the issues often raised in debates over tax legislation is whether the corporate AMT should be repealed. Among the topics discussed are the revenue generated, the related compliance costs, and the number of corporations subject to the AMT.

According to the IRS, nearly 6 million corporate tax returns were filed for tax year 2012. Of these returns, under 12,000 included any AMT liability, totaling over $5 billion.

Proponents of the corporate AMT argue that these statistics show that the AMT is being paid by corporations

targeted by the law (i.e., large corporations). Opponents argue that the same statistics show that the compliance costs borne by the mass of corporations do not justify the continuation of this tax system.

The exemption from the AMT for small corporations may be providing the needed solution. Large corporations must make minimal Federal income tax payments when the AMT applies. Most C corporations no longer need to compute the tax.

TAX IN THE NEWS: Drawn from today's business and popular press, **Tax in the News** features enliven class discussions by presenting current issues that illustrate the chapter material and applying them to real life.

In addition, editors offer weekly updates for instructors designed for use in the classroom with links, assignments, and activities inlcuded. See the **SWFT** blog at **https://taxintherealworld. wordpress.com.**

Take your students from Motivation to Mastery with CengageNOWv2

CengageNOWv2 is a powerful course management tool and online homework resource that elevates student thinking by providing superior content designed with the entire student workflow in mind.

- ■ **MOTIVATION:** engage students and better prepare them for class
- ■ **APPLICATION:** help students learn problem-solving behavior and skills in order to complete taxation problems on their own
- ■ **MASTERY:** help students make the leap from memorizing concepts to actual critical thinking

Motivation —

Many instructors find that students come to class unmotivated and unprepared. To help with engagement and preparedness, CengageNOWv2 for SWFT offers the following features:

- ■ **"Tax Drills" test students on key concepts and applications.** With three to five questions per learning objective, these "quick-hit" questions help students prepare for class lectures or review prior to an exam.

Application —

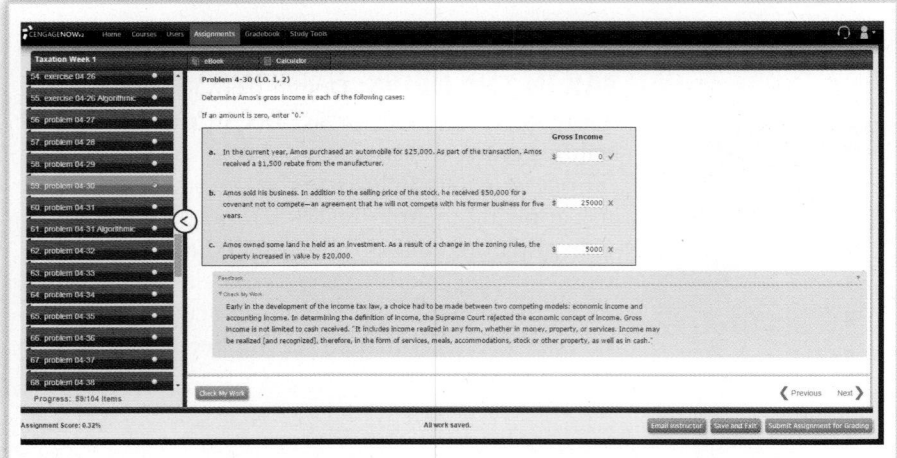

Students need to learn problem-solving behavior and skills in order to complete taxation problems on their own. However, as students try to work through homework problems, sometimes they become stuck and need guidance. To help reinforce concepts and keep students on the right track, CengageNOWv2 for SWFT offers the following:

- ■ **End-of-chapter homework from the text** is expanded and enhanced to follow the workflow a professional would use to solve various client scenarios. These enhancements better engage students and encourage them to think like a tax professional.

- **Algorithmic versions** of end-of-chapter homework are available for computational exercises and at least 15 problems per chapter.

- **"Check My Work" Feedback.** Homework questions include immediate feedback so students can learn as they go. Levels of feedback include an option for "check my work" prior to submission of an assignment.

- **Post-Submission Feedback.** After submitting an assignment, students receive even more extensive feedback explaining why their answers were incorrect. Instructors can decide how much feedback their students receive and when, including the full solution.

- **Built-in Test Bank** for online assessment.

Mastery —

- **NEW! Tax Form Problems** are *NEW* to CengageNOWv2. Students can now complete the Cumulative H&R Block Problems found in the end-of-chapter manually in a digital environment.

- **"What-If" Questions** allow students to develop a deeper understanding of the material as they are challenged to use their prior knowledge of the tax situations and critically think through new attributes to determine how the outcome will change.

- **An Adaptive Study Plan** comes complete with an eBook, practice quizzes, crossword puzzle, glossary, and flashcards. It is designed to help give students additional support and prepare them for the exam.

CengageNOWv2 Instant Access Code ISBN: 978-1-305-87496-1

Contact your Cengage Learning Consultant about different bundle options.

EXTENSIVELY REVISED. DEFINITIVELY UP TO DATE.

Each year the **South-Western Federal Taxation** series is updated with thousands of changes to each text. Some of these changes result from the feedback we receive from instructors and students in the form of reviews, focus groups, web surveys, and personal e-mail correspondence to our authors and team members. Other changes come from our careful analysis of the evolving tax environment. **We make sure that every tax law change relevant to the introductory taxation course was considered, summarized, and fully integrated into the revision of text and supplementary materials.**

The **South-Western Federal Taxation** authors have made every effort to keep all materials up to date and accurate. All chapters contain the following general changes for the 2017 Edition.

- Updated materials to reflect changes made by the Protecting Americans from Tax Hikes (PATH) Act of 2015 and other Public Laws of 2015.
- Streamlined chapter content (where applicable) to clarify material and make it easier for students to understand.
- Revised numerous materials as the result of changes caused by indexing of statutory amounts.
- Revised Problem Materials, Computational Exercises, and CPA Exam problems.
- Updated *Tax in the News* items with coverage of recent events.
- Updated Chapter Outlines to provide an overview of the material and to make it easier to locate specific topics.
- Revised *Financial Disclosure Insights* and *Global Tax Issues* as to current developments.

In addition, the following materials are available online.

- An appendix that helps instructors broaden and customize coverage of important tax provisions of the Affordable Care Act. (Instructor Companion Website at **www.cengage.com/login**)
- The Depreciation and the Accelerated Cost Recovery System (ACRS) appendix. (Instructor Companion Website at **www.cengage.com/login**)
- The Taxation in the Real World weekly blog posts for instructors. (**https://taxintherealworld.wordpress.com**)

Chapter 1

- Updated materials to reflect inflation indexation including the unified transfer tax credit and exemption amount, annual gift tax exclusion amount, and FICA base amount.
- Revised and updated statistics about Federal income tax paid by income classes, Federal budget receipts and collections, national excise taxes on gasoline and cigarettes consumption, and Tax Freedom Day.
- Added a Concept Summary on the major types of taxes imposed in the United States and the political jurisdictions that impose these taxes.

Chapter 2

- Updated references and citations throughout the chapter.
- Updated materials on administrative tax law sources and commercial tax services.

Chapter 3

- Updated the discussion of Schedule UTP and current filing statistics for Schedule UTP.
- Revised the computational templates for annual changes in deferred tax assets and liabilities.
- Added citations to certain GAAP rules in accounting for income taxes.
- Added example for ASC 740–10 (FIN 48).

Chapter 4

- Updated references and citations throughout the chapter.
- Reordered topics under specific items of gross income.
- Added cancellation of debt exercises.
- Modified exercises, where appropriate, to have students look up present values in appendix rather than be given the present and future value amounts.

Chapter 5

- Revised and clarified text and examples throughout the chapter. Modified materials as needed to reflect inflation indexation changes.
- Moved the domestic production activity deduction materials into a separate chapter section.
- Revised *Tax in the News* feature on executive compensation.
- Revised the materials on related-party transactions and charitable contributions.
- Added a Concept Summary on MACRS (class lives, methods, and conventions), enhanced the exhibit on cost recovery periods for personalty, and revised and updated text and examples throughout the chapter.
- Streamlined material on MACRS special rules.
- Updated materials to reflect tax extender legislation involving additional first-year depreciation and § 179 expense election.

Chapter 6

- Updated references and citations throughout the chapter.
- Changed § 469 references from passive to passive activity.
- Updated *Tax in the News* feature about virtual currency.

Chapter 7

- Added a Concept Summary (and related examples) on the wash sale rules.
- Clarified the discussion of the tax implications of easements.
- Revised and clarified text and examples throughout the chapter.

Chapter 8

- Updated qualified small business stock materials to reflect changes made by the PATH Act of 2015.
- Revised and clarified text and examples throughout the chapter.

Chapter 9

- Reorganized materials on filing status and related filing requirements.
- Revised and expanded the Concept Summary related to dependency exemption tests.
- Updated for 2016 inflation adjustments and legislative changes.

Chapter 10

- Updated for 2016 inflation adjustments and legislative changes.
- Added new *Tax in the News* features on complying with documentation requirements and the future of itemized deductions.
- Updated scholarship example to illustrate tax effect of cost of attendance scholarship that many student-athletes receive today.
- Updated for inflation and transitional changes to Affordable Care Act provisions.

Chapter 11

- Updated chapter materials for 2016 inflation adjustments and legislative changes.
- Added a Concept Summary on employee vs. independent contractor.
- Revised and clarified examples throughout the chapter.
- Updated the summary dealing with the many tax provisions involving education.
- Updated various retirement contribution amounts for inflation.

Chapter 12

- Added a Concept Summary comparing the tax attributes of various forms of business entities.
- Updated the *Tax in the News* feature that describes ways in which local and state jurisdictions compete to attract new businesses and employers in exchange for tax breaks.
- Added a Concept Summary on Schedule M–1 (Form 1120).
- Updated text to reflect new filing due dates for corporations.
- Updated text and examples throughout the chapter.

Chapter 13

- Enhanced and expanded the chapter examples on determining corporate E & P and allocating E & P to distributions.

- Updated *Tax Fact* feature "Who Pays Dividends?"

- Revised and clarified text and examples throughout the chapter.

Chapter 14

- Updated text to reflect new filing due dates for partnerships.

- Made minor revisions, updates, and clarifications throughout the chapter.

Chapter 15

- Updated S corporation filing statistics (including industry type).

- Enhanced and updated material concerning recognition period for built-in gains tax.

- Revised and clarified text and examples throughout the chapter.

Chapter 16

- Updated *Tax Fact* on tax rates in selected countries.

- Modified format of Exhibit 16.3 on computing state income tax liability.

Chapter 17

- Revised and clarified text and examples throughout the chapter, including changes made by the PATH Act of 2015.

- Updated chapter materials for inflation adjustments and for various computational formulas and amounts.

- Added *Tax in the News* feature on revenues raised by the corporate AMT.

- Revised and clarified text and examples throughout the chapter.

Chapter 18

- Updated data and statistics on number of business entities, their major industries, and profitability.

- Added return due dates, updated for 2015 law changes.

- Standardized uses of the terms *conduit perspective* and *entity perspective* and reorganized materials on these topics.

- Reorganized materials addressing entity effects of single and double taxation.

- Expanded materials concerning special allocations.

TAX LAW OUTLOOK

From your SWFT Series Editors:

Concerns about income inequity and job creation will keep income tax issues at the forefront of tax-related discussions throughout 2016 and 2017. Candidates and office holders will focus tax proposals on middle-class tax relief and tax increases for the wealthy. Federal tax treatments of income from overseas sources also may be reviewed. While a comprehensive "tax reform" bill is not likely, there will be serious consideration of various proposals, especially involving college tuition relief and the taxation of capital gains.

Congress may consider Federal corporate tax law changes during 2016–2017, including a decrease in the top tax rate and a move toward a territorial system in taxing income from overseas sources. Tax deferrals for unrepatriated global profits also may receive congressional and regulatory attention. Corporate tax reform remains difficult to craft, though, as so many businesses operate using pass-through structures. State and local governments also have budget problems, and they are looking for new revenue sources, including an adoption of the unitary concept and a broadening of the income and sales/use tax bases.

SUPPLEMENTS SUPPORT STUDENTS AND INSTRUCTORS

Built around the areas students and instructors have identified as the most important, our integrated supplements package offers more flexibility than ever before to suit the way instructors teach and students learn.

Online and Digital Resources for Students

CengageNOWv2 is a powerful course management and online homework tool that provides robust instructor control and customization to optimize the student learning experience and meet desired outcomes.

CengageNOWv2 Instant Access Code ISBN: 978-1-305-87496-1

Contact your Cengage Learning Consultant about different bundle options.

THOMSON REUTERS

CHECKPOINT®

Checkpoint® Student Edition from Thomson Reuters is the leading online tax research database used by professionals. There are three simple ways Checkpoint® helps introduce students to tax research:

- Intuitive web-based design makes it fast and simple to find what you need.

- Checkpoint® provides a comprehensive collection of primary tax law, cases, and rulings along with analytical insight you simply can't find anywhere else.

- Checkpoint® has built-in productivity tools such as calculators to make research more efficient—a resource more tax pros use than any other.

Six months' access to Checkpoint® Student Edition (after activation) is packaged automatically with every NEW copy of the textbook.*

More than software: Put the experience of H&R Block® tax professionals on your side.

- A step-by-step interview guides you through a customized process.

- Accurate calculations and 100% satisfaction—guaranteed.

- Worry-free Audit Support™ and tax advice from an H&R Block® tax professional.

Online access to H&R Block® Premium & Business software is offered with each NEW copy of the textbook—at no additional cost to students.*

CENGAGEbrain.com   Students can use **CengageBrain.com** to select this textbook and access Cengage Learning content, empowering them to choose the most suitable format and giving them a better chance of success in the course. Buy printed materials, eBooks, and digital resources directly through Cengage Learning and save at **CengageBrain.com.**

Online Student Resources

Students can go to **www.cengagebrain.com** for free resources to help them study as well as the opportunity to purchase additional study aids. These valuable free study resources will help students earn a better grade:

- Flashcards use chapter terms and definitions to aid students in learning tax terminology for each chapter.

- Online glossary for each chapter provides terms and definitions from the text in alphabetical order for easy reference.

- Learning objectives can be downloaded for each chapter to help keep students on track.

- Tax tables used in the textbook are downloadable for reference.

Printed Resources for Students

Looseleaf Edition (978-1-305-87484-8)

This version provides all the pages of the text in an unbound, three-hole punched format for portability and ease of use. Online access to H&R Block® Premium & Business software is included with every NEW textbook as well as Checkpoint® Student Edition from Thomson Reuters.*

---

*Checkpoint® Student Edition is not available with the Professional Editions of South-Western Federal Taxation texts. For all other editions, all NEW printed copies of the textbook are automatically packaged with access to Checkpoint® Student Edition and H&R Block® tax software. If students purchase the eBook, they will not automatically receive access to Checkpoint® Student Edition and H&R Block® software. They must purchase the tax media pack offering both of these products. The ISBN is 978-1-305-87432-9 and can be purchased at **www.cengagebrain.com.**

Comprehensive Supplements Support Instructors' Needs

CengageNOWv2 is a powerful course management and online homework tool that provides robust instructor control and customization to optimize the student learning experience and meet desired outcomes. In addition to the features and benefits mentioned earlier for students, CengageNOWv2 includes these features for instructors:

- **Learning Outcomes Reporting** and the ability to analyze student work from the gradebook. Each exercise and problem is tagged by topic, learning objective, level of difficulty, estimated completion time, and business program standards to allow greater guidance in developing assessments and evaluating student progress.

- **Built-in Test Bank for online assessment.** The Test Bank files are included in CengageNOWv2 so that they may be used as additional homework or tests.

Solutions Manual (978-1-305-87490-9)

Written by the **South-Western Federal Taxation** editors and authors, the Solutions Manual features solutions arranged in accordance with the sequence of chapter material.

Solutions to all homework items are tagged with their Estimated Time to Complete, Level of Difficulty, and Learning Objective(s), as well as the AACSB's and AICPA's core competencies—giving instructors more control than ever in selecting homework to match the topics covered. The Solutions Manual also contains the lettered answers (only) to the end-of-chapter Roger CPA Review Questions. **Available in print and on Instructor Companion Website at www.cengage.com/login.**

PowerPoint® Lectures with Notes

The Instructor PowerPoint® Lectures contain more than 30 slides per chapter, including outlines and instructor guides, concept definitions, alternate figures, and key points. **Available on Instructor Companion Website at www.cengage.com/login.**

Test Bank

Written by the **South-Western Federal Taxation** editors and authors, the Test Bank contains approximately 2,200 items and solutions arranged in accordance with the sequence of chapter material.

Each test item is tagged with its Estimated Time to Complete, Level of Difficulty, and Learning Objective(s),

as well as the AACSB's and AICPA's core competencies—for easier instructor planning and test item selection. The 2017 Test Bank is available in Cengage's test generator software, Cognero.

Cengage Learning Testing Powered by Cognero is a flexible, online system that allows you to:

- author, edit, and manage Test Bank content from multiple Cengage Learning solutions

- create multiple test versions in an instant

- deliver tests from your LMS, your classroom, or wherever you want

- create tests from school, home, the coffee shop—anywhere with Internet access. (No special installs or downloads needed.)

Test Bank files in Word format as well as versions to import into your LMS are available on the Instructor Companion Website. **Cognero Test Banks available via single sign-on (SSO) account at www.cengage.com/login.**

Other Instructor Resources

All of the following instructor course materials are available online at www.cengage.com/login. Once logged into the site, instructors should select this textbook to access the online Instructor Resources.

- Instructor Guide

- Edition-to-edition correlation grids by chapter

- Detailed answer feedback for the end-of-chapter Roger CPA Review Questions in Word format (Lettered answers only are available in the Solutions Manual.)

- An appendix that helps instructors broaden and customize coverage of important tax provisions of the Affordable Care Act

- The Depreciation and the Accelerated Cost Recovery System (ACRS) appendix (formerly Appendix G in SWFT *Individual Income Taxes*)

Custom Solutions

Cengage Learning Custom Solutions develops personalized solutions to meet your taxation education needs. Consider the following for your adoption of **South-Western Federal Taxation 2017 Edition**:

- Remove chapters you do not cover or rearrange their order to create a streamlined and efficient text.

- Add your own material to cover new topics or information.

- Add relevance by including sections from Smith's *Internal Revenue Code and Regulations*, Raabe/Whittenburg/Sanders/Sawyers' *Federal Tax Research*, or your state's tax laws and regulations.

ACKNOWLEDGMENTS

We want to thank all the adopters and non-adopters who participated in numerous online surveys as well as the following individuals who provided content reviews and feedback in the development of the ***South-Western Federal Taxation*** 2017 titles.

William A. Raabe / David M. Maloney / James C. Young / Annette Nellen

Lindsay G. Acker, *University of Wisconsin-Madison*

Deborah S. Adkins, *Nperspective, LLC*

Mark P. Altieri, *Kent State University*

Amy An, *University of Iowa*

Susan E. Anderson, *Elon University*

Henry M. Anding, *Woodbury University*

Jennifer A. Bagwell, *Ohio University*

George Barbi, *Lanier Technical College*

Terry W. Bechtel, *Texas A&M University – Texarkana*

Chris Becker, *LeMoyne College*

John G. Bell

Tamara Berges, *UCLA*

Ellen Best, *University of North Georgia*

Tim Biggart, *Berry College*

Rachel Birkey, *Illinois State University*

Patrick M. Borja, *Citrus College / California State University, Los Angeles*

Dianne H. Boseman, *Nash Community College*

Cathalene Bowler, *University of Northern Iowa*

Madeline Brogan, *Lone Star College – Montgomery*

Darryl L. Brown, *Illinois Wesleyan University*

Timothy G. Bryan, *University of Southern Indiana*

Robert S. Burdette, *Salt Lake Community College*

Ryan L. Burger, *Concordia University Nebraska*

Lisa Busto, *William Rainey Harper College*

Julia M. Camp, *Providence College*

Al Case, *Southern Oregon University*

Machiavelli W. Chao, *Merage School of Business University of California, Irvine*

Eric Chen, *University of Saint Joseph*

Christine Cheng, *Louisiana State University*

James Milton Christianson, *Southwestern University and Austin Community College*

Wayne Clark, *Southwest Baptist University*

Ann Burstein Cohen, *University at Buffalo, The State University of New York*

Ciril Cohen, *Fairleigh Dickinson University*

Dixon H. Cooper, *University of Arkansas*

Rick L. Crosser, *Metropolitan State University of Denver*

John P. Crowley, *Castleton University*

Susan E. M. Davis, *South University*

Dwight E. Denman, *Newman University*

James M. DeSimpelare, *Ross School of Business at the University of Michigan*

John Dexter, *Northwood University*

James Doering, *University of Wisconsin – Green Bay*

Michael P. Donohoe, *University of Illinois at Urbana Champaign*

Deborah A. Doonan, *Johnson & Wales University*

Monique O. Durant, *Central Connecticut State University*

Wayne L. Edmunds, *Virginia Commonwealth University*

Dr. Rafi Efrat, *California State University, Northridge*

Charles R. Enis, *The Pennsylvania State University*

Frank J. Faber, *St. Joseph's College*

A. Anthony Falgiani, *University of South Carolina, Beaufort*

Jason Fiske, *Thomas Jefferson School of Law*

John Forsythe, *Eagle Gate College*

Alexander L. Frazin, *University of Redlands*

Carl J. Gabrini, *College of Coastal Georgia*

Kenneth W. Gaines, *East-West University, Chicago, Illinois*

Carolyn Galantine, *Pepperdine University*

Sheri Geddes, *Hope College*

Alexander Gelardi, *University of St. Thomas*

Daniel J. Gibbons, *Waubonsee Community College*

Martie Gillen, *University of Florida*

Charles Gnizak, *Fort Hays State University*

Prof. J. David Golub, *Northeastern University*

George G. Goodrich, *John Carroll University*

Dr. Marina Grau, *Houston Community College – Houston, TX*

Vicki Greshik, *University of Jamestown College*

Jeffrey S. Haig, *Santa Monica College*

Marcye S. Hampton, *University of Central Florida*

June Hanson, *Upper Iowa University*

Donald Henschel, *Benedictine University*

Susanne Holloway, *Salisbury University*

Susan A. Honig, *Herbert H. Lehman College*

Jeffery Hoopes, *The Ohio State University*

Christopher R. Hoyt, *University of Missouri (Kansas City) School of Law*

Marsha M. Huber, *Youngstown State University*

Carol Hughes, *Asheville-Buncombe Technical Community College*

Dr. Helen Hurwitz, *Saint Louis University*

Richard R. Hutaff, *Wingate University*

Zite Hutton, *Western Washington University*

Brad Van Kalsbeek, *University of Sioux Falls*

John E. Karayan, *Woodbury University*

Carl Keller, *Missouri State University*

Cynthia Khanlarian, *Concord University*

Bob Kilpatrick, *Northern Arizona University*

Gordon Klein, *Lecturer, UCLA Anderson School*

Taylor Klett, *Sam Houston State University*

Aaron P. Knape, *Peru State College*

Cedric Knott, *Colorado State University – Global Campus*

Ausher M. B. Kofsky, *Western New England University*

Emil Koren, *Saint Leo University*

Jack Lachman, *Brooklyn College – CUNY*

Richard S. Leaman, *University of Denver*

Adena LeJeune, *Louisiana College*

Gene Levitt, *Mayville State University*

Teresa Lightner, *University of North Texas*

Sara Linton, *Roosevelt University*

Roger Lirely, *The University of Texas at Tyler*

Jane Livingstone, *Western Carolina University*

Heather Lynch, *Northeast Iowa Community College*

Michael J. MacDonald, *University of Wisconsin-Whitewater*

Mabel Machin, *Florida Institute of Technology*

Maria Alaina Mackin, *ECPI University*

Anne M. Magro, *George Mason University*

Richard B. Malamud, *California State University, Dominguez Hills*

Harold J. Manasa, *Winthrop University*

Barry R. Marks, *University of Houston – Clear Lake*

Dewey Martin, *Husson University*

Anthony Masino, *East Tennessee State University*

Norman Massel, *Louisiana State University*

Bruce W. McClain, *Cleveland State University*

Allison M. McLeod, *University of North Texas*

Meredith A. Menden, *Southern New Hampshire University*

John G. Miller, *Skyline College*

Tracie L. Miller-Nobles, *Austin Community College*

Jonathan G. Mitchell, *Stark State College*

Richard Mole, *Hiram College*

Lisa Nash, *CPA, MA, Vincennes University*

Mary E. Netzler, *Eastern Florida State College*

Joseph Malino Nicassio, *Westmoreland County Community College*

Mark R. Nixon, *Bentley University*

Garth Novack, *Pantheon Heavy Industries & Foundry*

Claude R. Oakley, *DeVry University, Georgia*

Al Oddo, *Niagara University*

Sandra Owen, *Indiana University – Bloomington*

Vivian J. Paige, *Old Dominion University*

Carolyn Payne, *University of La Verne*

Ronald Pearson, *Bay College*

Thomas Pearson, *University of Hawaii at Manoa*

Nichole L. Pendleton, *Friends University*

Chuck Pier, *Angelo State University*

Lincoln M. Pinto, *DeVry University*

Sonja Pippin, *University of Nevada – Reno*

Steve Platau, *The University of Tampa*

Walfyette Powell, *Strayer University*

Dennis Price, *Samford University*

Darlene Pulliam, *West Texas A&M University*

John S. Repsis, *University of Texas at Arlington*

John D. Rice, *Trinity University*

Jennifer Hardwick Robinson, *Trident Technical College*

Shani N. Robinson, *Sam Houston State University*

Donald Roth, *Dordt College*

Richard L. Russell, *Jackson State University*

Robert L. Salyer, *Northern Kentucky University*

Rhoda Sautner, *University of Mary*

Dr. Bunney L. Schmidt, *Keiser University*

Eric D. Schwartz, *LaRoche College*

Tony L. Scott, *Norwalk Community College*

Randy Serrett, *University of Houston – Downtown*

Wayne Shaw, *Southern Methodist University*

Paul A. Shoemaker, *University of Nebraska – Lincoln*

Kimberly Sipes, *Kentucky State University*

Georgi Smatrakalev, *Florida Atlantic University*

Randy Smit, *Dordt College*

Leslie S. Sobol, *California State University Northridge*

Marc Spiegel, *University of California, Irvine*

Teresa Stephenson, *University of Wyoming*

Beth Stetson, *Oklahoma City University*

Debra Stone, *Eastern New Mexico University*

Frances A. Stott, *Bowling Green State University*

Todd S. Stowe, *Southwest Florida College*

Martin Stub, *DeVry University*

James Sundberg, *Eastern Michigan University*

Kent Swift, *University of Montana*

Robert L. Taylor, *Lees-McRae College*

Francis C. Thomas, *Richard Stockton College of New Jersey*

Randall R. Thomas, *Upper Iowa University*

Ronald R. Tidd, *Central Washington University*

MaryBeth Tobin, *Bridgewater State University*

James P. Trebby, *Marquette University*

James M. Turner, *Georgia Institute of Technology*

Anthony W. Varnon, *Southeast Missouri State University*

Adria Palacios Vasquez, *Texas A&M University – Kingsville*

Terri Walsh, *Seminole State College of Florida*

Marie Wang

Natasha R. Ware, *Southeastern University*

Mark Washburn, *Sam Houston State University*

Bill Weispfenning, *University of Jamestown (ND)*

Andrew L. Whitehair

Kent Williams, *Indiana Wesleyan University*

Candace Witherspoon, *Valdosta State University*

Sheila Woods, *DeVry University, Houston, TX*

Xinmei Xie, *Woodbury University*

Thomas Young, *Lone Star College – Tomball*

SPECIAL THANKS

We are grateful to the faculty members who have diligently worked through the problems and test questions to ensure the accuracy of the ***South-Western Federal Taxation*** homework, solutions manuals, test banks, and comprehensive tax form problems. Their comments and corrections helped us focus on clarity as well as accuracy and tax law currency.

Sandra A. Augustine, *Hilbert College*

Bradrick M. Cripe, *Northern Illinois University*

Debra M. Johnson, *Montana State University, Billings*

Stephanie Lewis, *The Ohio State University*

Kate Mantzke, *Northern Illinois University*

Ray Rodriguez, *Murray State University*

George R. Starbuck, *McMurry University*

Donald R. Trippeer, *State University of New York College at Oneonta*

Raymond Wacker, *Southern Illinois University, Carbondale*

Michael Weissenfluh, *Tillamook Bay Community College*

Marvin J. Williams, *University of Houston, Downtown*

We are also grateful for the editorial assistance of **Bonnie Hoffman**, CPA, on many of the chapters. We also wish to thank Thomson Reuters for its permission to use Checkpoint® with the text.

The South-Western Federal Taxation Series

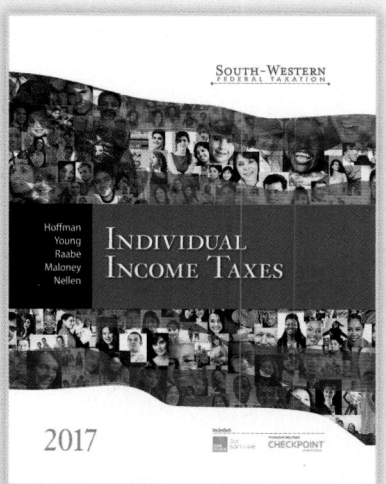

INDIVIDUAL INCOME TAXES, 2017 EDITION

(HOFFMAN, YOUNG, RAABE, MALONEY, NELLEN, Editors) provides accessible, comprehensive, and authoritative coverage of the relevant tax code and regulations as they pertain to the individual taxpayer, as well as coverage of all major developments in Federal taxation.

(ISBN 978-1-305-87398-8)

CORPORATIONS, PARTNERSHIPS, ESTATES & TRUSTS, 2017 EDITION

(HOFFMAN, RAABE, MALONEY, YOUNG, Editors) covers tax concepts as they affect corporations, partnerships, estates, and trusts. The authors provide accessible, comprehensive, and authoritative coverage of relevant tax code and regulations, as well as all major developments in Federal income taxation. This market-leading text is intended for students who have had a previous course in tax.

(ISBN 978-1-305-87433-6)

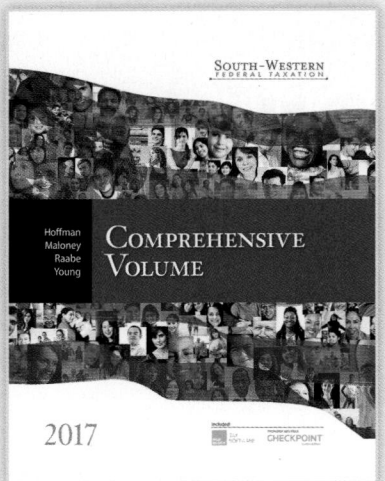

COMPREHENSIVE VOLUME, 2017 EDITION

(HOFFMAN, MALONEY, RAABE, YOUNG, Editors)
Combining the number one individual tax text with the number one corporations text, *Comprehensive Volume, 2017 Edition* is a true winner. An edited version of the first two **South-Western Federal Taxation** textbooks, this book is ideal for undergraduate or graduate levels. This text works for either a one-semester course in which an instructor wants to integrate coverage of individual and corporate taxation or for a two-semester sequence in which the use of only one book is desired.

(ISBN 978-1-305-87416-9)

ESSENTIALS OF TAXATION: INDIVIDUALS AND BUSINESS ENTITIES, 2017 EDITION

(RAABE, MALONEY, YOUNG, NELLEN, Editors) emphasizes tax planning and the multidisciplinary aspects of taxation. Formerly titled *Taxation of Business Entities*, this text is designed with the AICPA Model Tax Curriculum in mind, presenting the introductory Federal taxation course from a business entity perspective. Its **Tax Planning Framework** helps users fit tax planning strategies into an innovative pedagogical framework. The text is an ideal fit for programs that offer only one course in taxation where users need to be exposed to individual taxation, as well as corporate and other business entity taxation. This text assumes no prior course in taxation has been taken.

(ISBN 978-1-305-87482-4)

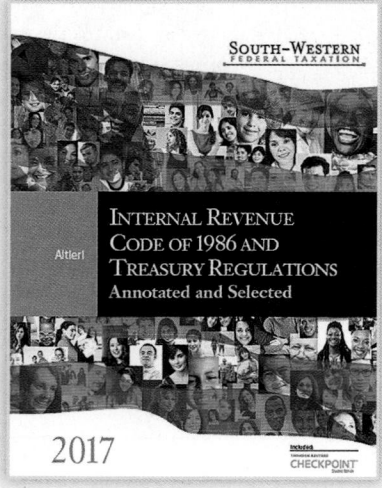

INTERNAL REVENUE CODE OF 1986 AND TREASURY REGULATIONS *Annotated and Selected, 2017 Edition*

(MARK ALTIERI) An ideal alternative to the traditional, bulky, and expensive multivolume set of code and regulations, this single-volume reference provides a useful selection of code and regulations sections and clear annotations in the form of editorial summaries that explain, analyze, and cross-reference topics to help students fully understand the intricacies of the tax code. The text is a perfect supplement for any **South-Western Federal Taxation** text as well as an excellent primary text for a Federal taxation course that stresses a code and regulations approach.

2017 Edition coming in July 2016 (ISBN 978-1-305-94320-9)

FEDERAL TAX RESEARCH, 10E

(SAWYERS, RAABE, WHITTENBURG, AND GILL) *Federal Tax Research*, Tenth Edition, offers hands-on tax research analysis and fully covers computer-oriented tax research tools. The tenth edition offers a new chapter on Financial Accounting Research that, when combined with their study of tax research, will equip students with the valuable research skills they need to be marketable to future employers. Also included in this edition is coverage on international tax research, an expanded review of tax ethics, and many new real-life cases to help foster a true understanding of Federal tax law.

(ISBN 978-1-285-43939-6)

ABOUT THE EDITORS

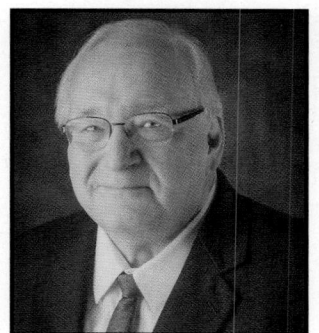

William A. Raabe, Ph.D., CPA, was the Wisconsin Distinguished Professor of Taxation. He taught at Ohio State, Arizona State, the Capital University (OH) Law School, and the Universities of Wisconsin – Milwaukee and Whitewater. A graduate of Carroll University (Wisconsin) and the University of Illinois, Dr. Raabe's teaching and research interests include international and multistate taxation, technology in tax education, personal financial planning, and the economic impact of sports teams and fine arts groups. Dr. Raabe also writes the PricewaterhouseCoopers Tax Case Studies. He has written extensively about book-tax differences in financial reporting. Dr. Raabe has been a visiting tax faculty member for a number of public accounting firms, bar associations, and CPA societies. He has received numerous teaching awards, including the Accounting Educator of the Year award from the Wisconsin Institute of CPAs. He has been the faculty adviser for student teams in the Deloitte Tax Case Competition (national finalists at three different schools) and the PricewaterhouseCoopers Extreme Tax policy competition (national finalist). For more information about Dr. Raabe, visit BillRaabeTax .com and BillRaabeTax on YouTube and Twitter.

David M. Maloney, Ph.D., CPA, is the Carman G. Blough Professor of Accounting Emeritus at the University of Virginia's McIntire School of Commerce. He completed his undergraduate work at the University of Richmond and his graduate work at the University of Illinois at Urbana-Champaign. Upon joining the Virginia faculty in January 1984, Dr. Maloney taught Federal taxation in the graduate and undergraduate programs and was a recipient of major research grants from the Ernst & Young and KPMG Foundations. Dr. Maloney has published work in numerous professional journals, including *Journal of Taxation, The Tax Adviser, Tax Notes, Corporate Taxation, Accounting Horizons, Journal of Taxation of Investments,* and *Journal of Accountancy.*

James C. Young is the Crowe Horwath Professor of Accountancy at Northern Illinois University. A graduate of Ferris State University (B.S.) and Michigan State University (M.B.A. and Ph.D.), Jim's research focuses on taxpayer responses to the income tax using archival data. His dissertation received the PricewaterhouseCoopers/American Taxation Association Dissertation Award and his subsequent research has received funding from a number of organizations, including the Ernst & Young Foundation Tax Research Grant Program. His work has been published in a variety of academic and professional journals, including the *National Tax Journal, The Journal of the American Taxation Association,* and *Tax Notes.* Jim is a Northern Illinois University Distinguished Professor, received the Illinois CPA Society Outstanding Accounting Educator Award in 2012, and has received university teaching awards from Northern Illinois University, George Mason University, and Michigan State University.

Annette Nellen, CPA, CGMA, Esquire, directs San José State University's graduate tax program (MST) and teaches courses in tax research, tax fundamentals, accounting methods, property transactions, state taxation, employment tax, ethics, and tax policy. Professor Nellen is a graduate of CSU Northridge, Pepperdine (MBA), and Loyola Law School. Prior to joining SJSU in 1990, she was with a Big 4 firm and the IRS. At SJSU, Professor Nellen is a recipient of the Outstanding Professor and Distinguished Service Awards. Professor Nellen is an active member of the tax sections of the AICPA and American Bar Association. In 2013, she received the AICPA Arthur J. Dixon Memorial Award, the highest award given by the accounting profession in the area of taxation. Professor Nellen is the author of *BloombergBNA Tax Portfolio, Amortization of Intangibles,* and the *BloombergBNA Internet Law Resource Center, Overview of Internet Taxation Issues.* She has published numerous articles in the *AICPA Tax Insider, Tax Adviser, State Tax Notes,* and *The Journal of Accountancy.* She has testified before the House Ways & Means and Senate Finance Committees and other committees on Federal and state tax reform. Professor Nellen maintains the 21st Century Taxation website and blog (www.21stcenturytaxation.com) as well as websites on tax reform and state tax issues (www.sjsu.edu/people/annette.nellen/).

Brief Contents

Part 5: Business Entities

Part 6: Special Business Topics

Contents

Part 2: Structure of the Federal Income Tax

Part 3:   Property Transactions

CHAPTER 7
PROPERTY TRANSACTIONS: BASIS, GAIN AND LOSS, AND NONTAXABLE EXCHANGES   7-1

CHAPTER 8
PROPERTY TRANSACTIONS: CAPITAL GAINS AND LOSSES, SECTION 1231, AND RECAPTURE PROVISIONS   8-1

Part 4: Taxation of Individuals

Part 5: Business Entities

CHAPTER 12
CORPORATIONS: ORGANIZATION, CAPITAL STRUCTURE, AND OPERATING RULES

CHAPTER 13
CORPORATIONS: EARNINGS & PROFITS AND DISTRIBUTIONS

Part 6: Special Business Topics

PART 1

THE WORLD OF TAXATION

Part 1 provides an introduction to taxation in the United States. Various taxes imposed by Federal, state, and local governments are discussed. A unique tax planning framework is presented that is applied throughout the book in developing tax planning strategies for both business entities and individual taxpayers. The tax research process, including the relevance of the legislative, administrative, and judicial sources of the tax law, is also discussed. Part 1 concludes with a chapter on accounting for income taxes, as a bridge to materials discussed in other accounting courses and an introduction to the financial disclosure effects of the tax law.

Introduction to Taxation

LEARNING OBJECTIVES: *After completing Chapter 1, you should be able to:*

LO.1 Define and illustrate the components of a tax.

LO.2 Identify the various taxes affecting business enterprises.

LO.3 Describe the basic tax formula for individuals and taxable business entities.

LO.4 State and explain the relationship between business entities and their owners.

LO.5 Identify tax planning opportunities and apply a general framework for tax planning.

LO.6 Explain the economic, social, equity, and political considerations that underlie the tax law.

LO.7 Describe the role played by the IRS and the courts in the evolution of the Federal tax system.

CHAPTER OUTLINE

TAX TALK *How many people were taxed, who was taxed, and what was taxed tell more about a society than anything else.* —CHARLES ADAMS

A Typical Tax Year for a Modern Family

Travis and Betty Carter are married and live in a state that imposes both a sales tax and an income tax. They have two children, April (age 17) and Martin (age 18). Travis is a mining engineer who specializes in land reclamation. After several years with a mining corporation, Travis established a consulting practice that involves a considerable amount of travel.

Betty is a registered nurse who, until recently, was a homemaker. In November of the current year, she decided to reenter the job market and accepted a position with a medical clinic.

The Carters live only a few blocks from Ernest and Mary Walker, Betty Carter's parents. The Walkers are retired and live on interest, dividends, and Social Security benefits.

The following developments with current year and possible future tax ramifications occurred.

- The ad valorem property taxes on the Carters' residence increased, while those on the Walkers' residence decreased.

- When Travis registered an automobile that was purchased last year in another state, he had to pay a sales tax to his home state.

- As an anniversary present, the Carters gave the Walkers a recreational vehicle (RV).

- When Travis made a consulting trip to Chicago, the client withheld Illinois state income tax from the payment made to Travis for his services.

- Travis employed his children to draft blueprints and prepare scale models for use in his work. Both April and Martin have had training in drafting and topography.

- Early in the year, the Carters were audited by the state on an income tax return filed several years ago. Later in the year, they were audited by the IRS on a Form 1040 they filed for the same year. In each case, a tax deficiency and interest were assessed.

- The Walkers were audited by the IRS. Unlike the Carters, they did not have to deal with a revenue agent, but settled the matter by mail.

Explain these developments and resolve any tax issues raised.

Read the chapter and formulate your response.

Taxes have a pervasive impact on our lives. They affect every individual in the United States from birth to death, and even beyond death (through taxation of an individual's estate). Taxes likewise affect every business from formation of the business entity to its operations, distribution of profits to owners, and ultimate disposition or liquidation.

Despite the wide-ranging impact of taxes, most studies of the tax law overemphasize the provisions applying to individual taxpayers and ignore much of the tax law relevant to business. That approach fails to address the role of taxes in *business decisions*, and it fails to provide the broad knowledge base necessary to succeed in today's business environment. This text adopts a more balanced approach; it introduces the tax laws that apply to individuals, and those rules applicable to all business entities, and it surveys the tax rules specific to each type of taxpayer. It also recognizes that both tax and nontax considerations are important in personal and business affairs.

LO.1

Define and illustrate the components of a tax.

1-1 THE STRUCTURE OF TAX SYSTEMS

Most taxes have two components: a tax rate and a tax base (such as income, wages, value, or sales price). Tax liability is computed by multiplying these two components. Taxes vary by the structure of their rates and by the base subject to tax.

1-1a Tax Rates

Tax rates can be progressive, proportional, or regressive. A tax rate is *progressive* if it increases as the tax base increases. The Federal income tax is structured so as to be progressive. For example, the Federal income tax rates for corporations range from 15 to 39 percent. These rates increase with increases in taxable income.

Refer to the corporate tax rate schedule inside the front cover of this text. If Abel Corporation records taxable income of $5,000, its income tax is $750 and its average tax rate is 15% ($750/$5,000, or the ratio of tax liability to the tax base).

If, however, Abel's taxable income is $200,000, its income tax is $61,250 [$22,250 + .39 ($200,000 − $100,000)] and its average tax rate is 30.63% ($61,250/$200,000). The tax is *progressive* because the average tax rate increases with increases in the tax base (income).

A tax is *proportional* if the rate of tax is constant, regardless of the size of the tax base. State retail **sales taxes** are proportional. Proportional tax rates also underlie the various "flat tax" proposals recently in the news.[1]

Bob purchases an automobile for $6,000. If the sales tax on automobiles is 7% in Bob's state, he will pay a $420 tax. Alternatively, if Bob pays $20,000 for a car, his sales tax will be $1,400 (still 7% of the sales price). Because the average tax rate does not change with the tax base (sales price), the sales tax is *proportional*.

Finally, *regressive* tax rates decrease as the tax base increases. Federal **employment taxes**, such as FICA and FUTA, are regressive. When the tax base and the taxpayer's ability to pay generally are positively correlated (i.e., when they move in the same direction), many tax pundits view regressive tax rates as unfair. This is because the tax burden decreases as a *percentage* of the taxpayer's ability to pay.

In 2016, the combined Social Security and Medicare tax rate levied on the wages of employees is 7.65% up to a maximum of $118,500 and 1.45% on all wages over $118,500. Sarah earns a salary of $30,000. She pays FICA taxes of $2,295, an average tax rate of 7.65%. Alternatively, if Sarah earns $150,000, she pays $9,522 [(.0765 × $118,500) + .0145 × ($150,000 − $118,500)], an average tax rate of 6.35%.

Once the FICA base exceeds the maximum amount subject to the Social Security part of FICA, the FICA tax becomes *regressive* because the average tax rate decreases as the tax base increases.

---

[1]Flat tax proposals call for a new tax with one low proportional rate (usually between 15% and 20%). Such a tax would have a very broad base, taxing almost all forms of income with few deductions. To avoid taxing those with lower incomes, large personal exemptions would be provided (e.g., $50,000 for a family of four).

TAX FACT Carrying the Tax Burden

Data from the IRS indicate that the progressive nature of the Federal income tax is quite severe, in that upper-income taxpayers are liable for taxes at a rate that is higher than their share of income reported.

Annual median adjusted gross income (defining the upper and lower one-half of citizens) is about $36,850. Income of about $428,000 puts a taxpayer in the top 1 percent of filers, and effective Federal taxes for the top 10 percent of earners have increased faster than their incomes. The following table shows the share of taxes paid by various income categories.

Income Category	Share of Adjusted Gross Income	Share of Federal Income Taxes Paid
Top 1%	19%	38%
Top 5%	34%	59%
Bottom 50%	11%	3%

Additional observations include the following.

- Individuals earning less than $50,000 per year can pay zero Federal income tax, and their payroll and gasoline taxes may be partly rebated through the earned income credit as well.

- When considering income, sales, payroll, property, and other taxes that are levied by U.S. governmental bodies of all sizes, taxpayers at nearly all income levels pay about 30 percent of their income in taxes.

- Due to additional taxes that are designated to pay for the Obamacare system, the degree of progressivity of the Federal income tax increases even further.

- The 400 individual Forms 1040 with the highest taxable income pay only about a 20 percent average Federal income tax rate, due chiefly to tax incentives that apply to investment income.

Under all three tax rate structures, the *amount* of taxes due increases as the tax base increases. The structure of tax rates only affects the *rate* of increase (i.e., progressive taxes increase at an increasing rate, proportional taxes increase at a constant rate, and regressive taxes increase at a decreasing rate).

1-1b Tax Bases

Most taxes are levied on one of four kinds of tax bases.

- Transactions [including sales or purchases of goods and services, and transfers of wealth (e.g., by gift or at death)].
- Property or wealth (including ownership of specific kinds of property).
- Privileges and rights (including the ability to do business as a corporation, the right to work in a certain profession, and the ability to move goods between countries).
- Income on a gross or net-of-expenses basis.

Because the Federal income tax usually has the most significant influence on business decisions, it is the principal focus of this text. Other taxes can play an important role, however, so it is important to have at least some familiarity with them. The next section introduces many of the taxes imposed on individuals and businesses in the United States.

In-depth coverage can be found on this book's companion website: www.cengagebrain.com | **1** DIGGING DEEPER

1-1c Incidence of Taxation

The degree to which various segments of society share the total tax burden is difficult to assess. Assumptions must be made concerning who absorbs the burden of paying the tax. For example, because dividend payments to shareholders are not deductible by a corporation and generally are taxable to shareholders, the same income is subject to a form of double taxation.

Concern over the potential for double taxation of the same income is valid to the extent that corporations are *not* able to shift the corporate tax to the consumer through higher prices and lower wages. But many research studies have shown that corporations are able to shift the corporate income tax burden (i.e., so that it is borne by both employees and the ultimate purchasers of goods), thereby avoiding any double taxation on the same income.

The progressiveness of the Federal income tax rate structure for individuals has varied over the years. In 1986, for example, there were 15 rates, ranging from 0 to 50 percent. These later were reduced to two rates of 15 and 28 percent. Currently, there are seven rates ranging from 10 to 39.6 percent.

LO.2

Identify the various taxes affecting business enterprises.

1-2 TYPES OF TAXES

After taxes on income, the various transaction taxes usually play the most important role in business (and personal) contexts. In many countries, transaction taxes are even more important than income taxes. There are three types of transaction taxes: sales and certain `excise taxes`, employment taxes, and taxes on the transfer of wealth (as gifts and at death).

1-2a Taxes on the Production and Sale of Goods

Sales tax and some excise taxes are imposed on the production, sale, or consumption of commodities or the use of services. Excise taxes and general sales taxes differ by the breadth of their bases. An excise tax base is limited to a specific kind of good or service, while a general sales tax is broad-based (e.g., it might be levied on all retail sales). All levels of government impose excise taxes, while state and local governments make heavy use of the general sales tax.

Federal Excise Taxes

Together with customs duties, excise taxes served as the principal source of revenue for the United States during its first 150 years of existence. Since World War II, the role of excise taxes in the Federal government's fund-raising efforts has steadily declined, falling from about 30 to 40 percent of revenues just prior to the war to about 3 percent now. During this time, the Federal government came to rely upon income and employment taxes as its principal sources of funds.

Despite the decreasing contribution of excise taxes to the Federal government, they continue to have a significant impact on specific industries. Currently, trucks, trailers, tires, liquor, tobacco, firearms, certain sporting equipment, and air travel all are subject to Federal excise taxes. In the past, the sale and manufacture of a variety of other goods, including furs, jewelry, boats, luxury automobiles, and theater tickets, have been taxed. Excise taxes extend beyond sales transactions. They also are levied on privileges and rights, as discussed below.

The bases used for Federal excise taxes are as diverse as the goods that are taxed. Fuels are taxed by the gallon, vaccines by the dose, air travel by the price paid for the ticket, water travel by the passenger, coal by the ton extracted or by the sales price, insurance by the premiums paid, and the gas guzzler tax by the mileage rating on the automobile produced. Some of these taxes are levied on producers, some on resellers, and some on consumers. In almost every circumstance, the tax rate structure is proportional.

With the exception of Federal excise taxes on alcohol, tobacco, and firearms, Federal excise taxes are due at least quarterly, when the Federal excise tax return (Form 720) is filed.

State Excise Taxes

Many states levy excise taxes on the same items taxed by the Federal government. For example, most states have excise taxes on gasoline, liquor, and tobacco. However, the tax on specific goods can vary dramatically among states. Compare New York's $4.35 tax on each pack of 20 cigarettes to Missouri's $.17 tax. These differences at the state level provide ample incentive for smuggling between states and for state-line enterprises specializing in taxed goods.[2]

Other goods and services subject to state and local excise taxes include admission to amusement facilities; hotel occupancy; rental of other facilities; and sales of playing cards, oleomargarine products, and prepared foods. Most states impose a tax on

---

[2]Some excise taxes are referred to as "sin" taxes (because goods such as liquor, marijuana, and tobacco are subject to the tax). Although it is commonly believed that these taxes are imposed for the purpose of discouraging consumption, evidence frequently fails to show this effect.

transfers of property that require recording of documents (such as real estate sales and sales of stock and securities).

Local Excise Taxes

Over the last few years, two types of excise taxes imposed at the local level have become increasingly popular. These are the hotel occupancy tax and the rental car "surcharge." Because they tax the visitor who cannot vote, they are a political windfall and serve as a means of financing special projects that generate civic pride (e.g., convention centers and state-of-the-art sports arenas).

General Sales Tax

The broad-based general sales tax is a major source of revenue for most state and local governments. It is used in all but five states (Alaska, Delaware, Montana, New Hampshire, and Oregon). The Federal government does not levy a general sales tax.

While specific rules vary from state to state, the sales tax typically employs a proportional tax rate and includes retail sales of tangible personal property (and occasionally personal services) in the base. Some states exempt medicine and food from the base (or tax these items at a lower rate), and sometimes tax rates vary with the good being sold (e.g., the sales tax rate for automobiles may differ from the rate on other goods). The sales tax is collected by the retailer and then paid to the state government.

Local general sales taxes, over and above those levied by the state, are common. It is not unusual to find taxpayers living in the same state who pay different general sales tax rates based on the city or county where they make their purchases.

For various reasons, some jurisdictions suspend the application of a general sales tax. The prevalent justification for these sales tax holidays involves the purchase of back-to-school items. Granted by approximately 15 states, the exemption typically is available in early August and covers modest expenditures for clothing and school supplies. Some states have used sales tax holidays to encourage the purchase of energy-conserving appliances (e.g., Maryland, Missouri, and Texas) and hurricane preparedness items (e.g., Louisiana and Virginia).

Use Taxes

One obvious approach to avoiding state and local sales taxes is to purchase goods in a state that has little or no sales tax and then transport the goods back to one's home state. Another alternative is to purchase goods from an out-of-state Internet-based vendor

 GLOBAL TAX ISSUES **Why Is Gasoline Expensive? It Depends on Where You Live**

In the United States, unlike other countries, the price of gasoline largely is attributable to the cost of crude oil; as U.S. production of crude has increased sharply, gasoline prices have fallen during this decade. In January 2016, the average price per gallon of gasoline in the United States was about $1.50.

In other countries, the real culprit is the amount of tax imposed. Consider the following situations.

Country	Average Price per Gallon (U.S. $)
Hong Kong	$6.91
United Kingdom	5.70
Germany	5.19
China	3.93
Saudi Arabia	0.87
Venezuela	0.06

While other factors may contribute to the various gasoline prices, the primary factor is the amount of tax charged in those countries. For example, in the United Kingdom, approximately 60 percent of the cost of gasoline is attributable to taxes. The equivalent rate for the United States is 20 percent.

(e.g., Amazon) that then ships the goods directly to the purchaser. **Use taxes** exist to prevent this tax reduction ploy. The use tax is a value-based tax, usually imposed at the same rate as the sales tax, on the use, consumption, or storage of tangible property. Every state that imposes a general sales tax levied on the consumer also applies a use tax.

The Big Picture

EXAMPLE 4

Return to the facts of *The Big Picture* on p. 1-1. The payment Travis made when he registered the car is probably a use tax. When the car was purchased in another state, likely no (or a lesser) sales tax was levied. The current payment makes up for the amount of sales tax he would have paid had the car been purchased in his home state.

The use tax is difficult to enforce for many purchases; therefore, the purchaser often does not pay it. Most states are taking steps to curtail this loss of revenue, especially by attempting to collect use taxes that relate to sales conducted on the Internet.

Value Added Tax

The **value added tax (VAT)** is a variation of a sales tax; it is levied at each stage of production on the value added by the producer. VAT is in widespread use in many countries around the world (most notably in the European Union and in Canada). The tax typically serves as a major source of revenue for governments that use it.[3]

EXAMPLE 5

Farmer Brown sells wheat to a flour mill for $100. If the wheat cost $65 for Brown to produce and if the VAT rate is 10%, then Brown will owe a VAT of $3.50 [.10($100 − $65)]. If the mill sells the flour for $200 to a baker, and if it cost the mill $120 to make the flour (including the cost of Brown's wheat), then it will pay a VAT of $8 [.10($200 − $120)]. If the baker sells the 200 loaves of bread made from the flour for $400, and if it cost the baker $280 to make the bread, then the baker pays a VAT of $12 [.10($400 − $280)].

The consumers who buy the bread will not pay any VAT directly. It is likely, however, that some or all of the total VAT paid of $23.50 ($3.50 + $8 + $12) will be paid by the consumers in the form of higher prices for the bread.

1-2b Employment Taxes

Both Federal and state governments tax the salaries and wages paid to employees. On the Federal side, employment taxes represent a major source of funds. For example, the **FICA tax** accounts for more than one-third of revenues in the Federal budget, second only to the income tax in its contribution.

The Federal government imposes two kinds of employment tax. The Federal Insurance Contributions Act (FICA) imposes a tax on self-employed individuals, employees, and employers. The proceeds of the tax are used to finance Social Security and Medicare benefits. The Federal Unemployment Tax Act (FUTA) imposes a tax on employers only. The **FUTA tax** provides funds to state unemployment benefit programs. Most state employment taxes are similar to the FUTA tax, with proceeds used to finance state unemployment benefit payments.

FICA Taxes

The FICA tax has two components: old age, survivors, and disability insurance payments (commonly referred to as Social Security) and Medicare health insurance payments. The Social Security tax rate is 6.2 percent for the employee and 6.2 percent for the employer, and the Medicare tax rate is 1.45 percent for both the employer and the employee. The maximum base for the Social Security tax is $118,500 for 2016 and 2015. There is no ceiling on the base amount for the Medicare tax. The employer withholds the FICA tax from an employee's wages.

---

[3]Some proposals to reduce the Federal government's reliance on the employment and income taxes have focused on VAT as an alternative tax system.

Payments usually are made through weekly or monthly electronic payments or deposits to a Federal depository. Employers must also file Form 941, Employer's Quarterly Federal Tax Return, by the end of the first month following each quarter of the calendar year (e.g., by July 31 for the quarter ending on June 30) and pay any remaining amount of employment taxes due for the previous quarter. Failure to pay can result in large penalties.

FICA tax is not assessed on all wages paid. For example, wages paid to children under the age of 18 who are employed in a parent's trade or business are exempt from the tax.

The Big Picture

EXAMPLE
6

Return to the facts of *The Big Picture* on p. 1-1. Presuming that April and Martin perform meaningful services for Travis (which the facts seem to imply), they are legitimate employees. April is not subject to Social Security tax because she is under the age of 18. However, Martin is 18, and Travis needs to collect and pay FICA taxes for him.

Furthermore, recall that Betty Carter now is working and is subject to the Social Security and Medicare taxes. Travis, as an independent contractor, is subject to self-employment tax, discussed in the next section.

An additional .9 percent Medicare tax is imposed on earned income (including self-employment income) *above* $200,000 (single filers) or $250,000 (married filing jointly). Unlike the Social Security tax of 6.2 percent and the regular Medicare portion of 1.45 percent, an employer does not match the employees' .9 percent additional Medicare tax.

Similarly, an additional 3.8 percent Medicare tax is assessed on the investment income of individuals whose modified adjusted gross income exceeds $200,000 or $250,000, as above. For this purpose, investment income includes interest, dividends, net capital gains, and income for similar portfolio items.

The Big Picture

EXAMPLE
7

Return to the facts of *The Big Picture* on p. 1-1. The combined income of Travis and Betty Carter may be large enough to trigger one or both of the additional Medicare taxes. The marginal tax rate[4] of "upper-income" taxpayers is higher than that of other individuals because of these taxes. Congress has designated these taxes to cover a portion of Federal health care costs. Betty would have considered these taxes when making her decision to re-enter the workforce.

Self-Employment Tax

Self-employed individuals also pay into the FICA system in the form of a self-employment (SE) tax (determined on Schedule SE, filed with Form 1040, U.S. Individual Income Tax Return). Self-employed individuals are required to pay both the employer and the employee portion of the FICA taxes. Therefore, the 2016 SE tax rate is 15.3 percent on self-employment income up to $118,500 and 2.9 percent on all additional self-employment income. Self-employed individuals deduct half of the SE tax—the amount normally deductible by an employer as a business expense. Self-employment income is discussed in more detail in Chapter 11.

Unemployment Taxes

For 2016, FUTA applies at a rate of 6.0 percent on the first $7,000 of covered wages paid during the year to each employee. As with FICA, this represents a regressive rate structure. The Federal government allows a credit for unemployment tax paid (or allowed under a merit rating system)[5] to the state. The credit cannot exceed 5.4 percent of the

---

[4]A taxpayer's *marginal tax rate* (or *marginal tax bracket*) is the rate that would be paid on an additional dollar of taxable income.

[5]States follow a policy of reducing unemployment tax on employers with stable employment. Thus, an employer with no employee turnover might face state unemployment tax rates as low as .1% or, in some cases, zero. This *merit rating system* explicitly accounts for the savings generated by steady employment.

covered wages. Thus, the amount required to be paid to the IRS could be as low as .6 percent (6.0% − 5.4%).

FUTA and state unemployment taxes differ from FICA in that the tax is imposed only on the employer.

1-2c **Taxes at Death**

The transfer of property upon the death of the owner may be a taxable event. If the tax is imposed on the transferor at death, it is called an estate tax. If it taxes the recipient of the property, it is termed an inheritance tax. As is typical of other types of transaction taxes, the value of the property transferred provides the base for determining the amount of the tax at death.

The Federal government imposes an estate tax. A few state governments, however, levy their own additional inheritance taxes, estate taxes, or both.

At the time of her death, Wilma lived in a state that imposes an inheritance tax but not an estate tax. Mary, one of Wilma's heirs, lives in the same state. Wilma's estate is subject to the Federal estate tax, and Mary is subject to the state inheritance tax.

The Federal Estate Tax

Never designed to generate a large amount of revenue, the Federal estate tax was intended to prevent large concentrations of wealth from being kept within a family for many generations. Whether this objective has been accomplished is debatable, because estate taxes can be substantially reduced (or deferred for decades) through careful tax planning activities.

Determination of the estate tax base begins with the *gross estate*, which includes property the decedent owned at the time of death. It also includes property interests, such as life insurance proceeds paid to the estate or to a beneficiary other than the estate if the deceased-insured had any ownership rights in the policy. Most property included in the gross estate is valued at fair market value as of the date of death.

Deductions from the gross estate in arriving at the *taxable estate* include funeral and administration expenses, certain taxes, debts of the decedent, and transfers to charitable organizations. A *marital deduction* is available for amounts passing to a surviving spouse (a widow or widower).

When Luis died, he owned $10 million in various securities, real estate, and personal effects. Under his will, Luis gave $1 million to the local art museum and provided $2 million to his surviving wife Angelina. Luis's executor computes a Federal estate tax on the $7 million taxable estate.

Once the taxable estate has been determined and certain taxable gifts have been added to it, one must determine a tentative tax liability. The tentative liability is reduced by a variety of credits to arrive at the amount due.

In most cases, the first $5 million of a U.S. decedent's estate effectively is excluded from the estate tax, with a maximum 40 percent tax rate on any excess. Spouses can share a $10 million estate tax exclusion. The $5 million and $10 million amounts are indexed for inflation.[6]

State Taxes at Death

States usually levy an inheritance tax, an estate tax, or both. The two forms of tax differ according to whether the liability is imposed on the heirs or on the estate.

Typically, an inheritance tax divides the heirs into classes based on their relationship to the decedent. The more closely related the heir, the lower the rates imposed and the greater the exemption allowed. Some states completely exempt amounts passing to a surviving spouse from taxation.

---

[6]For 2016, the indexed exemption amount for each individual is $5.45 million, and spouses share a $10.9 million Federal estate tax exclusion.

1-2d Gift Tax

Like estate and inheritance taxes, the Federal **gift tax** is an excise tax levied on the right to transfer property. In this case, however, the tax is imposed on transfers made during the owner's life rather than at death. The tax applies only to transferred amounts that are not supported by full and adequate consideration (i.e., gifts).

Carl sells property worth $20,000 to his daughter for $1,000. Although property worth $20,000 has been transferred, only $19,000 represents a gift, because this is the portion not supported by full and adequate consideration.

EXAMPLE 10

The Federal gift tax is intended to complement the estate tax. The gift tax base is the sum of all taxable gifts made *during one's lifetime*. Gifts are valued at the fair market value of the property on the date of the gift. To compute the tax due in a year, the tax rate schedule is applied to the sum of all lifetime taxable gifts. The resulting tax is then reduced by gift taxes paid in prior years.

The Federal gift tax and the Federal estate tax are *unified*.[7] The transfer of assets by a decedent at death effectively is treated as a final gift under the tax law. Thus, the $5 million exclusion (as indexed) and the 40 percent top tax rate for the estate tax also is available to calculate the tax liability generated by lifetime gifts. If the exclusion is exhausted during one's lifetime against taxable gifts, it is not available to reduce the estate tax liability. The same tax rate schedule applies to both lifetime gifts and the estate tax.

Before his death, Ben makes taxable gifts equivalent to the $5 million exclusion (as indexed). Because the unified transfer tax exclusion was used up during his life to offset the tax due on these gifts, no further amount is left to reduce Ben's estate tax liability.

EXAMPLE 11

Annual taxable gifts are determined by reducing the fair market value of gifts given by an *annual exclusion* of $14,000 per donee. A married couple can elect *gift splitting*, which enables them to transfer twice the annual exclusion ($28,000) per donee per year.

Taxable gifts are reduced by deductions for gifts to charity and to one's spouse (the *marital deduction*). Gifts for medical and educational purposes may be exempt from the gift tax as well.

Gift Tax Exclusion and Deductions

Marco made the following gifts: $500,000 to his wife Irena, $100,000 to their daughter Anita, and $100,000 to the San Mateo Church.

The marital and charitable deductions offset the gifts to Irena and the church. The $14,000 per donee annual exclusion reduces the taxable gift to Anita. Another $14,000 of the taxable gift could be eliminated if Irena agrees to a gift-splitting election.

EXAMPLE 12

On December 31, Vera gives $14,000 to each of her four married children, their spouses, and her eight grandchildren. On January 3 of the following year, she repeats the procedure.

Due to the annual exclusion, Vera has *not* made a taxable gift, although she transferred $224,000 [$14,000 × 16 (the number of donees)] twice, in a matter of days, for a total of $448,000.

If Vera had been married, she could have given twice as much ($896,000) tax-free, by electing gift splitting with her spouse.

EXAMPLE 13

Unlike death, the timing of which usually is involuntary, the making of a gift is a voluntary parting of ownership. Thus, the ownership of a business or a plot of land can be transferred gradually without incurring drastic and immediate tax consequences.

1-2e Property Taxes

A property tax can be a tax on the ownership of property or a tax on wealth, depending on the base used. Any measurable characteristic of the property being taxed can be

---

[7]§§ 2010 and 2505.

used as a base (e.g., weight, size, number, or value). Most property taxes in the United States are taxes on wealth; they use value as a base. These value-based property taxes are known as ad valorem taxes . Property taxes generally are administered by state and local governments, where they serve as a significant source of revenue.

Taxes on Realty

Property taxes on realty are used chiefly by states and their local political subdivisions such as cities, counties, and school districts. They represent a major source of revenue for local governments, but their importance at the state level is limited.

How realty is defined can have an important bearing on which assets are subject to tax. This is especially true in jurisdictions that do not impose ad valorem taxes on personalty (all assets that are not realty, discussed in the next section). Realty generally includes real estate and any capital improvements that are classified as fixtures. A fixture is something so permanently attached to the real estate that its removal will cause irreparable damage. A built-in bookcase might be a fixture, whereas a movable bookcase is not. Certain items such as electrical wiring and plumbing change from personalty to realty when installed in a building.

The following are some of the characteristics of ad valorem taxes on realty.

- Some states partially exempt the homestead, or personal residence, portion of property from taxation.
- Lower taxes may apply to a residence owned by a taxpayer age 65 or older.
- Some jurisdictions extend immunity from tax for a specified period of time (a tax holiday) to new or relocated businesses.
- Some states provide for lower valuations on property dedicated to agricultural use or other special uses (e.g., wildlife sanctuaries).

The Big Picture

EXAMPLE 14

Return to the facts of *The Big Picture* on p. 1-1. Why did the Walkers' taxes decrease while those of the Carters increased?

A likely explanation is that one (or both) of the Walkers achieved senior citizen status. In the case of the Carters, the assessed value of their property probably increased. Perhaps they made significant home improvements (e.g., kitchen/bathroom renovation, addition of a sundeck).

Taxes on Personalty

Personalty includes all assets that are not realty. It may be helpful to distinguish between the classification of an asset (realty or personalty) and the use to which it is put. Realty and personalty can be either business-use or personal-use property. Examples include a residence (personal-use realty), an office building (business-use realty), surgical instruments (business-use personalty), and the family car (personal-use personalty).

Personalty also can be classified as tangible property or intangible property. For property tax purposes, intangible personalty includes stocks, bonds, and various other securities (e.g., bank shares).

The following generalizations may be made concerning the property taxes on personalty.

- Particularly with personalty devoted to personal use (e.g., jewelry, household furnishings), taxpayer compliance ranges from poor to zero. Some jurisdictions do not even enact or attempt to enforce the tax on these items. For automobiles devoted to personal use, many jurisdictions have converted from value as the tax base to a tax based on the weight of the vehicle, or on the miles per gallon that it is estimated to achieve. Some jurisdictions also consider the vehicle's age (e.g., automobiles six years or older are not subject to the tax because they are presumed to have little value).
- For personalty devoted to business use (e.g., inventories, trucks, machinery, equipment), taxpayer compliance and enforcement procedures are notably better.
- Some jurisdictions impose an ad valorem property tax on intangibles.

TAX FACT **A Profile of Tax Collections**

Federal budget receipts as estimated for fiscal 2016 indicate a dependence to a great extent on payroll and individual income taxes. Corporate income tax collections likely are far below what the general public might expect.

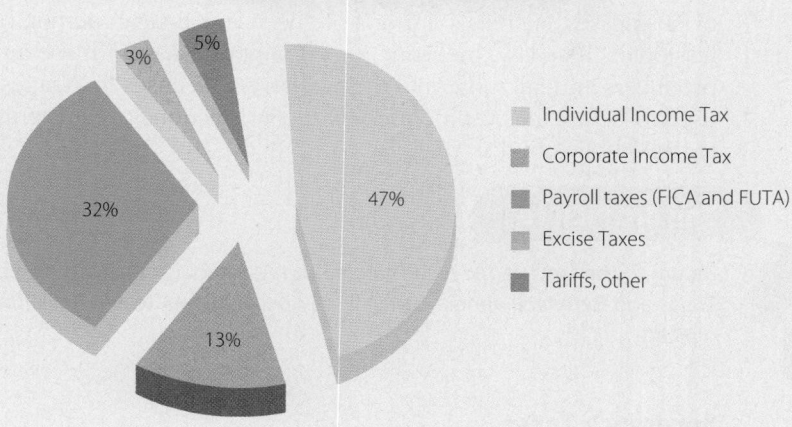

Federal Tax Collections

- Individual Income Tax
- Corporate Income Tax
- Payroll taxes (FICA and FUTA)
- Excise Taxes
- Tariffs, other

47%
32%
13%
5%
3%

In-depth coverage can be found on this book's companion website: www.cengagebrain.com

2 DIGGING DEEPER

1-2f **Taxes on Privileges and Rights**

Taxes on privileges and rights are usually considered excise taxes. The most important of these taxes are reviewed here.

Federal Customs Duties

Customs duties or tariffs can be characterized as a tax on the right to move goods across national borders. These taxes, together with selective excise taxes, provided most of the revenues needed by the Federal government during the nineteenth century. For example, tariffs and excise taxes alone paid off the national debt in 1835 and enabled the U.S. Treasury to pay a surplus of $28 million to the states. Today, however, customs duties account for only 1 percent of revenues in the Federal budget.

In recent years, tariffs have acted more as an instrument for carrying out protectionist policies than as a means of generating revenue. Thus, a particular U.S. industry might be saved from economic disaster, so the argument goes, by placing customs duties on the importation of foreign goods that can be sold at lower prices. Protectionists contend that the tariff therefore neutralizes the competitive edge held by the offshore producer of the goods.[8] But tariffs often lead to retaliatory action on the part of the nation or nations affected.

TAX IN THE NEWS **The Backdoor Tax Increase**

Can a landowner's property taxes increase even though the tax rate has not changed? Yes, if the assessed value of the property is increased! Known as a "backdoor tax increase," this procedure allows the taxing authority to generate additional revenue without having to secure voter approval for an increase in the tax rate.

Even more aggravating for the property owner is an increase in assessed value that is based on past market values and does not reflect the property's true current value. Under these conditions, increases in assessed value are likely to cause considerable taxpayer dissatisfaction and lead to proposals for legislative relief, such as a freeze on upward property assessments.

---

[8]The North American Free Trade Agreement (NAFTA) substantially reduces the tariffs on trade between Canada, Mexico, and the United States.

Franchise Taxes and Occupational Taxes

A **franchise tax** is a tax on the privilege of doing business in a state or local jurisdiction. Typically, the tax is imposed by states on corporations, but the tax base varies from state to state. While some states use a measure of corporate net income as part of the base, most states base the tax on the capitalization of the corporation (with or without certain long-term debt).

Closely akin to the franchise tax are **occupational taxes** applicable to various trades or businesses, such as a liquor store license, a taxicab permit, or a fee to practice a profession such as law, medicine, or accounting. Most of these are not significant revenue producers and fall more into the category of licenses than taxes. The revenue derived is used to defray the cost incurred by the jurisdiction to regulate the business or profession for the public good.

The Big Picture

EXAMPLE 15

Return to the facts of *The Big Picture* on p. 1-1. Although the facts do not mention the matter, both Travis and Betty will almost certainly pay occupational fees—Travis for engineering and Betty for nursing.

Severance Taxes

Severance taxes are based on the extraction of natural resources (e.g., oil, gas, iron ore, and coal). They are an important source of revenue for many states; Alaska does not levy either a state-level income or sales/use tax, because the collections from its severance taxes typically are quite large.

1-2g Income Taxes

Income taxes are levied by the Federal government, most states, and some local governments. In recent years, the trend in the United States has been to place greater reliance on this method of taxation while other countries are relying more heavily on transactions taxes such as the VAT.

Income taxes generally are imposed on individuals, corporations, and certain fiduciaries (estates and trusts). Most jurisdictions attempt to ensure the collection of income taxes by requiring certain pay-as-you-go procedures, including withholding requirements for employees and estimated tax prepayments for all taxpayers.

LO.3

Describe the basic tax formula for individuals and taxable business entities.

The Structure of the Federal Income Tax

Although some variations exist, the basic Federal income tax formula is similar for all taxable entities. This formula is shown in Exhibit 1.1.

EXHIBIT 1.1	Basic Formula for Federal Income Tax
Income (broadly defined)	$xxx,xxx
Less: Exclusions (income that is not subject to tax)	(xx,xxx)
Gross income (income that is subject to tax)	$xxx,xxx
Less: Deductions	(xx,xxx)
Taxable income	$xxx,xxx
Federal income tax on taxable income (see Tax Rate Schedules inside front cover of text)	$ xx,xxx
Less: Tax credits (including Federal income tax withheld and other prepayments of Federal income taxes)	(x,xxx)
Tax owed (or refund)	$ xxx

The income tax is based on the doctrine known as *legislative grace*: all income is subject to tax, and no deductions are allowed unless specifically provided for in the law. Some types of income are excluded on the basis of various economic, social, equity, and political considerations. Examples of such exclusions from the income tax base include gifts, inheritances, life insurance proceeds received by reason of death, and interest income from state and local bonds.

All entities are allowed to deduct business expenses from gross income, but a number of limitations and exceptions are applied. A variety of credits against the tax are also allowed, again on the basis of economic, social, equity, or political goals of Congress.

Income tax rates for all entities are progressive. The corporate rates effectively range from 15 percent on the lowest level of taxable income to 35 percent on the highest level. Individual rates range from 10 percent to 39.6 percent. Estates and trusts are also subject to income taxation, with rates ranging from 15 percent to 39.6 percent. Additional Medicare taxes (discussed previously) apply on top of these rates for certain upper-income taxpayers.

Partnerships, qualifying small business corporations, and some limited liability companies are not taxable entities, but must file information returns. Owners of these business entities then are taxed on the net taxable income of the enterprise, proportionate to their holdings.

For individuals, deductions are separated into two categories—deductions *for* adjusted gross income (AGI) and deductions *from* AGI. Generally, deductions *for* AGI are related to business activities, while deductions *from* AGI often are personal in nature (e.g., medical expenses, mortgage interest and property taxes on a personal residence, charitable contributions, and personal casualty losses) or are related to investment activities. Deductions *from* AGI take the form of *itemized deductions* and personal and dependency exemptions. Individuals may take a *standard deduction* (a specified amount based on filing status) rather than itemize actual deductions. An overview of the individual income tax formula is provided in Exhibit 1.2.

In-depth coverage can be found on this book's companion website: www.cengagebrain.com | **3 DIGGING DEEPER**

EXHIBIT 1.2	Federal Income Tax Formula for Individuals

Income (broadly defined)	$xx,xxx
Less: Exclusions (income that is not subject to tax)	(x,xxx)
Gross income (income that is subject to tax)	$xx,xxx
Less: Certain business and investment deductions (usually referred to as deductions *for* adjusted gross income)	(x,xxx)
Adjusted gross income	$xx,xxx
Less: The greater of certain personal and employee deductions (usually referred to as *itemized deductions*)	
or	
The standard deduction (including any *additional* standard deduction)	(x,xxx)
Less: Personal and dependency exemptions	(x,xxx)
Taxable income	$xx,xxx
Federal income tax on taxable income (see Tax Rate Schedules inside front cover of text)	$ x,xxx
Less: Tax credits (including Federal income tax withheld and other prepayments of Federal income taxes)	(xxx)
Tax owed (or refund)	$ xxx

State Income Taxes

Most states (except Alaska, Florida, Nevada, South Dakota, Texas, Washington, and Wyoming) impose a traditional income tax on individuals. Tennessee and New Hampshire tax only certain dividend and interest income. Most states also impose either a corporate income tax or a franchise tax based in part on corporate income. The following additional points can be made about state income taxes.

- State income tax laws usually rely on Federal income tax laws to some degree—the states use Federal taxable income (or Federal adjusted gross income) as a base, with a few adjustments (e.g., a few states allow an exclusion for interest income earned on Federal securities).

- Most states require withholding of state income tax from salaries and wages and estimated payments by corporations and self-employed individuals.

- Most states have their own set of rates, exemptions, and credits.

- Many states allow a credit for taxes paid to other states.

- Virtually all state income tax returns provide checkoff boxes for donations to various causes. Many are dedicated to medical research and wildlife programs, but special projects are not uncommon. For example, Oklahoma uses a checkoff to retire the debt incurred for its capitol dome addition, while a Wisconsin checkoff financed part of the renovations of Lambeau Field (home of the Green Bay Packers). These checkoff boxes have been criticized as adding complexity to the returns and misleading taxpayers.

Local Income Taxes

Cities imposing an income tax include Baltimore, Cincinnati, Cleveland, Columbus (OH), Denver, Detroit, Kansas City (MO), New York, Philadelphia, San Francisco, and St. Louis, among others. City income taxes usually apply to anyone who earns income in a city. They are designed to collect contributions for government services from those who live in the suburbs but work in the city, as well as from local residents.

Concept Summary 1.1 provides an overview of the major taxes existing in the United States and specifies which political jurisdiction imposes them.

DIGGING DEEPER 4   In-depth coverage can be found on this book's companion website: www.cengagebrain.com

TAX FACT   What Is the U.S. Tax Burden?

One popular measure of the burden of taxes in the U.S. economy is the Tax Foundation's "Tax Freedom Day." This statistic is a determination of the day upon which an individual has completed the entire year's obligation to governmental units (i.e., if all earnings were paid as taxes to this point, annual taxes would be paid up and one would now begin to "work for his or her own account").

Being "free from taxes" may bring about a feeling of relief, but in reality, tax burdens vary greatly from state to state. And as the U.S. economy has evolved and develops a more complex tax structure, adding emphasis on income and sales/use taxes and reducing the relative reliance on tariffs and excise taxes, year-to-year comparisons become difficult. Nonetheless, as a rough measure of the presence of government in our lives, Tax Freedom Day carries some importance.

If one is in need of consolation, Tax Freedom Day in Canada was June 10, 2015.

Year	Tax Freedom Day
1902	1/31
1930	2/12
1945	4/4
1960	4/15
1970	4/26
1990	5/1
1999	5/11
2000	5/3
2010	4/12
2015	4/24

BRIDGE DISCIPLINE **Bridge to Political Science and Sociology**

The tax law and its effects on citizens and businesses of the United States are included in many other academic disciplines. Tax burdens are part of American fiction, family studies, and minority issues, as well as economics, finance, and management courses.

In the Bridge feature found in most chapters of this text, we relate the concerns of other disciplines to a more specific review of tax law, as presented here. With the topical knowledge obtained in this text, the reader can better understand the issues raised by other disciplines, sometimes to support beliefs held by others and sometimes to refute them.

For instance, the structure of the U.S. tax system raises many issues of equity and fairness. Politicians and journalists discuss these issues freely, often without the requisite tax knowledge to draw proper conclusions.

- Should the property tax on real estate be used to finance the local public education system? Why should elderly taxpayers with grown children or parents who send their children to private schools continue to pay for public schools through these taxes?

- Would the lack of a charitable contribution deduction impair the ability of charities to raise operating and capital funds?

- Does a regressive sales/use tax fall harder on individuals of color?

- Is the tax law "friendly" to marriage and families with children?

- How should the tax law be used to encourage investments in "green" energy products? In improving access speeds for the Internet?

Concept Summary 1.1

Overview of Taxes in the United States

Type of Tax	Imposed by Jurisdiction		
	Federal	State	Local
Property taxes			
Ad valorem on realty	No	Yes	Yes
Ad valorem on personalty	No	Yes	Yes
Transaction taxes			
Excise	Yes	Yes	Few
General sales	No	Most	Some
Severance	Yes	Some	No
Estate	Yes	Few	No
Inheritance	No	Few	Few
Gift	Yes	Few	No
Income taxes			
Corporations	Yes	Most	Few
Individuals	Yes	Most	Few
Employment taxes			
FICA	Yes	No	No
FUTA	Yes	Yes	No
Other taxes			
Customs duties	Yes	No	No
Franchise taxes	No	Yes	No
Occupational taxes or fees	Yes	Yes	Yes

Most business taxpayers keep at least "two sets of books," in that they report one amount of "income" for financial accounting purposes and another amount of "taxable income" as required by various taxing jurisdictions—the definition that will be used throughout this book. In fact, "income" might be defined in many different ways, depending on the recipient of the income reports of the enterprise. For instance, a business entity might prepare markedly different income reports for lenders, employee unions, managers in operating divisions, and international agencies.

Financial accounting income guidance is provided for U.S. businesses by the Financial Accounting Standards Board (FASB), using the accumulated Generally Accepted Accounting Principles (GAAP) for the reporting period. When an entity conducts business outside the United States,

the International Financial Reporting Standards (IFRS) of the International Accounting Standards Board (IASB) also may apply.

Throughout this book, we point out some of the effects that Federal income tax provisions can have on the taxpayer's financial accounting results for the tax year. The vast majority of an entity's business transactions receive identical treatment under GAAP, IFRS, and the Federal tax law. But when the applicable provisions differ, "income" can be reported as different amounts—accounting professionals often refer to these as "book-tax differences."

A tax professional must be able to identify and explain the various constructs of "income" so that the business entity's operating results will be accurately reflected in its stock price, loan covenants, and cash-flow demands.

1-3 INCOME TAXATION OF BUSINESS ENTITIES

1-3a Proprietorships

The simplest form of business entity is a proprietorship, which is not a separate taxable entity. Instead, the proprietor reports the net profit of the business on his or her own individual tax return.

Individuals who own proprietorships (e.g., "Jenny's Fruit Stand") often have specific tax goals with regard to their financial interactions with the business. Because a proprietorship is, by definition, owned by an individual, the individual has great flexibility in structuring the entity's transactions in a way that will minimize his or her marginal income tax rate (or, in some cases, the marginal income tax rates of the family unit).

A proprietorship itself is not a taxpaying entity. The owner of the proprietorship reports the income and deductions of the business on a Schedule C (Profit or Loss from Business) and the net profit (or loss) of the proprietorship on his or her Form 1040 (U.S. Individual Income Tax Return). Specific issues related to the taxation of sole proprietorships are presented in detail in Chapter 11.

1-3b C Corporations

Some corporations pay tax on corporate taxable income, while others pay no tax at the corporate level. Corporations that are separate taxable entities are referred to as C corporations, because they are governed by Subchapter C of the Internal Revenue Code. C corporations are addressed in Chapters 12 and 13.

A C corporation is required to file a tax return (Form 1120) and is subject to the Federal income tax. The shareholders then pay income tax on the dividends they receive when the corporation distributes its profits. Thus, the profits of the corporation can be seen as subject to double taxation, first at the corporate level and then at the shareholder level.

EXAMPLE 16

Joseph is the president and sole shareholder of Falcon Corporation. Falcon's taxable income is $50,000, and its tax liability is $7,500.

If Joseph has the corporation pay all of its after-tax income to him as a dividend, he will receive $42,500 and pay Federal income tax on that amount as an individual taxpayer. In this case, most of Falcon's $50,000 income has been subjected to Federal income tax twice.

1-3c **Partnerships**

A partnership is not a separate taxable entity. The partnership is required to file a tax return (Form 1065) on which it summarizes the financial results of the business. Each partner then reports his or her share of the net income or loss and other special items that were reported on the partnership return.

Cameron and Connor form a partnership in which they are equal partners. The partnership reports a $100,000 net profit on its tax return, but is not subject to the Federal income tax. Cameron and Connor each report $50,000 net income from the partnership on their separate individual income tax returns.

1-3d **S Corporations**

Corporations that meet certain requirements and pay no tax at the corporate level are referred to as S corporations, because they are governed by Subchapter S of the Code. S corporations are discussed in detail in Chapter 15.

An S corporation is treated like a C corporation for all nontax purposes. Shareholders have limited liability, shares are freely transferable, the entity uses centralized management (vested in the board of directors), and there can be an unlimited continuity of life (i.e., the corporation continues to exist after the withdrawal or death of a shareholder).

With regard to tax factors, however, an S corporation is more like a partnership. The S corporation is not subject to the Federal *income tax*. Like a partnership, it does file a tax return (Form 1120S), but the shareholders report their share of net income or loss and other special items on their own tax returns.

Kay and Dawn form a corporation and elect to treat it as an S corporation. Kay owns 60% of the stock of the corporation, and Dawn owns 40%. The S corporation reports a $100,000 net profit on its tax return, but is not subject to the income tax. Kay reports $60,000 net income from the S corporation on her individual income tax return, and Dawn reports $40,000 on her tax return.

1-3e **Limited Liability Companies and Limited Liability Partnerships**

Limited liability companies (LLCs) and limited liability partnerships (LLPs) offer limited liability and some (but not all) of the other nontax features of corporations. Both forms usually are treated as partnerships for tax purposes.

The S corporation, limited liability company, and partnership forms of organization, which are referred to as *flow-through* entities, avoid the double taxation problem associated with the C corporation.

1-3f **Dealings between Individuals and Entities**

Many of the provisions in the tax law deal with the relationships between owners and the business entities they own. The following are some of the major interactions between owners and business entities.

- Owners put assets into a business when they establish a business entity (e.g., a proprietorship, partnership, or corporation).
- Owners take assets out of the business during its existence in the form of salary, dividends, withdrawals, redemptions of stock, etc.
- Through their entities, owner-employees set up retirement plans for themselves, including IRAs, Keogh plans, and qualified pension plans.
- Owners dispose of all or part of a business entity.

FINANCIAL DISCLOSURE INSIGHTS Book-Tax Differences

"Income" is defined differently for Federal income tax and financial accounting purposes. Financial accounting income (FAI) is designed to indicate the profitability of the business entity for the reporting period, in a fair and understandable way, to shareholders, creditors, and other parties who are interested in the results. Taxable income is a device used by Congress to raise revenue; stimulate or stabilize the economy; and accomplish other economic, social, and political goals in an equitable manner. In general, FAI recognizes *revenue* and *expenses*, while taxable income includes *gross income* and *deductions*.

The taxable income of a business taxpayer is not identical to FAI to the extent that *temporary* and *permanent* book-tax differences exist. Broadly, book-tax differences result when:

- Tax benefits are accelerated or deferred relative to their recognition for book purposes, for example, when cost recovery deductions are claimed earlier than depreciation expenses are allowed.

- Tax benefits are not recognized at all for book purposes (e.g., there is no book expense item corresponding to the domestic production activities deduction).

As a result of temporary book-tax differences, income tax payable (the amount due on the tax return, referred to by many tax professionals as the "cash tax") is not equal to the income tax expense on the book income statement. The income statement reflects the full income tax burden for the FAI of the reporting period, under the GAAP matching principle, but it is broken into the components *current income tax expense* and *deferred income tax expense*.

When a tax benefit is delayed for book purposes, such as for accelerated cost recovery deductions, a **deferred tax liability** is created on the entity's balance sheet. Taxable income will be greater than FAI in a subsequent year.

When a tax benefit is delayed for tax purposes, such as when a bad debt allowance is used for accounts receivable but is not permissible on the tax return, a **deferred tax asset** is created on the balance sheet. Taxable income will be less than FAI in a subsequent year.

Permanent book-tax differences, such as the exclusion for interest income from a state bond, do not affect the balance sheet. But because FAI and taxable income differ in this amount, the **effective tax rate** of the taxpayer is higher or lower than might be expected. The financial statement footnotes reconcile the statutory and effective tax rates of the entity, in dollar and/or percentage amounts.

The balance sheet accounts for deferred taxes can be sizable. For instance, in most years, Citigroup's deferred tax assets make up about one-third of its tangible equity capital.

Every major transaction that occurs between an owner and a business entity has important tax ramifications. The following are a few of the many tax issues that arise.

- How to avoid taxation at both the owner level and the entity level (i.e., the multiple taxation problem).
- How to get assets into the business with the least adverse tax consequences.
- How to get accumulated profits and assets out of the business with the least adverse tax consequences.
- How to dispose of the business entity with the least adverse tax consequences.

 DIGGING DEEPER 5 | In-depth coverage can be found on this book's companion website: www.cengagebrain.com

LO.5

Identify tax planning opportunities and apply a general framework for tax planning.

1-4 TAX PLANNING FUNDAMENTALS

1-4a Overview of Tax Planning and Ethics

Taxpayers generally attempt to minimize their tax liabilities, and it is perfectly acceptable to do so using legal means. It is a long-standing principle that taxpayers have no obligation to pay more than their fair share of taxes. The now-classic words of Judge Learned Hand in *Commissioner v. Newman* reflect the true values a taxpayer should have.

> Over and over again courts have said that there is nothing sinister in so arranging one's affairs as to keep taxes as low as possible. Everybody does so, rich or poor; and all do right, for nobody owes any public duty to pay

more than the law demands; taxes are enforced exactions, not voluntary contributions. To demand more in the name of morals is mere cant.[9]

Tax Planning: Avoidance Versus Evasion

Minimizing taxes legally is referred to as tax avoidance . On the other hand, some tax-payers attempt to *evade* income taxes through illegal actions. There is a major distinction between tax avoidance and tax evasion . Although eliminating or reducing taxes is also a goal of tax evasion, the term *evasion* implies the use of subterfuge and fraud as a means to this end. Tax avoidance is legal, while tax evasion subjects the taxpayer to numerous civil and criminal penalties, including prison sentences.

Clients expect tax professionals to provide advice to help them minimize their tax costs. This part of the tax practitioner's practice is referred to as *tax planning*. To structure a sound tax plan, a practitioner first must have a thorough knowledge of the tax law. Tax planning skill is based on knowledge of tax saving provisions in the tax law, as well as provisions that contain costly pitfalls for the unwary.

Thorough study of the remainder of this text will provide a solid base of the knowledge required to recognize opportunities and avoid pitfalls. Tax planning requires the practitioner to have in mind both a framework for planning and an understanding of the tax planning implications of a client's situation.

The Ethics of Tax Planning

Tax planning (avoidance) is a fully ethical activity by the taxpayer and the tax professional, but tax evasion (fraud) is not. The tax adviser's actions are limited by the codes of conduct of various professional organizations, such as the American Institute of CPAs or the pertinent state bar association.

Other formal restrictions and directives concerning the conduct of the tax professional can be found in two broad forms.

- Penalties and interest may apply to the taxpayer when a tax liability is understated. Examples include penalties for filing a tax return after its due date, understating gross income amounts, and underpaying withholding or estimated taxes that are due.

- Sanctions are used for tax preparers who disregard the tax law. The Treasury issues a regulation known as *Circular 230* to provide guidance to tax return preparers. Tax penalties also apply when the tax preparer fails to sign a tax return that he or she has worked on or takes an improper filing position on a tax return.

In-depth coverage can be found on this book's companion website: **www.cengagebrain.com** **6 DIGGING DEEPER**

1-4b A General Framework for Income Tax Planning

★ **Tax Planning Framework**

The primary goal of tax planning is to design a transaction so as to minimize its tax costs, while meeting the other nontax objectives of the client. Generally, this means that the client attempts to maximize the present value of its after-tax income and assets. Selecting a specific form of transaction solely for the sake of tax minimization often leads to a poor business decision. Effective tax planning requires careful consideration of the nontax issues involved in addition to the tax consequences.

Careful analysis of the tax formula (refer to Exhibit 1.1) reveals a series of tax minimization strategies. Through creative tax planning that also takes into consideration a client's nontax concerns, each component of the tax formula can be managed in a way that will help to minimize the client's tax liability. The General Framework for Income Tax Planning in Exhibit 1.3 lists each element in the income tax formula, develops tax planning strategies designed to minimize taxes, and provides brief summaries of specific examples of tax planning. The framework is followed by a discussion of the tax planning strategies, along with detailed examples of how the strategies can be applied. In Chapters 4 through 18 of this book, these strategies and their tax formula components provide the framework for Tax Planning Strategies features.

---

[9]47–1 USTC ¶9175, 35 AFTR 857, 159 F.2d 848 (CA–2, 1947).

EXHIBIT 1.3	General Framework for Income Tax Planning	

Tax Formula	Tax Planning Strategy	Tax Planning Examples
Income and exclusions	➢ **Avoid income recognition.**	Compensate employees with nontaxable fringe benefits (see Example 19).
	➢ **Postpone recognition of income to achieve tax deferral.**	Postpone sale of assets (see Example 20).
− Deductions	➢ **Maximize deductible amounts.**	Invest in stock of another corporation (see Example 21).
	➢ **Accelerate recognition of deductions to achieve tax deferral.**	Elect to deduct charitable contribution in year of pledge rather than in year of payment (see Example 22).
= Taxable income		
× Tax rate	➢ **Shift net income from high-bracket years to low-bracket years.**	Postpone recognition of income to a low-bracket year (see Example 23).
		Postpone recognition of deductions to a high-bracket year (see Example 24).
	➢ **Shift net income from high-bracket taxpayers to low-bracket taxpayers.**	Pay children to work in the family business (see Example 25).
	➢ **Shift net income from high-tax jurisdictions to low-tax jurisdictions.**	Establish subsidiary operations in countries with low tax rates (see Examples 26 and 27).
	➢ **Control the character of income and deductions.**	Hold assets long enough to qualify for long-term capital gain rates before selling them (see Example 28).
	➢ **Avoid double taxation.**	Operate as a flow-through entity rather than a C corporation (see Example 29).
		Maximize deductible expenses paid by a C corporation to a shareholder/employee (see Example 30).
= Federal income tax		
− Tax credits	➢ **Maximize tax credits.**	Make structural changes to a building where the expenditures qualify for the rehabilitation tax credit (see Example 31).
= Tax owed (or refund)		

1-4c Tax Minimization Strategies Related to Income

★ **Framework Focus: Income**

➢ *Tax Planning Strategy*

➢ *Avoid Income Recognition.* Section 61(a) defines gross income as "all income from whatever source derived." However, the Code contains provisions that allow various types of income to be excluded from the tax base. Numerous exclusions are available for individuals, but very few are available for corporations. However, a corporation can provide excludible income for its owners at no tax cost to the corporation.

EXAMPLE 19

The average employee of Penguin Corporation is a 25% bracket taxpayer. In negotiations with the employees' union, Penguin proposes that it will increase the amount it spends on nontaxable fringe benefits by an average of $3,000 per employee in lieu of granting a $3,000 average salary increase. The average employee will be better off by $750 if the union accepts Penguin's offer.

	Salary Increase	Fringe Benefit Increase
Value of compensation received	$3,000	$3,000
Tax on employee's compensation	(750)	(–0–)
After-tax increase in compensation	$2,250	$3,000

Although the average employee receives a $750 benefit, there is no tax cost to Penguin because both fringe benefits and salaries are deductible by the corporation.

➤ *Postpone Recognition of Income to Achieve Tax Deferral.* The tax law requires that both income and expenses be reported in the proper tax year. If not for this requirement, taxpayers could freely shift income and expenses from year to year to take advantage of tax rate differentials, or they could defer tax liabilities indefinitely, thereby achieving a time value of money advantage. Although various rules limit the shifting of income and deductions across time periods, some opportunities still exist.

➤ *Tax Planning Strategy*

In 2010, Turquoise Corporation acquired land for investment purposes at a cost of $500,000. In November 2016, Turquoise is negotiating to sell the land to Aqua Corporation for $800,000. Aqua insists that the transaction be completed in 2016, but Turquoise wants to delay the sale until 2017 to defer the tax on the gain. In an effort to compromise, Turquoise agrees to sell the land in November 2016 and asks Aqua to pay for the land in two installments, $400,000 in December 2016 and $400,000 in January 2017. This enables Turquoise to use the installment method for recognizing the gain, under which Turquoise will report $150,000 of the gain in 2016 and the remaining $150,000 in 2017.

By electing the installment method, Turquoise defers the payment of tax on $150,000 of the gain for one year. If the marginal tax rate for Turquoise is 35%, this tax deferral strategy provides $52,500 ($150,000 × 35%) to be invested or used in the business for another year.

1-4d Tax Minimization Strategies Related to Deductions

➤ *Maximize Deductible Amounts.* A corporation that owns stock in another corporation is eligible for a *dividends received deduction (DRD)*. The DRD is equal to a specified percentage of the dividends received. The percentage is based on the amount of stock that the investor corporation owns in the investee corporation.

★ **Framework Focus: Deductions**

➤ *Tax Planning Strategy*

- 70 percent deduction for ownership of less than 20 percent.
- 80 percent deduction for ownership of 20 percent or more but less than 80 percent.
- 100 percent deduction for ownership of 80 percent or more.

Falcon Corporation invests in bonds of Sparrow Corporation and receives interest of $20,000. Red Hawk Corporation acquires 15% of the stock of Pheasant Corporation and receives a $20,000 dividend.

Falcon's taxable income is increased by $20,000 of interest received. Red Hawk's income is increased by $20,000 in dividend income, but it is allowed a $14,000 dividends received deduction, thus increasing taxable income by only $6,000.

Example 21 demonstrates the *tax* advantage of dividend income versus interest income. However, it is also important to consider *nontax* factors. Is the investment in bonds safer than the investment in stock? Does the potential growth in the value of stock outweigh the possible risk of investing in stock versus bonds?

➤ *Accelerate Recognition of Deductions to Achieve Tax Deferral.* Both corporate and noncorporate taxpayers may deduct charitable contributions if the recipient is a qualified charitable organization. Generally, a deduction is allowed only for the year in which the payment is made. However, an important exception is available for *accrual basis corporations*. They may claim the deduction in the year *preceding* payment if two requirements are met. First, the contribution must be authorized by the board of directors by the end of that year. Second, the contribution must be paid on or before the fifteenth day of the third month of the next year.

➤ *Tax Planning Strategy*

Blue, Inc., a calendar year, accrual basis corporation, wants to make a $10,000 donation to the Atlanta Symphony Association (a qualified charitable organization), but does not have adequate funds to make the contribution in 2016. On December 28, 2016, Blue's board of directors *authorizes* a $10,000 contribution to the Association. The donation is made on March 14, 2017. Because Blue is an accrual basis corporation, it may claim the $10,000 donation as a deduction for tax year 2016, even though payment is not made until 2017.

Blue was able to take advantage of a tax provision and reduce 2016 taxable income by $10,000. If Blue is in the 35% marginal bracket, the corporation defers payment of $3,500 in Federal income tax. The $3,500 can be invested or used in the business for another tax year.

TAX FACT **The Rewards of Tax Planning**

Federal tax law does not fall equally on all taxpayers. Congress has allowed numerous tax incentives by which the taxpayer can manage long-term tax liabilities, when sound and ethical tax planning techniques are used. Here are some observations about the context in which the tax professional works with the taxpayer.

- The Federal income tax law provides over $1.4 trillion in credits, exemptions, exclusions, and deductions. The average individual reduces his or her tax liability by about $4,000 when these tax reductions are claimed.

- The most popular important Federal tax incentives for individuals include the following.

Tax Provision	Estimated Revenue Loss ($B)
Exclusions for Social Security and retirement plan income	$195
Exclusions, deductions for health care costs	155
Low tax rates on capital gains and dividends	155
Earned income, child credits	131
Deduction for home mortgage interest	71
Deduction for gifts to charity	42

- The most important tax incentives for corporate taxpayers include the following. Corporations claim about 10 percent of all tax expenditures.

Tax Provision	Estimated Revenue Loss ($B)
Deferral of overseas income not repatriated	$99
Accelerated depreciation deductions	25
Deduction for domestic manufacturing profits	12
Credit, deduction for research activities	11
Credit for providing low-income housing	7

★ **Framework Focus: Tax Rates**

➤ *Tax Planning Strategy*

1-4e **Tax Minimization Strategies Related to Tax Rates**

➤ *Shift Net Income from High-Bracket Years to Low-Bracket Years.* One objective of shifting income is to defer the payment of income tax (refer to Example 20). A second time-shifting strategy is to shift *net* income from high-tax to low-tax years. This can be accomplished by shifting income from high-bracket years to low-bracket years or by shifting deductions from low-bracket years to high-bracket years.

Shift Income to Low-Bracket Years

EXAMPLE 23

Egret Corporation, a calendar year taxpayer, is in the 34% bracket in 2016, but expects to be in the 25% bracket in 2017. The corporation, which is negotiating a $10,000 service contract with a client, decides to wait until 2017 to sign the contract and perform the services. The client is indifferent as to when the contract is completed. Thus, Egret saves $900 in income tax by deferring the service contract income to 2017, when it will be taxed at the 25% rate instead of the current 34% rate.

In this case, the income-shifting strategy is used to accomplish two tax planning objectives. First, shifting the income defers the payment of income tax from 2016 to 2017. Second, the shifting strategy results in the income being taxed at a rate of 25% rather than 34%.

EXAMPLE 24

Macaw Corporation has been sued for $125,000 damages by a customer, and the parties decided to settle out of court for $100,000. Macaw expects to be in the 25% bracket in 2016 and the 35% bracket in 2017. Macaw will save $10,000 in income tax if it finalizes the agreement in January 2017 rather than December 2016 [$100,000 × (35% − 25%)].

➤ *Tax Planning Strategy*

➤ *Shift Net Income from High-Bracket Taxpayers to Low-Bracket Taxpayers.* Individual income tax rates range from 10 percent to 39.6 percent (before considering the additional Medicare taxes on certain high-income individuals). Although several provisions in the tax law prevent shifting income from high-bracket taxpayers to low-bracket tax-payers, many opportunities to do so remain. Business entities can be effective vehicles for shifting income to low-bracket taxpayers.

> **EXAMPLE 25**
>
> Bill Gregory is the president and sole shareholder of Grayhawk, Inc., an S corporation. He projects that Grayhawk will earn $400,000 this year. Bill is taxed on this income at a 35% marginal rate. Bill and his wife have four teenage children, all of whom are dependents. The Gregorys record no other taxable income; they file a joint return.
>
> Bill employs the children as part-time workers throughout the year and pays them $11,000 each. This reduces Bill's income from Grayhawk by $44,000 and reduces his Federal income tax by $15,400 ($44,000 × 35%).
>
> The salaries paid to the children will be subject to their lower Federal income tax rates. The salaries also might be exempt from the FICA and other payroll taxes, so the family unit's total tax liability has been reduced by shifting taxable income to the children.

> **Tax Planning Strategy**

> **Shift Net Income from High-Tax Jurisdictions to Low-Tax Jurisdictions.**
A choice of the state or country where income is earned (or where a deduction is incurred) can have a large effect on an entity's overall tax liability. Hence, shifting income from high-tax jurisdictions to low-tax jurisdictions or shifting deductions from low-tax jurisdictions to high-tax jurisdictions is an important tax planning strategy.

Shifting Tax Jurisdictions

> **EXAMPLE 26**
>
> Gold International owns a sales subsidiary in Texas and a manufacturing subsidiary in Ireland (which imposes a 12.5% tax rate on certain types of business income). The Irish subsidiary makes drill presses and sells them for $4 million to the Texas subsidiary, which then modifies them and offers them for sale to businesses in the United States for $8.4 million. The cost of manufacturing and modifying each drill press is $3 million.
>
> Of the $5.4 million of profit earned, $1 million is attributable to the Irish corporation (which is subject to a 12.5% tax rate), and $4.4 million is attributable to the U.S. corporation (which is subject to a 34% tax rate). Gold's total tax liability is $1,621,000 [($1,000,000 × 12.5%) + ($4,400,000 × 34%)].

> **EXAMPLE 27**
>
> Assume the same facts as in the previous example, except that $5 million of the profit is attributable to the Irish corporation and $400,000 is attributable to the U.S. corporation, as the result of an effective tax planning arrangement. In this case, Gold's total tax liability is $761,000 [($5,000,000 × 12.5%) + ($400,000 × 34%)]. Thus, by altering the amount of work done in each of the two subsidiaries and the amount of income generated by each, Gold's tax liability is decreased by $860,000 ($1,621,000 − $761,000).

> **Tax Planning Strategy**

> **Control the Character of Income and Deductions.** For various policy reasons, Congress has chosen to treat certain categories of income and losses more favorably than others. For instance, the provisions that apply to most individuals and tax long-term capital gains at a maximum rate of 20 percent, compared to a top 39.6 percent rate on ordinary income, were enacted to encourage individuals to make long-term invest-ments of capital in the economy.

> **EXAMPLE 28**
>
> Lisa is the proprietor of Designer Enterprises. Because a proprietorship is a flow-through entity, Lisa reports all of Designer's transactions on her individual income tax return. On October 9, 2016, Lisa invested $25,000 of Designer's excess cash in Lavender Corporation stock. On October 1, 2017, the stock was worth $35,000.
>
> Lisa's marginal tax rate is 33% for ordinary income and 15% for long-term capital gain. She has decided to sell the stock and use the cash to increase Designer's inventory. She must hold the stock until October 10, 2017, for the gain to qualify as long term (held more than a year). If Lisa sells the stock before October 10, 2017, the gain is taxed as short term and she pays 33% tax on the gain. If she sells the stock after October 9, 2017, the gain is long term and she will pay 15% tax on the gain.

> **Tax Planning Strategy**

> **Avoid Double Taxation.** The owners of a corporation can choose between two entity forms. A C corporation is a taxable entity that pays tax on corporate profits. Shareholders also pay tax on dividends received from a C corporation, resulting in what is commonly referred to as *double taxation* (refer to Example 16). Note, however, as discussed in Chapter 4, that the dividends may be eligible for a beneficial tax rate.

Shareholders can avoid double taxation by electing that a corporate entity become an S corporation. Unlike a C corporation, an S corporation is not a taxable entity. Instead, the profits and losses of the S corporation flow through to the shareholders and are reported on their tax returns (see Chapter 15).

EXAMPLE 29

Chickadee, Inc., a C corporation with net income of $100,000, pays Carl, its sole shareholder, a $77,750 dividend. Chickadee must pay corporate income tax of $22,250 on the net income of $100,000, and Carl must pay tax on the $77,750 dividend. Sparrow, Inc., an S corporation, also earns $100,000. Sparrow is not a taxable entity, so it pays no income tax on the $100,000 net income. Sam, who is the sole shareholder of Sparrow, includes $100,000 in computing his taxable income.

Other entity choices can be used to avoid double taxation, including partnerships and limited liability companies. Partnerships and limited liability companies, like S corporations, are flow-through entities rather than taxable entities (see Chapter 14).

Choosing to operate as a **flow-through entity** is not the only way to avoid double taxation. Double taxation can be avoided or minimized by having the corporation make payments, such as salaries, rent, and interest to the shareholders.

EXAMPLE 30

Walt is the president and sole shareholder of Meadowlark, Inc., a C corporation. Meadowlark's taxable income before any payment to Walt is $600,000. Walt, a skilled manager, is primarily responsible for the profitability of the corporation. If Meadowlark pays Walt a dividend of $400,000, the corporation must pay Federal income tax on $600,000 and Walt must include the $400,000 dividend in gross income. However, if Meadowlark pays Walt a salary of $400,000, the salary is deductible and the corporation has only $200,000 of taxable income. Walt must include the $400,000 salary in gross income.

In either case, Walt includes $400,000 in gross income (the dividends may be eligible for a beneficial tax rate). Meadowlark, on the other hand, reports $400,000 less taxable income if the payment to Walt is a salary payment rather than a dividend payment.

In considering this plan, Meadowlark should examine the effects of employment taxes on Walt and the corporation as well.

1-4f **Tax Minimization Strategies Related to Credits**

➤ *Maximize Tax Credits.* Congress uses the tax credit provisions of the Internal Revenue Code liberally in implementing tax policy. It is important to understand the difference between a credit and a deduction, both of which reduce a taxpayer's tax liability. A deduction reduces taxable income, which results in a reduction of the tax paid. The tax benefit of the deduction depends on the amount of the qualifying expenditure and the taxpayer's tax rate. A tax credit reduces the tax liability dollar for dollar and is not affected by the taxpayer's tax rate.

> **★ Framework Focus: Credits**
>
> ➤ *Tax Planning Strategy*

EXAMPLE 31

Oriole Corporation, which is in the 25% marginal bracket, has a $6,000 deduction for expenditures made to repair a machine. The deduction reduces taxable income by $6,000 and results in a tax liability reduction of $1,500 ($6,000 deduction × 25% marginal rate).

Oriole also incurred expenditures of $6,000 to rehabilitate a building, which qualifies the corporation for a tax credit of $600 ($6,000 rehabilitation expenditures × 10% rate for the credit). The rehabilitation expenditures credit results in a $600 reduction of Oriole's tax liability. In addition, Oriole's depreciable basis for the building increases by $5,400 ($6,000 expenditures − $600 credit).

Had Oriole instead been subject to a 35% marginal tax rate, the repair deduction would have been worth more to the entity (now, $6,000 × 35% = $2,100). The rehabilitation credit still would be worth $600 to Oriole.

1-4g **Thinking Outside the Framework**

Although the General Framework for Income Tax Planning in Exhibit 1.3 is broad and covers most tax planning strategies, some strategies fall outside the framework. In addition, other planning ideas can supplement the strategies in the framework. Some of these ideas are discussed below.

Determining the Tax Burden

To engage in effective tax planning, one must be able to identify the relevant tax rate that will be applied to a transaction. There are at least three kinds of tax rates to consider in making a financial decision. A taxpayer's *marginal* tax rate is paid on an additional dollar of taxable income. Referring to the corporate income tax rate schedule on the inside front cover of this text, a C corporation's marginal tax rate on its first dollar of income is 15 percent. Similarly, the marginal tax rate faced by a corporation with $100,001 of income is 39 percent.

The *average* tax rate is the ratio of taxes paid to the tax base. Thus, a corporation with $100,000 of taxable income is subject to an average tax rate of 22.25 percent ($22,250 in tax divided by $100,000 in taxable income).

A third kind of tax rate computation, the *effective* tax rate, can be seen as either (1) the ratio of taxes paid to financial net income before tax or (2) the sum of currently payable and deferred tax expense divided by the book net income before tax. Of these approaches to determining a taxpayer's tax rate, the marginal tax rate is most appropriate for tax planning purposes.

EXAMPLE 32

Azure Corporation reports taxable income of $80,000. Azure also received $10,000 of tax-free interest income from Rock Township bonds. Using the corporate tax rate schedule on the inside front cover of this text, one can determine that the company's tax liability is $15,450.

If Azure were to earn an additional dollar in taxable income, it would pay an extra $.34 in tax. Thus, the company's marginal tax rate is 34%. Azure's average tax rate is the ratio of taxes paid to book income, or 19.3% ($15,450/$80,000). Finally, the company has an effective rate of tax of 17.2% ($15,450/$90,000), the ratio of taxes paid to book net income before tax (here, the sum of taxable income and tax-free income).

The actual tax paid may not always be apparent. For example, the amount of taxes paid should include both current taxes and the present value of future taxes generated by a transaction. Present value and future value tables are included in Appendix F of this text.

EXAMPLE 33

Magenta Corporation is a publishing company that specializes in electronic media. It is a new corporation that was formed on January 1, 2015. During that year, it generated a net operating loss (NOL) of $300,000. The NOL can be carried forward to offset future years' taxable income and thereby reduce Magenta's future tax liabilities. Magenta expects to earn $100,000 of income each year over the next four years. The NOL should completely offset the company's taxable income for the first three of these years.

At the beginning of 2016, Magenta must decide whether to invest in a project that will earn an additional $40,000 of taxable income during 2016 or in a project that will generate $36,000 of tax-free income. The company's president reasons that because the company has an NOL carryforward, the applicable tax rate is 0%, so the taxable project should be chosen.

The president's reasoning is incorrect, because an additional $40,000 of income now will result in $40,000 of taxable income in 2018 (because there will be $40,000 less NOL available in that year).

	2016	2017	2018	2019
Alternative 1 (tax-free investment)				
Pre-NOL taxable income	$ 100,000	$ 100,000	$ 100,000	$100,000
NOL carryforward (from 2015)	(300,000)	(200,000)	(100,000)	–0–
Taxable income	$ –0–	$ –0–	$ –0–	$100,000
Alternative 2 (taxable investment)				
Pre-NOL taxable income	$ 140,000	$ 100,000	$ 100,000	$100,000
NOL carryforward (from 2015)	(300,000)	(160,000)	(60,000)	–0–
Taxable income	$ –0–	$ –0–	$ 40,000	$100,000

The tax cost of the $40,000 project equals the discounted value of the tax due for 2018. Assuming a 10% after-tax internal rate of return and a 15% corporate tax rate, the present value of taxes deferred for three years is $4,508 and the discounted tax rate is 11.27%. Thus, the after-tax proceeds on the taxable project are $35,492, or $508 *less* than the $36,000 earnings on the tax-free project.

BRIDGE DISCIPLINE   Bridge to Political Science, Economics, Health Care

When the tax law is used to accomplish goals other than revenue collection, fiscal "winners" and "losers" can be created. The distribution is not equal across income levels for Federal tax expenditures and other Federal benefits. For this purpose, "Federal benefits" include retirement, health care, and poverty reduction programs that trigger payments to individuals.

"Federal tax breaks" usually do not involve an appropriation and payment by Congress. Instead, they represent tax reductions from individuals' exemptions, the standard deduction, itemized deductions (e.g., for payments of home mortgage interest), and lower tax rates on investment income.

The adjacent tables trace the distribution of Federal tax benefits and Federal tax breaks by taxpayer income levels, for a recent Federal fiscal year.

Federal Benefits Received

Income Quintile	$ Received per Family Unit	$B in Benefits Received	% of Total Benefits Received
Lowest	$18,007	$666	33%
2	17,755	551	27
3	13,003	349	17
4	10,780	246	12
Highest	10,087	203	10

Federal Tax Breaks Received

Income Quintile	$ Received per Family Unit	$B in Benefits Received	% of Total Benefits Received
Lowest	$ 1,110	$ 40	4%
2	2,149	74	7
3	2,757	91	8
4	5,021	152	14
Highest	24,693	723	67

1-5 UNDERSTANDING THE FEDERAL TAX LAW

LO.6

Explain the economic, social, equity, and political considerations that underlie the tax law.

The Federal tax law is a mosaic of statutory laws, administrative pronouncements, and court decisions. Anyone who has attempted to work with these provisions would admit to their complexity. For the person who has to trudge through a mass of rules to find the solution to a tax problem, it may be of some consolation to know that the law's complexity generally can be explained. Whether sound or not, there are reasons for the formulation of every rule. Recognizing these reasons, therefore, is an important step toward understanding the Federal tax law.

1-5a Revenue Needs

The foundation of the income tax system is the raising of revenue to cover the cost of government operations. Ideally, annual outlays should not exceed anticipated revenues, thereby leading to a balanced budget with no resulting deficit. Many states have achieved this objective by passing laws or constitutional amendments precluding deficit spending.

The U.S. Constitution allows deficit spending, and politicians often find it hard to resist the temptation to spend more than the tax system collects currently. Congress uses several approaches to reduce a tax bill's net revenue loss. When tax reductions are involved, the full impact of the legislation can be phased in over a period of years. Or as an alternative, the tax reduction can be limited to a period of years. When the period expires, Congress can then renew or not renew the provision in light of budget considerations.

1-5b Economic Considerations

Using the tax system in an effort to accomplish economic objectives has become increasingly popular in recent years. Generally, proponents of this approach use tax legislation to promote measures designed to help control the economy or encourage certain economic activities and businesses.

Encouragement of Certain Activities

Without passing judgment on the wisdom of any such choices, it is clear that the tax law encourages certain types of economic activity or segments of the economy. For example, the favorable treatment allowed research and development expenditures (immediate deduction vs. capitalization and amortization) can be explained by the desire to foster technological progress. Further, given the time value of money, the tax savings from a current deduction usually is preferable to capitalizing the cost with a write-off over the estimated useful life of the asset created.

Similarly, Congress has used depreciation deductions as a means of encouraging investment in business capital. Theoretically, shorter asset lives and accelerated methods should encourage additional investment in depreciable property acquired for business use. Conversely, longer asset lives and the required use of the straight-line method of depreciation dampen the tax incentive for capital outlays.

Ecological considerations justify a tax provision that permits a more rapid expensing of the costs of installing pollution control facilities. This provision may aid in maintaining a clean air environment and conserving energy resources; thus, it also can be justified under social considerations.

Is it wise to stimulate U.S. exports of goods and services? Considering the pressing and continuing problem of a deficit in the U.S. balance of payments, the answer should be clear. In an international setting, Congress has deemed it advisable to establish incentives for U.S. citizens who accept employment overseas.

Is saving desirable for the economy? Saving leads to capital formation and thereby makes funds available to finance home construction and industrial expansion. The tax law encourages saving by according preferential treatment to private retirement plans.

GLOBAL TAX ISSUES   Outsourcing of Tax Return Preparation

The use of foreign nationals to carry out certain job assignments for U.S. businesses is an increasingly popular practice. Outsourcing such activities as telemarketing to India, for example, usually produces the same satisfactory result but at a much lower cost.

Now outsourcing also is being applied to the preparation of tax returns. Not only can this practice be expected to continue, but it probably will increase in volume. Outsourcing tax return preparation does not violate Federal law, and the practice is compatible with accounting ethical guidelines as long as three safeguards are followed: First, the practitioner must make sure that client confidentiality is maintained. Second, the practitioner must verify the accuracy of the work that has been outsourced. Third, the practitioner must gain the consent of clients when any offshore third-party contractor is used to provide professional services.

Tax professionals justify tax preparation outsourcing as a means of conserving time and effort that can be applied toward more meaningful tax planning on behalf of their clients.

Sources: Reg. § 301.7216–2(c)(2); AICPA Ethics Interpretation 1.700.040.

Not only are deductions allowed for contributions to certain retirement plans and Individual Retirement Accounts (IRAs), but income on the contributions might not be taxed until withdrawn.

Encouragement of Certain Industries

A sound agricultural base is necessary for a well-balanced national economy. Undoubtedly, this explains why farmers are accorded special treatment under the Federal income tax system. Among the benefits available to farmers are the election to expense rather than capitalize certain soil and water conservation expenditures and fertilizers and the election to defer the recognition of gain on the receipt of crop insurance proceeds.

To stimulate the manufacturing industry, Congress enacted the domestic production activities deduction. The provision creates a tax benefit in the form of a deduction for profits derived from manufacturing activities conducted within the United States. By restricting the deduction to manufacturing income attributable to wages reportable to the IRS, new U.S. jobs will result and the outsourcing of labor is discouraged. Thus, the tax system is used to encourage both domestic manufacturing and job growth.

Encouragement of Small Business

It seems that in the United States, a consensus exists that what is good for small business is good for the economy as a whole. This assumption has led to a definite bias in the tax law favoring small business. Several income tax provisions can be explained by the desire to benefit small business, including the low marginal tax rates applied to the first dollars of the entity's income.

1-5c Social Considerations

Some provisions of the Federal tax law, particularly those dealing with the income tax of individuals, can be explained by a desire to encourage certain social results.

- Certain benefits provided to employees through accident and health insurance plans financed by employers are nontaxable to employees. Encouraging such plans is considered socially desirable because they provide medical benefits in the event of an employee's illness or injury.

- A contribution made by an employer to a qualified pension or profit sharing plan for an employee may receive special treatment. The contribution and any income it generates are not taxed to the employee until the funds are distributed. Such an arrangement also benefits the employer by allowing a tax deduction when the contribution is made to the qualified plan. Various types of retirement plans are encouraged to supplement the subsistence income level the employee otherwise would obtain under the Social Security system.

- A deduction is allowed for contributions to qualified charitable organizations. The deduction attempts to shift some of the financial and administrative burden of socially desirable programs from the public (government) to the private (citizens) sector.

- Various tax credits, deductions, and exclusions are designed to encourage taxpayers to obtain or extend their level of education.

- A tax credit is allowed for amounts spent to furnish care for certain minor or disabled dependents to enable the taxpayer to seek or maintain gainful employment.

- A tax deduction is denied for certain expenditures deemed to be contrary to public policy. This disallowance extends to items such as fines, penalties, illegal kickbacks, bribes to government officials, and gambling losses in excess of gains. Social considerations dictate that the tax law should not encourage these activities by permitting a deduction.

1-5d Equity Considerations

The concept of equity is relative. Reasonable persons can, and often do, disagree about what is fair or unfair. In the tax area, moreover, equity is most often tied to a particular taxpayer's personal situation. To illustrate, compare the tax positions of those who rent their personal residences with those who own their homes. Renters may not take a Federal income tax deduction for the rent they pay. For homeowners, however, a large portion of the house payments they make may qualify for the Federal mortgage interest and property tax deductions. Although renters may have difficulty understanding this difference in tax treatment, the encouragement of home ownership can be justified on both economic and social grounds.

In many other parts of the law, however, equity concerns are evident. The concept of equity appears in tax provisions that alleviate the effect of multiple taxation and postpone the recognition of gain when the taxpayer lacks the ability or wherewithal to pay the tax. Provisions that mitigate the effect of the application of the annual accounting period concept also reflect equity considerations.

Alleviating the Effect of Multiple Taxation

The income earned by a taxpayer may be subject to taxes imposed by different taxing authorities. If, for example, the taxpayer is a resident of New York City, income might be subject to Federal, state of New York, and city of New York income taxes. To compensate for this apparent inequity, the Federal tax law allows a taxpayer to claim a deduction for state and local income taxes.

Equity considerations also can explain the Federal tax treatment of certain income from non-U.S. sources, allowing deductions, credits, and exclusions where a taxpayer's income might be subject to tax by two or more countries.

The Wherewithal to Pay Concept

The wherewithal to pay concept recognizes the inequity of taxing a transaction when the taxpayer lacks the means to pay the tax. The wherewithal to pay concept underlies a provision in the tax law dealing with the treatment of gain resulting from an involuntary conversion. An involuntary conversion occurs when property is destroyed by casualty or taken by a public authority through condemnation. If gain results from the conversion, it need not be recognized immediately if the taxpayer replaces the property within a specified time period. The replacement property must be similar or related in service or use to that involuntarily converted.

EXAMPLE 34

Ron, a rancher, owns some pasture land that is condemned by the state for use as a game pre-serve. The condemned pasture land cost Ron $120,000, but the state pays him $150,000 (its fair market value). Shortly thereafter, Ron buys more pasture land for $150,000.

Ron has a realized gain of $30,000 [$150,000 (condemnation award) − $120,000 (cost of land)]. It would be inequitable to require Ron to pay a tax on this gain for two reasons. First, without disposing of the property acquired (the new land), Ron would be hard-pressed to pay the tax. Second, his economic position has not changed.

What if Ron reinvests only $140,000 of the award in new pasture land? Now Ron recognizes a $10,000 taxable gain in the current year. Instead of ending up with only replacement property, Ron now holds the new land and $10,000 in cash.

Mitigating the Effect of the Annual Accounting Period Concept

Federal income tax returns are due for every tax year of the taxpayer. The application of this annual accounting period concept can lead to dissimilar tax treatment for taxpayers who are, from a long-range standpoint, in the same economic position.

EXAMPLE 35

José and Alicia, both unmarried sole proprietors, experienced the following results during the indi-cated tax years.

	Profit (or Loss)	
Year	José	Alicia
2015	$50,000	$150,000
2016	60,000	60,000
2017	60,000	(40,000)

Although José and Alicia have the same total profit of $170,000 over the period from 2015 through 2017, the annual accounting period concept places Alicia at a disadvantage for tax purposes, both in terms of the time value of money and due to the higher tax rates that will apply to Alicia under the progressive rate structure.

However, the net operating loss deduction generated in 2017 offers Alicia some relief by allow-ing her to carry back some or all of her 2017 loss to the earlier profitable years (in this case, 2015). Thus, with an NOL carryback, Alicia can obtain an immediate refund for some of the taxes she paid on the $150,000 profit reported for 2015.

1-5e Political Considerations

A large segment of the Federal tax law is made up of statutory provisions. Because these statutes are enacted by Congress, is it any surprise that political considerations influence tax law?

Special Interest Legislation

Certain provisions of the tax law largely can be explained by the political influence some groups have had on Congress. For example, is there any other realistic reason that prepaid subscription and dues income is not taxed until earned, while prepaid rents are taxed to the landlord in the year received?

State and Local Government Influences

State law has had an influence in shaping our present Federal tax law. One example of this effect is the evolution of Federal tax law in response to states with community property sys-tems. The states with community property systems are Louisiana, Texas, New Mexico, Arizona, California, Washington, Idaho, Nevada, and Wisconsin. Spouses in Alaska can elect community property treatment. The rest of the states are common law jurisdictions.

The difference between common law and community property systems centers around the property rights held by married persons. In a common law system, each spouse owns whatever he or she earns. Under a community property system, one-half of the earnings of each spouse is considered owned by the other spouse.

EXAMPLE
36

Al and Fran are husband and wife, and their only income is the $80,000 annual salary Al receives. If they live in New Jersey (a common law state), the $80,000 salary belongs to Al.

If, however, they live in Arizona (a community property state), the $80,000 is divided equally, in terms of ownership, between Al and Fran.

At one time, the tax position of the residents of community property states was so advantageous that many common law states adopted community property systems. Needless to say, the political pressure placed on Congress to correct the disparity in tax treatment was considerable. To a large extent, this was accomplished in 1948 when the law extended many of the community property tax advantages to residents of common law jurisdictions.

The major advantage extended was the provision allowing married taxpayers to file joint returns and compute the tax liability as if one-half of the income had been earned by each spouse. This result is automatic in a community property state because half of the income earned by one spouse belongs to the other spouse. The income-splitting benefits of a joint return are incorporated as part of the tax rates applicable to married taxpayers. A similar motivation can be seen for the gift-splitting provisions of the Federal gift tax and the marital deduction of the Federal estate and gift taxes.

1-5f Influence of the Internal Revenue Service

LO.7

Describe the role played by the IRS and the courts in the evolution of the Federal tax system.

The influence of the IRS on tax law is apparent in many areas beyond its role in issuing the administrative pronouncements that make up a considerable portion of our tax law. The IRS has been instrumental in securing the passage of much legislation designed to curtail the most flagrant tax avoidance practices (to "close tax loopholes"). In addition, the IRS has sought and obtained legislation to make its own job easier (to attain administrative feasibility).

Closing Perceived Tax Loopholes

Certain tax provisions are intended to prevent a loophole from being used to avoid the tax consequences intended by Congress. Working within the letter of existing law, taxpayers and their advisers devise techniques that accomplish indirectly what cannot be accomplished directly. As a consequence, legislation is enacted to close the loopholes that taxpayers have located and exploited. Some tax law can be explained in this fashion and is discussed in the chapters to follow.

Administrative Feasibility

Some tax law is justified on the grounds that it simplifies the task of the IRS in collecting the revenue and administering the law. With regard to collecting the revenue, the IRS long ago realized the importance of placing taxpayers on a pay-as-you-go basis. Elaborate withholding procedures apply to wages, and accrual basis taxpayers often must pay taxes on prepaid income in the year received and not when earned. The approach may be contrary to generally accepted accounting principles, but it is consistent with the wherewithal to pay concept.

One of the keys to an effective administration of our tax system is the audit process conducted by the IRS. To carry out this function, the IRS is aided by provisions that reduce the chance of taxpayer error or manipulation and therefore reduce the audit effort that is necessary. An increase in the amount of the standard deduction, for example, reduces the number of individual taxpayers who will choose the alternative of itemizing their personal deductions. With fewer deductions to check, the audit function is simplified.

1-5g **Influence of the Courts**

In addition to interpreting statutory provisions and the administrative pronouncements issued by the IRS, the Federal courts have influenced tax law in two other respects. First, the courts have formulated certain judicial concepts that serve as guides in the application of various tax provisions. Second, certain key decisions have led to changes in the Internal Revenue Code.

Judicial Concepts Relating to Tax

Particularly in dealings between related parties, the courts test transactions by looking to whether the taxpayers acted in an arm's length manner. The question to be asked is: Would unrelated parties have handled the transaction in the same way?

EXAMPLE 37

Rex, the sole shareholder of Silver Corporation, leases property to the corporation for a yearly rent of $6,000. To test whether the corporation should be allowed a rent deduction for this amount, the IRS and the courts will apply the arm's length concept. Would Silver have paid $6,000 a year in rent if it had leased the same property from an unrelated party (rather than from Rex)?

Suppose it is determined that an unrelated third party would have charged an annual rent for the property of only $5,000. Under these circumstances, Silver can deduct only $5,000. The other $1,000 it paid for the use of the property represents a *nondeductible dividend*. Rex is treated as having received rent income of $5,000 and dividend income of $1,000.

Judicial Influence on Statutory Provisions

Some court decisions have been of such consequence that Congress has incorporated them into statutory tax law. For example, many years ago, the courts found that stock dividends distributed to the shareholders of a corporation were not gross income and therefore were not subject to tax. This result largely was accepted by Congress, and a provision in the tax statutes now addresses the issue.

1-6 **SUMMARY**

Tax laws are pervasive in today's global economy. Individuals and businesses must contend with complex rules in planning their personal and professional activities. Taxes can fall on income, wealth, asset transfers, consumer expenditures, and other events.

Tax planning is a means by which to manage the amount and timing of tax liabilities to accomplish one's long-term objectives. The conduct of tax practitioners is regulated by professional associations, lawmakers, and the taxing agencies.

Taxing systems are designed to provide revenues for governments to accomplish the common goals of citizens. In addition to its necessary revenue-raising objective, the Federal tax law has developed in response to several other factors.

- *Economic considerations.* Tax provisions can help to regulate the economy and encourage certain activities and types of businesses.

- *Social considerations.* Some tax provisions are designed to encourage (or discourage) socially desirable (or undesirable) practices.

- *Equity considerations.* Tax provisions can alleviate the effect of multiple taxation, recognize the wherewithal to pay concept, and mitigate the effect of the annual accounting period concept.

- *Political considerations.* Tax provisions can represent special interest legislation and reflect the effect of state and local law.

- *Influence of the IRS.* Many tax provisions are intended to aid the IRS in the collection of revenue and the administration of the tax law.

- *Influence of the courts.* Court decisions have established a body of judicial concepts relating to tax law and have, on occasion, led Congress to enact statutory provisions to either clarify or negate their effect.

REFOCUS ON THE BIG PICTURE

A TYPICAL TAX YEAR FOR A MODERN FAMILY

The explanation given for the difference in the ad valorem property taxes—the Carters' increase and the Walkers' decrease—seems reasonable. It is not likely that the Carters' increase was due to a *general* upward assessment in valuation, as the Walkers' taxes on their residence (located nearby) dropped. More business use of the Carters' residence (presuming that Travis conducts his consulting practice from his home) might be responsible for the increase, but capital improvements appear to be a more likely cause.

The imposition of the use tax when Travis registered the new automobile illustrates one of the means by which a state can preclude the avoidance of its sales tax (see Example 4).

When gifts between family members are material in amount (e.g., an RV) and exceed the annual exclusion, a gift tax return needs to be filed. Even though no gift tax may be due because of the availability of the unified transfer tax exclusion ($5.45 million for 2016, as indexed), the filing of a return starts the running of the statute of limitations.

The imposition of the "jock tax" on nonathletes is unusual but not improper. The Carters must recognize that some of their income is subject to income taxes in two states and take advantage of whatever relief is available to mitigate the result.

Significant Federal income tax savings might be available if Travis were to hire the children to work in the consulting practice.

What If?

Because of the double audit (i.e., both state and Federal) and the deficiency assessed, the Carters need to make sure that future returns do not contain similar errors. As the text suggests, taxpayers with prior deficiencies are among those whose returns may be selected for audit.

Suggested Readings

Jill Lepore, "Tax Time: Why We Pay," *The New Yorker*, November 26, 2012.

Donald Marron, "Should Governments Tax Unhealthy Foods and Drinks?," **http://tinyurl.com/obese-tax**.

Mark Robyn, Micah Cohen, and Joseph Henchman, "Sales Tax Holidays: Politically Expedient but Poor Tax Policy," July 24, 2013 working paper, **www.taxfoundation.org**.

Joseph J. Thorndike, "The Tenacity of Tax Complexity," December 2001 working paper, **www.taxhistory.org**.

Key Terms

Ad valorem taxes, 1-10

C corporations, 1-16

Deferred tax asset, 1-18

Deferred tax liability, 1-18

Effective tax rate, 1-18

Employment taxes, 1-2

Estate tax, 1-8

Excise taxes, 1-4

FICA tax, 1-6

Financial Accounting Standards Board (FASB), 1-16

Flow-through entity, 1-24

Franchise tax, 1-12

FUTA tax, 1-6

Generally Accepted Accounting Principles (GAAP), 1-16

Gift tax, 1-9

Inheritance tax, 1-8

International Accounting Standards Board (IASB), 1-16

International Financial Reporting Standards (IFRS), 1-16

Occupational taxes, 1-12

Personalty, 1-10

Proprietorship, 1-16

Realty, 1-10

S corporations, 1-17

Sales taxes, 1-2

Tax avoidance, 1-19

Tax evasion, 1-19

Use taxes, 1-6

Value added tax (VAT), 1-6

Wherewithal to pay, 1-29

Problems

Issue ID   1. **LO.1, 2, 5** James Corporation believes that it will have a better distribution location for its product if it relocates the corporation to another state. What considerations (both tax and nontax) should James weigh before making a decision on whether to make the move?

2. **LO.1** Distinguish between taxes that are *proportional* and those that are *progressive*.

Issue ID   3. **LO.2** Several years ago, Ethan purchased the former parsonage of St. James Church to use as a personal residence. To date, Ethan has not received any ad valorem property tax bills from either the city or the county tax authorities.

   a.   What is a reasonable explanation for this oversight?
   b.   What should Ethan do?

Critical Thinking   4. **LO.1, 6** In terms of Adam Smith's canon of economy, how does the Federal income tax fare?

Issue ID   5. **LO.2** Jim, a resident of Washington (which imposes a general sales tax), goes to Oregon (which does not impose a general sales tax) to purchase his automobile. Will Jim successfully avoid the Washington sales tax? Explain.

Issue ID   6. **LO.2** The Irontown Independent School District wants to sell a parcel of unimproved land that it does not need. Its three best offers are as follows: from the State Department of Public Safety (DPS), $4.3 million; from Trinity Lutheran Church,

$4.2 million; and from Baker Motors, $3.9 million. DPS would use the property for a new state highway patrol barracks, Trinity would start a church school, and Baker would open a car dealership. As the financial adviser for the school district, which offer would you prefer? Why?

7. **LO.2** What is the difference between an excise tax and a general sales tax?
   a. Do all states impose a general sales tax?
   b. Does the Federal government impose a general sales tax?

8. **LO.2** Sophia lives several blocks from her parents in the same residential subdivision. Sophia is surprised to learn that her ad valorem property taxes for the year were raised, while those of her parents were lowered. What is a possible explanation for the difference?   Issue ID

9. **LO.4, 5** Marco and Cynthia have decided to go into business together. They will operate a burrito delivery business. They expect to have a loss in the first and second years of the business and subsequently expect to make a substantial profit.   Decision Making
   Communications

   Marco and Cynthia are concerned about potential liability if a customer ever gets sick after eating one of their products. They have called your office and asked for advice about whether they should run their business as a partnership or as a corporation. Write a letter to Cynthia Clay, at 1206 Seventh Avenue, Fort Worth, TX 76101, describing the alternative forms of business they can select. In your letter, explain what form or forms of business you recommend and why.

10. **LO.4, 5** Ashley runs a small business in Boulder, Colorado, that makes snow skis. She expects the business to grow substantially over the next three years. Because she is concerned about product liability and is planning to take the company public in 2016, she is currently considering incorporating the business. Financial data are as follows.   Decision Making

	2015	2016	2017
Sales revenue	$150,000	$320,000	$600,000
Tax-free interest income	5,000	8,000	15,000
Deductible cash expenses	30,000	58,000	95,000
Tax depreciation	25,000	20,000	40,000

   Ashley expects her combined Federal and state marginal income tax rate to be 35% over the next three years before any profits from the business are considered. Her after-tax cost of capital is 12%.
   a. Compute the present value of the future cash flows for 2015 to 2017 assuming that Ashley incorporates the business and pays all after-tax income as dividends (for Ashley's dividends that qualify for the 15% rate).
   b. Compute the present value of the future cash flows for 2015 to 2017 assuming that Ashley continues to operate the business as a sole proprietorship.
   c. Should Ashley incorporate the business this year? Why or why not?

11. **LO.3, 5** Mauve Supplies, Inc., reports total income of $120,000. The corporation's taxable income is $105,000. What are Mauve's marginal, average, and effective tax rates?

12. **LO.2** Franklin County is in dire financial straits and is considering a number of sources for additional revenue. Evaluate the following possibilities in terms of anticipated taxpayer compliance.   Issue ID
   a. A property tax on business inventories.
   b. A tax on intangibles (i.e., stocks and bonds) held as investments.
   c. A property tax on boats used for recreational purposes.

13. **LO.6** Discuss the probable justification for each of the following provisions of the tax law.

   a. A tax credit allowed for electricity produced from renewable sources.

   b. A tax credit allowed for the purchase of a motor vehicle that operates on alternative energy sources (e.g., nonfossil fuels).

   c. A deduction for state and local income taxes.

   d. The deduction for personal casualty losses that is subject to computational limitations.

   e. Favorable treatment accorded to research and development expenditures.

   f. A deduction allowed for income resulting from U.S. production (manufacturing) activities.

   g. The deduction allowed for contributions to qualified charitable organizations.

   h. An election that allows certain corporations to avoid the corporate income tax and pass losses through to their shareholders.

14. **LO.6** Discuss the probable justification for each of the following aspects of the tax law.

   a. A tax credit is allowed for amounts spent to furnish care for minor children while the parent works.

   b. Deductions for interest on home mortgage and property taxes on one's personal residence.

   c. The income-splitting benefits of filing a joint return.

   d. Gambling losses in excess of gambling gains.

   e. Net operating losses of a current year can be carried back to profitable years.

   f. A taxpayer who sells property on an installment basis can recognize gain on the sale over the period the payments are received.

   g. The exclusion from Federal tax of certain interest income from state and local bonds.

   h. Prepaid income is taxed to the recipient in the year it is received and not in the year it is earned.

Critical Thinking   15. **LO.2** Contrast a value added tax (VAT) with a national sales tax in terms of anticipated taxpayer compliance.

Critical Thinking
Communications   16. **LO.2** Go to **www.taxfoundation.org**, and determine Tax Freedom Day for your state and a neighboring state, for the years 1950, 1960, 1970, 1980, 1990, 2000, and 2010. Report your results as a line graph.

Critical Thinking
Communications   17. **LO.5** Although the Federal income tax law is complex, most individual taxpayers are able to complete their tax returns without outside assistance. Gather data as to the accuracy of this statement. Summarize your comments in an e-mail to your instructor.

Ethics and Equity   18. **LO.5** President Franklin D. Roosevelt once said, "I am wholly unable to figure out the amount of tax," and wrote to the Federal Commissioner of Revenue, "may I ask that [the agency] let me know the amount of the balance due."

   When a friend of FDR was ordered to pay $420,000 in tax penalties, the President called the Commissioner within earshot of reporters and told him to cut the penalties to $3,000. One listener, journalist David Brinkley, recalled years later: "Nobody seemed to think it was news or very interesting." Evaluate the President's comments and actions.

BRIDGE DISCIPLINE

1. Discuss with respect to the Federal policy for reducing poverty:

   a. The individual income tax.

   b. The Social Security tax.

2. Prepare a two-page paper titled "How I Would Apply Federal Income Tax Law to Encourage the Availability of Universal Broadband in This Community" to submit to your economics professor.   Communications

3. Prepare an outline for a 10-minute speech to give to your government class. The speech is titled "If You Don't Pay Federal Taxes, You Can't Vote."   Communications

4. When taxes are "too high," taxpayers start to cheat on their taxes and dangerous consequences can result. Evaluate this statement. Give at least two examples to illustrate your conclusions.

5. Some tax rules can be justified on multiple grounds (e.g., economic or social). In this connection, comment on the possible justification for the rules governing the following.

   a. Pension plans.

   b. Education.

   c. Home ownership.

Working with the Tax Law

LEARNING OBJECTIVES: *After completing Chapter 2, you should be able to:*

LO.1 Describe the statutory, administrative, and judicial sources of the tax law and the purpose of each source.

LO.2 Locate and work with the tax law and explain the tax research process.

LO.3 Communicate the results of the tax research process in a client letter and a tax file memorandum.

LO.4 Employ a strategy of how best to use a computer when performing tax research and in taking the CPA exam.

CHAPTER OUTLINE

TAX TALK *The less people know about how sausages and laws are made, the better they'll sleep at night.* —OTTO VON BISMARCK

THE BIG PICTURE

RESEARCHING TAX QUESTIONS

Early in December, Fred and Megan Samuels review their financial and tax situation with their son, Sam, and daughter-in-law, Dana. Currently, Sam and Dana live with Fred and Megan. Fred and Megan are in the 28 percent tax bracket. Both Sam and Dana are age 21.

Sam, a student at a nearby university, owns some publicly traded stock that he inherited from his grandmother. A current sale would result in $8,000 of gross income ($19,000 amount realized − $11,000 basis).

At this point, Fred and Megan provide about 55 percent of Sam and Dana's support. Although neither is now employed, Sam earned $960 and Dana earned $900 earlier in the year. The problem: Should the stock be sold before the end of the year? If the stock were sold, would the sale prohibit Fred and Megan from claiming Sam and Dana as dependents? Would the stock sale result in a tax liability for Sam and Dana?

Read the chapter and formulate your responses.

F ederal tax law is a mixture of statutory provisions, administrative pronouncements, and court decisions. Anyone who has attempted to work with this body of knowledge is familiar with its complexity. Tax research provides the vehicle by which one makes sense out of this complexity.

2-1 TAX LAW SOURCES

LO.1

Describe the statutory, administrative, and judicial sources of the tax law and the purpose of each source.

Understanding taxation requires a mastery of the sources of the *rules of tax law*. These sources include not only legislative provisions in the form of the Internal Revenue Code but also congressional Committee Reports, Treasury Department Regulations, other Treasury Department pronouncements, and court decisions. Thus, the *primary sources* of tax information include pronouncements from all three branches of government: legislative, executive, and judicial.

In addition to being able to locate and interpret the sources of the tax law, a tax professional must understand the relative weight of authority that each source carries. The tax law is of little significance, however, until it is applied to a specific set of facts and circumstances. This chapter, therefore, both introduces the statutory, administrative, and judicial sources of the tax law *and* explains how the law is applied to business and individual transactions. It further explains how to apply research techniques effectively.

Tax research is necessary because the application of the law to a specific situation sometimes is not clear. As complicated as the Internal Revenue Code is, it cannot clearly address every conceivable situation. Accordingly, the tax professional must search other sources (such as administrative rulings and judicial decisions) to determine the most likely tax treatment of a transaction.

Working with such knowledge, a tax professional then can advise the client about the tax consequences of several possible courses of action. Tax research, in other words, is of critical importance not only in properly characterizing completed events but also in planning proposed transactions.

2-1a Statutory Sources of the Tax Law

Statutory sources of law include the Constitution (Article I, Sections 7, 8, and 10), tax treaties (agreements between countries to mitigate the double taxation of taxpayers subject to the tax laws of those countries), and the Internal Revenue Code. The Constitution grants Congress the power to impose and collect taxes, and it authorizes the creation of treaties with other countries. The Internal Revenue Code is the statutory basis for arriving at solutions to all tax questions.

Origin of the Internal Revenue Code

Before 1939, the statutory provisions relating to taxation were contained in the individual revenue acts enacted by Congress every year or two. The inconvenience and uncertainty that resulted from dealing with many separate acts led Congress to codify all of the Federal tax laws in 1939. Known as the Internal Revenue Code of 1939, this codification arranged all Federal tax provisions in a logical sequence and placed them in a separate part of the Federal statutes. A further rearrangement took place in 1954 and resulted in the Internal Revenue Code of 1954, which continued in effect until it was replaced by the Internal Revenue Code of 1986.[1]

Statutory amendments to the tax law are integrated into the existing Code. Thus, subsequent tax legislation, such as the American Taxpayer Relief Act of 2012 and the Protecting Americans from Tax Hikes of 2015, became part of the Internal Revenue Code of 1986.

---

[1]Aside from changes due to a large tax act, the organization of the Internal Revenue Code of 1986 is not substantively different from the organization of the 1954 Code. In contrast, the numbering scheme of sections in the 1939 Code differs from that used in the 1954 Code.

TAX FACT **Scope of the U.S. Tax System**

Although it started out in 1913 as a tax on only the uppermost-income individuals, the tax system today is pervasive in our lives.

- In the typical tax year, the IRS receives about 25 million Forms 1040EZ and about 40 million Forms 1040A.

- The typical Form 1040 requires 7.25 hours to gather records and assemble the return, and 6.25 hours to prepare the form and attachments. The estimated cost of complying with tax rules is $425 billion per year.

- The Internal Revenue Code is about 1 million words (2,650 pages) long, and the Regulations require another 4 million words (9,000 pages). Amazingly, these documents are more than twice the combined length of the *Harry Potter* series, *War and Peace*, and the King James Bible.

The Legislative Process

Federal tax legislation generally originates in the House of Representatives, where it first is considered by the House Ways and Means Committee. (Tax bills also can originate in the Senate if they are attached as riders to other legislative proposals.) If acceptable to the committee, the proposed bill is referred to the entire House of Representatives for approval or disapproval. Approved bills are sent to the Senate, where they initially are considered by the Senate Finance Committee.

The next step is referral from the Senate Finance Committee to the entire Senate. Assuming no disagreement between the House and Senate, passage by the Senate means referral to the President for approval or veto. If the bill is approved or if the President's veto is overridden, the bill becomes law and part of the Internal Revenue Code.

When the Senate version of the bill differs from that passed by the House, the Conference Committee, which includes members of both the House Ways and Means Committee and the Senate Finance Committee, is called upon to resolve the differences.

House and Senate versions of major tax bills frequently differ. One reason bills often are changed in the Senate is that, under the usual rules of Congress, each senator has considerable latitude to make amendments when the Senate as a whole is voting on a bill referred to it by the Senate Finance Committee. On the contrary, in most years the entire House of Representatives either accepts or rejects what is proposed by the House Ways and Means Committee, and changes from the floor are rare.

The deliberations of the Conference Committee usually produce a compromise between the two versions, which then is voted on by both the House and the Senate. If both bodies accept the revised bill, it is referred to the President for approval or veto. The typical legislative process dealing with tax bills is summarized in Exhibit 2.1.

The role of the Conference Committee indicates the importance of compromise in the legislative process. As an example of the practical effect of the compromise process, consider what happened with amendments to the refundability provisions of the child tax credit (see Exhibit 2.2).

Referrals from the House Ways and Means Committee, the Senate Finance Committee, and the Conference Committee usually are accompanied by *Committee Reports*. These Committee Reports often explain the provisions of the proposed legislation and are a valuable source for ascertaining the *intent of Congress*. What Congress had in mind when it considered and enacted tax legislation is the key to interpreting legislation. Because Regulations interpreting new legislation normally are not issued immediately after a statute is enacted, tax researchers and the courts look to Committee Reports to determine congressional intent.

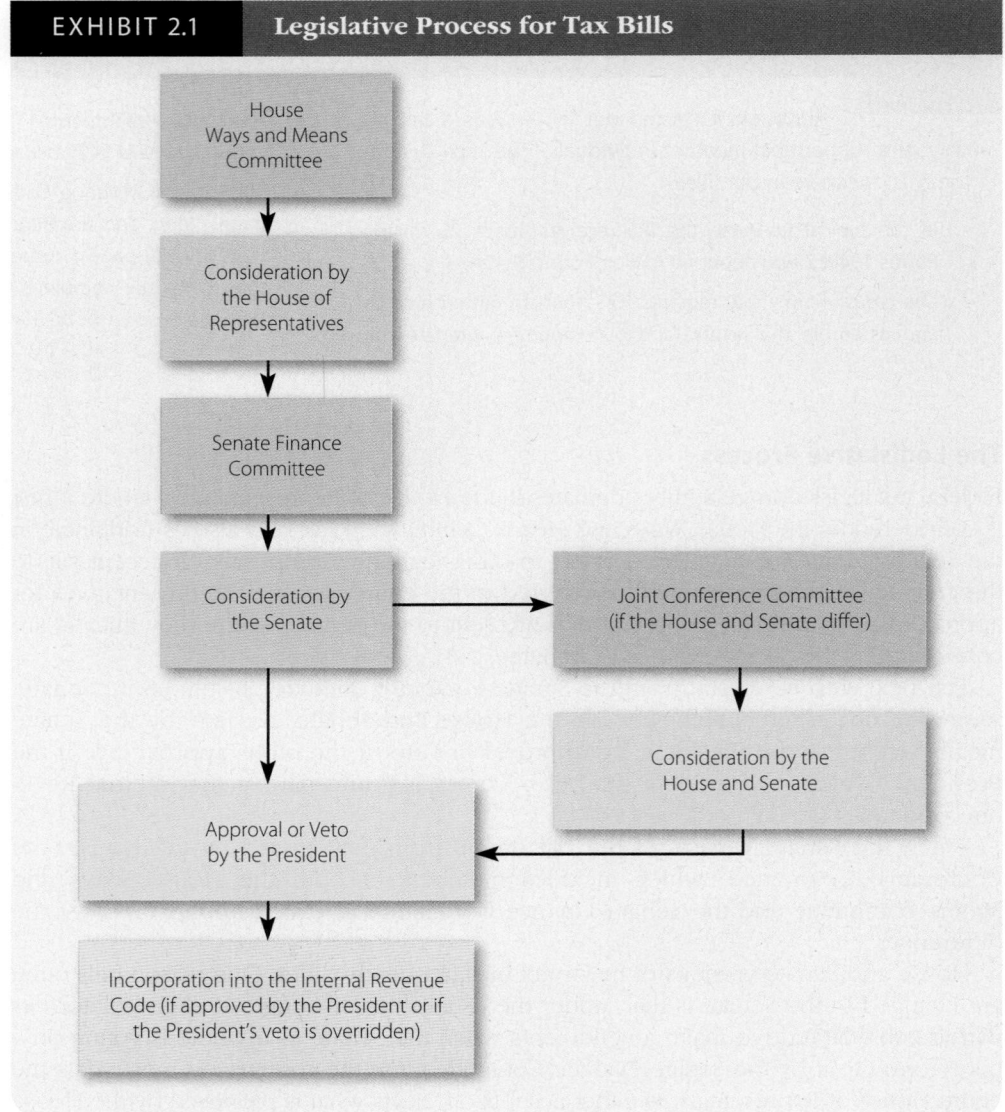

EXHIBIT 2.1   **Legislative Process for Tax Bills**

Arrangement of the Internal Revenue Code

The Internal Revenue Code is found in Title 26 of the U.S. Code. Here is a partial table of contents.

> Subtitle A. Income Taxes
>   Chapter 1. Normal Taxes and Surtaxes
>   Subchapter A. Determination of Tax Liability
>   Part I. Tax on Individuals
>   Sections 1–5
>   Part II. Tax on Corporations
>   Sections 11–12

In referring to a provision of the Code, the tax professional usually cites the Section number. In referring to § 2(a) (dealing with the status of a surviving spouse), for example, it is unnecessary to include Subtitle A, Chapter 1, Subchapter A, and Part I. Merely mentioning § 2(a) suffices because the Section numbers run consecutively and do not begin again with each new Subtitle, Chapter, Subchapter, or Part. Not all Code Section

EXHIBIT 2.2 **Example of Compromise in the Conference Committee**

House Version
For years beginning in 2009, the child tax credit is refundable at a rate of 15% of earned income in excess of $0 (rather than $12,550).

Senate Version
For years beginning in 2009, the child tax credit is refundable at a rate of 15% of earned income in excess of $8,100 (rather than $12,550).

Joint Conference Committee Result
For years beginning in 2009, the child tax credit is refundable at a rate of 15% of earned income in excess of $3,000 (rather than $12,550).

numbers are used, however. Part I ends with § 5, and Part II starts with § 11 (at present, there are no §§ 6, 7, 8, 9, and 10).[2]

Tax professionals commonly refer to certain areas of income tax law by Subchapter designation. Some of the more common Subchapter designations include Subchapter C ("Corporate Distributions and Adjustments"), Subchapter K ("Partners and Partnerships"), and Subchapter S ("Tax Treatment of S Corporations and Their Shareholders"). Particularly in the last situation, it is more convenient to describe the effect of the applicable Code provisions (§§ 1361–1379) as "Subchapter S" than as the "Tax Treatment of S Corporations and Their Shareholders."

Citing the Code

Code Sections often are broken down into subparts.[3] Section 2(a)(1)(A) serves as an example.

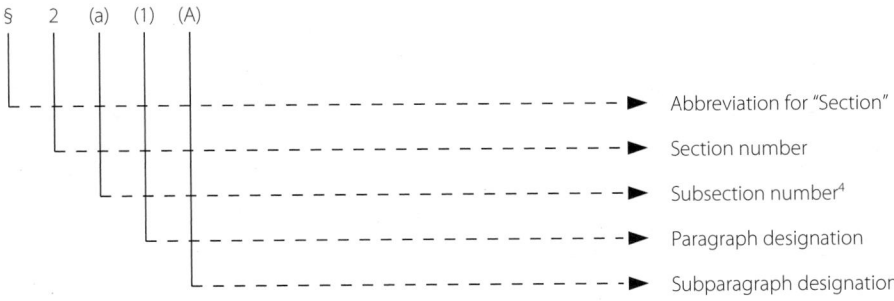

§ 2 (a) (1) (A)

— ► Abbreviation for "Section"

— ► Section number

— ► Subsection number[4]

— ► Paragraph designation

— ► Subparagraph designation

---

[2]When the Code was drafted, Section numbers were intentionally omitted so that later changes could be incorporated into the Code without disrupting its organization. When Congress does not leave enough space, subsequent Code Sections are given A, B, C, etc., designations. A good example is the treatment of §§ 280A through 280H.

[3]Some Code Sections do not have subparts. See, for example, §§ 211 and 241.

[4]Some Code Sections omit the subsection designation and use, instead, the paragraph designation as the first subpart. See, for example, §§ 212(1) and 1222(1).

Broken down by content, a citation for Code § 2(a)(1)(A) appears as follows.

§ 2	Definitions and special rules (relating to the income tax imposed on individuals).
(a)	Definition of a surviving spouse.
(1)	For purposes of § 1 (the determination of the applicable rate schedule), a surviving spouse must meet certain conditions.
(A)	One of the conditions necessary to qualify as a surviving spouse is that the taxpayer's spouse must have died during either of his or her two taxable years immediately preceding the present taxable year.

Throughout the text, references to the Code Sections are in the form shown previously. The symbols "§" and "§§" are used in place of "Section" and "Sections," respectively. The following table illustrates the format used in the text.

Complete Reference	Text Reference
Section 2(a)(1)(A) of the Internal Revenue Code of 1986	§ 2(a)(1)(A)
Sections 1 and 2 of the Internal Revenue Code of 1986	§§ 1 and 2
Section 2 of the Internal Revenue Code of 1954	§ 2 of the Internal Revenue Code of 1954
Section 12(d) of the Internal Revenue Code of 1939[5]	§ 12(d) of the Internal Revenue Code of 1939

Effect of Treaties

The United States signs certain tax treaties (sometimes called tax conventions) with foreign countries to render mutual assistance in tax enforcement and to avoid double taxation. These treaties affect transactions involving U.S. persons and entities operating or investing in a foreign country, as well as persons and entities of a foreign country operating or investing in the United States. Although these bilateral agreements are not codified in any one source, they are published at **www.irs.gov**, as well as in various commercial tax services.

Neither a tax law nor a tax treaty automatically takes precedence. When there is a direct conflict, the most recent item prevails. With certain exceptions, a taxpayer must disclose on the tax return any filing position for which a treaty overrides a tax law.[6] There is a $1,000 per *failure to disclose* penalty for individuals and a $10,000 per failure to disclose penalty for C corporations.[7]

---

[5] Section 12(d) of the Internal Revenue Code of 1939 is the predecessor to § 2 of the Internal Revenue Codes of 1954 and 1986.

[6] § 7852(d).

[7] § 6712(a).

2-1b Administrative Sources of the Tax Law

The administrative sources of the Federal tax law can be grouped as follows: Treasury Department Regulations, Revenue Rulings and Revenue Procedures, and various other administrative pronouncements (see Exhibit 2.3). All are issued by either the U.S. Treasury Department or its subsidiary agency, the IRS.

Treasury Department Regulations

Regulations are issued by the U.S. Treasury Department under authority granted by Congress.[8] Usually interpretive by nature, they provide taxpayers with considerable guidance on the meaning and application of the Code and often include examples. Regulations carry considerable authority as the official interpretation of tax statutes. They are an important resource to consider in complying with the tax law.

Treasury Regulations are arranged in the same sequence as the Code. A number is added at the beginning, however, to indicate the type of tax or other matter to which they relate. For example, the prefix 1 designates the Regulations under the income tax law. Thus, the Regulations under Code § 2 would be cited as Reg. § 1.2, with subparts added for further identification. The numbering pattern of these subparts often has no correlation with the Code subsections. The prefix 20 designates estate tax Regulations, 25 addresses gift tax Regulations, 31 relates to employment taxes, and 301 refers to procedure and administration. This list is not all-inclusive. Reg. § 1.351–1(a)(2) is an example of such a citation.

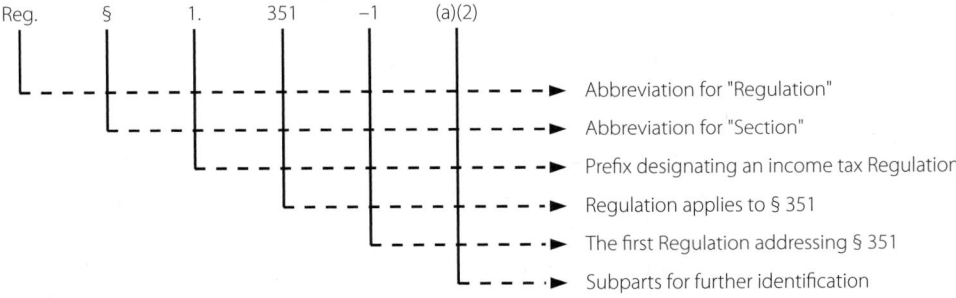

New Regulations and changes in existing Regulations usually are issued in proposed form before they are finalized. The interval between the proposal of a Regulation and its finalization permits taxpayers and other interested parties to comment on the propriety of the proposal. These comments usually are provided in writing, but oral comments can be offered at hearings held by the IRS on the Regulations in question pursuant to a public notice. This practice of notice-and-comment is a major distinction between Regulations and other forms of Treasury guidance such as Revenue Rulings, Revenue Procedures, and the like.

Proposed Regulations under Code § 2, for example, are cited as Prop.Reg. § 1.2. The Tax Court indicates that Proposed Regulations carry little weight in the litigation process.[9]

The Treasury Department issues **Temporary Regulations** relating to matters where immediate guidance is important. These Regulations are issued without the comment period required for Proposed Regulations. Temporary Regulations have the same authoritative value as final Regulations and may be cited as precedents. However, Temporary Regulations also are issued as Proposed Regulations and automatically expire within three years after the date of their issuance.[10]

Proposed, Temporary, and **Final Regulations** are published in the *Federal Register*, the *Internal Revenue Bulletin*, and major tax services.

---

[8]§ 7805.

[9]*F. W. Woolworth Co.*, 54 T.C. 1233 (1970); *Harris M. Miller*, 70 T.C. 448 (1978); and *James O. Tomerlin Trust*, 87 T.C. 876 (1986).

[10]§ 7805(e).

EXHIBIT 2.3	Administrative Sources	

Source	Locations (Selected)	Authority
Regulations	*Federal Register* *Internal Revenue Bulletin*	Force and effect of law. May be cited as precedent.
Temporary Regulations	*Federal Register* *Internal Revenue Bulletin*	May be cited as a precedent.
Proposed Regulations	*Federal Register* *Internal Revenue Bulletin*	Preview of final Regulations. Not yet a precedent.
Revenue Rulings Revenue Procedures Treasury Decisions Actions on Decisions	*Internal Revenue Bulletin*	IRS interpretation only. Weak precedent.
Determination Letters Technical Advice Memoranda	Tax Analysts' *Tax Notes* Thomson Reuters *Checkpoint* Commerce Clearing House *IntelliConnect*	IRS interpretation only. Weak precedent.
Letter Rulings	Thomson Reuters and CCH tax services	Applicable only to taxpayer addressed. May not be cited as precedent.

Regulations may also be classified as *legislative, interpretive,* or *procedural.* This classification scheme is discussed later in the chapter.

Revenue Rulings and Revenue Procedures

Revenue Rulings are official pronouncements of the National Office of the IRS.[11] Like Regulations, they are designed to provide interpretation of the tax law. However, they do not carry the same legal force and effect as Regulations and usually deal with more restricted problems. In addition, Regulations are approved by the Secretary of the Treasury, whereas Revenue Rulings generally are not.

Both Revenue Rulings and Revenue Procedures serve an important function in providing *guidance* to IRS personnel and taxpayers in handling routine tax matters. Revenue Rulings and Revenue Procedures generally apply retroactively and may be revoked or modified by subsequent rulings or procedures, Regulations, legislation, or court decisions.

Revenue Rulings typically provide one or more examples of how the IRS would apply a law to specific fact situations. Revenue Rulings may arise from technical advice memoranda of the IRS, court decisions, suggestions from tax practitioner groups, and various tax publications. A Revenue Ruling also may arise from a specific taxpayer's request for a letter ruling. If the IRS believes that a taxpayer's request for a letter ruling deserves official publication due to its widespread effect, the letter ruling is converted into a Revenue Ruling and issued for the information and guidance of taxpayers, tax professionals, and IRS personnel. Names, identifying descriptions, and money amounts are changed to conceal the identity of the requesting taxpayer.

Revenue Procedures are issued in the same manner as Revenue Rulings, but deal with the internal management practices and procedures of the IRS. Familiarity with these procedures increases taxpayer compliance and helps make the administration of the tax laws more efficient.

---

[11] § 7805(a).

Some recent Revenue Procedures dealt with the following matters.

- Procedures for issuing determination letters on the qualified status of employee pension plans.
- Procedures for requesting a filing date extension when electing S corporation status.
- Inflation-adjusted amounts for various Code provisions.

Revenue Rulings and Revenue Procedures are published weekly by the U.S. Government in the *Internal Revenue Bulletin* (I.R.B.).

The proper form for citing Revenue Rulings is as follows. Revenue Procedures are cited in the same manner, except that "Rev.Proc." is substituted for "Rev.Rul."

Rev.Rul. 2015–9, 2015–21 I.R.B. 972.

Explanation: Revenue Ruling Number 9, beginning at page 972 of the 21st weekly issue of the *Internal Revenue Bulletin* for 2015.

Revenue Rulings and other tax resources may be found at the IRS website **www.irs.gov**.[12]

Letter Rulings

Letter rulings are issued for a fee upon a taxpayer's request. They describe how the IRS will treat a *proposed* transaction for tax purposes. Letter rulings can be useful for taxpayers who want to be certain of how a transaction will be taxed before proceeding with it. Letter rulings allow taxpayers to avoid unexpected tax costs.

Requesting a ruling can be quite cumbersome, although it sometimes is the most effective way to carry out tax planning. The IRS limits the issuance of letter rulings to restricted, pre-announced areas of taxation; it generally will not rule on situations that are fact-intensive. Thus, a ruling may not be obtained on many of the problems that are particularly troublesome to taxpayers.[13]

The IRS makes letter rulings available for public inspection after identifying details are deleted.[14] Published digests of private letter rulings are found in Bloomberg BNA's *Daily Tax Reports* and Tax Analysts' *Tax Notes. IRS Letter Rulings Reports* (published by Commerce Clearing House) contains both digests and full texts of all letter rulings. In addition, computerized databases of letter rulings are available through several commercial publishers.

Letter rulings are issued multidigit file numbers that indicate the year and week of issuance as well as the number of the ruling during that week. Consider, for example, Ltr.Rul. 201503010, examining whether an entity is to be classified as a real estate investment trust.

2015	03	010
Year 2015	3rd week of 2015	10th ruling issued during the 3rd week

Other Administrative Pronouncements

Treasury Decisions (TDs) are issued by the Treasury Department to promulgate new Regulations, amend or otherwise change existing Regulations, or announce the position of the Government on selected court decisions. Like Revenue Rulings and Revenue Procedures, TDs are published in the *Internal Revenue Bulletin*.

---

[12]Commercial sources for Revenue Rulings and Revenue Procedures are available, usually requiring a subscription fee. Older Revenue Rulings and Revenue Procedures usually were cited as being published in the *Cumulative Bulletin* (C.B.) rather than the *Internal Revenue Bulletin* (I.R.B.).

[13]The first *Internal Revenue Bulletin* issued each year contains a list of areas in which the IRS will not issue advance rulings. This list may be modified throughout the year. See, for example, Rev.Proc. 2016–3, 2016–1 I.R.B. 126.

[14]§ 6110(c).

The IRS publishes other administrative communications in the *Internal Revenue Bulletin*, such as Announcements, Notices, Proposed Regulations, Termination of Exempt Organization Status, Practitioner Disciplinary Actions, and Prohibited Transaction Exemptions.

Like letter rulings, **determination letters** are issued at the request of taxpayers and provide guidance on the application of the tax law. They differ from letter rulings in that the issuing source is an IRS executive, rather than the National Office of the IRS. Further, determination letters usually involve *completed* (as opposed to proposed) transactions. Determination letters are not published regularly, and they are released officially only to the party making the request.

Difference between Letter Rulings and Determination Letters

EXAMPLE 1

The shareholders of Red Corporation and Green Corporation want assurance that the consolidation of their corporations into Blue Corporation will be a nontaxable reorganization. The proper approach is to ask the National Office of the IRS to issue a letter ruling concerning the income tax effect of the proposed transaction.

EXAMPLE 2

Chris operates a salon in which he employs eight barbers. To comply with the rules governing income tax and payroll tax withholdings, Chris wants to know whether the barbers working for him are employees or independent contractors. The proper procedure is to request a determination letter on their status from the IRS.

The National Office of the IRS releases **Technical Advice Memoranda (TAMs)** weekly. TAMs resemble letter rulings in that they give the IRS's determination of an issue. Letter rulings, however, are responses to requests by taxpayers, whereas TAMs are issued by the National Office of the IRS in response to questions raised by IRS field personnel during audits. TAMs deal with completed rather than proposed transactions and often are requested for questions relating to exempt organizations and employee plans.[15]

 DIGGING DEEPER 1 | **In-depth coverage can be found on this book's companion website: www.cengagebrain.com**

2-1c Judicial Sources of the Tax Law

After a taxpayer has exhausted some or all of the remedies available within the IRS (no satisfactory settlement has been reached at the agent level or at the Appeals Division level), a dispute can be taken to the Federal courts. The dispute first is considered by a **court of original jurisdiction** (known as a trial court), with any appeal (either by the taxpayer or the IRS) taken to the appropriate appellate court. In most situations, the taxpayer has a choice of four trial courts: a **District Court**, the **Court of Federal Claims**, the **Tax Court**, or the **Small Cases Division** of the Tax Court. The court system for Federal tax litigation is illustrated in Exhibit 2.4.

The broken line between the Tax Court and the Small Cases Division indicates that there is no appeal from the Small Cases Division, by either party to the case. Decisions from the Small Cases Division have no precedential value. Some of these cases are found on the U.S. Tax Court website. They may not be relied upon by other taxpayers, or even by the taxpayer itself in subsequent years. The jurisdiction of the

---

[15]Determination letters and technical advice memoranda may constitute substantial authority for purposes of the § 6662 accuracy-related penalty. Notice 90–20, 1990–1 C.B. 328.

EXHIBIT 2.4	**Federal Judicial System**

* No appeal from this court.

Small Cases Division is limited to cases involving tax, interest, and penalty amounts of $50,000 or less.

In-depth coverage can be found on this book's companion website: www.cengagebrain.com

2 DIGGING DEEPER

Knowledge of several terms is important in understanding court decisions. The plaintiff is the party requesting action in a court, and the defendant is the party against whom the suit is brought. Sometimes a court uses the terms *petitioner* and *respondent*. In general, *petitioner* is a synonym for *plaintiff*, and *respondent* is a synonym for *defendant*. At the trial court level, a taxpayer usually is the plaintiff (or petitioner), and the government is the defendant (or respondent). If the taxpayer wins and the Government appeals as the new petitioner (or appellant), the taxpayer now is the respondent.

Trial Courts

The differences among the various trial courts (courts of original jurisdiction) can be summarized as follows.

- *Number of courts.* There is only one Court of Federal Claims and only one Tax Court, but there are many District Courts. The taxpayer does not select the District Court that will hear the dispute, but must sue in the one that has jurisdiction where the taxpayer resides.

- *Number of judges.* A case tried in a District Court is heard before only 1 judge. The Court of Federal Claims has 16 judges, and the Tax Court has 19 regular judges. The entire Tax Court, however, reviews a case (the case is heard *en banc*), thereby taking on a more compelling authority, when important or novel tax issues are involved. Most cases, though, are heard and decided by only 1 of the 19 regular judges.

- *Location.* The Court of Federal Claims meets most often in Washington, D.C., while a District Court meets at a prescribed seat for the particular district. Each state has at least one District Court, and the more populous states have more than one District Court. Choosing the District Court usually minimizes the inconvenience and expense of traveling for the taxpayer and his or her counsel. The Tax Court is based in Washington, D.C., but its judges regularly travel to different parts of the country and hear cases at predetermined locations and dates. This procedure eases the distance problem for the taxpayer, but it can mean a delay before the case comes to trial.

• *Jurisdiction of the Court of Federal Claims.* The Court of Federal Claims has jurisdiction over any claim against the United States that is based upon the Constitution, any Act of Congress, or any Regulation of an executive department. Thus, the Court of Federal Claims hears nontax litigation as well as tax cases.

• *Jurisdiction of the Tax Court and District Courts.* The Tax Court hears only tax cases and is the most frequently used forum for tax cases. The District Courts hear a wide variety of nontax cases, including drug crimes and other Federal violations, as well as tax cases. For this reason, some people suggest that the Tax Court has more expertise in tax matters.

• *Jury trial.* The only court in which a taxpayer can obtain a jury trial is a District Court. Juries can decide only questions of fact and not questions of law. If a jury trial is not elected, the judge decides all issues. A District Court decision applies only in the district in which the court has jurisdiction.

• *Payment of deficiency.* Before the Court of Federal Claims or a District Court can have jurisdiction, the taxpayer must pay the tax deficiency assessed by the IRS and then sue for a refund. If the taxpayer wins (assuming no successful appeal by the Government), the tax paid plus appropriate interest is recovered. Jurisdiction in the Tax Court, however, usually is obtained without first paying the assessed tax deficiency.

 DIGGING DEEPER 3 | In-depth coverage can be found on this book's companion website: www.cengagebrain.com

• *Appeals.* Appeals from a District Court or a Tax Court decision go to the Court of Appeals for the circuit in which the taxpayer resides. Appeals from the Court of Federal Claims go to the Court of Appeals for the Federal Circuit. Few Tax Court cases are appealed, and when appeals are made, most are filed by the taxpayer rather than the IRS.

• *Bankruptcy.* When a taxpayer files a bankruptcy petition, the IRS, like other creditors, is prevented from taking action against the taxpayer. Sometimes a bankruptcy court settles a tax claim.

For a summary of several attributes of the Federal trial courts, see Concept Summary 2.1.

Concept Summary 2.1

Federal Judicial System: Trial Courts

Issue	Tax Court	District Court	Court of Federal Claims
Number of judges per court	19	1 per case	16
Payment of deficiency before trial	No	Yes	Yes
Jury trial available	No	Yes	No
Types of dispute	Tax cases only	Mostly criminal and civil issues	Claims against the United States
Jurisdiction	Nationwide	Location of taxpayer	Nationwide
IRS acquiescence policy	Yes	Yes	Yes
Appeal is to	U.S. Court of Appeals	U.S. Court of Appeals	Court of Appeals for the Federal Circuit

Appellate Courts

The losing party can appeal a trial court decision to a **Circuit Court of Appeals**. The 11 geographic circuits, the circuit for the District of Columbia, and the Federal Circuit[16] are shown in Exhibit 2.5.

Process and Outcomes If the government loses at the trial court level (District Court, Tax Court, or Court of Federal Claims), it need not (and frequently does not) appeal. The fact that an appeal is not made, however, does not indicate that the IRS agrees with the result and will not litigate similar issues in the future. The IRS may decide not to appeal for a number of reasons. First, its current litigation load may be heavy. As a consequence, the IRS may decide that available personnel should be assigned to other more important cases. Second, the IRS may not appeal for strategic reasons. For example, the taxpayer may be in a sympathetic position, or the facts may be particularly strong in his or her favor. In that event, the IRS may wait for a weaker case to test the legal issues involved. Third, if the appeal is from a District Court or the Tax Court, the Court of Appeals of jurisdiction could have some bearing on whether the IRS decides to pursue an appeal. Based on past experience and precedent, the IRS may conclude that the chance for success on a particular issue might be more promising in another Court of Appeals. If so, the IRS will wait for a similar case to arise in a different jurisdiction.

The role of appellate courts is limited to a review of the record of the case that was compiled by the trial courts. Thus, the appellate process usually involves a determination of whether the trial court applied the proper law in arriving at its decision, rather than a consideration of the trial court's factual findings.

EXHIBIT 2.5	The Federal District Courts and Circuit Courts of Appeals

ADMINISTRATIVE OFFICE OF THE UNITED STATES SUPREME COURT
APRIL 1988

---

[16]The Court of Appeals for the Federal Circuit hears decisions appealed from the Court of Federal Claims.

An appeal can have any of a number of possible outcomes. The appellate court may let stand (affirm) or overturn (reverse) the lower court's finding, or it may send the case back for further consideration (remand). When many issues are involved, a mixed result is not unusual. Thus, the lower court may be affirmed (*aff'd.*) on Issue A and reversed (*rev'd.*) on Issue B, while Issue C is remanded (*rem'd.*) for additional fact finding.

When more than one judge is involved in the decision-making process, disagreements are not uncommon. In addition to the majority view, one or more judges may concur (agree with the result reached but not with some or all of the reasoning) or dissent (disagree with the result). In any one case, the majority view controls. But concurring and dissenting views can influence other courts or, at some subsequent date when the composition of the court has changed, even when involving the same court.

Other Rules and Strategies   The Federal Circuit at the appellate level provides a taxpayer with an alternative forum to the Court of Appeals of his or her home circuit. When a particular circuit has issued an adverse decision for a case that is similar in facts, the taxpayer may prefer the Court of Federal Claims, because any appeal will be to the Court of Appeals for the Federal Circuit.

District Courts, the Tax Court, and the Court of Federal Claims must abide by the `precedents` set by the Court of Appeals of their jurisdiction. A particular Court of Appeals need not follow the decisions of another Court of Appeals. All courts, however, must follow decisions of the `Supreme Court` .

This pattern of appellate precedents raises an issue for the Tax Court. Because the Tax Court is a national court, it decides cases from all parts of the country. Appeals from its decisions, however, go to all of the Courts of Appeals except the Court of Appeals for the Federal Circuit. Accordingly, identical Tax Court cases might be appealed to different circuits with different results. As a result of *Golsen*,[17] the Tax Court will not follow its own precedents in a subsequent case if the Court of Appeals with jurisdiction over the taxpayer in question has previously reversed the Tax Court on the specific issue at hand.

EXAMPLE 3	Emily lives in Texas and sues in the Tax Court on Issue A. The Fifth Circuit Court of Appeals is the appellate court with jurisdiction. The Fifth Circuit already has decided, in a case involving similar facts but a different taxpayer, that Issue A should be resolved against the Government. Although the Tax Court maintains that the Fifth Circuit is wrong, under its *Golsen* policy, it will render judgment for Emily.

Shortly thereafter, in a comparable case, Rashad, a resident of New York, sues in the Tax Court on Issue A. The Second Circuit Court of Appeals, the appellate court with jurisdiction in New York, never has expressed itself on Issue A. Presuming that the Tax Court has not reconsidered its position on Issue A, it will decide against Rashad.

Thus, it is possible for two taxpayers suing in the same court to end up with opposite results merely because they live in different parts of the country.

Appeal to the Supreme Court is not automatic. One applies to be heard via a `Writ of Certiorari` . If the Court agrees to hear the case, it will grant the Writ (*Cert. granted*). Most often, it declines to hear the case (*Cert. denied*). In fact, the Supreme Court rarely hears tax cases. The Court usually grants certiorari to resolve a conflict among the Courts of Appeals (e.g., two or more appellate courts have opposing positions on a particular issue) or where the tax issue is extremely important. The granting of a *Writ of Certiorari* indicates that at least four of the nine members of the Supreme Court believe that the issue is of sufficient importance to be heard by the full Court.

---

[17] *Jack E. Golsen*, 54 T.C. 742 (1970).

Judicial Citations

Court decisions are an important source of tax law. The ability to locate a case and to cite it is a must in working with the tax law. Judicial citations usually follow a standard pattern: case name, volume number, reporter series, page or paragraph number, court (where necessary), and year of decision.

Judicial Citations—The Tax Court The Tax Court issues two types of decisions: Regular and Memorandum. The Chief Judge decides whether the opinion is issued as a Regular or Memorandum decision. The distinction between the two involves both substance and form. In terms of substance, *Memorandum* decisions deal with situations necessitating only the application of already established principles of law. *Regular* decisions involve novel issues of the tax law that have not previously been resolved by the court. In actual practice, however, this distinction is not always so clear. Be that as it may, both Regular and Memorandum decisions represent the position of the Tax Court and, as such, can be relied on by others.

Regular and Memorandum decisions issued by the Tax Court also differ in form. Memorandum decisions are not published officially, while Regular decisions are published by the U.S. Government in a series called *Tax Court of the United States Reports* (T.C.). Each volume of these *Reports* covers a six-month period (January 1 through June 30 and July 1 through December 31) and is given a succeeding volume number. But there is usually a time lag between the date a decision is rendered and the date it appears in official form. A temporary citation often is used to help the researcher locate a recent Regular decision. Consider, for example, the temporary and permanent citations for *MoneyGram International, Inc. and Subsidiaries*, a decision filed on January 7, 2015.

Temporary Citation ⎰ *MoneyGram International, Inc. and Subsidiaries*, 144 T.C. ___, No. 1 (2015).
⎱ *Explanation:* Page number left blank because not yet known.

Permanent Citation ⎰ *MoneyGram International, Inc. and Subsidiaries*, 144 T.C. 1 (2015).
⎱ *Explanation:* Page number now available.

The temporary citation tells us that the case ultimately will appear in Volume 144 of the *Tax Court of the United States Reports*. Until this volume becomes available to the general public, however, the page number is left blank. Instead, the temporary citation identifies the case as being the 1st Regular decision issued by the Tax Court since Volume 143 ended. With this information, the decision easily can be located at the Tax Court website or in the Tax Court services published by Commerce Clearing House (CCH) and Thomson Reuters *Checkpoint*. Once Volume 144 is released, the permanent citation is substituted, and the number of the case is dropped. Regular decisions and Memorandum decisions are published and searchable at **www.ustaxcourt.gov**.

Before 1943, the Tax Court was called the Board of Tax Appeals, and its decisions were published as the *United States Board of Tax Appeals Reports* (B.T.A.). These 47 volumes cover the period from 1924 to 1942. For example, the citation *Karl Pauli*, 11 B.T.A. 784 (1928) refers to the 11th volume of the *Board of Tax Appeals Reports*, page 784, issued in 1928.

If the IRS loses a decision, it may indicate whether it agrees or disagrees with the results reached by the court by publishing an **acquiescence** ("A" or "*Acq.*") or **nonacquiescence** ("NA" or "*Nonacq.*"), respectively.

The acquiescence or nonacquiescence is published in the *Internal Revenue Bulletin* as an *Action on Decision*. After the announcement is made by the IRS, the acquiescence status of the case is added to the citation for the decision. Examples of such announcements include A.O.D. 2012-007, 2013-25 I.R.B. (an acquiescence), and A.O.D. 2014-001, 2014-38 I.R.B. (a nonacquiescence). The IRS can revoke an acquiescence retroactively.

DIGGING DEEPER 4   In-depth coverage can be found on this book's companion website: www.cengagebrain.com

As noted earlier, Memorandum decisions are found at **www.ustaxcourt.gov**. Memorandum decisions also are published by CCH and Thomson Reuters. Consider, for example, the ways that a Tax Court Memorandum case can be cited.

> *Nick R. Hughes*, T.C.Memo. 2009–94.
> *Explanation:* The 94th Memorandum decision issued by the Tax Court in 2009.

> *Nick R. Hughes*, 97 TCM 1488 (2009).
> *Explanation:* Page 1488 of Volume 97 of the CCH *Tax Court Memorandum Decisions.*

The second citation requires a parenthetical reference to the year in which the case was published. The first citation does do not need this reference, as the publication date is included elsewhere in the citation.

The citation to a decision changes when the IRS issues an acquiescence or a nonacquiescence. For example, a proper citation appears as follows for a case after the A.O.D. is issued.

> *Estate of Martinez*, T.C.Memo. 2004-1501, *nonacq.*, A.O.D. 2015-001.

U.S. Tax Court Summary Opinions relate to decisions of the Tax Court's Small Cases Division. These opinions are published commercially, and on the U.S. Tax Court website, with the warning that they may not be treated as precedent for any other case. For example, a Small Cases decision can be cited as follows.

> *Darrel W. Wyatt*, T.C. Summary Opinion 2015–31 (April 20, 2015).

Judicial Citations—The District Courts, Court of Federal Claims, and Courts of Appeals District Court, Court of Federal Claims, and Court of Appeals decisions dealing with Federal tax matters are reported in both the *U.S. Tax Cases* (USTC) and the *American Federal Tax Reports* (AFTR) series.

District Court decisions, dealing with *both* tax and nontax issues, are also published in the *Federal Supplement Series* (F.Supp.). Volume 999, published in 1998, was the last volume of the Federal Supplement Series. The *Federal Supplement Second Series* (F.Supp.2d) now is used. A District Court case can be cited in three different forms.

> *Turner v. U.S.*, 2004–1 USTC ¶60,478 (D.Ct. N.Tex.).
>
> *Explanation:* Reported in the first volume of the *U.S. Tax Cases* (USTC) for calendar year 2004 (2004–1) and located at paragraph 60,478 (¶60,478).

> *Turner v. U.S.*, 93 AFTR 2d 2004–686 (D.Ct. N.Tex.).
>
> *Explanation:* Reported in the 93rd volume of the second series of the *American Federal Tax Reports* (AFTR 2d) beginning on page 686.

> *Turner v. U.S.*, 306 F.Supp.2d 668 (D.Ct. N.Tex., 2004).
>
> *Explanation:* Reported in the 306th volume of the *Federal Supplement Second Series* (F.Supp.2d) beginning on page 668. The date reference is needed, as it is not found elsewhere in the citation.

In all of the preceding citations, the names of both of the parties to the case are listed. This is a common practice in virtually all legal citations, with the name of the plaintiff or petitioner listed first. But in a Tax Court citation, because all such cases are brought by the taxpayer, no reference to the government is needed (i.e., "*v. Commissioner*" is omitted).

Decisions of the Courts of Appeals are published in the USTCs, the AFTRs, and the *Federal Second Series* (F.2d). Volume 999, published in 1993, was the last volume of the *Federal Second Series*. The *Federal Third Series* (F.3d) now is used. Decisions of the Court of Federal Claims are published in the USTCs, the AFTRs, and the *Claims Court Reporter* (abbreviated as Cl.Ct.).

Gribauskas is a decision rendered by the Second Circuit Court of Appeals in 2003 (CA–2, 2003), while *Apollo Computer, Inc.* was issued by the Court of Federal Claims in 1994 (Fed.Cl., 1994), but not published in the USTC until 1995.

In-depth coverage can be found on this book's companion website: www.cengagebrain.com **5 DIGGING DEEPER**

Judicial Citations—The Supreme Court Like all other Federal tax decisions (except those rendered by the Tax Court), Supreme Court decisions dealing with Federal tax matters are published in the USTCs and in the AFTRs. The U.S. Government Printing Office publishes all Supreme Court decisions in the *United States Supreme Court Reports* (U.S.). Such decisions also are found in the *Supreme Court Reporter* (S.Ct.) and the *United States Reports, Lawyer's Edition* (L.Ed.).

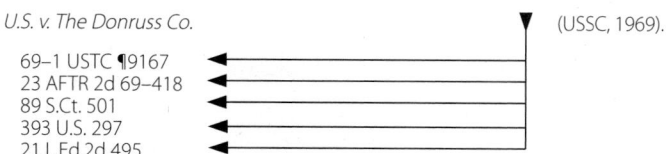

The parenthetical reference (USSC, 1969) identifies the decision as having been rendered by the U.S. Supreme Court in 1969. In this text, the citations of Supreme Court decisions are limited to the USTC, AFTR, and S.Ct. versions.

LO.2

Locate and work with the tax law and explain the tax research process.

2-2 WORKING WITH THE TAX LAW—TAX RESEARCH

Tax research is undertaken to determine the best available solution to a situation that has tax consequences. In the case of a completed transaction, the objective of the research is to determine the tax result of what has already taken place. For example, is the expenditure incurred by the taxpayer deductible or not deductible for tax purposes? When dealing with proposed transactions, tax research is concerned with the determination of possible alternative tax consequences to facilitate effective tax planning.

Tax research involves the following procedures.

- Identifying and refining the problem.
- Locating the appropriate tax law sources.
- Assessing the tax law sources.
- Arriving at the solution or at alternative solutions while giving due consideration to nontax factors.
- Effectively communicating the solution to the taxpayer or the taxpayer's representative.
- Following up on the solution (where appropriate) in light of new developments.

This process is depicted schematically in Exhibit 2.6. The broken lines indicate steps of particular interest when tax research is directed toward proposed, rather than completed, transactions.

EXHIBIT 2.6   Tax Research Process

2-2a **Identifying the Problem**

Problem identification starts with a compilation of the relevant facts involved. In this regard, *all* of the facts that may have a bearing on the problem must be gathered, as any omission could modify the solution reached. To illustrate, consider what appears to be a very simple problem.

EXAMPLE

4

In reviewing their tax and financial situation, Joan and Richard, a married couple, notice that Joan's investment in Airways stock has declined from its purchase price of $8,000 to a current market value of $5,500. Joan wants to sell this stock now and claim the $2,500 loss ($5,500 value − $8,000 cost) as a deduction this year. Richard, however, believes that Airways will yet prosper and does not want to part with the stock. Their daughter Margaret suggests that they sell the Airways stock to Maple, Inc., a corporation owned equally by Joan and Richard. That way, they can claim the deduction this year but still hold the stock through their corporation. Will this suggestion work?

2-2b **Refining the Problem**

Joan and Richard in Example 4 face three choices.

1. Sell the Airways stock through their regular investment broker and get a deduction in the current year (Joan's plan).
2. Continue to hold the Airways stock (Richard's plan).
3. Sell the Airways stock to a corporation owned 50–50 by Joan and Richard (Margaret's suggestion).

The tax consequences of plans (1) and (2) are clear, but the question that Joan and Richard want to resolve is whether plan (3) will work as anticipated. Refining the problem further, can shareholders deduct a loss from the sale of an asset to a corporation that they control? Section 267(a)(1) indicates that losses from the sale of property between persons specified in § 267(b) are not deductible. This subsection lists 12 different relationships, including in § 267(b)(2): "an individual and a corporation more than 50 percent in value of the outstanding stock of which is owned, directly or indirectly, by or for such individual."

Thus, if Joan and Richard each own 50 percent of Maple, neither owns *more than* 50 percent, as § 267(b) requires. Accordingly, the loss disallowance rule would not apply to Joan, and Margaret's suggestion would appear to be sound.

The language of the statute, however, indicates that any stock owned *directly or indirectly* by an individual is counted toward the 50 percent test. Might Richard's stock be considered owned "indirectly" by Joan? Further research is necessary.

Section 267(c) contains rules for determining "constructive ownership of stock," or when stock owned by one person will be attributed to someone else. One of the rules in this subsection declares that an individual is considered to own any stock that is owned by that person's *family*, and family is defined in § 267(c)(4) as including a person's *spouse*, among others.

Therefore, Richard's Maple stock will be attributed to Joan, so that Joan is treated as owning all of the stock of Maple, Inc. As a result, § 267(a) would indeed apply, and no loss would be deductible if Joan sells the Airways stock to Maple. In short, we must conclude that Margaret's suggestion will not work.

2-2c **Locating the Appropriate Tax Law Sources**

Once the problem is clearly defined, what is the next step? While it is a matter of individual judgment, most tax research begins with a keyword search using an online tax service. If the problem is not complex, the researcher may bypass the tax service and turn directly to the Internal Revenue Code and the Treasury Regulations. For the beginner, the latter procedure saves time and solves many of the more basic problems. If the researcher does not have a personal copy of the Code or Regulations, access to the

BRIDGE DISCIPLINE   Bridge to Business Law

U.S. income tax laws change daily by the action of Congress, tax administrators, and the courts. This process matches the three-branch structure of the rest of the government, with the legislative, executive, and judicial branches each having a say in making tax law. But this distinction among the functions of government is perhaps less clear when it involves the tax law.

- Presidential vetoes of tax legislation are rare.

- The Tax Court is a creation of the Congress in the Internal Revenue Code, not of the U.S. Constitution.

- The cost of tax litigation and the time it takes for a case to work its way through the judicial system render the courts unavailable to most taxpayers.

Under the U.S. Constitution, legislation involving government revenues must start in the House of Representatives. This provision likely was included so that the public would have greater control over those who want greater access to their pocketbooks. Several recent pieces of tax legislation, though, have been initiated as bills in the Senate. And most bills introduced in both houses of Congress are required to be "revenue-neutral" (i.e., they must include provisions by which the legislation's new programs will be paid for). In both houses, this has resulted in amendments to the Internal Revenue Code being attached to legislation involving clean air and water standards, child care programs, and product import and export limitations.

In a few cases, the courts considered a taxpayer challenge to the way that specific tax legislation was crafted. But so far the courts have failed to overturn any tax provisions solely because they were initiated outside of the House and its committee processes. The courts' rationale for this seemingly unconstitutional position is that (1) the House and its committees heard a full discussion of the proposal and (2) too much time has passed since adoption of the legislation to easily unwind it and undertake a refund procedure.

appropriate volume(s) of a tax service or an online service is necessary.[18] A partial list of the major tax services and their publishers are:

CCH IntelliConnect, Commerce Clearing House. Includes the *Standard Federal Tax Reporter*.

Thomson Reuters Checkpoint, Research Institute of America. Includes RIA's *Federal Tax Coordinator 2d*.

Parker Tax Pro Library, formerly Kleinrock *Tax Expert*.

Tax Management Portfolios, Bloomberg BNA.

Westlaw services, Thomson Reuters. Includes access to *Tax Management Portfolios* and *Federal Tax Coordinator 2d*.

TaxCenter, LexisNexis, primary law sources and various materials taken from CCH, Kleinrock, and Bloomberg BNA.

Federal Research Library, Tax Analysts (a nonprofit organization), primary law sources including treaties, with newsletters and commentaries.

DIGGING DEEPER 6   In-depth coverage can be found on this book's companion website: www.cengagebrain.com

Tax Services

In this text, it is not feasible to explain the use of any particular tax service—this ability can be obtained with further study and professional experience. However, several important observations about the use of tax services cannot be overemphasized. First, always check for current developments. Online tax services are updated several times a day, and tax newsletters often feature highlights of recent tax law developments. Second, there is no substitute for the original source. Do not base a conclusion solely on a tax service's commentary. If a Code Section, Regulation, or case is vital to the research, read it.

---

[18]Several of the major tax services publish paperback editions of the Code and Treasury Regulations that can be purchased at modest prices. These editions are usually revised twice each year. For an annotated and abridged version of the Code and Regulations that is published annually, see Mark Altieri, *South-Western Federal Taxation: Internal Revenue Code of 1986 and Treasury Regulations: Annotated and Selected* (Cengage Learning, 2017).

Tax Commentary

Various tax publications are another source of relevant information. The use of tax editorial commentary in these publications often can shorten the research time needed to resolve a tax issue. If an article or a posting is relevant to the issue at hand, it may provide the references needed to locate the primary sources of the tax law that apply (e.g., citations to judicial decisions, Regulations, and other IRS pronouncements). Thus, the researcher obtains a "running start" in arriving at a solution to the problem.

The following are some of the more useful tax publications.

Journal of Taxation
Journal of International Taxation
Practical Tax Strategies
Estate Planning
Corporate Taxation
Business Entities
Taxation of Exempts
Real Estate Taxation
ria.thomsonreuters.com/journals

The Tax Executive
www.tei.org

The Tax Adviser
aicpa.org/pubs/taxadv

The Tax Lawyer
www.law.georgetown.edu/journals/tax

The ATA Journal of Legal Tax Research
aaajournals.org/loi/jltr

Trusts and Estates
wealthmanagement.com/te-home

Journal of Passthrough Entities
TAXES—The Tax Magazine
tax.cchgroup.com/books

Tax Notes
taxanalysts.com

2-2d Assessing Tax Law Sources

Once a source has been located, the next step is to assess it in light of the problem at hand. Proper assessment involves careful interpretation of the tax law and consideration of its relevance and significance.

Interpreting the Internal Revenue Code

The language of the Code often is difficult to comprehend fully. Contrary to many people's suspicions, the Code is not written deliberately to confuse its readers. Nevertheless, it often has that effect. The Code is intended to apply to more than 320 million citizens, most of whom are willing to exploit any linguistic imprecision to their benefit—to find a "loophole," in popular parlance. Moreover, many of the Code's provisions are limitations or restrictions involving two or more variables. Expressing such concepts algebraically would be more direct; using words to accomplish this task instead is often quite cumbersome.

Nevertheless, the Code is the governing law, the only source of tax law (other than treaties) that has received the actual approval of Congress and the President. Accordingly, it is usually the first source to be consulted, and often it is the only source needed.

Assessing the Significance of a Treasury Regulation

Treasury Regulations are the official interpretation of the Code and are entitled to great deference. Occasionally, however, a court will invalidate a Regulation or a portion thereof on the grounds that the Regulation is contrary to the intent of Congress. Usually, courts do not question the validity of Regulations because of the belief that "the first administrative interpretation of a provision as it appears in a new act often expresses the general understanding of the times or the actual understanding of those who played an important part when the statute was drafted."[19]

---

[19]*Augustus v. Comm.*, 41–1 USTC ¶9255, 26 AFTR 612, 118 F.2d 38 (CA–6, 1941).

Keep in mind the following observations when assessing the significance of a Regulation.

- IRS agents *must* give the Code and any related Regulations equal weight when dealing with taxpayers and their representatives.

- Proposed Regulations provide a preview of future final Regulations, but they are not binding on the IRS or taxpayers.

- In a challenge, the burden of proof is on the taxpayer to show that a Regulation varies from the language of the statute and has no support in the Committee Reports.

- Final Regulations can be classified as procedural, interpretive, or legislative. Procedural Regulations neither establish tax laws nor attempt to explain tax laws. Procedural Regulations often include procedural instructions, indicating information that taxpayers should provide the IRS, as well as information about the internal management and conduct of the IRS itself.

- Interpretive Regulations rephrase and elaborate what Congress stated in the Committee Reports that were issued when the tax legislation was enacted. If the language has gone through the public notice and comment procedures discussed earlier in the chapter, interpretive Regulations are *hard and solid* and almost impossible to overturn unless they do not clearly reflect the intent of Congress.

- In some Code Sections, Congress has given the *Treasury Secretary or a delegate* the specific authority to prescribe Regulations to carry out the details of administration or to otherwise create rules not included in the Code. Under such circumstances, Congress effectively is delegating its legislative powers to the Treasury Department. Regulations issued pursuant to this type of authority possess the force and effect of law and often are called Legislative Regulations (e.g., consolidated return Regulations).

DIGGING DEEPER 7   In-depth coverage can be found on this book's companion website: **www.cengagebrain.com**

Assessing the Significance of Other Administrative Sources of the Tax Law

Revenue Rulings issued by the IRS carry much less weight than Treasury Department Regulations. Revenue Rulings are important, however, in that they reflect the position of the IRS on tax matters. In any dispute with the IRS on the interpretation of tax law, taxpayers should expect agents to follow the results reached in applicable Revenue Rulings. It is not unusual, however, for courts to overturn Revenue Rulings as incorrect applications of the law to the facts presented.

The Big Picture

EXAMPLE

5

Return to the facts of *The Big Picture* on p. 2-1. Tax law involving the sale of investment assets is found largely in the Internal Revenue Code. The Samuels family will find incontrovertible law for these transactions in the Code.

Rules concerning dependency exemptions chiefly are found in Regulations, Revenue Rulings, and instructions to IRS forms. With respect to these tax law sources, the authority of each is less than that of the Code, and the Regulations carry much more weight than the form instructions.

Assessing the Significance of Judicial Sources of the Tax Law

The judicial process as it relates to the formulation of tax law has been described. How much reliance can be placed on a particular decision depends upon the following factors.

- *The level of the court.* A decision rendered by a trial court (e.g., a District Court) carries less weight than one issued by an appellate court (e.g., the Fifth Circuit Court of Appeals). Until Congress changes the Code, decisions by the U.S. Supreme Court represent the last word on any tax issue.

- *The legal residence of the taxpayer.* If, for example, a taxpayer lives in Texas, a decision of the Fifth Circuit Court of Appeals means more than one rendered by the Second Circuit Court of Appeals. This is the case because any appeal from a District Court or the Tax Court would be to the Fifth Circuit and not to the Second Circuit.

- *The type of decision.* A Tax Court Regular decision carries more weight than a Memorandum decision; the Tax Court does not consider Memorandum decisions to have precedential value.[20]

- *The weight of the decision.* A decision that is supported by cases from other courts carries more weight than a decision that is not supported by other cases.

- *Subsequent events.* Was the decision affirmed or overruled on appeal?

In connection with the last two factors, a citator is helpful to tax research.[21] A **citator** provides the history of a case, including the authority relied on (e.g., other judicial decisions) in reaching the result. Reviewing the references listed in the citator discloses whether the decision was appealed and, if so, with what result (e.g., affirmed, reversed, remanded). It also reveals other cases with the same or similar issues and how they were decided. Thus, a citator reflects on the validity of a case and may lead to other relevant judicial material. If one plans to rely on a judicial decision to any significant degree, "running" the case through a citator is imperative.

The Big Picture

EXAMPLE 6

Return to the facts of *The Big Picture* on p. 2-1. Assume that on the Samuels' joint return a dependency exemption is claimed for both Sam and Dana. The IRS challenges these exemptions after an audit. The likelihood of a successful challenge to the IRS's position in this dispute will turn on several factors.

- Was an appellate court ruling in their favor issued by the Federal circuit in which they live? If so, that decision is controlling law. If not and the Samuels' circuit has not ruled to the contrary on the issue but another circuit has ruled in their favor in a parallel case, the taxpayers could use that decision as support for their side of the argument.

- Assume that a Revenue Ruling also is found that supports the taxpayers' claim of the exemptions. But how long ago were the Revenue Ruling and appellate decision issued? A legal precedent generally is stronger if it was issued more recently.

- If the Samuels' circuit has ruled favorably, have other courts discussed the appellate court holding? Were those discussions favorable or unfavorable to the Samuels' position? The more courts that follow a holding and cite it favorably, the stronger the legal precedent of the holding. Information of this sort can be found by reviewing the case history of the decision or by consulting a citator.

Understanding Judicial Opinions

Reading judicial opinions can be more productive if certain conventions of usage are understood. Some courts, including the Tax Court, apply the terms *petitioner* and *respondent* to the plaintiff and defendant, respectively, particularly when the case does not involve an appellate proceeding. Appellate courts often use the terms *appellant* and *appellee* instead.

---

[20]*Severino R. Nico, Jr.*, 67 T.C. 647 (1977).

[21]The major citators are published by CCH, Thomson Reuters, WESTLAW, and Shepard's Citations, Inc.

It also is important to distinguish between a court's final determination, or *holding*, and passing comments made in the course of its opinion. These latter remarks, examples, and analogies, often collectively termed *dicta*, are not part of the court's conclusion and do not have precedential value. Nevertheless, they often facilitate one's understanding of the court's reasoning and can enable a tax adviser to better predict how the court might resolve some future tax case.

DIGGING DEEPER 8   In-depth coverage can be found on this book's companion website: www.cengagebrain.com

Assessing the Significance of Other Sources

Primary sources of tax law include the Constitution, legislative history materials (e.g., Committee Reports), statutes, treaties, Treasury Regulations, IRS pronouncements, and judicial decisions. In general, the IRS regards only primary sources as substantial authority. However, reference to *secondary materials* such as tax publications, treatises, legal opinions, and written determinations may be useful. In general, secondary sources do not constitute tax authority.

Although the statement that the IRS regards only primary sources as substantial authority is generally true, there is one exception. Substantial authority *for purposes of the accuracy-related penalty* in § 6662 includes a number of secondary materials (e.g., letter rulings).[22] "Authority" does not include conclusions reached in treatises, textbooks and Web postings by tax commentators, and written opinions rendered for compensation by tax professionals.

A letter ruling or determination letter can be relied upon *only* by the taxpayer to whom it is issued, except as noted previously with respect to the accuracy-related penalty.

DIGGING DEEPER 9   In-depth coverage can be found on this book's companion website: www.cengagebrain.com

2-2e Arriving at the Solution or at Alternative Solutions

Example 4 raises the question of whether taxpayers would be denied a loss deduction from the sale of stock to a corporation that they own. The solution depends, in part, on the relationship of the corporation's shareholders to each other. Because Richard and Joan are married to each other, § 267(c)(2) attributes Richard's Maple stock to Joan in applying the "more than 50 percent" test of § 267(b)(2). Accordingly, Joan and Maple, Inc., are considered related parties under § 267(a), and a sale between them does not produce a deductible loss. If Richard and Joan were not related to each other, the constructive stock ownership rules would not apply and a loss could be deducted on a sale by Joan to Maple.

If Maple, Inc., were a *partnership* instead of a corporation, § 267 would not apply.[23] However, a different Code Section, namely § 707, produces the same result: no deduction is allowed for the loss from a sale between a "more than 50 percent" partner and the partnership. This additional research prevents the couple from erroneously selling their Airways stock to a related partnership in hopes of obtaining a loss deduction from the sale. Accordingly, Joan still must sell the Airways stock to an unrelated party to deduct the loss.

Because Richard still wants to own Airways stock, he might consider purchasing new Airways Co. stock to replace the stock that Joan sells to the unrelated party. Additional research reveals that for the loss on the sale to be deductible, the "wash sale" rule requires that more than 30 days elapse between the purchase of the new stock and the sale of the old stock.[24] This rule applies to purchases and sales of *substantially identical*

---

[22]Reg. § 1.6661–3(b)(2).
[23]Reg. § 1.267(b)–1(b)(1).

[24]§ 1091.

stock or securities. As a result, to deduct the loss on the Airways stock, Richard either must wait more than 30 days after Joan sells the shares to buy new Airways stock or acquire stock in a different company at any time. This new company can even be in the same general business as Airways.[25]

2-2f Communicating Tax Research

Once the problem has been researched adequately, a memorandum, a letter, or a speech setting forth the result may need to be prepared. The form the communication takes could depend on a number of considerations. For example, does an employer or instructor recommend a particular procedure or format for tax research memos? Is the memo to be given directly to the client, or will it first go to the preparer's employer? If the communication is a speech, who is the audience? How long should one speak?[26] Whatever form it takes, a good research communication should contain the following elements.

LO.3

Communicate the results of the tax research process in a client letter and a tax file memorandum.

- A clear statement of the issue.
- In more complex situations, a short review of the fact pattern that raises the issue.
- A review of the pertinent tax law sources (e.g., Code, Regulations, Revenue Rulings, and judicial authority).
- Any assumptions made in arriving at the solution.
- The solution recommended and the logic or reasoning supporting it.
- The references consulted in the research process.

A memo to the tax file is a collection of thoughts resulting from a current tax research project. It is shared with others who have access to the memo files so that they do not need to duplicate the current work at a later date. The file memo is written by a tax professional, to be read by another tax professional, so it features citations in good form to the Code, Regulations, and other sources of the law, often hyperlinking directly to the underlying document. A file memo is organized so as to list the pertinent facts, open tax issues, a brief conclusion, and a discussion of the research findings and underlying tax logic. A file memo seldom exceeds two pages in length.

A letter to the client is written to convey the results of a research engagement and to identify the next steps for the taxpayer to consider. Because most clients have little knowledge or experience in working with tax source documents, citations typically are not used. If the recipient of the letter is a tax executive or other colleague, a more technical approach might be taken in the letter. The letter typically does not exceed a page or two, and it sometimes is supplemented with an attached spreadsheet or chart. It includes various social graces and any needed regulatory language.

Illustrations of the memo for the tax file and the client letter associated with Example 4 appear in Exhibits 2.7 and 2.8.

2-2g Following Up

Because tax research may involve a proposed (as opposed to a completed) transaction, a change in the tax law (legislative, administrative, or judicial) could alter the original conclusion. Additional research may be necessary to test the solution in light of current developments (refer to the broken lines at the right in Exhibit 2.6).

2-2h Conducting Online Tax Research

Computer-based tax research tools dominate the tax practice. Electronic tax resources allow the tax library to reflect the tax law's dynamic and daily changes. Nevertheless, using a computer to locate tax law sources cannot substitute for developing and maintaining a thorough knowledge of the tax law or for careful analysis when addressing tax research issues.

LO.4

Employ a strategy of how best to use a computer when performing tax research and in taking the CPA exam.

---

[25]Rev.Rul. 59–44, 1959–1 C.B. 205.

[26]See W. A. Raabe and G. E. Whittenburg, "Talking Tax: How to Make a Tax Presentation," *The Tax Adviser*, March 1997, pp. 179–182.

EXHIBIT 2.7 **Tax File Memorandum**

August 26, 2017

TAX FILE MEMORANDUM

FROM   Gillian J. Jones

SUBJECT Joan and Richard Taxpayer
             Engagement

Today I talked with Joan concerning her August 14, 2017 letter requesting tax assistance. Joan wants to know if she can sell some stock in Airways Co. to Maple, Inc., and deduct the $2,500 loss realized.

FACTS Maple, Inc., is owned 50% by Richard and 50% by Joan. Richard wants to continue holding Airways stock in anticipation of a rebound in its value, but Joan wants to sell her shares and deduct the realized loss. They have asked about a proposed sale of this stock to Maple.

ISSUE Can shareholders deduct a loss on the sale of an asset to a corporation, all of whose stock they own?

CONCLUSION Joan should *not* sell the Airways stock to Maple if the couple wants to deduct the realized loss in the current tax year. Instead, Joan should sell this stock to a third party. Then the couple should either acquire new Airways stock more than 30 days before or after the date of sale, or acquire stock of a similar company.

ANALYSIS Section 267(a) provides that no loss is deductible on a sale or exchange between certain related parties. One of these relationships involves a corporation and a shareholder who owns "more than 50 percent" of that corporation's stock [see § 267(b)(2)]. Although Richard owns only 50% of Maple, Inc., his wife, Joan, owns the other 50%. The constructive ownership rule of § 267(c)(2) attributes stock held by family members, and a spouse is part of a taxpayer's family for this purpose, according to § 267(c)(4). Consequently, Richard's Maple stock is attributed to Joan, who is then treated as owning 100% of Maple, Inc. The related-party disallowance rule then applies to the loss from Joan's selling the Airways stock to Maple. Accordingly, Joan must sell this stock to an unrelated party to make the realized loss deductible.

Because Richard wants to retain an investment in Airways, he can purchase replacement stock either before or after Joan sells the original Airways stock. Section 1091(a), however, requires that more than 30 days elapse between the purchase and the sale, or the sale and the purchase, as the case may be. Moreover, for this purpose, an option to buy the stock is treated as equivalent to the stock itself. As a result, Richard must wait more than 30 days between transactions and cannot utilize stock options in the interim to minimize his stock price exposure.

A final alternative might be to replace the Airways stock with securities of a comparable company in the same industry. Although no two companies are exactly alike, there may be another company whose management philosophy, marketing strategy, and financial data are sufficiently similar to Airways to provide an equivalent return on investment. Under this alternative, Richard could acquire the new company's shares immediately, without waiting the 30 days mandated by § 1091(a). Despite the two companies' investment similarity, they would not be treated as "substantially identical" for this purpose (see Rev.Rul. 59–44, 1959–1 C.B. 205), and the Airways realized loss could be recognized.

Most computer-based tax services allow a user to retrieve documents in order of relevance, or in the order listed by database sources. Although this can be useful, even though a document is placed high on the relevance list, it still may not constitute valid law. Reading the primary sources, validating their authority, and checking the citator are essential in reaching a correct answer.

Electronic Tax Services

Usually, tax professionals use one of the following strategies when performing computer-based tax research.

- *Search* various databases using keywords that are likely to be found in the underlying documents, as written by Congress, the judiciary, or administrative sources.

- *Link* to tax documents for which all or part of the proper citation is known.

- *Browse* the tax databases, examining various tables of contents and indexes in a traditional manner or using cross-references in the documents to jump from one tax law source to another.

Virtually all of the major commercial tax publishers and most of the primary sources of the law itself, such as the Supreme Court and some of the Courts of Appeals, provide tax material in a variety of electronic formats.

EXHIBIT 2.8	**Client Letter**

Raabe, Maloney, Young, & Nellen, CPAs
5191 Natorp Boulevard
Mason, OH 45040

August 30, 2017

Mr. and Ms. Richard Taxpayer
111 Tragg Boulevard
Williamsburg, VA 23185

Dear Joan and Richard:

It was good to see you last week at our firm's golf outing. I'm glad that your children are doing so well in college and that our work to build up their education funds was so effective in providing the needed cash flow!

I am responding to your request to review your family's financial and tax situation. Our conclusions are based upon the facts as outlined in your August 14 letter. Any change in the facts may affect our conclusions.

Joan owns stock in Airways Co. that has declined in value, but Richard would like to retain this stock in anticipation of a rebound in its value. You have proposed a sale of this stock at its current market value to Maple, Inc., a corporation owned 50–50 by the two of you. Such a sale, however, would not permit the loss to be deducted.

A better approach would be to sell the Airways stock to a third party before year-end and repurchase this stock in the market. Please understand that the loss will not be deductible unless more than 30 days elapse between the sale and the repurchase of the stock. You can sell the old stock first and then buy the new stock, or you can buy the new stock first and then sell the old stock; the ordering of the transactions does not change the result. However, it is essential that more than 30 days elapse between the sale and purchase transactions. Using options during this 30-day period is ineffective and also will prevent the loss from being deducted in the current taxable year.

If the 30-day requirement is unacceptable, you might consider replacing the Airways stock with securities of some other company, perhaps even a company in the same general business as Airways. In that situation, your loss on the Airways stock can be deducted without regard to when you buy the new stock.

Let's meet to discuss this some more—and to allow me to show you our new office. Please e-mail me if I can clarify any of these points or if you have more information for me to consider. My work on this engagement is regulated by Treasury Circular 230.

Sincerely yours,

Gillian J. Jones, CPA
Partner

Online Commercial Services

Online tax research systems allow practitioners to obtain virtually instantaneous use of tax law sources by accessing databases via the Internet. Some online services may employ price-per-search cost structures, which can be as much as $200 per hour. Thus, unless a practitioner who is subject to this pricing structure can pass along related costs to clients or others, online searching generally is limited to the most important issues and to the researchers with the most experience and training in search techniques.

Other Web Sources

The Internet provides a wealth of tax information in several popular forms, sometimes at no direct cost to the researcher. Many tax professionals begin a research task with a simple online search. Other sources include the following.

- *The Web* provides access to a number of sites maintained by accounting and consulting firms, publishers, tax academics and libraries, and governmental bodies. The best sites offer links to other sites and direct contact to the site providers. Exhibit 2.9 lists some of the websites that may be most useful to tax researchers and their Internet addresses as of press date.

EXHIBIT 2.9	Tax-Related Websites	

Website	Web Address at Press Date	Description
Internal Revenue Service	**irs.gov**	News releases, downloadable forms and instructions, tables, Circular 230, and filing advice.
Tax Analysts	**taxanalysts.com**	Policy-oriented readings on tax laws and proposals to change it, moderated bulletins on various tax subjects.
Tax laws online	**law.cornell.edu/cfr**	Treasury Regulations.
	law.cornell.edu/uscode	Internal Revenue Code.
	uscode.house.gov	
Commercial tax publishers	For example, **cchgroup.com**	Information about products and services available by subscription and newsletter excerpts.
Accounting firms and professional organizations	For example, the AICPA's page is at **aicpa.org**, Ernst & Young is at **ey.com**, and KPMG is at **kpmg.com**	Tax planning newsletters, descriptions of services offered and career opportunities, and exchange of data with clients and subscribers.
Cengage Learning	**cengagebrain.com**	Informational updates, newsletters, support materials for students and adopters, and continuing education.

Caution: Web addresses change frequently.

- *Blogs and newsletters* provide a means by which information related to the tax law can be exchanged among taxpayers, tax professionals, and others who subscribe to the group's services. The tax professional can read the exchanges among other members and offer replies and suggestions to inquiries as desired. Discussions address the interpretation and application of existing law, analysis of proposals and new pronouncements, and reviews of tax software.

While tax information on the Internet is plentiful, public domain information never should be relied upon without referring to other, more reliable sources. Always remember that anyone can set up a website and that quality control can be difficult for the tax professional to ascertain.

In many situations, solutions to research problems benefit from or require the use of various electronic tax research tools. A competent tax professional must become familiar and proficient with these tools and be able to use them effectively to meet the expectations of clients and the necessities of work in the modern world.[27]

2-3 TAX RESEARCH ON THE CPA EXAMINATION

The CPA examination is computer-based, and it emphasizes information technology and general business knowledge. The 16-hour exam has four sections, and taxation is included in the Regulation section, which covers these topics.

- Federal tax procedures and accounting issues.
- Federal taxation of property transactions.
- Federal taxation—individuals.
- Federal taxation—entities.

Each exam section includes multiple-choice questions and case studies called simulations. At least 60 multiple-choice tax questions appear in the Regulation section

---

[27]For a more detailed discussion of the use of electronic tax research in a tax practice, see R. B. Sawyers, W. A. Raabe, G. E. Whittenburg, and S. L. Gill, *Federal Tax Research*, 10th ed. (Cengage Learning, 2015).

FINANCIAL DISCLOSURE INSIGHTS Where Does GAAP Come From?

As this chapter has described, the tax law is developed by many entities, including Congress, the legislators of other countries, the courts, and the IRS. Accounting principles also have many sources. Consequently, in reconciling the tax and financial accounting reporting of a transaction, the tax professional will need to know the hierarchy of authority of accounting principles—in particular, the level of importance to assign to a specific GAAP document. The diagram below presents the sources of GAAP arranged in a general order of authority from highest to lowest.[28] Note how many of these GAAP sources parallel those that have been discussed with respect to the tax law.

Professional research is conducted to find and analyze the sources of accounting reporting standards, in much the same way a tax professional conducts research concerning an open tax question. In fact, many of the publishers that provide tax research materials also can be used to find GAAP and IFRS documents. The Financial Accounting Standards Board (FASB) also makes its standards and interpretations available by subscription.

Highest Authority
- Financial Accounting Standards and Interpretations of the FASB.
- Pronouncements of bodies that preceded the FASB, such as the Accounting Principles Board (APB).

- FASB Technical Bulletins.
- Audit and Accounting Guides, prepared by the American Institute of CPAs (AICPA) and cleared by the FASB.
- Practice Bulletins, prepared by the American Institute of CPAs (AICPA) and cleared by the FASB.

- Interpretation Guides of the FASB Staff.
- Accounting Interpretations of the AICPA.
- IASB Accounting Standards.
- FASB Concepts Standards.
- Widely accepted accounting practices, professional journals, accounting textbooks, and treatises.

of the exam. Simulations are small case studies designed to test a candidate's tax knowledge and skills using real-life work-related situations. Simulations include a four-function pop-up calculator, a blank spreadsheet with some elementary functionality, and authoritative literature for the candidate to research in completing the tax case study simulations (e.g., Internal Revenue Code, Regulations, IRS publications, and Federal tax forms). Examples of such simulations follow.

CPA Exam Simulation Example

EXAMPLE 7

The tax *citation type* simulation requires the candidate to research the Internal Revenue Code and enter a Code Section and subsection citation. For example, Amber Company is considering using the simplified dollar-value method of pricing its inventory for purposes of the LIFO method that is available to certain small businesses. What Internal Revenue Code Section is the relevant authority to which you should turn to determine whether the taxpayer is eligible to use this method? To be successful, the candidate needs to find § 474.

---

[28]See Chapter 10 of Sawyers, et al., cited in footnote 27, for a discussion of strategies and techniques used in conducting research with financial accounting resources.

BRIDGE DISCIPLINE **Bridge to Regulation and Oversight**

The interests of the public are represented by Federal, state, and local governments, as they oversee the various economic transactions carried out by individuals and businesses. Control of the financial sector is assigned to the Treasury and the Securities and Exchange Commission, among other agencies.

Most citizens assume that attorneys and CPAs hold broad high-level skills in working with the tax laws. But the nature of today's economy dictates that professionals working in law and accounting instead develop narrower specialties that clients will find valuable in the marketplace. Only a subset of CPAs and attorneys practice regularly with the tax law, but all such professionals must hold and maintain broad-based skills in taxation.

Tax law is the subject of only one of the sections of the CPA exam, and only a portion of those questions relate to specific provisions of the tax law. The exam also tests the candidate's research and communication skills, and because it is administered with computer software, the candidate must have some technological facility as well.

The depth and variety of the skills that are required of an effective tax professional almost certainly are not measured well by the CPA or bar examinations. The integrity of the taxing system may be at risk when one can attain credible professional certification with only entry-level skills. It is likely that several further levels of specialty certifications, and rigorous, lifelong skill improvement, should be required of tax professionals.

CPA Exam Simulation Example

EXAMPLE

8

A *tax form completion* simulation requires the candidate to fill out a portion of a tax form. For example, Red is a limited liability company (LLC). Complete the income section of the Form 1065 for Red Company using the values found and calculated on previous tabs along with the following data.

Ordinary income from other partnerships	$ 5,200
Net gain (loss) from Form 4797	2,400
Management fee income	12,000

The candidate is provided with page 1 of Form 1065 on which to record the appropriate amounts.

Candidates can learn more about the CPA examination at **www.cpa-exam.org**. This online tutorial site reviews the exam's format, navigation functions, and tools. A 30- to 60-minute sample exam will familiarize a candidate with the types of questions on the examination.

REFOCUS ON THE BIG PICTURE

RESEARCHING TAX QUESTIONS

Fred and Megan will need you to conduct some rigorous tax research concerning the proper treatment of the stock sale and to determine the correct number of dependency exemptions for the year. Your work will entail a review of primary sources of the tax law and some computations for them, using a spreadsheet to illustrate your findings.

Communications with your clients will include a variety of phone and e-mail exchanges; a memo for your tax file; and a letter to them, summarizing your findings and recommendations.

Your research likely will be complete using Code sections and several IRS rulings, but you must convey your results to the clients in a manner that is understandable to them, as they likely are untrained in the tax law.

What If?

It is not uncommon that you later will receive additional information from Fred and Megan about the affected transactions. This may occur if additional facts are discovered by them, if Fred and Megan gave you incomplete information because they did not understand which of the facts were relevant in determining the tax outcome, or if your original interviews and data collection from them were incomplete.

If this new information changes the conclusions and recommendations that you already had developed, you should make certain that the taxpayers understand that your original work no longer is valid and that they should not depend on it.

Suggested Readings

Sheldon I. Banoff and Richard M. Lipton, Editors' Shop Talk, "Is Wikipedia Good Authority in the Tax Court?," *Journal of Taxation*, April 2007.

"Can Treasury and the IRS Write Rules in 'Plain' Language?," *Journal of Taxation*, December 2010.

Cara Griffith, "Why Do We Still Have Unpublished Opinions?," *Tax Analysts Blog*, October 30, 2015.

T. S. Rose and J. Temares, "Tax Research Tips to Solve Tax Problems," *CPA Magazine*, **tinyurl.com/tax-research-tips**.

"Writing Skills for the Tax Professional," **www2.gsu.edu/~accerl/home.html**.

Key Terms

Acquiescence, 2-15	Interpretive Regulations, 2-22	Revenue Rulings, 2-8
Circuit Court of Appeals, 2-13	Legislative Regulations, 2-22	Small Cases Division, 2-10
Citator, 2-23	Letter rulings, 2-9	Supreme Court, 2-14
Court of Federal Claims, 2-10	Nonacquiescence, 2-15	Tax Court, 2-10
Court of original jurisdiction, 2-10	Precedents, 2-14	Technical Advice Memoranda (TAMs), 2-10
Determination letters, 2-10	Procedural Regulations, 2-22	Temporary Regulations, 2-7
District Court, 2-10	Proposed Regulations, 2-7	Writ of Certiorari, 2-14
Final Regulations, 2-7	Revenue Procedures, 2-8	

Problems

1. **LO.1** What precedents must each of these courts follow?
   a. U.S. Tax Court.
   b. U.S. Court of Federal Claims.
   c. U.S. District Court.

2. **LO.1, 3** Butch Bishop operates a small international firm named Tile, Inc. A new treaty between the United States and Spain conflicts with a Section of the Internal Revenue Code. Butch asks you for advice. If he follows the treaty position, does he need to disclose this on this year's tax return? If he is required to disclose, are there any penalties for failure to disclose? Prepare a letter in which you respond to Butch. Tile's address is 100 International Drive, Tampa, FL 33620. *Communications*

3. **LO.1** Distinguish between the following.
   a. Treasury Regulations and Revenue Rulings.
   b. Revenue Rulings and Revenue Procedures.
   c. Revenue Rulings and letter rulings.
   d. Letter rulings and determination letters.

4. **LO.1, 2** Rank the following items from the lowest to highest authority in the Federal tax law system.
   a. Interpretive Regulation.
   b. Legislative Regulation.
   c. Letter ruling.
   d. Revenue Ruling.
   e. Internal Revenue Code.
   f. Proposed Regulation.

5. **LO.1** Interpret each of the following citations.

    a.   Temp.Reg. § 1.956–2T.

    b.   Rev.Rul. 2012–15, 2012–23 I.R.B. 975.

    c.   Ltr.Rul. 200204051.

6. **LO.1** List an advantage and a disadvantage of using the U.S. Court of Federal Claims as the trial court for Federal tax litigation.

Communications   7. **LO.1, 3** Eddy Falls is considering litigating a tax deficiency of approximately $229,030 in the court system. He asks you to provide him with a short description of his litigation alternatives, indicating the advantages and disadvantages of each. Prepare your response to Eddy in the form of a letter. His address is 200 Mesa Drive, Tucson, AZ 85714.

8. **LO.1** A taxpayer lives in Michigan. In a controversy with the IRS, the taxpayer loses at the trial court level. Describe the appeal procedure for each of the following trial courts.

    a.   Small Cases Division of the Tax Court.

    b.   Tax Court.

    c.   District Court.

    d.   Court of Federal Claims.

9. **LO.1** For the Tax Court, the District Court, and the Court of Federal Claims, indicate the following.

    a.   Number of regular judges per court.

    b.   Availability of a jury trial.

    c.   Whether the deficiency must be paid before the trial.

10. **LO.1** A taxpayer living in the following states would appeal a decision of the U.S. District Court to which Court of Appeals?

    a.   Wyoming.

    b.   Nebraska.

    c.   Idaho.

    d.   Louisiana.

    e.   Illinois.

Critical Thinking   11. **LO.1** What is meant by the term *petitioner*?

12. **LO.1, 2** In assessing the validity of a prior court decision, discuss the significance of the following on the taxpayer's issue.

    a.   The decision was rendered by the U.S. District Court of Wyoming. Taxpayer lives in Wyoming.

    b.   The decision was rendered by the Court of Federal Claims. Taxpayer lives in Wyoming.

    c.   The decision was rendered by the Second Circuit Court of Appeals. Taxpayer lives in California.

    d.   The decision was rendered by the Supreme Court.

    e.   The decision was rendered by the Tax Court. The IRS has acquiesced in the result.

    f.   Same as part (e), except that the IRS has nonacquiesced in the result.

13. **LO.1** What is the difference between a Regular decision, a Memorandum decision, and a Summary Opinion of the Tax Court?

14. **LO.1** Explain the following abbreviations.

a. CA–2.	f. *Cert. denied.*	k. F.3d.
b. Fed.Cl.	g. *acq.*	l. F.Supp.
c. *aff'd.*	h. B.T.A.	m. USSC.
d. *rev'd.*	i. USTC.	n. S.Ct.
e. *rem'd.*	j. AFTR.	o. D.Ct.

15. **LO.2** Referring to the citation only, determine which tax law source issued these documents.
    a. 716 F.2d 693 (CA–9, 1983).
    b. 92 T.C 400 (1998).
    c. 70 U.S. 224 (1935).
    d. 3 B.T.A. 1042 (1926).
    e. T.C.Memo. 1957–169.
    f. 50 AFTR 2d 92–6000 (Cl.Ct., 1992).
    g. Ltr.Rul. 9046036.
    h. 111 F.Supp.2d 1294 (S.D.N.Y., 2000).
    i. 98–50, 1998–1 C.B. 10.

16. **LO.2** Interpret each of the following citations.
    a. 14 T.C. 74 (1950).
    b. 592 F.2d 1251 (CA–5, 1979).
    c. 95–1 USTC ¶ 50,104 (CA–6, 1995).
    d. 75 AFTR 2d 95–110 (CA–6, 1995).
    e. 223 F.Supp. 663 (W.D. Tex., 1963).

17. **LO.2** Which of the following items may be found in the *Internal Revenue Bulletin*?
    a. Action on Decision.
    b. Small Cases Division of the Tax Court decision.
    c. Letter ruling.
    d. Revenue Procedure.
    e. Final Regulation.
    f. Court of Federal Claims decision.
    g. Acquiescences to Tax Court decisions.
    h. U.S. Circuit Court of Appeals decision.

18. **LO.2** Answer the following questions based upon this citation: *United Draperies, Inc. v. Comm.*, 340 F.2d 936 (CA–7, 1964), *aff'g* 41 T.C. 457 (1963), *cert. denied* 382 U.S. 813 (1965).
    a. In which court did this decision first appear?
    b. Did the appellate court uphold the trial court?
    c. Who was the plaintiff?
    d. Did the Supreme Court uphold the appellate court decision?

19. **LO.2, 4** For her tax class, Yvonne is preparing a research paper discussing the tax aspects of child support payments. Explain to Yvonne how she can research the provisions on this topic.   Issue ID

20. **LO.1, 2** Tom, an individual taxpayer, has been audited by the IRS and, as a result, has been assessed a substantial deficiency (which has not yet been paid) in additional income taxes. In preparing his defense, Tom advances the following possibilities.
    a. Although a resident of Kentucky, Tom plans to sue in a U.S. District Court in Oregon that appears to be more favorably inclined toward taxpayers.
    b. If part (a) is not possible, Tom plans to take his case to a Kentucky state court where an uncle is the presiding judge.
    c. Because Tom has found a B.T.A. decision that seems to help his case, he plans to rely on it under alternative (a) or (b).
    d. If he loses at the trial court level, Tom plans to appeal either to the U.S. Court of Federal Claims or to the U.S. Second Circuit Court of Appeals because he has relatives in both Washington, D.C., and New York. Staying with these relatives could save Tom lodging expense while his appeal is being heard by the court selected.
    e. Whether or not Tom wins at the trial court or appeals court level, he feels certain of success on an appeal to the U.S. Supreme Court.

    Evaluate Tom's notions concerning the judicial process as it applies to Federal income tax controversies.

21. **LO.1** Using the legend provided, classify each of the following statements (more than one answer per statement may be appropriate).

   Legend

   D = Applies to the District Court
   T = Applies to the Tax Court
   C = Applies to the Court of Federal Claims
   A = Applies to the Circuit Court of Appeals
   U = Applies to the Supreme Court
   N = Applies to none of the above

   a.   Decides only Federal tax matters.
   b.   Decisions are reported in the F.3d Series.
   c.   Decisions are reported in the USTCs.
   d.   Decisions are reported in the AFTRs.
   e.   Appeal is by *Writ of Certiorari*.
   f.   Court meets most often in Washington, D.C.
   g.   Offers the choice of a jury trial.
   h.   Is a trial court.
   i.   Is an appellate court.
   j.   Allows appeal to the Court of Appeals for the Federal Circuit and bypasses the taxpayer's own Circuit Court of Appeals.
   k.   Has a Small Cases Division.
   l.   Is the only trial court where the taxpayer does not have to first pay the tax assessed by the IRS.

22. **LO.1, 2** Using the legend provided, classify each of the following citations as to the type of court.

   Legend

   D = District Court
   T = Tax Court
   C = Court of Federal Claims
   A = Circuit Court of Appeals
   U = Supreme Court
   N = None of the above

   a.   Rev.Rul. 2009–34, 2009–42 I.R.B. 502.
   b.   *Joseph R. Bolker*, 81 T.C. 782 (1983).
   c.   *Magneson*, 753 F.2d 1490 (CA–9, 1985).
   d.   *Lucas v. Ox Fibre Brush Co.*, 281 U.S. 115 (1930).
   e.   *Ashtabula Bow Socket Co.*, 2 B.T.A. 306 (1925).
   f.   *BB&T Corp.*, 97 AFTR 2d 2006–873 (D.Ct. Mid.N.Car., 2006).
   g.   *Choate Construction Co.*, T.C.Memo. 1997–495.
   h.   Ltr.Rul. 200940021.
   i.   *John and Rochelle Ray*, T.C. Summary Opinion 2006–110.

23. **LO.1, 2** Using the legend provided, classify each of the following tax sources.

   Legend

   P = Primary tax source
   S = Secondary tax source
   B = Both
   N = Neither

a. Sixteenth Amendment to the U.S. Constitution.

b. Tax treaty between the United States and India.

c. Revenue Procedure.

d. Chief Counsel Advice (issued 2009).

e. U.S. District Court decision.

f. *Yale Law Journal* article.

g. Temporary Regulations (issued 2014).

h. U.S. Tax Court Memorandum decision.

i. Small Cases Division of the U.S. Tax Court decision.

j. House Ways and Means Committee report.

24. **LO.1** In which Subchapter of the Internal Revenue Code would one find information about corporate distributions?

a. Subchapter S.

b. Subchapter C.

c. Subchapter P.

d. Subchapter K.

e. Subchapter M.

25. **LO.1, 2** To locate an IRS Revenue Procedure that was issued during the past week, which source would you consult?

a. *Federal Register.*

b. *Internal Revenue Bulletin.*

c. Internal Revenue Code.

d. Some other source. Identify it.

26. **LO.1, 2** In the citation *Schuster's Express, Inc.*, 66 T.C. 588 (1976), *aff'd* 562 F.2d 39 (CA–2, 1977), *nonacq.*, to what do the 66, 39, and *nonacq.* refer?

27. **LO.1** Is there an automatic right to appeal to the U.S. Supreme Court? If so, what is the process?

28. **LO.2** An accountant friend of yours tells you that he "almost never" does any tax   Ethics and Equity
research because he believes that "research usually reveals that some tax planning idea has already been thought up and shot down." Besides, he points out, most tax returns are never audited by the IRS. Can a tax adviser who is dedicated to reducing his client's tax liability justify the effort to engage in tax research? Do professional ethics *demand* such efforts? Which approach would a client probably prefer?

29. **LO.1, 4** Go to the U.S. Tax Court website.   Communications

a. What different types of cases can be found on the site?

b. What is a Summary Opinion? Find one.

c. What is a Memorandum decision? Find one.

d. Find the court's Rules of Practice and Procedures.

e. Is the site user-friendly? E-mail suggested improvements to the site's webmaster.

30. **LO.2, 3** Locate the following Code provisions, and give a brief description of each   Critical Thinking
in an e-mail to your instructor.   Communications

a. § 61(a)(13).

b. § 643(a)(2).

c. § 2503(g)(2)(A).

BRIDGE DISCIPLINE

1. Comment on these statements.
   a. The tax law is created and administered in the same way as other Federal provisions.
   b. Most taxpayers find it too expensive and time-consuming to sue the government in a tax dispute.

Communications   2. Using the title "The Federal Taxing System Operates Outside the U.S. Constitution," write a two-page paper to submit in your Government Policy course. Do not address "tax protester" issues (e.g., that the income tax is unconstitutional or that one's taxes should be measured using only the gold standard). Instead, concentrate on how Federal tax law is made and interpreted and how the process measures up to other governmental standards.

Communications   3. Develop an outline from which you will deliver a 10-minute talk to the local Chamber of Commerce, with the title "Regulation of the Tax Profession in the 21st Century." Use no more than four PowerPoint slides for your talk, and discuss what the business community now needs with respect to oversight of a stable, yet productive revenue-raising system. Include administrative developments of the last two years in your research.

Ethics and Equity   4. A friend of yours, who is a philosophy major, has overheard the conversation described in Problem 28 and declares that all tax research is "immoral." She says that tax research enables people with substantial assets to shift the burden of financing public expenditures to those who "get up every morning, go to work, play by the rules, and pay their bills." How do you respond?

Research Problems

Note: Solutions to Research Problems can be prepared by using the Checkpoint® Student Edition online research product, which is available to accompany this text. It is also possible to prepare solutions to the Research Problems by using tax research materials found in a standard tax library.

Communications   **Research Problem 1.** Locate the following items, and e-mail to your professor a brief summary of the results.
   a. *Charles Y. Choi*, T.C.Memo. 2002–183.
   b. Ltr.Rul. 200231003.
   c. Action on Decision, 2000–004, May 10, 2000.

Research Problem 2. Locate the following Code citations, and give a brief topical description of each.
   a. § 708(a).
   b. § 1371(a).
   c. § 2503(a).

Communications   **Research Problem 3.** Locate the following Regulations, and give a brief topical description of each. Summarize your comments in an e-mail to your instructor.
   a. Reg. § 1.170A–4A(b)(2)(ii)(C).
   b. Reg. § 1.672(b)–1.
   c. Reg. § 20.2031–7(f).

Research Problem 4. Determine the missing data in these court decisions and rulings.

   a. *Higgins v. Comm.*, 312 U.S._____ (1941).

   b. *Talen v. U.S.*, 355 F.Supp.2d 22 (D.Ct. D.C., _____).

   c. Rev.Rul. 2008–18, 2008–13 I.R.B._____.

   d. *Pahl v. Comm.*, 150 F.3d 1124 (CA–9, _____).

   e. *Veterinary Surgical Consultants PC*, 117 T.C.____ (2001).

   f. *Yeagle Drywall Co.*, T.C.Memo. 2001_____.

Research Problem 5. Locate the following Tax Court case: *Thomas J. Green, Jr.*, 59 T.C. 456 (1972). Briefly describe the issue in the case, and explain what the Tax Court said about using IRS publications to support a research conclusion.

Research Problem 6. Can a Tax Court Small Cases decision be treated as a precedent by other taxpayers? Explain.

Partial list of research aids:
§ 7463(b).
Maria Antionette Walton Mitchell, T.C. Summary Opinion 2004–160.

Research Problem 7. Find *Kathryn Bernal*, 120 T.C. 102 (2003), and answer the following questions.

   a. What was the docket number?

   b. When was the dispute filed?

   c. Who is the respondent?

   d. Who was the attorney for the taxpayers?

   e. Who was the judge who wrote the opinion?

   f. What was the disposition of the dispute?

Research Problem 8. This year, Frank lived with and supported Daisy, an unrelated 20-year-old woman to whom he was not married. Frank lives in a state that has a statute that makes cohabitation a misdemeanor for a man and a woman who are not married to each other. May Frank claim Daisy as a dependent, assuming that he meets all of the applicable tests to claim the exemption? Should Frank and Daisy move to another state? Describe your research path in a PowerPoint presentation for your classmates.

Decision Making

Communications

Partial list of research aids:
§ 152(f)(3).
John T. Untermann, 38 T.C. 93 (1962).

Use the tax resources of the Internet to address the following questions. Do not restrict your search to the Web, but include a review of newsgroups and general reference materials, practitioner sites and resources, primary sources of the tax law, chat rooms and discussion groups, and other opportunities.

Internet Activity

Research Problem 9. Find three blogs related to tax practice. On one PowerPoint slide, list the URLs for each blog and the general topical areas addressed at each. Send your slide to the others in your course.

Communications

Research Problem 10. Find one instance of each of the following using a nonsubscription site on the Web or an online library at your school. In an e-mail to your professor, give a full citation for the document and describe how you found it.

Communications

   a. Letter Ruling.
   b. Action on Decision.
   c. IRS Notice.
   d. Revenue Ruling.
   e. Revenue Procedure.

   f. Code Section.
   g. Tax Regulation.
   h. Tax treaty.
   i. Tax Court Summary Opinion.
   j. Tax Court Regular decision.

Taxes on the Financial Statements

LEARNING OBJECTIVES: *After completing Chapter 3, you should be able to:*

LO.1 Enumerate the differences between book and tax methods of computing income tax expense.

LO.2 Compute a corporation's book income tax expense.

LO.3 Describe the purpose of the valuation allowance.

LO.4 Interpret the disclosure information contained in the financial statements.

LO.5 Identify the GAAP treatment concerning tax uncertainties and unrepatriated foreign earnings.

LO.6 Use financial statement income tax information to benchmark a company's tax position.

CHAPTER OUTLINE

TAX TALK *Truth is, figuring out how much tax a company actually pays is impossible.... Tax disclosure is just inscrutable.* —ROBERT WILLENS

THE BIG PICTURE

TAXES ON THE FINANCIAL STATEMENTS

Raymond Jones, the CEO of Arctic Corporation, would like some help reconciling the amount of income tax expense on Arctic's financial statements with the amount of income tax reported on the company's corporate income tax return for its first year of operations. Mr. Jones does not understand why he can't simply multiply the financial statement income by the company's 35 percent marginal tax rate to get the financial tax expense. While the financial statements show book income before tax of $25 million, the reported Federal tax expense is only $7.7 million. In addition, the corporate tax return reports taxable income of $19 million and Federal income taxes payable of $6.65 million ($19 million × 35%).

Without knowing the specifics of the company's financial statements, does Arctic's situation look reasonable? Why is Arctic's financial tax expense not equal to $8.75 million ($25 million × 35%)? What causes the $1.05 million difference between the taxes shown on the financial statements and the taxes due on the tax return?

Read the chapter and formulate your response.

The ultimate result of the many tax planning ideas, advice, and compliance efforts provided by tax professionals to their clients is captured in a simple summary number—income tax expense. A U.S. corporation's tax expense is reported in its annual Federal tax return, its financial statements, and other regulatory filings and is often the starting point for state and local tax returns. As it turns out, however, deriving a corporation's income tax expense (i.e., its "provision" for income taxes) is not so simple.

A corporation may report millions of dollars in tax expense in its financial statements and yet pay virtually nothing to the U.S., state, or foreign governments. Alternatively, a corporation may pay substantial amounts to the U.S., state, and foreign governments and report very little income tax expense in its financial statements. Why do such differences exist? Which income tax expense is the "correct" number? How can data regarding a corporation's income tax provision render valuable information for the corporation, its competitors, and tax professionals assisting in the planning function? This chapter addresses these questions.

3-1 BOOK-TAX DIFFERENCES

LO.1

Enumerate the differences between book and tax methods of computing income tax expense.

A significant difference may exist between a corporation's Federal income tax liability as reported on its Form 1120 (tax) and the corporation's income tax expense as reported on its financial statements (book) prepared using generally accepted accounting principles (GAAP). This book-tax difference is caused by one or more of the following.

- Differences in reporting entities included in the calculation.
- Different definition of taxes included in the income tax expense amount.
- Different accounting methods.

A corporation's activities are captured in its accounting records, producing general ledger results. At the end of the year, these records are summarized to produce a trial balance. Adjustments to these accounting data may be necessary to produce both the corporation's financial statements and its corporate income tax return. These book and tax adjustments rarely match. Different entities may be included in the reports, and the book and tax rules can be quite different. For instance, GAAP includes a materiality principle, under which some items can be ignored if they are insignificant in amount. The tax law includes no similar materiality threshold: all items are material in computing taxable income.

On a tax return, Schedule M–1 or M–3 reconciles the differences between an entity's book income and its taxable income. See Exhibit 3.1.

3-1a Different Reporting Entities

A corporate group must consolidate all U.S. and foreign subsidiaries within a single financial statement for book purposes when the parent corporation controls more than 50 percent of the voting power of those subsidiaries.[1] In cases where the parent corporation owns between 20 and 50 percent of another corporation, the parent uses the equity method to account for the earnings of the subsidiary. Under the equity method, the parent currently records its share of the subsidiary's income or loss for the year.[2] Corporations that own less than 20 percent of other corporations typically use the *cost method* to account for income from these investments and include income only when actual dividends are received.

---

[1]*Consolidation,* ASC Topic 810 (formerly *Consolidation of All Majority Owned Subsidiaries,* Statement of Financial Accounting Standards No. 94). Certain adjustments are made to reduce book income for the after-tax income related to minority shareholders.

[2]*Investments—Equity Method and Joint Ventures,* ASC Topic 323 (formerly *The Equity Method of Accounting for Investments in Common Stock,* Accounting Principles Board Opinion No. 18).

EXHIBIT 3.1	**Flow of Accounting Data**

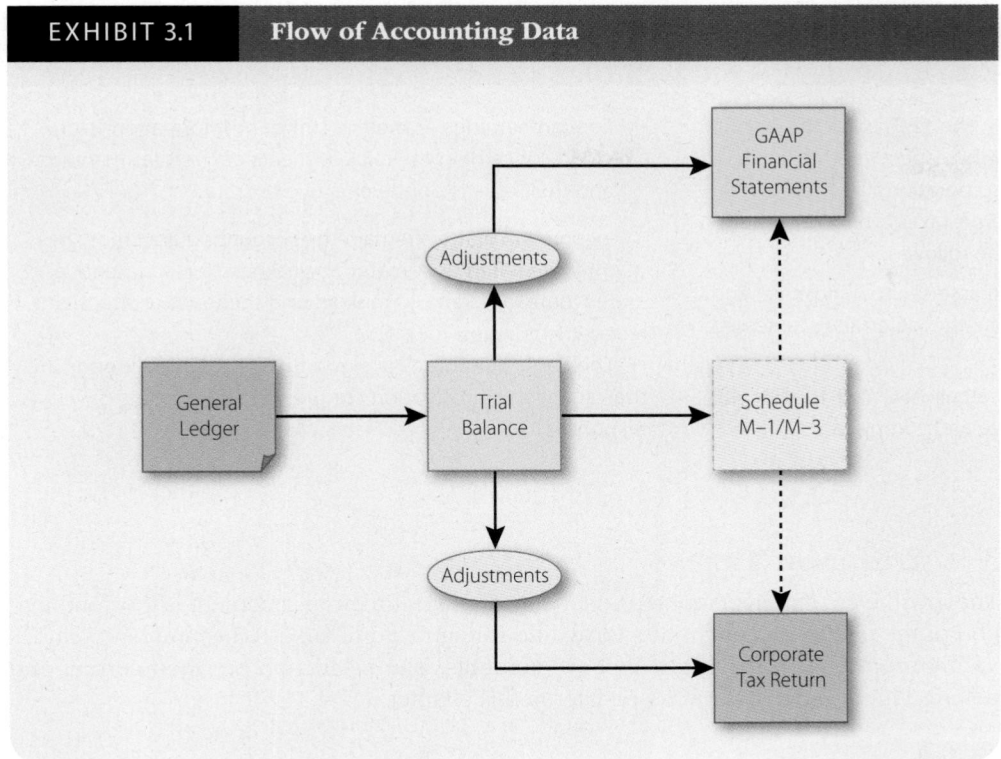

The Big Picture

EXAMPLE 1

Return to the facts of *The Big Picture* on p. 3-1. Arctic Corporation owns 100% of Gator, Inc., a domestic corporation; 100% of Hurricane, Ltd., a foreign corporation; and 40% of Beach, Inc., a domestic corporation. Arctic's combined financial statement includes its own net income and the net income of both Gator and Hurricane. In addition, Arctic's financial statement includes its 40% share of Beach's net income. Arctic's financial statement includes the income of these subsidiaries regardless of whether Arctic receives any actual profit distributions from its subsidiaries.

For Federal income tax purposes, a U.S. corporation may elect to include in its consolidated U.S. tax return any *domestic* subsidiaries that are 80 percent or more owned.[3] On the other hand, the income of non-U.S. subsidiaries and less than 80 percent owned domestic subsidiaries is not included in the consolidated tax return.

The Big Picture

EXAMPLE 2

Return to the facts of *The Big Picture* on p. 3-1. Also assume the facts presented in Example 1. If Arctic elects to include Gator as part of its consolidated Federal income tax return, Arctic's return includes its own taxable income and the taxable income generated by Gator. Hurricane's taxable income is not included in the consolidated return because it is a non-U.S. corporation. Beach, although a domestic corporation, cannot be consolidated with Arctic because Arctic owns only 40% of the stock. Income from Hurricane and Beach will be included in Arctic's U.S. taxable income only when Arctic receives actual or constructive dividends from those two companies.

---

[3]§§ 1501–1504. An election to consolidate an 80% or more owned subsidiary
 generally can be changed only with the permission of the IRS.

TAX IN THE NEWS   **The Watchdog Is Watching**

A recent report by the SEC listed the watchdog agency's areas of focus with respect to the financial statements of publicly traded corporations as they pertain to issues in accounting for income taxes. The most important of the focus areas include the following.

- Realizability of deferred tax assets—how positive and negative evidence supporting the deferrals is assessed by the taxpayer.

- Uncertain tax positions—whether ASC 740-10 (FIN 48) disclosures are comprehensive and complete.

- Foreign earnings—whether sufficient information is provided concerning the reinvestments of overseas earnings and their effects on the effective tax rate.

Income tax matters remain the accounting area most frequently identified as a material weakness for large entities, and income taxes always rank among the ten most frequent restatement issues.

The Edgar database[4] is a good place to follow trends in the agency's information requests and the taxpayer's responses.

3-1b **Different Taxes**

The income tax expense reported on a corporation's financial statement is the combination of the entity's Federal, state, local, and foreign income taxes. This number includes both current and deferred tax expense amounts. The distinction between current and deferred income taxes is discussed later in this chapter.

The Big Picture

EXAMPLE 3

Return to the facts of *The Big Picture* on p. 3-1. Also assume the facts presented in Example 1. For book purposes, Arctic, Gator, and Hurricane combine their income and expenses into a single financial statement. The book tax expense for the year includes all Federal, state, local, and foreign income taxes paid or accrued by these three corporations. In addition, the book tax expense amount includes any future Federal, state, local, or foreign income tax expenses (or tax savings) on income reported in the current income statement.

The income tax provision computed on the Federal income tax return is only the U.S. *Federal* income tax expense. This amount is based on the U.S. corporation's taxable income. State and local income taxes are reported on the Federal tax return, but as deductions in arriving at taxable income.

The Big Picture

EXAMPLE 4

Return to the facts of *The Big Picture* on p. 3-1. Also assume the facts presented in Examples 1 and 2. Arctic and Gator file a consolidated Federal tax return. The tax expense reported on the Form 1120 is only the U.S. Federal income tax expense for the consolidated taxable income of Arctic and Gator. This tax expense does not include the income taxes that Arctic and its subsidiaries paid to state, local, or foreign governments.

3-1c **Different Methods**

Many differences exist between book and tax accounting methods. Some are **temporary differences**, with income and expenses appearing in *both* the financial statement and the tax return, but in different reporting periods (i.e., a timing difference). Others are **permanent differences**, with items appearing in *either* the financial statement or the tax return, but not both.

---

[4]See **http://edgar.sec.gov/edgar.shtml**.

Temporary differences include the following.

- *Depreciation on fixed assets.* Taxpayers may use an accelerated depreciation method under the modified accelerated cost recovery system (MACRS) rules but a straight-line method for book purposes. Even if identical methods are used, the period over which the asset is depreciated may differ between book and tax.

- *Compensation-related expenses.* Generally, the tax law does not allow for the use of estimates or reserves, as is common under GAAP. For example, under GAAP, corporations accrue the future expenses related to providing postretirement benefits other than pensions (e.g., health insurance coverage). However, these expenses are deductible for tax purposes only when paid.

- *Accrued income and expenses.* Although most income and expense items are recognized for tax and book purposes in the same period, a number of items potentially appear in different periods. For example, warranty expenses are accrued for book purposes but are not deductible for tax purposes until incurred. Inventory write-offs are accrued for book but are not deductible for tax until incurred. Similarly, different methods regarding the timing of income recognition may create temporary differences. For instance, GAAP recognizes income and loss when the *fair value* of most investment assets changes during the year, while tax rules recognize such realized gain or loss only upon a sale or other taxable disposition of the asset.

- *Net operating losses.* Taxable income for the year cannot be less than zero; thus, operating losses from one tax year may be used to offset taxable income in another tax year. As a result, the losses incurred in one year for book purposes may be used as a deduction for tax purposes in a different year. No such loss carryovers are used under GAAP; GAAP losses are reported as negative income amounts in the year incurred.

- *Intangible assets.* Goodwill and some other intangibles are not amortizable for book purposes. However, GAAP requires an annual determination of whether the intangible asset has suffered a reduction in value (i.e., impairment). If an intangible has suffered an impairment, a current expense is required to reduce the asset's book value to the lower level. For tax purposes, certain intangibles (including goodwill) can be amortized over 15 years.[5]

Permanent differences include the following.

- *Nontaxable income.* A common example is municipal bond interest, which is income for book purposes but is not taxable.

- *Nondeductible expenses.* The disallowed portion of meals and entertainment expense and certain penalties are not deductible for tax purposes, but they are expensed in arriving at book income.[6]

- *Special tax deductions.* GAAP does not allow expenses for certain income tax deductions, such as the domestic production activities deduction (DPAD) and the dividends-received deduction.

- *Tax credits.* Credits such as the research activities credit reduce the Federal income tax liability, but have no corresponding book treatment. Tax credits are discussed in Chapter 17.

In-depth coverage can be found on this book's companion website: www.cengagebrain.com   **1 DIGGING DEEPER**

---

[5]See § 197 and *Intangibles—Goodwill and Other*, ASC Topic 350 (formerly *Goodwill and Other Intangible Assets*, Statement of Financial Accounting Standards No. 142).

[6]Federal income tax liabilities are another example of this type of permanent book-tax difference.

FINANCIAL DISCLOSURE INSIGHTS   **Supersized Goodwill**

When a balance sheet includes an asset value for goodwill, the company's total valuation is seen to exceed the aggregate value of its physical assets, such as cash and equipment. Goodwill typically is created as the result of the takeover of a target entity in an acquisition transaction.

GAAP rules concerning goodwill and its impairment evolved in a context of stable market values and managed income. But when goodwill gets to be so large that it is a major asset in itself, are GAAP impairment write-downs sure to follow?

An impairment write-down often is an indication that an acquiror overpaid for the target entity in a takeover transaction. Thus, conglomerates that grow by a series of acquisitions may be doubly exposed to goodwill write-downs. Accordingly, goodwill and its impairment can become an outsized element of the financial statements for many companies.

In a recent year, the following data concerning recorded goodwill were reported.

Company	Goodwill as a Percentage of Total Value
Frontier Communications	165.7%
Republic Services	108.8%
Time Warner	80.8%
Kraft Foods	54.3%
Dow Chemical	34.2%
Dr Pepper Snapple Group	32.2%
Starbucks Corporation	0.8%
Netflix	0.0%

EXAMPLE 5

Wise, Inc., reported the following results for the current year.

Book income (before tax)	$ 685,000
Tax depreciation in excess of book	(125,000)
Nondeductible warranty expense	65,000
Municipal bond interest income	(35,000)
Taxable income (Form 1120)	$ 590,000

Wise reports net income before tax of $685,000 on its financial statement but must adjust this amount for differences between book and tax income.

Tax depreciation in excess of book is a tax deduction not currently expensed for book purposes, and warranty expense is deductible for book purposes but not yet deductible for tax. Both of these items are temporary differences, because they eventually reverse (with book depreciation eventually exceeding tax depreciation and the warranty expense ultimately deducted for tax when incurred).

The municipal bond interest is a permanent difference because this income will never be subject to tax.

3-1d Tax Return Disclosures

Book-tax differences are reported in the Federal income tax returns of most business entities.

Exhibit 3.2 contains the **Schedule M–1** from Form 1120, the corporate income tax return. The purpose of Schedule M–1 is to reconcile book income to the taxable income as reported on the tax return. Line 1 is the net income or loss per books, and line 2 adds back the book tax expense to get back to book income before tax.[7] The remainder of Schedule M–1 contains adjustments for both temporary and permanent differences, until arriving at taxable income on line 10.[8]

Schedule M–3 is required for a C corporation or consolidated tax group with total year-end assets of $10 million or more. The Schedule M–3 provides the IRS with more detailed information than is provided in the Schedule M–1. In addition, the

---

[7]Line 1, "Net income (loss) per books," is not defined in the instructions to the form, and corporations can use various starting points in the Schedule M–1 (e.g., only the book income from U.S. members of the group). The Schedule M–3 is more specific in defining book income.

[8]Form 1120, page 1, line 28 represents corporate taxable income before subtracting the net operating loss and dividends-received deductions.

EXHIBIT 3.2	Schedule M–1

Schedule M-1   **Reconciliation of Income (Loss) per Books With Income per Return**

Note: The corporation may be required to file Schedule M-3 (see instructions).

1	Net income (loss) per books			7	Income recorded on books this year not included on this return (itemize):		
2	Federal income tax per books				Tax-exempt interest $ _____		
3	Excess of capital losses over capital gains .						
4	Income subject to tax not recorded on books this year (itemize): _____						
				8	Deductions on this return not charged against book income this year (itemize):		
5	Expenses recorded on books this year not deducted on this return (itemize):			a	Depreciation . . $ _____		
a	Depreciation . . . . $ _____			b	Charitable contributions $ _____		
b	Charitable contributions . $ _____						
c	Travel and entertainment . $ _____						
				9	Add lines 7 and 8		
6	Add lines 1 through 5			10	Income (page 1, line 28)—line 6 less line 9		

Schedule M–3 requires identification of whether a book-tax difference is temporary or permanent.

Schedule M–1 or M–3 typically is the starting point for IRS audits of corporations. Identifying large differences between book and taxable income may offer the IRS auditor insights into tax saving strategies (some perhaps questionable) employed by the taxpayer. See Chapter 12 for additional discussion of the Schedules M–1 and M–3. Concept Summary 3.1 summarizes the sources of typical corporate book-tax differences.

In-depth coverage can be found on this book's companion website: www.cengagebrain.com   **2**   DIGGING DEEPER

Concept Summary 3.1

Income Reporting: Book versus Tax

Financial Statement	U.S. Federal Income Tax Return
Reporting entities	**Reporting entities**
• 50% or more owned domestic and foreign subsidiaries *must* be consolidated.	• 80% or more owned domestic subsidiaries *may* be consolidated.
• Share of income from 20 to 50% owned domestic and foreign corporations included in current income.	• Share of income from other corporations reported only when actual or constructive dividends are received.
Income tax expense	**Income tax expense**
• Federal income taxes.	• Federal income taxes.
• State income taxes.	• Current only.
• Local income taxes.	
• Foreign income taxes.	
• Current and deferred.	
Methods	**Methods**
• Temporary differences.	• Temporary differences.
• Permanent differences.	• Permanent differences.
• Income tax note reconciliation.	• Schedule M–1 or M–3 reconciliation.

Uncertain Tax Positions

The IRS requires that large corporations list the tax return positions they have taken that may not be fully supported by the law. Schedule UTP ("uncertain tax positions") is added to the Form 1120 for all corporations with assets of at least $10 million.

Some tax professionals feel that the Schedule UTP alerts the IRS to specific items that will be most vulnerable to audit adjustments. The public does not have access to a corporation's Schedule UTP because tax returns are confidential documents.

Disclosures on the Schedule UTP include a list of tax return positions for the current and prior tax years where:

- The taxpayer or a related party recorded a reserve against the Federal income tax expense on its audited financial statements, or
- There was no recorded tax reserve based on its analysis of expected litigation with the IRS. This means that, in the taxpayer's view, the probability of settling the issue with the IRS in the taxpayer's favor is less than 50 percent, and the taxpayer determines that it is *more likely than not* (a greater than 50 percent likelihood) to prevail on the merits of the issue in litigation.

Disclosures are not required for items that are immaterial under GAAP rules, or for which the filing position is sufficiently certain that no financial accounting reserve is required.

The IRS maintains that it will limit releases of the Schedule UTP to other taxing jurisdictions, and that it will not use Schedule UTP data to usurp the attorney-client and tax practitioner privileges of confidentiality or the work-product doctrine. Taxpayers are not required to disclose the amounts of any reserves or the precise nature of the tax planning technique that led to the reserve for the filing position.

For some taxpayers, tax filing positions reported on Schedules UTP are few in number because they are "less aggressive" in making filing decisions, or because they negotiate with the IRS before filing a return as to certain deductions and credits.

IRS statistics show that about 5,200 uncertain tax positions are reported in the typical year, involving about 2,200 taxpayers. About 80 percent of taxpayers filing a Schedule UTP submitted the schedule in a previous year. Over half of the Schedule UTP filers are publicly traded, and about half of the filers report only one uncertain tax position.

The most commonly reported uncertain tax positions on a Schedule UTP involve the research credit (about 30 percent of all UTP disclosures), transfer pricing computations (about 20 percent), and the domestic production activities deduction (about 5 percent).[9]

LO.2

Compute a corporation's book income tax expense.

3-2 INCOME TAXES IN THE FINANCIAL STATEMENTS

3-2a GAAP Principles

As mentioned earlier, a corporation's financial statements are prepared in accordance with GAAP. The purpose and objectives of these statements are quite different from the objective of the corporation's income tax return.

The ASC 740 (SFAS 109) approach produces a total income tax expense (also called the income tax provision) for the income currently reported on a corporation's combined financial statement.[10] This approach follows the matching principle, where all of the expenses related to earning income are reported in the same period as the

---

[9]**www.irs.gov/Businesses/Corporations/UTPFilingStatistics**

[10]*Income Taxes*, ASC Topic 740 (formerly *Accounting for Income Taxes*, Statement of Financial Accounting Standards No. 109).

FINANCIAL DISCLOSURE INSIGHTS   **The Book-Tax Income Gap**

According to one study, 115 companies in the Standard and Poor's stock index incurred a Federal and state income tax rate of less than 20 percent. In fact, the rate for 39 of those companies was less than 10 percent.

At least 30 of the Fortune 500 companies paid zero or negative Federal corporate income taxes over a recent three-year period. These companies included General Electric, American Electric Power, FedEx, Honeywell, Pfizer, Verizon, Boeing, and PG&E. Pepco Holdings reported an effective Federal income tax rate of *negative* 57.6 percent!

The firms maintained that they had paid all of their required tax liabilities, and that effective income tax planning had resulted in their zero or negative effective tax rates.

Corporations further maintain that the large differences in book and tax income are a function of the different rules and objectives of GAAP for financial statements and the Internal Revenue Code for tax returns.

Low effective tax rates often are traceable to one or more of the following.

- Use of NOL carryovers.

- Large investments in depreciable assets.

- Use of state, local, federal, and international tax incentives (e.g., to encourage new companies and targeted industries such as high-tech, energy, and domestic manufacturing).

- Use of temporary tax provisions (e.g., stimulus, anti-recession, or other targeted rules designed to stimulate the economy via tax cuts).

- Negotiations and settlements with revenue agencies.[11]

- Application of legal tax planning techniques.

income without regard to when the expenses are actually paid. If an entity fails to follow GAAP in reporting its tax provision and related accounts, the SEC could respond with a comment letter indicating a material weakness in the financial statements, or the agency might require a full restatement of them.

EXAMPLE

6

PanCo, Inc., earns $100,000 in book income before tax and is subject to a 35% marginal Federal income tax rate. PanCo records a single temporary difference. Tax depreciation exceeds book depreciation by $20,000. Accordingly, PanCo's taxable income is $80,000 ($100,000 − $20,000 additional tax deduction).

On its income tax return, PanCo reports a current Federal tax liability of $28,000 ($80,000 × 35%). On its financial statement, PanCo reports a total tax provision of $35,000 ($100,000 × 35%). This $7,000 book-tax difference relates to the difference between the book and tax basis of the depreciable asset times the current corporate tax rate ($7,000 = $20,000 × 35%).

Although PanCo did not actually pay the $7,000 tax this year, in future years when the book-tax depreciation difference reverses, the $7,000 eventually will be paid. As a result, the *future* income tax expense is matched to the related book income and is reported in the GAAP statements for the current year.

The total book tax expense under ASC 740 (SFAS 109) is made up of both current and deferred components. The **current tax expense** theoretically represents the taxes actually payable to (or refund receivable from) the governmental authorities for the current period.[12]

One might think of this amount as the actual check the taxpayer writes to the government (or refund received) for the current year; some tax professionals refer to this as the "cash tax" amount. Exhibit 3.3 summarizes the computation of a corporation's current tax expense.

---

[11]For instance, AstraZeneca reduced its effective tax rate after settling an audit with U.S. and U.K. tax authorities about its transfer pricing policies (see Chapter 16). The taxpayer's liability after the settlement was less than the tax reserve it had set aside on its GAAP statements with respect to the audit.

[12]ASC 740-10-10-1(a).

EXHIBIT 3.3	Current Tax Expense (Simplified)

	Pretax book income
±	Schedule M–1/M–3 adjustments
	Taxable income before NOLs
−	NOL carryforwards
	Taxable income
×	Applicable tax rate
	Current tax expense (provision) before tax credits
−	Tax credits
	Current tax expense (tax provision)

The deferred component of the book tax expense is called the **deferred tax expense** or **deferred tax benefit**. This component represents the future tax cost (or savings) connected with income reported in the current-period financial statement.[13] Deferred tax expense or benefit is created as a result of temporary differences. More technically, ASC 740 (SFAS 109) adopts a **balance sheet approach** to measuring deferred taxes. Under this approach, the deferred tax expense or benefit is the change from one year to the next in the entity's net, cumulative **deferred tax liability** or **deferred tax asset**.

A deferred tax liability is the expected future tax liability related to current income (measured using enacted tax rates and rules). A deferred tax liability is created in the following situations.

- An item is deductible for tax in the current period but is not expensed for book until some future period.

- Income is includible currently for book purposes but is not includible in taxable income until a future period.

In essence, a deferred tax liability is created when the book basis of an asset exceeds its tax basis. The opposite condition creates a deferred tax asset.

GLOBAL TAX ISSUES   **Accounting for Income Taxes in International Standards**

The FASB and the International Accounting Standards Board (IASB) have worked to move the GAAP and IFRS treatment of income taxes closer together in light of the proposed convergence of GAAP and IFRS. Both ASC 740 (SFAS 109) and IAS 12 (the IFRS guidance for income taxes) are based on a balance sheet approach.

Nevertheless, several significant differences exist between the two standards. These include the thresholds for recognition and approach to valuation allowances, the treatment of foreign subsidiaries and undistributed earnings, and the measurement of uncertain tax positions.[14] The IRS looks for comments on the Federal tax aspects of these convergence projects.[15]

---

[13]ASC 740-10-10-1(b).

[14]One can keep up with the FASB and the IASB's work on income tax reporting by visiting the FASB website at **www.fasb.org** and searching for the "Technical Agenda" section under "Projects."

[15]See, for example, Notice 2015–40, 2015-24 I.R.B. 1057, as to the IFRS revenue recognition projects.

Deferred Tax Expense

EXAMPLE 7

PJ Enterprises earns net income before depreciation of $500,000 in 2016 and $600,000 in 2017. PJ uses equipment acquired in 2016 for $80,000. For tax purposes, assume that PJ uses an accelerated method and deducts $60,000 in depreciation expense for the first year and $20,000 in depreciation expense for the second year. For book purposes, PJ depreciates the asset on a straight-line basis over two years ($40,000 in depreciation expense per year).

2016

	Beginning of Year			End of Year			Change in Basis Difference This Year	Tax Rate	Change in Deferred Tax Liability
	Book Basis	Tax Basis	Basis Differences, Book to Tax	Book Basis	Tax Basis	Basis Differences, Book to Tax			
Equipment	$—	$—	$—	$40,000	$20,000	$20,000	$20,000	35%	$7,000

A $7,000 deferred tax liability is created in 2016, due to the timing difference for the equipment depreciation.

2017

	Beginning of Year			End of Year			Change in Basis Difference This Year	Tax Rate	Change in Deferred Tax Liability
	Book Basis	Tax Basis	Basis Differences, Book to Tax	Book Basis	Tax Basis	Basis Differences, Book to Tax			
Equipment	$40,000	$20,000	$20,000	$—	$—	$—	($20,000)	35%	($7,000)

The book-tax difference in the asset basis reverses in 2017, with a resulting reduction of the deferred tax liability account.

EXAMPLE 8

Continue with the facts in Example 7. The following journal entries record the book tax expense (provision) for each year. The book total tax expense combines the current amount (income tax payable) and the future amount (deferred tax liability).

2016 Journal Entry

Income tax expense (provision)	$161,000*	
Income tax payable		$154,000**
Deferred tax liability		7,000

2017 Journal Entry

Income tax expense (provision)	$196,000*	
Deferred tax liability	7,000	
Income tax payable		$203,000**

At the end of 2016, the PJ balance sheet reflects a net deferred tax liability of $7,000. At the end of 2017, the PJ balance sheet contains a zero deferred tax liability; the temporary difference that created the deferred tax liability has reversed itself.

* 2016: ($500,000 − $40,000) × 35%   ** 2016: ($500,000 − $60,000) × 35%
  2017: ($600,000 − $40,000) × 35%   2017: ($600,000 − $20,000) × 35%

A deferred tax asset is the expected future tax benefit related to current book income (measured using enacted tax rates and rules). A deferred tax asset is created in the following situations.

- An expense is claimed for book purposes in the current period but is not deductible for tax until some future period.
- Income is includible in taxable income currently but is not recorded as book income until a future period.

Deferred Tax Assets

EXAMPLE 9

MollCo, Inc., earns net income before warranty expense of $400,000 in 2016 and $450,000 in 2017. In 2016, MollCo deducts $30,000 in warranty expense for book purposes related to expected warranty repairs. This warranty expense is not deductible for tax purposes until actually incurred. Assume that the $30,000 warranty obligation is paid in 2017, and that this is MollCo's only temporary difference.

2016	Beginning of Year			End of Year					
	Book Basis	Tax Basis	Basis Differences, Book to Tax	Book Basis	Tax Basis	Basis Differences, Book to Tax	Change in Basis Difference This Year	Tax Rate	Change in Deferred Tax Liability
Warranty	$—	$—	$—	$—	$30,000	($30,000)	($30,000)	35%	($10,500)

A $10,500 deferred tax asset is created in 2016, due to the timing difference for the warranty obligations.

2017	Beginning of Year			End of Year					
	Book Basis	Tax Basis	Basis Differences, Book to Tax	Book Basis	Tax Basis	Basis Differences, Book to Tax	Change in Basis Difference This Year	Tax Rate	Change in Deferred Tax Asset
Warranty	$—	$30,000	($30,000)	$—	$—	$—	$30,000	35%	$10,500

The book-tax difference in the warranty expense payable reverses in 2017, with a resulting reduction of the deferred tax asset account.

EXAMPLE 10

Continue with the facts in Example 9. The following journal entries record the book tax expense (provision) for each year. The book total tax expense combines the current amount (income tax payable) and the future amount (deferred tax asset).

2016 Journal Entry

Income tax expense (provision)	$129,500	
Deferred tax asset	10,500	
Income tax payable		$140,000

2017 Journal Entry

Income tax expense (provision)	$157,500	
Deferred tax asset		$ 10,500
Income tax payable		147,000

At the end of 2016, the MollCo balance sheet reflects a net deferred tax asset of $10,500. At the end of 2017, the MollCo balance sheet contains a zero deferred tax asset; the temporary difference that created the deferred tax asset has reversed itself.

Deferred tax assets and liabilities are reported on the balance sheet just like any other asset or liability is reported. However, the interpretation of these assets and liabilities is quite different. Typically, an asset is "good" because it represents a claim on something of value, and a liability is "bad" because it represents a future claim against the corporation's assets. In the case of deferred tax assets and liabilities, the interpretation is reversed. Deferred tax liabilities are "good" because they represent an amount that may be paid to the government in the future.

In essence, deferred tax liabilities are like an interest-free loan from the government with a due date perhaps many years in the future. Deferred tax assets, on the other hand, are future tax benefits and thus are similar to a receivable from the government that may not be received until many years in the future.

3-2b Valuation Allowance

Much of GAAP is based on the conservatism principle . That is, accounting rules are designed to provide assurance that assets are not overstated and liabilities are not understated. Current recognition of deferred tax liabilities does not require significant professional judgment because future tax liabilities always are expected to be settled in full. However, under ASC 740 (SFAS 109), deferred tax assets are recognized only when it is *more likely than not* (a greater than 50 percent likelihood) that the future tax benefits will be realized.

LO.3

Describe the purpose of the valuation allowance.

EXAMPLE
11

Warren, Inc., reported book income before tax of $2 million in 2017. Warren's taxable income also is $2 million (i.e., there are no temporary or permanent differences). Warren reports a current U.S. income tax liability for 2017 of $700,000 before tax credits ($2 million × 35%). During 2017, Warren paid $100,000 in foreign income taxes that it is not able to use as a credit on its 2017 tax return because of the foreign tax credit (FTC) limitation (see Chapter 16).

Warren's auditors believe it is *more likely than not* that Warren will be able to use the $100,000 in FTCs within the next 10 years (i.e., in a period before they expire unused). Consequently, the future tax benefit of the FTCs is accounted for in the current-year book tax expense as a $100,000 future tax benefit.

The current and deferred tax expense are calculated as follows.

	Book	Tax
Income tax expense/payable	$600,000	$700,000
Current tax expense	$700,000	
Deferred tax expense (benefit)	($100,000)	

Warren records the following journal entry for the book income tax expense and deferred tax asset related to the expected use of the FTCs.

Income tax expense (provision)	$600,000	
Deferred tax asset	100,000	
Income tax payable		$700,000

Because Warren is able to record the benefit of the future FTCs, its effective tax rate is 30% ($600,000 tax expense/$2 million book income before tax).

When a deferred tax asset does not meet the *more likely than not* threshold for recognition, ASC 740 (SFAS 109) requires that a valuation allowance be created. The valuation allowance is a contra-asset account that offsets all or a portion of the deferred tax asset.

EXAMPLE
12

Assume that the auditors in Example 11 believe that Warren will be able to use only $40,000 of the FTCs, with the remaining $60,000 expiring unused. In this case, the future tax benefit recognized currently should be only $40,000 rather than the full $100,000. To implement this reduction in the deferred tax asset, Warren records a valuation allowance of $60,000, resulting in a book tax expense of $660,000.

	Book	Tax
Income tax expense/payable	$660,000	$700,000
Current tax expense	$700,000	
Deferred tax expense (benefit)	($ 40,000)	

continued

Warren records the following journal entry for the book income tax expense and deferred tax asset related to the expected use of the FTCs.

Income tax expense (provision)	$660,000	
Deferred tax asset	100,000	
Valuation allowance		$ 60,000
Income tax payable		700,000

Warren reduces the deferred tax asset by $60,000, which increases its effective tax rate to 33% ($660,000 tax expense/$2 million book income before tax), compared with the 30% effective tax rate in Example 11.

To determine whether a valuation allowance is required, both positive and negative evidence must be evaluated. Negative evidence (i.e., evidence suggesting that the deferred tax asset will not be realized) includes the following.

- History of losses.
- Expected future losses.
- Short carryback/carryforward periods.
- History of tax credits expiring unused.

Positive evidence (i.e., support for realizing the current benefit of future tax savings) includes the following.

- Strong earnings history.
- Existing contracts.
- Unrealized appreciation in assets.
- Sales backlog of profitable orders.

The valuation allowance is examined for appropriateness each year. The allowance may be increased or decreased in subsequent reporting periods if facts and circumstances change.

The Big Picture

EXAMPLE 13

Return to the facts of *The Big Picture* on p. 3-1. Arctic Corporation has recorded a $3 million deferred tax asset for an NOL carryforward. The deferred tax asset has been offset by a $1 million valuation allowance, due to doubts over the levels of future sales and profitability.

But this year, Arctic completed improvements to its inventory management system that are likely to increase the contribution margin of every product that Arctic sells. In addition, two of Arctic's largest customers have secured financing that will relieve the financial difficulties that have restricted them. In fact, Arctic just received purchase orders from those customers that will increase unit sales by 20% over the next 18 months. As a result, Arctic's auditors now support a release of $200,000 of the valuation allowance in the current quarter.

DIGGING DEEPER 3   In-depth coverage can be found on this book's companion website: www.cengagebrain.com

TAX PLANNING STRATEGIES Releasing Valuation Allowances

FRAMEWORK FOCUS: DEDUCTIONS

Strategy: Maximize Deductible Amounts.

When a corporation records a valuation allowance, it loses the ability to recognize the benefit of future tax savings in the current period. However, all is not lost if the taxpayer can demonstrate that facts and circumstances have changed. For example, if a taxpayer generates a net operating loss (NOL), it records a deferred tax asset for the future tax savings related to using the NOL. However, if the evidence suggests that it is *more likely than not* that the NOL will expire unused, a valuation allowance must be recorded.

To reduce this valuation allowance, the taxpayer must demonstrate that there will be future taxable income sufficient to absorb the NOL within the carryforward period. Sources of future taxable income include reversals of temporary differences that will produce future taxable income and other sources of future profits. Taxpayers also may demonstrate that the adoption of new tax planning strategies will allow the use of deferred tax assets.

For example, assume that Warren, Inc., from Example 12, adopts new planning strategies in 2018 that will allow it ultimately to use all $100,000 of its FTC carryforward. Warren earns $2.3 million in book income before tax and reports $2.3 million in taxable income in 2018 (i.e., there are no permanent or temporary differences). The current tax expense is $805,000 ($2.3 million × 35%).

Based on new evidence (implementation of tax planning strategies), the auditors determine that the entire $100,000

in FTCs will be used in the future before expiration. Accordingly, the $60,000 valuation allowance from 2017 is "released," and the tax benefit of this release affects the 2018 financial results as follows.

	Book	Tax
Income tax expense/payable	$745,000	$805,000
Current tax expense	$805,000	
Deferred tax expense	($ 60,000)	

Warren makes the following journal entry to record the book income tax expense and valuation allowance release related to the expected use of the FTCs.

Income tax expense (provision)	$745,000	
Valuation allowance	60,000	
Income tax payable		$805,000

Warren's effective tax rate for 2018 is 32.4 percent ($745,000/$2.3 million). Without the valuation allowance release, Warren's effective tax rate would have been 35 percent ($805,000/$2.3 million). This tax rate benefit is realized even though the $100,000 in FTC carryforwards have yet to be used in Warren's tax return.

3-2c Tax Disclosures in the Financial Statements

As illustrated earlier, any temporary differences create deferred tax liabilities or deferred tax assets, and these amounts appear in the corporation's balance sheet.

LO.4

Interpret the disclosure information contained in the financial statements.

FINANCIAL DISCLOSURE INSIGHTS Tax Losses and the Deferred Tax Asset

Although a current-year net operating loss (NOL) represents a failure of an entity's business model to some, others see it as an immediate tax refund. But when an NOL hits the balance sheet as a deferred tax asset, the story is not over. The NOL creates or increases a deferred tax asset that may or may not be used in future financial accounting reporting periods. The key question for a financial analyst is whether the entity will generate enough net revenue in future years to create a

positive tax liability that can be offset by the NOL carryover amount.

IFRS rules do not allow for a valuation allowance. Under IAS 12, a deferred tax asset is recorded only when it is "probable" (a higher standard than GAAP's "more likely than not") that the deferred tax amount will be realized, and then only to the extent of that probable amount. Thus, no offsetting valuation allowance is needed.

The Balance Sheet

As with any asset or liability, these accounts are classified as either current or noncurrent, based on the assets or liabilities that created the temporary difference.[16] If the deferred tax liability or asset is not related to any asset, then the classification is based on the expected reversal period.

EXAMPLE 14

JenCo, Inc., holds a deferred tax liability generated because tax depreciation exceeds book depreciation on manufacturing equipment. Because the equipment is a noncurrent asset, the deferred tax liability also is noncurrent. JenCo also reports a deferred tax asset related to bad debt expenses deductible for book purposes but not yet deductible for tax purposes. Because the bad debt expense is related to accounts receivable, a current asset, the associated deferred tax asset is classified as current.

If JenCo incurs an NOL, a deferred tax asset is created, because of the future tax benefit provided by the NOL deduction. The NOL is not related to any specific asset or liability. Accordingly, the deferred tax asset is classified based on when the corporation expects to use the NOL. If the expected use is more than one year in the future, the deferred tax asset is classified as noncurrent.

A corporation may hold both deferred tax assets and liabilities, current and noncurrent. The corporation reports the *net* current deferred tax assets or liabilities and the *net* noncurrent deferred tax assets or liabilities.[17]

The Big Picture

EXAMPLE 15

Return to the facts of *The Big Picture* on p. 3-1. Arctic Corporation holds the following deferred tax asset and liability accounts for the current year.

Current deferred tax assets	$50,000
Current deferred tax liabilities	72,000
Noncurrent deferred tax assets	93,000
Noncurrent deferred tax liabilities	28,000

On its balance sheet, Arctic reports a $22,000 current net deferred tax liability ($72,000 − $50,000) and a $65,000 noncurrent net deferred tax asset ($93,000 − $28,000).

FINANCIAL DISCLOSURE INSIGHTS **Valuation Allowances for NOLs**

Financial analysts use the valuation allowance system to help them determine an entity's expected future cash flows. Some critics of the GAAP rules for valuation allowances maintain that the process allows management to manipulate profits and earnings per share in an arbitrary fashion.

Only a few of the largest business entities, supported by going-concern assumptions and access to worldwide debt and equity capital, need to record a sizable valuation allowance. But valuation allowances also often are found in the financial reports of smaller entities and those in volatile industries, whose future profitability is likely to present questions.

In a recent reporting year, for instance, the following telecommunications businesses reported a valuation allowance related to expectations that their NOLs (for Federal and/or state taxing jurisdictions) would expire unused.

	Deferred Tax Assets ($ in 000's)	Valuation Allowance ($ in 000's)
Verizon	$17,852	$1,841
Sprint Corporation	11,353	8,880
AT&T	13,804	1,142

Establishing a valuation allowance does not affect the entity's internal cash balances, but it might have an effect on the stock price. Valuation allowances can be "released" by management when evidence develops that the carryforwards are more likely to be used in the future, for example, if profitability improves and appears to be sustainable.

---

[16]ASC 740-10-45-4.

[17]ASC 740-10-45-6.

TAX FACT Effective Tax Rates for Selected Fortune 100 Companies

Here are some recent provisions for income taxes (state, federal, and international) made by selected major corporations, as a percentage of their book income before taxes. Recall that the top statutory Federal tax rate is 35 percent. State and local taxes generally add another 5 percentage points to that rate.

Aetna	34.9%	Disney	33.3%
Apple	24.2%	ExxonMobil	44.0%
Boeing	34.0%	Ford	28.8%
Chevron	43.2%	General Electric	14.4%
Citigroup	0.3%	Google	19.4%
		IBM	24.2%
		JPMorgan Chase	24.6%
		Pfizer	21.2%
		United Health Group	35.9%
		Wal-Mart	32.6%
		Yahoo!	20.7%

The Income Statement

In its GAAP income statement, a corporation reports a total income tax expense that consists of both the current tax expense (or benefit) and the deferred tax expense (or benefit). The tax expense is allocated among income from continuing operations, discontinued operations, extraordinary items, prior-period adjustments, and the cumulative effect of accounting changes. Additional disclosures are required for the tax expense allocated to income from continuing operations (e.g., current versus deferred, benefits of NOL deductions, and changes in valuation allowances).

Financial Statement Footnotes

The income tax footnote contains a wealth of information, including the following.

- Breakdown of income between domestic and foreign.
- Analysis of the provision for income tax expense.
- Analysis of deferred tax assets and liabilities.
- Effective tax rate reconciliation (dollar amount or percentage).
- Information on use of ASC 740-30 (APB 23) for the earnings of foreign subsidiaries.
- Discussion of significant tax matters.

The steps in determining a corporation's income tax expense for book purposes are summarized in Concept Summary 3.2.

Rate Reconciliation

The purpose of the rate reconciliation is to demonstrate how a corporation's actual book effective tax rate relates to its "hypothetical tax rate" (i.e., as if the book income were taxed at the U.S. corporate rate of 35 percent).[18] Although similar to Schedule M–1 or M–3, the tax footnote rate reconciliation generally reports only differences triggered by permanent differences. An analysis of the rate reconciliation can provide substantial indicators as to the tax planning strategies adopted (or not adopted) by a company; see text Section 3-3: Benchmarking.

---

[18]ASC 740-10-50-12.

Concept Summary 3.2

Steps in Determining the Book Tax Expense

Start with the corporation's book income after permanent differences.

↓

Determine the corporation's temporary differences.

↓

Compute the corporation's current tax provision.

↓

Compute the corporation's deferred tax provision.

↓

Determine whether a valuation allowance is required.

↓

Prepare the income tax note disclosures.

Rate Reconciliations

EXAMPLE 16

BoxCo, Inc., a domestic corporation, owns 100% of PaperCo, Ltd., an Erasmus corporation. BoxCo's U.S. corporate tax rate is 35% and its Erasmus rate is 10%. As discussed later in the chapter, BoxCo reports book but not taxable income for PaperCo's overseas profits under ASC 740-30 (APB 23). Book income, permanent and temporary differences, and current tax expense are computed as follows.

	BoxCo	PaperCo
Book income before tax	$300,000	$200,000
Permanent differences		
Meals and entertainment expense	20,000	—
Municipal bond interest income	(50,000)	—
Book income after permanent differences	$270,000	$200,000
Temporary differences		
Tax > book depreciation	(50,000)	—
Book > tax bad debt expense	10,000	—
Taxable income	$230,000	$200,000
Tax rate	× 35%	× 10%
Current tax expense	$ 80,500	$ 20,000

continued

Specifically, basis amounts and current deductions for the two assets are reported as follows.

	Book Basis, Beginning of Year	Tax Basis, Beginning of Year	Basis Difference, Beginning of Year	Current-Year Book Expense	Current-Year Tax Deduction
Depreciable assets	$900,000	$750,000	$150,000	$40,000	$90,000
Receivables	800,000	850,000	(50,000)	15,000	5,000

Thus, the beginning-of-the-year deferred tax liability is $35,000 [($150,000 − $50,000) × 35%].

To determine the deferred tax expense (benefit) for the current year, the change in the balance sheet amounts for these temporary differences from the beginning to the end of the year must be determined and then multiplied by the appropriate tax rate.

	Beginning of Year			End of Year			Change in Basis Difference This Year	Tax Rate	Change in Deferred Tax Liability/ (Asset)
	Book Basis	Tax Basis	Basis Differences, Book to Tax	Book Basis	Tax Basis	Basis Differences, Book to Tax			
Depreciation	$900,000	$750,000	$150,000	$860,000	$660,000	$200,000	$ 50,000	35%	$17,500
Receivables	800,000	850,000	(50,000)	785,000	845,000	(60,000)	(10,000)	35%	(3,500)

The deferred tax liability increased by $14,000 for the year. Consequently, BoxCo's total tax provision for book purposes is $114,500.

Current tax expense

Domestic	$ 80,500
Foreign	20,000

Deferred tax expense

Domestic	14,000
Foreign	—
Total tax expense	$114,500

The journal entry to record the book income tax expense is constructed as follows.

Income tax expense (provision)	$114,500	
Income tax payable		$100,500
Deferred tax liability		14,000

BoxCo's book income is $500,000 (the combined book income of both BoxCo and PaperCo). The effective tax rate reconciliation is based on this book income, with the dollar amounts in the table representing the tax expense (benefit) related to the item and the percentage representing the tax expense (benefit) as a percentage of book income. For example, the municipal bond interest of $50,000 reduces tax liability by $17,500 ($50,000 × 35%). This $17,500 as a percentage of the $500,000 book income is 3.5%.

	Effective Tax Rate Reconciliation	
	$	%
Hypothetical tax at U.S. rate	$175,000	35.0%
Disallowed meals and entertainment expense	7,000	1.4
Municipal bond interest	(17,500)	(3.5)
Foreign income taxed at less than U.S. rate	(50,000)*	(10.0)
Income tax expense (provision)	$114,500	22.9%

*$200,000 × (35% − 10%).

Only permanent differences appear in the rate reconciliation. Temporary differences do not affect the *total* book income tax expense; they simply affect the amount of the tax expense that is current versus deferred.

TAX FACT   Effective Tax Rates Examined

A U.S. Government Accountability Office (GAO) study examined the tax returns of profitable U.S. corporations for a recent tax year; the data came from an analysis of corporate Schedules M–3. Some of the most interesting findings from the study include the following.

- The effective tax rate for these entities was 12.6 percent of worldwide income. Including income tax obligations to state, local, and non-U.S. governments, the effective tax rate became 16.9 percent. The statutory Federal tax rate for these entities was 35 percent.

- Some of the largest reported book-tax differences included:
  - Interest deductions that were deferred for tax purposes.
  - Cost recovery deductions that were accelerated.
  - Retirement plan contributions that were accelerated.
  - Tax deductions for current non-U.S. income that were allowed.

Source: **www.gao.gov/assets/660/654957.pdf**.

Rate Reconciliations

EXAMPLE 17

Assume the same facts as Example 16, except that a new income tax law is enacted before the end of the current year that will increase the U.S. corporate tax rate to 40% beginning next year. In this case, multiply the year-end total temporary differences of $140,000 by 40% rather than 35%. This results in an increase in the deferred tax liability of $21,000.

Basis Differences, Book to Tax	Beginning of Year	End of Year	Effect of Rate Change
Depreciation	$150,000	$200,000	
Receivables	(50,000)	(60,000)	
Total temporary differences	$100,000	$140,000	
Tax rate	× 35%	× 40%	
Deferred tax liability	$ 35,000	$ 56,000	$21,000

The current-year deferred tax liability is a function of both the change in temporary differences at the enacted rate ($40,000 × 40%) and the additional 5% tax on the beginning temporary differences [$100,000 × (40% − 35%)].

3-2d Special Issues

LO.5

Identify the GAAP treatment concerning tax uncertainties and unrepatriated foreign earnings.

Financial Accounting for Tax Uncertainties

Companies take positions in their tax returns that may not ultimately survive the scrutiny of the IRS or other tax authorities. If a taxpayer loses the benefit of a favorable tax position after an audit, there may be an unfavorable effect on the company's financial statement tax expense in that year. The additional tax cost will become part of the current tax expense, yet the income that this tax is related to would have been reported in a previous year. This result can wreak havoc with a company's effective tax rate.

To avoid such an increase in effective tax rate, companies may record a book reserve (or "cushion") for the uncertain tax position in the year the position is taken. That is, rather than book the entire tax benefit (and thus reduce tax expense in the current year), the company may book only a portion (or none) of the tax benefit. If the company later loses the actual tax benefit upon audit, to the extent the additional tax imposed is charged against the reserve, the additional tax does not affect the future-year tax expense. If the company's tax position is not challenged in the future (or the company successfully defends any challenge), the reserve can be released. This release reduces the current tax expense in the future (release) year, and it lowers the company's effective tax rate in that year.

TAX PLANNING STRATEGIES Tax Savings Are Not Always Created Equal

FRAMEWORK FOCUS: THINKING OUTSIDE THE FRAMEWORK

Many different types of tax planning strategies can produce tax savings. Yet, even when planning ideas produce identical current cash-flow effects, some ideas may have an edge. CEOs and CFOs of public companies are focused on the bottom line—the company's net income after tax and related earnings per share. A CFO is likely to be just as interested in an idea's effect on the company's bottom line income as on the cash tax savings.

For example, consider two tax planning ideas that each produce $700,000 of current tax savings. The first idea generates its $700,000 in tax savings by increasing tax depreciation relative to book depreciation by $2 million ($700,000 = $2 million × 35%). The second idea produces

research activities tax credits of $700,000, thus reducing current-year tax by $700,000.

Idea 1 produces its current tax savings via a temporary difference. Accordingly, the book tax expense will not reflect the $700,000 in tax savings. Instead, this $700,000 simply moves from the current tax category to the deferred tax category. Even if the book-tax difference is not expected to reverse in the next 30 years (effectively generating "permanent" savings), the book tax expense does not reflect this savings.

In contrast, idea 2 produces its current tax savings via a permanent difference. Thus, the book tax expense also declines by $700,000. This item appears in the income tax note rate reconciliation.

To add more structure to the accounting for tax reserves, the FASB released an interpretation, "Accounting for Uncertainty in Income Taxes" **[ASC 740-10 (FIN 48)]**. The approach required under this interpretation results in significantly more disclosure about uncertain tax positions by companies.

When ASC 740-10 (FIN 48) applies, uncertain tax positions effectively are defined as those material items not fully certain by the taxpayer to be sustainable upon a later review based on technical merits. Such tax positions result in a permanent reduction of income taxes payable, a deferral of income taxes otherwise currently payable to future years, or a change in the expected realizability of deferred tax assets.

Application of the ASC 740-10 (FIN 48) rules essentially is a two-step process—recognition and measurement. These steps are illustrated in Concept Summary 3.3.

Concept Summary 3.3

Disclosures Under ASC 740-10 (FIN 48)

RECOGNITION

Regarding the uncertain tax position, is it *more likely than not* that the tax benefit will be recognized?

MEASUREMENT

Determine the recognized amount of the tax benefit.

FINANCIAL STATEMENT DISCLOSURE

Reassess for every reporting period.

First, a tax benefit from an uncertain tax position may be *recognized* in the financial statements only if it is *more likely than not* (a greater than 50 percent likelihood) that the position would be sustained on its technical merits. In this regard, audit or detection risk cannot be considered. This first step determines whether any of the tax benefit is recognized.

If the *more likely than not* standard is failed, no financial statement disclosure is required. If the uncertain tax position meets the *more likely than not* threshold, the second step is to determine the amount of the tax benefit to report.

Measurement of the amount of the tax benefit to be disclosed then occurs. This computation is based on the probabilities associated with the position not being challenged, or with it being challenged using a negotiated settlement or litigation.

A probability table is constructed, considering all of the possible post-audit and post-settlement outcomes for the tax benefit from the filing position. The filing position is recorded (i.e., the income or deduction amount is recognized for GAAP purposes) as the largest amount of the related tax benefit that is *more likely than not* (a greater than 50 percent probability) to be agreeable to the taxing authority, assuming that the agency has full knowledge of all relevant information.[19]

EXAMPLE

18

StarksCo has adopted certain aggressive transfer pricing strategies with related parties overseas. StarksCo estimates that it will reduce its Federal income tax liability by $100,000 as a result of these strategies but that the IRS is likely to challenge the pricing structure in an audit. After negotiating and settling with the IRS, StarksCo estimates that the tax benefit may be reduced (amounts as indicated with related probabilities); StarksCo constructs a table of these probabilities and results.

Resulting Estimated Tax Benefit	Probability of Agreement Between StarksCo and IRS	Cumulative Probability Computed
$100,000	40%	40%
80,000	35%	75%
45,000	20%	95%
—0—	5%	100%

Assume that StarksCo recorded a book tax provision of $250,000, *including* the $100,000 tax benefit from this tax uncertainty. In light of the requirements of ASC 740-10 (FIN 48), StarksCo instead should record an $80,000 tax benefit for this item. That amount is the estimated tax benefit that first exceeds a 50% cumulative probability of agreement with the IRS (here, a 75% chance of acceptance exists).

The journal entry that StarksCo records for this computation is as follows, increasing the tax provision by $20,000, the amount dictated by ASC 740-10 (FIN 48) = $100,000 − $80,000.

Current income tax expense	$20,000	
Income tax payable		$20,000

The entry for the new $20,000 payable is classified as a current liability only if it is expected that the negotiations with the IRS on this matter will be resolved within 12 months.

The recognition and measurement of uncertain tax positions is reassessed at each reporting date. ASC 740-10 (FIN 48) requires a reconciliation of the beginning and ending balances of the unrecognized tax benefits and a discussion of potential changes in these unrecognized tax benefits that might occur over the next 12 months.

Earnings of Foreign Subsidiaries

As discussed earlier, a corporate group's financial statements include both domestic and foreign controlled subsidiaries. However, foreign corporations, even those controlled by U.S. shareholders, are not part of a U.S. consolidated tax return (see Chapter 16).

---

[19]ASC 740-10-30-7.

Consequently, U.S. taxpayers can achieve deferral of current U.S. taxes on foreign income if they operate their overseas activities through foreign subsidiary corporations in jurisdictions with lower tax rates than those of the United States (see Chapter 16). Although the *actual* U.S. taxes on foreign corporations' profits are deferred, the reported effective tax rate for financial statement purposes may not reflect this deferral, because ASC 740 (SFAS 109) requires that a corporate group report both current and deferred income tax expense.

USCo, a domestic corporation, operates a manufacturing facility in Singapore through a Singapore corporation. USCo's U.S. tax rate is 35% and its Singapore tax rate is 6%. For the current year, USCo earns $600,000 in taxable income. The Singapore corporation earns $400,000 in taxable income from its operations, pays $24,000 in taxes to Singapore, and makes no distributions to its U.S. parent. The Singapore corporation is not taxed in the United States because it is not a U.S. entity, and it conducts no activities in the United States.

USCo is not taxed on the Singapore profits because it has not received any distributions of these profits. Accordingly, USCo has achieved deferral and reduced its worldwide cash tax costs.

However, for financial statement purposes, the USCo group includes the $400,000 in Singapore profits in its net income. It reports both the Singapore tax and any *potential* U.S. tax (after allowable FTCs) as its total tax expense.

U.S. Tax Return		Potential U.S. Tax on Non-U.S. Income	
Income	$600,000	Income	$400,000
Tax rate	× 35%	Tax rate	× 35%
U.S. tax	$210,000	Total tax	$140,000
		Foreign tax credit	(24,000)
		Net U.S. tax	$116,000

Consequently, the total tax expense for financial statement purposes is $350,000. The financial statement effective tax rate on USCo's global income is 35% ($350,000 total tax expense/ $1,000,000 net income). Thus, although USCo paid only $234,000 in taxes, its after-tax book income does not reflect the savings generated from operating in Singapore, a low-tax country.

Current U.S. tax	$210,000
Current foreign tax	24,000
Deferred U.S. tax	116,000
Total tax expense	$350,000

ASC 740-30 (APB 23) provides an exception to ASC 740 (SFAS 109) for income from foreign subsidiaries.[20] If a corporation documents that it is permanently reinvesting the earnings of its foreign subsidiaries outside the United States, the corporation does not record as an expense any future U.S. income tax the corporation may pay on such earnings.

USCo, in Example 19, uses ASC 740-30 (APB 23) to avoid reporting the $116,000 in deferred taxes. Because USCo plans to reinvest its Singapore earnings indefinitely outside the United States, it is not required to include the deferred U.S. taxes as part of its total tax expense.

USCo's total financial statement income remains $1 million, but its total tax expense is only $234,000 (the taxes currently paid to the United States and Singapore). The resulting financial statement effective tax rate is 23.4% ($234,000/$1,000,000), and the USCo group's after-tax book income reflects the Singapore tax savings.

ASC 740-30 (APB 23) is a major issue only when the foreign subsidiary is taxed at rates below the applicable U.S. tax rate. Otherwise, there is no potential for tax deferral.

Using ASC 740-30 (APB 23) is not an "all or nothing" decision. It can be adopted in some years and not others. Even within a year, it may be used for only a portion of foreign subsidiary earnings.

---

[20]Formerly *Opinion No. 23—Accounting for Income Taxes—Special Areas,* Accounting Principles Board.

FINANCIAL DISCLOSURE INSIGHTS   Corporate Tax Rate Cuts: Be Careful What You Wish For

Many lawmakers, businesses, and think tanks are calling for a reform to the U.S. corporate income tax, including a cut in the top tax rate from the current 35 percent to perhaps 25 percent—a reduction in the top rate of almost 30 percent. The lower rate would match that used by most other developed countries, and a rate cut might make U.S. entities more competitive in the global marketplace. A rate cut would be paid for by repealing or capping various deductions and credits that corporations use to reduce their average and effective tax rates.

But for those corporations that hold deferred tax assets (e.g., NOL and credit carryforwards), the corresponding GAAP results might not be so attractive. Deferred tax assets (DTAs) would be written down for book purposes (because lower tax rates will apply in the future, the deferred deductions and credits will produce lower tax savings). Such write-downs of the DTAs thus would reduce current book income—perhaps by dramatic amounts. That cannot be good for stock prices and executive bonuses.

A corporation's specific DTAs are not publicly disclosed, but a 30 percent cut in the U.S. corporate income tax rates would, on average, trigger a 30 percent DTA write-down. Could the GAAP consequences of a corporate income tax rate reduction be so negative as to move businesses to block the cut itself?

The Big Picture

EXAMPLE 21

Return to the facts of *The Big Picture* on p. 3-1. Recall from Example 1 that Arctic Corporation has a wholly owned foreign subsidiary, Hurricane, Ltd. Assume that Arctic also owns 100% of another foreign corporation, Typhoon, Ltd.

Arctic can choose to apply ASC 740-30 (APB 23) to both of its foreign subsidiaries in year 1 and to only Hurricane in year 2. In year 3, Arctic can choose to use ASC 740-30 (APB 23) for 40% of Hurricane's earnings and 80% of Typhoon's earnings.

Under these rules, an assertion by management that foreign earnings will remain overseas indefinitely converts a temporary book-tax difference into a permanent difference. This can result in a significant decrease in the entity's book effective tax rate.

EXAMPLE 22

Raven is a U.S. corporation that is subject to a 35% U.S. income tax rate. Its 100% owned subsidiary Cuervo operates in Despina, a country that does not levy an income tax. Cuervo makes no distributions to Raven during the tax year.

Raven's book-tax differences and effective tax rate are computed as follows. If Raven's management asserts that Cuervo's profits are to be permanently invested in Despina, the book effective tax rate decreases by about one-third.

	Cuervo Earnings Are "Permanently Reinvested" in Despina ($ in 000's)	Cuervo Earnings Are *Not* "Permanently Reinvested" in Despina ($ in 000's)
Pretax U.S. book income	$100,000	$100,000
Pretax Despina book income	50,000	50,000
Total pretax book income	$150,000	$150,000
Temporary book-tax difference: Despina earnings		(50,000)
Permanent book-tax difference: Despina earnings	(50,000)	
Taxable income	$100,000	$100,000
U.S. income tax	$ 35,000	$ 35,000
Deferred income tax expense		17,500
Total income tax expense	$ 35,000	$ 52,500
GAAP effective tax rate	23.3%	35.0%

TAX PLANNING STRATEGIES **Reducing Effective Tax Rates with ASC 740-30 (APB 23) Can Backfire**

FRAMEWORK FOCUS: DEDUCTIONS

Strategy: Maximize Deductible Amounts.

Because ASC 740-30 (APB 23) allows for higher reported book earnings (no deferred U.S. tax expense is recorded), its use may be reflected in higher stock prices and increased shareholder wealth. Many U.S. multinationals with foreign subsidiaries use ASC 740-30 (APB 23) to avoid reporting U.S. deferred taxes on foreign earnings.

The "permanent reinvestment" exception should not be employed unless the corporation truly expects to keep its foreign earnings outside the United States. Using ASC 740-30 (APB 23) and then repatriating foreign profits after all can cause extreme spikes in a corporation's effective tax rate.

USCo, a domestic corporation, owns 100% of Shamrock, Ltd., an Atlantis corporation. Its U.S. tax rate is 35%, and its Atlantis tax rate is 10%. In 2016, USCo earns $100,000 in taxable income and pays $35,000 to the United States. Shamrock earns $400,000 in taxable income and pays $40,000 in taxes to Atlantis. Shamrock makes no distributions to its U.S. parent and is not taxed in the United States because it is not a U.S. entity and has no activities in the United States.

USCo is not taxed on the Atlantis profits because it has not received any distributions of these profits. Furthermore, USCo uses ASC 740-30 (APB 23) to avoid recording any deferred U.S. income tax expense on its financial statements. Accordingly, USCo has achieved deferral and reduced its worldwide cash tax costs and book income tax expense.

USCo's total income tax provision for financial statement purposes is $75,000.

Current U.S. tax	$35,000
Current foreign tax	40,000
Total tax expense	$75,000

EXAMPLE

23

The financial statement effective tax rate on USCo's global income is 15% ($75,000 total tax expense/$500,000 net income). Thus, the USCo group has achieved higher after-tax book income and earnings per share.

In 2017, USCo earns $200,000 in taxable income and pays $70,000 to the United States. Shamrock breaks even for the year and pays no taxes to Atlantis. At the same time, USCo decides that Shamrock should pay it a dividend of $360,000.

U.S. Tax Return	
U.S. income	$200,000
Foreign dividend*	400,000
Taxable income	$600,000
Tax rate	× 35%
	$210,000
FTC	(40,000)
Net U.S. tax	$170,000

*The total gross income is the $360,000 cash dividend grossed up by the $40,000 potential FTC (see Chapter 16).

For book purposes, USCo reports only $200,000 in net income (the $400,000 in Atlantis income was included in book income in 2016 and is not included again). The 2017 total tax expense for financial statement purposes is $170,000.

Current U.S. tax	$170,000
Current foreign tax	—0—
Total tax expense	$170,000

The financial statement effective tax rate on USCo's global income is 85% ($170,000 total tax expense/$200,000 net income). This extremely high effective rate is caused by the mismatching of the Atlantis income (reported in 2016) and the U.S. taxes on the Atlantis income (reported in 2017).

TAX IN THE NEWS **The APB 23 Deferral**

Multinational corporations tend to leave off-shore the cash resulting from their profitable overseas activities, deferring both book and tax income recognition thereof. This is not "idle cash" by any means, as the funds typically are used to finance growth in the non-U.S. operations of the entity. Furthermore, if the offshore cash were "brought home" to the United States (e.g., to create U.S. jobs or pay cash dividends to U.S. investors), book and taxable income would be triggered, and stock prices might suffer.

Here are recent estimates of the overseas cash holdings and the related deferred U.S. corporate income tax of several prominent entities.

Corporation	Overseas Cash ($ in billions)	Deferred Federal Corporate Income Tax ($ in billions)
Bank of America	$ 17.2	$ 4.5
Citigroup	43.8	11.6
Microsoft	92.9	29.6
Apple	157.8	51.6

In fact, when a U.S. corporation desires to make a dividend payment to its shareholders, it can borrow funds to provide the necessary liquidity, using the overseas cash as collateral for the loan; free cash results, but the tax deferral continues. Apple and other corporations have used this technique in the recent past.

But sometimes, corporations bring the cash back to implement strategic plans. General Electric (GE) repatriated about $36 billion in overseas cash as part of its plan to sell off GE Capital. The repatriation triggered an additional Federal income tax liability of about $6 billion. For GE, the taxes paid were simply the cost of exiting a complex and highly-regulated business. GE used the remaining cash to help fund a $50 billion stock buyback.

3-2e **Summary**

The tax department of a business often is charged with constructing the entity's tax strategies (*tax planning*) and filing all required tax returns (*tax compliance*) while preparing for subsequent audit and litigation activity (*tax controversy*). Tax professionals often work closely with those who prepare the entity's financial statements, especially concerning the tax footnote, tax deferral accounts, and tax rate reconciliations. Professional tax and accounting research underlies all of this work.

The efforts of a modern tax department are depicted in Exhibit 3.4. Tax professionals must be proficient in all of the indicated areas, so that they can meet the demands placed upon the entity by shareholders, regulators, and taxing agencies. If the tax professional grasps both the tax and financial statement effects of various tax planning and compliance activities, he or she brings great value to the entity through the tax department.

EXHIBIT 3.4	Functions of a Tax Department (by Percent of Time Spent)

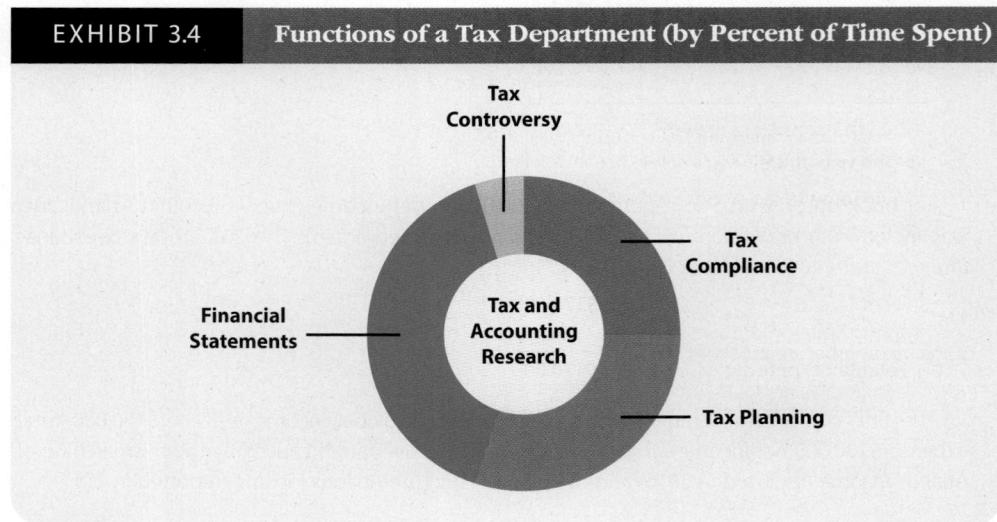

3-3 BENCHMARKING

LO.6

Use financial statement income tax information to benchmark a company's tax position.

An entity's income tax expense amount may appear to be of little interest to anyone beyond the taxpayer that makes the payment and the government agencies that collect it. The tax year is over, the transactions are completed, and the final costs have been tallied. Still, this historical tax information may prove valuable. A company's income tax expense is one of the single largest expense items on its income statement, and understanding the components of this expense is a critical activity for the tax professional.

Consider a typical baseball game. Two teams meet, interact following a specific set of rules, and ultimately complete the game, generating a final score. Of course, the final score is of immediate interest to the teams and the fans, but once the game is over, the score and associated statistics (runs, hits, and errors) are relegated to the history books. Yet, these statistics still can be quite useful. A team coach may use the game statistics to evaluate the strengths and weaknesses of the players to assist in improving performance. Other teams may use the statistics to develop strategies for upcoming games. Players can use the statistics to "benchmark" themselves against their own performance in prior games or against players on other teams. In short, there is a wealth of information in these historical data.

A taxpayer's reported income tax expense likewise is a valuable source of information for the company, its tax advisers, and its competitors. The reported information provides clues about a company's operational and tax planning strategies.

Companies may benchmark their tax situation to other years' results or to other companies in the same industry. The starting point for a **benchmarking** exercise usually is the data from the income tax note rate reconciliation.

3-3a Dynamic Benchmarking

Exhibit 3.5 shows the tax rate reconciliation information from the income tax notes for two recent years of Sears Holding Corporation (Sears) and Wal-Mart Stores, Inc. (Wal-Mart). Both companies are listed on the New York Stock Exchange, are in the same industry, and operate both inside and outside the United States. Although the income and tax expense amounts of both companies are quite different in magnitude, the tax amounts are converted to percentage of income numbers for comparability purposes. In year 1, Sears reported an effective tax rate that was 12 percentage points higher than Wal-Mart's rate. In year 2, Sears's effective tax rate was 4.9 points below

EXHIBIT 3.5	Tax Rate Reconciliation for Sears and Wal-Mart			
	Sears		**Wal-Mart**	
	Year 2	**Year 1**	**Year 2**	**Year 1**
Hypothetical tax (benefit) at U.S. Federal rate	35.0%	35.0%	35.0%	35.0%
State and local income taxes, net of Federal benefit	6.0	7.2	1.9	1.7
Tax credits	(3.0)	(6.3)		
Resolution of income tax matters	(6.2)	(6.8)		
Basis difference in domestic subsidiary	—	(30.2)		
Non-U.S. income taxed at different rates	(0.9)	(2.3)	(1.7)	(1.6)
Nondeductible goodwill	—	50.0		
Other	(1.6)	(0.4)	(1.0)	(1.0)
	29.3%	46.2%	34.2%	34.1%
Book income before tax (in millions)	$420.0	$184.0	$20,898.0	$20,158.0

BRIDGE DISCIPLINE   **Bridge to Financial Analysis**

Financial analysts perform an important function for the capital markets in their detailed analyses of companies. The analyst combs through the financial reports and other information about a company to produce an informed opinion on how a company is performing. Analysts' earnings forecasts often constitute an important metric to examine when making decisions about investing in companies.

An experienced financial analyst typically will have a good handle on interpreting financial statement informa-

tion. However, even experienced analysts often will "punt" when it comes to interpreting the tax information contained in a financial statement, preferring to look at net income before taxes (or even EBITDA, earnings before interest, taxes, depreciation, and amortization).

A great deal of useful information about a business is contained in its tax footnote, and analysts might have an edge if they work at understanding the mysteries of taxes in the financial statements.

Wal-Mart's rate. What factors created these differences? Rate reconciliation information can provide clues.

Sears reported a higher effective tax rate in year 1 because its state and local income tax burden was higher, and because it suffered a goodwill impairment (the goodwill write-off is not tax deductible). These increase items were offset by reductions caused by certain basis differences in a domestic subsidiary, larger benefits from tax credits, and a larger benefit from a favorable resolution of tax matters.

When comparing effective tax rates, it is important to consider which components of the effective tax rate produce one-time effects, and which will be observed permanently. For example, for year 2, the effective tax rates of both companies were more similar (Sears was about 5 percentage points lower than Wal-Mart). In particular, without the large effects of nondeductible goodwill and the domestic subsidiary basis difference, Sears approaches the effective tax rate of Wal-Mart.

Consequently, it appears that there are no long-term structural differences in the tax burdens faced by the two companies. This is not surprising, given that both companies are incorporated in the United States, perform in the same industry, and operate in many of the same jurisdictions.

However, items such as the nondeductible goodwill difference do indicate that there may be potential fundamental differences in how Sears's management deals with growth via expansion rather than acquisitions. It is acquired goodwill rather than the homegrown sort that faces potential impairment. The Sears example shows that the results of past and current strategic decisions eventually may show up in the income tax footnote.

3-3b **Refining the Analysis**

In addition to comparing effective tax rates, companies can compare levels of deferred tax assets and liabilities.

EXAMPLE

24

Akiko Enterprises reports a net deferred tax liability of $280,000. Erde, Inc., a company in the same industry, reports a net deferred tax liability of $860,000. The presence of deferred tax liabilities on the balance sheet indicates that both companies are benefiting from deferring actual tax payments (essentially, an interest-free loan from the government).

At first glance, it may appear that Erde is doing better in this regard. However, what if Akiko holds total assets of $2.6 million and Erde's assets total $19.2 million? This information indicates that Akiko has 10.8% ($280,000/$2.6 million) of its total assets "financed" with an interest-free loan from the government, while Erde has only 4.5% ($860,000/$19.2 million) of its assets "financed" with its deferred tax liabilities.

A company may do a more refined benchmarking analysis by examining each component of its deferred tax assets and liabilities as a percentage of total assets. For example, an observer can examine how the deferred tax assets or liabilities related to property, plant, and equipment compare with those of its competitors. The nature of the components of deferred tax liabilities and deferred tax assets becomes quite important in a benchmarking analysis.

Benchmarking Financial Results

EXAMPLE 25

LinCo reports total book income before taxes of $10 million and a total tax provision of $3.2 million, producing a 32% effective tax rate. TuckCo also reports book income before taxes of $10 million. TuckCo's total tax expense is $3.1 million, producing an effective tax rate of 31%. At first glance, it appears that both companies are similar with regard to effective tax rates. The total tax expense divided between current and deferred is as follows.

	LinCo	TuckCo
Current tax expense	$4,100,000	$ 4,200,000
Deferred tax benefit	(900,000)	(1,100,000)
Total tax expense	$3,200,000	$ 3,100,000

Again, it appears that both companies have created deferred tax assets in the current year that are expected to produce tax savings in the future. Knowing the nature of the underlying deferred tax assets will add greatly to one's interpretation of the effective tax rates.

The deferred tax asset generating LinCo's $900,000 expected future tax savings is the use of an NOL. The deferred tax asset generating TuckCo's expected future tax savings is generated by different book and tax methods in accounting for warranty expense. This additional information reveals that LinCo previously has incurred losses, and it is critical that it earn future taxable income in order to use the NOL.

This is quite different from TuckCo's situation, which reveals only that common differences in accounting methods exist. Although the tax positions of LinCo and TuckCo seem very similar on the surface, a closer look reveals a striking difference.

EXAMPLE 26

WageCo and SalaryCo operate in the same industry, and they both report a 38% effective tax rate. Their book income and current, deferred, and total tax expense were reported as follows.

	WageCo	SalaryCo
Book income before tax	$1,500,000	$2,300,000
Current tax expense	$ 980,000	$ 24,000
Deferred tax expense (benefit)	(410,000)	850,000
Total tax expense	$ 570,000	$ 874,000
Effective tax rate	38%	38%

WageCo's total tax expense is highly dependent on the current recognition of future tax savings of $410,000. SalaryCo appears to be deferring a substantial portion of its tax expense to future years. Although both companies report a 38% effective tax rate, the details indicate that the two companies face very different tax situations.

3-3c Sustaining the Tax Rate

It is important in benchmarking exercises to remove the effect of one-time items in comparing sustainable effective tax rates across time or companies. Examples of one-time items include restructuring costs, legal settlements, and IRS or other tax liability settlements. A one-time item may seem beneficial or detrimental to a company's effective tax rate. But the very nature of such an item implies that it has little to do with the company's long-term sustainable tax costs.

EXAMPLE

27

MetalCo and IronCo operate in the same industry, and they report the following tax rate reconciliations in their tax footnotes.

	MetalCo	IronCo
Hypothetical tax at U.S. rate	35.0%	35.0%
State and local taxes	2.2	2.1
Foreign income taxed at less than U.S. rate	(6.2)	(6.1)
Tax Court settlement on disputed tax issue	(18.6)	—
Effective tax rate	12.4%	31.0%

Although it appears that MetalCo has a significantly lower effective tax rate (12.4%) than IronCo (31.0%), removing MetalCo's one-time item related to the court settlement indicates that both companies may operate under a 31% effective tax rate (12.4% + 18.6% = 31%).

3-3d Uses of Benchmarking Analysis

Benchmarking is part science and part art. A useful analysis requires both an accountant's knowledge of how the underlying financial statements are constructed, including arriving at the appropriate tax expense, and a detective's sense of where to look and what questions to ask. Concept Summary 3.4 summarizes the most typical uses of benchmarking in an analysis of an entity's financial results.

Concept Summary 3.4

Benchmarking Analysis

A benchmarking analysis can be helpful in comparing the tax positions of two or more business entities. One might consider the following aspects of the taxpayers' financial disclosures in this regard. This list is not all-inclusive; benchmarking also includes the judgment and experience of the parties conducting the analysis.

- Compare the effective tax rates of the entities.

- Explain the differences in effective rates. Are these differences sustainable over time?

- Apply the analysis to both the tax dollars involved and the underlying net assets of the entities.

- Discount (but do not ignore) any one-time tax benefits/detriments that are observed.

REFOCUS ON THE BIG PICTURE

TAXES ON THE FINANCIAL STATEMENTS

Raymond Jones should understand that the tax expense reported on the company's financial statements and the tax payable on the company's income tax returns often differ as a result of differences in the reporting entities used in the calculation and the different accounting methods used for book purposes and tax purposes. The use of different accounting methods may result in both temporary and permanent differences in financial statement income and taxable income. Examples of permanent differences include nontaxable income such as municipal bond interest and tax credits. Temporary differences include depreciation differences and other amounts that are affected by the timing of a deduction or an inclusion, but they ultimately result in the same amount being reflected in the financial statements and income tax returns.

Permanent differences such as municipal bond interest cause Arctic's book income to be greater than its taxable income. In calculating the tax provision shown on the financial statements, Arctic's book income must be adjusted for these permanent differences.

continued

This results in an effective tax rate for financial statement purposes (30.8 percent) that is below the top U.S. statutory corporate income tax rate of 35 percent.

In this case, Arctic's income tax expense of $7.7 million is higher than the current Federal income tax payable. This results from timing differences and creates a $1.05 million deferred tax liability that is reported on the company's balance sheet. Unlike other liabilities, deferred tax liabilities are "good" in the sense that they represent an amount that may be paid to the government in the future rather than today.

What If?

Mr. Jones is concerned about a newspaper article that said that companies reporting less tax on their tax returns than on their financial statements were cheating the IRS. Is this an accurate assessment?

While differences in income taxes payable to the IRS and financial tax expense can result from aggressive and illegal tax shelters, differences also result from different methods of accounting that are required for financial statement reporting using GAAP and tax laws enacted by Congress.

Suggested Readings

Cheryl Anderson, "Creating Value in the Corporate Tax Function Through Benchmarking," *AICPA Tax Adviser*, September 2008.

J. O. Everett, C. J. Hennig, and W. A. Raabe, *Schedule M–3 Compliance*, 2nd ed., Commerce Clearing House, 2008.

J. Richard Harvey, "Schedule UTP—Why So Few Disclosures?" *Tax Notes*, April 1, 2013.

C. J. Hennig, W. A. Raabe, and J. O. Everett, "FIN 48 Compliance," *AICPA Tax Adviser*, January 2008.

Floyd Norris, "The Islands Treasured by Offshore Tax Avoiders," *Wall Street Journal*, June 5, 2014.

Key Terms

ASC 740 (SFAS 109), 3-8

ASC 740-10 (FIN 48), 3-21

ASC 740-30 (APB 23), 3-23

Balance sheet approach, 3-10

Benchmarking, 3-27

Conservatism principle, 3-13

Current tax expense, 3-9

Deferred tax asset, 3-10

Deferred tax benefit, 3-10

Deferred tax expense, 3-10

Deferred tax liability, 3-10

Equity method, 3-2

Generally accepted accounting principles (GAAP), 3-2

Income tax provision, 3-8

Permanent differences, 3-4

Permanently reinvesting, 3-23

Rate reconciliation, 3-17

Schedule M–1, 3-6

Schedule M–3, 3-6

Temporary differences, 3-4

Valuation allowance, 3-13

Problems

1. **LO.2** Ovate, Inc., earns $140,000 in book income before tax and is subject to a 35% marginal Federal income tax rate. Ovate records a single temporary difference: Warranty expenses deducted for book purposes are $8,000, of which only $2,000 are deductible for tax purposes. Determine the amount of Ovate's deferred tax asset or liability.

2. **LO.3** Ion Corporation reports an income tax expense/payable for book purposes of $200,000 and $250,000 for tax purposes. According to Ion's management

and financial auditors, Ion will only be able to use $30,000 of any deferred tax asset, with the balance expiring unused. Determine the amount of Ion's deferred tax asset and valuation allowance from this year's activities, and construct Ion's related journal entry for these items.

3. **LO.4** RadioCo, a domestic corporation, owns 100% of TVCo, a manufacturing facility in the European country Adagio. TVCo has no operations or activities in the United States. The U.S. tax rate is 35%, and the Adagio tax rate is 12.5%.

For the current year, RadioCo earns $200,000 in taxable income from its U.S. operations. TVCo earns $800,000 in taxable income from its operations, pays $100,000 in taxes to Adagio, and makes no distributions to RadioCo. Determine RadioCo's effective tax rate for book purposes with and without the permanent reinvestment assumption of ASC 740-30 (APB 23).

4. **LO.2** Prance, Inc., earns pretax book net income of $800,000 in 2016. Prance acquires a depreciable asset that year, and first-year tax depreciation exceeds book depreciation by $80,000. Prance reported no other temporary or permanent book-tax differences. The pertinent U.S. tax rate is 35%.

a.   Compute Prance's total income tax expense, current income tax expense, and deferred income tax expense.

b.   Determine the 2016 end-of-year balance in Prance's deferred tax asset and deferred tax liability balance sheet accounts.

Ethics and Equity 5. **LO.1** Evaluate the following statement: For most business entities, book income differs from taxable income because "income" has different meanings for the users of the data in the income computation.

6. **LO.1** Parent, a domestic corporation, owns 100% of Block, a foreign corporation, and Chip, a domestic corporation. Parent also owns 45% of Trial, a domestic corporation. Parent receives no distributions from any of these corporations. Which of these entities' net income is included in Parent's income statement for current-year financial reporting purposes?

7. **LO.1** Parent, a domestic corporation, owns 100% of Block, a foreign corporation, and Chip, a domestic corporation. Parent also owns 45% of Trial, a domestic corporation. Parent receives no distributions from any of these corporations. Which of these entities' taxable income is included in Parent's current-year Form 1120, U.S. income tax return? Parent consolidates all eligible subsidiaries for Federal income tax purposes.

Communications 8. **LO.1** Marcellus Jackson, the CFO of Mac, Inc., notices that the tax liability reported on Mac's tax return is less than the tax expense reported on Mac's financial statements. Provide a letter to Jackson outlining why these two tax expense numbers differ. Mac's address is 482 Linden Road, Paris, KY 40362.

Issue ID 9. **LO.1** Define the terms *temporary difference* and *permanent difference* as they pertain to the financial reporting of income tax expenses. Describe how these two book-tax differences affect the gap between book and taxable income. How are permanent and temporary differences alike? How are they different?

Communications 10. **LO.1** In no more than three PowerPoint slides, list several commonly encountered temporary and permanent book-tax differences. The slides will be used in your presentation next week to your school's Future CPAs Club.

11. **LO.2** Prance, in Problem 4, reports $600,000 of pretax book net income in 2017. Prance's book depreciation exceeds tax depreciation that year by $20,000. Prance reports no other temporary or permanent book-tax differences. Assuming that the pertinent U.S. tax rate is 35%, compute Prance's total income tax expense, current income tax expense, and deferred income tax expense.

12. **LO.2** Using the facts of Problem 11, determine the 2017 end-of-year balance in Prance's deferred tax asset and deferred tax liability balance sheet accounts.

13. **LO.2** Mini, Inc., earns pretax book net income of $750,000 in 2016. Mini deducted $20,000 in bad debt expense for book purposes. This expense is not yet deductible for tax purposes. Mini records no other temporary or permanent differences. Assuming that the U.S. tax rate is 35%, compute Mini's total income tax expense, current income tax expense, and deferred income tax expense.

14. **LO.2** Using the facts of Problem 13, determine the 2016 end-of-year balance in Mini's deferred tax asset and deferred tax liability balance sheet accounts.

15. **LO.2** Mini, in Problem 13, reports $800,000 of pretax book net income in 2017. For that year, Mini did not deduct any bad debt expense for book purposes but did deduct $15,000 in bad debt expense for tax purposes. Mini records no other temporary or permanent differences. Assuming that the U.S. tax rate is 35%, compute Mini's total income tax expense, current income tax expense, and deferred income tax expense.

16. **LO.2** Using the facts of Problem 15, determine the 2017 end-of-year balance in Mini's deferred tax asset and deferred tax liability balance sheet accounts.

17. **LO.3** You saw on the online Business News Channel that YoungCo has "released one-third of its valuation allowances because of an upbeat forecast for sales of its tablet computers over the next 30 months." What effect does such a release likely have on YoungCo's current-year book effective tax rate? Be specific.

18. **LO.6** Jill is the CFO of PorTech, Inc. PorTech's tax advisers have recommended two tax planning ideas that will each provide $5 million of current-year cash tax savings. One idea is based on a timing difference and is expected to reverse in full 10 years in the future. The other idea creates a permanent difference that never will reverse.

   Determine whether these ideas will allow PorTech to reduce its reported book income tax expense for the current year. Illustrate in a table or timeline your preference for one planning strategy over the other. Which idea will you recommend to Jill?

   Decision Making
   Communications

19. **LO.4** Underwood, the CFO of TechCo, Inc., has used ASC 740-30 (APB 23) to avoid reporting any U.S. deferred tax expense on $50 million of the earnings of TechCo's foreign subsidiaries. All of these subsidiaries operate in countries with lower tax rates than in the United States. Underwood wants to bring to the United States $10 million in profits from these foreign subsidiaries in the form of dividends. How will this profit repatriation affect TechCo's book effective tax rate?

   Issue ID

20. **LO.4** BuildCo, Inc., a domestic C corporation, has used ASC 740-30 (APB 23) to avoid reporting any U.S. deferred tax expense on $100 million of the earnings of BuildCo's foreign subsidiaries. All of these subsidiaries operate in countries with higher tax rates than the ones that apply under U.S. law. Jaime, BuildCo's CFO, wants to bring back to the United States $30 million in profits from these foreign subsidiaries in the form of dividends. How will this profit repatriation affect BuildCo's book effective tax rate?

   Issue ID

21. **LO.6** RoofCo reports total book income before taxes of $20 million and a total tax expense of $8 million. FloorCo reports book income before taxes of $30 million and a total tax expense of $12 million. The companies' breakdown between current and deferred tax expense (benefit) is as follows.

	RoofCo	FloorCo
Current tax expense	$10.0	$13.0
Deferred tax benefit	(2.0)	(1.0)
Total tax expense	$ 8.0	$12.0

RoofCo's deferred tax benefit is from a deferred tax asset created because of differences in book and tax depreciation methods for equipment. FloorCo's deferred tax benefit is created by the expected future use of an NOL. Compare and contrast these two companies' effective tax rates. How are they similar? How are they different?

Communications   22. **LO.6** LawnCo and TreeCo operate in the same industry, and both report a 30% effective tax rate. Their book income and current, deferred, and total tax expense are reported below.

	LawnCo	TreeCo
Book income before tax	$500,000	$650,000
Current tax expense	$200,000	$ 20,000
Deferred tax expense (benefit)	(50,000)	175,000
Total tax expense	$150,000	$195,000
Effective tax rate	30%	30%

ShrubCo is a competitor of both of these companies. Prepare a letter to Laura Collins, VP-Taxation of ShrubCo, outlining your analysis of the other two companies' effective tax rates, using only the preceding information. ShrubCo's address is 9979 West Third Street, Peru, IN 46970.

23. **LO.6** HippCo and HoppCo operate in the same industry and report the following tax rate reconciliations in their tax footnotes. Compare and contrast the effective tax rates of these two companies.

	HippCo	HoppCo
Hypothetical tax at U.S. rate	35.0%	35.0%
State and local taxes	2.7	3.9
Foreign income taxed at less than U.S. rate	(12.5)	(7.8)
Tax Court settlement on disputed tax issue	6.0	—
Effective tax rate	31.2%	31.1%

Ethics and Equity   24. **LO.6** In the current year, Dickinson, Inc., reports an effective tax rate of 36%, and Badger, Inc., reports an effective tax rate of 21%. Both companies are domestic and operate in the same industry. Your initial examination of the financial statements of the two companies indicates that Badger apparently is doing a better job with its tax planning, explaining the difference in effective tax rates. Consequently, all else being equal, you decide to invest in Badger.

In a subsequent year, it comes to light that Badger had used some very aggressive tax planning techniques to reduce its reported tax expense. After an examination by the IRS, Badger loses the tax benefits and reports a very large tax expense in that year. Over this multiple-year period, it turns out that Dickinson had the lower effective tax rate after all.

Do you believe Badger was ethical in not fully disclosing the aggressiveness of its tax positions in its current financial statements? How does ASC 740-10 (FIN 48) affect Badger's disclosure requirement? Does ASC 740-10 (FIN 48) still leave room for ethical decision making by management in determining how to report uncertain tax positions? Explain.

25. **LO.2** Phillips, Inc., a cash basis C corporation, completes $100,000 in sales for year 1, but only $75,000 of this amount is collected during year 1. The remaining $25,000 from these sales is collected promptly during the first quarter of year 2. The applicable income tax rate for year 1 and thereafter is 30%. Compute Phillips's year 1 current and deferred income tax expense.

26. **LO.2** Continue with the results of Problem 25. Prepare the GAAP journal entries for Phillips's year 1 income tax expense.

27. **LO.2** Britton, Inc., an accrual basis C corporation, sells widgets on credit. Its book and taxable income for year 1 totals $60,000 before accounting for bad debts. Britton's book allowance for uncollectible accounts increased for year 1 by $10,000,

but none of the entity's bad debts received a specific write-off for tax purposes. The applicable income tax rate for year 1 and thereafter is 30%. Compute Britton's year 1 current and deferred income tax expense.

28. **LO.2** Continue with the results of Problem 27. Prepare the GAAP journal entries for Britton's year 1 income tax expense.

29. **LO.2** Rubio, Inc., an accrual basis C corporation, reports the following amounts for the tax year. The applicable income tax rate is 30%. Compute Rubio's taxable income.

Book income, including the items below	$80,000
Increase in book allowance for anticipated warranty costs	5,000
Interest income from City of Westerville bonds	10,000
Bribes paid to Federal inspectors	17,000

30. **LO.2** Continue with the results of Problem 29. Determine Rubio's income tax expense and GAAP income for the year.

31. **LO.2** Willingham, Inc., an accrual basis C corporation, reports pretax book income of $1.6 million. At the beginning of the tax year, Willingham reported no deferred tax accounts on its balance sheet. It is subject to a 35% U.S. income tax rate in the current year and for the foreseeable future.

Willingham's book-tax differences include the following. Compute the entity's current and deferred income tax expense for the year.

Addition to the book reserve for uncollectible receivables (no specific write-offs occurred; therefore, a zero income tax deduction)	$4,000,000
Tax depreciation in excess of book	3,000,000
Book gain from installment sale of nonbusiness asset, deferred for tax	2,000,000
Interest income from school district bonds	200,000

32. **LO.2** Continue with the results of Problem 31. Prepare the GAAP journal entries for Willingham's income tax expense.

33. **LO.2** Relix, Inc., is a domestic corporation with the following balance sheet for book and tax purposes at the end of the year. Based on this information, determine Relix's net deferred tax asset or net deferred tax liability at year-end. Assume a 34% corporate tax rate and no valuation allowance.

	Tax Debit/(Credit)	Book Debit/(Credit)
Assets		
Cash	$ 500	$ 500
Accounts receivable	8,000	8,000
Buildings	750,000	750,000
Accumulated depreciation	(450,000)	(380,000)
Furniture & fixtures	70,000	70,000
Accumulated depreciation	(46,000)	(38,000)
Total assets	$332,500	$410,500
Liabilities		
Accrued litigation expense	$ –0–	($ 50,000)
Note payable	(78,000)	(78,000)
Total liabilities	($ 78,000)	($128,000)
Stockholders' Equity		
Paid-in capital	($ 10,000)	($ 10,000)
Retained earnings	(244,500)	(272,500)
Total liabilities and stockholders' equity	($332,500)	($410,500)

34. **LO.2** Based on the facts and results of Problem 33 and the beginning-of-the-year book-tax basis differences listed below, determine the change in Relix's deferred tax assets for the current year.

	Beginning of Year
Accrued litigation expense	$34,000
Subtotal	$34,000
Applicable tax rate	× 34%
Gross deferred tax asset	$11,560

35. **LO.2** Based on the facts and results of Problem 33 and the beginning-of-the-year book-tax basis differences listed below, determine the change in Relix's deferred tax liabilities for the current year.

	Beginning of Year
Building—accumulated depreciation	($57,000)
Furniture & fixtures—accumulated depreciation	(4,200)
Subtotal	($61,200)
Applicable tax rate	× 34%
Gross deferred tax liability	($20,808)

36. **LO.2** Based on the facts and results of Problems 33–35, determine Relix's change in net deferred tax asset or net deferred tax liability for the current year. Provide the journal entry to record this amount.

37. **LO.2** In addition to the temporary differences identified in Problems 33–36, Relix reported two permanent differences between book and taxable income. It earned $2,375 in tax-exempt municipal bond interest, and it incurred $780 in nondeductible meals and entertainment expense. Relix's book income before tax is $4,800. With this additional information, calculate Relix's current tax expense.

38. **LO.2** Provide the journal entry to record Relix's current tax expense as determined in Problem 37.

39. **LO.2** Based on the facts and results of Problems 33–38, calculate Relix's total provision for income tax reported in its financial statements, and determine its book net income after tax.

40. **LO.2** Based on the facts and results of Problems 33–39, provide the income tax footnote rate reconciliation for Relix.

41. **LO.2** Kantner, Inc., is a domestic corporation with the following balance sheet for book and tax purposes at the end of the year. Based on this information, determine Kantner's net deferred tax asset or net deferred tax liability at year-end. Assume a 34% corporate tax rate and no valuation allowance.

	Tax Debit/(Credit)	Book Debit/(Credit)
Assets		
Cash	$ 1,000	$ 1,000
Accounts receivable	9,000	9,000
Buildings	850,000	850,000
Accumulated depreciation	(700,000)	(620,000)
Furniture & fixtures	40,000	40,000
Accumulated depreciation	(10,000)	(8,000)
Total assets	$190,000	$272,000

	Tax Debit/(Credit)	Book Debit/(Credit)
Liabilities		
Accrued warranty expense	$ –0–	($ 40,000)
Note payable	(16,000)	(16,000)
Total liabilities	($ 16,000)	($ 56,000)
Stockholders' Equity		
Paid-in capital	($ 50,000)	($ 50,000)
Retained earnings	(124,000)	(166,000)
Total liabilities and stockholders' equity	($190,000)	($272,000)

42. **LO.2** Based on the facts and results of Problem 41 and the beginning-of-the-year book-tax basis differences listed below, determine the change in Kantner's deferred tax assets for the current year.

	Beginning of Year
Accrued warranty expense	$30,000
Subtotal	$30,000
Applicable tax rate	× 34%
Gross deferred tax asset	$10,200

43. **LO.2** Based on the facts and results of Problem 41 and the beginning-of-the-year book-tax basis differences listed below, determine the change in Kantner's deferred tax liabilities for the current year.

	Beginning of Year
Building—accumulated depreciation	($62,000)
Furniture & fixtures—accumulated depreciation	(400)
Subtotal	($62,400)
Applicable tax rate	× 34%
Gross deferred tax liability	($21,216)

44. **LO.2** Based on the facts and results of Problems 41–43, determine Kantner's change in net deferred tax asset or net deferred tax liability for the current year. Provide the journal entry to record this amount.

45. **LO.2** In addition to the temporary differences identified in Problems 41–44, Kantner reported two permanent book-tax differences. It earned $7,800 in tax-exempt municipal bond interest, and it reported $850 in nondeductible meals and entertainment expense. Kantner's book income before tax is $50,000. With this additional information, calculate Kantner's current tax expense.

46. **LO.2** Provide the journal entry to record Kantner's current tax expense as determined in Problem 45.

47. **LO.2** Based on the facts and results of Problems 41–46, calculate Kantner's total provision for income tax expense reported on its financial statement and its book net income after tax.

48. **LO.2** Based on the facts and results of Problems 41–47, provide the income tax footnote rate reconciliation for Kantner.

49. **LO.3** Does the taxpayer's effective tax rate increase or decrease when:

   a. It creates a valuation allowance against the deferred tax asset for a net operating loss?

   b. It releases a valuation allowance against the deferred tax asset for a net operating loss?

50. **LO.3** Identify whether each of the following items constitute *positive* or *negative* evidence when a taxpayer assesses whether a valuation allowance is required or should be adjusted.

   a. Product orders are increasing.

   b. Only two years remain for the taxpayer's net operating loss carryforward.

   c. Book income for the past three years totals to a negative amount.

   d. Investment assets held by the taxpayer show a realized gain.

   e. The industry in which the taxpayer operates is in a down cycle.

   f. The entity's tax plan includes a switch from MACRS accelerated depreciation to straight-line.

51. **LO.3** GinnyCo reports a $100,000 income tax payable in the current year. In the current year, GinnyCo paid $40,000 in income taxes to another country. GinnyCo cannot use the foreign tax credit this year, and its auditors maintain that one-fourth of the credit carryforward will expire unused. Construct the journal entry to report these items.

52. **LO.4** KellerCo reports $5 million of U.S. taxable income, and it is subject to a 34% Federal income tax rate. Its book-tax differences include the following.

Nondeductible meals and entertainment costs	$ 400,000
Domestic production activities deduction	2,100,000
Tax depreciation in excess of book depreciation	1,500,000

   Construct KellerCo's tax rate reconciliation for its GAAP tax footnote. Use either dollars or percentages in your reconciliation.

53. **LO.5** LaceCo has adopted certain aggressive policies for deducting, rather than capitalizing, its repair costs. The entity estimates that it will reduce its Federal income tax liability by $400,000 as a result of these strategies, but that the IRS is likely to challenge the policies in an audit.

   After negotiating and settling with the IRS, LaceCo estimates that the tax benefit may be reduced (amounts as indicated with related probabilities); LaceCo constructs a table of these probabilities and results.

Resulting Estimated Tax Benefit	Probability of Agreement Between LaceCo and IRS	Cumulative Probability Computed
$400,000	10%	10%
300,000	35%	45%
250,000	40%	85%
—0—	15%	100%

   LaceCo recorded a book-tax provision of $600,000, *including* the $400,000 tax benefit from this tax uncertainty.

   a. Determine the amount that LaceCo should record for the tax benefit from this item, under GAAP rules and ASC 740-10 (FIN 48).

   b. Construct the journal entry that LaceCo should record for these items.

BRIDGE DISCIPLINE

1. Locate summary financial information for two companies in the same industry. Compare and contrast the following items across the two companies: debt-to-equity ratio, return on assets, return on equity, inventory turnover ratio, and effective tax rate.

2. Locate news or other items reporting financial analysts' forecasts or other information regarding two different companies. Determine whether the analyst appears to use any tax information in the report. For example, does the analyst use pretax or after-tax earnings in the analysis? Draft an e-mail to your instructor describing your findings.

   Communications

3. Using the annual reports or 10-Ks of two different public companies in the same industry, locate information regarding the compensation paid to their executives. Prepare a table comparing the compensation levels (cash and noncash) of top executives across the two companies, and send the table to your instructor. Illustrate the relationship between executive compensation and company performance by comparing the compensation to other company information such as net income.

   Communications

Research Problems

Use the tax resources of the Internet to address the following questions. Do not restrict your search to the Web, but include a review of newsgroups and general reference materials, practitioner sites and resources, primary sources of the tax law, chat rooms and discussion groups, and other opportunities.

Internet Activity

Research Problem 1. Locate the web page of Citizens for Tax Justice. Find the report "Corporate Taxpayers and Corporate Tax Dodgers, 2008-10." In no more than four PowerPoint slides for your classmates, summarize the following.

Communications

- Methodology, motivation, and background of the study.
- Five notable companies, their book income and their effective Federal income tax rates, and where those rates are zero or negative.
- Five industries, their effective tax rates, and the dollar amounts of the tax subsidies they receive.
- Five notable companies, their effective domestic effective Federal income tax rate, and the effective tax rate on their overseas profits.

Research Problem 2. Locate the most recent financial statements of two companies in the same industry using the companies' websites or the SEC's website (**www.sec.gov**). Perform a benchmarking analysis of the two companies' effective tax rates, components of the effective tax rate reconciliation, levels of deferred tax assets and liabilities, and other relevant data. Summarize this information in an e-mail to your instructor.

Research Problem 3. Locate articles or other discussions regarding the key differences between ASC 740 (SFAS 109) and International Accounting Standard No. 12 (related to income taxes). Summarize these key differences in an e-mail to your instructor. Make certain you have found the most current information for this comparison. Provide the URL for each of your sources.

Communications

WWW   **For the latest in changes to tax legislation, visit www.cengagebrain.com.**

Communications **Research Problem 4.** Locate the financial statements of three different companies that report information in the income tax footnote regarding uncertain tax positions under ASC 740-10 (FIN 48). Create a schedule that compares and contrasts the changes in uncertain tax positions reported by the three companies. E-mail the schedule to your instructor.

Communications **Research Problem 5.** Locate the financial statements of three different companies. Review the income tax footnote information on deferred tax assets (DTAs) and deferred tax liabilities (DTLs). Create a schedule that compares and contrasts the end-of-the-year amounts of DTAs and DTLs, including any valuation allowances. E-mail the schedule to your instructor.

Research Problem 6. Locate summary financial information for two companies in the same industry. Compare and contrast the following items across the two companies: debt-to-equity ratio, return on assets, shareholder yield, return on equity, inventory turnover ratio, and effective tax rate. In your comparison, include the Federal, state/local, and international effective rates for the entities. Summarize in one paragraph the key reasons why the effective tax rates are similar (or different).

Roger CPA Review Questions

1. Identify the correct answer about the purposes of Schedules M–1 and M–3.

	Reconciles Book Income (Loss) with Income per Return	Distinguishes Between Permanent and Temporary Differences
a.	Both Schedule M–1 and Schedule M–3	Neither Schedule M–1 nor M–3
b.	Both Schedule M–1 and Schedule M–3	Schedule M–1 Only
c.	Schedule M–1 Only	Both Schedule M–1 and Schedule M–3
d.	Both Schedule M–1 and Schedule M–3	Schedule M–3 Only

2. Kelsey Corp. is an accrual-basis, calendar-year domestic corporation which is not part of a consolidated group. In the current tax year, Kelsey recorded over $10 million in gross receipts and ended the year with $9 million in total assets. Which reconciliation schedule—M–1 or M–3—should Kelsey file along with its corporate tax return for the current year?
   a. Only Schedule M–1 can be filed.
   b. Schedule M–3 is required.
   c. Depends on how many years the corporation has been in existence.
   d. Only Schedule M–1 is required, but Schedule M–3 may be elected instead.

3. Indicate for each of the following financial statement items whether it would cause no adjustment or whether its absolute value would be either added to or subtracted from net income per books when computing taxable income on the Schedule M–1.

	Municipal Bond Interest Earned	Excess of Capital Losses Over Capital Gains	Interest Expense Associated with Purchase of Municipal Bonds
a.	Subtracted from	No adjustment	No adjustment
b.	Added to	No adjustment	Subtracted from
c.	Subtracted from	Added to	Added to
d.	Subtracted from	No adjustment	Added to

4. Indicate for each of the following financial statement items whether it would cause no adjustment or whether its absolute value would be either added to or subtracted from net income per books when computing taxable income on the Schedule M–1.

	Premiums Paid on Key Employee Life Insurance	Excess of Book vs. Tax Depreciation	Accrued Warranty Expense
a.	No adjustment	No adjustment	No adjustment
b.	No adjustment	No adjustment	Subtracted from
c.	Subtracted from	Added to	Subtracted from
d.	Added to	Added to	Added to

5. Kookaburra Corp. reports net income per books of $575,000 for the current tax year. Included in this amount are the following items.

Item	Amount
Accrued vacation expense	$50,000
Meals and entertainment expense	40,000
Depreciation expense	35,000
Inventory shrinkage (accrual based on a percentage of total sales)	5,000

Depreciation reported on the current year tax return is $40,000.

Considering only the above information, what is Kookaburra Corp.'s taxable income for the current tax year?

a. $655,000
b. $650,000
c. $640,000
d. $645,000

PART 2

STRUCTURE OF THE FEDERAL INCOME TAX

CHAPTER **4**
Gross Income

CHAPTER **5**
Business Deductions

CHAPTER **6**
Losses and Loss Limitations

Part 2 introduces the components of the Federal income tax model. The gross income component, including the effect of exclusions, the accounting period, and accounting methods, is presented. This is followed by an analysis of business deductions, including amounts allowed and disallowed and the proper timing for such deductions. Tax provisions are addressed concerning the amounts and timing of deductions that result from losses, including the use of carryovers and the proper financial accounting treatment of the resulting tax amounts.

CHAPTER 4

Gross Income

LEARNING OBJECTIVES: *After completing Chapter 4, you should be able to:*

LO.1 Explain the concepts of gross income and realization and distinguish between the economic, accounting, and tax concepts of gross income.

LO.2 Explain when the cash, accrual, and hybrid methods of accounting are used and how they are applied.

LO.3 Identify who should pay the tax on an item of income.

LO.4 Apply the statutory authority as to when to exclude an item from gross income.

LO.5 Describe the general tax consequences of property transactions.

LO.6 Explain and apply the tax provision that excludes interest on state and local government obligations from gross income.

LO.7 Determine the extent to which life insurance proceeds are excluded from gross income.

LO.8 Describe when income must be reported from the discharge of indebtedness.

LO.9 Determine the extent to which receipts can be excluded under the tax benefit rule.

LO.10 Apply the tax provisions on loans made at below-market interest rates.

LO.11 Use the tax rules concerning the exclusion of leasehold improvements from gross income.

CHAPTER OUTLINE

TAX TALK *The first nine pages of the Internal Revenue Code define income. The remaining 1,100 pages spin the web of exceptions and preferences.* —WARREN G. MAGNUSON

© TYLER OLSON/SHUTTERSTOCK.COM

JUST WHAT IS INCLUDED IN GROSS INCOME?

At the beginning of the year, Dr. Cliff Payne, age 27, opened his new dental practice as a personal service corporation. The entity uses a December 31 year-end and the accrual method of accounting. During the year, the corporation billed patients and insurance companies for $385,000 of dental services. At the end of the year, $52,000 of this amount had not been collected. The entity earned $500 interest on a money market account held at the local bank and another $500 interest on an investment in bonds issued by the Whitehall School District.

Dr. Payne's salary from his corporation is $10,000 per month. However, he did not cash his December payroll check until January. To help provide funds to invest in the new business, Dr. Payne's parents loaned him $150,000 and did not charge him any interest. He also owns stock that has increased in value from $7,000 at the beginning of the year to more than $25,000 at the end of the year.

Although Dr. Payne took several accounting classes in college, he would like your help in calculating the correct amounts of his own gross income and the gross income of the corporation.

Read the chapter and formulate your response.

The first step in computing an income tax liability is the determination of the amount of income that is subject to tax. In completing that step, some of the following questions must be answered. We will address these and other concerns in this chapter.

- *What:* What is income?
- *When:* In which tax period is the income recognized?
- *Who:* Who is taxed on the income?

4-1 THE TAX FORMULA

The basic income tax formula was introduced in Chapter 1 and summarized in Exhibit 1.1. This chapter, together with Chapters 5 through 8, examines the elements of this formula in detail. However, before embarking on a detailed study of the income tax, a brief introduction of each component of the tax formula, which follows, is provided as an overview.

4-1a Components of the Tax Formula

Income (Broadly Defined)

This includes all of the taxpayer's income, both taxable and nontaxable. Although it essentially is equivalent to gross receipts, it does not include a return of capital or borrowed funds.

Exclusions

For various reasons, Congress has chosen to exclude certain types of income from the income tax base. The principal income exclusions that apply to all entities (e.g., life insurance proceeds received by reason of death of the insured and state and local bond interest) are discussed later in this chapter, while exclusions that are unique to individuals are addressed in Chapters 9 through 11.

Gross Income

Section 61 of the Internal Revenue Code provides the following definition of gross income.

> Except as otherwise provided in this subtitle, gross income means all income from whatever source derived.

This language is based on the Sixteenth Amendment to the Constitution. The "except as otherwise provided" phrase refers to exclusions.

Supreme Court decisions have made it clear that *all* sources of income are subject to tax unless Congress specifically excludes the type of income received.

> The starting point in all cases dealing with the question of the scope of what is included in "gross income" begins with the basic premise that the purpose of Congress was to use the full measure of its taxing power.[1]

---

[1] *James v. U.S.*, 61–1 USTC ¶9449, 7 AFTR 2d 1361, 81 S.Ct. 1052 (USSC, 1961).

GLOBAL TAX ISSUES From "All Sources" Is a Broad Definition

When § 61 refers to "income from whatever source derived," the taxing authorities are reaching far beyond the borders of the United States. Although one interpretation of "source" in this context is type of income (e.g., wages, interest, etc.), a broader interpretation revolves around the place where the income is generated. In this context, citizens and residents of the United States are subject to taxation on income earned from sources both inside and outside the country. This "worldwide income" tax base can cause potential double taxation problems, with other countries also taxing income earned within their borders, but mechanisms such as the foreign tax credit can alleviate these tax burdens.

Recently, a few prominent U.S. corporations have reorganized in other countries to avoid the higher U.S. tax rates on income earned abroad. About 3,000 individuals undergo a tax-motivated renunciation of U.S. citizenship every year. Chapter 16 discusses the Federal government's worldwide taxation of the income of a U.S. person.

While it is clear that income is to be broadly construed, the statutory law fails to provide a satisfactory definition of the term and lists only a small set of items that are specifically included in income, including:

- Compensation for services.
- Business income.
- Gains from sales and other disposition of property.
- Interest.
- Dividends.
- Rents and royalties.
- Certain income arising from discharge of indebtedness.
- Income from partnerships.

Deductions

Generally, all ordinary and necessary trade or business expenses are deductible by taxpaying entities. Such expenses include the cost of goods sold, salaries, wages, operating expenses (such as rent and utilities), research and development expenditures, interest, taxes, depreciation, amortization, and depletion.

As noted in Chapter 1, individuals can use two categories of deductions—deductions *for* AGI and deductions *from* AGI. In addition, individuals are unique among taxpaying entities in that they are permitted to deduct a variety of personal expenses (i.e., expenses unrelated to business or investment), they are allowed a standard deduction if this amount exceeds the deductible personal expenses, and they can claim a deduction for personal and dependency exemptions.

Determining the Tax

Taxable income is determined by subtracting deductions (after any applicable limitations) from gross income. The tax rates (located on the inside front cover of this text) then are applied to determine the tax. Finally, tax prepayments (such as Federal income tax withholding on salaries and estimated tax payments) and a wide variety of credits are subtracted from the tax to determine the amount due to the Federal government or the refund due to the taxpayer. This formula is summarized on the inside back cover of this text, and in text Exhibits 1.1 and 1.2.

4-2 GROSS INCOME—WHAT IS IT?

4-2a Concepts of Income

As noted above, Congress failed to provide in the Code a clear definition of income. Instead, it was left to the judicial and administrative branches of government to determine the meaning of the term. As the income tax law developed, two competing

LO.1

Explain the concepts of gross income and realization and distinguish between the economic, accounting, and tax concepts of gross income.

FINANCIAL DISCLOSURE INSIGHTS   What Does "Income" Mean to You?

Accountants use a definition of income that relies on the realization principle.[2] **Accounting income** is not recognized until it is realized. For realization to occur:

- An exchange of goods or services must take place between the entity and some independent, external party, and

- The goods or services received by the entity must be capable of being objectively valued.[3]

Thus, an increase in the fair market value of an asset before its sale or other disposition is not sufficient to trigger the recognition of accounting income. Similarly, the imputed savings that arise when an entity creates assets for its own use (e.g., feed grown by a farmer for his or her livestock) do not constitute accounting income because no exchange has occurred.

Business taxpayers often reconcile their annual income computations for financial accounting and tax law purposes. Taxpayers required to prepare audited financial statements must explain in the footnotes to the statements (1) the most important accounting principles used in computing book income and (2) the most important tax elections and other consequences of the tax law on earnings per share.

models of income were considered by these agencies: economic income and accounting income.

The term **income** is used in the Code but is defined very broadly. Early in the history of our tax laws, the courts were required to interpret "the commonly understood meaning of the term which must have been in the minds of the people when they adopted the Sixteenth Amendment."[4]

Economists measure income (**economic income**) by determining the change (increase or decrease) in the fair market value of the entity's assets (net of liabilities) from the beginning to the end of the year. This focus on change in *net worth* as a measure of income (or loss) requires no disposition of assets. For *individual* taxpayers, one then adds the value of the year's personal consumption of goods and services (e.g., food, the rental value of owner-occupied housing, etc.).[5]

EXAMPLE 1

Helen's economic income is calculated by comparing her net worth at the end of the year (December 31) with her net worth at the beginning of the year (January 1) and adding the amount of her personal consumption.

Fair market value of Helen's assets on December 31	$220,000	
Less liabilities on December 31	(40,000)	
Net worth on December 31		$ 180,000
Fair market value of Helen's assets on January 1	$200,000	
Less liabilities on January 1	(80,000)	
Net worth on January 1		(120,000)
Increase in net worth		$ 60,000
Consumption		
Food, clothing, and other personal expenditures	$ 25,000	
Imputed rental value of the home Helen owns and occupies	12,000	
Total consumption		37,000
Economic income		$ 97,000

The tax law relies to some extent on net worth as a measure of income.[6] Potentially, anything that increases net worth is income, and anything that decreases net worth is

---

[2]See the American Accounting Association Committee Report on the "Realization Concept," *The Accounting Review* (April 1965): 312–322.

[3]Valuation is carried out in the local currency of the reporting entity.

[4]*Merchants Loan and Trust Co. v. Smietanka*, 1 USTC ¶42, 3 AFTR 3102, 41 S.Ct. 386 (USSC, 1921).

[5]See Henry C. Simons, *Personal Income Taxation* (Chicago: University of Chicago Press, 1933), Chapters 2–3.

[6]*Comm. v. Glenshaw Glass Co.*, 55–1 USTC ¶9308, 47 AFTR 162, 348 U.S. 426 (USSC, 1955).

deductible (if permitted by statute). Thus, *windfall income* such as buried treasure found in one's backyard is taxable, under the theory that net worth has increased.[7] Likewise, a lender does *not* recognize gross income on receipt of loan principal repayments. The lender's investment simply changes from a loan receivable to cash, so net worth does not change.

Because the strict application of a tax based on economic income would require taxpayers to determine the value of their assets annually, compliance would be burdensome. Controversies between taxpayers and the IRS inevitably would arise under an economic approach to income determination because of the subjective nature of valuation in many circumstances. In addition, using market values to determine income for tax purposes could result in liquidity problems. That is, a taxpayer's assets could increase in value but not be easily converted into the cash needed to pay the resulting tax (e.g., increases in the value of commercial real estate).[8] Thus, the IRS, Congress, and the courts have rejected broad application of the economic income concept as impractical.

The Big Picture

Return to the facts of *The Big Picture* on p. 4-1. Dr. Payne's portfolio has increased in value by more than 250% during the tax year, and that additional value constitutes economic income to him. But the Federal income tax law does not include the value increase in Dr. Payne's gross income, even though the taxpayer could convert some of those gains to cash through, say, a margin loan from his broker.

EXAMPLE

2

4-2b **Comparing Accounting and Tax Concepts of Income**

Although income tax rules frequently parallel financial accounting measurement concepts, differences do exist. Of major significance, for example, is the fact that unearned (prepaid) income received by an accrual basis taxpayer often is taxed in the year of receipt. For financial accounting purposes, such prepayments are not treated as income until earned. Because of this and other differences, many corporations report financial accounting income that is substantially different from the amounts reported for tax purposes.

The Supreme Court provided an explanation for some of the variations between accounting and taxable income in a decision involving inventory and bad debt adjustments.

> The primary goal of financial accounting is to provide useful information to management, shareholders, creditors, and others properly interested; the major responsibility of the accountant is to protect these parties from being misled. The primary goal of the income tax system, in contrast, is the equitable collection of revenue.... Consistently with its goals and responsibilities, financial accounting has as its foundation the principle of conservatism, with its corollary that "possible errors in measurement [should] be in the direction of understatement rather than overstatement of net income and net assets." In view of the Treasury's markedly different goals and responsibilities, understatement of income is not destined to be its guiding light....
>
> Financial accounting, in short, is hospitable to estimates, probabilities, and reasonable certainties; the tax law, with its mandate to preserve the revenue, can give no quarter to uncertainty.[9]

---

[7]*Cesarini v. U.S.*, 69–1 USTC ¶9270, 23 AFTR 2d 69–997, 296 F.Supp. 3 (D.Ct. N.Oh., 1969), *aff'd* 70–2 USTC ¶9509, 26 AFTR 2d 70–5107, 428 F.2d 812 (CA–6, 1970); Rev.Rul. 61, 1953–1 C.B. 17.

[8]In Chapter 1, this was identified as a justification of the wherewithal to pay concept.

[9]*Thor Power Tool Co. v. Comm.*, 79–1 USTC ¶9139, 43 AFTR 2d 79–362, 99 S.Ct. 773 (USSC, 1979).

4-2c Form of Receipt

Gross income is not limited to cash received. "It includes income realized in any form, whether in money, property, or services. Income may be realized [and recognized], therefore, in the form of services, meals, accommodations, stock or other property, as well as in cash."[10]

EXAMPLE 3

Ostrich Corporation allows Cameron, an employee, to use a company car for his vacation. Cameron realizes income equal to the rental value of the car for the time and mileage.

EXAMPLE 4

Donna is a CPA specializing in individual tax return preparation. Her neighbor, Jill, is a dentist. Each year, Donna prepares Jill's tax return in exchange for two dental checkups. Jill and Donna both have gross income equal to the fair market value of the services they receive.

Concept Summary 4.1

Gross Income Concepts

Taxable income is computed using a specific form of income statement, i.e., one created by Congress. Taxable income can be seen as similar but not identical to both economic income and the income computation that is required by generally accepted accounting principles (GAAP).

1. Economic income is not appropriate for computing taxable income. Economic income depends on annual measures of market value and consumption, both of which would be difficult to apply on a short tax-filing deadline.

2. Many of the same accounting methods that are allowed by GAAP also can be used in computing gross income and tax deductions, as the tax law largely follows the realization principle of financial accounting.

4-3 YEAR OF INCLUSION

4-3a Taxable Year

The annual accounting period or **taxable year** is a basic component of our tax system. Generally, a taxpayer uses the *calendar year* to report gross income. However, a *fiscal year* (a period of 12 months ending on the last day of any month other than December) can be adopted if the taxpayer maintains adequate books and records.[11] In most cases, this fiscal year option generally is not available to partnerships, S corporations, and personal service corporations (i.e., one performing services in health, law, engineering, architecture, accounting, actuarial science, performing arts, or consulting).

Determining the tax year in which the income is recognized is important in determining the tax consequences of the income.

- With a progressive tax rate system, a taxpayer's marginal tax rate can change from year to year.
- Congress may change the tax rates.
- The relevant rates may change because of a change in the entity's status (e.g., a proprietorship may incorporate).
- Several provisions in the Code require computations using the taxpayer's income for the year (e.g., the charitable contribution deduction).
- The taxpayer wants to reduce the present value of any tax that is owed. In this regard, income recognition in a later year is preferred; the longer payment of the tax can be postponed, the lower the present value of the tax.

---

[10]Reg. § 1.61–1(a).   [11]§ 441; Reg. § 1.441–1.

TAX IN THE NEWS **Academy Awards Participants Have a Tax Problem**

Movie stars and other film industry luminaries who appear at various awards ceremonies can receive "gift baskets" for participating in the event. The gift baskets might include expense-paid vacations, pearls, chocolates, clothing, and a variety of other items. The IRS has estimated that the value of some of the baskets has exceeded $230,000.

The IRS has put Hollywood on notice that "movie stars face the same obligation as ordinary Americans." Thus, the presenters must include the value of the basket contents in gross income.

4-3b Accounting Methods

LO.2

Explain when the cash, accrual, and hybrid methods of accounting are used and how they are applied.

The year in which an item of income is subject to tax often depends upon the accounting method the taxpayer employs. The three primary methods of accounting are (1) the cash receipts and disbursements method, (2) the accrual method, and (3) the hybrid method. Most individuals use the cash receipts and disbursements method of accounting, while most larger businesses use the accrual method. Because the Regulations require the accrual method for determining purchases and sales when inventory is an income-producing factor,[12] some businesses employ a hybrid method that is a combination of the cash and accrual methods.

In addition to these overall accounting methods, specialized tax accounting methods are available for certain items or transactions. For instance, a taxpayer may spread the gain from an installment sale of property over the collection period by using the *installment method* of income recognition. Contractors may either spread profits from contracts over the period in which the work is done (the *percentage of completion method*) or defer all profit until the year in which the project is completed (the *completed contract method*) in limited circumstances.[13]

The IRS can prescribe the accounting method to be used by the taxpayer. The IRS holds broad powers to determine whether an accounting method *clearly reflects income.*

> If no method of accounting has been regularly used by the taxpayer, or if the method used does not clearly reflect income, the computation of taxable income shall be made under such method as, in the opinion of the Secretary ... does clearly reflect income.[14]

Cash Receipts Method

Under the cash receipts method, property or services received are included in the taxpayer's gross income in the year of actual or constructive receipt by the taxpayer or agent, regardless of whether the income was earned in that year.[15] The income received need not be reduced to cash in the same year. All that is necessary for income recognition is that property or services received be measurable by a fair market value.[16]

Thus, a cash basis taxpayer that receives a note in payment for services recognizes gross income in the year of receipt equal to the fair market value of the note. However, a creditor's mere promise to pay (e.g., an account receivable), with no supporting note, usually is not considered to have a fair market value.[17] Thus, the cash basis taxpayer defers income recognition until the account receivable is collected.

---

[12]Reg. § 1.446–1(c)(2)(i).

[13]§§ 453 and 460.

[14]§ 446(b).

[15]*Julia A. Strauss*, 2 B.T.A. 598 (1925). The doctrine of *constructive receipt* holds that if income is unqualifiedly available although not physically in the taxpayer's possession, it is subject to the income tax. An example is

accrued interest on a savings account. Under the doctrine of constructive receipt, the interest is taxed to a depositor in the year available, rather than the year actually withdrawn. The fact that the depositor uses the cash basis of accounting for tax purposes is irrelevant. Reg. § 1.451–2.

[16]Reg. §§ 1.446–1(a)(3) and (c)(1)(i).

[17]*Bedell v. Comm.*, 1 USTC ¶359, 7 AFTR 8469, 30 F.2d 622 (CA–2, 1929).

EXAMPLE 5

Finch & Thrush, a CPA firm, uses the cash receipts method of accounting. In 2016, the firm performs an audit for Orange Corporation and bills the client for $5,000, which is collected in 2017. In 2016, the firm also performs an audit for Blue Corporation. Because of Blue's precarious financial position, Finch & Thrush requires Blue to issue an $8,000 secured negotiable note in payment of the fee. The note has a fair market value of $6,000. The firm collects $8,000 on the note in 2017. Finch & Thrush reports the following gross income for the two years.

	2016	2017
Fair market value of note received from Blue	$6,000	
Cash received		
From Orange on account receivable		$ 5,000
From Blue on note receivable		8,000
Less: Recovery of capital	–0–	(6,000)
Total gross income	$6,000	$ 7,000

Generally, a cash basis taxpayer recognizes gross income when a check is received in payment for goods or services rendered in a business setting. This is true even if the taxpayer receives the check after banking hours. But if the person paying with the check requests that the check not be cashed until a subsequent date, the cash basis income is deferred until the date the check can be cashed.[18]

Certain taxpayers are not permitted to use the cash method of accounting. Specifically, the accrual basis must be used to report the income earned by (1) C corporations, (2) partnerships with a corporate partner (other than an S corporation), (3) business taxpayers that carry inventories, and (4) tax shelters. A number of other businesses usually still can use the cash method.[19]

- A farming business (other than certain corporations).
- A qualified personal service corporation.
- A corporation, or a partnership with a corporate partner, whose average annual gross receipts for all prior three-year periods are $5 million or less.
- Certain small taxpayers that carry inventories.[20]

TAX PLANNING STRATEGIES **Cash Receipts Method**

FRAMEWORK FOCUS: INCOME

Strategy: Postpone Recognition of Income to Achieve Tax Deferral.

FRAMEWORK FOCUS: TAX RATE

Strategy: Shift Net Income from High-Bracket Years to Low-Bracket Years.

The timing of income from services often can be controlled through the cash method of accounting. The usual lag between billings and collections (e.g., December's billings collected in January) can result in a deferral of some income until the last year of operations.

As another example, before rendering services, a corporate officer approaching retirement may contract with the corporation to defer a portion of his or her compensation to the lower tax bracket retirement years.

---

[18]*Charles F. Kahler*, 18 T.C. 31 (1952); *Bright v. U.S.*, 91–1 USTC ¶50,142, 67 AFTR 2d 91–673, 926 F.2d 383 (CA–5, 1991).

[19]§§ 441, 448(a), 448, 471.

[20]Rev.Procs. 2002–28, 2002–1 C.B. 815; 2001–10, 2001–1 C.B. 272.

BRIDGE DISCIPLINE **Bridge to Economics and Finance**

Nontaxable Economic Benefits

Home ownership is the prime example of economic income from capital that is not subject to tax. If the taxpayer uses his or her capital to purchase investments but pays rent on a personal residence, the taxpayer pays tax on the income from the investments but cannot deduct the rent payment.

However, if the taxpayer purchases a personal residence instead of the investments, he or she removes the investment income from the tax return but incurs no other form of gross income. A homeowner "pays rent to himself," but such rent is not subject to income tax. Thus, the homeowner has substituted nontaxable for taxable income.

Tax Deferral

Because deferred taxes are tantamount to interest-free loans from the government, the deferral of taxes is a worthy goal of the tax planner. However, the tax planner also must consider the tax rates for the years the income is shifted from and to. For example, a one-year deferral of income from a year in which the taxpayer's tax rate was 28 percent to a year in which the tax rate will be 35 percent would not be advisable if the taxpayer expects to earn less than a 7 percent after-tax return on the deferred tax dollars. Text Appendix F provides tables by which to compute the present and future values of gross income, deductions, and tax liabilities.

The taxpayer often can defer the recognition of income from appreciated property by postponing the event triggering realization (e.g., the final closing on a sale or exchange of property). If the taxpayer needs cash, obtaining a loan by using the appreciated property as collateral may be the least costly alternative. When the taxpayer anticipates reinvesting the proceeds, a sale may be inadvisable.

EXAMPLE 6

Ira owns 100 shares of Pigeon Company common stock with a cost of $20,000 and a fair market value of $50,000. Although the stock's value has increased substantially in the past three years, Ira thinks the growth cycle for the stock is over. If he sells the Pigeon stock, Ira will invest the proceeds from the sale in other common stock. Assuming that Ira's marginal tax rate on the sale is 20%, he keeps only $44,000 [$50,000 − .20($50,000 − $20,000)] to reinvest. The alternative investment must substantially outperform Pigeon in the future for the sale to be beneficial.

Accrual Method

Under the **accrual method**, an item generally is included in gross income for the year in which it is earned, regardless of when the income is collected. The income is earned when (1) all the events have occurred that fix the right to receive the income and (2) the amount to be received can be determined with reasonable accuracy.[21]

Generally, the taxpayer's rights to the income accrue when title to property passes to the buyer or the services are performed for the customer or client.[22] If the rights to the income have accrued but are subject to a potential refund claim (e.g., under a product warranty), the income is reported in the year of sale and a deduction is allowed in subsequent years when actual claims accrue.[23]

Where the taxpayer's rights to the income are being contested (e.g., when a contractor fails to meet specifications), gross income is recognized only when payment has been received.[24] If the payment is received before the dispute is settled, however, the

---

[21]Reg. § 1.451–1(a).

[22]*Lucas v. North Texas Lumber Co.*, 2 USTC ¶484, 8 AFTR 10276, 50 S.Ct. 184 (USSC, 1930).

[23]*Brown v. Helvering*, 4 USTC ¶1222, 13 AFTR 851, 54 S.Ct. 356 (USSC, 1933).

[24]*Burnet v. Sanford and Brooks*, 2 USTC ¶636, 9 AFTR 603, 51 S.Ct. 150 (USSC, 1931).

court-made **claim of right doctrine** requires the taxpayer to recognize the income in the year of receipt.[25]

If Finch & Thrush in Example 5 uses the accrual basis of accounting, it recognizes $13,000 ($8,000 + $5,000) income in 2016, the year its rights to the income accrue.

EXAMPLE 7

Tangerine Construction, Inc., completes construction of a building at the end of the year and presents a bill to the customer. The customer refuses to pay the bill and claims that Tangerine has not met specifications. A settlement with the customer is not reached until the next year.

No gross income accrues to Tangerine until the second year.

Hybrid Method

The accrual method is used to determine sales and cost of goods sold. To simplify record keeping, some taxpayers account for inventory using the accrual method but use the cash method for all other income and deduction items. This approach, called the **hybrid method**, is used primarily by small businesses when the cash method otherwise is not available.

4-3c Special Rules for Cash Basis Taxpayers

Constructive Receipt

Income that has not actually been received by the taxpayer is taxed as though it had been received—the income is constructively received—under the following conditions.

- The amount is made readily available to the taxpayer.
- The taxpayer's actual receipt is not subject to substantial limitations or restrictions.[26]

The rationale for the **constructive receipt** doctrine is that if the income is available, the taxpayer should not be allowed unilaterally to postpone income recognition. For instance, a taxpayer is not permitted to defer income for December services by refusing to accept payment until January.

Constructive Receipt

EXAMPLE 8

Rob, a physician, conducts his medical practice as a sole proprietorship. Rob is also a member of a barter club. This year, Rob provided medical care for other club members and earned 3,000 points. Each point entitles him to $1 in goods and services sold by other members of the club; the points can be used at any time. Rob exchanged his points for a new high-definition TV in the next year, but he recognizes $3,000 gross income in the first year, i.e. when the 3,000 points were credited to his account.[27]

EXAMPLE 9

On December 31, an employer issued a bonus check to an employee but asked her to hold it for a few days until the company could make deposits to cover the check. The income was not constructively received on December 31 because the issuer did not have sufficient funds in its account to pay the debt.[28]

EXAMPLE 10

Mauve, Inc., an S corporation, owned interest coupons that matured on December 31. The coupons can be converted to cash at any bank at maturity. Thus, the income was constructively received on December 31, even though Mauve failed to cash in the coupons until the following year.[29]

---

[25]*North American Oil Consolidated Co. v. Burnet*, 3 USTC ¶943, 11 AFTR 16, 52 S.Ct. 613 (USSC, 1932).

[26]Reg. § 1.451–2(a).

[27]Rev.Rul. 80–52, 1980–1 C.B. 100.

[28]*L. M. Fischer*, 14 T.C. 792 (1950).

[29]Reg. § 1.451–2(b).

TAX IN THE NEWS **Congress Rescues Lottery Winners from Constructive Receipt Problems**

Under the general rules of constructive receipt, a lottery winner who elected to receive the winnings in installments could face horrendous tax problems. If the winner had the right to receive the entire amount but elected to be paid in installments, tax could be due on the present value of the amounts to be received in the future as well as the amount received currently. Frequently, the winner made the election without being aware of the tax consequences.

To protect poorly advised, or unadvised, lottery winners, Congress changed the tax law so that the constructive receipt doctrine does not apply to "qualified prizes," a term crafted specifically to address the lottery and prize-winner's situation. Thus, lottery winnings can be received in installments and included in gross income as the installments are received.

Constructive Receipt

Flamingo Company mails dividend checks on December 31. The checks will not be received by the shareholders until January. The shareholders do not realize gross income until January.[30]

EXAMPLE 11

The constructive receipt doctrine does not reach income the taxpayer is not yet entitled to receive, even though the taxpayer could have contracted to receive the income

Murphy offers to pay Peach Corporation (a cash basis taxpayer) $100,000 for land in December 2017. Peach Corporation refuses, but offers to sell the land to Murphy on January 1, 2018, when the corporation will be in a lower tax bracket. If Murphy accepts Peach's offer, the gain is taxed to Peach in 2018, when the sale is completed.[31]

EXAMPLE 12

In-depth coverage can be found on this book's companion website: www.cengagebrain.com

1 DIGGING DEEPER

Original Issue Discount

Lenders frequently make loans that require a payment at maturity of more than the amount of the original loan. The difference between the amount due at maturity and the amount of the original loan is actually interest but is referred to as **original issue discount**. In these circumstances, the Code requires the original issue discount to be reported when it is earned, regardless of the taxpayer's accounting method.[32] The *interest earned* is calculated by the effective interest rate method.

On January 1, year 1, Blue and White, a cash basis partnership, pays $92,456 for a 24-month certificate of deposit. The certificate is priced to yield 4% (the effective interest rate) with interest compounded annually. No interest is paid until maturity, when Blue and White receives $100,000.

The partnership's gross income from the certificate is $7,544 ($100,000 − $92,456). Blue and White calculates income earned each year as follows.

EXAMPLE 13

Year 1 (.04 × $92,456) =	$3,698
Year 2 [.04($92,456 + $3,698)] =	3,846
	$7,544

---

[30]Reg. § 1.451–2(b).

[31]*Cowden v. Comm.*, 61–1 USTC ¶9382, 7 AFTR 2d 1160, 289 F.2d 20 (CA–5, 1961).

[32]§§ 1272(a)(3) and 1273(a).

The original issue discount rules do not apply to U.S. savings bonds or to obligations with a maturity date of one year or less from the date of issue.[33]

Amounts Received under an Obligation to Repay

The receipt of funds with an obligation to repay that amount in the future is the essence of borrowing. The taxpayer's assets and liabilities increase by the same amount, so no income is realized when the borrowed funds are received.

A landlord receives a damage deposit from a tenant. The landlord does not recognize income until the deposit is forfeited because the landlord has an obligation to repay the deposit if no damage occurs.[34] However, if the deposit is in fact a prepayment of rent, it is taxed in the year of receipt.

4-3d Special Rules for Accrual Basis Taxpayers

Prepaid Income

For financial reporting purposes, advance payments received from customers are reflected as prepaid income and as a liability of the seller. For tax purposes, however, the prepaid income often is taxed in the year of receipt.

In December 2016, Jared's sole proprietorship pays its January 2017 rent of $1,000. Jared's calendar-year, accrual basis landlord includes the $1,000 in 2016 gross income for tax purposes, although $1,000 unearned rent income is reported as a liability on the landlord's financial accounting balance sheet for December 31, 2016.

Deferral of Advance Payments for Goods

Generally, an accrual basis taxpayer can elect to defer recognition of income from advance payments for goods if the method of accounting for the sale is the same for tax and financial reporting purposes.[35]

Brown Company ships goods only after payment for the goods has been received. In December 2016, Brown receives a $10,000 payment for goods that are not shipped until January 2017. Assuming that a proper election is in place, Brown reports the income in 2017 for tax purposes, assuming that the company reports the income in that year for financial reporting purposes.

Deferral of Advance Payments for Services

When payments are received for services that will be performed in a later tax year, an accrual basis taxpayer can defer for one year the recognition of income for the services that will be performed later.[36] This method of accounting may also be used for advance payments received for goods, as well as licensing of intellectual property, and the sale, lease, or license of software.

Advance payments for prepaid rent or prepaid interest, however, always are taxed in the year of receipt, as illustrated in Example 15.

---

[33]§ 1272(a)(2).
[34]*John Mantell*, 17 T.C. 1143 (1952).

[35]Reg. § 1.451–5(b). The election covers the current and all future tax years, unless the IRS allows the taxpayer to terminate it. See Reg. § 1.451–5(c) for exceptions to this deferral opportunity.
[36]Rev.Proc. 2004–34, 2004–1 C.B. 991.

Yellow Corporation, an accrual basis calendar-year taxpayer, sells its computer consulting services under 12-month, 24-month, and 36-month contracts. The corporation provides services to each customer every month. On May 1, year 1, Yellow sold the following contracts.

EXAMPLE 17

Length of Contract	Total Proceeds
12 months	$3,000
24 months	4,800
36 months	7,200

Yellow may defer until year 2 all of the income that will be reported on its financial statements after year 1.

Length of Contract	Income Recorded in Year 1	Income Recorded in Year 2
12 months	$2,000 ($3,000 × 8/12)	$1,000 ($3,000 × 4/12)
24 months	1,600 ($4,800 × 8/24)	3,200 ($4,800 × 16/24)
36 months	1,600 ($7,200 × 8/36)	5,600 ($7,200 × 28/36)

TAX PLANNING STRATEGIES **Prepaid Income**

FRAMEWORK FOCUS: INCOME

Strategy: Postpone Recognition of Income to Achieve Tax Deferral.

The accrual basis taxpayer who receives advance payments from customers should adopt the available tax accounting income deferral methods. It then should structure the transactions using those rules, so as to avoid a payment of tax on income before the time the income actually is earned.

In addition, both cash and accrual basis taxpayers sometimes can defer income by stipulating that the payments are deposits rather than prepaid income. For example, a tax-savvy landlord might consider requiring an equivalent damage deposit rather than prepayment of the last month's rent.

Concept Summary 4.2

Income Tax Accounting

Tax accounting methods often parallel those used for financial accounting, especially those that affect the timing of the tax recognition of income and deduction items. Certain exceptions do exist, however.

1. Businesses may be able to adopt the cash, accrual, or hybrid method of accounting. The tax law allows certain businesses to use either the cash or hybrid method, while others may be required to use the accrual method. For instance, the accrual method typically is required if the taxpayer holds inventories or is a C corporation with over $5 million of gross receipts (other than a qualified personal service corporation).

2. Other tax accounting methods parallel those of financial accounting, such as the installment method and the treatment of long-term contracts.

3. Special rules apply when the taxpayer has control, but not possession, of funds that have been earned.

4. Tax accounting method rules may allow the deferral of income recognition concerning prepayments for the sale of goods and services.

4-4 INCOME SOURCES

LO.3

Identify who should pay the tax on an item of income.

4-4a Personal Services

It is a well-established principle of taxation that income from personal services must be included in the gross income of the person who performs the services. This principle was first established in a Supreme Court decision, *Lucas v. Earl*.[37] Mr. Earl entered into a binding agreement with his wife under which Mrs. Earl was to receive one-half of Mr. Earl's salary. Justice Holmes used the celebrated **fruit and tree metaphor** to explain that the fruit (income) must be attributed to the tree from which it came (Mr. Earl's services). A mere **assignment of income** to another party does not shift the liability for the tax.

Services of an Employee

Services performed by an employee for the employer's customers are considered performed by the employer. Thus, the employer is taxed on the income from the services provided to the customer, and the employee is taxed on any compensation received from the employer.[38]

The Big Picture

EXAMPLE 18

Return to the facts of *The Big Picture* on p. 4-1. Dr. Payne has entered into an employment contract with his corporation and receives a salary. All patients contract to receive their dental services from the corporation, and those services are provided through the corporation's employee, Dr. Payne.

Thus, the corporation earned the income from patients' services and must include the patients' fees in its gross income. Payne includes his salary in his own gross income. The corporation claims a deduction for the reasonable salary paid to Payne.

DIGGING DEEPER 2   In-depth coverage can be found on this book's companion website: www.cengagebrain.com

4-4b Income from Property

Income earned from property (e.g., interest, dividends, rent) is included in the gross income of the owner of the property. If a shareholder clips interest coupons from bonds shortly before the interest payment date and transfers the coupons to his or her solely owned corporation, the interest still is taxed to the shareholder.

Often income-producing property is transferred after income from the property has accrued but before the income is recognized under the transferor's method of accounting. The IRS and the courts have developed rules to allocate the income between the transferor and the transferee. These allocation rules are addressed below. Other allocation rules address income in community property states.

DIGGING DEEPER 3   In-depth coverage can be found on this book's companion website: www.cengagebrain.com

Interest

According to the tax law, interest accrues daily. Therefore, the interest for the period that includes the date of an asset transfer is allocated between the transferor and the transferee based on the number of days during the period that each owned the property.

---

[37] 2 USTC ¶496, 8 AFTR 10287, 50 S.Ct. 241 (USSC, 1930).

[38] *Sargent v. Comm.*, 91–1 USTC ¶50,168, 67 AFTR 2d 91–718, 929 F.2d 1252 (CA–8, 1991).

Of the 147 million individual income tax returns filed for the 2013 tax year, 83 percent included wage or salary income, and about 35 percent included some amount of interest income. But except for these two categories, no other type of income was found in even a quarter of the returns filed. Sales of business assets were found on fewer than 1.5 percent of the returns, and about 6 percent of the returns included flow-through income or loss from partnerships and S corporations. Capital gains showed up on about 17 percent of the returns, but only when distributions from mutual fund investments were included.

Floyd, a cash basis taxpayer, gives his son, Seth, corporate bonds with a face amount of $12,000 and a 5% stated annual interest rate. The interest is payable on the last day of each quarter. Floyd makes the gift to Seth on February 28. Floyd recognizes $100 interest income at the time of the gift ($12,000 × 5% × 3/12 interest for the quarter × 2/3 months in the quarter earned before the gift).

EXAMPLE 19

For the transferor, the timing of the recognition of gross income from the property depends upon the pertinent accounting method and the manner in which the property was transferred. In the case of a gift of income-producing property, the donor's share of the accrued income is recognized at the time it would have been recognized had the donor continued to own the property.[39] If the transfer is a sale, however, the transferor recognizes the accrued income at the time of the sale, because the accrued amount is included in the sales proceeds.

Mia purchased a corporate bond at its face amount on January 1 for $10,000. The bond paid 5% interest each December 31. On March 31, Mia sold the bond for $10,600. Mia recognizes $125 interest income, accrued as of the date of the sale (5% × $10,000 × 3/12 months before the sale). She also recognizes a $475 capital gain from the sale of the bond, computed as follows.

EXAMPLE 20

Amount received from sale	$ 10,600
Accrued interest income already recognized	(125)
Selling price of bond, less interest	$ 10,475
Less cost of the bond	(10,000)
Capital gain recognized on sale	$ 475

Dividends

A corporation is taxed on its earnings, and the shareholders are taxed on the dividends paid to them from the corporation's after-tax earnings.

Partial relief from the double taxation of dividends has been provided in that *qualified dividends* are taxed at the same marginal rate that is applicable to a net capital gain. Distributions that are not qualified dividends are taxed at the rates that apply to ordinary income.[40]

Tax Rate That Applies to the Taxpayer's Ordinary Income	Tax Rate That Applies to Dividend Income
0, 10, or 15%	0%
25, 28, 33, or 35%	15%
39.6%	20%

---

[39]Rev.Rul. 72–312, 1972–1 C.B. 22.

[40]§ 1(h)(11). Qualified dividends are not treated as capital gains in the gains and losses netting process; thus, they are *not* reduced by capital losses. For certain high-income individuals, the additional Medicare tax on net investment income also may apply to dividends, interest, net capital gains, and the like. See Chapter 9.

GLOBAL TAX ISSUES   Which Foreign Dividends Get the Discounted Rate?

A dividend from a non-U.S. corporation is eligible for qualified dividend status only if one of the following requirements is met: (1) the foreign corporation's stock is traded on an established U.S. securities market or (2) the foreign corporation is eligible for the benefits of a comprehensive income tax treaty or information-sharing agreement between its country of incorporation and the United States.[41]

Because the beneficial tax rate is intended to mitigate double taxation, only certain dividends are eligible for the beneficial treatment. Excluded are certain dividends from non-U.S. corporations, dividends from tax-exempt entities, and dividends that do not satisfy the holding period requirement.

Corporations that are shareholders (that is, they own stock in another corporation) may be allowed a deduction to offset some or all of their dividend income. See Chapter 12.

A holding period requirement must be satisfied for the lower tax rates to apply: the stock that paid the dividend must have been held for more than 60 days during the 121-day period beginning 60 days before the ex-dividend date.[42] The purpose of this requirement is to prevent the taxpayer from buying the stock shortly before the dividend is paid, receiving the dividend, and then selling the stock at a short-term capital loss after the stock goes ex-dividend. A stock's price often declines after the stock goes ex-dividend.

Qualified Dividends

EXAMPLE 21

Green Corporation pays a dividend of $1.50 on each share of its common stock. Madison and Daniel, two unrelated shareholders, each own 1,000 shares of the stock. Consequently, each receives a dividend of $1,500 (1,000 shares × $1.50). Assume that Daniel satisfies the 60/120-day holding period rule, but Madison does not.

The $1,500 that Daniel receives is subject to the lower rates on qualified dividends. The $1,500 that Madison receives, however, is not. Because Madison did not comply with the holding period rule, her dividend is not a *qualified dividend*; it is taxed at ordinary income rates.

EXAMPLE 22

Assume that both Madison and Daniel in Example 21 are in the 35% Federal income tax bracket. Consequently, Madison pays a tax of $525 (35% × $1,500) on her dividend, while Daniel pays a tax of $225 (15% × $1,500) on his. The $300 saving that Daniel enjoys underscores the advantages of receiving a qualified dividend.

A distribution by a corporation to its shareholders is classified as a dividend only if it is paid from the entity's *earnings and profits* (E & P). If the distribution is not made from E & P, it is treated as a return of the shareholder's investment and generally is not taxed at the time of the distribution. See Chapter 13.

Unlike interest, dividends do not accrue on a daily basis; the declaration of a dividend is at the discretion of the corporation's board of directors. Generally, dividends are taxed to the person who is entitled to receive them—the shareholder of record as of the corporation's record date.[43] Thus, if a taxpayer sells stock after a dividend has been declared but before the record date, the dividend generally is taxed to the purchaser.

If a donor makes a gift of stock to someone (e.g., a family member) after the declaration date but before the record date, the donor does not shift the dividend income to

---

[41]§§ 1(h)(11)(C)(i), (ii).

[42]The ex-dividend date is the date before the record date on which the corporation finalizes the list of shareholders who will receive the dividends.

[43]Reg. § 1.61–9(c). The record date is the cutoff for determining the shareholders who are entitled to receive the dividend.

TAX FACT Business Income and Loss

Sole proprietors reporting net business income or loss on Form 1040 constitute over 12 percent of all returns filed. About 4 percent of all Forms 1040 show income from rentals or farming operations. And more than 1 percent of individuals report winnings from gambling activities!

the donee. The *fruit* has ripened sufficiently as of the declaration date to tax the dividend income to the donor of the stock.[44]

EXAMPLE 23

On June 20, the board of directors of Black Corporation declares a $10 per share dividend. The dividend is payable on June 30 to shareholders of record on June 25. As of June 20, Kathleen owns 200 shares of Black stock. On June 21, Kathleen sells 100 of the shares to Jon for their fair market value and gives 100 of the shares to Andrew (her son). Both Jon and Andrew are shareholders of record as of June 25.

Jon (the purchaser) is taxed on $1,000 because he is entitled to receive the dividend. However, Kathleen (the donor) is taxed on the $1,000 received by Andrew (the donee) because the gift was made after the declaration date but before the record date of the dividend.

In-depth coverage can be found on this book's companion website: www.cengagebrain.com

4 DIGGING DEEPER

4-4c Income Received by an Agent

Income received by the taxpayer's agent is considered to be received by the taxpayer. A cash basis principal must recognize the income at the time it is received by the agent.[45]

EXAMPLE 24

Longhorn, Inc., a cash basis corporation, delivers cattle to the auction barn in late December. The auctioneer, acting as the corporation's agent, sells the cattle and collects the proceeds in December. The auctioneer does not pay Longhorn until the following January. Longhorn includes the sales proceeds in its gross income in the year the auctioneer received the funds.

TAX PLANNING STRATEGIES Techniques for Reducing Investment Income

FRAMEWORK FOCUS: INCOME

Strategy: Postpone Recognition of Income to Achieve Tax Deferral.

FRAMEWORK FOCUS: TAX RATE

Strategy: Control the Character of Income

Because no tax is due until a gain has been recognized, the law favors investments that yield appreciation rather than annual income, and it favors capital gains over interest income.

Vera can buy a low-rated corporate bond or an acre of land for $10,000. The bond pays $1,000 of interest (10%) each year, and Vera expects the land to increase in value 10% each year for the next 10 years. She is in the 40% (combined Federal and state) tax bracket for ordinary income and 26% for qualifying capital gains. If the bond would mature or the land would be sold in 10 years and

EXAMPLE 25

continued

---

[44]*M. G. Anton*, 34 T.C. 842 (1960).

[45]Rev.Rul. 79–379, 1979–2 C.B. 204.

Vera would reinvest the interest at a 10% before-tax return, she would accumulate the following amounts at the end of 10 years. See text Appendix F.

		Bond	Land
Original investment		$10,000	$ 10,000
Annual income	$ 1,000		
Less tax	(400)		
	$ 600		
Compound amount reinvested for 10 years at 6% after-tax	×13.1808	7,908	
Future value		$17,908	
Compound amount, 10 years at 10%			× 2.5937
			$ 25,937
Less tax on sale: 26%($25,937 − $10,000)			(4,143)
Future value			$ 21,794

Therefore, the value of the deferral that results from investing in the land rather than in the bond is $3,886 ($21,794 − $17,908). The income then would be subject to Vera's tax rates, namely, ordinary rates on interest income and capital gain rates on the land sale.

LO.4

Apply the statutory authority as to when exclude an item from gross income.

4-5 SPECIFIC ITEMS OF GROSS INCOME

The all-inclusive principles of gross income determination as applied by the IRS and the courts have, on occasion, been expanded or modified by Congress through legislation. This legislation generally provides more specific rules for determining gross income from certain sources. Most of these special rules appear in §§ 71–90 of the Code.

In addition to provisions describing how specific sources of gross income are to be taxed, several specific rules *exclude* items from gross income. Authority for excluding specific items is provided in §§ 101–150 and in various other provisions in the Code.

Many statutory exclusions are unique to *individual taxpayers* (e.g., gifts and inheritances,[46] scholarships,[47] and a variety of fringe benefits paid to *employees*). These exclusions are discussed in Chapters 9 through 11. Other exclusions are broader and apply to all entities. These exclusions include interest on state and local bonds (§ 103), life insurance proceeds received by reason of death of the insured (§ 101), the fair market value of leasehold improvements received by the lessor when a lease is terminated (§ 109),[48] and income from discharge of indebtedness (§ 108).

Taxpayers can recognize gross income when there is a sale or other disposition of a nonbusiness asset. These transactions are discussed in more detail in Chapters 7 and 8, but this section includes an introduction to the tax rules that apply in the most common situations. Some of the broadly applied statutory rules describing inclusions and exclusions are discussed next.

---

[46]§ 102.

[47]§ 117.

[48]If the tenant made the improvements in lieu of rent payments, the value of the improvements is not eligible for exclusion.

4-5a **Gains and Losses from Property Transactions**

LO.5

Describe the general tax consequences of property transactions.

When property is sold or otherwise disposed of, gain or loss may result. Such gain or loss has an effect on the gross income of the party making the sale or other disposition when the gain or loss is *realized* and *recognized* for tax purposes. The concept of realized gain or loss is expressed as follows.

$$\begin{matrix} \text{Amount realized} \\ \text{from the sale} \end{matrix} - \begin{matrix} \text{Adjusted basis of} \\ \text{the property} \end{matrix} = \begin{matrix} \text{Realized gain} \\ \text{(or loss)} \end{matrix}$$

The *amount realized* is the selling price of the property less any costs of disposition (e.g., brokerage commissions) incurred by the seller. The *adjusted basis* of the property is determined as follows.

Cost (or other original basis) at date of acquisition[49]
Add: Capital additions
Subtract: Depreciation (if appropriate) and other capital recoveries (see Chapter 5)
Equals: Adjusted basis at date of sale or other disposition

Without realized gain or loss, generally, there can be no recognized (taxable) gain or loss. All realized gains are recognized unless some specific part of the tax law provides otherwise. Realized losses may or may not be recognized (deductible) for tax purposes, depending on the circumstances involved. For example, losses realized from the disposition of personal-use property (property held by individuals and not used for business or investment purposes) are not recognized.

During the current year, Ted sells his sailboat (adjusted basis of $4,000) for $5,500. Ted also sells one of his personal automobiles (adjusted basis of $8,000) for $5,000. Ted's realized gain of $1,500 from the sale of the sailboat is recognized. The $3,000 realized loss on the sale of the automobile, however, is not recognized. Thus, the gain is taxable, but the loss is not deductible.

EXAMPLE 26

Once it has been determined that the disposition of property results in a recognized gain or loss, that amount is included in Adjusted Gross Income. The next step is to classify the gain or loss as capital or ordinary. Although ordinary gain is fully taxable and ordinary loss is fully deductible, the same is not true for capital gains and capital losses.

Capital Gains and Losses

Gains and losses from the disposition of capital assets receive special tax treatment. Capital assets are defined in the Code as any property held by the taxpayer *other than*, among other things, inventory, accounts receivable, and depreciable property or real estate used in a business. The sale or exchange of assets in these categories usually results in ordinary income or loss treatment (see Chapter 8). The sale of any other asset generally creates a capital gain or loss.

Cardinal, Inc., owns a pizza parlor. During the current year, Cardinal sells an automobile. The automobile, which had been used as a pizza delivery car for three years, was sold at a loss of $1,000. Because this automobile was a depreciable asset used in its business, Cardinal reports an ordinary loss of $1,000, rather than a capital loss. Cardinal also sold securities held for investment during the current year. The securities were sold for a gain of $800. The securities are capital assets. Therefore, Cardinal has a capital gain of $800.

EXAMPLE 27

---

[49]Cost usually means purchase price plus expenses related to the acquisition of the property and incurred by the purchaser (e.g., brokerage commis-

sions). For the basis of property acquired by gift or inheritance and other basis rules, see Chapter 7.

Computing the Net Capital Gain/Loss To ascertain the appropriate tax treatment of capital gains and losses, a netting process first is applied.

1. Capital gains and losses are classified as:
   a. short term, if the sold asset was held for one year or less, or
   b. long term, if the sold asset was held for more than one year.
2. Capital gains and losses then are netted within these two classifications. Specifically, short-term capital losses (STCL) are offset against short-term capital gains (STCG), resulting in either a net short-term capital loss (NSTCL) or a net short-term capital gain (NSTCG).
3. Similarly, long-term capital losses (LTCL) are offset against long-term capital gains (LTCG), resulting in either a net long-term capital gain (NLTCG) or a net long-term capital loss (NLTCL).
4. If the resulting amounts are of opposite signs (i.e., there remains a gain and a loss), those amounts are netted against each other. This produces the taxpayer's net capital gain or loss for the tax year. It is entirely long- or short-term, as dictated by the number that was larger in steps 2 and 3.

EXAMPLE 28

Colin is subject to a 35% marginal tax rate and reports the following capital gains (losses) from asset sales during the year.

Penguin Corporation stock (held for 7 months)	$ 1,000
Owl Corporation stock (held for 9 months)	(3,000)
Flamingo Corporation bonds (held for 14 months)	2,000
Land (held for 3 years)	4,000

SHORT TERM: The Penguin gain of $1,000 is offset by the Owl loss of $3,000. This results in a $2,000 NSTCL.

LONG TERM: Netting the results of the sales of the bonds and the land, a $6,000 NLTCG is computed.

CONTINUE NETTING: Because there remains a gain and a loss, net these amounts against each other. A $4,000 net long-term capital gain results.

Taxing the Net Capital Gain/Loss Individuals and corporations are taxed differently on their net capital gains and losses. An individual's *net capital gain* is subject to the following *maximum* tax rates.[50] Certain upper-income taxpayers also may incur the additional Medicare tax on net investment income with respect to net capital gains. See Chapter 9.

	Maximum Rate[51]
Short-term gains	39.6%
Long-term gains	20%

A C corporation's net capital gain does not receive any beneficial tax treatment. It is taxed as ordinary income.

The net capital losses of individuals can be used to offset up to $3,000 of ordinary income each year. Any remaining capital loss is carried forward indefinitely until it is exhausted.

C corporations may deduct capital losses only to the extent of capital gains. Capital losses of C corporations in excess of capital gains may not be deducted against ordinary income.

---

[50]§ 1(h).

[51]Certain assets, such as collectibles (e.g., art, antiques, stamps, etc.) and some real estate, receive special treatment. When the 15% or 20% long-term capital gains tax rate otherwise applies, the collectibles gain is taxed at a maximum rate of 28%, and certain real estate gains are taxed at a maximum tax rate of 25%. See Chapter 8.

Such unused capital losses are carried back three years and then carried forward five years to offset capital gains in those years.[52]

EXAMPLE

29

Jones records a short-term capital loss of $5,000 during 2017 and no capital gains. If Jones is an individual, she can deduct $3,000 of this amount as an ordinary loss. The remaining $2,000 loss is carried forward to 2018 and thereafter, until it is fully deducted against ordinary income or netted against other capital gains and losses.

If Jones is a C corporation, none of the capital loss is deductible in 2017. All of the $5,000 loss is carried back and offset sequentially against capital gains in 2014, 2015, and 2016 (generating an immediate tax refund). Any remaining capital loss is carried forward and offset against capital gains in tax years 2018 to 2022.

In-depth coverage can be found on this book's companion website: www.cengagebrain.com

5 DIGGING DEEPER

4-5b Interest on Certain State and Local Government Obligations

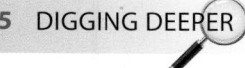

LO.6

Explain and apply the tax provision that excludes interest on state and local government obligations from gross income.

At the time the Sixteenth Amendment was ratified by the states, there was some question as to whether the Federal government possessed the constitutional authority to tax interest on state and local government obligations. Taxing such interest was thought to violate the doctrine of intergovernmental immunity because the tax would impair the ability of state and local governments to finance their operations.[53] Thus, interest on state and local government obligations was specifically exempted from Federal income taxation.[54] However, the Supreme Court has concluded that there is no constitutional prohibition against levying a nondiscriminatory Federal income tax on state and local government obligations.[55] Nevertheless, the statutory exclusion still exists.

The current exempt status applies solely to state and local government bonds. Thus, income received from the accrual of interest on a condemnation award or an overpayment of state tax is fully taxable.[56] Nor does the exemption apply to gains on the sale of tax-exempt securities.

BRIDGE DISCIPLINE **Bridge to Public Economics**

The exclusion granted by the Federal government for interest paid on state and local bonds costs the U.S. Treasury approximately $29 billion per year, according to the Office of Management and Budget. Such forgone revenue is referred to as a "tax expenditure." However, if the capital markets are working properly, the exclusion should produce cost savings to the state and local governments.

If the exclusion were eliminated, state and local governments would pay higher interest rates on their bonds; the investor would demand a higher interest rate to produce the same after-tax yield as that received from taxable bonds of comparable risk. Therefore, the exclusion operates as a form of revenue sharing to the benefit of the state and local governments; it can be seen as a less-visible alternative to a direct grant from the Federal government to the state or local agency. It also is clear that this "expenditure" by the Federal government disproportionately is received by upper-income, high-wealth bondholders.

---

[52]§§ 1211 and 1212.

[53]*Pollock v. Farmer's Loan & Trust Co.*, 3 AFTR 2602, 15 S.Ct. 912 (USSC, 1895).

[54]§ 103(a).

[55]*South Carolina v. Baker III*, 88–1 USTC ¶9284, 61 AFTR 2d 88–995, 108 S.Ct. 1355 (USSC, 1988).

[56]*Kieselbach v. Comm.*, 43–1 USTC ¶9220, 30 AFTR 370, 63 S.Ct. 303 (USSC, 1943); *U.S. Trust Co. of New York v. Anderson*, 3 USTC ¶1125, 12 AFTR 836, 65 F.2d 575 (CA–2, 1933).

EXAMPLE 30

Macaw Corporation purchases State of Virginia bonds for $10,000 on July 1. The bonds pay $400 interest each June 30 and December 31. Macaw excludes from gross income the $400 interest received on December 31.

On March 31 of the next year, Macaw sells the bonds for $10,500 plus $200 of accrued interest. Macaw recognizes a $500 taxable gain ($10,500 − $10,000), but the $200 accrued interest is exempt from taxation.

DIGGING DEEPER 6   In-depth coverage can be found on this book's companion website: www.cengagebrain.com

The interest exclusion reduces the cost of borrowing for state and local governments. A taxpayer with a 35 percent marginal tax rate requires only a 5.2 percent yield on a tax-exempt bond to obtain the same after-tax income as a taxable bond paying 8 percent interest [5.2% ÷ (1 − .35) = 8%].

Although the Internal Revenue Code excludes from Federal gross income the interest on state and local government bonds, the interest paid on U.S. government bonds is not excluded from the Federal tax base. Congress has decided, however, that if the Federal government is not to tax state and local bond interest, the state and local governments are prohibited from taxing interest on U.S. government bonds.[57] While this parity between the Federal and state and local governments exists with regard to taxing each others' obligations, the states are free to tax another's obligations. Thus, some states exempt the interest on the bonds they issue, but tax the interest on bonds issued by other states.

The Big Picture

EXAMPLE 31

Return to the facts of *The Big Picture* on p. 4-1. Dr. Payne includes in gross income the $500 of interest income from the bank's money market account, but not the $500 that is earned on the Whitehall School District bonds.

LO.7

Determine the extent to which life insurance proceeds are excluded from gross income.

4-5c Life Insurance Proceeds

Life insurance proceeds paid to the beneficiary because of the death of the insured are exempt from income tax.[58] Congress chose to exempt life insurance proceeds from gross income for several reasons, including the following.

- For family members, life insurance proceeds serve much the same purpose as a nontaxable inheritance.

- In a business context (as well as in a family situation), life insurance proceeds replace an economic loss suffered by the beneficiary.

Thus, Congress concluded that, in general, making life insurance proceeds exempt from income tax was a good policy.

EXAMPLE 32

Sparrow Corporation purchased an insurance policy on the life of its CEO and named itself as the beneficiary. Sparrow paid $24,000 in premiums. When the company's CEO died, Sparrow collected the insurance proceeds of $60,000. The $60,000 is excluded from Sparrow's gross income.

Exceptions to Exclusion Treatment

The income tax exclusion applies only when the insurance proceeds are received because of the death of the insured. If the owner cancels the policy and receives the

---

[57]31 U.S.C.A. § 742.   [58]*Estate of D. R. Daly*, 3 B.T.A. 1042 (1926).

cash surrender value, he or she must recognize gain to the extent of the excess of the amount received over the cost of the policy.[59]

Another exception to exclusion treatment applies if the policy is transferred after the insurance company issues it. If the policy is transferred for valuable consideration, the insurance proceeds are includible in the gross income of the transferee to the extent the proceeds received exceed the amount paid for the policy by the transferee plus any subsequent premiums paid.

Platinum Corporation pays premiums of $5,000 for an insurance policy with a face amount of $12,000 on the life of Beth, an officer of the corporation. Subsequently, Platinum sells the policy to Beth's husband, Jamal, for $5,500. On Beth's death, Jamal receives the proceeds of $12,000. Jamal excludes from gross income $5,500 plus any premiums he paid subsequent to the transfer. The remainder of the proceeds constitutes gross income to Jamal, as he acquired the policy for cash consideration.

There are several major exceptions to the consideration rule.[60] These exceptions permit exclusion treatment for transfers to the following parties. The first three exceptions facilitate the use of insurance contracts to fund **buy-sell agreements**.

1. A partner of the insured.
2. A partnership in which the insured is a partner.
3. A corporation in which the insured is an officer or shareholder.
4. A transferee whose basis in the policy is determined by reference to the transferor's basis, such as a gift or a transfer due to a divorce.
5. The insured party under the policy.

Rick and Sam are equal partners who have a buy-sell agreement that allows either partner to purchase the interest of a deceased partner for $500,000. Neither partner has sufficient cash to buy the other partner's interest, but each holds a life insurance policy on his own life in the amount of $500,000. Rick and Sam could exchange their policies (usually at little or no taxable gain), and upon the death of either partner, the surviving partner could collect tax-free insurance proceeds. The proceeds then could be used to purchase the decedent's interest in the partnership.

TAX PLANNING STRATEGIES **Life Insurance**

FRAMEWORK FOCUS: INCOME AND EXCLUSION

Strategy: Avoid Income Recognition.

Life insurance is a tax-favored investment. The annual increase in the cash surrender value of the policy is not taxable because it is subject to substantial restrictions (no income has been actually or constructively received). By borrowing on the policy's cash surrender value, the owner can receive the policy's increase in value in cash without recognizing any current gross income.

---

[59]*Landfield Finance Co. v. U.S.*, 69–2 USTC ¶9680, 24 AFTR 2d 69–5744, 418 F.2d 172 (CA–7, 1969).

[60]§ 101(a)(2).

Investment earnings arising from the reinvestment of life insurance proceeds generally are subject to income tax. For example, the beneficiary may elect to collect the insurance proceeds in installments that include taxable interest income. The interest portion of each installment is included in gross income.[61]

 DIGGING DEEPER 7   **In-depth coverage can be found on this book's companion website: www.cengagebrain.com**

LO.8

Describe when income must be reported from the discharge of indebtedness.

4-5d Income from Discharge of Indebtedness

Gross income usually is generated when a creditor cancels a borrower's debt or accepts a payment for less than the amount owed. Foreclosure by a creditor is treated as a sale or exchange of the property and usually triggers gross income.[62]

EXAMPLE 35

Juan owed State Bank $50,000 on a note secured by some investment land. When Juan's basis in the land was $20,000 and the land's fair market value was $50,000, the bank foreclosed on the loan and took title to the land. Juan recognizes a $30,000 gain on the foreclosure, as though he had sold the land directly to State Bank.

A creditor may cancel debt to ensure the viability of the debtor. In such cases, the debtor's net worth is increased by the amount of debt forgiven. Generally, the debtor recognizes gross income equal to the amount of debt canceled.[63]

Debt Cancellation and Gross Income

EXAMPLE 36

Brown Corporation is unable to meet the mortgage payments on its factory building. Both the corporation and the mortgage holder are aware of the depressed market for industrial property in the area. Foreclosure would only result in the creditor obtaining unsellable property.

To improve Brown's financial position and thus improve its chances of obtaining the additional credit necessary for survival from other lenders, the creditor agrees to forgive all amounts past due and to reduce the principal amount of the mortgage. Brown's gross income is increased by the amount of the debt that was forgiven *plus* the reduction in the remaining mortgage balance.

EXAMPLE 37

A corporation issues bonds with a face value of $500,000. Subsequently, the corporation repurchases the bonds in the market for $150,000. It has effectively canceled its $500,000 debt with a $150,000 payment, so it recognizes $350,000 in gross income.[64]

EXAMPLE 38

Keri borrowed $60,000 from National Bank to purchase a warehouse. Keri agreed to make monthly principal and interest payments for 15 years. The interest rate on the note was 3%.

When the balance on the note had been reduced through monthly payments to $48,000, the bank offered to accept $45,000 in full settlement of the note. The bank made the offer because interest rates had increased to 4.5%. Keri accepted the bank's offer. As a result, she recognizes $3,000 ($48,000 − $45,000) gross income.[65]

---

[61]Reg. §§ 1.72–7(c)(1), 1.101–7T.

[62]*Estate of Delman v. Comm.*, 73 T.C. 15 (1979).

[63]§ 61(a)(12).

[64]See *U.S. v. Kirby Lumber Co.*, 2 USTC ¶814, 10 AFTR 458, 52 S.Ct. 4 (USSC, 1931).

[65]Rev.Rul. 82–202, 1982–1 C.B. 35.

A discharge of indebtedness generally increases the taxpayer's gross income, but the reduction in debt is excluded in each of the following situations.[66]

1. Creditors' gifts.
2. Discharges that occur when the debtor is insolvent.
3. Discharges under Federal bankruptcy law.
4. Discharge of the farm debt of a solvent taxpayer.
5. Discharge of qualified real property business indebtedness.
6. A seller's cancellation of a buyer's indebtedness.
7. A shareholder's cancellation of a corporation's indebtedness.
8. Forgiveness of certain loans to students.
9. Discharge of acquisition indebtedness on the taxpayer's principal residence that occurs after 2006 and before 2017, and is the result of the financial condition of the debtor.

Creditors' Gifts

If the creditor reduces the debt as an act of *love, respect, or generosity*, the debtor has simply received a nontaxable gift (situation 1). Such motivations generally arise only on loans between friends or family members. Rarely will a gift be found to have occurred in a business context. A businessperson may settle a debt for less than the amount due, but only as a matter of business expediency (e.g., high collection costs or disputes as to contract terms) rather than generosity.[67]

Insolvency and Bankruptcy

Cancellation of indebtedness income is excluded when the debtor is insolvent (i.e., the debtor's liabilities exceed the fair market value of the assets) or when the cancellation of debt results from a bankruptcy proceeding (situations 2 and 3). The insolvency exclusion is limited to the amount of insolvency. The tax law permits this exclusion to avoid imposing undue hardship on the debtor (wherewithal to pay) and the debtor's limited resources.

The law imposes a cost for the insolvency and bankruptcy exclusion. More specifically, the debtor must decrease certain tax benefits (capital loss carryforwards, net operating loss carryforwards, some tax credits, and suspended passive activity losses)[68] by the amount of income excluded. In addition, if the amount of excluded income exceeds these tax benefits, the debtor reduces the basis in assets.[69] Thus, excluded cancellation of indebtedness income either accelerates recognition of future income (by reducing tax benefit carryforwards) or is deferred until the debtor's assets are sold (or depreciated).

EXAMPLE 39

Before any debt cancellation, Maroon Corporation holds assets with a fair market value of $500,000 and related liabilities of $600,000. A creditor agrees to cancel $125,000 of liabilities. Maroon excludes $100,000 of the debt cancellation income (the amount of insolvency) and is taxed on $25,000. Maroon also reduces any tax benefits and the basis of its assets by $100,000 (the excluded income).

Qualified Real Property Indebtedness

Taxpayers (other than C corporations) can elect to exclude income from cancellation of indebtedness if the canceled debt is secured by real property used in a trade or business (situation 5). The debt must have been used to acquire or improve real property in a trade or business to qualify for the exclusion.[70]

---

[66]§§ 108 and 1017.

[67]*Comm. v. Jacobson,* 49–1 USTC ¶9133, 37 AFTR 516, 69 S.Ct. 358 (USSC, 1949).

[68]See Chapter 6 for a discussion of net operating loss carryforwards and suspended passive losses. Chapter 8 discusses capital loss carryforwards. Chapter 17 discusses tax credits.

[69]§ 108(b).

[70]§ 108(a)(1)(D).

The amount of the exclusion is limited to the *lesser of* (1) the excess of the debt over the fair market value of the real property or (2) the adjusted basis of all depreciable real property held. In addition, the basis of all depreciable real property held by the debtor is reduced by the excluded amount.

Blue, Inc., (an S corporation) owns a warehouse worth $5 million, with a $3 million basis. The warehouse is subject to a $7 million mortgage that was incurred in connection with the acquisition of the warehouse. In lieu of foreclosure, the lender decides that it will reduce the mortgage to $4.5 million. Blue may elect to exclude $2 million from gross income ($7 million debt − $5 million value). If Blue makes the election, it reduces the aggregate basis of its depreciable realty by $2 million.

If the basis of the warehouse had been $1 million, and the warehouse was the only piece of depreciable realty that Blue owned, only $1 million of the debt cancellation income would be excluded.

Seller Cancellation

When a seller of property cancels debt previously incurred by a buyer in a purchase transaction, the cancellation generally does not trigger gross income to the buyer (situation 6). Instead, the reduction in debt is considered to be a reduction in the purchase price of the asset. Consequently, the basis of the asset is reduced in the hands of the buyer.[71]

Snipe, Inc., purchases a truck from Sparrow Autos for $10,000 in cash and a $25,000 note payable. Two days after the purchase, Sparrow announces a sale on the same model truck, with a sales price of $28,000. Snipe contacts Sparrow and asks to be given the sales price on the truck. Sparrow complies by canceling $7,000 of the note payable. The $7,000 is excluded from Snipe's gross income, and the basis of the truck to Snipe is $28,000.

Shareholder Cancellation

If a shareholder cancels the corporation's indebtedness to him or her (situation 7) and receives nothing in return, the cancellation usually is considered a contribution of capital to the corporation by the shareholder. Thus, the corporation recognizes no gross income. Instead, its paid-in capital is increased, and its liabilities are decreased by the same amount.[72]

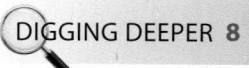

DIGGING DEEPER 8   In-depth coverage can be found on this book's companion website: www.cengagebrain.com

Student Loans

Many states make loans to students on the condition that the loan will be forgiven if the student practices a profession in the state upon completing his or her studies. The amount of the loan that is forgiven (situation 8) is excluded from gross income.[73]

4-5e Tax Benefit Rule

Determine the extent to which receipts can be excluded under the tax benefit rule.

Generally, if a taxpayer claims a deduction for an item in one year and in a later year recovers all or a portion of the prior deduction, the recovery is included in gross income in the year received.[74]

Accrual-basis MegaCorp deducted as a loss a $1,000 receivable from a customer when it appeared the amount would never be collected. The following year, the customer paid $800 on the receivable. MegaCorp reports the $800 as gross income in the year it is received.

---

[71]§ 108(e)(5).

[72]§ 108(e)(6).

[73]§ 108(f).

[74]§ 111(a).

However, the **tax benefit rule** limits income recognition when a deduction does not yield a tax benefit in the year it is taken. If MegaCorp in Example 42 reported the same Federal income tax liability in the year that the loss occurred, the $800 receipt would be excluded from gross income in the year of the recovery.

> **EXAMPLE 43**
>
> Before deducting a $1,000 loss from an uncollectible business receivable, Tulip Company reported taxable income of $200. The business bad debt deduction yields only a $200 tax benefit (assuming no loss carryback is made). That is, taxable income is reduced by only $200 (to zero) as a result of the bad debt deduction. Therefore, if the customer makes a payment on the previously deducted receivable in the following year, only the first $200 is a taxable recovery of a prior deduction. Any additional amount collected is nontaxable because only $200 of the loss yielded a reduction in taxable income (i.e., a tax benefit).

4-5f Imputed Interest on Below-Market Loans

LO.10

Apply the tax provisions on loans made at below-market interest rates.

As discussed earlier in the chapter, generally, no income is recognized unless it is realized. Realization usually occurs when the taxpayer performs services or sells goods, thus becoming entitled to a payment from the other party. It follows that no income is realized if the goods or services are provided at no charge. Under this prior-law interpretation of the realization requirement, interest-free loans were used to shift income between taxpayers.

> **EXAMPLE 44**
>
> Brown Corporation is in the 35% tax bracket and has $400,000 in a money market account earning 5% interest. Jack is the sole shareholder of Brown. He is in the 15% tax bracket and has no investment income. In view of the difference in tax rates, Jack believes that it would be better for him to receive and pay tax on the earnings from Brown's $400,000 investment. Jack does not want to receive the $400,000 from Brown as a dividend because that would trigger a tax.
>
> Under prior law, Jack could receive the money market account from Brown in exchange for a $400,000 non-interest-bearing note, payable on Brown's demand. As a result, Jack would receive the $20,000 annual earnings on the money market account, and the combined taxes of Brown and Jack would be decreased every year by $4,000.
>
> | | |
> |---|---|
> | Decrease in Brown's tax (.05 × $400,000) × .35 | ($7,000) |
> | Increase in Jack's tax (.05 × $400,000) × .15 | 3,000 |
> | Overall decrease in tax liability | ($4,000) |

The Federal income tax law no longer allows this income-shifting result. Brown Corporation in Example 44 is deemed to have received an interest payment from Jack even though no interest was actually paid.[75] This payment of imputed interest is taxable to Brown. Jack may be able to deduct the imaginary interest payment on his return as investment interest if he itemizes deductions. Brown then is deemed to return the interest to Jack in the form of a taxable dividend.

Imputed interest is calculated using rates that the Federal government pays on new borrowings and is compounded semiannually. The Federal rates are adjusted monthly and are published by the IRS.[76] There are three Federal rates: short-term (not over three years and including demand loans), mid-term (over three years but not over nine years), and long-term (over nine years).

If interest is charged on the loan but is less than the Federal rate, the imputed interest is the difference between the amount that would have been charged at the Federal rate and the amount actually charged.

[75]§ 7872(a)(1).

[76]§§ 7872(b)(2) and (f)(2).

EXAMPLE

45

Assume that the Federal rate applicable to the loan in the preceding example is 3.5% through June 30 and 4% from July 1 through December 31. Brown Corporation made the loan on January 1, and the loan is still outstanding on December 31. Brown recognizes interest income of $15,140, and Jack reports interest expense of $15,140. Brown is deemed to have paid a $15,140 dividend to Jack.

Interest Calculations	
January 1 to June 30 (.035 × $400,000) ($\frac{1}{2}$ year)	$ 7,000
July 1 to December 31 [.04($400,000 + $7,000)] ($\frac{1}{2}$ year)	8,140
	$15,140

If Brown had charged 3% interest under the terms of the note, compounded annually, the deemed interest amount would have been $3,140.

Interest at the Federal rate	$ 15,140
Less interest actually charged (.03 × $400,000)	(12,000)
Imputed interest	$ 3,140

The imputed interest rules apply to the following types of below-market loans.[77]

- Gift loans (made out of love, respect, or generosity).
- Compensation-related loans (employer loans to employees).
- Corporation-shareholder loans (a corporation's loans to its shareholders, as in Example 44).

The effects of these loans on the borrower and lender are summarized in Exhibit 4.1.

Exceptions and Limitations

No interest is imputed on total outstanding *compensation-related loans* or *corporation-shareholder loans* of $10,000 or less unless the purpose of the loan is tax avoidance.[78] This vague tax avoidance standard exposes practically all compensation-related and corporation-shareholder loans to possible imputed interest problems. Nevertheless, the $10,000 exception should apply when an employee's borrowing was necessitated by personal needs (e.g., to meet unexpected expenses) rather than tax considerations.

Similarly, no interest is imputed on outstanding *gift loans* of $10,000 or less between individuals, unless the loan proceeds are used to purchase income-producing property.[79] This exemption eliminates from these complex provisions immaterial amounts that do not result in sizable shifts of income.

EXHIBIT 4.1	Effect of Certain Below-Market Loans: Imputed Interest Income and Deductions		
Type of Loan		**Lender**	**Borrower**
Gift	Step 1	Interest income	Interest expense
	Step 2	Gift made*	Gift received
Compensation related	Step 1	Interest income	Interest expense
	Step 2	Compensation expense	Compensation income
Corporation to shareholder	Step 1	Interest income	Interest expense
	Step 2	Dividend paid	Dividend income

* The gift may be subject to the Federal gift tax (refer to Chapter 1).

[77] § 7872(c). Additional situations exist where these rules apply. See, e.g., §§ 7872(c)(1)(D), (E).

[78] § 7872(c)(3).

[79] § 7872(c)(2).

FINANCIAL DISCLOSURE INSIGHTS   **Loans to Executives Prohibited**

Interest-free loans have become a popular form of compensation for executives. Several examples of multimillion-dollar loans have come to light as a result of recent bankruptcies by large corporations. The board of directors often justifies the loans as necessary to enable the executive to be able to purchase a residence or to buy stock in the company.

Loans by publicly held corporations to their executives generally are prohibited by Federal law. The Sarbanes-Oxley provisions generally prohibit loans by corporations to their executives. However, an exception permits corporate loans to finance the acquisition of a personal residence for an executive.

On loans of $100,000 or less between individuals, the imputed interest cannot exceed the borrower's net investment income for the year (gross income from all investments less the related expenses).[80] Through the gift loan provision, the imputed interest rules are designed to prevent high-income individuals from shifting income to relatives in a lower marginal bracket. This shifting of investment income is considered to occur only to the extent that the borrower also recognizes net investment income. Thus, the income imputed to the lender is limited to the borrower's net investment income.

If the borrower's net investment income for the year does not exceed $1,000, no interest is imputed on loans of $100,000 or less. However, this exemption does not apply if a principal purpose of a loan is tax avoidance. In such a case, interest is imputed, and the imputed interest is not limited to the borrower's net investment income.[81]

These exceptions to the imputed interest rules are summarized in Exhibit 4.2.

The Big Picture

Return to the facts of *The Big Picture* on p. 4-1. Dr. Payne's loan from his parents likely is a *gift loan*, as his parents are not shareholders in the personal service corporation. Imputed interest must be computed annually with regard to this loan by both Dr. Payne and his parents, under two different tax rules: (1) the principal amount of the loan exceeds $100,000 and (2) the loan proceeds were invested in an income-producing asset.

EXAMPLE 46

Vicki made interest-free gift loans as follows.

EXAMPLE 47

Borrower	Amount	Borrower's Net Investment Income	Purpose
Susan	$ 8,000	$–0–	Education
Dan	9,000	500	Purchase of stock
Mai	25,000	–0–	Purchase of a business
Olaf	120,000	–0–	Purchase of a residence

Tax avoidance is not a principal purpose of any of the loans. The loan to Susan is not subject to the imputed interest rules because the $10,000 exception applies. The $10,000 exception does not apply to the loan to Dan because the proceeds were used to purchase income-producing assets. However, under the $100,000 exception, the imputed interest is limited to Dan's investment income ($500). Because the $1,000 exception also applies to this loan, no interest is imputed.

No interest is imputed on the loan to Mai because the $100,000 exception applies. None of the exceptions apply to the loan to Olaf because the loan was for more than $100,000; he recognizes imputed interest income related to his loan.

---

[80]§ 7872(d). The $100,000 provision applies only to gift loans.   [81]§ 7872 (d)(1)(B).

EXHIBIT 4.2	**Exceptions to the Imputed Interest Rules for Below-Market Loans**	
Exception	**Eligible Loans**	**Ineligible Loans and Limitations**
De minimis—aggregate loans of $10,000 or less	Gift loans	Proceeds are used to purchase income-producing assets.
	Employer-employee	Principal purpose is tax avoidance.
	Corporation-shareholder	Principal purpose is tax avoidance.
Aggregate loans of $100,000 or less	Gift loans between individuals	Principal purpose is tax avoidance. For all other loans, interest is imputed to the extent of the borrower's net investment income if it exceeds $1,000.

LO.11

Use the tax rules concerning the exclusion of leasehold improvements from gross income.

4-5g Improvements on Leased Property

When a real property lease expires, the landlord regains control of both the real property and any improvements to the property (e.g., buildings and landscaping) made by the tenant during the term of the lease. Any improvements made to the leased property are excluded from the landlord's gross income unless the improvement is made to the property in lieu of rent.[82]

EXAMPLE

48

Mahogany Corporation leases office space to Zink and Silver, Attorneys-at-Law. When the law firm took possession of the office space, it added wall partitions, a wireless computer network, and a variety of other improvements to the space. The improvements were not made in lieu of rent payments to Mahogany. When the lease expires and Mahogany regains possession of the space, the value of the improvements is excluded from Mahogany's gross income.

Concept Summary 4.3

Income Recognition Rules

Generally, realized income is recognized as gross income by the Federal tax law. Special rules apply for certain taxpayers and transactions.

1. Income from services and the use of property typically are taxed immediately as they are earned to the taxpayer that generated the income item.

2. Interest income is recognized as it is earned, and dividend income is taxed when the corporation makes a distribution to its shareholders from corporate E & P. Dividends can qualify for lower tax rates or offsetting deductions. Long-term capital gains also can qualify for lower tax rates.

3. Income exclusions are available for certain types of income, including life insurance proceeds received and interest

income received from the debt of U.S. government agencies at the state and local level.

4. Generally, gross income results for a borrower when a lender forgives an outstanding debt obligation. Certain taxpayers qualify for an exclusion of such income, though, e.g., in the context of a bankruptcy, a student loan, or a financially distressed residence.

5. Gross income may result when the taxpayer holds a debt investment that pays interest at a rate that is lower than the broader market would pay.

---

[82]§ 109.

REFOCUS ON THE BIG PICTURE

JUST WHAT IS INCLUDED IN GROSS INCOME?

Using the accrual method of accounting, the gross income recognized by Cliff Payne's corporation is $385,500. This includes the entire $385,000 of revenue earned from providing services to patients during the year and the $500 of interest income earned on the money market account. The $500 of school district bond interest is excluded from gross income.

Dr. Payne's own gross income includes $120,000 of salary earned during the year. Even though Cliff did not cash his December paycheck until January, he is considered to have constructively received the income, because it was readily available to him. Dr. Payne may be able to reduce his taxable income with a deduction in the amount of the imputed interest expense on the below-market loan from his parents. The increase in value on his stock does not result in gross income until he sells the stock and realizes a gain or loss.

What If?

Rather than electing the accrual method, what if Dr. Payne had chosen to use the cash method of accounting for his business? Using the cash method is acceptable for certain personal service corporations. While using the cash method would reduce the company's gross income from $385,000 to $333,000 ($385,000 amount billed less $52,000 still to be received), this is only part of the picture. Using the cash method also might result in some of the corporation's expenses not being deducted until they are paid in a future year.

Suggested Readings

Todd D. Keator, "Rental Real Estate and the Net Investment Income Tax," *Journal of Taxation*, August 2013.

Craig J. Langstraat and William G. Prascher, "Cancellation of Debt Income Exclusions for Individuals: Good and Bad News," *Practical Tax Strategies*, July 2010.

Richard Rubin and Carter Dougherty, "Bitcoin is Property, Not Currency, in Tax System: IRS," *Bloomberg.com*, March 25, 2014.

Sophia Yan, "Giving Up Your U.S. Passport? It's Going to Cost You," **money.cnn.com**, December 10, 2014.

Key Terms

Accounting income, 4-4

Accounting method, 4-7

Accrual method, 4-9

Assignment of income, 4-14

Buy-sell agreements, 4-23

Cash receipts method, 4-7

Claim of right doctrine, 4-10

Constructive receipt, 4-10

Economic income, 4-4

Fruit and tree metaphor, 4-14

Gross income, 4-2

Hybrid method, 4-10

Income, 4-4

Life insurance proceeds, 4-22

Original issue discount, 4-11

Qualified real property business indebtedness, 4-25

Tax benefit rule, 4-27

Taxable year, 4-6

Computational Exercises

1.   **LO.3** Champ received a $10,000 distribution from NeatCo, a U.S. C corporation. NeatCo's earnings and profits for the year totaled $6,000. How much dividend income does Champ recognize? What Federal income tax rate applies to the dividend if Champ's ordinary income is subject to a 15% tax rate? A 33% rate?

2.   **LO.5** Lefty completes the following capital asset transactions. By how much does Lefty's AGI increase as a result of these gains/losses?

Long-term gain	$10,000
Short-term gain	4,000
Short-term loss	25,000

3.   **LO.8** Before any debt cancellation, KuhnCo holds business equipment with a fair market value of $1 million and related liabilities of $1.25 million. The lender agrees to cancel $400,000 of the liabilities.

   a.   How much gross income does KuhnCo report as a result of the debt cancellation?

   b.   How would your answer change, if at all, had the lender cancelled $200,000 of the debt?

4.   **LO.8** Before any debt cancellation, PeppersCo holds business land with a $2.4 million fair market value, a $1 million tax basis, and a related mortgage of $3 million. In lieu of foreclosure, the lender reduces the mortgage principal by $1.3 million. What are the Federal income tax consequences of the debt cancellation?

5.   **LO.9** Leilei operates a sole proprietorship, using the accrual basis of tax accounting. Last year, she claimed a $10,000 bad debt deduction for a receivable from Jackie. But this year, Jackie sent her a check for $7,000, which Leilei accepted in full satisfaction of the receivable. How much gross income does Leilei record for the item this year?

6.   **LO.10** Lisbeth makes the following interest-free loans during the year. The relevant Federal interest rate is 5%, and none of the loans are motivated by tax avoidance. All of the loans were outstanding for the last six months of the tax year. Identify the Federal income tax effects of these loans.

Borrower	Amount	Borrower's Other Net Investment Income	Purpose of Loan
Richard	$ 5,000	$800	Gift
Woody	8,000	600	Stock purchase
Irene	105,000	0	Purchase principal residence

Problems

Issue ID   7.   **LO.1** Howard buys wrecked cars and stores them on his property. Recently, he purchased a 1990 Ford Taurus for $400. If he can sell all of the usable parts, his total proceeds from the Taurus will be over $2,500. As of the end of the year, he has sold only the radio for $75, and he does not know how many, if any, of the remaining parts will ever be sold. What are Howard's Federal income tax issues?

8.   **LO.1** Determine the taxpayer's current-year (1) economic income and (2) gross income for tax purposes from the following events.

a. Sam's employment contract as chief executive of a large corporation was terminated, and he was paid $500,000 not to work for a competitor of the corporation for five years.

b. Elliot, a 6-year-old child, was paid $5,000 for appearing in a television commercial. His parents put the funds in a savings account for the child's education.

c. Valerie found a suitcase that contained $100,000. She could not determine who the owner was.

d. Winn purchased a lottery ticket for $5 and won $750,000 from it.

e. Larry spent $1,000 to raise vegetables that he and his family consumed. The cost of the vegetables in a store would have been $2,400.

f. Dawn purchased an automobile for $1,500 that was worth $3,500. The seller was in desperate need of cash.

9. **LO.1** The roof of your corporation's office building recently suffered some damage as the result of a storm. You, the president of the corporation, are negotiating with a carpenter who has quoted two prices for the repair work: $600 if you pay in cash ("folding money") and $700 if you pay by check. The carpenter observes that the IRS can more readily discover his receipt of a check. Thus, he hints that he will report the receipt of the check (but not the cash).   Ethics and Equity

The carpenter holds another full-time job and will do the work after hours and on the weekend. He comments that he should be allowed to keep all he earns after regular working hours. Evaluate what you should do.

10. **LO.1** Dolly is a college student who works as a part-time server in a restaurant. Her usual tip is 20% of the price of the meal. A customer ordered a piece of pie and said that he would appreciate prompt service. Dolly fulfilled the customer's request. The customer's bill was $8, but the customer left a $100 bill on the table and did not ask for a receipt. Dolly gave the cashier $8 and pocketed the $100 bill.

Dolly concludes that the customer thought that he had left a $10 bill, although the customer did not return to correct the apparent mistake. The customer had commented about how much he appreciated Dolly's prompt service. Dolly thinks that a $2 tip would be sufficient and that the other $98 is like "found money." How much should Dolly include in her gross income concerning this customer?

11. **LO.2** Determine Amos's gross income in each of the following cases.

a. In the current year, Amos purchased an automobile for $25,000. As part of the transaction, Amos received a $1,500 rebate from the manufacturer.

b. Amos sold his business. In addition to the selling price of the stock, he received $50,000 for a covenant not to compete—an agreement that he will not compete directly with his former business for five years.

c. Amos owned some land he held as an investment. As a result of a change in the zoning rules, the property increased in value by $20,000.

12. **LO.2** The Bluejay Apartments, a new development, is in the process of structuring its lease agreements. The company would like to set the damage deposits high enough that tenants will keep the apartments in good condition. The company actually is more concerned about such damage than about tenants not paying their rent.   Decision Making

a. Discuss the tax effects of the following alternatives.

- $500 damage deposit and $500 rent for the final month of the lease.

- $1,000 rent for the final two months of the lease and no damage deposit.

- $1,000 damage deposit with no rent prepayment.

b. Which option do you recommend? Why?

13. **LO.2, 11** Julie is considering three alternative investments of $10,000. Julie is in the 25% marginal tax bracket for ordinary income and 15% for qualifying capital   Decision Making

gains in all tax years. The selected investment will be liquidated at the end of five years. The alternatives are:

- A taxable corporate bond yielding 5.333% before tax and the interest reinvested at 5.333% before tax.
- A tax-favored bond that will have a maturity value of $12,200 (a 4% pretax rate of return).
- Land that will increase in value.

The gain on the land is classified and taxed as a long-term capital gain. The interest from the bonds is taxed as ordinary income: the interest from the corporate bond as it is earned annually, but that from the tax-favored bond is recognized only upon redemption.

How much must the land increase in value to yield a greater after-tax return than either of the bonds? Use the future value tables in Appendix F as needed for your calculations and comparisons.

14. **LO.1** Determine the taxpayer's gross income for tax purposes in each of the following situations.

   a. Deb, a cash basis taxpayer, traded a corporate bond with accrued interest of $300 for corporate stock with a fair market value of $12,000 at the time of the exchange. Deb's cost of the bond was $10,000. The value of the stock had decreased to $11,000 by the end of the year.

   b. Deb needed $10,000 to make a down payment on her house. She instructed her broker to sell some stock to raise the $10,000. Deb's cost of the stock was $3,000. Based on her broker's advice, instead of selling the stock, she borrowed the $10,000 using the stock as collateral for the debt.

   c. Deb's boss gave her two tickets to the Rabid Rabbits rock concert because Deb met her sales quota. At the time Deb received the tickets, each ticket had a face price of $200 and was selling on eBay for $300 each. On the date of the concert, the tickets were selling for $250 each. Deb and her son attended the concert.

15. **LO.2** Al is a physician who conducts his practice as a sole proprietor. During 2016, he received cash of $280,000 for medical services. Of the amount collected, $40,000 was for services provided in 2015. At the end of 2016, Al held accounts receivable of $60,000, all for services rendered in 2016. In addition, at the end of the year, Al received $12,000 as an advance payment from a health maintenance organization (HMO) for services to be rendered in 2017. Compute Al's gross income for 2016:

   a. Using the cash basis of accounting.

   b. Using the accrual basis of accounting.

16. **LO.2** Selma operates a contractor's supply store. She maintains her books using the cash method. Selma wants to know whether the accrual basis of accounting would be preferable for her business.

   At the end of the year, Selma's accountant computes her accrual basis income that is used on her tax return. For 2016, Selma reported cash receipts of $1.4 million, which included $200,000 collected on accounts receivable from 2015 sales. It also included the proceeds of a $100,000 bank loan. At the end of 2016, she held $250,000 in accounts receivable from customers, all from 2016 sales.

   a. Compute Selma's accrual basis gross receipts for 2016.

   b. Selma paid cash for all of the purchases. The total amount paid for merchandise in 2016 was $1.3 million. At the end of 2015, she had merchandise on hand with a cost of $150,000. At the end of 2016, the cost of merchandise on hand was $300,000. Compute Selma's gross income from merchandise sales for 2016.

Communications   17. **LO.2** Trip Garage, Inc. (459 Ellis Avenue, Harrisburg, PA 17111), is an accrual basis taxpayer that repairs automobiles. In late December 2016, the company repaired Samuel Mosley's car and charged him $1,000. Samuel did not think the problem had been fixed, so he refused to pay; thus, Trip refused to release the automobile.

In early January 2017, Trip made a few adjustments under the hood; Trip then convinced Samuel that the automobile was working properly. At that time, Samuel agreed to pay only $900 because he did not have the use of the car for a week. Trip said "fine," accepted the $900, and released the automobile to Samuel.

An IRS agent thinks Trip, as an accrual basis taxpayer, should report $1,000 of income in 2016, when the work was done, and then deduct a $100 business loss in 2017. Prepare a memo to Susan Apple, the treasurer of Trip, with your recommended treatment for the disputed income.

18. **LO.1, 4** Each Saturday morning, Ted makes the rounds of the local yard sales. He has developed a keen eye for bargains, but he cannot use all of the items he thinks are "real bargains." Ted has found a way to share the benefits of his talent with others. If Ted spots something priced at $40 that he knows is worth $100, for example, he will buy it and list it on eBay for $70. **Ethics and Equity**

Ted does not include his gain in his gross income because he reasons that he is performing a valuable service for others (both the original sellers and the future buyers) and sacrificing profit he could receive. "Besides," according to Ted, "the IRS does not know about these transactions." Should Ted's ethical standards depend on his perception of his own generosity and the risk that his income-producing activities will be discovered by the IRS? Discuss.

19. **LO.2** Accounting students understand that the accrual method of accounting is superior to the cash method for measuring the income and expenses from an ongoing business for financial reporting purposes. Often, CPAs advise their clients to use the accrual method of accounting. Yet, CPA firms generally use the cash method to prepare their own tax returns. Are the CPAs being hypocritical? Explain. **Ethics and Equity**

20. **LO.2** Drake Appliance Company, an accrual basis taxpayer, sells home appliances and service contracts. Determine the effects of each of the following transactions on the company's 2016 gross income assuming that the company uses any available options to defer its taxes.

a. In December 2015, the company received a $1,200 advance payment from a customer for an appliance that Drake had special ordered from the manufacturer. The appliance did not arrive from the manufacturer until January 2016, and Drake immediately delivered it to the customer. The sale was reported in 2016 for financial accounting purposes.

b. In October 2016, the company sold a 6-month service contract for $240. The company also sold a 36-month service contract for $1,260 in July 2016.

c. On December 31, 2016, the company sold an appliance for $1,200. The company received $500 cash and a note from the customer for $700 and $260 interest, to be paid at the rate of $40 a month for 24 months. Because of the customer's poor credit record, the fair market value of the note was only $600. The cost of the appliance was $750.

21. **LO.2** Dr. Randolph, a cash basis taxpayer, knows that she will be in a lower marginal tax bracket next year. To take advantage of the expected decrease in the marginal tax rate, Randolph instructs her office manager to delay filing the medical insurance claims for services performed in November and December until January of the following year. This will ensure that the receipts will not be included in current gross income. Is Randolph abusing the cash method of accounting rules? Why or why not? **Ethics and Equity**

22. **LO.2** Your client is a new partnership, ARP Associates, which is an engineering consulting firm. Generally, ARP bills clients for services at the end of each month. Client billings are about $50,000 each month. On average, it takes 45 days to **Decision Making** **Communications**

collect the receivables. ARP's expenses are primarily for salary and rent. Salaries are paid on the last day of each month, and rent is paid on the first day of each month.

The partnership has a line of credit with a bank, which requires monthly financial statements. These must be prepared using the accrual method. ARP's managing partner, Amanda Sims, has suggested that the firm also use the accrual method for tax purposes and thus reduce accounting fees by $600.

The partners are in the 35% (combined Federal and state) marginal tax bracket. Write a letter to your client explaining why you believe it would be worthwhile for ARP to file its tax return on the cash basis even though its financial statements are prepared on the accrual basis. ARP's address is 100 James Tower, Denver, CO 80208.

23. **LO.3** Alva received dividends on her stocks as follows.

Amur Corporation (a French corporation whose stock is traded on an established U.S. securities market)	$60,000
Blaze, Inc., a Delaware corporation	40,000
Grape, Inc., a Virginia corporation	22,000

a. Alva purchased the Grape stock three years ago, and she purchased the Amur stock two years ago. She purchased the Blaze stock 18 days before it went ex-dividend and sold it 20 days later at a $5,000 loss. Alva reported no other capital gains and losses for the year. She is in the 35% marginal tax bracket. Compute Alva's tax on her dividend income.

b. Alva's daughter, Veda, who is age 25 and who is not Alva's dependent, reported taxable income of $10,000, which included $1,000 of dividends on Grape stock. Veda purchased the stock two years ago. Compute Veda's tax liability on the dividends.

Critical Thinking   24. **LO.3** Liz and Doug were divorced on July 1 of the current year after 10 years of marriage. Their current year's income received before the divorce included:

Doug's salary	$41,000
Liz's salary	55,000
Rent on apartments purchased by Liz 15 years ago	8,000
Dividends on stock Doug inherited from his mother 4 years ago	1,900
Interest on a savings account in Liz's name funded with her salary	2,400

Allocate the income to Liz and Doug assuming that they live in:

a. California.

b. Texas.

Decision Making   25. **LO.4, 10** Roy decides to buy a personal residence, and he goes to the bank for a $150,000 loan. The bank tells Roy that he can borrow the funds at 4% if his father will guarantee the debt. Roy's father, Hal, owns a $150,000 CD currently yielding 3.5%. The Federal rate is 3%. Hal agrees to either of the following.

- Roy borrows from the bank with Hal's guarantee provided to the bank.
- Cash in the CD (with no penalty) and lend Roy the funds at 2% interest.

Hal is in the 33% marginal tax bracket. Roy, whose only source of income is his salary, is in the 15% marginal tax bracket. The interest that Roy pays on the mortgage will be deductible by him. Which option will maximize the family's after-tax wealth?

26. **LO.5** During the year, Olivia recorded the following transactions involving capital assets.

Gain on the sale of unimproved land (held as an investment for 4 years)	$ 4,000
Loss on the sale of a camper (purchased 2 years ago and used for family vacations)	(5,000)
Loss on the sale of IBM stock (purchased 9 months ago as an investment)	(1,000)
Gain on the sale of a fishing boat and trailer (acquired 11 months ago at an auction and used for recreational purposes)	2,000

a. If Olivia is in the 33% bracket, how much Federal income tax results?

b. If Olivia is in the 15% bracket, how much Federal income tax results?

27. **LO.5** Andy reported the following gains and losses from the sale of capital assets.   Critical Thinking

Loss on Pigeon Corporation stock (held 9 months)	($14,000)
Gain on painting (held for 2 years as an investment)	5,000
Gain on unimproved land (held for 3 years as an investment)	3,000

a. If Andy is in the 35% tax bracket, determine the Federal income tax consequences of these transactions.

b. What if Andy is in the 15% tax bracket?

c. What if Andy is a C corporation in the 35% tax bracket?

28. **LO.6** Determine Hazel's Federal gross income from the following receipts for the year.

Gain on sale of Augusta County bonds	$800
Interest on U.S. government savings bonds	400
Interest on state income tax refund	200
Interest on Augusta County bonds	700

29. **LO.6** Tammy, a resident of Virginia, is considering whether to purchase a North Carolina bond that yields 4.6% before tax. She is in the 35% Federal marginal tax bracket and the 5% state marginal tax bracket.   Decision Making

Tammy is aware that State of Virginia bonds of comparable risk are yielding 4.5%. Virginia bonds are exempt from Virginia tax, but the North Carolina bond interest is taxable in Virginia.

Which of the two options will provide the greater after-tax return to Tammy? Tammy can deduct all state taxes paid on her Federal income tax return.

30. **LO.7** The Egret Company has a 40% combined Federal and state marginal tax rate. Egret's board estimates that, if its current president should die, the company would incur $200,000 in costs to find a suitable replacement. In addition, profits on various projects the president is responsible for would likely decrease by $300,000. The president has recommended that Egret purchase a $500,000 life insurance policy.   Decision Making

How much insurance should the company carry on the life of its president to compensate for the after-tax loss that would result from the president's death? Assume that the $200,000 costs of finding a president are deductible and the lost profits would have been taxable.

31. **LO.7** Ray and Carin are partners in an accounting firm. The partners have entered into an arm's length agreement requiring Ray to purchase Carin's partnership interest from Carin's estate if she dies before Ray. The price is set at 120% of the book value of Carin's partnership interest at the time of her death.   Decision Making

Ray purchased an insurance policy on Carin's life to fund this agreement. After Ray had paid $45,000 in premiums, Carin was killed in an automobile accident, and Ray collected $800,000 of life insurance proceeds. Ray used the life insurance proceeds to purchase Carin's partnership interest.

What amount should Ray include in his gross income from receiving the life insurance proceeds?

32. **LO.7** Laura recently was diagnosed with cancer and has begun chemotherapy treatments. A cancer specialist has given Laura less than one year to live. She has incurred sizable medical bills and other general living expenses and is in need of cash. Therefore, Laura is considering selling stock that cost her $35,000 in 2005 and now has a fair market value of $50,000. This amount would be sufficient to pay her medical bills.   Critical Thinking Decision Making

However, she has read about a company (VitalBenefits.com) that would purchase her life insurance policy for $50,000. To date, Laura has paid $30,000 in premiums on the policy.

a. Considering only the Federal income tax effects, would selling the stock or selling the life insurance policy result in more beneficial tax treatment?

b. Assume that Laura is a dependent child and that her mother owns the stock and the life insurance policy, which is on the mother's life. Which of the alternative means of raising the cash would result in more beneficial tax treatment?

33. **LO.8** Vic, who was experiencing financial difficulties, adjusted his debts as follows. Determine the Federal income tax consequences from these events.

a. Vic is an attorney. Vic owed his uncle $25,000. The uncle told Vic that if he serves as the executor of the uncle's estate, Vic's debt will be canceled in the uncle's will.

b. Vic borrowed $80,000 from First Bank. The debt was secured by land that Vic purchased for $100,000. Vic was unable to pay, and the bank foreclosed when the liability was $80,000, which was also the fair market value of the property.

c. The Land Company, which had sold land to Vic for $80,000, reduced the mortgage principal on the land by $12,000.

34. **LO.9** How does the tax benefit rule apply in the following cases?

a. In 2014, the Orange Furniture Store, an accrual method taxpayer, sold furniture on credit for $1,000 to Sammy. Orange's cost of the furniture was $600. In 2015, Orange took a bad debt deduction for the $1,000 because Sammy would not pay his bill.

   In 2016, Sammy inherited some money and paid Orange the $1,000 he owed. Orange was in the 35% marginal tax bracket in 2014, the 15% marginal tax bracket in 2015, and the 35% marginal tax bracket in 2016.

b. In 2015, Barb, a cash basis taxpayer, was in an accident and incurred $8,000 in medical expenses, which she claimed as an itemized deduction for medical expenses. Because of a limitation, though, the expense reduced her taxable income by only $3,000. In 2016, Barb successfully sued the person who caused the physical injury and collected $8,000 to reimburse her for the cost of her medical expenses. Barb was in the 15% marginal tax bracket in all tax years.

Issue ID   35. **LO.10** Brad is the president of the Yellow Corporation. He and other members of his family control the corporation. Brad has a temporary need for $50,000, and the corporation has excess cash. He could borrow the money from a bank at 5%, when Yellow is earning 3% on its temporary investments. Yellow has made loans to other employees on several occasions. Therefore, Brad is considering borrowing $50,000 from the corporation. He will repay the loan principal in two years plus interest at 5%. Identify the relevant tax issues for Brad and Yellow Corporation.

36. **LO.10** Ridge is a generous individual. During the year, she made interest-free loans to various family members when the Federal interest rate was 3%. What are the Federal tax consequences of the following loans by Ridge?

a. On June 30, Ridge loaned $12,000 to a cousin, Jim, to buy a used truck. Jim's only source of income was his wages on various construction jobs during the year.

b. On August 1, Ridge loaned $8,000 to a niece, Sonja. The loan was meant to enable Sonja to pay her college tuition. Sonja reported $1,200 interest income from CDs that her parents had given her.

c. On September 1, Ridge loaned $25,000 to a brother, Al, to start a business. Al reported only $220 of dividends and interest for the year.

d. On September 30, Ridge loaned $150,000 to her mother, Joan, so that Joan could pay the entrance fee at a retirement home. Joan's only receipts for the year were $9,000 in Social Security benefits and $500 interest income received.

37. **LO.10** Apply the imputed interest rules apply in the following situations.

   a. Mike loaned his sister Shonda $90,000 to buy a new home. Mike did not charge interest on the loan. The Federal rate was 4%. Shonda earned $900 of investment income for the year.

   b. Sam's employer maintains an emergency loan fund for its employees. During the year, Sam's wife Tina was very ill, and he incurred unusually large medical expenses. He borrowed $8,500 from his employer's emergency loan fund for six months. The Federal rate was 4%. Sam and Tina earned no investment income for the year.

   c. Jody borrowed $25,000 from her controlled corporation for six months. She used the funds to pay her daughter's college tuition. The corporation charged Jody 3% interest. The Federal rate was 4%. Jody earned $3,500 of investment income for the year.

   d. Kait loaned her son, Jake, $60,000 for six months. Jake used the $60,000 to pay off college loans. The Federal rate was 4%, and Kait did not charge Jake any interest. Jake earned dividend and interest income of $2,100 for the tax year.

BRIDGE DISCIPLINE

1. Find the audited financial statements of a major U.S. corporation.
   a. Summarize its most important financial accounting policies.
   b. Describe two elements of the Federal income tax law that significantly affected the corporation's earnings per share for the operating year.

2. For the same corporation, summarize three key tax accounting applications, and point out how they differ from book income principles. Summarize your findings, and present them to your classmates in no more than five PowerPoint slides.

   Communications

3. The exclusion of state and local bond interest from Federal income tax often is criticized as creating a tax haven for the wealthy. Critics, however, often fail to take into account the effect of market forces. In recent months, the long-term tax-exempt interest rate has been 2.5%, while the long-term taxable rate for bonds of comparable risk was approximately 3.75%. On the other hand, state and local governments do enjoy a savings in interest costs because of the tax-favored status of their bonds.

   To date, Congress has concluded that the benefits gained by the states and municipalities and their residents, such as the access to capital and the creation of jobs to construct and maintain critical infrastructure, outweigh any damages to our progressive income tax system. Do you agree with the proponents of the exclusion? Why or why not?

4. In a two-page paper, separately evaluate each of the following alternative proposals for taxing the income from property.
   a. All assets would be valued at the end of the year, any increase in value that occurred during the year would be included in gross income, and any decrease in value would be deductible from gross income.
   b. No gain or loss would be recognized until the taxpayer sold or exchanged the property.
   c. Increases or decreases in the value of property traded on a national exchange (e.g., the New York Stock Exchange) would be reflected in gross income for the years in which the changes in value occur. For all other assets, no gain or loss would be recognized until the owner disposes of the property.

   Critical Thinking

   Communications

Communications   5. Various Federal stimulus provisions were designed to assist state and local governments in borrowing funds, leveraging the gross income exclusion for such bond interest so that such jurisdictions would have increased access to funds. One of the justifications for these provisions was that state and local governments cannot run budget deficits and cannot "print money," so the recent recession put them in a difficult cash-flow position.

Audits of the use of these borrowed funds showed that some of the bond proceeds were used by the jurisdictions to participate in "public-private partnerships," where government funds were used to assist private entities in expanding in or relocating to the jurisdiction. Specifically, bond proceeds were found to have been used to provide targeted road-building and utility-construction projects to benefit large commercial entities.

Is this an appropriate use of the gross income exclusion for state and local bond interest? Summarize your comments in an e-mail to your instructor.

Research Problems

Note: Solutions to Research Problems can be prepared by using the Checkpoint® Student Edition online research product, which is available to accompany this text. It is also possible to prepare solutions to the Research Problems by using tax research materials found in a standard tax library.

Communications   **Research Problem 1.** Tranquility Funeral Home, Inc., your client, is an accrual basis taxpayer that sells "pre-need" funeral contracts. Under these contracts, the customer pays in advance for goods and services to be provided at the contract beneficiary's death. These payments are refundable at the contract purchaser's request, pursuant to state law, at any time until the goods and services are furnished. Tranquility, consistent with its financial accounting reporting, includes the payments in income for the year the funeral service is provided.

An IRS agent insists that the contract payments constitute prepaid income subject to tax in the year of receipt. Your client believes the amounts involved are tax-deferred customer deposits.

Write a letter to Tranquility that contains your tax advice about how the issue should be resolved. The client's address is 400 Rock Street, Memphis, TN 38152.

Communications   **Research Problem 2.** Clint, your client, owns a life insurance policy on his own life. He has paid $6,800 in premiums, and the cash surrender value of the policy is $30,000. Clint borrowed $30,000 from the insurance company, using the cash surrender value as collateral. He is considering canceling the policy in payment of the loan. Clint would like to know the Federal income tax consequences of canceling his policy. Summarize your findings in a brief research memo.

Communications   **Research Problem 3.** Your client, New Shoes Ltd., is a retailer that often issues store gift (debit) cards to customers in lieu of a cash refund. You recall that the IRS issued a revenue procedure that provided that the prepaid income rules in Revenue Procedure 2004–34 could be applied to the income from the gift cards. Locate a more recent revenue procedure that authorizes the deferral of gross income from gift cards. Outline the key points of this document, and send the outline to your instructor.

Research Problem 4. Your friend Hui is an investor in bitcoin. Indicate whether and how she is subject to Federal income taxation in the following circumstances.

a. Earns $1,000 in bitcoin from mining.

b. Purchases $1,000 in bitcoin from another friend.

c. Sells the purchase in part (b) in the market to a third party for $1,400.

d. Spends $1,000 of bitcoin to acquire an asset worth $1,500.

e. Spends $1,000 of bitcoin to acquire an asset worth $750.

f. Holds bitcoin that she bought in February for $1,000. On December 31, the bitcoin is worth $1,200.

Use the tax resources of the Internet to address the following questions. Do not restrict your search to the Web, but include a review of newsgroups and general reference materials, practitioner sites and resources, primary sources of the tax law, chat rooms and discussion groups, and other opportunities.

Internet Activity

Research Problem 5. Construct a chart for your state and four of its neighboring states. Provide "Yes/No" entries for each state in the following categories. Send the chart to your classmates by e-mail.

Communications

- Does the state exclude interest income from U.S. Treasury bonds?
- Does the state exclude interest income from Fannie Mae bonds?
- Does the state exclude interest income from bonds issued by governments in its own state?
- Does the state exclude interest income from bonds issued by governments in other states?

Research Problem 6. Determine the applicable Federal interest rate as of today for purposes of § 7872 below-market loans. In an e-mail to your professor, describe how the rate is determined and how you discovered the pertinent rules.

Communications

Roger CPA Review Questions

1. Stephen purchased a video game console five years ago for $500. To raise money for the "latest and greatest" console, Stephen sold his original console for $100. Because of advances in technology, Stephen can purchase the new console for $400. What is the tax treatment of Stephen's sale of his console?

   a. Stephen recognizes a $400 loss

   b. Stephen does not report the sale

   c. Stephen recognizes a $300 loss

   d. Stephen recognizes a $100 gain

2. Which of the following is excluded from gross income on an individual's 2016 tax return?

   a. January 2017 rent received in December 2016

   b. Value arising from personal use of company vehicle in 2016

   c. Dividends announced by a C Corporation in December 2015 and received in January 2016

   d. Refundable security deposit received in January 2016 for a lease ending in July 2017

CHAPTER 5

Business Deductions

LEARNING OBJECTIVES: *After completing Chapter 5, you should be able to:*

LO.1 Articulate the meaning and application of the ordinary, necessary, and reasonableness requirements for the deduction of business expenses.

LO.2 Describe the cash and accrual methods of accounting for business deductions.

LO.3 Apply a variety of Internal Revenue Code deduction disallowance provisions.

LO.4 State and apply the alternative tax treatments for research and experimental expenditures.

LO.5 Identify the activities eligible for the domestic production activities deduction and calculate the deduction.

LO.6 Identify and measure deductible charitable contributions, determine corporate limitations on the contribution deduction, and identify several other common business deductions.

LO.7 Determine the amount of cost recovery under MACRS and apply the § 179 expensing election and the deduction limitations on listed property and automobiles when making the MACRS calculation.

LO.8 Identify intangible assets that are eligible for amortization and calculate the amount of the deduction.

LO.9 Determine the amount of depletion expense and specify the alternative tax treatments for intangible drilling and development costs.

CHAPTER OUTLINE

TAX TALK *Last year I had difficulty with my income tax. I tried to take my analyst off as a business deduction. The Government said it was entertainment. We compromised finally and made it a religious contribution.* —WOODY ALLEN

CALCULATING DEDUCTIBLE EXPENSES

Michael Forney, owner of a small engine service and repair business, operates his business as a C corporation with a December 31 year-end. Using the accrual method of accounting, Mr. Forney reports the following expense information along with $435,500 of gross income.

Salaries and wages (including Michael's salary of $55,000 and Terry's salary of $3,000)	$150,000
Building rent	24,000
Depreciation of machinery and equipment*	13,000
Insurance (coverage for all assets of the business)	6,000
Consulting fees	6,000
Utilities	12,000
Taxes and licenses	6,000
Fine paid to city	2,500
Advertising	3,000
Interest expense	3,000
Charitable contributions	3,000
Dues paid to Small Engine Repair Institute	10,000
Political contributions	2,000

*$130,000 of new machinery and equipment were purchased this year. The financial reporting system depreciation is based on straight-line depreciation over 10 years. The MACRS cost recovery period for tax purposes is 7 years. Assume for purposes of this scenario that no depreciation may be claimed this year for assets acquired in prior years because they have been fully depreciated.

Michael would like to know the amount of his deductible expenses for tax purposes.

Mr. Forney owns 80 percent of the corporation's stock, while his wife (Kathleen) and his mother (Terry) each own 10 percent of the stock. Michael is a full-time employee at his business, and his mother helps out with the books for about two hours a week. At this time, Kathleen does not work at the business.

Michael would also like your advice on another matter. Because his business has been very profitable over the years, it has built up large cash reserves, and its cash flow continues to be strong. Even with the high levels of cash in the business, it has never paid any dividends to the shareholders. For next year, he is

continued

considering paying himself a salary of $140,000 and his mother a salary of $30,000. This would give them more cash to spend for planned vacations and home improvements.

Finally, during the year, Michael purchased another personal residence for $300,000 and converted his original residence to rental property. The original residence cost $250,000 five years ago and has a current market value of $180,000. Also during the year, he purchased a condo for $170,000, which he will rent to tenants. Michael holds these rental properties outside his small engine service and repair business. He would like to know the tax implications, if any, of these transactions.

Read the chapter and formulate your response.

The tax law has an all-inclusive definition of income; that is, income from whatever source derived is includible in gross income. Income cannot be excluded unless there is a specific statement to that effect in the Internal Revenue Code.

Conversely, deductions are disallowed unless a specific provision in the tax law permits them. However, the Code goes on to allow a deduction for most expenses incurred in a trade or business. This chapter discusses many of the common business deductions encountered by taxpayers that are specified in the Code.

Articulate the meaning and application of the ordinary, necessary, and reasonableness requirements for the deduction of business expenses.

5-1 OVERVIEW OF BUSINESS DEDUCTIONS

As just noted, an income tax deduction is not allowed under Federal law unless Congress creates a specific provision allowing it.[1] For businesses, trade or business deductions are allowed by statute, but only if they are both *ordinary and necessary* and *reasonable* in amount.[2]

5-1a Ordinary and Necessary Requirement

Section 162(a) permits a deduction for all ordinary and necessary expenses paid or incurred in carrying on a trade or business. Generally, a trade or business expense deductible under § 162 is allowed in full, without limitation or restriction. To understand the scope of this provision, it is critical to understand the meanings of the terms *ordinary* and *necessary*.

Neither ordinary nor necessary is defined in the Code or Regulations. The courts, therefore, have had to deal with these terms on numerous occasions.

An expense has been held to be *ordinary* if it is normal, usual, or customary in the type of business conducted by the taxpayer and is not capital in nature.[3] However, an expense need not be recurring to be deductible as ordinary. For example, a business may be in a situation that is a very rare occurrence and incur an expense. If other businesses in a similar situation are likely to incur a similar expense, then the expense can be ordinary, even though it is not recurring.

EXAMPLE 1

Zebra Corporation was engaged in a mail-order business. The post office judged that Zebra's advertisements were false and misleading. Under a fraud order, the post office stamped "fraudulent" on all letters addressed to Zebra's business and returned them to the senders. Zebra spent $30,000 on legal fees in an unsuccessful attempt to force the post office to stop. The legal fees (although not recurring) were ordinary business expenses because they were normal, usual, or customary under the circumstances.[4]

---

[1]§ 161(a).
[2]§ 162(a).

[3]*Deputy v. DuPont*, 40–1 USTC ¶9161, 23 AFTR 808, 60 S.Ct. 363 (USSC, 1940).
[4]*Comm. v. Heininger*, 44–1 USTC ¶9109, 31 AFTR 783, 64 S.Ct. 249 (USSC, 1943).

An expense has been held to be *necessary* if a prudent businessperson would incur the same expense and the expense is expected to be appropriate and helpful in the taxpayer's business.[5] But as Example 2 shows, no deduction will be allowed unless the expense is also ordinary.

Pat purchased a business that had just been adjudged bankrupt. Because the business had a poor financial rating, Pat wanted to restore its financial reputation. Consequently, he paid off some of the debts owed by the former owners that had been cancelled by the bankruptcy court. Because Pat had no legal obligation to make these payments, the U.S. Supreme Court decided that he was trying to generate goodwill. Although the payments were necessary (i.e., appropriate and helpful), they were *not* ordinary and their deduction *was not* allowed.[6]

5-1b Reasonableness Requirement

An expense must also be reasonable to be deductible. Although the Code applies the **reasonableness requirement** solely to salaries and other compensation for services, the courts have held that for any expense to be ordinary and necessary, it must also be reasonable in amount.[7]

What constitutes reasonableness is a question of fact.[8] If an expense is unreasonable, the excess amount is not allowed as a deduction. The question of reasonableness usually arises with respect to closely held corporations where there is no separation of ownership and management.

Transactions between shareholders and a closely held corporation may result in the disallowance of deductions for excessive salaries, rent, and other expenses paid by the corporation to the shareholders. The courts will view the reasonableness of a salary in light of all relevant circumstances and may find that an unusually large salary is reasonable despite its size. If excessive payments for salaries, rent, and other expenses are closely related to the percentage of stock owned by the recipients, the payments are generally treated as dividends.[9] Because dividends are not deductible by the corporation, the disallowance results in an increase in corporate taxable income. Deductions for reasonable salaries will not be disallowed solely because the corporation has paid insubstantial portions of its earnings as dividends to its shareholders.

The Big Picture

Return to the facts of *The Big Picture* on p. 5-1. The small engine service and repair business, a closely held C corporation, is owned by Michael Forney, his wife (Kathleen) and his mother (Terry). The company has been highly profitable over the years and has never paid dividends. Michael is the key employee of the business, while his mother plays a very minor role. Assuming that their current salaries of $55,000 and $3,000 are comparable to what they could earn at similar companies for the work they do, they are likely to be considered reasonable and, therefore, deductible.

If Mr. Forney's plan to more than double his salary and increase his mother's salary by tenfold is implemented, the amounts in excess of their current salaries may be deemed unreasonable; if that is the case, the excess would be disallowed as deductible salary. The disallowed amounts would then be treated as dividends rather than salary income to Michael and Terry. Salaries are deductible by the corporation, but dividends are not. Note, however, that the shareholders may benefit from this reclassification. Salaries would be taxed at ordinary income rates and are subject to payroll taxes. However, dividend income would be taxed at long-term capital gain rates if the dividends are qualified (see Chapter 13).

---

[5] *Welch v. Helvering*, 3 USTC ¶1164, 12 AFTR 1456, 54 S.Ct. 8 (USSC, 1933).

[6] *Welch v. Helvering*, cited in footnote 5.

[7] *Comm. v. Lincoln Electric Co.*, 49–2 USTC ¶9388, 38 AFTR 411, 176 F.2d 815 (CA–6, 1949).

[8] *Kennedy, Jr. v. Comm.*, 82–1 USTC ¶9186, 49 AFTR 2d 82–628, 671 F.2d 167 (CA–6, 1982), *rev'g* 72 T.C. 793 (1979).

[9] Reg. § 1.162–8.

Common Business Deductions

The language of § 162 is broad enough to permit the deduction of many different types of ordinary and necessary business expenses. Some of the more common deductions are listed in Exhibit 5.1.

LO.2

Describe the cash and accrual methods of accounting for business deductions.

5-2 THE TIMING OF EXPENSE RECOGNITION

A taxpayer's accounting method is a major factor in determining taxable income. The method used determines *when* an item is includible in income and *when* an item is deductible. Usually, the taxpayer's regular method of record keeping is used for income tax purposes.[10] The Code and Regulations require that the accounting method used must clearly reflect income and that items be handled consistently.[11] The most common methods of accounting are the cash method and the accrual method. If a taxpayer owns multiple businesses, it may be possible to use the cash method for some and the accrual method for others.

Throughout the portions of the Code dealing with deductions, the phrase *paid or incurred* is used. A cash basis taxpayer is generally allowed a deduction in the year an expense is *paid*. An accrual basis taxpayer is allowed a deduction in the year in which the liability for the expense is *incurred*.

EXHIBIT 5.1	Partial List of Business Deductions	
Advertising		Pension and profit sharing plans
Bad debts		Rent or lease payments
Commissions and fees		Repairs and maintenance
Depletion		Salaries and wages
Depreciation		Supplies
Employee benefit programs		Taxes and licenses
Insurance		Travel and transportation
Interest		Utilities

---

[10] § 446(a).   [11] §§ 446(b) and (e); Reg. § 1.446–1(a)(2).

5-2a Cash Method Requirements

The expenses of cash basis taxpayers are deductible only when they are actually paid with cash or other property. Promising to pay or issuing a note does not satisfy the actually paid requirement.[12] However, the payment can be made with borrowed funds. Thus, taxpayers are allowed to claim the deduction at the time they charge expenses on credit cards. They are deemed to have simultaneously borrowed money from the credit card issuer and constructively paid the expenses.[13]

Although the cash basis taxpayer must have actually or constructively paid the expense, payment does not ensure a current deduction. The Regulations require capitalization of any expenditure that creates an asset having a useful life that extends substantially beyond the end of the tax year.[14] Thus, taxpayers cannot take a current deduction for capital expenditures except through amortization, depletion, or depreciation over the tax life of the asset.

EXAMPLE 4

Redbird, Inc., a calendar year and cash basis taxpayer, rents property from Bluejay, Inc. On July 1, 2016, Redbird pays $24,000 rent for the 24 months ending June 30, 2018.

The prepaid rent extends 18 months after the close of the tax year—substantially beyond the year of payment. Therefore, Redbird must capitalize the prepaid rent and amortize the expense on a monthly basis. Redbird's deduction for 2016 is $6,000.

TAX PLANNING STRATEGIES Time Value of Tax Deductions

FRAMEWORK FOCUS: DEDUCTIONS

Strategy: Accelerate Recognition of Deductions to Achieve Tax Deferral.

Cash basis taxpayers often have the ability to make early payments for their expenses at the end of the tax year. This may permit the payments to be deducted in the year of payment instead of in the following tax year. Given the time value of money, a tax deduction this year may be worth more than the same deduction next year.

Before employing this strategy, the taxpayer must consider what next year's expected income and tax rates will be and whether a cash-flow problem may develop from early payments. Thus, a variety of considerations must be taken into account when planning the timing of tax deductions.

In-depth coverage can be found on this book's companion website: www.cengagebrain.com

1 DIGGING DEEPER

5-2b Accrual Method Requirements

An accrual basis taxpayer can deduct an expense when both the *all events test* and the *economic performance test* are met. The all events test is met when (1) all of the events have occurred to establish the existence of a legal liability and (2) the amount of the liability can be determined with reasonable accuracy. Further, the deduction is permitted only when economic performance has occurred. In situations in which a liability arises as a result of services being provided, or property being transferred, to the taxpayer, economic performance occurs when the service is provided or the property is acquired. If the liability is the result of the taxpayer being required to provide services or transfer property, economic performance occurs when the service is provided or the property is transferred.[15]

---

[12]*Page v. Rhode Island Trust Co., Exr.*, 37–1 USTC ¶9138, 19 AFTR 105, 88 F.2d 192 (CA–1, 1937).

[13]Rev.Rul. 78–39, 1978–1 C.B. 73. See also Rev.Rul. 80–335, 1980–2 C.B. 170, which applies to pay-by-phone arrangements.

[14]Reg. § 1.461–1(a).

[15]§ 461(h).

EXAMPLE 5

Robin, Inc., an entertainment business, sponsored a jazz festival in a rented auditorium at City College. Robin is responsible for cleaning up after the festival, which took place on December 22, 2016, and reinstalling the auditorium seats. Because the college is closed over the Christmas holidays, the company hired by Robin to perform the work did not begin these activities until January 3, 2017. Robin cannot deduct its $1,200 labor cost until 2017, when the services are performed.

DIGGING DEEPER 2   **In-depth coverage can be found on this book's companion website: www.cengagebrain.com**

An important consequence of the economic performance test is that many expenses that are estimated for financial reporting purposes, often by employing reserves or allowance accounts, are not immediately deductible for tax purposes. These expenses typically require estimation precisely because economic performance has not occurred. Instead, deductibility is deferred until economic performance has occurred.

EXAMPLE 6

Oriole Airlines is required by Federal law to test its engines after 3,000 flying hours. Aircraft cannot return to flight until the tests have been conducted. An unrelated aircraft maintenance company performs the tests. Oriole estimates that the tests will cost approximately $1,500 per engine.

For financial reporting purposes, the company accrues an expense based upon $.50 per hour of flight ($1,500 ÷ 3,000 hours) and credits an allowance account. The actual amounts paid for maintenance are offset against the allowance account.

For tax purposes, the economic performance test is not satisfied until the work has been done. Therefore, the reserve method cannot be used for tax purposes.

Note that the economic performance test does not require that an expense be paid before it is deductible. In Example 6, the economic performance test is met when the maintenance work is performed, even if the expense is not paid until the following year.

5-2c Expenses Accrued to Related Parties

Regardless of the taxpayer's general method of accounting, the Internal Revenue Code places restrictions on the deductibility of expenses accrued to *related parties*. Without these restrictions, related taxpayers who have control over both sides of a transaction would have the ability to enter into transactions that allow the immediate deduction of an expense by an accrual basis taxpayer while allowing the deferral of the related income by a cash basis taxpayer on the other side of the transaction. For example, an accrual basis, closely held corporation might borrow funds from a cash basis individual shareholder. At the end of the year, the corporation would accrue and deduct the interest expense, but the cash basis lender would not recognize interest income because no interest had been paid.

Section 267 specifically addresses related-party transactions and defers the deduction of an expense accrued to a related party until the related party is required to recognize the item in income; that is, when it is actually received by the cash basis taxpayer. Note that deferral is not required if both parties use the same general method of accounting. Likewise, deferral will not be required if the related party reporting income uses the accrual method and the related party taking the deduction uses the cash method.

Relationships and Constructive Ownership

For purposes of § 267, *related parties* include the following:

- Family members, including brothers and sisters (whether whole, half, or adopted), spouse, ancestors (parents and grandparents), and lineal descendants (children and grandchildren) of the taxpayer.

- Corporations and shareholders who own more than 50 percent (directly or indirectly) of the corporation's stock.

- Two corporations that are members of a controlled group (discussed in Chapter 9).

Constructive ownership provisions are applied to determine whether the taxpayers are related. Under these provisions, stock owned by related parties is deemed to be owned by the taxpayer for purposes of applying § 267. For example, a taxpayer is deemed to own not only his or her stock but also the stock owned by his or her lineal descendants, ancestors, brothers and sisters or half-brothers and half-sisters, and spouse.[16]

Related-Party Transactions

EXAMPLE 7

The stock of Sparrow Corporation is owned 20% by Ted, 30% by Ted's father, 30% by Ted's mother, and 20% by Ted's sister. Although Ted actually owns only 20% of Sparrow Corporation, he is *deemed* to own the stock owned by his father (30%), mother (30%), and sister (20%).

As a result, he directly and indirectly owns 100% of Sparrow, and Ted and Sparrow are related parties. The same outcome (100% direct and indirect ownership) results for all of the shareholders in this example.

EXAMPLE 8

Continue with the facts presented in Example 7. On July 1 of the current year, Ted loaned $10,000 to Sparrow Corporation at 6% annual interest, with principal and interest payable on demand. For tax purposes, Sparrow uses the accrual basis and Ted uses the cash basis. Both report on a calendar year basis.

Ted actually and constructively owns 100% of Sparrow; Ted and Sparrow are related parties. So, if Sparrow accrues the interest within the taxable year, no deduction can be taken until payment is made to Ted.

5-3 DISALLOWANCE POSSIBILITIES

LO.3

Apply a variety of Internal Revenue Code deduction disallowance provisions.

While most ordinary and necessary business expenses are deductible, the tax law contains provisions that disallow a deduction for certain expenditures. The most frequently encountered disallowance provisions are discussed below.

5-3a Public Policy Limitations

Certain disallowance provisions are a codification or extension of prior court decisions. For example, after the courts denied deductions for payments considered to be in violation of public policy, the tax law was changed to provide specific authority for the disallowance of these deductions.

Justification for Denying Deductions

The courts developed the principle that a payment in violation of public policy is not deductible.[17] Although the payment may be helpful to a business and even contribute to its success, a deduction would, in effect, represent an indirect governmental subsidy for taxpayer wrongdoing.

Under legislation enacted based on this principle, the following deductions are disallowed for specific types of expenditures that are considered contrary to public policy:

- Bribes and kickbacks illegal under either Federal or state law.
- Two-thirds of the treble damage payments made to claimants resulting from violation of antitrust law.[18]
- Fines and penalties paid to a government for violation of law.

The Big Picture

EXAMPLE 9

Refer to the facts of *The Big Picture* on p. 5-1. Michael Forney had not instituted proper procedures for disposing of used motor oil and other engine fluids from his business. During the current tax year, he was fined $2,500 by the city. Mr. Forney believes the fine should be deducted as an ordinary business expense. However, because the fine was assessed by and paid to a government for a law violation, the $2,500 is not deductible.

In-depth coverage can be found on this book's companion website: www.cengagebrain.com

3 DIGGING DEEPER

---

[16]While this provision applies to related parties as previously defined, note that it also applies to transactions between any partner (shareholder) and a partnership (S corporation), regardless of the ownership interest held by the partner or shareholder.

[17]*Tank Truck Rentals, Inc. v. Comm.*, 58–1 USTC ¶9366, 1 AFTR 2d 1154, 78 S.Ct. 507 (USSC, 1958).

[18]§§ 162(c), (f), and (g).

Expenses Related to an Illegal Business

Interestingly, the expenses of operating an illegal business (e.g., a money laundering operation) that are not inherently illegal themselves are deductible.[19] While allowing deductions for illegal activity may seem inappropriate, recall that the law taxes net income from a business operation, not gross revenue.

EXAMPLE 10

Grizzly, Inc., owns and operates a restaurant. In addition, Grizzly operates an illegal gambling establishment out of the restaurant's back room. In connection with the illegal activity, Grizzly has the following expenses during the year:

Rent	$ 60,000
Payoffs to police	40,000
Depreciation on equipment	100,000
Wages	140,000
Interest	30,000
Criminal fines	50,000
Illegal kickbacks	10,000
Total	$430,000

All of the usual expenses (rent, depreciation, wages, and interest) are deductible; payoffs, fines, and kickbacks are not deductible. Of the $430,000 spent, $330,000 is deductible and $100,000 is not.

An exception applies to expenses incurred in illegal trafficking in drugs.[20] Drug dealers are not allowed a deduction for ordinary and necessary business expenses incurred in their business. In arriving at gross income from the business, however, dealers may reduce total sales by the cost of goods sold.[21]

5-3b Political Contributions and Lobbying Activities

Political Contributions

No business deduction is permitted for direct or indirect payments for political purposes.[22] Historically, Congress has been reluctant to extend favorable tax treatment to political expenditures by businesses. Allowing deductions might encourage abuses and enable businesses to have undue influence on the political process.

---

[19]*Comm. v. Sullivan*, 58–1 USTC ¶9368, 1 AFTR 2d 1158, 78 S.Ct. 512 (USSC, 1958).

[20]§ 280E.

[21]Reg. § 1.61–3(a). Gross income is defined as sales minus cost of goods sold. Thus, while § 280E prohibits any deductions for drug dealers, it does not modify the normal definition of gross income.

[22]§ 276.

The Big Picture

Refer to the facts of *The Big Picture* on p. 5-1. Michael Forney's business made political contributions to the State Senate campaigns of Tom Smith and Virginia White. Mr. Forney made these contributions because he believed these candidates would be sensitive to the needs of small businesses. Therefore, he assumed that these would be deductible business expenses.

However, political contributions are not deductible, so he will receive no tax benefit from them.

EXAMPLE 11

Lobbying Expenditures

The Code places severe restrictions on the deductibility of expenses incurred in connection with lobbying activities.[23] These provisions deny deductions for expenditures incurred in connection with attempting to influence:

- State or Federal legislation and
- The actions of certain high-ranking public officials.

The disallowance also applies to a pro rata portion of the membership dues of trade associations and other groups that are involved in lobbying activities. There are three exceptions to the disallowance provisions. First, an exception is provided for influencing *local* legislation (e.g., city and county governments). Second, the disallowance provision does not apply to activities devoted solely to *monitoring* legislation. Third, a *de minimis* exception allows the deduction of up to $2,000 of annual *in-house expenditures* incurred by the taxpayer if the expenditures are not otherwise disallowed under the provisions discussed above. In-house lobbying expenditures are those paid or incurred directly by the taxpayer rather than amounts paid to professional lobbyists or other third parties. If in-house expenditures exceed $2,000, none of the in-house expenditures can be deducted.

The Big Picture

Refer to the facts of *The Big Picture* on p. 5-1. Mr. Forney's business made contributions to the Small Engine Repair Institute, a trade association for owners of similar-type businesses. The trade association estimates that 70% of its dues are allocated to lobbying activities. Thus, the deduction on the corporate tax return is limited to $3,000 ($10,000 × 30%).

EXAMPLE 12

5-3c **Excessive Executive Compensation**

The reasonableness requirement and its relevance to the deductibility of expenses paid by small businesses was discussed above. However, the reasonableness of other expenses, including those paid or incurred by larger businesses, has also gained the attention of Congress as well as the general public. Recall that allowing a deduction indirectly reduces the economic burden of an expense, allowing the taxpayer to share the cost with the larger taxpaying public. In response to concerns over the reasonableness of compensation paid to executives of large corporations, Congress enacted a limitation on the deductibility of such compensation.[24] Specifically, the Code limits the deductibility of the compensation paid to certain executives of publicly traded corporations to $1 million per year. Note that the provision does not limit the amount of compensation that can be paid but only the amount that is deductible.

The limitation does not apply to:

- Any compensation that is excludable from the executive's gross income (discussed in Chapter 11);
- Commissions based on performance;

---

[23]§ 162(e).

[24]§ 162(m).

TAX IN THE NEWS Do Deduction Limits Affect Executive Compensation?

Only $1 million of compensation can be deducted for the CEO, the CFO, and the three other highest-compensated executives of publicly traded companies. However, as noted previously, this limitation does not apply to *performance-based* compensation. One interesting issue is whether this exception is broad enough to allow publicly traded companies to pay substantial compensation to executives and still receive a tax deduction. The answer is clearly yes.

For example, in 2014, the CEO of Microsoft received a base salary of $918,917, which is just under the $1 million limitation. However, he received bonuses and stock incentives of over $80 million, which qualify to be deducted under the performance-based exception.

Fortune magazine recently reported that cash salaries account for only 10 percent of CEO compensation. The remaining 90 percent consists primarily of performance incentives. This indicates that the $1 million limit does have an influence on the base salary of CEOs. However, because of the performance-based exception, this tax law appears to have had very little impact on the escalation of executives' salaries.

Source: Based on Laura Lorenzetti, "Salaries for These CEOs Make Pay for Big Bank Bosses Look Modest," *Fortune*, September 2, 2015, **http://fortune.com/2015/09/02/pay-ratio-retail-ceos-banks/**.

- Other performance-based compensation as long as (1) the compensation formula is approved by a compensation committee comprised of at least two members of the board of directors who are not also employees of the company and a vote of the shareholders, and (2) the attainment of the performance goal is certified by the same compensation committee.

5-3d Investigation of a Business

Recall that § 162 allows a deduction for expenses incurred in carrying on a trade or business. However, expenses may be incurred to investigate the creation or acquisition of a business before the business is actually conducted by the taxpayer. Such costs might include travel, engineering and architectural surveys, marketing reports, and various legal and accounting services. How such expenses are treated for tax purposes depends on a number of variables, including the following:

- The current business, if any, of the taxpayer.
- The nature of the business being investigated.
- Whether the acquisition actually takes place.

If the taxpayer is in a business that is the *same as or similar* to that being investigated (i.e., the taxpayer is investigating the expansion of an existing trade or business), all investigation expenses are deductible in the year paid or incurred. The tax result is the same whether or not the taxpayer acquires the business being investigated.[25]

The Big Picture

EXAMPLE 13

Return to the facts of *The Big Picture* on p. 5-1. Michael Forney believes that his mechanical and business skills can be used to turn around other small engine businesses whose revenues have been declining. He investigates Southside Small Engine Services LLC, a nearby competitor that is for sale. Expenses paid to consultants and accountants as part of this investigation totaled $6,000. He determined that Southside Small Engine Services would not be a good investment, so he did not buy it.

The $6,000 spent to investigate this business is deductible as a business expense because Mr. Forney is already in the small engine service and repair business. Investigating new business opportunities in one's current trade or business is an ordinary and necessary business expense.

When the taxpayer is *not* in a business that is the same as or similar to the one being investigated, the tax result depends on whether the new business is acquired. If the business is not acquired, the investigation expenses generally are nondeductible.[26]

---

[25]*York v. Comm.*, 58–2 USTC ¶9952, 2 AFTR 2d 6178, 261 F.2d 421 (CA–4, 1958).

[26]Rev.Rul. 57–418, 1957–2 C.B. 143; *Morton Frank*, 20 T.C. 511 (1953); and *Dwight A. Ward*, 20 T.C. 332 (1953).

Lynn, president and sole shareholder of Marmot Corporation, incurs expenses when traveling from Rochester, New York, to California to investigate the feasibility of acquiring several auto care centers. Marmot is in the residential siding business. If no acquisition takes place, Marmot may not deduct any of the expenses.

If the taxpayer is *not* in a business that is the same as or similar to the one being investigated and actually acquires the new business, the expenses must be capitalized as <mark>startup expenditures</mark>. In general, startup expenditures are not deductible under § 162 because they are incurred *before* a business begins rather than in the course of operating a trade or business. However, the taxpayer may be able to deduct up to $5,000 of startup expenses in the month in which business begins. This immediate deduction is reduced dollar-for-dollar for expenses exceeding $50,000. As a result, the immediate deduction is totally phased out when total startup expenses reach $55,000. Therefore, the immediate deduction is targeted primarily to smaller businesses. Any expenses not eligible for an immediate deduction are amortized over 180 months, again beginning in the month in which business begins.[27]

Tina, a sole proprietor, owns and operates 10 restaurants located in various cities throughout the Southeast. She travels to Atlanta to discuss the acquisition of an auto dealership. In addition, she incurs legal and accounting costs associated with the potential acquisition. After incurring total investigation costs of $52,000, she acquires the auto dealership on October 1, 2016.

Tina may immediately deduct $3,000 [$5,000 − ($52,000 − $50,000)] and amortize the balance of $49,000 ($52,000 − $3,000) over a period of 180 months. For calendar year 2016, therefore, Tina can deduct $3,817 [$3,000 + ($49,000 × 3/180)].

Startup expenses include the following:

- Expenses incurred to investigate the creation or acquisition of a business by the taxpayer (e.g., market studies).
- Expenses incurred in creating or acquiring a business (e.g., professional fees, identifying suppliers, and obtaining licenses).
- Expenses incurred before the day the business begins that would otherwise have been deductible under § 162 (e.g., salaries, utilities, and advertising).

In-depth coverage can be found on this book's companion website: www.cengagebrain.com   **4 DIGGING DEEPER**

5-3e Transactions between Related Parties

As discussed previously, Code § 267 puts restrictions on the deductibility of expenses accrued to related parties. Section 267 also disallows the immediate recognition of any losses from sales or exchanges of property directly or indirectly between those same related parties.[28] Without this restriction, taxpayers would be able to recognize losses on property sales without effectively giving up control of the property itself.

Although the loss realized in a related-party sale is not immediately recognized, it may be used to offset any future gain recognized when the property is subsequently sold to an *unrelated* party (i.e., a right of offset is created). However, this loss offset is only available to the party who subsequently sells the property to an unrelated party, and *not* to the initial seller who realized the loss. Further, the right of offset cannot create or increase a loss. Any right of offset not used by the subsequent seller to offset some or all of the recognized gain is permanently lost.

---

[27]§ 195(b).   [28]§ 267(a)(1).

EXAMPLE 16

Donald owns real estate that he originally purchased in July 2012 for $1 million. In 2014, the property has a fair market value of $600,000. Donald believes the property will appreciate in value when a proposed shopping mall is built nearby and, therefore, does not want to lose control of it. In addition, he has realized a large gain on the sale of a different piece of property and would like to use the loss related to this parcel of real estate to offset the gain. So, at the end of 2014, Donald sells the property to his brother, Ben. In 2017, after the mall is built, Ben sells the land to a developer for $850,000.

Since Ben and Donald are related parties, Donald cannot recognize the $400,000 loss realized on the 2014 sale to Ben. However, when Ben subsequently sells the property to the developer in 2017, his $250,000 realized gain can be reduced, but not below zero, by Donald's $400,000 unrecognized loss. As a result, Ben does not recognize a gain on the sale. The remaining $150,000 loss not used by Ben is permanently lost.

The Big Picture

EXAMPLE 17

Return to the facts of *The Big Picture* on p. 5-1. Assume that Michael Forney, the 80% shareholder in his small engine service and repair business, sells a stock investment in his personal portfolio with a basis of $10,000 to his corporation for its fair market value of $8,000. Michael's $2,000 loss from the sale of the stock is disallowed because the sale is to a related party. The disallowed loss creates a $2,000 right of offset.

Michael's business sells the stock several years later for $11,000. However, only $1,000 of gain ($11,000 selling price − $8,000 basis − $2,000 right of offset) is taxable to the business upon the subsequent sale.

The Big Picture

EXAMPLE 18

Assume the same facts as Example 17, except that the corporation sells the stock for $9,000 to an unrelated party. The corporation's gain of $1,000 ($9,000 selling price − $8,000 basis) is not recognized because of the right of offset of $2,000 from Michael's sale.

The offset may result in only a partial tax benefit upon the subsequent sale (as in this case). If Michael originally had sold the stock to an unrelated party rather than to his corporation, he could have recognized a $2,000 loss. However, aggregating the effect to Michael and his corporation, they can benefit from only $1,000 of loss.

5-3f Expenses and Interest Related to Tax-Exempt Income

Certain income, such as interest on municipal bonds, is tax-exempt.[29] The law also allows the taxpayer to deduct expenses incurred for the production of income.[30] Together, these provisions could lead to unintended consequences.

EXAMPLE 19

Oriole, Inc., a corporation in the 35% income tax bracket, purchased $100,000 of 6% municipal bonds. At the same time, Oriole used the bonds as collateral on a bank loan of $100,000 at 8% interest. A positive cash flow would result from the tax benefit as follows:

Cash paid out on loan	($8,000)
Cash received from bonds	6,000
Net negative cash flow	($2,000)

Had the deduction of $8,000 been allowed for interest expense, this would have resulted in a tax benefit of $2,800 (35% × $8,000). In that case, a positive cash flow of $800 ($6,000 + $2,800 − $8,000) would have resulted.

---

[29]§ 103. [30]§ 212.

To prevent the type of tax arbitrage possibilities illustrated above, the Code generally disallows the deduction of expenses paid or incurred to generate tax-exempt income.[31] The disallowance applies to interest expense that is directly related to purchasing or carrying tax-exempt bonds as well as any other expense allocable to tax-exempt income.

EXAMPLE
20

In January of the current year, Crane Corporation borrowed $100,000 at 8% interest. Crane used the loan proceeds to purchase 5,000 shares of stock in White Corporation. In July, Crane sold the stock for $120,000 and reinvested the proceeds in City of Denver bonds, the income from which is tax-exempt.

Assuming that the $100,000 loan remained outstanding throughout the entire year, Crane cannot deduct the interest attributable to the period when the loan was used to carry the bonds.

In-depth coverage can be found on this book's companion website: www.cengagebrain.com

5 DIGGING DEEPER

5-3g **Other Disallowance Possibilities**

Other expenditures that are not deductible include capital expenditures and expenditures for which the taxpayer does not have adequate substantiation.

In-depth coverage can be found on this book's companion website: www.cengagebrain.com

6 DIGGING DEEPER

5-4 RESEARCH AND EXPERIMENTAL EXPENDITURES

LO.4
State and apply the alternative tax treatments for research and experimental expenditures.

Section 174 covers the treatment of research and experimental expenditures . The Regulations define research and experimental expenditures as follows:

> all such costs incident to the development or improvement of a product (including an experimental or pilot model, a plant process, a product, a formula, an invention, or similar property). The term includes the costs of obtaining a patent, such as attorneys' fees expended in making and perfecting a patent application. Expenditures represent research and development costs in the experimental or laboratory sense if they are for activities intended to discover information that would eliminate uncertainty concerning the development or improvement of a product. The term does not include expenditures such as those for the ordinary testing or inspection of materials or products for quality control or those for efficiency surveys, management studies, consumer surveys, advertising, or promotions.[32]

Expenses incurred in connection with the acquisition or improvement of land or depreciable property are not research and experimental expenditures. Rather, they increase the basis of the land or depreciable property. However, depreciation on a building used for research may be a research and experimental expense.

The law permits *three alternatives* for handling research and experimental expenditures.

- Deduct in the year paid or incurred.
- Defer and amortize.
- Capitalize.

The law also provides a credit for increasing research expenses over what the expense amount was in a base year or years. Two different formulas are available for computing the credit.[33]

---

[31]§ 265.

[32]Reg. § 1.174–2(a)(1), (2), and (3).

[33]§ 41. See Chapter 17 for a more detailed discussion of the research activities credit.

5-4a **Expense Method**

A taxpayer can deduct all of the research and experimental expenditures incurred in the current year and all subsequent years. The consent of the IRS is not required if the method is adopted for the first taxable year in which such expenditures were paid or incurred. Once this method is adopted, the taxpayer must continue to deduct all qualifying expenditures unless a request for a change is made to, and approved by, the IRS. In certain instances, a taxpayer may incur research and experimental expenditures before actually engaging in any trade or business activity. In such instances, the Supreme Court has applied the liberal standard of deductibility crafted by Congress in § 174 and permitted a deduction in the year of incurrence.[34]

5-4b **Deferral and Amortization Method**

Alternatively, research and experimental expenditures may be deferred and amortized if the taxpayer makes an election.[35] Under the election, research and experimental expenditures are amortized ratably over a period of not less than 60 months. A deduction is allowed beginning with the month in which the taxpayer first realizes benefits from the research and experimental expenditures.[36] The election is binding; a change requires permission from the IRS.

EXAMPLE
21

Gold Corporation decides to develop a new line of adhesives. The project begins in 2016. Gold incurs the following expenses in 2016 and 2017 in connection with the project.

	2016	2017
Salaries	$25,000	$18,000
Materials	8,000	2,000
Depreciation on machinery	6,500	5,700

The benefits from the project will be realized starting in March 2018. If Gold Corporation elects a 60-month deferral and amortization period, there is no deduction prior to March 2018, the month benefits from the project begin to be realized. The deduction for 2018 is $10,867, computed as follows:

Salaries ($25,000 + $18,000)	$43,000
Materials ($8,000 + $2,000)	10,000
Depreciation ($6,500 + $5,700)	12,200
Total	$65,200
2018: $65,200 × (10 months/60 months)	$10,867

Costs that are neither deducted immediately nor treated as deferred expenses must be capitalized. These costs are not deductible until the research project is abandoned or is deemed worthless. Given the time value of money, it is generally preferable to deduct research and development costs immediately. The option to treat research and experimental expenditures as a deferred expense is usually employed when a company does not have sufficient income to offset the research and experimental expenses. Rather than create net operating loss carryovers that might not be utilized because of the 20-year limitation on such carryovers, the deferral and amortization method may be used. The deferral of research and experimental expenditures should also be considered if the taxpayer expects higher tax rates in the future.

LO.5

Identify the activities eligible for the domestic production activities deduction and calculate the deduction.

5-5 **DOMESTIC PRODUCTION ACTIVITIES DEDUCTION**

Although most deductions relate to expenditures made by the taxpayer, the **domestic production activities deduction (DPAD)** is instead based on the nature of a taxpayer's income. A number of years ago, Congress replaced certain tax provisions that our world

---

[34]*Snow v. Comm.*, 74–1 USTC ¶9432, 33 AFTR 2d 74–1251, 94 S.Ct. 1876 (USSC, 1974).

[35]§ 174(b)(2).

[36]Section 59(e) allows a taxpayer to elect to capitalize research and development expenditures and amortize them over a period of 10 years beginning in the year the expenditures are made.

trading partners regarded as allowing unfair advantage to U.S. exports. As part of these changes, Congress created a deduction based on the income from U.S. manufacturing activities (designated as *production activities*).

5-5a Calculation of the Domestic Production Activities Deduction

The DPAD is based on the following formula:[37]

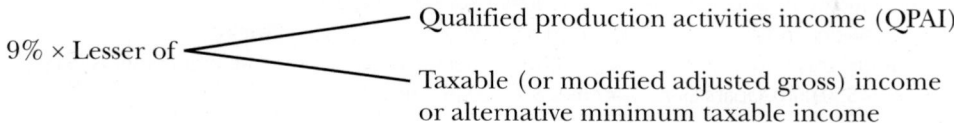

$$9\% \times \text{Lesser of} \begin{cases} \text{Qualified production activities income (QPAI)} \\ \text{Taxable (or modified adjusted gross) income} \\ \text{or alternative minimum taxable income} \end{cases}$$

5-5b Qualified Production Activities Income

Qualified production activities income (QPAI) is the excess of domestic production gross receipts (DPGR) over the sum of:

- The cost of goods sold allocated to such receipts.
- Other deductions, expenses, or losses allocable to such receipts.[38]

In other words, the deduction is based on the net income from qualifying activities.

QPAI is determined on an item-by-item basis—not on a division-by-division or a transaction-by-transaction basis. Because all items must be netted in the calculation, the final QPAI amount can be either positive or negative. The effect of the netting rule is to preclude taxpayers from selecting only profitable product lines or profitable transactions when calculating QPAI.

EXAMPLE 22

A taxpayer manufactures pants and shirts with the following QPAI results: $5 for one pair of pants and a negative $2 for one shirt. Because the two items are netted, the QPAI amount that controls is $3 ($5 − $2).

Five specific categories of DPGR qualify for the DPAD.[39]

- The lease, license, sale, exchange, or other disposition of qualified production property (QPP) that was manufactured, produced, grown, or extracted (MPGE) by the taxpayer in the United States.
- Qualified films (i.e., motion picture film or video tape) largely created in the United States.
- The production of electricity, natural gas, or potable water.
- Construction (but not self-construction) performed in the United States.
- Engineering and architectural services for domestic construction.

The sale of food and beverages prepared by a taxpayer at a retail establishment and the transmission or distribution of electricity, natural gas, or potable water are specifically excluded from the definition of DPGR.

The deduction is limited to 9 percent of the taxpayer's taxable income. Taxable income is determined without regard to the DPAD. In the case of an individual (a sole proprietorship or an owner of a flow-through entity), modified adjusted gross income is substituted for taxable income.[40]

The taxable income limitation is determined after the application of any net operating loss (NOL) deduction for the tax year (NOLs are explained in Chapter 6). Thus, a company with an NOL carryforward for a tax year is ineligible for the DPAD if the carryforward eliminates current taxable income. Further, a taxpayer that has an NOL

---

[37]§ 199(a).

[38]§ 199(c).

[39]§ 199(c)(4).

[40]§ 199(d)(2). Generally, modified AGI is AGI before any DPAD.

carryback may lose part or all of the DPAD benefit for that year. If qualified production activities income (QPAI) cannot be used in a particular year due to the taxable income limitation (see the preceding formula), it is lost forever. (The calculation of QPAI is explained in the next section.)

DPAD: Calculation Using QPAI and Taxable Income

EXAMPLE 23

Opal, Inc., manufactures and sells costume jewelry. It also sells costume jewelry purchased from other manufacturers. During 2016, Opal had a *profit* of $200,000 (QPAI) from the sale of its own manufactured jewelry and a *loss* of $50,000 from the sale of the purchased jewelry.

Based on this information, Opal's QPAI is $200,000 and its taxable income is $150,000 ($200,000 − $50,000). Opal's DPAD becomes $13,500 [9% of the lesser of $200,000 (QPAI) or $150,000 (taxable income)].

EXAMPLE 24

Assume the same facts as in the previous example, except that Opal also has an NOL carryover from 2015 of $300,000.

As taxable income for 2016 is zero ($200,000 − $50,000 − $300,000), there is no DPAD.

Another important limitation is that the amount of the DPAD cannot exceed 50 percent of certain **W–2 wages** paid by the taxpayer during the tax year.[41] If no W–2 wages are paid, no DPAD will be allowed. So, part of the rationale behind this limitation is to preserve U.S. manufacturing jobs and discourage their outsourcing.

An employer's W–2 wages include the sum of the aggregate amount of wages and elective deferrals required to be included on the W–2 wage statements for certain employees during the employer's taxable year. Elective deferrals include those amounts deferred under § 457 plans and Roth IRA contributions. An employer previously included wages paid to all workers during a tax year and not just the wages of the employees engaged in qualified production activities. However, as a result of a recent statutory change, an employer is permitted to include only those W–2 wages paid to employees engaged in qualified production activities.

DPAD: W–2 Limitation

EXAMPLE 25

In 2016, Red, Inc., a calendar year taxpayer, has QPAI of $2 million and taxable income of $2.1 million. Because Red outsources much of its work to independent contractors, its W–2 wage base, which for Red is related entirely to production activities, is $80,000.

Although Red's DPAD normally would be $180,000 [9% of the lesser of $2 million (QPAI) or $2.1 million (taxable income)], it is limited to $40,000 [50% of $80,000 (W–2 wages)].

EXAMPLE 26

Assume the same facts as in the previous example, except that Red also pays salaries of $50,000 related to its *nonproduction* activities.

Because these wages are not paid to employees engaged in production activities, the wage limitation on the DPAD remains at $40,000 [50% of $80,000 ($80,000 + $0)].

5-5c Eligible Taxpayers

The deduction is available to all taxpayers. The QPAI of pass-through entities, as well as the related wages that may limit the deduction, flow through to the entities' owners.

---

[41]§ 199(b).

5-6 CHARITABLE CONTRIBUTIONS

LO.6

Identify and measure deductible charitable contributions, determine corporate limitations on the contribution deduction, and identify several other common business deductions.

Though charitable contributions are neither ordinary nor necessary business expenses, Congress allows all taxpayers to deduct certain contributions. By allowing a deduction, the government encourages taxpayers to support organizations that provide social welfare needs to communities (while reducing the costs that the government would incur to provide these services).[42] However, as most expenses deductible under § 162 are allowed without limitation or restriction, Congress expressly precludes contributions from falling under § 162 and instead addresses them separately, so as to define precisely what types of contributions are encouraged and how much encouragement will be provided.

A deduction is only available for contributions made to qualified organizations.[43] Qualified organizations include:

- A state or possession of the United States or any subdivisions thereof.

- A corporation, trust, or community chest, fund, or foundation that is situated in the United States and is organized and operated exclusively for religious, charitable, scientific, literary, or educational purposes or for the prevention of cruelty to children or animals.

In no case is a deduction allowed for a contribution made to an individual.

In-depth coverage can be found on this book's companion website: www.cengagebrain.com   **7 DIGGING DEEPER**

To qualify as a **charitable contribution**, a payment must be made with donative intent and with no expectation of a benefit or consideration being received from the organization. These requirements have potential consequences for the timing of the deduction. Recall that an accrual basis taxpayer may generally only deduct an expense when both the all events and economic performance tests are met. As no consideration results from a contribution, a contribution can never meet the economic performance test. Rather, contributions are only deductible when *paid* (regardless of the accounting method used by the taxpayer). However, an *accrual basis corporation* may claim the deduction in the year preceding payment if two requirements are met. First, the contribution must be *authorized* by the board of directors by the end of that year. Second, it must be *paid* on or before the due date of the corporation's tax return (i.e., the fifteenth day of the fourth month following the close of its taxable year).[44]

EXAMPLE

27

On December 29, 2016, Blue Company, a calendar year, accrual basis partnership, authorizes a $5,000 donation to the Atlanta Symphony Association (a qualified charitable organization). The donation is made on April 11, 2017. Because Blue Company is a partnership, the contribution can be deducted only in 2017.[45]

However, if Blue Company is a corporation and the December 29, 2016 authorization was made by its board of directors, Blue may claim the $5,000 donation as a deduction for calendar year 2016.

5-6a Property Contributions

A deduction is available for contributions of cash as well as noncash property. How a noncash contribution is measured depends on the type of property contributed. For this purpose, property must be identified as capital gain property or ordinary income property. **Capital gain property** is property that, if sold, would result in long-term capital gain or § 1231 gain for the taxpayer. Such property generally must be a capital asset and must be held for the long-term holding period (more than one year). **Ordinary income property** is property that, if sold, would result in ordinary income for the taxpayer. Examples of ordinary income property include inventory and capital assets held short term (one year or less). Refer to

---

[42]§ 170.

[43]§ 170(c).

[44]§ 170(a)(2). Previously, the due date was the fifteenth day of the *third* month following the close of the corporation's tax year. In general, the new due date is effective for tax years beginning after 2015.

[45]Each partner will report an allocable portion of the charitable contribution deduction as of December 31, 2017 (the end of the partnership's tax year). See Chapter 14.

Chapter 4 for a brief introduction to the distinction between capital and ordinary assets and Chapter 8 for a complete discussion of the nature of capital and § 1231 assets.

A contribution of noncash property is generally measured by the property's fair market value. This potentially allows taxpayers to include in the deduction any amount by which the property may have appreciated without also recognizing that appreciation as income.

EXAMPLE 28

During the current year, Mallard Corporation donates a parcel of land (a capital asset) to Oakland Community College. Mallard acquired the land five years ago for $60,000, and the fair market value on the date of the contribution is $100,000.

The corporation's charitable contribution is measured by the asset's fair market value of $100,000, even though the $40,000 of appreciation on the land has never been included in Mallard's income.

In some situations, the measurement of a noncash contribution is limited to its adjusted basis (i.e., it must be measured without regard to any appreciation). These situations include the following:

- Contributions of ordinary income property (e.g., inventory), and
- Contributions of capital gain property that is also tangible and personal, but only if the property is *not* used by the organization in activities related to its tax-exempt purpose.[46]

Contributions of Tangible Personal Property

EXAMPLE 29

White Corporation donates a painting worth $200,000 to Western States Art Museum (a qualified charity), which exhibits the painting. White had acquired the painting in 2000 for $90,000.

Because the museum put the painting to a related use, White is allowed to deduct $200,000, the fair market value of the painting.

EXAMPLE 30

Assume the same facts as in the previous example, except that White Corporation donates the painting to the American Cancer Society, which sells the painting and deposits the $200,000 proceeds in the organization's general fund.

White's deduction is limited to the $90,000 basis because it contributed tangible personal property that was put to an unrelated use by the charitable organization.

EXAMPLE 31

Black Corporation donates a painting worth $90,000 to the American Cancer Society which sells the painting and deposits the $90,000 proceeds into the organization's general fund. Black acquired the painting several years ago for $200,000.

Black's contribution is measured by the fair market value of the painting, but limited to its adjusted basis. As the painting's adjusted basis is greater than its fair market value, Black's contribution is $90,000. Further, Black recognizes no loss on the depreciation of the painting. Rather than contributing a depreciated asset to a qualified charity, a taxpayer should consider selling the asset, recognizing the loss, and donating the proceeds.

As a general rule, the deduction for a contribution of ordinary income property is limited to the basis of the property. On certain contributions of inventory by *corporations*, however, the amount of the deduction is equal to the lesser of (1) the sum of the property's basis plus 50 percent of the appreciation on the property or (2) twice the property's basis. The following inventory contributions qualify for this increased contribution amount.

- Inventory contributed to a charitable organization that uses the inventory to care for the ill, needy, or infants.

---

[46]The measurement of capital gain property contributed to certain private nonoperating foundations (defined in §§ 4942 and 509) is also limited to the basis of the property.

- Tangible personal research property constructed by the corporation and given to a qualified educational or scientific organization that uses the property for research or research training.

Lark Corporation, a clothing retailer, donates children's clothing to the Salvation Army to be used to attire homeless children. Lark's basis in the clothes is $2,000, and the fair market value (the sales price to customers) is $3,000. Lark's deduction is $2,500 [$2,000 basis + 50% × ($3,000 − $2,000)].

If, instead, the fair market value of the clothes is $7,000, Lark's deduction is $4,000 (2 × $2,000 basis).

5-6b **Limitations Imposed on Charitable Contribution Deductions**

Both corporations and individuals are subject to limitations on the charitable contribution deduction.[47] The complex limitations for individual taxpayers are covered in Chapter 10.

For any tax year, a corporate taxpayer's contribution deduction is limited to 10 percent of taxable income. For this purpose, taxable income is computed without regard to the charitable contribution deduction, any net operating loss carryback or capital loss carryback, the dividends received deduction, and the domestic production activities deduction. Any contributions in excess of the 10 percent limitation may be carried forward to the five succeeding tax years. Any carryforward must be added to subsequent contributions and will be subject to the 10 percent limitation. In applying this limitation, the current year's contributions must be deducted first, with carryover amounts from previous years deducted in order of time.[48]

Annual Limitation and Carryover Rules Illustrated

During 2016, Orange Corporation (a calendar year taxpayer) had the following income and expenses.

Income from operations	$140,000
Expenses from operations	110,000
Dividends received	10,000
Charitable contributions made in May 2016	6,000

For purposes of the 10% limitation only, Orange Corporation's taxable income is $40,000 ($140,000 − $110,000 + $10,000). Consequently, the allowable charitable contribution deduction for 2016 is $4,000 (10% × $40,000). The $2,000 unused portion of the contribution can be carried forward to 2017, 2018, 2019, 2020, and 2021 (in that order) until exhausted.

Assume the same facts as in the previous example. In 2017, Orange Corporation has taxable income (for purposes of the 10% limitation) of $50,000 and makes a charitable contribution of $4,500. The maximum deduction allowed for 2017 is $5,000 (10% × $50,000). The entire 2017 contribution of $4,500 and $500 of the 2016 charitable contribution carryforward are currently deductible. The remaining $1,500 of the 2016 contribution may be carried over until it is used (or the 5-year carryforward period ends).

5-7 **OTHER BUSINESS EXPENSES**

In addition to the provisions related to charitable contributions and research and experimental expenditures, a variety of other expenses are subject to special rules and limitations. Some of these rules are noted briefly in the paragraphs that follow.

---

[47]The percentage limitations applicable to individuals and corporations are identified in § 170(b).

[48]The carryover rules relating to all taxpayers are in § 170(d).

5-7a **Interest Expense**

Generally, taxpayers are not limited in the amount of business interest expense they may deduct. However, the deductibility of expenses (including interest) from certain activities may be limited.[49] Further, the deductibility of interest by individuals depends on the activity to which the interest relates.[50]

Because the deductibility of interest expense associated with certain activities is limited, the IRS provides rules for allocating interest expense among activities. Under these rules, interest is allocated in the same manner as the debt with respect to which the interest is paid, and debt is allocated by tracing disbursements of the debt proceeds to specific expenditures. The interest tracing rules are complex and depend on whether loan proceeds are commingled with other cash and the length of time the loan proceeds are held before they are spent.

5-7b **Taxes**

As with interest expense, tax payments in a business or investment context are generally deductible. However, most Federal taxes are not deductible.

The deductibility of real estate taxes in the year in which property is purchased or sold may also raise issues. Real estate taxes for the entire year are apportioned between the buyer and seller based on the number of days the property was held by each during the real property tax year. This apportionment is required whether the tax is paid by the buyer or the seller or is prorated according to the purchase agreement. The apportionment determines who is entitled to deduct the real estate taxes in the year of sale. The required apportionment prevents the shifting of the deduction for real estate taxes from buyer to seller, or vice versa. In making the apportionment, the assessment date and the lien date are disregarded. The date of sale counts as a day the property is owned by the buyer.

EXAMPLE 35

A county's real property tax year runs from January 1 to December 31. Nuthatch Corporation, the owner on January 1 of real property located in the county, sells the real property to Crane, Inc., on June 30. Crane owns the real property from June 30 through December 31. The tax for the real property tax year, January 1 through December 31, is $3,650.

Assuming that this is not a leap year, the portion of the real property tax treated as imposed upon Nuthatch, the seller, is $1,800 [(180/365) × $3,650, January 1 through June 29], and $1,850 [(185/365) × $3,650, June 30 through December 31] of the tax is treated as imposed upon Crane, the purchaser.

If the actual real estate taxes are not prorated between the buyer and seller as part of the purchase agreement, adjustments are required. The adjustments are necessary to determine the amount realized by the seller and the basis of the property to the buyer. If the buyer pays the entire amount of the tax, it effectively has paid the seller's portion of the real estate tax and has therefore paid more for the property than the actual purchase price. Thus, the amount of real estate tax that is apportioned to the seller (for Federal income tax purposes) and paid by the buyer is added to the buyer's basis. The seller must increase the amount realized on the sale by the same amount.

EXAMPLE 36

Seth sells real estate on October 3 for $400,000. The buyer, Winslow Company, pays the real estate taxes of $3,650 for the calendar year, which is the real estate property tax year. Assuming that this is not a leap year, $2,750 (for 275 days) is apportioned to and is deductible by the seller, Seth, and $900 (for 90 days) of the taxes is deductible by Winslow. The buyer has paid Seth's real estate taxes of $2,750 and has therefore paid $402,750 for the property. Winslow's basis is increased to $402,750, and the amount realized by Seth from the sale is increased to $402,750.

---

[49]See, for example, the discussion of the passive activity limits in Chapter 6.

[50]See Chapter 10 for a more detailed discussion of the deductibility of interest by individuals.

The opposite result occurs if the seller (rather than the buyer) pays the real estate taxes. In this case, the seller reduces the amount realized from the sale by the amount that has been apportioned to the buyer. The buyer is required to reduce his or her basis by a corresponding amount.

Finally, the deductibility of state income taxes may raise at least two issues. The first relates to when state income taxes are deductible. A tax is generally defined as a required payment to a government for which there is no direct benefit. The lack of a direct benefit suggests that the liability for income taxes can never meet the economic performance test. Therefore, like contributions, taxes are generally deductible when paid regardless of a taxpayer's accounting method.[51] As discussed in Chapter 2, a corporation may recognize in its financial statements an expense for both current and deferred taxes. A deduction for current taxes may be allowed in the year they are accrued under the recurring item exception discussed previously. Deferred taxes, however, are *not* eligible for the recurring item exception.

The second issue relates to the state income taxes of individuals. All state income taxes are considered to be the personal liability of the taxpayer. Therefore, even though a portion of an individual's income taxes may be allocable to a business (i.e., a sole proprietorship), an individual's income taxes will never be considered a business expense under § 162.[52]

5-8 COST RECOVERY ALLOWANCES

LO.7

Determine the amount of cost recovery under MACRS and apply the § 179 expensing election and the deduction limitations on listed property and automobiles when making the MACRS calculation.

5-8a Overview

Taxpayers may deduct, or recover, the cost of certain assets that are used in a trade or business or held for the production of income. A deduction may take the form of a *cost recovery allowance* (depreciation under prior law), *depletion*, or *amortization*. Generally, the costs of tangible assets, other than natural resources, are recovered through cost recovery allowances. The costs of natural resources are recovered through *depletion*, and the costs of intangible assets are recovered through *amortization*. Generally, no deduction is allowed for an asset that does not have a determinable useful life.

The tax rules for recovering the cost of business assets differ from the accounting rules. Several methods are available for determining depreciation for accounting purposes, including the straight-line, declining-balance, and sum-of-the-years' digits methods. Historically, *depreciation* for tax purposes was computed using variations of these accounting methods. Congress completely overhauled the depreciation rules in 1981 by creating the accelerated cost recovery system (ACRS), which shortened the period over which costs are recovered and allowed accelerated methods. In 1986, Congress made substantial modifications to ACRS, which resulted in the modified accelerated cost recovery system (MACRS).

Although the terms depreciation and cost recovery are often used interchangably, the former refers to the allocation of costs over the periods they benefit for financial reporting purposes while the latter refers to the recovery of cost for tax purposes. This portion of the chapter focuses on the MACRS rules because they cover acquisitions after 1986.

5-8b Cost Recovery: In General

Cost recovery is available only with respect to qualifying assets held for business use or for the production of income. Thus, identifying the particular assets that qualify and their basis is critical to determining the appropriate cost recovery deduction.

---

[51] § 1.461–4(g)(6).

[52] § 1.162–1T(d); Douglas H. Tanner (1965) 45 T.C. 145; Rev.Rul. 70–40, 1970–1 C.B. 50; Rev.Rul. 58–142, 1958–1 C.B. 147.

Nature of Property

MACRS provides separate cost recovery periods and methods for realty (real property) and personalty (personal property). *Realty* generally includes land and buildings permanently affixed to the land. *Personalty* is defined as any asset that is not realty. Personalty includes furniture, machinery, equipment, and any other asset that is movable, or not permanently affixed to land. Personalty should not be confused with personal-use property. Personal-use property is any property (realty or personalty) that is held for personal use rather than for use in a trade or business or an income-producing activity. Cost recovery deductions are not allowed for personal-use assets.

In summary, both realty and personalty can be either business-use/income-producing property or personal-use property. Examples include:

- A residence (realty that is personal use),
- An office building (realty that is business use),
- A dump truck (personalty that is business use), and
- Common wearing apparel (personalty that is personal use).

Finally, assets used in a trade or business or for the production of income (e.g., an automobile that the taxpayer rents to third parties) are eligible for cost recovery only if they are subject to wear and tear, decay or decline from natural causes, or obsolescence. Assets that do not decline in value on a predictable basis or that do not have a determinable useful life (e.g., land, stock, and antiques) are not eligible for cost recovery.

Placed in Service Requirement

Cost recovery begins on the date an asset is placed in service rather than when an asset is purchased. This distinction is particularly important for an asset that is purchased near the end of the tax year, but not placed in service until the following tax year.

Cost Recovery Allowed or Allowable

To prevent the recovery of the same cost more than once (i.e., through periodic cost recovery and on the sale of the asset), the basis of property is reduced by any cost recovery deductions allowed. Furthermore, the adjusted basis of property is reduced by at least the amount of cost recovery that was allowable, or the amount that could have been taken under the applicable cost recovery method. Therefore, even if a taxpayer fails to claim any allowable cost recovery in a given year, the basis of the property is still reduced by the amount of cost recovery that should have been claimed.

BRIDGE DISCIPLINE **Bridge to Finance**

For many business entities, success in producing goods for sale is dependent on the efficient use of fixed assets, such as machinery and equipment. An important question for such businesses to resolve is how they should gain access to the required complement of fixed assets: that is, whether the assets should be purchased or leased. To answer this question, the taxpayer must determine which alternative is more cost-effective. Critical to this assessment is quantifying the after-tax cost (including the associated tax benefits) of each option.

Purchasing productive assets for business use often necessitates an immediate cash outflow. However, the tax savings resulting from the available depreciation expense deductions mitigate the impact of that outflow by reducing the taxpayer's taxable income and the income tax paid for the year. Consequently, the tax savings from the depreciation calculation associated with the purchase of an asset reduce the after-tax cost of employing the asset. The analysis can be refined further by evaluating the tax savings from the depreciation deductions in present value terms by quantifying the tax savings from the depreciation expense over the life of the asset. The asset's purchase also can be financed with debt.

Taxpayers who lease rather than buy an asset benefit by not giving up the use of funds that otherwise would have gone to purchase the asset. Lessees also forgo the opportunity to claim depreciation deductions; however, they reduce the cost of the leasing option by claiming the lease expense as a deduction against their tax base.

EXAMPLE 37

On March 15 in year 1, Heron, Inc., purchased, for $10,000, a copier, to use in its business. The copier is 5-year property, and Heron elected to use the straight-line method of cost recovery. Heron made the election because its business was new, and Heron reasoned that in the first few years of the business, a large cost recovery deduction was not needed.

Because the business was doing poorly, Heron did not even claim any cost recovery deductions in years 3 and 4. In years 5 and 6, Heron deducted the proper amount of cost recovery. Therefore, the allowed cost recovery (cost recovery actually deducted) and the allowable cost recovery are computed as follows:[53]

	Cost Recovery Allowed	Cost Recovery Allowable
Year 1	$1,000	$ 1,000
Year 2	2,000	2,000
Year 3	–0–	2,000
Year 4	–0–	2,000
Year 5	2,000	2,000
Year 6	1,000	1,000
Totals	$6,000	$10,000

The adjusted basis of the copier at the end of year 6 is $0 ($10,000 cost – $10,000 *allowable* cost recovery). If Heron sells the copier for $800 in year 7, it will recognize an $800 gain ($800 amount realized – $0 adjusted basis).

Cost Recovery Basis for Personal-Use Assets Converted to Business or Income-Producing Use

If personal-use assets are converted to business or income-producing use, the basis for cost recovery and for loss is the lower of the adjusted basis or the fair market value at the time the property was converted. As a result of this basis rule, losses that occurred while the property was personal-use property are not recognized for tax purposes through the cost recovery of the property.

---

[53]The cost recovery allowances are based on the half-year convention, which allows a half-year's cost recovery in the first and last years of the recovery period.

The Big Picture

EXAMPLE 38

Return to the facts of *The Big Picture* on p. 5-1. Five years ago, Michael Forney purchased a personal residence for $250,000. In the current year, with the housing market down, Michael found an attractively priced larger home that he acquired for his personal residence. Because of the downturn in the housing market, however, he was not able to sell his original residence and recover his purchase price of $250,000. The residence was appraised at $180,000.

Instead of continuing to try to sell the original residence, he converted it to rental property. The basis for cost recovery of the rental property is $180,000 because the fair market value is less than the adjusted basis. The $70,000 decline in value is deemed to be personal (because it occurred while the property was held for Michael's personal use) and therefore nondeductible.

5-8c Modified Accelerated Cost Recovery System (MACRS)

The IRS issues tables that provide annual cost recovery allowances based on the recovery periods, methods, and conventions specified in the Internal Revenue Code. Those tables are based on depreciation methods and conventions that should be familiar to most accounting students. These methods and conventions are discussed below and summarized in Concept Summary 5.1.

Concept Summary 5.1

MACRS: Class Lives, Methods, and Conventions

	Personalty	Realty
Class lives	3 to 20 years	Residential: 27.5 years Nonresidential: 39 years
Method	200% declining balance for property with class lives less than 15 years; 150% declining balance for property with 15- or 20-year class lives	Straight-line
Convention	Half-year or mid-quarter	Mid-month

5-8d MACRS for Personal Property

MACRS provides that the basis of eligible personalty (and certain realty) is recovered over 3, 5, 7, 10, 15, or 20 years.[54] Property included in the different cost recovery categories is shown in Exhibit 5.2.[55] Notice that the 3-, 10-, 15-, and 20-year categories tend to apply to assets used for special purposes or in specific industries. Most general purpose assets have recovery periods of five or seven years.

Cost recovery of personalty in all but the 15- and 20-year classes is based on double-declining-balance depreciation, switching to straight-line when appropriate. Cost recovery of property in the 15- and 20-year categories is based on the 150 percent declining-balance method.

Cost recovery of all personalty generally incorporates the **half-year convention**; that is, cost recovery in the year the asset is placed in service, as well as the year it is removed from service, is based on the assumption that the asset was used for exactly one-half of the year, allowing a half-year of cost recovery.[56] Thus, for example, the statutory recovery period for property with a class life of three years begins in the middle of the year the asset is placed in service and ends three years later. In practical terms, this means that the cost is actually recovered over 4, 6, 8, 11, 16, and 21 tax years.

---

[54]Personalty is assigned to recovery classes based on asset depreciation range (ADR) midpoint lives provided by the IRS (Rev.Proc. 87–56, 1987–2 C.B. 674). ADR lives generally represent estimates of an asset's useful economic life.

[55]§ 168(e) provides the ADR ranges included in Exhibit 5.2.
[56]§ 168(d)(4)(A).

EXHIBIT 5.2	Cost Recovery Periods/Classes: Personalty

Class	Generally Includes Assets with the Following ADR Lives	Examples
3-year	4 years or less	Tractor units for use over-the-road
		Any horse that is not a racehorse and is more than 12 years old at the time it is placed in service
		Special tools used in the manufacturing of motor vehicles, such as dies, fixtures, molds, and patterns
5-year	More than 4 years and less than 10 years	Automobiles and taxis
		Light and heavy general-purpose trucks
		Calculators and copiers
		Computers and peripheral equipment
7-year	10 years or more and less than 16 years	Office furniture, fixtures, and equipment
		Agricultural machinery and equipment
10-year	16 years or more and less than 20 years	Vessels, barges, tugs, and similar water transportation equipment
		Assets used for petroleum refining or for the manufacture of grain and grain mill products, sugar and sugar products, or vegetable oils and vegetable oil products
		Single-purpose agricultural or horticultural structures
15-year	20 years or more and less than 25 years	Land improvements
		Assets used for industrial steam and electric generation and/or distribution systems
		Assets used in the manufacture of cement
20-year	25 years or more	Farm buildings except single-purpose agricultural and horticultural structures
		Water utilities

As mentioned above, the appropriate methods and conventions are built into the tables provided by the IRS. Therefore, it is generally not necessary to perform any calculations. To determine the amount of the cost recovery allowance, simply identify the asset by class and go to the appropriate table. The only calculation required is the application of the part-year convention in a year in which an asset is removed from service. The MACRS percentages for personalty are shown in Exhibit 5.4 (MACRS tables are located at the end of the chapter prior to the problem materials).

Taxpayers may *elect* the straight-line method to compute cost recovery allowances for each of these classes of property. Certain property is not eligible for accelerated cost recovery and must be depreciated under an alternative depreciation system (ADS). Both the straight-line election and ADS are discussed later in the chapter.

Half-Year Convention

Robin Corporation acquires a 5-year class asset on April 10, 2016, for $30,000. Robin's cost recovery deduction for 2016 is computed as follows:

MACRS calculation based on Exhibit 5.4 ($30,000 × .20)	$6,000

EXAMPLE

39

Half-Year Convention

EXAMPLE 40

Assume the same facts as in the previous example. Robin sells the asset on March 5, 2018. Robin's cost recovery deduction for 2018 is $2,880 [$30,000 × ½ × .192 (Exhibit 5.4)].

Mid-Quarter Convention

The half-year convention arises from the simplifying presumption that assets generally will be acquired evenly throughout the tax year. However, Congress was concerned that taxpayers might override that presumption by placing large amounts of property in service toward the end of the taxable year (and, by doing so, still receive a half-year's cost recovery allowance).

To inhibit this behavior, Congress added the **mid-quarter convention** that applies if more than 40 percent of the value of property other than eligible real estate[57] is placed in service during the last quarter of the year.[58] Under this convention, property acquisitions are grouped by the quarter when they were acquired for cost recovery purposes. Acquisitions during the first quarter are allowed 10.5 months (three and one-half quarters) of cost recovery; the second quarter, 7.5 months (two and one-half quarters); the third quarter, 4.5 months (one and one-half quarters); and the fourth quarter, 1.5 months. The percentages are shown in Exhibit 5.5.

EXAMPLE 41

Silver Corporation puts into service the following new 5-year class property in 2016.

Acquisition Dates	Cost
February 15	$ 200,000
July 10	400,000
December 5	600,000
Total	$1,200,000

Under the statutory percentage method, Silver's cost recovery allowances for the first two years are computed as follows. Because more than 40% ($600,000/$1,200,000 = 50%) of the acquisitions are in the last quarter, the mid-quarter convention applies.

2016	Mid-Quarter Convention Depreciation (Exhibit 5.5)		Total Depreciation
February 15	$200,000 × .35	=	$ 70,000
July 10	$400,000 × .15	=	60,000
December 5	$600,000 × .05	=	30,000
Total			$160,000

2017			
February 15	$200,000 × .26	=	$ 52,000
July 10	$400,000 × .34	=	136,000
December 5	$600,000 × .38	=	228,000
Total			$416,000

Without the mid-quarter convention, Silver's 2016 MACRS deduction would have been $240,000 [$1,200,000 × .20 (Exhibit 5.4)]. The mid-quarter convention slows down the taxpayer's available cost recovery deductions.

---

[57]See MACRS for Real Estate on the following page for a discussion of eligible real estate.

[58]§ 168(d)(3).

When "mid-quarter" property is sold, the property is treated as though it were sold at the midpoint of the quarter. So in the quarter when sold, cost recovery is allowed for one-half of the quarter.

> **EXAMPLE 42**
>
> Assume the same facts as in the previous example, except that Silver Corporation sells the $400,000 asset on November 30, 2017. The cost recovery allowance for 2017 is computed as follows (Exhibit 5.5):
>
> | | | | |
> |---|---|---|---|
> | February 15 | $200,000 × .26 | = | $ 52,000 |
> | July 10 | $400,000 × .34 × (3.5/4) | = | 119,000 |
> | December 5 | $600,000 × .38 | = | 228,000 |
> | Total | | | $399,000 |

5-8e MACRS for Real Estate

Under MACRS, the cost of most real property is recovered using the straight-line method. The recovery period for residential rental real estate is 27.5 years. **Residential rental real estate** includes property where 80 percent or more of the gross rental revenues are from residential units (e.g., an apartment building). Hotels, motels, and similar establishments are not residential rental property. Most nonresidential real estate is recovered over 39 years.[59]

All MACRS real estate is depreciated using the **mid-month convention**.[60] Regardless of when the property is placed in service, it is deemed to have been placed in service at the middle of the month. This allows for one-half month's cost recovery for the month the property is placed in service. If the property is sold before the end of the recovery period, one-half month's cost recovery is permitted for the month of sale (no matter when the property is sold).

Like personalty, the IRS provides tables to help determine cost recovery on real property. Cost recovery is computed by multiplying the applicable rate by the cost recovery basis. The MACRS real property rates are provided in Exhibit 5.6.

> **Real Estate Cost Recovery**
>
> **EXAMPLE 43**
>
> Badger Rentals, Inc., acquired a building on April 1, 1999, for $800,000. If the building is classified as residential real estate, the cost recovery deduction for 2016 is $29,088 (.03636 × $800,000).
>
> If the building is sold on October 7, 2016, the cost recovery deduction for 2016 is $23,028 [.03636 × (9.5/12) × $800,000].
>
> If the building is acquired on March 2, 1993, for $1 million and is classified as nonresidential real estate, the cost recovery deduction for 2016 is $31,740 (.03174 × $1,000,000).
>
> If the building is sold on January 5, 2016, the cost recovery deduction for 2016 is $1,323 [.03174 × (.5/12) × $1,000,000]. (See the first two sections of Exhibit 5.6 for the percentages.)

> **EXAMPLE 44**
>
> Oakenwood Properties, Inc., acquired a building on November 19, 2016, for $1.2 million. If the building is classified as nonresidential real estate, the cost recovery deduction for 2016 is $3,852 (.00321 × $1,200,000). The cost recovery deduction for 2017 is $30,768 (.02564 × $1,200,000).
>
> If the building is sold on May 21, 2017, the cost recovery deduction for 2017 is $11,538 [.02564 × (4.5/12) × $1,200,000]. (See the last section of Exhibit 5.6 for the percentages.)

In-depth coverage can be found on this book's companion website: www.cengagebrain.com

 8 DIGGING DEEPER

---

[59] §§ 168(b), (c), and (e). A 31.5-year life is used for such property placed in service before May 13, 1993. Certain leasehold improvements can be recovered over a 15-year period.

[60] § 168(d)(1).

5-8f **Straight-Line Election**

Although MACRS requires straight-line depreciation for all eligible real estate, the taxpayer may *elect* to use the straight-line method for depreciable personal property.[61] The property is depreciated using the class life (recovery period) of the asset with a half-year convention or a mid-quarter convention, whichever applies. The election is available on a class-by-class and year-by-year basis. The percentages for the straight-line election with a half-year convention appear in Exhibit 5.7.

Straight-Line Election

EXAMPLE 45

Terry puts into service a new 10-year class asset on August 4, 2016, for $100,000. He elects the straight-line method of cost recovery. Terry's cost recovery deduction for 2016 is $5,000 ($100,000 × .05). His cost recovery deduction for 2017 is $10,000 ($100,000 × .10). (See Exhibit 5.7 for the percentages.)

EXAMPLE 46

Assume the same facts as in the previous example, except that Terry sells the asset on November 21, 2017. His cost recovery deduction for 2017, which is subject to the half-year convention, is $5,000 [$100,000 × .10 × ½ (Exhibit 5.7)].

5-8g **Additional First-Year Depreciation**

As noted in Chapter 1, Congress uses the tax system to stimulate the economy—especially in challenging economic times. Such is the case with **additional first-year depreciation** (also referred to as "bonus depreciation"). Under this provision, taxpayers can take an additional 50 percent cost recovery in the year qualified property is placed in service.[62]

Qualified property includes tangible personal property, computer software, and qualified improvement property. The taxpayer must be the first to use the property (i.e., the property must be *new*). Qualified improvement property includes most improvements made to the interior of nonresidential real property.

The additional first-year depreciation is taken in the year in which the qualifying property is placed in service. This amount may be claimed in addition to otherwise available depreciation deductions. After the additional first-year depreciation is determined, the standard MACRS cost recovery allowance is calculated by multiplying the cost recovery basis (original cost recovery basis less additional first-year depreciation) by the percentage that reflects the applicable cost recovery method and convention.

A taxpayer may elect *not* to claim additional first-year depreciation. Examples 46 and 47 reflect the tax treatment for 2016.

Bonus Depreciation

EXAMPLE 47

Morgan acquires, for $50,000, and places in service a 5-year class asset on March 20, 2016. Morgan's total 2016 cost recovery deduction is:

50% additional first-year depreciation ($50,000 × .50)	$25,000
MACRS cost recovery [($50,000 − $25,000) × .20 (Exhibit 5.4)]	5,000
Total cost recovery	$30,000

EXAMPLE 48

Assume the same facts as in the previous example. Morgan disposes of the asset on October 22, 2017. Morgan's 2017 cost recovery deduction for the asset is $4,000 [$25,000 × ½ year × .32 (Exhibit 5.4)].

---

[61] § 168(b)(5).

[62] § 168(k). Additional first-year depreciation is allowed for qualified property placed in service after 2011 and before 2020. The additional first-year depreciation percentage decreases from 50% to 40% in 2018 and then to 30% in 2019. No bonus depreciation will be allowed after 2019. Different rules applied between 2008 and 2011.

5-8h **Election to Expense Assets (§ 179)**

Section 179 (Election to Expense Certain Depreciable Business Assets) permits a taxpayer to elect to immediately recover up to $500,000 of the acquisition cost of § 179 property used in a trade or business.[63] Amounts that are expensed under § 179 are not eligible for additional first-year depreciation or cost recovery under MACRS.

The **§ 179 expensing election** is an annual election that applies to the acquisition cost of property placed in service that year. The immediate expense election generally is not available for real property or for property used for the production of income.[64]

Any elected § 179 expense is taken *before* additional first-year and any other cost recovery is computed. The base for calculating both any additional first-year cost recovery and the standard MACRS deduction is determined net of the § 179 expense.

EXAMPLE 49

Kodiak Corporation acquires and places in service equipment (5-year class asset) on February 1, 2016, at a cost of $525,000. It elects to expense $500,000 under § 179. Kodiak also claims the 50 percent additional first-year cost recovery deduction for 2016. As a result, the total deduction for the year is calculated as follows:

§ 179 expense	$500,000
50% additional first-year depreciation [($525,000 − $500,000) × 50%]	12,500
Standard MACRS amount [($525,000 − $500,000 − $12,500) × .20]	2,500
Total cost recovery claimed	$515,000

---

[63]Section 179 property includes tangible personal property, computer software, qualified real property (leasehold improvements that qualify for 15-year cost recovery), and heating and air conditioning units. The annual expense and phaseout amounts ($500,000 and $2 million, respectively) apply to 2010 and subsequent years. These amounts are adjusted for inflation beginning in 2016 and rounded to the nearest $10,000 multiple.

[64]§§ 179(b) and (d). Generally, property used for the production of income is property that is held in a capacity or function where income is generated, but where it is not used by a trade or business.

Annual Limitations

Two additional limitations apply to the amount deductible under § 179. First, the annual maximum allowance available is reduced dollar for dollar when § 179 property placed in service during the taxable year exceeds a maximum amount ($2,010,000 in 2016; $2 million in 2015). Second, the § 179 deduction cannot exceed the taxpayer's trade or business taxable income, computed without regard to the § 179 amount.

Any § 179 deduction in excess of taxable income is carried forward to future taxable years and added to other amounts eligible for expensing. For 2016, the § 179 amount eligible for expensing in a carryforward year is limited to the *lesser* of (1) the appropriate statutory dollar amount ($500,000) reduced by the cost of § 179 property placed in service in excess of $2,010,000 in the carryforward year or (2) business taxable income in the carryforward year.

EXAMPLE 50

Jill owns a computer service business and operates it as a sole proprietorship. In 2016, taxable income is $138,000 before considering any § 179 deduction. If Jill spends $2.3 million on new equipment, her § 179 expense deduction for the year is computed as follows:

§ 179 deduction before adjustment	$ 500,000
Less: Dollar limitation reduction ($2,300,000 − $2,010,000)	(290,000)
Remaining § 179 deduction	$ 210,000
Business income limitation	$ 138,000
§ 179 deduction allowed	$ 138,000
§ 179 deduction carryforward ($210,000 − $138,000)	$ 72,000

Effect on Basis

The basis of the property for cost recovery purposes is reduced by the § 179 amount after accounting for the current-year amount of property placed in service in excess of the threshold amount ($2,010,000 in 2016). This adjusted amount does not reflect any business income limitation.

EXAMPLE 51

Assume the same facts as in Example 49. Jill's adjusted basis in the equipment for cost recovery purposes is $2,090,000 ($2.3 million cost less the $210,000 § 179 expense amount before the business income limitation). If any portion of the $72,000 carryover (due to the income limitation) is not deducted before the equipment is sold, this amount may be added back to the basis of the equipment in determining its adjusted basis.

BRIDGE DISCIPLINE   Bridge to Economics and the Business Cycle

Congress has passed several stimulus packages intended to stabilize and accelerate the economy. One provision, additional first-year depreciation, increased the amount of certain fixed asset acquisition costs that could be expensed rather than depreciated. Given that some sectors of the economy are still struggling, however, many companies are not able to take advantage of the increased deductions because they cannot afford to purchase new assets. Businesses do not purchase assets simply to save on taxes.

Source: Based on Joyce Rosenberg, "Deduction Dilemma Hits Companies," *Telegraph Herald* (Dubuque, Iowa), November 9, 2008, p. B2.

5-8i **Business and Personal Use of Automobiles and Other Listed Property**

Limits exist on cost recovery deductions for automobiles and other listed property used for both personal and business purposes.[65] These limits would apply, for example, to an automobile used by a sole proprietor partly for business purposes and partly for personal use.

Listed property is not eligible for the accelerated methods built into MACRS, § 179 expense, nor bonus depreciation unless it is predominantly used for business purposes. Rather, if not used predominantly for business, the cost of listed propriety must be recovered using the straight-line method (see Exhibit 5.7). The straight-line method must continue to be used even if, at some later date, the business usage of the property increases to more than 50 percent. Listed property includes:[66]

- Any passenger automobile.
- Any other property used as a means of transportation (e.g., trucks and airplanes).
- Any property of a type generally used for purposes of entertainment, recreation, or amusement.
- Any computer or peripheral equipment, with the exception of equipment used exclusively at a regular business establishment, including a qualifying home office.
- Any other property specified in the Regulations.

Automobiles and Other Listed Property Used Predominantly in Business

For listed property to be considered as *predominantly used in business*, its *business usage* must exceed 50 percent.[67] The use of listed property for production of income does not qualify as business use for purposes of the more-than-50% test. However, both production-of-income and business-use percentages are used to compute the cost recovery deduction.

On September 1, 2016, Emma acquires and places in service listed 5-year recovery property. The property cost $10,000. Emma does not claim any available additional first-year cost recovery.

If Emma uses the property 40% for business and 25% for the production of income, the property is not considered as predominantly used for business. The asset cost is recovered using the straight-line method. Emma's cost recovery allowance for the year is $650 ($10,000 × .10 × .65).

If, however, Emma uses the property 60% for business and 25% for the production of income, the property is considered as used predominantly for business. Therefore, she may use the MACRS tables. Emma's cost recovery allowance for the year is $1,700 ($10,000 × .20 × .85).

EXAMPLE
52

In determining the percentage of business usage for listed property, a mileage-based percentage is used for automobiles. For other listed property, one employs the most appropriate unit of time (e.g., hours) for which the property actually is used (rather than its availablility for use).[68]

Limits on Cost Recovery for Automobiles

The law places further limitations on the annual cost recovery deductions for *passenger automobiles*.[69] These statutory dollar limits were imposed on passenger automobiles because of the belief that the tax system was being used to underwrite automobiles whose cost and luxury features far exceeded what was needed for the taxpayer's business use. Any cost otherwise recoverable but limited by the annual limitation may be recovered in later years subject to the limit applicable to the subsequent year.

---

[65]§§ 280F and 168(k)(2)(D).
[66]§ 280F(d)(4).
[67]§ 280F(b)(3).

[68]Reg. § 1.280F–6T(e).
[69]§ 280F(d)(5).

The following "luxury auto" depreciation limits apply.[70]

Date Placed in Service	First Year	Second Year	Third Year	Fourth and Later Years
2014–2015*	$3,160	$5,100	$3,050	$1,875
2012–2013	$3,160	$5,100	$3,050	$1,875
2010–2011	$3,060	$4,900	$2,950	$1,775

*Because the 2016 indexed amounts are not yet available, the 2015 amounts are used in the examples and end-of-chapter problem materials.

For an automobile placed in service prior to 2010, the limitation for subsequent years' cost recovery is based on the limits for the year the automobile was placed in service.[71] If a new passenger automobile otherwise qualifies for additional first-year depreciation, the *luxury auto* limitation increases by $8,000.[72] Therefore, for acquisitions made in 2015, the initial-year cost recovery limitation increases from $3,160 to $11,160 ($3,160 + $8,000).

There are also separate cost recovery limitations for trucks and vans and for electric automobiles. Because these limitations are applied in the same manner as those imposed on passenger automobiles, these additional limitations are not discussed further in this chapter.

The luxury auto limits must be reduced proportionally for any personal use of the auto. In addition, the limitation in the first year includes any amount the taxpayer elects to expense under § 179.[73] If the passenger automobile is used partly for personal use, the personal-use percentage is ignored for the purpose of determining the unrecovered cost available for deduction in later years.

EXAMPLE 53

On July 1, 2016, Dan acquires and places in service a new automobile that cost $40,000. He does not elect § 179 expensing and he elects not to take any available additional first-year depreciation. The car is used 80% for business and 20% for personal purposes in each tax year. Dan chooses the MACRS 200% declining-balance method of cost recovery (the auto is a 5-year asset; see Exhibit 5.4).

The depreciation computation for 2016 through 2021 is summarized in the table below. The cost recovery allowed is the lesser of the MACRS amount or the recovery limitation.

Year	MACRS Amount	Recovery Limitation	Depreciation Allowed	Depreciation Deferred	Cumulative Deferred Depreciation
2016	$6,400 ($40,000 × .2000 × 80%)	$2,528 ($3,160 × 80%)	$2,528	$3,872	$ 3,872
2017	$10,240 ($40,000 × .3200 × 80%)	$4,080 ($5,100 × 80%)	$4,080	$6,160	$10,032
2018	$6,144 ($40,000 × .1920 × 80%)	$2,440 ($3,050 × 80%)	$2,440	$3,704	$13,736
2019	$3,686 ($40,000 × .1152 × 80%)	$1,500 ($1,875 × 80%)	$1,500	$2,186	$15,922
2020	$3,686 ($40,000 × .1152 × 80%)	$1,500 ($1,875 × 80%)	$1,500	$2,186	$18,108
2021	$1,843 ($40,000 × .0576 × 80%)	$1,500 ($1,875 × 80%)	$1,500	$ 343	$18,451

If Dan continues to use the car after 2021, his cost recovery is limited to the lesser of the recoverable basis or the recovery limitation (i.e., $1,875 × business-use percentage). For this purpose, the recoverable basis is computed as if the full cost recovery limitation was allowed, even if the full deduction was not claimed. Thus, the recoverable basis as of January 1, 2022, is $23,065 ($40,000 − $3,160 − $5,100 − $3,050 − $1,875 − $1,875 − $1,875).

If Dan takes additional first-year depreciation in 2016, the calculated amount of additional first-year depreciation is $16,000 ($40,000 × 80% × 50%). However, the deduction for the year would be limited to $8,928 [($8,000 + $3,160) × 80%].

---

[70]§ 280F(a)(1); Rev.Proc. 2014–21, 2014–11 I.R.B. 641.

[71]Cost recovery limitations for years prior to 2009 are found in IRS Publication 463.

[72]§ 168(k)(2)(F). The $8,000 amount will decrease to $6,400 in 2018 and $4,800 in 2019. No increase in the first-year recovery limitation will be allowed after 2019.

[73]§ 280F(d)(1).

Realize the cost recovery limitations are maximum amounts. If the regular MACRS calculation produces a lesser amount of cost recovery, the lesser amount is used.

On April 2, 2016, Gail places in service a pre-owned automobile that cost $10,000. The car is always used 70% for business and 30% for personal use.

The cost recovery allowance for 2016 is $1,400 ($10,000 × .20 × 70%), and not $2,212 (the $3,160 passenger auto maximum × 70%).

Limitation for SUVs

Some sport utility vehicles (SUVs) are not considered passenger automobiles and, therefore, are not subject to the luxury automobile limitations. However, a $25,000 limit applies to the § 179 deduction when the luxury auto limits do not apply. The limit is in effect for SUVs with an unloaded gross vehicle weight (GVW) rating of more than 6,000 pounds and not more than 14,000 pounds.[74]

During 2016, Jay acquires and places in service a new SUV that cost $70,000 and has a GVW of 8,000 pounds. Jay uses the vehicle 100% of the time for business purposes. The total deduction for 2016 with respect to the SUV is computed as follows:

§ 179 expense, as limited	$25,000
50% additional first-year depreciation [($70,000 − $25,000) × 50%]	22,500
Standard MACRS amount [($70,000 − $25,000 − $22,500) × .20 (Exhibit 5.4)]	4,500
Total cost recovery claimed	$52,000

Change from Predominantly Business Use

If the business-use percentage of listed property falls to 50 percent or less after the year the property is placed in service, the property is subject to *cost recovery recapture*. The amount required to be recaptured and included in the taxpayer's ordinary income is the excess cost recovery. *Excess cost recovery* is the excess of the cost recovery deduction taken in prior years using the statutory percentage method over the amount that would have been allowed if the straight-line method had been used since the property was placed in service.[75]

After the business usage of the listed property drops below the more-than-50% level, the straight-line method must be used for the remaining life of the property.

Concept Summary 5.2 illustrates the cost recovery rules for various types of listed property.

Leased Automobiles

Taxpayers who lease, rather than purchase, a passenger automobile for business purposes are not subject to the luxury auto limits. To prevent taxpayers from circumventing the luxury auto limits by deducting the lease payments associated with a luxury automobile leased for business, the Code requires these taxpayers to report an *inclusion amount* in gross income. The inclusion amount is computed from an IRS table for each taxable year for which the taxpayer leases the automobile.

The inclusion amount is based on the fair market value of the automobile; it is prorated for the number of days the auto is used during the taxable year. The prorated dollar amount then is multiplied by the business and income-producing usage percentage.[76] The taxpayer deducts the lease payments, multiplied by the business and income-producing usage percentage. In effect, the taxpayer's annual deduction for the lease payment is reduced by the inclusion amount.

---

[74]§ 179(b)(6).

[75]§ 280F(b)(2).

[76]Reg. § 1.280F–7(a).

Concept Summary 5.2

Listed Property Cost Recovery

EXAMPLE

56

On April 1, 2016, Jim leases and places in service a passenger automobile worth $52,400. The lease is to be for a period of five years. During the taxable years 2016 and 2017, Jim uses the automobile 70% for business and 30% for personal use.

Assuming that the inclusion amounts from the IRS table for 2016 and 2017 are $53 and $115, respectively, Jim includes in gross income:

2016: $53 × (275/366) × .70 = $28
2017: $115 × (366/365) × .70 = $81

In each year, Jim still can deduct 70% of the lease payments made, related to his business use of the auto.

BRIDGE DISCIPLINE **Bridge to Finance and Economics**

A new car, on average, loses a much larger portion of its value during the first five years through economic depreciation than it loses during later years. Depreciation accounts for about 35 percent of the ownership costs of a car during this 5-year period.

Leasing a car will not eliminate the problem because the monthly lease payments are determined, in part, by the projected value of the car at the end of the lease. Because a new car loses its value faster in the earlier years, the shorter the lease, the higher the economic cost of depreciation.

Substantiation Requirements

Listed property is subject to the substantiation requirements of § 274. This means that the taxpayer must prove for any business usage the amount of expense or use, the time and place of use, the business purpose for the use, and the business relationship to the taxpayer of persons using the property.

Substantiation requires adequate records or sufficient evidence corroborating the taxpayer's statement. However, these substantiation requirements do not apply to vehicles that, by reason of their nature, are not likely to be used more than a *de minimis* amount for personal purposes.[77]

5-8j Alternative Depreciation System (ADS)

The **alternative depreciation system (ADS)** must be used:[78]

- To calculate the portion of depreciation treated as an alternative minimum tax (AMT) adjustment (see Chapter 17).[79]
- To compute depreciation allowances for property:
  - Used predominantly outside the United States.
  - Leased or otherwise used by a tax-exempt entity.
  - Financed with the proceeds of tax-exempt bonds.
  - Imported from foreign countries that maintain discriminatory trade practices or otherwise engage in discriminatory acts.
- To compute depreciation allowances as part of earnings and profits (see Chapter 13).

Exhibits 5.8, 5.9, and 5.10 provide cost recovery rates under the ADS method. Generally, personal property is depreciated under the ADS using the appropriate asset class life (e.g., 5- or 7-year) and the 150 percent declining-balance method. ADS uses straight-line depreciation for all realty, over a 40-year class life.

5-9 AMORTIZATION

LO.8
Identify intangible assets that are eligible for amortization and calculate the amount of the deduction.

Taxpayers can recover the costs of certain intangible assets through an **amortization** deduction. The amount of the deduction is determined by amortizing the adjusted basis of such intangibles ratably over a 15-year period beginning in the month in which the intangible is acquired.[80]

Section 197 covers the amortization of most intangibles. Amortizable *§ 197 intangibles* include most intangibles acquired after August 10, 1993, and acquired in connection with the acquisition of a business including goodwill, going-concern value, franchises, trademarks, copyrights, patents, and covenants not to compete. Generally, self-created intangibles are not § 197 intangibles.

The 15-year amortization period applies regardless of the actual useful life of an amortizable § 197 intangible. No other depreciation or amortization deduction is permitted with respect to any amortizable § 197 intangible except those permitted under the 15-year amortization rules.

On June 1, Sally purchased and began operating the Falcon Café. Of the purchase price, $90,000 is allocated to goodwill.

The year's § 197 amortization deduction is $3,500 [($90,000 ÷ 15) × (7/12)].

EXAMPLE
57

---

[77]§§ 274(d) and (i).

[78]§ 168(g).

[79]This AMT adjustment applies for real and personal property placed in service before 1999. However, it continues to apply for personal property

placed in service after 1998 if the taxpayer uses the 200% declining-balance method for regular income tax purposes. See Chapter 17.

[80]§ 197(a).

TAX PLANNING STRATEGIES   **Structuring the Sale of a Business**

FRAMEWORK FOCUS: TAX RATE

Strategy: Control the Character of Income and Deductions.

On the sale of a sole proprietorship where the sales price exceeds the fair market value of the tangible assets and stated intangible assets, a planning opportunity may exist for both the seller and the buyer.

The seller's preference is for the excess amount to be allocated to *goodwill* because goodwill is a capital asset whose sale may result in favorably taxed long-term capital gain. Amounts received for a *covenant not to compete,* however, produce ordinary income, which is not subject to favorable long-term capital gain rates.

Because a covenant and goodwill both are amortized over a statutory 15-year period, the tax results of a covenant not to compete versus goodwill are the same for the *buyer.* However, the buyer should recognize that an allocation to goodwill rather than a covenant may provide a tax benefit to the seller. Therefore, the buyer, in negotiating the purchase price, should factor in the tax benefit to the seller of having the excess amount labeled goodwill rather than a covenant not to compete. Of course, if the noncompetition aspects of a covenant are important to the buyer, a portion of the excess amount can be assigned to a covenant.

LO.9

Determine the amount of depletion expense and specify the alternative tax treatments for intangible drilling and development costs.

5-10 DEPLETION

Natural resources (e.g., oil, gas, coal, gravel, and timber) are subject to **depletion**, a form of cost recovery applicable to natural resources. Land generally cannot be depleted. Although all natural resources are subject to depletion, oil and gas wells are used as an example in the following paragraphs to illustrate the related costs and issues.

In developing an oil or gas well, the producer typically makes four types of expenditures:

- Natural resource costs.
- Intangible drilling and development costs.
- Tangible asset costs.
- Operating costs.

Natural resources are physically limited, and the costs to acquire them (e.g., oil under the ground) are, therefore, recovered through depletion. Costs incurred in making the property ready for drilling, such as the cost of labor in clearing the property, erecting derricks, and drilling the hole, are **intangible drilling and development costs (IDCs)**. These costs generally have no salvage value and are a lost cost if the well is not productive (dry).

Costs for tangible assets such as tools, pipes, and engines are capitalized and recovered through depreciation (cost recovery). Costs incurred after the well is producing are operating costs. These costs include expenditures for items such as labor, fuel, and supplies. Operating costs are deductible as trade or business expenses. Intangible drilling and development costs and depletable costs receive different treatment.

5-10a **Intangible Drilling and Development Costs (IDCs)**

Intangible drilling and development costs can be handled in one of two ways at the option of the taxpayer. They can be either charged off as an expense in the year in which they are incurred or capitalized and written off through depletion. The taxpayer makes the election in the first year such expenditures are incurred, either by taking a deduction on the return or by adding them to the depletable basis.

Once made, the election is binding on both the taxpayer and the IRS for all such expenditures in the future. If the taxpayer fails to elect to expense IDCs, on the original timely filed return for the first year in which such expenditures are incurred, an irrevocable election to capitalize them has been made.

As a general rule, it is more advantageous to expense IDCs. The obvious benefit of an immediate write-off (as opposed to a deferred write-off through depletion) is not the only advantage. Because a taxpayer can use percentage depletion, which is calculated without reference to basis, the IDCs may be completely lost as a deduction if they are capitalized.

5-10b Depletion Methods

There are two methods of calculating depletion. *Cost depletion* can be used on any wasting asset (and is the only method allowed for timber). *Percentage depletion* is subject to a number of limitations, particularly for oil and gas deposits. Depletion should be calculated both ways, and the method that results in the larger deduction should be used. The choice between cost depletion and percentage depletion is an annual decision; the taxpayer can use cost depletion in one year and percentage depletion in the following year.

Cost Depletion

Cost depletion resembles units-of-production depreciation.[81] The basis is divided by the estimated recoverable units of the asset (e.g., barrels and tons) to arrive at the depletion per unit. This amount then is multiplied by the number of units sold (not the units produced) during the year to arrive at the cost depletion allowed.

On January 1, 2016, Pablo purchases the rights to a mineral interest for $1 million. At that time, the remaining recoverable units in the mineral interest are estimated to be 200,000. The depletion per unit is $5 [$1,000,000 (adjusted basis) ÷ 200,000 (estimated recoverable units)].

If 60,000 units are mined and 25,000 are sold, the cost depletion is $125,000 [$5 (depletion per unit) × 25,000 (units sold)].

EXAMPLE 58

If the taxpayer later discovers that the original estimate was incorrect, the depletion per unit for future calculations is redetermined, using the revised estimate.[82]

Assume the same facts as in the previous example. In 2017, Pablo realizes that an incorrect estimate was made. The remaining recoverable units now are determined to be 400,000. Based on this new information, the revised depletion per unit is $2.1875 [$875,000 (adjusted basis) ÷ 400,000 (estimated recoverable units)]. The adjusted basis is the original cost ($1,000,000) reduced by the depletion claimed in 2016 ($125,000).

If 30,000 units are sold in 2017, the depletion for the year is $65,625 [$2.1875 (depletion per unit) × 30,000 (units sold)].

EXAMPLE 59

Percentage Depletion

Percentage depletion (also referred to as statutory depletion) uses a specified percentage provided by the Code. The percentage varies according to the type of mineral interest involved. A sample of these percentages is shown in Exhibit 5.3. The rate is applied to the gross income from the property, but in no event may percentage depletion exceed 50 percent of the taxable income from the property before the allowance for depletion.[83]

CarrolCo reports gross income of $100,000 and other property-related expenses of $60,000 and uses a depletion rate of 22%. CarrollCo's depletion allowance is determined as follows:

Gross income	$100,000
Less: Other expenses	(60,000)
Taxable income before depletion	$ 40,000
Depletion allowance [the lesser of $22,000 (22% × $100,000) or $20,000 (50% × $40,000)]	(20,000)
Taxable income after depletion	$ 20,000

EXAMPLE 60

The adjusted basis of CarrollCo's property is reduced by $20,000, the depletion deduction allowed. If the other expenses had been only $55,000, the full $22,000 could have been deducted, and the adjusted basis would have been reduced by $22,000.

Note that percentage depletion is based on a percentage of the gross income from the property and makes no reference to cost. All other cost recovery deductions detailed in this chapter are a function of the adjusted basis (cost) of the property. Thus, when

---

[81]§ 612.

[82]§ 611(a).

[83]§ 613(a). Special rules apply for certain oil and gas wells (e.g., the 50% ceiling is replaced with a 100% ceiling, and the percentage depletion may not exceed 65% of the taxpayer's taxable income from all sources before the allowance for depletion). § 613A.

EXHIBIT 5.3	**Sample of Percentage Depletion Rates**

22% Depletion

Cobalt	Sulfur
Lead	Tin

15% Depletion

Copper	Oil and gas
Gold	Silver

10% Depletion

Coal	Perlite

5% Depletion

Gravel	Sand

percentage depletion is used, it is possible to claim aggregate depletion deductions that exceed the original cost of the property. If percentage depletion is used, however, the adjusted basis of the property (for computing cost depletion in a future tax year) is reduced by any depletion deducted, until the basis reaches zero.

TAX PLANNING STRATEGIES   **Switching Depletion Methods**

FRAMEWORK FOCUS: DEDUCTIONS

Strategy: Maximize Deductible Amounts.

As long as the basis of a depletable asset remains above zero, cost depletion or percentage depletion, whichever method the taxpayer elects, is used. When the basis of the asset is exhausted, percentage depletion still can be taken.

EXAMPLE 61

Warbler Company reports the following related to its sulfur mine:

Remaining depletable basis	$ 11,000
Gross income (10,000 units)	100,000
Expenses (other than depletion)	30,000
Percentage depletion rate	22%

Because cost depletion is limited to the remaining depletable basis of $11,000, Warbler would choose percentage depletion of $22,000 [lesser of ($100,000 × 22%) or ($70,000 × 50%)]. The basis in the mine then becomes zero.

In future years, however, Warbler can continue to use percentage depletion; percentage depletion is computed without reference to the remaining asset basis.

5-11 COST RECOVERY TABLES

Summary of Cost Recovery Tables (continued)

Exhibit 5.4   MACRS statutory percentage table for personalty.
Applicable depreciation methods: 200 or 150 percent declining-balance switching to straight-line.
Applicable recovery periods: 3, 5, 7, 10, 15, 20 years.
Applicable convention: half-year.

Exhibit 5.5   MACRS statutory percentage table for personalty.
Applicable depreciation method: 200 percent declining-balance switching to straight-line.

Summary of Cost Recovery Tables

	Applicable recovery periods: 3, 5, 7 years.
	Applicable convention: mid-quarter.
Exhibit 5.6	MACRS straight-line table for realty.
	Applicable depreciation method: straight-line.
	Applicable recovery periods: 27.5, 31.5, 39 years.
	Applicable convention: mid-month.
Exhibit 5.7	MACRS optional straight-line table for personalty.
	Applicable depreciation method: straight-line.
	Applicable recovery periods: 3, 5, 7, 10, 15, 20 years.
	Applicable convention: half-year.
Exhibit 5.8	ADS for alternative minimum tax: 150 percent declining-balance table for personalty.
	Applicable depreciation method: 150 percent declining-balance switching to straight-line.
	Applicable recovery periods: 3, 5, 7, 9.5, 10, 12 years.
	Applicable convention: half-year.
Exhibit 5.9	ADS straight-line table for personalty.
	Applicable depreciation method: straight-line.
	Applicable recovery periods: 5, 10, 12 years.
	Applicable convention: half-year.
Exhibit 5.10	ADS straight-line table for realty.
	Applicable depreciation method: straight-line.
	Applicable recovery period: 40 years.
	Applicable convention: mid-month.

EXHIBIT 5.4 — MACRS Accelerated Depreciation for Personal Property Assuming Half-Year Convention

For Property Placed in Service after December 31, 1986

Recovery Year	3-Year (200% DB)	5-Year (200% DB)	7-Year (200% DB)	10-Year (200% DB)	15-Year (150% DB)	20-Year (150% DB)
1	33.33	20.00	14.29	10.00	5.00	3.750
2	44.45	32.00	24.49	18.00	9.50	7.219
3	14.81*	19.20	17.49	14.40	8.55	6.677
4	7.41	11.52*	12.49	11.52	7.70	6.177
5		11.52	8.93*	9.22	6.93	5.713
6		5.76	8.92	7.37	6.23	5.285
7			8.93	6.55*	5.90*	4.888
8			4.46	6.55	5.90	4.522
9				6.56	5.91	4.462*
10				6.55	5.90	4.461
11				3.28	5.91	4.462
12					5.90	4.461
13					5.91	4.462
14					5.90	4.461
15					5.91	4.462
16					2.95	4.461
17						4.462
18						4.461
19						4.462
20						4.461
21						2.231

*Switchover to straight-line depreciation.

| EXHIBIT 5.5 | MACRS Accelerated Depreciation for Personal Property Assuming Mid-Quarter Convention |

For Property Placed in Service after December 31, 1986 (Partial Table*)

	3-Year			
Recovery Year	First Quarter	Second Quarter	Third Quarter	Fourth Quarter
1	58.33	41.67	25.00	8.33
2	27.78	38.89	50.00	61.11

	5-Year			
Recovery Year	First Quarter	Second Quarter	Third Quarter	Fourth Quarter
1	35.00	25.00	15.00	5.00
2	26.00	30.00	34.00	38.00

	7-Year			
Recovery Year	First Quarter	Second Quarter	Third Quarter	Fourth Quarter
1	25.00	17.85	10.71	3.57
2	21.43	23.47	25.51	27.55

*The figures in this table are taken from the official tables that appear in Rev.Proc. 87–57, 1987–2 C.B. 687. Because of their length, the complete tables are not presented.

| EXHIBIT 5.6 | MACRS Straight-Line Depreciation for Real Property Assuming Mid-Month Convention* |

For Property Placed in Service after December 31, 1986: 27.5-Year Residential Real Property

Recovery Year(s)	The Applicable Percentage Is (Use the Column for the Month in the First Year the Property Is Placed in Service):											
	1	2	3	4	5	6	7	8	9	10	11	12
1	3.485	3.182	2.879	2.576	2.273	1.970	1.667	1.364	1.061	0.758	0.455	0.152
2–18	3.636	3.636	3.636	3.636	3.636	3.636	3.636	3.636	3.636	3.636	3.636	3.636
19–27	3.637	3.637	3.637	3.637	3.637	3.637	3.637	3.637	3.637	3.637	3.637	3.637
28	1.970	2.273	2.576	2.879	3.182	3.485	3.636	3.636	3.636	3.636	3.636	3.636
29	0.000	0.000	0.000	0.000	0.000	0.000	0.152	0.455	0.758	1.061	1.364	1.667

For Property Placed in Service after December 31, 1986, and before May 13, 1993: 31.5-Year Nonresidential Real Property

Recovery Year(s)	The Applicable Percentage Is (Use the Column for the Month in the First Year the Property Is Placed in Service):											
	1	2	3	4	5	6	7	8	9	10	11	12
1	3.042	2.778	2.513	2.249	1.984	1.720	1.455	1.190	0.926	0.661	0.397	0.132
2–19	3.175	3.175	3.175	3.175	3.175	3.175	3.175	3.175	3.175	3.175	3.175	3.175
20–31	3.174	3.174	3.174	3.174	3.174	3.174	3.174	3.174	3.174	3.174	3.174	3.174
32	1.720	1.984	2.249	2.513	2.778	3.042	3.175	3.175	3.175	3.175	3.175	3.175
33	0.000	0.000	0.000	0.000	0.000	0.000	0.132	0.397	0.661	0.926	1.190	1.455

For Property Placed in Service after May 12, 1993: 39-Year Nonresidential Real Property

Recovery Year(s)	The Applicable Percentage Is (Use the Column for the Month in the First Year the Property Is Placed in Service):											
	1	2	3	4	5	6	7	8	9	10	11	12
1	2.461	2.247	2.033	1.819	1.605	1.391	1.177	0.963	0.749	0.535	0.321	0.107
2–39	2.564	2.564	2.564	2.564	2.564	2.564	2.564	2.564	2.564	2.564	2.564	2.564
40	0.107	0.321	0.535	0.749	0.963	1.177	1.391	1.605	1.819	2.033	2.247	2.461

*The official tables contain a separate row for each year. For ease of presentation, certain years are grouped in these tables. In some instances, this will produce a difference of .001 for the last digit when compared with the official tables.

EXHIBIT 5.7	MACRS Straight-Line Depreciation for Personal Property Assuming Half-Year Convention*

For Property Placed in Service after December 31, 1986

MACRS Class	% First Recovery Year	Other Recovery Years		Last Recovery Year	
		Years	%	Year	%
3-year	16.67	2–3	33.33	4	16.67
5-year	10.00	2–5	20.00	6	10.00
7-year	7.14	2–7	14.29	8	7.14
10-year	5.00	2–10	10.00	11	5.00
15-year	3.33	2–15	6.67	16	3.33
20-year	2.50	2–20	5.00	21	2.50

*The official table contains a separate row for each year. For ease of presentation, certain years are grouped in this table. In some instances, this will produce a difference of .01 for the last digit when compared with the official table.

EXHIBIT 5.8	ADS for Alternative Minimum Tax: 150% Declining-Balance for Personal Property Assuming Half-Year Convention

For Property Placed in Service after December 31, 1986 (Partial Table*)

Recovery Year	3-Year 150%	5-Year 150%	7-Year 150%	9.5-Year 150%	10-Year 150%	12-Year 150%
1	25.00	15.00	10.71	7.89	7.50	6.25
2	37.50	25.50	19.13	14.54	13.88	11.72
3	25.00**	17.85	15.03	12.25	11.79	10.25
4	12.50	16.66**	12.25**	10.31	10.02	8.97
5		16.66	12.25	9.17**	8.74**	7.85
6		8.33	12.25	9.17	8.74	7.33**
7			12.25	9.17	8.74	7.33
8		6.13	9.17	8.74	7.33
9				9.17	8.74	7.33
10				9.16	8.74	7.33
11					4.37	7.32
12						7.33
13						3.66

*The figures in this table are taken from the official table that appears in Rev.Proc. 87–57, 1987–2 C.B. 687. Because of its length, the complete table is not presented.
**Switchover to straight-line depreciation.

EXHIBIT 5.9	ADS Straight-Line for Personal Property Assuming Half-Year Convention

For Property Placed in Service after December 31, 1986 (Partial Table*)

Recovery Year	5-Year Class	10-Year Class	12-Year Class
1	10.00	5.00	4.17
2	20.00	10.00	8.33
3	20.00	10.00	8.33
4	20.00	10.00	8.33
5	20.00	10.00	8.33
6	10.00	10.00	8.33
7		10.00	8.34
8		10.00	8.33
9		10.00	8.34
10		10.00	8.33
11		5.00	8.34
12			8.33
13			4.17

*The figures in this table are taken from the official table that appears in Rev.Proc. 87–57, 1987–2 C.B. 687. Because of its length, the complete table is not presented. The tables for the mid-quarter convention also appear in Rev.Proc. 87–57.

EXHIBIT 5.10	ADS Straight-Line for Real Property Assuming Mid-Month Convention

For Property Placed in Service after December 31, 1986

Recovery Year(s)	Month Placed in Service											
	1	2	3	4	5	6	7	8	9	10	11	12
1	2.396	2.188	1.979	1.771	1.563	1.354	1.146	0.938	0.729	0.521	0.313	0.104
2–40	2.500	2.500	2.500	2.500	2.500	2.500	2.500	2.500	2.500	2.500	2.500	2.500
41	0.104	0.312	0.521	0.729	0.937	1.146	1.354	1.562	1.771	1.979	2.187	2.396

REFOCUS ON THE BIG PICTURE

CALCULATING DEDUCTIBLE EXPENSES

In general, the expenses incurred in Michael Forney's small engine service and repair business are deductible as long as they are ordinary and necessary expenses. In addition, the salaries and wages paid must be reasonable. However, his plan to increase salaries radically next year for himself and his mother probably should not be pursued, because most or all of the increase could be considered unreasonable. Charitable contributions generally are limited to 10 percent of taxable income before the charitable contribution deduction, and political contributions and the fine are not deductible. The dues paid to Small Engine Repair Institute are not fully deductible because 70 percent of the organization's efforts relate to lobbying activities. However, the amount paid to consultants to investigate a new business opportunity is fully deductible as an ordinary and necessary business expense.

Michael can elect to expense the costs of the machinery and equipment under the provisions of § 179. For the current year, assume the § 179 deduction is limited to $500,000 and cannot exceed the taxable income derived from the business (before the § 179 deduction). In this case, the entire purchase price of $130,000 is deductible.

continued

Gross income	$ 435,500
Less: Salaries and wages	(150,000)
Building rent	(24,000)
§ 179 deduction	(130,000)
Insurance	(6,000)
Consulting fees	(6,000)
Utilities	(12,000)
Taxes and licenses	(6,000)
Advertising	(3,000)
Interest expense	(3,000)
Dues paid to Small Engine Repair Institute	(3,000)
Taxable income before the charitable contribution deduction	$ 92,500
Less: Charitable contributions	(3,000)
Taxable income	$ 89,500

As to Michael's rental properties, he will be required to report all associated rent income and expenses, including depreciation on the house he converted from personal use to rental use and on the rental condo he purchased.

What If?

Instead assume that Mr. Forney purchased and placed in service this year $142,000 of new machinery and equipment of the type that qualifies for the § 179 deduction. In addition, Michael thinks that he can justify increasing his salary to $115,500 because of special expertise he developed recently, which will increase total salaries and wages to $210,500. Michael still can elect to expense all $142,000 of the cost of the machinery and equipment under § 179. In other words, the machinery and equipment will not be depreciated using the additional first-year depreciation or regular MACRS rules. As a result of the increased salary and § 179 deductions, the charitable contribution deduction now is limited to $2,000. The remainder ($1,000) is carried over to the next tax year.

Gross income	$ 435,500
Less: Salaries and wages	(210,500)
Building rent	(24,000)
§ 179 deduction	(142,000)
Insurance	(6,000)
Consulting fees	(6,000)
Utilities	(12,000)
Taxes and licenses	(6,000)
Advertising	(3,000)
Interest expense	(3,000)
Dues paid to Small Engine Repair Institute	(3,000)
Taxable income before the charitable contribution deduction	$ 20,000
Less: Charitable contributions (limited to 10% of taxable income)	(2,000)
Taxable income	$ 18,000

Suggested Readings

Bradley T. Borden and Cali A. Lieberman, "Section 179(f) Deductions and Recapture of Costs of Qualified Real Property," *Journal of Taxation,* January 2014.

Wilton B. Hyman, "Finding Breaks for Business in the American Taxpayer Relief Act of 2012," *Business Entities,* July/August 2013.

Robert W. Jamison and Christopher W. Hesse, "Controlled Groups and the Sec. 179 Election for S Corporations," *The Tax Adviser,* November 2013.

John M. Malloy, Craig J. Langstraat, and James M. Plečnik, "Major Developments in Cost Segregation," *The Tax Adviser*, April 2014.

Kreig D. Mitchell, "The R&D Tax Credit for Start-Up Companies," *Practical Tax Strategies*, February 2012.

Debra T. Sinclair and Britton A. McKay, "Excess Compensation and the Independent Investor Test," *Practical Tax Strategies*, April 2013.

Key Terms

§ 179 expensing election, 5-29

Accelerated cost recovery system (ACRS), 5-21

Additional first-year depreciation, 5-28

Alternative depreciation system (ADS), 5-35

Amortization, 5-35

Capital gain property, 5-17

Charitable contribution, 5-17

Cost depletion, 5-37

Cost recovery, 5-21

Depletion, 5-36

Depreciation, 5-21

Domestic production activities deduction (DPAD), 5-14

Domestic production gross receipts (DPGR), 5-15

Half-year convention, 5-24

Intangible drilling and development costs (IDCs), 5-36

Listed property, 5-31

Mid-month convention, 5-27

Mid-quarter convention, 5-26

Modified accelerated cost recovery system (MACRS), 5-21

Modified adjusted gross income, 5-15

Ordinary and necessary, 5-2

Ordinary income property, 5-17

Percentage depletion, 5-37

Qualified production activities income (QPAI), 5-15

Reasonableness requirement, 5-3

Related-party transactions, 5-6

Research and experimental expenditures, 5-13

Residential rental real estate, 5-27

Startup expenditures, 5-11

W–2 wages, 5-16

Computational Exercises

1. **LO.2** Glenda, a calendar year and cash basis taxpayer, rents property from Janice. As part of the rental agreement, Glenda pays $8,400 rent on April 1, 2016, for the 12 months ending March 31, 2017.
   a. How much is Glenda's deduction for rent expense in 2016?
   b. Assume the same facts, except that the $8,400 is for 24 months rent ending March 31, 2018. How much is Glenda's deduction for rent expense in 2016?

2. **LO.3** Vella owns and operates an illegal gambling establishment. In connection with this activity, he has the following expenses during the year:

Rent	$ 24,000
Bribes	40,000
Travel expenses	4,000
Utilities	18,000
Wages	230,000
Payroll taxes	13,800
Property insurance	1,600
Illegal kickbacks	22,000

   What are Vella's total deductible expenses for tax purposes?

3. **LO.3** Stanford owns and operates two dry cleaning businesses. He travels to Boston to discuss acquiring a restaurant. Later in the month, he travels to New York to discuss acquiring a bakery. Stanford does not acquire the restaurant but does purchase the bakery on November 1, 2016. Stanford incurred the following expenses:

Total investigation costs related to the restaurant	$28,000
Total investigation costs related to the bakery	51,000

   What is the maximum amount Stanford can deduct in 2016 for investigation expenses?

4. **LO.4** Sandstorm Corporation decides to develop a new line of paints. The project begins in 2016. Sandstorm incurs the following expenses in 2016 in connection with the project:

Salaries	$85,000
Materials	30,000
Depreciation on equipment	12,500

The benefits from the project will be realized starting in July 2017. If Sandstorm Corporation chooses to defer and amortize its research and experimental expenditures over a period of 60 months, what are its related deductions in 2016 and 2017?

5. **LO.6** Tabitha sells real estate on March 2 for $260,000. The buyer, Ramona, pays the real estate taxes of $5,200 for the calendar year, which is the real estate property tax year. Assume that this is not a leap year.

   a. Determine the real estate taxes apportioned to and deductible by the seller, Tabitha, and the amount of taxes deductible by Ramona.

   b. Calculate Ramona's basis in the property and the amount realized by Tabitha from the sale.

6. **LO.7** Hamlet acquires a 7-year class asset on November 23, 2016, for $100,000. Hamlet does not elect immediate expensing under § 179. He does not claim any available additional first-year depreciation. Calculate Hamlet's cost recovery deductions for 2016 and 2017.

7. **LO.7** Lopez acquired a building on June 1, 2011, for $1 million. Calculate Lopez's cost recovery deduction for 2016 if the building is:

   a. Classified as residential rental real estate.

   b. Classified as nonresidential real estate.

8. **LO.7** In 2016, McKenzie purchased qualifying equipment for his business that cost $212,000. The taxable income of the business for the year is $5,600 before consideration of any § 179 deduction. Calculate McKenzie's § 179 expense deduction for 2016 and any carryover to 2017.

9. **LO.7** On April 5, 2016, Kinsey places in service a new automobile that cost $36,000. He does not elect § 179 expensing, and he elects not to take any available additional first-year depreciation. The car is used 70% for business and 30% for personal use in each tax year.

   Kinsey chooses the MACRS 200% declining-balance method of cost recovery (the auto is a 5-year asset). Assume the following luxury automobile limitations: year 1: $3,160; year 2: $5,100. Compute the total depreciation allowed for 2016 and 2017.

10. **LO.9** Jebali Company reports gross income of $340,000 and other property-related expenses of $229,000 and uses a depletion rate of 14%. Calculate Jebali's depletion allowance for the current year.

Problems

11. **LO.2** Duck, an accrual basis corporation, sponsored a rock concert on December 29, 2016. Gross receipts were $300,000. The following expenses were incurred and paid as indicated:

Expense		Payment Date
Rental of coliseum	$ 25,000	December 21, 2016
Cost of goods sold:		
Food	30,000	December 30, 2016
Souvenirs	60,000	December 30, 2016

Expense		Payment Date
Performers	$100,000	January 5, 2017
Cleaning of coliseum	10,000	February 1, 2017

Because the coliseum was not scheduled to be used again until January 15, the company with which Duck had contracted did not perform the cleanup until January 8–10, 2017.

Calculate Duck's net income from the concert for tax purposes for 2016.

12. **LO.2** Which of the following are related parties under § 267?

Father
Brother
Niece
Uncle
Cousin
Grandson
Corporation and a 45% shareholder
Corporation and a 55% shareholder

13. **LO.2, 3** The Robin Corporation is owned as follows:

Isabelle	26%
Peter, Isabelle's husband	19%
Sonya, Isabelle's mother	15%
Reggie, Isabelle's father	25%
Quinn, an unrelated party	15%

Robin is on the accrual basis, and Isabelle and Peter are on the cash basis. Isabelle and Peter each loaned the Robin Corporation $40,000 out of their separate funds. On December 31, 2016, Robin accrued interest at 7% on both loans. The interest was paid on February 4, 2017. What is the tax treatment of this interest expense/income to Isabelle, Peter, and Robin?

Decision Making

Communications

14. **LO.2, 3** Brittany Callihan sold stock (basis of $184,000) to her son, Ridge, for $160,000, the fair market value.

a. What are the tax consequences to Brittany?

b. What are the tax consequences to Ridge if he later sells the stock for $190,000? For $152,000? For $174,000?

c. Write a letter to Brittany in which you inform her of the tax consequences if she sells the stock to Ridge for $160,000. Explain how a sales transaction could be structured that would produce better tax consequences for her. Brittany's address is 32 Country Lane, Lawrence, KS 66045.

15. **LO.2, 3** For each of the following independent transactions, calculate the recognized gain or loss to the seller and the adjusted basis to the buyer.

a. Bonnie sells Parchment, Inc. stock (adjusted basis $17,000) to Phillip, her brother, for its fair market value of $12,000.

b. Amos sells land (adjusted basis $85,000) to his nephew, Boyd, for its fair market value of $70,000.

c. Susan sells a tax-exempt bond (adjusted basis $20,000) to her wholly owned corporation for its fair market value of $19,000.

d. Ron sells a business truck (adjusted basis $20,000) that he uses in his sole proprietorship to his cousin, Agnes, for its fair market value of $18,500.

e. Martha sells her partnership interest (adjusted basis $175,000) in Pearl Partnership to her adult daughter, Kim, for $220,000.

16. **LO.2, 3** Lupe, a cash basis taxpayer, owns 55% of the stock of Jasper Corporation, a calendar year accrual basis C corporation. On December 31, 2016, Jasper accrues a performance bonus of $100,000 to Lupe that it pays to him on January 15,

2017. In which year can Jasper deduct the bonus? In which year must Lupe include the bonus in gross income?

17. **LO.2, 3** Broadbill Corporation, a calendar year C corporation, has two unrelated cash method shareholders: Marcia owns 51% of the stock, and Zack owns the remaining 49%. Each shareholder is employed by the corporation at an annual salary of $240,000. During 2016, Broadbill paid each shareholder-employee $220,000 of his or her annual salary, with the remaining $20,000 paid in January 2017. How much of the 2016 salaries for Marcia and Zack is deductible by Broadbill in 2016 if the corporation is:

a. A cash method taxpayer?

b. An accrual method taxpayer?

18. **LO.3** Ted, an agent for Waxwing Corporation, which is an airline manufacturer,   Issue ID
is negotiating a sale with a representative of the U.S. government and with a representative of a developing country. Waxwing has sufficient capacity to handle only one of the orders. Both orders will have the same contract price. Ted believes that if Waxwing authorizes a $500,000 payment to the representative of the foreign country, he can guarantee the sale. He is not sure that he can obtain the same result with the U.S. government. Identify the relevant tax issues for Waxwing.

19. **LO.3** Linda operates an illegal gambling operation and incurs the following expenses. Which of these expenses can reduce her taxable income?

a. Bribes paid to city employees.

b. Salaries to employees.

c. Security cameras.

d. Kickbacks to police.

e. Rent on an office.

f. Depreciation on office furniture and equipment.

g. Tenant's casualty insurance.

h. Utilities.

20. **LO.3** Cardinal Corporation is a trucking firm that operates in the mid-Atlantic   Ethics and Equity
states. One of Cardinal's major customers frequently ships goods between Charlotte and Baltimore. Occasionally, the customer sends last-minute shipments that are outbound for Europe on a freighter sailing from Baltimore. To satisfy the delivery schedule in these cases, Cardinal's drivers must substantially exceed the speed limit. Cardinal pays for any related speeding tickets. During the past year, two drivers had their licenses suspended for 30 days each for driving at such excessive speeds. Cardinal continues to pay each driver's salary during the suspension periods.

Cardinal believes that it is necessary to conduct its business in this manner if it is to be profitable, maintain the support of the drivers, and maintain the goodwill of customers. Evaluate Cardinal's business practices.

21. **LO.3** Quail Corporation anticipates that being positively perceived by the individual who is elected mayor will be beneficial for business. Therefore, Quail contributes to the campaigns of both the Democratic and Republican candidates. The Republican candidate is elected mayor. Can Quail deduct any of the political contributions it made? Explain.

22. **LO.3** Melissa, the owner of a sole proprietorship, does not provide health insurance for her 20 employees. She plans to spend $1,500 lobbying in opposition to legislation that would require her to provide such insurance. Discuss the tax advantages and disadvantages of paying the $1,500 to a professional lobbyist rather than spending the $1,500 on in-house lobbying expenditures.

Issue ID   23. **LO.3** Ella owns 60% of the stock of Peach, Inc. The stock has declined in value since she purchased it five years ago. She is going to sell 5% of the stock to a relative. Ella is also going to make a gift of 10% of the stock to another relative. Identify the relevant tax issues for Ella.

24. **LO.3** Jarret owns City of Charleston bonds with an adjusted basis of $190,000. During the year, he receives interest payments of $3,800. Jarret partially financed the purchase of the bonds by borrowing $100,000 at 5% interest. Jarret's interest payments on the loan this year are $4,900, and his principal payments are $1,100.

a. Should Jarret report any interest income this year? Explain.

b. Can Jarret deduct any interest expense this year? Explain.

25. **LO.3** Egret Corporation, a calendar year C corporation, was formed on March 6, 2016, and opened for business on July 1, 2016. After its formation but prior to opening for business, Egret incurred the following expenditures:

Accounting	$ 7,000
Advertising	14,500
Employee payroll	11,000
Rent	8,000
Utilities	1,000

What is the maximum amount of these expenditures that Egret can deduct in 2016?

26. **LO.3** Nancy, the owner of a very successful hotel chain in the Southeast, is exploring the possibility of expanding the chain into a city in the Northeast. She incurs $35,000 of expenses associated with this investigation. Based on the regulatory environment for hotels in the city, she decides not to expand. During the year, she also investigates opening a restaurant that will be part of a national restaurant chain. Her expenses for this are $53,000. The restaurant begins operations on September 1. Determine the amount Nancy can deduct in the current year for investigating these two businesses.

27. **LO.4** Blue Corporation, a manufacturing company, decided to develop a new line of merchandise. The project began in 2016. Blue had the following expenses in connection with the project:

	2016	2017
Salaries	$500,000	$600,000
Materials	90,000	70,000
Insurance	8,000	11,000
Utilities	6,000	8,000
Cost of inspection of materials for quality control	7,000	6,000
Promotion expenses	11,000	18,000
Advertising	–0–	20,000
Equipment depreciation	15,000	14,000
Cost of market survey	8,000	–0–

The new product will be introduced for sale beginning in July 2018. Determine the amount of the deduction for research and experimental expenditures for 2016, 2017, and 2018 if:

a. Blue Corporation elects to expense the research and experimental expenditures.

b. Blue Corporation elects to amortize the research and experimental expenditures over 60 months.

28. **LO.5** Sarah Ham, operating as a sole proprietor, manufactures printers in the United States. For 2016, the proprietorship has QPAI of $400,000. Sarah's modified AGI was $350,000. The W–2 wages paid by the proprietorship to employees engaged in the qualified domestic production activity were $60,000. Calculate Sarah's DPAD for 2016.

29. **LO.5** In 2016, Rose, Inc., has QPAI of $4 million and taxable income of $3 million. Rose pays independent contractors $500,000. Rose's W–2 wages are $600,000, but only $400,000 of the wages are paid to employees engaged in qualified domestic production activities.

    a. Calculate the DPAD for Rose, Inc., for 2016.

    b. What suggestions could you make to enable Rose to increase its DPAD?

Decision Making

30. **LO.6** In 2016, Gray Corporation, a calendar year C corporation, holds a $75,000 charitable contribution carryover from a gift made in 2011. Gray is contemplating a gift of land to a qualified charity in either 2016 or 2017. Gray purchased the land as an investment five years ago for $100,000 (current fair market value is $250,000).

    Before considering any charitable deduction, Gray projects taxable income of $1 million for 2016 and $1.2 million for 2017. Should Gray make the gift of the land to charity in 2016 or in 2017? Provide support for your answer.

Decision Making

31. **LO.6** Dan Simms is the president and sole shareholder of Simms Corporation, 1121 Madison Street, Seattle, WA 98121. Dan plans for the corporation to make a charitable contribution to the University of Washington, a qualified public charity. He will have the corporation donate Jaybird Corporation stock, held for five years, with a basis of $11,000 and a fair market value of $25,000. Dan projects a $310,000 net profit for Simms Corporation in 2016 and a $100,000 net profit in 2017. Dan calls you on December 11, 2016, and asks whether Simms should make the contribution in 2016 or 2017. Write a letter advising Dan about the timing of the contribution.

Decision Making

Communications

32. **LO.6** On December 23, 2016, the directors of Partridge Corporation, an accrual basis calendar year taxpayer, authorized a cash contribution of $10,000 to the American Cancer Association. The payment is made on April 14, 2017. Can Partridge deduct the charitable contribution in 2016? Explain.

33. **LO.6** Aquamarine Corporation, a calendar year C corporation, makes the following donations to qualified charitable organizations during the current year:

	Adjusted Basis	Fair Market Value
Painting held four years as an investment, to a church, which sold it immediately	$15,000	$25,000
Apple stock held two years as an investment, to United Way, which sold it immediately	40,000	90,000
Canned groceries held one month as inventory, to Catholic Meals for the Poor	10,000	17,000

Determine the amount of Aquamarine Corporation's charitable deduction for the current year. (Ignore the taxable income limitation.)

34. **LO.6** Joseph Thompson is president and sole shareholder of Jay Corporation. In December 2016, Joe asks your advice regarding a charitable contribution he plans to have the corporation make to the University of Maine, a qualified public charity. Joe is considering the following alternatives as charitable contributions in December 2016:

Decision Making

Communications

	Fair Market Value
(1) Cash donation	$200,000
(2) Unimproved land held for six years ($110,000 basis)	200,000
(3) Maize Corporation stock held for eight months ($140,000 basis)	200,000
(4) Brown Corporation stock held for nine years ($360,000 basis)	200,000

Joe has asked you to help him decide which of these potential contributions will be most advantageous taxwise. Jay Corporation's taxable income is $3.5 million before considering the contribution. Rank the four alternatives and write a letter to Mr. Thompson communicating your advice. The corporation's address is 1442 Main Street, Freeport, ME 04032.

35. **LO.7** On November 4, 2014, Blue Company acquired an asset (27.5-year residential real property) for $200,000 for use in its business. In 2014 and 2015, respectively, Blue took $642 and $5,128 of cost recovery. These amounts were incorrect; Blue applied the wrong percentages (i.e., those for 39-year rather than 27.5-year property). Blue should have taken $910 and $7,272 of cost recovery in 2014 and 2015, respectively.

     On January 1, 2016, the asset was sold for $180,000. Calculate the gain or loss on the sale of the asset for that year.

36. **LO.7** Juan, a sole proprietor, acquires a new 5-year class asset on March 14, 2016, for $200,000. This is the only asset Juan acquired during the year. He does not elect immediate expensing under § 179. Juan does not claim any available additional first-year depreciation. On July 15, 2017, Juan sells the asset.

    a. Determine Juan's cost recovery for 2016.

    b. Determine Juan's cost recovery for 2017.

37. **LO.7** Debra acquired the following new assets during 2016:

Date	Asset	Cost
April 11	Furniture	$40,000
July 28	Trucks	40,000
November 3	Computers	70,000

Determine Debra's cost recovery deductions for the current year. Debra does not elect immediate expensing under § 179. She does not claim any available additional first-year depreciation.

38. **LO.7** On May 5, 2016, Christy purchased and placed in service a hotel. The hotel cost $10.8 million. Calculate Christy's cost recovery deductions for 2016 and for 2026.

39. **LO.7** Janice acquired an apartment building on June 4, 2016, for $1.6 million. The value of the land is $300,000. Janice sold the apartment building on November 29, 2022.

    a. Determine Janice's cost recovery deduction for 2016.

    b. Determine Janice's cost recovery deduction for 2022.

Decision Making   40. **LO.7** Lori, who is single, purchased 5-year class property for $200,000 and 7-year class property for $400,000 on May 20, 2016. Lori expects the taxable income derived from her business (without regard to the amount expensed under § 179) to be about $800,000. Lori wants to elect immediate § 179 expensing, but she doesn't know which asset she should expense under § 179. She does not claim any available additional first-year depreciation.

    a. Determine Lori's total deduction if the § 179 expense is first taken with respect to the 5-year class asset.

    b. Determine Lori's total deduction if the § 179 expense is first taken with respect to the 7-year class asset.

    c. What is your advice to Lori?

    d. Assume that Lori is in the 25% marginal tax bracket and that she uses § 179 on the 7-year asset. Determine the present value of the tax savings from the depreciation deductions for both assets. See Appendix F for present value factors, and assume a 6% discount rate.

    e. Assume the same facts as in part (d), except that Lori decides not to use § 179 on either asset. What is the present value of the tax savings generated by using the § 179 deduction on the 7-year asset?

41. **LO.7** Olga is the proprietor of a small business. In 2016, the business's income, before consideration of any cost recovery or § 179 deduction, is $250,000.

     Olga spends $600,000 on new 7-year class assets and elects to take the § 179 deduction on them. She does not claim any available additional first-year depreciation. Olga's cost recovery deduction for 2016, except for the cost recovery with respect to the new 7-year assets, is $95,000. Determine Olga's total cost recovery for 2016 with respect to the 7-year class assets and the amount of any § 179 carryforward.

42. **LO.7** On June 5, 2015, Dan purchased and placed in service a 7-year class asset costing $550,000. Determine the maximum deductions that Dan can claim with respect to this asset in 2015 and 2016.

43. **LO.7** Jabari Johnson is considering acquiring an automobile at the beginning of 2016 that he will use 100% of the time as a taxi. The purchase price of the automobile is $35,000. Johnson has heard of cost recovery limits on automobiles and wants to know the maximum amount of the $35,000 he can deduct in the first year.
    Write a letter to Jabari in which you present your calculations. Also prepare a memo for the tax files, summarizing your analysis. Johnson's address is 100 Morningside, Clinton, MS 39058.

Communications

44. **LO.7** On October 15, 2016, Jon purchased and placed in service a used car. The purchase price was $25,000. This was the only business-use asset Jon acquired in 2016. He used the car 80% of the time for business and 20% for personal use. Jon used the MACRS statutory percentage method. Calculate the total deduction Jon may take for 2016 with respect to the car.

45. **LO.7** On June 5, 2015, Leo purchased and placed in service a new car that cost $20,000. The business-use percentage for the car is always 100%. Leo claims any available additional first-year depreciation. Compute Leo's cost recovery deduction for 2015 and 2016.

46. **LO.7** On May 28, 2016, Mary purchased and placed in service a new $20,000 car. The car was used 60% for business, 20% for production of income, and 20% for personal use in 2016. In 2017, the usage changed to 40% for business, 30% for production of income, and 30% for personal use. Mary did not elect immediate expensing under § 179. She did not claim any available additional first-year depreciation. Compute Mary's cost recovery deduction and any cost recovery recapture in 2017.

Critical Thinking

47. **LO.7** In 2016, Muhammad purchased a new computer for $16,000. The computer is used 100% for business. Muhammad did not make a § 179 election with respect to the computer. He does not claim any available additional first-year depreciation. If Muhammad uses the MACRS statutory percentage method, determine his cost recovery deduction for 2016 for computing taxable income and for computing his alternative minimum tax.

48. **LO.7** Jamie purchased $100,000 of new office furniture for her business in June of the current year. Jamie understands that if she elects to use ADS to compute her regular income tax, there will be no difference between the cost recovery for computing the regular income tax and the AMT.

    a.   Jamie wants to know the present value of the *tax cost*, after three years, of using ADS rather than MACRS. Assume that Jamie does not elect § 179 expensing, she does not claim any additional first-year depreciation, and her marginal tax rate is 28%. See Appendix F for present value factors, and assume a 6% discount rate.

    b.   What is the present value of the *tax savings/costs* that result over the life of the asset if Jamie uses MACRS rather than ADS?

Decision Making

49. **LO.8** Mike Saxon is negotiating the purchase of a business. The final purchase price has been agreed upon, but the allocation of the purchase price to the assets is still being discussed. Appraisals on a warehouse range from $1,200,000 to $1,500,000. If a value of $1,200,000 is used for the warehouse, the remainder of the purchase price, $800,000, will be allocated to goodwill. If $1,500,000 is allocated to the warehouse, goodwill will be $500,000.
    Mike wants to know what effect each alternative will have on cost recovery and amortization during the first year. Under the agreement, Mike will take over the business on January 1 of next year. Write a letter to Mike in which you present your calculations and recommendation. Also prepare a memo for the tax files. Mike's address is 200 Rolling Hills Drive, Shavertown, PA 18708.

Decision Making

Communications

Ethics and Equity   50. **LO.9** Sam Jones owns a granite stone quarry. When he acquired the land, Sam allocated $800,000 of the purchase price to the quarry's recoverable mineral reserves, which were estimated at 10 million tons of granite stone. Based on these estimates, the cost depletion was $.08 per ton. In April of the current year, Sam received a letter from the State Department of Highways notifying him that part of his property was being condemned so that the state could build a new road. At that time, the recoverable mineral reserves had an adjusted basis of $600,000 and 7.5 million tons of granite rock. Sam estimates that the land being condemned contains about 2 million tons of granite. Therefore, for the current year, Sam has computed his cost depletion at $.11 per ton [$600,000/(7,500,000 − 2,000,000)]. Evaluate the appropriateness of what Sam is doing.

51. **LO.9** Wes acquired a mineral interest during the year for $10 million. A geological survey estimated that 250,000 tons of the mineral remained in the deposit. During the year, 80,000 tons were mined, and 45,000 tons were sold for $12 million. Other related expenses amounted to $5 million. Assuming that the mineral depletion rate is 22%, calculate Wes's lowest taxable income, after any depletion deductions.

BRIDGE DISCIPLINE

Decision Making   1. Sparrow Corporation is considering the acquisition of an asset for use in its business over the next five years. However, Sparrow must decide whether it would be better served by leasing the asset or buying it. An appropriate asset could be purchased for $15,000, and it would qualify as a three-year asset under the MACRS classification. Assume that the election to expense assets under § 179 is not available, that any available additional first-year depreciation is not claimed, and that the asset is not expected to have a salvage value at the end of its use by Sparrow. Alternatively, Sparrow could lease the asset for a $3,625 annual cost over the 5-year period. If Sparrow is in the 34% tax bracket, would you recommend that Sparrow buy or lease the asset? In your calculations, assume that 10% is an appropriate discount factor.

Decision Making   2. Lark Corporation is considering the acquisition of an asset for use in its business over the next five years. However, Lark must decide whether it would be better served by leasing the asset or buying it. An appropriate asset could be purchased for $15,000, and it would qualify as a three-year asset under the MACRS classification. Assume that the election to expense assets under § 179 is made, but any available additional first-year depreciation is not claimed, and that the asset is not expected to have a salvage value at the end of its use by Lark. Alternatively, Lark could lease the asset for a $3,625 annual cost over the 5-year period. If Lark is in the 34% tax bracket, would you recommend that Lark buy or lease the asset? In your calculations, assume that 10% is an appropriate discount factor.

3. Wayside Fruit Company is a sole proprietorship owned by Neil Stephenson. The company's records reflect the following:

Sales revenue	$185,000
Operating expenses	125,000
Depreciation expense for book	13,000
Cost recovery allowance for tax	17,500
Loss on the sale of delivery truck to Neil's brother	5,000
Amount paid to fruit inspector to overlook below-standard fruit shipped to various vendors	3,000

Compute the net income before tax for book purposes and the amount of taxable income for Wayside Fruit Company.

Research Problems

Note: Solutions to Research Problems can be prepared by using the Checkpoint® Student Edition online research product, which is available to accompany this text. It is also possible to prepare solutions to the Research Problems by using tax research materials found in a standard tax library.

THOMSON REUTERS
CHECKPOINT®
Student Edition

Research Problem 1. Gray Chemical Company manufactured pesticides that were toxic. Over the course of several years, the toxic waste contaminated the air and water around the company's plant. Several employees suffered toxic poisoning, and the Environmental Protection Agency cited the company for violations. In court, the judge found Gray guilty and imposed fines of $15 million. The company voluntarily set up a charitable fund for the purpose of bettering the environment and funded it with $8 million. The company incurred legal expenses in setting up the foundation and defending itself in court. The court reduced the fine from $15 million to $7 million.

Communications

Gray deducted the $8 million paid to the foundation and the legal expenses incurred. The IRS disallowed both deductions on the grounds that the payment was, in fact, a fine and in violation of public policy.

Gray's president, Ted Jones, has contacted you regarding the deductibility of the $7 million fine, the $8 million payment to the foundation, and the legal fees. Write a letter to Mr. Jones that contains your advice, and prepare a memo for the tax files. Gray's address is 200 Lincoln Center, Omaha, NE 68182.

Partial list of research aids:
§§ 162(a) and (f).
Reg. § 1.162–21(b).

Research Problem 2. In 2012, Jed James began planting a vineyard. The costs of the land preparation, labor, rootstock, and planting were capitalized. The land preparation costs do not include any nondepreciable land costs. In 2016, when the plants became viable, Jed placed the vineyard in service. Jed wants to know whether he can claim a deduction under § 179 on his 2016 income tax return for the 2012 costs for planting the vineyard.

Research Problem 3. Juan owns a business that acquires exotic automobiles that are high-tech, state-of-the-art vehicles with unique design features or equipment. The exotic automobiles are not licensed, nor are they set up to be used on the road. Rather, the cars are used exclusively for car shows or related promotional photography. With respect to the exotic automobiles, can Juan take a cost recovery deduction on his Federal income tax return? Prepare an outline for your classmates addressing this issue.

Communications

Partial list of research aids:
Bruce Selig, 70 TCM 1125, T.C.Memo. 1995–519.

Use the tax resources of the Internet to address the following questions. Do not restrict your search to the Web, but include a review of newsgroups and general reference materials, practitioner sites and resources, primary sources of the tax law, chat rooms and discussion groups, and other opportunities.

Internet Activity

Research Problem 4. Many states that have corporate income taxes "piggyback" onto the Federal corporate income tax calculation. In other words, these states' corporate income tax calculations incorporate many of the Federal calculations and deductions to make both compliance and verification of tax liability easier. However, some state legislatures were concerned that the domestic production activities deduction, if allowed for state tax purposes, would result in significant revenue losses. Determine whether states with corporate income taxes allow or disallow the domestic production activities deduction in the calculation of the state's corporate income tax liability. Be sure to state the sources for your answer.

Communications   **Research Problem 5.** Changes to depreciation systems often are discussed by policy-makers and observers of the tax system. Outline the terms and policy objectives of one of the changes currently proposed by the Treasury, a member of Congress, or a tax policy think tank.

Roger CPA Review Questions

1. Regarding the tax treatment of a business's research and experimental (R&E) expenditures, which of the following statements is true?

    a. A common reason for electing tax deferral for such expenses is the expectation of lower tax rates in the future.

    b. Expenses associated with the acquisition of land upon which a purpose-built R&E facility is constructed are considered R&E expenditures for tax purposes.

    c. Companies generally prefer to expense R&E costs immediately, but may elect instead to defer and amortize such costs over a minimum of 60 months.

    d. Companies may elect to immediately expense R&E costs incurred in the first applicable taxable year and all future years through an appropriate filing with the IRS.

2. Identify the correct statement below regarding the domestic production activities deduction (DPAD).

    a. Qualified production activities income (QPAI) is calculated by applying a percentage to net income from an IRS rate table based on specific criteria.

    b. The DPAD cannot exceed attributable W–2 wages paid.

    c. A sole proprietorship cannot claim the DPAD, but a partnership or an S corporation with more than one shareholder can.

    d. Taxable income for the purposes of calculating or amending the DPAD includes any net operating loss (NOL) deduction, such as an NOL carryforward or NOL carryback.

3. Newton, a business owner, signed a ten-year lease beginning in July of 2015, and immediately paid rent for the remainder of 2015, all of 2016, and all of 2017. How much of the rent paid at the lease signing can be declared as a business expense on Schedule C of Newton's 2016 tax return?

    a. All of it

    b. The July 2015–June 2016 portion only

    c. None of it

    d. The 2015 portion only

4. A sale between which of the following could trigger a gain or a loss for Federal tax purposes?

    a. Husband and wife

    c. Majority shareholder and corporation

    b. Cousin and cousin

    d. Ancestor and descendent

5. Quanti Co., a calendar year taxpayer, purchased equipment for $5,000 on December 21, 2016, representing the company's **only** purchase of tangible personal property that took place during 2016. On its 2016 tax return, how many months of MACRS depreciation may Quanti Co. claim on the tools?

    a. One and a half months

    c. Six months

    b. One month

    d. None

6. Which of the following is **correct** about depreciation under Federal tax law?

   I.   The recovery period is longer than the useful life of the asset.
   II. There are different recovery periods for new and used property.
   III. Salvage values are ignored.

   a. I and II only   c. III only
   b. II only   d. I, II, and III

7. Joe purchased a van on February 1, 2016, for use in his business, Crew Airport Transport. The van was purchased for $30,000, has an estimated useful life of 10 years, and has a salvage value of $2,000. No other assets were put into service that year. What is Joe's MACRS depreciation for the van in 2016?

   a. $2,567   c. $10,500
   b. $6,000   d. $10,267

8. Dolly purchased and placed into service qualifying depreciable property in 2016 at a total cost of $2,250,000. Dolly has elected to take the § 179 deduction. What is Dolly's § 179 deduction for 2016?

   a. $0   c. $500,000
   b. $260,000   d. $1,750,000

9. In 2016, Christa purchased and placed into service five-year assets at a total cost of $2,250,000. If Christa elects both the § 179 deduction and additional first-year bonus depreciation, but does not elect the straight-line method, what is Christa's depreciation expense for tax purposes for the year, assuming a half-year convention?

   a. $260,000   c. $1,250,000
   b. $500,000   d. $1,454,000

10. Orange, Inc., a calendar year C corporation, has $800,000 of qualified production activities income (QPAI) and $950,000 of total taxable income in 2016. All of the QDPAI was produced by Orange's manufacturing plant, which relies mainly on a temporary employment agency for its workforce, employing only two W–2 employees who in aggregate earned $140,000 in 2016. Orange also has an office in Mexico, which is unrelated to its domestic manufacturing plant and which employs one W–2 employee, who earned $75,000 in 2016. What amount of domestic production activities deduction may Orange claim on its 2016 corporate tax return?

    a. $73,350
    b. $72,000
    c. Depends on wages paid by employment agency
    d. $70,000

Losses and Loss Limitations

LEARNING OBJECTIVES: *After completing Chapter 6, you should be able to:*

LO.1 Determine the amount, classification, and timing of the bad debt deduction.

LO.2 State and illustrate the tax treatment of worthless securities, including § 1244 stock.

LO.3 Identify a casualty and determine the amount, classification, and timing of casualty and theft losses.

LO.4 Describe the impact of the net operating loss carryback and carryover provisions on previous and subsequent years' taxable income.

LO.5 Explain the tax shelter problem and the reasons for at-risk and passive activity loss limitations.

LO.6 Describe how the at-risk limitation and the passive activity loss rules limit deductions for losses and identify taxpayers subject to these restrictions.

LO.7 Discuss the definitions of activity, material participation, and rental activity under the passive activity loss rules.

LO.8 Determine the relationship between the at-risk and passive activity loss limitations.

LO.9 Explain the special treatment available to real estate activities.

LO.10 Determine the consequences of the disposition of passive activities.

CHAPTER OUTLINE

TAX TALK *The income tax has made more liars out of the American people than golf has. Even when you make a tax form out on the level, you don't know when it's through if you are a crook or a martyr.* —WILL ROGERS

THE BIG PICTURE

RECEIVING TAX BENEFITS FROM LOSSES

Robyn, an unmarried, cash basis and calendar year taxpayer, is nearing the end of a year that she would like to forget. Several years ago, she loaned $25,000 to her friend Jamil to enable him to start a business. Jamil had made scheduled payments of $7,000 (including $1,000 of interest) when he suddenly died in January. At the time of his death, he was insolvent, and Robyn's attempts to collect the debt were fruitless.

Last year, Robyn invested $60,000 by purchasing stock in Owl Corporation, a closely held small business corporation started by her brother. However, the company declared bankruptcy in May of this year, and the bankruptcy trustee informed the shareholders that they should not expect to receive anything from the company.

Robyn has owned and operated a bookstore as a sole proprietorship for the past 10 years. The bookstore has been profitable, producing annual taxable income of approximately $75,000. However, due to the growth of online vendors and e-books, the business lost $180,000 this year.

In September, a tornado caused a large oak tree to blow over onto Robyn's house. The cost of removing the tree and making repairs to the house was $32,000. Robyn received a check for $25,000 from her insurance company. Her adjusted basis for the house was $280,000.

Finally, Robyn invested $20,000 for a 10 percent interest in a limited partnership that owns and operates orange groves in Florida. Due to a hard freeze that damaged much of the fruit, the partnership lost $200,000 and allocated $20,000 of ordinary loss to Robyn.

Robyn has come to you for tax advice and would like to know the tax ramifications of each of the events and transactions listed above.

Read the chapter and formulate your response.

Chapter 5 introduced rules governing the deductibility of trade or business expenses. This chapter extends the notion of deductibility to losses occurring in the course of business operations. In particular, special rules concerning the tax treatment of bad debts, casualty losses, and operating losses are reviewed. In addition, tax shelters and the rules that limit their usefulness as tax avoidance strategies are discussed.

Determine the amount, classification, and timing of the bad debt deduction.

6-1 BAD DEBTS

If a taxpayer lends money or purchases a debt instrument and the debt is not repaid, a **bad debt** deduction is allowed. Similarly, if an accrual basis taxpayer sells goods or provides services on credit and the account receivable subsequently becomes worthless, a bad debt deduction is permitted.[1] No deduction is allowed, however, for a bad debt arising from the sale of a product or service when the taxpayer is on the cash basis because no income is reported until the cash has been collected. Permitting a bad debt deduction for a cash basis taxpayer would amount to a double deduction because the expenses of the product or service rendered are deducted when payments are made to suppliers and to employees or when the sale is made.

> **EXAMPLE 1**
>
> Ella, a sole proprietor, operates a business named Executive Accounting and Tax Services. Last year, Pat hired Ella to help him with the accounting for his small business. Ella also prepared the S corporation income tax return for the business and Pat's personal income tax return. Ella billed Pat $8,000 for the services she performed. Pat has never paid the bill, his business no longer exists, and his whereabouts are unknown.
>
> If Ella is an *accrual basis taxpayer*, she includes the $8,000 in income when the services are performed. When she determines that Pat's account will not be collected, she deducts the $8,000 as a bad debt.
>
> If Ella is a *cash basis taxpayer*, she does not include the $8,000 in income until payment is received. When she determines that Pat's account will not be collected, she cannot deduct the $8,000 as a bad debt expense because it was never recognized as income.

> **The Big Picture**
>
> **EXAMPLE 2**
>
> Return to the facts of *The Big Picture* on p. 6-1. Because Robyn is a cash basis taxpayer, she cannot take as a bad debt deduction any unpaid accrued interest on the loan to her friend, Jamil, because it was never recognized as income.

6-1a Specific Charge-Off Method

Most taxpayers are required to use the **specific charge-off method** when accounting for bad debts. However, some financial institutions are permitted to use an alternative **reserve method** for computing bad debt deductions.

A taxpayer using the specific charge-off method may claim a deduction when a specific *business* debt becomes either partially or wholly worthless or when a specific *nonbusiness* debt becomes wholly worthless.[2] For a business debt, the taxpayer must have evidence that the debt is partially worthless and must demonstrate the amount of worthlessness.

If a business debt previously deducted as partially worthless becomes totally worthless in a future year, only the remainder not previously deducted can be deducted in the future year.

In the case of total worthlessness, a deduction is allowed for the entire amount in the year that the debt becomes worthless. The amount of the deduction depends on the taxpayer's basis in the bad debt. If the debt arose from the sale of services or products and the face amount was previously included in income, that amount is deductible. If the

[1] Reg. § 1.166–1(e). [2] § 166(a).

TAX FACT Just How Good Is Your Credit?

To be successful, a business must generate sales among customers who are willing and able to pay their obligations. Nonetheless, if a sale is made and it is determined that the related account receivable is uncollectible, an accrual method business is allowed to claim a bad debt deduction. Recently, corporations claimed bad debt deductions of nearly $194 billion against business receipts of about $26 trillion.

Source: 2012 Corporation Income Tax Returns; Table 2—Balance Sheet, Income Statement, and Selected Other Items, by Size of Total Assets; 2015.

taxpayer purchased the debt, the deduction equals the amount the taxpayer paid for the debt instrument.

Determining when a bad debt becomes worthless can be a difficult task. Legal proceedings need not be initiated against the debtor when the surrounding facts indicate that such action will not result in collection.

EXAMPLE 3

In 2014, Partridge Company lent $1,000 to Kay, who agreed to repay the loan in two years. In 2016, Kay disappeared after the note became delinquent. If a reasonable investigation by Partridge indicates that Kay cannot be found or that a suit against Kay would not result in collection, Partridge can deduct the $1,000 in 2016.

Bankruptcy is generally an indication of at least partial worthlessness of a debt. Bankruptcy may create worthlessness before the settlement date. If this is the case, the deduction may be taken in the year of worthlessness.

EXAMPLE 4

In Example 3, assume that Kay filed for personal bankruptcy in 2015 and that the debt is a business debt. At that time, Partridge learned that unsecured creditors (including Partridge) were ultimately expected to receive 20 cents on the dollar. In 2016, settlement is made, and Partridge receives only $150. Partridge should deduct $800 ($1,000 loan − $200 expected settlement) in 2015 and $50 in 2016 ($200 balance − $150 proceeds).

If a receivable is written off (deducted) as uncollectible and is subsequently collected during the same tax year, the write-off entry is reversed. If a receivable has been written off (deducted) as uncollectible, collection in a later tax year may result in income being recognized. Income will result if the deduction yielded a tax benefit in the year it was taken (the tax benefit rule).

Concept Summary 6.1 provides a summary of the tax treatment of bad debts using the specific charge-off method.

Concept Summary 6.1

The Tax Treatment of Bad Debts Using the Specific Charge-Off Method

	Business Bad Debts	Nonbusiness Bad Debts
Timing of deduction	A deduction is allowed when the debt becomes either partially or wholly worthless.	A deduction is allowed *only* when the debt becomes wholly worthless.
Character of deduction	The bad debt may be deducted as an ordinary loss.	The bad debt is classified as a short-term capital loss, subject to the $3,000 capital loss limitation for individuals.
Recovery of amounts previously deducted	If the account recovered was written off during the current tax year, the write-off entry is reversed. If the account was written off in a previous tax year, income is created subject to the tax benefit rule.	If the account recovered was written off during the current tax year, the write-off entry is reversed. If the account was written off in a previous tax year, income is created subject to the tax benefit rule.

6-1b **Business versus Nonbusiness Bad Debts**

The nature of a debt depends upon whether the lender is engaged in the business of lending money or whether there is a proximate relationship between the creation of the debt and the *lender's* trade or business. Where either of these conditions is true, a bad debt is classified as a `business bad debt`. If these conditions are not met, a bad debt is classified as a `nonbusiness bad debt`. The use to which the borrowed funds are put is of no consequence when making this classification decision.

The Big Picture

Return to the facts of *The Big Picture* on p. 6-1. Robyn loaned her friend Jamil $25,000. Jamil used the money to start a business, which subsequently failed. When Jamil died after having made principal payments of $6,000 on the loan, he was insolvent.

Even though the proceeds of the loan were used in a business, the loan is a nonbusiness bad debt because the business was Jamil's, not Robyn's, and Robyn is not in the business of lending money.

The nonbusiness bad debt provisions are *not* applicable to a business entity (e.g., a corporation or partnership). It is assumed that any loans made by a business are related to its trade or business. Therefore, any bad debts resulting from loans made by a business are automatically business bad debts.

EXAMPLE 6

Horace operates a sole proprietorship that sells premium electronic equipment. Horace uses the accrual method to account for sales of the electronic equipment. During the year, he sold $4,000 of equipment to Herbie on credit. Later that year, the account receivable becomes worthless. The loan is a business bad debt, because the debt was related to Horace's business.

The distinction between a business bad debt and a nonbusiness bad debt is important. A business bad debt is deductible as an ordinary loss in the year incurred, whereas a nonbusiness bad debt is always treated as a short-term capital loss. Thus, regardless of the age of a nonbusiness bad debt, the deduction may be of limited benefit due to the $3,000 capital loss limitation for individuals (refer to the discussion in Chapter 4).

6-1c **Loans between Related Parties**

Loans between related parties raise the issue of whether the transaction was a *bona fide* loan or some other type of transfer, such as a gift, a disguised dividend payment, or a contribution to capital. The Regulations state that a bona fide debt arises from a debtor-creditor relationship based on a valid and enforceable obligation to pay a fixed or determinable sum of money. Thus, individual circumstances must be examined to determine whether advances between related parties are loans. Some considerations are these:

- Was a note properly executed?
- Was there a reasonable rate of interest?
- Was collateral provided?
- What collection efforts were made?
- What was the intent of the parties?

Ted, who is the sole shareholder of Penguin Corporation, lends the corporation $10,000 so that it can continue business operations. The note specifies a 2% interest rate and is payable on demand. Penguin has shown losses in each year of its five-year existence. The corporation also has liabilities greatly in excess of its assets. It is likely that Ted's transfer to the corporation would be treated as a contribution to capital rather than a liability. Consequently, no bad debt deduction would be allowed upon default by Penguin.

DIGGING DEEPER 1 | In-depth coverage can be found on this book's companion website: www.cengagebrain.com

6-2 WORTHLESS SECURITIES AND SMALL BUSINESS STOCK LOSSES

LO.2

State and illustrate the tax treatment of worthless securities, including § 1244 stock.

6-2a Worthless Securities

A loss is allowed for securities that become *completely* worthless during the year (**worthless securities**).[3] Such securities are shares of stock, bonds, notes, or other evidence of indebtedness issued by a corporation or government. The losses generated are treated as capital losses (refer to Chapter 4) deemed to have occurred on the *last day* of the tax year. By treating losses as having occurred on the last day of the tax year, a loss that would otherwise have been classified as short term (if the date of worthlessness were used) may be classified as long term.

The Big Picture

EXAMPLE 8

Return to the facts of *The Big Picture* on p. 6-1. Robyn owned stock in Owl Corporation that she acquired as an investment on October 1, 2015, at a cost of $60,000. On May 31, 2016, the stock became worthless when the company declared bankruptcy.

Because the stock is deemed to have become worthless as of December 31, 2016, Robyn has a capital loss from an asset held for more than one year (a long-term capital loss). Alternatively, if the stock is § 1244 small business stock (see the following section), she has a $50,000 ordinary loss and a $10,000 long-term capital loss.

6-2b Small Business Stock (§ 1244 Stock) Losses

The general rule is that shareholders receive capital loss treatment for losses from the sale or exchange of corporate stock. As noted in Chapter 4, the deductibility of capital losses is limited. However, it is possible to avoid capital loss limitations if the loss is sustained on **small business stock (§ 1244 stock)**. Such a loss could arise from a sale of the stock or from the stock becoming worthless. Only *individuals*[4] who acquired the stock *from* the issuing corporation are eligible to receive ordinary loss treatment under § 1244. The ordinary loss treatment is limited to $50,000 ($100,000 for married individuals filing jointly) per year. Losses on § 1244 stock in excess of the statutory limits are treated as capital losses.

The issuing corporation must meet certain requirements under § 1244 for the loss on the stock to be treated as an *ordinary*—rather than a capital—loss. The principal requirement is that the total capitalization of the corporation is limited to a maximum of $1 million. This capital limit includes all money and other property received by the corporation for stock and all capital contributions made to the corporation. The $1 million test is made at the time the stock is issued. There are no requirements regarding the kind of stock issued. Section 1244 stock can be either common or preferred.

Section 1244 applies only to losses. If § 1244 stock is sold at a gain, the provision does not apply and the gain is capital gain (which, for individuals, may be subject to preferential tax treatment, as discussed in Chapter 4).

EXAMPLE 9

Iris, a single individual, was looking for an investment that would give some diversification to her stock portfolio. A friend suggested that she acquire some stock in Eagle Corporation, a new startup company. On July 1, 2014, Iris purchased 100 shares of Eagle Corporation for $100,000. At the time Iris acquired her stock from Eagle Corporation, the corporation had $700,000 of paid-in capital. As a result, the stock qualified as § 1244 stock. On June 20, 2016, Iris sold all of her Eagle stock to Michael for $20,000 producing an $80,000 loss ($20,000 − $100,000). Because the Eagle stock is § 1244 stock, Iris has a $50,000 ordinary loss and a $30,000 long-term capital loss.

If Michael were to sell the stock later for $8,000 in a taxable transaction, the $12,000 loss ($8,000 − $20,000) would not qualify for ordinary loss treatment under § 1244 because Eagle Corporation had not issued the stock to him.

---

[3]§ 165(g).

[4]The term *individuals* for this purpose does not include a trust or an estate (but could include a partnership or an LLC).

TAX PLANNING STRATEGIES   **Maximizing the Benefits of Small Business (§ 1244 Stock) Losses**

FRAMEWORK FOCUS: TAX RATE

Strategy: Control the Character of Income and Deductions.

Because § 1244 limits the amount of loss classified as ordinary loss on a yearly basis, a taxpayer might maximize the benefits of § 1244 by selling the stock in more than one taxable year.

EXAMPLE 10

Mitch, a single individual, acquired small business stock in 2014 for $150,000 (150 shares at $1,000 per share). On December 20, 2016, the stock is worth $60,000 (150 shares at $400 per share). Mitch wants to sell the stock at this time. He earns a salary of $80,000 a year, has no other capital transactions, and does not expect any in the future.

If Mitch sells all of the small business stock in 2016, his recognized loss will be $90,000 ($60,000 selling price − $150,000 cost). The loss will be characterized as a $50,000 ordinary loss and a $40,000 long-term capital loss. In computing taxable income for 2016, Mitch could deduct the $50,000 ordinary loss but could deduct only $3,000 of the capital loss (assuming that he has no capital gains). The remainder of the capital loss could be carried over and used in future years subject to the capital loss limitations in those years.

Alternatively, if Mitch sells 82 shares in 2016, he will recognize an ordinary loss of $49,200 [82 × ($400 − $1,000)]. If Mitch then sells the remainder of the shares in 2017, he will recognize an ordinary loss of $40,800 [68 × ($400 − $1,000)], successfully avoiding the capital loss limitation. Mitch could deduct the $49,200 ordinary loss in computing 2016 taxable income and the $40,800 ordinary loss in computing 2017 taxable income.

LO.3

Identify a casualty and determine the amount, classification, and timing of casualty and theft losses.

6-3 CASUALTY AND THEFT LOSSES

Losses on business property are deductible, whether attributable to casualty, theft, or some other cause (e.g., rust, termite damage). While all *business* property losses are generally deductible, the amount and timing of casualty and theft losses are determined using special rules. Furthermore, for individual taxpayers, who may deduct casualty losses on personal-use (nonbusiness) property as well as on business and investment property (held in partnerships and S corporations or in an individual capacity), a set of special limitations applies. Casualty gains are also afforded special consideration in the tax law.

6-3a Definition of Casualty

The term *casualty* generally includes *fire, storm, shipwreck*, and *theft*. In addition, losses from *other casualties* are deductible. Such losses generally include any loss resulting from an event that is (1) identifiable; (2) damaging to property; and (3) sudden, unexpected, and unusual in nature. The term also includes accidental loss of property provided the loss qualifies under the same rules as any other casualty.

A *sudden event* is an event that is swift and precipitous and not gradual or progressive. An *unexpected event* is one that is ordinarily unanticipated and occurs without the intent of the taxpayer who suffers the loss. An *unusual event* is an event that is extraordinary and nonrecurring and does not commonly occur during the activity in which the taxpayer was engaged when the destruction occurred.[5] Examples include auto accidents, sonic booms, vandalism, and mine cave-ins. A taxpayer can take a deduction for a casualty loss from an automobile accident if the accident is not attributable to the taxpayer's willful act or willful negligence. Weather that causes damage (e.g., drought) must be unusual and severe for the particular region to qualify as a casualty. Furthermore, damage must be to the *taxpayer's* property to be deductible.

---

[5]Rev.Rul. 72–592, 1972–2 C.B. 101.

Events That Are Not Casualties

Not all acts of nature are treated as casualty losses for income tax purposes. Because a casualty must be sudden, unexpected, and unusual, progressive deterioration (such as erosion due to wind or rain) is not a casualty because it does not meet the suddenness test.

An example of an event that generally does not qualify as a casualty is insect damage. When termites caused damage over a period of several years, some courts have disallowed a casualty loss deduction.[6] On the other hand, some courts have held that termite damage over periods of up to 15 months after infestation constituted a sudden event and was, therefore, deductible as a casualty loss.[7] Despite the existence of some judicial support for the deductibility of termite damage as a casualty loss, the current position of the IRS is that termite damage is not deductible.[8]

Other examples of events that are not casualties are losses resulting from a decline in value rather than an actual loss of the property. For example, a taxpayer was allowed a loss for the actual flood damage to his property but not for the decline in market value due to the property being in a flood-prone area.[9] Similarly, a decline in value of an office building due to fire damage to nearby buildings is not deductible as a casualty.

6-3b Deduction of Casualty Losses

Generally, a casualty loss is deducted in the year the loss occurs. However, no casualty loss is permitted if a reimbursement claim with a reasonable *prospect of full recovery* exists.[10] If the taxpayer has a partial claim, only part of the loss can be claimed in the year of the casualty and the remainder is deducted in the year the claim is settled.

Fuchsia Corporation's new warehouse was completely destroyed by fire in 2016. Its cost and fair market value were $250,000. Fuchsia's only claim against the insurance company was on a $70,000 policy and was not settled by year-end. The following year, 2017, Fuchsia settled with the insurance company for $60,000. Fuchsia is entitled to a $180,000 deduction in 2016 and a $10,000 deduction in 2017.

If a taxpayer receives reimbursement for a casualty loss sustained and deducted in a previous year, an amended return is not filed for that year. Instead, the taxpayer must include the reimbursement in gross income on the return for the year in which it is received to the extent the previous deduction resulted in a tax benefit (refer to Chapter 4).

Golden Hawk, Inc., had a deductible casualty loss of $15,000 on its 2015 tax return. Golden Hawk's taxable income for 2015 was $60,000 after deducting the $15,000 loss. In June 2016, the corporation is reimbursed $13,000 for the prior year's casualty loss.

Golden Hawk includes the entire $13,000 in gross income for 2016 because the deduction in 2015 produced a tax benefit.

Disaster Area Losses

An exception to the general rule for the time of deduction is allowed for disaster area losses, which are casualties or disaster-related business losses sustained in an area designated as a disaster area by the President of the United States.[11] In such cases, the taxpayer may *elect* to treat the loss as having occurred in the taxable year immediately *preceding* the taxable year in which the disaster actually occurred. The rationale for this exception is to provide immediate relief to disaster victims in the form of accelerated tax benefits.

If the due date, plus extensions, for the prior year's return has not passed, a taxpayer makes the election to claim the disaster area loss on the prior year's tax return. If a disaster area is designated after the prior year's return has been filed, it is necessary to file

[6]*Fay v. Helvering*, 41–2 USTC ¶9494, 27 AFTR 432, 120 F.2d 253 (CA–2, 1941); *U.S. v. Rogers*, 41–1 USTC ¶9442, 27 AFTR 423, 120 F.2d 244 (CA–9, 1941).

[7]*Rosenberg v. Comm.*, 52–2 USTC ¶9377, 42 AFTR 303, 198 F.2d 46 (CA–8, 1952); *Shopmaker v. U.S.*, 54–1 USTC ¶9195, 45 AFTR 758, 119 F.Supp. 705 (D.Ct. Mo., 1953).

[8]Rev.Rul. 63–232, 1963–2 C.B. 97.
[9]*S. L. Solomon*, 39 TCM 1282, T.C.Memo. 1980–87.
[10]Reg. § 1.165–1(d)(2)(i).
[11]§ 165(h).

Strategy: Maximize Deductible Amounts.

Because the validity of loans between related taxpayers might be questioned, adequate documentation is needed to substantiate a bad debt deduction if the loan subsequently becomes worthless. Documentation should include proper execution of the note (legal form) and the establishment of a bona fide purpose for the loan. In addition, it is desirable to stipulate a reasonable rate of interest and a fixed maturity date.

Because a theft loss deduction is not permitted for misplaced items, a police report and evidence of the value of the property (e.g., appraisals, pictures of the property, and purchase receipts) are necessary to document a theft.

Similar documentation of the value of property should be provided to support a casualty loss deduction because the amount of loss is measured, in part, by the decline in fair market value of the property.

Casualty loss deductions must be reported on Form 4684.

either an amended return or a refund claim. In any case, the taxpayer must show clearly that such an election is being made.

The Big Picture

EXAMPLE 13

Return to the facts of *The Big Picture* on p. 6-1. On September 28, 2016, Robyn's personal residence was damaged when a tornado caused an oak tree to fall on the house. The amount of her uninsured casualty loss was $7,000 ($32,000 loss − $25,000 insurance recovery). Due to the extent of the damage in the area, the President of the United States designated the area a disaster area. Because Robyn's loss is a disaster area loss, she may elect to file an amended return for 2015 and take the loss in that year.

If Robyn elects this course of action, the amount of the loss will be reduced first by $100 (the materiality amount in 2015) and then by 10% of her 2015 AGI.

If Robyn forgoes the election, she may take the loss on her 2016 income tax return. The amount of the loss will be reduced first by $100 (the materiality amount in 2016) and then by 10% of her 2016 AGI. The advantage to Robyn of claiming the deduction in the earlier year is to receive the tax relief sooner.

6-3c Definition of Theft

Theft includes, but is not necessarily limited to, larceny, embezzlement, and robbery.[12] Theft does not include misplaced items.[13]

Theft losses are treated like other casualty losses, but the *timing* of recognition of the loss differs. A theft loss is deducted in the *year of discovery*, which may not be the same as the year of the theft. If in the year of the discovery a claim exists (e.g., against an insurance company) and there is a reasonable expectation of recovering the adjusted basis of the asset from the insurance company, no deduction is permitted.[14] If in the year of settlement the recovery is less than the asset's adjusted basis, a deduction may be available. If the recovery is greater than the asset's adjusted basis, *casualty gain* may be recognized.

EXAMPLE 14

Sakura, Inc., owned a computer that was stolen from its offices in December 2015. The theft was discovered on June 3, 2016, and the corporation filed a claim with its insurance company that was settled on January 30, 2017.

Assuming that there is a reasonable expectation of full recovery, no deduction is allowed in 2016. A deduction may be available in 2017 if the actual insurance proceeds are less than the adjusted basis of the asset. (Loss measurement rules are discussed later in this chapter.)

---

[12]Reg. § 1.165–8(d).

[13]*Mary Francis Allen*, 16 T.C. 163 (1951).

[14]Reg. §§ 1.165–1(d)(2) and 1.165–8(a)(2).

TAX IN THE NEWS The Tax Consequences of Lost Bitcoins

In Notice 2014–21 (2014–16 I.R.B. 938), the Internal Revenue Service provided initial guidance on transactions involving virtual currency (including bitcoins). Specifically, the IRS indicates that bitcoin is *not* currency; rather, it is property. As such, gain and losses on the disposition of bitcoins will not be treated in a manner similar to other currencies (e.g., euros and British pounds). This is a disappointment to taxpayers who lost money in bitcoin investments and may have hoped that the losses would be classified as currency losses (and, as such, ordinary losses). Taxpayers who have disposed of appreciated investment positions in bitcoins may enjoy capital gains treatment. Taxpayers who hold bitcoin as inventory will be subject to ordinary gains and losses upon disposition.

But what happens if the hard drive on which bitcoins are stored crashes and the data are not recoverable? Is this a "sudden, unexpected, and unusual event" that could qualify for a casualty loss? One might argue that failure to back up the data on the hard drive might be deemed carelessness (and so none of the loss would be allowed). And, certainly, no loss would be allowed until the taxpayer could confirm that there was no chance of recovery.

What if the taxpayer inadvertently deletes keys to bitcoins he or she previously mined? In general, one cannot take a loss for lost or misplaced property. In this case, no loss would be allowed due to carelessness on the part of the taxpayer. So the bottom line is this: Always back up your digital files.

6-3d Loss Measurement

The rules for determining the amount of a loss depend in part on whether business, investment, or personal-use (nonbusiness) property was involved. Another factor that must be considered is whether the property was partially or completely destroyed.

If business property or investment property (e.g., rental property) is *completely destroyed*, the loss is equal to the adjusted basis[15] (typically cost less depreciation) of the property at the time of destruction.

A different measurement rule applies for *partial destruction* of business and investment property and for *partial* or *complete destruction* of personal-use property held by individuals. In these situations, the loss is the *lesser* of:

- The adjusted basis of the property, or
- The difference between the fair market value of the property before the event and the fair market value immediately after the event.

EXAMPLE 15

Wynd and Rain, a law firm, owned an airplane that was used only for business purposes. The airplane was damaged in an accident. On the date of the accident, the fair market value of the plane was $52,000, and its adjusted basis was $32,000. After the accident, the plane was appraised at $24,000.

The law firm's loss deduction is $28,000 (the lesser of the adjusted basis or the decrease in fair market value). If instead the airplane had been completely destroyed in the accident, the loss deduction would have been $32,000 (the adjusted basis of the airplane).

Any insurance recovery reduces the loss for business, investment, and personal-use losses. In fact, a taxpayer may realize a gain if the insurance proceeds exceed the adjusted basis of the property. Chapter 8 discusses the treatment of net gains and losses on business property and income-producing property.

A special rule on insurance recovery applies to *personal-use property*. In particular, individuals are not permitted to deduct a casualty loss for damage to insured personal-use property unless an insurance claim is filed. This rule applies whether the insurance provides partial or full reimbursement for the loss.[16]

---

[15]See Chapter 7 for a detailed discussion of basis rules.
[16]§ 165(h)(5)(E).

Generally, an appraisal before and after the casualty is needed to measure the amount of loss. However, the *cost of repairs* to the damaged property generally is acceptable as a method of establishing the loss in value.[17]

DIGGING DEEPER 2 | In-depth coverage can be found on this book's companion website: **www.cengagebrain.com**

Multiple Losses

When multiple casualty losses occur during the year, the amount of each loss is computed separately. The rules for computing loss deductions where multiple losses have occurred are illustrated in Example 16.

EXAMPLE
16

During the year, Swan Enterprises had the following business casualty losses:

		Fair Market Value of the Asset		
Asset	Adjusted Basis	Before the Casualty	After the Casualty	Insurance Recovery
A	$900	$600	$–0–	$400
B	300	800	250	150

The following losses are allowed:

- Asset A: $500. The complete destruction of a business asset results in a deduction of the adjusted basis of the property (reduced by any insurance recovery), regardless of the asset's fair market value.

- Asset B: $150. The partial destruction of a business asset results in a deduction equal to the lesser of the adjusted basis ($300) or the decline in value ($550), reduced by any insurance recovery ($150).

6-3e Casualty and Theft Losses of Individuals

Recall from Chapters 1 and 4 that the individual income tax formula distinguishes between deductions *for* AGI and deductions *from* AGI. Casualty and theft losses incurred by an individual in connection with a business or with rental and royalty activities are deductible *for* AGI and are limited only by the rules previously discussed.[18] Losses from most other investment activities and personal-use losses are generally deducted *from* AGI. Investment casualty and theft losses (e.g., the theft of a security) are classified as other miscellaneous itemized deductions (not subject to a 2%-of-AGI floor as explained in Chapter 10). Casualty and theft losses of personal-use property are subject to special limitations discussed next.

Personal-Use Property

In addition to the valuation rules discussed previously, casualty and theft loss deductions from personal-use property must be reduced by a $100-*per-event* floor and a 10%-of-AGI *aggregate* floor.[19] The $100 floor applies separately to each casualty or theft and applies to the entire loss from each casualty or theft (e.g., if a storm damages both a taxpayer's residence and automobile, only $100 is subtracted from the total amount of the loss). All personal-use losses incurred during the year (net of the $100 floor for each event) are then added together, and the total is reduced by 10 percent of the taxpayer's AGI. The resulting amount is the taxpayer's itemized deduction for personal-use casualty and theft losses.

---

[17]Reg. § 1.165–7(a)(2)(ii).
[18]§ 62(a)(1).

[19]§§ 165(c)(3) and (h).

EXAMPLE

17

Rocky, who had AGI of $30,000, was involved in a motorcycle accident in 2016. His motorcycle, which was used only for personal use and had a fair market value of $12,000 and an adjusted basis of $9,000, was completely destroyed. He received $5,000 from his insurance company.

Rocky's casualty loss deduction is $900 [$9,000 basis − $5,000 insurance recovery − $100 floor − $3,000 (.10 × $30,000 AGI)]. The $900 casualty loss is an itemized deduction (*from* AGI).

Where there are both casualty and theft gains and losses from personal-use property, special netting rules apply. Generally, if casualty and theft gains exceed losses during the year, the gains and losses are treated as capital gains and losses. Alternatively, if losses exceed gains, the casualty and theft gains (and losses to the extent of gains) are treated as ordinary gains and losses. Any excess losses are deductible as personal-use casualty and theft losses.

See Concept Summary 6.2 for a review of the tax treatment of casualty gains and losses.

Concept Summary 6.2

Casualty Gains and Losses

	Business-Use or Income-Producing Property	Personal-Use Property
Event creating the loss	Any event.	Casualty or theft.
Amount	The lesser of the decline in fair market value or the adjusted basis, but always the adjusted basis if the property is totally destroyed.	The lesser of the decline in fair market value or the adjusted basis.
Insurance	Insurance proceeds received reduce the amount of the loss.	Insurance proceeds received (or for which there is an unfiled claim) reduce the amount of the loss.
$100 floor	Not applicable.	Applicable per event.
Gains and losses	Gains and losses are netted (see detailed discussion in Chapter 8).	Personal casualty and theft gains and losses are netted.
Gains exceeding losses	See Chapter 8.	The gains and losses are treated as gains and losses from the sale of capital assets.
Losses exceeding gains	See Chapter 8.	The gains—and the losses to the extent of gains—are treated as ordinary items in computing AGI. The losses in excess of gains, to the extent that they exceed 10% of AGI, are itemized deductions (*from* AGI).

In-depth coverage can be found on this book's companion website: www.cengagebrain.com

3 DIGGING DEEPER

6-4 NET OPERATING LOSSES

LO.4

Describe the impact of the net operating loss carryback and carryover provisions on previous and subsequent years' taxable income.

A **net operating loss (NOL)** in a particular tax year would produce no tax benefits if the Code did not provide for the carryback and carryforward of such losses to profitable years.

6-4a Introduction

The requirement that every taxpayer file an annual income tax return (whether on a calendar year or a fiscal year) can lead to inequities for taxpayers who experience uneven income over a series of years. These inequities result from the application of progressive tax rates to taxable income determined on an annual basis.

EXAMPLE 18

Orange, Inc., realizes the following taxable income or loss over a five-year period: year 1, $50,000; year 2, ($30,000); year 3, $100,000; year 4, ($200,000); and year 5, $380,000. Blue Corporation has taxable income of $60,000 every year. Note that both corporations have total taxable income of $300,000 over the five-year period. Assume that there is no provision for carryback or carryover of net operating losses. Orange and Blue would have the following five-year tax liabilities:

Year	Orange's Tax	Blue's Tax
1	$ 7,500	$10,000
2	–0–	10,000
3	22,250	10,000
4	–0–	10,000
5	129,200	10,000
	$158,950	$50,000

Note: The computation of tax is made without regard to any NOL benefit. Rates applicable to 2016 are used to compute the tax.

Even though Orange and Blue realized the same total taxable income ($300,000) over the five-year period, Orange would have to pay taxes of $158,950, while Blue would pay taxes of only $50,000.

To provide partial relief from this inequitable tax treatment, a deduction is allowed for net operating losses (NOLs).[20] This provision permits an NOL for any one year to offset taxable income in other years. The NOL provision provides relief only for losses from the operation of a trade or business or from casualty and theft.

Only C corporations and individuals are permitted an NOL deduction because losses of partnerships and S corporations pass through to their owners. For C corporations, the NOL equals any negative taxable income for the year, with an adjustment for the dividends received deduction (see Chapter 12). In addition, deductions for prior-year NOLs are not allowed when determining a current-year NOL.

6-4b Carryback and Carryover Periods

The mechanism providing a tax benefit from the NOL is the provision that allows a loss deduction in profitable years of the business activity. The loss may be carried back to earlier years and/or carried over to future years.

General Rules

A current-year NOL is usually carried back and deducted against income over the two preceding tax years.[21] It is carried back first to the second year before the loss year and then to the year immediately preceding the loss year (until it fully offsets income). If the loss is not completely used against income in the carryback period, it is carried forward for 20 years following the loss year. NOLs that are not used within the 20-year carry-forward period are lost. Thus, an NOL sustained in 2016 is used first in 2014 and then 2015. Then the loss is carried forward and offsets income in 2017 through 2036.

When an NOL is carried back, the taxpayer requests an immediate refund of prior years' taxes by filing an amended return for the previous two years. Alternatively, a form for a quick refund may be filed (Form 1139 for corporations or Form 1045 for individuals). When an NOL is carried forward, the current return shows an NOL deduction for the prior year's loss. Thus, a struggling business with an NOL can receive rapid cash-flow assistance.

---

[20]§ 172.

[21]A three-year carryback period is available for any portion of an individual's NOL resulting from a casualty or theft loss. The three-year carryback rule also applies to NOLs that are attributable to Presidentially declared disaster areas that are incurred by a small business. For purposes of this provision, a small business is a business whose average annual gross receipts for a three-year period are $5 million or less. See § 172(b)(1)(F).

NOLs from Multiple Tax Years

When the taxpayer has NOLs in two or more years, the earliest year's loss is used first. Later years' losses can then be used until they offset income or are lost. Thus, one year's return could show NOL carryovers from two or more years. Each loss is computed and applied separately.

Election to Forgo Carryback

A taxpayer can *irrevocably elect* not to carry back an NOL. The election is made on a corporate tax return (Form 1120) by checking the appropriate box. Individuals can make the election by attaching a statement to their tax return. If the election is made, the loss can *only* be carried forward for 20 years. This election may be desirable in circumstances where marginal tax rates in future years are expected to exceed rates in prior years.

6-5 THE TAX SHELTER PROBLEM

LO.5

Explain the tax shelter problem and the reasons for at-risk and passive activity loss limitations.

Before Congress enacted legislation to reduce their effectiveness, tax shelters provided a popular way to avoid or defer taxes, as they could generate losses and other benefits to offset income from other sources. Because of the tax avoidance potential of many tax shelters, they were attractive to wealthy taxpayers with high marginal tax rates. Many tax shelters merely provided an opportunity for "investors" to buy deductions and credits in ventures that were not expected to generate a profit, even in the long run.

Although it may seem odd that a taxpayer would intentionally invest in an activity that was designed to produce losses, there is a logical explanation. The typical tax shelter operated as a partnership and relied heavily on nonrecourse financing.[22] Accelerated depreciation and interest expense deductions generated large losses in the early years of the activity. At the very least, the tax shelter deductions deferred the recognition of any net income from the venture until the activity was sold. In the best of situations, the investor could realize additional tax savings by offsetting other income (e.g., salary, interest, dividends) with losses flowing from the tax shelter. Ultimately, the sale of the investment would result in *tax-favored* capital gain. The following example illustrates what was possible *before* Congress enacted legislation to curb tax shelter abuses.

EXAMPLE
19

Bob, who earned a salary of $400,000 as a business executive and dividend income of $15,000, invested $20,000 for a 10% interest in a cattle-breeding tax shelter. He did not participate in the operation of the business. Through the use of $800,000 of nonrecourse financing and available cash of $200,000, the partnership acquired a herd of an exotic breed of cattle costing $1 million. Depreciation, interest, and other deductions related to the activity resulted in a loss of $400,000, of which Bob's share was $40,000. Bob was allowed to deduct the $40,000 loss even though he had invested and stood to lose only $20,000 if the investment became worthless. The net effect of the $40,000 deduction from the partnership was that a portion of Bob's salary and dividend income was "sheltered," and as a result, he was required to calculate his tax liability on only $375,000 of income [$415,000 (salary and dividends) − $40,000 (deduction)] rather than $415,000. If this deduction were available under current law and if Bob was in a combined Federal and state income tax bracket of 40%, a tax savings of $16,000 ($40,000 × 40%) would be generated in the first year alone!

---

[22]Nonrecourse debt is an obligation for which the borrower is not personally liable. An example of nonrecourse debt is a liability on real estate acquired by a partnership without the partnership or any of the partners assuming any liability for the mortgage. The acquired property generally is pledged as collateral for the loan.

BRIDGE DISCIPLINE   **Bridge to Finance**

An overarching requirement to maximizing wealth is to reduce the present value cost of taxation. One way to reduce the cost of taxation in present value terms is to defer the payment of a tax into the future for as long as possible. This can be accomplished by reducing the tax-payer's tax base (i.e., taxable income) either by deferring the recognition of income or by accelerating the timing of deductions. As a result, to the extent that the tax cost associated with an investment alternative is reduced, the after-tax benefit from that investment and the investor's wealth position are enhanced.

For example, a common attribute of many tax-advantaged investments is the availability of tax losses that investors may claim on their own income tax returns. Many times, these tax losses are the result of investment-level deductions, such as interest and depreciation expenses, that are bunched in the early years of the life of the investment rather than being due to economic woes of the investment itself.

Through the at-risk limitations and the passive activity loss rules, the tax law works to scale back the ability of tax-payers to claim tax losses flowing from certain investments. These limitations have a direct impact on *when* investors can claim loss deductions flowing from affected investments. The typical result of these provisions is that the loss deductions are deferred. Therefore, when evaluating competing investment alternatives, taxpayers must address the impact of these tax limitations in projecting the after-tax benefits that can be expected to follow.

A review of Example 19 shows that the taxpayer took a two-for-one write-off ($40,000 deduction, $20,000 amount invested). In the heyday of these types of tax shelters, promoters often promised tax deductions for the investor well in excess of the amount invested.

The first major provision aimed at tax shelters is the at-risk limitation. Its objective is to limit a taxpayer's deductions to the amount that the taxpayer could actually lose from the investment (the amount "at risk") if it becomes worthless. Thus, in Example 19, the at-risk rule limits Bob's loss to $20,000—the amount at risk.

The second major attack on tax shelters came with the passage of the passive activity loss rules. The passive activity loss rules require the taxpayer to segregate all income and losses into three categories: active, portfolio, and passive. (These categories are defined in text Section 6-7.) In general, the passive activity loss limits *disallow* the deduction of passive activity losses against *active or portfolio income* even when the taxpayer is at risk to the extent of the loss. In general, passive activity losses can only offset passive activity income.

Thus, in Example 19, the passive activity loss rules disallow a current deduction for any of the loss. The loss from the tax shelter is a passive activity loss because Bob does not materially participate in the activity. Therefore, the $20,000 loss that is allowed under the at-risk rules is disallowed under the passive activity loss rules because Bob does not report any passive activity income for the year—he reports only active and portfolio income. Consequently, Bob's current-year income must reflect his nonpassive activity income of $415,000. As explained later in the chapter, the disallowed $20,000 passive activity loss is suspended and may be deducted in a future year under certain conditions.

The following two sections explore the nature of the at-risk limits and the passive activity loss rules and their impact on investors. Congress intentionally structured these rules so that investors evaluating potential investments must consider mainly the *economics* of the venture instead of the *tax benefits* or tax avoidance possibilities that an investment may generate.

LO.6

Describe how the at-risk limitation and the passive activity loss rules limit deductions for losses and identify taxpayers subject to these restrictions.

6-6 AT-RISK LIMITATIONS

The at-risk provisions limit the deductibility of losses from business and income-producing activities. These provisions, which apply to individuals and closely held corporations, are designed to prevent taxpayers from deducting losses in excess of their actual economic investment in an activity. In the case of an S corporation or a partnership, the at-risk limits apply at the owner level. Under the at-risk rules, a taxpayer's deductible loss from an activity for any taxable year is limited to the amount the taxpayer has at risk at the end of the taxable year (i.e., the amount the taxpayer could actually lose in the activity).

While the amount at risk generally vacillates over time, the initial amount considered at risk consists of the following:[23]

- The amount of cash and the adjusted basis of property contributed to the activity by the taxpayer.
- Amounts borrowed for use in the activity for which the taxpayer is personally liable.
- The adjusted basis of property pledged as security that is not used in the activity.

This amount usually is increased each year by the taxpayer's share of income and is decreased by the taxpayer's share of deductible losses and withdrawals from the activity. In addition, because *general partners* are jointly and severally liable for recourse debts of the partnership, their at-risk amounts are increased when the partnership increases its debt and are decreased when the partnership reduces its debt. However, a taxpayer generally is not considered at risk with respect to borrowed amounts if either of the following is true:

- The taxpayer is not personally liable for repayment of the debt (e.g., non-recourse debt).
- The lender has an interest (other than as a creditor) in the activity.

An important exception provides that in the case of an activity involving the holding of real property, a taxpayer is considered at risk for his or her share of any *qualified nonrecourse financing* that is secured by real property used in the activity.[24]

Subject to the passive activity loss rules discussed later in the chapter, a taxpayer may deduct a loss as long as the at-risk amount is positive. However, once the at-risk amount is exhausted, any remaining loss cannot be deducted until a later year. Any losses disallowed for any given taxable year by the at-risk rules may be deducted in the first succeeding year in which the rules do not prevent the deduction—that is, when there is, and to the extent of, a positive at-risk amount.

EXAMPLE 20

In 2016, Sue invests $40,000 in an oil partnership. The partnership incurs a first-year net loss, of which $60,000 is her share. Assume that Sue's interest in the partnership is subject to the at-risk limits but is not subject to the passive activity loss limits. Because Sue has only $40,000 of capital at risk, she cannot deduct more than $40,000 against her other income and must reduce her at-risk amount to zero ($40,000 at-risk amount − $40,000 loss deducted). The nondeductible loss of $20,000 ($60,000 loss generated − $40,000 loss allowed) can be carried over to 2017.

In 2017, Sue has taxable income of $15,000 from the oil partnership and invests an additional $10,000 in the venture. Her at-risk amount is now $25,000 ($0 beginning balance + $15,000 taxable income + $10,000 additional investment). This enables Sue to deduct the $20,000 carryover loss and requires her to reduce her at-risk amount to $5,000 ($25,000 at-risk amount − $20,000 carryover loss allowed).

Complicating the at-risk rule is the fact that previously allowed losses must be recaptured as income to the extent the at-risk amount is reduced below zero.[25] This rule applies in situations such as those when the amount at risk is reduced below zero by distributions to the taxpayer or when the status of indebtedness changes from recourse to nonrecourse.

Calculation of at-risk amount is reviewed in Concept Summary 6.3.

---

[23]§ 465(b)(1).

[24]Section 465(b)(6) defines *qualified nonrecourse financing*. See also the related discussion in Chapter 14.

[25]§ 465(e).

Concept Summary 6.3

Calculation of At-Risk Amount

Increases to a taxpayer's at-risk amount:

- Cash and the adjusted basis of property contributed to the activity.
- Amounts borrowed for use in the activity for which the taxpayer is personally liable.
- The adjusted basis of property pledged as security that is not used in the activity.
- Taxpayer's share of amounts borrowed for use in the activity that are qualified nonrecourse financing.
- Taxpayer's share of the activity's income.

Decreases to a taxpayer's at-risk amount:

- Withdrawals from the activity.
- Taxpayer's share of the activity's deductible loss.
- Taxpayer's share of any reductions of debt for which recourse against the taxpayer exists or any reductions of qualified nonrecourse debt.

6-7 PASSIVE ACTIVITY LOSS LIMITS

This section identifies and explains a number of key issues that are pertinent when applying the passive activity loss limits.

- The limits apply only to passive activity losses incurred by certain types of taxpayers.
- Losses are limited under these rules only if they are generated by a passive activity.
- Special rules exist for interests in real estate activities.
- Benefits may arise when a disposition of a passive activity occurs.

6-7a Classification and Impact of Passive Activity Income and Loss

The passive activity loss rules operate by requiring taxpayers to classify their income and losses into various categories. Then the rules limit the extent to which losses in the passive category can be used to offset income in the other categories.

Classification

The passive activity loss rules require income and loss to be classified into one of three categories: *active, portfolio,* or *passive*. **Active income** includes the following:

- Wages, salary, commissions, bonuses, and other payments for services rendered by the taxpayer.
- Profit from a trade or business in which the taxpayer is a material participant (material participation is described later in the chapter).

Portfolio income includes the following:

- Interest, dividends, annuities, and royalties not derived in the ordinary course of a trade or business.
- Gain or loss from the disposition of property that produces portfolio income or is held for investment purposes.

Section 469 provides that passive activity income or loss arises from activities that are treated as passive, which include:

- Any trade or business or income-producing activity in which the taxpayer does not materially participate.
- Subject to certain exceptions (discussed later in the chapter), all rental activities, whether or not the taxpayer materially participates.

General Impact

Losses or expenses generated by passive activities can only be deducted to the extent of income from passive activities. Any excess loss may not be used to offset income from

TAX IN THE NEWS **"Passive" under the Tax Law May Not Be "Passive" in the Real World**

As the real estate market continues to strengthen from the economic depths of several years ago, more Americans are interested in buying and managing rental property as a sideline. Many such investors quickly learn that holding rental property invariably is more involved than simply collecting rent every month.

Managing rental property can be a time-consuming business venture. Screening potential renters, routinely maintaining and upgrading the property, managing the books and accounting records, and responding to calls from the renters at any hour of the day or night concerning property issues are but a few of the tasks that rental property owners face regularly.

Then at the end of the year when the tax preparer mentions to the taxpayer that the rental property is a passive activity, the taxpayer is mystified by the disconnect between reality and the terminology of the tax law. But the more significant sting may arise from the application of the passive activity loss restrictions that apply under the tax law.

active or portfolio income. Instead, any unused passive activity losses are suspended and carried forward to future years to offset passive activity income generated in those years. Otherwise, suspended losses may be used only when a taxpayer disposes of his or her entire interest in an activity. In that event, generally, all current and suspended passive activity losses related to the activity may offset active and portfolio income.

The Big Picture

EXAMPLE 21

Return to the facts of *The Big Picture* on p. 6-1. Recall that Robyn invested $20,000 in the Florida orange grove limited partnership, which produced an allocable $20,000 loss for her this year. Assume that Robyn earns a salary of $100,000 along with $12,000 in dividends and interest from various portfolio investments. Because her at-risk basis in the partnership is $20,000, the current $20,000 loss is not limited by the at-risk rules. However, because the loss is a passive activity loss, it is not deductible against her other income. The loss is suspended and is carried over to the future. If Robyn has passive activity income from this investment or from other passive activities in the future, she can offset the suspended loss against that passive activity income. If she does not have passive activity income to offset this suspended loss in the future, she will be allowed to offset the loss against other types of income when she eventually disposes of her investment in the passive activity.

Impact of Suspended Losses

The actual economic gain or loss from a passive investment (including any suspended losses) can be determined when a taxpayer disposes of his or her entire interest in the investment. As a result, under the passive activity loss rules described above, upon a fully taxable disposition, any overall loss realized from the taxpayer's activity is recognized and can be offset against passive, active, and portfolio income.

A fully taxable disposition generally involves a sale of the property to a third party at arm's length and thus, presumably, for a price equal to the property's fair market value. As presented in the following example, a gain recognized upon the transfer of an interest in a passive activity generally is treated as passive and is first offset by the suspended passive activity losses from that activity.

EXAMPLE 22

Rex sells an apartment building, a passive activity, with an adjusted basis of $100,000 for $180,000. In addition, he has suspended passive activity losses of $60,000 associated with the building. His total gain, $80,000, and his taxable gain, $20,000, are calculated as follows:

Net sales price	$ 180,000
Less: Adjusted basis	(100,000)
Total gain	$ 80,000
Less: Suspended losses	(60,000)
Taxable gain (passive)	$ 20,000

If current and suspended losses of the passive activity exceed the gain realized from the sale or if the sale results in a realized loss, the amount of

- any loss from the activity for the tax year (including losses suspended in the activity disposed of)

in excess of

- net income or gain for the tax year from all passive activities (without regard to the activity disposed of)

is treated as a loss that is not from a passive activity. In computing the loss from the activity for the year of disposition, any gain or loss recognized is included in the calculation.

Dean sells an apartment building, a passive activity, with an adjusted basis of $100,000 for $150,000. In addition, he has current and suspended passive activity losses of $60,000 associated with the building and has no other passive activities. His total gain of $50,000 and his deductible loss of $10,000 are calculated as follows:

Net sales price	$ 150,000
Less: Adjusted basis	(100,000)
Total gain	$ 50,000
Less: Suspended losses	(60,000)
Deductible loss (not passive)	($ 10,000)

The $10,000 loss can be deducted against Dean's active and portfolio income. Even if the building is sold for a loss (i.e., the adjusted basis exceeds the sales price), the total loss, including the suspended losses, is deductible as a nonpassive activity loss.

Carryovers of Suspended Losses

The preceding examples assumed that the taxpayer had an interest in only one passive activity; as a result, the suspended loss was related exclusively to the activity that was disposed of. However, taxpayers often own more than one passive activity, in which case any suspended losses must be allocated among those passive activities that generated losses. The allocation to an activity is made by multiplying the disallowed passive activity loss from all activities using the following fraction:

$$\frac{\text{Loss from one passive activity}}{\text{Sum of losses for taxable year from all passive activities having losses}}$$

Diego has investments in three passive activities with the following income and losses for 2015:

Activity A	($30,000)
Activity B	(20,000)
Activity C	25,000
Net passive activity loss	($25,000)
Net passive activity loss of $25,000 allocated to:	
Activity A [$25,000 × ($30,000/$50,000)]	($15,000)
Activity B [$25,000 × ($20,000/$50,000)]	(10,000)
Total suspended losses	($25,000)

Suspended losses are carried over indefinitely and are offset in the future, first against any passive activity income from the activities to which they relate and then against passive activity income from other passive activities.[26] Taxpayers subject to the passive activity loss limitation rule must maintain records to track the suspended losses and the activities to which they belong.

---

[26]§ 469(b).

Assume that the facts are the same as in the preceding example and that in 2016, Activity A produces $10,000 of income. Diego may use $10,000 of Activity A's suspended loss of $15,000 from 2015 to offset the $10,000 income from this activity. If Diego sells Activity A in early 2017, the remaining $5,000 suspended loss is used to offset any income from the activity reported by Diego in 2017 and to determine his final gain or loss.

EXAMPLE 25

Passive Activity Credits

Credits (such as the low-income housing credit and rehabilitation credit—discussed in Chapter 17) that arise from passive activities are limited in much the same way as passive activity losses. Passive activity credits can be utilized only against regular tax attributable to passive activity income,[27] which is calculated by comparing the tax on all income (including passive activity income) with the tax on income excluding passive activity income.

Sam owes $50,000 of tax, disregarding net passive activity income, and $80,000 of tax, considering both net passive activity and other taxable income (disregarding the credits in both cases). The amount of tax attributable to the passive activity income is $30,000.

EXAMPLE 26

In the preceding example, Sam can claim a maximum of $30,000 of passive activity credits; the excess credits are carried over. These passive activity credits can be used only against the *regular* tax attributable to passive activity income. If a taxpayer has a net loss from passive activities during a given year, no credits can be used.

Carryovers of Passive Activity Credits

Tax credits attributable to passive activities can be carried forward indefinitely, much like suspended passive activity losses. Unlike passive activity losses, however, passive activity credits are permanently lost when the activity is disposed of in a taxable transaction where loss is recognized. Credits are allowed on dispositions only when there is sufficient tax on passive activity income to absorb them.

Use of Passive Activity Credits upon Disposition of an Activity

Alicia sells a passive activity for a gain of $10,000. The activity had suspended losses of $40,000 and suspended credits of $15,000. The $10,000 gain is offset by $10,000 of the suspended losses, and the remaining $30,000 of suspended losses is deductible against Alicia's active and portfolio income. The suspended credits are permanently lost because the sale of the activity did not generate any tax after the effect of the suspended losses was considered.

EXAMPLE 27

If Alicia in the preceding example had realized a $100,000 gain on the sale of the passive activity, the suspended credits could have been used to the extent of the regular tax attributable to the net passive activity income.

EXAMPLE 28

Gain on sale	$100,000
Less: Suspended losses	(40,000)
Net gain	$ 60,000

If the tax attributable to the net gain of $60,000 is $15,000 or more, the entire $15,000 of suspended credits can be used. If the tax attributable to the gain is less than $15,000, the excess of the suspended credits over the tax attributable to the gain is lost.

When a taxpayer has sufficient regular tax liability from passive activities to trigger the use of suspended credits, the credits lose their character as passive activity credits. They are reclassified as regular tax credits and made subject to the same limits as other credits (see Chapter 17).

---

[27]§ 469(d)(2).

Passive Activity Changes to Active

If a formerly passive activity becomes active, suspended losses are allowed to the extent of income from the now active business.[28] If any of the suspended loss remains, it continues to be treated as a loss from a passive activity. The excess suspended loss can be deducted against passive activity income or carried over to the next tax year and deducted to the extent of income from the now active business in the succeeding year(s).

EXAMPLE 29

For several years, Rebecca has owned an interest in a passive activity that has produced losses of $80,000 during that period. Because she did not have passive activity income from other sources, she could not deduct any of the activity's passive activity losses. In the current year, she has become a material participant in the activity and her share of the business profits total $25,000. As a result, she may use $25,000 of the suspended passive activity loss to offset the current business profits. Rebecca's remaining suspended passive activity loss from the activity is $55,000 ($80,000 − $25,000), which is carried over to future years and used to offset income from the formerly passive activity or income from other passive activities.

6-7b Taxpayers Subject to the Passive Activity Loss Rules

The passive activity loss rules apply to individuals, estates, trusts, personal service corporations, and closely held C corporations.[29] Passive activity income or loss from investments in partnerships or S corporations (see Chapters 14 and 15) flows through to the owners, and the passive activity loss rules are applied at the owner level. Consequently, it is necessary to understand how the passive activity rules apply to both entities *and* their owners (including individual taxpayers).

Personal Service Corporations

Determination of whether a corporation is a **personal service corporation** is based on rather broad definitions. A personal service corporation is a regular (or C) corporation that meets both of the following conditions:

- The principal activity is the performance of personal services.
- Such services are substantially performed by owner-employees.

---

[28]§ 469(f).   [29]§ 469(a).

Generally, personal service corporations include those in the fields of health, law, engineering, architecture, accounting, actuarial science, performing arts, and consulting.[30]

Application of the passive activity loss limitations to personal service corporations is intended to prevent taxpayers from sheltering personal service income by creating personal service corporations and acquiring passive activities at the corporate level.

Two tax accountants who earn an aggregate of $200,000 a year in their individual practices agree to work together in a newly formed personal service corporation. Shortly after its formation, the corporation invests in a passive activity that produces a $200,000 loss during the year. Because the passive activity loss rules apply to personal service corporations, the corporation may not deduct the $200,000 passive activity loss against the $200,000 of active income.

In-depth coverage can be found on this book's companion website: www.cengagebrain.com   **4 DIGGING DEEPER**

Closely Held C Corporations

Application of the passive activity loss rules to closely held (nonpersonal service) C corporations is also intended to prevent individuals from incorporating to avoid the passive activity loss limitations. A corporation is classified as a **closely held C corporation** if at any time during the taxable year, more than 50 percent of the value of its outstanding stock is owned, directly or indirectly, by or for five or fewer individuals. Closely held C corporations (other than personal service corporations) may use passive activity losses to offset *active* income but *not portfolio* income.

Silver Corporation, a closely held (nonpersonal service) C corporation, has a $500,000 passive activity loss from a rental activity, $400,000 of active income, and $100,000 of portfolio income. The corporation may offset $400,000 of the $500,000 passive activity loss against the $400,000 of active business income but may not offset the remainder against the $100,000 of portfolio income. Thus, $100,000 of the passive activity loss is suspended ($500,000 passive activity loss − $400,000 offset against active income).

Application of the passive activity loss limitations to closely held C corporations prevents shareholders from transferring their portfolio investments to such corporations to offset passive activity losses against portfolio income.

6-7c Rules for Determining Passive Activities

Identifying what constitutes an activity is a necessary first step in applying the passive activity loss limitation. The rules used to delineate an activity state that in general, a taxpayer can treat one or more trade or business activities or rental activities as a single activity if those activities form an *appropriate economic unit* for measuring gain or loss. The Regulations provide guidelines for identifying appropriate economic units.[31] These guidelines are designed to prevent taxpayers from arbitrarily combining different businesses in an attempt to circumvent the passive activity loss limitation. For example, combining a profitable active business and a passive business generating losses into one activity would allow the taxpayer to offset passive activity losses against active income.

LO.7

Discuss the definitions of activity, material participation, and rental activity under the passive activity loss rules.

In-depth coverage can be found on this book's companion website: www.cengagebrain.com   **5 DIGGING DEEPER**

To determine which ventures form an appropriate economic unit, all of the relevant facts and circumstances must be considered. However, special rules restrict the grouping of rental and nonrental activities.[32] The following example, adapted from the Regulations, illustrates the application of the activity grouping rules.[33]

---

[30]§ 448(d)(2)(A).
[31]Reg. § 1.469–4.

[32]Reg. § 1.469–4(d).
[33]Reg. § 1.469–4(c)(3).

EXAMPLE 32

George owns a men's clothing store and an Internet café in Chicago. He also owns a men's clothing store and an Internet café in Milwaukee. Reasonable methods of applying the facts and circumstances test may result in any of the following groupings:

- All four businesses may be grouped into a single activity because of common ownership and control.
- The clothing stores may be grouped into an activity, and the Internet cafés may be grouped into an activity.
- The Chicago businesses may be grouped into an activity, and the Milwaukee businesses may be grouped into an activity.
- Each of the four businesses may be treated as a separate activity.

Once a set of activities has been grouped by the taxpayer using the above rules, the grouping cannot be changed unless a material change in the facts and circumstances occurs or the original grouping was clearly inappropriate. In addition, the Regulations also grant the IRS the right to regroup activities when one of the primary purposes of the taxpayer's grouping is to avoid the passive activity loss limitation and the grouping fails to reflect an appropriate economic unit.[34]

6-7d **Material Participation**

As indicated previously, if a taxpayer materially participates in a nonrental trade or business activity, any loss from that activity is treated as an active loss that can offset active or portfolio income. (Participation is defined later in the chapter.) If a taxpayer does not materially participate, however, the loss is treated as a passive activity loss, which can only offset passive activity income. Therefore, controlling whether a particular activity is treated as active or passive is an important part of the tax strategy of a taxpayer who owns an interest in one or more businesses. Consider the following examples.

Implications of Material Participation Status

EXAMPLE 33

Cameron, a corporate executive, earns a salary of $600,000 per year. In addition, he owns a separate business in which he participates. The business produces a loss of $100,000 during the year. If Cameron materially participates in the business, the $100,000 loss is an active loss that may offset his active income from his corporate employer. If he does not materially participate, the loss is passive and is suspended unless he has other passive activity income. Cameron may use the suspended loss in the future only when he has passive activity income or disposes of the activity.

EXAMPLE 34

Connor, an attorney, earns $350,000 a year in his law practice. In addition, he owns interests in two activities, A and B, in which he participates. Activity A, in which he does not *materially* participate, produces a loss of $50,000. Connor has not yet met the material participation standard, described below, for Activity B, which produces income of $80,000. However, he can meet the material participation standard if he spends an additional 50 hours in Activity B during the year. Should Connor attempt to meet the material participation standard for Activity B? If he continues working in Activity B and becomes a material participant, the $80,000 of income from the activity is active and the $50,000 passive activity loss from Activity A must be suspended. A more favorable tax strategy is for Connor *not to meet* the material participation standard for Activity B, thus making the income from that activity passive. This enables him to offset the $50,000 passive activity loss from Activity A against most of the passive activity income from Activity B.

It is possible to devise numerous scenarios in which the taxpayer could control the tax outcome by increasing or decreasing participation in different activities. Examples 33 and 34 demonstrate two of the possibilities. The conclusion reached in most analyses of

---

[34]Reg. § 1.469–4(f).

this type is that taxpayers will benefit by having profitable activities classified as passive so that any passive activity losses can be used to offset that passive activity income. If the activity produces a loss, however, the taxpayer will benefit if it is classified as active so that the loss is not subject to the passive activity loss limitations.

Temporary Regulations[35] provide seven tests (listed in Concept Summary 6.4) that serve to determine when **material participation** is achieved.

Concept Summary 6.4

Tests to Determine Material Participation

Tests Based on Current Participation

1. The individual participates in the activity for more than 500 hours during the year.

2. The individual's participation in the activity for the taxable year constitutes substantially all of the participation in the activity of all individuals (including nonowner employees) for the year.

3. The individual participates in the activity for more than 100 hours during the year, and this participation is not less than that participation of any other individual (including nonowner employees) for the year.

4. The activity is a **significant participation activity** (where the person's participation *exceeds* 100 hours during the year), and the hours for all significant participation activities during the year is more than 500 hours.

Tests Based on Prior Participation

5. The individual materially participated in the activity for any 5 taxable years during the 10 taxable years that immediately precede the current taxable year.

6. The activity is a personal service activity, and the individual materially participated in the activity for any three preceding taxable years.

Test Based on Facts and Circumstances

7. Based on all of the facts and circumstances, the individual participates in the activity on a regular, continuous, and substantial basis during the year.

In-depth coverage can be found on this book's companion website: www.cengagebrain.com   **6 DIGGING DEEPER**

Participation Defined

Participation generally includes any work done by an individual in an activity that he or she owns. Participation does not include work if it is of a type not customarily done by owners *and* if one of its principal purposes is to avoid the disallowance of passive activity losses or credits. Work done in an individual's capacity as an investor (e.g., reviewing financial reports in a nonmanagerial capacity) is not counted in applying the material participation tests. However, participation by an owner's spouse counts as participation by the owner.[36]

EXAMPLE

35

Tom, a partner in a CPA firm, owns a computer store that operated at a loss during the year. To offset this loss against the income from his CPA practice, Tom would like to avoid having the computer business classified as a passive activity. During the year, he worked 480 hours in the business in management and selling activities and 30 hours doing janitorial chores. In addition, Tom's wife participated 40 hours as a salesperson. It is likely that Tom's 480 hours of participation in management and selling activities will count as participation in work customarily done by owners, but the 30 hours spent doing janitorial chores will not. However, the 40 hours of participation by his wife will count. Assuming that none of the participation's principal purposes is to avoid the allowance of passive activity losses or credits, Tom will qualify as a material participant under the more-than-500-hour rule (480 + 40 = 520).

---

[35]Temp.Reg. § 1.469–5T(a).   [36]§ 469(h)(5) and Temp.Reg. § 1.469–5T(f)(3).

Limited Partners

A *limited* partner is a partner whose liability to third-party creditors of the partnership is limited to the amount the partner has invested in the partnership. Such a partnership must have at least one *general* partner who is fully liable in an individual capacity for the debts of the partnership to third parties. Generally, a *limited partner* is not considered a material participant unless he or she qualifies under Test 1, 5, or 6 as shown in Concept Summary 6.4. However, a *general partner* may qualify as a material participant by meeting any of the seven tests. If a general partner also owns a limited interest in the same limited partnership, all interests are treated as a general interest.[37]

Corporations

Personal service corporations and closely held C corporations cannot directly participate in an activity. However, a corporation is deemed to materially participate if its owners materially participate in an activity of the corporation. Together, the participating owners must own directly or indirectly more than 50 percent of the value of the outstanding stock of the corporation.[38] Alternatively, a closely held C corporation may be deemed to materially participate in an activity if, during the entire year, it has at least one full-time employee actively managing the business and at least three full-time non-owner employees working for the business. In addition, the corporation's trade or business expenses must exceed, by 15 percent, the gross income from that business for the year.[39]

6-7e Rental Activities

Subject to certain exceptions, all rental activities are treated as passive activities.[40] A rental activity is defined as any activity where payments are received principally for the use of tangible (real or personal) property.[41] Importantly, an activity classified as a rental activity is subject to the passive activity loss rules even if the taxpayer meets a material participation test.

[37]§ 469(h)(2) and Temp.Reg. § 1.469–5T(e)(3)(ii). Under Prop.Reg. § 1.469–5, however, material participation status for owners of LLCs and LLPs is dependent on the taxpayer's general involvement in the business.

[38]Temp.Reg. § 1.469–1T(g)(3)(i)(A).

[39]Temp.Reg. § 1.469–1T(g)(3)(i)(B).

[40]§ 469(c)(2).

[41]§ 469(j)(8).

Sarah owns a fleet of automobiles that are held for rent, and she spends an average of 60 hours a week in the activity. Assuming that her automobile business is classified as a rental activity, it is automatically subject to the passive activity rules even though Sarah spends more than 500 hours a year in its operation.

EXAMPLE
36

Certain rentals of real and personal property might be classified under the passive activity loss rules as nonrental activities.[42] In these situations, assuming that the activity is a trade or business, the material participation tests shown in Concept Summary 6.4 must be applied to determine whether the activity is a passive activity.

In-depth coverage can be found on this book's companion website: www.cengagebrain.com

7 DIGGING DEEPER

Dan owns a bicycle rental business at a nearby resort. Because the average period of customer use is seven days or less, Dan's business is not treated as a rental activity.

EXAMPLE
37

This exception to the definition of a rental activity is based on the presumption that a person who rents property for seven days or less is generally required to provide significant services to the customer. Providing such services supports a conclusion that the person is engaged in a service business rather than a rental business.

If Dan in Example 37 is a material participant, the business is treated as active. If he is not a material participant, it is treated as a passive activity. For additional discussion of the rental exceptions, see IRS Publication 925 (*Passive Activity and At-Risk Rules*).

The general rules relating to passive activity losses are reviewed in Concept Summary 6.5.

Concept Summary 6.5

Passive Activity Loss Rules: Key Issues and Answers

What is the fundamental passive activity rule?	Passive activity losses may be deducted only against passive activity income and gains. Losses not allowed are suspended and used in future years.
Who is subject to the passive activity rules?	Individuals.
	Estates.
	Trusts.
	Personal service corporations.
	Closely held C corporations.
What is a passive activity?	Trade or business or income-producing activity in which the taxpayer does not materially participate during the year or rental activities, subject to certain exceptions, regardless of the taxpayer's level of participation.
What is an activity?	One or more trades or businesses or rental activities that comprise an appropriate economic unit.
How is an appropriate economic unit determined?	Based on a reasonable application of the relevant facts and circumstances.
What is material participation?	In general, the taxpayer participates on a regular, continuous, and substantial basis. More specifically, when the taxpayer meets the conditions of one of the seven tests provided in the Regulations.
What is a rental activity?	In general, an activity where payments are received for the use of tangible property. Special rules apply to rental real estate.

---

[42]Temp.Reg. § 1.469–1T(e)(3).

LO.8

Determine the relationship between the at-risk and passive activity loss limitations.

6-7f Interaction of At-Risk and Passive Activity Loss Limits

The determination of whether a loss is suspended under the passive activity loss rules is made *after* application of the at-risk rules, as well as other provisions relating to the measurement of taxable income. A loss that is not allowed for the year because the taxpayer is not at risk with respect to it is suspended under the at-risk provisions, not under the passive activity loss rules. Further, a taxpayer's at-risk basis is reduced by the losses (but not below zero) even if the deductions are not currently usable because of the passive activity loss rules. The following examples illustrate these points.

At-Risk and Passive Activity Loss Interactions

EXAMPLE 38

Jack's adjusted basis in a passive activity is $10,000 at the beginning of 2015. His loss from the activity in 2015 is $4,000. Because Jack has no passive activity income, the $4,000 cannot be deducted. At year-end, Jack has an adjusted basis and an at-risk amount of $6,000 in the activity and a suspended passive activity loss of $4,000.

EXAMPLE 39

Jack in the preceding example has a loss of $9,000 in the activity in 2016. Because the $9,000 exceeds his at-risk amount ($6,000) by $3,000, that $3,000 loss is disallowed by the at-risk rules. If Jack has no passive activity income, the remaining $6,000 is suspended under the passive activity rules. At year-end, he has:

- A $3,000 loss suspended under the at-risk rules.
- $10,000 of suspended passive activity losses ($4,000 from 2015 and $6,000 from 2016).
- An adjusted basis and at-risk amount in the activity of zero.

EXAMPLE 40

Jack in Example 39 realizes $1,000 of passive activity income from the activity in 2017. Because the $1,000 increases his at-risk amount, $1,000 of the $3,000 unused loss from 2016 is reclassified as a passive activity loss. If he has no other passive activity income, the $1,000 income is offset by $1,000 of suspended passive activity losses. At the end of 2017, Jack has:

- No taxable passive activity income.
- $2,000 ($3,000 − $1,000) of suspended losses under the at-risk rules.
- $10,000 of (reclassified) suspended passive activity losses ($10,000 + $1,000 of reclassified suspended at-risk losses − $1,000 of passive activity losses offset against passive activity income).
- An adjusted basis and an at-risk amount in the activity of zero.

EXAMPLE 41

In 2018, Jack has no gain or loss from the activity in Example 40. He contributes $5,000 more to the passive activity. Because the $5,000 contribution increases his at-risk amount, the $2,000 of losses suspended under the at-risk rules is reclassified as passive. Jack gets no passive activity loss deduction in 2018. At year-end, he has:

- No suspended losses under the at-risk rules.
- $12,000 of suspended passive activity losses ($10,000 + $2,000 of reclassified suspended at-risk losses).
- An adjusted basis and an at-risk amount of $3,000 ($5,000 additional investment − $2,000 of reclassified losses).

See Concept Summary 6.6 for the interactions of the at-risk and passive activity loss limits.

Concept Summary 6.6

Treatment of Losses Subject to the At-Risk and Passive Activity Loss Limitations

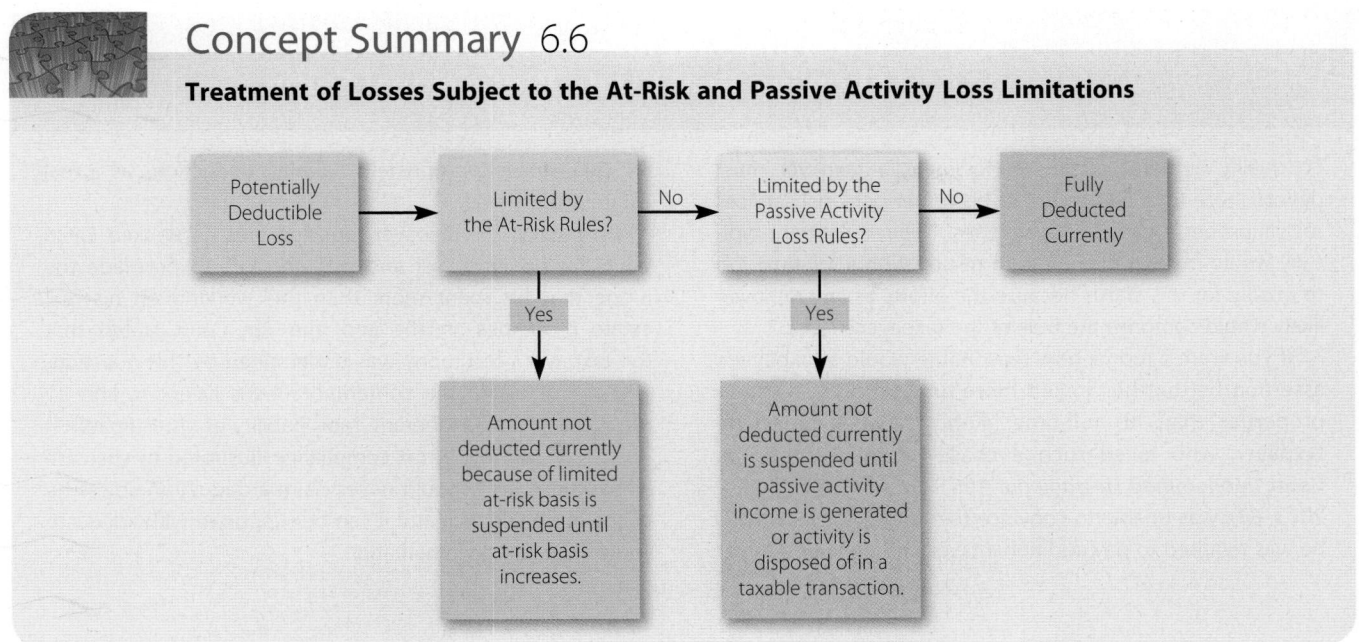

6-7g Special Rules for Real Estate

The passive activity loss rules contain two exceptions related to real estate activities. These exceptions allow all or part of real estate rental losses to offset active or portfolio income even though the activity otherwise is defined as a passive activity.

LO.9

Explain the special treatment available to real estate activities.

Real Estate Professionals

The first exception allows certain real estate professionals to avoid passive activity loss treatment for losses from real estate rental activities.[43] To qualify for nonpassive treatment, a taxpayer must satisfy both of the following requirements:

- More than half of the personal services that the taxpayer performs in trades or businesses are performed in real property trades or businesses in which the taxpayer materially participates.
- The taxpayer performs more than 750 hours of services in these real property trades or businesses as a material participant.

Taxpayers who do not satisfy the above requirements must continue to treat income and losses from real estate rental activities as passive activity income and losses.

EXAMPLE 42

During the current year, Della performs personal service activities as follows: 900 hours as a personal financial planner, 550 hours in a real estate development business, and 600 hours in a real estate rental activity. Any loss Della incurs in either real estate activity will not be subject to the passive activity loss rules. Being a nonrental business, the real estate development business is deemed active under the more-than-500-hour material participation test. The real estate rental activity is active because Della meets the two requirements to be a real estate professional [more than 50% of her personal services are devoted to real property trades or businesses (i.e., the development and rental) and these hours exceed 750]. Thus, she is allowed to apply the material participation tests to the real estate rental activity, and she meets one of these tests (the more than 500 hours test). Hence, any losses from either real estate activity can offset active and portfolio income. Likewise, any income from these activities is nonpassive (active) income.

As discussed earlier, a spouse's work is taken into consideration in satisfying the material participation requirement. However, the hours worked by a spouse are not

---

[43]§ 469(c)(7).

To qualify as a real estate professional, a taxpayer must devote more than 50 percent of his or her personal services to real property trades or businesses. This requirement typically would make it difficult for a person with a full-time job to qualify for this status because the efforts as an employee likely would comprise the bulk of the taxpayer's labor.

If you were a judge, how reasonable would a taxpayer's assertion be that he worked more time on his real estate properties than his full-time, 40-hour-a-week job? One taxpayer, who faced such a challenge before the Tax Court (*Mohammad Hassanipour* 105 TCM 1542, T.C.Memo. 2013–88), was unable to convince the judge. Consequently, he was required to pay additional taxes and penalties—over

$45,000—for inappropriately claiming deductions as a real estate professional.

Essentially, the taxpayer reported that he worked 1,936 hours for his employer and was not able to persuade the judge that he spent more than this working on his real estate properties. In the end, the Tax Court stated that the taxpayer's testimony was undermined by "his questionable claims about the contemporaneous calendar, and by the vagueness and inherent improbability of his estimates."

A basic premise of tax compliance illustrated by the case is that a taxpayer should never claim a deduction unless he or she is entitled to it and it can be supported with adequate and convincing documentation.

taken into account when ascertaining whether a taxpayer has worked for more than 750 hours in real property trades or businesses during a year. Services performed by an employee are not treated as being related to a real estate trade or business unless the employee performing the services owns more than a 5 percent interest in the employer. In addition, a closely held C corporation may also qualify for the passive activity loss relief if more than 50 percent of its gross receipts for the year are derived from real property trades or businesses in which it materially participates.[44]

Rental Real Estate with Active Participation

The second exception to the passive activity loss limits is more significant in that it is not restricted to real estate professionals. This exception allows individuals to deduct up to $25,000 of losses from real estate rental activities against active and portfolio income.[45] The potential annual $25,000 deduction is reduced by 50 percent of the taxpayer's adjusted gross income (AGI) in excess of $100,000. Thus, the entire deduction is phased out at $150,000 of AGI. If married individuals file separately, the $25,000 deduction is reduced to zero unless they lived apart for the entire year, in which case the loss amount is $12,500 each and the phaseout begins at $50,000 of AGI.

To qualify for the $25,000 exception, a taxpayer must meet both of the following requirements:[46]

- *Actively participate* in the real estate rental activity.
- Own 10 percent or more (in value) of all interests in the activity during the entire taxable year (or shorter period during which the taxpayer held an interest in the activity).

The difference between *active participation* and *material participation* is that the former can be satisfied without regular, continuous, and substantial involvement in operations as long as the taxpayer participates in making management decisions in a significant and bona fide sense. In this context, relevant management decisions include decisions such as approving new tenants, deciding on rental terms, and approving capital or repair expenditures.

The $25,000 allowance is available after all active participation rental losses and gains are netted and applied to other passive activity income. If a taxpayer has a

---

[44]§ 469(c)(7)(B) and Reg. § 1.469–9. In *Frank Aragona Trust*, 142 T.C. 165 (2014), the Tax Court found that a trust also could qualify for the real estate professional rule.

[45]§ 469(i).
[46]§ 469(i)(6).

real estate rental loss in excess of the amount that can be deducted under the real estate rental exception, that excess is treated as a passive activity loss, usable in future years.

Brad has $90,000 of AGI before considering rental activities. Brad also has $85,000 of losses from a real estate rental activity in which he actively participates. He also actively participates in another real estate rental activity from which he has $30,000 of income. He has other passive activity income of $36,000. Of the net rental loss of $55,000 ($30,000 − $85,000), $36,000 is absorbed by the passive activity income, leaving $19,000 that can be deducted against active or portfolio income because of the availability of the $25,000 allowance.

The $25,000 offset allowance is an aggregate of both deductions and credits in deduction equivalents. The deduction equivalent of a passive activity credit is the amount of deductions that reduces the tax liability for the taxable year by an amount equal to the credit.[47] A taxpayer with $5,000 of credits and a marginal tax rate of 25 percent would have a deduction equivalent of $20,000 ($5,000 ÷ 25%).

If total deductions and deduction equivalents exceed $25,000, the taxpayer must allocate the benefit on a pro rata basis. First, the allowance must be allocated among the losses (including real estate rental activity losses suspended in prior years) and then to credits.

Deduction Equivalent Considerations

Kevin is an active participant in a real estate rental activity that produces $8,000 of income, $26,000 of deductions, and $1,500 of credits. Kevin, whose marginal tax rate is 25%, may deduct the net passive activity loss of $18,000 ($8,000 − $26,000). After deducting the loss, he has an available deduction equivalent of $7,000 ($25,000 − $18,000 passive activity loss). Because the actual credits produce a deduction equivalent ($1,500 ÷ 25% = $6,000) that is less than $7,000, Kevin may claim the entire $1,500 credit.

Kelly, whose marginal tax rate is 25%, actively participates in three separate real estate rental activities. The relevant tax results for each activity are as follows:

- Activity A: $20,000 of losses.
- Activity B: $10,000 of losses.
- Activity C: $4,200 of credits.

Kelly's deduction equivalent from the credits is $16,800 ($4,200 ÷ 25%). Therefore, the total passive activity deductions and deduction equivalents are $46,800 ($20,000 + $10,000 + $16,800), which exceeds the maximum allowable amount of $25,000. Consequently, Kelly must allocate pro rata first from among losses and then from among credits. Deductions from losses are limited as follows:

- Activity A: $25,000 × [$20,000/($20,000 + $10,000)] = $16,667.
- Activity B: $25,000 × [$10,000/($20,000 + $10,000)] = $8,333.

Because the amount of passive activity deductions exceeds the $25,000 maximum, the deduction balance of $5,000 and passive activity credits of $4,200 must be carried forward. Kelly's suspended losses and credits by activity are as follows:

	Total	Activity		
		A	**B**	**C**
Allocated losses	$ 30,000	$ 20,000	$10,000	$ –0–
Allocated credits	4,200	–0–	–0–	4,200
Utilized losses	(25,000)	(16,667)	(8,333)	–0–
Suspended losses	5,000	3,333	1,667	–0–
Suspended credits	4,200	–0–	–0–	4,200

---

[47]§ 469(j)(5).

LO.10

Determine the consequences of the disposition of passive activities.

6-7h Disposition of Passive Activities

Recall from an earlier discussion that if a taxpayer disposes of an entire interest in a passive activity, any suspended losses (and in certain cases, suspended credits) may be utilized when calculating the final economic gain or loss on the investment. In addition, if a loss ultimately results, that loss can offset other types of income. However, the consequences may differ if the activity is disposed of in a transaction that is not fully taxable. The following sections discuss the treatment of suspended passive activity losses in two such dispositions.

Disposition of a Passive Activity at Death

When a transfer of a taxpayer's interest occurs because of the taxpayer's death, suspended losses are allowed (to the decedent) to the extent they exceed the amount, if any, of the allowed step-up in basis.[48] Suspended losses that are equal to or less than the amount of the basis increase are, however, lost. The losses allowed generally are reported on the final return of the deceased taxpayer.

Disposition of Suspended Losses at Death

EXAMPLE
46

Alyson dies with passive activity property having an adjusted basis of $40,000, suspended losses of $10,000, and a fair market value at the date of her death of $75,000. The increase (i.e., step-up) in basis (see Chapter 7) is $35,000 (fair market value at date of death in excess of adjusted basis). None of the $10,000 suspended loss is deductible on Alyson's final return or by the beneficiary. The suspended losses ($10,000) are lost because they do not exceed the step-up in basis ($35,000).

EXAMPLE
47

Assume the same facts as in the previous example except that the property's fair market value at the date of Alyson's death is $47,000. Because the step-up in basis is only $7,000 ($47,000 − $40,000), the suspended losses allowed are limited to $3,000 ($10,000 suspended loss at time of death − $7,000 increase in basis). The $3,000 loss available to Alyson is reported on her final income tax return.

Disposition of a Passive Activity by Gift

In a disposition of a taxpayer's interest in a passive activity by gift, the suspended losses are added to the basis of the property.[49]

As such, the suspended losses become permanently nondeductible to both the donor and the donee. Nonetheless, a tax *benefit* may be available to the donee for another reason. Due to the increase in the property's basis, greater depreciation deductions can result and there will be less gain (or more loss) on a subsequent sale of the property. The side benefits of increased basis do not materialize if the recipient is a charity, as such organizations generally are not subject to income taxation.

EXAMPLE
48

Carlton makes a gift to Yolanda of passive activity property having an adjusted basis of $40,000, suspended losses of $10,000, and a fair market value at the date of the gift of $100,000. Carlton cannot deduct the suspended losses in the year of the disposition. However, the suspended losses of $10,000 transfer with the property and are added to the adjusted basis of the property, thus becoming $50,000 in Yolanda's hands. Assuming that Yolanda is able to sell the property for $105,000 soon after she receives the gift, her taxable gain would be $55,000 ($105,000 − $50,000), which reflects the benefit from the increased basis.

---

[48]§ 469(g)(2).

[49]§ 469(j)(6).

TAX PLANNING STRATEGIES Utilizing Passive Activity Losses

FRAMEWORK FOCUS: TAX RATE

Strategy: Control the Character of Income and Deductions.

Perhaps the biggest challenge individuals face with the passive activity loss rules is to recognize the potential impact of the rules and then to structure their affairs to minimize this impact. Taxpayers who have passive activity losses (PALs) should adopt a strategy of generating passive activity income that can be sheltered by existing passive activity losses. One approach is to buy an interest in a passive activity that is generating income (referred to as a passive income generator, or PIG). Then the PAL can offset income from the PIG. From a tax perspective, it would be foolish to buy a loss-generating passive activity unless one has passive activity income to shelter or the activity is rental real estate that can qualify for the $25,000 exception or the exception available to real estate professionals.

If a taxpayer does invest in an activity that produces losses subject to the passive activity loss rules, the following strategies may help minimize the loss of current deductions:

- If money is borrowed to finance the purchase of a passive activity, the associated interest expense is generally treated as part of any passive activity loss. Consequently, by using more available (i.e., not borrowed) cash to purchase the passive investment, the investor will need less debt and will incur less interest expense. By incurring less interest expense, a possible suspended passive activity loss deduction is reduced.

- If the investor does not have sufficient cash readily available for the larger down payment, cash can be obtained by borrowing against the equity in his or her personal residence. The interest expense on such debt will be deductible under the qualified residence interest provisions (see Chapter 10) and will not be subject to the passive activity loss limitations. Thus, the taxpayer avoids the passive activity loss limitation and secures a currently deductible interest expense.

As explained earlier, unusable passive activity losses often accumulate and provide no current tax benefit because the taxpayer has no passive activity income. When the taxpayer disposes of the entire interest in a passive activity, however, any suspended losses from that activity are used to reduce the taxable gain. If any taxable gain still remains, it can be offset by losses from other passive activities. As a result, the taxpayer should carefully select the year in which to dispose of a passive activity. It is to the taxpayer's advantage to wait until sufficient passive activity losses have accumulated to offset any gain recognized on the asset's disposition.

EXAMPLE
49

Bill, a calendar year taxpayer, owns interests in two passive activities: Activity A, which he plans to sell in December of this year at a gain of $100,000, and Activity B, which he plans to keep indefinitely. Current and suspended losses associated with Activity B total $60,000, and Bill expects losses from the activity to be $40,000 next year. If Bill sells Activity A this year, the $100,000 gain can be offset by the current and suspended losses of $60,000 from Activity B, producing a net taxable gain of $40,000. However, if Bill delays the sale of Activity A until January of next year, the $100,000 gain will be fully offset by the $100,000 of losses generated by Activity B ($60,000 current and prior losses + $40,000 next year's loss). Consequently, by postponing the sale by one month, he could avoid recognizing $40,000 of gain that would otherwise result.

Taxpayers with passive activity losses should consider the level of their involvement in all other trades or businesses in which they have an interest. If they show that they do not materially participate in a profitable activity, the activity becomes a passive activity. Current and suspended passive activity losses then could shelter any income generated by the profitable business. Family partnerships in which certain members do not materially participate would qualify. The silent partner in any general partnership engaged in a trade or business would also qualify.

continued

EXAMPLE

50

Gail has an investment in a limited partnership that produces annual passive activity losses of approximately $25,000. She also owns a newly acquired interest in a convenience store where she works. Her share of the store's income is $35,000. If she works enough to be classified as a material participant, her $35,000 share of income is treated as active income. This results in $35,000 being subject to tax every year, while her $25,000 loss is suspended. However, if Gail reduces her involvement at the store so that she is not a material participant, the $35,000 of income receives passive treatment. Consequently, the $35,000 of income can be offset by the $25,000 passive activity loss, resulting in only $10,000 being subject to tax. Thus, by reducing her involvement, Gail ensures that the income from the profitable trade or business receives passive treatment and can then be used to absorb passive activity losses from other passive activities.

The passive activity loss rules can have a dramatic effect on a taxpayer's ability to claim passive activity losses currently. As a result, it is important to keep accurate records of all sources of income and losses, particularly any suspended passive activity losses and credits and the activities to which they relate, so that their potential tax benefit will not be lost.

The passive activity rules can also affect planning for individuals subject to the Net Investment Income Tax (Chapter 9).

REFOCUS ON THE BIG PICTURE

RECEIVING TAX BENEFITS FROM LOSSES

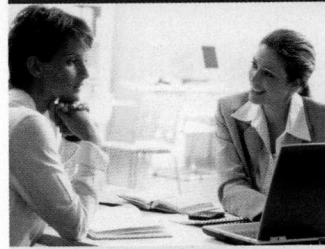

While Robyn's circumstances were unfortunate, the good news is that she will be able to receive some tax benefits from the losses.

- *Bad debt.* Based on the facts provided, it appears that Robyn's loan to her friend, Jamil, was a bona fide nonbusiness bad debt. The amount of the loss deduction is the unpaid principal balance of $19,000 ($25,000 − $6,000). As a nonbusiness bad debt, the loss is classified as a short-term capital loss (see Example 5).

- *Loss from stock investment.* Likewise, the $60,000 loss on the Owl Corporation stock investment is deductible. If Robyn purchased the stock directly from the company, the stock may qualify as small business stock under § 1244. If this is the case, the first $50,000 of the loss is an ordinary loss and the remaining $10,000 loss is treated as a long-term capital loss. If the stock is not § 1244 stock, the entire $60,000 loss is treated as a long-term capital loss (see Example 8).

- *Loss from bookstore.* The $180,000 loss from the bookstore is reported on Schedule C of Robyn's Form 1040. It is an ordinary loss and qualifies for net operating loss (NOL) treatment if she does not have enough other taxable income this year against which the loss could be offset. Any NOL can be carried back 2 years or carried forward for the next 20 years to produce refunds of taxes paid from prior years or to reduce taxes owed on taxable income earned in the future.

- *Casualty loss.* The loss from the damage to Robyn's personal residence is a personal casualty loss. Using the cost of repairs method, the amount of the casualty loss is $7,000 ($32,000 loss − $25,000 insurance recovery). However, this amount must be reduced by the statutory amount of $100 and 10 percent of AGI (see Example 13).

- *Passive activity loss.* The $20,000 loss on the limited partnership is not deductible currently due to the passive activity loss limitation. However, the loss can be carried forward and utilized in the future to offset any passive activity income generated from the venture or other passive activities (see Example 21).

continued

What If?

What if instead of operating orange groves, the partnership was a general partnership that owns and rents apartments to college students and Robyn actively participates in the venture? In this case, Robyn may qualify for a $20,000 ordinary loss deduction under the rental real estate with active participation exception.

Suggested Readings

Sharon Burnett and Darlene Pulliam, "LLC Principal At-Risk Amounts for Guaranteed Debt," *Practical Tax Strategies*, April 2015.

John O. Everett, Cherie J. Hennig, William A. Raabe, and Blaise M. Sonnier, "How Effective Planning Can Increase the Tax Benefits of Corporate NOLs," *Journal of Taxation*, February 2014.

James R. Hamill, "The Section 1411 Surtax and the Real Estate Professional," *Practical Tax Strategies*, March 2014.

William C. Hood, "Deducting Ponzi Losses," *Practical Tax Strategies*, March 2014.

David H. Kirk and Vinny Satchit "Peeling the Onion: Passive Loss Regrouping in Light of Section 1411," *Business Entities*, March/April 2015.

Key Terms

Active income, 6-16	Material participation, 6-23	Reserve method, 6-2
At-risk limitation, 6-14	Net operating loss (NOL), 6-11	Significant participation activity, 6-23
Bad debt, 6-2	Nonbusiness bad debt, 6-4	Small business stock (§ 1244 stock), 6-5
Business bad debt, 6-4	Passive activity loss, 6-14	Specific charge-off method, 6-2
Casualty losses, 6-7	Personal service corporation, 6-20	Tax shelters, 6-13
Closely held C corporation, 6-21	Portfolio income, 6-16	Theft losses, 6-8
Disaster area losses, 6-7	Rental activity, 6-24	Worthless securities, 6-5

Computational Exercises

1. **LO.1** Last year Jane identified $50,000 as a nonbusiness bad debt. In that tax year, before considering the tax implications of the nonbusiness bad debt, Jane had $100,000 of taxable income, of which $5,000 consisted of short-term capital gains. This year Jane collected $10,000 of the amount she had previously identified as a bad debt. Determine Jane's tax treatment of the $10,000 received in the current tax year.

2. **LO.1** Bob owns a collection agency. He purchases uncollected accounts receivable from other businesses at 60% of their face value and then attempts to collect these accounts. During the current year, Bob collected $60,000 on an account with a face value of $80,000. Determine the amount of Bob's bad debt deduction.

3. **LO.2** On May 9, 2014, Calvin acquired 250 shares of stock in Aero Corporation, a new startup company, for $68,750. Calvin acquired the stock directly from Aero, and it is classified as § 1244 stock (at the time Calvin acquired his stock, the corporation had $900,000 of paid-in capital). On January 15, 2016, Calvin sold all of his Aero stock for $7,000. Assuming that Calvin is single, determine his tax consequences as a result of this sale.

4. **LO.3** Mary's diamond ring was stolen in 2015. She originally paid $8,000 for the ring, but it was worth considerably more at the time of the theft. Mary filed an insurance claim for the stolen ring, but the claim was denied. Because the insurance claim was denied, Mary took a casualty loss deduction for the stolen ring on her 2015 tax return. In 2015, Mary had AGI of $40,000. In 2016, the insurance company had a "change of heart" and sent Mary a check for $5,000 for the stolen ring. Determine the proper tax treatment of the $5,000 Mary received from the insurance company in 2016.

5. **LO.3** Determine the treatment of a loss on rental property under the following facts:

Basis	$650,000
FMV before the loss	800,000
FMV after the loss	200,000

6. **LO.6** In the current year, Ed invests $30,000 in an oil partnership. He has taxable income for the current year of $2,000 from the oil partnership and withdraws $10,000. What is Ed's at-risk amount at the end of the year?

7. **LO.6** Lucy sells her partnership interest, a passive activity, with an adjusted basis of $305,000 for $330,000. In addition, she has current and suspended losses of $28,000 associated with the partnership and has no other passive activities. Calculate Lucy's total gain and her current deductible loss. Describe the type of income that the deductible loss may offset.

8. **LO.8** Rhonda has an adjusted basis and an at-risk amount of $7,500 in a passive activity at the beginning of the year. She also has a suspended passive activity loss of $1,500 carried over from the prior year. During the current year, she has a loss of $12,000 from the passive activity. Rhonda has no passive activity income from other sources this year. Determine the following items relating to Rhonda's passive activity as of the end of the year.
   a. Adjusted basis and at-risk amount in the passive activity.
   b. Loss suspended under the at-risk rules.
   c. Suspended passive activity loss.

9. **LO.9** Noah, who has $62,000 of AGI before considering rental activities, has $70,000 of losses from a real estate rental activity in which he actively participates. He also actively participates in another real estate rental activity from which he has $33,000 of income. He has other passive activity income of $20,000. What amount of rental loss can Noah use to offset active or portfolio income in the current year?

10. **LO.10** Rose dies with passive activity property having an adjusted basis of $65,000, suspended losses of $13,000, and a fair market value at the date of her death of $90,000. Of the $13,000 suspended loss existing at the time of Rose's death, how much is deductible on her final return or by the beneficiary?

Problems

Communications   11. **LO.1** Several years ago, Loon Finance Company, which is in the lending business, loaned Sara $30,000 to purchase an automobile to be used for personal purposes. In August of the current year, Sara filed for bankruptcy, and Loon was notified that it could not expect to receive more than $4,000. As of the end of the current year, Loon has received $1,000. Loon has contacted you about the possibility of taking a bad debt deduction for the current year.

Write a letter to Loon Finance Company that contains your advice as to whether it can claim a bad debt deduction for the current year. Also prepare a memo for the tax files. Loon's address is 100 Tyler Lane, Erie, PA 16563.

12. **LO.1** Monty loaned his friend Ned $20,000 three years ago. Ned signed a note and made payments on the loan. Last year, when the remaining balance was $11,000, Ned filed for bankruptcy and notified Monty that he would be unable to pay the balance on the loan. Monty treated the $11,000 as a nonbusiness bad debt. Last year, before considering the tax implications of the nonbusiness bad debt, Monty had capital gains of $4,000 and taxable income of $20,000. During the current year, Ned paid Monty $10,000 in satisfaction of the debt. Determine Monty's tax treatment for the $10,000 received in the current year.

13. **LO.2** Many years ago, Jack purchased 400 shares of Canary stock. During the current year, the stock became worthless. It was determined that the company "went under" because several corporate officers embezzled a large amount of company funds. Identify the relevant tax issues for Jack.

    Issue ID

14. **LO.1** Jake and Mary Snow are residents of the state of New York. They are cash basis taxpayers and file a joint return for the calendar year. Jake is a licensed master plumber. Two years ago, Jake entered into a contract with New York City to perform plumbing services. During the current year, Jake was declared to be in breach of the contract, and he ceased performing plumbing services. Jake received a Form W–2 that reported $50,000 for wages paid. He also maintains that the city has not paid him $35,000 for work he performed. Jake is considering claiming a $35,000 business bad debt on his tax return. Evaluate Jake's plan.

    Ethics and Equity

15. **LO.1, 2** Mable and Jack file a joint return. For the current year, they had the following items:

Salaries	$120,000
Loss on sale of § 1244 stock acquired two years ago	105,000
Gain on sale of § 1244 stock acquired six months ago	20,000
Nonbusiness bad debt	19,000

    Determine the impact of the above items on Mable and Jack's income for the current year.

16. **LO.2** Mary, a single taxpayer, purchased 10,000 shares of § 1244 stock several years ago at a cost of $20 per share. In November of the current year, Mary receives an offer to sell the stock for $12 per share. She has the option of either selling all of the stock now or selling half of the stock now and half of the stock in January of next year. Mary's salary is $80,000 for the current year, and it will be $90,000 next year. Mary has long-term capital gains of $8,000 for the current year and will have $10,000 next year. If Mary's goal is to minimize her AGI for the two years, determine whether she should sell all of her stock this year or half of her stock this year and half next year.

    Decision Making

17. **LO.3** Olaf lives in the state of Minnesota. A tornado hit the area and damaged his home and automobile. Applicable information is as follows:

    Decision Making

Item	Adjusted Basis	FMV before	FMV after	Insurance Proceeds
Home	$350,000	$500,000	$100,000	$280,000
Auto	60,000	40,000	10,000	20,000

    Because of the extensive damage caused by the tornado, the President designated the area a disaster area.

    Olaf and his wife, Anna, always file a joint return. Their 2015 tax return shows AGI of $180,000 and taxable income of $140,000. In 2016, their return shows AGI of $300,000 and taxable income (exclusive of the casualty loss deduction) of $215,000.

    Determine the amount of Olaf and Anna's loss and the year in which they should take the loss.

Issue ID   18. **LO.3** In 2013, John opened an investment account with Randy Hansen, who held himself out to the public as an investment adviser and securities broker. John contributed $200,000 to the account in 2013. John provided Randy with a power of attorney to use the $200,000 to purchase and sell securities on John's behalf. John instructed Randy to reinvest any gains and income earned. In 2013, 2014, and 2015, John received statements of the amount of income earned by his account and included these amounts in his gross income for these years. In 2016, it was discovered that Randy's purported investment advisory and brokerage activity was in fact a fraudulent investment arrangement known as a Ponzi scheme. In reality, John's account balance was zero, the money having been used by Randy in his scheme. Identify the relevant tax issues for John.

Critical Thinking   19. **LO.4** Mary, a single taxpayer with two dependent children, has the following items of income and expense during 2016:

Gross receipts from business	$144,000
Business expenses	180,000
Alimony received	22,000
Interest income	3,000
Itemized deductions (no casualty or theft)	24,000

     a.   Determine Mary's taxable income for 2016.

     b.   Determine Mary's NOL for 2016.

20. **LO.6** In 2015, Fred invested $50,000 in a general partnership. Fred's interest is not considered to be a passive activity. If his share of the partnership losses is $35,000 in 2015 and $25,000 in 2016, how much can he deduct in each year?

Communications   21. **LO.6** In the current year, Bill Parker (54 Oak Drive, St. Paul, MN 55164) is considering making an investment of $60,000 in Best Choice Partnership. The prospectus provided by Bill's broker indicates that the partnership investment is not a passive activity and that Bill's share of the entity's loss in the current year will likely be $40,000, while his share of the partnership loss next year will probably be $25,000. Write a letter to Bill in which you indicate how the losses would be treated for tax purposes in the current year and the following year.

22. **LO.6** A number of years ago, Kay acquired an interest in a partnership in which she is not a material participant. Kay's basis in her partnership interest at the beginning of 2015 is $40,000. Kay's share of the partnership loss is $35,000 in 2015, while her share of the partnership income is $15,000 in 2016. How much may Kay deduct in 2015 and 2016, assuming that she owns no other passive activities?

Decision Making   23. **LO.6** Jorge owns two passive investments, Activity A and Activity B. He plans to dispose of Activity A in the current year or next year. Juanita has offered to buy Activity A this year for an amount that would produce a taxable passive activity gain to Jorge of $115,000. However, if the sale, for whatever reason, is not made to Juanita, Jorge believes that he could find a buyer who would pay about $7,000 less than Juanita. Passive activity losses and gains generated (and expected to be generated) by Activity B follow:

Two years ago	($35,000)
Last year	(35,000)
This year	(8,000)
Next year	(30,000)
Future years	Minimal profits

All of Activity B's losses are suspended. Should Jorge close the sale of Activity A with Juanita this year, or should he wait until next year and sell to another buyer? Jorge is in the 28% tax bracket.

24. **LO.6** Sarah has investments in four passive activity partnerships purchased several years ago. Last year, the income and losses were as follows:

Activity	Income (Loss)
A	$ 30,000
B	(30,000)
C	(15,000)
D	(5,000)

In the current year, she sold her interest in Activity D for a $10,000 gain. Activity D, which had been profitable until last year, had a current loss of $1,500. How will the sale of Activity D affect Sarah's taxable income in the current year?

25. **LO.6** Leon sells his interest in a passive activity for $100,000. Determine the tax effect of the sale based on each of the following independent facts:
    a. Adjusted basis in this investment is $35,000. Losses from prior years that were not deductible due to the passive activity loss restrictions total $40,000.
    b. Adjusted basis in this investment is $75,000. Losses from prior years that were not deductible due to the passive activity loss restrictions total $40,000.
    c. Adjusted basis in this investment is $75,000. Losses from prior years that were not deductible due to the passive activity loss restrictions total $40,000. In addition, suspended credits total $10,000.

26. **LO.6** In the current year, White, Inc., earns $400,000 from operations and receives $36,000 of interest income from various portfolio investments. White also pays $150,000 to acquire a 20% interest in a passive activity that produces a $200,000 loss.
    a. Assuming that White is a personal service corporation, how will these transactions affect its taxable income?
    b. Same as part (a), except that White is closely held but not a personal service corporation.

27. **LO.7** John, an engineer, operates a separate business that he acquired eight years ago. If he participates 85 hours in the business and it incurs a loss of $34,000, under what circumstances can John claim an active loss?

28. **LO.7** Rene retired from public accounting after a long and successful career of 45 years. As part of her retirement package, she continues to share in the profits and losses of the firm, albeit at a lower rate than when she was working full-time. Because Rene wants to stay busy during her retirement years, she has invested and works in a local hardware business, operated as a partnership. Unfortunately, the business has recently gone through a slump and has not been generating profits. Identify relevant tax issues for Rene.

Issue ID

29. **LO.6, 8** Kristin Graf (123 Baskerville Mill Road, Jamison, PA 18929) is trying to decide how to invest a $10,000 inheritance. One option is to make an additional investment in Rocky Road Excursions in which she has an at-risk basis of $0, suspended losses under the at-risk rules of $7,000, and suspended passive activity losses of $1,000. If Kristin makes this investment, her share of the expected profits this year will be $8,000. If her investment stays the same, her share of profits from Rocky Road Excursions will be $1,000. Another option is to invest $10,000 as a limited partner in the Ragged Mountain Winery; this investment will produce passive activity income of $9,000. Write a letter to Kristin to review the tax consequences of each alternative. Kristin is in the 28% tax bracket.

Decision Making

Communications

30. **LO.8** The end of the year is approaching, and Maxine has begun to focus on ways of minimizing her income tax liability. Several years ago, she purchased an

Decision Making

investment in Teal Limited Partnership, which is subject to the at-risk and the passive activity loss rules. (Last year, Maxine sold a different investment that was subject to these rules and that produced passive activity income.) She believes that her investment in Teal has good long-term economic prospects. However, it has been generating tax losses for several years in a row. In fact, when she was discussing last year's income tax return with her tax accountant, he said that unless "things change" with respect to her investments, she would not be able to deduct losses this year.

a.   What was the accountant referring to in his comment?

b.   You learn that Maxine's current at-risk basis in her investment is $1,000 and that her share of the current loss is expected to be $13,000. Based on these facts, how will her loss be treated?

c.   After reviewing her situation, Maxine's financial adviser suggests that she invest at least an additional $12,000 in Teal to ensure a full loss deduction in the current year. How do you react to his suggestion?

d.   What would you suggest Maxine consider as she attempts to maximize her current-year deductible loss?

31. **LO.8** A number of years ago, Lee acquired a 20% interest in the BlueSky Partnership for $60,000. The partnership was profitable through 2015, and Lee's amount at risk in the partnership interest was $120,000 at the beginning of 2016. BlueSky incurred a loss of $400,000 in 2016 and reported income of $200,000 in 2017. Assuming that Lee is not a material participant, how much of his loss from BlueSky Partnership is deductible in 2016 and 2017? Consider the at-risk and passive activity loss rules, and assume that Lee owns no other investments.

32. **LO.6** Grace acquired an activity four years ago. The loss from the activity is $50,000 in the current year (at-risk basis of $40,000 as of the beginning of the year). Without considering the loss from the activity, she has gross income of $140,000. If the activity is a convenience store and Grace is a material participant, what is the effect of the activity on her taxable income?

33. **LO.5, 6, 8** Jonathan, a physician, earns $200,000 from his practice. He also receives $18,000 in dividends and interest from various portfolio investments. During the year, he pays $45,000 to acquire a 20% interest in a partnership that produces a $300,000 loss. Compute Jonathan's AGI assuming that:

a.   He does not participate in the operations of the partnership.

b.   He is a material participant in the operations of the partnership.

34. **LO.5, 6, 8** Five years ago, Gerald invested $150,000 in a passive activity, his sole investment venture. On January 1, 2015, his amount at risk in the activity was $30,000. His shares of the income and losses were as follows:

Year	Income (Loss)
2015	($40,000)
2016	(30,000)
2017	50,000

Gerald holds no suspended at-risk or passive activity losses at the beginning of 2015. How much can Gerald deduct in 2015 and 2016? What is his taxable income from the activity in 2017? Consider the at-risk rules as well as the passive activity loss rules.

Ethics and Equity

Communications

35. **LO.5, 6, 7** You have just met with Scott Myers (603 Pittsfield Drive, Champaign, IL 61821), a successful full-time real estate developer and investor. During your meeting, you discussed his tax situation because you are starting to prepare his current Federal income tax return. During your meeting, Scott mentioned that he and his wife, Susan, went to great lengths to maximize their participation in an apartment complex that they own and manage. In particular, Scott included the following activities in the 540 hours of participation for the current year:

- Time spent thinking about the rentals.
- Time spent by Susan on weekdays visiting the apartment complex to oversee operations of the buildings (i.e., in a management role).
- Time spent by both Scott and Susan on weekends visiting the apartment complex to assess operations. Scott and Susan always visited the complex together on weekends, and both counted their hours (i.e., one hour at the complex was two hours of participation).
- Time spent on weekends driving around the community looking for other potential rental properties to purchase. Again, both Scott's hours and Susan's hours were counted, even when they drove together.

After reviewing Scott's records, you note that the apartment complex generated a significant loss this year. Prepare a letter to Scott describing your position on the deductibility of the loss.

36. **LO.6, 9** Bonnie and Jake (ages 35 and 36, respectively) are married with no dependents and live in Montana (not a community property state). Because Jake has large medical expenses, they seek your advice about filing separately to save taxes. Their income and expenses for 2016 are as follows:

Decision Making

Bonnie's salary	$ 42,500
Jake's salary	26,000
Interest income (joint)	1,500
Rental loss from actively managed rental property	(23,000)
Jake's unreimbursed medical expenses	8,500
All other itemized deductions:*	
Bonnie	9,000
Jake	3,400

*None subject to limitations.

Determine whether Bonnie and Jake should file jointly or separately for 2016.

37. **LO.9** During the current year, Gene, a CPA, performs services as follows: 1,800 hours in his tax practice and 50 hours in an apartment leasing operation in which he has a 15% interest. Because of his oversight duties, Gene is considered to be an active participant. He expects that his share of the loss realized from the apartment leasing operation will be $30,000 and that his tax practice will show a profit of approximately $80,000. Gene is single and has no other income. Discuss the character and treatment of the income and losses generated by these activities.

38. **LO.9** Ida, who has AGI of $80,000 before considering rental activities, is active in three separate real estate rental activities. Ida has a marginal tax rate of 28%. She has $12,000 of losses from Activity A, $18,000 of losses from Activity B, and income of $10,000 from Activity C. She also has $2,100 of tax credits from Activity A. Calculate the deductions and credits that she is allowed and the suspended losses and credits.

39. **LO.9** Ella has $105,000 of losses from a real estate rental activity in which she actively participates. She has other rent income of $25,000 and other passive activity income of $32,000. Her AGI before considering these items of income and loss is $95,000. How much rental loss can Ella deduct against active and portfolio income (ignoring the at-risk rules)? Does she have any suspended losses to carry over? Explain.

40. **LO.5, 6, 10** In the current year, Abe gives an interest in a passive activity to his daughter, Andrea. The value of the interest at the date of the gift is $25,000, and its adjusted basis to Abe is $13,000. During the time that Abe owned the investment, losses of $3,000 could not be deducted because of the passive activity loss limitations. What is the tax treatment of the suspended passive activity losses to Abe and Andrea?

BRIDGE DISCIPLINE

1. Marketplace, Inc., has recognized over time that a certain percentage of its customer accounts receivable will not be collected. To ensure the appropriate matching of revenues and expenditures in its financial reports, Marketplace uses the reserve method for bad debts. Records show the following pertaining to its treatment of bad debts.

Beginning allowance for bad debts	$120,000
Ending allowance for bad debts	123,000
Bad debts written off during the year	33,000

   a. What was the bad debt expense for financial accounting purposes during the year?

   b. What was the bad debt expense for income tax purposes during the year?

   c. Assuming that the before-tax net income for financial accounting purposes was $545,000, what is the taxable income for the year if the treatment of bad debts is the only book-tax difference?

Decision Making   2. Heather wants to invest $40,000 in a relatively safe venture and has discovered two alternatives that would produce the following ordinary income and loss over the next three years:

Year	Alternative 1 Income (Loss)	Alternative 2 Income (Loss)
1	($20,000)	($48,000)
2	(28,000)	32,000
3	72,000	40,000

   She is interested in the after-tax effects of these alternatives over a three-year horizon. Assume that:

   - Heather's investment portfolio produces sufficient passive activity income to offset any potential passive activity loss that may arise from these alternatives.

   - Heather's marginal tax rate is 25%, and her cost of capital is 6% (see Appendix F for the present value factors).

   - Each investment alternative possesses equal growth potential and comparable financial risk.

   - In the loss years for each alternative, there is no cash flow from or to the investment (i.e., the loss is due to depreciation), while in those years when the income is positive, cash flows to Heather equal the amount of the income.

   Based on these facts, compute the present value of these two investment alternatives and determine which option Heather should choose.

Decision Making   3. Emily has $100,000 that she wants to invest and is considering the following two options:

   - Option A: Investment in Redbird Mutual Fund, which is expected to produce interest income of $8,000 per year.

- Option B: Investment in Cardinal Limited Partnership (buys, sells, and operates wine vineyards). Emily's share of the partnership's ordinary income and loss over the next three years would be as follows:

Year	Income (Loss)
1	($ 8,000)
2	(2,000)
3	34,000

Emily is interested in the after-tax effects of these alternatives over a three-year horizon. Assume that Emily's investment portfolio produces ample passive activity income to offset any passive activity losses that may be generated. Her cost of capital is 8% (see Appendix F for the present value factors), and she is in the 28% tax bracket. The two investment alternatives possess equal growth potential and comparable financial risk. Based on these facts, compute the present value of these two investment alternatives and determine which option Emily should choose.

Research Problems

**Note: Solutions to Research Problems can be prepared by using the Checkpoint®
Student Edition online research product, which is available to accompany this text. It
is also possible to prepare solutions to the Research Problems by using tax research
materials found in a standard tax library.**

THOMSON REUTERS
CHECKPOINT®
Student Edition

Research Problem 1. Esther owns a large home on the East Coast. Her home is surrounded by large, mature oak trees that significantly increase the value of her home. In August 2015, a hurricane damaged many of the trees surrounding her home. In September 2015, Esther engaged a local arborist to evaluate and treat the trees, but five of the largest trees were seriously weakened by the storm. These trees died from disease in 2016. Esther has ascertained that the amount of the casualty loss from the death of the five trees is $25,000; however, she is uncertain in which year to deduct this loss. Discuss whether the casualty loss should be deducted in the calculation of Esther's 2015 or 2016 taxable income.

Partials list of research aids:
Reg. § 1.165–1.
Oregon Mesabi Corporation, 39 B.T.A. 1033 (1939).

Research Problem 2. Five years ago, Bridget decided to purchase a limited partnership interest in a fast-food restaurant conveniently located near the campus of Southeast State University. The general partner of the restaurant venture promised her that the investment would prove to be a winner. During the process of capitalizing the business, $2 million was borrowed from Northside Bank; however, each of the partners was required to pledge personal assets as collateral to satisfy the bank loan in the event that the restaurant defaulted. Bridget pledged shares of publicly traded stock (worth $200,000, basis of $75,000) to satisfy the bank's requirement.

The restaurant did a good business until just recently, when flagrant health code violations were discovered and widely publicized by the media. As a result, business has declined to a point where the restaurant's continued existence is doubtful. In addition, the $2 million loan is now due for payment. Because the restaurant cannot pay, the bank has called for the collateral provided by the partners to be used to satisfy the debt. Bridget sells the pledged stock for $200,000 and forwards the proceeds to the bank. Bridget believes that her share of the restaurant's current and suspended passive activity losses can offset the $125,000 gain from the stock sale. As a result, after netting the passive activity losses against the gain, none of the gain is subject to tax.

How do you react to Bridget's position?

Research Problem 3. During 2016, John was the chief executive officer and a shareholder of Maze, Inc. He owned 60% of the outstanding stock of Maze. In 2013, John and Maze, as co-borrowers, obtained a $100,000 loan from United National Bank. This loan was secured by John's personal residence. Although Maze was listed as a co-borrower, John repaid the loan in full in 2016. On Maze's Form 1120 tax returns, no loans from shareholders were reported. Discuss whether John is entitled to a bad debt deduction for the amount of the payment on the loan.

Partial list of research aids:
U.S. v. Generes, 405 U.S. 93 (1972).
Dale H. Sundby, T.C.Memo. 2003–204.
Arrigoni v. Comm., 73 T.C. 792 (1980).
Estate of Herbert M. Rapoport, T.C.Memo. 1982–584.
Clifford L. Brody and Barbara J. DeClerk, T.C. Summary Opinion, 2004–149.

Internet Activity

Use the tax resources of the Internet to address the following questions. Do not restrict your search to the Web, but include a review of newsgroups and general reference materials, practitioner sites and resources, primary sources of the tax law, chat rooms and discussion groups, and other opportunities.

Research Problem 4. Find a newspaper article that discusses tax planning for casualty losses when a disaster area designation is made. Does the article convey the pertinent tax rules correctly? Then list all of the locations identified by the President as Federal disaster areas in the last two years.

Research Problem 5. Investment advisers and tax professionals are continuously striving to create sophisticated transactions and investment vehicles (i.e., tax-advantaged investments) that are designed to provide economic benefits to investors by reducing their taxes. These professionals might like to patent such schemes. Identify whether patenting a tax shelter is a legal possibility.

Roger CPA Review Questions

ROGER
CPA Review

1. Glenn and Mary's house was damaged by a hurricane in 2016. The fair value of their home before the hurricane was $150,000. After the hurricane, the fair value of their home was $125,000. They received $10,000 from their homeowner's insurance policy. What is their casualty loss deduction for 2016 if their adjusted gross income was $40,000?

   a. $10,900   c. $14,900
   b. $11,000   d. $15,000

2. Hank's home is burglarized on December 22, 2016. Personal property with a fair market value of $40,000 and an adjusted basis to Hank of $25,000 is stolen. Hank paid an independent appraiser $700 on December 29 to determine the fair market value of the property at the time of the break-in. Hank's homeowner's insurance policy leads him to believe he is entitled to receive $15,000 in reimbursement for the event, but no settlement has been made with the insurance company by year-end. Hank's AGI in 2016 is $30,000. How much may Hank deduct from AGI as a result of these facts on his 2016 tax return? Assume Hank itemizes, and assume there has still been no settlement with the insurance company at the time of filing.

   a. $7,000   c. $6,900
   b. $21,900   d. $22,000

3. On the night of October 14, 2016, a hurricane caused serious damage to Paige's personal vehicle and to the roof of her personal residence, a townhome. Just prior to the hurricane, Paige had a $200,000 basis in her home and a $12,000 basis in her vehicle, which had a fair market value just prior to the hurricane of $10,000. The damage to the roof is appraised at $7,000, and the fair market value of the vehicle immediately after the hurricane is appraised at $5,000. Paige is uninsured and has a 2016 AGI of $40,000. What amount of casualty loss deduction may Paige claim on her 2016 tax return as a result of the hurricane?

   a. $9,800
   b. $7,900
   c. $9,900
   d. $7,800

4. Lee, a married individual, is an employee with three rental properties in which Lee does not actively participate. In 2016, Property 1 had a net loss of $10,000, Property 2 had a net gain of $25,000, and Property 3 had a net loss of $5,000. Lee's W–2 income in 2016 was $110,000. Considering only the foregoing facts, what is Lee's 2016 adjusted gross income?

   a. $120,000
   b. $125,000
   c. $110,000
   d. $135,000

5. Anscomb is an employee who also solely owns and actively participates in a rental activity which produced a $20,000 loss in the current year. Anscomb's W–2 income in the current year is $115,000. Considering only the foregoing facts, what should Anscomb's adjusted gross income be for the current year?

   a. $97,500
   b. $115,000
   c. $107,500
   d. $102,500

6. Lewis is not an active participant in three rental activities which have turned profits in recent years. The following profit and losses apply to the current year for Lewis:

	Gain or (Loss)
Rental Activity 1	($10,000)
Rental Activity 2	12,000
Rental Activity 3	(8,000)
Total	($ 6,000)

   What amount of the suspended loss should Lewis allocate to Rental Activity 3?
   a. $4,500
   b. $2,667
   c. $0
   d. Suspended losses may be allocated according to the taxpayer's preference

7. Smith bought a rental property in year 1 for $100,000. In year 1, Smith's adjusted gross income (AGI) was $125,000, and Smith sustained a $30,000 loss on the property. In year 2, Smith's AGI was $175,000, and Smith sustained a $20,000 loss on the property. In year 3, Smith sold the property for $155,000. What amount of gain or loss must Smith report on Smith's year 3 tax return as a result of the sale? Assume Smith actively participated in the rental activity in all three years but is not considered a real estate professional for tax purposes.

   a. $17,500 gain
   b. $0 (no gain or loss)
   c. $22,500 gain
   d. $20,000 gain

8. Patel bought a rental property in year 1 for $150,000. In year 1, Patel's adjusted gross income (AGI) was $100,000, and Patel sustained a $15,000 loss on the property. In year 2, Patel's AGI was $140,000, and Patel sustained a $10,000 loss on the property. In year 3, Patel sold the property for $175,000. What amount of gain or loss must

Patel report on Patel's year 3 tax return as a result of the sale? Assume Patel did not actively participate in the rental activity in any of the three years.

a. $25,000   c. $5,000

b. $0 (no income or loss)   d. $20,000

9. The following chart applies to Bettelli, an investor who owns two rental activities, Property A and Property B, and has no other involvement in passive activities:

	Property	Income (Loss)
Year 1	A	($12,000)
	B	5,000
Year 2	A	(6,000)
	B	1,000

Bettelli met the requirements for active participation in year 1 but not in year 2. Bettelli's AGI in year 1 was $140,000; in year 2, $180,000. In year 3, Bettelli sells Property A for a $15,000 gain. How much of the gain must Bettelli report on Bettelli's year 3 tax return?

a. $0   c. $8,000

b. $3,000   d. $13,000

CHAPTER 7

Property Transactions: Basis, Gain and Loss, and Nontaxable Exchanges

CHAPTER 8

Property Transactions: Capital Gains and Losses, Section 1231, and Recapture Provisions

Part 3 presents the tax treatment of sales, exchanges, and other dispositions of property. Topics discussed include the determination of the realized gain or loss, recognized gain or loss, and the classification of the recognized gain or loss as capital or ordinary. The topic of basis is evaluated both in terms of its effect on the calculation of the gain or loss, and in the determination of the basis of any other transfers of property.

CHAPTER

7

Property Transactions: Basis, Gain and Loss, and Nontaxable Exchanges

LEARNING OBJECTIVES: *After completing Chapter 7, you should be able to:*

LO.1 State and explain the computation of realized gain or loss on property dispositions.

LO.2 Distinguish between realized and recognized gain or loss.

LO.3 Understand and illustrate how basis is determined for various methods of asset acquisition.

LO.4 Describe various loss disallowance provisions.

LO.5 Apply the nonrecognition provisions and basis determination rules for like-kind exchanges.

LO.6 Explain the nonrecognition provisions available on the involuntary conversion of property.

LO.7 Identify other nonrecognition provisions contained in the Code.

CHAPTER OUTLINE

TAX TALK *To base all of your decisions on tax consequences is not necessarily to maintain the proper balance and perspective on what you are doing.* —BARBER CONABLE

THE BIG PICTURE

CALCULATING BASIS AND RECOGNIZED GAIN FOR PROPERTY TRANSACTIONS

Alice owns land that she received from her father 10 years ago as a gift. The land was purchased by her father in 1993 for $2,000 and was worth $10,000 at the time of the gift. Alice's father did not owe gift taxes upon making the transfer. The property is currently worth about $50,000. Alice is considering selling the land and purchasing a piece of undeveloped property in the mountains.

Alice also owns 500 shares of AppleCo stock, 300 of which were acquired as an inheritance when her grandfather died in 1997. Alice's grandfather paid $12,000 for the shares, and the shares were worth $30,000 at the time of his death. The other 200 shares of AppleCo were purchased by Alice two months ago for $28,000. The stock is currently worth $120 per share, and Alice is considering selling the shares.

In addition, Alice owns a house that she inherited from her grandmother two years ago. Her grandmother lived in the house for over 50 years. Alice has many fond memories associated with the house because she spent many summer vacations there, and she has been reluctant to sell the house. However, a developer has recently purchased several homes in the area and has offered Alice $600,000 for the property. Based on the estate tax return, the fair market value of the house at the date of her grandmother's death was $475,000. According to her grandmother's attorney, her grandmother's basis for the house was $275,000. Alice is considering selling the house. She expects any selling expenses to be minimal because she already has identified a buyer for the property.

The building Alice used in her business was destroyed by a fire on October 5, 2016. Fortunately, the building (adjusted basis of $50,000) was insured and on November 17, 2016, she receives an insurance reimbursement of $100,000 for the loss. Alice intends to invest $80,000 in a new building and use the other $20,000 of insurance proceeds to pay off credit card debt.

Alice has come to you for tax advice with respect to the property she owns. What is the recognized gain or loss for the land, stock, and house if they are sold? What tax consequences arise with respect to the involuntary conversion of her business building? Can Alice avoid paying taxes on any of the sales? Alice's objectives are to minimize the recognition of any realized gain and to maximize the recognition of any realized loss.

Read the chapter and formulate your response.

This chapter and the following chapter explain the income tax consequences of property transactions, including the sale or other disposition of property. Specifically, the following questions are considered:

- Is there a realized gain or loss?
- If so, is that gain or loss recognized for tax purposes?
- If that gain or loss is recognized, is it ordinary or capital?
- What is the basis of any replacement property that is acquired?

This chapter discusses the determination of realized and recognized gain or loss and the basis of property. The next chapter covers the classification of recognized gain or loss as ordinary or capital.

For the most part, the rules discussed in Chapters 7 and 8 apply to all types of taxpayers. Individuals, partnerships, closely held corporations, limited liability companies, and publicly held corporations all own assets for use in business activities or as investments in entities that themselves conduct business activities. Individuals, however, are unique among taxpayers because they also own assets that are used in daily life, which have no significant business or investment component. Because of that possibility, some property transaction concepts may apply somewhat differently to individual taxpayers. Thus, the material that follows pertains to taxpayers generally, except where otherwise noted.

7-1 DETERMINATION OF GAIN OR LOSS

To determine the tax consequences of a property transaction, the taxpayer must first determine the amount of gain or loss realized. Then the taxpayer must determine whether the realized gain or loss is recognized. Not all realized gains or losses are recognized for tax purposes.

LO.1

State and explain the computation of realized gain or loss on property dispositions.

7-1a Realized Gain or Loss

For tax purposes, gain or loss is the difference between the *amount realized* from the sale or other disposition of property and the property's *adjusted basis* on the date of disposition. If the amount realized exceeds the property's adjusted basis, the result is a realized gain . Conversely, if the property's adjusted basis exceeds the amount realized, the result is a realized loss .[1]

EXAMPLE 1

Lavender, Inc., sells Swan Corporation stock with a basis of $3,000 for $5,000. Lavender's realized gain is $2,000. If Lavender had sold the stock for $2,000, it would have had a realized loss of $1,000.

Sale or Other Disposition

The term *sale or other disposition* is defined broadly to include virtually any disposition of property. Thus, trade-ins, casualties, condemnations, thefts, and bond retirements are all treated as dispositions of property. The most common disposition of property is a sale or an exchange. Usually, the key factor in determining whether a disposition has taken place is whether an identifiable event has occurred[2] as opposed to a mere fluctuation in the value of the property.[3]

EXAMPLE 2

Heron & Associates owns Tan Corporation stock that cost $3,000. The stock has appreciated in value by $2,000 since Heron purchased it. Heron has no realized gain because mere fluctuation in value is not a disposition or an identifiable event for tax purposes. Nor would Heron have a realized loss had the stock declined in value.

---

[1]§ 1001(a) and Reg. § 1.1001–1(a).
[2]Reg. § 1.1001–1(c)(1).

[3]*Lynch v. Turrish,* 1 USTC ¶18, 3 AFTR 2986, 38 S.Ct. 537 (USSC, 1918).

Amount Realized

The amount realized from a sale or other disposition of property is the sum of any money received plus the fair market value of other property received. The amount realized also includes any real property taxes treated as imposed on the seller that are actually paid by the buyer.[4] The reason for including these taxes in the amount realized is that by paying the taxes, the purchaser is, in effect, paying an additional amount to the seller for the property.

The amount realized also includes any liability on the property disposed of, such as mortgage debt, if the buyer assumes the mortgage or the property is sold subject to the mortgage.[5] The amount of the liability is included in the amount realized, even if the debt is nonrecourse and even if the amount of the debt is greater than the fair market value of the mortgaged property.[6]

Bunting & Co. sells property to Orange, Inc., for $50,000 cash. There is a $20,000 mortgage on the property. Bunting's amount realized from the sale is $70,000 if Orange assumes the mortgage or takes the property subject to the mortgage.

EXAMPLE 3

The fair market value of property received in a sale or other disposition has been defined by the courts as the price at which the property will change hands between a willing seller and a willing buyer when neither is compelled to sell or buy.[7] Fair market value is determined by considering the relevant factors in each case.[8] An expert appraiser is often required to evaluate these factors in arriving at fair market value. When the fair market value of the property received cannot be determined, the value of the property given up by the taxpayer may be used.[9]

In calculating the amount realized, selling expenses (such as advertising, commissions, and legal fees) relating to the disposition are deducted. The amount realized is the net amount the taxpayer received directly or indirectly, in the form of cash or anything else of value, from the disposition of the property.

Adjusted Basis

The adjusted basis of property disposed of is the property's original basis adjusted to the date of disposition.[10] Original basis is the cost or other basis of the property on the date the property is acquired by the taxpayer. Considerations involving original basis are discussed later in this chapter. *Capital additions* increase and *recoveries of capital* decrease the original basis so that on the date of disposition, the adjusted basis reflects the unrecovered cost or other basis of the property.[11] Adjusted basis is determined as follows:

Cost (or other adjusted basis) on date of acquisition
+ Capital additions
− Capital recoveries
= Adjusted basis on date of disposition

Capital Additions

Capital additions include the cost of capital improvements and betterments made to the property by the taxpayer. These expenditures are distinguishable from expenditures for the ordinary repair and maintenance of the property, which are neither capitalized nor added to the original basis (refer to Chapter 5). The latter expenditures are deductible in

---

[4]§ 1001(b) and Reg. § 1.1001–1(b). Refer to Example 35 in Chapter 5 for a discussion of this subject.

[5]*Crane v. Comm.*, 47–1 USTC ¶9217, 35 AFTR 776, 67 S.Ct. 1047 (USSC, 1947). Although a legal distinction exists between the direct assumption of a mortgage and the taking of property subject to a mortgage, the tax consequences in calculating the amount realized are the same.

[6]*Comm. v. Tufts*, 83–1 USTC ¶9328, 51 AFTR 2d 83–1132, 103 S.Ct. 1826 (USSC, 1983).

[7]*Comm. v. Marshman*, 60–2 USTC ¶9484, 5 AFTR 2d 1528, 279 F.2d 27 (CA–6, 1960).

[8]*O'Malley v. Ames*, 52–1 USTC ¶9361, 42 AFTR 19, 197 F.2d 256 (CA–8, 1952).

[9]*U.S. v. Davis*, 62–2 USTC ¶9509, 9 AFTR 2d 1625, 82 S.Ct. 1190 (USSC, 1962).

[10]§ 1011(a) and Reg. § 1.1011–1.

[11]§ 1016(a) and Reg. § 1.1016–1.

the current taxable year if they are related to business or income-producing property. Amounts representing real property taxes treated as imposed on the seller but paid or assumed by the buyer are part of the cost of the property.[12] Any liability on property that is assumed by the buyer is also included in the buyer's original basis of the property. The same rule applies if property is acquired subject to a liability. In a similar fashion, amortization of the discount on bonds increases the adjusted basis of the bonds.[13]

EXAMPLE 4

Bluebird Corporation purchased some manufacturing equipment for $25,000. Whether Bluebird uses $25,000 from the business's cash account to pay for this equipment or uses $5,000 from that account and borrows the remaining $20,000, the basis of this equipment will be the same—namely, $25,000. Moreover, it does not matter whether Bluebird borrowed the $20,000 from the equipment's manufacturer, from a local bank, or from any other lender.

Capital Recoveries

Capital recoveries decrease the adjusted basis of property. The prominent types of capital recoveries are discussed below.

Depreciation and Cost Recovery Allowances The original basis of depreciable property is reduced by the annual depreciation charges (or cost recovery allowances) while the property is held by the taxpayer. The amount of depreciation that is subtracted from the original basis is the greater of the *allowed* or *allowable* depreciation calculated on an annual basis.[14] In most circumstances, the allowed and allowable depreciation amounts are the same (refer to Chapter 5).

Casualties and Thefts A casualty or theft may result in the reduction of the adjusted basis of property.[15] The adjusted basis is reduced by the amount of the deductible loss. In addition, the adjusted basis is reduced by the amount of insurance proceeds received. However, the receipt of insurance proceeds may result in a recognized gain rather than a deductible loss. The gain increases the adjusted basis of the property.[16]

Capital Recoveries: Casualties and Thefts

EXAMPLE 5

An insured truck owned by Falcon Corporation is destroyed in an accident. At the time of the accident, the adjusted basis was $8,000, and the fair market value was $6,500. Falcon receives insurance proceeds of $6,500.

The amount of the casualty *loss* is $1,500 ($6,500 insurance insurance proceeds − $8,000 adjusted basis). The truck's adjusted basis becomes $0 ($8,000 pre-accident adjusted basis − $1,500 casualty loss − $6,500 of insurance proceeds received).

EXAMPLE 6

Osprey, Inc., owned an insured truck that was destroyed in an accident. At the time of the accident, the adjusted basis and fair market value of the truck were $6,500 and $8,000, respectively. Osprey receives insurance proceeds of $8,000.

The amount of the casualty *gain* is $1,500 ($8,000 insurance proceeds − $6,500 adjusted basis). The truck's adjusted basis is increased by the $1,500 casualty gain and is reduced by the $8,000 of insurance proceeds received ($6,500 basis before casualty + $1,500 casualty gain − $8,000 insurance proceeds = $0 ending adjusted basis).

---

[12]Reg. §§ 1.1001–1(b)(2) and 1.1012–1(b). Refer to Chapter 5 for a discussion of this subject.

[13]See Chapter 4 for a discussion of original issue discount.

[14]§ 1016(a)(2) and Reg. § 1.1016–3(a)(1)(i).

[15]Refer to Chapter 6 for the discussion of casualties and thefts.

[16]Reg. § 1.1016–6(a).

BRIDGE DISCIPLINE **Bridge to Financial Accounting**

Certain property transactions discussed later in this chapter are treated differently for tax purposes than for financial accounting purposes. For example, the category of transactions generally referred to as "nontaxable exchanges," such as like-kind exchanges and involuntary conversions, gives taxpayers the opportunity to defer the recognition of gain on the disposition of property in qualifying transactions. The gains or losses deferred under tax law, however, are not deferred for financial reporting purposes. Instead, the actual gain or loss realized is reflected in the entity's financial reports.

Identifying and calculating the book-tax differences that arise from *taxable* dispositions of certain other property may not be so easy. For example, as discussed in Chapter 5, cost recovery (i.e., depreciation) rules provided by the tax law specify various ways in which an asset's cost may be recovered over time. These methods often differ from the methods used to depreciate an asset for book purposes. Consequently, the annual book-tax differences in these depreciation expense calculations are noted in the financial reports. But in addition, these cumulative differences, as reflected in the accumulated depreciation account, will also produce a book-tax difference on the asset's disposition. That is, because an asset's accumulated depreciation may differ for book and tax purposes, its adjusted basis will also differ. Consequently, when the asset is sold, the amount of gain or loss for book purposes will differ from that recognized for tax purposes.

Certain Corporate Distributions A corporate distribution to a shareholder that is not taxable is treated as a return of capital, and it reduces the basis of the shareholder's stock in the corporation.[17] Once the basis of the stock is reduced to zero, the amount of any subsequent distributions is a capital gain if the stock in the hands of the shareholder is a capital asset. See Chapter 13 for additional discussion.

Amortizable Bond Premium The basis in a bond purchased at a premium is reduced by the amortizable portion of the bond premium.[18] Investors in taxable bonds may *elect* to amortize the bond premium.[19] The amount of the amortized premium on taxable bonds is allowed as an interest deduction. Therefore, the election enables the taxpayer to take an annual interest deduction to offset ordinary income in exchange for a larger capital gain or smaller capital loss on the disposition of the bond (due to the basis reduction).

In-depth coverage can be found on this book's companion website: www.cengagebrain.com	**1 DIGGING DEEPER**

In contrast to the treatment of taxable bonds, the premium on tax-exempt bonds *must* be amortized, and no interest deduction is permitted. Furthermore, the basis of tax-exempt bonds is reduced even though the amortization is not allowed as a deduction. No amortization deduction is permitted on tax-exempt bonds because the interest income is exempt from tax, and the amortization of the bond premium merely represents an adjustment of the effective amount of such income.

EXAMPLE 7

Navy, Inc., purchases Eagle Corporation taxable bonds with a face value of $100,000 for $110,000, thus paying a premium of $10,000. The annual interest rate is 7%, and the bonds mature 10 years from the date of purchase. The annual interest income is $7,000 (7% × $100,000).

If Navy elects to amortize the bond premium, the $10,000 premium is deducted over the 10-year period. Navy's basis for the bonds is reduced each year by the amount of the amortization deduction.

If the bonds were tax-exempt, amortization of the bond premium and the basis adjustment would be mandatory and no deduction would be allowed for the amortization.

---

[17]§ 1016(a)(4) and Reg. § 1.1016–5(a).

[18]§ 1016(a)(5) and Reg. § 1.1016–5(b). The accounting treatment of bond premium amortization is the same as for tax purposes. The amortization results in a decrease in the bond investment account.

[19]§ 171(c).

TAX IN THE NEWS   Tax Implications of Virtual Currency (Bitcoin)

In Notice 2014–21 (2014–16 I.R.B. 938), the Internal Revenue Service (IRS), through a series of questions and answers, describes how existing tax principles apply to transactions using virtual currency.

Background. Bitcoin is a decentralized virtual store of value that is beginning to gain greater acceptance as a medium of exchange in the mainstream marketplace. Notice 2014–21 describes virtual currencies such as Bitcoin as follows:

"[A] digital representation of value that functions as a medium of exchange, a unit of account, and/or a store of value.... Virtual currency that has an equivalent value in real currency, or that acts as a substitute for real currency, is referred to as 'convertible' virtual currency...."

Bitcoin derives value not from governmental backing or a link to an underlying commodity, but purely from its finite nature, the effort required to generate new Bitcoin, and the value its users place on it and its acceptance as a medium of exchange in certain segments of the market. Bitcoin supply is finite (the maximum number of Bitcoin that will ever exist is approximately 21 million). A good summary of fundamental questions and answers surrounding Bitcoin can be found at **https://bitcoin.org/en/faq**.

IRS Guidance. Notice 2014–21 provides answers to frequently asked questions (FAQs) on virtual currency such as Bitcoin. These FAQs provide basic information on the U.S. Federal tax implications of transactions in, or transactions that use, virtual currency. In some environments, virtual currency operates like "real" currency (e.g., the coin and paper money of the United States) but it does not have legal tender status in any jurisdiction.

In its guidance, the IRS indicates that Bitcoin is *not* currency; rather, virtual currency is treated as *property* for U.S. Federal tax purposes. General tax principles that apply to property transactions apply to transactions using virtual currency. Among other things, this means that:

- Wages paid to employees using virtual currency are taxable to the employee, must be reported by an employer on a Form W–2, and are subject to Federal income tax withholding and payroll taxes.

- Payments using virtual currency made to independent contractors and other service providers are taxable, and self-employment tax rules generally apply. Payers are subject to the same information reporting requirements as any other payer (so, for example, a Form 1099–MISC must be issued to an independent contractor if Bitcoin payments exceed $600 per year).

- The character of gain or loss from the sale or exchange of virtual currency depends on whether the virtual currency is a capital asset in the hands of the taxpayer.

- A payment made using virtual currency is subject to information reporting to the same extent as any other payment made in property.

The full set of 16 questions and answers provided by the IRS can be found at **www.irs.gov/pub/irs-drop/n-14-21.pdf**.

Easements An easement is the legal right to use another's land for a special purpose. Historically, easements were commonly used to obtain rights-of-way for utility lines, roads, and pipelines. In recent years, grants of conservation easements have become a popular means of obtaining charitable contribution deductions and reducing the value of real estate for transfer tax (i.e., estate and gift) purposes. Likewise, scenic easements are used to reduce the value of land as assessed for ad valorem property tax purposes.

The amount received for granting an easement is subtracted from the basis of the property. If the taxpayer does not retain any right to the use of the land, all of the basis is assigned to the easement. However, if the use of the land is only partially restricted, an allocation of some of the basis to the easement is appropriate. If, however, it is impossible or impractical to separate the basis of the part of the property on which the easement is granted, the basis of the whole property is reduced by the amount received. If the amount received for the easement exceeds the basis, a taxable gain results.[20]

7-1b Recognized Gain or Loss

LO.2

Distinguish between realized and recognized gain or loss.

Recognized gain is the amount of the realized gain that is included in the taxpayer's gross income.[21] A recognized loss, on the other hand, is the amount of a realized loss that is deductible for tax purposes.[22] As a general rule, the entire amount of a realized gain or loss is recognized when it is realized.[23]

---

[20]See Rev.Rul. 68–291, 1968–1 C.B. 351 and Rev.Rul. 77–414, 1977–2 C.B. 299.

[21]§ 61(a)(3) and Reg. § 1.61–6(a).

[22]§ 165(a) and Reg. § 1.165–1(a).

[23]§ 1001(c) and Reg. § 1.1002–1(a).

Concept Summary 7.1 summarizes the realized gain or loss and recognized gain or loss concepts.

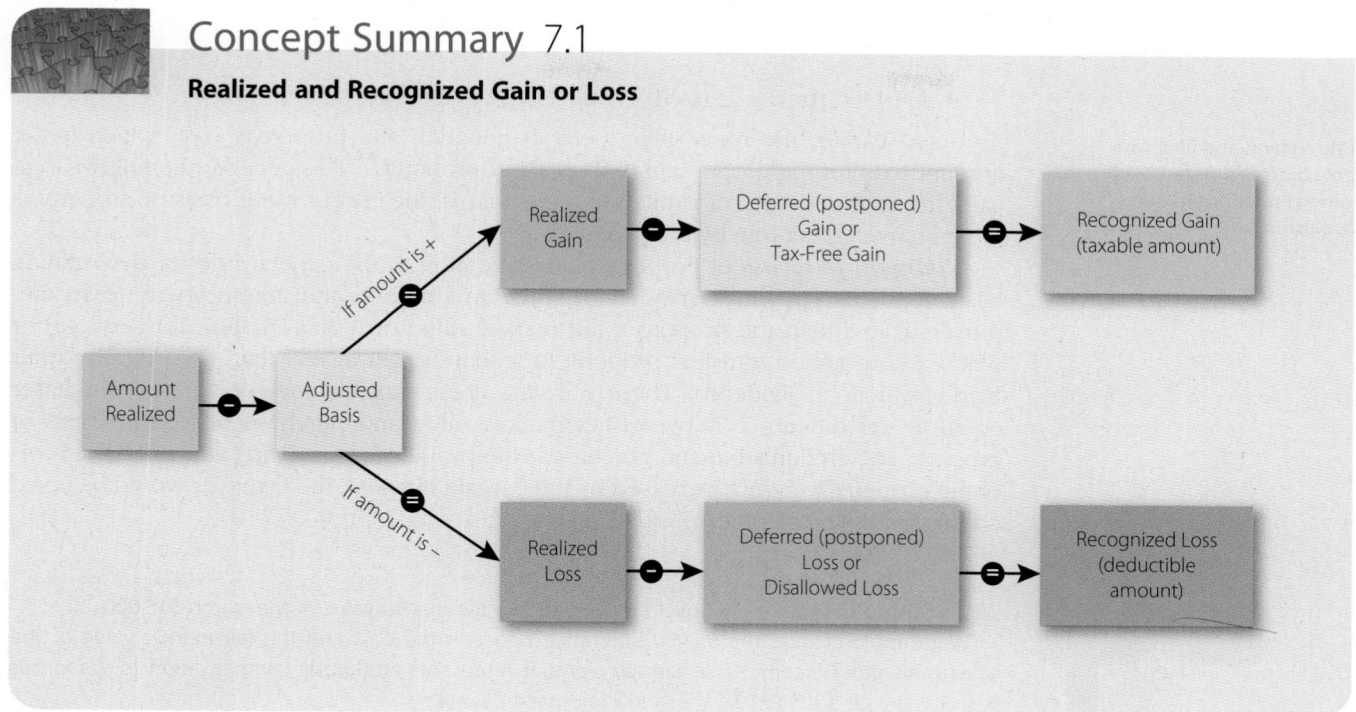

Concept Summary 7.1
Realized and Recognized Gain or Loss

7-1c **Nonrecognition of Gain or Loss**

In certain cases, a realized gain or loss is not recognized upon the sale or other disposition of property. One such case involves nontaxable exchanges, which are covered later in this chapter. In addition, realized losses from the sale or exchange of property between certain related parties are not recognized.[24]

Dispositions of Personal-Use Assets

For individual taxpayers, special rules apply to *personal-use* assets (i.e., assets such as a residence or an automobile that are not used in any business or investment activity). A loss from the sale, exchange, or condemnation of such assets is not recognized for tax purposes. An exception exists for casualty or theft losses from personal-use assets (refer to Chapter 6). In contrast, any gain realized from the disposition of personal-use assets is generally taxable.

Freda sells an automobile, which she has held exclusively for personal use, for $6,000. The basis of the automobile is $5,000. Freda has a realized and recognized gain of $1,000.

   If she sold this automobile for $4,500, she would have a realized loss of $500, but the loss would not be recognized for tax purposes.

EXAMPLE

8

In-depth coverage can be found on this book's companion website: www.cengagebrain.com

2 DIGGING DEEPER

---

[24]§ 267(a)(1).

7-2 BASIS CONSIDERATIONS

A key element in calculating gain or loss from a property transaction is the asset's basis at the time of the transaction. Various methods for determining basis apply, depending on how the asset was acquired.

Understand and illustrate how basis is determined for various methods of asset acquisition.

7-2a Determination of Cost Basis

As noted earlier, the basis of property is generally the property's cost, which is the amount paid for the property in cash or other property.[25] This general rule follows logically from the recovery of capital doctrine; that is, the cost or other basis of property is to be recovered tax-free by the taxpayer.

A *bargain purchase* of property is an exception to the general rule for determining basis. A bargain purchase may result when an employer transfers property to an employee at less than the property's fair market value (as compensation for services) or when a corporation transfers property to a shareholder at less than the property's fair market value (a dividend). These transfers create taxable income for the purchaser equal to the difference between fair market value and purchase price. The basis of property acquired in a bargain purchase is the property's fair market value.[26] If the basis of the property were not increased by the bargain element, the taxpayer would be taxed on this amount again at disposition.

> **EXAMPLE 9**
>
> Wade buys land from his employer for $10,000. The fair market value of the land is $15,000.
>
> Wade must include the $5,000 difference between the cost and the fair market value of the land in his gross income. The bargain element represents additional compensation to Wade. His basis for the land is $15,000, the land's fair market value.

Identification Problems

Sometimes, it can be difficult to determine the cost of an asset being sold. This problem is frequently encountered in sales of corporate stock, because a taxpayer may purchase separate lots of a company's stock on different dates and at different prices. When the stock is sold, if the taxpayer cannot identify the specific shares being sold (specific identification), the stock sold is determined on a first-in, first-out (FIFO) basis. Thus, the holding period and cost of the stock sold are determined by referring to the purchase date and cost of the first lot of stock acquired.[27] But if the stock being sold can be adequately identified, then the basis and holding period of the specific stock sold are used in determining the nature and amount of gain or loss.[28] Thus, to avoid FIFO treatment when the sold securities are held by a broker, it is often necessary to provide specific instructions and receive written confirmation of the securities being sold. Brokers and others in similar enterprises are now required to provide investors with an annual report on the cost basis of their stocks sold during the year (to be included on Form 1099–B and reported to the IRS).

> **EXAMPLE 10**
>
> Pelican, Inc., purchases 100 shares of Olive Corporation stock on July 1, 2014, for $5,000 ($50 a share) and another 100 shares of Olive stock on July 1, 2015, for $6,000 ($60 a share). Pelican sells 50 shares of the stock on January 2, 2016.
>
> The cost of the stock sold, assuming that Pelican cannot adequately identify the shares, is $50 a share (from shares purchased on July 1, 2014), or $2,500. This is the cost Pelican will compare with the amount realized in determining the gain or loss from the sale.

---

[25]§ 1012 and Reg. § 1.1012–1(a).

[26]Reg. §§ 1.61–2(d)(2)(i) and 1.301–1(j). See the discussion in Chapter 11 of the circumstances under which what appears to be a taxable bargain purchase is an excludible qualified employee discount (text Section 11-2j).

[27]*Kluger Associates, Inc.*, 69 T.C. 925 (1978).

[28]Reg. § 1.1012–1(c)(1).

Allocation Problems

When a taxpayer acquires *several assets in a lump-sum purchase*, the total cost must be allocated among the individual assets.[29] Allocation is necessary for several reasons:

- Some of the assets acquired may be depreciable (e.g., buildings), while others may not be (e.g., land).
- Only a portion of the assets acquired may be sold.
- Some of the assets may be capital or depreciable assets that receive special tax treatment upon subsequent sale or other disposition.

The lump-sum cost is allocated on the basis of the fair market values of the individual assets acquired.

EXAMPLE 11

Magenta Corporation purchases a building and land for $800,000. Because of the depressed nature of the industry in which the seller was operating, Magenta was able to negotiate a very favorable purchase price. Appraisals of the individual assets indicate that the fair market value of the building is $600,000 and that of the land is $400,000.

Magenta's basis for the building is $480,000 [($600,000/$1,000,000) × $800,000], and its basis for the land is $320,000 [($400,000/$1,000,000) × $800,000].

If a business is purchased and **goodwill** is involved, a special allocation applies. Initially, the purchase price is assigned to the assets, excluding goodwill, to the extent of their total fair market value. This assigned amount is allocated among the assets on the basis of the fair market value of the individual assets acquired. Goodwill is then assigned the residual amount of the purchase price. The resultant allocation is applicable to both the buyer and the seller.[30]

EXAMPLE 12

Roadrunner, Inc., sells its business to Coyote Corporation. The two companies agree that the values of the specific assets are as follows:

Marketable securities	$ 5,000
Inventory	35,000
Building	500,000
Land	200,000

After negotiations, Roadrunner and Coyote agree on a sales price of $1 million. Applying the residual method, the residual purchase price is allocated to goodwill, resulting in the following basis of assets to Coyote Corporation:

Marketable securities	$ 5,000
Inventory	35,000
Building	500,000
Land	200,000
Goodwill	260,000

In the case of *nontaxable stock dividends*, the allocation depends on whether the dividend is a common stock dividend on common stock or a preferred stock dividend on common stock. If the stock dividend is common on common, the cost of the original common shares is allocated to the total shares owned after the dividend.[31]

EXAMPLE 13

Yellow, Inc., owns 100 shares of Sparrow Corporation common stock for which it paid $1,100. Yellow receives a 10% common stock dividend, giving it a new total of 110 shares. Before the stock dividend, Yellow's basis was $11 per share ($1,100 ÷ 100 shares). The basis of each share after the stock dividend is $10 ($1,100 ÷ 110 shares).

---

[29]Reg. § 1.61–6(a).

[30]§ 1060. In most cases, the seller's recognized gain associated with the goodwill is classified as capital (as discussed in Chapter 8).

[31]§§ 305(a) and 307(a). The holding period of the new shares includes the holding period of the old shares. § 1223(5) and Reg. § 1.1223–1(e). See Chapter 8 for a discussion of the importance of the holding period.

If the nontaxable stock dividend is preferred stock on common, the cost of the original common shares is allocated between the common and preferred shares on the basis of their relative fair market values on the date of distribution.[32]

EXAMPLE 14

Brown Company owns 100 shares of Cardinal Corporation common stock for which it paid $1,000. Brown receives a nontaxable stock dividend of 50 shares of preferred stock on the Cardinal common stock. The fair market values on the date of distribution of the preferred stock dividend are $30 a share for common stock and $40 a share for preferred stock.

Fair market value of common ($30 × 100 shares)	$3,000
Fair market value of preferred ($40 × 50 shares)	2,000
	$5,000
Basis of common: 3/5 × $1,000	$ 600
Basis of preferred: 2/5 × $1,000	$ 400

The basis per share for the common stock is $6 ($600/100 shares). The basis per share for the preferred stock is $8 ($400/50 shares).

7-2b Gift Basis

Although business entities can neither make nor receive gratuitous transfers, ownership interests in such entities are frequently the subject of lifetime and testamentary gifts. Partnership interests, stock in closely or publicly held corporations, and other assets are regularly passed from one generation of owners to another for a variety of family and business reasons. Special basis rules apply to such transfers.

When a taxpayer receives property as a gift, there is no cost to the donee (recipient). Thus, under the cost basis provision, the donee's basis would be zero. With a zero basis, if the donee sold the property, the entire amount realized would be treated as taxable gain. Instead, the Code[33] assigns a basis to the property received that depends upon the following:

- The date of the gift.
- The basis of the property to the donor.
- The fair market value of the property.
- The amount of the gift tax paid, if any.

Gift Basis Rules If No Gift Tax Is Paid

If a property's fair market value on the date of the gift exceeds the donor's basis in the property, the donor's basis carries over to the new owner.[34] This basis is called a *carryover basis* and is used in determining the donee's gain or loss.

The Big Picture

EXAMPLE 15

Return to the facts of *The Big Picture* on p. 7-1. Alice's father purchased the land in 1993 for $2,000. He gave the land to Alice 10 years ago, when the fair market value was $10,000. No gift tax was paid on the transfer. Alice is considering selling the land, which is currently worth $50,000.

If she sells the property for $50,000, Alice will have a realized gain of $48,000 ($50,000 amount realized − $2,000 basis in the land).

---

[32]Reg. § 1.307–1(a).

[33]§ 1015(a).

[34]§ 1015(a) and Reg. § 1.1015–1(a)(1). See Reg. § 1.1015–1(a)(3) for cases in which the facts necessary to determine the donor's adjusted basis are unknown. See Example 18 for the effect of depreciation deductions by the donee.

If the property's fair market value on the date of the gift is *lower* than the donor's basis in the property, the donee's basis cannot be determined until the donee disposes of the property. For the purpose of determining *gain*, the donor's basis will carry over, as in the preceding example. But for determining *loss*, the property's basis will be its fair market value when the gift was made.

The Big Picture

EXAMPLE 16

Return to the facts of *The Big Picture* on p. 7-1. Instead, assume that Alice's father had purchased the land in 1993 for $12,000. He gave the land to Alice 10 years ago, when the fair market value was $10,000. No gift tax was paid on the transfer.

If Alice sells the property for $50,000, she has a realized gain of $38,000 ($50,000 amount realized − $12,000 basis in the land).

However, if the property has declined in value because of the discovery of contaminants on the property and Alice is able to sell the land for only $7,000, she will realize a loss of $3,000 ($7,000 amount realized − $10,000 basis in the land).

Note that this loss basis rule prevents the donee from receiving a tax benefit from a decline in value that occurred while the donor held the property. Therefore, in the preceding example, Alice has a loss of only $3,000 rather than a loss of $5,000 ($7,000 − $12,000). The $2,000 difference represents the decline in value that occurred while Alice's father held the property. Ironically, however, a donee might be subject to income tax on the appreciation that occurred while the donor held the property, as illustrated in Example 15.

In any case, the operation of this dual basis rule produces a curious anomaly: if the sales proceeds fall *between* the donor's adjusted basis and the property's fair market value at the date of gift, no gain or loss is recognized.

The Big Picture

EXAMPLE 17

Return to the facts of *The Big Picture* on p. 7-1. Instead, assume that Alice's father had purchased the land in 1993 for $12,000. He gave the land to Alice 10 years ago, when the fair market value was $10,000. No gift tax was paid on the transfer. Now Alice plans to sell the property for $11,000.

To calculate gain, she would use a basis of $12,000, her father's basis. But when a $12,000 basis is compared with the $11,000 sales proceeds, a *loss* is produced. Yet in determining loss, Alice must use the property's fair market value at the date of gift—namely, $10,000. When a $10,000 basis is compared to sales proceeds of $11,000, a *gain* is produced. Accordingly, no gain or loss is recognized on this transaction.

Adjustment for Gift Tax

Because of the size of the unified estate and gift tax exemption ($5.45 million in 2016), basis adjustments for gift taxes paid are rare. If, however, gift taxes are paid by the donor, the portion of the gift tax paid that is related to any appreciation is taken into account in determining the donee's gain basis.[35]

For *gifts made before 1977*, the full amount of the gift tax paid is added to the donor's basis, with basis capped at the donor's fair market value at the date of the gift.

---

[35]§ 1015(d)(6) and Reg. § 1.1015–5(c)(2). Examples illustrating these rules can be found in Reg. § 1.1015–5(c)(5) and IRS Publication 551 (*Basis of Assets*), p. 9.

TAX PLANNING STRATEGIES   **Gift Planning**

FRAMEWORK FOCUS: TAX RATE

Strategy: Shift Net Income from High-Bracket Taxpayers to Low-Bracket Taxpayers.

FRAMEWORK FOCUS: DEDUCTIONS

Strategy: Maximize Deductible Amounts.

Gifts of *appreciated property* can produce tax savings if the donee is in a lower tax bracket than the donor. The carryover basis rule effectively shifts the tax on the property's appreciation to the new owner, even if all of the appreciation arose while the property was owned by the donor.

On the other hand, donors should generally avoid making gifts of property that are worth less than the donor's adjusted basis (loss property). The operation of the basis rule for losses may result in either (1) a realized loss that is not deductible by either the donor or the donee or (2) reduced tax benefits when the loss is recognized by a donee facing lower marginal tax rates. Unless the property is expected to rebound in value before it is sold, a donor would be better advised to sell the property that has declined in value, deduct the resulting loss, and then transfer the proceeds to the prospective donee.

Holding Period

The **holding period** for property acquired by gift begins on the date the donor acquired the property,[36] unless the special circumstance requiring use of the property's fair market value at the date of gift applies. If so, the holding period starts on the date of the gift.[37] The significance of the holding period for capital assets is discussed in Chapter 8.

Basis for Depreciation

The basis for depreciation on depreciable gift property is the donee's basis for determining gain.[38] This rule is applicable even if the donee later sells the property at a loss and uses the property's fair market value at the date of gift in calculating the amount of the realized loss.

EXAMPLE 18

Vito gave a machine to Tina earlier this year. At that time, the adjusted basis was $32,000 (cost of $40,000 − accumulated depreciation of $8,000), and the fair market value was $26,000. No gift tax was due. Tina's basis for determining gain is $32,000, and her loss basis is $26,000. During this year, Tina deducts depreciation (cost recovery) of $6,400 ($32,000 × 20%). (Refer to Chapter 5 for the cost recovery tables.) At the end of this year, Tina's basis determinations are calculated as follows:

	Gain Basis	Loss Basis
Donor's basis or fair market value	$32,000	$26,000
Depreciation	(6,400)	(6,400)
	$25,600	$19,600

---

[36]§ 1223(2) and Reg. § 1.1223–1(b).

[37]Rev.Rul. 59–86, 1959–1 C.B. 209.

[38]§ 1011 and Reg. §§ 1.1011–1 and 1.167(g)–1.

7-2c **Property Acquired from a Decedent**

For a taxpayer who has received property from a deceased individual (i.e., decedent) and later disposes of that property, the property's basis must be determined. Typically, a favorable rule may be applied.

General Rules

The basis of property acquired from a decedent is generally the property's fair market value at the date of death (referred to as the *primary valuation amount*).[39] The property's basis is the fair market value six months after the date of death if the executor or administrator of the estate *elects* the alternate valuation date for estate tax purposes. This amount is referred to as the *alternate valuation amount*.

In-depth coverage can be found on this book's companion website: www.cengagebrain.com	**3 DIGGING DEEPER**

> **EXAMPLE 19**
>
> Linda and various other family members inherited stock in a closely held corporation from Linda's father, who died earlier this year. At the date of death, her father's basis for the stock Linda inherited was $35,000. The stock's fair market value at the date of death was $50,000. The alternate valuation date was not elected.
>
> Linda's basis for income tax purposes is $50,000. This is commonly referred to as a *stepped-up basis*.
>
> If, instead, the stock's fair market value at the date of death was $20,000, Linda's basis would be $20,000. This is commonly referred to as a *stepped-down basis*.

> **The Big Picture**
>
> **EXAMPLE 20**
>
> Return to the facts of *The Big Picture* on p. 7-1. Alice owns 500 shares of AppleCo stock, 300 of which were inherited from her grandfather. Her grandfather's cost basis in the stock was $12,000 (i.e., its purchase price), but the shares were worth $30,000 at the time of his death. Alice purchased the other 200 shares for $28,000.
>
> Therefore, the basis in her 500 AppleCo shares is $58,000: the 300 shares received as an inheritance take a stepped-up basis of $30,000, and the 200 shares purchased take a cost basis of $28,000.

The alternate valuation date and amount are only available to estates for which an estate tax return must be filed [generally, estates with a valuation in excess of $5.45 million in 2016 ($5.43 million in 2015)]. Even if an estate tax return is filed and the executor elects the alternate valuation date, the six-months-after-death date is available only for property that the executor has not distributed before this date.[40]

The alternate valuation date can be elected *only if*, as a result of the election, *both* the value of the gross estate and the estate tax liability are lower than they would have been if the primary valuation date had been used.[41]

In-depth coverage can be found on this book's companion website: www.cengagebrain.com	**4 DIGGING DEEPER**

---

[39]§ 1014(a) and § 1022.

[40]§ 2032(a)(1) and Rev.Rul. 56–60, 1956–1 C.B. 443. For any property distributed by the executor during the six-month period preceding the alternate valuation date, the basis to the beneficiary will equal the fair market value on the date of distribution.

[41]§ 2032(c). This provision prevents the alternate valuation election from being used to increase the basis of the property to the beneficiary for income tax purposes without simultaneously increasing the estate tax liability (because of estate tax deductions or credits).

TAX PLANNING STRATEGIES   Property Acquired from a Decedent

FRAMEWORK FOCUS: INCOME

Strategy: Avoid Income Recognition.

FRAMEWORK FOCUS: DEDUCTIONS

Strategy: Maximize Deductible Amounts.

If a taxpayer *retains appreciated property* until death, the property's basis will be "stepped up" to its fair market value at that time. Thus, no income tax will be paid on the property's appreciation by either the former owner (the decedent) or the new owner (the heir).

Alternatively, *depreciated property should be sold* prior to death. Otherwise, the property's basis in the heir's hands will be its declined fair market value, and neither the decedent nor the heir will be able to deduct the loss that occurred while the property was owned by the decedent.

Holding Period of Property Acquired from a Decedent

The holding period of property acquired from a decedent is *deemed to be long term* (held for the required long-term holding period). This provision applies regardless of whether the property is disposed of at a gain or at a loss.[42]

7-2d Disallowed Losses

In certain situations, losses that normally would be recognized are disallowed. Such disallowance commonly occurs in transactions between related parties and in wash sales.

Related Taxpayers

LO.4

Describe various loss disallowance provisions.

Section 267 provides that realized losses from sales or exchanges of property between certain related parties are not recognized. This loss disallowance provision applies to several types of related-party transactions.[43] The most common involve (1) members of a family and (2) an individual and a corporation in which the individual owns, directly or indirectly, more than 50 percent in value of the corporation's outstanding stock. Section 707 provides a similar loss disallowance provision where the related parties are a partner and a partnership in which the partner owns, directly or indirectly, more than 50 percent of the capital interests or profits interests in the partnership. Neither provision, however, prevents the recognition of *gains* between related parties. The rules governing the relationships covered by § 267 were discussed in Chapter 5.

If income-producing or business property is transferred to a related party and a loss is disallowed, the basis of the property to the recipient is the property's cost to the transferee. However, if a subsequent sale or other disposition of the property by the original transferee results in a realized gain, the amount of gain is reduced by the loss that was previously disallowed. This *right of offset* is not applicable if the original sale involved the sale of a personal-use asset (e.g., a personal residence). Furthermore, the right of offset is available only to the original transferee (the related-party buyer). See Examples 16 through 18 in Chapter 5.

DIGGING DEEPER 5   In-depth coverage can be found on this book's companion website: www.cengagebrain.com

Wash Sales

Section 1091 stipulates that in certain cases, a realized loss on the sale or exchange of stock or securities is not recognized. Specifically, if a taxpayer sells or exchanges stock

---

[42]§ 1223(11).   [43]§ 267(b).

or securities and within 30 days before *or* after the date of the sale or exchange acquires *substantially identical* stock or securities, any loss realized from the sale or exchange is not recognized because the transaction is a **wash sale**.[44] The term *acquire* means acquire by purchase or in a taxable exchange and includes an option to purchase substantially identical securities. *Substantially identical* means the same in all important particulars. Corporate bonds and preferred stock normally are not considered substantially identical to a corporation's common stock. However, if the bonds and preferred stock are convertible into common stock, they may be considered substantially identical under certain circumstances.[45] Attempts to avoid the application of the wash sale rules by having a related taxpayer repurchase the securities have been unsuccessful.[46] The wash sale provisions do *not* apply to gains. Concept Summary 7.2 provides an overview of the wash sale rules.

Concept Summary 7.2

Wash Sale Rules

Recognition of the loss is disallowed because the taxpayer is considered to be in substantially the same economic position after the sale and repurchase as before. This disallowance rule does not apply to taxpayers engaged in the business of buying and selling securities.[47] Investors, however, are not allowed to create losses through wash sales to offset income for tax purposes.

---

[44]§ 1091(a) and Reg. §§ 1.1091–1(a) and (f).

[45]Rev.Rul. 56–406, 1956–2 C.B. 523.

[46]*McWilliams v. Comm.*, 47–1 USTC ¶9289, 35 AFTR 1184, 67 S.Ct. 1477 (USSC, 1947).

[47]Reg. § 1.1091–1(a).

A realized loss that is not recognized is added to the *basis* of the substantially identical stock or securities whose acquisition resulted in the nonrecognition of loss.[48] In other words, the basis of the replacement stock or securities is increased by the amount of the unrecognized loss. If the loss were not added to the basis of the newly acquired stock or securities, the taxpayer would never recover the entire basis of the old stock or securities. As a result, the wash sale rule operates to *defer* the recognition of the taxpayer's loss.

EXAMPLE 21

Oriole Manufacturing Company sold 50 shares of Green Corporation stock (basis of $10,000) for $8,000. Ten days later, Oriole purchased 50 shares of the same stock for $7,000.

Oriole's realized loss of $2,000 ($8,000 amount realized − $10,000 basis) is not recognized because it resulted from a wash sale. Oriole's basis in the newly acquired stock is $9,000 ($7,000 purchase price + $2,000 unrecognized loss from the wash sale).

The basis of the new stock or securities includes the unrecovered portion of the basis of the formerly held stock or securities. Therefore, the *holding period* of the new stock or securities begins on the date of acquisition of the old stock or securities.[49]

A taxpayer may acquire fewer shares than the number sold in a wash sale. In this case, the loss from the sale is prorated between recognized and unrecognized loss on the basis of the ratio of the number of shares acquired to the number of shares sold.[50]

TAX PLANNING STRATEGIES Avoiding Wash Sales

FRAMEWORK FOCUS: DEDUCTIONS

Strategy: Maximize Deductible Amounts.

The wash sale restriction can be avoided by replacing the sold security with a *similar* but not "substantially identical" security. For example, if IBM common stock is sold to claim an unrealized loss, the taxpayer could immediately acquire Dell common stock without triggering the wash sale rule, even though both entities are computer companies.

Nontax considerations must also come into play, however, because IBM and Dell are two different companies with different investment prospects. Although both securities will be affected by many of the same factors, they will also be subject to different factors that may be even more significant than the ones they share.

7-2e Conversion of Property from Personal Use to Business or Income-Producing Use

As discussed previously, losses from the sale of personal-use assets are not recognized for tax purposes, but losses from the sale of business and income-producing assets are deductible. Can a taxpayer convert a personal-use asset that has declined in value to business or income-producing use and then sell the asset to recognize a business or income-producing loss? The tax law prevents this practice by specifying that the *basis for determining loss* on personal-use assets converted to business or income-producing use is the *lower* of the property's adjusted basis or its fair market value on the date of conversion.[51] The *gain basis* for converted property is the property's adjusted basis on the date of conversion, regardless of whether the property's use is business, income-producing, or personal in nature.

---

[48]§ 1091(d) and Reg. § 1.1091–2(a).

[49]§ 1223(4) and Reg. § 1.1223–1(d).

[50]§ 1091(b) and Reg. § 1.1091–1(c).

[51]Reg. § 1.165–9(b)(2).

TAX IN THE NEWS   Triple the Misery!

Although short sales have traditionally involved stocks, today the term *short sale* also refers to the sale of a personal residence by a homeowner who is "underwater," owing more on the home than it is worth. In a short sale, the homeowner sells the residence for its fair market value, which is less than the mortgage (or mortgages) on the property. One possible result of this transaction is that the taxpayer realizes a loss—the selling price is less than his or her basis in the property. Unfortunately, the realized loss cannot be recognized because a residence is a personal use asset. To add to the trauma of losing the home in a nondeductible loss sale, the mortgage company may require the taxpayer to keep paying on the portion of the mortgage still outstanding (i.e., the amount of the mortgage in excess of the net sales price). Thus, the taxpayer has triple misery: no home, a non-deductible loss, and an outstanding debt to pay.

Diane's personal residence has an adjusted basis of $175,000 and a fair market value of $160,000. When she converts the personal residence to residential rental property on January 1, her basis for determining loss is $160,000 (lower of $175,000 adjusted basis and fair market value of $160,000). The $15,000 decline in value is a personal loss and can never be recognized for tax purposes. Diane's basis for determining gain is $175,000.

 EXAMPLE 22

The basis for determining loss is also the *basis for depreciating* the converted property.[52] This is an exception to the general rule that the basis for depreciation is the basis for determining gain (e.g., property received by gift). This exception prevents the taxpayer from recovering a personal loss indirectly through depreciation of the higher original basis. Once property is converted, both its basis for loss and its basis for gain are adjusted for depreciation deductions from the date of conversion to the date of disposition.

Assume the same facts as in Example 22. The MACRS cost recovery deduction for the current year is $5,576 ($160,000 × 3.485%). Thus, at the end of the current year, Diane's adjusted basis for gain for the rental property is $169,424 ($175,000 − $5,576), and her adjusted basis for loss is $154,424 ($160,000 − $5,576).

 EXAMPLE 23

In-depth coverage can be found on this book's companion website: www.cengagebrain.com

6, 7   DIGGING DEEPER

7-2f Summary of Basis Adjustments

Some of the more common items that either increase or decrease the basis of an asset appear in Concept Summary 7.3.

In discussing the topic of basis, a number of specific techniques for determining basis have been presented. Although the various techniques are responsive to and mandated by transactions occurring in the marketplace, they possess enough common characteristics to be categorized as follows:

- The basis of the asset may be determined by its cost.
- The basis of the asset may be determined by the basis of another asset.
- The basis of the asset may be determined by its fair market value.
- The basis of the asset may be determined by the basis of the asset in the hands of another taxpayer.

---

[52]Reg. § 1.167(g)–1.

Concept Summary 7.3

Adjustments to Basis

Item	Effect	Refer to Chapter	Explanation
Amortization of bond discount	Increase	7	Amortization is mandatory for certain taxable bonds and elective for tax-exempt bonds.
Amortization of bond premium	Decrease	7	Amortization is mandatory for tax-exempt bonds and elective for taxable bonds.
Amortization of covenant not to compete	Decrease	5	Covenant must be for a definite and limited time period. The amortization period is a statutory period of 15 years.
Amortization of intangibles	Decrease	5	Intangibles are amortized over a 15-year period.
Bad debts	Decrease	6	Most taxpayers must use the specific charge-off method.
Capital additions	Increase	7	Certain items, at the taxpayer's election, can be capitalized or deducted.
Casualty	Decrease	7	For a casualty loss, the amount of the adjustment is the sum of the deductible loss and the insurance proceeds received. For a casualty gain, the amount of the adjustment is the insurance proceeds received reduced by the recognized gain.
Condemnation	Decrease	7	See casualty explanation.
Cost recovery	Decrease	5	Section 168 is applicable to tangible assets placed in service after 1980 whose useful life is expressed in terms of years.
Depletion	Decrease	5	Use the greater of cost or percentage depletion. Percentage depletion can be deducted even when the basis is zero.
Depreciation	Decrease	5	Section 167 is applicable to tangible assets placed in service before 1981 and to tangible assets not depreciated in terms of years.
Easement	Decrease	7	If the taxpayer does not retain any use of the land, all of the basis is allocable to the easement transaction. However, if only part of the land is affected by the easement, only part of the basis is allocable to the easement transaction.
Improvements by lessee to lessor's property	Increase	4	Adjustment occurs only if the lessor is required to include the fair market value of the improvements in gross income under § 109.
Imputed interest	Decrease		Amount deducted is not part of the cost of the asset.
Inventory: lower of cost or market	Decrease		Not available if the LIFO method is used.
Limited expensing under § 179	Decrease	5	Occurs only if the taxpayer elects § 179 treatment.
Medical capital expenditure deducted as a medical expense	Decrease	10	Adjustment is the amount of the deduction (the effect on basis is to increase it by the amount of the capital expenditure net of the deduction).
Real estate taxes: apportionment between the buyer and seller	Increase or decrease	5	To the extent the buyer pays the seller's pro rata share, the buyer's basis is increased. To the extent the seller pays the buyer's pro rata share, the buyer's basis is decreased.
Rebate from manufacturer	Decrease		Because the rebate is treated as an adjustment to the purchase price, it is not included in the buyer's gross income.
Stock dividend	Decrease	7	Adjustment occurs only if the stock dividend is nontaxable. While the basis per share decreases, the total stock basis does not change.
Stock rights	Decrease	13	Adjustment to stock basis occurs only for nontaxable stock rights and only if the fair market value of the rights is at least 15% of the fair market value of the stock, or if less than 15%, the taxpayer elects to allocate the basis between the stock and the rights.
Theft	Decrease	6	See casualty explanation.

7-3 GENERAL CONCEPT OF A NONTAXABLE EXCHANGE

A taxpayer who is going to replace a productive asset (e.g., machinery) used in a trade or business may structure the transaction as a sale of the old asset and the purchase of a new asset. When this approach is used, any realized gain or loss on the sale of the old asset is recognized. The basis of the new asset is its cost. Alternatively, the taxpayer may be able to trade the old asset for the new asset. This exchange of assets may produce beneficial tax consequences as a nontaxable exchange.

The tax law recognizes that nontaxable exchanges result in a change in the *form* but not the *substance* of a taxpayer's relative economic position. The replacement property received in the exchange is viewed as essentially a continuation of the old investment.[53] Additional justification for nontaxable treatment is that this type of transaction does not provide the taxpayer with the wherewithal to pay the tax on any realized gain.

The nonrecognition provisions for nontaxable exchanges do not apply to realized losses from the sale or exchange of personal-use assets. Such losses are never recognized (i.e., they are disallowed) because they are personal in nature.

In contrast, in a **nontaxable exchange**, recognition of gains or losses is *postponed* (i.e., deferred) until the new property received in the nontaxable exchange is subsequently disposed of in a taxable transaction. This is accomplished by assigning a carryover basis to the replacement property.

> **EXAMPLE**
> **24**
>
> Starling Management Company completes a *nontaxable exchange* of property with an adjusted basis of $10,000 and a fair market value of $12,000 for property with a fair market value of $12,000.
>
> Starling has a realized gain of $2,000 ($12,000 amount realized − $10,000 adjusted basis). Its recognized gain is $0. Starling's basis in the replacement property is a carryover basis of $10,000.
>
> Assume that the replacement property is nondepreciable and that Starling subsequently sells it for $12,000. The realized and recognized gain will be the $2,000 gain that was postponed (deferred) in the nontaxable transaction. If the replacement property is depreciable, the carryover basis of $10,000 is used in calculating depreciation.

In some nontaxable exchanges, only some of the property involved in the transaction qualifies for nonrecognition treatment. If the taxpayer receives cash or other nonqualifying property, part or all of the realized gain from the exchange is recognized. In these situations, gain is recognized because the taxpayer has changed or improved its relative economic position and has the wherewithal to pay income tax to the extent of cash or other property received.

It is important to distinguish between a nontaxable disposition (or nonrecognition transaction, as the term is used in the statute) and a tax-free transaction. As previously mentioned, the term *nontaxable* refers to postponement of recognition via some version of carryover basis. In a *tax-free* transaction, the nonrecognition is permanent (e.g., see the discussion later in this chapter of the exclusion of gain from the sale of a principal residence).

Either way, nontaxable and tax-free transactions must be understood as exceptions to the Code's general rule that gains and losses are recognized when they are realized. These exceptions have their own sets of requirements, limitations, and restrictions, all of which must be satisfied for a transaction to be characterized as nontaxable or tax-free. Otherwise, the general rule of recognition applies to the gain or loss at hand.

7-4 LIKE-KIND EXCHANGES—§ 1031

LO.5

Apply the nonrecognition provisions and basis determination rules for like-kind exchanges.

Section 1031 provides for nontaxable exchange treatment if the following requirements are satisfied:[54]

- The form of the transaction is an exchange.
- Both the property transferred and the property received are held either for productive use in a trade or business or for investment.
- The property is like-kind property.

---

[53]Reg. § 1.1002–1(c).

[54]§ 1031(a) and Reg. § 1.1031(a)–1(a).

Qualifying like-kind exchanges include exchanges of business for business, business for investment, investment for business, and investment for investment property. Property held for personal use does not qualify under the like-kind exchange provisions. Thus, the purpose for which the property is held by the taxpayer in question is critical. For example, if Janet uses a small truck in her trade or business, it may qualify for like-kind treatment, but if she uses this truck as her personal-use vehicle, it is ineligible for nonrecognition treatment under § 1031.

Some assets are excluded from like-kind treatment by statute. These excluded assets include a taxpayer's inventory or "stock in trade," as well as most forms of investment other than real estate. Thus, stocks, bonds, partnership interests (whether general or limited), and other securities, even though held for investment, do not qualify for like-kind exchange treatment.

The nonrecognition provision for like-kind exchanges is *mandatory* rather than elective. A taxpayer who wants to recognize a realized gain or loss will have to structure the transaction in a form that does not satisfy the statutory requirements for a like-kind exchange.

TAX PLANNING STRATEGIES Like-Kind Exchanges

FRAMEWORK FOCUS: DEDUCTIONS

Strategy: Maximize Deductible Amounts.

Because nonrecognition of gain or loss is mandatory in like-kind exchanges, a taxpayer must affirmatively *avoid such exchanges* if nonrecognition treatment is not desired. If an asset is worth less than its adjusted basis, a *loss would result* from its disposition. Accordingly, the taxpayer should sell this property outright to ensure the deductibility of the loss, assuming it would otherwise be deductible.

Even if *disposition would result in a gain*, a taxpayer might want to recognize this gain in the current taxable year. If so,

a like-kind exchange should be avoided. Circumstances suggesting this strategy include:

- Unused capital loss carryovers, especially if the taxpayer is a corporation for which such carryovers are limited in duration (see Chapters 4 and 8).
- Unused net operating loss carryovers (see Chapter 6).
- Unused general business credit carryovers (see Chapter 17).
- Suspended or current passive activity losses (see Chapter 6).

7-4a Like-Kind Property

The term *like-kind* is explained in the Regulations as follows: "The words 'like-kind' refer to the nature or character of the property and not to its grade or quality. One kind or class of property may not … be exchanged for property of a different kind or class."[55] The Regulations go on to explain that although real estate can be exchanged only for other real estate, the definition of real estate is quite broad. *Real estate* (or realty) includes principally rental buildings, office and store buildings, manufacturing plants, warehouses, and land. It is immaterial whether real estate is improved or unimproved. Thus, unimproved land can be exchanged for an apartment house. Alternatively, real property located in the United States exchanged for foreign real property (and vice versa) does not qualify as like-kind property. A similar provision applies to exchanges of foreign and domestic personalty.

In any case, real estate cannot be exchanged in a like-kind transaction for personalty. *Personalty* includes tangible assets other than real estate, such as machinery, equipment, trucks, automobiles, furniture, and fixtures. Thus, an exchange of a machine (personalty) for a small office building (realty) is not a like-kind exchange. Finally, the Code mandates that livestock of different sexes are not like-kind property.

---

[55]Reg. § 1.1031(a)–1(b).

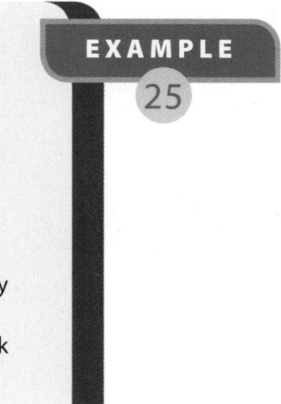

EXAMPLE 25

Pheasant, Inc., made the following exchanges during the taxable year:

(a) Inventory for a machine used in business.
(b) Land held for investment for a building used in business.
(c) Stock held for investment for equipment used in business.
(d) A light-duty business truck for a light-duty business truck.
(e) Livestock for livestock of a different sex.
(f) Land held for investment in New York for land held for investment in London.

Exchanges (b), investment real property for business real property, and (d), business personalty for business personalty, qualify as exchanges of like-kind property.

The other exchanges do not qualify because they involve (a), inventory; (c), stock; (e), livestock of different sexes; and (f), U.S. and foreign real estate.

In-depth coverage can be found on this book's companion website: www.cengagebrain.com | **8 DIGGING DEEPER**

Special Rule for Depreciable Tangible Personal Property

The Regulations dealing with § 1031 like-kind exchanges provide greater specificity when determining whether depreciable tangible personalty is of a like kind. Such property held for productive use in a business is of like kind only if the exchanged property is within the same *general business asset class* (as specified by the IRS in Rev.Proc. 87–57 or as subsequently modified) or the same *product class* (as specified by the Department of Commerce). Property included in a general business asset class is evaluated exclusively under the Revenue Procedure, rather than under the product class system. (See Chapter 2 for a discussion of the nature and authority of Revenue Procedures.)

The following are examples of general business asset classes:

- Office furniture, fixtures, and equipment.
- Information systems (computers and peripheral equipment).
- Airplanes.
- Automobiles and taxis.
- Buses.
- Light general-purpose trucks.
- Heavy general-purpose trucks.

These Regulations narrow the range of depreciable tangible personalty qualifying for § 1031 like-kind exchange treatment. For example, the exchange of office equipment for a computer does not qualify as an exchange of like-kind property. Even though both assets are depreciable tangible personalty, they are not like-kind property because they are in different general business asset classes. Accordingly, any realized *gain or loss* on the office equipment would be recognized currently.

In-depth coverage can be found on this book's companion website: www.cengagebrain.com | **9 DIGGING DEEPER**

7-4b Exchange Requirement

The transaction must generally involve a direct exchange of property to qualify as a like-kind exchange. The sale of old property and the purchase of new property, even though like kind, is not an exchange. However, the Code does provide a limited procedure for real estate to be exchanged for qualifying property that is acquired subsequent to the exchange.[56]

Of course, the taxpayer may want to avoid nontaxable exchange treatment. Recognition of gain gives the taxpayer a higher basis for depreciation. To the extent that such gains would, if recognized, either receive favorable capital gain treatment or be passive

---

[56]§ 1031(a)(3).

activity income that could be offset by passive activity losses, it might be preferable to avoid the nonrecognition provisions through an indirect exchange transaction. For example, a taxpayer may sell property to one company, recognize the gain, and subsequently purchase similar property from another company. The taxpayer may also want to avoid nontaxable exchange treatment so that a realized loss can be recognized.

DIGGING DEEPER 10 | **In-depth coverage can be found on this book's companion website: www.cengagebrain.com**

7-4c **Boot**

If the taxpayer in a like-kind exchange gives or receives some property that is not like-kind property, recognition may occur. Property that is not like-kind property, including cash, is often referred to as **boot**. Although the term *boot* does not appear in the Code, tax practitioners commonly use it rather than saying "property that does not qualify as like-kind property."

The *receipt* of boot will trigger recognition of gain if there is realized gain. The amount of the recognized gain is the *lesser* of the boot received or the realized gain (realized gain serves as the ceiling on recognition).

Implications of Boot Received

EXAMPLE 26

Blue, Inc., and White Corporation exchange machinery, and the exchange qualifies as like kind under § 1031. Because Blue's machinery (adjusted basis of $20,000) is worth $24,000 and White's machine has a fair market value of $19,000, White also gives Blue cash of $5,000.

Blue's recognized gain is $4,000, the lesser of the realized gain of $4,000 ($24,000 amount realized — $20,000 adjusted basis) or the fair market value of the boot received of $5,000.

EXAMPLE 27

Assume the same facts as in the preceding example, except that White's machine is worth $21,000 (not $19,000). Under these circumstances, White gives Blue cash of $3,000 to make up the difference.

Blue's recognized gain is $3,000, the lesser of the realized gain of $4,000 ($24,000 amount realized — $20,000 adjusted basis) or the fair market value of the boot received of $3,000.

The receipt of boot does not result in recognition if there is realized loss.

Implications of Boot Received

EXAMPLE 28

Assume the same facts as in Example 26, except that the adjusted basis of Blue's machine is $30,000.

Blue's realized loss is $6,000 ($24,000 amount realized — $30,000 adjusted basis). The receipt of the boot of $5,000 does not trigger recognition of Blue's loss.

The *giving* of boot does not trigger recognition if the boot consists solely of cash.

Implications of Boot Given

EXAMPLE 29

Flicker, Inc., and Gadwall Corporation exchange equipment in a like-kind exchange. Flicker receives equipment with a fair market value of $75,000 and transfers equipment worth $63,000 (adjusted basis of $45,000) and cash of $12,000.

Flicker's realized gain is $18,000 ($75,000 amount realized — $45,000 adjusted basis of equipment transferred — $12,000 cash), none of which is recognized.

If, however, the boot given is appreciated or depreciated property, gain or loss is recognized to the extent of the difference between the adjusted basis and the fair market value of the boot. For this purpose, *appreciated or depreciated property* is property with an adjusted basis that differs from fair market value.

Implications of Boot Given

EXAMPLE 30

Assume the same facts as in the preceding example, except that Flicker transfers equipment worth $30,000 (adjusted basis of $36,000) and boot worth $45,000 (adjusted basis of $27,000). Flicker's net gain on this exchange is $12,000 [$75,000 amount realized − adjusted basis of $63,000 ($36,000 + $27,000)]. But Flicker is transferring two pieces of property: equipment (like-kind property) with a built-in realized loss of $6,000 ($30,000 fair market value − $36,000 adjusted basis) and non-like-kind property (boot) with a built-in realized gain of $18,000 ($45,000 fair market value − $27,000 adjusted basis).

In this case, the $6,000 realized loss on the like-kind property is *deferred* (not recognized) and the $18,000 realized gain on the non-like-kind property is recognized. In other words, the realized loss on the like-kind property *cannot* be used to offset the realized gain on the boot given up as part of the transaction.

7-4d Basis and Holding Period of Property Received

If an exchange does not qualify as nontaxable under § 1031, gain or loss is recognized and the basis of property received in the exchange is the property's fair market value. If the exchange qualifies for nonrecognition, the basis of property received must be adjusted to reflect any postponed (deferred) gain or loss. The *basis of like-kind property* received in the exchange is the property's fair market value less postponed gain or plus postponed loss. The *basis* of any *boot* received is the boot's fair market value.

Basis of Like-Kind Property Received

EXAMPLE 31

Vireo Property Management Company exchanges a building (used in its business) with an adjusted basis of $300,000 and a fair market value of $380,000 for land with a fair market value of $380,000. The land is to be held as an investment. The exchange qualifies as like kind (an exchange of business real property for investment real property).

The basis of the land is $300,000 (land's fair market value of $380,000 − $80,000 postponed gain on the building). If the land is later sold for its fair market value of $380,000, the $80,000 postponed gain is recognized.

EXAMPLE 32

Assume the same facts as in the preceding example, except that the building has an adjusted basis of $480,000 and a fair market value of only $380,000.

The basis in the newly acquired land is $480,000 (fair market value of $380,000 + $100,000 postponed loss on the building). If the land is later sold for its fair market value of $380,000, the $100,000 postponed loss is recognized.

The Code provides an alternative approach for determining the basis of like-kind property received:

Adjusted basis of like-kind property surrendered
+ Adjusted basis of boot given
+ Gain recognized
− Fair market value of boot received
− Loss recognized
= *Basis of like-kind property received*

This approach accords with the recovery of capital doctrine. That is, the unrecovered cost or other basis is increased by additional cost (boot given) or decreased by cost recovered (boot received). Any gain recognized is included in the basis of the new property. The taxpayer has been taxed on this amount and is now entitled to recover it tax-free. Any loss recognized is deducted from the basis of the new property because the taxpayer has already received a tax benefit on that amount.

The holding period of the property surrendered in the exchange carries over and *tacks on* to the holding period of the like-kind property received.[57] This rule derives from the basic concept that the new property is a continuation of the old investment. The boot received has a new holding period (from the date of exchange) rather than a carryover holding period.

Depreciation recapture potential carries over to the property received in a like-kind exchange.[58] See Chapter 8 for a discussion of this topic.

DIGGING DEEPER 11 | **In-depth coverage can be found on this book's companion website: www.cengagebrain.com**

If the taxpayer either assumes a liability or takes property subject to a liability, the amount of the liability is treated as boot given. For the taxpayer whose liability is assumed or whose property is taken subject to the liability, the amount of the liability is treated as boot received. The following example illustrates the effect of such a liability. In addition, the example illustrates the tax consequences for both parties involved in the like-kind exchange.

EXAMPLE

33

Jaeger & Company and Lark Enterprises, Inc., exchange real estate investments. Jaeger gives up property with an adjusted basis of $250,000 (fair market value of $420,000) that is subject to a mortgage of $80,000 (assumed by Lark). In return for this property, Jaeger receives property with a fair market value of $340,000 (Lark's adjusted basis in the property is $200,000). Jaeger's and Lark's realized and recognized gains and their basis in the like-kind property received are computed as follows:[59]

	Jaeger	Lark
Amount realized:		
Like-kind property received	$ 340,000	$ 420,000
Boot received:		
Cash		
Mortgage assumed	80,000	
	$ 420,000	$ 420,000
Adjusted basis:		
Like-kind property given	(250,000)	(200,000)
Boot given:		
Cash		
Mortgage assumed		(80,000)
Realized gain	$ 170,000	$ 140,000
Recognized gain	80,000*	–0–**
Deferred gain	$ 90,000	$ 140,000
Basis of property transferred:		
Like-kind property	$ 250,000	$ 200,000
Cash		
Mortgage assumed		80,000
	$ 250,000	$ 280,000
Plus: Gain recognized	80,000	
Less: Boot received	(80,000)	
Basis of new property	$ 250,000	$ 280,000

*Lesser of boot received ($80,000 mortgage assumed) or realized gain ($170,000).
**No boot received. Therefore, no gain is recognized.

---

[57]§ 1223(1) and Reg. § 1.1223–1(a). For like-kind exchanges after March 1, 1954, the tacked-on holding period applies only if the like-kind property surrendered was either a capital asset or § 1231 property.

[58]Reg. §§ 1.1245–2(a)(4) and 1.1250–2(d)(1).

[59]Example (2) of Reg. § 1.1031(d)–2 illustrates a special situation in which both the buyer and the seller transfer liabilities that are assumed by the other party or both parties acquire property that is subject to a liability.

BRIDGE DISCIPLINE **Bridge to Economics**

One can assert that the "tax variable" is neutralized in nontaxable exchanges when taxable gains or losses do not arise. Neutralizing potential tax consequences can have a positive result given that tax costs tend to dampen economic activity. For example, in a like-kind exchange, a taxpayer can exchange one asset for another asset of like kind without having to recognize a gain or pay a tax. The justification for the tax deferral is that the taxpayer is viewed as having an equivalent economic investment after the transaction as before the transaction. But the tax-neutral result changes when the taxpayer receives property that is not "like kind" because the taxpayer's economic standing has changed.

If, for example, the taxpayer receives investment land *and* cash in exchange for investment land, her ownership in the land given up has, at least in part, been converted to cash, and to that degree, her investment has substantively changed. That is, the taxpayer's economic investment has changed from an ownership exclusively in land to ownership in land *and* cash. Alternatively, if the taxpayer gives up her investment in land for corporate stock in a high-tech venture, the nature of her investment also would substantively change as a result of the transaction. These differences in the taxpayer's economic position after the transaction lead to the transactions being taxed.

7-5 INVOLUNTARY CONVERSIONS—§ 1033

LO.6

Explain the nonrecognition provisions available on the involuntary conversion of property.

Section 1033 provides that a taxpayer who suffers an involuntary conversion of property may postpone recognition of *gain* realized from the conversion. The objective of this provision is to provide relief to the taxpayer who has suffered hardship and does not have the wherewithal to pay the tax on any gain realized from the conversion. Postponement of realized gain is permitted to the extent that the taxpayer *reinvests* the amount realized from the conversion in replacement property. If the amount reinvested in replacement property is *less than* the amount realized, realized gain *is recognized* to the extent of the deficiency.

By its terms, § 1033 generally is *elective*. A taxpayer need not postpone recognition of gain, even if replacement property is acquired. In essence, a taxpayer has three options:

- Reinvest the proceeds and elect § 1033's nonrecognition of gain.

- Reinvest the proceeds and not elect § 1033, thereby triggering recognition of realized gain under the usual rules applicable to property transactions.

- Not reinvest the proceeds and recognize the realized gain accordingly.

If a *loss* occurs on an involuntary conversion, § 1033 does not apply and the general rules for loss recognition are effective. See Chapter 6 for the discussion of the deduction of losses.

7-5a Involuntary Conversion Defined

An **involuntary conversion** results from the destruction (complete or partial), theft, seizure, requisition or condemnation, or sale or exchange under threat or imminence of requisition or condemnation of the taxpayer's property.[60] This description includes fires (other than arson),[61] tornadoes, hurricanes, earthquakes, floods, and other natural disasters. In these circumstances, *gain* can result from insurance proceeds received in an amount that exceeds the taxpayer's historical cost of the property, especially if depreciation deductions have lowered the property's adjusted basis.

For requisitions and condemnations, the amount realized includes the compensation paid by the public authority acquiring the taxpayer's property. To prove the existence of a threat or imminence of condemnation, the taxpayer must obtain confirmation that there has been a decision to acquire the property for public use.

---

[60]§ 1033(a) and Reg. §§ 1.1033(a)–1(a) and −2(a).   [61]Rev.Rul. 82–74, 1982–1 C.B. 110.

In addition, the taxpayer must have reasonable grounds to believe the property will be taken.[62] The property does not have to be sold to the authority threatening to condemn it to qualify for § 1033 postponement. If the taxpayer satisfies the confirmation and reasonable grounds requirements, he or she can sell the property to another party.[63] Likewise, the sale of property to a condemning authority by a taxpayer who acquired the property from its former owner with the knowledge that the property was under threat of condemnation also qualifies as an involuntary conversion under § 1033.[64]

DIGGING DEEPER 12 | In-depth coverage can be found on this book's companion website: www.cengagebrain.com

7-5b **Replacement Property**

The requirements for replacement property under the involuntary conversion rules generally are more restrictive than those for like-kind property under § 1031. The basic requirement is that the replacement property be similar or related in service or use to the involuntarily converted property.[65]

Different interpretations of the phrase *similar or related in service or use* apply depending on whether the involuntarily converted property is held by an *owner-user* or by an *owner-investor* (e.g., lessor). For an owner-investor, the *taxpayer use test* applies, and for an owner-user, the *functional use test* applies. Furthermore, a special test applies in the case of involuntary conversions that result from condemnations.

Functional Use Test

Under this test, a taxpayer's use of the replacement property and of the involuntarily converted property must be the same. Replacing a manufacturing plant with a wholesale grocery warehouse does not meet this test. Instead, the plant must be replaced with another facility of similar functional use.

Taxpayer Use Test

The taxpayer use test for owner-investors provides the taxpayer with more flexibility in terms of what qualifies as replacement property than does the functional use test for owner-users. Essentially, the properties must be used by the taxpayer (the owner-investor) in similar endeavors. For example, rental property held by an owner-investor qualifies if replaced by other rental property, regardless of the type of rental property involved. The test is met when an investor replaces a manufacturing plant with a wholesale grocery warehouse if both properties are held for the production of rental income.[66] The replacement of a rental residence with a personal residence does not meet the test.[67]

Special Rule for Condemnations

In addition to the functional and taxpayer use tests, the Code provides a special rule for business or investment real property *that is condemned*. This rule applies the broad like-kind classification for real estate to such circumstances. Accordingly, improved real property can be replaced with unimproved real property.

The rules concerning the nature of replacement property are illustrated in Concept Summary 7.4.

---

[62]Rev.Rul. 63–221, 1963–2 C.B. 332 and *Joseph P. Balistrieri*, 38 TCM 526, T.C.Memo. 1979–115.

[63]Rev.Rul. 81–180, 1981–2 C.B. 161.

[64]Rev.Rul. 81–181, 1981–2 C.B. 162.

[65]§ 1033(a) and Reg. § 1.1033(a)–1.

[66]*Loco Realty Co. v. Comm.*, 62–2 USTC ¶9657, 10 AFTR 2d 5359, 306 F.2d 207 (CA–8, 1962).

[67]Rev.Rul. 70–466, 1970–2 C.B. 165.

Concept Summary 7.4

Involuntary Conversions: Replacement Property Tests

Type of Property and User	Taxpayer Use Test	Functional Use Test	Special Rule for Condemnations*
An investor's rented shopping mall is destroyed by fire; the mall may be replaced with other rental properties (e.g., an apartment building).	X		
A manufacturing plant is destroyed by fire; replacement property must consist of another manufacturing plant that is functionally the same as the property converted.		X	
Personal residence of a taxpayer is condemned by a local government authority; replacement property must consist of another personal residence.		X	
Land used by a manufacturing company is condemned by a local government authority.			X
Apartment and land held by an investor are sold due to the threat or imminence of condemnation.			X

*Applies the same test as in the case of like-kind exchanges.

7-5c Time Limitation on Replacement

The taxpayer normally has a two-year period after the close of the taxable year in which gain is realized from an involuntary conversion to replace the property.[68] This rule affords as much as three years from the date of realization of gain to replace the property if the realization of gain took place on the first day of the taxable year.[69]

> Magpie, Inc.'s building is destroyed by fire on December 16, 2015. The adjusted basis is $325,000. Magpie receives $400,000 from the insurance company on January 10, 2016. The company is a calendar year and cash method taxpayer.
>
> The latest date for replacement is December 31, 2018 (the end of the taxable year in which realized gain occurred plus two years). The critical date is not the date the involuntary conversion occurred, but rather the date of gain realization (when the insurance proceeds are received).

EXAMPLE 34

In the case of a condemnation of real property used in a trade or business or held for investment, the Code substitutes a three-year period for the normal two-year period. In this case, a taxpayer might have as many as four years from the date of realization of gain to replace the property.

> Assume the same facts as in the preceding example, except that Magpie's building is condemned. On November 1, 2015, Magpie receives notification of the future condemnation, which occurs on December 16, 2015. The condemnation proceeds are received on January 10, 2016.
>
> The latest date for replacement is December 31, 2019 (the end of the taxable year in which realized gain occurred plus three years).

EXAMPLE 35

The *earliest date* for replacement typically is the date the involuntary conversion occurs. However, if the property is condemned, it is possible to replace the condemned property before this date. In this case, the earliest date is the date of the threat or imminence of requisition or condemnation of the property. The purpose of this provision is to enable the taxpayer to make an orderly replacement of the condemned property.

---

[68]§§ 1033(a)(2)(B) and (g)(4) and Reg. § 1.1033(a)–2(c)(3). The two-year period is extended to a four-year period if the property is located in a Presidentially-declared disaster area.

[69]A taxpayer can apply for an extension of this time period anytime before its expiration [Reg. § 1.1033(a)–2(c)(3)]. Also, the period for filing the application for extension can be extended if a taxpayer shows reasonable cause.

7-5d **Nonrecognition of Gain**

Nonrecognition of gain can be either mandatory or elective, depending on whether the conversion is direct (into replacement property) or indirect (into money).

Direct Conversion

If the conversion is directly into replacement property rather than into money, nonrecognition of realized gain is *mandatory*. In this case, the basis of the replacement property is the same as the adjusted basis of the converted property. Direct conversion is rare in practice and usually involves condemnations.

EXAMPLE 36

Oak, Inc.'s property, with an adjusted basis of $20,000, is condemned by the state. Oak receives property with a fair market value of $50,000 as compensation for the property taken.

Because the nonrecognition of realized gain is mandatory for direct conversions, Oak's realized gain of $30,000 is not recognized and the basis of the replacement property is $20,000 (adjusted basis of the condemned property).

Conversion into Money

If the conversion is into money, the realized gain is recognized only to the extent the amount realized from the involuntary conversion exceeds the cost of the qualifying replacement property.[70] This is the usual case, and nonrecognition (postponement) is *elective*. If the election is not made, the realized gain is recognized.

The basis of the replacement property is the property's cost less any postponed (deferred) gain.[71] If the election to postpone gain is made, the holding period of the replacement property includes the holding period of the converted property.

Section 1033 applies *only to gains* and *not to losses*. Losses from involuntary conversions are recognized if the property is held for business or income-producing purposes. Personal casualty losses are recognized, but condemnation losses related to personal use assets (e.g., a personal residence) are neither recognized nor postponed.

The Big Picture

EXAMPLE 37

Return to the facts of *The Big Picture* on p. 7-1. Alice's building (used in her trade or business), with an adjusted basis of $50,000, is destroyed by a fire on October 5, 2016. Alice is a calendar year taxpayer. On November 17, 2016, she receives an insurance reimbursement of $100,000 for the loss. Assume that Alice goes ahead with her plan to invest $80,000 in a new building and to use the other $20,000 of insurance proceeds to pay off credit card debt.

- Alice has until December 31, 2018, to make the new investment and qualify for the nonrecognition election.
- Alice's realized gain is $50,000 ($100,000 insurance proceeds received − $50,000 adjusted basis of old building).
- Assuming that the replacement property qualifies as similar or related in service or use, Alice's recognized gain is $20,000. Because she reinvested $20,000 less than the insurance proceeds received ($100,000 proceeds − $80,000 reinvested), her realized gain is recognized to that extent.
- Alice's basis in the new building is $50,000. This is the building's cost of $80,000 less the postponed gain of $30,000 (realized gain of $50,000 − recognized gain of $20,000).

The Big Picture

EXAMPLE 38

Return to the facts of *The Big Picture* on p. 7-1. Assume the same facts as in the previous example, except that Alice receives only $45,000 of insurance proceeds. She has a realized and recognized loss of $5,000. The basis of the new building is the building's cost of $80,000.

---

[70]§ 1033(a)(2)(A) and Reg. § 1.1033(a)–2(c)(1).   [71]§ 1033(b).

TAX PLANNING STRATEGIES **Recognizing Involuntary Conversion Gains**

FRAMEWORK FOCUS: TAX RATE

Strategy: Shift Net Income from High-Bracket Years to Low-Bracket Years.

FRAMEWORK FOCUS: DEDUCTIONS

Strategy: Maximize Deductible Amounts.

Sometimes, a taxpayer may prefer to *recognize a gain from an involuntary conversion* and will choose not to elect § 1033, even though replacement property is acquired. Circumstances suggesting this strategy would include:

- The taxpayer realized the gain in a low-bracket tax year, quite possibly because of the events that caused the involuntary conversion, such as a flood and its aftermath that seriously disrupted the business.

- The taxpayer has an expiring net operating loss carry-over that can offset most, if not all, of the gain from the involuntary conversion.

- The replacement property is depreciable, and the tax-payer would prefer an unreduced basis for this asset to maximize depreciation deductions in future years.

Nontax considerations might also come into play, perhaps suggesting that the property not be replaced at all. Even before the event that produced the involuntary conversion, the tax-payer might have been wanting to downsize the business or ter-minate it outright. In any case, the taxpayer might prefer to recognize the gain, pay the tax involved, and thereby free up the remaining proceeds for other uses—business, investment, or even personal—especially if the gain is small compared to the amount of proceeds received.

7-6 OTHER NONRECOGNITION PROVISIONS

LO.7

Identify other nonrecognition provisions contained in the Code.

Several additional nonrecognition provisions are treated briefly in the remainder of this chapter.

7-6a Transfer of Assets to Business Entity—§§ 351 and 721

Taxpayers can transfer assets to corporations in exchange for stock without recognizing gain or loss on the transfer according to § 351. See Chapter 12 for the applicable restrictions and corresponding basis adjustments for the stock acquired. A similar provision (§ 721) allows the nontaxable transfer of assets to a partnership in exchange for an interest in that partnership. See Chapter 14 for a description of § 721.

7-6b Exchange of Stock for Property—§ 1032

Under § 1032, a corporation does not recognize gain or loss on the receipt of money or other property in exchange for its stock (including treasury stock). In other words, a corporation does not recognize gain or loss when it deals in its own stock. This provi-sion accords with the accounting treatment of such transactions. See Chapter 12 for additional discussion.

7-6c Certain Exchanges of Insurance Policies—§ 1035

Under § 1035, no gain or loss is recognized from the exchange of certain insurance con-tracts or policies. The rules relating to exchanges not solely in kind (i.e., with boot) and the basis of the property acquired are the same as under § 1031. Exchanges qualifying for nonrecognition include the following:

- The exchange of life insurance contracts.

- The exchange of a life insurance contract for an endowment or annuity contract.

- The exchange of an endowment contract for another endowment contract that provides for regular payments beginning at a date not later than the date pay-ments would have begun under the contract exchanged.

- The exchange of an endowment contract for an annuity contract.
- The exchange of annuity contracts.

7-6d Exchange of Stock for Stock of the Same Corporation—§ 1036

Section 1036 provides that a shareholder does not recognize gain or loss on the exchange of common stock solely for common stock in the same corporation or from the exchange of preferred stock for preferred stock in the same corporation. Exchanges between individual shareholders as well as between a shareholder and the corporation are included under this nonrecognition provision. The rules relating to exchanges not solely in kind and the basis of the property acquired are the same as under § 1031. For example, a nonrecognition exchange occurs when common stock with different rights, such as voting for nonvoting, is exchanged. A shareholder usually recognizes gain or loss from the exchange of common for preferred or preferred for common even though the stock exchanged is in the same corporation.

7-6e Rollovers into Specialized Small Business Investment Companies—§ 1044

Section 1044 provides a postponement opportunity associated with the sale of publicly traded securities. If the amount realized is reinvested in the common stock or partnership interest of a specialized small business investment company (SSBIC), the realized gain is not recognized. Gain will be recognized, however, to the extent of any amount not reinvested. To qualify, the taxpayer must reinvest the proceeds within 60 days of the date of sale.

7-6f Sale of a Principal Residence—§ 121

Section 121 allows individual taxpayers to exclude gain from the sale of a *principal residence*. This provision applies to the first $250,000 of realized gain, or $500,000 on certain joint returns. For this purpose, the residence must have been owned and used by the taxpayer as the primary residence for at least two of the five years preceding the date of sale. In addition, the exclusion is not available for sales occurring within two years of its last use. This exclusion can be prorated, however, if a taxpayer failed to meet one or more of these time period requirements due to a change in his or her place of employment or health. Moreover, a surviving spouse counts the ownership and usage periods of the decedent spouse in meeting the two-year test. This provision applies only to gains; losses on residences, like those of other personal-use assets, are not recognized for tax purposes.

DIGGING DEEPER 13, 14, 15 | In-depth coverage can be found on this book's companion website: www.cengagebrain.com

7-6g Transfers of Property between Spouses or Incident to Divorce—§ 1041

Section 1041 provides for nontaxable exchange treatment on property transfers *between spouses during marriage*. The basis to the recipient spouse is a carryover basis.

Section 1041 also provides that transfers of property *between spouses or former spouses incident to divorce* are nontaxable transactions. Therefore, the basis to the recipient is a carryover basis. To be treated as incident to the divorce, the transfer must be related to the cessation of marriage or must occur within one year after the date on which the marriage ceases.

REFOCUS ON THE BIG PICTURE

CALCULATING BASIS AND RECOGNIZED GAIN FOR PROPERTY TRANSACTIONS

Alice's basis in the land acquired as a gift is a carryover basis of $2,000. If Alice sells the land outright, she will realize and recognize a gain of $48,000. However, if she replaces the property with other real property, she should be able to qualify for favorable like-kind exchange treatment under § 1031 and defer the gain on the property disposition. However, if Alice receives any cash as a part of the exchange transaction, realized gain would be recognized to the extent of the cash (boot) received.

Alice's basis in the 300 shares of stock received as an inheritance is the property's $30,000 fair market value at the date of her grandfather's death. If Alice sells the 300 shares, she will realize and recognize a $6,000 gain [$36,000 sales price (300 shares × $120) − $30,000 basis].

Alice's basis in the 200 shares of stock purchased is her purchase price of $28,000. Those shares are currently worth $24,000 (200 shares × $120). Consequently, if she sells those shares, she will realize and recognize a $4,000 loss.

You advise Alice that her basis in the house is its $475,000 fair market value on the date of her grandmother's death. If Alice sells the house for $600,000, her realized and recognized gain would be $125,000.

Regarding the fire-related involuntary conversion of Alice's business building, a $50,000 realized gain occurs upon the receipt of the $100,000 of insurance proceeds. Because she intends to invest only $80,000 of the insurance proceeds in a qualifying property, Alice's recognized gain will be $20,000 ($100,000 proceeds − $80,000 reinvested). Therefore, her realized gain would be recognized to that extent (see Example 37).

What If?

Alice is leaning toward selling the house. However, she knows that her grandmother would not want her to have to pay income taxes on the sale. Alice asks whether there is any way she could avoid paying taxes on the sale.

You inform Alice of the exclusion provision under § 121. Alice can qualify for this exclusion of up to $250,000 of realized gain if she owns and occupies the house as her principal residence for at least two of the five years prior to a sale.

From a tax planning perspective, what can Alice do so that none of the $50,000 of realized gain from the involuntary conversion is recognized? To have full postponement of the $50,000 realized gain, Alice would have to reinvest all of the $100,000 of insurance proceeds received in another qualified building. Under this circumstance, the basis of the replacement building would be $50,000 ($100,000 cost of replacement building − $50,000 deferred gain).

Suggested Readings

Mary Cunningham, "Accomplishing Section 1031 Tax-Deferred Exchanges," *Practical Tax Strategies*, August 2014.

Mary B. Foster, "A Checklist For Like-Kind Real Estate Exchanges," *Journal of Real Estate Taxation*, Second Quarter 2015.

James R. Hamill, "Preserving the Residence Sale Exclusion for Mixed Use Property," *Practical Tax Strategies*, June 2013.

Christian J. Kenefick, "What Is a $10 Gold Coin Worth? Basis, FMV, and Realization Issues Abound," *Journal of Taxation*, February 2013.

Edward J. Schnee, "Like-Kind Exchange Rules: Continued Evolution," *The Tax Adviser,* July 2014.

Timothy M. Todd, "Whose Goodwill Is It? The Taxation of Goodwill in Owner-Entity Transactions," *Journal of Taxation,* February 2015.

Key Terms

Adjusted basis, 7-3

Amount realized, 7-3

Boot, 7-22

Fair market value, 7-3

Goodwill, 7-9

Holding period, 7-12

Involuntary conversion, 7-25

Like-kind exchanges, 7-20

Nontaxable exchange, 7-19

Realized gain, 7-2

Realized loss, 7-2

Recognized gain, 7-6

Recognized loss, 7-6

Wash sale, 7-15

Computational Exercises

1. **LO.3** Luciana, a nonshareholder, purchases a condominium from her employer for $85,000. The fair market value of the condominium is $120,000. What is Luciana's basis in the condominium and the amount of any income as a result of this purchase?

2. **LO.3** Sebastian purchases two pieces of equipment for $100,000. Appraisals of the equipment indicate that the fair market value of the first piece of equipment is $72,000 and that of the second piece of equipment is $108,000. What is Sebastian's basis in these two assets?

3. **LO.2, 4** Lisa sells business property with an adjusted basis of $130,000 to her son, Alfred, for its fair market value of $100,000.

    a. What is Lisa's realized and recognized gain or loss?

    b. What is Alfred's recognized gain or loss if he subsequently sells the property for $138,000? For $80,000?

4. **LO.4** Arianna's personal residence has an adjusted basis of $230,000 and a fair market value of $210,000. Arianna converts the personal residence to rental property. What is Arianna's gain basis? What is her loss basis?

Critical Thinking 5. **LO.1, 4** Peyton sells an office building and the associated land on May 1, 2016. Under the terms of the sales contract, Peyton is to receive $1,600,000 in cash. The purchaser is to assume Peyton's mortgage of $950,000 on the property. To enable the purchaser to obtain adequate financing, Peyton is to pay the $9,000 in points charged by the lender. The broker's commission on the sale is $75,000. The purchaser agrees to pay the $24,000 in property taxes for the entire year. What is Peyton's amount realized?

6. **LO.2, 5** Logan and Johnathan exchange land, and the exchange qualifies as like kind under § 1031. Because Logan's land (adjusted basis of $85,000) is worth $100,000 and Johnathan's land has a fair market value of $80,000, Johnathan also gives Logan cash of $20,000.

    a. What is Logan's recognized gain?

    b. Assume instead that Johnathan's land is worth $90,000 and he gives Logan $10,000 cash. Now what is Logan's recognized gain?

7. **LO.2, 6** Camilo's property, with an adjusted basis of $155,000, is condemned by the state. Camilo receives property with a fair market value of $180,000 as compensation for the property taken.

    a. What is Camilo's realized and recognized gain?

    b. What is the basis of the replacement property?

8. **LO.2, 7** Constanza, who is single, sells her current personal residence (adjusted basis of $165,000) for $450,000. She has owned and lived in the house for 30 years. Her selling expenses are $22,500. What is Constanza's realized and recognized gain? **Critical Thinking**

Problems

9. **LO.1** If a taxpayer sells property for cash, the amount realized consists of the net proceeds from the sale. For each of the following, indicate the effect on the amount realized:
   a. The property is sold on credit.
   b. A mortgage on the property is assumed by the buyer.
   c. A mortgage on the property of the buyer is assumed by the seller.
   d. The buyer acquires the property subject to a mortgage of the seller.
   e. Stock that has a basis to the purchaser of $6,000 and a fair market value of $10,000 is received by the seller as part of the consideration.

10. **LO.1, 2** Pam owns a personal-use boat that has a fair market value of $35,000 and an adjusted basis of $45,000. Pam's AGI is $100,000. Calculate the realized and recognized gain or loss if:
    a. Pam sells the boat for $35,000.
    b. Pam exchanges the boat for another boat worth $35,000.
    c. The boat is stolen and Pam receives insurance proceeds of $35,000.
    d. Would your answer in part (a) change if the fair market value and the selling price of the boat were $48,000?

11. **LO.1, 2** Yancy's personal residence is condemned as part of an urban renewal project. His adjusted basis for the residence is $480,000. He receives condemnation proceeds of $460,000 and invests the proceeds in stocks and bonds.
    a. Calculate Yancy's realized and recognized gain or loss.
    b. If the condemnation proceeds are $505,000, what are Yancy's realized and recognized gain or loss?
    c. What are Yancy's realized and recognized gain or loss in part (a) if the house was rental property?

12. **LO.1, 2, 3** Finch, Inc., purchases 1,000 shares of Bluebird Corporation stock on October 3, 2016, for $300,000. On December 12, 2016, Finch purchases an additional 750 shares of Bluebird stock for $210,000. According to market quotations, Bluebird stock is selling for $285 per share on December 31, 2016. Finch sells 500 shares of Bluebird stock on March 1, 2017, for $162,500.
    a. What is the adjusted basis of Finch's Bluebird stock on December 31, 2016?
    b. What is Finch's recognized gain or loss from the sale of Bluebird stock on March 1, 2017, assuming that the shares sold are from the shares purchased on December 12, 2016?
    c. What is Finch's recognized gain or loss from the sale of Bluebird stock on March 1, 2017, assuming that Finch cannot adequately identify the shares sold?

Communications 13. **LO.2, 3** Rod Clooney purchases Agnes Mitchell's sole proprietorship for $990,000 on August 15, 2016. The assets of the business are as follows:

Asset	Agnes's Adjusted Basis	FMV
Accounts receivable	$ 70,000	$ 70,000
Inventory	90,000	100,000
Equipment	150,000	160,000
Furniture and fixtures	95,000	130,000
Building	190,000	250,000
Land	25,000	75,000
Total	$620,000	$785,000

a. Calculate Agnes's realized and recognized gain.
b. Determine Rod's basis for each of the assets.
c. Write a letter to Rod informing him of the tax consequences of the purchase. His address is 300 Riverview Drive, Delaware, OH 43015.

14. **LO.1, 2, 3** Roberto has received various gifts over the years. He has decided to dispose of the following assets he received as gifts:

a. In 1951, he received land worth $32,000. The donor's adjusted basis was $35,000. Roberto sells the land for $95,000 in 2016.
b. In 1956, he received stock in Gold Company. The donor's adjusted basis was $19,000. The fair market value on the date of the gift was $34,000. Roberto sells the stock for $40,000 in 2016.
c. In 1962, he received land worth $15,000. The donor's adjusted basis was $20,000. Roberto sells the land for $9,000 in 2016.
d. In 2003, he received stock worth $30,000. The donor's adjusted basis was $42,000. Roberto sells the stock for $38,000 in 2016.

What is the recognized gain or loss from each of the preceding transactions? Assume for each of the gift transactions that no gift tax was paid.

15. **LO.1, 2, 3** Nicky receives a car from Sam as a gift. Sam paid $48,000 for the car. He had used it for business purposes and had deducted $10,000 for depreciation up to the time he gave the car to Nicky. The fair market value of the car is $33,000.

a. Assuming that Nicky uses the car for business purposes, what is her basis for depreciation?
b. Assume that Nicky deducts depreciation of $6,500 and then sells the car for $32,500. What is her recognized gain or loss?
c. Assume that Nicky deducts depreciation of $6,500 and then sells the car for $20,000. What is her recognized gain or loss?

Issue ID 16. **LO.3** Simon owns stock that has declined in value since acquired. He has decided either to give the stock to his nephew, Fred, or to sell it and give Fred the proceeds. If Fred receives the stock, he will sell it to obtain the proceeds. Simon is in the 15% tax bracket, while Fred's bracket is 25%. In either case, the holding period for the stock will be short-term. Identify the tax issues relevant to Simon in deciding whether to give the stock or the sale proceeds to Fred.

17. **LO.3** On September 18, 2016, Gerald received land and a building from Frank as a gift. Frank's adjusted basis and the fair market value at the date of the gift are as follows:

Asset	Adjusted Basis	FMV
Land	$100,000	$212,000
Building	80,000	100,000

No gift tax was paid on the transfer.

a. Determine Gerald's adjusted basis for the land and building.

b. Assume instead that the fair market value of the land was $87,000 and that of the building was $65,000. Determine Gerald's adjusted basis for the land and building.

18. **LO.3** Dan bought a hotel for $2,600,000 in January 2012. In May 2016, he died and left the hotel to Ed. While Dan owned the hotel, he deducted $289,000 of cost recovery. The fair market value in May 2016 was $2,800,000. The fair market value six months later was $2,850,000.

a. What is the basis of the property to Ed?

b. What is the basis of the property to Ed if the fair market value six months later was $2,500,000 (not $2,850,000) and the objective of the executor was to minimize the estate tax liability?

19. **LO.4** Sheila sells land to Elane, her sister, for the fair market value of $40,000. Six months later when the land is worth $45,000, Elane gives it to Jacob, her son. (No gift tax resulted.) Shortly thereafter, Jacob sells the land for $48,000.

a. Assuming that Sheila's adjusted basis for the land is $24,000, what are Sheila's and Jacob's recognized gain or loss on the sales?

b. Assuming that Sheila's adjusted basis for the land is $60,000, what are Sheila's and Jacob's recognized gain or loss on the sales?

20. **LO.1, 2, 3, 4** Tyneka inherited 1,000 shares of Aqua, Inc. stock from Joe. Joe's basis was $35,000, and the fair market value on July 1, 2016 (the date of death), was $45,000. The shares were distributed to Tyneka on July 15, 2016. Tyneka sold the stock on July 30, 2017, for $33,000. After giving the matter more thought, she decides that Aqua is a good investment and purchases 1,000 shares for $30,000 on August 20, 2017.   Decision Making

a. What is Tyneka's basis for the 1,000 shares purchased on August 20, 2017?

b. Could Tyneka have obtained different tax consequences in part (a) if she had sold the 1,000 shares on December 27, 2016, and purchased the 1,000 shares on January 5, 2017? Explain.

21. **LO.4** Sam owns 1,500 shares of Eagle, Inc., stock that he purchased over 10 years ago for $80,000. Although the stock has a current market value of $52,000, Sam still views the stock as a solid long-term investment. He has sold other stock during the year with overall gains of $30,000, so he would like to sell the Eagle stock and offset the $28,000 loss against these gains—but somehow keep his Eagle investment. He has devised a plan to keep his Eagle investment by using funds in his traditional IRA to purchase 1,500 Eagle shares immediately after selling the shares he currently owns. Evaluate Sam's treatment of these stock transactions. Can his plan work? Explain.   Ethics and Equity

22. **LO.1, 2, 4** Abby's home had a basis of $360,000 ($160,000 attributable to the land) and a fair market value of $340,000 ($155,000 attributable to the land) when she converted 70% of it to business use by opening a bed-and-breakfast. Four years after the conversion, Abby sells the home for $500,000 ($165,000 attributable to the land).

a. Calculate Abby's basis for gain, loss, and cost recovery for the portion of her personal residence that was converted to business use.

b. Calculate the cost recovery deducted by Abby during the four-year period of business use assuming that the bed-and-breakfast is opened on January 1 of year 1 and the house is sold on December 31 of year 4.

c. What is Abby's recognized gain or loss on the sale of the business-use portion?

Critical Thinking
Decision Making

23. **LO.4** Surendra's personal residence originally cost $340,000 (ignore land). After living in the house for five years, he converts it to rental property. At the date of conversion, the fair market value of the house is $320,000. As to the rental property, calculate Surendra's basis for:

    a.   Loss.

    b.   Depreciation.

    c.   Gain.

    d.   Could Surendra have obtained better tax results if he had sold his personal residence for $320,000 and then purchased another house for $320,000 to hold as rental property? Explain.

24. **LO.5** Sue exchanges a sport-utility vehicle (adjusted basis of $16,000; fair market value of $19,500) for cash of $2,000 and a pickup truck (fair market value of $17,500). Both vehicles are for business use. Sue believes that her basis for the truck is $17,500. In calculating her basis, what has Sue failed to consider?

Issue ID

25. **LO.6** A warehouse owned by M&S (a partnership) and used in its business (i.e., to store inventory) is being condemned by the city to provide a right-of-way for a highway. The warehouse has appreciated by $180,000 based on an estimate of fair market value. In the negotiations, the city is offering $35,000 less than what M&S believes the property is worth. Alan, a real estate broker, has offered to purchase the property for $20,000 more than the city's offer. The partnership plans to invest the proceeds it will receive in an office building that it will lease to various tenants.

    a.   Identify the relevant tax issues for M&S.

    b.   Would the answer in part (a) change if M&S's warehouse was property being held for investment rather than being used in its business? Explain.

Decision Making
Communications

26. **LO.5** Tanya Fletcher owns undeveloped land (adjusted basis of $80,000 and fair market value of $92,000) on the East Coast. On January 4, 2016, she exchanges it with Martin (an unrelated party) for undeveloped land on the West Coast and $3,000 cash. Martin has an adjusted basis of $72,000 for his land, and its fair market value is $89,000. As the real estate market on the East Coast is thriving, on September 1, 2017, Martin sells the land he acquired for $120,000.

    a.   What are Tanya's recognized gain or loss and adjusted basis for the West Coast land on January 4, 2016?

    b.   What are Martin's recognized gain or loss and adjusted basis for the East Coast land on January 4, 2016?

    c.   What is Martin's recognized gain or loss from the September 1, 2017 sale?

    d.   What effect does Martin's 2017 sale have on Tanya?

    e.   Write a letter to Tanya advising her of the tax consequences of this exchange. Her address is The Corral, El Paso, TX 79968.

27. **LO.5** Starling Corporation exchanges a yellow bus (used in its business) for Robin Corporation's gray bus and some garage equipment (used in its business). The assets have the following characteristics:

	Adjusted Basis	Fair Market Value
Yellow bus	$6,000	$15,000
Gray bus	3,000	11,000
Equipment	2,000	4,000

    a.   What are Starling's recognized gain or loss and basis for the gray bus and garage equipment?

    b.   What are Robin's recognized gain or loss and basis for the yellow bus?

28. **LO.5** Maple Company owns a machine (adjusted basis of $90,000; fair market value of $125,000) that it uses in its business. Maple exchanges it for another machine (worth $100,000) and stock (worth $25,000). Determine Maple's:
   a. Realized and recognized gain or loss on the exchange.
   b. Basis in the new machine.
   c. Basis in the stock Maple received.

29. **LO.5** Tulip, Inc., would like to dispose of some land it acquired four years ago   Issue ID
   because the land will not continue to appreciate. Its value has increased by $50,000 over the four-year period. The company also intends to sell stock that has declined in value by $50,000 during the six months since its purchase. Tulip has four offers to acquire the stock and land:

   Buyer 1: Exchange land.
   Buyer 2: Purchase land for cash.
   Buyer 3: Exchange stock.
   Buyer 4: Purchase stock for cash.

   Identify the tax issues relevant to Tulip in disposing of this land and stock.

30. **LO.5** What is the basis of the new property in each of the following exchanges?
   a. Apartment building held for investment (adjusted basis of $145,000) for office building to be held for investment (fair market value of $225,000).
   b. Land and building used as a barbershop (adjusted basis of $190,000) for land and building used as a grocery store (fair market value of $350,000).
   c. Office building (adjusted basis of $45,000) for bulldozer (fair market value of $42,000), both held for business use.
   d. IBM common stock (adjusted basis of $20,000) for ExxonMobil common stock (fair market value of $28,000).
   e. Rental house (adjusted basis of $90,000) for mountain cabin to be held for personal use (fair market value of $225,000).
   f. General partnership interest (adjusted basis of $400,000) for a limited partnership interest (fair market value of $580,000).

31. **LO.1, 2, 5** Rose Company owns Machine A (adjusted basis of $12,000 and fair market value of $15,000), which it uses in its business. Rose sells Machine A for $15,000 to Aubry (a dealer) and then purchases Machine B for $15,000 from Joan (also a dealer). Machine B would normally qualify as like-kind property.
   a. What are Rose Company's realized and recognized gain on the sale of Machine A?
   b. What is Rose's basis for Machine B?
   c. What factors would motivate Rose to sell Machine A and purchase Machine B rather than exchange one machine for the other?
   d. Assume that the adjusted basis of Machine A is $15,000 and the fair market value of both machines is $12,000. Respond to parts (a) through (c).

32. **LO.5** Cardinal Properties, Inc., exchanges real estate used in its business along with stock for real estate to be held for investment. The stock transferred has an adjusted basis of $45,000 and a fair market value of $50,000. The real estate transferred has an adjusted basis of $85,000 and a fair market value of $190,000. The real estate acquired has a fair market value of $240,000.
   a. What is Cardinal's realized gain or loss?
   b. Its recognized gain or loss?
   c. The basis of the newly acquired real estate?

33. **LO.5** Tom and Frank are brothers. Each owns investment property in the other's   Decision Making
   hometown. To make their lives easier, they decide to exchange the

investment properties legally. Under the terms of the exchange, Frank will transfer realty (adjusted basis of $52,000; fair market value of $80,000) and Tom will exchange realty (adjusted basis of $60,000; fair market value of $92,000). Tom's property is subject to a mortgage of $12,000 that will be assumed by Frank.

a.   What are Frank's and Tom's recognized gains?

b.   What are their adjusted bases?

c.   As an alternative, Frank has proposed that rather than assuming the mortgage, he will transfer cash of $12,000 to Tom. Tom would use the cash to pay off the mortgage. Advise Tom on whether this alternative would be beneficial to him from a tax perspective.

34. **LO.5** Determine the realized, recognized, and postponed gain or loss and the new basis for each of the following like-kind exchanges:

	Adjusted Basis of Old Asset	Boot Given	Fair Market Value of New Asset	Boot Received
a.	$ 7,000	$ –0–	$12,000	$4,000
b.	14,000	2,000	15,000	–0–
c.	3,000	7,000	8,000	500
d.	15,000	–0–	29,000	–0–
e.	10,000	–0–	11,000	1,000
f.	17,000	–0–	14,000	–0–

35. **LO.5** Turquoise Realty Company owns an apartment house that has an adjusted basis of $760,000 but is subject to a mortgage of $192,000. Turquoise transfers the apartment house to Dove, Inc., and receives from Dove $120,000 in cash and an office building with a fair market value of $780,000 at the time of the exchange. Dove assumes the $192,000 mortgage on the apartment house.

a.   What is Turquoise's realized gain or loss?

b.   What is its recognized gain or loss?

c.   What is the basis of the newly acquired office building?

Critical Thinking
Ethics and Equity

36. **LO.5** Randall owns an office building (adjusted basis of $250,000) that he has been renting to a group of physicians. During negotiations over a new seven-year lease, the physicians offer to purchase the building for $900,000. Randall accepts the offer with the stipulation that the sale be structured as a delayed § 1031 transaction. Consequently, the sales proceeds are paid to a qualified third-party intermediary on the closing date of September 30, 2016. On October 2, 2016, Randall properly identifies an office building that he would like to acquire. Unfortunately, on November 10, 2016, the property Randall selected is withdrawn from the market. Working with the intermediary, on November 12, 2016, Randall identifies another office building that meets his requirements. The purchase of this property closes on December 15, 2016, and the title is transferred to Randall. Randall treats the transaction as a § 1031 like-kind exchange. Even though the original office building identified was not acquired, Randall concludes that in substance, he has satisfied the 45-day rule. He identified the acquired office building as soon as the negotiations ceased on his first choice. Should the IRS accept Randall's attempt to comply? Explain.

37. **LO.6** Howard's roadside vegetable stand (adjusted basis of $275,000) is destroyed by a tractor-trailer accident. He receives insurance proceeds of $240,000 ($300,000 fair market value – $60,000 coinsurance). Howard immediately uses the proceeds plus additional cash of $45,000 to build another roadside vegetable stand at the same location. What are the tax consequences to Howard?

38. **LO.6** For each of the following involuntary conversions, indicate whether the property acquired qualifies as replacement property, the recognized gain, and the basis for the property acquired.

a. A warehouse is destroyed by a tornado. The space in the warehouse was rented to various tenants. The adjusted basis was $470,000. The owner of the warehouse uses all of the insurance proceeds of $700,000 to build a shopping mall in a neighboring community where no property has been damaged by tornadoes. The shopping mall is rented to various tenants.

b. A warehouse is destroyed by fire. The adjusted basis is $300,000. Because of economic conditions in the area, the owner decides not to rebuild the warehouse. Instead, it uses all of the insurance proceeds of $400,000 to build a warehouse in another state.

c. Ridge's personal residence is condemned as part of a local government project to widen the highway from two lanes to four lanes. The adjusted basis is $170,000. Ridge uses all of the condemnation proceeds of $200,000 to purchase another personal residence.

d. Swallow Fashions, Inc., owns a building that is destroyed by a hurricane. The adjusted basis is $250,000. Because of an economic downturn in the area caused by the closing of a military base, Swallow decides to rent space for its retail outlet rather than replace the building. It uses all of the insurance proceeds of $300,000 to buy a four-unit apartment building in another city. A realtor in that city will handle the rental of the apartments.

e. Susan and Rick's personal residence is destroyed by a tornado. They had owned it for 15 months. The adjusted basis was $170,000. Because they would like to travel, they decide not to acquire a replacement residence. Instead, they invest all of the insurance proceeds of $200,000 in a duplex, which they rent to tenants.

f. Ellen and Harry's personal residence (adjusted basis of $245,000) is destroyed in a flood. They had owned it for 18 months. Of the insurance proceeds of $350,000, they reinvest $342,000 in a replacement residence four months later.

39. **LO.6** Edith's warehouse (adjusted basis of $450,000) is destroyed by a hurricane in October 2016. Edith, a calendar year taxpayer, receives insurance proceeds of $525,000 in January 2017. Calculate Edith's realized gain or loss, recognized gain or loss, and basis for the replacement property if she:

a. Acquires a new warehouse for $550,000 in January 2017.

b. Acquires a new warehouse for $500,000 in January 2017.

c. Does not acquire replacement property.

40. **LO.7** Wesley, who is single, listed his personal residence with a real estate agent on March 3, 2016, at a price of $390,000. He rejected several offers in the $350,000 range during the summer. Finally, on August 16, 2016, he and the purchaser signed a contract to sell for $363,000. The sale (i.e., closing) took place on September 7, 2016. The closing statement showed the following disbursements: Critical Thinking

Real estate agent's commission	$ 21,780
Appraisal fee	600
Exterminator's certificate	300
Recording fees	800
Mortgage to First Bank	305,000
Cash to seller	34,520

Wesley's adjusted basis for the house is $200,000. He owned and occupied the house for seven years. On October 1, 2016, Wesley purchases another residence for $325,000.

a. Calculate Wesley's recognized gain on the sale.

b. What is Wesley's adjusted basis for the new residence?

c. Assume instead that the selling price is $800,000. What is Wesley's recognized gain? His adjusted basis for the new residence?

Critical Thinking

Decision Making

41. **LO.7** Roby and James have been married for nine years. Roby sells Plum, Inc. stock that she has owned for four years to James for its fair market value of $180,000. Her adjusted basis is $200,000.

a.   Calculate Roby's recognized gain or recognized loss.

b.   Calculate James's adjusted basis for the stock.

c.   How would the tax consequences in parts (a) and (b) differ if Roby had made a gift of the stock to James? Which form of the transaction would you recommend?

 BRIDGE DISCIPLINE   **Bridge Discipline**

1. In April of the current year, Blue Corporation purchased an asset to be used in its manufacturing operations for $100,000. Blue's management expects the asset to ratably provide valuable services in the production process for eight years and have a salvage value of $12,000. The asset is a five-year asset for tax purposes. Blue has adopted the half-year convention for book purposes in the year of acquisition and disposition; Blue uses MACRS for tax purposes.
   a. Compute the depreciation expense in the year of acquisition for book and tax purposes.
   b. Identify the book-tax difference related to the depreciation expense in the year of acquisition.

2. Refer to the facts in the preceding problem. Assume that Blue Corporation disposes of the manufacturing asset at the beginning of year 7 for $40,000. Compute the amount of gain or loss recognized for book and tax purposes. What is the book-tax difference in the year of disposition?

3. Identify whether the taxpayer's economic position has changed in the following exchanges such that they are subject to current taxation. That is, identify whether the following qualify as like-kind exchanges under § 1031.
   a. Improved for unimproved real estate.
   b. Vending machine (used in business) for inventory.
   c. Rental house for personal residence.
   d. Business equipment for securities.
   e. Warehouse for office building (both used for business).
   f. Truck for computer (both used in business).
   g. Rental house for land (both held for investment).
   h. Ten shares of stock in Blue Corporation for 10 shares of stock in Red Corporation.
   i. Office furniture for office equipment (both used in business).
   j. Unimproved land in Jackson, Mississippi, for unimproved land in Toledo, Spain.
   k. General partnership interest for a general partnership interest.

Research Problems

Student Edition

Note: Solutions to Research Problems can be prepared by using the Checkpoint® Student Edition online research product, which is available to accompany this text. It is also possible to prepare solutions to the Research Problems by using tax research materials found in a standard tax library.

Communications

Research Problem 1. Ruth Ames died on January 10, 2016. In filing the estate tax return, her executor, Melvin Sims, elects the primary valuation date and amount (fair market value on the date of death). On March 12, 2016, Melvin invests $30,000 of cash that Ruth had in her money market account in acquiring 1,000 shares of Orange, Inc. ($30 per share). On January 10, 2016, Orange was selling for $29 per share. The stock is distributed to a beneficiary, Annette Rust, on June 1, 2016, when it is selling for $33 per share. Melvin wants you to determine the amount at which the Orange shares should appear on the estate tax return and the amount of Annette's adjusted basis for the stock. Write a letter to Melvin in which you respond to his inquiry, and prepare a memo for the tax files. His address is 100 Center Lane, Miami, FL 33124.

Research Problem 2. Terry owns real estate with an adjusted basis of $600,000 and a fair market value of $1.1 million. The amount of the nonrecourse mortgage on the property is $2.5 million. Because of substantial past and projected future losses associated with the real estate development (occupancy rate of only 37% after three years), Terry deeds the property to the creditor.

a. What are the tax consequences to Terry?

b. Assume that the data are the same, except that the fair market value of the property is $2,525,000. Therefore, when Terry deeds the property to the creditor, she also receives $25,000 from the creditor. What are the tax consequences to Terry?

Research Problem 3. Ted and Marvin Brown purchased an apartment building in 2005 as equal tenants in common. After a hectic decade of co-ownership, the brothers decided that their business association should be terminated. This led to the sale of the apartment building and a division of the proceeds.

Critical Thinking

The realized gain on the sale of the apartment building for each brother was $350,000. Ted recognized gain on his share and used the net proceeds to invest in stock. Marvin wanted to defer any recognized gain, so he worked with a realtor to identify property that would be eligible for § 1031 like-kind exchange treatment. After one prospect failed, the realtor identified a single-family home on Lake Tahoe that was currently being rented by the owner. Marvin agreed with the choice and acquired the single-family house, using the proceeds from the apartment building. Because the single-family house qualified as like-kind property, Marvin deferred all of his realized gain.

After attempting to rent the property for eight months without success, Marvin concluded that he could not continue to make the mortgage payments on his primary residence and this rental property. To ease his financial liquidity problem, Marvin sold his principal residence for a realized gain of $190,000 and moved into the Lake Tahoe house. He reported no recognized gain on the sale of his principal residence as the sale qualified for § 121 exclusion treatment.

The IRS issued a deficiency notice to Marvin associated with the sale of the apartment building. The position of the IRS was that Marvin did not hold the single-family residence for investment purposes as required by § 1031. Instead, his intention was personal—to use it as a replacement for his current residence that he planned on selling.

Who should prevail?

Use the tax resources of the Internet to address the following questions. Do not restrict your search to the Web, but include a review of newsgroups and general reference materials, practitioner sites and resources, primary sources of the tax law, chat rooms and discussion groups, and other opportunities.

Internet Activity

Research Problem 4. Many see the "step-up in basis at death" rule of § 1014 as an expensive tax loophole enjoyed by the wealthy. Find the latest estimates of the revenue loss to the Treasury that is attributable to this rule.

Communications

a. How does Canada's tax law determine the basis of property acquired from a decedent?

b. Send an e-mail to a member of the House Ways and Means Committee expressing a preference for the preservation of the current § 1014 rule or the modifications made to it by the Tax Relief Reconciliation Act of 2001 and the Tax Relief Act of 2010.

Research Problem 5. In general, the 45-day identification period and the 180-day exchange period for like-kind exchanges cannot be extended. Does this rule change if the like-kind property or the taxpayer involved in the exchange is located in a Presidentially-declared disaster area? Use the IRS's website (**www.irs.gov**) to find the answer.

Roger CPA Review Questions

1. Kellye purchased her home in 2011 for $140,000. After living in it for five years, she sold it in 2016 for $170,000, its market value. What is the tax treatment of the sale of Kellye's home?

   a. A $30,000 gain is recognized, but not reported.

   b. A $30,000 gain is recognized and reported.

   c. A $30,000 gain is carried forward.

   d. The transaction is not reported.

2. Ike, a single taxpayer, is reassigned for his job and must move to a new state. While searching for a place to live, he encounters a person who is selling her home in order to move to Ike's current city. The two agree to trade their properties to each other without any further consideration. Ike's house has a fair market value of $200,000 and basis of $130,000. He has lived in the house for one year. The house he is acquiring in the trade has a fair market value of $300,000. What gain will Ike recognize for Federal tax purposes?

   a. $50,000   c. $0

   b. $100,000   d. $300,000

3. Mikhail owns real estate with a basis of $400,000 and a fair market value of $650,000. He exchanges it for other real estate with a fair market value of $480,000. In addition, Mikhail is relieved of a mortgage on the old property of $200,000, assumes a mortgage on the new property of $100,000, and receives $70,000 in cash. Under Code Section 1031, what is Mikhail's recognized gain on the exchange?

   a. $170,000   c. $70,000

   b. $270,000   d. $350,000

4. Stephen purchased a video game console five years ago for $500. In order to raise money for the "latest and greatest" console, Stephen sold his console for $100. Because of advances in technology, Stephen can purchase the new console for $400. What is the tax treatment of Stephen's sale of his console?

   a. Stephen recognizes a $400 loss.

   b. Stephen does not report the sale.

   c. Stephen recognizes a $300 loss.

   d. Stephen recognizes a $100 gain.

5. Uncle Ubb gave his nephew, Leroy Lamprey, a gift of stock worth $10,000. Uncle Ubb's basis in the stock was $15,000. Leroy sold the stock to an unrelated party for $11,000. What amount of gain or loss should Leroy report as a result of this sale?

   a. $0   c. $200 gain

   b. $4,000 loss   d. $1,000 gain

6. On June 1, 2016, Gary gave Gertrude a gift of stock worth $10,000, paying no gift tax on the transaction. Gary had purchased the stock for $7,500 in 2012. On October 1,

2016, Gertrude sold the stock to an unrelated party for $11,000. What is the amount and character of Gertrude's gain upon the sale?

a. $1,000 short-term capital gain

b. $3,500 long-term capital gain

c. $1,000 long-term capital gain

d. $3,500 short-term capital gain

7. Shomit purchases 100 shares of stock in Classy Corporation for $500 in year 1. On December 20 of year 2, he purchases an additional 100 shares in the company for $400. On December 27 of year 2, Shomit sells the 100 shares acquired in year 1 for $410. What is Shomit's resulting basis in the shares acquired on December 20 of year 2?

a. $400   c. $490

b. $500   d. $410

8. Sengupta died on February 1, 2015, and bequeathed two different assets to a beneficiary, Roberts. Asset One was distributed to Roberts on April 24, 2015; Asset Two was distributed to Roberts on October 25, 2015. The executor of Sengupta's estate makes a qualified alternate valuation date election. The basis of each bequeathed asset will thus be the fair market value on which date?

	Asset One	Asset Two
a.	August 1, 2015	August 1, 2015
b.	April 24, 2015	August 1, 2015
c.	April 24, 2015	October 25, 2015
d.	August 1, 2015	October 25, 2015

CHAPTER

8

Property Transactions: Capital Gains and Losses, Section 1231, and Recapture Provisions

LEARNING OBJECTIVES: *After completing Chapter 8, you should be able to:*

LO.1 Explain the general scheme of taxation for capital gains and losses and distinguish capital assets from ordinary assets.

LO.2 State and explain the relevance of a sale or exchange to classification as a capital gain or loss.

LO.3 Determine the applicable holding period for a capital asset.

LO.4 Describe the tax treatment of capital gains and losses for noncorporate taxpayers.

LO.5 Describe the tax treatment of capital gains and losses for corporate taxpayers.

LO.6 Distinguish § 1231 assets from ordinary and capital assets and calculate § 1231 gain or loss.

LO.7 Determine when recapture provisions apply and derive their effects.

TAX TALK *Governments likely to confiscate wealth are unlikely to find much wealth to confiscate in the long run.* —THOMAS SOWELL

THE BIG PICTURE

CAPITAL GAINS AND LOSSES, § 1231 GAINS AND LOSSES, AND RECAPTURE

Alice owns land that she received from her father 10 years ago as a gift. The land was purchased by her father in 1993 for $2,000 and was worth $10,000 at the time of the gift. The property is currently worth about $50,000. If Alice sells the land, you previously determined in Chapter 7 that she would have a taxable gain of $48,000.

Alice also owns 500 shares of AppleCo stock, 300 of which were acquired as an inheritance when Alice's grandfather died in 1997. Alice's grandfather paid $12,000 for the AppleCo shares, and they were worth $30,000 at the time of his death. If Alice sells those shares for $120 each, you previously determined that she would have a $6,000 taxable gain. The other 200 shares were purchased by Alice two months ago for $28,000. If Alice sells those shares for $120 each, you determined that she would have a recognized loss of $4,000.

Nine months ago, Alice purchased 100 shares of Eagle Company stock for $5,000. Also on the same day, Alice invested $50,000 in a 50 percent interest in a patent that Kathy, a former college roommate who is an unemployed inventor, had obtained for a special battery she had developed to power "green" cars. To date, Kathy has been unable to market the battery to an auto manufacturer or supplier, but she has high hopes of doing so in the future.

In addition, Alice purchased a franchise from Orange, Inc., for $100,000, which she subsequently sells to Maurve, Inc., for $101,000 nine months later.

Alice also owns a house that she inherited from her grandmother two years ago. Based on the estate tax return, the fair market value of the house at the date of her grandmother's death was $475,000, and Alice will recognize a $125,000 gain on the sale of the property.

Finally, Alice's new husband, Jeff, sold depreciable equipment used in his sole proprietorship. The business purchased the equipment for $50,000 and deducted $35,000 of depreciation before selling it for $60,000.

Now Alice would like to know more about the gains and losses and the tax liability that she and her husband can expect from these transactions.

Read the chapter and formulate your response.

Historically, for Federal income tax purposes, gains from capital assets have received preferential treatment in the form of either partial exclusion, lower rates, or a maximum tax rate. Losses from capital assets, however, have received less desirable treatment than losses from other assets. In addition, the Code has imposed limitations on when capital losses can be deducted to prevent taxpayers from manipulating their tax liability excessively.

During World War II, capital asset treatment was extended to other assets. These assets are now called "§ 1231 assets" after the Code Section that prescribes their special treatment. Later, Congress believed that this special treatment was no longer entirely warranted. Instead of repealing § 1231, however, Congress left that section in place but eroded many—but not all—of its benefits through *recapture provisions* in § 1245 and § 1250. Together, these Code Sections constitute one of the most complicated areas of tax law affecting both individual taxpayers and business entities.

Because taxpayers can time the realization of gains and losses by choosing when or even whether to sell the asset in question, preferential treatment is given for capital gains. The nature of this preferential treatment is discussed later in this chapter, but the essential point for now is that preferential treatment is confined to the excess of net long-term capital gains over net short-term capital losses. In addition, the tax law requires taxpayers to separate their capital asset transactions from their transactions involving noncapital assets. It further requires taxpayers to separate their long-term (i.e., more than one year) transactions from their short-term (i.e., one year or less) transactions. Moreover, certain types of capital assets (principally real estate and "collectibles") receive specific treatment apart from the rates generally applicable to capital assets.

8-1 GENERAL SCHEME OF TAXATION

LO.1

Explain the general scheme of taxation for capital gains and losses and distinguish capital assets from ordinary assets.

Recognized gains and losses must be properly classified. Proper classification depends upon three characteristics.

- The tax status of the property, including the specific type of asset.
- The manner of the property's disposition.
- The holding period of the property.

The three possible tax statuses are capital asset, § 1231 asset, and ordinary asset. Property disposition may be by sale, exchange, casualty, theft, or condemnation. The two relevant holding periods are one year or less (short-term) and more than one year (long-term).

8-2 CAPITAL ASSETS

Investments comprise the most typical category of capital assets and include corporate stocks and bonds, mutual funds, partnership interests, government securities, and vacant land. These assets can be held by any type of taxpayer—individuals; partnerships; limited liability companies; and corporations, whether closely held or publicly held. In addition, individuals own certain capital assets that are part of their daily life, such as residences, automobiles, furniture, and artwork. The classification of these *personal-use* assets as capital assets is relevant only when their disposition produces a recognized gain. Losses from the disposition of personal-use assets are not recognized for tax purposes, as explained in the preceding chapter. For businesses, goodwill is often the only capital asset.

DIGGING DEEPER 1   In-depth coverage can be found on this book's companion website: www.cengagebrain.com

8-2a Definition of a Capital Asset

Capital assets are not directly defined in the Code. Instead, § 1221(a) defines what is *not* a capital asset. In general, a capital asset is property *other than* inventory, accounts and notes receivable, supplies, and most fixed assets of a business.

Specifically, the Code defines a capital asset as property held by the taxpayer that is *not* any of the following.

- Inventory or property held primarily for sale to customers in the ordinary course of a business. The Supreme Court, in *Malat v. Riddell*,[1] defined *primarily* as meaning "of first importance or principally."

- Accounts and notes receivable acquired from the sale of inventory or acquired for services rendered in the ordinary course of business.

- Depreciable property or real estate used in a business.

- Certain copyrights; literary, musical, or artistic compositions; or letters, memoranda, or similar property held by (1) a taxpayer whose efforts created the property; (2) in the case of a letter, memorandum, or similar property, a taxpayer for whom it was produced; or (3) a taxpayer who received the property as a lifetime gift from someone described in (1) or (2). When a sale or exchange involves musical compositions or copyrights in musical works either (1) created by the taxpayer's personal efforts or (2) having a basis determined by reference to the basis in the hands of a taxpayer whose personal efforts created the compositions or copyrights, the taxpayer may elect to treat the sale or exchange as the disposition of a capital asset.[2]

- U.S. government publications that are (1) received by a taxpayer from the U.S. government other than by purchase at the price at which they are offered for sale to the public or (2) held by a taxpayer who received the publication as a lifetime gift from someone described in (1).

- Supplies of a type regularly used or consumed in the ordinary course of a business.

Inventory

What constitutes inventory is determined by reference to the taxpayer's business.

Inventory Determination

Green Company buys and sells used automobiles. Its automobiles are inventory. Therefore, Green's gains from the sale of the cars are ordinary income.

EXAMPLE 1

Soong sells her personal-use automobile at a $500 gain. The automobile is a personal-use asset and, therefore, a capital asset. Soong's gain is a capital gain.

EXAMPLE 2

No asset is inherently capital or ordinary. If Soong in Example 2 sells her capital asset automobile to Green Company in Example 1, that very same automobile loses its capital asset status, because it is inventory to Green Company. Similar transformations can occur if, for example, an art dealer sells a painting (inventory, *not* a capital asset) to a private collector (now a capital asset). Whether an asset is capital or ordinary, therefore, depends entirely on the relationship of *that asset* to the taxpayer who sold it. This classification dilemma is but one feature of capital asset treatment that makes this area so confusing and perennially complicated.

---

[1]66–1 USTC ¶9317, 17 AFTR 2d 604, 86 S.Ct. 1030 (USSC, 1966).   [2]§ 1221(b)(3).

Accounts and Notes Receivable

Collection of an accrual basis account receivable usually does not result in a gain or loss because the amount collected equals the receivable's basis. The *sale* of an account or note receivable may generate a gain or loss, however, because it will probably be sold for more or less than its basis. That gain or loss will be ordinary because the receivable is not a capital asset. A cash basis account receivable has no basis; so sale of such a receivable generates a gain, and that gain is ordinary income. Collection of a cash basis receivable also generates ordinary income.

Oriole Company, an *accrual basis taxpayer*, has accounts receivable of $100,000. Gross income of $100,000 was recorded, and a $100,000 basis was established when the receivable was created. Because Oriole needs working capital, it sells the receivables for $83,000 to a financial institution. Accordingly, it has a $17,000 ordinary loss.

   If Oriole is a *cash basis taxpayer*, it has $83,000 of ordinary income because it would not have recorded any income earlier and the receivable would have no tax basis.

Business Fixed Assets

Depreciable personal property and real estate (both depreciable and nondepreciable) used by a business are not capital assets. Thus, *business fixed assets* are not capital assets. Business fixed assets can sometimes be treated as capital assets pursuant to § 1231, however, as discussed later in this chapter.

Copyrights and Creative Works

Generally, the person whose efforts led to the copyright or creative work has an ordinary asset, not a capital asset. This rule makes the creator comparable to a taxpayer whose customary activity (salary, business profits) is taxed as ordinary income. *Creative works* include the works of authors, composers, and artists. Also, the person for whom a letter, a memorandum, or another similar property was created has an ordinary asset. Finally, a person receiving a copyright, creative work, a letter, a memorandum, or similar property by lifetime gift from the creator or the person for whom the work was created also has an ordinary asset. As mentioned earlier, a taxpayer may elect to treat the sale or exchange of a musical composition or a copyright of a musical work as the disposition of a capital asset.

Creative Works

Wanda is a part-time music composer. A music publisher purchases one of her songs for $5,000.

   Wanda has a $5,000 ordinary gain from the sale of an ordinary asset unless she elects to treat the gain as a capital gain.

Ed received a letter from the President of the United States in 1994. In the current year, Ed sells the letter to a collector for $300.

   Ed has a $300 ordinary gain from the sale of an ordinary asset (because the letter was created for Ed).

Isabella gives her son a song she composed. Her son sells the song to a music publisher for $5,000.

   Her son has a $5,000 ordinary gain from the sale of an ordinary asset unless he elects to treat the gain as a capital gain.

   If he inherits the song from Isabella, his basis for the song is its fair market value at Isabella's death. In this situation, the song is a capital asset because the son's basis is not related to Isabella's basis for the song (i.e., the song was not a *lifetime* gift).

U.S. Government Publications

U.S. government publications received from the U.S. government (or its agencies) for a reduced price (i.e., below that at which it is available to the general public) are *not* capital assets. This prevents a taxpayer from later donating the publications to charity and claiming a charitable contribution deduction equal to the fair market value of the publications. A charitable contribution of a capital asset generally yields a deduction equal to the asset's fair market value. If such property is received by gift from the original purchaser, the property is not a capital asset to the donee. (For a more comprehensive explanation of charitable contributions of property, refer to Chapter 5.)

In-depth coverage can be found on this book's companion website: www.cengagebrain.com

2 DIGGING DEEPER

8-2b Statutory Expansions

Because of the uncertainty often associated with capital asset status, Congress has occasionally enacted Code Sections to clarify the definition in particular circumstances. These statutory expansions of the capital asset definition are discussed in this section.

Dealers in Securities

As a general rule, securities (stocks, bonds, and other financial instruments) held by a dealer are considered to be inventory and are, therefore, not subject to capital gain or loss treatment. A *dealer in securities* is a merchant (e.g., a brokerage firm) that regularly engages in the purchase and resale of securities to customers. However, under the following circumstances, a dealer will have capital gain or capital loss.

If a dealer clearly identifies certain securities as held for investment purposes by the close of business on the acquisition date, gain from the securities' sale will be capital gain. The gain will be ordinary if the dealer ceases to hold the securities for investment prior to the sale. Losses are capital losses if at any time the securities have been clearly identified by the dealer as held for investment.

In-depth coverage can be found on this book's companion website: www.cengagebrain.com

3 DIGGING DEEPER

Real Property Subdivided for Sale

Substantial real property development activities may result in the owner being considered a dealer for tax purposes. If so, income from the sale of real estate property lots will be treated as the sale of inventory and therefore will be taxed as ordinary income. However, § 1237 allows real estate investors to claim capital gain treatment if they engage *only* in *limited* development activities. To be eligible for § 1237 treatment, the following requirements must be met.

- The taxpayer is not a corporation.
- The taxpayer is not a real estate dealer.
- No substantial improvements have been made to the lots sold. *Substantial* generally means more than a 10 percent increase in the value of a lot. Shopping centers and other commercial or residential buildings are considered substantial, while filling, draining, leveling, and clearing operations are not.
- The taxpayer has held the lots sold for at least 5 years, except for inherited property. The substantial improvements test is less stringent if the property is held at least 10 years.

If the preceding requirements are met, all gain is capital gain until the taxable year in which the *sixth* lot is sold. Sales of contiguous lots to a single buyer in the same transaction count as the sale of one lot. Beginning with the taxable year in which the *sixth* lot is sold, 5 percent of the revenue from lot sales is potential ordinary income. That potential ordinary income is offset by any selling expenses from the lot sales. Practically, sales commissions often are at least 5 percent of the sales price, so usually none of the gain is treated as ordinary income.

Section 1237 does not apply to losses. A loss from the sale of subdivided real property is ordinary loss unless the property qualifies as a capital asset under § 1221. The following example illustrates the application of § 1237.

EXAMPLE 7

Ahmed owns a large tract of land and subdivides it for sale. Assume that Ahmed meets all of the requirements of § 1237 and during the tax year sells the first 10 lots to 10 different buyers for $10,000 each. Ahmed's basis in each lot sold is $3,000, and he incurs total selling expenses of $4,000 on the sales. Ahmed's gain is computed as follows.

Selling price (10 × $10,000)	$100,000	
Less: Selling expenses	(4,000)	
Amount realized		$ 96,000
Basis (10 × $3,000)		(30,000)
Realized and recognized gain		$ 66,000
Classification of recognized gain:		
Ordinary income		
Five percent of selling price (5% × $100,000)	$ 5,000	
Less: Selling expenses	(4,000)	
Ordinary gain		1,000
Capital gain		$ 65,000

A portion of the gain recognized is given ordinary treatment because the *sixth* lot is sold in the current year.

8-3 SALE OR EXCHANGE

LO.2

State and explain the relevance of a sale or exchange to classification as a capital gain or loss.

Recognition of capital gain or loss usually requires a **sale or exchange** of a capital asset. The Code uses the term *sale or exchange*, but does not define it. Generally, a property sale involves the receipt of money by the seller and/or the assumption by the purchaser of the seller's liabilities. An exchange involves the transfer of property for other property. Thus, an involuntary conversion (casualty, theft, or condemnation) is not a sale or exchange. In several situations, the determination of whether or when a sale or exchange has taken place has been clarified by the enactment of Code Sections that specifically provide for sale or exchange treatment. These situations are discussed below.

Recognized gains or losses from the cancellation, lapse, expiration, or any other termination of a right or obligation with respect to personal property (other than stock) that is or would be a capital asset in the hands of the taxpayer are capital gains or losses.[3] See the discussion under Options (text Section 8-3c) for more details.

8-3a Worthless Securities and § 1244 Stock

Occasionally, securities such as stocks and bonds may become worthless due to the insolvency of their issuer. If the security is a capital asset, the loss is deemed to have occurred as the result of a sale or exchange on the *last day* of the tax year.[4] This last-day rule may have the effect of converting a short-term capital loss into a long-term capital loss. (See Capital Losses later in this chapter.) Worthless securities are discussed in Chapter 6.

Section 1244 allows an *ordinary* deduction on disposition of stock at a loss. The stock must be that of a small business corporation, and the ordinary deduction is limited to $50,000 ($100,000 for married individuals filing jointly) per year.

---

[3] § 1234A.

[4] § 165(g)(1).

TAX IN THE NEWS   Bankruptcy and Worthless Stock

During 2009, General Motors went into bankruptcy, was reorganized, and emerged from bankruptcy. However, the common shareholders of the General Motors that went into bankruptcy were not the common shareholders of the General Motors that emerged from bankruptcy.

The original common shareholders lost their entire investment because their stock became worthless. The holding period of their stock ended for tax purposes on December 31, 2009, because of the worthless stock rules. They had a capital loss equal to whatever their basis was for the worthless shares.

The debtors of General Motors accepted common shares in the General Motors that emerged from bankruptcy. Generally, the exchange of debt for common shares in a bankruptcy reorganization is not a taxable transaction, and the basis of the debt becomes the basis for the shares.

8-3b **Retirement of Corporate Obligations**

A debt obligation (e.g., a bond or note payable) may have a tax basis different from its redemption value because it may have been acquired at a premium or discount (see Chapter 7 for a discussion of bond amortization). Consequently, the collection of the redemption value may result in a loss or a gain. Generally, the collection of a debt obligation is treated as a sale or exchange.[5] Therefore, any loss or gain is capital because a sale or exchange has taken place.

Osprey, Inc., purchases $1,000 of Golden Eagle Corporation bonds for $1,020 in the open market.

If the bonds are held to maturity and the bond premium is not amortized, the $20 difference between Osprey's collection of the $1,000 redemption value and its cost of $1,020 is treated as capital loss.

EXAMPLE 8

In-depth coverage can be found on this book's companion website: www.cengagebrain.com

4 DIGGING DEEPER

8-3c **Options**

Frequently, a potential buyer of property wants to defer a final purchase decision, but wants to control the sale and/or the sale price in the meantime. **Options** are used to achieve such control. The potential purchaser (grantee) pays the property owner (grantor) for an option on the property. The grantee then becomes the option holder. An option, which usually sets the price at which a grantee can buy the property, expires after a specified period of time.

Sale of an Option

In addition to exercising an option or letting it expire, a grantee can often arrange for its sale or exchange. Such a sale or exchange generally results in capital gain or loss if the option property is (or would be) a capital asset to the grantee.[6]

Robin & Associates wants to buy some vacant land for investment purposes, but currently cannot afford the full purchase price. Instead, Robin & Associates (grantee) pays the landowner (grantor) $3,000 for an option to buy the land for $100,000 anytime in the next two years. The option is a capital asset to Robin because if the firm actually purchased the land (the option property), the land would be a capital asset.

Three months after purchasing the option, Robin sells it for $7,000. The firm has a $4,000 ($7,000 − $3,000) capital gain on this sale.

EXAMPLE 9

---

[5]§ 1271.

[6]§ 1234(a) and Reg. § 1.1234–1(a)(1).

Failure to Exercise Options

If an option holder (grantee) fails to exercise the option, the lapse of the option is considered a sale or exchange on the option expiration date. Thus, the resulting loss is a capital loss if the property subject to the option is (or would be) a capital asset in the hands of the grantee.

The grantor of an option on *stocks, securities, commodities, or commodity futures* receives short-term capital gain treatment upon the expiration of the option.[7] For example, an individual investor who owns stock (a capital asset) may sell a call option, entitling the buyer of the option to acquire the stock at a specified price higher than the stock's value at the date the option is granted. The writer of the call (the grantor) receives a premium for writing the option. If the price of the stock does not increase during the option period, the option will expire unexercised. Upon the expiration of the option, the grantor must recognize a short-term capital gain equal to the premium received (whereas the grantee recognizes a loss, the character of which depends on the underlying asset). These provisions do not apply to options held for sale to customers (the inventory of a securities dealer).

Options on property *other than* stocks, securities, commodities, or commodity futures (for instance, vacant land) result in ordinary income to the grantor when the option expires. For instance, the landowner in the preceding example would have ordinary income of $3,000 if Robin (the grantee) had allowed the option to expire.

Exercise of Options by Grantee

If an option is exercised, the amount paid for the option is added to the optioned property's selling price. This increases the gain (or reduces the loss) to the grantor resulting from the sale of the property. The grantor's gain or loss is capital or ordinary depending on the tax status of the property. The grantee adds the cost of the option to the basis of the property purchased.

The Big Picture

EXAMPLE 10

Return to the facts of *The Big Picture* on p. 8-1. On February 1, 2016, Alice purchases 100 shares of Eagle Company stock for $5,000. On April 1, 2016, she writes a call option on the stock, giving the grantee the right to buy the stock for $6,000 during the following six-month period. Alice (the grantor) receives a call premium of $500 for writing the call.

- If the call is exercised by the grantee on August 1, 2016, Alice has $1,500 ($6,000 + $500 − $5,000) of short-term capital gain from the sale of the stock. The grantee has a $6,500 basis for the stock ($500 option premium + $6,000 purchase price).

- Investors sometimes get nervous and want to "lock in" gains or losses.
  - Assume that, prior to the grantee's exercise of the call, Alice decides to sell her stock for $6,000 and enters into a closing transaction by purchasing a call on 100 shares of Eagle Company stock for $5,000.
  - Because the Eagle stock is selling for $6,000, Alice must pay a call premium of $1,000.
  - She recognizes a $500 short-term capital loss [$500 (call premium received) − $1,000 (call premium paid)] on the closing transaction.
  - On the actual sale of the Eagle stock, Alice has a short-term capital gain of $1,000 [$6,000 (selling price) − $5,000 (cost)].
  - The original grantee is not affected by Alice's closing transaction. The original option is still in existence, and the grantee's tax consequences depend on what action the grantee takes—exercising the option, letting the option expire, or selling the option.

- Assume that the original option expired unexercised. Alice has a $500 short-term capital gain equal to the call premium received for writing the option. This gain is not recognized until the option expires. The grantee has a loss from expiration of the option. The nature of the loss will depend upon whether the option was a capital asset or an ordinary asset.

[7]§ 1234(b)(1).

Concept Summary 8.1 sets out the consequences of various transactions involving options, to both the grantor and grantee.

Concept Summary 8.1

Options: Consequences to the Grantor and Grantee

Event	Effect on	
	Grantor	**Grantee**
Option is granted.	Receives value and has a contract obligation (a liability).	Pays value and has a contract right (an asset).
Option expires.	Has a short-term capital gain if the option property is stocks, securities, commodities, or commodity futures. Otherwise, gain is ordinary income.	Has a loss (capital loss if option property would have been a capital asset for the grantee).
Option is exercised.	Amount received for option increases proceeds from sale of the option property.	Amount paid for option becomes part of the basis of the option property purchased.
Option is sold or exchanged by grantee.	Result depends upon whether option later expires or is exercised (see above).	Could have gain or loss (capital gain or loss if option property would have been a capital asset for the grantee).

8-3d Patents

Transfer of a **patent** is treated as the sale or exchange of a long-term capital asset when *all substantial rights* to the patent (or an undivided interest that includes all such rights) are transferred by a *holder*.[8] The transferor/holder may receive payment in virtually any form. Lump-sum or periodic payments are most common. The amount of the payments may also be contingent on the transferee/purchaser's productivity, use, or disposition of the patent. If the transfer meets these requirements, any gain or loss is *automatically a long-term* capital gain or loss. Whether the asset was a capital asset for the transferor, whether a sale or exchange occurred, and how long the transferor held the patent are all irrelevant. Copyrights for authors, composers, and artists are not capital assets, as discussed earlier. Example 11 illustrates the special treatment for patents.

Substantial Rights

As noted previously, to receive favorable capital gain treatment, *all substantial rights* to the patent (or an undivided interest in it) must be transferred. All substantial rights to a patent means all rights that are valuable at the time the patent rights (or an undivided interest in the patent) are transferred. All substantial rights have not been transferred when the transfer is limited geographically within the issuing country or when the transfer is for a period less than the remaining legal life of the patent. The circumstances of the entire transaction, rather than merely the language used in the transfer instrument, are to be considered in deciding whether all substantial rights have been transferred.[9]

---

[8]§ 1235.   [9]Reg. § 1.1235–2(b)(1).

The Big Picture

EXAMPLE

11

Return to the facts of *The Big Picture* on p. 8-1. Kathy transfers her remaining 50% share of the rights in the battery patent to the Green Battery Company in exchange for a lump-sum payment of $1 million plus $.50 for each battery sold.

Assuming that Kathy has transferred all substantial rights, the question of whether the transfer is a sale or exchange of a capital asset is not relevant. Kathy automatically has a long-term capital gain from both the lump-sum payment received and the per battery royalty to the extent that those proceeds exceed her basis for the patent.

Kathy also had an automatic long-term capital gain when she sold the other 50% of her rights in the patent to Alice, because Kathy transferred an undivided interest that included all substantial rights in the patent.

Whether Alice gets long-term capital gain treatment on a transfer to Green Battery will depend on whether she is a holder (see the following discussion and Example 12).

Holder Defined

The *holder* of a patent must be an *individual* and is usually the invention's creator. A holder may also be an individual who purchases the patent rights from the creator before the patented invention has been reduced to practice. However, the creator's employer and certain parties related to the creator do not qualify as holders. Thus, in the common situation where an employer has all rights to an employee's inventions, the employer is not eligible for long-term capital gain treatment. More than likely, the employer will have an ordinary asset because the patent was developed as part of its business.

The Big Picture

EXAMPLE

12

Continuing with the facts of Example 11, Kathy is clearly a holder of the patent because she is the inventor and was not an employee when she invented the battery. When Alice purchased a 50% interest in the patent nine months ago, she became a holder if the patent had not yet been reduced to practice. Because batteries were apparently not being manufactured at the time of the purchase, the patent had not been reduced to practice.

Consequently, Alice is also a holder, and she has an automatic long-term capital gain or loss when she transfers all substantial rights in her interest in the patent to Green Battery Company. Alice's basis for her share of the patent is $50,000, and the proceeds from the transfer of her share of the patent are $1 million plus $.50 for each battery sold. Thus, Alice will have a long-term capital gain even though she has not held her interest in the patent for more than one year.

8-3e Franchises, Trademarks, and Trade Names

A mode of operation, a widely recognized brand name (trade name), and a widely known business symbol (trademark) are all valuable assets. These assets may be licensed (commonly known as *franchising*) by their owner for use by other businesses. Many fast-food restaurants (such as McDonald's and Taco Bell) are franchises. The franchisee usually pays the owner (franchisor) an initial fee plus a contingent fee. The contingent fee is often based upon the franchisee's sales volume.

For Federal income tax purposes, a franchise is an agreement that gives the franchisee the right to distribute, sell, or provide goods, services, or facilities within a specified area.[10] A franchise transfer includes the grant of a franchise, a transfer by one franchisee to another person, or the renewal of a franchise.

---

[10]§ 1253(b)(1).

Section 1253 provides that a transfer of a franchise, trademark, or trade name is *not* a sale or exchange of a capital asset when the transferor retains any significant power, right, or continuing interest in the property transferred.

In-depth coverage can be found on this book's companion website: www.cengagebrain.com

5 DIGGING DEEPER

Significant Power, Right, or Continuing Interest

Significant powers, rights, or continuing interests include control over assignment of the franchise, trademark, or trade name, as well as the quality of the transferee's products or services. The following rights also are included.

- Right to require the transferee to sell or advertise *only* the transferor's products or services.
- Right to require the transferee to purchase substantially all supplies and equipment from the transferor.
- Right to receive substantial contingent payments.
- Right to terminate the franchise, trademark, or trade name at will.

In the unusual case where no significant power, right, or continuing interest is retained by the transferor, a sale or exchange may occur, and capital gain or loss treatment may be available. For capital gain or loss treatment to be available, the asset transferred must still qualify as a capital asset.

The Big Picture

EXAMPLE 13

Return to the facts of *The Big Picture* on p. 8-1. Alice sells for $101,000 to Mauve, Inc., the franchise purchased from Orange, Inc., nine months ago. The $101,000 received by Alice is not contingent, and all significant powers, rights, and continuing interests are transferred.

The $1,000 gain ($101,000 proceeds − $100,000 basis) is a short-term capital gain because Alice has held the franchise for only nine months.

Noncontingent Payments

When the transferor retains a significant power, right, or continuing interest, the transferee's noncontingent payments to the transferor are ordinary income to the transferor. The franchisee capitalizes the payments and amortizes them over 15 years. If the franchise is sold, amortization is subject to recapture under § 1245, as discussed later in this chapter.

EXAMPLE 14

Grey Company signs a 10-year franchise agreement with DOH Donuts. Grey (the franchisee) makes payments of $3,000 per year for the first 8 years of the franchise agreement—a total of $24,000. Grey cannot deduct $3,000 per year as the payments are made. Instead, Grey must amortize the $24,000 total over 15 years. Thus, Grey may deduct $1,600 per year for each of the 15 years of the amortization period.

The same result would occur if Grey had made a $24,000 lump-sum payment at the beginning of the franchise period. Assuming that DOH Donuts (the franchisor) retains significant powers, rights, or a continuing interest, it will have ordinary income when it receives the payments from Grey.

Contingent Payments

The contingent franchise payments are ordinary income for the franchisor and an ordinary deduction for the franchisee when the transferor retains a significant power, right, or continuing interest.

EXAMPLE 15

TAK, a spicy chicken franchisor, transfers an 8-year franchise to Egret Corporation. TAK retains a significant power, right, or continuing interest. Egret, the franchisee, agrees to pay TAK 15% of sales. This contingent payment is ordinary income to TAK and a business deduction for Egret as the payments are made.

Concept Summary 8.2 reviews the effects of transactions involving franchises on both the franchisor and franchisee.

Concept Summary 8.2

Franchises: Consequences to the Franchisor and Franchisee

Event	Effect on	
	Franchisor	Franchisee
Franchisor Retains Significant Powers and Rights		
Noncontingent payment	Ordinary income.	Capitalized and amortized over 15 years as an ordinary deduction; if franchise is sold, amortization is subject to recapture under § 1245.
Contingent payment	Ordinary income.	Ordinary deduction.
Franchisor Does *Not* Retain Significant Powers and Rights		
Noncontingent payment	Ordinary income if franchise rights are an ordinary asset; capital gain if franchise rights are a capital asset (unlikely).	Capitalized and amortized over 15 years as an ordinary deduction; if the franchise is sold, amortization is subject to recapture under § 1245.
Contingent payment	Ordinary income.	Ordinary deduction.

8-3f Lease Cancellation Payments

The tax treatment of payments received for canceling a lease depends on whether the recipient of the payments is the **lessor** or the **lessee** and whether the lease is a capital asset.

Lessee Treatment

Lease cancellation payments received by a lessee (the tenant) are treated as an exchange.[11] Thus, these payments are capital gains if the lease is a capital asset. Generally, a lessee's lease is a capital asset if the property (either personalty or realty) is used for the lessee's personal use (e.g., his or her residence). A lease held one year or less is an ordinary income asset if the property is used in the lessee's trade or business.[12]

EXAMPLE 16

Merganser, Inc., owns an apartment building that it is going to convert into an office building. Vicki is one of the apartment tenants who receives $1,000 from Merganser to cancel the lease.

Vicki has a capital gain of $1,000 (which is long term or short term depending upon how long she has held the lease). Merganser has an ordinary deduction of $1,000.

---

[11]§ 1241 and Reg. § 1.1241–1(a).

[12]Reg. § 1.1221–1(b) and PLR 200045019. If the lease was held for more than one year before cancellation, it is a § 1231 asset.

Lessor Treatment

Payments received by a lessor (the landlord) for a lease cancellation are always ordinary income because they are considered to be in lieu of rental payments.[13]

Finch & Company owns an apartment building near a university campus. Hui-Fen is one of the tenants. Hui-Fen is graduating early and offers Finch $800 to cancel the apartment lease. Finch accepts the offer.

Finch has ordinary income of $800. Hui-Fen has a nondeductible payment because the apartment was personal-use property.

EXAMPLE 17

8-4 HOLDING PERIOD

LO.3

Determine the applicable holding period for a capital asset.

Property must be held more than one year to qualify for long-term capital gain or loss treatment.[14] Property not held for the required long-term period results in short-term capital gain or loss. To compute the **holding period**, start counting on the day after the property was acquired and include the day of disposition.

The Big Picture

Return to the facts of *The Big Picture* on p. 8-1. Assume that Alice purchased the 200 shares of AppleCo stock on January 15, 2015. If she sells them on January 16, 2016, Alice's holding period is more than one year and the gain or loss is long term.

If instead Alice sells the stock on January 15, 2016, the holding period is exactly one year and the gain or loss is short term.

EXAMPLE 18

To be held for more than one year, a capital asset acquired on the last day of any month must not be disposed of until on or after the first day of the thirteenth succeeding month.[15]

Purple, Inc., purchases a capital asset on March 31, 2015. If Purple sells the asset on March 31, 2016, the holding period is one year and Purple will have a short-term capital gain or loss.

If Purple sells the asset on April 1, 2016, the holding period is more than one year and it will have a long-term capital gain or loss.

EXAMPLE 19

8-4a Special Holding Period Rules

There are several special holding period rules.[16] The application of these rules varies depending upon the type of asset involved and how it was acquired.

Nontaxable Exchanges

The holding period of property received in a like-kind exchange (and certain other qualified nontaxable exchanges) includes the holding period of the former asset if the property that was exchanged was either a capital asset or a § 1231 asset.

Holding Period Rules

Red Manufacturing Corporation exchanges some vacant real estate it owns (a capital asset) for land closer to its factory.

The transaction is a like-kind exchange, so the holding period of the new land includes the holding period of the old land.

EXAMPLE 20

A lightning strike destroyed Vireo Company's generator (a § 1231 asset) in March. Vireo uses all of the insurance proceeds it received to acquire a comparable generator.

The holding period of the new generator includes the holding period of the old generator because this is a nontaxable involuntary conversion.

EXAMPLE 21

---

[13]Reg. § 1.61–8(b).
[14]§ 1222(3).

[15]Rev.Rul. 66–7, 1966–1 C.B. 188.
[16]§ 1223.

Nontaxable Transactions Involving Carryover of Another Taxpayer's Basis

If a transaction is nontaxable and the former owner's basis carries over to the present owner (e.g., a gift), the former owner's holding period is included in ("tacked on" to) the present owner's holding period. A donor's adjusted basis carries over to the donee when the property's fair market value at the date of the gift is greater than the donor's adjusted basis. See the discussion of nontaxable transactions in Chapter 7.

Carryover Basis

EXAMPLE 22

Kareem acquired 100 shares of Robin Corporation stock for $1,000 on December 31, 2012. He transferred the shares by gift to Megan on December 31, 2015, when the stock was worth $2,000. Kareem's basis of $1,000 becomes the basis for determining gain or loss on a subsequent sale by Megan. Megan's holding period begins with the date the stock was acquired by Kareem.

EXAMPLE 23

Assume the same facts as in the preceding example, except that the fair market value of the shares was only $800 on the date of the gift. If Megan sells the stock for a loss, its value on the date of the gift is her basis. Accordingly, the tacked-on holding period rule does not apply, and Megan's holding period begins with the date of the gift.

So if she sells the shares for $500 on April 1, 2016, Megan has a $300 recognized capital loss, the holding period is from December 31, 2015, to April 1, 2016, and the loss is short term.

Disallowed Loss Transactions

Under several Code provisions, realized losses are disallowed. When a loss is disallowed, there is no carryover of holding period. Losses can be disallowed under § 267 (sale or exchange between related taxpayers) and § 262 (sale or exchange of personal-use assets) as well as other Code Sections. Taxpayers who acquire property in a disallowed loss transaction begin a new holding period and have a basis equal to the purchase price.

EXAMPLE 24

Janet sells her personal automobile at a loss. She may not deduct the loss because it arises from the sale of personal-use property. Janet purchases a replacement automobile for more than the selling price of her former automobile. Janet has a basis equal to the cost of the replacement automobile, and her holding period begins when she acquires the replacement automobile.

Inherited Property

The holding period for inherited property is treated as long term no matter how long the property is actually held by the heir. The holding period of the decedent or the decedent's estate is not relevant to the heir's holding period.

EXAMPLE 25

Shonda inherits Blue Company stock from her father, who died in 2016. She receives the stock on April 1, 2016, and sells it on November 1, 2016. Even though Shonda did not hold the stock for more than one year, she receives long-term capital gain or loss treatment on the sale.

8-4b Short Sales

A short sale occurs when a taxpayer sells borrowed property and repays the lender with substantially identical property either held on the date of the sale or purchased after the sale. Short sales typically involve corporate stock. The seller's objective is to make a profit in anticipation of a decline in the stock's price. If the price declines, the seller in a short sale recognizes a profit equal to the difference between the sales price of the borrowed stock and the price paid for its replacement.

Section 1233 provides that a short sale gain or loss is a capital gain or loss to the extent the short sale property constitutes a capital asset of the taxpayer. This gain or loss is not recognized until the short sale is closed. Generally, the holding period of the short sale property is determined by how long the property used to close the short sale was held.

Short Sales

On January 4, Green & Associates sold short 100 shares of Osprey Corporation for $1,500. Green closed the transaction on July 28 of the same year by purchasing 100 shares of Osprey for $1,000 and delivering them to the broker from whom the securities were borrowed. Because this stock was held less than one year (actually, less than a day), Green's $500 gain ($1,500 sale price − $1,000 basis) is short term.

EXAMPLE 26

Assume the same facts as in the preceding example, except that the January 4 short sale was not closed until January 28 of the *following* year. The result is the same, because the stock was acquired and used to close the transaction on the same day; that is, it was not held more than a year.

EXAMPLE 27

If a taxpayer owns securities that are "substantially identical" to those sold short, § 1259 subjects the short sale to potential *constructive sale treatment*, and the taxpayer recognizes gain (but not loss) as of that date. If the taxpayer has not closed the short sale by delivering the short sale securities to the broker from whom the securities were borrowed before January 31 of the year following the short sale, the short sale is deemed to have closed on the short sale date. The holding period in such circumstances is determined by how long the securities in question were held.

Assume the same facts as in Example 26, except that Green & Associates owned 100 shares of Osprey Corporation when it sold short 100 shares on January 4. Green does not close the short sale before January 31 of the following year. Green must recognize any gain on its 100 shares of Osprey as of January 4 of the current year. If Green owned those shares more than one year as of that date, the gain is long term.

EXAMPLE 28

TAX PLANNING STRATEGIES Timing Capital Gains

FRAMEWORK FOCUS: INCOME AND EXCLUSIONS

Strategy: Postpone Recognition of Income to Achieve Tax Deferral.

FRAMEWORK FOCUS: DEDUCTIONS

Strategy: Maximize Deductible Amounts.

Taxpayers have considerable control over the timing of their capital gains through the mechanism of realization. Accordingly, a taxpayer might want to defer recognizing a large capital gain in a year with *substantial itemized deductions*, such as large personal casualty losses or miscellaneous itemized deductions. In so doing, the taxpayer minimizes the loss of such deductions due to AGI limitations. See additional discussion in Chapter 10.

Nontax considerations, of course, often dictate when assets are sold. If a particular stock is peaking in popularity, selling it might be a wise investment strategy, even if the taxpayer's current tax situation is not optimal.

Similarly, if a taxpayer needs cash to start a business, purchase a home, or pay for a child's education or medical costs, the capital asset might need to be sold at a time when investment *and* tax considerations counsel otherwise. In these circumstances, however, a taxpayer might choose to *borrow* the money required and use the capital asset as collateral for the loan, rather than sell the asset. A loan does not trigger tax consequences, and the taxpayer can continue to hold the asset until a more opportune time—albeit at the cost of paying interest, which may be nondeductible.

LO.4

Describe the tax treatment of capital gains and losses for noncorporate taxpayers.

8-5 TAX TREATMENT OF CAPITAL GAINS AND LOSSES OF NONCORPORATE TAXPAYERS

This section discusses how capital gains and losses are taxed to noncorporate taxpayers; that is, individuals, trusts, and estates. The rules applicable to corporations are considered in the following section of this chapter.

8-5a Capital Gains

Gains from the sale or exchange of capital assets are taxed at various rates, depending upon the holding period, the taxpayer's regular tax rate, and the type of asset involved.

Short-Term Gains

Gains on capital assets held one year or less are taxed as *ordinary income.* Accordingly, the applicable tax rates vary from 10 percent to 39.6 percent. Although short-term capital gains receive no preferential tax treatment compared to ordinary income, they do have one advantage: they can absorb capital losses without limit. As discussed later in this section, *capital losses* are deducted first against capital gains (without limit) and then against ordinary income, but only up to $3,000 per year.[17] Thus, someone with a large capital loss will find short-term capital gains attractive, even though such gains do not qualify for lower tax rates.

Long-Term Gains

Gains on capital assets held more than one year are classified as *long-term* gains and are eligible for a special 20 percent tax rate (for taxpayers in the 39.6 percent bracket), 15 percent tax rate (for taxpayers in the 25, 28, 33, or 35 percent tax bracket), or 0 percent rate (for taxpayers in the 10 or 15 percent tax bracket). Thus, the benefit of these long-term capital gain tax rates can be significant, with as much as a 20 percentage point tax rate differential (i.e., for a taxpayer whose ordinary rate is 35 percent and who benefits from the 15 percent capital gains rate).

TAX PLANNING STRATEGIES   Gifts of Appreciated Securities

FRAMEWORK FOCUS: TAX RATE

Strategy: Shift Net Income from High-Bracket Taxpayers to Low-Bracket Taxpayers.

Persons with appreciated securities that have been held over one year may reduce the tax due on their sale by giving the securities to someone (often a child) who is in the *lowest tax bracket.* The donor's holding period carries over, along with his or her basis, and the donee's lower tax rate applies when the securities are sold. As a result, the gain could be taxed at the donee's 0 percent, rather than the donor's 15 or 20 percent. The donee should be at least age 19 (or 24 in the case of a full-time student) by year-end, however, or the *kiddie tax* will nullify most of the tax advantage being sought. The kiddie tax subjects the gain to the parents' tax rate. See Chapter 9.

Such gifts usually bear no gift tax due to the $14,000 annual exclusion. But once the property is transferred by the donor, it belongs to the donee. It is not available to the donor, nor may it be used to pay a parent's essential support obligations. Moreover, these assets may affect a child's eligibility for need-based financial aid when applying to college.

In point of fact, relatively few capital gains are realized by persons in the 10 or 15 percent tax bracket. In addition, there are relatively few taxpayers who are in the highest

---

[17]§ 1211(b).

income tax bracket and subject to the 20 percent rate. Thus, the tax rate that generally applies to long-term capital gains is 15 percent.

There are two major exceptions, however, to this general treatment. The first exception relates to so-called *28% property*, which consists of the following items.

- **Collectibles** (works of art, rugs, antiques, gems, coins, stamps, and alcoholic beverages) held more than one year.[18]

- The taxable portion of the gain on sales of *qualified small business stock* (see the end of this section).

These assets are labeled *28% property*, because the gains they produce are taxed at 28 percent. But this 28 percent rate is a *maximum* rate, so a taxpayer in a lower tax bracket would pay at that lower rate. As a result, the benefit of the applicable tax rates for gains on *28% property* is as follows.

Ordinary Income Tax Rates	Applicable Tax Rates	Differential (Percentage Points)
10%	10%	None
15%	15%	None
25%	25%	None
28%	28%	None
33%	28%	5%
35%	28%	7%
39.6%	28%	11.6%

Note that gains on *28% property* receive preferential tax treatment only when realized by taxpayers in the top three tax brackets.

The second major exception involves depreciable real estate that has been held more than one year. Some—but not all—of the gain attributable to depreciation deductions on real estate such as apartments, office buildings, shopping centers, and warehouses is taxable at 25 percent rather than 0, 15, or 20 percent. The amount that is taxed in this manner depends upon how much depreciation is "recaptured" as ordinary income under § 1250, as explained later in this chapter. Accordingly, these gains are called *unrecaptured § 1250 gain*. The 25 percent rate is a *maximum* rate; so the benefit of this tax rate for gains from the sale of depreciable real estate really only impacts taxpayers in the 28 percent to 39.6 percent tax brackets, and saves them from 3 percentage points to a maximum of 14.6 percentage points.

Concept Summary 8.3 reviews the tax treatment given to capital gains recognized by noncorporate taxpayers.

---

[18]§ 408(m) and Reg. § 1.408–10(b).

Concept Summary 8.3

Capital Gains of Noncorporate Taxpayers

Type of Asset	Applicable Rate
Held not more than one year (short-term).	10%–39.6%, same as ordinary income.
Collectibles held more than one year (*28% property*).	10%/15%/25% for lowest-bracket taxpayers, 28% for all others.
Taxable portion (50%, 25%, or 0%) of gain on qualified small business stock held more than five years (*28% property*; see Section 8-5d for a detailed explanation of the special treatment given to "qualified small business stock").	10%/15%/25% for lowest-bracket taxpayers, 28% for all others.
Unrecaptured § 1250 gain on depreciable real estate held more than one year.	10%/15% for two lowest-bracket taxpayers, 25% for all others.
Other capital assets held more than one year (regular long-term).	0% for two lowest-bracket taxpayers, 20% for taxpayers in the highest bracket, 15% for all others.

8-5b Capital Losses

As explained previously, capital gains can be classified into four general categories.

- Short term—taxed as ordinary income.
- *28% property*—taxed at no more than 28 percent.
- *Unrecaptured § 1250 gain*—taxed at no more than 25 percent.
- Regular long term—taxed at 0 percent, 15 percent, or 20 percent.

A taxpayer can also have losses from capital assets in *three* of these four categories. The *unrecaptured § 1250 gain* category applies only to gain.

8-5c Capital Gain and Loss Netting Process

When both gains and losses occur in the year, they must be netted against each other in the following order.

Step 1. Group all gains and losses into short-term, *28% property*, *unrecaptured § 1250*, and regular long-term categories.

Step 2. Net the gains and losses within each category to obtain net short-term, *28% property*, *unrecaptured § 1250*, and regular long-term gain or loss.

Step 3. Offset the net *28% property* and *unrecaptured § 1250* amounts if they are of opposite sign. Add them if they have the same sign. Then offset the resulting amount against the regular net long-term amount if they are of opposite sign, or add the amounts if they have the same sign.

Step 4. Offset the result of step 3 with the net short-term gain *or loss* from step 2 if they are of opposite sign.

These netting rules offset net short-term capital loss against the *highest-taxed gain first*. Consequently, if there is a net short-term capital loss, it first offsets any net *28% property gain*, any remaining loss offsets *unrecaptured § 1250 gain*, and then any remaining loss offsets regular long-term gain.

If the result of step 4 is *only* a short-term capital gain, the taxpayer is not eligible for a reduced tax rate. If the result of step 4 is a loss, a **net capital loss** exists and the taxpayer may be eligible for a *capital loss deduction* (discussed later in this chapter). If there was no offsetting in step 4 because the short-term and step 3 results were both gains *or* if the result of the offsetting is a *28% property*, an *unrecaptured § 1250 property*, and/or a regular long-term gain, a **net capital gain** exists and the taxpayer may be eligible for a reduced tax rate. The net capital gain may consist of regular long-term gain, *unrecaptured § 1250 gain*, and/or *28% property gain*. Each of these gains may be taxed at a different rate.

Special Tax Rates and Capital Gain and Loss Netting Process

Joe is in the 35% Federal income tax bracket. He is taxed as follows.

Ordinary income	35%
Unrecaptured § 1250 gain	25%
28% gain	28%
Short-term capital gain	35%
Other long-term capital gain	15%

EXAMPLE 29

This example shows how a *net long-term capital loss* is applied.

Step	Short-Term	28% Gain	Unrecaptured § 1250 Gain	Regular Long-Term	Comment
1	$ 3,000	$ 1,000		$ 3,000	
				(8,000)	
2	$ 3,000	$ 1,000		($ 5,000)	
3		(1,000)	→	1,000	Netted because of opposite sign.
		$ –0–		($ 4,000)	
4	(3,000)	→	→	3,000	The net short-term gain is netted against the net regular long-term loss, and the remaining loss is eligible for the capital loss deduction.
	$ –0–			($ 1,000)	

EXAMPLE 30

This example shows how *net short-term* and *regular long-term capital losses* are applied.

Step	Short-Term	28% Gain	Unrecaptured § 1250 Gain	Regular Long-Term	Comment
1	$ 3,000	$15,000	$4,000	$ 3,000	
	(5,000)	(7,000)		(8,000)	
2	($ 2,000)	$ 8,000	$4,000	($ 5,000)	
3		(5,000)	←	5,000	Net regular long-term loss is netted against *28% gain* first.
		$ 3,000		$ –0–	
4	2,000 →	(2,000)			Short-term loss is netted against *28% gain* next.
	$ –0–	$ 1,000	$4,000		
		Net *28%* gain	Net *25%* gain		

EXAMPLE 31

If a net loss remains after applying these rules for offsetting losses, a noncorporate taxpayer may deduct up to $3,000 of that loss against ordinary income.[19] Losses in excess of $3,000 are carried over to future years where they are applied first against capital gains and then deducted up to $3,000 per year. Capital loss carryovers expire, however, when the taxpayer dies.

---

[19]§ 1211(b)(1). Married persons filing separate returns are limited to a $1,500 deduction per tax year.

Use of Capital Loss Carryovers

EXAMPLE 32

James incurred a $10,000 loss on his only capital asset transaction in 2016. If he has no other capital asset transactions from that point on, his $10,000 loss is deducted as follows.

Year	Deduction
2016	$3,000
2017	3,000
2018	3,000
2019	1,000

EXAMPLE 33

Assume the same facts as in the preceding example, except that James realizes a capital gain of $4,500 in 2018. At that time, his remaining capital loss carryover is $4,000 ($10,000 − $6,000 deducted previously). Because his capital gain in 2018 (i.e., $4,500) exceeds this loss carryforward, James can deduct the entire $4,000 against that year's capital gain.

EXAMPLE 34

Assume the same facts as in Example 32, except that James died in late 2017. His remaining capital loss carryforward of $4,000 ($10,000 − $6,000 deducted in 2016 and 2017) expires unused.

When a taxpayer's capital loss exceeds $3,000 and derives from more than one category, it is used in the following order: first, short-term; then, *28% property*; then, *unrecaptured § 1250 property*; and finally, regular long-term. Unused losses are carried forward as follows: short-term losses carry forward as short-term losses, and long-term losses carry forward as long-term losses.

TAX PLANNING STRATEGIES   Matching Gains with Losses

FRAMEWORK FOCUS: INCOME AND EXCLUSIONS

Strategy: Avoid Income Recognition.

A taxpayer who has already realized a large capital gain may want to *match this gain* with an *offsetting capital loss*. Doing so will shelter the capital gain from taxation and will also free up an asset that has declined in value. Without the capital gain, after all, the taxpayer might hesitate to sell a loss asset, because the resulting capital loss may be deductible only in $3,000 annual increments.

Similarly, a taxpayer with a large realized capital loss might use the occasion to sell some appreciated assets. Doing so would enable the taxpayer to use the capital loss immediately and at the same time realize the benefit of the asset appreciation at little or no tax cost.

On the other hand, matching capital losses and long-term capital gains means that the taxpayer utilizes the capital loss

against income that would otherwise qualify for a preferential tax rate of 0, 15, or 20 percent. If the taxpayer's ordinary income is taxed at a higher rate, he or she might prefer to deduct the loss against that higher taxed income, even on a schedule of $3,000 per year. However, the *time value of money* must be considered; a current-year deduction at 0, 15, or 20 percent might be worth more than a series of annual deductions at higher rates spread over several years.

Nontax considerations, such as investment prospects for the assets in question, are also important. Future investment prospects are often unknowable or at least highly speculative, while tax effects can be determined with relative certainty—which explains some of the late December selling activity in publicly traded securities and mutual funds.

Nancy incurs a long-term capital loss of $8,500 this year, of which $3,000 is deducted against her ordinary income. The remaining $5,500 ($8,500 loss − $3,000 deducted) carries forward as a long-term capital loss.

EXAMPLE
35

In-depth coverage can be found on this book's companion website: www.cengagebrain.com

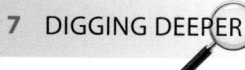

7 DIGGING DEEPER

8-5d **Small Business Stock**

A special *exclusion* is available to noncorporate taxpayers who derive capital gains from the sale or exchange of qualified small business stock.[20] Any amount not excluded from income is taxed at a maximum rate of 28 percent (as noted earlier). The exclusion amount varies, depending on when the qualified small business stock was acquired:

- 100 percent of the gain is excluded for qualified stock acquired after September 27, 2010.
- 75 percent of the gain is excluded for qualified stock acquired after February 17, 2009, and before September 28, 2010.
- 50 percent of the gain is excluded for qualified stock acquired before February 18, 2009.

As a result, the maximum effective tax rate on gains from the sale of qualified small business stock is 0 percent (28% × 0%), 7 percent (28% × 25%), or 14 percent (28% × 50%).

Yolanda realized a $100,000 gain on the sale of qualified small business stock that she acquired in 2005. Yolanda is subject to the 33% marginal tax rate without considering this gain. As the stock was acquired before February 18, 2009, $50,000 of this gain (50%) is excluded from gross income, and the other $50,000 is taxed at the maximum rate of 28%. As a result, Yolanda owes Federal income tax of $14,000 on the stock sale ($50,000 × 28%), an effective tax rate of 14% on the entire $100,000 gain.

If, instead, Yolanda acquired the stock in January 2011 and sold it in March 2016, she would exclude 100% of the gain.

EXAMPLE
36

Given this very favorable treatment of gains, Congress imposed additional restrictions to ensure that the gain exclusion only applied in very specific situations. These restrictions include the following.

- The stock must have been newly issued *after* August 10, 1993.
- The taxpayer must have held the stock *more than five years*.
- The issuing corporation must use at least 80 percent of its assets, determined by their value, in the *active conduct* of a trade or business.
- When the stock was issued, the issuing corporation's assets must not have exceeded $50 million, at adjusted basis, including the proceeds of the stock issuance.
- The corporation does not engage in banking, financing, insurance, investing, leasing, farming, mineral extraction, hotel or motel operations, restaurant operations, or any business whose principal asset is the *reputation or skill* of its employees (such as accounting, architecture, health, law, engineering, or financial services).

Even if each of these requirements is met, the amount of gain eligible for the exclusion is limited to the *greater* of 10 times the taxpayer's basis in the stock or $10 million per taxpayer per company,[21] computed on an aggregate basis.

Vanita purchased $100,000 of qualified small business stock when it was first issued in October 2001. This year, she sold the stock for $4 million. Her gain is $3.9 million ($4,000,000 − $100,000). Although this amount exceeds 10 times her basis ($100,000 × 10 = $1,000,000), it is *less* than $10 million; so the entire $3.9 million gain is eligible for a 50% exclusion.

EXAMPLE
37

---

[20]§ 1202(a).

[21]For married persons filing separately, the limitation is $5 million.

Transactions that fail to satisfy *any one* of the applicable requirements are taxed as capital gains (and losses) realized by noncorporate taxpayers generally.

Gains are also eligible for *nonrecognition* treatment if the sale proceeds are invested in other qualified small business stock within 60 days.[22] To the extent that the sale proceeds are not so invested, gain is recognized, but the exclusion still applies. To be eligible for this treatment, the stock sold must have been held more than six months.

EXAMPLE 38

Assume the same facts as in the preceding example, except that Vanita sold her stock in January 2017 and used $3.5 million of the sale proceeds to purchase other qualified small business stock one month later. Vanita's gain is recognized to the extent that the sale proceeds were not reinvested—namely, $500,000 ($4,000,000 sale proceeds − $3,500,000 reinvested). A 50% exclusion will apply, however, to the $500,000.

DIGGING DEEPER 8   In-depth coverage can be found on this book's companion website: **www.cengagebrain.com**

LO.5

Describe the tax treatment of capital gains and losses for corporate taxpayers.

8-6 TAX TREATMENT OF CAPITAL GAINS AND LOSSES OF CORPORATE TAXPAYERS

The treatment of a corporation's net capital gain or loss differs dramatically from the rules for noncorporate taxpayers discussed in the preceding section. Briefly, the differences are as follows.

- Capital gains are taxed at the ordinary income tax rates.[23]
- Capital losses offset only capital gains. No deduction of capital losses is permitted against other taxable income.
- There is a three-year carryback and a five-year carryforward period for net capital losses.[24] Capital loss carrybacks and carryforwards are always treated as short-term, regardless of their original nature.

Note that with the treatment given to corporate capital gains and losses, no substantive advantage results to the taxpayer. In fact, capital asset designation often can lead to a detriment (e.g., a delay or the ultimate loss of a capital loss deduction).

EXAMPLE 39

Sparrow Corporation has a $15,000 long-term capital loss for the current year and $57,000 of other taxable income. Sparrow may not offset the $15,000 long-term capital loss against its other income by taking a capital loss deduction.

The $15,000 long-term capital loss becomes a $15,000 short-term capital loss for carryback and carryforward purposes. This amount may offset capital gains in the three-year carryback period or, if not absorbed there, offset capital gains in the five-year carryforward period. Any amount remaining after this carryforward period expires is permanently lost.

LO.6

Distinguish § 1231 assets from ordinary and capital assets and calculate § 1231 gain or loss.

8-7 SECTION 1231 ASSETS

Businesses own many assets that are used in the business rather than held for resale. In financial accounting, such assets are known as "fixed assets." For example, a foundry's 30,000-pound stamping machine is a fixed asset. It is also a depreciable asset. The

---

[22]§ 1045(a).

[23]§ 1201. The alternative tax rate of 35% produces no beneficial results.

[24]§ 1212(a)(1).

TAX FACT Capital Gains for the Wealthy?

Economists and other observers of society often accuse the Code of favoring those with higher levels of income and wealth, despite a fairly substantial progressivity in the Federal income tax rate structure. The claim is that the wealthy are the primary owners of capital assets and that capital gains and qualified dividends from those assets are subject to highly favorable tax treatment. Most recently available tax return data may confirm those assertions.

Source: Based on Justin Bryan, "Individual Income Tax Returns, 2011," *SOI Bulletin,* Fall 2013, Figure F.

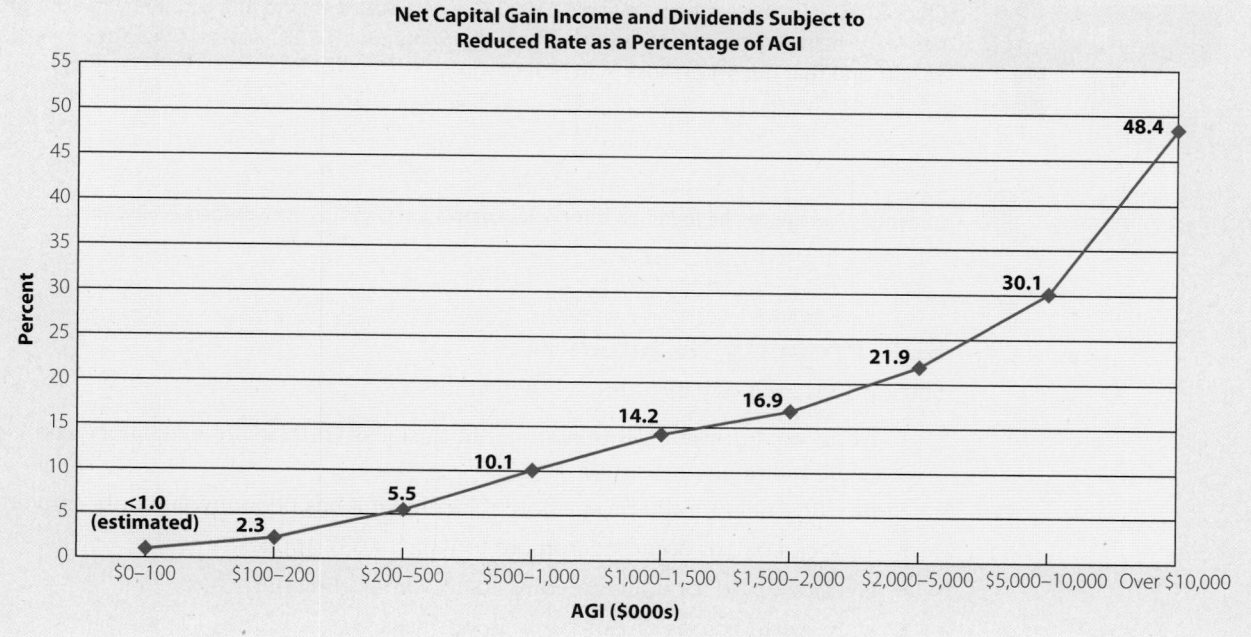

Net Capital Gain Income and Dividends Subject to Reduced Rate as a Percentage of AGI

8-7a Relationship to Capital Assets

At first glance, the *classification of fixed assets* ought to be straightforward. Section 1221(a)(2) specifically excludes from the capital asset definition any property that is depreciable or that is real estate "used in a trade or business." Accordingly, the foundry's stamping machine and the building housing the foundry described earlier are not capital assets. Therefore, one would expect gains to be taxed as ordinary income and losses to be deductible as ordinary losses. Since World War II, however, certain business assets have received more favorable treatment.

Section 1231 provides that business assets held for more than one year can receive the best of both worlds: capital gain treatment on gains and ordinary loss treatment on losses. More specifically, this provision requires that gains and losses from § 1231 property be aggregated at the end of the taxable year; the *net result* is then classified as capital gain if a net gain is produced, or as ordinary loss if a net loss is produced. As a result, a particular disposition's character as capital or ordinary is not determined until the taxable year has concluded and all of the taxpayer's § 1231 gains and losses are tabulated.

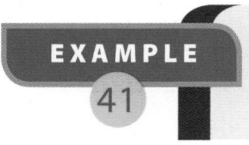

Section 1231 Treatment

EXAMPLE 40

Brown & Co. sells a building at a $5,000 gain and equipment at a $3,000 loss. Both properties were § 1231 assets because they were used in Brown's trade or business and held for the long-term holding period (more than one year). Brown's net gain is $2,000, and that net gain *may* (depending on various recapture rules discussed later in this chapter) be treated as a long-term capital gain under § 1231.

EXAMPLE 41

Chickadee, Inc., sells equipment at a $10,000 loss and business land at a $2,000 gain. Both properties were held for more than one year and, therefore, are § 1231 assets. Chickadee's net loss is $8,000, and that net § 1231 loss is an ordinary loss.

DIGGING DEEPER 9   In-depth coverage can be found on this book's companion website: www.cengagebrain.com

8-7b Property Included

Section 1231 property includes the following.

- Depreciable or real property used in business (principally machinery and equipment, buildings, and land).
- Property held for the production of income if it has been involuntarily converted.
- Timber, coal, or domestic iron ore to which § 631 applies.
- Livestock held for draft, breeding, dairy, or sporting purposes.
- Unharvested crops on land used in business.
- Certain *purchased* intangible assets (such as patents and goodwill) that are eligible for amortization.

DIGGING DEEPER 10, 11   In-depth coverage can be found on this book's companion website: www.cengagebrain.com

8-7c Property Excluded

Section 1231 property generally does *not* include the following.

- Property not held more than one year. Livestock must be held at least 12 months (24 months in some cases). Unharvested crops do not have to be held for more than one year, but the land must be so held.
- Business-use property, where casualty losses exceed casualty gains for the taxable year. If a taxpayer has a net casualty loss, the casualty gains and losses are treated as ordinary gains and losses.
- Inventory and property held primarily for sale to customers.
- Copyrights; literary, musical, or artistic compositions, etc.; and certain U.S. government publications.
- Accounts receivable and notes receivable arising in the ordinary course of the trade or business.

TAX IN THE NEWS   Loss from Cattle Rustling

A newspaper in "cattle country" reported that rustlers had stolen 20 head of prime milk cows from a local ranch. The rancher never recovered the cows. According to the article, the rancher had no insurance on the cows and was upset because he had no way of recovering his loss.

A CPA might advise the rancher that he could be entitled to a special "theft loss" deduction for tax purposes because the theft loss rules apply to § 1231 assets such as cattle held for 24 months or more.

8-7d Casualty or Theft and Nonpersonal-Use Capital Assets

When § 1231 assets are disposed of by casualty or theft, a special netting rule is applied. For simplicity, the term *casualty* is used to mean both casualty and theft dispositions. First, the casualty gains and losses from § 1231 assets *and* the casualty gains and losses from long-term nonpersonal-use capital assets are determined. For business entities, virtually any capital asset is a nonpersonal-use capital asset, because partnerships, limited liability companies, and corporations are incapable of using assets *personally*. This classification, therefore, is most significant to individual taxpayers who might use certain capital assets as part of their daily life.

Casualties and thefts are *involuntary conversions*, it should be recalled, and gains from such conversions need not be recognized if the proceeds are timely reinvested in similar property. Thus, the netting process described in the next section would not consider any casualty and theft gains that are being deferred because insurance proceeds were reinvested according to the requirements of § 1033 (see Chapter 7). Section 1231, in other words, has no effect on whether a *realized* gain or loss is recognized. Instead, § 1231 merely dictates how a *recognized* gain will be classified.

This special netting process for casualties and thefts does not apply to *condemnation* gains and losses. As a result, if a § 1231 asset is disposed of by condemnation, any resulting gain or loss will get § 1231 treatment.

8-7e General Procedure for § 1231 Computation

To determine the tax treatment of § 1231 gains and losses, specific steps of a rather complex *netting* procedure must be followed. Concept Summary 8.4 may be used as a guide to better understand these netting rules.

Step 1: Casualty Netting

Net all recognized long-term gains and losses from casualties of § 1231 assets and nonpersonal-use capital assets. This casualty netting is beneficial because if there is a net gain, the gain may receive long-term capital gain treatment. If there is a net loss, it receives ordinary loss treatment.

a.   If the casualty gains exceed the casualty losses, add the net gain to the other § 1231 gains for the taxable year.

b.   If the casualty losses exceed the casualty gains, exclude all casualty losses and gains from further § 1231 computation. The casualty gains are ordinary income, and the casualty losses are deductible. For individual taxpayers, the casualty losses must be classified further. For individual taxpayers, § 1231 asset casualty losses are deductible *for* AGI, while other casualty losses are deductible *from* AGI (see Chapter 10).

Step 2: § 1231 Netting

After adding any net casualty gain from step 1(a) on the previous page to the other § 1231 gains and losses (including *recognized* § 1231 asset condemnation gains and losses), net all § 1231 gains and losses.

a. If the gains exceed the losses, the net gain is offset by the "lookback" nonrecaptured § 1231 losses (see step 3).
b. If the losses exceed the gains, the net loss is deducted against ordinary income. For individual taxpayers only, the gains are ordinary income, the § 1231 asset losses are deductible *for* AGI, and the other casualty losses are deductible *from* AGI.

Concept Summary 8.4

Section 1231 Netting Procedure

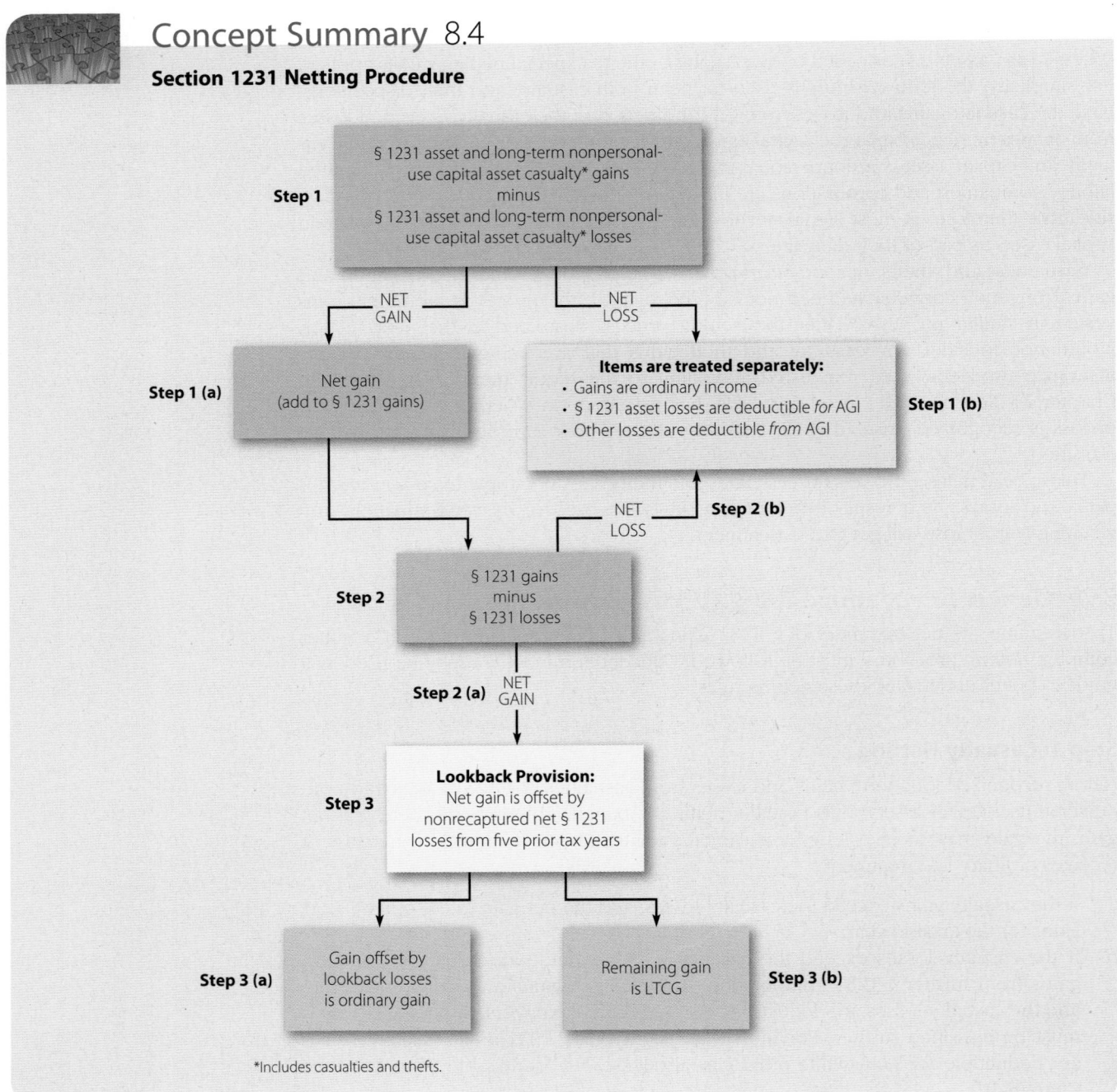

*Includes casualties and thefts.

Section 1231 Computations

EXAMPLE

42

Falcon Management, Inc., recognized the following gains and losses this year.

Capital Gains and Losses	
Long-term capital gain	$3,000
Long-term capital loss	(400)
Short-term capital gain	1,000
Short-term capital loss	(200)

Casualties	
Gain from insurance recovery on fire loss to building, owned five years	$ 1,200
Loss from theft of computer (uninsured), owned two years	(1,000)

§ 1231 Gains and Losses from Sale of Depreciable Business Assets Held Long Term	
Asset A	$ 300
Asset B	1,100
Asset C	(500)

Gains and Losses from Sale of Depreciable Business Assets Held Short Term	
Asset D	$ 200
Asset E	(300)

Falcon had no net § 1231 losses in prior tax years.

Disregarding the recapture of depreciation (discussed later in this chapter), Falcon's gains and losses receive the following tax treatment.

- **Step 1:** The casualty netting of the § 1231 and nonpersonal-use capital assets contains two items—the $1,200 gain from the business building and the $1,000 loss from the computer. Consequently, there is a $200 net gain and that gain is treated as a § 1231 gain (added to the § 1231 gains).

- **Step 1 (a):** The gains from § 1231 transactions (Assets A and B and the § 1231 asset casualty gain) exceed the losses (Asset C) by $1,100 ($1,600 − $500). This excess is a long-term capital gain and is added to Falcon's other long-term capital gains.

- **Step 2:** Falcon's net long-term capital gain is $3,700 ($3,000 + $1,100 from § 1231 transactions − $400 long-term capital loss). Its net short-term capital gain is $800 ($1,000 − $200). The result is capital gain income of $4,500, which will be taxed at ordinary rates. If Falcon were an individual rather than a corporation, the $3,700 net long-term capital gain portion would be eligible for preferential capital gain treatment and the $800 net short-term capital gain would be taxed as ordinary income.

- Falcon treats the gain and loss from Assets D and E as ordinary gain and loss because § 1231 does not apply unless the assets have been held more than one year.[25]

Results of the Gains and Losses on Falcon's Tax Computation	
Net long-term capital gain	$3,700
Net short-term capital gain	800
Ordinary gain from sale of Asset D	200
Ordinary loss from sale of Asset E	(300)
Gross income	$4,400

---

[25]§ 1231(b)(1).

EXAMPLE 43

Assume the same facts as in the preceding example, except that the loss from Asset C was $1,700 instead of $500.

- The treatment of the casualty gains and losses is the same.
- **Step 1 (b):** The losses from § 1231 transactions now exceed the gains by $100 ($1,700 − $1,600). As a result, the net loss is deducted in full as an ordinary loss.
- Capital gain income is $3,400 ($2,600 long-term + $800 short-term).

Results of the Gains and Losses on Falcon's Tax Computation	
Net long-term capital gain	$2,600
Net short-term capital gain	800
Net ordinary loss on Assets A, B, and C and § 1231 casualty gain	(100)
Ordinary gain from sale of Asset D	200
Ordinary loss from sale of Asset E	(300)
Gross income	$3,200

Step 3: § 1231 Lookback Provision

The net § 1231 gain from step 2(a) is offset by the nonrecaptured net § 1231 losses for the five preceding taxable years.[26] For transactions in 2016, the lookback years are 2011, 2012, 2013, 2014, and 2015.

a. To the extent of the nonrecaptured net § 1231 loss, the current-year net § 1231 gain is ordinary income. The *nonrecaptured net § 1231 losses* are losses that have not already been used to offset net § 1231 gains.

b. Only the net § 1231 gain exceeding this net § 1231 loss carryforward is given long-term capital gain treatment. The § 1231 lookback provision reduces the taxpayer's ability to gain a tax advantage by "timing" sales artificially.

EXAMPLE 44

Komodo Manufacturing Corporation sold used equipment and some business real estate during 2016 for a net § 1231 gain of $25,000. During 2015, Komodo had no § 1231 transactions, but in 2014, it had a net § 1231 loss of $17,000. This loss causes $17,000 of the 2016 gain to be classified as ordinary income. The remaining 2016 gain of $8,000 ($25,000 of § 1231 gain − $17,000 nonrecaptured loss) is § 1231 gain.

EXAMPLE 45

Assume the same facts as in the preceding example, except that Komodo had a net § 1231 loss of $37,000 in 2014 and a net § 1231 gain of $10,000 in 2015.

- The 2014 net § 1231 loss of $37,000 would cause the net § 1231 gain of $10,000 in 2015 to be classified as ordinary income, and $27,000 ($37,000 loss − $10,000 recaptured) would carry over to 2016.

- The remaining nonrecaptured § 1231 loss of $27,000 from 2014 completely offsets the § 1231 gain of $25,000 from 2016, making that entire gain ordinary income.

- The remaining nonrecaptured § 1231 loss from 2014 is $2,000 ($27,000 nonrecaptured § 1231 loss carried to 2016 − $25,000 recaptured in 2016). This recapture potential carries over to 2017.

---

[26]§ 1231(c).

8-8 SECTION 1245 RECAPTURE

As explained earlier, when Congress determined that § 1231 was unduly generous, it chose to *recapture* some of § 1231's benefits rather than repeal that section altogether. This recapture phenomenon applies exclusively to the gain side of § 1231; the ordinary loss feature applicable to § 1231 property is not affected by the Code's recapture provisions. In essence, recapture takes part—often all—of the gain from the sale or exchange of a § 1231 asset and classifies it as *ordinary income* before the netting process of § 1231 begins. Accordingly, recaptured gain is computed *first*, without considering the other § 1231 transactions that occurred during the taxable year. This section discusses the § 1245 recapture rules, and the next section discusses the § 1250 recapture rules.

Section 1245 requires taxpayers to treat all gain as ordinary gain unless the property is sold for more than its original cost. This result is accomplished by requiring that all gain be treated as ordinary gain to the extent of the depreciation taken on the property disposed of. Section 1231 gain results only if the property is disposed of for more than its original cost. The excess of the sales price over the original cost is § 1231 gain. As described more completely in the next section, § 1245 applies primarily to personalty such as machinery, trucks, and office furniture.

The Big Picture

EXAMPLE 46

Return to the facts of *The Big Picture* on p. 8-1. Recall that Alice's husband, Jeff, had purchased, for $50,000, depreciable equipment for use in his business and had deducted $35,000 of depreciation.

If Jeff sold the equipment for $45,000, his gain would be $30,000 [$45,000 amount realized − $15,000 adjusted basis ($50,000 cost − $35,000 depreciation taken)]. Section 1245 treats as ordinary income (not as § 1231 gain) any gain to the extent of depreciation taken. In this example, the entire $30,000 gain would be ordinary income.

The Big Picture

EXAMPLE 47

Continue with the facts of *The Big Picture* on p. 8-1. If Jeff sold the business equipment for $60,000, he would have a gain of $45,000 ($60,000 amount realized − $15,000 adjusted basis). The § 1245 gain would be $35,000 (equal to the depreciation taken), and the remaining gain of $10,000 (equal to the excess of the sales price over the original cost) would be § 1231 gain.

The Big Picture

EXAMPLE 48

Continue with the facts of Example 47, except that Jeff sold the equipment for $8,000 instead of $45,000. Jeff would have a loss of $7,000 ($8,000 amount realized − $15,000 adjusted basis). Because there is a loss, there is no depreciation recapture. All of the loss is § 1231 loss.

Section 1245 recapture applies to the portion of *recognized* gain from the sale or other disposition of § 1245 property that represents depreciation, including § 167 depreciation, § 168 cost recovery, § 179 immediate expensing, § 168(k) additional first-year depreciation, and § 197 amortization. Section 1245 merely *classifies* gain as ordinary income; it does not cause gain to be recognized. Thus, in Example 46, Jeff recaptures as ordinary income only the $30,000 of actual gain, not the entire $35,000 of depreciation taken. In other words, § 1245 recaptures the *lesser* of the depreciation taken or the gain recognized.

The method of depreciation (e.g., accelerated or straight-line) does not matter. All depreciation taken is potentially subject to recapture. Thus, § 1245 recapture is often referred to as *full recapture*. Any remaining gain after subtracting the amount recaptured as ordinary income will usually be § 1231 gain. The remaining gain is casualty

The essence of much of the tax code is to create definitions that discriminate among certain types of income or expenditures so that special tax treatment can be afforded to one of the definitional groups. For instance, municipal bond interest might be favored over corporate bond interest income, long-term capital gains over short-term capital gains or ordinary income, and processing fees to bribes. In each case, the former generally allows a reduction of taxable income or the tax liability and helps the taxpayer meet its goal of maximizing the available after-tax income that it generates.

Maximizing net income also is a goal of financial accounting, at least from the viewpoint of current and potential shareholders. In the long run, stock prices may advance solely because of the positive earnings that the corporation generates relative to the rest of the capital markets. The greater the net earnings, the greater the increase in stock price and private wealth.

But financial accounting makes far fewer distinctions when classifying the reporting entity's revenues and expenses. Most of the tax code's definitions and distinctions are politically or economically motivated means designed to reduce the effective tax rate of the taxpayer, perhaps without affecting its nominal rate.

The preferential treatment of long-term capital gains is one of the most long-lived of these tax fictions. The "best of both worlds" § 1231 treatment is over 70 years old itself. Whereas the gain or loss generated by the sale of a business or investment asset is merely included in the body of the income statement of the reporting entity, § 1221 and § 1231 can reduce the taxpayer's effective tax rate and § 1245 and § 1250 can increase it.

Differences in classification of income and deductions created solely by the tax code constitute most of the items to be reconciled in the Schedule M–1 or M–3 of the C corporation, S corporation, partnership, and limited liability entity. Many of these items must be reported as permanent or temporary differences in the Deferred Tax Liability account regulated by ASC 740 (SFAS 109).

gain, however, if the asset is disposed of in a casualty event. For example, if the equipment in Example 47 had been disposed of by casualty and the $60,000 received had been an insurance recovery, Jeff would still have a gain of $45,000, and $35,000 of that gain would still be recaptured by § 1245 as ordinary gain. The other $10,000 of gain, however, would be casualty gain.

If § 1245 property is disposed of in a transaction other than a sale, exchange, or involuntary conversion, the maximum amount recaptured is the excess of the property's fair market value over its adjusted basis. See the discussion under Exceptions to §§ 1245 and 1250 later in this chapter.

8-8a Section 1245 Property

Generally, § 1245 property includes all depreciable personal property (e.g., machinery and equipment), including livestock. Buildings and their structural components usually are not § 1245 property. The following property is *also* subject to § 1245 treatment.

- Amortizable personal property such as goodwill, patents, copyrights, and leaseholds of § 1245 property.
- Professional baseball and football player contracts.
- Expensed costs to remove architectural and transportation barriers that restrict the handicapped and/or elderly.
- Section 179 immediately expensed depreciable tangible personal property.
- Certain depreciable tangible real property (other than buildings and their structural components) employed as an integral part of certain activities such as manufacturing and production. For example, a natural gas storage tank where the gas is used in the manufacturing process is § 1245 property.
- Pollution control facilities, railroad grading and tunnel bores, on-the-job training facilities, and child care facilities on which amortization is taken.
- Single-purpose agricultural and horticultural structures and petroleum storage facilities (e.g., a greenhouse or silo).

8-8b Observations on § 1245

- In most instances, the total depreciation taken will exceed the recognized gain. Therefore, the disposition of § 1245 property usually results in ordinary income rather than § 1231 gain (refer to Example 46).

- Recapture applies to the total amount of depreciation allowed or allowable regardless of the depreciation method used (i.e., full recapture).

- Recapture applies regardless of the holding period of the property. Of course, the entire recognized gain would be ordinary income if the property was not held more than one year, because then § 1231 would not apply.

- Section 1245 does not apply to losses, which receive § 1231 treatment.

- Gains from the disposition of § 1245 assets may also be treated as passive activity gains (refer to Chapter 6).

TAX PLANNING STRATEGIES **Depreciation Recapture and § 179**

FRAMEWORK FOCUS: DEDUCTIONS

Strategy: Accelerate Recognition of Deductions to Achieve Tax Deferral.

Section 1245 recapture applies to all types of depreciation, including § 179 *immediate expensing*. Expensing under § 179, however, is elective and entirely within the discretion of the taxpayer. Choosing this option accelerates depreciation on the affected property but increases the potential recapture as well. Therefore, if a taxpayer anticipates that an asset will generate a gain when it is sold and that such sale will occur in the early years of the asset's life, the taxpayer might decide to forgo electing the additional depreciation under § 179.

On the other hand, electing § 179 remains attractive if little or no gain is anticipated upon an asset's disposition. After all, § 1245 recapture applies only to the extent gain is actually realized. Moreover, even if a substantial gain is anticipated upon an asset's disposition, the *time value of money* might suggest that § 179 be elected if the disposition is expected to be many years away. In any case, the taxpayer can usually control when an asset is sold or exchanged and can thereby extend the time before the taxes saved by electing § 179 must be returned as § 1245 recapture.

8-9 SECTION 1250 RECAPTURE

Some depreciable property that is not subject to § 1245 recapture faces a separate recapture computation mechanism in § 1250. For the most part, § 1250 applies to *depreciable real property* (principally buildings and their structural components), such as apartments, office buildings, factories, stores, and warehouses. Intangible real property, such as leaseholds of §1250 property, also is included.

Section 1250 recapture is less onerous than § 1245 recapture. Section 1250 recaptures only a property's *additional depreciation*, which is the excess of the depreciation actually deducted over the amount that would have been allowed under the straight-line method of depreciation. For this reason, § 1250 recapture is often referred to as *partial recapture*, in contrast to § 1245's full recapture.

Because § 1250 recaptures only the excess over straight-line depreciation, the concept does not apply to properties that were depreciated using the straight-line method (unless they were held for one year or less). Real property placed in service *after 1986* can only be depreciated using the straight-line method, so there is *no § 1250 recapture* upon the disposition of such properties that are held for longer than one year. Finally, § 1250 does not affect the § 1231 treatment of realized losses.

TAX IN THE NEWS   **Building or Tangible Personal Property?**

Many taxpayers have "cost-segregated" their buildings. This means that an engineering study is done to determine whether some of a building's cost can be segregated into tangible personal property (generally a 5-year or 7-year MACRS life with accelerated depreciation) rather than real property (a 27.5-year or 39-year MACRS life with straight-line depreciation). The faster depreciation for the tangible personal property yields significant tax savings.

However, there is a downside. When the property is sold, the tangible personal property gains are taxable as ordinary income due to § 1245 depreciation recapture, whereas the gain from the sale of the building is not subject to full recapture, is a § 1231 gain, and may receive long-term capital gain treatment.

EXAMPLE

49

Sanjay Enterprises, Ltd., acquires a residential rental building on January 1, 2015, for $300,000. Sanjay receives an offer of $450,000 for the building and sells it on December 23, 2016.

- Sanjay takes $20,909 [($300,000 × .03485) + ($300,000 × .03636 × $^{11.5}/_{12}$) = $20,909] of total depreciation for 2015 and 2016. The adjusted basis of the property is $279,091 ($300,000 − $20,909).

- Sanjay's recognized gain is $170,909 ($450,000 − $279,091).

- All of the gain is § 1231 gain.

Concept Summary 8.5 compares and contrasts the § 1245 and § 1250 depreciation recapture rules.

Concept Summary 8.5

Comparison of § 1245 and § 1250 Depreciation Recapture

	§ 1245	§ 1250
Property affected	All depreciable personal property, including items such as § 179 expense and § 197 amortization of intangibles such as goodwill, patents, and copyrights.	Nonresidential real property acquired after 1969 and before 1981, on which accelerated depreciation was taken. Residential rental real property acquired after 1975 and before 1987, on which accelerated depreciation was taken.
Depreciation recaptured	Potentially all depreciation taken. If the selling price is greater than or equal to the original cost, all depreciation is recaptured. If the selling price is between the adjusted basis and the original cost, only some depreciation is recaptured.	Normally, there is no depreciation recapture, but in the special situations listed above, there can be § 1250 depreciation recapture of additional depreciation (the excess of accelerated depreciation over straight-line depreciation). All depreciation taken if property disposed of in first year.
Limit on recapture	Lesser of depreciation taken or gain recognized.	Lesser of additional depreciation or gain recognized.
Treatment of gain exceeding recapture gain	Usually § 1231 gain.	Usually § 1231 gain.
Treatment of loss	No depreciation recapture; loss is usually § 1231 loss.	No depreciation recapture; loss is usually § 1231 loss.

8-9a Unrecaptured § 1250 Gain (Real Estate 25% Gain)

As noted previously in the chapter, *noncorporate taxpayers* pay tax at a maximum rate of 25 percent on their **unrecaptured § 1250 gain**. This gain represents that part of the gain on § 1250 property that is attributable to depreciation that was not recaptured by § 1250.

The procedure for computing this amount involves three distinct steps.

Step 1. Determine the part of the recognized gain that is attributable to *depreciation deductions* claimed in prior years.

Step 2. Apply § 1250 to determine the portion of the gain calculated in step 1 that is recaptured as ordinary income (if any).

Step 3. Subtract the gain recaptured under § 1250 (step 2) from the gain derived in step 1. This amount is the *unrecaptured § 1250 gain.*

Recall that for property placed in service after 1986, § 1250 generally does not apply, because such property is depreciated using the straight-line method under MACRS. As a result, *all* of the gain attributable to depreciation on such assets is *unrecaptured § 1250 gain.*

Linda placed two apartment buildings in service at a cost of $100,000 each. On each building, she claimed depreciation deductions of $78,000. Thus, her adjusted basis for each building is $22,000 ($100,000 cost − $78,000 depreciation deducted). Because the buildings were depreciated using the straight-line method, there is no § 1250 recapture. She now sells these buildings for $96,000 and $110,000, respectively, and computes her gain as follows.

EXAMPLE 50

	Building A	Building B
Amount realized	$ 96,000	$110,000
Adjusted basis	(22,000)	(22,000)
Recognized gain	$ 74,000	$ 88,000
Depreciation recaptured by § 1250	(–0–)	(–0–)
Remaining gain	$ 74,000	$ 88,000
Unrecaptured § 1250 gain	(74,000)	(78,000)
§ 1231 gain	None	$ 10,000

8-9b Additional Recapture for Corporations

Although depreciation recapture is generally the same for all taxpayers, corporations that sell depreciable real estate face an additional amount of depreciation recapture. Section 291(a)(1) requires recapture of 20 percent of the excess of the amount that would be recaptured under § 1245 (had § 1245 applied) over the amount actually recaptured under § 1250.

Red Corporation purchases nonresidential real property on May 1, 2001, for $800,000. Straight-line depreciation is taken in the amount of $316,239 before the property is sold on October 8, 2016, for $1.2 million.

EXAMPLE 51

First, determine the recognized gain:

Sales price		$1,200,000
Less: Adjusted basis—		
Cost of property	$ 800,000	
Less: Cost recovery	(316,239)	(483,761)
Recognized gain		$ 716,239

Second, determine the § 1245 recapture potential. This is the lesser of $716,239 (recognized gain) or $316,239 (cost recovery claimed).

Third, determine the normal § 1250 recapture amount:

Cost recovery taken	$ 316,239
Less: Straight-line cost recovery	(316,239)
§ 1250 ordinary income	$ –0–

continued

Fourth, because the taxpayer is a corporation, determine the additional § 291 amount:

§ 1245 recapture potential	$ 316,239
Less: § 1250 recapture amount	(–0–)
Excess § 1245 recapture potential	$ 316,239
Apply § 291 percentage	× 20%
Additional ordinary income under § 291	$ 63,248

Red Corporation's recognized gain of $716,239 is accounted for as follows:

Ordinary income under § 1250	$ –0–
Ordinary income under § 291	63,248
§ 1231 gain	652,991
Total recognized gain	$ 716,239

TAX PLANNING STRATEGIES   **Selling Depreciable Real Estate**

FRAMEWORK FOCUS: DEDUCTIONS

Strategy: Maximize Deductible Amounts.

FRAMEWORK FOCUS: TAX RATE

Strategy: Control the Character of Income and Deductions.

A building depreciated on an accelerated method eventually generates annual allowances that are smaller than the amount the straight-line method would have produced. Beyond that "cross-over" point, the *cumulative* amount of "additional depreciation" is reduced every year the asset is used. Doing so effectively converts gain for an individual taxpayer that would otherwise be subject to § 1250 recapture into "*unrecaptured § 1250 gain*," enabling the taxpayer to save the difference between the applicable tax rate on ordinary income and 25 percent.

Continuing to use the building, however, brings forth an array of important *nontax considerations*. Each year a building is used subjects it to additional maintenance expenses to keep it in operating condition. Moreover, a building's appeal to current and prospective tenants tends to decline over time as newer structures appear offering more modern amenities, such as wireless high-speed Internet access, and other conveniences. Finally, local real estate developments might produce lower resale prices that offset much, if not all, of the tax advantage obtained by holding the property for the additional time.

8-10 EXCEPTIONS TO §§ 1245 AND 1250

Recapture under §§ 1245 and 1250 does not apply to the following transactions.

8-10a Gifts

Depreciation recapture potential carries over to the donee.[27]

EXAMPLE 52

Wade gives his daughter, Helen, § 1245 property with an adjusted basis of $1,000. The amount of recapture potential is $700. Helen uses the property in her business and claims further depreciation of $100 before selling it for $1,900.

Helen's recognized gain is $1,000 [$1,900 amount realized − $900 adjusted basis ($1,000 carryover basis − $100 depreciation taken by Helen)], of which $800 is recaptured as ordinary income ($100 depreciation taken by Helen + $700 recapture potential carried over from Wade). The remaining gain of $200 is § 1231 gain. Even if Helen had used the property for personal purposes, the $700 recapture potential would have carried over.

---

[27]§§ 1245(b)(1) and 1250(d)(1) and Reg. §§ 1.1245–4(a)(1) and 1.1250–3(a)(1).

8-10b **Death**

Although not an attractive tax planning approach, death eliminates all recapture potential.[28] Depreciation recapture potential does not carry over from a decedent to an estate or an heir.

Assume the same facts as in the preceding example, except that Helen receives the property as a result of Wade's death and the property has a fair market value of $1,700 when Wade dies. The $700 recapture potential from Wade is extinguished at his death. Helen has a basis in the property equal to its fair market value at Wade's death ($1,700).

Helen will have a $300 gain when the property is sold because the selling price ($1,900) exceeds the property's adjusted basis of $1,600 ($1,700 basis to Helen − $100 depreciation) by $300. Because of § 1245, Helen has ordinary income of $100. The remaining gain of $200 is § 1231 gain.

8-10c **Charitable Transfers**

Depreciation recapture potential reduces the amount of any charitable contribution deduction.[29]

Bullfinch Corporation donates to a museum § 1245 property with a fair market value of $10,000 and an adjusted basis of $7,000. Assume that the depreciation recapture potential associated with this property is $2,000 (the amount of recapture that would occur if the property were sold).

The company's charitable contribution deduction (subject to the limitations discussed in Chapter 5) is $8,000 ($10,000 fair market value − $2,000 recapture potential).

8-10d **Certain Nontaxable Transactions**

In certain transactions, the transferor's adjusted basis for the property carries over to the transferee. If this is the case, any depreciation recapture potential also carries over to the transferee.[30] Included in this category are the following transfers of property:

- Nontaxable incorporations under § 351 (see Chapter 12).
- Certain liquidations of subsidiary corporations under § 332 (see Chapter 13).
- Nontaxable contributions to a partnership under § 721 (see Chapter 14).
- Nontaxable corporate reorganizations.

Gain may be recognized in these transactions if boot is received. If gain is recognized, it is treated as ordinary income to the extent of the recapture potential or the recognized gain, whichever is lower.[31]

8-10e **Like-Kind Exchanges and Involuntary Conversions**

As explained in Chapter 7, realized gain is recognized to the extent of boot received in a like-kind exchange. Realized gain is also recognized to the extent the proceeds from an involuntary conversion are not reinvested in similar property. Such recognized gain is subject to recapture as ordinary income under §§ 1245 and 1250. Any remaining recapture potential carries over to the property received in the exchange.

---

[28]§§ 1245(b)(2) and 1250(d)(2).

[29]§ 170(e)(1)(A) and Reg. § 1.170A–4(b)(1). In certain circumstances, § 1231 gain also reduces the amount of the charitable contribution. See § 170(e)(1)(B).

[30]§§ 1245(b)(3) and 1250(d)(3); Reg. §§ 1.1245–2(a)(4) and (c)(2), 1.1245–4(c), 1.1250–2(d)(1) and (3).

[31]§§ 1245(b)(3) and 1250(d)(3); Reg. §§ 1.1245–4(c) and 1.1250–3(c).

EXAMPLE 55

Crane Corporation exchanges § 1245 property with an adjusted basis of $300 for § 1245 property with a fair market value of $6,000 plus $1,000 cash (boot). The exchange qualifies as a like-kind exchange under § 1031. Crane's realized gain is $6,700 ($7,000 amount realized − $300 adjusted basis of property).

Because Crane received boot of $1,000, it recognizes gain to this extent. Assuming that the recapture potential is $7,500, Crane recognizes § 1245 gain of $1,000. The remaining recapture potential of $6,500 carries over to the like-kind property received.

DIGGING DEEPER 12   In-depth coverage can be found on this book's companion website: www.cengagebrain.com

8-11 REPORTING PROCEDURES

Noncapital gains and losses are reported on Form 4797 (Sales of Business Property). However, before Form 4797 is filled out, Part B of Form 4684 (Casualties and Thefts) must be completed to determine whether any casualties will enter into the § 1231 computation procedure. Recall that recognized gains from § 1231 asset casualties may be recaptured by § 1245 or § 1250. These gains do not appear on Form 4684. The § 1231 gains and nonpersonal-use long-term capital gains are netted against § 1231 and nonpersonal-use long-term capital losses on Form 4684 to determine whether there is a net gain to transfer to Form 4797, Part I.

DIGGING DEEPER 13   In-depth coverage can be found on this book's companion website: www.cengagebrain.com

TAX PLANNING STRATEGIES   Timing of Recapture

FRAMEWORK FOCUS: TAX RATE

Strategy: Shift Net Income from High-Bracket Years to Low-Bracket Years.
Shift Net Income from High-Bracket Taxpayers to Low-Bracket Taxpayers.

Because recapture is usually not triggered until the property is sold or disposed of, it may be possible to plan for recapture in low-bracket or loss years. If a taxpayer has net operating loss carryovers that are about to expire, the recognition of ordinary income from recapture may be advisable to absorb the loss carryovers.

EXAMPLE 56

Angel Corporation has a $15,000 net operating loss carryover that will expire this year. It owns a machine that it plans to sell in the early part of next year. The expected gain of $17,000 from the sale of the machine will be recaptured as ordinary income under § 1245. Angel sells the machine before the end of this year and offsets $15,000 of the ordinary income by the net operating loss carryover.

It is also possible to postpone recapture or to shift the burden of recapture to others. For example, recapture is avoided upon the disposition of a § 1231 asset if the taxpayer replaces the property by entering into a like-kind exchange. In this instance, recapture potential is merely carried over to the newly acquired property (refer to Example 55).

Recapture can be shifted to others through the gratuitous transfer of § 1245 or § 1250 property to family members. A subsequent sale of such property by the donee will trigger recapture to the donee rather than the donor (refer to Example 52). This technique is advisable when the donee is in a lower income tax bracket than the donor.

REFOCUS ON THE BIG PICTURE

CAPITAL GAINS AND LOSSES, § 1231 GAINS AND LOSSES, AND RECAPTURE

The land, stock, franchise, and home owned by Alice are all capital assets and will produce capital gain or loss when sold. Accordingly, Alice will have a long-term capital gain of $48,000 from the sale of the land, a long-term capital gain of $6,000 from the sale of 300 shares of inherited AppleCo stock, a short-term capital loss of $4,000 from the sale of the other 200 shares of AppleCo stock, a short-term capital gain of $1,000 from the sale of the franchise, and a $125,000 long-term capital gain from the sale of the house. The treatment given to the Eagle stock will depend on the nature of its disposition (see Example 10).

For the patent, because Alice is a "holder" of the patent, it will qualify for the beneficial capital gain rate regardless of the holding period if the patent should produce income in excess of her $50,000 investment. However, if Alice loses money on the investment, she will be able to deduct only $3,000 of the loss per year against her ordinary income (assuming that there are no offsetting capital gains in the year of a sale).

The depreciable property owned by Alice's husband is § 1231 property. The $45,000 gain from the sale of the property ($60,000 amount realized − $15,000 adjusted basis) is subject to depreciation recapture under § 1245. Accordingly, the first $35,000 of the gain (up to the amount of depreciation taken on the property) is taxed as ordinary income. The remaining $10,000 is § 1231 gain and is given long-term capital gain treatment.

As a result of these transactions where the amount of gain or loss is determined, Alice and her husband have a net long-term capital gain of $189,000 ($48,000 + $6,000 + $125,000 + $10,000) and a net short-term capital loss of $3,000 ($1,000 gain − $4,000 loss). The long-term capital gain and short-term capital loss are netted, so the final result is a net capital gain of $186,000, which is taxed at the 15 or 20 percent tax rate. Alice and her husband also report $35,000 of ordinary income on their joint income tax return because of the depreciation recapture provisions.

What If?

What if the depreciable business property was worth only $10,000 when it was sold? In this case, there is no depreciation recapture, and the $5,000 loss is deductible as an ordinary loss under § 1231.

Suggested Readings

Tom Crice, "The Perils of Winning: Settlement Payments, Trade Secrets, and Taxes," *Practical Tax Strategies*, September 2012.

Melanie James, "Factors Influencing Reduction in Value for Potential Capital Gains Tax," *Practical Tax Strategies*, April 2014.

Timothy R. Koski, "Bitcoin—Tax Planning in the Uncertain World of Virtual Currency," *Practical Tax Strategies*, December 2014.

"LLC Members Received Capital Gains Income from Sale of LLC's Assets," *Practical Tax Strategies*, October 2012.

John Przybylski, "Managing Capital Gain to Minimize the Pain," *Practical Tax Strategies*, July 2015.

Key Terms

Capital assets, 8-2	Long-term nonpersonal-use capital assets, 8-25	Section 1231 lookback, 8-28
Capital gains, 8-2	Net capital gain, 8-18	Section 1231 property, 8-23
Capital losses, 8-2	Net capital loss, 8-18	Section 1245 property, 8-30
Collectibles, 8-17	Options, 8-7	Section 1245 recapture, 8-29
Franchise, 8-10	Patent, 8-9	Section 1250 property, 8-31
Holding period, 8-13	Qualified small business stock, 8-21	Section 1250 recapture, 8-31
Lessee, 8-12	Sale or exchange, 8-6	Short sale, 8-14
Lessor, 8-12	Section 1231 gains and losses, 8-23	Unrecaptured § 1250 gain, 8-32

Computational Exercises

1. **LO.1** Dexter owns a large tract of land and subdivides it for sale. Assume that Dexter meets all of the requirements of § 1237 and during the tax year sells the first eight lots to eight different buyers for $22,000 each. Dexter's basis in each lot sold is $15,000, and he incurs total selling expenses of $900 on each sale. What is the amount of Dexter's capital gain and ordinary income?

Critical Thinking 2. **LO.2** Shelia purchases $50,000 of newly issued Gingo Corporation bonds for $45,000. The bonds have original issue discount (OID) of $5,000. After Sheila amortized $2,300 of OID and held the bonds for four years, she sold the bonds for $48,000. What is the amount and character of her gain or loss?

3. **LO.2** Olivia wants to buy some vacant land for investment purposes. She currently cannot afford the full purchase price. Instead, Olivia pays the landowner $8,000 to obtain an option to buy the land for $175,000 anytime in the next four years. Fourteen months after purchasing the option, Olivia sells the option for $10,000. What is the amount and character of Olivia's gain or loss?

4. **LO.4** Coline has the following capital gain and loss transactions for 2016.

Short-term capital gain	$ 5,000
Short-term capital loss	(2,100)
Long-term capital gain (28%)	6,000
Long-term capital gain (15%)	2,000
Long-term capital loss (28%)	(10,500)

After the capital gain and loss netting process, what is the amount and character of Coline's gain or loss?

5. **LO.4** Elliott has the following capital gain and loss transactions for 2016.

Short-term capital gain	$ 1,500
Short-term capital loss	(3,600)
Long-term capital gain (28%)	12,000
Long-term capital gain (25%)	4,800
Long-term capital gain (15%)	6,000
Long-term capital loss (28%)	(4,500)
Long-term capital loss (15%)	(9,000)

After the capital gain and loss netting process, what is the amount and character of Elliott's gain or loss?

6. **LO.6, 7** Renata Corporation purchased equipment in 2014 for $180,000 and has taken $83,000 of regular MACRS depreciation. Renata Corporation sells the equipment in 2016 for $110,000. What is the amount and character of Renata's gain or loss?

7. **LO.6, 7** Jacob purchased business equipment for $56,000 in 2013 and has taken $35,000 of regular MACRS depreciation. Jacob sells the equipment in 2016 for $26,000. What is the amount and character of Jacob's gain or loss?

8. **LO.6, 7** Sissie owns two items of business equipment. Both were purchased in 2012 for $100,000, both have a 7-year MACRS recovery period, and both have an adjusted basis of $37,490. Sissie is considering selling these assets in 2016. One of them is worth $60,000, and the other is worth $23,000. Because both items were used in her business, Sissie simply assumes that the loss on one will offset the gain from the other and that the net gain or loss will increase or reduce her business income. What is the amount and character of Sissie's gain or loss?

9. **LO.7** An apartment building was acquired in 2007. The depreciation taken on the building was $123,000, and the building was sold for a $34,000 gain. What is the maximum amount of *25% gain*?

10. **LO.7** In a § 1031 like-kind exchange, Rafael exchanges equipment that originally cost $200,000. On the date of the exchange, the equipment given up has an adjusted basis of $85,000 and a fair market value of $110,000. Rafael pays $15,000 and receives equipment with a fair market value of $125,000. What is the amount and character of Rafael's gain or loss?

11. **LO.7** Gaston Corporation distributes § 1245 property as a dividend to its share-holders. The property's fair market value is $580,000, and the adjusted basis is $560,000. In addition, the amount of the recapture potential is $55,000. What is the amount and character of Gaston's gain or loss?

Critical Thinking

Problems

12. **LO.1** An individual taxpayer sells some used assets at a garage sale. Why are none of the proceeds taxable in most situations?

Issue ID

13. **LO.1** Alison owns a painting that she received as a gift from her aunt 10 years ago. The aunt created the painting. Alison has displayed the painting in her home and has never attempted to sell it. Recently, a visitor noticed the painting and offered Alison $5,000 for it. If Alison decides to sell the painting, what tax issues does she face?

Issue ID

14. **LO.1** During the year, Eugene had the four property transactions summarized below. Eugene is a collector of antique glassware and occasionally sells a piece to get funds to buy another. What are the amount and nature of the gain or loss from each of these transactions?

Property	Date Acquired	Date Sold	Adjusted Basis	Sales Price
Antique vase	06/18/05	05/23/16	$37,000	$42,000
Blue Growth Fund (100 shares)	12/23/07	11/22/16	22,000	38,000
Orange bonds	02/12/08	04/11/16	34,000	42,000*
Green stock (100 shares)	02/14/16	11/23/16	11,000	13,000

*The sales price included $750 of accrued interest income.

15. **LO.1** Rennie owns a video game arcade. He buys vintage video games from estates, often at much less than the retail value of the property. He usually installs the vintage video games in a special section of his video game arcade that appeals to players of "classic" video games. Recently, Rennie sold a classic video game that a

Decision Making

customer "just had to have." Rennie paid $11,250 for it, owned it for 14 months, and sold it for $18,000. Rennie had suspected that this particular classic video game would be of interest to collectors; so he had it refurbished, put it on display in his video arcade, and listed it for sale on the Internet. No customers in the arcade had played it other than those testing it before considering it for purchase. Rennie would like the gain on the sale of the classic video game to be a long-term capital gain. Did he achieve that objective? Why or why not?

16. **LO.1** George is the owner of numerous classic automobiles. His intention is to hold the automobiles until they increase in value and then sell them. He rents the automobiles for use in various events (e.g., antique automobile shows) while he is holding them. In 2016, he sold a classic automobile for $1.5 million. He had held the automobile for five years, and it had a tax basis of $750,000. Was the automobile a capital asset? Why or why not?

Communications 17. **LO.1** Hyacinth, Inc., is a dealer in securities. The firm has spotted a fast-rising company and would like to buy and hold its stock for investment. The stock is currently selling for $2 per share, and Hyacinth thinks it will climb to $40 a share within two years. How can Hyacinth ensure that any gain it realizes will be taxed as long-term capital gain? Draft a letter responding to Hyacinth's inquiry. The firm's address is 200 Catamon Drive, Great Falls, MT 59406.

18. **LO.1** Eagle Partners meets all of the requirements of § 1237 (subdivided realty). In 2016, Eagle Partners begins selling lots and sells four separate lots to four different purchasers. Eagle Partners also sells two contiguous lots to another purchaser. The sales price of each lot is $30,000. The partnership's basis for each lot is $15,000. Selling expenses are $500 per lot.
    a.   What are the realized and recognized gain?
    b.   Explain the nature of the gain (i.e., ordinary income or capital gain).
    c.   Would your answers change if, instead, the lots sold to the fifth purchaser were not contiguous? If so, how?

Critical Thinking 19. **LO.1, 2** Benny purchased $400,000 of Peach Corporation face value bonds for $320,000 on November 13, 2015. The bonds had been issued with $80,000 of original issue discount because Peach was in financial difficulty in 2015. On December 3, 2016, Benny sold the bonds for $283,000 after amortizing $1,000 of the original issue discount. What are the nature and amount of Benny's gain or loss?

20. **LO.2** Carla was the owner of vacant land that she was holding for investment. She paid $2 million for the land in 2014. Raymond was an investor in vacant land. He thought Carla's land might be the site of an exit ramp from a new freeway. Raymond gave Carla $836,000 for an option on her land in 2015. The option was good for two years and gave Raymond the ability to purchase Carla's land for $4,765,000. The freeway was not approved by the government, and Raymond's option expired in 2016. Does Carla have $836,000 of long-term capital gain upon the expiration of the option? Explain.

Decision Making 21. **LO.2, 3, 4** Mac, an inventor, obtained a patent on a chemical process to clean old aluminum siding so that it can be easily repainted. Mac has a $50,000 tax basis in the patent. Mac does not have the capital to begin manufacturing and selling this product, so he has done nothing with the patent since obtaining it two years ago.

Now a group of individuals has approached him and offered two alternatives. Under one alternative, they will pay Mac $600,000 (payable evenly over the next 15 years) for the exclusive right to manufacture and sell the product. Under the other, they will form a business and contribute capital to it to begin manufacturing and selling the product; Mac will receive 20% of the company's shares of stock in exchange for all of his patent rights. Discuss which alternative is better for Mac.

22. **LO.2** Blue Corporation and Fuchsia Corporation are engaged in a contract negotiation over the use of Blue's trademarked name, DateSiteForSeniors. For a one-time payment of $45,000, Blue licensed Fuchsia to use the name DateSiteForSeniors, and the license requires that Fuchsia pay Blue a royalty every time a new customer signs up on Fuchsia's website. Blue is a developer of "website ideas" that it then licenses to other companies such as Fuchsia. Did Fuchsia purchase a franchise right from Blue, or did Fuchsia purchase the name DateSiteForSeniors from Blue?

23. **LO.2** Freys, Inc., sells a 12-year franchise to Red Company. The franchise contains many restrictions on how Red may operate its store. For instance, Red cannot use less than Grade 10 Idaho potatoes; must fry the potatoes at a constant 410 degrees; must dress store personnel in Freys-approved uniforms; and must have a Freys sign that meets detailed specifications on size, color, and construction. When the franchise contract is signed, Red makes a noncontingent $160,000 payment to Freys. During the same year, Red pays Freys $300,000—14% of Red's sales. How does Freys treat each of these payments? How does Red treat each of the payments?

24. **LO.3** Maria held vacant land that qualified as an investment asset. She purchased the vacant land on April 10, 2012. She exchanged the vacant land for a rental house in a qualifying like-kind exchange on January 22, 2016. Maria was going to hold the house for several years and then sell it. However, she got an "offer she could not refuse" and sold it on November 22, 2016, for a substantial gain. What was Maria's holding period for the house?

25. **LO.3** Thrasher Corporation sells short 100 shares of ARC stock at $20 per share on January 15, 2016. It buys 200 shares of ARC stock on April 1, 2016, at $25 per share. On May 2, 2016, Thrasher closes the short sale by delivering 100 of the shares purchased on April 1.   Critical Thinking

    a. What are the amount and nature of Thrasher's loss upon closing the short sale?

    b. When does the holding period for the remaining 100 shares begin?

    c. If Thrasher sells (at $27 per share) the remaining 100 shares on January 20, 2017, what will be the nature of its gain or loss?

26. **LO.1, 3, 4** Elaine Case (single with no dependents) has the following transactions in 2016:   Communications

AGI (exclusive of capital gains and losses)	$240,000
Long-term capital gain	22,000
Long-term capital loss	(8,000)
Short-term capital gain	19,000
Short-term capital loss	(23,000)

    What is Elaine's net capital gain or loss? Draft a letter to Elaine describing how the net capital gain or loss will be treated on her tax return. Assume that Elaine's income from other sources puts her in the 39.6% bracket. Elaine's address is 300 Ireland Avenue, Shepherdstown, WV 25443.

27. **LO.4** Sally has taxable income of $160,000 as of November 30 of this year. She wants to sell a Rodin sculpture that has appreciated $90,000 since she purchased it six years ago, but she does not want to pay more than $15,000 of additional tax on the transaction. Sally also owns various stocks, some of which are currently worth less than their basis. How can she achieve her desired result?   Decision Making

28. **LO.5** Platinum, Inc., has determined its taxable income as $215,000 before considering the results of its capital gain or loss transactions. Platinum has a short-term capital loss of $24,000, a long-term capital loss of $38,000, and a short-term capital gain of $39,000. What is Platinum's taxable income? What (if any) are the amount and nature of its capital loss carryover?

Ethics and Equity 29. **LO.1, 4** The taxpayer is an antiques collector and is going to sell an antique purchased many years ago for a large gain. The facts and circumstances indicate that the taxpayer might be classified as a dealer rather than an investor in antiques. The taxpayer will save $40,000 in taxes if the gain is treated as long-term capital gain rather than as ordinary income. The taxpayer is considering the following options as ways to ensure the $40,000 tax savings.

- Give the antique to his daughter, who is an investment banker, to sell.
- Merely assume that he has held the antique as an investment.
- Exchange the antique in a like-kind exchange for another antique he wants.

One of the tax preparers the taxpayer has contacted has said that he would be willing to prepare the return under the second option. Would you? Why or why not? Evaluate the other options.

Communications 30. **LO.1, 4** In 2016, Bertha Jarow had a $28,000 loss from the sale of a personal residence. She also purchased from an individual inventor for $7,000 (and resold in two months for $18,000) a patent on a rubber bonding process. The patent had not yet been reduced to practice. Bertha purchased the patent as an investment. In addition, she had the following capital gains and losses from stock transactions:

Long-term capital loss	($ 6,000)
Long-term capital loss carryover from 2015	(12,000)
Short-term capital gain	21,000
Short-term capital loss	(7,000)

What is Bertha's net capital gain or loss? Draft a letter to Bertha explaining the tax treatment of all of these transactions. Assume that Bertha's income from other sources puts her in the 28% bracket. Bertha's address is 1120 West Street, Ashland, OR 97520.

Issue ID 31. **LO.1, 3, 4** Bridgette is known as the "doll lady." She started collecting dolls as a child, always received one or more dolls as gifts on her birthday, never sold any dolls, and eventually owned 600 dolls. She is retiring and moving to a small apartment and has decided to sell her collection. She lists the dolls on an Internet auction site and, to her great surprise, receives an offer from another doll collector of $45,000 for the entire collection. Bridgette sells the entire collection, except for five dolls she purchased during the last year. She had owned all of the dolls sold for more than a year. What tax factors should Bridgette consider in deciding how to report the sale?

Critical Thinking 32. **LO.1, 2, 4** Two years ago, Harriet Company (an unincorporated entity) developed a process for preserving doughnuts that gives the doughnuts a much longer shelf life. The process is not patented or copyrighted, and only Harriet knows how it works. A conglomerate has approached Harriet with an offer to purchase the formula for the process. Specifically, the offer allows Harriet to choose between the following. Which option should Harriet accept?

Decision Making

- $650,000 cash for the formula and a 10-year covenant not to compete, paying Harriet $65,000 per year for 10 years.
- $650,000 cash for a 10-year covenant not to compete, and an annual $65,000 royalty for the formula, payable for 10 years.

Communications 33. **LO.6** A sculpture that Tulip & Co. held for investment was destroyed in a flood. The sculpture was insured, and Tulip had a $60,000 gain from this casualty. It also had a $17,000 loss from an uninsured antique vase that was destroyed by the flood. The vase was also held for investment. Tulip had no other property transactions during the year and has no nonrecaptured § 1231 losses from prior years. Both the sculpture and the vase had been held for more than one year when the flood occurred. Compute Tulip's net gain or loss, and identify how it would be treated. Write a letter to Tulip, explaining the nature of the gain or loss. Tulip's address is 2367 Meridian Road, Hannibal, MO 63401.

34. **LO.6** Harold, a CPA, has a new client who recently moved to town. Harold pre-pares the client's current-year tax return, which shows a net § 1231 gain. Harold calls the client to request copies of the returns for the preceding five years to determine if there are any § 1231 lookback losses. The client says that the returns are "still buried in the moving mess somewhere" and cannot be found. The client also says that he does not remember any § 1231 net losses on the prior year returns. What should Harold do? Justify your answer.

Ethics and Equity

35. **LO.6** Geranium, Inc., has the following net § 1231 results for each of the years shown. What is the nature of the net gain in 2015 and 2016?

Tax Year	Net § 1231 Loss	Net § 1231 Gain
2011	$18,000	
2012	33,000	
2013	42,000	
2014		$41,000
2015		30,000
2016		41,000

36. **LO.6** Delphinium Company owns two parcels of land (§ 1231 assets). One parcel can be sold at a loss of $60,000, and the other parcel can be sold at a gain of $70,000. The company has no nonrecaptured § 1231 losses from prior years. The parcels could be sold at any time because potential purchasers are abundant. The company has a $35,000 short-term capital loss carryover from a prior tax year and no capital assets that could be sold to generate long-term capital gains. Both land parcels have been held more than one year. What should Delphinium do based upon these facts? (Assume that tax rates are constant, and ignore the present value of future cash flows.)

Decision Making

37. **LO.6, 7** Siena Industries (a sole proprietorship) sold three § 1231 assets on October 10, 2016. Data on these property dispositions are as follows.

Asset	Cost	Acquired	Depreciation	Sold for
Rack	$100,000	10/10/12	$62,000	$85,000
Forklift	35,000	10/16/13	23,000	5,000
Bin	87,000	03/12/15	34,000	60,000

a. Determine the amount and the character of the recognized gain or loss from the disposition of each asset in 2016.

b. Assuming that Siena has no nonrecaptured net § 1231 losses from prior years, how much of the recognized gains are treated as long-term capital gains?

38. **LO.6, 7** On December 1, 2014, Lavender Manufacturing Company (a corporation) purchased another company's assets, including a patent. The patent was used in Lavender's manufacturing operations; $49,500 was allocated to the patent, and it was amortized at the rate of $275 per month. On July 30, 2016, Lavender sold the patent for $95,000. Twenty months of amortization had been taken on the pat-ent. What are the amount and nature of the gain Lavender recognizes on the dispo-sition of the patent? Write a letter to Lavender, discussing the treatment of the gain. Lavender's address is 6734 Grover Street, Boothbay Harbor, ME 04538. The letter should be addressed to Bill Cubit, Controller.

Communications

39. **LO.6, 7** Larry is the sole proprietor of a trampoline shop. During 2016, the following transactions occurred.

- Unimproved land adjacent to the store was condemned by the city on February 1. The condemnation proceeds were $15,000. The land, acquired in 1986, had an allocable basis of $40,000. Larry has additional parking across the street and plans to use the condemnation proceeds to build his inventory.
- A truck used to deliver trampolines was sold on January 2 for $3,500. The truck was purchased on January 2, 2012, for $6,000. On the date of sale, the adjusted basis was zero.
- Larry sold an antique rowing machine at an auction. Net proceeds were $4,900. The rowing machine was purchased as used equipment 17 years ago for $5,200 and is fully depreciated.
- Larry sold an apartment building for $300,000 on September 1. The rental property was purchased on September 1, 2013, for $150,000 and was being depreciated over a 27.5-year MACRS life using the straight-line method. At the date of sale, the adjusted basis was $124,783.
- Larry's personal yacht was stolen on September 5. The yacht had been purchased in August at a cost of $25,000. The fair market value immediately preceding the theft was $19,600. Larry was insured for 50% of the original cost, and he received $12,500 on December 1.
- Larry sold a Buick on May 1 for $9,600. The vehicle had been used exclusively for personal purposes. It was purchased on September 1, 2012, for $20,800.
- Larry's trampoline stretching machine (owned two years) was stolen on May 5, but the business's insurance company will not pay any of the machine's value because Larry failed to pay the insurance premium. The machine had a fair market value of $8,000 and an adjusted basis of $6,000 at the time of theft.
- Larry had AGI of $102,000 from sources other than those described above.
- Larry has no nonrecaptured § 1231 lookback losses.

   a. For each transaction, what are the amount and nature of recognized gain or loss?
   b. What is Larry's 2016 AGI?

Critical Thinking 40. **LO.6, 7** A business building on which straight-line depreciation of $13,000 was taken is sold on the installment basis for $100,000 with $20,000 down and four yearly installments of $20,000 plus interest. The adjusted basis for the building is $35,000 at the time of the sale. The building had been held for more than 12 months. What are the amount and nature of the recognized gain?

41. **LO.7** Nicholas owns business equipment with a $155,000 adjusted basis; he paid $200,000 for the equipment, and it is currently worth $173,000. Nicholas dies suddenly, and his son Alvin inherits the property. What is Alvin's basis for the property? What happens to the § 1245 depreciation recapture potential?

BRIDGE DISCIPLINE

1. Using an online research service, find the audited financial statements of a major U.S. corporation.
   a. List some of the items that the corporation reports as having different treatment for tax and financial accounting purposes. These items often are mentioned in the footnotes to the statements.
   b. List two or more such items that seem to increase the taxpayer's after-tax income and two or more that seem to decrease it.

Research Problems

Note: Solutions to Research Problems can be prepared by using the Checkpoint® Student Edition online research product, which is available to accompany this text. It is also possible to prepare solutions to the Research Problems by using tax research materials found in a standard tax library.

Research Problem 1. Clyde had worked for many years as the chief executive of Red Industries, Inc., and had been a major shareholder. Clyde and the company had a falling out, and Clyde was terminated. Clyde and Red executed a document under which Clyde's stock in Red would be redeemed and Clyde would agree not to compete against Red in its geographic service area. After extensive negotiations between the parties, Clyde agreed to surrender his Red stock in exchange for $600,000. Clyde's basis in his shares was $143,000, and he had held the shares for 17 years. The agreement made no explicit allocation of any of the $600,000 to Clyde's agreement not to compete against Red. How should Clyde treat the $600,000 payment on his 2016 tax return?

Research Problem 2. Ali owns 100 shares of Brown Corporation stock. He purchased the stock at five different times and at five different prices per share as indicated.

Decision Making

Share Block	Number of Shares	Per-Share Price	Purchase Date
A	10	$60	10/10/1999
B	20	20	08/11/2000
C	15	15	10/24/2001
D	35	30	04/23/2002
E	20	25	07/28/2003

On April 28, 2016, Ali will sell 40 shares of Brown stock for $40 per share. All of Ali's shares are held by his stockbroker. The broker's records track when the shares were purchased. May Ali designate the shares he sells? If so, which shares should he sell? Assume that Ali wants to maximize his gain because he has a capital loss carryforward.

Research Problem 3. Siva Nathaniel owns various plots of land in Fulton County, Georgia. He acquired the land at various times during the last 20 years. About every fourth year, Siva subdivides into lots one of the properties he owns. He then has water, sewer, natural gas, and electricity hookups put in each lot and paves new streets. Siva has always treated his sales of such lots as sales of capital assets. His previous tax returns were prepared by an accountant whose practice you recently purchased. Has the proper tax treatment been used on the prior tax returns? Explain.

Partial list of research aids:
§§ 1221 and 1237.
Jesse W. and Betty J. English, 65 TCM 2160, T.C.Memo. 1993–111.

Use the tax resources of the Internet to address the following questions. Do not restrict your search to the Web, but include a review of newsgroups and general reference materials, practitioner sites and resources, primary sources of the tax law, chat rooms and discussion groups, and other opportunities.

Internet Activity

Research Problem 4. Find a website, other than the IRS website, that discusses the taxation of short sales of securities.

Research Problem 5. Perform a Google search to find information about capital gains tax rates worldwide (and across U.S. states). Try searching for: "capital gains rate by country (state)." What jurisdiction has the highest capital gains tax rate? What U.S. states have high capital gains tax rates?

Roger CPA Review Questions

1. Identify which of the following is a capital asset:

   I.   A canvas painting of a portrait client, in the painter's hands
   II. Depreciable fixtures in a business parking lot
   III. Office supplies held by a business

   a. II only
   b. II and III only
   c. III only
   d. None of the above

2. On January 15 of the current year, Kreutzer, an individual, received as an inheritance from Gladstone's estate shares of stock worth $25,000. Gladstone had purchased the shares in June of the previous year for $20,000, and the shares were worth $25,000 at Gladstone's date of death in November of the previous year. The executor of Gladstone's estate did not elect to use the alternate valuation date. In March of the current year, Kreutzer sold the shares for $27,000. As a result of the sale, what is the amount and type of gain reported by Kreutzer?

   a. $7,000 long-term capital gain
   b. $2,000 short-term capital gain
   c. $7,000 short-term capital gain
   d. $2,000 long-term capital gain

3. In 2016, Colossus Corporation incurred a net capital loss in the amount of $25,000. Colossus had the following net capital gains in the previous five years:

   2015: $7,000
   2014: $2,000
   2013: $5,000
   2012: $4,000
   2011: $3,000

   How much of the 2016 net capital loss may Colossus carry over to 2017?

   a. $0
   b. $25,000
   c. $11,000
   d. $4,000

4. The following facts apply to Eliot, an individual, in the current year:

   April 2: Sold shares of stock, purchased on April 1 of the previous year, for a $2,000 gain.

   May 15: Sold equipment used in Eliot's business, which had been purchased in July of the previous year, for a $2,000 gain.

   July 12: Sold shares of stock, purchased in February of the previous year, for a $7,000 gain.

   November 3: Sold equipment used in Eliot's business, which had been purchased in January of the current year, for a $1,000 loss.

   December 9: Sold shares of stock, purchased on February 22 of the current year, for a $3,000 loss.

   Considering only the above facts, what is Eliot's net capital gain for the current year?

   a. $7,000 long-term capital gain
   b. $9,000 long-term capital gain
   c. $5,000 long-term capital gain
   d. $6,000 long-term capital gain

5. Joe purchased a van for $30,000 on February 1, 2014, for use with his business, Crew Airport Transport. Joe elected to take the § 179 deduction for the entire cost. On January 1, 2016, Joe sold the van for $20,000. What were the tax effects of this transaction?

    a. $10,000 loss

    b. $20,000 capital gain

    c. $20,000 ordinary gain

    d. $10,000 capital gain, $10,000 ordinary gain

6. In year 3, Daniels, an individual, sold depreciable equipment for $21,000 that had an adjusted basis of $12,000, resulting in a $9,000 gain. The property had cost Daniels $20,000 when purchased in year 1, and $8,000 of MACRS depreciation had been taken. How should Daniels report the gain on Daniels' year 3 tax return?

    a. As a long-term capital gain of $9,000

    b. As an ordinary gain of $1,800 and a § 1231 gain of $7,200

    c. As an ordinary gain of $8,000 and a § 1231 gain of $1,000

    d. As an ordinary gain of $7,200 and a § 1231 gain of $1,800

7. Cowabunga Corp. had a highly profitable year 4, during which it purchased $1,000,000 in tangible personal property and elected to claim the highest depreciation expense allowed for tax purposes under § 179. In year 6, Cowabunga sells the tangible personal property, which now has an adjusted basis of $200,000 as a result of the heavy depreciation taken in years 4 and 5. Had only MACRS depreciation been taken on the property, its adjusted basis at the time of sale would have been $800,000. At a sales price of $930,000, how much of the $730,000 realized gain must be reported as ordinary gain for tax purposes?

    a. $720,000

    b. $600,000

    c. $0

    d. $730,000

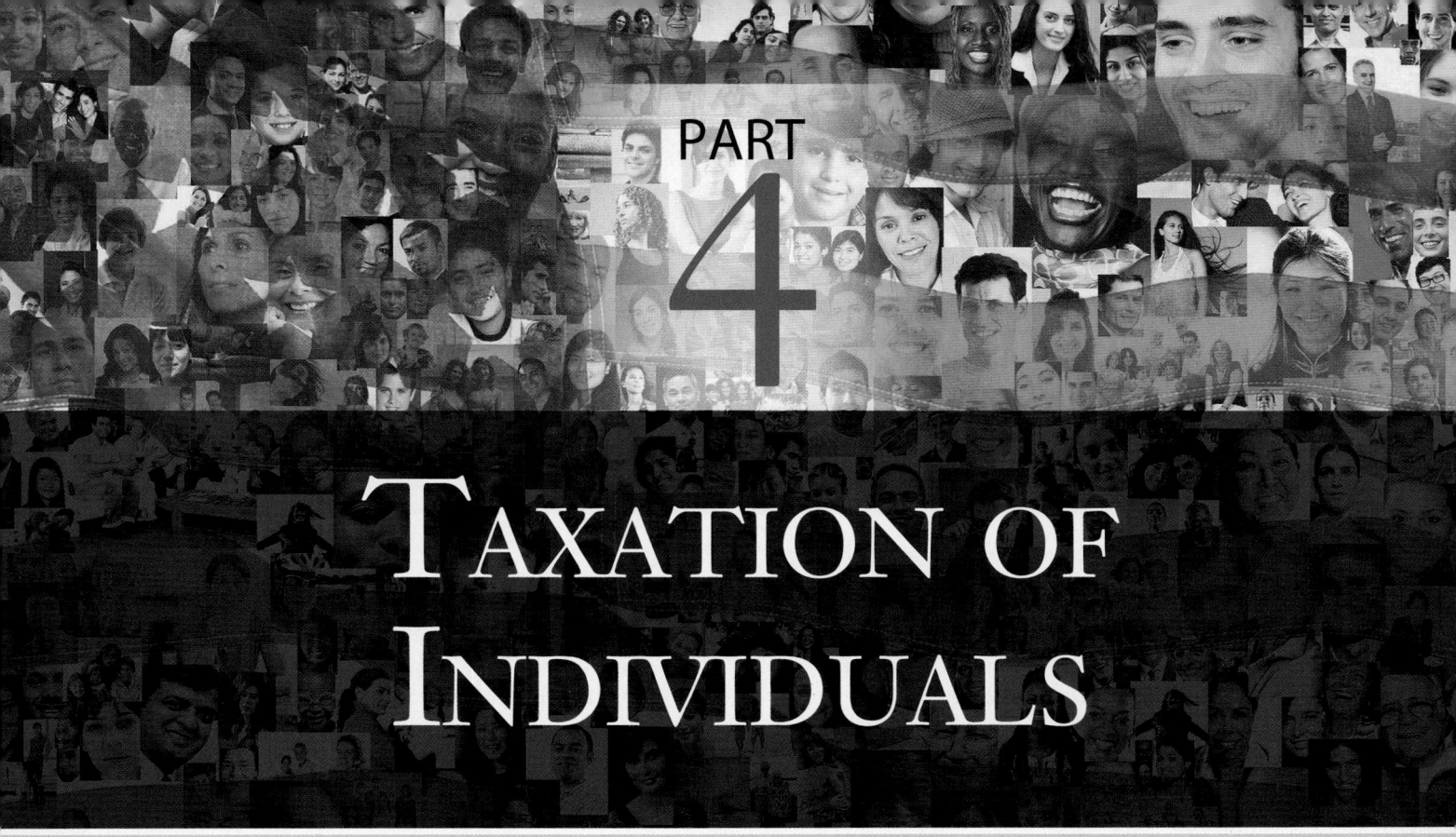

PART 4

TAXATION OF INDIVIDUALS

Part 4 focuses on numerous tax concepts and rules for individuals. The topics are unique to individual taxpayers, including personal exemptions, filing status, itemized deductions, sole proprietorship provisions, and the kiddie tax. Then we discuss various education credits, the earned income credit, and relevant provisions of the Affordable Care Act.

Individuals as the Taxpayer

LEARNING OBJECTIVES: *After completing Chapter 9, you should be able to:*

LO.1 Describe and apply the components of the Federal income tax formula for individuals.

LO.2 Explain the standard deduction and evaluate its choice in arriving at taxable income.

LO.3 Apply the rules for arriving at personal exemptions.

LO.4 Explain the rules for determining dependency exemptions.

LO.5 Choose the proper filing status and identify the related filing requirements.

LO.6 Demonstrate the proper procedures for determining the tax liability.

LO.7 Identify and report kiddie tax situations.

CHAPTER OUTLINE

TAX TALK *I'm proud of paying taxes in the United States. The only thing is—I could be just as proud for half the money.* —Arthur Godfrey

THE BIG PICTURE

A DIVIDED HOUSEHOLD

Polly maintains a household in which she lives with her unemployed husband (Nick), stepdaughter (Paige), and a family friend (Maude). She provides more than one-half of the support for both Paige and Maude. Maude was fatally injured in an automobile accident in February, and Polly paid for her hospitalization and funeral expenses. Paige, an accomplished gymnast, graduated from high school last year. Paige has a part-time job but spends most of her time training and looking for an athletic scholarship to the "right" college. In March, Nick left for parts unknown and has not been seen or heard from since. Polly was more surprised than distressed over Nick's unexpected departure.

Based on these facts, what are Polly's income tax concerns for the current year?

Read the chapter and formulate your response.

The individual income tax accounts for approximately 47 percent of Federal budget receipts, compared with approximately 13 percent for the corporate income tax. The tax laws affecting individuals have become increasingly complex in recent years as the government adds new laws to protect or increase this important source of revenue. Taxpayers respond to each new tax act with techniques to exploit loopholes, and the government responds with loophole-closing provisions, making the individual income tax law even more complex.[1]

Describe and apply the components of the Federal income tax formula for individuals.

9-1 THE INDIVIDUAL TAX FORMULA

Individuals are subject to Federal income tax based on taxable income. This chapter explains how taxable income and the income tax of an individual taxpayer are determined. To compute taxable income, it is necessary to understand the tax formula in Concept Summary 9.1.

Concept Summary 9.1

Individual Income Tax Formula

Income (broadly defined)	$xx,xxx
Less: Exclusions	(x,xxx)
Gross income	$xx,xxx
Less: Deductions *for* adjusted gross income	(x,xxx)
Adjusted gross income (AGI)	$xx,xxx
Less: The greater of—	
Total itemized deductions *or* standard deduction	(x,xxx)
Less: Personal and dependency exemptions	(x,xxx)
Taxable income	$xx,xxx
Tax on taxable income (see Tax Tables or Tax Rate Schedules)	$ x,xxx
Less: Tax credits (including income taxes withheld and prepaid)	(xxx)
Tax due (or refund)	$ xxx

Although this formula is rather simple, determining an individual's taxable income can be quite complex because of the numerous provisions that govern the determination of gross income and allowable deductions.

After taxable income is computed, an individual's filing status must be determined because different tax rates apply for single, married, and heads of household taxpayers. The individual tax rate structure is progressive, with rates for 2016 ranging from 10 percent to 39.6 percent.[2] For comparison, the lowest rate structure, which was in effect from 1913 to 1915, ranged from 1 to 7 percent, and the highest, in effect during 1944 to 1945, ranged from 23 to 94 percent.

Once the individual's tax has been computed, prepayments and credits are subtracted to determine whether the taxpayer owes additional tax or is entitled to a refund.

9-1a Components of the Tax Formula

Before the application of the tax formula is illustrated, a brief discussion of each of its components is helpful.

---

[1]Refer to the discussion of tax complexity in Chapter 1.

[2]The current Tax Rate Schedules that apply to individuals are shown on the inside front cover of the text.

Income (Broadly Defined)

In the tax formula, "income" is broadly defined and includes all of the taxpayer's income, both taxable and nontaxable. In general, the courts have defined "income" as any realized increase in wealth.[3] Income does not include a return of capital, receipt of borrowed funds, or unrealized appreciation in the value of a taxpayer's assets.

EXAMPLE 1

When Dan's apartment lease ends, he decides to buy a house. Consequently, the owner of the apartment building returns to Dan the $600 damage deposit he previously made. To make a down payment on the house, Dan sells stock for $20,000 (original cost of $8,000) and borrows $150,000 from a bank.

Only the $12,000 gain from the sale of the stock is income to Dan. The $600 damage deposit and the $8,000 cost of the stock are a return of capital. The $150,000 bank loan is not income as Dan has an obligation to repay that amount (the loan does not increase his wealth).

Gross Income

The Internal Revenue Code defines gross income broadly as "except as otherwise provided ..., all income from whatever source derived."[4] The "except as otherwise provided" phrase refers to exclusions. Gross income includes, but is not limited to, the items in Exhibit 9.1.

Exclusions

For various reasons, Congress has chosen to exclude certain types of income from the income tax base. The principal income exclusions are listed in Exhibit 9.2. The exclusions most commonly encountered by individual taxpayers (employee fringe benefits) are discussed in detail in Chapter 11.

EXHIBIT 9.1	Partial List of Gross Income Items
Alimony	Interest
Bargain purchase from employer	Jury duty fees
Bonuses	Partnership income
Breach of contract damages	Pensions
Business income	Prizes (with some exceptions)
Commissions	Professional fees
Compensation for services	Punitive damages
Debts forgiven (with some exceptions)	Rents
Dividends	Rewards
Embezzled funds	Royalties
Farm income	Salaries
Fees	Severance pay
Gains from illegal activities	Strike and lockout benefits
Gains from sale of property	Tips and gratuities
Gambling winnings	Treasure trove (found property)
Hobby income	Wages

---

[3]*Comm. v. Glenshaw Glass Co.*, 55–1 USTC ¶9308, 47 AFTR 162, 348 U.S. 426 (USSC, 1955).

[4]§ 61(a).

EXHIBIT 9.2	Partial List of Exclusions from Gross Income

Accident and health insurance proceeds

Annuity payments (to the extent proceeds represent a recovery of the taxpayer's investment)

Child support payments

Damages for personal injury or sickness

Fringe benefits of employees:

- Educational assistance payments provided by employer
- Employer-provided accident and health insurance
- Group term life insurance (for coverage up to $50,000)
- Meals and lodging (if furnished for convenience of employer)
- Tuition reductions for employees of educational institutions
- Miscellaneous benefits

Gains from sale of principal residence (subject to statutory ceiling)

Gifts and inheritances received

Interest from state and local bonds

Life insurance paid upon death of insured

Scholarship grants (to a limited extent)

Social Security benefits (to a limited extent)

Workers' compensation benefits

EXAMPLE 2

Beth received the following amounts during the year:

Salary	$30,000
Interest on savings account	900
Gift from her aunt	10,000
Prize won in state lottery	1,000
Alimony from ex-husband	12,000
Child support from ex-husband	6,000
Damages for injury in auto accident	25,000
Ten $50 bills in an unmarked envelope found in an airport lounge (airport authorities could not locate anyone who claimed ownership)	500
Federal income tax refund for last year's tax overpayment	120

In addition, her stock investments increased in value by $5,000.

Review Exhibits 9.1 and 9.2 to determine the amount Beth must include in the computation of taxable income and the amount she may exclude. Then check your answer in footnote 5.[5]

Deductions *for* Adjusted Gross Income

Individual taxpayers have two categories of deductions: (1) deductions *for* adjusted gross income (deductions from gross income to arrive at adjusted gross income) and (2) deductions *from* adjusted gross income. Deductions *for* adjusted gross income (AGI) include the following:[6]

- Ordinary and necessary expenses incurred in a trade or business.
- Part of the self-employment tax paid.

---

[5]Beth must include $44,400 in computing taxable income ($30,000 salary + $900 interest + $1,000 lottery prize + $12,000 alimony + $500 found property). She can exclude $41,000 ($10,000 gift from aunt + $6,000 child support + $25,000 damages). The $120 Federal income tax refund is excluded because it represents an adjustment (i.e., overpayment) of a nondeductible expenditure made in the previous year. The unrealized gain of $5,000 on the stock held for investment is not included in gross income. Such gain will be included in gross income only when it is realized upon disposition of the stock.

[6]See § 62 for a comprehensive list of items that are deductible *for* AGI. Deductions *for* AGI are sometimes known as *above-the-line* deductions because on the tax return, they are taken before the "line" designating AGI.

- Alimony payments.
- Certain payments to traditional Individual Retirement Accounts and Health Savings Accounts.
- Moving expenses.
- The capital loss deduction (limited to $3,000).

The effect on AGI of deductions *for* AGI is illustrated below.

Mason, age 45, earned a salary of $78,000 in the current year. He contributed $4,000 to his traditional Individual Retirement Account (IRA), sold stock held as an investment for a short-term capital loss of $2,000, and paid $4,600 in alimony to his ex-wife. His AGI is determined as follows:

Gross income		
Salary		$ 78,000
Less: Deductions *for* AGI		
IRA contribution	$4,000	
Capital loss	2,000	
Alimony paid	4,600	(10,600)
AGI		$ 67,400

EXAMPLE 3

Deductions *from* Adjusted Gross Income

As a general rule, personal expenditures are disallowed as deductions in arriving at taxable income; however, Congress allows specified personal expenses as deductions *from* AGI (commonly referred to as itemized deductions). Itemized deductions are discussed in Chapter 10.

AGI is an important subtotal that serves as the basis for computing percentage limitations on certain itemized deductions such as medical expenses, charitable contributions, and certain casualty losses. For example, medical expenses are deductible only to the extent they exceed 10 percent of AGI (or 7.5 percent through 2016 if either spouse is age 65 or older), and charitable contribution deductions may not exceed 50 percent of AGI. These limitations might be described as a percentage *floor* under the medical expense deduction and a 50 percent *ceiling* on the charitable contribution deduction.

Assume the same facts as in Example 3, except that Mason also had unreimbursed medical expenses of $8,000. Medical expenses may be included in his itemized deductions to the extent they exceed 10% of AGI. In computing his itemized deductions, Mason may include medical expenses of $1,260 [$8,000 medical expenses − $6,740 (10% × $67,400 AGI)].

EXAMPLE 4

Trade or business expenses, which are deductions *for* AGI, must be incurred in connection with a trade or business. Nonbusiness expenses, on the other hand, are expenses incurred in connection with an income-producing activity that does not qualify as a trade or business. Such expenses are itemized deductions.

Leo is the owner and operator of a video game arcade. All allowable expenses that he incurs in connection with the arcade business are deductions *for* AGI. In addition, Leo paid mortgage interest, state income tax, and charitable contributions. These personal expenses are allowable as itemized deductions.

EXAMPLE 5

Standard Deduction

In lieu of claiming itemized deductions, taxpayers will use the standard deduction . As discussed later in the chapter, the standard deduction amount varies depending on filing status, age, and blindness. Each year, as required by law, the IRS adjusts the standard deduction amount for the effects of inflation.

Personal and Dependency Exemptions

Exemptions, another type of deduction, are allowed for the taxpayer, the taxpayer's spouse, and each dependent of the taxpayer. Like the standard deduction, personal and dependency exemptions (discussed later) are adjusted each year for inflation. The exemption amount for 2016 is $4,050 (up from $4,000 in 2015).

Taxable Income

The determination of taxable income is illustrated in Example 6.

EXAMPLE 6

Grace, age 25, is single and has her disabled and dependent mother living with her. This qualifies Grace for head-of-household filing status and a standard deduction of $9,300 in 2016. In 2016, Grace earned a $42,000 salary as a high school teacher. Her other income consisted of $1,100 interest on a certificate of deposit (CD) and $500 of nontaxable interest on municipal bonds she had received as a graduation gift in 2011. During 2016, she sustained a deductible capital loss of $1,000 from the sale of stock. Her itemized deductions are $9,500. Grace's taxable income for the year is computed as follows:

Income (broadly defined)		
Salary		$42,000
Interest on a CD		1,100
Interest on municipal bonds		500
Total income		$43,600
Less: Exclusion—		
Interest on municipal bonds		(500)
Gross income		$43,100
Less: Deduction *for* adjusted gross income—capital loss		(1,000)
Adjusted gross income (AGI)		$42,100
Less: The *greater* of—		
Total itemized deductions	$9,500	
or the standard deduction for head of household	9,300	(9,500)
Less: Personal and dependency exemptions (2 × $4,050)		(8,100)
Taxable income		$24,500

Note that the exclusion of $500 (i.e., interest from municipal bonds) is subtracted in determining gross income. The capital loss of $1,000 from a property transaction is classified as a deduction *for* AGI. Grace chose to itemize her deductions *from* AGI as they exceed the standard deduction (see Exhibit 9.3). Grace's income tax is determined later in this chapter in Example 36.

9-2 STANDARD DEDUCTION

LO.2

Explain the standard deduction and evaluate its choice in arriving at taxable income.

A major component of the tax formula is the standard deduction. The effect of the standard deduction is to exempt part of a taxpayer's income from Federal income tax liability. In the past, Congress has attempted to set the tax-free amount represented by the standard deduction approximately equal to an estimated poverty level,[7] but it has not always been consistent in doing so.

9-2a Basic and Additional Standard Deduction

The standard deduction is the sum of two components: the *basic* standard deduction and the *additional* standard deduction.[8] Exhibit 9.3 lists the basic standard deduction allowed for taxpayers in each filing status. All taxpayers allowed a *full* standard

---

[7]S.Rep. No. 92–437, 92nd Cong., 1st Sess., 1971, p. 54. Another purpose of the standard deduction was discussed in Chapter 1 under Influence of the Internal Revenue Service—Administrative Feasibility. The size of the standard deduction has a direct bearing on the number of taxpayers who are in a position to itemize deductions. Reducing the number of taxpayers who itemize also reduces the audit effort required from the IRS.

[8]§ 63(c)(1).

EXHIBIT 9.3	Basic Standard Deduction Amounts	
Filing Status	**2015**	**2016**
Single	$ 6,300	$ 6,300
Married, filing jointly	12,600	12,600
Surviving spouse	12,600	12,600
Head of household	9,250	9,300
Married, filing separately	6,300	6,300

deduction are entitled to the applicable amount listed in Exhibit 9.3. The standard deduction amounts are subject to adjustment for inflation each year.

Certain taxpayers are not allowed to claim *any* standard deduction, and the standard deduction is *limited* for others. These provisions are discussed later in the chapter.

A taxpayer who is age 65 or over *or* blind in 2016 qualifies for an *additional standard deduction* of $1,250 or $1,550, depending on filing status (see amounts in Exhibit 9.4). Two additional standard deductions are allowed for a taxpayer who is age 65 or over *and* blind. The additional standard deduction provisions also apply for a qualifying spouse who is age 65 or over or blind, but a taxpayer may not claim an additional standard deduction for a dependent.

To determine whether to itemize, the taxpayer compares the *total* standard deduction (the sum of the basic standard deduction and any additional standard deductions) with total itemized deductions. Taxpayers are allowed to deduct the *greater* of itemized deductions or the standard deduction. The choice is elective. Undoubtedly, some taxpayers claim the standard deduction because they do not want to bother completing the Schedule A required for itemizing deductions *from* AGI. Likewise, the choice is an annual one, and a taxpayer is not bound by what was done on returns filed for past years. For example, many taxpayers who have previously claimed the standard deduction will switch to itemizing after purchasing a home (because of the mortgage interest and property tax deductions). In other circumstances, the reverse could be true—the taxpayer will switch from itemizing to taking the standard deduction. As illustrated in the next example, age can make a difference.

Prior to 2016, Sara, who is single, had always chosen to itemize. In 2016, however, she reaches age 65. Her itemized deductions for 2016 are $6,500, but her total standard deduction is $7,850 [$6,300 (basic standard deduction) + $1,550 (additional standard deduction)].

Sara should compute her taxable income for 2016 using the standard deduction ($7,850) because it exceeds her itemized deductions ($6,500).

EXAMPLE

7

In-depth coverage can be found on this book's companion website: www.cengagebrain.com

1 DIGGING DEEPER

EXHIBIT 9.4	Amount of Each Additional Standard Deduction	
Filing Status	**2015**	**2016**
Single	$1,550	$1,550
Married, filing jointly	1,250	1,250
Surviving spouse	1,250	1,250
Head of household	1,550	1,550
Married, filing separately	1,250	1,250

9-2b **Special Limitations on the Standard Deduction for Dependents**

Special rules apply to the standard deduction and personal exemption of an individual who can be claimed as a dependent on another person's tax return.

When filing his or her own tax return, a *dependent's* basic standard deduction in 2016 is limited to the greater of $1,050 or the sum of the individual's earned income for the year plus $350.[9] However, if the sum of the individual's earned income plus $350 exceeds the normal standard deduction, the standard deduction is limited to the appropriate amount shown in Exhibit 9.3. These limitations apply only to the basic standard deduction. A dependent who is 65 or over or blind or both is also allowed the additional standard deduction amount on his or her own return (refer to Exhibit 9.4).

Dependent Standard Deduction

EXAMPLE 8

Susan, who is 17 years old and single, is claimed as a dependent on her parents' tax return. During 2016, she received $1,200 of interest (unearned income) on a savings account. She also earned $400 from a part-time job. When Susan files her own tax return, her standard deduction is $1,050 (the greater of $1,050 or the sum of earned income of $400 plus $350).

EXAMPLE 9

Assume the same facts as in Example 8, except that Susan is 67 years old and is claimed as a dependent on her son's tax return. In this case, when Susan files her own tax return, her standard deduction is $2,600 [$1,050 (see Example 8) + $1,550 (the additional standard deduction allowed because Susan is age 65 or over)].

EXAMPLE 10

Peggy, who is 16 years old and single, earned $800 from a summer job and had no unearned income during 2016. She is claimed as a dependent on her parents' tax return. Her standard deduction is $1,150 (the greater of $1,050 or the sum of earned income of $800 plus $350).

EXAMPLE 11

Jack, who is 20 years old, single, and a full-time college student, is claimed as a dependent on his parents' tax return. He worked as a musician during the summer of 2016, earning $6,500. Jack's standard deduction is $6,300 (the greater of $1,050 or the sum of earned income of $6,500 plus $350, but limited to the $6,300 standard deduction for a single taxpayer).

LO.3

Apply the rules for arriving at personal exemptions.

9-3   PERSONAL EXEMPTIONS

The use of exemptions in the tax system is based in part on the idea that a taxpayer with a small amount of income should be exempt from income taxation. An exemption frees a specified amount of income from tax ($4,050 in 2016 and $4,000 in 2015). The exemption amount is adjusted annually for inflation.

Exemptions that are allowed for the taxpayer and spouse are designated as **personal exemptions**. Those exemptions allowed for the care and maintenance of other persons are called dependency exemptions and are discussed in the next section.

An individual cannot claim a personal exemption if he or she is claimed as a dependent by another.

---

[9] § 63(c)(5). Both the $1,050 amount and the $350 amount are subject to adjustment for inflation each year. In 2015, the amounts were $1,050 and $350.

EXAMPLE

12

Assume the same facts as in Example 11. On his own income tax return,[10] Jack's taxable income is determined as follows:

Gross income	$ 6,500
Less: Standard deduction	(6,300)
Personal exemption	(–0–)
Taxable income	$ 200

Jack is not allowed a personal exemption because he is claimed as a dependent by his parents.

When a married couple file a joint return, they may claim two personal exemptions. However, when separate returns are filed, a married taxpayer cannot claim an exemption for his or her spouse *unless* the spouse has no gross income and is not claimed as the dependent of another taxpayer.[11]

The determination of marital status generally is made at the end of the taxable year, except when a spouse dies during the year. Spouses who enter into a legal separation under a decree of divorce or separate maintenance before the end of the year are considered to be unmarried at the end of the taxable year.

The amount of the exemption is not reduced due to the taxpayer's death. The same rule applies to dependency exemptions. As long as an individual qualified as a dependent at the time of death, the full amount of the exemption can be claimed.

9-4 DEPENDENCY EXEMPTIONS

LO.4

Explain the rules for determining dependency exemptions.

As is the case with personal exemptions, a taxpayer is permitted to claim an exemption of $4,050 in 2016 ($4,000 in 2015) for each person who qualifies as a dependent. A dependency exemption is available for either a qualifying child or a qualifying relative and must not run afoul of certain other rules (i.e., joint return or nonresident alien prohibitions).

9-4a Qualifying Child

In the interest of uniformity and simplicity, Congress has tried to establish a uniform definition of a qualifying child. The qualifying child definition applies to the following tax provisions:

- Dependency exemption.
- Head-of-household filing status.
- Earned income tax credit.
- Child tax credit.
- Credit for child and dependent care expenses.

A qualifying child must meet the relationship, abode, age, and support tests.[12] For dependency exemption purposes, a qualifying child must also satisfy the joint return test and the citizenship or residency test (see Other Rules for Dependency Exemptions later in the chapter).

Relationship Test

The relationship test includes a taxpayer's child (son or daughter), adopted child, stepchild, eligible foster child, brother, sister, half brother, half sister, stepbrother, stepsister, or a *descendant* of any of these parties (e.g., grandchild, nephew, and niece). Note that *ancestors* of any of these parties (e.g., uncles and aunts) and in-laws (e.g., son-in-law and brother-in-law) *are not included*.

An adopted child includes a child lawfully placed with the taxpayer for legal adoption even though the adoption is not final. An eligible foster child is a child who is placed with the taxpayer by an authorized placement agency or by a judgment decree or other order of any court of competent jurisdiction.

---

[10]As noted on p. 9–21 (Filing Requirements for Dependents), Jack will be required to file an income tax return.

[11]§ 151(b).

[12]§ 152(c).

Abode Test

A qualifying child must live with the taxpayer for more than half of the year. For this purpose, temporary absences (e.g., school, vacation, medical care, military service, detention in a juvenile facility) are disregarded. Special rules apply in the case of certain kidnapped children.[13]

Age Test

By the end of the tax year, a qualifying child must be under age 19 or under age 24 in the case of a student. A student is a child who, during any part of five months of the year, is enrolled full-time at a school or government-sponsored on-farm training course.[14] Also, an individual cannot be older than the taxpayer claiming him or her as a qualifying child (e.g., a brother cannot claim his older sister as a qualifying child). The age test does not apply to a child who is disabled during any part of the year.[15]

The Big Picture

EXAMPLE 13

Return to the facts of *The Big Picture* on p. 9-1. Does Paige meet the requirements of a qualifying child as to Polly? Paige satisfies the relationship and abode tests, but the answer to the age test remains unclear. Because she is not a full-time student or disabled, she must be under 19 to meet the age test. Unfortunately, the facts given do not provide Paige's age.

Support Test

To be a qualifying child, the individual must not be self-supporting (i.e., provide more than one-half of his or her own support). In the case of a child who is a full-time student, scholarships are not considered to be support.[16]

EXAMPLE 14

Shawn, age 23, is a full-time student and lives with his parents and an older cousin. During 2016, Shawn receives his support from the following sources: 30% from a part-time job, 30% from a scholarship, 20% from his parents, and 20% from the cousin.

Shawn is not self-supporting and can be claimed by his parents as a dependent even though his parents contribute only 20% of his support. (Note: Shawn cannot be a qualifying child as to his cousin due to the relationship test.)

Tiebreaker Rules

In some situations, a child may be a qualifying child to more than one person. In this event, the tax law specifies which person has priority in claiming the dependency exemption.[17] Called "tiebreaker rules," these rules are summarized in Concept Summary 9.2.

Concept Summary 9.2

Tiebreaker Rules for Claiming Qualifying Child

Persons Eligible to Claim Exemption	Person Prevailing
One of the persons is the parent.	Parent
Both persons are the parents, and the child lives longer with one parent.	Parent with the longer period of residence
Both persons are the parents, and the child lives with each the same period of time.	Parent with the higher adjusted gross income (AGI)
None of the persons are the parent.	Person with highest AGI

---

[13]§ 152(f)(6).

[14]§ 152(f)(2).

[15]Within the meaning of § 22(e)(3) for purposes of the credit for the elderly or disabled.

[16]§ 152(f)(5).

[17]§ 152(c)(4).

In-depth coverage can be found on this book's companion website: www.cengagebrain.com

2 DIGGING DEEPER

9-4b Qualifying Relative

In addition to the category of a qualifying child, there is a second category of dependency exemption designated as the **qualifying relative**.

A qualifying relative must meet the following relationship, gross income, and support tests.[18] As in the case of the qualifying child category, qualifying relative status also requires that the joint return and nonresident alien restrictions be avoided (see Other Rules for Dependency Exemptions later in the chapter).

Relationship Test

The relationship test for a qualifying relative is more expansive than for a qualifying child. Also included are the following relatives:

- Lineal ascendants (e.g., parents and grandparents).
- Collateral ascendants (e.g., uncles and aunts).
- Certain in-laws (e.g., son-, daughter-, father-, mother-, brother-, and sister-in-law).[19]

Children who do not satisfy the qualifying child definition may meet the qualifying relative criteria.

> **EXAMPLE 15**
>
> Inez provides more than half of the support of her son, age 20, who is neither disabled nor a full-time student. The son is not a qualifying child due to the age test, but is a qualifying relative if the gross income test is met. Consequently, Inez may claim a dependency exemption for her son.

The relationship test also includes individuals who are "members of the household" (i.e., live with the taxpayer for the entire year). These individuals can be related or unrelated. For example, cousins are not "qualifying relatives" (cousins are not on the list above), but a cousin can meet the relationship test if a "member of the household." Member-of-the-household status is not available for anyone whose relationship with the taxpayer violates local law or anyone who was a spouse during any part of the year.[20] However, an ex-spouse can qualify as a member of the household in a year following the divorce.

As the relationship test indicates, the category designation of "qualifying relative" is somewhat misleading since persons other than relatives can qualify as dependents. Furthermore, not all relatives will qualify (although relatives that are not listed could be a "member of the household").

The Big Picture

> **EXAMPLE 16**
>
> Return to the facts of *The Big Picture* on p. 9-1. Although Maude is unrelated to Polly, she qualifies as Polly's dependent by being a member of the household. Because Maude is a dependent, Polly can also claim the medical expenses she paid on Maude's behalf. The funeral expenses are not deductible. Although Maude lived for only two months, the full amount of the dependency exemption is allowed and does not have to be apportioned.

Gross Income Test

A dependent's gross income must be *less* than the exemption amount—$4,050 in 2016 and $4,000 in 2015. Gross income is determined by the income that is taxable. In the

---

[18]§ 152(d).

[19]Once established by marriage, in-law status continues to exist and survives divorce.

[20]§§ 152(d)(2)(H) and (f)(3).

case of scholarships, for example, include the taxable portion (e.g., amounts received for room and board) and exclude the nontaxable portion (e.g., amounts received for books and tuition). See the discussion of scholarships in Chapter 10.

Gross Income Test

Elsie provides more than half of the support of her son, Tom, who does not live with her. Tom, age 26, is a full-time student in medical school, earns $3,000 from a part-time job, and receives a $12,000 scholarship covering his tuition.

Elsie may claim Tom as a dependent because he meets the gross income test and is a qualifying relative. (Note: Tom is not a qualifying child; he fails both the abode and the age test.)

Aaron provides more than half of the support of his widowed aunt, Myrtle, who does not live with him. Myrtle's income for the year is as follows: dividend income of $1,100, earnings from pet sitting of $1,200, nontaxable Social Security benefits of $6,000, and nontaxable interest from City of Milwaukee bonds of $8,000.

Because Myrtle's gross income is only $2,300 ($1,100 + $1,200), she meets the gross income test and can be claimed as Aaron's dependent.

The Big Picture

Return to the facts of *The Big Picture* on p. 9-1. Assuming that Paige is not a qualifying child (see Example 13), can she be a qualifying relative for dependency exemption purposes? She meets the relationship and support tests, but what about the gross income test?

If her income from her part-time job is less than $4,050 (the 2016 exemption amount), she does qualify and can be claimed by Polly as a dependent.

Support Test

Over one-half of the support of the qualifying relative must be furnished by the taxpayer. Support includes food, shelter, clothing, toys, medical and dental care, and education. However, a scholarship (both taxable and nontaxable portions) received by a student is not included for purposes of determining whether the taxpayer furnished more than half of the relative's support.

Hal contributed $3,400 (consisting of food, clothing, and medical care) toward the support of his nephew, Sam, who lives with him. Sam earned $1,300 from a part-time job and received $2,000 from a student loan to attend a local university. Assuming that the other dependency tests are met, Hal can claim Sam as a dependent because Hal has contributed more than half of Sam's support (i.e., Hal contributed $3,400 and Sam contributed $3,300).

If an individual does not spend funds that have been received from any source, the unspent amounts are not counted for purposes of the support test.

Emily contributed $3,000 to her father's support during the year. In addition, her father received $2,400 in Social Security benefits, $200 of interest, and wages of $600. Her father deposited the Social Security benefits, interest, and wages in his own savings account and did not use any of the funds for his support. Thus, the Social Security benefits, interest, and wages are not considered to be support provided by Emily's father. Emily may claim her father as a dependent if the other tests are met.

An individual's own funds, however, must be taken into account if applied toward support. In this regard, the source of the funds so used is not relevant.

Frank contributes $8,000 toward his parents' total support of $20,000. The parents, who do not live with Frank, obtain the other $12,000 from savings and a home equity loan on their residence. Although the parents have no income, their use of savings and borrowed funds are counted as part of their support. Because Frank does not satisfy the support test, he cannot claim his parents as dependents.

EXAMPLE 22

Capital expenditures for items such as furniture, appliances, and automobiles are included for purposes of the support test if the item does, in fact, constitute support.

Norm purchased a television costing $950 and gave it to his mother, who lives with him. The television was placed in the mother's bedroom and was used exclusively by her. Norm should include the cost of the television in determining the support of his mother.

EXAMPLE 23

Multiple Support Agreements An exception to the support test involves a `multiple support agreement`. A multiple support agreement permits one of a group of taxpayers who furnish support for a qualifying relative to claim a dependency exemption for that individual even if no one person provides more than 50 percent of the support.[21] The group together must provide more than 50 percent of the support. Any person who contributed *more than 10 percent* of the support is entitled to claim the exemption if each person in the group who contributed more than 10 percent files a written consent. This provision frequently enables one of the children of aged dependent parents to claim an exemption when none of the children meets the 50 percent support test.

Each person who is a party to the multiple support agreement must meet all other requirements (except the support requirement) for claiming the exemption. A person who does not meet the relationship or member-of-the-household test, for instance, cannot claim the dependency exemption under a multiple support agreement. It does not matter if he or she contributes more than 10 percent of the individual's support.

Wanda, who resides with her son, Adam, received $12,000 from various sources during the year. This constituted her entire support for the year. She received support from the following individuals:

EXAMPLE 24

	Amount	Percentage of Total
Adam, a son	$ 5,760	48%
Bob, a son	1,200	10
Carol, a daughter	3,600	30
Diane, a friend	1,440	12
	$12,000	100%

If Adam and Carol file a multiple support agreement, either may claim the dependency exemption for Wanda. Bob may not claim Wanda because he did not contribute *more than 10%* of her support. Bob's consent is not required for Adam and Carol to file a multiple support agreement. Diane does not meet the relationship or member-of-the-household test and cannot be a party to the agreement. The decision as to who claims Wanda rests with Adam and Carol. It is possible for Carol to claim Wanda, even though Adam furnished more of Wanda's support.

In-depth coverage can be found on this book's companion website: www.cengagebrain.com

3 DIGGING DEEPER

---

[21]§ 152(d)(3).

TAX PLANNING STRATEGIES   Multiple Support Agreements and the Medical Expense Deduction

FRAMEWORK FOCUS: DEDUCTIONS

Strategy: Maximize Deductible Amounts.

Generally, medical expenses are deductible only if they are paid on behalf of the taxpayer, his or her spouse, and their dependents.[22] Because deductibility may rest on dependency status, planning is important in arranging multiple support agreements.

EXAMPLE 25

During the year, Suzanne will be supported by her two sons (Gary and Alan) and her daughter (Maria). Each will furnish approximately one-third of the required support. If the parties decide that the dependency exemption should be claimed by Maria under a multiple support agreement, any medical expenses incurred by Suzanne should be paid by Maria.

In planning a multiple support agreement, take into account which of the parties is most likely to have total medical expenses that exceed the 10 percent (7.5 percent if at least 65) of AGI limitation. In Example 25, for instance, Maria might be a poor choice if she and her family do not expect to incur many medical expenses of their own.

Children of Divorced or Separated Parents Another exception to the support test applies when parents with children are divorced or separated under a decree of separate maintenance. For unmarried parents, living apart (for the last six months of the year) will suffice. Special rules apply if the parents meet the following conditions:

- They would have been entitled to the dependency exemption(s) had they been married and filed a joint return.
- They have custody (either jointly or singly) of the child (or children) for more than half of the year.

Under the general rule, the parent having custody of the child (children) for the greater part of the year (i.e., the custodial parent) is entitled to the dependency exemption(s). The general rule does not apply if a multiple support agreement is in effect. It also does not apply if the custodial parent agrees to a waiver in favor of the noncustodial parent.[23]

DIGGING DEEPER 4   In-depth coverage can be found on this book's companion website: www.cengagebrain.com

9-4c   Other Rules for Dependency Exemptions

In addition to fitting into either the qualifying child or the qualifying relative category, a dependent must meet the joint return and the citizenship or residency tests.

Joint Return Test

If a dependent is married, the supporting taxpayer (e.g., the parent of a married child) generally is not permitted a dependency exemption if the married individual files a joint return with his or her spouse.[24] The joint return rule does not apply, however, if the following conditions are met:

- The reason for filing is to claim a refund for tax withheld.
- No tax liability would exist for either spouse on separate returns.
- Neither spouse is required to file a return.

---

[22]See the discussion of medical expenses in Chapter 10.

[23]See Reg. § 1.152–4T and §§ 152(e)(2) and (5).

[24]§ 152(b)(2).

Paul provides over half of the support of his son, Quinn. He also provides over half of the support of Vera, who is Quinn's wife. During the year, both Quinn and Vera had part-time jobs. To recover the taxes withheld, they file a joint return. If Quinn and Vera have income low enough that they are not *required* to file a return, Paul is allowed to claim both as dependents.

EXAMPLE
26

TAX PLANNING STRATEGIES **Problems with a Joint Return**

FRAMEWORK FOCUS: DEDUCTIONS

Strategy: Maximize Deductible Amounts.

A married person who files a joint return generally cannot be claimed as a dependent by another taxpayer. If a joint return has been filed, the damage may be undone if separate returns are substituted on a timely basis (on or before the due date of the return).

While preparing a client's 2015 income tax return on April 2, 2016, a tax practitioner discovered that the client's daughter had filed a joint return with her husband in late January 2016. Presuming that the daughter otherwise qualifies as the client's dependent, the exemption is not lost if she and her husband file separate returns on or before April 18, 2016.

EXAMPLE
27

Citizenship or Residency Test

To be a dependent, the individual must be a U.S. citizen, a U.S. resident, or a resident of Canada or Mexico for some part of the calendar year in which the taxpayer's tax year begins.[25]

9-4d Comparison of Categories for Dependency Exemptions

Concept Summary 9.3 identifies the tests for the two categories of dependency exemptions. In contrasting the two categories, the following observations are in order:

- As to the relationship tests, the qualifying relative category is considerably more expansive. Besides including those prescribed under the qualifying child grouping, other relatives are added. Nonrelated persons who are members of the household are also included.

- The support tests are entirely different. In the case of a qualifying child, support is not necessary. What is required is that the child not be self-supporting.

- The qualifying child category has no gross income limitation, whereas the qualifying relative category has no age restriction.

9-4e Phaseout of Exemptions

Several provisions of the tax law are intended to increase the tax liability of more affluent taxpayers who might otherwise enjoy some benefit from certain deductions and credits. One such provision phases out certain itemized deductions and is discussed in Chapter 10. Another provision phases out personal and dependency exemptions.[26] The exemption phaseout occurs as AGI exceeds specified threshold amounts (indexed annually for inflation). The phaseout begins when AGI exceeds the following:

Filing Status	2015	2016
Married, filing jointly	$309,900	$311,300
Head of household	284,050	285,350
Single	258,250	259,400
Married, filing separately	154,950	155,650

---

[25]§ 152(b)(3).

[26]§ 151(d)(3).

Concept Summary 9.3

Tests for Dependency Exemption

Test	Qualifying Child	Qualifying Relative
Relationship:		
• Children (natural, step, or adopted) and their *descendants*, and siblings and stepsiblings and their *descendants*.	X	
• Children (natural, step, or adopted) and their *descendants*, siblings and their children, parents and their *ascendants*, uncles and aunts, stepparents and step-siblings, and certain in-laws.		X
• Member of the household (live with taxpayer for *entire* year; relative or non-relative).		X
Abode	X	
Age	X	
Support:		
• Not self-supporting ("child" furnishes one-half or less of his or her support).	X	
• Taxpayer furnishes over one-half of the support of potential dependent.		X
Gross income *less* than the exemption amount		X
Joint return (potential dependent cannot file joint return)	X	X
Citizenship or residency (potential dependent must meet test)	X	X

Exemptions are phased out by 2 percent for each $2,500 (or fraction thereof) by which the taxpayer's AGI exceeds the threshold amounts. For a married taxpayer filing separately, the phaseout is 2 percent for each $1,250 (or fraction thereof). The allowable exemption amount can be determined with the following steps:

1. AGI − threshold amount = excess amount.
2. Excess amount ÷ $2,500 = reduction factor [rounded up to the next whole number (e.g., 18.1 = 19)] × 2 = phaseout percentage.
3. Phaseout percentage (from step 2) × exemption amount = phaseout amount.
4. Exemption amount − phaseout amount = allowable exemption deduction.

EXAMPLE 28

Brad files as a single individual in 2016. His AGI is $292,050. He is entitled to one personal exemption. Brad's allowable exemption amount is determined as follows:

1. $292,050 − $259,400 = $32,650 excess amount.
2. [($32,650 ÷ $2,500) = 13.06; rounded to 14]; 14 × 2 = 28% (phaseout percentage).
3. 28% × $4,050 = $1,134 phaseout amount.
4. $4,050 − $1,134 = $2,916 allowable exemption deduction.

LO.5

Choose the proper filing status and identify the related filing requirements.

9-5 FILING STATUS AND FILING REQUIREMENTS

Once taxable income has been ascertained, a two-step process is used in determining income tax due (or refund available). First, the taxpayer's filing status and then whether a tax return must be filed must be determined. Second, the tax has to be computed and adjusted for available tax credits—see Concept Summary 9.1 and the tax formula. This section deals with the filing status and filing requirements. Text Section 9-6 covers

TAX IN THE NEWS **How to Subtly Pluck the Chicken**

No government likes to admit that it is enacting new taxes or even raising the rates on existing taxes. Needless to say, this is particularly true of the U.S. Congress. But there are more subtle ways to raise revenue (or to curtail revenue loss). The most popular way is to use a so-called *stealth tax*. A stealth tax is not really a tax at all. Instead, it is a means of reducing the benefits of certain tax provisions to higher-income taxpayers.

The heart and soul of the stealth tax is the phaseout approach. As income increases, the tax benefit thought to be derived from a particular provision decreases. Because the phaseout usually is gradual and not drastic, many affected taxpayers are unaware of what has happened.

The tax law is rampant with phaseouts. One of the most prominent phaseouts limits the deductibility of personal and dependency exemptions (which was discussed on the previous page). In addition, here are some other examples of these stealth taxes, each of which is discussed in Chapter 10:

- Child tax credit.
- Social Security benefits.
- Interest deduction on student loans.
- Itemized deductions.
- Education tax credits.
- Earned income credit.
- Premium tax credit.

the tax computation procedures. Text Section 9-7 covers tax return filing procedures (including selecting the correct form and determining when and how the tax return should be filed).

9-5a Filing Status

Every year, taxpayers must determine their **filing status**. The taxpayer's filing status is used to determine:

- The taxpayer's standard deduction;
- Whether the taxpayer must file a tax return;
- The taxpayer's tax liability; and
- Reductions of exemptions, itemized deductions, and certain tax credits.
- Eligibility for certain provisions (e.g., some credits are not available when the married, filing separately status is used).

There are five filing statuses, and all taxpayers will file a return based on the filing status selected:

- Single
- Married, filing jointly
- Married, filing separately
- Surviving spouse (qualifying widow or widower)
- Head of household.

The amount of tax will vary considerably depending on which filing status is used. This is illustrated in the following example.

EXAMPLE 29

The following amounts of tax are computed using the 2016 Tax Rate Schedules for a taxpayer (or taxpayers in the case of a joint return) with $60,000 of taxable income (see Appendix A).

Filing Status	Amount of Tax
Single	$10,771
Married, filing jointly	8,073
Married, filing separately	10,771
Head of household	9,298

Besides the effect from the tax rates that will apply, filing status also has an impact on the amount of the standard deduction that is allowed—see Exhibits 9.3 and 9.4 earlier in the chapter.

Single Taxpayers

A taxpayer who is unmarried or separated from his or her spouse by a decree of divorce or separate maintenance and does not qualify for another filing status must use the rates for single taxpayers. Marital status is determined as of the last day of the tax year, except when a spouse dies during the year. In that case, marital status is determined as of the date of death.

Married Individuals

The joint return was originally enacted to establish equity between married taxpayers in common law states and those in community property states. Before the joint return rates were enacted, taxpayers in community property states were in an advantageous position relative to taxpayers in common law states because they could split their income.

Taxpayers in common law states did not have this income-splitting option, so their taxable income was subject to higher marginal rates. This inconsistency in treatment was remedied by the joint return provisions. The progressive rates in the joint return Tax Rate Schedule are constructed based on the assumption that income is earned equally by the two spouses.

A same-sex couple who is legally married in a state or jurisdiction that recognizes same-sex marriage is treated as married for Federal tax purposes (no matter where they live). According to the IRS, registered domestic partners, though, are not "spouses" under Federal law. Therefore, they cannot file Federal tax returns using married filing jointly or married filing separately status. The same rule applies to same-sex partners in civil unions.[27]

If married individuals elect to file separate returns, each reports only his or her own income, exemptions, deductions, and credits, and each must use the Tax Rate Schedule applicable to married taxpayers filing separately. In a community property state, each individual must report his or her half of the community property income.[28] It is generally advantageous for married individuals to file a joint return because the combined amount of tax is lower. However, special circumstances (e.g., significant medical expenses incurred by one spouse subject to the 10 percent limitation) may warrant the election to file separate returns. It may be necessary to compute the tax under both assumptions to determine the most advantageous filing status. Filing a joint return carries the potential disadvantage of joint and several liability. This means that the IRS can pursue the collection of the tax due for that year against either spouse.

Marriage Penalty When Congress enacted the rate structure available to those filing joint returns, it generally favored married taxpayers. In certain situations, however, the parties would incur less tax if they were not married and filed separate returns. The additional tax that a joint return caused, commonly called the **marriage penalty**, usually developed when *both* spouses had large taxable incomes.

DIGGING DEEPER 5 | In-depth coverage can be found on this book's companion website: www.cengagebrain.com

Surviving Spouse The joint return rates also apply for two years following the death of one spouse if the surviving spouse maintains a household for a dependent child. The child must be a son, stepson, daughter, or stepdaughter who qualifies as a dependent of the taxpayer. This is referred to as **surviving spouse** status.[29]

---

[27]Rev.Rul. 2013–17, 2013–38 I.R.B. 201 and *U.S. v. Windsor*, 2013–2 USTC ¶50,400, 111 AFTR 2d 2013–2385, 133 S.Ct. 2675; **www.irs.gov/uac/ Answers-to-Frequently-Asked-Questions-for-Registered-Domestic-Partners-and-Individuals-in-Civil-Unions**.

[28]Form 8958 (Allocation of Tax Amounts Between Certain Individuals in Community Property States) is used for this purpose.

[29]§ 2(a). The IRS label for surviving spouse status is "qualifying widow(er) with dependent child."

Much has been made in the press and in political circles over the years concerning the so-called marriage penalty tax. This marriage penalty refers to the additional income tax that married couples pay over and above the aggregate amount two single individuals would pay with equal amounts of income. The marriage penalty arose because of the nature of the income tax rate structure that applies to individual taxpayers.

Relevant policy and ethical issues related to this dilemma are:

- Should the income tax system contain a bias against marriage?

- Should the income tax system require two people of economic means equal to that of two other people to pay a different amount of income taxes?

- Should the income tax system encourage two individuals to cohabit outside the commitment of marriage?

Long aware of the inequity of the marriage penalty, Congress reduced the effect of the problem by increasing the standard deduction available to married filers to 200 percent of that applicable to single persons and increasing the 15 percent bracket for joint filers to 200 percent of the size of that bracket applicable to single filers.

Head of Household

Unmarried individuals who maintain a household for a dependent (or dependents) are generally entitled to use the **head-of-household** rates.[30] The tax liability using the head-of-household rates falls between the liability using the joint return Tax Rate Schedule and the liability using the Tax Rate Schedule for single taxpayers.

To qualify for head-of-household rates, a taxpayer must pay more than half the cost of maintaining a household as his or her home. The household must also be the principal home of a dependent. Except for temporary absences (e.g., school, hospitalization), the dependent must live in the taxpayer's household for over half the year.

The Big Picture

EXAMPLE 30

Return to the facts of *The Big Picture* on p. 9-1. Assuming that Polly can be treated as single (i.e., not married), can Maude qualify Polly for head-of-household filing status? The answer is no. Even though Maude can be claimed as Polly's dependent (see Example 16), she does not meet the relationship test.

In-depth coverage can be found on this book's companion website: www.cengagebrain.com

6 DIGGING DEEPER

Abandoned Spouse Rules

Congress has enacted provisions that allow married taxpayers, commonly referred to as abandoned spouses, to file as a head of household if the following conditions are satisfied:

- The taxpayer does not file a joint return.

- The taxpayer paid more than one-half the cost of maintaining his or her home for the tax year.

- The taxpayer's spouse did not live in the home during the last six months of the tax year.

- The home was the principal residence of the taxpayer's son, daughter, stepson, stepdaughter, foster child, or adopted child for more than half the year, and the child can be claimed as a dependent.[31]

The resulting tax burden using the relatively favorable head-of-household status is lower than when using the married filing separately rate schedule.

---

[30]§ 2(b).   [31]§ 7703(b).

John Garth is a U.S. citizen and resident, but he spends much of his time in London, where his employer sends him on frequent assignments. John is married to Victoria, a citizen and resident of the United Kingdom.

Can John and Victoria file a joint return for U.S. Federal income tax purposes? Although § 6013(a)(1) specifically precludes the filing of a joint return if one spouse is a nonresident alien, another Code provision permits an exception. Under § 6013(g), the parties can elect to treat the nonqualifying spouse as a "resident" of the United States. This election would allow John and Victoria to file jointly.

But should John and Victoria make this election? If Victoria has considerable income of her own (from non-U.S. sources), the election could be ill-advised. As a nonresident alien, Victoria's non-U.S. source income *would not* be subject to the U.S. income tax. If she is treated as a U.S. resident, however, her non-U.S. source income *will be subject to U.S. tax.* Under the U.S. worldwide approach to taxation, all income (regardless of where earned) of anyone who is a *resident* or *citizen* of the United States is subject to tax.

The Big Picture

EXAMPLE

31

Return to the facts of *The Big Picture* on p. 9-1. Can Polly qualify as an abandoned spouse? Yes, if she can claim Paige as a dependent—either as a qualifying child (see Example 13) or as a qualifying relative (see Example 19). If so, Polly can use head-of-household filing status. If not, her filing status is married filing separately.

9-5b **Filing Requirements**

General Rules

An individual must file a tax return if certain minimum amounts of gross income have been received. The general rule is that a tax return is required for every individual who has gross income that equals or exceeds the sum of the exemption amount plus the applicable standard deduction.[32] For example, a single taxpayer under age 65 must file a tax return in 2016 if gross income equals or exceeds $10,350 ($4,050 exemption plus $6,300 standard deduction). Because the exemption and standard deduction amounts are subject to an annual inflation adjustment, the gross income thresholds for determining whether a tax return must be filed normally change every year.

DIGGING DEEPER **7** | In-depth coverage can be found on this book's companion website: **www.cengagebrain.com**

The additional standard deduction for being age 65 or older is considered in determining the gross income filing requirements. For example, the 2016 filing requirement for a single taxpayer age 65 or older is $11,900 ($6,300 basic standard deduction + $1,550 additional standard deduction + $4,050 exemption).

A self-employed individual with net earnings of $400 or more from a business or profession must file a tax return regardless of the amount of gross income.

Even though an individual has gross income below the filing level amounts and therefore does not owe any tax, he or she must file a return to obtain a tax refund of amounts withheld. A return is also necessary to obtain the benefits of the earned income credit (see Chapter 10) allowed to taxpayers with little or no tax liability. In addition, an individual who needs to reconcile the amount of premium tax credit received in advance during the year or owed to them (to help pay for health insurance obtained through the Marketplace) must file a return (see Chapter 10).

---

[32]§ 6012(a)(1).

Filing Requirements for Dependents

Computation of the gross income filing requirement for an individual who can be claimed as a dependent on another person's tax return is subject to more complex rules. For example, such an individual must file a return if he or she has earned income only and gross income that is more than the total standard deduction (including any additional standard deduction) the individual is allowed for the year.

In-depth coverage can be found on this book's companion website: www.cengagebrain.com   **8 DIGGING DEEPER**

9-6 TAX DETERMINATION

LO.6

Demonstrate the proper procedures for determining the tax liability.

The computation of income tax due (or refund) involves applying the proper set of tax rates to taxable income and then adjusting the liability for available credits. In certain cases, however, the application of the kiddie tax will cause a modification of the means by which the tax is determined.

9-6a Tax Table Method

The tax liability is computed using either the Tax Table method or the Tax Rate Schedule method. Most taxpayers compute their tax using the **Tax Table**. Eligible taxpayers compute taxable income (as shown in Concept Summary 9.1) and *must* determine their tax by reference to the Tax Table.

In-depth coverage can be found on this book's companion website: www.cengagebrain.com   **9 DIGGING DEEPER**

Although the Tax Table is derived from the Tax Rate Schedules (discussed next), the tax calculated using the two methods may vary slightly. This variation occurs because the tax for a particular income range in the Tax Table is based on the midpoint amount.

Linda is single and has taxable income of $30,000 for calendar year 2015. To determine Linda's tax using the Tax Table (see Appendix A),[33] find the $30,000 to $30,050 income line. The tax of $4,043 is actually the tax the Tax Rate Schedule for 2015 (see Appendix A) would yield on taxable income of $30,025 (i.e., the midpoint amount between $30,000 and $30,050).

EXAMPLE

32

9-6b Tax Rate Schedule Method

Taxpayers who do not use the Tax Tables use the **Tax Rate Schedules**. The 2016 rate schedule for single taxpayers is reproduced in Exhibit 9.5.[34] This schedule is used to illustrate the tax computations in Examples 33 and 34.

Pat is single and had $5,870 of taxable income in 2016. His tax is $587 ($5,870 × 10%).

EXAMPLE

33

Several terms are used to describe tax rates. The rates in the Tax Rate Schedules are often referred to as *statutory* (or nominal) rates. The *marginal* rate is the tax rate that would be assessed on the next dollar of income for a particular taxpayer. In Example 33, the statutory rate and the marginal rate are both 10 percent.

---

[33]The 2016 Tax Table was not available from the IRS at the date of publication of this text. The Tax Table for 2015 is located at **www.irs.gov** and is used to illustrate this computation.

[34]Individual tax rates are found in § 1.

EXHIBIT 9.5	2016 Tax Rate Schedule for Single Taxpayers		

If Taxable Income Is			
Over	**But Not Over**	**The Tax Is:**	**Of the Amount Over**
$ –0–	$ 9,275	10%	$ –0–
9,275	37,650	$ 927.50 + 15%	9,275
37,650	91,150	5,183.75 + 25%	37,650
91,150	190,150	18,558.75 + 28%	91,150
190,150	413,350	46,278.75 + 33%	190,150
413,350	415,050	119,934.75 + 35%	413,350
415,050		120,529.75 + 39.6%	415,050

EXAMPLE 34

Chris is single and had taxable income of $92,000 in 2016. Her tax is $18,796.75 [$18,558.75 + 28% ($92,000 − $91,150)].

The *average* rate is equal to the tax liability divided by taxable income. In Example 34, Chris has statutory rates of 10 percent, 15 percent, 25 percent, and 28 percent and a marginal rate of 28 percent. Chris's average rate is 20.4 percent ($18,796.75 tax liability ÷ $92,000 taxable income).

A tax is *progressive* (or graduated) if a higher rate of tax applies as the tax base increases. The progressive nature of the Federal income tax on individuals is illustrated by computing the tax in Example 34 utilizing each rate bracket.

Tax on first $9,275 at 10%	$ 927.50
Tax on $37,650 − $9,275 at 15%	4,256.25
Tax on $91,150 − $37,650 at 25%	13,375.00
Tax on $92,000 − $91,150 at 28%	238.00
Total tax on taxable income of $92,000	$18,796.75

A special computation limits the effective tax rate on qualified dividends (see Chapter 4) and net long-term capital gains (see Chapter 8).

TAX PLANNING STRATEGIES Shifting Income and Deductions across Time

FRAMEWORK FOCUS: TAX RATE

Strategy: Shift Net Income from High-Bracket Years to Low-Bracket Years.

It is natural for taxpayers to be concerned about the tax rates that apply to them. What might a tax practitioner suggest to clients about tax rate planning? There are several possibilities. For example, a taxpayer who is in the 15 percent bracket this year and expects to be in the 28 percent bracket next year should, if possible, defer payment of deductible expenses until next year to maximize the tax benefit of the deduction.

A note of caution is in order with respect to shifting income and expenses between years. Congress has recognized the tax planning possibilities of such shifting and has enacted many provisions to limit a taxpayer's ability to do so. Some of these limitations on the shifting of income and deductions are discussed in Chapters 4 through 6.

9-6c Computation of Net Taxes Payable or Refund Due

The pay-as-you-go feature of the Federal income tax system requires payment of all or part of the taxpayer's income tax liability during the year. These payments take the form of Federal income tax withheld by employers or estimated tax paid by

TAX IN THE NEWS Same-Sex Couples May Face a Tax Filing Nightmare

In *U.S. v. Windsor*, the Supreme Court struck down portions of the Defense of Marriage Act. Specifically, this decision invalidated a Federal definition of marriage as between one man and one woman. Guidance from the IRS (Rev.Rul. 2013–17) provides that a same-sex couple possessing a marriage license from any U.S. state or other jurisdiction will be considered married for Federal income tax purposes (no matter where they live). However, this interpretation of marriage does not extend to "domestic partnerships" or "civil unions." Couples in these relationships are still regarded as *single* by the IRS.

As far as income taxes are concerned, have these new rules resolved the prior difficulties of same-sex couples? The answer depends on where they live and whether such location imposes an income tax. Consider the following possibilities as to residence.

1. No state or local income taxes imposed.
2. State and local income taxes imposed and jurisdiction recognizes same-sex marriages.
3. State and local income taxes imposed but jurisdiction does not recognize same-sex marriages.

Category (1) was never a problem, and Category (2) was resolved via *U.S. v. Windsor*. Thus, the filing status used for state and local purposes (e.g., married filing jointly) will also be available for Federal purposes. With the Supreme Court decision in *Obergefell v. Hodges* (135 S.Ct. 2584), Category (3) has been resolved as each state must now accept same-sex marriages (no matter where licensed).

However, challenges remain for persons in a domestic partnership or civil union. They could be treated as married for state purposes but single for Federal tax law.

the taxpayer or both.[35] The payments are applied against the tax from the Tax Table or Tax Rate Schedules to determine whether the taxpayer will get a refund or pay additional tax.

Employers are required to withhold income tax on compensation paid to their employees and to pay this tax to the government. The employer notifies the employee of the amount of income and income tax withheld on Form W–2 (Wage and Tax Statement). The employee should receive this form by January 31 after the year in which the income tax is withheld.

If taxpayers receive income that is not subject to withholding or income from which insufficient tax is withheld, they may have to pay estimated tax. These individuals must file Form 1040–ES (Estimated Tax for Individuals) and pay in quarterly installments the income tax and self-employment tax estimated to be due.

The income tax from the Tax Table or the Tax Rate Schedules also is reduced by the individual's tax credits. There is an important distinction between tax credits and tax deductions. Tax credits (including tax withheld) reduce the tax liability dollar for dollar. Tax deductions reduce taxable income on which the tax liability is based.

EXAMPLE 35

Gail is a taxpayer in the 25% tax bracket. As a result of incurring $1,000 in child care, she is entitled to a $200 credit for child and dependent care expenses ($1,000 child care expenses × 20% credit rate). She also contributed $1,000 to the American Cancer Society and included this amount in her itemized deductions.

The credit for child and dependent care expenses results in a $200 reduction of Gail's tax liability for the year. The contribution to the American Cancer Society reduces taxable income by $1,000 and results in a $250 reduction in Gail's tax liability ($1,000 reduction in taxable income × 25% tax rate).

Selected tax credits for individuals are discussed in Chapter 10. Following are some of the more common credits available to individuals:

- Child tax credit.
- Credit for child and dependent care expenses.
- Earned income credit.
- Premium tax credit.

The computation of net taxes payable or refund due can be illustrated by returning to the facts of Example 6.

---

[35]See § 3402 for withholding and § 6654 for estimated payments.

EXAMPLE 36

Grace is single and has her disabled and dependent mother living with her. Recall that Example 6 established that Grace has taxable income of $24,500. Further assume that she has the following income tax withheld, $2,500; estimated tax payments, $600; and a credit for dependent care expenses, $200. Grace's net taxes payable (refund due) is computed as follows:

Income tax (from 2016 Tax Rate Schedule for head of household)		$3,013 (rounded)
Less: Tax credits and prepayments—		
Credit for dependent care expenses	$ 200	
Income tax withheld	2,500	
Estimated tax payments	600	(3,300)
Net taxes payable (refund due, if negative)		($ 287)

9-6d Additional Taxes for Certain Individuals

A review of page 2 of Form 1040 shows that an individual may owe taxes in addition to the income tax. These other taxes include the following:

- Alternative minimum tax (see discussion in Chapter 17)
- Self-employment tax (see discussion in Chapter 11)
- Taxes from Forms 8959 and 8960 (discussed below)

The taxes computed on Forms 8959 and 8960 were created as part of the Affordable Care Act. The tax reported on Form 8959 is the Additional Medicare Tax. This tax is computed at a rate of .9 percent on wages and self-employment income in excess of threshold amounts. For married taxpayers, the threshold amount is $250,000 ($125,000 if married filing separately) and $200,000 for all other taxpayers. An employer must withhold the .9% tax on wages paid to any employee that exceed $200,000 for the year (regardless of the employee's filing status). The Additional Medicare Tax is imposed only on the employee, not also the employer.

Form 8960 reports an individual's Net Investment Income Tax (NIIT). This tax is imposed at a rate of 3.8 percent of the lesser of:

- Net investment income, or
- The excess of modified adjusted gross income (MAGI) over $250,000 for married taxpayers filing a joint return ($125,000 if married filing separately) and $200,000 for all other taxpayers.

In general, "net investment income" includes interest, dividends, annuities, royalties, rents, income from passive activities, and net gains from the sale of investment property, reduced by deductions allowed in generating such income. For purposes of computing the NIIT, MAGI is defined as AGI increased by any foreign earned income exclusion (adjusted for related deductions). See Chapter 11 for discussion of the foreign earned income exclusion.

A high-income individual may be subject to both the 3.8 percent NIIT as well as the .9 percent Additional Medicare Tax on wages or self-employment income. The effect of the NIIT and Additional Medicare Tax is to increase the individual's marginal tax rate.

EXAMPLE 37

Rajiv is single and has the following income for 2016: wages of $220,000, interest income of $6,000, and capital gain of $28,000. Rajiv owes Additional Medicare Tax of $180 [.9% × ($220,000 − $200,000)]. In addition, he owes NIIT of $1,292 computed as follows:

3.8% × the lesser of:

- Net investment income of $34,000 ($6,000 + $28,000), or
- Modified adjusted gross income of $254,000 ($220,000 + $6,000 + $28,000) over $200,000, or $54,000

Unlike many threshold amounts, the ones for the NIIT and the Additional Medicare Tax are not adjusted annually for inflation. These additional taxes must be paid during the year through income tax withholdings or estimated tax payments.

9-6e Kiddie Tax—Unearned Income of Children Taxed at Parents' Rate

LO.7

Identify and report kiddie tax situations.

Most individuals compute taxable income using the tax formula shown in Concept Summary 9.1. Special provisions govern the computation of taxable income and the tax liability for certain children who have unearned income in excess of specified amounts.

Recall that individuals who are claimed as dependents by other taxpayers cannot claim an exemption on their own return. This prevents parents from shifting the tax on investment income (such as interest and dividends) to a child by transferring ownership of the assets producing the income. Without this provision, the child would pay no tax on the income to the extent it was sheltered by the child's exemption and standard deduction amounts.

Current tax law also reduces or eliminates the possibility of saving taxes by shifting income from parents to children by taxing the net unearned income of these children as if it were the parents' income. Unearned income includes taxable interest, dividends, capital gains, rents, royalties, the taxable portion of scholarships, pension and annuity income, and income (other than earned income) received as the beneficiary of a trust.

This provision, commonly referred to as the kiddie tax, applies to any child who is under age 19 (or under age 24 if a full-time student) and has unearned income of more than $2,100 in 2015 (also $2,100 in 2014).[36] The kiddie tax does not apply if the child has earned income that exceeds half of his or her support, if the child is married and files a joint return, or if both parents are deceased.

Net Unearned Income

In 2016, net unearned income of a dependent child is computed as follows:

Unearned income
Less: $1,050
Less: The *greater* of
$1,050 of the standard deduction *or*
The amount of allowable itemized deductions directly connected with the production of the unearned income
Equals: Net unearned income

If net unearned income is not a positive amount, the child's tax is computed without using the parents' rate. If the amount of net unearned income (regardless of source) is positive, the net unearned income will be taxed at the parents' rate. The child's remaining taxable income (known as nonparental source income) is taxed at the child's rate. The $1,050 amounts in the preceding formula are subject to adjustment for inflation each year.

In-depth coverage can be found on this book's companion website: www.cengagebrain.com

10 DIGGING DEEPER

Election to Report Certain Unearned Income on Parents' Return

In 2016, if a child who is subject to the kiddie tax is required to file a tax return and meets all of the following requirements, the parents may elect to report the child's unearned income that exceeds $2,100 (same in 2015) on the parents' own tax return.

- Gross income is from interest and dividends only.

- Gross income is more than $1,050 but less than $10,500 (for 2015, these amounts are the same).

- No estimated tax has been paid in the name and Social Security number of the child, and the child is not subject to backup withholding.

---

[36]§ 1(g)(2).

If the parental election is made, the child is treated as having no gross income and is not required to file a tax return. In this case, Form 8814 (Parents' Election to Report Child's Interest and Dividends) must be filed as part of the parents' tax return.

The parent(s) must also pay an additional tax equal to the smaller of $105 or 10 percent of the child's gross income over $1,050. Parents who have substantial itemized deductions based on AGI may find that making the parental election increases total taxes for the family unit. Taxes should be calculated both with and without the parental election to determine the appropriate choice.

TAX PLANNING STRATEGIES Income of Certain Children

FRAMEWORK FOCUS: TAX RATE

Strategy: Shift Net Income from High-Bracket Taxpayers to Low-Bracket Taxpayers.

Taxpayers can use several strategies to avoid or minimize the effect of the rules that tax the unearned income of certain children at the parents' rate. With the cutoff age being 19 (under 24 for full-time students), many children are vulnerable to the application of the kiddie tax. Parents should consider giving a younger child assets that defer the inclusion in gross income until the child reaches a nonvulnerable age. For example, U.S. government Series EE savings bonds can be used to defer income until the bonds are cashed in.

Growth stocks typically pay little in the way of dividends. However, the unrealized appreciation on an astute investment may more than offset the lack of dividends. The child can hold the growth stock until he or she reaches a safe age. If the stock is sold then at a profit, the profit is taxed at the child's low rates.

Taxpayers in a position to do so can employ their children in their business and pay them a reasonable wage for the work they actually perform (e.g., light office help such as filing). The child's earned income is sheltered by the standard deduction, and the parents' business is allowed a deduction for the wages. The kiddie tax rules have no effect on earned income, even if it is earned from the parents' business.

9-7 TAX RETURN FILING PROCEDURES

9-7a Selecting the Proper Form

Although a variety of forms are available to individual taxpayers, the use of some of these forms is restricted. For example, Form 1040–EZ cannot be used if:

- Taxpayer claims any dependents,
- Taxpayer (or spouse) is 65 or older or blind,
- Taxable income is $100,000 or more, or
- Taxpayer claims the premium tax credit.

Taxpayers who want to itemize deductions *from* AGI cannot use Form 1040–A, but must file Form 1040.

TAX FACT What Form of Tax Compliance Is Right for You?

Based on recent projections from the IRS, when preparing about 154 million individual income tax returns expected to be filed in 2017, taxpayers will be using relatively fewer paper Forms 1040, 1040A, and 1040–EZ. As a result, the IRS expects the level of electronically filed returns to be at or near an all-time high.

	Percentage
Paper individual returns	12%
Electronically filed individual returns	88
	100%

Source: Fiscal Year Return Projections for the United States: 2015–2022, IRS, Document 6292, Fall 2015 Update, Table 1.

9-7b **The E-File Approach**

The e-file program is an increasingly popular approach (and is mandatory for most tax return preparers). The required tax information is transmitted to the IRS electronically either directly from the taxpayer (i.e., an "e-file online return") or indirectly through an electronic return originator (ERO). EROs are tax professionals who have been accepted into the electronic filing program by the IRS. Such parties hold themselves out to the general public as "authorized IRS e-file providers." Providers often are the preparers of the return as well.

Through prearrangement with the IRS, a number of software providers offer free e-filing services. These services generally are available only to taxpayers who have AGI of $60,000 or less. A list of these providers and their eligibility requirements can be obtained through the IRS website.

The e-file approach has two major advantages over paper filing. First, compliance with the format required by the IRS eliminates many errors that would otherwise occur. Second, the time required for processing a refund usually is reduced to three weeks or less.

9-7c **When and Where to File**

Tax returns of individuals are due on or before the fifteenth day of the fourth month following the close of the tax year. For the calendar year taxpayer, the usual filing date is on or before April 15 of the following year.[37] When the due date falls on a Saturday, Sunday, or legal holiday, the last day for filing falls on the next business day.

If a taxpayer is unable to file the return by the specified due date, a six-month extension of time can be obtained by filing Form 4868 (Application for Automatic Extension of Time to File U.S. Individual Income Tax Return).[38]

Although obtaining an extension excuses a taxpayer from a penalty for failure to file, it does not insulate against the penalty for failure to pay. If more tax is owed, the filing of Form 4868 should be accompanied by an additional payment to cover the balance due. The return should be sent or delivered to the IRS Regional Service Center listed in the instructions for each type of return or contained in software applications.[39]

9-7d **Modes of Payment**

Payments of taxes due can be made by check, money order, IRS Direct Pay (electronic funds withdrawal from a bank account), the Electronic Federal Tax Payment System (EFTPS), and a number of major credit cards. The use of a credit or debit card results in a charge to the taxpayer.

REFOCUS ON THE BIG PICTURE

A DIVIDED HOUSEHOLD

Of major concern to Polly is her filing status. If she qualifies as an abandoned spouse, she is entitled to file as head of household. If not, she is considered to be a married person filing separately. Moreover, to be an abandoned spouse, Polly must be able to claim Paige as a dependent. To be a dependent, Paige must meet the requirements of a qualifying child or a qualifying relative.

For qualifying child purposes, Paige must meet either the age (i.e., under age 19) or the full-time student (under age 24) test. (A disabled child exception seems highly unlikely.) Because Paige currently is not a full-time student, is she under age 19? If so, she is a qualifying child (see Example 13). If Paige is not a qualifying child, is she a qualifying relative? Here, the answer depends on meeting the gross income test (see Example 19). How much did Paige earn from her part-time job? If her

continued

© RUDIYANTO WIJAYA/GETTY IMAGES

---

[37]§ 6072(a).

[38]Reg. § 1.6081–4. See also *Your Federal Income Tax* (IRS Publication 17).

[39]The appropriate Regional Service Center address can be found at **www.irs.gov/uac/Where-To-File-Addresses-for-Tax-Professionals**.

earnings are under $4,000, she satisfies the gross income test. Thus, if Paige can be claimed as a dependent under either the qualifying child or the qualifying relative category, Polly is an abandoned spouse entitled to head-of-household filing status (see Example 31). If not, she is a married person filing separately.

Maude can be claimed as Polly's dependent because she is a member of the household. It does not matter that she died in February, and the dependency exemption amount need not be apportioned and is allowed in full. Because Maude is her dependent, Polly can claim the medical expenses she paid on Maude's behalf. The funeral expenses, however, are not deductible (see Example 16).

Does Maude qualify Polly for head-of-household filing status? No—although she is a dependent, Maude does not meet the relationship test (see Example 30).

What If?

Assume that Nick left for parts unknown in August (not March). Now Polly cannot qualify as an abandoned spouse. Her spouse lived in the home during part of the last six months of the year. Consequently, Polly is treated as married and cannot qualify for head-of-household filing status. She must file as a married person filing separately. The change in when Nick left will not affect the dependency issue regarding Paige, however.

Suggested Readings

David R. Baldwin, Lawrence H. Carlton, Donna Haim, Jonathan Horn, Kenneth L. Rubin, Kaye F. Sheridan, David E. Taylor, and Donald J. Zidik Jr., "Directions in Individual Taxation," *The Tax Adviser*, September 2015.

Andrew Lafond and Bruce A. Leauby, "Help Wanted: Hire Your Kids for Tax Savings," *Practical Tax Strategies*, October 2013.

M. Jill Lockwood, Britton McKay, and Michael Wiggins, "Tax Planning for Divorce: Avoiding the Pitfalls," *Practical Tax Strategies,* September 2012.

Key Terms

Dependency exemption, 9-9

E-file, 9-27

Filing status, 9-17

Head-of-household, 9-19

Itemized deductions, 9-5

Kiddie tax, 9-25

Marriage penalty, 9-18

Multiple support agreement, 9-13

Personal exemptions, 9-8

Qualifying child, 9-9

Qualifying relative, 9-11

Standard deduction, 9-5

Surviving spouse, 9-18

Tax Rate Schedules, 9-21

Tax Table, 9-21

Unearned income, 9-25

Computational Exercises

Issue ID   1.   **LO.2** Sam and Abby are dependents of their parents, and each has income of $2,100 for the year. Sam's standard deduction for the year is $1,050, while Abby's is $2,450. As their income is the same, what causes the difference in the amount of the standard deduction?

2. **LO.2** Compute the 2016 standard deduction for the following taxpayers.   Critical Thinking

   a. Margie is 15 and claimed as a dependent by her parents. She has $800 in dividend income and $1,400 in wages from a part-time job.

   b. Ruby and Woody are married and file a joint tax return. Ruby is age 66, and Woody is 69. Their taxable retirement income is $10,000.

   c. Shonda is age 68 and single. She is claimed by her daughter as a dependent. Her earned income is $500, and her interest income is $125.

   d. Frazier, age 55, is married but is filing a separate return. His wife itemizes her deductions.

3. **LO.4** In 2016, Dominique and Felix are married and file a joint tax return. Their AGI is $314,050 and they claim three exemptions. Determine their total exemption amount for 2016.

4. **LO.5** Paul and Sonja, who are married, had itemized deductions of $8,200 and   Issue ID
$400, respectively, during 2016. Paul suggests that they file separately—he will itemize his deductions *from* AGI, and she will claim the standard deduction.

   a. Evaluate Paul's suggestion.

   b. What should they do?

5. **LO.6** Compute the 2016 tax liability and the marginal and average tax rates for the following taxpayers (use the 2016 tax rate schedules in Appendix A for this purpose).

   a. Chandler, who files as a single taxpayer, has taxable income of $93,000.

   b. Lazare, who files as a head of household, has taxable income of $56,000.

6. **LO.6** George and Aimee are married. George has wage income of $190,000, and Aimee has a sole proprietorship that generated net income of $85,000. They also have interest and dividend income of $21,000. Compute any NIIT and Additional Medicare Tax they owe for the current year.

7. **LO.7** In 2016, Simon, age 12, has interest income of $800 and dividend income of   Critical Thinking
$4,000. He has no investment expenses. His parents have taxable income of $80,200 and file a joint tax return. Assume that no parental election is made. Determine Simon's net unearned income, allocable parental tax, and total tax liability.

Problems

8. **LO.1, 5** During the year, Addison is involved in the following transactions: Issue ID

   a. Lost money gambling on a recent trip to a casino.

   b. Helped pay for her neighbor's dental bills. The neighbor is a good friend who is unemployed.

   c. Received from the IRS a tax refund due to Addison's overpayment of last year's Federal income taxes.

   d. Paid a traffic ticket received while double parking to attend a business meeting.

   e. Contributed to the mayor's reelection campaign. The mayor had promised Addison to have some of her land rezoned. The mayor was reelected and got Addison's land rezoned.

   f. Borrowed money from a bank to make a down payment on an automobile.

   g. Sold a houseboat and a camper on eBay. Both were personal use items, and the gain from one offset the loss from the other.

   h. Her dependent grandfather died on June 3 of the year.

   i. Paid for dependent grandfather's funeral expenses.

   j. Paid premiums on her dependent son's life insurance policy.

What are the possible income tax ramifications of these transactions?

9. **LO.1** Which of the following items are *inclusions* in gross income?

a. During the year, stock that the taxpayer purchased as an investment doubled in value.

b. Amount an off-duty motorcycle police officer received for escorting a funeral procession.

c. While his mother was in the hospital, the taxpayer sold her jewelry and gave the money to his girlfriend.

d. Child support payments received.

e. A damage deposit the taxpayer recovered when he vacated the apartment he had rented.

f. Interest received by the taxpayer on an investment in general purpose bonds issued by IBM.

g. Amounts received by the taxpayer, a baseball "Hall of Famer," for autographing sports equipment (e.g., balls and gloves).

h. Tips received by a bartender from patrons. (Taxpayer is paid a regular salary by the cocktail lounge that employs him.)

i. Taxpayer sells his Super Bowl tickets for three times what he paid for them.

j. Taxpayer receives a new BMW from his grandmother when he passes the CPA exam.

10. **LO.1** Which of the following items are *exclusions* from gross income?

a. Alimony payments received.

b. Damages award received by the taxpayer for personal physical injury—none were for punitive damages.

c. A new golf cart won in a church raffle.

d. Amount collected on a loan previously made to a college friend.

e. Insurance proceeds paid to the taxpayer on the death of her uncle—she was the designated beneficiary under the policy.

f. Interest income on City of Chicago bonds.

g. Jury duty fees.

h. Stolen funds the taxpayer had collected for a local food bank drive.

i. Reward paid by the IRS for information provided that led to the conviction of the taxpayer's former employer for tax evasion.

j. An envelope containing $8,000 found (and unclaimed) by the taxpayer in a bus station.

Decision Making   11. **LO.1** In late 2016, the Polks come to you for tax advice. They are considering selling some stock investments for a loss and making a contribution to a traditional IRA. In reviewing their situation, you note that they have large medical expenses and a casualty loss, neither of which is covered by insurance. What advice would you give the Polks?

12. **LO.1, 2, 3, 4** Compute the taxable income for 2016 in each of the following independent situations:

a. Drew and Meg, ages 40 and 41, respectively, are married and file a joint return. In addition to four dependent children, they have AGI of $65,000 and itemized deductions of $15,000.

b. Sybil, age 40, is single and supports her dependent parents, who live with her, as well as her grandfather, who is in a nursing home. She has AGI of $80,000 and itemized deductions of $8,000.

c. Scott, age 49, is a surviving spouse. His household includes two unmarried stepsons who qualify as his dependents. He has AGI of $75,000 and itemized deductions of $10,100.

d. Amelia, age 33, is an abandoned spouse who maintains a household for her three dependent children. She has AGI of $58,000 and itemized deductions of $9,500.

e. Dale, age 42, is divorced but maintains the home in which he and his daughter, Jill, live. Jill is single and qualifies as Dale's dependent. Dale has AGI of $64,000 and itemized deductions of $9,900.

13. **LO.1, 2, 3, 4** Compute the taxable income for 2016 for Emily on the basis of the following information. Her filing status is single.

Salary	$85,000
Interest income from bonds issued by Xerox	1,100
Alimony payments received	6,000
Contribution to traditional IRA	5,500
Gift from parents	25,000
Short-term capital gain from stock investment	2,000
Amount lost in football office pool	500
Number of potential dependents (two cousins, who live in Canada)	?
Age	40

14. **LO.1, 2, 3, 4** Compute the taxable income for 2016 for Aiden on the basis of the following information. Aiden is married but has not seen or heard from his wife since 2014.

Salary	$ 80,000
Interest on bonds issued by the City of Boston	3,000
Interest on CD issued by Wells Fargo Bank	2,000
Cash dividend received on Chevron common stock	2,200
Life insurance proceeds paid on death of aunt (Aiden was the designated beneficiary of the policy)	200,000
Inheritance received upon death of aunt	100,000
Jackson (a cousin) repaid a loan Aiden made to him in 2009 (no interest was provided for)	5,000
Itemized deductions (state income tax, property taxes on residence, interest on home mortgage, and charitable contributions)	9,700
Number of dependents (children, ages 17 and 18, and mother-in-law, age 70)	3
Age	43

15. **LO.2** In choosing between the standard deduction and itemizing deductions *from*   Issue ID
AGI, what effect, if any, does each of the following have?

a. The age of the taxpayer(s).

b. The health (i.e., physical condition) of the taxpayer.

c. Whether taxpayers rent or own their residence.

d. Taxpayer's filing status (e.g., single, married, filing jointly).

e. Whether married taxpayers decide to file separate returns.

f. The taxpayer's uninsured personal residence was recently destroyed by fire.

g. The number of personal and dependency exemptions the taxpayer can claim.

16. **LO.2, 3, 5** David is age 78, is a widower, and is being claimed as a dependent by his son. How does this situation affect the following?

a. David's own individual filing requirement.

b. David's personal exemption.

c. The standard deduction allowed to David.

d. The availability of any additional standard deduction.

17. **LO.2** Determine the amount of the standard deduction allowed for 2016 in the following independent situations. In each case, assume that the taxpayer is claimed as another person's dependent.

    a. Curtis, age 18, has income as follows: $700 interest from a certificate of deposit and $6,100 from repairing cars.

    b. Mattie, age 18, has income as follows: $600 cash dividends from a stock investment and $4,700 from handling a paper route.

    c. Mel, age 16, has income as follows: $675 interest on a bank savings account and $800 for painting a neighbor's fence.

    d. Lucy, age 15, has income as follows: $400 cash dividends from a stock investment and $500 from grooming pets.

    e. Sarah, age 67 and a widow, has income as follows: $500 from a bank savings account and $3,200 from babysitting.

18. **LO.4** Analyze each of the characteristics in considering the indicated test for dependency as a qualifying child or qualifying relative. In the last two columns, after each listed test (e.g. gross income), state whether the particular test is Met, Not Met or Not Applicable (NA).

	Characteristic	Qualifying Child Test	Qualifying Relative Test
a.	Taxpayer's son has gross income of $7,000	Gross income	Gross income
b.	Taxpayer's niece has gross income of $3,000	Gross income	Gross income
c.	Taxpayer's uncle lives with him	Relationship	Relationship
d.	Taxpayer's daughter is 25 and disabled	Age	Age
e.	Taxpayer's daughter is age 18, has gross income of $8,000, and does not live with him	Abode, Gross income	Gross income
f.	Taxpayer's cousin does not live with her	Relationship, Abode	Relationship
g.	Taxpayer's brother does not live with her	Abode	Relationship
h.	Taxpayer's sister has dropped out of school, is age 17, and lives with him	Relationship, Abode, Age	Relationship
i.	Taxpayer's older nephew is age 23 and a full-time student	Relationship, Age	Relationship
j.	Taxpayer's grandson lives with her and has gross income of $7,000	Relationship, Abode	Relationship, Gross income

19. **LO.4** Caden and Lily are divorced on March 3, 2015. For financial reasons, however, Lily continues to live in Caden's apartment and receives her support from him. Caden does not claim Lily as a dependent on his 2015 Federal income tax return but does so on his 2016 return. Explain.

20. **LO.3, 4** For tax year 2016, determine the number of personal and dependency exemptions in each of the following independent situations:

    a. Leo and Amanda (ages 48 and 46, respectively) are husband and wife and furnish more than 50% of the support of their two children, Elton (age 18) and Trista (age 24). During the year, Elton earns $4,500 providing transportation for elderly persons with disabilities, and Trista receives a $5,000 scholarship that is used entirely for tuition at the law school she attends.

    b. Audry (age 45) was divorced this year. She maintains a household in which she, her ex-husband (Clint), and his mother (Olive) live and furnishes more than 50% of their support. Olive is age 91 and blind.

    c. Crystal, age 45, furnishes more than 50% of the support of her married son, Andy (age 18), and his wife, Paige (age 19), who live with her. During the year, Andy earned $8,200 from a part-time job. All parties live in Iowa (a common law state).

    d. Assume the same facts as in part (c), except that all parties live in Washington (a community property state).

21. **LO.3, 4** Sam and Elizabeth Jefferson file a joint return and have three children—all of whom qualify as dependents. If the Jeffersons have AGI of $333,400, what is their allowable deduction for personal and dependency exemptions for 2016?

22. **LO.4** Wesley and Myrtle (ages 90 and 88, respectively) live in an assisted care facility and for 2015 and 2016 received their support from the following sources:

	Percentage of Support
Social Security benefits	16%
Son	20
Niece	29
Cousin	12
Brother	11
Family friend (not related)	12

   a. Which persons are eligible to claim the dependency exemptions under a multiple support agreement?

   b. Must Wesley and Myrtle be claimed by the same person(s) for both 2015 and 2016? Explain.

   c. Who, if anyone, can claim their medical expenses?

23. **LO.2, 7** Taylor, age 18, is claimed as a dependent by her parents. For 2016, she has the following income: $4,000 of wages from a summer job, $1,800 of interest from a money market account, and $2,000 of interest from City of Boston bonds.   *Critical Thinking*

   a. What is Taylor's taxable income for 2016?

   b. What is Taylor's tax for 2016? [Her parents file a joint return and have taxable income of $130,000 (no dividends or capital gains)].

24. **LO.4** Walter and Nancy provide 60% of the support of their daughter (age 18) and son-in-law (age 22). The son-in-law (John) is a full-time student at a local university, while the daughter (Irene) holds various part-time jobs from which she earns $11,000. Walter and Nancy engage you to prepare their tax return for 2016. During a meeting with them in late March 2017, you learn that John and Irene have filed a joint return. What tax advice would you give based on the following assumptions: *Issue ID*   *Decision Making*

   a. All parties live in Louisiana (a community property state).

   b. All parties live in New Jersey (a common law state).

25. **LO.1, 4, 6** Charlotte (age 40) is a surviving spouse and provides all of the support of her four minor children who live with her. She also maintains the household in which her parents live and furnished 60% of their support. Besides interest on City of Miami bonds in the amount of $5,500, Charlotte's father received $2,400 from a part-time job. Charlotte has a salary of $80,000, a short-term capital loss of $2,000, a cash prize of $4,000 from a church raffle, and itemized deductions of $10,500. Using the Tax Rate Schedules, compute the 2016 tax liability for Charlotte.

26. **LO.1, 2, 3, 4, 5, 6** Morgan (age 45) is single and provides more than 50% of the support of Rosalyn (a family friend), Flo (a niece, age 18), and Jerold (a nephew, age 18). Both Rosalyn and Flo live with Morgan, but Jerold (a French citizen) lives in Canada. Morgan earns a salary of $95,000, contributes $5,000 to a traditional IRA, and receives sales proceeds of $15,000 for an RV that cost $60,000 and was used for vacations. She has $8,200 in itemized deductions. Using the Tax Rate Schedules, compute the 2016 tax liability for Morgan.

WWW For the latest in changes to tax legislation, visit **www.cengagebrain.com.**

Ethics and Equity   27. **LO.5** Bob and Carol have been in and out of marital counseling for the past few years. Early in 2016, they decide to separate. However, because they are barely able to get by on their current incomes, they cannot afford separate housing or the legal costs of a divorce. So Bob moves out of their house in March and takes up residence in their detached garage (which has an enclosed workshop and bathroom). Carol stays in the house with their two children and pays more than half of the costs of maintaining their residence. Bob does not enter the house for the remainder of the year. Can Carol qualify as an abandoned spouse? Explain.

Critical Thinking   28. **LO.5** Which of the following individuals are required to file a tax return for 2016? Should any of these individuals file a return even if filing is not required? Why or why not?

   a.   Patricia, age 19, is a self-employed single individual with gross income of $5,200 from an unincorporated business. Business expenses amounted to $4,900.

   b.   Mike is single and is 67 years old. His gross income from wages was $10,800.

   c.   Ronald is a dependent child under age 19 who received $6,500 in wages from a part-time job.

   d.   Sam is married and files a joint return with his spouse, Lana. Both Sam and Lana are 67 years old. Their combined gross income was $24,250.

   e.   Quinn, age 20, is a full-time college student who is claimed as a dependent by his parents. For 2016, Quinn has taxable interest and dividends of $2,500.

Decision Making   29. **LO.5, 6** Roy and Brandi are engaged and plan to get married. During 2016, Roy is a full-time student and earns $9,000 from a part-time job. With this income, student loans, savings, and nontaxable scholarships, he is self-supporting. For the year, Brandi is employed and has wages of $61,000. How much income tax, if any, can Brandi save if she and Roy marry in 2016 and file a joint return?

   30. **LO.6** Jayden calculates his 2016 income tax by using both the Tax Tables and the Tax Rate Schedules. Because the Tax Rate Schedules yield a slightly lower tax liability, he plans to pay this amount.

   a.   Why is there a difference?

   b.   Is Jayden's approach permissible? Why or why not?

Critical Thinking   31. **LO.1, 3, 7** Paige, age 17, is claimed as a dependent on her parents' 2016 return, on which they report taxable income of $120,000 (no qualified dividends or capital gains). Paige earned $3,900 pet sitting and $4,100 in interest on a savings account. What are Paige's taxable income and tax liability for 2016?

Critical Thinking   32. **LO.1, 3, 7** Terri, age 16, is claimed as a dependent on her parents' 2016 return. During the year, Terri earned $5,000 in interest income and $3,000 from part-time jobs.

   a.   What is Terri's taxable income?

   b.   How much of Terri's income is taxed at her rate? At her parents' rate?

   c.   Can the parental election be made? Why or why not?

Comprehensive Tax Return Problems

Tax Return Problem

H&R BLOCK

TAX SOFTWARE

1.   Lance H. and Wanda B. Dean are married and live at 431 Yucca Drive, Santa Fe, NM 87501. Lance works for the convention bureau of the local Chamber of Commerce, while Wanda is employed part-time as a paralegal for a law firm.

   During 2015, the Deans had the following receipts:

Salaries ($60,000 for Lance, $41,000 for Wanda)		$101,000
Interest income—		
City of Albuquerque general purpose bonds	$1,000	
Ford Motor Company bonds	1,100	
Ally Bank certificate of deposit	400	2,500
Child support payments from John Allen		7,200
Annual gifts from parents		26,000
Settlement from Roadrunner Touring Company		90,000
Lottery winnings		600
Federal income tax refund (for tax year 2014)		400

Wanda was previously married to John Allen. When they divorced several years ago, Wanda was awarded custody of their two children, Penny and Kyle. (Note: Wanda has never issued a Form 8332 waiver.) Under the divorce decree, John was obligated to pay alimony and child support—the alimony payments were to terminate if Wanda remarried.

In July, while going to lunch in downtown Santa Fe, Wanda was injured by a tour bus. As the driver was clearly at fault, the owner of the bus, Roadrunner Touring Company, paid her medical expenses (including a one-week stay in a hospital). To avoid a lawsuit, Roadrunner also transferred $90,000 to her in settlement of the personal injuries she sustained.

The Deans had the following expenditures for 2015:

Medical expenses (not covered by insurance)		$7,200
Taxes—		
Property taxes on personal residence	$3,600	
State of New Mexico income tax (includes amount withheld from wages during 2015)	4,200	7,800
Interest on home mortgage		6,000
Paid church pledge		3,600
Life insurance premiums (policy on Lance's life)		1,200
Contribution to traditional IRA (on Wanda's behalf)		5,000
Traffic fines		300
Contribution to the reelection campaign fund of the mayor of Santa Fe		500
Funeral expenses for Wayne Boyle		6,300

The life insurance policy was taken out by Lance several years ago and designates Wanda as the beneficiary. As a part-time employee, Wanda is excluded from coverage under her employer's pension plan. Consequently, she provides for her own retirement with a traditional IRA obtained at a local trust company. Because the mayor is a member of the local Chamber of Commerce, Lance felt compelled to make the political contribution.

The Deans' household includes the following, for whom they provide more than half of the support:

	Social Security Number*	Birth Date
Lance Dean (age 42)	123-45-6786	12/16/1973
Wanda Dean (age 40)	123-45-6787	08/08/1975
Penny Allen (age 19)	123-45-6788	10/09/1996
Kyle Allen (age 17)	123-45-6789	05/03/1998
Wayne Boyle (age 75)	123-45-6785	06/15/1940

*In the interest of privacy and to protect against taxpayer identification misuse, Social Security numbers used throughout the textbook have been replaced with fictitious numbers.

Penny graduated from high school on May 9, 2015, and is undecided about college. During 2015, she earned $8,500 (placed in a savings account) playing a harp in the lobby of a local hotel. Wayne is Wanda's widower father, who died on January 20, 2015. For the past few years, Wayne qualified as a dependent of the Deans.

Federal income tax withheld is $5,200 (Lance) and $3,100 (Wanda). The proper amount of Social Security and Medicare tax was withheld.

Determine the Federal income tax for 2015 for the Deans on a joint return by completing the appropriate forms. They do not want to contribute to the Presidential Election Campaign Fund. All members of the family had health care coverage for all of 2015. If an overpayment results, it is to be refunded to them. Suggested software: H&R BLOCK Tax Software.

Tax Return Problem

Decision Making

Communications

TAX SOFTWARE

2. Logan B. Taylor is a widower whose wife, Sara, died on June 6, 2013. He lives at 4680 Dogwood Lane, Springfield, MO 65801. He is employed as a paralegal by a local law firm. During 2015, he had the following receipts:

Salary		$ 80,000
Interest income—		
Money market account at Omni Bank	$ 300	
Savings account at Boone State Bank	1,100	
City of Springfield general purpose bonds	3,000	4,400
Inheritance from Daniel		60,000
Life insurance proceeds		200,000
Amount from sale of St. Louis lot		80,000
Proceeds from estate sale		9,000
Federal income tax refund (for 2014 tax overpayment)		700

Logan inherited securities worth $60,000 from his uncle, Daniel, who died in 2015. Logan also was the designated beneficiary of an insurance policy on Daniel's life with a maturity value of $200,000. The lot in St. Louis was purchased on May 2, 2010, for $85,000 and held as an investment. As the neighborhood has deteriorated, Logan decided to cut his losses and sold the lot on January 5, 2015, for $80,000. The estate sale consisted largely of items belonging to Sara and Daniel (e.g., camper, boat, furniture, and fishing and hunting equipment). Logan estimates that the property sold originally cost at least twice the $9,000 he received and has declined or stayed the same in value since Sara and Daniel died.

Logan's expenditures for 2015 include the following:

Medical expenses (including $10,500 for dental)		$11,500
Taxes—		
State of Missouri income tax (includes withholdings during 2015)	$3,200	
Property taxes on personal residence	4,500	7,700
Interest on home mortgage		4,600
Contribution to church (paid pledges for 2015 and 2016)		4,800

Logan and his dependents are covered by his employer's health insurance policy for all of 2015. However, he is subject to a deductible, and dental care is not included. The $10,500 dental charge was for Helen's implants. Helen is Logan's widowed mother, who lives with him (see below). Logan normally pledges $2,400 ($200 per month) each year to his church. On December 5, 2015, upon the advice of his pastor, he prepaid his pledge for 2016.

Logan's household, all of whom he supports, includes the following:

	Social Security Number	Birth Date
Logan Taylor (age 48)	123-45-6787	08/30/1967
Helen Taylor (age 70)	123-45-6780	01/13/1945
Asher Taylor (age 23)	123-45-6783	07/18/1992
Mia Taylor (age 22)	123-45-6784	02/16/1993

Helen receives a modest Social Security benefit. Asher, a son, is a full-time student in dental school and earns $4,500 as a part-time dental assistant. Mia, a daughter, does not work and is engaged to be married.

Part 1—Tax Computation

Using the appropriate forms and schedules, compute Logan's income tax for 2015. Federal income tax of $5,500 was withheld from his wages. If Logan has any over-payment on his income tax, he wants the refund sent to him. Assume that the proper amounts of Social Security and Medicare taxes were withheld. Logan does not want to contribute to the Presidential Election Campaign Fund. Suggested software: H&R BLOCK Tax Software.

Part 2—Follow-Up Advice

In early 2016, the following take place:

- Helen decides that she wants to live with one of her daughters and moves to Arizona.
- Asher graduates from dental school and joins an existing practice in St. Louis.
- Mia marries, and she and her husband move in with his parents.
- Using the insurance proceeds he received on Daniel's death, Logan pays off the mortgage on his personal residence.

Logan believes that these events may have an effect on his tax position for 2016. Therefore, he requests your advice.

Write a letter to Logan explaining in general terms the changes that will occur for tax purposes. Assume that Logan's salary and other factors not mentioned (e.g., property and state income taxes) will remain the same. Use the Tax Rate Schedules in projecting Logan's tax for 2016.

Research Problems

Note: Solutions to Research Problems can be prepared by using the Checkpoint® Student Edition online research product, which is available to accompany this text. It is also possible to prepare solutions to the Research Problems by using tax research materials found in a standard tax library.

Research Problem 1. Kathy and Brett Ouray married in 1998. They began to experience marital difficulties in 2012 and, in the current year, although they are not legally separated, consider themselves completely estranged. They have contemplated getting a divorce. However, because of financial concerns and because they both want to remain involved in the lives of their three sons, they have not yet filed for divorce. In addition, their financial difficulties have meant that Kathy and Brett cannot afford to live in separate residences. So although they consider themselves emotionally estranged, they and their three sons all reside in a single-family home in Chicago, Illinois.

Communications

Although Brett earns significantly more than Kathy, both contribute financially to maintaining their home and supporting their teenage sons. In one of their few and brief conversations this year, they determined that Brett had contributed far more than Kathy to the maintenance of their home and the support of their sons. Thus, Brett has decided that for the current tax year, they will file separate Federal income tax returns and that he will claim head-of-household filing status. While they live under the same roof, Brett believes that he and Kathy should maintain separate households. Given this fact and the fact that he provides significantly more for the support of his and Kathy's sons, he believes that he is eligible for head-of-household filing status. Advise Brett on which filing status is most appropriate for him in the current year. His address is 16 Lahinch, Chicago, IL 60608.

Decision Making

Research Problem 2. John and Janet Baker are husband and wife and maintain a household in which the following persons live: Calvin and Florence Carter and Darin, Andrea, and Morgan Baker.

- Calvin and Florence are Janet's parents, who are retired. During the year, they receive $19,000 in nontaxable funds (e.g., disability income, interest on municipal bonds, and Social Security benefits). Of this amount, $8,000 is spent equally between them for clothing, transportation, and recreation (e.g., vacation) and the balance of $11,000 is invested in tax-exempt securities. Janet paid $1,000 for her mother's dental work and paid the $1,200 premium on an insurance policy her father owned on his own life. Calvin also had medical expenses, but he insisted on paying for them with his own funds.

- Darin is the Bakers' 18-year-old son who is not a student but operates a pool-cleaning service on a part-time basis. During the year, he earns $14,000 from the business, which he places in a savings account for later college expenses.

- Andrea is the Bakers' 19-year-old daughter who does not work or go to school. Tired of the inconvenience of borrowing and sharing the family car, during the year, she purchased a Camaro for $21,000. Andrea used funds from a savings account she had established several years ago with an inheritance from her paternal grandfather.

- Morgan is the Bakers' 23-year-old daughter. To attend graduate school at a local university, she applied for and obtained a student loan of $20,000. She uses the full amount to pay her college tuition.

The Bakers' fair rental value of their residence, including utilities, is $14,000, while their total food expense for the household is $10,500.

a. How many dependency exemptions are the Bakers entitled to claim for the year? Explain your answer.

b. From a planning standpoint, how might the Bakers have improved the tax result?

Partial list of research aids:
Reg. §§ 1.152–1(a) and –1(c).
Your Federal Income Tax (IRS Publication 17), Chapter 3.

Internet Activity

Use the tax resources of the Internet to address the following questions. Do not restrict your search to the Web, but include a review of newsgroups and general reference materials, practitioner sites and resources, primary sources of the tax law, chat rooms and discussion groups, and other opportunities.

Research Problem 3. Locate IRS Form 2120 (at **www.irs.gov**), and answer the following questions.

a. Who must sign the form?

b. Who must file the form?

c. Can it be used for someone who is not related to the taxpayer? Explain.

Research Problem 4. What purpose is served by Form 8857? Read the directions to the form, and see IRS Publication 971 for additional information.

Research Problem 5. A nonresident alien earns money in the United States that is subject to Federal income tax. What guidance does the IRS provide about what tax form needs to be used and when it should be filed? In terms of the proper filing date, does it matter whether the earnings were subject to income tax withholding? Explain.

Roger CPA Review Questions

1. Keller is a single individual who in 2016 qualified for a foreign earned income exclusion of $80,000. Keller's 2016 net investment income was $25,000, and Keller's 2016 adjusted gross income prior to the foreign earned income exclusion was $220,000. Given a 3.8% Unearned Income Medicare Contribution Tax rate, what is Keller's 2016 liability for this surtax?

   a. $760   c. $950
   b. $0   d. $570

2. Walters, an individual, received the following in 2016:

W–2 income	$10,000
Federal tax refund for 2015	1,250
Scholarship stipend, in return for teaching assistant duties performed	25,000
Cash inheritance from deceased great-uncle	5,000

   Considering only the above, what is Walters' 2016 gross income?

   a. $35,000   c. $15,000
   b. $36,250   d. $16,250

3. For "qualifying widow(er)" filing status, which of the following requirements must be met?

   I.   The surviving spouse does not remarry before the end of the current year.
   II. The surviving spouse was eligible to file a joint tax return in the year of the spouse's death.
   III. The surviving spouse maintains the cost of the principal residence for six months.

   a. I, II, and III   c. I and III, but not II
   b. I and II, but not III   d. I only

4. Parker and his wife Marie would have been filing a joint tax return for 2014; however, Marie died in October of 2014. Parker has not remarried and continues to maintain a home for himself and his two children during 2014, 2015, 2016, and 2017. Which of the following are Parker's filing statuses for 2014, 2015, 2016, and 2017?

	2014	2015	2016	2017
a.	Qualifying widower	Married filing joint return	Qualifying widower	Head of household
b.	Married filing joint return	Married filing joint return	Head of household	Qualifying widower
c.	Married filing joint return	Qualifying widower	Qualifying widower	Head of household
d.	Qualifying widower	Qualifying widower	Head of household	Qualifying widower

CHAPTER

10

Individuals: Income, Deductions, and Credits

LEARNING OBJECTIVES: *After completing Chapter 10, you should be able to:*

LO.1 Identify specific income inclusions and exclusions applicable to individuals.

LO.2 Determine an individual's allowable itemized deductions.

LO.3 Explain and illustrate the adoption expenses credit, child tax credit, education tax credits, credit for

child and dependent care expenses, and earned income credit.

LO.4 Explain some of the key tax provisions of the Affordable Care Act.

CHAPTER OUTLINE

TAX TALK *A tax loophole is something that benefits the other guy. If it benefits you, it is tax reform.* —Russell B. Long

THE BIG PICTURE

THE TAX IMPLICATIONS OF LIFE!

Donna and David Steele, ages 35 and 37, respectively, recently married and have come to you for tax advice. They have several questions about their tax situation. Both are employed, and they expect to have combined wages from all sources of $70,000 for the current year.

During the year, Donna worked as an intern in the compliance area at a CPA firm. She was paid well enough for her work that she was able to save some money for school. The CPA firm was so pleased with Donna's work that, at the conclusion of her internship, she was given a bonus of $1,500 more than the firm had agreed to pay her. The extra amount was intended to help with her graduate school expenses in the masters of accounting program at State University. Because of her excellent academic record, the university awarded Donna a graduate assistantship that waived her tuition of $6,000 per semester and paid her $400 per month. In exchange, Donna was required to teach a principles of accounting course each semester. She used the cash she received each month for books and incidental fees. Donna also paid $250 of interest during the year on student loans still outstanding from her undergraduate years.

Donna and David received a wedding gift of $10,000 from her grandmother, and the couple earned $250 of interest on a savings account they opened with the money. David sold stock for $1,000 that was purchased two years ago for $5,000.

Late in the year, Donna was crossing a street in the pedestrian crosswalk when a delivery van struck her. The driver of the truck had a blood alcohol level of .12. She suffered a severe injury to her right arm that required her to miss work for a month. The delivery company's insurance company settled the case by paying damages as follows:

Compensatory damages:	
Medical expenses	$ 30,000
Injury to Donna's right arm	100,000
Pain and suffering	50,000
Loss of income	10,000
Legal fees	25,000
Punitive damages	160,000
	$375,000

continued

This is David's second marriage, and he pays alimony to his ex-wife. He has custody of his 15-year-old son, Stephen, who lives with Donna and David for nine months each year. The Steeles rent their home, paid $3,500 of state income taxes, paid a $412 motor vehicle registration tax on their personal car, incurred additional medical expenses of $25,000, and made $2,500 of charitable contributions.

Without calculating Donna and David's tax liability, what are the tax implications of the transactions noted above? Are there other tax deductions or credits for which they may qualify or other tax issues about which they should be made aware?

Read the chapter and formulate your response.

This chapter focuses on the computation of taxable income for individual taxpayers. Recall that taxable income is the base on which the tax liability is calculated. In the simplest of terms, taxable income is determined by reducing *gross income* by allowable *tax deductions*. Prior chapters discussed these terms in a general sense. This chapter describes rules that apply specifially to individual taxpayers, with respect to both income and deduction items. In addition, the chapter discusses key individual tax credits that may further reduce an individual's tax liability. The chapter concludes by describing key components of the Affordable Care Act that might impact an individual's tax computation.

LO.1

Identify specific income inclusions and exclusions applicable to individuals.

10-1 OVERVIEW OF INCOME PROVISIONS APPLICABLE TO INDIVIDUALS

As indicated in Chapter 9, the definition of gross income is broad enough to include almost all receipts of money, property, or services. However, the tax law provides for exclusion of certain types of income.[1] The following income *inclusions* and *exclusions*, which apply to all taxpayers (including individuals), were discussed in Chapter 4:

- Interest from state and local bonds (exclusion).
- Life insurance paid on death of the insured (exclusion).
- Imputed interest on below-market loans (inclusion).
- Income from discharge of indebtedness (inclusion unless a specific exclusion applies).
- Income included under the tax benefit rule (inclusion).

Most *exclusions* available only to individuals are for *fringe benefits* received by *employees* (refer to Exhibit 9.1 in Chapter 9). Fringe benefits are discussed in Chapter 11. Other specific inclusions and exclusions for individuals are discussed next.

10-2 SPECIFIC INCLUSIONS APPLICABLE TO INDIVIDUALS

The general principles governing the determination of gross income have occasionally yielded results that Congress found unacceptable. Thus, Congress has provided more

---

[1]See §§ 101–140.

BRIDGE DISCIPLINE **Bridge to Economics and Finance**

As is the case for business entities, a primary financial goal for individual taxpayers should entail maximizing the *after-tax value* of their assets over time. This approach requires not only selecting the best investment alternatives but also choosing those investments with the most favorable tax attributes. Fundamental to this notion is recognizing the key role the government plays in all economic activity through its taxing authority. As a result, an investor should consider economically sound strategies that minimize the extent to which the government can stake a claim to his or her success. For example, taxpayers can reduce the government's share of their wealth accumulations by deferring the payment of taxes until future years and by taking advantage of investment strategies for which tax incentives are available. Taxpayers should choose the investment alternatives that provide the best after-tax return over time and not necessarily the ones that lead to the least amount of taxation.

These points can be illustrated by examining two classic strategies. One of the best ways for individuals to maximize their personal wealth is to invest to the extent possible in qualified retirement savings programs [e.g., traditional Individual Retirement Accounts, § 401(k) accounts]. Not only do current additions to such accounts provide a current tax deduction, but earnings in the account are not subject to taxation until they are withdrawn, which, in most cases, is during the retirement years of the owner. Postponing the tax in these two ways reduces the present value of the tax cost, which increases the after-tax value of the investment. Another strategy involves investing in tax-free municipal bonds, which produce interest income that is free of Federal income tax. The returns from such investments, however, should be compared with the after-tax returns flowing from taxable debt securities. For example, a relevant question is how the implicit tax (see Chapter 1) associated with a municipal bond compares with the explicit tax associated with a taxable bond.

specific rules for determining the amount of gross income from certain sources. The following provisions applicable to individuals are covered in this chapter:

- Alimony and separate maintenance payments.
- Prizes and awards.
- Unemployment compensation.
- Social Security benefits.

10-2a **Alimony and Separate Maintenance Payments**

When a married couple divorces or becomes legally separated, state law generally requires a division of the property accumulated during the marriage. In addition, one spouse may have a legal obligation to provide support to the other spouse. The Code distinguishes between the support payments (alimony or separate maintenance) and the property division in terms of the tax consequences. Further, if payments are made that are intended to provide for the support of a child, the law is clear that these payments are distinguishable from both alimony and property settlements.

Alimony and separate maintenance payments are deductible by the party making the payments and are includible in the gross income of the party receiving the payments.[2] Thus, taxation of the income is shifted from the income earner to the income beneficiary.

EXAMPLE
1

Pete and Tina are divorced, and Pete is required to pay Tina $15,000 of alimony each year. Pete earns $61,000 a year. The tax law presumes that because Tina receives the $15,000, she is better able than Pete to pay the tax on that amount. Therefore, Tina must include the $15,000 in her gross income, and Pete is allowed to deduct $15,000 from his gross income.

Property Settlements

A transfer of property other than cash to a former spouse under a divorce decree or agreement is not a taxable event. The transferor is not entitled to a deduction and does

---

[2]§§ 71 and 215.

not recognize gain or loss on the transfer. The transferee does not recognize income and has a cost basis equal to the transferor's basis.[3]

EXAMPLE 2

Paul transfers stock to Rosa this year as part of a divorce settlement. The cost of the stock to Paul was $12,000, and the stock's fair market value at the time of the transfer is $15,000. Rosa later sells the stock for $16,000. Paul is not required to recognize gain from the transfer of the stock to Rosa, and Rosa has a realized *and* recognized gain of $4,000 ($16,000 − $12,000) when she sells the stock.

Requirements for Alimony

To classify payments as support obligations (alimony), as opposed to property of the other spouse (property settlements) or child support obligations, Congress developed the following objective rules. Payments made under agreements and decrees are *classified as alimony* only if the following conditions are satisfied:

- The payments are in cash. (This clearly distinguishes alimony from a property division.)
- The agreement or decree does not specify that the payments are not alimony. (This allows the parties to determine by agreement whether the payments will be alimony.)
- The payor and payee are not members of the same household at the time the payments are made. (This ensures the payments are for maintaining two households.)
- There is no liability to make the payments for any period after the death of the payee.[4]

DIGGING DEEPER 1   In-depth coverage can be found on this book's companion website: **www.cengagebrain.com**

Child Support

While alimony is taxable, a taxpayer does *not* realize income from the receipt of child support payments made by his or her former spouse. This result occurs because the money is received subject to the duty to use the money for the child's benefit. The payor is not allowed to deduct the child support payments because the payments are made to satisfy the payor's legal obligation to support the child.

In many cases, it may be difficult to determine whether the payments are intended to be alimony or child support. The tax law resolves this issue in many cases with the following rule: If the amount of the payments would be reduced upon the happening of a contingency related to a child (e.g., the child attains age 21 or dies), the amount of the future reduction in the payment is deemed child support.[5] The rule is applied even though the divorce agreement specifies other amounts for the support of the child.[6]

EXAMPLE 3

Under their divorce agreement, Matt is required to make periodic alimony payments of $500 per month to Grace. However, when Matt and Grace's child reaches age 21, marries, or dies (whichever occurs first), the payments will be reduced to $300 per month. Because the required contingency is the cause for the reduction in the payments, from $500 to $300, child support payments are $200 per month and alimony is $300 per month.

---

[3]Section 1041 was added to the Code in 1984 to repeal the rule of *U.S. v. Davis*, 62–2 USTC ¶9509, 9 AFTR 2d 1625, 82 S.Ct. 1190 (USSC, 1962). Under the *Davis* rule, which applied to pre-1985 divorces, a property transfer incident to divorce was a taxable event.

[4]See *Divorced or Separated Individuals* (IRS Publication 504) for additional information on alimony.

[5]§ 71(c)(2).

[6]*Johnson v. Comm.*, T.C.Memo. 2014–67.

TAX IN THE NEWS **Social Security Benefits as a Source of Federal Revenue**

Recipients' Social Security benefits are indexed for inflation, but the base amounts used in the formula to calculate the taxable portion of the benefits are not indexed. (For a complete discussion of this formula, see the materials associated with Digging Deeper 2.) The $25,000 and $32,000 base amounts were established in 1984. If they were indexed for inflation, these nontaxable amounts would have doubled by 2010. Thus, as income and Social Security benefits rise with inflation, taxable income increases more than the related increase in "real" benefits.

10-2b Prizes and Awards

The fair market value of prizes and awards must be included in gross income.[7] Therefore, lottery winnings, magazine publisher prizes, door prizes, and awards from an employer to an employee in recognition of performance are fully taxable to the recipient.

A narrow exception permits a prize or an award to be excluded from gross income if *all* of the following requirements are satisfied:

- The prize or award is received in recognition of religious, charitable, scientific, educational, artistic, literary, or civic achievement (e.g., Nobel Prize, Pulitzer Prize, or faculty teaching award).

- The recipient was selected without taking any action to enter the contest or proceeding.

- The recipient is not required to render substantial future services as a condition for receiving the prize or award.[8]

- The recipient transfers the prize or award to a qualified governmental unit or non-profit organization.

A taxpayer can also avoid including prizes and awards in gross income by refusing to accept the prize or award.[9]

Another exception is provided to allow exclusion of certain employee achievement awards in the form of tangible personal property (e.g., a gold watch). The awards must be made in recognition of length of service or safety achievement. Generally, the ceiling on the excludible amount for an employee is $400 per taxable year. However, if the award is a *qualified plan award*, the ceiling on the exclusion is $1,600 per taxable year.[10]

10-2c Unemployment Compensation

The unemployment compensation program is sponsored and operated by the states and Federal government to provide a source of income for people who have been employed and are temporarily out of work. In a series of rulings over a period of 40 years, the IRS exempted unemployment benefits from tax. These payments were considered social benefit programs for the promotion of the general welfare. In 1986, in order to reduce the unemployment compensation recipient's disincentive to work, Congress amended the Code to make these benefits taxable.[11]

10-2d Social Security Benefits

If a taxpayer's income exceeds a specified base amount, as much as 85 percent of Social Security retirement benefits must be included in gross income. The taxable amount of benefits is determined through the application of one of two formulas described in § 86.

In-depth coverage can be found on this book's companion website: www.cengagebrain.com

2 DIGGING DEEPER

---

[7] § 74.
[8] § 74(b).
[9] See Rev.Rul. 57-374, 1957-2 C.B. 69 and Rev.Proc. 87-54, 1987-2 C.B. 669.

[10] §§ 74(c) and 274(j).
[11] § 85.

10-3 SPECIFIC EXCLUSIONS APPLICABLE TO INDIVIDUALS

If an income item is within the all-inclusive definition of gross income, the item can be excluded only if the taxpayer can locate specific authority for doing so. The discussion that follows focuses on common exclusion items provided in the law that are available to individual taxpayers.

10-3a Gifts and Inheritances

Beginning with the Income Tax Act of 1913 and continuing to the present, Congress has allowed the recipient of a gift to exclude the value of the property from gross income. The exclusion applies to gifts made during the life of the donor (*inter vivos* gifts) and transfers that take effect upon the death of the donor (bequests and inheritances).[12] However, the recipient of a gift of income-producing property is subject to tax on the income subsequently earned from the property. Also, as discussed in Chapter 1, the donor or the decedent's estate may be subject to gift or estate taxes on such transfers.

In numerous cases, "gifts" are made in a business setting. For example, a salesperson gives a purchasing agent free samples, an employee receives cash from his or her employer upon retirement, or a corporation makes payments to employees who were victims of a natural disaster. In these and similar instances, it is frequently unclear whether the payment was a gift or represents compensation for past, present, or future services.

The courts have defined a gift as "a voluntary transfer of property by one to another without adequate consideration or compensation therefrom."[13] If the payment is intended to be for services rendered, it is not a gift, even though the payment is made without legal or moral obligation and the payor receives no economic benefit from the transfer. To qualify as a gift, the payment must be made "out of affection, respect, admiration, charity or like impulses."[14] Thus, the cases on this issue have been decided on the basis of the donor's intent.[15]

In the case of cash or other property received by an employee from his or her employer, Congress has eliminated any ambiguity. Transfers from an employer to an employee cannot be excluded as a gift.[16]

The Big Picture

EXAMPLE 4

Return to the facts of *The Big Picture* on p. 10-1. The $1,500 bonus paid to Donna by the CPA firm was compensation for her services rather than a gift, even though the employer had not contracted to pay this additional amount. This results because the payment was most likely not motivated by the employer's generosity, but rather was made as a result of business considerations. Even if the payment had been made out of generosity, because the payment was received from her employer, Donna could not exclude the "gift."

DIGGING DEEPER 3   In-depth coverage can be found on this book's companion website: **www.cengagebrain.com**

---

[12]§ 102.

[13]*Estate of D. R. Daly*, 3 B.T.A. 1042 (1926).

[14]*Robertson v. U.S.*, 52–1 USTC ¶9343, 41 AFTR 1053, 72 S.Ct. 994 (USSC, 1952).

[15]See, for example, *Comm. v. Duberstein*, 60–2 USTC ¶9515, 5 AFTR 2d 1626, 80 S.Ct. 1190 (USSC, 1960).

[16]§ 102(c). But see § 139 for qualified disaster situations.

TAX IN THE NEWS Complying with Documentation Requirements Is Critical, Even for IRS Agents

The income tax law is clear that a taxpayer bears the burden to show that he or she is entitled to claim a deduction for a gift made to a qualified charity. Some may argue that the documentation and substantiation rules written by the IRS are overly strict. Nonetheless, if a taxpayer wants to take a deduction for charitable gifts, the best recommendation would be to follow the rules carefully and be able to provide credible support if requested by the IRS.

One taxpayer, a 28-year employee of the IRS, was denied charitable deductions in two years because she was unable to provide convincing evidence that she had made cash gifts of over $20,000 to a New York church (*Margaret Payne*,

T.C. Summary Opinion 2013–64). The evidence Payne provided to support the deduction, a statement on church letterhead, was characterized as a "cut and paste job" that was apparently signed by one of Payne's children. The Tax Court ultimately denied the deduction stating that the "record was full of inconsistencies, contradicting testimony, fabricated documents, and simple untruths."

So if any lessons can be gleaned from this experience, they may be that tax rules apply equally to IRS agents and regular citizens alike, and if a cash gift is made to one's favorite charity, whether it be for $20,000 or $20, legitimate and convincing documentation must be gathered to support it.

10-3b Scholarships

General Information

Payments or benefits received by a student at an educational institution may be (1) compensation for services, (2) a gift, or (3) a scholarship. If the payments or benefits are received as compensation for services (past or present), the fact that the recipient is a student generally does not render the amounts received nontaxable.[17] Thus, a university teaching or research assistant is usually considered an employee, and his or her stipend is taxable compensation for services rendered. On the other hand, athletic scholarships largely are nontaxable when the individual is not required to participate in the sport.[18] In general, amounts received to be used for educational purposes (other than amounts received from family members) cannot be excluded as gifts because conditions attached to the receipt of the funds mean that the payments were not made out of "detached generosity."

As an exception to the compensation for services, nonprofit educational institutions can provide qualified tuition reduction plans for their employees and the employees can exclude the tuition from their gross income. The exclusion also applies to tuition reductions granted to the employee's spouse and the employee's dependent children.[19]

The scholarship rules are intended to provide exclusion treatment for education-related benefits that cannot qualify as gifts but are not compensation for services. According to the Regulations, "a scholarship is an amount paid or allowed to, or for the benefit of, an individual to aid such individual in the pursuit of study or research."[20] The recipient must be a candidate for a degree at an educational institution.[21]

The Big Picture

Return to the facts of *The Big Picture* on p. 10-1. State University waives tuition for all graduate teaching assistants. The tuition waived is intended as compensation for services and is therefore included in the graduate assistants' gross income. Therefore, the $6,000 Donna received in the form of a tuition waiver each semester is compensation for her services. The $400 she received each month also is compensation for services. The fact that she used the funds for educational expenses does not change the tax treatment of the compensation.

EXAMPLE
5

---

[17]Reg. § 1.117–2(a). See *C. P. Bhalla*, 35 T.C. 13 (1960), for a discussion of the distinction between a scholarship and compensation. See also *Bingler v. Johnson*, 69–1 USTC ¶9348, 23 AFTR 2d 1212, 89 S.Ct. 1439 (USSC, 1969). For potential exclusion treatment, see the discussion of qualified tuition reductions in Chapter 11.

[18]Rev.Rul. 77–263, 1977–2 C.B. 47.
[19]§ 117(d).
[20]Prop.Reg. § 117–6(c)(3)(i).
[21]§ 117(a).

Terry enters a contest sponsored by a local newspaper. Each contestant is required to submit an essay on local environmental issues. The prize is one year's tuition at State University. Terry wins the contest. The newspaper has a legal obligation to Terry (as the contest winner). Thus, the benefit is not a gift. However, because the tuition payment aids Terry in pursuing her studies and is not compensation for services, the payment is a scholarship.

A scholarship recipient may exclude from gross income the amount used for tuition and related expenses (fees, books, supplies, and equipment required for courses), provided the conditions of the grant do not require that the funds be used for other purposes.[22]

Kelly received an athletic scholarship from State University. The scholarship pays her tuition, $9,000, and books and supplies, $2,400. She also received $4,500 a year for costs of attendance, which she uses to pay for housing, food, laundry, and transportation. The tuition and the cost of books and supplies are excluded from gross income as a scholarship. The $4,500 received as costs of attendance does not qualify for the scholarship exclusion; therefore, Kelly must include that amount in her gross income.

Timing Issues

Frequently, the scholarship recipient is a cash basis taxpayer who receives the money in one tax year but pays the educational expenses in a subsequent year. The amount eligible for exclusion may not be known at the time the money is received. In that case, the transaction is held open until the educational expenses are paid.[23]

In August 2016, Sanjay received $10,000 as a scholarship for the academic year 2016–2017. Sanjay's expenditures for tuition, books, and supplies were as follows:

August–December 2016	$3,000
January–May 2017	4,500
	$7,500

Sanjay's gross income for 2017 includes $2,500 ($10,000 − $7,500) that is not excludible as a scholarship. None of the scholarship is included in his gross income in 2016.

Disguised Compensation

Some employers make scholarships available solely to the children of key employees. The tax objective of these plans is to provide a nontaxable fringe benefit to the executives by making the payment to the child in the form of an excludible scholarship. However, the IRS has ruled that the payments are generally includible in the gross income of the parent-employee.[24]

10-3c **Damages**

A person who suffers harm caused by another is often entitled to **compensatory damages**. The tax consequences of the receipt of damages depend on the type of harm the taxpayer has experienced. The taxpayer may seek recovery for (1) a loss of income, (2) expenses incurred, (3) property destroyed, or (4) personal injury.

Generally, reimbursement for a loss of income is taxed in the same manner as the income replaced (see the exception under Personal Injury below). Damages that are a recovery of expenses previously deducted by the taxpayer are generally taxable under the tax benefit rule (refer to Chapter 4).

---

[22]§ 117(b).

[23]Prop.Reg. § 1.117–6(b)(2).

[24]Rev.Rul. 75–448, 1975–2 C.B. 55 and *Richard T. Armantrout*, 67 T.C. 996 (1977).

A payment for damaged or destroyed property is treated as an amount received in a sale or exchange of the property. Thus, the taxpayer has a realized gain if the damages payments received exceed the property's basis. Damages for personal injuries receive special treatment under the Code.

Personal Injury

The legal theory of personal injury damages is that the amount received is intended "to make the plaintiff (the injured party) whole as before the injury."[25] It follows that if the damages payments received were subject to tax, the after-tax amount received would be less than the actual damages incurred and the injured party would not be "whole as before the injury." With regard to personal injury damages, a distinction is made between compensatory damages and **punitive damages** .

Compensatory damages are intended to compensate the taxpayer for the damages incurred. Only those compensatory damages received on account of *physical personal injury or sickness* can be excluded from gross income.[26] Such exclusion treatment includes amounts received for loss of income associated with the physical personal injury or physical sickness. Compensatory damages awarded on account of emotional distress are not received on account of physical injury or sickness and thus cannot be excluded from gross income (except to the extent of any amount received for medical care). Likewise, any amounts received for age discrimination or injury to one's reputation cannot be excluded.

Punitive damages are amounts the party that caused the harm must pay to the victim as punishment for outrageous conduct. Punitive damages are not intended to compensate the victim, but rather to punish the party who caused the harm. Thus, it follows that amounts received as punitive damages may actually place the victim in a better economic position than before the harm was experienced. Thus, punitive damages are included in gross income.

These rules are set forth in Concept Summary 10.1.

Concept Summary 10.1

Taxation of Damages

Type of Claim	Taxation of Award or Settlement
Breach of contract (generally loss of income)	Taxable.
Property damages	Recovery of cost; gain to the extent of the excess over basis. A loss is deductible for business property and investment property to the extent of basis over the amount realized. A loss may be deductible for personal-use property (see discussion of casualty losses in Chapter 6).
Personal injury	
Physical	All compensatory amounts are excluded unless previously deducted (e.g., medical expenses). Amounts received as punitive damages are included in gross income.
Nonphysical	Compensatory damages and punitive damages are included in gross income.

The Big Picture

Return to the facts of *The Big Picture* on p. 10-1. The damages Donna received were awarded as a result of a physical personal injury. Therefore, all of the compensatory damages can be excluded. Note that even the compensation for the loss of income of $10,000 can be excluded. The punitive damages Donna received, however, must be included in her gross income.

EXAMPLE
9

---

[25] *C. A. Hawkins*, 6 B.T.A. 1023 (1928).   [26] § 104(a)(2).

10-3d **Workers' Compensation**

State workers' compensation laws require the employer to pay fixed amounts for specific job-related injuries. The state laws were enacted so that the employee would not have to go through the ordeal of a lawsuit (and possibly not collect damages because of some defense available to the employer) to recover the damages. Although the payments are intended, in part, to compensate for a loss of future income, Congress has specifically exempted workers' compensation benefits from inclusion in gross income.[27]

10-3e **Accident and Health Insurance Benefits**

The income tax treatment of accident and health insurance benefits depends on whether the policy providing the benefits was purchased by the taxpayer or the taxpayer's employer. Benefits collected under an accident and health insurance policy purchased by the taxpayer are excludible even though the payments are a substitute for income.[28]

Bonnie purchases a medical and disability insurance policy. The insurance company pays Bonnie $1,000 per week to replace wages she loses while in the hospital. Although the payments serve as a substitute for income, the amounts received are tax-exempt benefits collected under Bonnie's insurance policy.

A different set of rules applies if the accident and health insurance protection was purchased by the individual's employer, as discussed in Chapter 11.

10-3f **Educational Savings Bonds**

The cost of a college education has risen dramatically during the past 15 years. According to U.S. Department of Education estimates, the cost of attending a publicly supported university for four years now commonly exceeds $60,000. For a private university, the cost often exceeds $200,000. Consequently, Congress has attempted to assist low- to middle-income parents in saving for their children's college education.

One of the ways that Congress assists such families is through an interest income exclusion on educational savings bonds.[29] The interest on U.S. government Series EE savings bonds may be excluded from gross income if the bond proceeds are used to pay qualified higher education expenses.

Qualified higher education expenses consist of tuition and fees paid to an eligible educational institution for the taxpayer, spouse, or dependent. If the redemption proceeds (both principal and interest) exceed the qualified higher education expenses, only a pro rata portion of the interest will qualify for exclusion treatment.

Tracy's redemption proceeds from qualified savings bonds during the taxable year are $6,000 (principal of $4,000 and interest of $2,000). Tracy's qualified higher education expenses are $5,000. Because the redemption proceeds exceed the qualified higher education expenses, only $1,667 [($5,000/$6,000) × $2,000] of the interest is excludible.

The exclusion is limited by the application of the wherewithal to pay concept. That is, once the *modified AGI (MAGI)* exceeds a threshold amount, the phaseout of the exclusion begins. The threshold amounts are adjusted for inflation each year. For 2016, the phaseout begins at $77,550 ($116,300 on a joint return).[30] The phaseout is completed when MAGI exceeds the threshold amount by more than $15,000 ($30,000 on a joint return). The otherwise excludible interest is reduced by the amount calculated as follows:

$$\frac{\text{MAGI} - \$77,550}{\$15,000} \times \frac{\text{Excludible interest}}{\text{before phaseout}} = \frac{\text{Reduction in}}{\text{excludible interest}}$$

---

[27]§ 104(a)(1).

[28]§ 104(a)(3).

[29]§ 135.

[30]The indexed amounts for 2015 were $77,200 and $115,750.

On a joint return, $116,300 is substituted for $77,550 (in 2016), and $30,000 is substituted for $15,000.

Assume the same facts as in Example 11, except that Tracy's MAGI for 2016 is $80,000. Tracy is single. The phaseout results in Tracy's interest exclusion being reduced by $272 {[($80,000 − $77,550)/$15,000] × $1,667}. Therefore, Tracy's exclusion is $1,395 ($1,667 − $272).

EXAMPLE 12

10-4 ITEMIZED DEDUCTIONS

LO.2

Determine an individual's allowable itemized deductions.

Taxpayers are allowed to deduct *from* AGI specified expenditures as itemized deductions. Itemized deductions, which are reported on Schedule A, can be classified as follows:

- Expenses that are purely *personal* in nature.
- Expenses incurred by *employees* in connection with their employment activities.
- Expenses related to (1) the *production or collection of income* and (2) the *management of property* held for the production of income.[31]

Expenses in the third category, sometimes referred to as *nonbusiness expenses*, differ from trade or business expenses (discussed previously). Trade or business expenses, which are deductions *for* AGI, must be incurred in connection with a trade or business. Nonbusiness expenses, on the other hand, are expenses incurred in connection with an income-producing activity that does not qualify as a trade or business. If the nonbusiness expense is incurred in connection with rent or royalty property, it is classified as a deduction *for* AGI. Otherwise, it is classified as a deduction *from* AGI. Itemized deductions include, but are not limited to, the expenses listed in Exhibit 10.1.

The election to itemize is appropriate when total itemized deductions exceed the standard deduction based on the taxpayer's filing status (see Chapter 9). The more commonly encountered itemized deductions are discussed next.

EXHIBIT 10.1	Partial List of Itemized Deductions

Personal Expenditures

Medical expenses in excess of 10% (7.5% if at least age 65) of AGI

State and local income taxes or sales taxes

Real estate taxes

Personal property taxes

Interest on home mortgage

Charitable contributions (limited to a maximum of 50% of AGI)

Casualty and theft losses (in excess of 10% of AGI)

Tax return preparation fee (subject to the 2%-of-AGI floor)

Expenditures Related to Employment (subject to the 2%-of-AGI floor)

Union dues

Professional dues and subscriptions

Certain educational expenses

Unreimbursed employee business expenses

Expenditures Related to Income-Producing Activities

Investment interest (to the extent of net investment income)

Investment counsel fees (subject to the 2%-of-AGI floor)

Other investment expenses (subject to the 2%-of-AGI floor)

[31]§ 212.

10-4a **Medical Expenses**

Medical expenses paid for the care of the taxpayer, spouse, and dependents are allowed as an itemized deduction to the extent the expenses are not reimbursed. The medical expense deduction is limited to the amount by which such expenses exceed a threshold percentage of the taxpayer's AGI. Under current law, the threshold percentage is 10 percent for most taxpayers. For taxpayers age 65 and older, however, the threshold is 7.5 percent of AGI until 2017, when it increases to 10 percent.[32]

The Big Picture

EXAMPLE 13

Return to the facts of *The Big Picture* on p. 10-1. In addition to the medical expenses incurred associated with Donna's accident that were later reimbursed by the delivery company's insurance company, the Steeles had other qualifying medical expenses. Assuming that their AGI for the year is $200,000, they will need to itemize their deductions and have more than $20,000 ($200,000 × 10%) in unreimbursed medical expenses to receive a tax benefit from those expenses. Thus, the deductible amount would be whatever qualifying medical expenses were incurred that exceeded the $20,000 threshold.

Medical Expenses Defined

The term *medical care* includes expenditures incurred for the "diagnosis, cure, mitigation, treatment, or prevention of disease, or for the purpose of affecting any structure or function of the body."[33] Medical expense also includes premiums paid for health care insurance, prescribed drugs and insulin, and lodging while away from home for the purpose of obtaining medical care. Examples of deductible and nondeductible medical expenses appear in Exhibit 10.2.

Cosmetic Surgery

Amounts paid for unnecessary cosmetic surgery are not deductible medical expenses. However, if cosmetic surgery is deemed necessary, it is deductible as a medical expense. Cosmetic surgery is necessary when it improves the effects of (1) a deformity arising from a congenital abnormality, (2) a personal injury, or (3) a disfiguring disease.

EXHIBIT 10.2	Examples of Deductible and Nondeductible Medical Expenses Paid by Taxpayer

Deductible	Nondeductible
Medical (including dental, mental, and hospital) care	Funeral, burial, or cremation expenses
Prescription drugs and insulin	Nonprescription drugs (except insulin)
Special equipment	Bottled water
Wheelchairs	Toiletries, cosmetics
Crutches	Diaper service, maternity clothes
Artificial limbs	Programs for the general improvement of health
Eyeglasses (including contact lenses)	Weight reduction
Hearing aids	Health spas
Transportation for medical care	Social activities (e.g., dancing and swimming lessons)
Medical and hospital insurance premiums	Unnecessary cosmetic surgery
Long-term care insurance premiums (subject to limitations)	
Cost of alcohol and drug rehabilitation	
Certain costs to stop smoking	
Weight reduction programs related to obesity	

---

[32]Prior to 2013, the percentage threshold for regular income tax purposes was 7.5 percent of AGI for all taxpayers.

[33]§ 213(d)(1)(A).

Nursing Home Care

The cost of care in a nursing home or home for the aged, including meals and lodging, can be included in deductible medical expenses if the primary reason for being in the home is to get medical care. If the primary reason for being there is personal, any costs for medical or nursing care can be included in deductible medical expenses, but the cost of meals and lodging must be excluded.

Capital Expenditures

When capital expenditures are incurred for medical purposes, they must be deemed medically necessary by a physician, the facility must be used primarily by the patient alone, and the expense must be reasonable. Examples of such expenditures include dust elimination systems,[34] elevators,[35] and vans specially designed for wheelchair-bound taxpayers. Other examples of expenditures that may qualify are swimming pools if the taxpayer does not have access to a neighborhood pool and air conditioners if they do not become permanent improvements (e.g., window units).[36]

Both a capital expenditure for a permanent improvement and expenditures made for the operation or maintenance of the improvement may qualify as medical expenses. The allowable cost of such qualified medical expenditures is deductible in the year incurred. Although depreciation is required for most other capital expenditures, it is not required for those qualifying for medical purposes.

Medical Expenses for Spouse and Dependents

In computing the medical expense deduction, a taxpayer may include medical expenses for a spouse and for a person who was a dependent at the time the expenses were paid or incurred. Of the requirements that normally apply in determining dependency status, neither the gross income nor the joint return test applies in determining dependency status for medical expense deduction purposes.

Transportation and Lodging

Payments for transportation to and from a hospital or other medical facility for medical care are deductible as medical expenses (subject to the AGI 10% or 7.5% floor). These costs include bus, taxi, train, or plane fare; charges for ambulance service; and out-of-pocket expenses for the use of an automobile. A mileage allowance of 19 cents per mile for 2016 may be used instead of actual out-of-pocket automobile expenses.[37] Whether the taxpayer chooses to claim out-of-pocket automobile expenses or the 19 cents per mile automatic mileage option, related parking fees and tolls can also be deducted. Also included are transportation expenditures for someone such as a parent or nurse who must accompany the patient. The cost of meals while en route to obtain medical care is not deductible.

In-depth coverage can be found on this book's companion website: www.cengagebrain.com   **4   DIGGING DEEPER**

Health Savings Accounts

Qualifying individuals may make deductible contributions to a **Health Savings Account (HSA)**. An HSA is a qualified trust or custodial account administered by a qualified HSA trustee, which can be a bank, an insurance company, or another IRS-approved trustee.[38] A taxpayer can use an HSA in conjunction with a high-deductible medical insurance policy to help reduce the overall cost of medical coverage. The high-deductible policy provides coverage for extraordinary medical expenses (in excess of the deductible), and expenses not covered by the policy can be paid with funds withdrawn tax-free from the HSA.

---

[34]Ltr.Rul. 7948029.

[35]*Riach v. Frank*, 62–1 USTC ¶9419, 9 AFTR 2d 1263, 302 F.2d 374 (CA–9, 1962).

[36]Reg. § 1.213–1(e)(1)(iii).

[37]This amount is adjusted periodically. The allowance was 23 cents per mile for 2015.

[38]§ 223.

In an era of large government deficits and debt ceiling debates, many have concluded that the Federal government needs to learn to live within its means. In simplest of terms, to bring the government's spending in line with its revenues, more revenues must be raised, expenditures must be decreased, or some combination of the two must occur. During these debates, some continue to argue that "tax reform" should occur simultaneously with the search for increased tax revenues, and such reform should lead to certain tax deductions being either repealed or scaled back. They observe that if the tax code were simplified by no longer allowing certain popular itemized deductions, billions of dollars of additional tax revenue would be collected because taxable income would be higher.

Currently, popular tax deductions "cost" the government billions by virtue of the fact that they reduce taxable income. These deductions are often referred to as "tax expenditures." Recently, the Joint Committee on Taxation estimated the cost during 2016 of allowing the following itemized deductions for individuals:

Deduction	Cost in Billions of Dollars
Medical expenses	$12.4
Mortgage interest on owner-occupied housing	81.6
Interest on student loans	1.9
Charitable contributions	47.0
State and local income, sales, and personal property taxes	63.0
Property tax on real property	6.4

Arguably, by repealing these deductions, government revenues would increase by significant amounts. While repealing all of these deductions may not be feasible for political, economic, or other reasons, be aware that certain politicians or policy wonks will push to reform, limit, or scale back these deductions to all or certain taxpayers in the future.

Source: Joint Committee on Taxation, "Estimates of Federal Tax Expenditures for Fiscal Years 2014–2018," (JCX-97-14), August 5, 2014, Table 1.

EXAMPLE 14

Sanchez, who is married and has three dependent children, carries a high-deductible medical insurance policy with a deductible of $4,400. He establishes an HSA and contributes the maximum allowable amount to the HSA in 2016. During 2016, the Sanchez family incurs medical expenses of $7,000. The high-deductible policy covers $2,600 of the expenses ($7,000 expenses − $4,400 deductible). Sanchez may withdraw $4,400 from the HSA to pay the medical expenses not covered by the high-deductible policy.

High-Deductible Plans High-deductible policies are less expensive than low-deductible policies, so taxpayers with low medical costs can benefit from the lower premiums and use funds from the HSA to pay costs not covered by the high-deductible policy. A plan must meet two requirements to qualify as a high-deductible plan.[39]

1. The annual deductible in 2016 is not less than $1,300 for self-only coverage ($2,600 for family coverage).
2. The annual limit in 2016 on total out-of-pocket costs (excluding the premiums) under the plan does not exceed $6,550 for self-only coverage ($13,100 for family coverage).

Tax Treatment of HSA Contributions and Distributions To establish an HSA, a taxpayer contributes funds to a tax-exempt trust.[40] As illustrated in the preceding example, funds can be withdrawn from an HSA to pay medical expenses that are not covered by the high-deductible policy. The following general tax rules apply to HSAs:

1. Contributions made by the taxpayer to an HSA are deductible from gross income to arrive at AGI (deduction *for* AGI). Thus, the taxpayer does not need to itemize to take the deduction.

---

[39]§ 223(c)(2).   [40]§ 223(d).

2. Earnings on HSAs are not subject to taxation unless distributed, in which case tax-ability depends on the way the funds are used.[41]

- Distributions from HSAs are excluded from gross income if they are used to pay for medical expenses not covered by the high-deductible policy.

- Distributions that are not used to pay for medical expenses are included in gross income and are subject to an additional 20 percent penalty if made before age 65, death, or disability. Such distributions made by reason of death or disability and distributions made after the HSA beneficiary becomes eligible for Medicare are taxed but not penalized.

HSAs have at least two other attractive features. First, an HSA is portable. Taxpayers who switch jobs can take their HSAs with them. Second, anyone under age 65 who has a high-deductible plan and is not covered by another policy that is not a high-deductible plan can establish an HSA.

Deductible Amount The annual deduction for contributions to an HSA is limited to the sum of the monthly limitations. The monthly limitation is calculated for each month the individual is an eligible individual. The monthly deduction is not allowed after the individual becomes eligible for Medicare coverage.

The amount of the monthly limitation for an individual who has self-only coverage in 2016 is one-twelfth of $3,350, while the monthly limitation for an individual who has family coverage in 2016 is one-twelfth of $6,750. These amounts are subject to annual cost-of-living adjustments.[42] An eligible taxpayer who has attained the age of 55 by the end of the tax year may make an additional annual contribution in 2016 of up to $1,000.

Determining the Maximum HSA Contribution Deduction

Liu (age 45), who is married and self-employed, carries a high-deductible medical insurance pol-icy with family coverage and an annual deductible of $4,000. In addition, he has established an HSA. Liu's maximum annual contribution to the HSA in 2016 is $6,750.

EXAMPLE 15

During 2016, Adam, who is self-employed, made 12 monthly payments of $1,200 for an HSA con-tract that provides medical insurance coverage with a $3,600 deductible. The plan covers Adam, his wife, and their two children. Of the $1,200 monthly fee, $675 was for the high-deductible pol-icy, and $525 was deposited into an HSA. The monthly deductible contribution to the HSA is calcu-lated as follows:

EXAMPLE 16

Maximum annual deduction for family coverage	$6,750.00
Monthly limitation (1/12 of $6,750)	$ 562.50

Because Adam is *self-employed*, he can deduct $8,100 of the amount paid for the high-deductible policy ($675 per month × 12 months) as a deduction *for* AGI (refer to Chapter 11). In addition, he can deduct the $6,300 ($525 × 12) paid to the HSA as a deduction *for* AGI. Note that the $6,300 HSA deduction does not exceed the $6,750 ceiling.

10-4b **Taxes**

A deduction is allowed for certain state and local taxes paid or accrued by a taxpayer.[43] The deduction was created to relieve the burden of multiple taxation upon the same source of revenue.

Deductible taxes must be distinguished from nondeductible fees. Fees for special privileges or services are not deductible as itemized deductions if personal in nature.

---

[41] § 223(f).

[42] § 223(b)(2). The annual limits were $3,350 and $6,650 in 2015.

[43] Most deductible taxes are listed in § 164, while the nondeductible items are included in § 275.

Examples include fees for dog licenses, automobile inspections, automobile titles and registration, hunting and fishing licenses, bridge and highway tolls, drivers' licenses, parking meter deposits, and postage. These items, however, could be deductible if incurred as a business expense or for the production of income (refer to Chapter 5). Deductible and nondeductible taxes for purposes of computing itemized deductions are summarized in Exhibit 10.3.

Personal Property Taxes

Deductible personal property taxes must be *ad valorem* (assessed in relation to the value of the property). Therefore, a motor vehicle tax based on weight, model, year, or horsepower is not an ad valorem tax. In contrast, a motor vehicle tax based on the value of the car is deductible.

The Big Picture

EXAMPLE 17

Return to the facts of *The Big Picture* on p. 10-1. In Donna and David Steele's state, assume that the government imposes a motor vehicle registration tax equal to 2% of the value of the vehicle plus 40 cents per hundred pounds. The Steeles own a car having a value of $20,000 and weighing 3,000 pounds. They pay an annual registration tax of $412. Of this amount, $400 (2% × $20,000 of value) is deductible as a personal property tax if they itemize their deductions. The remaining $12, based on the weight of the car, is not deductible.

Real Estate Taxes

Real estate taxes of individuals are generally deductible. Taxes on personal-use property and investment property are deductible as itemized deductions. Taxes on business property are deductible as business expenses. Real property taxes on property that is sold during the year must be allocated between the buyer and the seller (refer to Chapter 5).

State and Local Income Taxes and Sales Taxes

The position of the IRS is that state and local *income* taxes imposed upon an individual are deductible only as itemized deductions, even if the taxpayer's sole source of income is from a business, rents, or royalties.

Cash basis taxpayers are entitled to deduct state income taxes withheld by the employer in the year the taxes are withheld. In addition, estimated state income tax payments are deductible in the year the payment is made by cash basis taxpayers even if the payments relate to a prior or subsequent year.[44] If the taxpayer overpays state

EXHIBIT 10.3	Deductible and Nondeductible Taxes
Deductible	**Nondeductible**
State, local, and foreign real property taxes	Federal income taxes
State and local personal property taxes	FICA taxes imposed on employees
State and local income taxes *or* sales/use taxes*	Employer FICA taxes paid on domestic household workers
Foreign income taxes	Estate, inheritance, and gift taxes
	Federal, state, and local excise taxes (e.g., gasoline, tobacco, and spirits)
	Taxes on real property to the extent such taxes are to be apportioned and treated as imposed on another taxpayer
	Special assessments for streets, sidewalks, curbing, and other similar improvements

*The sales/use tax deduction was made permanent by the Protecting Americans from Tax Hikes Act (Public Law 114–113; Dec. 18, 2015).

---

[44]Rev.Rul. 71–190, 1971–1 C.B. 70. See also Rev.Rul. 82–208, 1982–2 C.B. 58, where a deduction is not allowed when the taxpayer cannot, in good faith, reasonably determine that there is additional state income tax liability.

income taxes because of excessive withholdings or estimated tax payments, the refund received is included in gross income of the following year to the extent the deduction reduced the taxable income in the prior year.

EXAMPLE 18

Leona, a cash basis, unmarried taxpayer, had $800 of state income tax withheld during 2016. Also in 2016, Leona paid $100 that was due when she filed her 2015 state income tax return and made estimated payments of $300 toward her 2016 state income tax liability. When Leona files her 2016 Federal income tax return in April 2017, she elects to itemize deductions, which amount to $8,500, including the $1,200 of state income tax payments and withholdings. The itemized deductions reduce her taxable income.

As a result of overpaying her 2016 state income tax, Leona receives a refund of $200 early in 2017. She will include this amount in her 2017 gross income in computing her Federal income tax. It does not matter whether Leona received a check from the state for $200 or applied the $200 toward her 2017 state income tax.

Individuals can elect to deduct either their state and local income taxes *or* their sales/use taxes paid as an itemized deduction on Schedule A of Form 1040. The annual election can reflect actual sales/use tax payments *or* an amount from an IRS table. The amount from the table may be increased by sales tax paid on the purchase of motor vehicles, boats, and other specified items. Most often, the sales tax deduction will be elected by those living in states with no individual income tax. In 2015, this provision was made a permanent part of the Code.

TAX PLANNING STRATEGIES **Timing the Payment of Deductible Taxes**

FRAMEWORK FOCUS: DEDUCTIONS

Strategy: Accelerate Recognition of Deductions to Achieve Tax Deferral.

It is sometimes possible to defer or accelerate the payment of certain deductible taxes, such as state income tax, real property tax, and personal property tax. For instance, the final installment of estimated state income tax is generally due after the end of a given tax year. However, accelerating the payment of the final installment could result in larger itemized deductions for the current year.

10-4c **Interest**

For Federal income tax purposes, interest must be divided into five categories: business interest, personal interest, interest on qualified student loans, investment interest, and qualified residence interest. Business interest is fully deductible as an ordinary and necessary expense. Most personal (consumer) interest such as interest paid on credit cards and car loans is not deductible. However, interest on qualified student loans, investment interest, and qualified residence (home mortgage) interest are deductible, subject to the limits discussed below.

Interest on Qualified Student Loans

Taxpayers who pay interest on a qualified student loan may be able to deduct the interest as a deduction *for* AGI. The deduction is allowable only to the extent the proceeds of the loan are used to pay qualified education expenses. The maximum annual deduction is $2,500. However, in 2016, the deduction is phased out for taxpayers with modified AGI (MAGI) between $65,000 and $80,000 ($130,000 and $160,000 on joint returns). The deduction is not available for taxpayers who are claimed as dependents or for married taxpayers filing separately.[45]

EXAMPLE 19

In 2016, Curt and Rita, who are married and file a joint return, paid $3,000 of interest on a qualified student loan. Their MAGI was $137,500. Their maximum potential deduction for qualified student loan interest is $2,500, but it must be reduced by $625 as a result of the phaseout rules.

$$\$2,500 \text{ interest} \times \frac{\$137,500 \text{ (MAGI)} - \$130,000 \text{ (phaseout floor)}}{\$30,000 \text{ (phaseout range)}} = \$625 \text{ reduction}$$

Curt and Rita are allowed a student loan interest deduction of $1,875 ($2,500 maximum deduction − $625 reduction = $1,875 deduction *for* AGI).

Investment Interest

Years ago, wealthy taxpayers used the interest deduction in the tax law to create wealth. By borrowing to purchase investments that would appreciate in the future, the interest on the debt was claimed as an ordinary deduction when paid. Later, when the asset was sold at a gain, only a capital gains tax was due on the appreciation. Thus, today's interest deduction could lead to tomorrow's capital gain.

In response, Congress limited the deductibility of **investment interest**, which is interest paid on debt borrowed for the purpose of purchasing or continuing to hold investment property. The deduction for investment interest allowed during the tax year is limited to the lesser of the investment interest paid or net investment income.[46]

Net investment income, which serves as the ceiling on the deductibility of investment interest, is the excess of investment income over investment expenses. Investment income includes gross income from interest, annuities, and royalties not derived in the ordinary course of a trade or business.

Investment expenses are those deductible expenses directly connected with the production of investment income, such as brokerage and investment counsel fees. Investment expenses do not include interest expense.

After net investment income is determined, the allowable deductible investment interest expense is calculated.

EXAMPLE 20

Ethan's financial records for the year reflect the following:

Interest income from bank savings account	$10,000
Taxable annuity receipts	5,500
Investment counsel fee	1,100
Safe deposit box rental (to hold annuity documents)	200
Investment interest expense	17,000

Ethan's investment income amounts to $15,500 ($10,000 + $5,500), and investment expenses total $1,300 ($1,100 + $200). Therefore, his net investment income is $14,200 ($15,500 − $1,300). Consequently, the investment interest deduction is limited to $14,200, the lesser of investment interest expense ($17,000) or net investment income.

The amount of investment interest disallowed is carried over to future years. No limit is placed on the length of the carryover period.

DIGGING DEEPER 5   In-depth coverage can be found on this book's companion website: www.cengagebrain.com

---

[45]§ 221. See § 221(b)(2)(C) for the definition of MAGI. For 2015, the MAGI threshold amounts also were $65,000 and $80,000 ($130,000 and $160,000 on joint returns).

[46]§ 163(d)(1).

Qualified Residence Interest

Qualified residence interest is interest paid or accrued during the taxable year on indebtedness (subject to limitations) secured by any property that is a qualified residence of the taxpayer. Qualified residence interest falls into two categories: (1) interest on **acquisition indebtedness** and (2) interest on **home equity loans**. Before each of these categories is discussed, however, the term *qualified residence* must be defined.

A qualified residence includes the taxpayer's principal residence and one other residence of the taxpayer or spouse. The principal residence is one that meets the requirement for nonrecognition of gain upon sale under § 121 (see Chapter 7). The one other residence, or second residence, refers to one that is used as a residence if not rented or, if rented, meets the requirements for a personal residence under the rental of vacation home rules of § 280A. A taxpayer who has more than one second residence can make the selection each year as to which one is the qualified second residence. A residence includes, in addition to a house in the ordinary sense, cooperative apartments, condominiums, and mobile homes and boats that have living quarters (sleeping accommodations and toilet and cooking facilities).

Although in most cases interest paid on a home mortgage is fully deductible, there are limitations.[47] Interest paid or accrued during the tax year on aggregate acquisition indebtedness of $1 million or less ($500,000 for married persons filing separate returns) is deductible as qualified residence interest. *Acquisition indebtedness* refers to amounts incurred in acquiring, constructing, or substantially improving a qualified residence of the taxpayer.

Qualified residence interest also includes interest on home equity loans. These loans utilize the personal residence of the taxpayer as security, typically in the form of a second mortgage. Because the funds from home equity loans can be used for personal purposes (e.g., auto purchases and medical expenses), what would otherwise have been nondeductible personal interest becomes deductible qualified residence interest. However, interest is deductible only on the portion of a home equity loan that does not exceed the lesser of:

- The fair market value of the residence, reduced by the acquisition indebtedness, or
- $100,000 ($50,000 for married persons filing separate returns).

EXAMPLE 21

Larry owns a personal residence with a fair market value of $450,000 and an outstanding first mortgage of $420,000. Therefore, his equity in his home is $30,000 ($450,000 − $420,000). Larry issues a second mortgage on the residence and in return borrows $15,000 to purchase a new family automobile. All interest on the $435,000 of first and second mortgage debt is treated as qualified residence interest.

Under current law, mortgage insurance premiums paid by the taxpayer on a qualified residence may be deducted (treated as qualified residence interest). However, the deduction begins to phase out for taxpayers with AGI in excess of $100,000 ($50,000 for married taxpayers filing separately). The deduction is fully phased out when AGI exceeds $109,000 ($54,500 for married taxpayers filing separately).[48]

Interest Paid for Services Mortgage loan companies commonly charge a fee, often called a loan origination fee, for finding, placing, or processing a mortgage loan. Loan origination fees are typically nondeductible amounts included in the basis of the acquired property. Other fees, sometimes called **points** and expressed as a percentage of the loan amount, are paid to reduce the interest rate charged over the term of the loan. Essentially, the payment of points is a prepayment of interest and is considered

---

[47]§ 163(h)(3).

[48]§§ 163(h)(3)(E)(i) and (ii). This provision is scheduled to expire as of December 31, 2016.

compensation to a lender solely for the use or forbearance of money. To be deductible, points must be in the nature of interest and cannot be a form of service charge or payment for specific services.[49]

Points must be capitalized and are amortized and deductible ratably over the life of the loan. A special exception, however, permits the purchaser of a principal residence to deduct qualifying points in the year of payment.[50] The exception also covers points paid to obtain funds for home improvements.

Points paid to refinance an existing home mortgage cannot be immediately deducted, but must be capitalized and amortized as an interest deduction over the life of the new loan.[51]

EXAMPLE 22

Sandra purchased her residence many years ago, obtaining a 30-year mortgage at an annual interest rate of 8%. In the current year, Sandra refinances the mortgage to reduce the interest rate to 4%. To obtain the refinancing, she has to pay points of $2,600. Therefore, the $2,600, which is considered prepayment of interest, must be capitalized and amortized over the life of the mortgage.

Prepayment Penalty

When a mortgage or loan is paid off in full in a lump sum before its term, the lending institution may require an additional payment of a certain percentage applied to the unpaid amount at the time of prepayment. This is known as a prepayment penalty and is considered to be interest (e.g., personal, investment, qualified residence) in the year paid. The general rules for deductibility of interest also apply to prepayment penalties.

Interest Paid to Related Parties

Nothing prevents the deduction of interest paid to a related party as long as the payment actually took place and the interest meets the requirements for deductibility. However, a special rule applies for related taxpayers when the debtor is on the accrual basis and the related creditor is on the cash basis. If this rule is applicable, interest that has been accrued but not paid at the end of the debtor's tax year is not deductible until payment is made and the income is reportable by the cash basis recipient.

Tax-Exempt Securities

The tax law provides that no deduction is allowed for interest on debt incurred to purchase or carry tax-exempt securities.[52] A major problem for the courts has been to determine what is meant by the words *to purchase or carry*. Refer to Chapter 5 for a detailed discussion of these issues.

Prepaid Interest

Accrual method reporting is imposed on cash basis taxpayers for interest prepayments that extend beyond the end of the taxable year.[53] Such payments must be allocated to the tax years to which the interest payments relate. These provisions are intended to prevent cash basis taxpayers from *manufacturing* tax deductions before the end of the year by prepaying interest.

Classification of Interest Expense

Whether interest is deductible *for* AGI or as an itemized deduction (*from* AGI) depends on whether the indebtedness has a business, investment, or personal purpose. If the indebtedness is incurred in relation to a business (other than performing services as an employee) or for the production of rent or royalty income, the interest is deductible *for* AGI. If the indebtedness is incurred for personal use, such as qualified residence interest, any deduction allowed is taken *from* AGI and is reported on Schedule A of Form 1040 if

---

[49]Rev.Rul. 69–188, 1969–1 C.B. 54.
[50]§ 461(g)(2).
[51]Rev.Rul. 87–22, 1987–1 C.B. 146.

[52]§ 265(a)(2).
[53]§ 461(g)(1).

the taxpayer elects to itemize. Note, however, that interest on a student loan is deductible *for* AGI. If the taxpayer is an employee who incurs debt in relation to his or her employment, the interest is considered to be personal, or consumer, interest and is not deductible. Business expenses appear on Schedule C of Form 1040, and expenses related to rents or royalties are reported on Schedule E. Concept Summary 10.2 reviews the tax treatment given to the various types of interest expense incurred by individual taxpayers.

Concept Summary 10.2

Deductibility of Personal, Student Loan, Investment, and Mortgage Interest

Type	Deductible	Comments
Personal (consumer) interest	No	Includes any interest that is not qualified residence interest, interest on qualified student loans, investment interest, or business interest. Examples include interest on car loans and credit card debt.
Qualified student loan interest	Yes	Deduction *for* AGI; subject to limitations.
Investment interest (*not* related to rental or royalty property)	Yes	Itemized deduction; limited to net investment income for the year; disallowed interest can be carried over to future years.
Investment interest (related to rental or royalty property)	Yes	Deduction *for* AGI; limited to net investment income for the year; disallowed interest can be carried over to future years.
Qualified residence interest on acquisition indebtedness	Yes	Deductible as an itemized deduction; limited to indebtedness of $1 million.
Qualified residence interest on home equity indebtedness	Yes	Deductible as an itemized deduction; limited to indebtedness equal to lesser of $100,000 or FMV of residence minus acquisition indebtedness.

10-4d **Charitable Contributions**

As noted in Chapter 5, § 170 allows individuals to deduct contributions made to qualified domestic organizations. Contributions to qualified charitable organizations serve certain social welfare needs and thus relieve the government of the cost of providing these needed services to the community.

Criteria for a Gift

A charitable contribution is defined as a gift made to a qualified organization.[54] The major elements needed to qualify a contribution as a gift are a donative intent, the absence of consideration, and acceptance by the donee. Consequently, the taxpayer has the burden of establishing that the transfer was made from motives of disinterested generosity as established by the courts.[55] This test is quite subjective and has led to problems of interpretation (refer to the discussion of gifts earlier in this chapter).

Benefit Received Rule

When a donor derives a tangible benefit from a contribution, he or she cannot deduct the value of the benefit.

Ralph purchases a ticket at $100 for a special performance of the local symphony (a qualified charity). If the price of a ticket to a symphony concert is normally $35, Ralph is allowed only $65 as a charitable contribution. Even if Ralph does not attend the concert, his deduction is limited to $65.

If, however, he does *not* accept the ticket from the symphony (or returns it prior to the event), he can deduct the full $100.

EXAMPLE 23

---

[54]§ 170(c).
[55]*Comm. v. Duberstein*, 60–2 USTC ¶9515, 5 AFTR 2d 1626, 80 S.Ct. 1190 (USSC, 1960).

An exception to this benefit rule provides for the deduction of an automatic percentage of the amount paid for the right to purchase athletic tickets from colleges and universities.[56] Under this exception, 80 percent of the amount paid to or for the benefit of the institution qualifies as a charitable contribution deduction.

EXAMPLE
24

Janet donates $5,000 to State University's athletic department. The payment guarantees that she will have preferred seating on the 50-yard line at football games. Subsequently, Janet buys four $50 game tickets. Under the exception to the benefit rule, she is allowed a $4,000 (80% of $5,000) charitable contribution deduction for the taxable year.

If, however, Janet's $5,000 donation includes four $50 tickets, that portion [$200 ($50 × 4)] and the remaining portion of $4,800 ($5,000 − $200) are treated as separate amounts. Thus, Janet is allowed a charitable contribution deduction of $3,840 (80% of $4,800).

Contribution of Services

No deduction is allowed for the value of one's services contributed to a qualified charitable organization. However, unreimbursed expenses related to the services rendered may be deductible. For example, the cost of a uniform (without general utility) that is required to be worn while performing services may be deductible, as are certain out-of-pocket transportation costs incurred for the benefit of the charity. In lieu of these out-of-pocket costs for an automobile, a standard mileage rate of 14 cents per mile is allowed.[57] Deductions are permitted for transportation, reasonable expenses for lodging, and the cost of meals while away from home that are incurred in performing the donated services. The travel expenses are not deductible if the travel involves a significant element of personal pleasure, recreation, or vacation.[58]

Nondeductible Items

In addition to the benefit received rule and the restrictions placed on the contribution of services, the following items may not be deducted as charitable contributions:

- Dues, fees, or bills paid to country clubs, lodges, fraternal orders, or similar groups.
- Cost of raffle, bingo, or lottery tickets.
- Cost of tuition.
- Value of blood given to a blood bank.
- Donations to homeowners associations.
- Gifts to individuals.
- Rental value of property used by a qualified charity.

Time of Deduction

A charitable contribution generally is deducted in the year the payment is made. This rule applies to both cash and accrual basis individuals. A contribution is ordinarily deemed to have been made on the date of delivery of the property to the donee. A contribution made by check is considered delivered on the date of mailing. Thus, a check mailed on December 31, 2016, is deductible on the taxpayer's 2016 tax return. If the contribution is charged on a credit card, the date the charge is made determines the year of deduction.

Record-Keeping Requirements

No deduction is allowed for a charitable contribution made to a qualified organization unless the taxpayer gathers (and, in some cases, supplies to the IRS) the appropriate documentation and substantiation. The specific type of documentation required depends on the amount of the contribution and whether the contribution is made in

---

[56]§ 170(l).

[57]§ 170(i).

[58]§ 170(j).

GLOBAL TAX ISSUES **Choose the Charity Wisely**

Maiya, a U.S. citizen of Nepali descent, was distressed by the damage caused by a major earthquake in Nepal. She donated $100,000 to the Earthquake Victims' Relief Fund, a Nepali charitable organization that was set up to help victims of the earthquake. Raju, also a U.S. citizen of Nepali descent, donated $100,000 to help with the relief effort. However, Raju's contribution went to his church, which sent the proceeds of a fund drive to the Earthquake Victims' Relief Fund in Nepal. Maiya's contribution is not deductible, but Raju's is. Why? Contributions to charitable organizations are not deductible unless the organization is a U.S. charity.

cash or noncash property.[59] For example, for a single contribution of $250 or more, no charitable deduction is allowed unless the taxpayer receives written acknowledgment of the donation from the charity that notes the donation and states whether the donor received anything in return from the donee. In addition, special rules may apply to gifts of certain types of property (e.g., used automobiles) where Congress has noted taxpayer abuse in the past. Further, for certain gifts of noncash property, Form 8283 (Noncash Charitable Contributions) must be attached to the taxpayer's return.

The required substantiation must be obtained before the earlier of (1) the due date (including extensions) of the return for the year the contribution is claimed or (2) the date the return is filed. Failure to comply with the reporting rules may result in disallowance of the charitable contribution deduction. In addition, significant overvaluation exposes the taxpayer to stringent penalties.

Valuation Requirements

Property donated to a charity is generally valued at fair market value at the time the gift is made. The Code and Regulations give very little guidance on the measurement of the fair market value except to say, "The fair market value is the price at which the property would change hands between a willing buyer and a willing seller, neither being under any compulsion to buy or sell and both having reasonable knowledge of relevant facts."

Generally, charitable organizations do not attest to the fair market value of the donated property. Nevertheless, the taxpayer must maintain reliable written evidence of the value of the donation.

In-depth coverage can be found on this book's companion website: **www.cengagebrain.com**   **6 DIGGING DEEPER**

Limitations on Charitable Contribution Deduction

The potential charitable contribution deduction is the total of all donations, both money and property, that qualify for the deduction. After this determination is made, the actual amount of the charitable contribution deduction that is allowed for individuals for the tax year is limited as follows:

- If the qualifying contributions for the year total 20 percent or less of AGI, they are fully deductible.
- If the qualifying contributions are more than 20 percent of AGI, the deductible amount may be limited to 20 percent, 30 percent, or 50 percent of AGI, depending on the type of property given and the type of organization to which the donation is made.
- In any case, the maximum charitable contribution deduction may not exceed 50 percent of AGI for the tax year.

The following sections explain when the 50 percent, 30 percent, and 20 percent limitations apply.

---

[59]The specific documentation thresholds and requirements are provided in § 170(f).

To correctly calculate the amount of a charitable contribution deduction, it is also necessary to understand the distinction between capital gain property and ordinary income property . These rules, which were discussed in Chapter 5, are summarized in Concept Summary 10.3.

Concept Summary 10.3

Determining the Deduction for Contributions of Property by Individuals

If the Type of Property Contributed Is:	And the Property Is Contributed to:	The Contribution Is Measured by:	But the Deduction Is Limited to:
Capital gain property	A 50% organization	Fair market value of the property	30% of AGI
Ordinary income property	A 50% organization	The basis of the property*	50% of AGI
Capital gain property (and the property is tangible personal property put to an unrelated use by the donee)	A 50% organization	The basis of the property*	50% of AGI
Capital gain property	A private nonoperating foundation that is not a 50% organization	The basis of the property*	The lesser of: 1. 20% of AGI 2. 50% of AGI minus other contributions to 50% organizations

*If the FMV of the property is less than the adjusted basis (i.e., the property has declined in value instead of appreciating), the FMV is used.

Fifty Percent Ceiling

Contributions made to public charities may not exceed 50 percent of an individual's AGI for the year. The 50 percent ceiling on contributions applies to public charities such as churches; schools; hospitals; and Federal, state, or local governmental units. The 50 percent ceiling also applies to contributions to private operating foundations and certain private nonoperating foundations.

In the remaining discussion of charitable contributions, public charities and private foundations (both operating and nonoperating) that qualify for the 50 percent ceiling will be referred to as 50 percent organizations.

Thirty Percent Ceiling

A 30 percent ceiling applies to contributions of cash and ordinary income property to private nonoperating foundations that are not 50 percent organizations. The 30 percent ceiling also applies to contributions of appreciated capital gain property to 50 percent organizations.[60]

In the event the contributions for any one tax year involve both 50 percent and 30 percent property, the allowable deduction comes first from the 50 percent property.

EXAMPLE 25

During the year, Lisa makes the following donations to her church: cash of $2,000 and unimproved land worth $30,000. Lisa had purchased the land four years ago for $22,000 and held it as an investment. Therefore, it is capital gain property. Lisa's AGI for the year is $60,000. Disregarding percentage limitations, Lisa's potential deduction is $32,000 [$2,000 (cash) + $30,000 (fair market value of land)].

continued

---

[60]Under a special election, a taxpayer may choose to permanently forgo a deduction of the appreciation on capital gain property. Referred to as the reduced deduction election, this enables the taxpayer to move from the 30% limitation to the 50% limitation. See § 170(b)(1)(C)(iii).

In applying the percentage limitations, however, the current deduction for the land is limited to $18,000 [30% (limitation applicable to capital gain property) × $60,000 (AGI)]. Thus, the total current deduction is $20,000 ($2,000 cash + $18,000 land). Note that the total deduction does not exceed $30,000, which is 50% of Lisa's AGI.

Twenty Percent Ceiling

A 20 percent ceiling applies to contributions of appreciated capital gain property to private nonoperating foundations that are not 50 percent organizations. Also recall from Chapter 5 that only the basis of the contributed property is allowed as a deduction.

In-depth coverage can be found on this book's companion website: www.cengagebrain.com   **7 DIGGING DEEPER**

Contribution Carryovers

Contributions that exceed the percentage limitations for the current year can be carried over for five years.[61] In the carryover process, such contributions do not lose their identity for limitation purposes. Thus, if the contribution originally involved 30 percent property, the carryover will continue to be classified as 30 percent property in the carryover year.

Assume the same facts as in Example 25. Because only $18,000 of the $30,000 value of the land is deducted in the current year, the balance of $12,000 may be carried over to the following year. But the carryover will still be treated as capital gain property and will be subject to the 30%-of-AGI limitation.

EXAMPLE 26

In applying the percentage limitations, current charitable contributions must be claimed first before any carryovers can be considered. If carryovers involve more than one year, they are utilized in a first-in, first-out order.

10-4e Miscellaneous Itemized Deductions Subject to 2 Percent Floor

In general, no deduction is allowed for personal, living, or family expenses.[62] However, a taxpayer may incur a number of deductible expenditures related to employment. If an employee or outside salesperson incurs unreimbursed business expenses or expenses that are reimbursed under a nonaccountable plan (see Chapter 11), including travel and transportation, the expenses are deductible as **miscellaneous itemized deductions**.[63] Certain other expenses also fall into the special category of miscellaneous itemized deductions. Some are deductible only to the extent they exceed 2 percent of the taxpayer's AGI. These miscellaneous itemized deductions include the following:

- Professional dues to membership organizations.
- Cost of uniforms or other clothing that cannot be used for normal wear.
- Fees incurred for the preparation of one's tax return or fees incurred for tax litigation before the IRS or the courts.
- Job-hunting costs.
- Fee paid for a safe deposit box used to store papers and documents relating to taxable income-producing investments.
- Investment expenses that are deductible under § 212 as discussed previously in this chapter.

---

[61]§ 170(d); Reg. § 1.170A–10.
[62]§ 262.

[63]Actors and performing artists who meet certain requirements are not subject to this rule. See § 62(a)(2)(B).

- Appraisal fees to determine the amount of a casualty loss or the fair market value of donated property.
- Hobby losses up to the amount of hobby income (see Chapter 11).
- Unreimbursed employee expenses (refer to Chapter 11).

Certain employee business expenses that are reimbursed are not itemized deductions, but are deducted *for* AGI. Employee business expenses are discussed in depth in Chapter 11.

10-4f Other Miscellaneous Deductions

Certain expenses and losses do not fall into any category of itemized deductions already discussed but are nonetheless deductible. The following expenses and losses are deductible on Schedule A as Other Miscellaneous Deductions. These are not subject to the 2%-of-AGI floor.

- Gambling losses up to the amount of gambling winnings.
- Impairment-related work expenses of a handicapped person.
- Federal estate tax on income in respect of a decedent.

10-4g Overall Limitation on Certain Itemized Deductions

Similar in effect to the exemption phaseout described in Chapter 9, high-income taxpayers also are subject to a limitation on the tax benefits from certain itemized deductions. In 2016, the phaseout of itemized deductions (also referred to as a *cutback adjustment*) applies to married taxpayers filing jointly whose AGI exceeds $311,300 ($259,400 for single filers).[64] Phaseouts of this type are sometimes referred to as "stealth taxes."

The limitation applies to the following frequently encountered itemized deductions:

- Taxes.
- Home mortgage interest, including points.
- Charitable contributions.
- Unreimbursed employee expenses subject to the 2%-of-AGI floor.
- All other expenses subject to the 2%-of-AGI floor.

The following are *not* subject to the limitation on itemized deductions:

- Medical expenses.
- Investment interest expense.
- Nonbusiness casualty and theft losses.
- Gambling losses.

Taxpayers subject to the limitation must reduce itemized deductions by the *lesser* of:

- 3 percent of the amount by which AGI exceeds $311,300 ($259,400 if single).
- 80 percent of itemized deductions that are affected by the limit.

The overall limitation is applied after applying all other limitations to those itemized deductions that are affected by the overall limitation. For example, other limitations apply to charitable contributions, certain meals and entertainment expenses, and certain miscellaneous itemized deductions.

---

[64]§ 68. The AGI thresholds are $285,350 for heads of household and $155,650 for married taxpayers filing separately. In 2015, the phaseouts applied to married taxpayers filing jointly whose AGI exceeded $309,900 ($258,250 for single taxpayers, $284,050 for heads of household, and $154,950 for married taxpayers filing separately).

Gavin, who is single and age 45, had AGI of $275,000 for 2016. He incurred the following expenses and losses during the year:

Medical expenses before 10%-of-AGI limitation	$29,500
State and local income taxes	3,200
Real estate taxes	2,800
Home mortgage interest	7,200
Charitable contributions	2,000
Casualty loss before 10% limitation (after $100 floor)	29,000
Unreimbursed employee expenses (subject to 2%-of-AGI limitation)	5,800
Gambling losses (Gavin had $3,000 of gambling income)	7,000

Gavin's itemized deductions *before* the overall limitation are computed as follows:

Medical expenses [$29,500 − (10% × $275,000)]	$ 2,000
State and local income taxes	3,200
Real estate taxes	2,800
Home mortgage interest	7,200
Charitable contributions	2,000
Casualty loss [$29,000 − (10% × $275,000)]	1,500
Unreimbursed employee expenses [$5,800 − (2% × $275,000)]	300
Gambling losses ($7,000 loss limited to $3,000 of gambling income)	3,000
Total itemized deductions before overall limitation	$22,000

Gavin's itemized deductions subject to the overall limitation are as follows:

State and local income taxes	$ 3,200
Real estate taxes	2,800
Home mortgage interest	7,200
Charitable contributions	2,000
Unreimbursed employee expenses	300
Total	$15,500

Gavin must reduce the amount by the lesser of the following:

• 3% × ($275,000 AGI − $259,400)	$ 468
• 80% of itemized deductions subject to limitation ($15,500 × .80)	12,400

Therefore, the amount of the reduction is $468, and Gavin has $21,532 of deductible itemized deductions, computed as follows:

Deductible itemized deductions subject to overall limitation ($15,500 − $468)	$15,032
Itemized deductions not subject to overall limitation:	
Medical expenses	2,000
Casualty loss	1,500
Gambling losses	3,000
Deductible itemized deductions	$21,532

TAX PLANNING STRATEGIES Effective Utilization of Itemized Deductions

FRAMEWORK FOCUS: DEDUCTIONS

Strategy: Maximize Deductible Amounts.

An individual may use the standard deduction in one year and itemize deductions in another year. Therefore, it is possible to obtain tax benefits by shifting itemized deductions from one year to another. For example, if a taxpayer's itemized deductions and the standard deduction are approximately the same for each year of a two-year period, the taxpayer should use the standard deduction in one year and shift itemized deductions (to the extent permitted by law) to the other year. The individual could, for example, prepay a church pledge for a particular year or avoid paying end-of-the-year medical expenses to shift the deduction to the following year.

LO.3

Explain and illustrate the adoption expenses credit, child tax credit, education tax credits, credit for child and dependent care expenses, and earned income credit.

10-5 INDIVIDUAL TAX CREDITS

A tax credit should not be confused with an income tax deduction. Recall from the discussion of the individual income tax formula in Chapter 1 that the tax benefit received from a tax deduction depends on the taxpayer's tax rate, while a tax credit is not affected by the tax rate. Instead, a credit is a dollar-for-dollar reduction in a taxpayer's tax liability. Several commonly encountered tax credits available to individuals are discussed in this section.

10-5a Adoption Expenses Credit

Adoption expenses paid or incurred by a taxpayer may give rise to the **adoption expenses credit**.[65] The provision is intended to assist taxpayers who incur nonrecurring costs directly associated with the adoption process, such as adoption fees, attorney fees, court costs, social service review costs, and transportation costs.

In 2016, up to $13,460 of costs incurred to adopt an eligible child qualify for the credit. An eligible child is one who is:

- Under 18 years of age at the time of the adoption, or
- Physically or mentally incapable of taking care of himself or herself.

A taxpayer may claim the credit in the year qualifying expenses were paid or incurred if they were paid or incurred during or after the tax year in which the adoption was finalized. For qualifying expenses paid or incurred in a tax year prior to the year the adoption was finalized, the credit must be claimed in the tax year following the tax year during which the expenses are paid or incurred. A married couple must file a joint return to claim the credit.

EXAMPLE 28

In late 2015, Sam and Martha pay $4,000 in legal fees, adoption fees, and other expenses directly related to the adoption of an infant daughter, Susan. In 2016, the year in which the adoption becomes final, they pay an additional $10,000. Sam and Martha are eligible for a $13,460 credit in 2016 (for expenses of $14,000, limited by the $13,460 ceiling, paid in 2015 and 2016).

The amount of the credit that is otherwise available is subject to phaseout for taxpayers whose AGI (modified for this purpose) exceeds $201,920 in 2016, and it is phased out completely when AGI reaches $241,920. The resulting credit is calculated by reducing the allowable credit (determined without this reduction) by the amount determined using the following formula:

$$\text{Allowable credit} \times \frac{\text{AGI} - \$201,920}{\$40,000}$$

EXAMPLE 29

Assume the same facts as in the previous example, except that Sam and Martha's AGI is $226,920 in 2016. As a result, their available credit in 2016 is reduced from $13,460 to $5,048 {$13,460 − [$13,460 × ($25,000/$40,000)]}.

The credit is nonrefundable. However, any unused adoption expenses credit may be carried forward for up to five years, being utilized on a first-in, first-out basis.

10-5b Child Tax Credit

The **child tax credit** provision allows individual taxpayers to take a tax credit based solely on the *number* of their qualifying children. This credit is one of several "family-friendly" provisions that currently are part of our tax law. To be eligible for the credit, the child must be under age 17, must be a U.S. citizen, and must be claimed as a dependent on the taxpayer's return.

---

[65]§ 23.

Maximum Credit and Phaseouts

Under current law, the maximum credit available is $1,000 per child.[66] The available credit is phased out for higher-income taxpayers beginning when AGI reaches $110,000 for joint filers ($55,000 for married taxpayers filing separately) and $75,000 for single taxpayers. The credit is phased out by $50 for each $1,000 (or part thereof) of AGI above the threshold amounts.[67] Because the maximum credit available to taxpayers depends on the number of qualifying children, the income level at which the credit is phased out completely also depends on the number of children qualifying for the credit.[68]

EXAMPLE 30

Juanita and Alberto are married and file a joint tax return claiming their two children, ages 6 and 8, as dependents. Their AGI is $122,400. Juanita and Alberto's maximum child tax credit is $2,000 ($1,000 × 2 children). Because Juanita and Alberto's AGI is in excess of the $110,000 threshold, the maximum credit must be reduced by $50 for every $1,000 (or part thereof) above the threshold amount {$50 × [($122,400 − $110,000)/$1,000]}. Thus, the credit reduction equals $650 [$50 × 13 (rounded up from 12.4)]. Therefore, Juanita and Alberto's child tax credit is $1,350 ($2,000 − $650).

10-5c Credit for Child and Dependent Care Expenses

The **credit for child and dependent care expenses** mitigates the inequity felt by working taxpayers who must pay for child care services to work outside the home.[69] This credit is a specified percentage of expenses incurred to enable the taxpayer to work or to seek employment. Expenses on which the credit for child and dependent care expenses is based are subject to limitations.

Eligibility

To be eligible for the credit, an individual must have either of the following:

- A dependent under age 13.
- A dependent or spouse who is physically or mentally incapacitated and who lives with the taxpayer for more than one-half of the year.

Generally, married taxpayers must file a joint return to obtain the credit.

Eligible Employment-Related Expenses

Eligible expenses include amounts paid for household services and care of a qualifying individual that are incurred to enable the taxpayer to be employed. Child and dependent care expenses include expenses incurred in the home, such as payments for a housekeeper. Out-of-the-home expenses incurred for the care of a dependent under the age of 13 also qualify for the credit.

Out-of-the-home expenses incurred for an older dependent or spouse who is physically or mentally incapacitated qualify for the credit if that person regularly spends at least eight hours each day in the taxpayer's household. This makes the credit available to taxpayers who keep handicapped older children and elderly relatives in the home instead of institutionalizing them.

Out-of-the-home expenses incurred for services provided by a dependent care center qualify only if the center complies with all applicable laws and regulations of a state or unit of local government.

Child care payments to a relative are eligible for the credit unless the relative is a child (under age 19) of the taxpayer.

---

[66]§ 24.

[67]AGI is modified for purposes of this calculation. The threshold amounts are *not* indexed for inflation. See §§ 24(a) and (b).

[68]The child tax credit generally is refundable to the extent of 15% of the taxpayer's earned income in excess of $3,000.

[69]§ 21.

Earned Income Ceiling

Qualifying employment-related expenses are limited to an individual's earned income. For married taxpayers, this limitation applies to the spouse with the lesser amount of earned income. Special rules are provided for taxpayers with nonworking spouses who are disabled or are full-time students. If a nonworking spouse is physically or mentally disabled or is a full-time student, he or she is deemed to have earned income for purposes of this limitation. The deemed amount is $250 per month if there is one qualifying individual in the household (e.g., a dependent child under age 13) or $500 per month if there are two or more qualifying individuals in the household. In the case of a student-spouse, the student's income is treated as earned only for the months the student is enrolled on a full-time basis at an educational institution.[70]

Calculation of the Credit

In general, the credit is equal to a percentage of unreimbursed employment-related expenses up to $3,000 for one qualifying individual and $6,000 for two or more individuals. The credit rate varies between 20 percent and 35 percent, depending on the taxpayer's AGI (see Exhibit 10.4).

EXAMPLE 31

Nancy, who has two children under age 13, worked full-time while her spouse, Ron, attended college for 10 months during the year. Nancy earned $22,000 and incurred $6,200 of child care expenses. Ron is deemed to be fully employed and to have earned $500 for each of the 10 months (or a total of $5,000).

Because Nancy and Ron report AGI of $22,000, they are allowed a credit rate of 31%. Nancy and Ron are limited to $5,000 in qualified child care expenses ($6,000 maximum expenses, limited to Ron's deemed earned income of $5,000). Therefore, they are entitled to a tax credit of $1,550 (31% × $5,000) for the year.

EXHIBIT 10.4	Child and Dependent Care Credit Computations	

Adjusted Gross Income		
Over	**But Not Over**	**Applicable Rate of Credit**
$ 0	$15,000	35%
15,000	17,000	34%
17,000	19,000	33%
19,000	21,000	32%
21,000	23,000	31%
23,000	25,000	30%
25,000	27,000	29%
27,000	29,000	28%
29,000	31,000	27%
31,000	33,000	26%
33,000	35,000	25%
35,000	37,000	24%
37,000	39,000	23%
39,000	41,000	22%
41,000	43,000	21%
43,000	No limit	20%

[70] § 21(d).

10-5d Education Tax Credits

The **American Opportunity credit** and the **lifetime learning credit**[71] are available to help qualifying low- and middle-income individuals defray the cost of higher education. The credits are available for qualifying tuition and related expenses incurred by students pursuing undergraduate or graduate degrees or vocational training. Books and other course materials are eligible for the American Opportunity credit (but not the lifetime learning credit).[72] Room and board are ineligible for both credits.

Maximum Credit

The American Opportunity credit permits a maximum credit of $2,500 per year (100 percent of the first $2,000 of tuition expenses plus 25 percent of the next $2,000 of tuition expenses) for the *first four years* of postsecondary education. The lifetime learning credit permits a credit of 20 percent of qualifying expenses (up to $10,000 per year) incurred in a year in which the American Opportunity credit is not claimed with respect to a given student. Generally, the lifetime learning credit is used for individuals who are beyond the first four years of postsecondary education.

Eligible Individuals

Both education credits are available for qualified expenses incurred by a taxpayer, taxpayer's spouse, or taxpayer's dependent. The American Opportunity credit is available per eligible student, while the lifetime learning credit is calculated per taxpayer. To be eligible for the American Opportunity credit, a student must take at least one-half of the full-time course load for at least one academic term at a qualifying educational institution. No comparable requirement exists for the lifetime learning credit. Therefore, taxpayers who are seeking new job skills or maintaining existing skills through graduate training or continuing education are eligible for the lifetime learning credit. Taxpayers who are married must file a joint return to claim either education credit. To claim these education credits, the individual must have received Form 1098–T, Tuition Statement, from the educational institution.

Income Limitations and Refundability

Both education credits are subject to income limitations, which differ between the two credits. Forty percent of the American Opportunity credit is refundable, and it can be used to offset a taxpayer's alternative minimum tax (AMT) liability (the lifetime learning credit is neither refundable nor an AMT liability offset).[73]

The American Opportunity credit amount is phased out beginning when the taxpayer's AGI (modified for this purpose) reaches $80,000 ($160,000 for married taxpayers filing jointly).[74] The credit is reduced by the extent to which AGI exceeds $80,000 ($160,000 for married taxpayers filing jointly) as a percentage of a $10,000 phaseout range ($20,000 for married taxpayers filing jointly). As a result, the credit is eliminated when modified AGI reaches $90,000 ($180,000 for married taxpayers filing jointly).

For 2016, the lifetime learning credit amount is phased out beginning when the taxpayer's AGI (modified for this purpose) reaches $55,000 ($111,000 for married taxpayers filing jointly). The credit is reduced by the extent to which AGI exceeds $55,000 ($111,000 for married filing jointly) as a percentage of a $10,000 ($20,000 for married filing jointly) phaseout range. The credit equals zero when AGI reaches $65,000 ($131,000 for married filing jointly).

---

[71]§ 25A.

[72]§ 25A(i)(3).

[73]If the credit is claimed for a taxpayer subject to § 1(g) (the "kiddie tax"), the credit is not refundable.

[74]These amounts are not adjusted for inflation.

American Opportunity Credit: Calculation and Limitation

Tom and Jennifer are married; file a joint tax return; have modified AGI of $158,000; and have two children, Lora and Sam. Tom and Jennifer paid $7,500 of tuition and $8,500 for room and board for Lora (a freshman) and $8,100 of tuition plus $7,200 for room and board for Sam (a junior). Both Lora and Sam are full-time students and are Tom and Jennifer's dependents.

Lora's tuition and Sam's tuition are qualified expenses for the American Opportunity credit. For 2016, Tom and Jennifer may claim a $2,500 American Opportunity credit for both Lora's and Sam's expenses [(100% × $2,000) + (25% × $2,000)]; in total, they qualify for a $5,000 American Opportunity credit.

Assume the same facts as in Example 32, except that Tom and Jennifer's modified AGI for 2016 is $172,000, instead of $158,000. In this case, Tom and Jennifer can claim a $2,000 American Opportunity credit for 2016 (rather than a $5,000 credit).

The potential $5,000 American Opportunity credit is reduced because their modified AGI exceeds the $160,000 limit for married taxpayers. The reduction is computed as the amount by which modified AGI exceeds the limit, expressed as a percentage of the phaseout range, or [($172,000 − $160,000)/$20,000], resulting in a 60% reduction. Therefore, the maximum available credit for 2016 is $2,000 ($5,000 × 40% allowable portion).

Restrictions on Double Tax Benefit

Taxpayers are prohibited from receiving a double tax benefit associated with qualifying educational expenses. Therefore, taxpayers who claim an education credit may not deduct the expenses, nor may they claim the credit for amounts that are otherwise excluded from gross income (e.g., scholarships and employer-paid educational assistance).

10-5e Earned Income Credit

The **earned income credit** is used by Congress as a means of providing income tax equity to the working poor. In addition, the credit has been designed to help offset other Federal taxes, such as the gasoline tax, that impose a relatively larger burden on low-income taxpayers. Further, the credit is intended to encourage economically disadvantaged individuals to become contributing members of the workforce.[75]

Eligibility Requirements

Eligibility for the credit depends not only on whether the taxpayer meets the earned income and AGI thresholds but also on whether he or she has a qualifying child. The term *qualifying child* generally has the same meaning here as it does for purposes of determining who qualifies as a dependent.

In addition to being available for taxpayers with qualifying children, the earned income credit is also available to certain workers without children. However, this provision is available only to such taxpayers ages 25 through 64 who cannot be claimed as a dependent on another taxpayer's return.

Amount of the Credit

The earned income credit is determined by multiplying a maximum amount of earned income by the appropriate credit percentage. Generally, earned income includes employee compensation and net earnings from self-employment; it excludes items such as interest, dividends, pension benefits, nontaxable employee compensation, and

---

[75]§ 32. The earned income credit is not available if the taxpayer's unearned income (e.g., interest and dividends) exceeds $3,400 in 2016 (the same as in 2015). See § 32(i).

alimony. If a taxpayer has children, the credit percentage used in the calculation depends on the number of qualifying children.

In 2016, the maximum earned income credit is $3,373 ($9,920 × 34%) for a taxpayer with one qualifying child, $5,572 ($13,930 × 40%) for a taxpayer with two qualifying children, and $6,269 ($13,930 × 45%) for a taxpayer with three or more qualifying children. However, the maximum earned income credit is phased out completely if the taxpayer's earned income or AGI exceeds certain thresholds. To the extent the greater of earned income or AGI exceeds $23,740 in 2016 for married taxpayers filing a joint return ($18,190 for other taxpayers), the difference, multiplied by the appropriate phaseout percentage, is subtracted from the maximum earned income credit.

It is not necessary for the taxpayer to actually compute the earned income credit. To simplify the compliance process, the IRS issues an Earned Income Credit Table for determining the appropriate amount of the credit. This table and a worksheet are included in the instructions for the Form 1040.

10-6 AFFORDABLE CARE ACT PROVISIONS

LO.4

Explain some of the key tax provisions of the Affordable Care Act.

Some of the most sweeping new legislation in the last decade is known as the Affordable Care Act (ACA) or "ObamaCare." The ACA was enacted to increase the quality and affordability of health insurance, reduce the number of uninsured individuals in the United States by expanding public and private insurance coverage, and lower health care costs for individuals and the government. Included in the ACA are a number of tax provisions, two of which are discussed briefly below. The Net Investment Income Tax (NIIT) and Additional Medicare tax, also part of the ACA, were covered in Chapter 9.

10-6a Individual Shared Responsibility Payment

The ACA's "individual mandate"—which has been deemed a "tax" by the U.S. Supreme Court[76]—requires all individuals not covered by an employer-sponsored health plan, Medicare, Medicaid, or other public insurance programs to secure a private insurance policy or pay a penalty for each month they do not have health coverage. The penalty is the **individual shared responsibility payment (ISRP)**.[77]

Under this provision, individuals without coverage in 2016 will pay an ISRP of the greater of a flat amount of $695 per adult and $347.50 per child up to a maximum of $2,085 per family, or 2.5 percent of household income. (In 2015, the ISRP was $325 per adult and $162.50 per child, or 2.0 percent of household income.) After 2016, the flat dollar amounts will be increased annually by a cost-of-living adjustment. The ISRP cannot be greater than the national average cost of a bronze-level health plan ($207 per month per individual in 2015).[78]

Exemptions are granted for financial hardship, religious objections, Native Americans, those without coverage for less than three consecutive months, undocumented immigrants, incarcerated individuals, those for whom the lowest cost plan option exceeds a specified percentage of household income, and those with incomes below the tax filing threshold (in 2016, the percentage is 8.13 percent and the income threshold for taxpayers under age 65 is $10,350 for singles and $20,700 for couples).[79]

10-6b Premium Tax Credit

Individuals and families whose household incomes are at least 100 percent but no more than 400 percent of the Federal poverty level (also called the Federal poverty line; FPL) may be eligible to receive a Federal subsidy [the **premium tax credit (PTC)**] if they purchase insurance via the Health Insurance Marketplace (the Marketplace).[80] Individuals whose income exceeds 400 percent of the FPL are not eligible for a PTC. For 2016 tax

---

[76]*National Federation of Independent Business v. Sebelius*, 132 S.Ct. 2566 (2012).

[77]§ 5000A.

[78]Rev.Proc. 2015–15, 2015–5 I.R.B. 564.

[79]Rev.Proc. 2014–62, 2014–50 I.R.B. 948. Individuals eligible for an exemption are to report it on Form 8965 (Health Coverage Exemptions). This form also includes worksheets for calculating any ISRP owed.

[80]§ 36B. Also see Rev.Proc. 2014–37, 2014–33 I.R.B. 363.

returns, the FPL for claiming a PTC is $11,770 for a single person (an additional $4,160 is added to that amount for each person in the household). [81]

Individuals can choose to receive their PTC in advance, and the Marketplace will send the money directly to the insurer to reduce the monthly insurance payments. Alternatively, individuals can receive the PTC as a refundable credit when they file their tax return for the year. Most individuals choose to receive their PTC in advance. In either case, however, taxpayers will be required to complete Form 8962 (Premium Tax Credit) when their tax return is filed. Taxpayers who claim the premium tax credit cannot use Form 1040EZ (they must use either Form 1040A or Form 1040).

Taxpayers who enrolled in health care coverage via the Marketplace will receive information necessary to complete Form 8962 by the end of January each year [Form 1095–A (Health Insurance Marketplace Statement)]. Included in this information statement are monthly health insurance premium payments and any premium tax credit received in advance. This information also is reported to the IRS.

Taxpayers who received the credit in advance must reconcile the actual credit based on actual income that year with the amounts that were subsidized through the Marketplace. They will receive a refund (if the advance credit was too low) or owe an additional tax obligation (if the advance credit was too large).

REFOCUS ON THE BIG PICTURE

THE TAX IMPLICATIONS OF LIFE!

While Donna and David's wages and salaries of $70,000 are taxable, they should be aware that their employers may have provided them with a number of tax-free fringe benefits. In addition, if Donna and David paid monthly premiums for accident and health care plans or contributed to a flexible spending account, those amounts may reduce their taxable income (these items are discussed more fully in Chapter 11). The good news is that the $10,000 gift received from Donna's grandmother can be excluded from gross income. However, the $250 of interest earned on the money is taxable, as is the $1,500 bonus Donna earned at the CPA firm.

Donna's tuition waiver of $6,000 and the related payments of $400 per month are intended as a form of compensation. Therefore, she must include both of these in her gross income. However, insofar as the damages awards are concerned, all of the compensatory damages of $215,000 can be excluded from gross income because they relate to personal physical injury or sickness. However the punitive damages of $160,000 must be included in Donna's gross income.

Donna and David have several deductions *for* adjusted gross income. In addition to the alimony paid by David, $3,000 of the capital loss from the stock sale is deductible *for* AGI and interest on the qualified student loan is deductible *for* AGI (subject to a phaseout).

While medical expenses, state income taxes, personal property taxes, and charitable contributions are deductible *from* AGI, Donna and David should claim the standard deduction for a married couple as it appears to exceed their itemized deductions.

Donna and David will claim three personal and dependency exemptions—one for each spouse and one for David's son. They will determine their tax liability using the tax rate schedule for married couples filing a joint return.

continued

---

[81]80 FR 3236. Different amounts apply for Alaska and Hawaii. For 2015 tax returns, these amounts were $11,670 and $4,060, respectively.

Donna and David may be eligible for one or more tax credits, including the child tax credit and an education tax credit related to the tuition paid by Donna. If Stephen has unearned income in excess of certain thresholds, Donna and David should be made aware of the potential "kiddie" tax problem.

If Donna and David did not have affordable health coverage from their employers and purchased insurance in the Marketplace, they might be eligible for the PTC (if their household income is no more than 400 percent of the FPL). If they did not have health insurance for any portion of the year and did not meet any exemption, they will owe the ISRP. One of the questions on the Federal income tax form is whether they had health coverage for every month of the year (line 61 of the 2015 Form 1040).

What If?

What if Donna and David purchase a house in the current year? What are the likely tax implications of owning a new home? If Donna and David purchase a new home, mortgage interest and property taxes paid on the home are treated as additional itemized deductions. Depending on the amount of these deductions, Donna and David's itemized deductions might then exceed the standard deduction amount, giving them a larger tax deduction and reducing their tax liability even more.

Suggested Readings

Seth M. Colwell, "What's New? Pell Grants and the American Opportunity Tax Credit," *Practical Tax Strategies*, December 2015.

John Gregory, "Managing an EIC Audit," *Practical Tax Strategies*, February 2015.

J. Russell Hardin and Thomas G. Noland, "The Tax Impact of Home Mortgage Modification Programs," *Practical Tax Strategies*, August 2014.

Mark Jackson, "Unintended Consequences of the Earned Income Tax Credit," *Practical Tax Strategies*, February 2013.

Eric Smith, "Distinguishing 'Live-Burn' and 'Deconstruction' Donations," *Practical Tax Strategies*, April 2014.

Key Terms

Accident and health insurance benefits, 10-10

Acquisition indebtedness, 10-19

Adoption expenses credit, 10-28

Alimony and separate maintenance payments, 10-3

American Opportunity credit, 10-31

Capital gain property, 10-24

Charitable contribution, 10-21

Child tax credit, 10-28

Compensatory damages, 10-8

Credit for child and dependent care expenses, 10-29

Earned income credit, 10-32

Educational savings bonds, 10-10

Health Savings Account (HSA), 10-13

Home equity loans, 10-19

Individual shared responsibility payment (ISRP), 10-33

Investment interest, 10-18

Lifetime learning credit, 10-31

Medical expenses, 10-12

Miscellaneous itemized deductions, 10-25

Net investment income, 10-18

Ordinary income property, 10-24

Points, 10-19

Premium tax credit (PTC), 10-33

Punitive damages, 10-9

Qualified residence interest, 10-19

Scholarship, 10-7

Computational Exercises

1. **LO.1** Casper and Cecile are divorced this year. As part of the divorce settlement, Casper transferred stock to Cecile. Casper purchased the stock for $25,000, and it had a market value of $43,000 on the date of the transfer. Cecile sold the stock for $40,000 a month after receiving it. In addition, Casper is required to pay Cecile $1,500 a month in alimony. He made five payments to her during the year. What are the tax consequences for Casper and Cecile regarding these transactions?

   a. How much gain or loss does Casper recognize on the transfer of the stock?
   b. Does Casper receive a deduction for the $7,500 alimony paid?
   c. How much income does Cecile have from the $7,500 alimony received?
   d. When Cecile sells the stock, how much gain or loss does she report?

Critical Thinking   2. **LO.1** Sarah, who is single, is retired. She would like to take on a part-time job to supplement her Social Security benefits. Any income Sarah earns will not reduce her Social Security benefits because she has reached retirement age. However, in her situation, this additional income will cause 85% of these benefits to be included in her income. Should Sarah be discouraged from taking a part-time job in order to reduce the amount of her Social Security benefits subject to income tax?

3. **LO.1** Jarrod receives a scholarship of $18,500 from Riggers University to be used to pursue a bachelor's degree. He spends $12,000 on tuition, $1,500 on books and supplies, $4,000 for room and board, and $1,000 for personal expenses. How much may Jarrod exclude from his gross income?

4. **LO.2** Pierre, a cash basis, unmarried taxpayer, had $1,400 of state income tax withheld during 2016. Also in 2016, Pierre paid $455 that was due when he filed his 2015 state income tax return and made estimated payments of $975 toward his 2016 state income tax liability. When Pierre files his 2016 Federal income tax return in April 2017, he elects to itemize deductions, which amount to $10,650, including the state income tax payments and withholdings, all of which reduce his taxable income.

   a. What is Pierre's 2016 state income tax deduction?
   b. As a result of overpaying his 2016 state income tax, Pierre receives a refund of $630 early in 2017. The standard deduction for single taxpayers for 2016 was $6,300. How much of the $630 will Pierre include in his 2017 gross income?

5. **LO.2** Troy's financial records for the year reflect the following:

Interest income from bank savings account	$ 900
Taxable annuity receipts	1,800
Safe deposit box rental (to hold annuity documents)	125
Investment interest expense	3,200

   Calculate Troy's net investment income and his current investment interest deduction. Assume that Troy does not itemize his personal deductions. How is any potential excess investment interest deduction treated?

6. **LO.2** Miller owns a personal residence with a fair market value of $195,000 and an outstanding first mortgage of $157,500. Miller gets a second mortgage on the residence and in return borrows $10,000 to purchase new jet skis. How much of the first and second mortgage debt is treated as qualified residence indebtedness?

7. **LO.2** Donna donates stock in Chipper Corporation to the American Red Cross on September 10, 2016. She purchased the stock for $18,100 on December 28, 2015, and it had a fair market value of $27,000 when she made the donation.

   a. What is Donna's charitable contribution deduction?
   b. Assume instead that the stock had a fair market value of $15,000 (rather than $27,000) when it was donated to the American Red Cross. What is Donna's charitable contribution deduction?

8. **LO.2** Issac has AGI of $73,400 and incurred the following expenses. How much of the business and personal expenditures are deductible (after any limitation) either as miscellaneous itemized deductions or as other itemized deductions?

Cost of uniforms	$ 535
Tax return preparation fees	600
Fee paid for a safe deposit box used to store papers and documents relating to taxable income-producing investments	65
Job-hunting costs	1,100

9. **LO.2** Pedro, who is a single taxpayer, had AGI of $328,000 for 2016. He incurred the following expenses during the year:

Medical expenses before 10%-of-AGI limitation	$12,000
State and local income taxes	8,900
Real estate taxes	1,600
Home mortgage interest	16,000
Charitable contributions	2,200
Deductible investment interest expense	1,700

Compute the amount of Pedro's itemized deductions after any applicable reductions.

10. **LO.3** In late 2015, Randy and Rachel Erwin paid $7,000 in legal fees, adoption fees, and other expenses directly related to the adoption of an infant son, Jameson. In 2016, the year in which the adoption becomes final, they pay an additional $8,000. Their AGI in 2016 is $135,000.

    a. Determine the amount of the Erwins' adoption tax credit in 2016.

    b. Instead, assume that the Erwins' 2016 AGI is $210,000. Determine the amount of the Erwins' adoption tax credit in 2016.

11. **LO.3** Santiago and Amy are married and file a joint tax return claiming their three children, ages 12, 14, and 18, as dependents. Their AGI is $140,000. Determine the amount of the couple's child tax credit.

12. **LO.3** Ivanna, who has three children under age 13, worked full-time while her spouse, Sergio, was attending college for nine months during the year. Ivanna earned $28,000 and incurred $9,100 of child care expenses. Determine Ivanna and Sergio's child and dependent care credit.

Problems

13. **LO.1** William and Abigail, who live in San Francisco, have been experiencing problems with their marriage. They have a 3-year-old daughter, April, who stays with William's parents during the day because both William and Abigail are employed. Abigail worked to support William while he attended medical school, and now she has been accepted by a medical school in Mexico. Abigail has decided to divorce William and attend medical school. April will stay in San Francisco because of her strong attachment to her grandparents and because they can provide her with excellent day care. Abigail knows that William will expect her to contribute to the cost of raising April. Abigail also believes that to finance her education, she must receive cash for her share of the property they accumulated during their marriage. In addition, she believes that she should receive some reimbursement for her contribution to William's support while he was in medical school. She expects the divorce proceedings to take several months. Identify the relevant tax issues for Abigail.

    Issue ID

14. **LO.1** Patrick and Eva are planning to divorce. Patrick has offered to pay Eva $12,000 each year until their 11-year-old daughter reaches age 21. Alternatively, Patrick

    Decision Making

will transfer to Eva common stock that he owns with a fair market value of $100,000. What factors should Eva and Patrick consider in deciding between these two options?

15. **LO.1** For each of the following, determine the amount that should be included in gross income:

a. Peyton was selected the most valuable player in the Super Bowl. In recognition of this, he was awarded an automobile with a value of $60,000. Peyton did not need the automobile, so he asked that the title be put in his parents' names.

b. Jacob was awarded the Nobel Peace Prize. When he was presented the check for $1.4 million, Jacob said, "I do not need the money. Give it to the United Nations to use toward the goal of world peace."

c. Linda won the Craig County Fair beauty pageant. She received a $10,000 scholarship that paid her $6,000 for tuition and $4,000 for meals and housing for the academic year.

16. **LO.1** Herbert was employed for the first six months of 2016 and earned $90,000 in salary. During the next six months, he collected $8,800 of unemployment compensation, borrowed $12,000 (using his personal residence as collateral), and withdrew $2,000 from his savings account (including $60 of interest). He received dividends of $550. His luck was not all bad, for in December, he won $1,500 in the lottery on a $5 ticket. Calculate Herbert's gross income.

17. **LO.1** Adrian was awarded an academic scholarship to State University for the 2016–2017 academic year. He received $6,500 in August and $7,200 in December 2016. Adrian had enough personal savings to pay all expenses as they came due. Adrian's expenditures for the relevant period were as follows:

Tuition, August 2016	$3,700
Tuition, January 2017	3,750
Room and board	
August–December 2016	2,800
January–May 2017	2,500
Books and educational supplies	
August–December 2016	1,000
January–May 2017	1,200

Determine the effect on Adrian's gross income for 2016 and 2017.

18. **LO.1** Determine the effect on gross income in each of the following cases:

a. Eloise received $150,000 in settlement of a sex discrimination case against her former employer.

b. Nell received $10,000 for damages to her personal reputation. She also received $40,000 in punitive damages.

c. Beth received $10,000 in compensatory damages and $30,000 in punitive damages in a lawsuit she filed against a tanning parlor for severe burns she received from using its tanning equipment.

d. Joanne received compensatory damages of $75,000 and punitive damages of $300,000 from a cosmetic surgeon who botched her nose job.

Communications   19. **LO.2** Emma Doyle, age 55, is employed as a corporate attorney. For calendar year 2016, she had AGI of $100,000 and paid the following medical expenses:

Medical insurance premiums	$3,700
Doctor and dentist bills for Bob and April (Emma's parents)	6,800
Doctor and dentist bills for Emma	5,200
Prescription medicines for Emma	400
Nonprescription insulin for Emma	350

Bob and April would qualify as Emma's dependents, except that they file a joint return. Emma's medical insurance policy does not cover them. Emma filed a claim for reimbursement of $2,800 of her own expenses with her insurance company in

December 2016 and received the reimbursement in January 2017. What is Emma's maximum allowable medical expense deduction for 2016? Prepare a memo for your firm's tax files in which you document your conclusions.

20. **LO.2** Reba, who is single and age 45, does a lot of business entertaining at home. Lawrence, Reba's 84-year-old dependent grandfather, lived with Reba until this year, when he moved to Lakeside Nursing Home because he needs medical and nursing care. During the year, Reba made the following payments on behalf of Lawrence:

Room at Lakeside	$11,000
Meals for Lawrence at Lakeside	2,200
Doctor and nurse fees at Lakeside	1,700
Cable TV service for Lawrence's room at Lakeside	380
Total	$15,280

Lakeside has medical staff in residence. Disregarding the 10%-of-AGI floor, how much, if any, of these expenses qualifies for a medical expense deduction by Reba?

21. **LO.2** Paul, age 62, suffers from emphysema and severe allergies and, upon the recommendation of his physician, has a dust elimination system installed in his personal residence. In connection with the system, Paul incurs and pays the following amounts during 2016.

Doctor and hospital bills	$ 2,500
Dust elimination system	10,000
Increase in utility bills due to the system	450
Cost of certified appraisal	300

In addition, Paul pays $750 for prescribed medicines.

The system has an estimated useful life of 20 years. The appraisal was to determine the value of Paul's residence with and without the system. The appraisal states that his residence was worth $350,000 before the system was installed and $356,000 after the installation. Paul's AGI for the year was $50,000. How much of the medical expenses qualify for the medical expense deduction in 2016?

22. **LO.2** Norma, who is single and uses the cash method of accounting, lives in a state that imposes an income tax. In April 2016, she files her state income tax return for 2015 and pays an additional $1,000 in state income taxes. During 2016, her withholdings for state income tax purposes amount to $7,400, and she pays estimated state income tax of $700. In April 2017, she files her state income tax return for 2016, claiming a refund of $1,800. Norma receives the refund in August 2017.

   a. Assuming that Norma itemized deductions in 2016, how much may she claim as a deduction for state income taxes on her Federal return for calendar year 2016 (filed in April 2017)?

   b. Assuming that Norma itemized deductions in 2016, how will the refund of $1,800 that she received in 2017 be treated for Federal income tax purposes?

   c. Assume that Norma itemized deductions in 2016 and that she elects to have the $1,800 refund applied toward her 2017 state income tax liability. How will the $1,800 be treated for Federal income tax purposes?

   d. Assuming that Norma did not itemize deductions in 2016, how will the refund of $1,800 received in 2017 be treated for Federal income tax purposes?

23. **LO.2** In 2016, Kathleen Tweardy incurs $30,000 of interest expense related to her investments. Her investment income includes $7,500 of interest, $6,000 of qualified dividends, and a $12,000 net capital gain on the sale of securities. Kathleen asks you to compute the amount of her deduction for investment interest, taking into consideration any options she might have. In addition, she wants your suggestions as to any tax planning alternatives that are available. Write a letter to her that contains your advice. Kathleen lives at 11934 Briarpatch Drive, Midlothian, VA 23113.

Decision Making

Communications

Critical Thinking

Critical Thinking   24. **LO.2** Helen borrowed $150,000 to acquire a parcel of land to be held for investment purposes. During 2016, she paid interest of $12,000 on the loan. She had AGI of $90,000 for the year. Other items related to Helen's investments include the following:

Investment income	$11,000
Long-term capital gain on sale of stock	3,500
Investment counsel fees	200

Helen is single and does not itemize her deductions.

a.   Determine Helen's investment interest deduction for 2016.

b.   Discuss the treatment of the portion of Helen's investment interest that is disallowed in 2016.

25. **LO.2** Ten years ago, Liam, who is single, purchased a personal residence for $340,000 and took out a mortgage of $200,000 on the property. In May of the current year, when the residence had a fair market value of $440,000 and Liam owed $140,000 on the mortgage, he took out a home equity loan for $220,000. He used the funds to purchase a recreational vehicle, which he uses 100% for personal use. What is the maximum amount on which Liam can deduct home equity interest?

Decision Making   26. **LO.2** In December of each year, Eleanor Young contributes 10% of her gross income to the United Way (a 50% organization). Eleanor, who is in the 28% marginal tax bracket, is considering the following alternatives for satisfying the contribution.

Communications

Critical Thinking

	Fair Market Value
(1) Cash donation	$23,000
(2) Unimproved land held for six years ($3,000 basis)	23,000
(3) Blue Corporation stock held for eight months ($3,000 basis)	23,000
(4) Gold Corporation stock held for two years ($28,000 basis)	23,000

Eleanor has asked you to help her decide which of the potential contributions listed above will be most advantageous taxwise. Evaluate the four alternatives, and write a letter to Eleanor to communicate your advice to her. Her address is 2622 Bayshore Drive, Berkeley, CA 94709.

Decision Making   27. **LO.2** Ramon had AGI of $180,000 in 2016. He is considering making a charitable contribution this year to the American Heart Association, a qualified charitable organization. Determine the current allowable charitable contribution deduction in each of the following independent situations, and indicate the treatment for any amount that is not deductible currently.

Critical Thinking

a.   A cash gift of $95,000.

b.   A gift of OakCo stock worth $95,000 on the contribution date. Ramon acquired the stock as an investment two years ago at a cost of $84,000.

c.   A gift of a painting worth $95,000 that Ramon purchased three years ago for $60,000. The charity has indicated that it would sell the painting to generate cash to fund medical research.

28. **LO.2** Linda, age 37, who files as a single taxpayer, had AGI of $280,000 for 2016. She incurred the following expenses and losses during the year:

Medical expenses (before the 10%-of-AGI limitation)	$33,000
State and local income taxes	4,500
State sales tax	1,300
Real estate taxes	4,000
Home mortgage interest	5,000
Automobile loan interest	750
Credit card interest	1,000
Charitable contributions	7,000
Casualty loss (before 10% limitation but after $100 floor)	34,000
Unreimbursed employee expenses subject to the 2%-of-AGI limitation	7,600

Calculate Linda's allowable itemized deductions for the year.

29. **LO.3** Ann and Bill were on the list of a local adoption agency for several years, seeking to adopt a child. Finally, in 2015, good news came their way, and an adoption seemed imminent. They paid qualified adoption expenses of $5,000 in 2015 and $11,000 in 2016. Assume that the adoption becomes final in 2016. Ann and Bill always file a joint income tax return.

    a. Determine the amount of the adoption expenses credit available to Ann and Bill, assuming that their combined annual income is $120,000. In what year(s) will they benefit from the credit?

    b. Assuming that Ann and Bill's modified AGI in 2015 and 2016 is $220,000, calculate the amount of the adoption expenses credit.

30. **LO.3** Paul and Karen are married, and both are employed (Paul earns $44,000 and Karen earns $9,000 during 2016). Paul and Karen have two dependent children, both under the age of 13. So they can work outside the home, Paul and Karen pay $3,800 to various unrelated parties to care for their children while they are working. Assuming that Paul and Karen file a joint return, what, if any, is their tax credit for child and dependent care expenses?

31. **LO.3** Jim and Mary Jean are married and have two dependent children under the age of 13. Both parents are employed outside the home and during 2016 earn salaries as follows: $16,000 (Jim) and $5,200 (Mary Jean). To care for their children while they work, they pay Eleanor (Jim's mother) $5,600. Eleanor does not qualify as a dependent of Jim and Mary Jean. Assuming that Jim and Mary Jean file a joint tax return, what, if any, is their credit for child and dependent care expenses?

32. **LO.3** Bernadette, a longtime client of yours, is an architect and the president of the local Rotary chapter. To keep up to date with the latest developments in her profession, she attends continuing education seminars offered by the architecture school at State University. During 2016, Bernadette spends $2,000 on course tuition to attend such seminars. She also spends another $400 on architecture books during the year.

    Bernadette's son, Pablo, is a senior majoring in engineering at the University of the Midwest. During the 2016 calendar year, Pablo incurs the following expenses: $8,200 for tuition ($4,100 per semester) and $750 for books and course materials. Pablo, who Bernadette claims as a dependent, lives at home while attending school full-time. Bernadette is married, files a joint return, and reports a combined AGI with her husband of $113,000.

    a. Calculate Bernadette's education tax credit for 2016.

    b. In her capacity as president of the local Rotary chapter, Bernadette has asked you to make a 30- to 45-minute speech outlining the different ways the tax law helps defray (1) the cost of higher education and (2) the cost of continuing education once someone is in the workforce. Prepare an outline of possible topics for presentation. A tentative title for your presentation is "How Can the Tax Law Help Pay for College and Continuing Professional Education?"

    Communications

33. **LO.3** Mark and Lisa are approaching an exciting time in their lives as their oldest son, Austin, graduates from high school and moves on to college. What are some of the tax issues Mark and Lisa should consider as they think about paying for Austin's college education?

    Issue ID

34. **LO.3** Joyce, a widow, lives in an apartment with her two minor children (ages 8 and 10), whom she supports. Joyce earns $33,000 during 2016. She uses the standard deduction.

    Critical Thinking

    a. Calculate the amount, if any, of Joyce's earned income credit.

    b. During the year, Joyce is offered a new job that has greater future potential than her current job. If she accepts the job offer, her earnings for the year will be $39,000; however, she is afraid she will not qualify for as much of the earned income credit. Using after-tax cash-flow calculations, determine whether Joyce should accept the new job offer.

    Decision Making

Comprehensive Tax Return Problems

TAX SOFTWARE

1. Alice J. and Bruce M. Byrd are married taxpayers who file a joint return. Their Social Security numbers are 123-45-6789 and 111-11-1112, respectively. Alice's birthday is September 21, 1968, and Bruce's is June 27, 1967. They live at 473 Revere Avenue, Lowell, MA 01850. Alice is the office manager for Lowell Dental Clinic, 433 Broad Street, Lowell, MA 01850 (employer identification number 98-765432). Bruce is the manager of a Super Burgers fast-food outlet owned and operated by Plymouth Corporation, 1247 Central Avenue, Hauppauge, NY 11788 (employer identification number 11-1111111).

The following information is shown on their Wage and Tax Statements (Form W–2) for 2015.

Line	Description	Alice	Bruce
1	Wages, tips, other compensation	$58,000	$62,100
2	Federal income tax withheld	4,500	6,300
3	Social Security wages	58,000	62,100
4	Social Security tax withheld	3,596	3,850
5	Medicare wages and tips	58,000	62,100
6	Medicare tax withheld	841	900
15	State	Massachusetts	Massachusetts
16	State wages, tips, etc.	58,000	62,100
17	State income tax withheld	2,950	3,100

The Byrds provide over half of the support of their two children, Cynthia (born January 25, 1991, Social Security number 123-45-6788) and John (born February 7, 1995, Social Security number 123-45-6786). Both children are full-time students and live with the Byrds except when they are away at college. Cynthia earned $4,200 from a summer internship in 2015, and John earned $3,800 from a part-time job.

During 2015, the Byrds provided 60% of the total support of Bruce's widower father, Sam Byrd (born March 6, 1939, Social Security number 123-45-6787). Sam lived alone and covered the rest of his support with his Social Security benefits. Sam died in November, and Bruce, the beneficiary of a policy on Sam's life, received life insurance proceeds of $1,600,000 on December 28.

The Byrds had the following expenses relating to their personal residence during 2015:

Property taxes	$5,000
Qualified interest on home mortgage	8,700
Repairs to roof	5,750
Utilities	4,100
Fire and theft insurance	1,900

The Byrds had the following medical expenses for 2015:

Medical insurance premiums	$4,500
Doctor bill for Sam incurred in 2014 and not paid until 2015	7,600
Operation for Sam	8,500
Prescription medicines for Sam	900
Hospital expenses for Sam	3,500
Reimbursement from insurance company, received in 2015	3,600

The medical expenses for Sam represent most of the 60% that Bruce contributed toward his father's support.

Other relevant information follows:

- When they filed their 2014 state return in 2015, the Byrds paid additional state income tax of $900.

- During 2015, Alice and Bruce attended a dinner dance sponsored by the Lowell Police Disability Association (a qualified charitable organization). The Byrds paid $300 for the tickets. The cost of comparable entertainment would normally be $50.

- The Byrds contributed $5,000 to Lowell Presbyterian Church and gave used clothing (cost of $1,200 and fair market value of $350) to the Salvation Army. All donations are supported by receipts, and the clothing is in very good condition.
- In 2015, the Byrds received interest income of $2,750, which was reported on a Form 1099–INT from Second National Bank.
- Alice's employer requires that all employees wear uniforms to work. During 2015, Alice spent $850 on new uniforms and $566 on laundry charges.
- Bruce paid $400 for an annual subscription to the *Journal of Franchise Management* and $741 for annual membership dues to his professional association.
- Neither Alice's nor Bruce's employer reimburses for employee expenses.
- The Byrds do not keep the receipts for the sales taxes they paid and had no major purchases subject to sales tax.
- Everyone in the Byrd family had health care coverage for all months of 2015.
- Alice and Bruce paid no estimated Federal income tax. Neither Alice nor Bruce wants to designate $3 to the Presidential Election Campaign Fund.

Part 1—Tax Computation
Compute net tax payable or refund due for Alice and Bruce Byrd for 2015. If they have overpaid, they want the amount to be refunded to them. If you use tax forms for your computations, you will need Forms 1040 and 2106 and Schedules A and B. Suggested software: H&R BLOCK Tax Software.

Part 2—Tax Planning
Alice and Bruce are planning some significant changes for 2016. They have provided you with the following information and asked you to project their taxable income and tax liability for 2016.

The Byrds will invest the $1,600,000 of life insurance proceeds in short-term certificates of deposit (CDs) and use the interest for living expenses during 2016. They expect to earn total interest of $32,000 on the CDs.

Bruce has been promoted to regional manager, and his salary for 2016 will be $88,000. He estimates that state income tax withheld will increase by $4,000 and the Social Security tax withheld will be $5,456.

Alice, who has been diagnosed with a serious illness, will take a leave of absence from work during 2016. The estimated cost for her medical treatment is $15,400, of which $6,400 will be reimbursed by their insurance company in 2016. Their medical insurance premium will increase to $9,769. Property taxes on their residence are expected to increase to $5,100. The Byrds' home mortgage interest expense and charitable contributions are expected to be unchanged from the prior year.

John will graduate from college in December 2015 and will take a job in New York City in January 2016. His starting salary will be $46,000.

Assume that all of the information reported in 2015 will be the same in 2016 unless other information has been presented.

2. Paul and Donna Decker are married taxpayers, ages 44 and 42, respectively, who file a joint return for 2016. The Deckers live at 1121 College Avenue, Carmel, IN 46032. Paul is an assistant manager at Carmel Motor Inn, and Donna is a teacher at Carmel Elementary School. They present you with W–2 forms that reflect the following information:

Tax Computation Problem

	Paul	Donna
Salary	$68,000	$56,000
Federal tax withheld	6,770	6,630
State income tax withheld	900	800
FICA (Social Security and Medicare) withheld	5,202	4,284
Social Security numbers	111-11-1111	123-45-6789

Donna is the custodial parent of two children from a previous marriage who reside with the Deckers through the school year. The children, Larry and Jane Parker, reside with their father, Bob, during the summer. Relevant information for the children follows:

	Larry	Jane
Age	17	18
Social Security numbers	123-45-6788	123-45-6787
Months spent with Deckers	9	9

Under the divorce decree, Bob pays child support of $150 per month per child during the nine months the children live with the Deckers. Bob says that he spends $200 per month per child during the three summer months they reside with him. Donna and Paul can document that they provide $2,000 of support per child per year. The divorce decree is silent as to which parent can claim the exemptions for the children.

In August, Paul and Donna added a suite to their home to provide more comfortable accommodations for Hannah Snyder (Social Security number 123-45-6786), Donna's mother, who had moved in with them in February 2015 after the death of Donna's father. Not wanting to borrow money for this addition, Paul sold 300 shares of Acme Corporation stock for $50 per share on May 3, 2016, and used the proceeds of $15,000 to cover construction costs. The Deckers had purchased the stock on April 29, 2011, for $25 per share. They received dividends of $750 on the jointly owned stock a month before the sale.

Hannah, who is 66 years old, received $7,500 in Social Security benefits during the year, of which she gave the Deckers $2,000 to use toward household expenses and deposited the remainder in her personal savings account. The Deckers determine that they have spent $2,500 of their own money for food, clothing, medical expenses, and other items for Hannah. They do not know what the rental value of Hannah's suite would be, but they estimate it would be at least $300 per month.

Interest paid during the year included the following:

Home mortgage interest (paid to Carmel Federal Savings and Loan)	$7,890
Interest on an automobile loan (paid to Carmel National Bank)	1,660
Interest on Citibank Visa card	620

In July, Paul hit a submerged rock while boating. Fortunately, he was uninjured after being thrown from the boat and landing in deep water. However, the boat, which was uninsured, was destroyed. Paul had paid $25,000 for the boat in June 2015, and its value was appraised at $18,000 on the date of the accident.

The Deckers paid doctor and hospital bills of $10,700 and were reimbursed $2,000 by their insurance company. They spent $640 for prescription drugs and medicines and $5,904 for premiums on their health insurance policy. They have filed additional claims of $1,200 with their insurance company and have been told they will receive payment for that amount in January 2017. Included in the amounts paid for doctor and hospital bills were payments of $380 for Hannah and $850 for the children. All members of the Decker family had health insurance coverage for all of 2016.

Additional information of potential tax consequence follows:

Real estate taxes paid	$3,850
Sales taxes paid (per table)	1,379
Contributions to church	1,950
Appraised value of books donated to public library	740
Paul's unreimbursed employee expenses to attend hotel management convention:	
Airfare	340
Hotel	170
Meals	95
Registration fee	340
Refund of state income tax for 2015 (the Deckers itemized on their 2015 Federal tax return)	1,520

Compute net tax payable or refund due for the Deckers for 2016. Ignore the child tax credit in your computations. If the Deckers have overpaid, the amount is to be credited toward their taxes for 2017.

BRIDGE DISCIPLINE

1. George comes to you asking for your advice. He wants to invest $10,000 either in a debt security or in an equity investment. His choices are shown below.

   • Redbreast Corporation bond, annual coupon rate of 7.50%.

   • City of Philadelphia general obligation bond, coupon rate of 6.00%.

   • Blue Corporation 7.50% preferred stock (produces qualified dividend income).

   These alternatives are believed to carry comparable risk. Assuming that George is in the 35% marginal tax bracket, which investment alternative could be expected to produce the superior annual after-tax rate of return?

2. Assume the same facts as in Problem 1, except that George is a C corporation rather than an individual and is in the 34% marginal tax bracket. Which investment strategy would maximize George, Inc.'s annual return?

Research Problems

Note: Solutions to Research Problems can be prepared by using the Checkpoint® Student Edition online research product, which is available to accompany this text. It is also possible to prepare solutions to the Research Problems by using tax research materials found in a standard tax library.

THOMSON REUTERS
CHECKPOINT®
Student Edition

Research Problem 1. Jane suffers from a degenerative spinal disorder. Her physician said that swimming could help prevent the onset of permanent paralysis and recommended the installation of a swimming pool at her residence for her use. Jane's residence had a market value of approximately $500,000 before the swimming pool was installed. The swimming pool was built, and an appraiser estimated that the value of Jane's home increased by $98,000 because of the addition.

   The pool cost $194,000, and Jane claimed a medical expense deduction of $96,000 ($194,000 − $98,000) on her tax return. Upon audit of the return, the IRS determined that an adequate pool should have cost $70,000 and would increase the value of her home by only $31,000. Thus, the IRS claims that Jane is entitled to a deduction of only $39,000 ($70,000 − $31,000).

   a. Is there any ceiling limitation on the amount deductible as a medical expense? Explain.

   b. Can capital expenditures be deductible as medical expenses? Explain.

   c. What is the significance of a "minimum adequate facility"? Should aesthetic or architectural qualities be considered in the determination? Why or why not?

Research Problem 2. Ken and Mary Jane Blough, your neighbors, have asked you for advice after receiving correspondence in the mail from the IRS. You learn that the IRS is asking for documentation in support of the itemized deductions the Bloughs claimed on a recent tax return. The Bloughs tell you that their income in the year of question was $75,000. Because their record-keeping habits are poor, they felt justified in claiming itemized deductions equal to the amounts that represent the average claimed by other taxpayers in their income bracket. These averages are calculated and reported by the IRS annually based on actual returns filed in an earlier year. Accordingly, they claimed medical expenses of $7,102, taxes of $6,050, interest of $10,659, and charitable contributions of $2,693. What advice do you give the Bloughs?

Partial list of research aids:
Cheryl L. de Werff, T.C. Summary Opinion, 2011–29.

Research Problem 3. Ashby and Curtis, a professional couple, have a 2-year-old son, Jason. Curtis works full-time as an electrical engineer, but Ashby has not worked outside the home since Jason was born. As Jason is getting older, Ashby thinks that Jason would benefit from attending nursery school several times a week, which would give her an opportunity to reinvigorate her love of painting at a nearby art studio. Ashby thinks that if she is lucky, the proceeds from the sale of her paintings will pay for the nursery school tuition. But in addition, she is planning to claim the credit for child and dependent care expenses because the care provided Jason at the nursery school is required for her to pursue her art career. Can Ashby and Curtis claim the credit for child and dependent care expenses for the nursery school expenditure? Why or why not?

Internet Activity

Use the tax resources of the Internet to address the following questions. Do not restrict your search to the Web, but include a review of newsgroups and general reference materials, practitioner sites and resources, primary sources of the tax law, chat rooms and discussion groups, and other opportunities.

Research Problem 4. Go to the web page of a consulting firm that offers counseling services to individuals as they negotiate the terms of a divorce. What specific tax-related services do these firms offer? Suggest a new tax-related service the consulting firm could offer.

Research Problem 5. The cutback adjustment that limits the amount of itemized deductions for some taxpayers is otherwise known as the Pease limitation. This limitation is named after former Congressman Donald Pease and was first in effect for tax years after December 31, 1990. The purpose of this limitation is to raise additional tax revenue by limiting some popular and common itemized deductions incurred by high-income taxpayers. One such deduction is the charitable contribution deduction. Search Google or a business press database to see what tax law analysts speculated the consequences would be of limiting charitable contribution deductions. Also determine whether such speculation has materialized.

Research Problem 6. Taxpayers who purchase health insurance coverage through the Health Insurance Marketplace may be eligible for the premium tax credit under § 36B. Use the IRS's website (**www.irs.gov**) to read about this provision and determine which taxpayers are eligible for the credit.

Roger CPA Review Questions

ROGER
CPA Review

1. Walters, an individual, received the following in 2016:

W–2 income	$10,000
Federal tax refund for 2015	1,250
Scholarship stipend, in return for teaching assistant duties performed	25,000
Cash inheritance from deceased great-uncle	5,000

   Considering only the above, what is Walters' 2016 gross income?

   a. $35,000   c. $15,000
   b. $36,250   d. $16,250

2. Smith, an individual, is required to pay Goode yearly alimony of $6,000 and yearly child support of $18,000. Smith paid Goode $20,000 in 2016. Smith's 2016 W–2

income was $50,000. Considering only the foregoing facts, what should Smith's adjusted gross income be for 2016?

a. $30,000   c. $48,000
b. $45,000   d. $50,000

3. Pierce, a married individual, received the following in 2016:

Worker's compensation award	$25,000
W–2 income	20,000
Unemployment compensation	4,800
Damages awarded for emotional distress experienced as a result of workplace bodily injury	10,000

Considering only the above, what is Pierce's 2016 gross income?

a. $49,800   c. $30,000
b. $34,800   d. $24,800

4. Kellye, a teacher, volunteers for eight hours per week at a school for high-risk children, a qualified charitable organization. Kellye's normal rate for teaching is $30 per hour. Kellye's out-of-pocket costs in 2016 were $250 for supplies, and she spent $20 each week in transportation getting to and from the school. Kellye made no cash contributions to charity in 2016. If Kellye volunteered every week in 2016, what is her charitable contribution deduction?

a. $0   c. $1,290
b. $250   d. $13,770

5. Aaron, age 55, has an adjusted gross income in 2016 of $30,000. His expenses are as follows:

Non-prescription medicine	$ 100
Prescription medicine	500
Doctor visits	500
Weekly meal preparation for a diet plan	2,000
Removal of a benign facial mole	400
Contact lenses	500
Eyeglasses	200
Dental services	300

What is Aaron's itemized deduction for medical expenses?

a. $0   c. $2,000
b. $1,500   d. $4,500

6. Which of the following deductions for taxes paid may be taken in the same year?
   a. Real estate taxes, state income taxes, state sales taxes
   b. Real estate taxes, property taxes, state income taxes
   c. Property taxes, state income taxes, state sales taxes
   d. Real estate taxes, property taxes, state income taxes, state sales taxes

7. Zunilda is a 77-year-old individual with an AGI of $25,000 in 2016. She began living in a nursing home in 2016 upon the recommendation of her primary care physician in order to receive medical care for a specific condition. She had the following unreimbursed expenses in 2016:

Expense	Amount
Nursing home health care costs	$5,000
Nursing home meal and lodging costs	8,000
Prescription drugs	1,500

As a result of these unreimbursed expenses, how much may Zunilda deduct from AGI on her 2016 tax return? Assume Zunilda elects to itemize deductions.

a. $12,000

c. $12,625

b. $4,000

d. $4,625

8. Which of the following credits is *not* refundable?
   a. Child Tax Credit
   b. Child and Dependent Care Credit
   c. American Opportunity Tax Credit
   d. Earned Income Credit

9. Which of the following credits is refundable?
   a. Child Tax Credit
   b. Child and Dependent Care Credit
   c. Lifetime Learning Credit
   d. Foreign Tax Credit

10. Which of the following education-related expenses can be used to claim an education credit?

	Tuition	Fees	Room and Board	Meals
a.	Yes	Yes	Yes	Yes
b.	Yes	Yes	Yes	No
c.	Yes	Yes	No	Yes
d.	Yes	Yes	No	No

11. Michael and Kathy have one dependent, Dustin, who is in his third year of college. Additionally, Michael is taking classes in the evening towards an MBA. What credits can Michael and Kathy claim as to these amounts?

   I. American Opportunity Tax Credit
   II. Lifetime Learning Credit

   a. I only

   c. I and II

   b. II only

   d. I or II

12. Which of the following best describes the effect of a tax credit?
   a. It reduces a person's gross income.
   b. It reduces a person's adjusted gross income.
   c. It reduces a person's taxable income.
   d. It reduces a person's tax liability.

CHAPTER

11

Individuals as Employees and Proprietors

LEARNING OBJECTIVES: *After completing Chapter 11, you should be able to:*

LO.1 Distinguish between employee and self-employed status.

LO.2 State and explain the exclusions from income available to employees who receive fringe benefits.

LO.3 Apply the rules for computing deductible expenses of employees, including transportation, travel, moving, education, and entertainment expenses.

LO.4 Explain the difference between accountable and nonaccountable employee plans.

LO.5 Understand the opportunities available to build wealth through Individual Retirement Accounts.

LO.6 State and explain the tax provisions applicable to proprietors.

LO.7 Distinguish between business and hobby activities and apply the rules limiting the deduction of hobby losses.

CHAPTER OUTLINE

TAX TALK *The taxpayer—that's someone who works for the Federal government but doesn't have to take a civil service examination.* —RONALD REAGAN

© ISTOCKPHOTO.COM/NEUSTOCKIMAGES

SELF-EMPLOYED VERSUS EMPLOYEE—WHAT'S THE DIFFERENCE?

Mark and Mary Herman come to you for tax advice. Mark Herman is a self-employed consultant. Last year, Mark's business generated revenue of $165,000 and incurred expenses of $18,000 for rent and utilities for an office. Mark also spent $8,000 purchasing depreciable equipment used in the business and paid a part-time secretary $12,000 for administrative work performed during the year. He hired Ellen, an assistant to help him in his consulting practice, and paid her $40,000.

Mark paid $3,000 for his own health insurance and $500 for term life insurance; he did not contribute to any retirement plans. Mary (Mark's wife) also works as a consultant, but is employed by a large firm. Her salary last year was $85,000. Mary's employer paid $3,000 of premiums for her health insurance and provided $50,000 of group term life insurance to each of its employees. Mary is not covered by a qualified retirement plan at work, but she contributed $5,500 to a traditional IRA.

Mary routinely travels for her job and was reimbursed by her employer for all travel expenses. In addition, Mary spent $500 on other employee business expenses that were not reimbursed by her employer.

What are the tax consequences of these items? Can Mark and Mary deduct the expenses they incurred? Are there other tax planning opportunities the couple may be missing or tax issues of which they should be aware?

Read the chapter and formulate your response.

Generally, individuals earn business income as employees or through self-employment. Self-employed individuals are described variously as freelancers, independent contractors, external consultants, micro-business owners, entrepreneurs, and proprietors.

In many cases, properly categorizing an individual as an employee or as self-employed for tax purposes is a complex determination. This chapter begins with a discussion of the factors that must be considered in determining whether an individual is an employee or is self-employed. This is followed by a discussion of tax provisions applicable to employees and then by a discussion of tax provisions related to self-employed individuals.

11-1 EMPLOYEE VERSUS SELF-EMPLOYED

LO.1

Distinguish between employee and self-employed status.

When one person performs services for another person or for an entity, the person performing the services either is an employee or is self-employed (i.e., an **independent contractor**). Globalization, advances in technology, and economic factors have led to increases in self-employment. Some individuals view self-employment as a way to be their own boss, have a flexible work schedule, and do work they truly love. Employers often see hiring self-employed individuals (rather than employees) as a means to achieve greater workforce flexibility and control costs. As a result, the proper determination of employment status is important and is often scrutinized.

From an employer's perspective, misclassification of an individual as self-employed rather than as an employee is not uncommon. This misclassification can be unintentional, resulting from the difficulty in applying a complex set of rules related to employee versus independent contractor status. However, classifying someone as a contractor instead of as an employee may be an intentional strategy to avoid certain costs. Unlike employees, self-employed individuals need not be included in various fringe benefit programs and retirement plans. Further, employers are not required to pay FICA and unemployment taxes (refer to Chapter 1) on compensation paid to independent contractors.

From the worker's perspective, categorization as an employee may avoid certain risks associated with self-employment that employees generally do not assume. For example, a self-employed individual assumes responsibility for employment-related tax obligations and assumes the legal responsibilities associated with performing the job. From a tax perspective, a self-employed individual is responsible for both the employee and the employer share of FICA and unemployment taxes. However, allowable business expenses of self-employed taxpayers are generally classified as deductions *for* AGI and are reported on Schedule C (Profit or Loss from Business) of Form 1040.[1] With the exception of reimbursement under an **accountable plan** (covered later in the chapter), expenses of employees are deductions *from* AGI. They are reported on Form 2106 (Employee Business expenses) and Schedule A (Itemized Deductions) of Form 1040.[2]

Failure to categorize an individual's work status correctly can have serious tax consequences; tax deficiencies as well as interest and penalties may result for the employer and the employee. The next section discusses those factors that are considered in the proper classification of an individual as an employee or as a self-employed person.

11-1a Factors Considered in Classification

The pivotal issue in classifying an individual as an independent contractor or an employee is whether an employer-employee relationship exists. The common law definition of an employee originated in judicial case law and is summarized in various IRS documents; one of them lists 20 factors that can be used in determining whether a worker is a common law employee or an independent contractor (and, thus, self-employed).[3]

---

[1] §§ 62(a)(1) and 162(a). In simple situations, a Schedule C–EZ can be used. In that case, a Schedule SE (Self-Employment Tax) must be filed.

[2] § 67(a). In simple situations, a Form 2106–EZ (Unreimbursed Employee Business Expenses) can be used.

[3] Rev.Rul. 87–41, 1987–1 C.B. 296. Also see IRS Publication 1779 (*Independent Contractor or Employee*).

BRIDGE DISCIPLINE Bridge to Equity or Fairness and Business Law

Max performs services for Calico, Inc. Amy performs services for Amber, Inc. Max and Amy's work products are very similar. Yet, Max is classified as an employee, and Amy is classified as an independent contractor. Does such a legal classification produce equitable results in terms of the effects it has on Max and Amy?

In distinguishing between an employee and an independent contractor, the overriding theme of common law is that the employee is subject to the will and control of the employer as to what is to be done and how it is to be done. Put in tax law terminology, an employer has the right to control and direct the individual who performs the services, not only as to the result to be accomplished by the work but also as to the details and means by which the result is accomplished. Among the factors generally considered in determining whether this right exists are the following.

- Degree of control exercised over the details of the work.
- Provision of facilities used in the work.
- Opportunity for profit or loss.
- Right to discharge.
- Whether work is part of regular business.
- Permanency of the relationship.
- Relationship that the parties believe they are creating.
- Manner of payment (e.g., by the job or by the hour).
- Skill required.
- Offering of the services to the general public rather than to one individual or entity.
- Distinct occupation or recognized trade or calling involved.
- Custom in the trade.

A common law employee-employer relationship exists when the employer specifies the end result and the ways and means by which that result is to be attained.[4] This means that an employee is subject to the will and control of the employer with respect not only to what shall be done but also to how it shall be done. If the individual is subject to the direction or control of another only to the extent of the end result but not as to the means of accomplishment, an employee-employer relationship does not exist.

Certain factors indicate a common law employee-employer relationship. These include the performance of the following by the employer.

- Furnishing tools or equipment and a place to work.
- Providing support services, including the hiring of assistants to help do the work.
- Making training available to provide needed job skills.
- Allowing participation in various workplace fringe benefits (e.g., accident and health plans, group life insurance, and retirement plans).
- Paying for services based on time rather than the task performed.

Each case is tested on its own merits, and the right to control the means and methods of accomplishment is the definitive test. Generally, physicians, attorneys, dentists, contractors, subcontractors, and others who offer services to the public are not classified as employees.

In-depth coverage can be found on this book's companion website: www.cengagebrain.com   **1 DIGGING DEEPER**

The Big Picture

EXAMPLE 1

Return to the facts of *The Big Picture* on p. 11-1. Mark is a consultant whose major client accounts for 60% of his billings. He does the routine consulting work at the client's request. He is paid a monthly retainer in addition to amounts charged for extra work. Mark is a self-employed individual. Even though most of his income comes from one client, he still has the right to determine *how* the end result of his work is attained.

[4]Reg. § 31.3401(c)–1(b).

EXAMPLE 2

Return to the facts of *The Big Picture* on p. 11-1. Ellen is a recent MBA graduate hired by Mark to assist him in the performance of services for the client mentioned in Example 1. Ellen is under Mark's supervision; he reviews her work and pays her an hourly fee. Ellen is Mark's employee.

DIGGING DEEPER 2 In-depth coverage can be found on this book's companion website: www.cengagebrain.com

TAX PLANNING STRATEGIES Self-Employed Individuals

FRAMEWORK FOCUS: DEDUCTIONS

Strategy: Maximize Deductible Amounts.

Some taxpayers, such as real estate agents and consultants, might be classified as either employees or self-employed individuals. These taxpayers should consider all factors and not automatically assume that self-employed status is preferable.

It is advantageous to deduct one's business expenses *for* AGI and avoid the 2 percent floor for miscellaneous itemized deductions. However, a self-employed individual may incur additional expenses such as local gross receipts taxes, license fees, franchise fees, personal property taxes, and occupation taxes. Record-keeping and filing requirements can also be quite burdensome.

One of the most expensive considerations is the **self-employment tax** imposed on independent contractors and other self-employed individuals. A self-employed person is required to pay twice the amount of Social Security and Medicare taxes that are imposed on an employee with the same amount of earned income (wages). Even though a deduction *for* AGI is allowed for one-half of the self-employment tax paid, an employee and a self-employed individual are not in the same tax position on equal amounts of earnings.

LO.2

State and explain the exclusions from income available to employees who receive fringe benefits.

11-2 EXCLUSIONS AVAILABLE TO EMPLOYEES

Several gross income exclusions that are available to *all taxpayers* were discussed in Chapter 4; these include interest income on obligations of state and local governments, life insurance proceeds, and income from discharge of indebtedness. Other exclusions, available only to *individuals*, were discussed in Chapter 10; these include gifts and inheritances, scholarships, and compensation for injuries and sickness.

Another class of exclusions available only to *employees* is referred to as qualified fringe benefits. The popularity of fringe benefits is attributable to the fact that the cost of such benefits is deductible by employers and excludible from income by employees. The next sections discuss several of the most popular fringe benefits available to employees.

EXAMPLE 3

Cardinal Corporation, which has a marginal tax rate of 35%, provides health insurance coverage to employees at a cost of $1,000 per employee. Because Cardinal can deduct the health insurance premiums paid to provide this coverage, the net cost to the corporation is $650 per employee ($1,000 cost − $350 tax savings). The employee excludes the value of this fringe benefit, so there is no tax cost to the employee.

The average employee of Cardinal Corporation is in the 28% bracket. If Cardinal did not provide the health insurance coverage and the employee paid a $1,000 premium, the employee would use after-tax dollars to acquire the coverage. The employee then must earn $1,389 to pay for the coverage [$1,389 wages − ($1,389 × 28% tax)]. The after-tax cost to the corporation of $1,389 in wages is $903 ($1,389 wages − $486 corporate tax savings). Thus, the cost of health insurance coverage is $253 less per employee ($903 − $650) if it is a qualified fringe benefit, because the insurance is both deductible by the corporation and excludible by the employee.

11-2a **Employer-Sponsored Accident and Health Plans**

Congress encourages employers to provide employees, retired former employees, and their dependents with accident and health benefits, disability insurance, and long-term care plans. The *premiums* are deductible by the employer and are excluded from the employee's gross income.[5] Although § 105(a) provides the general rule that the employee has includible income when he or she collects the insurance *benefits*, two exceptions are provided.

Section 105(b) generally excludes payments received for medical care of the employee, spouse, and dependents. However, if the payments are for expenses that do not meet the Code's definition of medical care,[6] the amount received is included in gross income. In addition, the taxpayer includes in gross income any amounts received for medical expenses that were deducted by the taxpayer on a prior return.

Tab's employer-sponsored health insurance plan paid $4,000 for hair transplants that did not meet the Code's definition of medical care. As a result, Tab includes $4,000 in his gross income.

EXAMPLE 4

Section 105(c) excludes payments for the permanent loss or the loss of the use of a member or function of the body or the permanent disfigurement of the employee, the spouse, or a dependent. However, payments that are a substitute for salary (e.g., related to the period of time absent from work) are included in income.

Jill loses an eye in an automobile accident unrelated to her work. As a result of the accident, Jill incurs $2,000 of medical expenses, which she deducts on her return. She collects $10,000 from an accident insurance policy carried by her employer. The benefits are paid according to a schedule of amounts that varies with the part of the body injured (e.g., $10,000 for loss of an eye and $20,000 for loss of a hand).

Because the payment is for loss of a *member or function of the body*, the $10,000 is excluded from Jill's gross income. Jill was absent from work for a week as a result of the accident. Her employer also provides her with insurance for the loss of income due to illness or injury. Jill collects $500, which is includible in her gross income.

EXAMPLE 5

11-2b **Medical Reimbursement Plans**

In lieu of providing an employee with insurance coverage for hospital and medical expenses, the employer may agree to reimburse the employee for these expenses. The amounts received through the insurance coverage (insured plan benefits) are excluded from gross income under § 105 (as previously discussed).

Insurance companies that issue this type of policy usually require a broad coverage of employees. An alternative is to have a plan that is not funded with insurance (a self-insured arrangement). Under a self-insured plan, the employer reimburses employees directly for any medical expenses. The benefits received under a self-insured plan can be excluded from the employee's gross income if the plan does not discriminate in favor of highly compensated employees.[7]

There is also an alternative means of accomplishing a medical reimbursement plan. The employer can purchase a medical insurance plan with a high deductible (e.g., the employee is responsible for the first $2,600 of the family's medical expenses) and then make contributions to the employee's **Health Savings Account (HSA)**.[8] The employer can make contributions each month up to the maximum contribution of 100 percent of the deductible amount. The monthly deductible amount is limited to one-twelfth of $3,350 under a high-deductible plan for self-only coverage. The monthly amount for an individual who has family coverage is limited to one-twelfth of $6,750 under a high-deductible plan.

---

[5]§ 106, Reg. § 1.106–1, and Rev.Rul. 82–196, 1982–2 C.B. 53.

[6]See the discussion of medical care in Chapter 10.

[7]§ 105(h). Also see § 106 and Rev.Rul. 61–146, 1961–2 C.B. 25. Employers should make sure that such reimbursement plans fall within the require-

ments of the Affordable Care Act to avoid an excise tax. See § 4980D, Notice 2013–54, 2013–40 I.R.B. 287, and Notice 2015–17, 2015–10 I.R.B. 845.

[8]§§ 106(d) and 223. See additional coverage in Chapter 10.

Withdrawals from the HSA must be used to reimburse the employee for the medical expenses paid by the employee that are not covered under the high-deductible plan. The employee is not taxed on the employer's contributions to the HSA, the earnings on the funds in the account, or the withdrawals made for medical expenses.[9]

11-2c Long-Term Care Insurance Benefits

Generally, long-term care insurance, which covers expenses such as the cost of care in a nursing home, is treated the same as accident and health insurance benefits. Thus, the employee does not recognize gross income when the employer pays the premiums. An individual who purchases his or her own policy can exclude the benefits from gross income. However, statutory limitations (indexed for inflation) exist for the following amounts.

- Premiums paid by the employer.
- Benefits collected under the employer's plan.
- Benefits collected from the individual's policy.

The employer or insurance company generally provides the employee with information about the amount of his or her taxable benefits. The maximum amount excluded must be reduced by any amount received from other third parties (e.g., Medicare, Medicaid).[10]

EXAMPLE 6

Hazel, who suffers from Alzheimer's disease, is a patient in a nursing home for the last 30 days of 2016. While in the nursing home, she incurs total costs of $7,600. Medicare pays $3,500 of the costs. Hazel receives $7,000 from her long-term care insurance policy, which pays while she is in the facility.

The amount Hazel may exclude is calculated as follows.

Greater of:		
2015 statutory amount	$10,200	
Actual cost of the care	7,600	$10,200
Less: Amount received from Medicare		(3,500)
Amount of exclusion		$ 6,700

Therefore, Hazel reports gross income of $300 ($7,000 − $6,700) for the long-term care benefits received.

---

[9]§§ 106(d), 223(b), and 223(d). The amounts for 2015 were $3,350 and $6,650.

[10]§ 7702B and § 213(d)(10). See IRS Publication 525 for the taxable and nontaxable amounts that the employer is required to report on the employee's Form W–2.

11-2d Meals and Lodging Furnished for the Convenience of the Employer

Under the following conditions, the value of meals and lodging provided to the employee and the employee's spouse and dependents are excluded from gross income.[11]

- The meals and/or lodging are *furnished by the employer*, on the employer's *business premises*, for the *convenience of the employer*.

- In the case of lodging, the *employee is required* to accept the lodging as a condition of employment.

Furnished by the Employer

The courts have raised two questions with regard to the *furnished by the employer* requirement.

- Who is considered an *employee*?
- What is meant by *furnished*?

The IRS and some courts have reasoned that because a partner is not an employee, the exclusion does not apply to a partner. However, the Tax Court and the Fifth Circuit Court of Appeals have ruled in favor of the taxpayer on this issue.[12]

The Supreme Court held that a *cash meal allowance* was ineligible for the exclusion because the employer did not actually furnish the meals.[13] Similarly, one court denied the exclusion where the employer paid for the food and supplied the cooking facilities but the employee prepared the meal.[14]

On the Employer's Business Premises

The *on the employer's business premises* requirement, applicable to both meals and lodging, has resulted in much litigation. The Regulations define business premises as simply "the place of employment of the employee."[15] Thus, the Sixth Circuit Court of Appeals held that a residence, owned by the employer and occupied by an employee, located two blocks from the motel that the employee managed was not part of the business premises.[16] However, the Tax Court considered an employer-owned house located across the street from the hotel that was managed by the taxpayer to be on the business premises of the employer.[17]

Perhaps these two cases can be reconciled by comparing the distance from the lodging facilities to the place where the employer's business was conducted. Apparently, the closer the lodging is to the business operations, the more likely the convenience of the employer is served.

For the Convenience of the Employer

The *convenience of the employer* test is intended to focus on the employer's motivation for furnishing the meals and lodging rather than on the benefits received by the employee. If the employer furnishes the meals and lodging primarily to enable the employee to perform his or her duties properly, it does not matter that the employee considers these benefits to be a part of his or her compensation.

---

[11]§ 119(a). The value of meals and lodging is also excluded from FICA and FUTA tax. *Rowan Companies, Inc. v. U.S.*, 81–1 USTC ¶9479, 48 AFTR 2d 81–5115, 101 S.Ct. 2288 (USSC, 1981).

[12]Rev.Rul. 80, 1953–1 C.B. 62; *Comm. v. Doak*, 56–2 USTC ¶9708, 49 AFTR 1491, 234 F.2d 704 (CA–4, 1956); but see *G. A. Papineau*, 16 T.C. 130 (1951); *Armstrong v. Phinney*, 68–1 USTC ¶9355, 21 AFTR 2d 1260, 394 F.2d 661 (CA–5, 1968).

[13]*Comm. v. Kowalski*, 77–2 USTC ¶9748, 40 AFTR 2d 77–6128, 98 S.Ct. 315 (USSC, 1977).

[14]*Tougher v. Comm.*, 71–1 USTC ¶9398, 27 AFTR 2d 71–1301, 441 F.2d 1148 (CA–9, 1971).

[15]Reg. § 1.119–1(c)(1).

[16]*Comm. v. Anderson*, 67–1 USTC ¶9136, 19 AFTR 2d 318, 371 F.2d 59 (CA–6, 1966).

[17]*J. B. Lindeman*, 60 T.C. 609 (1973).

The tests for excluding meals are satisfied in the following cases.[18]

- A restaurant requires its service staff to eat their meals on the premises during the busy lunch and breakfast hours.
- A bank furnishes meals on the premises for its tellers, to limit the time the employees are away from their booths during the busy hours.
- A worker is employed at a construction site in a remote part of Alaska. The employer must furnish meals and lodging due to the inaccessibility of other facilities.

Required as a Condition of Employment

The *employee is required to accept* test applies only to lodging. If the employee's use of the housing would serve the convenience of the employer but the employee is not required to use the housing, the exclusion is not available.

EXAMPLE 7

VEP, a utilities company, has all of its service personnel on 24-hour call for emergencies. The company encourages its employees to live near the plant so that they can respond quickly to emergency calls. Company-owned housing is available rent-free. Only 10 of the employees live in company housing because it is not perceived as suitable for families.

VEP employees are not required to use the company-provided housing. Therefore, the employees who live in company housing must include its value in gross income.

In addition, if the employee has the option of accepting a benefit of cash or lodging, the employer-required test is not satisfied.

EXAMPLE 8

Khalid is the manager of a large apartment complex. The employer requires Khalid to live on the premises but does not charge him rent. The rental value of his apartment is $9,600 a year. Although Khalid considers the rent-free housing a significant benefit, he is not required to include the value of the housing in his gross income.

Other housing exclusions are available for certain employees of educational institutions, ministers of the gospel, and military personnel.

11-2e Group Term Life Insurance

An employee can claim a limited exclusion for group term life insurance benefits that are provided by the employer. The premiums paid by the employer for a reasonable amount of group term life insurance protection are excludible from the employee's gross income.

The benefits of this exclusion are available only to employees. Proprietors and partners are not considered employees. Moreover, only a broad-scale coverage of employees satisfies the group requirement (e.g., shareholder-employees would not constitute a qualified group). The exclusion applies only to term insurance (protection for a period of time but with no cash surrender value) and not to ordinary life insurance (lifetime protection plus a cash surrender value that can be drawn upon before death).

The exclusion applies to the first $50,000 of group term life insurance protection. For each $1,000 of coverage in excess of $50,000, the employee must include the amounts indicated in Exhibit 11.1 in gross income.[19]

DIGGING DEEPER 3 | In-depth coverage can be found on this book's companion website: www.cengagebrain.com

---

[18]Reg. § 1.119–1(f). [19]Reg. § 1.79–3(d)(2).

Finch Corporation provides its employees with a group term life insurance policy with coverage equal to the employee's annual salary. Keith, age 52, is president of the corporation and receives an annual salary of $350,000. Keith must include $828 in gross income from the insurance protection for the year.

EXAMPLE 9

$$\frac{\$350,000 - \$50,000}{\$1,000} \times \$.23 \times 12 \text{ months} = \$828$$

If the plan discriminates in favor of certain key employees (e.g., officers), the key employees are not eligible for the exclusion.[20] In such a case, the key employees include in gross income the *greater* of actual premiums paid by the employer or the amount calculated from the Uniform Premiums table in Exhibit 11.1.

11-2f Qualified Tuition Reduction Plans

Employees (including retired and disabled former employees) of nonprofit educational institutions can exclude from gross income a tuition waiver that is provided pursuant to a qualified tuition reduction plan. The exclusion applies to tuition reductions granted to the employee, the employee's spouse, and the employee's dependent children.[21]

11-2g Other Employee Fringe Benefits

Employees can qualify for some other fringe benefits, which are excluded from gross income.

- The employee does not include in gross income the value of child and dependent care services paid for by the employer and incurred to enable the employee to work. The exclusion cannot exceed $5,000 per year ($2,500 if married and filing separately). For a married couple, the annual exclusion cannot exceed the earned income of the spouse who has the lesser amount. For an unmarried taxpayer, the exclusion cannot exceed the taxpayer's earned income.[22]

EXHIBIT 11.1	Uniform Premiums for $1,000 of Group Term Life Insurance Protection	

Attained Age on Last Day of Employee's Tax Year	Cost of $1,000 of Protection for a One-Month Period*
Under 25	$ .05
25–29	.06
30–34	.08
35–39	.09
40–44	.10
45–49	.15
50–54	.23
55–59	.43
60–64	.66
65–69	1.27
70 and above	2.06

*Reg. § 1.79–3.

[20]§ 79(d).
[21]§ 117(d).

[22]§ 129. The exclusion applies to the same types of expenses that, if paid by the employee (and not reimbursed by the employer), would be eligible for the credit for child and dependent care expenses, discussed in Chapter 10.

- The value of the use of a gymnasium or other athletic facilities by employees, their spouses, and their dependent children is excluded from an employee's gross income. The facilities must be on the employer's premises, and substantially all of the use of the facilities must be by employees and their family members.[23]

- A scholarship recipient may exclude from gross income the amount used for tuition and related expenses (fees, books, supplies, and equipment required for courses), provided the conditions of the grant do not require that the funds be used for other purposes.[24]

EXAMPLE 10

Kelly receives a scholarship of $9,500 from State University to be used to pursue a bachelor's degree. She spends $4,000 on tuition, $3,000 on books and supplies, and $2,500 for room and board. Kelly may exclude $7,000 ($4,000 + $3,000) from gross income. The $2,500 spent for room and board is included in Kelly's gross income.

- Qualified employer-provided educational assistance (tuition, fees, books, and supplies) at the undergraduate and graduate levels is excludible from gross income. The exclusion does not cover meals, lodging, transportation costs, and educational payments for courses involving sports, games, or hobbies. The exclusion is subject to an annual statutory ceiling of $5,250 per employee.[25]

- The employee can exclude from gross income up to $13,460 of expenses incurred to adopt a child, where the adoption expenses are paid or reimbursed by the employer under a qualified adoption assistance program.[26] For 2016, the exclusion is phased out as adjusted gross income increases from $201,920 to $241,920.

11-2h Cafeteria Plans

Generally, if an employee is offered a choice between cash and some other form of compensation, the employee has constructively received the cash even when the noncash option is elected. Thus, the employee recognizes gross income regardless of the option chosen.

An exception to this constructive receipt treatment is provided under the cafeteria plan rules. Under such a plan, the employee can choose between cash and nontaxable benefits (e.g., group term life insurance, health and accident protection, child care). If the employee chooses the otherwise nontaxable benefits, the cafeteria plan rules allow the benefits to be excluded from the employee's gross income.[27]

Cafeteria plans provide tremendous flexibility in tailoring the employee pay package to fit individual needs. Some employees (usually the younger group) prefer cash, while others (usually the older group) will opt for the fringe benefit program. However, long-term care insurance cannot be part of a cafeteria plan. Thus, an employer that wants to provide long-term care benefits must provide such benefits separate from the cafeteria plan.[28]

---

[23]§ 132(j)(4).

[24]§ 117(b).

[25]§ 127.

[26]§ 137. A credit relating to the expenditures of the parents also is available under § 23, as discussed in Chapter 10.

[27]§ 125.

[28]§ 125(f).

Hawk Corporation offers its employees (on a nondiscriminatory basis) a choice of any one or all of the following benefits.

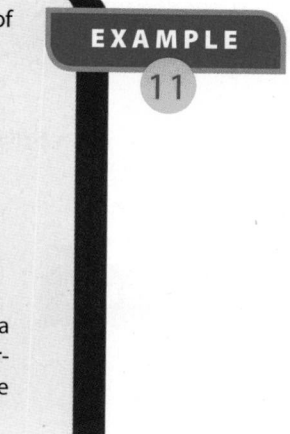

EXAMPLE 11

Benefit	Cost
Group term life insurance	$ 200
Hospitalization insurance for family members	2,400
Child care payments	1,800
	$4,400

If a benefit is not selected, the employee receives cash equal to the cost of the benefit. Kay, a Hawk employee, has a spouse who works for another employer that provides hospitalization insurance but no child care payments. Kay elects to receive the group term life insurance, the child care payments, and $2,400 of cash. Only the $2,400 is included in Kay's gross income.

11-2i Flexible Spending Plans

Flexible spending plans (often referred to as flexible benefit plans) operate much like cafeteria plans. Under these plans, the employee accepts lower cash compensation (as much as $2,550) in return for the employer's agreement to pay certain costs without the employee recognizing gross income. For example, assume that the employer's health insurance policy does not cover dental expenses. The employee could estimate his or her dental expenses for the upcoming year and agree to a salary reduction equal to the estimated dental expenses. The employer then pays or reimburses the employee for the actual dental expenses incurred, up to the amount of the salary reduction. If the employee's actual dental expenses are less than the reduction in cash compensation, the employee cannot recover the difference. Hence, these plans often are referred to as *use or lose* plans. To avoid forfeiture of unpaid amounts, the IRS allows a payment until March 15 of the following year to count. As is the case for cafeteria plans, flexible spending plans cannot be used to pay long-term care insurance premiums.

Concept Summary 11.1 reviews the exclusions discussed to this point in the chapter.

Concept Summary 11.1

Employee Fringe Benefits

Type of Benefit	Exclusion
Accident, health, and long-term care insurance and medical reimbursement (§§ 105 and 106)	Insurance premiums paid by the employer and benefits collected
High-deductible health insurance and contributions to employee's Health Savings Account (§§ 106 and 223)	Employer premiums on high-deductible medical insurance plus contributions to Health Savings Account (statutory limits, indexed for inflation)
Meals and lodging furnished for the convenience of the employer (§ 119)	Value of meals and lodging on the employer's premises
Group term life insurance (§ 79)	Premiums on up to $50,000 of protection
Qualified tuition reduction [§ 117(d)]	Value of tuition waiver
Child care provided by the employer or reimbursement for employee's cost (§ 129)	Services provided or reimbursement of expenses up to $5,000 a year
Athletic facilities on the employer's premises (§ 132)	Value of services
Educational assistance for tuition, fees, books, and supplies (§ 127)	Limited to $5,250 annually
Adoption assistance (§ 137)	Expenses up to $13,460
Flexible spending plans (§ 125)	Limited to $2,550 annually

11-2j **General Classes of Excluded Benefits**

An employer can confer numerous forms and types of economic benefits to its employees. Under the all-inclusive concept of income, the benefits are taxable unless one of the provisions previously discussed specifically excludes the item from gross income. The amount of the resulting gross income is the fair market value of the benefit. This reasoning can lead to results that are unsatistfactory, as illustrated in the following example.

Ryan is employed in New York as a ticket clerk for Trans National Airlines. Ryan's mother is ill in Miami, but Ryan has no money with which to purchase plane tickets. Trans National offers daily flights from New York to Miami that often leave with empty seats. The cost of a round-trip ticket is $400. If Trans National allows Ryan to fly without charge to Miami, under the general gross income rules, Ryan recognizes income equal to the value of a ticket.

Because Congress believed that taxing fringe benefits often yielded harsh results, it established seven broad classes of nontaxable employee benefits. The value of the benefits that the employer provides are excluded from the employee's gross income under certain circumstances.[29]

- No-additional-cost services.
- Qualified employee discounts.
- Working condition fringes.
- *De minimis* fringes.
- Qualified transportation fringes.
- Qualified moving expense reimbursements.
- Qualified retirement planning services.

No-Additional-Cost Services

The circumstances of Example 12 illustrate the reason for the **no-additional-cost service** fringe benefit. The value of the services received is excluded from an employee's gross income if all of the following conditions are satisfied.

- The employee receives services, as opposed to property.
- The employer does not incur substantial additional costs, including forgone revenue, in providing the services to the employee.
- The services are offered to customers in the ordinary course of the business in which the employee works.[30]

In Example 12, although the airplane may burn slightly more fuel because Ryan is aboard and Ryan may receive the same meal or snacks as paying customers, the additional costs to the airline would not be substantial. Thus, the trip could qualify as a no-additional-cost service.

On the other hand, assume that Ryan is given a reserved seat on a flight that is frequently full. The employer would be forgoing revenue to allow Ryan to fly. This forgone revenue would be a substantial additional cost, and the benefit would be taxable to Ryan.

DIGGING DEEPER 4   **In-depth coverage can be found on this book's companion website:** www.cengagebrain.com

---

[29]See, generally, § 132.   [30]Reg. § 1.132–2.

The no-additional-cost exclusion extends to the employee's spouse and dependent children and to retired and disabled former employees.[31] However, the exclusion is not extended to highly compensated employees unless the benefit is available on a nondiscriminatory basis.

Qualified Employee Discounts

When the employer sells goods or services (other than no-additional-cost benefits just discussed) to the employee for a price that is less than the price charged to regular customers, the employee recognizes gross income equal to the discount. However, a qualified employee discount can be excluded from the gross income of the employee under the following conditions and limitations.

- The exclusion is not available for discounted sales of real property (e.g., a house) or for personal property of the type commonly held for investment (e.g., common stocks).

- The property or services must be from the same line of business in which the employee works.

- In the case of *property*, the exclusion is limited to the *gross profit component* of the price to customers.

- In the case of *services*, the exclusion is limited to 20 percent of the customer price.

EXAMPLE 14

Silver Corporation, which operates a department store, sells a television to its employee Kylie for $300. The regular customer price is $500, and the gross profit rate is 25%. Silver also sells Kylie a service contract for $120. The regular customer price for the contract is $150.

Customer price for property	$ 500	
Less: Gross profit (25%)	(125)	
Employee price	(300)	
Excess discount		$75
Customer price for service contract	$ 150	
Less: 20% maximum exclusion	(30)	
Employee price	(120)	
Excess discount		0
Kylie's gross income recognized		$75

As in the case of no-additional-cost benefits, the exclusion applies to employees, an employee's spouse and dependent children, an employee's surviving spouse, and retired and disabled former employees.

Working Condition Fringes

Generally, an employee may exclude from gross income the cost of property or services provided by the employer if the employee could deduct the cost of those items if he or she had actually paid for them. These benefits are called working condition fringes.

EXAMPLE 15

Mitch is a CPA employed by an accounting firm. The employer pays Mitch's annual dues to professional organizations. Mitch is not required to include the payment of the dues in gross income because if he had paid the dues, he would deduct the amount as an employee business expense (as discussed later in this chapter).

---

[31]Reg. § 1.132–1(b).

In many cases, this exclusion merely avoids reporting income and an offsetting deduction. Unlike the other fringe benefits discussed previously, working condition fringes can be made available on a discriminatory basis and still qualify for the exclusion.

De Minimis Fringes

As the term suggests, de minimis fringe benefits are so small in amount that accounting for them is impractical. Examples of *de minimis* fringes include the following.

- Occasional personal use of a company copying machine, occasional company cocktail parties or picnics for employees, occasional supper money or taxi fare for employees because of overtime work, and certain holiday gifts of property with a low fair market value are excluded.

- The value of meals consumed in a subsidized eating facility (e.g., an employees' cafeteria) operated by the employer is excluded if the facility is located on or near the employer's business premises, if the facility's revenue equals or exceeds direct operating costs, and if nondiscrimination requirements are met.

When taxpayers venture beyond established norms, there is obviously room for disagreement as to what is *de minimis*. According to the IRS, cash or gift cards never are considered *de minimis*.[32]

In Notice 2011–72, the IRS addressed the question of whether the personal use of cell phones provided by the employer could be excluded from the employee's gross income. Generally, the value of personal use of the cell phone is excluded if the device is provided primarily for business reasons, such as to enable the employee to be in contact with clients when the employee is away from the office.

Qualified Transportation Fringes

The intent of the exclusion for qualified transportation fringes is to encourage employees to use mass transit for commuting to and from work. Qualified transportation fringes include the following.

1. Transportation in a commuter highway vehicle, like a dedicated bus or van, between the employee's residence and the place of employment.
2. A transit pass.
3. Qualified parking.
4. Qualified bicycle commuting reimbursement.

Statutory dollar limits are placed on the amount of the exclusion. Categories (1) and (2) above are combined for purposes of applying the limit. For 2016, the inflation adjusted limit for categories (1) and (2) combined, as well as for category (3), is $255 per month ($250 in 2015).

Qualified parking includes the following.

- Parking provided to an employee on or near the employer's business premises.

- Parking provided to an employee on or near a location from which the employee commutes to work via mass transit, in a commuter highway vehicle, or in a carpool.

The *qualified bicycle commuting reimbursement* enables an employee to exclude up to $20 per month received from an employer as reimbursement for the cost of commuting by bicycle (i.e., bicycle purchase, improvement, repair, and storage).

Qualified transportation fringes may be provided directly by the employer or may be in the form of cash reimbursements.

---

[32]TAM 200437030 (9/10/04) and IRS Publication 15B (2015), *Employer's Tax Guide to Fringe Benefits*, p. 8.

Gray Corporation's offices are located in the center of a large city. The company pays for parking spaces to be used by the company officers. Emma, a vice president, receives $300 of such benefits each month during 2016. The parking space rental qualifies as a qualified transportation fringe. Of the $300 benefit received each month, $255 is excludible from gross income. The balance of $45 is included in Emma's gross income. The same result would occur if Emma paid for the parking and was reimbursed by her employer.

Qualified Moving Expense Reimbursements

Qualified moving expenses that are reimbursed or paid by the employer are excludible from gross income. A qualified moving expense is an expense that would be deductible under § 217. See the discussion of moving expenses later in this chapter.

Qualified Retirement Planning Services

Qualified retirement planning services include any retirement planning advice or information that an employer who maintains a qualified retirement plan provides to an employee or the employee's spouse. Such an exclusion should motivate more employers to provide retirement planning services to their employees.

Nondiscrimination Provisions

For no-additional-cost services, qualified employee discounts, and qualified retirement planning services that are discriminatory in favor of *highly compensated employees*, exclusion treatment is denied. However, any non-highly compensated employees still can exclude these benefits.[33]

Dove Company's officers are allowed to purchase goods from the company at a 25% discount. All other employees are allowed only a 15% discount. The company's gross profit margin on these goods is 30%. Because the officers receive more favorable discounts, the plan is discriminatory in favor of the officers. With regard to all other employees, the discount is "qualified" because it is available to all employees (other than the officers who receive a more favorable discount) and the discount is less than the company's gross profit.

Peggy, an officer in the company, purchased goods from the company for $750 when the price charged to customers was $1,000. Peggy reports $250 in gross income because the plan is discriminatory.

Mason, an employee of the company who is not an officer, purchased goods for $850 when the customer price was $1,000. Mason is not required to recognize gross income because he received a qualified employee discount.

De minimis fringe benefits (except for subsidized eating facilities) and working condition fringe benefits can be provided on a discriminatory basis. Likewise, the qualified transportation fringe and the qualified moving expense reimbursement can be provided on a discriminatory basis.

A review of employee fringe benefits is set forth in Concept Summary 11.2.

In-depth coverage can be found on this book's companion website: www.cengagebrain.com   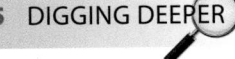 **5 DIGGING DEEPER**

---

[33]§§ 132(j)(1) and 132(m)(2).

Concept Summary 11.2

General Classes of Fringe Benefits

Benefit	Description and Examples	Coverage Allowed	Effect of Discrimination
1. No-additional-cost services	The employee takes advantage of the employer's excess capacity (e.g., free passes for airline employees).	Current, retired, and disabled employees; their spouses and dependent children; spouses of deceased employees. Partners are treated as employees.	No exclusion for highly compensated employees.
2. Qualified discounts on goods	The employee is allowed a discount no greater than the gross profit margin on goods sold to customers.	Same as (1) above.	Same as (1) above.
3. Qualified discounts on services	The employee is allowed a discount (maximum of 20%) on services the employer offers to customers.	Same as (1) above.	Same as (1) above.
4. Working condition fringes	Expenses paid by the employer that would be deductible if paid by the employee (e.g., a mechanic's tools). Also includes auto salesperson's use of a car held for sale.	Current employees, partners, directors, and independent contractors.	No effect.
5. *De minimis* items	Expenses so immaterial that accounting for them is not warranted (e.g., occasional supper money, personal use of the copy machine).	Any recipient of a fringe benefit.	No effect.
6. Qualified transportation fringes	Transportation benefits provided by the employer to employees, including a commute in a commuter highway vehicle, a transit pass, qualified parking, and qualified bicycle commuting.	Current employees.	No effect.
7. Qualified moving expense reimbursements	Qualified moving expenses that are paid or reimbursed by the employer. A qualified moving expense is one that would be deductible under § 217.	Current employees.	No effect.
8. Qualified retirement planning services	Qualified retirement planning services that are provided by the employer.	Current employees and spouses.	Same as (1) above.

11-2k Foreign Earned Income

The United States uses a global tax system as opposed to a territorial system. Under this global system, a U.S. citizen is generally subject to U.S. tax on his or her income regardless of the income's geographic origin. In countries where a territorial system is used, one's gross income is taxed only in the country in which the income was earned. Under a global system, a U.S. citizen who earns income in another country could experience double taxation: the same income would be taxed in the United States and in the foreign country.

Out of a sense of fairness and so as not to discourage U.S. citizens from working abroad, Congress has provided alternative forms of relief from taxes on foreign earned income. The taxpayer can elect *either* (1) to include the foreign income in his or her taxable income and then claim a credit for foreign taxes paid or (2) to exclude the foreign earnings from his or her U.S. gross income (the **foreign earned income exclusion**).[34]

---

[34] § 911(a).

The foreign tax credit option is discussed in Chapter 17, but as is apparent from the following discussion, most taxpayers choose the exclusion.

Foreign earned income consists of the earnings from the individual's personal services rendered in a foreign country (other than as an employee of the U.S. government). Such an employee often is referred to as an "expatriate." To qualify for the exclusion, the taxpayer must be either of the following.

- A bona fide resident of the foreign country (or countries).

- Present in a foreign country (or countries) for at least 330 days during any 12 consecutive months.

> **EXAMPLE 18**
>
> Sandra's trip to and from a foreign country in connection with her work encompassed the following dates:
>
> | Arrived in Foreign Country | Returned to the United States |
> | --- | --- |
> | March 10, 2015 | February 15, 2016 |
>
> During the 12 consecutive months ending on March 10, 2016, Sandra was present in the foreign country for at least 330 days (366 days less 14 days in February and 10 days in March 2016). Therefore, all income earned in the foreign country through March 10, 2016, is eligible for the exclusion.

The exclusion is limited to an indexed amount of $101,300 for 2016 ($100,800 in 2015). For married persons, both of whom have foreign earned income, the exclusion is computed separately for each spouse. If all of the days in the tax year are not qualifying days (i.e., days present in the other country), the taxpayer must compute the maximum exclusion on a daily basis ($101,300 divided by the number of days in the entire year and multiplied by the number of qualifying days).

> **EXAMPLE 19**
>
> Keith qualifies for the foreign earned income exclusion. He was present in France for all of 2016. Keith's salary for 2016 is $120,000. Because all of the days in 2016 are qualifying days, Keith can exclude $101,300 of his $120,000 salary.
>
> Assume instead that only 339 days were qualifying days. Then Keith's exclusion is computed as follows.
>
> $$\$101,300 \times \frac{339 \text{ days outside the U.S.}}{366 \text{ days in the year}} = \$93,827$$

11-3 EMPLOYEE EXPENSES

LO.3

Apply the rules for computing deductible expenses of employees, including transportation, travel, moving, education, and entertainment expenses.

Once the employment relationship is established, employee expenses fall into one of the following categories.

- Transportation.
- Travel.
- Moving.

- Education.
- Entertainment.
- Other employee expenses.

Deductions for these expenses are not necessarily limited to employees. A deduction for business transportation, for example, is equally available to taxpayers who are self-employed.

11-3a Transportation Expenses

An employee may deduct unreimbursed employment-related **transportation expenses** as an itemized deduction *from* AGI. Transportation expenses include only the cost of transporting the employee from one place to another in the course of employment when the employee is not away from home in travel status. Such costs include taxi fares, automobile expenses, tolls, and parking.

Commuting Expenses

Commuting between home and one's place of employment is a personal, nondeductible expense. The fact that one employee drives 30 miles to work and another employee walks six blocks is of no significance.[35] However, the expenses of getting from one job to another job or from one workstation to another workstation are deductible transportation expenses rather than nondeductible commuting expenses.

DIGGING DEEPER **6** | In-depth coverage can be found on this book's companion website: www.cengagebrain.com

---

EXAMPLE

20

In the current year, Cynthia holds two jobs, a full-time job with Blue Corporation and a part-time job with Wren Corporation. Cynthia customarily leaves home at 7:30 A.M. and drives 30 miles to the Blue plant, where she works until 5:00 P.M. After dinner at a nearby café, Cynthia drives 20 miles to Wren and works from 7:00 to 11:00 P.M. The distance from the second job to Cynthia's home is 40 miles. Her deduction is based on 20 miles (the distance between jobs).

Referring back to Example 20, assume that Cynthia has an office in the home that qualifies as a principal place of business. In this circumstance, the transportation between home and various work locations is not a deductible commuting expense.

Computation of Automobile Expenses

A taxpayer has two choices in computing deductible automobile expenses. The first alternative is to use the actual operating cost, which includes depreciation (refer to Chapter 5), fuel, oil, repairs, licenses, and insurance costs. Records must be kept that document the automobile's personal and business use. Only the percentage allocable to business transportation and travel is allowed as a deduction.

The second alternative is the **automatic mileage method**. For 2016, the deduction is based on 54 cents per mile for business miles (57.5 cents for 2015).[36] Parking fees and tolls are allowed in addition to expenses computed using the automatic mileage method.

Generally, a taxpayer may elect either method for any particular year. However, the following restrictions apply:

- The vehicle is owned or leased by the taxpayer.
- The vehicle is not used for hire (e.g., taxicab).
- If five or more vehicles are in use (for business purposes) at the *same* time (not alternately), a taxpayer may not use the automatic mileage method.
- A taxpayer may not switch to the automatic mileage method if the MACRS statutory percentage method or the election to expense under § 179 has been used.

DIGGING DEEPER **7** | In-depth coverage can be found on this book's companion website: www.cengagebrain.com

11-3b Travel Expenses

An itemized deduction is allowed for *unreimbursed* **travel expenses** related to a taxpayer's employment. Travel expenses are more broadly defined in the Code than are

---

[35]*U.S. v. Tauferner*, 69–1 USTC ¶9241, 23 AFTR 2d 69–1025, 407 F.2d 243 (CA–10, 1969).

[36]Notice 2016–1, 2016–2 I.R.B 265, and Rev.Proc. 2010–51, 2010–51 I.R.B. 883.

transportation expenses. Travel expenses include transportation expenses and meals and lodging while away from home in the pursuit of a trade or business. Meals cannot be lavish or extravagant. A deduction for meals and lodging is available only if the tax-payer is away from his or her tax home. Deductible travel expenses also include reasonable laundry and incidental expenses.

In-depth coverage can be found on this book's companion website: www.cengagebrain.com **8 DIGGING DEEPER**

Away-from-Home Requirement

The crucial test for the deductibility of travel expenses is whether the employee is away from home overnight. "Overnight" need not be a 24-hour period, but it must be a period substantially longer than an ordinary day's work and must require rest, sleep, or a relief-from-work period.[37] Thus, a one-day business trip is not travel, and meals and lodging for such a trip are not deductible.

Temporary Assignments

The employee must be away from home for a temporary period. If the taxpayer-employee is reassigned to a new post for an indefinite period of time, that new post becomes his or her tax home. Temporary indicates that the assignment's termination is expected within a reasonably short period of time. The position of the IRS is that the tax home is the business location, post, or station of the taxpayer. Thus, travel expenses are not deductible if a taxpayer is reassigned for an indefinite period and does not move his or her place of residence to the new location.

Temporary Becomes Permanent

Malcolm's employer opened a branch office in San Diego. Malcolm was assigned to the new office for three months to train a new manager and to assist in setting up the new office. He tried commuting from his home in Los Angeles for a week and decided that he could not continue driving several hours a day. He rented an apartment in San Diego, where he lived during the week. He spent weekends with his wife and children at their home in Los Angeles.

Malcolm's rent, meals, laundry, incidentals, and automobile expenses in San Diego are deductible. To the extent that Malcolm's transportation expense related to his weekend trips home exceeds what his cost of meals and lodging would have been, the excess is personal and nondeductible.

EXAMPLE 21

Assume that Malcolm in Example 21 was transferred to the new location to become the new manager permanently. His wife and children continued to live in Los Angeles until the end of the school year. Malcolm is no longer "away from home" because the assignment is not temporary. His travel expenses are not deductible.

EXAMPLE 22

To curtail controversy in this area, the Code specifies that a taxpayer "shall not be treated as temporarily away from home during any period of employment if such period exceeds 1 year."[38]

In-depth coverage can be found on this book's companion website: www.cengagebrain.com **9 DIGGING DEEPER**

---

[37]*U.S. v. Correll*, 68–1 USTC ¶9101, 20 AFTR 2d 5845, 88 S.Ct. 445 (USSC, 1967); Rev.Rul. 75–168, 1975–1 C.B. 58.

[38]§ 162(a).

Determining the Tax Home

Under ordinary circumstances, determining the location of a taxpayer's tax home does not present a problem. The tax home is the area in which the taxpayer derives his or her principal source of income; when the taxpayer has more than one place of employment, the tax home is based on the amount of time spent in each location.

It is possible for a taxpayer never to be away from his or her tax home. In other words, the tax home follows the taxpayer. Under such circumstances, all meals and lodging remain personal and are not deductible.

Jim is single and works full-time as a long-haul truck driver. He lists his mother's home as his address and stays there during holidays. However, he contributes nothing toward its maintenance. Because Jim has no regular place of duty or place where he regularly lives, his tax home is where he works (i.e., on the road). As an itinerant (transient), he is never away from home, and all of his meals and lodging while on the road are personal and not deductible.

The result reached in Example 23 is justified on the grounds that there is no duplication of living expenses in the case of itinerant taxpayers.[39]

Combined Business and Pleasure Travel

Deductible travel expenses need not be incurred in the performance of specific job functions. Travel expenses incurred to attend a professional convention are deductible by an employee if attendance is connected with services as an employee. For example, an employee of a law firm can deduct travel expenses incurred to attend a meeting of the American Bar Association.

To limit the possibility of a taxpayer claiming a tax deduction for what is essentially a personal vacation, several provisions have been enacted to restrict deductions associated with combined business and pleasure trips. If the business/pleasure trip is from one point in the United States to another point in the United States (*domestic travel*), the transportation expenses are deductible only if the trip is primarily for business.[40] Meals, lodging, and other expenses are allocated between business and personal days. If the trip is primarily for pleasure, no transportation expenses qualify as a deduction.

🔍 DIGGING DEEPER 10   In-depth coverage can be found on this book's companion website: www.cengagebrain.com

In the current year, Hana travels from Seattle to New York primarily for business. She spends five days conducting business and three days sightseeing and attending shows. Her plane and taxi fare amounts to $1,160. Her meals amount to $200 per day, and lodging and incidental expenses are $350 per day.

Hana can deduct the transportation expenses of $1,160 because the trip is primarily for business (five days of business versus three days of sightseeing). Deductible meals are limited to five days and are subject to the 50% cutback (discussed later in the chapter) for a total of $500 [5 days × ($200 × 50%)], and other deductions are limited to $1,750 (5 days × $350). If Hana is an employee, the unreimbursed travel expenses are miscellaneous itemized deductions subject to the 2%-of-AGI floor.

When the trip is outside the United States (*foreign travel*), special rules apply.[41] Transportation expenses must be allocated between business and personal days *unless* (1) the taxpayer is away from home for seven days or less or (2) less than 25 percent of the time was for personal purposes. No allocation is required if the taxpayer has no

[39]Rev.Rul. 73–539, 1973–2 C.B. 201 and *James O. Henderson*, 70 TCM 1407, T.C.Memo. 1995–559, *aff'd* by 98–1 USTC ¶50,375, 81 AFTR 2d 98–1748, 143 F.3d 497 (CA–9, 1998).

[40]Reg. § 1.162–2(b)(1).

[41]§ 274(c) and Reg. § 1.274–4. For purposes of the seven-days-or-less exception, the departure travel day is not counted.

substantial control over arrangements for the trip or the desire for a vacation is not a major factor in taking the trip. If the trip is primarily for pleasure, no transportation charges are deductible. Days devoted to travel are considered business days. Weekends, legal holidays, and intervening days are considered business days, provided that both the preceding and succeeding days were business days.

In-depth coverage can be found on this book's companion website: www.cengagebrain.com

11 DIGGING DEEPER

EXAMPLE 25

In the current year, Robert takes a trip from New York to Japan primarily for business purposes. He is away from home from June 10 through June 19. He spends three days vacationing and seven days (including two travel days) conducting business. His airfare is $4,000, his meals amount to $200 per day, and lodging and incidental expenses are $300 per day.

Because Robert is away from home for more than seven days and more than 25% of his time is devoted to personal purposes, only 70% (7 days business/10 days total) of the transportation is deductible. His deductions are computed as follows.

Transportation (70% × $4,000)		$2,800
Lodging ($300 × 7)		2,100
Meals ($200 × 7)	$1,400	
Less: 50% cutback (discussed later in this chapter)	(700)	700
Total deductions		$5,600

If Robert was gone the same period of time but spent only two days vacationing, no allocation of transportation would be required. Because the pleasure portion of the trip was less than 25% of the total, all of the airfare qualifies for the travel deduction.

The foreign convention rules do not operate to bar a deduction to an employer if the expense is *compensatory* in nature. For example, a trip to Rome won by a top salesperson is included in the gross income of the employee and is fully deductible by the employer.

TAX PLANNING STRATEGIES Transportation and Travel Expenses

FRAMEWORK FOCUS: DEDUCTIONS

Strategy: Maximize Deductible Amounts.

Adequate detailed records of all transportation and travel expenses should be kept. Because the automatic (standard) mileage allowance often is modest in amount, a new, expensive automobile used primarily for business may generate a higher expense based on actual cost. The election to expense part of the cost of the automobile under § 179, MACRS depreciation, insurance, repairs and maintenance, automobile club dues, and other related costs may result in

automobile expenses greater than the automatic mileage allowance.

If a taxpayer wants to sightsee or vacation on a business trip, it would be beneficial to schedule business on both a Friday and a Monday to turn the weekend into business days for allocation purposes. It is especially crucial to schedule appropriate business days when foreign travel is involved.

11-3c **Moving Expenses**

Moving expenses are deductible for moves in connection with the commencement of work at a new principal workplace.[42] Both employees and self-employed individuals

---

[42]§ 217(a).

can deduct these expenses. To be eligible for a moving expense deduction, a taxpayer must meet two basic tests: distance and time.

Distance Test

To meet the distance test, the taxpayer's new job location must be at least 50 miles farther from the taxpayer's old residence than the old residence was from the former place of employment. In this regard, the location of the new residence is not relevant. This eliminates a moving expense deduction for (1) taxpayers who purchase a new home in the same general area without changing their place of employment and (2) taxpayers who accept a new job in the same area as their old job.

If an individual is not employed before the move, the new job must be at least 50 miles from the former residence. Concept Summary 11.3 illustrates the application of the distance test.

Concept Summary 11.3

Meeting and Not Meeting the Distance Test

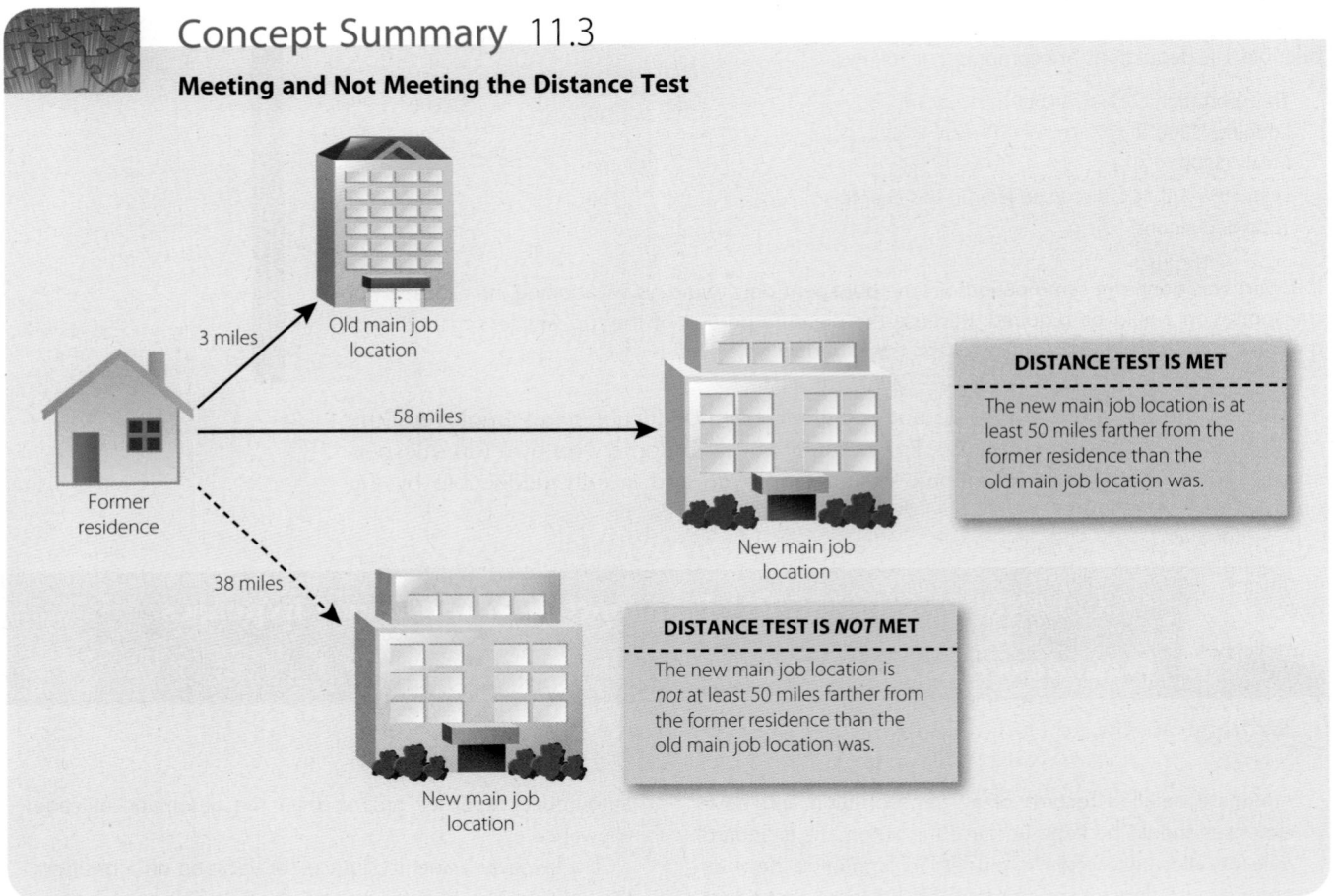

DISTANCE TEST IS MET

The new main job location is at least 50 miles farther from the former residence than the old main job location was.

DISTANCE TEST IS *NOT* MET

The new main job location is *not* at least 50 miles farther from the former residence than the old main job location was.

Time Test

To meet the time test, an employee must be employed on a full-time basis at the new location for 39 weeks in the 12-month period following the move. If the taxpayer is a self-employed individual, he or she must work in the new location for 78 weeks during the 24 months following the move; the first 39 weeks must be in the first 12 months. The time test is disregarded if the taxpayer dies, becomes disabled, or is discharged (other than for willful misconduct) or transferred by the employer.

DIGGING DEEPER **12**   In-depth coverage can be found on this book's companion website: www.cengagebrain.com

GLOBAL TAX ISSUES   Expatriates and the Moving Expense Deduction

Expatriates, U.S. persons who accept work assignments overseas, enjoy several favorable tax advantages regarding foreign moves. First, the cost of storing household goods qualifies as a moving expense. This could lead to a major tax saving because expatriates typically do not ship most of their household effects to the foreign location. Furthermore, the cost of storage, particularly in a climate-controlled facility, is not insignificant.

The second advantage expatriates may enjoy is an exemption from the time test. Those who return to the United States to retire are absolved from the 39-week or 78-week work requirement. Thus, the return home expenses are treated as qualified moving expenses.

Treatment of Moving Expenses

Qualified moving expenses include reasonable expenses of:

- Moving household goods and personal effects.
- Traveling from the former residence to the new residence.

For this purpose, traveling includes lodging, but not meals, for the taxpayer and members of the household.[43] The taxpayer can elect to use actual auto expenses (no depreciation is allowed) or the automatic mileage method. In this case, moving expense mileage is limited in 2016 to 19 cents per mile for each car (23 cents for 2015). These expenses also are limited by the reasonableness standard. For example, if a person moves from Texas to Florida via Maine and takes six weeks to do so, some of the expenditures will be nondeductible personal expenses.

EXAMPLE 26

Jill is transferred by her employer from the Atlanta office to the San Francisco office. In this connection, she spends the following amounts.

Cost of moving furniture	$4,800
Transportation	700
Meals	450
Lodging	600

Jill's total qualified moving expense is $6,100 ($4,800 + $700 + $600), which includes all costs listed above except for the cost of meals.

The moving expense deduction is allowed regardless of whether the employee is transferred by the existing employer or is employed by a new employer. It is allowed if the employee moves to a new area and obtains employment or switches from self-employed status to employee status (and vice versa). The moving expense deduction also is allowed for an individual who was unemployed before obtaining employment in a new area.

What Is Not Included

The moving expense deduction does *not* include the following costs.

- Meals consumed while en route to the new location.
- New car tags and driver's licenses.
- Loss on the sale of a residence or penalty for breaking a lease.

---

[43]§ 217(b).

- Forfeiture of security deposits and loss from disposing of club memberships.
- Pre-move house-hunting expenses.
- Temporary living expenses.

 DIGGING DEEPER 13 | In-depth coverage can be found on this book's companion website: www.cengagebrain.com

TAX PLANNING STRATEGIES **Moving Expenses**

FRAMEWORK FOCUS: DEDUCTIONS

Strategy: Maximize Deductible Amounts.

Persons who retire and move to a new location incur personal nondeductible moving expenses. If the retired person accepts a full-time job in the new location before moving and meets the time and distance requirements, the moving expenses are deductible.

EXAMPLE
27

At the time of his retirement from the national office of a major accounting firm, Gordon had an annual salary of $480,000. He moves from New York City to Seattle to retire and accepts a full-time teaching position at a Seattle junior college at an annual salary of $42,000. If Gordon satisfies the 39-week test, his moving expenses are deductible. The disparity between the two salaries (previous and current) is of no consequence.

11-3d **Education Expenses**

Employees *and* self-employed individuals can deduct expenses incurred for education as ordinary and necessary business expenses, provided the expenses are incurred to either:

- Meet the express requirements of the employer or the requirements imposed by law to retain his or her employment status; or
- Maintain or improve existing skills required in the present job.

Education expenses are not deductible if the education is for either of the following purposes (except as discussed in text Section 11-3e).

- To meet the minimum educational standards for qualification in the taxpayer's existing job; or
- To qualify the taxpayer for a new trade or business.[44]

Thus, fees incurred for professional exams (the bar exam, for example) and fees for review courses (such as a CPA review course) generally are not deductible.[45] If the education incidentally results in a promotion or raise, the deduction is allowed as long as the education maintained and improved existing skills and did not qualify the person for a new trade or business.

A change in duties does not by itself make the education expense nondeductible (i.e., if the worker's new duties involve the same general work). For example, the IRS has ruled that a practicing dentist's education expenses incurred to become an orthodontist are deductible.[46]

---

[44]Reg. §§ 1.162–5(b)(2) and (3).
[45]Reg. § 1.212–1(f) and Rev.Rul. 69–292, 1969–1 C.B. 84.

[46]Rev.Rul. 74–78, 1974–1 C.B. 44.

Requirements Imposed by Law or by the Employer for Retention of Employment

Taxpayers can deduct education expenses if additional courses are required by the employer or are imposed by law. Many states require a minimum of a bachelor's degree and a specified number of additional courses to retain a teaching job. In addition, some public school systems have imposed a master's degree requirement and require teachers to make satisfactory progress toward a master's degree to keep their positions. If the required education is the minimum degree required for the job, no deduction is allowed.

Expenses incurred for education required by law for various professions (e.g., medicine, law, and accounting) also qualify for deduction.

| In-depth coverage can be found on this book's companion website: www.cengagebrain.com | 14 DIGGING DEEPER |

Maintaining or Improving Existing Skills

The *maintaining or improving existing skills* requirement in the Code has been difficult for both taxpayers and the courts to interpret. For example, a business executive may be permitted to deduct the costs of obtaining an MBA on the grounds the advanced management education is undertaken to maintain and improve existing management skills. The executive is eligible to deduct the costs of specialized, nondegree management courses that are taken for continuing education or for maintaining or improving existing skills. Expenses incurred by the executive to obtain a law degree are not deductible, however, because the education constitutes training for a new trade or business. The Regulations specifically deny a self-employed accountant a deduction for expenses relating to law school.[47]

TAX PLANNING STRATEGIES   Education Expenses

FRAMEWORK FOCUS: DEDUCTIONS

Strategy: Maximize Deductible Amounts.

Education expenses are treated as nondeductible personal items unless the individual is employed or is engaged in a trade or business. A temporary leave of absence for further education is one way to ensure that the taxpayer is still treated as being engaged in a trade or business. An individual was permitted to deduct education expenses even though he resigned from his job, returned to school full-time for two years, and accepted another job in the same field upon graduation. The court held that the student had merely suspended active participation in his field.[48]

If the time out of the field is too long, education expense deductions are disallowed. For example, a teacher who left the field for four years to raise her child and curtailed her employment searches and writing activities was denied a deduction for education expenses. She was no longer actively engaged in the trade or business of being an educator.[49]

Classification of Specific Items

Education expenses include books and supplies, tuition, transportation (e.g., from the office to night school), and travel (e.g., meals and lodging while away from home at summer school).

---

[47]Reg. § 1.162–5(b)(3)(ii) Example (1).

[48]*Stephen G. Sherman*, 36 TCM 1191, T.C.Memo. 1977–301.

[49]*Brian C. Mulberin*, 42 TCM 834, T.C.Memo. 1981–454; *George A. Baist*, 56 TCM 778, T.C.Memo. 1988–554.

Sherry, who holds a bachelor of education degree, is a secondary education teacher in the Charleston school system. The school board recently raised its education requirement for new teachers from four years of college training to five. A transition clause allows teachers with only four years of college to continue to qualify if they show satisfactory progress toward a graduate degree.

Sherry enrolls at the University of South Carolina during the summer and takes two graduate courses. Her unreimbursed expenses for this purpose are as follows.

Books and tuition	$3,600
Lodging while in travel status (June–August)	2,150
Meals while in travel status	1,100
Laundry while in travel status	220
Transportation	900

Sherry's education expense deduction is computed as follows.

Books and tuition	$3,600
Lodging	2,150
Meals less 50% cutback (discussed later in this chapter)	550
Laundry	220
Transportation	900
	$7,420

11-3e Targeted Tuition Deduction

One of the major shortcomings of the education deduction, discussed previously, is that it is unavailable for taxpayers obtaining a basic skill (i.e., to meet the minimum standards required for the taxpayer's current job). This shortcoming has been partly resolved with the **deduction for qualified tuition and related expenses**.

A deduction *for* AGI is allowed for qualified tuition and related expenses involving higher education (i.e., postsecondary). The deduction is the lesser of the qualifying amount spent or the maximum amount allowed by § 222. The maximum deductions allowed are shown in Exhibit 11.2.[50]

EXHIBIT 11.2	Limitations for Targeted Tuition Deduction	
Filing Status	**MAGI Limit**	**Maximum Deduction Allowed**
Single	$ 65,000	$4,000
Married	130,000	
Single	65,001 to 80,000*	2,000
Married	130,001 to 160,000*	2,000

*No deduction is available if MAGI exceeds this amount.

---

[50]MAGI is modified adjusted gross income as defined in § 222(b)(2)(C). Examples of some of these modifications include adding back to regular AGI the foreign earned income exclusion and the domestic production activities deduction. See IRS Publication 970 (*Tax Benefits for Education*).

The § 222 limitations are not indexed for inflation.[51] Various aspects of the targeted higher education tuition deduction are summarized as follows.

- *Qualified tuition and related expenses* include whatever is required for enrollment at the institution. Usually, student activity fees, books, and room and board are not included.[52]
- The expense need not be employment-related, although it can be.
- The deduction is available for a taxpayer's spouse or anyone who can be claimed as a dependent and is an eligible student.
- The deduction is not available for married persons who file separate returns.
- To avoid a "double benefit," the deduction must be coordinated with other education provisions (e.g., American Opportunity and lifetime learning credits as discussed in Chapter 10). Along this same line, no deduction is allowed for a taxpayer who qualifies as another's dependent.[53]

EXAMPLE 29

Tina is single and a full-time employee of a CPA firm. During the current year, she attends law school at night and incurs the following expenses: $4,200 for tuition and $340 for books and supplies. Presuming that she satisfies the MAGI limitation (see Exhibit 11.2), she can claim $4,000 as a deduction *for* AGI. If she itemizes her deductions for the year, can she claim the $540 not allowed under § 222 ($200 tuition in excess of $4,000 + $340 for books and supplies) as an education expense eligible for itemized deduction treatment? No, because obtaining a law degree leads to a new trade or business.

The deduction for qualified tuition and related expenses can be determined by completing Form 8917 (Tuition and Fees Deduction). The form should be attached to Form 1040 (or Form 1040A). In addition, the taxpayer must have received a Form 1098–T (Tuition Statement) from a higher education institution to claim the deduction.

Another deduction item relating to education is the limited deduction of interest on student loans, which is covered in Chapter 10.[54]

11-3f Entertainment Expenses

Many taxpayers attempt to deduct personal **entertainment expenses** as business expenses. For this reason, the tax law restricts the deductibility of entertainment expenses. The Code contains strict record-keeping requirements and provides restrictive tests for the deduction of certain types of entertainment expenses.

The Fifty Percent Cutback

Only 50 percent of business-related meal and entertainment expenses is deductible.[55] The limitation applies in the context of employment and self-employment status. The 50 percent cutback applies to the one who pays (economically) for the meals or entertainment.

In-depth coverage can be found on this book's companion website: www.cengagebrain.com | **15 DIGGING DEEPER**

EXAMPLE 30

Jane, an employee of Pato Corporation, entertains one of her clients. If Pato Corporation does not reimburse Jane, her expenses are subject to the cutback. If, however, Pato Corporation reimburses Jane (or pays for the entertainment directly), Pato suffers the cutback.

---

[51]Section 222 is scheduled to expire December 31, 2016.

[52]Section 222(d) refers to § 25A(f), which addresses the American Opportunity and lifetime learning credits (see Chapter 10). Student activity fees and prescribed course-related books may be allowed if they are a condition for enrollment.

[53]§ 222(c).

[54]§ 221.

[55]§ 274(n).

Transportation expenses are not affected by the cutback rule—only meals and entertainment expenses are reduced. The 50 percent cutback also applies to taxes and tips relating to meals and entertainment, as well as cover charges, parking fees at an entertainment location, and room rental fees for a meal or cocktail party.

 DIGGING DEEPER 16 | In-depth coverage can be found on this book's companion website: **www.cengagebrain.com**

EXAMPLE 31

Joe pays a $40 cab fare to meet his client for dinner. The meal costs $150, and Joe leaves a $30 tip at the restaurant. His deduction is $130 [($150 meal costs + $30 tip) × 50% + $40 cab fare].

Classification of Expenses

Entertainment expenses are classified either as *directly related* to business or *associated with* business.[56] Directly related expenses are related to an actual business meeting or discussion. These expenses are distinguished from entertainment expenses that are incurred to promote goodwill, such as maintaining existing customer relations. To obtain a deduction for directly related entertainment, it is not necessary to show that actual benefit resulted from the expenditure as long as there was a reasonable expectation of benefit.

To qualify as directly related, the expense should be incurred in a business setting. If there is little possibility of engaging in the active conduct of a trade or business due to the nature of the social facility, it is difficult to qualify the expenditure as directly related to business.

Expenses associated with, rather than directly related to, business entertainment must serve a specific business purpose, such as obtaining new business or continuing existing business. These expenditures qualify only if the expenses directly precede or follow a bona fide business discussion. Entertainment occurring on the same day as the business discussion is considered associated with business.

EXAMPLE 32

Jerry, a manufacturer's representative, took his client to play a round of golf during the afternoon. They had dinner the same evening, during which time business was discussed. After dinner, they went to a nightclub to have drinks and listen to a jazz band. The business dinner qualifies as directly related entertainment. The golf outing and the visit to the nightclub qualify as associated with entertainment.

 TAX PLANNING STRATEGIES **Entertainment Expenses**

FRAMEWORK FOCUS: DEDUCTIONS

Strategy: Maximize Deductible Amounts.

Taxpayers should maintain detailed records of amounts, time, place, business purpose, and business relationships. A credit card receipt details the place, date, and amount of the expense. A notation made on the receipt of the names of the person(s) attending, the business relationship, and the topic of discussion should constitute sufficient documentation.[57] Failure to provide sufficient documentation could lead to disallowance of entertainment expense deductions.

Associated with or goodwill entertainment requires a business discussion to be conducted immediately before or after the entertainment. Furthermore, a business purpose must exist for the entertainment. Taxpayers should arrange for a business discussion before or after such entertainment. They also must document the business purpose, such as obtaining new business from a prospective customer.

---

[56]§ 274(a)(1)(A).

[57]*Kenneth W. Guenther,* 54 TCM 382, T.C.Memo. 1987–440.

Restrictions upon Deductibility of Business Meals

The expense for a business meal is deductible only if all of the following are true.[58]

- The meal is directly related to or associated with the active conduct of a trade or business.
- The expense is not lavish or extravagant under the circumstances.
- The taxpayer (or an employee) is present at the meal.

A business meal with a business associate or customer is not deductible unless business is discussed before, during, or after the meal. This requirement does not apply to meals consumed while away from home on business.

Taxpayer Presence at Business Meals

Lacy travels to San Francisco for a business convention. She pays for dinner with three colleagues and is not reimbursed by her employer. They do not discuss business. She can deduct 50% of the cost of her meal. However, she cannot deduct the cost of her colleagues' meals.

EXAMPLE 33

Lance, a party to a contract negotiation, buys dinner for other parties to the negotiation but does not attend the dinner. No deduction is allowed because Lance was not present.

EXAMPLE 34

Restrictions upon Deductibility of Club Dues

The Code provides that "No deduction shall be allowed … for amounts paid or incurred for membership in any club organized for business, pleasure, recreation, or other social purpose."[59] Although this prohibition seems quite broad, it does not apply to clubs whose primary purpose is public service and community volunteerism (e.g., Kiwanis, Lions, and Rotary). Although *dues* are not deductible, actual entertainment at a club may qualify.

During the current year, Vincent spent $1,400 on business lunches at the Lakeside Country Club. The annual membership fee was $6,000, and Vincent used the facility 60% of the time for business. Presuming that the lunches meet the business meal test, Vincent may claim $700 (50% cutback × $1,400) as a deduction. None of the club dues are deductible.

EXAMPLE 35

In-depth coverage can be found on this book's companion website: www.cengagebrain.com

17 DIGGING DEEPER

Business Gifts

Although not subject to a cutback adjustment, business gifts are deductible only to the extent of $25 per donee per year.[60] An exception is made for gifts costing $4 or less (e.g., pens with the employee's or company's name on them) or promotional materials; such items are not treated as business gifts subject to the $25 limitation. In addition, incidental costs such as engraving of jewelry and nominal charges for gift-wrapping, mailing, and delivery are not included in the cost of the gift in applying the limitation. Gifts to superiors and employers are not deductible. Records must be maintained to substantiate business gifts.

---

[58]§ 274(k).

[59]§ 274(a)(3).

[60]§ 274(b)(1).

11-3g **Other Employee Expenses**

In addition to those expenses discussed previously, the Code provides for the deduction of a number of other job-related expenses. The home office deduction, educator expenses, miscellaneous employee expenses, and job hunting expenses are discussed in this section.

Office in the Home

Employees and self-employed individuals are not allowed a deduction for **office in the home expenses** unless a portion of the residence is used *exclusively and on a regular basis* as either:

- The principal place of business for any trade or business of the taxpayer.
- A place of business used by clients, patients, or customers.

Employees must meet an additional test: the use must be for the convenience of the employer rather than merely being "appropriate and helpful."[61]

The precise meaning of "principal place of business" has been the subject of considerable controversy.[62] The term *principal place of business* includes a place of business that satisfies the following requirements.[63]

- The office is used by the taxpayer to conduct administrative or management activities of a trade or business.
- There is no other fixed location of the trade or business where the taxpayer conducts these activities.

EXAMPLE 36

Ken is a self-employed anesthesiologist. During the year, he spends 30 to 35 hours per week administering anesthesia and postoperative care to patients in three hospitals, none of which provides him with an office. He also spends two or three hours per day in a room in his home that he uses exclusively as an office. Ken does not meet patients there, but he performs a variety of tasks related to his medical practice (e.g., contacting surgeons, doing bookkeeping, and reading medical journals).

A deduction for this office in the home is allowed because Ken conducts administrative or management activities there, and he has no other fixed location where these activities can be carried out.

The exclusive use requirement means that a specific part of the home must be used solely for business purposes. A deduction, if permitted, requires an allocation of total expenses of operating the home between business and personal use based on floor space or number of rooms.

DIGGING DEEPER 18 In-depth coverage can be found on this book's companion website: **www.cengagebrain.com**

Even if the taxpayer meets the above requirements, the allowable home office expenses cannot exceed the gross income from the business less all other business expenses attributable to the activity. That is, the home office deduction cannot create a loss. Furthermore, the home office expenses that are allowed as itemized deductions anyway (e.g., mortgage interest and real estate taxes) must be deducted first.

All home office expenses of an employee are miscellaneous itemized deductions, except those (such as interest and taxes) that qualify as other personal itemized deductions. Home office expenses of a self-employed individual are trade or business expenses and are deductible *for* AGI. Any disallowed home office expenses are carried forward and used in future years subject to the same limitations.

---

[61]§ 280A(c)(1).

[62]See the restrictive interpretation arrived at in *Comm. v. Soliman*, 93–1 USTC ¶50,014, 71 AFTR 2d 93–463, 113 S.Ct. 701 (USSC, 1993).

[63]§ 280A(c)(1).

Rick is a certified public accountant employed by a regional CPA firm as a tax manager. He operates a separate business in which he refinishes furniture in his home. For this business, he uses two rooms in the basement of his home exclusively and regularly. The floor space of the two rooms is 240 square feet, which constitutes 10% of the total floor space of his 2,400-square-foot residence. Gross income from the business totals $8,000. Expenses of the business (other than home office expenses) are $6,500. Rick incurs the following home office expenses.

Real property taxes on residence	$ 4,000
Interest expense on residence	7,500
Operating expenses of residence (including homeowners insurance)	2,000
Depreciation on residence (based on 10% business use)	350

Rick's deductions are determined as follows.

Business income		$ 8,000
Less: Other business expenses		(6,500)
Net income from the business (before the office in the home deduction)		$ 1,500
Less: Allocable taxes ($4,000 × 10%)	$400	
Allocable interest ($7,500 × 10%)	750	(1,150)
Subtotal		$ 350
Less: Allocable operating expenses of the residence ($2,000 × 10%)		(200)
Subtotal		$ 150
Less: Allocable depreciation ($350, limited to remaining income)		(150)
Remaining home office expenses		$ –0–

Rick now holds a carryover deduction of $200 (the unused excess depreciation). Because he is self-employed, the allocable taxes and interest ($1,150), the other deductible office expenses ($200 + $150), and $6,500 of other business expenses are deductible *for* AGI.

Educator Expenses

Many elementary and secondary school teachers pay for professional development courses or purchase school supplies for classroom use and are not reimbursed by their employer. Such teachers may deduct the costs they incur for books, supplies, professional development courses, computer equipment and related software and services, other equipment, and supplementary materials they use in the classroom. The annual ceiling on this *for* AGI deduction is $250.[64]

Miscellaneous Employee Expenses

Deductible miscellaneous employee expenses include special clothing and its upkeep, union dues, and professional expenses. Also deductible are professional dues, professional meetings, and employment agency fees for seeking new employment in the taxpayer's current trade or business, whether or not a new job is secured.

To be deductible, *special clothing* must be both specifically required as a condition of employment and not adaptable for regular wear. For example, a police officer's uniform is not suitable for off-duty activities. No deduction is allowed for clothing that takes the place of regular clothing (e.g., some military uniforms).

Captain Roberts is on active duty in the U.S. Army. The cost of his regular uniforms is not deductible because such clothing is suitable for regular wear. Captain Roberts, however, spends over $1,100 to purchase "dress blues." Under military regulations, dress uniforms may be worn only during ceremonial functions (e.g., official events, parades). The $1,100 cost, to the extent it exceeds any clothing allowance, qualifies as a deduction.

---

[64]§ 62(a)(2)(D). The deduction ceiling is indexed to inflation.

Job Hunting

Expenses incurred in *seeking employment* are deductible if the taxpayer is seeking employment in the same trade or business. The deduction is allowed whether or not the attempts to secure employment are successful. Individuals seeking their first job or seeking employment in a new trade or business are not allowed a deduction for job-hunting expenses.

11-3h Classification of Employee Expenses

LO.4

Explain the difference between accountable and nonaccountable employee plans.

The classification of employee expenses depends on whether they are reimbursed by the employer under an accountable plan. If so, then they are not reported by the employee at all. In effect, this result is equivalent to reporting the reimbursement as income and treating the expenses as deductions *for* AGI.[65] Alternatively, if the expenses are reimbursed under a nonaccountable plan or are not reimbursed at all, they are classified as deductions *from* AGI and can be claimed only if the employee-taxpayer itemizes (subject to the 2%-of-AGI floor).

Accountable Plans

An accountable plan requires the employee to satisfy these two requirements.

- Adequately account for (substantiate) the expenses. An employee renders an *adequate accounting* by submitting a record, with receipts and other substantiation, to the employer.[66]
- Return any excess reimbursement or allowance. An "excess reimbursement or allowance" is any amount the employee does not adequately account for as an ordinary and necessary business expense.

The law provides that no deduction is allowed for any travel, entertainment, business gift, or listed property (automobiles and computers) expenditure unless properly substantiated by adequate records. The records should contain the following information:[67]

- The amount of the expense.
- The time and place of travel or entertainment (or date of gift).
- The business purpose of the expense.
- The business relationship of the taxpayer to the person entertained (or receiving the gift).

This means that the taxpayer must maintain an account book or diary in which the above information is recorded at the time of the expenditure. Documentary evidence such as an itemized receipt is required to support any expenditure for lodging while traveling away from home and for any other expenditure of $75 or more. If a taxpayer fails to keep adequate records, each expense must be established by a written or oral statement of the exact details of the expense and by other corroborating evidence.[68]

DIGGING DEEPER 19 | In-depth coverage can be found on this book's companion website: www.cengagebrain.com

Nonaccountable Plans

A **nonaccountable plan** is a plan in which an adequate accounting or return of excess amounts, or both, is not required. All reimbursements of expenses are reported in full as wages on the employee's Form W–2. Any allowable expenses are deductible in the same manner as unreimbursed expenses.

If an employer offers an accountable plan and requires employees to return excess reimbursements or allowances, but an employee fails to follow the rules of the plan, the expenses and reimbursements are subject to nonaccountable plan treatment.

---

[65]§ 62(a)(2).
[66]Reg. § 1.162–17(b)(4).

[67]§ 274(d).
[68]Reg. § 1.274–5T(c)(3).

Unreimbursed Employee Expenses

Unreimbursed employee expenses are treated in a straightforward manner. Meals and entertainment expenses are subject to the 50 percent limit. Total unreimbursed employee business expenses usually are reported as miscellaneous itemized deductions subject to the 2%-of-AGI floor (refer to Chapter 10). If the employee could have received, but did not seek, reimbursement for whatever reason, none of the employment-related expenses are deductible.

TAX PLANNING STRATEGIES **Unreimbursed Employee Business Expenses**

FRAMEWORK FOCUS: DEDUCTIONS

Strategy: Maximize Deductible Amounts.

The 2 percent floor for unreimbursed employee business expenses offers a tax planning opportunity for married couples. If one spouse has high miscellaneous expenses subject to the floor, it may be beneficial for the couple to file separate returns. If they file jointly, the 2 percent floor is based on the adjusted gross incomes of both. Filing separately lowers the reduction to 2 percent of only one spouse's adjusted gross income.

Other provisions of the law should be considered, however. For example, filing separately could cost a couple losses of up to $25,000 from rental activities under the passive activity loss rules (discussed in Chapter 6).

Another possibility is to negotiate a salary reduction with one's employer in exchange for the 100 percent reimbursement of employee expenses. The employee is better off because the 2 percent floor does not apply. The employer is better off because certain expense reimbursements are not subject to Social Security and other payroll taxes.

In-depth coverage can be found on this book's companion website: www.cengagebrain.com

20 DIGGING DEEPER

11-3i **Contributions to Individual Retirement Accounts**

LO.5

Traditional and Roth Individual Retirement Accounts, or IRAs, are commonly used retirement plans, designed by Congress to encourage individual savings. They can be simple to create and maintain. The tax rules that govern deductible contributions, taxable distributions, age requirements, and possible penalties for early withdrawals or excess contributions are discussed in the following section.

Understand the opportunities available to build wealth through Individual Retirement Accounts.

Traditional IRAs

An individual can contribute to a traditional **Individual Retirement Account (IRA)** assuming that the person (or spouse) has earned income and is under age 70½. These contributions may be deductible, depending upon income level and access to another work-related retirement plan. For 2016, the contribution ceiling is the lesser of $5,500 (or $11,000 for spousal IRAs) or 100 percent of compensation.[69] An individual who attains the age of 50 by the end of the tax year can make an additional "catch-up" IRA contribution of up to $1,000 in 2016.

If the taxpayer is an active participant in a qualified plan, the traditional IRA deduction limitation is phased out *proportionately* between certain AGI ranges, as shown in Exhibit 11.3.[70] If AGI is above the phaseout range, no IRA deduction is allowed.

---

[69]§§ 219(b)(1) and (c)(2). The limit is adjusted annually for inflation in $500 increments.

[70]§ 219(g).

AGI is calculated taking into account any passive activity losses and taxable Social Security benefits and ignoring any foreign income exclusion, savings bonds interest exclusion, and the IRA deduction itself. The IRA deduction limitation cannot be less than $200.

IRA Deduction Calculation

Dan, who is single, reports compensation income of $67,000 in 2016. He is an active participant in his employer's qualified retirement plan. Dan contributes $5,500 to a traditional IRA. The deductible amount is reduced from $5,500 by $3,300 because of the phaseout mechanism (see Exhibit 11.3).

$$\frac{\$6,000}{\$10,000} \times \$5,500 = \$3,300 \text{ reduction}$$

Therefore, of the $5,500 contribution, Dan can deduct only $2,200 ($5,500 − $3,300).

Bonnie, an unmarried individual, is an active participant in her employer's qualified retirement plan in 2016. With AGI of $70,800, Bonnie's IRA deduction limit would be $110 {$5,500 − [($70,800 − $61,000)/$10,000 × $5,500]}. However, she is allowed a $200 IRA deduction.

An individual is not considered an active participant in a qualified plan merely because the individual's spouse is an active participant in such a plan for any part of a plan year. Thus, even when filing jointly, the nonparticipating individual may take a full $5,500 deduction regardless of the participation status of his or her spouse, unless the couple has AGI above $184,000. If their AGI is above $184,000, the phaseout of the deduction begins at $184,000 and ends at $194,000 (phaseout over the $10,000 range) rather than beginning and ending at the phaseout amounts in Exhibit 11.3.[71]

EXAMPLE 41

Nell is covered by a qualified employer retirement plan at work. Her husband, Nick, is not an active participant in a qualified plan. If Nell and Nick's combined AGI is $135,000, Nell cannot make a deductible IRA contribution because she exceeds the income threshold for an active participant. However, because Nick is not an active participant and their combined AGI does not exceed $184,000, he can make a fully deductible contribution of $5,500 to an IRA.

To the extent an individual is ineligible to make a deductible contribution to an IRA, *nondeductible contributions* can be made to separate accounts. The nondeductible contributions are subject to the same dollar limits as deductible contributions ($5,500 of earned income, $11,000 for a spousal IRA). Income in the account accumulates tax-free until distributed. Only the account earnings are taxed upon distribution because the account basis equals the contributions made by the taxpayer.

EXHIBIT 11.3	Phaseout of Traditional IRA Deduction of an Active Participant in 2016	
AGI, Filing Status	**Phaseout Begins***	**Phaseout Ends***
Single and head of household	$61,000	$ 71,000
Married, filing joint return	98,000	118,000
Married, filing separate return	–0–	10,000

*These AGI amounts are indexed annually for inflation.

Roth IRAs

A Roth IRA is a *nondeductible* alternative to the traditional deductible IRA. Earnings inside a Roth IRA are not taxable, and all qualified distributions from a Roth IRA are tax-free.[72]

The maximum allowable annual contribution to a Roth IRA for 2016 is the lesser of $5,500 ($11,000 for spousal IRAs) or 100 percent of the individual's compensation for the year. Contributions to a Roth IRA must be made by the due date (excluding extensions) of the taxpayer's tax return. Contributions to a Roth IRA (unlike a traditional IRA) may continue beyond age 70½ so long as the person generates compensation income and is not barred by the AGI limits.

A taxpayer can make tax-free withdrawals from a Roth IRA after an initial five-year holding period if any of the following requirements are satisfied.

- The distribution is made on or after the date on which the participant attains age 59½.

- The distribution is made to a beneficiary (or the participant's estate) on or after the participant's death.

- The participant becomes disabled.

- The distribution is used for qualified first-time homebuyer's expenses (maximum $10,000).

Edith establishes a Roth IRA at age 42 and contributes $5,000 per year for 20 years. The account is now worth $149,400, consisting of $100,000 of nondeductible contributions and $49,400 in accumulated earnings that have not been taxed. Edith may withdraw the $149,400 tax-free from the Roth IRA because she is over age 59½ and has met the five-year holding period requirement.

If the taxpayer receives a distribution from a Roth IRA and does not satisfy the aforementioned requirements, some of the distribution may constitute gross income. If the distribution represents a return of capital, it is not taxable. Conversely, if the distribution represents a payout of earnings, it is taxable. Distributions are treated as first made from contributions (return of capital).

Assume the same facts as in the previous example, except that Edith is only age 50 and receives a distribution of $55,000. Because her basis for the Roth IRA is $100,000 (contributions made), the distribution is tax-free, and her basis in the account is reduced to $45,000 ($100,000 − $55,000).

Contributions to Roth IRAs are subject to income limits. In 2016, the maximum annual contribution of $5,500 is phased out beginning at AGI of $117,000 for single taxpayers and $184,000 for married couples who file a joint return. The phaseout range is $10,000 for married taxpayers filing jointly and $15,000 for single taxpayers. For a married taxpayer filing separately, the phaseout begins with AGI of $0 and is phased out over a $10,000 range.

Bev, who is single, would like to contribute $5,500 to her Roth IRA. Her AGI is $126,000. As a result, her contribution is limited to $1,833 ($5,500 − $3,667), calculated as follows.

$$\frac{\$10,000}{\$15,000} \times \$5,500 = \$3,667 \text{ reduction}$$

Rollovers and Conversions

Often when employees change jobs, they do not want to leave their retirement savings with their former employer. As a result, retirement savings in a qualified plan may be directly transferred from that plan to an IRA or may be "rolled over" into an IRA. Amounts that are directly transferred to another plan are not included in the owner's

---

[72]§ 408A.

gross income. Rollover distributions will not be included in gross income as long as the funds received are transferred to an IRA within 60 days of receipt.[73]

In addition, a traditional IRA may be rolled over or converted to a Roth IRA. The tax consequences depend on whether the contributions made to the traditional IRA were deductible or nondeductible. If deductible, the basis for the IRA is zero. Thus, the entire amount of the rollover or conversion is included in gross income. If nondeductible, the basis for the IRA is equal to the sum of the contributions. Thus, only the IRA earnings included in the rollover or conversion are included in gross income.

See Concept Summary 11.4 for an overview of some of the primary differences between traditional and Roth IRAs.

Concept Summary 11.4

Traditional IRAs and Roth IRAs Compared

	Traditional IRA	Roth IRA
Contribution limit	$5,500 or 100% of compensation, pre-tax dollars.	$5,500 or 100% of compensation, after-tax dollars.
Deduction limit	$5,500 or 100% of compensation.	No deduction.
Tax benefits	Tax-deferred growth of earnings.	Tax-free growth of earnings.
Taxation at withdrawal in retirement	Deductible contributions and earnings taxed as ordinary income.	Contributions and earnings withdrawn tax-free.
Taxation of withdrawals prior to retirement	10% penalty on withdrawals before 59½, except for withdrawals to pay for certain medical expenses and health insurance, qualified education expenses, and qualified first-time homebuyer expenses.	10% penalty on earnings withdrawn before age 59½. No penalty on contributions withdrawn after 5 years or where the distribution is used to pay for qualified first-time homebuyer's expenses.
Timing of contribution	Grace period up to due date of tax return (not including extensions).	Grace period up to due date of tax return (not including extensions).

LO.6

State and explain the tax provisions applicable to proprietors.

11-4 INDIVIDUALS AS PROPRIETORS

A sole proprietorship is *not* a taxable entity separate from the individual who owns the proprietorship. The owner reports the results of business operations of the proprietorship on Schedule C of Form 1040. The net profit or loss reported on the Schedule C is then transferred to the first page of the Form 1040. The proprietor reports all of the net profit or net loss from the business, regardless of the amount actually withdrawn from the proprietorship during the year.

Income and expenses of the proprietorship retain their character when reported by the proprietor. For example, ordinary income of the proprietorship is treated as ordinary income when reported by the proprietor, and capital gain of the proprietorship is treated as capital gain by the proprietor.

EXAMPLE 45

George is the sole proprietor of George's Bicycle Shop. Gross income of the business is $200,000, and operating expenses are $110,000. George also sells a capital asset held by the business for a $10,000 long-term capital gain. During the year, he withdraws $60,000 cash from the business for living expenses.

George reports the operating income and expenses of the business on Schedule C, resulting in net profit (ordinary income) of $90,000 ($200,000 − $110,000). Even though he withdrew from the business cash of only $60,000, George reports all of the $90,000 net profit from the business on Form 1040. He also reports a $10,000 long-term capital gain on his personal tax return (Schedule D of Form 1040).

11-4a Income of a Proprietorship

The broad definition of gross income in § 61(a) applies equally to individuals and business entities, including proprietorships, corporations, and partnerships. Thus, asset inflows into a proprietorship are to be treated as income unless a Code section provides for an exclusion from income (e.g., interest on state and local bonds, appreciation on investments). Refer to Chapter 4 for a detailed discussion of gross income.

11-4b Deductions Related to a Proprietorship

The provisions that govern business deductions also are general and not entity-specific. The § 162 requirement that trade or business expenses be *ordinary and necessary* (refer to Chapter 5) applies to proprietorships as well as corporations, partnerships, and other business entities. However, certain specific deductions are available only to self-employed taxpayers. These deductions are addressed next.

Health Insurance Premiums

A self-employed taxpayer may deduct *for* AGI any insurance premiums paid for medical coverage.[74] The deduction is allowed for premiums paid on behalf of the taxpayer, the taxpayer's spouse, and dependents of the taxpayer. The deduction is not allowed to any taxpayer who is eligible to participate in a subsidized health plan maintained by any employer of the taxpayer or of the taxpayer's spouse.

This deduction is reported in the Adjusted Gross Income section of Form 1040 rather than on Schedule C. Premiums paid for medical coverage of the *employees* of a self-employed taxpayer are deductible as business expenses on Schedule C, however.

Ellen, a sole proprietor of a restaurant, has two dependent children. This year, she paid health insurance premiums of $8,800 for her own coverage and $8,000 for coverage of her two children. Ellen can claim health insurance premiums of $16,800 as a deduction *for* AGI.

**EXAMPLE
46**

Self-Employment Tax

The tax on self-employment income is levied to provide Social Security and Medicare benefits (old age, survivors, and disability insurance and hospital insurance) for self-employed individuals. Individuals with net earnings of $400 or more from self-employment are subject to the self-employment tax.[75] For 2016, the combined self-employment (SE) tax rate is 15.3 percent (12.4 percent for Social Security and 2.9 percent for Medicare) and the tax is computed on self-employment earnings up to $118,500. This amount is adjusted annually for inflation. These amounts are unchanged from 2015.

Net SE earnings include gross income from a trade or business less allowable trade or business deductions, plus the taxpayer's distributive share of any business-related partnership income or loss, and any net income from rendering personal services as an independent contractor. This amount includes profits from sales of inventory.[76]

In computing the tax, net SE earnings are reduced by 7.65 percent (to 92.35 percent of the total), to reflect a deduction for the "employer's half" of the total 15.3 percent tax. Self-employed taxpayers are allowed a deduction *for* AGI equal to one-half of the self-employment tax liability.[77]

If an individual who is self-employed also receives wages subject to the FICA tax from working as an employee of another organization, the amount of the Social Security portion on which the self-employment tax is computed is reduced. However, a combination of FICA wages and self-employment earnings will not reduce the Medicare component of the self-employment tax, as there is no ceiling on this component of the tax.

---

[74]§ 162(l).

[75]§ 6017.

[76]§ 1402(a)(12).

[77]§ 164(f).

Computing Self-Employment Taxes

EXAMPLE 47

In 2016, Kelly recorded $76,000 of net earnings from a data imaging services business that she owns. During the year, she also received wages of $54,000 as an employee of a small accounting firm. The amount of Kelly's self-employment income subject to the Social Security tax (12.4%) is $64,500 ($118,500 − $54,000), producing a tax of $7,998 ($64,500 × 12.4%); note that $64,500 is less than Kelly's net SE income ($76,000 × .9235 = $70,186), so the smaller amount is used.

Although there is a limit on Social Security taxes ($118,500 maximum base in 2016), no such limit exists for the Medicare portion of the self-employment tax. Therefore, all of Kelly's net self-employment income ($76,000 × .9235 = $70,186) is subject to the 2.9% Medicare portion of the self-employment tax. Thus, Kelly's Medicare tax on this income is $2,035 ($70,186 × 2.9%).

EXAMPLE 48

Continue with the facts of Example 47. If Kelly's wages from working at the accounting firm were only $30,000, then her ceiling for Social Security taxation would be $88,500 ($118,500 − $30,000). Because her net self-employment income ($70,186) is less than this amount, Kelly would compute her self-employment tax on the full amount of the $70,186 net SE income.

11-4c **Retirement Plans for Self-Employed Individuals**

Individual Retirement Accounts (discussed earlier in this chapter) are available to both employees and self-employed individuals. Other options for self-employed individuals include, but are not limited to, H.R. 10 (Keogh) plans and SIMPLE plans, both of which are discussed next.

Keogh Plans

Self-employed individuals (e.g., partners and sole proprietors) can establish and receive qualified retirement benefits under Keogh plans (also known as H.R. 10 plans). Self-employed individuals who establish Keogh plans for themselves also must cover their *employees* under the plan.

Keogh investments can include a variety of funding vehicles, such as mutual funds, annuities, real estate shares, certificates of deposit, debt instruments, commodities, securities, and personal properties. When an individual decides to make all investment decisions for the plan's holdings, a *self-directed retirement plan* is established. Investment in most collectibles (e.g., coins or art) is not allowed in a self-directed plan.

A Keogh plan may be either a *defined contribution* plan or a *defined benefit* plan. In a defined contribution plan, the amount that can be contributed each year is subject to limitations. Retirement benefits depend on the amount contributed and the amount earned by the plan. In a defined benefit plan, the amount of retirement income is fixed and is determined on the basis of the employee's compensation while working, the number of years in the plan, and age upon retirement. Contributions are derived actuarially, to provide the benefits that are needed when withdrawals are made.

A self-employed individual may contribute the lesser of $53,000 (in 2016) or 100 percent of earned SE income to a defined contribution Keogh plan annually.[78] For a defined contribution plan, the contribution can be no more than 20 percent of SE earnings before accounting for transfers to the plan.[79]

Net earnings from self-employment means the gross income derived by an individual from any trade or business carried on by that individual, less appropriate deductions,[80] plus the distributive share of income or loss from a partnership.[81] Earned income is reduced by contributions to a Keogh plan on the individual's behalf and by 50 percent of any self-employment tax.[82]

---

[78]§ 415(c)(1).

[79]§ 415(b)(1). The amount is indexed annually.

[80]§ 401(c)(2).

[81]§ 1402(a).

[82]§§ 401(c)(2)(A)(v) and 164(f).

Pat, a partner, reports earned income of $150,000 in 2016 (after the deduction for one-half of self-employment tax, but before any Keogh contribution). The maximum contribution Pat may make to a defined contribution Keogh plan is $53,000, the lesser of $150,000 or $53,000.

EXAMPLE 49

TAX PLANNING STRATEGIES   Important Dates Related to IRAs and Keogh Plans

FRAMEWORK FOCUS: DEDUCTIONS

Strategy: Accelerate Recognition of Deductions to Achieve Tax Deferral.

A Keogh or IRA participant may make a deductible contribution for a tax year up to the time prescribed for filing the individual's tax return for that tax year. A Keogh plan must have been *established* by the end of the *prior* tax year (e.g., December 31, 2016) to obtain a deduction on the 2016 income tax return for the contribution made in the *current* year (2017). An individual can establish an IRA during the *current* tax year (up to the normal filing date) and still receive a deduction on the prior-year income tax return for the contribution made in the *current* year.

SIMPLE Plans

Employers with 100 or fewer employees who do not maintain another qualified retirement plan may establish a *savings incentive match plan for employees* (SIMPLE plan).[83] The plan can be in the form of a § 401(k) plan or an IRA. A SIMPLE § 401(k) plan is not subject to the nondiscrimination rules that apply to § 401(k) plans.

All employees who received at least $5,000 in compensation from the employer during any two preceding years and who reasonably expect to receive at least $5,000 in compensation during the current year must be eligible to participate in the plan. The decision to participate is up to the employee. A *self-employed individual* also may establish a SIMPLE plan.

The contributions made by the employee (a salary reduction is made) must be expressed as a percentage of compensation rather than as a fixed dollar amount. The SIMPLE plan must not permit the elective employee contribution for the year to exceed $12,500 (in 2016).[84] The SIMPLE elective deferral limit is increased under a "catch-up" provision for employees age 50 and over. The amount is $3,000 in 2016 and is indexed for inflation in $500 increments.

Generally, the employer must either match elective employee contributions up to 3 percent of the employee's compensation or provide nonmatching contributions of 2 percent of compensation for each eligible employee. Thus, for an employee under age 50, the maximum amount that may be contributed to the plan for 2016 is $20,450 [$12,500 employee contributions + $7,950 ($265,000 compensation ceiling × 3%) employer match].

No other contributions may be made to the plan other than the employee elective contribution and the required employer matching contribution (or nonmatching contribution under the 2 percent rule). All contributions are fully vested. An employer is required to make the required matching or nonmatching contributions to a SIMPLE § 401(k) plan once it is established, whereas an employer's contributions to a traditional § 401(k) plan generally may be discretionary.

An employer's deduction for contributions to a SIMPLE § 401(k) plan is limited to the greater of 25 percent of the compensation paid or accrued or the amount the employer is required to contribute to the plan. An employer is allowed a deduction for matching contributions only if the contributions are made by the due date (including extensions) for the employer's tax return.

---

[83]§ 408(p).

[84]§ 408(p)(2)(E)(i).

Contributions to a SIMPLE plan are excludible from the employee's gross income, and the SIMPLE plan itself is tax-exempt. A SIMPLE plan must be established by October 1 of a calendar tax year. Distributions cannot be made until the third year of the plan's existence.

TAX PLANNING STRATEGIES   Factors Affecting Retirement Plan Choices

FRAMEWORK FOCUS: DEDUCTIONS

Strategy: Maximize Deductible Amounts.

An IRA might not be the best retirement plan option for many self-employed taxpayers. The maximum amount that can be deducted is $5,500 per year ($11,000 for a spousal plan), which may be too low to provide funding for an adequate level of retirement income. Other options such as Keogh plans and SIMPLE plans allow larger contributions and larger deductions.

However, a self-employed individual who establishes either a Keogh or a SIMPLE plan is required to cover most employees of the business under such plans. This can result in substantial expenditures, not only for the required contributions but also for expenses of administering the plan. An advantage of an IRA is that coverage of employees is not required.

11-4d Accounting Periods and Methods

Proprietors may choose among various accounting methods, just as other business entities do (refer to Chapters 4 and 5). The cash method is commonly used by proprietorships that provide services, while the accrual or hybrid method generally is required if inventory is a material income-producing factor.

The accounting period rules for proprietorships generally are much simpler than the rules for partnerships and S corporations. Because a proprietorship is not an entity separate from the proprietor, the proprietorship must use the same tax year-end as the proprietor. This does not preclude the use of a fiscal year for a proprietorship, but most proprietorships use the calendar year.

11-4e Estimated Tax Payments

Although the following discussion largely centers on self-employed taxpayers, some of the procedures may be applicable to employed persons. In many cases, for example, employed persons may be required to pay estimated tax if they have income that is not subject to withholding (e.g., income from consulting work, rental property, dividends, or interest).

Estimated Tax for Individuals

Estimated tax is the amount of tax (including alternative minimum tax and self-employment tax) an individual expects to owe for the year after subtracting tax credits and income tax withheld. Any individual who is expected to owe Federal income tax for the year of $1,000 or more and whose withholding does not equal or exceed the required annual payment (discussed below) must make quarterly payments.[85] Otherwise, a penalty may be assessed.

No quarterly payments are required and no penalty will apply on an underpayment if the taxpayer's estimated tax is under $1,000. No penalty will apply if the taxpayer had a zero tax liability for the preceding tax year *and* the preceding tax year was a taxable year of 12 months *and* the taxpayer was a U.S. citizen or resident for the entire preceding tax year.

---

[85]§§ 6654(c)(1) and 6654(e)(1).

The required annual payment must first be computed. This is the smaller of:

- Ninety percent of the tax shown on the current year's return; or
- One hundred percent of the tax shown on the preceding year's return (the return must cover the full 12 months of the preceding year). If the AGI on the preceding year's return exceeds $150,000 ($75,000 if married filing separately), the 100 percent requirement is increased to 110 percent.

In general, one-fourth of this required annual payment is due on April 15, June 15, and September 15 of the tax year and January 15 of the following year. An equal part of withholding is deemed paid on each due date, even if a taxpayer's earnings fluctuate widely during the year. Payments are submitted with the payment voucher for the appropriate quarter from Form 1040–ES.

Penalty on Underpayments

A nondeductible penalty is imposed on the amount of underpayment of estimated tax. The rate for this penalty is adjusted quarterly to reflect changes in market interest rates.[86]

EXAMPLE 50

Marta made the following payments of estimated tax for 2016 and had no income tax withheld.

April 15, 2016	$1,400
June 15, 2016	2,300
September 15, 2016	1,500
January 17, 2017	1,800

Marta's actual tax for 2016 is $8,000, and her tax in 2015 was $10,000. Therefore, each installment should have been at least $1,800 [($8,000 × 90%) × 25%]. Of the payment on June 15, $400 will be credited to the unpaid balance of the first quarterly installment due on April 15,[87] thereby effectively stopping the underpayment penalty for the first quarterly period. Of the remaining $1,900 payment on June 15, $100 is credited to the September 15 payment, resulting in this third quarterly payment being $200 short. Then $200 of the January 17, 2017 payment is credited to the September 15 shortfall, ending the period of underpayment for that portion due. The January 17, 2017 installment is now underpaid by $200, and a penalty will apply from January 17, 2017, to April 17, 2017 (unless some tax is paid sooner).

In summary, Marta's underpayments for the periods of underpayment are determined as follows.

1st installment due:	$400 from April 15 to June 15, 2016
2nd installment due:	Paid in full
3rd installment due:	$200 from September 15, 2016, to January 17, 2017
4th installment due:	$200 from January 17 to April 17, 2017

If a possible underpayment of estimated tax is indicated, Form 2210 is filed to compute the penalty due or to justify that no penalty applies.

11-5 HOBBY LOSSES

LO.7

Distinguish between business and hobby activities and apply the rules limiting the deduction of hobby losses.

Expenses incurred by a self-employed taxpayer are deductible only if the taxpayer can show that the activity was entered into for the purpose of making a profit.[88]

Certain activities can have attributes that make it difficult to determine if the primary motivation for the activity is to make a profit or is for personal pleasure. Examples include raising horses and operating a farm that is also used as a weekend residence. While personal losses are not deductible, losses attributable to profit-seeking activities may be deducted and used to offset a taxpayer's other income. Activities that have both personal and profit-seeking motives are classified as hobbies, and the tax law limits the deductibility of hobby losses .

---

[86]§ 6654(b)(2).

[87]Payments are credited to unpaid installments in the order in which the installments are required to be paid. § 6654(b)(3).

[88]Reg. § 1.183–1(a).

The income and deductions from a hobby are reported separately on the tax return. Hobby income always is reported as *other income* on page 1 of Form 1040. The reporting of deductions is discussed below.

11-5a **General Rules**

If an individual can show that an activity has been conducted with the intent to earn a profit, losses from the activity are fully deductible. The hobby loss rules apply only if the activity is not engaged in for profit. Hobby expenses are deductible only to the extent of hobby income.[89]

The Regulations stipulate that the following nine factors should be considered in determining whether an activity is profit-seeking or a hobby.[90]

• Whether the activity is conducted in a businesslike manner.

• The expertise of the taxpayers or their advisers.

• The time and effort expended.

• The expectation that the assets of the activity will appreciate in value.

• The taxpayer's previous success in conducting similar activities.

• The history of income or losses from the activity.

• The relationship of profits earned to losses incurred.

• The financial status of the taxpayer (e.g., if the taxpayer does not have substantial amounts of other income, this may indicate that the activity is engaged in for profit).

• Elements of personal pleasure or recreation in the activity.

The presence or absence of a factor is not by itself determinative of whether the activity is profit-seeking or is a hobby. Rather, the decision is a subjective one that is based on an analysis of the facts and circumstances.

11-5b **Presumptive Rule of § 183**

The Code provides a rebuttable presumption that an activity is profit-seeking if the activity shows a profit in at least three of the previous five tax years.[91] If the activity involves horses, a profit in at least two of the previous seven tax years meets the presumptive rule. If these profitability tests are met, the activity is presumed to be a trade or business rather than a personal hobby. In this situation, the IRS bears the burden of proving that the activity is personal rather than trade- or business-related. On the other hand, if the three-year test (two for horses) is not met, then the activity is presumed to be a hobby and the taxpayer has the burden to prove that it is profit-seeking.

EXAMPLE 51

Camille and Walter are married taxpayers who enjoy a busy lifestyle. Camille, who is an executive for a large corporation, is paid a salary of $800,000. Walter is a collector of antiques. Several years ago he opened an antique shop in a local shopping center and spends most of his time buying and selling antiques. He occasionally earns a small profit from this activity but more frequently incurs substantial losses.

If Walter's losses are business-related, they are fully deductible against Camille's salary income on a joint return. To the contrary, hobby losses may not be fully deductible by Walter. In resolving this issue, consider the following.

• Initially determine whether Walter's antique activity has met the three-out-of-five years profit test.

• If the presumption is not met, the activity may nevertheless qualify as a business if Walter can show that the intent is to engage in a profit-seeking activity. It is not necessary to show actual profits.

• Attempt to fit the operation within the nine criteria prescribed in the Regulations listed previously.

---

[89]§ 183(b)(2).

[90]Reg. §§ 1.183–2(b)(1) through (9).

[91]§ 183(d).

11-5c **Determination of the Deductible Amount**

If an activity is deemed to be a hobby, the expenses are deductible only to the extent of the gross income from the hobby. These expenses are deducted in the following order.

1. Amounts deductible under other Code sections without regard to the nature of the activity, such as property taxes and home mortgage interest.
2. Amounts deductible under other Code sections as if the activity had been engaged in for profit, but only if those amounts do not affect adjusted basis. Examples include maintenance, utilities, and supplies.
3. Amounts that affect adjusted basis and would be deductible under other Code sections if the activity had been engaged in for profit.[92] Examples include depreciation, amortization, and depletion.

The last two categories of deductions are deductible *from* AGI as itemized deductions to the extent they exceed 2 percent of AGI.[93] If the taxpayer uses the standard deduction rather than itemizing, the hobby loss deductions generate no tax benefit.

EXAMPLE
52

Jim, the vice president of an oil company, reports AGI of $80,000. He decides to pursue painting in his spare time. He uses a home studio, comprising 10% of the home's square footage. During the current year, Jim incurs the following expenses.

Frames	$ 1,800
Art supplies	900
Fees paid to models	4,000
Home studio expenses	
Total home property taxes	2,000
Total home mortgage interest	10,000
Total home maintenance and utilities	4,600
Calculated depreciation on 10% of home	500

During the year, Jim sold paintings for a total of $8,660. If the activity is held to be a hobby, Jim is allowed deductions computed as follows.

Gross income		$ 8,660
Deduct: Taxes and interest (10% of $12,000)		(1,200)
Remainder		$ 7,460
Deduct: Frames	$1,800	
Art supplies	900	
Models' fees	4,000	
Maintenance and utilities (10%)	460	(7,160)
Remainder		$ 300
Depreciation ($500, but limited to $300)		(300)
Net income		$ –0–

Jim includes the $8,660 of income in AGI, making his AGI $88,660. The taxes and interest are itemized deductions, deductible in full. The remaining $7,460 of expenses are reduced by 2% of his AGI (2% × $88,660 = $1,773), so the net deduction is $5,687. All of these deductions are reported as itemized deductions on Schedule A. Because the property taxes and home mortgage interest are deductible even without the hobby, the net effect is a $2,973 ($8,660 − $5,687) increase in taxable income.

---

[92]Reg. § 1.183–1(b)(1).

[93]Reg. § 1.67–1T(a)(1)(iv) and Rev.Rul. 75–14, 1975–1 C.B. 90.

SELF-EMPLOYED VERSUS EMPLOYEE—WHAT'S THE DIFFERENCE?

Mark may deduct the ordinary and necessary business expenses incurred by his proprietorship. This includes the $18,000 for rent and utilities; the $12,000 paid to his secretary; and the $40,000 paid to Ellen, his assistant. The $8,000 paid for equipment can be depreciated or may qualify for immediate expensing under § 179. As a self-employed taxpayer, Mark may deduct the $3,000 of health insurance premiums paid, but only if he is not eligible to participate in the subsidized health plan maintained by Mary's employer. On the other hand, Mark cannot deduct the premiums of $500 paid for his life insurance policy.

Mark may want to consider contributing to his own IRA or establishing a Keogh plan or SIMPLE plan to allow for greater retirement contributions. Mark should be aware that in addition to paying income tax on the net income earned by his business, he also owes self-employment tax at a combined rate of 15.3 percent, but he can claim an income tax deduction for half of the self-employment tax paid.

While Mary will owe income tax on her $85,000 salary, the health insurance premiums of $3,000 and group term life insurance premiums paid by her employer qualify as tax-free fringe benefits. In addition, as long as Mary is required to substantiate her travel expenses as part of an accountable plan, none of the travel-related reimbursements need to be included in Mary's gross income. Because Mary is not covered by a qualified retirement plan at work, she can deduct the entire $5,500 contribution made to her traditional IRA.

While the $500 of employee business expenses are technically deductible, they provide a tax benefit to Mary only if they exceed 2 percent of the couple's AGI. While Mary is not subject to self-employment tax, she still incurred a 7.65 percent payroll tax related to Social Security and Medicare. Her employer paid an additional 7.65 percent.

What If?

Mary is considering entering an MBA program at a local college, to improve her skills in her present job. At the same time, to save money while Mary is in school, Mark is considering moving his office into a vacant room in their home. Are Mary's education expenses deductible? Can Mark deduct expenses associated with his home office? As long as the new degree is not required to meet the minimum requirements of her existing job and the degree does not qualify Mary for a new trade or business, Mary's books, tuition, and other related educational expenses are deductible as a miscellaneous itemized deduction. However, like the $500 of other employee business expenses mentioned earlier, the expenses provide a tax benefit only to the extent they exceed 2 percent of the couple's AGI.

As a self-employed individual, Mark is allowed to deduct the costs of a home office as long as the office is used exclusively and on a regular basis as either the principal place of business or a place of business used by his clients and customers. Deductible expenses would include a portion of mortgage interest and property taxes paid on the home; a portion of utilities, repairs and maintenance, and other household expenses; and depreciation on the business portion of the home.

Suggested Readings

G. Edgar Adkins Jr. and Jeffrey A. Martin, "Local Lodging Provided to an Employee: Whether to Include It in the Employee's Income," *The Tax Adviser*, February 2016.

Jeffrey Gramlich and Kimberly Houser. "Marijuana Business and Sec. 280E: Potential Pitfalls for Clients and Advisers," *The Tax Adviser*, July 2015.

Melanie James, "When are Commuting Costs Deductible?" *Practical Tax Strategies*, November 2014.

David L. Keligian, "Winning Independent Contractor Status," *Journal of Taxation*, November 2011.

Susan L. Megaard and Michael M. Megaard, "When Should the New Safe Harbor Method for Deducting Home-Office Expenses be Elected," *Journal of Taxation*, July 2013.

Richard Toolson, "The Health Savings Account as a Smart Savings Option for Retirement," *TAXES—The Tax Magazine*, December 2014.

Key Terms

Accountable plan, 11-2

Automatic mileage method, 11-18

Cafeteria plans, 11-10

De minimis fringe benefits, 11-14

Deduction for qualified tuition and related expenses, 11-26

Education expenses, 11-24

Entertainment expenses, 11-27

Estimated tax, 11-40

Flexible spending plans, 11-11

Foreign earned income exclusion, 11-16

Health Savings Account (HSA), 11-5

Hobby losses, 11-41

Independent contractor, 11-2

Individual Retirement Account (IRA), 11-33

Keogh plans, 11-38

Moving expenses, 11-21

No-additional-cost service, 11-12

Nonaccountable plan, 11-32

Office in the home expenses, 11-30

Qualified employee discount, 11-13

Qualified transportation fringes, 11-14

Self-employment tax, 11-4

Transportation expenses, 11-17

Travel expenses, 11-18

Working condition fringes, 11-13

Computational Exercises

1. **LO.2** Valentino is a patient in a nursing home for 45 days in 2016. While in the nursing home, he incurs total costs of $13,500. Medicare pays $8,000 of the costs. Valentino receives $15,000 from his long-term care insurance policy, which pays while he is in the facility. Assume that the daily Federal statutory amount for Valentino is $340. Of the $15,000, what amount may Valentino exclude from his gross income?

2. **LO.2** Mio was transferred from New York to Germany. He lived and worked in Germany for 340 days in 2016. Mio's salary for 2016 is $190,000. What is Mio's foreign earned income exclusion? (In your computation, round any division to four decimal places before converting to a percentage. For example, .473938 would be rounded to 47.39%.)

3. **LO.3** Michael holds a full-time job with Brown Company and a part-time job with Tan Corporation. During a workday, he drives 20 miles to Brown, returns home, eats a meal, and then drives 15 miles to Tan. Tan is located 12 miles from Brown. What is Michael's deductible mileage?

4. **LO.3** Fred travels from Denver to Miami primarily on business. He spends five days conducting business and two days sightseeing. His expenses are $400 (airfare), $150 per day (meals), and $300 per night (lodging). What are Fred's deductible expenses?

5. **LO.3** Brenda travels from Chicago to Barcelona (Spain) on business. She is gone for 10 days (including 2 days of travel), during which time she spends 5 days conducting business and 3 days sightseeing. Her expenses are $1,500 (airfare), $200 per day (meals), and $400 per night (lodging). Because Brenda stayed with relatives while sightseeing, she paid for only 5 nights of lodging.

   What is Brenda's deduction for:

   a. Airfare?

   b. Meals?

   c. Lodging?

6. **LO.3** Samantha recently was hired by an accounting firm. During the year, she spends $2,500 for a CPA exam review course and begins working on a law degree in night school. Her law school expenses were $4,200 for tuition and $450 for books (which are not a requirement for enrollment in the course). Samantha's AGI this year is $58,000. Assuming no reimbursement, how much can Samantha deduct for the:

   a. CPA exam review course?

   b. Law school expenses?

7. **LO.3** Robert entertains four key clients and their spouses at a nightclub. Substantive business discussions occurred over dinner and prior to the entertainment beginning. Expenses were $200 (limo charge), $120 (cover charge), $700 (drinks and dinner), and $140 (tips to servers). If Robert is self-employed, how much can he deduct for this event?

8. **LO.3** The CEO of Crimson, Inc., entertains seven clients at a skybox in Memorial Stadium for an athletic event. Substantive business discussions occurred at various times during the event.

   The box costs $2,000 per event and seats 10 people. (The cost of a regular seat at Memorial ranges from $55 to $100.) Refreshments served during the event totaled $700. How much of these costs may Crimson deduct?

9. **LO.6** In 2016, Miranda records net earnings from self-employment as an interior decorator of $146,000. She also earned a $50,000 salary from her work at a design studio. Determine the amount of Miranda's self-employment tax.

10. **LO.5** Myers, who is single, reports compensation income of $68,000 in 2016. He is an active participant in his employer's qualified retirement plan. Myers contributes $5,500 to a traditional IRA. Of the $5,500 contribution, how much can Myers deduct?

11. **LO.5** Meredith, who is single, would like to contribute $5,500 to her Roth IRA. What is the maximum amount that Meredith can contribute if her AGI is $118,000?

Problems

12. **LO.1** Mason performs various home repair services for Isabella. In determining whether Mason is an employee or an independent contractor, comment on the relevance of each of the factors listed below.

   a. Mason performs services only for Isabella and does not work for anyone else.

   b. Mason sets his own work schedule.

   c. Mason reports his job-related expenses on a Schedule C.

   d. Mason obtained his job skills from Isabella's training program.

   e. Mason performs the services at Isabella's business location.

   f. Mason is paid based on time worked rather than on task performed.

13. **LO.2** Rex, age 55, is an officer of Blue Company, which provides him with the following nondiscriminatory fringe benefits. Determine the amounts that Rex must include in gross income.

   • Hospitalization insurance premiums for Rex and his dependents. The cost of the coverage for Rex is $2,900 per year, and the additional cost for his dependents is $3,800 per year. The plan applies a $2,000 deductible, but his employer contributed $1,500 to Rex's Health Savings Account (HSA). Rex withdrew only $800 from the HSA, and the account earned $50 of interest during the year.

   • Insurance premiums of $840 for salary continuation payments. Under the plan, Rex will receive his regular salary in the event he is unable to work due to illness. Rex collected $4,500 on the policy to replace lost wages while he was ill during the year.

   • Rex is a part-time student working on his bachelor's degree in engineering. His employer reimbursed his $5,200 tuition under a plan available to all full-time employees.

14. **LO.2** Casey is in the 15% marginal tax bracket, and Jean is in the 35% marginal tax bracket. Their employer is experiencing financial difficulties and cannot continue to pay for the company's health insurance plan. The annual premiums are approximately $8,000 per employee.

   The employer has proposed to either (1) require the employee to pay the premiums or (2) reduce each employee's pay by $10,000 per year with the employer paying the premium. Which option is less objectionable to Casey, and which is less objectionable to Jean?

Decision Making

15. **LO.2** Belinda spent the last 60 days of the year in a nursing home. The cost of the services provided to her was $18,000 ($300 per day). Medicare paid $8,500 toward the cost of her stay. Belinda also received $5,500 of benefits under a long-term care insurance policy she had purchased. What is the effect of each of these items on Belinda's gross income?

16. **LO.2** Does the taxpayer recognize gross income in the following situations? Explain.

   a. Ava is a filing clerk at a large insurance company. She is permitted to leave the premises for her lunch, but she usually eats in the company's cafeteria because it is quick and she is on a tight schedule. On average, she pays $2 for a lunch that would cost $12 at a restaurant. However, if the prices in the cafeteria were not so low and the food was not so delicious, she would probably bring her own lunch at a cost of $3 per day.

   b. Scott is an executive for an international corporation located in New York City. Often he works late, taking telephone calls from the company's West Coast branches. Scott often stays in a company-owned condominium when he has a late-night work session. The condominium is across the street from the company office.

   c. Ira recently moved to take a new job. For the first month on the new job, Ira was searching for a home to purchase or rent. During this time, his employer permitted Ira to live in an apartment that the company maintains for customers during the buying season. The month that Ira occupied the apartment was not during the buying season, however, and the apartment would not otherwise have been occupied.

17. **LO.2** Tim is the vice president of western operations for Maroon Oil Company and is stationed in San Francisco. He is required to live in an employer-owned home, which is three blocks from his company office. The company-provided home is equipped with high-speed Internet access and several telephone lines. Tim receives telephone calls and e-mails that require immediate attention any time of

day or night because the company's business is spread all over the world. A full-time administrative assistant resides in the house to assist Tim with the urgent business matters.

Tim often uses the home for entertaining customers, suppliers, and employees. The fair market value of comparable housing is $9,000 per month. Tim also is provided with free parking at his company's office, a value of $350 per month. Calculate the amount associated with the company-provided housing and free parking that Tim must include in his gross income for 2016.

Communications   18. **LO.1, 4** Finch Construction Company provides the carpenters it employs with all required tools. However, the company believes that this has led to some employees not taking care of the tools, and to the mysterious disappearance of some of the tools.

The company is considering requiring all of its employees to provide their own tools. Employees' salaries would be increased by $1,500 to compensate for the additional costs. Write a letter to Finch's management, explaining the tax consequences of this plan to the carpenters. Finch's address is 300 Harbor Drive, Vermillion, SD 57069.

Decision Making   19. **LO.2** Rosa's employer has instituted a flexible benefits program. Rosa will use the plan to pay for her daughter's dental expenses and other medical expenses that are not covered by health insurance. Rosa is in the 28% marginal tax bracket and estimates that the medical and dental expenses not covered by health insurance will be within the range of $4,000 to $5,000. Her employer's plan permits her to set aside as much as $5,000 in the flexible benefits account. Rosa does not itemize her deductions.

a. Rosa puts $4,000 in her flexible benefits account, and her actual expenses are $5,000. What is her after-tax cost of underestimating the expenses?

b. Rosa puts $5,000 in her flexible benefits account, and her actual expenses are only $4,000. What is her after-tax cost of overestimating her expenses?

c. What is Rosa's cost of underfunding as compared with the cost of overfunding the flexible benefits account?

d. Does your answer in part (c) suggest that Rosa should fund the account closer to the low end or to the high end of her estimates?

20. **LO.2** Sparrow Corporation would like you to review its employee fringe benefits program with regard to the tax consequences of the plan for the company's president (Polly), who is also the majority shareholder.

a. Sparrow offers a qualified retirement plan. The company pays the cost of employees attending a retirement planning seminar. The employee must be within 10 years of retirement, and the cost of the seminar is $1,500 per attendee.

b. The company owns a parking garage that is used by customers, employees, and the general public. Only the general public is required to pay for parking. The charge to the general public for Polly's parking for the year would have been $3,600 (a $300 monthly rate).

c. All employees are allowed to use the company's fixed charge long-distance telephone services as long as the privilege is not abused. Although no one has kept track of the actual calls, Polly's use of the telephone had a value (what she would have paid on her personal telephone) of approximately $600 for the year.

d. The company owns a condominium at the beach, which it uses to entertain customers. Employees are allowed to use the facility without charge when the company has no scheduled events. Polly used the facility 10 days during the year. The dates of Polly's personal use had a rental value of $1,000.

e. Sparrow operates in the household moving business. Employees are allowed to ship goods without charge whenever there is excess space on a truck. Polly purchased a dining room suite for her daughter. Company trucks delivered the furniture to the daughter. Normal freight charges would have been $750.

f. The company has a storage facility for household goods. Officers are allowed a 20% discount on charges for storing their goods. All other employees are allowed a 10% discount. Polly's discounts for the year totaled $900.

21. **LO.2** Ted works for Azure Motors, an automobile dealership. All employees can buy a car at the company's cost plus 2%. The company does not charge employees the $300 dealer preparation fee that nonemployees must pay. Ted purchased an automobile for $29,580 ($29,000 + $580). The company's cost was $29,000. The price for a nonemployee would have been $33,900 ($33,600 + $300 preparation fee). What is Ted's gross income from the purchase of the automobile?

22. **LO.2** Several of Egret Company's employees have asked the company to create a hiking trail that employees could use during their lunch hours. The company owns vacant land that is being held for future expansion, but would have to spend approximately $50,000 if it were to make a trail. Nonemployees would be allowed to use the facility as part of the company's effort to build strong community support. What are the relevant tax issues for the employees?

Issue ID

23. **LO.2** Bluebird, Inc., does not provide its employees with any tax-exempt fringe benefits. The company is considering adopting a hospital and medical benefits insurance plan that will cost approximately $9,000 per employee. To adopt this plan, the company may need to reduce salaries and/or lower future salary increases. Bluebird is in the 35% (combined Federal and state rates) bracket.

Bluebird also is responsible for matching the Social Security and Medicare taxes withheld on employees' salaries (at the full 7.65% rate). The hospital and medical benefits insurance plan will not be subject to the Social Security and Medicare taxes, and the company is not eligible for the small business credit for health insurance. The employees generally fall into two marginal tax rate groups, specifically:

Income Tax	Social Security and Medicare Tax	Total
.15	.0765	.2265
.35	.0145	.3645

The company has asked you to assist in its financial planning for the hospital and medical benefits insurance plan by computing the following.

a. How much taxable compensation is the equivalent of $9,000 of exempt compensation for each of the two classes of employees?

b. What is the company's after-tax cost of the taxable compensation computed in part (a)?

c. What is the company's after-tax cost of the exempt compensation?

d. Briefly explain your conclusions from the preceding analysis.

24. **LO.2** George is a U.S. citizen who is employed by Hawk Enterprises, a global company. Beginning on June 1, 2016, George began working in London. He worked there until January 31, 2017, when he transferred to Paris. He worked in Paris the remainder of 2017. His salary for the first five months of 2016 was $100,000, and it was earned in the United States. His salary for the remainder of 2016 was $175,000, and it was earned in London.

George's 2017 salary from Hawk was $300,000, with part being earned in London and part being earned in Paris. What is George's gross income in 2016 and 2017 (assume that the 2017 indexed amount is the same as the 2016 indexed amount)?

Critical Thinking   25. **LO.3** Ella is the regional sales manager for a fast-food chain. She starts her work day by driving from home to the regional office, works there for several hours, and then visits the three sales outlets in her region. Relevant mileage is as follows.

Home to regional office	10 miles
Regional office to sales outlet 1	13
Sales outlet 1 to sales outlet 2	11
Sales outlet 2 to sales outlet 3	9
Sales outlet 3 to home	15

If Ella uses the automatic mileage method and works 240 days in 2016, what is her deduction for the year?

26. **LO.3** Kristen, the regional manager for a national hardware chain, is based in Atlanta. During March and April of the current year, she replaces the district manager in Jackson (Mississippi) temporarily. During this period, Kristen flies to Jackson on Sunday night, spends the week at the district office, and returns home to Atlanta on Friday afternoon. The cost of returning home is $550, while the cost of spending the weekend in Jackson would have been $490.

a. Presuming no reimbursement by her employer, how much, if any, of these weekend expenses may Kristen deduct?

b. Would your answer in part (a) change if the amounts involved were reversed (i.e., the trip home cost $490; staying in Jackson would have been $550)? Explain.

27. **LO.3** In June of this year, Dr. and Mrs. Bret Spencer traveled to Denver to attend a three-day conference sponsored by the American Society of Implant Dentistry. Bret, a practicing oral surgeon, participated in scheduled technical sessions dealing with the latest developments in surgical procedures. On two days, Mrs. Spencer attended group meetings where various aspects of family tax planning were discussed. On the other day, she went sightseeing. Mrs. Spencer does not work for her husband, but she does their tax returns and handles the family investments. Expenses incurred in connection with the conference are summarized as follows.

Airfare (two tickets)	$2,000
Lodging (single and double occupancy are the same rate—$250 each day)	750
Meals ($200 × 3 days)*	600
Conference registration fee (includes $120 for Family Tax Planning sessions)	620
Car rental	300

*Split equally between Dr. and Mrs. Spencer.

How much, if any, of these expenses can the Spencers deduct?

28. **LO.3** On Thursday, Justin flies from Baltimore (his home office) to Cadiz (Spain). He conducts business on Friday and Tuesday; vacations on Saturday, Sunday, and Monday (a legal holiday in Spain); and returns to Baltimore on Thursday. Justin was scheduled to return home on Wednesday, but all flights were canceled due to bad weather. Therefore, he spent Wednesday watching floor shows at a local casino.

a. For tax purposes, what portion of Justin's trip is regarded as being for business?

b. Suppose Monday had not been a legal holiday. Would this change your answer to part (a)? Explain.

c. Under either part (a) or (b), how much of Justin's airfare qualifies as a deductible business expense?

Ethics and Equity   29. **LO.3** Veronica is a key employee of Perdiz Corporation, an aerospace engineering concern located in Seattle. Perdiz would like to establish an office on the east coast of Florida and wants Veronica to be in charge of the branch. Veronica is hesitant about making the move because she fears she will have to sell her residence in Seattle at a loss. Perdiz buys the house from Veronica for $420,000, its cost to her. She has owned and occupied the house as her principal residence for eight years. One year later, Perdiz resells the property for $370,000.

Nothing regarding the sale of the residence is ever reflected on Veronica's income tax returns. Perdiz absorbs all of Veronica's moving expenses. As an ethical tax professional, do you have any qualms as to the way these matters have been handled for income tax purposes? Explain.

30. **LO.3** Upon losing his job as a plant manager in Quincy, Massachusetts, Anthony incurs $6,200 in job search expenses. Having no success in finding new employment in the same type of work, Anthony moves to Clearwater, Florida, in 2016 and begins a charter boat business. His expenses in connection with the move are summarized below. How much of these expenses may Anthony deduct?

Penalty for breaking lease on Quincy rented residence	$2,800
Forfeiture of membership in Quincy Country Club	2,200
Packing and moving van charges	7,100
Lodging during move (3 nights)	380
Meals during move	360
Mileage (total for two automobiles)	2,400 miles

31. **LO.3** Elijah is employed as a full-time high school teacher. The school district for   Issue ID
which he works recently instituted a policy requiring all of its teachers to start working on a master's degree. Pursuant to this new rule, Elijah spent most of the summer of 2016 taking graduate courses at an out-of-town university. His expenses include:

Tuition	$6,600
Books and course materials	1,500
Lodging	1,700
Meals	2,200
Laundry and dry cleaning	200
Campus parking	300

In addition, Elijah drove his personal automobile 2,200 miles in connection with the education. He uses the automatic mileage method.

a. How much, if any, of these expenses might qualify as a deduction *for* AGI?

b. How much, if any, of these expenses might qualify as a deduction *from* AGI?

32. **LO.3** In each of the following independent situations, determine how much, if any,   Issue ID
qualifies as a deduction *for* AGI under § 222 (targeted tuition and related expenses).

a. Lily is single and is employed as an architect. This year, she spent $4,100 in tuition to attend law school at night. Her MAGI is $64,000.

b. Liam is single and is employed as a pharmacist. During the year, he spent $2,400 ($2,100 for tuition and $300 for books) to take a course in herbal supplements at a local university. His MAGI is $81,000.

c. Hailey is married and is employed as a bookkeeper. She spends $5,200 for tuition and $900 for books and supplies to pursue a bachelor's degree in accounting. Her MAGI is $40,000 on the separate return that she files.

d. John spends $6,500 of his savings for tuition to attend Carmine State College. John is claimed as a dependent by his parents.

e. How much, if any, of the preceding amounts *not allowed under § 222* might otherwise qualify as a deduction *from* AGI?

Decision Making   33. **LO.3** During the year, Brenda has the following expenses related to her employment.

Airfare	$8,500
Meals	4,000
Lodging	4,900
Transportation while in travel status (taxis and limos)	940
Entertainment of clients	8,000

Although Brenda renders an adequate accounting to her employer, she is reimbursed for only $12,000 of the above expenses. What are Brenda's tax consequences based on the following assumptions?

a.   The $12,000 reimbursement does not designate which expenses are covered.

b.   The reimbursement specifically covers only the meals and entertainment expenses.

c.   The reimbursement covers any of the expenses other than meals and entertainment.

d.   If Brenda has a choice of reimbursement procedures [part (a), (b), or (c) above], which should she select? Why?

Critical Thinking   34. **LO.3, 4** Charles reports AGI of $94,000 during the year and the following expenses related to his employment.

Lodging while in travel status	$5,000
Meals during travel	4,000
Business transportation	6,000
Entertainment of clients	3,800
Professional dues and subscriptions	800

Charles is reimbursed $14,000 under his employer's accountable plan. What are his deductions *for* and *from* AGI?

35. **LO.5** Janet, age 29, is unmarried and is an active participant in a qualified retirement plan. Her modified AGI is $63,000 in 2016.

a.   Calculate the amount Janet can contribute to a traditional IRA and the amount she can deduct.

b.   Assume instead that Janet is a participant in a SIMPLE IRA and that she elects to contribute 4% of her compensation to the account, while her employer contributes 3%. What amount will be contributed for 2016? What amount will be vested?

36. **LO.5** Carri and Dane, ages 34 and 32, respectively, have been married for 11 years, and both are active participants in employer qualified retirement plans. Their total AGI in 2016 is $187,000, and they earn salaries of $87,000 and $95,000, respectively. What amount may Carri and Dane:

a.   Contribute to regular IRAs?

b.   Deduct for their contributions in part (a)?

c.   Contribute to Roth IRAs?

d.   Deduct for their contributions in part (c)?

37. **LO.6** In 2016, Susan's sole proprietorship earns $300,000 of self-employment net income (after the deduction for one-half of self-employment tax). Calculate the maximum amount Susan can deduct for contributions to a defined contribution Keogh plan.

38. **LO.6** Harvey is a self-employed accountant with earned income from the business of $120,000 (after the deduction for one-half of his self-employment tax). He has a profit sharing plan (e.g., defined contribution Keogh plan). What is the maximum amount Harvey can contribute to his retirement plan in 2016?

39. **LO.7** Alex, who is single, conducts an activity this year that is classified as a hobby. The activity produces the following revenues and expenses.

Revenue	$18,000
Property taxes	3,000
Materials and supplies	4,500
Utilities	2,000
Advertising	5,000
Insurance	750
Depreciation	4,000

Without regard to this activity, Alex's AGI is $42,000. Determine the amount of gross income that Alex must report, the amount of the expenses he is permitted to deduct, and his taxable income from the hobby.

Comprehensive Tax Return Problems

Tax Return Problem

TAX SOFTWARE

1. Beth R. Jordan lives at 2322 Skyview Road, Mesa, AZ 85201. She is a tax accountant with Mesa Manufacturing Company, 1203 Western Avenue, Mesa, AZ 85201 (employer identification number 11-1111111). She also writes computer software programs for tax practitioners and has a part-time tax practice. Beth is single and has no dependents. Beth's birthday is July 4, 1972, and her Social Security number is 123-45-6789. She wants to contribute $3 to the Presidential Election Campaign Fund.

    The following information is shown on Beth's Wage and Tax Statement (Form W–2) for 2015.

Line	Description	Amount
1	Wages, tips, other compensation	$65,000.00
2	Federal income tax withheld	10,500.00
3	Social Security wages	65,000.00
4	Social Security tax withheld	4,030.00
5	Medicare wages and tips	65,000.00
6	Medicare tax withheld	942.50
15	State	Arizona
16	State wages, tips, etc.	65,000.00
17	State income tax withheld	1,954.00

During the year, Beth received interest of $1,300 from Arizona Federal Savings and Loan and $400 from Arizona State Bank. Each financial institution reported the interest income on a Form 1099–INT. She received qualified dividends of $800 from Blue Corporation, $750 from Green Corporation, and $650 from Orange Corporation. Each corporation reported Beth's dividend payments on a Form 1099–DIV.

Beth received a $1,100 income tax refund from the state of Arizona on April 29, 2015. On her 2014 Federal income tax return, she reported total itemized deductions of $8,200, which included $2,200 of state income tax withheld by her employer.

Fees earned from her part-time tax practice in 2015 totaled $3,800. She paid $600 to have the tax returns processed by a computerized tax return service.

On February 8, 2015, Beth bought 500 shares of Gray Corporation common stock for $17.60 a share. On September 12, 2015, she sold the stock for $14 a share.

Beth bought a used sports utility vehicle for $6,000 on June 5, 2015. She purchased the vehicle from her brother-in-law, who was unemployed and was in need of cash. On November 2, 2015, she sold the vehicle to a friend for $6,500.

On January 2, 2015, she acquired 100 shares of Blue Corporation common stock for $30 a share. She sold the stock on December 19, 2015, for $55 a share.

During the year, Beth records revenues of $16,000 from the sale of a software program she developed. She incurred the following expenditures in connection with her software development business.

Cost of personal computer	$7,000
Cost of printer	2,000
Furniture	3,000
Supplies	650
Fee paid to computer consultant	3,500

Beth elected to expense the maximum portion of the cost of the computer, printer, and furniture allowed under the provisions of § 179. These items were placed in service on January 15, 2015, and used 100% in her business.

Although Mesa suggested that Beth attend a convention on current developments in corporate taxation, Beth was not reimbursed for the travel expenses of $1,420 she incurred in attending. The $1,420 included $200 for meals.

During the year, Beth paid $300 for prescription medicines and $2,875 for medical bills. Health insurance premiums were paid for her by her employer, covering her for the entire year.

Beth paid real property taxes of $1,766 on her home. Interest on her home mortgage was $3,845, and interest to credit card companies was $320. She contributed $30 each week to her church and $10 each week to the United Way. Professional dues and subscriptions totaled $350. Beth paid estimated Federal income taxes of $1,000.

Part 1—Tax Computation

Compute the net tax payable or refund due for Beth R. Jordan for 2015. If you use tax forms for your solution, you will need Forms 1040, 2106-EZ, and 4562 and Schedules A, B, C, D, and SE. Suggested software: H&R BLOCK Tax Software.

Part 2—Tax Planning

Beth is anticipating significant changes in her life in 2016, and she has asked you to estimate her taxable income and tax liability for 2016. She just received word that she has been qualified to adopt a 2-year-old daughter. Beth expects that the adoption will be finalized in 2016 and that she will incur approximately $2,000 of adoption expenses. In addition, she expects to incur approximately $3,500 of child and dependent care expenses relating to the care of her new daughter, which will enable her to keep her job at Mesa Manufacturing.

With the additional demands on her time because of her daughter, she has decided to discontinue her two part-time jobs (i.e., the part-time tax practice and her software business), and she will cease making estimated income tax payments. In your computations, assume that all other income and expenditures will remain at approximately the same levels as in 2015.

Tax Computation Problem

Communications

TAX SOFTWARE

2. David R. and Ella M. Cole (ages 39 and 38, respectively) are husband and wife who live at 1820 Elk Avenue, Denver, CO 80202. David is a regional sales manager for Wren Industries, a national wholesaler of plumbing and heating supplies, and Ella is a part-time dental hygienist for the Smile For Me chain of dental clinics.

- David is classified by Wren as a statutory employee with compensation for 2015 (based on commissions) of $95,000. He is expected to maintain his own office and pay for all business expenses from this amount. Wren does not require him to render any accounting as to the use of these funds. It does not withhold Federal and state income taxes but does withhold and account for the payroll taxes incurred (e.g., Social Security and Medicare). The Coles are adequately covered by Wren's noncontributory medical plan but have chosen not to participate in its § 401(k) retirement plan.

David's employment-related expenses for 2015 are summarized below.

Airfare	$8,800
Lodging	5,000
Meals (during travel status)	4,800
Entertainment	3,600
Ground transportation (e.g., limos, rental cars, and taxis)	800
Business gifts	900
Office supplies (includes postage, overnight delivery, and copying)	1,500

The entertainment involved business meals for purchasing agents, store owners, and building contractors. The business gifts consisted of $50 gift certificates to a national restaurant. These were sent by David during the Christmas holidays to 18 of his major customers.

In addition, David drove his 2013 Ford Expedition 11,000 miles for business and 3,000 for personal use during 2015. He purchased the Expedition on August 15, 2012; David always has used the automatic (standard) mileage method for tax purposes. Parking and tolls relating to business use total $340 in 2015.

• When the Coles purchased their present residence in April 2012, they devoted 450 of the 3,000 square feet of living space to an office for David. The property cost $440,000 ($40,000 of which is attributable to the land) and has since appreciated in value. Expenses relating to the residence in 2015 (except for mortgage interest and property taxes; see below) are as follows.

Insurance	$2,600
Repairs and maintenance	900
Utilities	4,700
Painting office area; area rugs and plants (in the office)	1,800

The Coles use the MACRS percentage tables applicable to 39-year nonresidential real property. As to depreciable personalty (e.g., office furniture), David tries to avoid capitalization and uses whatever method provides the fastest deduction for tax purposes.

• Ella works part-time as a substitute for whichever hygienist is ill or on vacation or when one of the clinics is particularly busy (e.g., prior to the beginning of the school year). Besides her transportation, she must provide and maintain her own uniforms. Her expenses for 2015 appear below.

Uniforms	$690
State and city occupational licenses	380
Professional journals and membership dues in the American Dental Hygiene Association	340
Correspondence study course (taken online) dealing with teeth whitening procedures	420

Ella's salary for the year is $42,000, and her Form W–2 for the year shows income tax withholdings of $4,000 (Federal) and $1,000 (state) and the proper amount of Social Security and Medicare taxes. Because Ella is a part-time employee, she is not included in her employer's medical or retirement plans.

• In addition to those items already mentioned, the Coles had the following receipts during 2015.

Interest income—		
State of Colorado general purpose bonds	$2,500	
IBM bonds	800	
Wells Fargo Bank CD	1,200	$ 4,500
Federal income tax refund for year 2014		510
Life insurance proceeds paid by Eagle Assurance Corporation		200,000
Inheritance of savings account from Sarah Cole		50,000
Sales proceeds from two ATVs		9,000

For several years, the Coles household has included David's divorced mother, Sarah, who has been claimed as their dependent. In late November 2015, Sarah unexpectedly died in her sleep. Unknown to Ella and David, Sarah owned a life insurance policy and a savings account (with David as the designated beneficiary of each).

In 2014, the Coles purchased two ATVs for $14,000. After several near mishaps, they decided that the sport was too dangerous. In 2015, they sold the ATVs to their neighbor.

- Additional expenditures for 2015 include:

Funeral expenses for Sarah		$ 4,500
Taxes—		
Real property taxes on personal residence	$6,400	
Colorado state income tax due (paid in April 2015		
for tax year 2014)	310	6,710
Mortgage interest on personal residence		6,600
Paid church pledge		2,400
Contributions to traditional IRAs for Ella and David		
($5,500 + $5,500)		11,000

In 2015, the Coles made quarterly estimated tax payments of $1,400 (Federal) and $500 (state) for a total of $5,600 (Federal) and $2,000 (state).

Part 1—Tax Computation
Using the appropriate forms and schedules, compute David and Ella's joint Federal income tax for 2015. Disregard the alternative minimum tax (AMT) and various education credits. Relevant Social Security numbers are:

David Cole	123-45-6788
Ella Cole	123-45-6787
Sarah Cole	123-45-6799

The Coles do not want to contribute to the Presidential Election Campaign Fund. They want any overpayment of tax refunded to them and *not* applied toward next year's tax liability. Suggested software: H&R BLOCK Tax Software.

Part 2—Follow-Up Advice
Ella has always wanted to pursue a career in nursing. To this end, she has earned a substantial number of college credits on a part-time basis. With Sarah no longer requiring home care, Ella believes that she now can complete her degree by attending college on a full-time basis.

David would like to know how Ella's plans will affect their income tax position. Specifically, he wants to know:

- How much Federal income tax they will save if Ella quits her job.
- Any tax benefits that might be available from the cost of the education.

Write a letter to David, addressing these concerns. In making your projections, assume that David's salary and expenses remain the same. Disregard any consideration of the educational tax credits (i.e., American Opportunity and lifetime learning).

BRIDGE DISCIPLINE

1. Justin performs services for Partridge, Inc., and receives compensation of $85,000 for the year. Determine the tax consequences of Social Security and Medicare on Justin's take-home pay if:
   a. Justin is classified as an employee of Partridge.
   b. Justin is classified as an independent contractor.

2. The Code contains provisions that are "friendly" to specific groups of taxpayers. Among these are the following:

   • Senior citizens.

   • Married taxpayers.

   • Employed taxpayers.

   • Taxpayers with children.

   • Self-employed taxpayers.

   Provide justification for the special treatment for each of the above groups, and give an example of such special treatment for each group.

Research Problems

Note: Solutions to Research Problems can be prepared by using the Checkpoint® Student Edition online research product, which is available to accompany this text. It is also possible to prepare solutions to the Research Problems by using tax research materials found in a standard tax library.

THOMSON REUTERS
CHECKPOINT
Student Edition

Research Problem 1. The employees of the city of Greenville must make mandatory contributions to the city's postretirement health benefit plan. The employees' contributions are placed in a trust and are used exclusively for the employees' benefits. The employees believe that because they are required to make the contributions from their base salaries, the result should be the same as if the employer made the contribution and had reduced their salaries by the amount of the contributions. Therefore, the employees believe they should be permitted to exclude the payments from gross income. The employees have asked you to research the issue.

Research Problem 2. Rick Beam has been an independent sales representative for various textile manufacturers for many years. His products consist of soft goods such as tablecloths, curtains, and drapes. Rick's customers are clothing store chains, department stores, and smaller specialty stores. The employees of these companies who are responsible for purchasing merchandise are known as buyers. These companies generally prohibit their buyers from accepting gifts from manufacturers' sales representatives.

Communications

Each year, Rick gives cash gifts (never more than $25) to most of the buyers who are his customers. Generally, he cashes a large check in November and gives the money personally to the buyers around Christmas. Rick says, "This is one of the ways that I maintain my relationship with my buyers." He maintains adequate substantiation of all of the gifts.

Rick's deductions for these gifts have been disallowed by the IRS based on § 162(c)(2). Rick is confused and comes to you, a CPA, for advice.

a. Write a letter to Rick concerning his tax position on this issue. Rick's address is 948 Octavia Street, Baton Rouge, LA 70821.

b. Prepare a memo for your files supporting the advice you have given.

Research Problem 3. Aaron, a resident of Minnesota, has been a driver for Green Delivery Service for the past six years. For this purpose, he leases a truck from Green, and his compensation is based on a percentage of the income resulting from his pickup and delivery services. Green allows its drivers to choose their 10-hour shifts and does not exercise any control on how these services are carried out (e.g., the route to be taken or the order in which parcels are delivered or picked up). Under Green's operating agreement with its drivers, Green can terminate the arrangement after 30 days' notice. In practice, however, Green allows its truckers to quit immediately without giving advance notice. The agreement also labels the drivers as independent contractors.

Green maintains no health or retirement plans for its drivers, and each year it reports their income by issuing Forms 1099–MISC (and not Forms W–2). Green requires its drivers to maintain a commercial driver's license and be in good standing with the state highway law enforcement division.

Citing the employment tax Regulations in §§ 31.3121(d)–1(c)(2) and 31.3306(i)–1(b), an IRS agent contends that Aaron is an independent contractor and, therefore, is subject to the self-employment tax. Based on *Peno Trucking, Inc.* (93 TCM 1027, T.C.Memo. 2007–66), Aaron disagrees and contends that he is an employee (i.e., not self-employed). Who is correct? Why?

Internet Activity

Use the tax resources of the Internet to address the following questions. Do not restrict your search to the Web, but include a review of newsgroups and general reference materials, practitioner sites and resources, primary sources of the tax law, chat rooms and discussion groups, and other opportunities.

Communications   **Research Problem 4.** In no more than four Powerpoint slides for a presentation to your school's Accounting Club, describe the operation of a "U.S. 801(k) plan." In general, who would use such a plan and why?

Research Problem 5. Sarah was contemplating making a contribution to her traditional IRA in 2015. She determined she would contribute $5,000 in December 2015, but forgot about making the contribution until she was preparing her 2015 tax return in February 2016. Use the website of any well-known IRA provider (e.g., Fidelity, Vanguard, T. Rowe Price) to determine if Sarah can make a deductible 2015 contribution to her IRA after the tax year has ended.

Communications   **Research Problem 6.** Taxpayers who purchase health insurance coverage through the Health Insurance Marketplace may be eligible for the premium tax credit under § 36B. Use the IRS's website (**www.irs.gov**) to read about this provision and determine which taxpayers are eligible for the credit. Summarize your findings in an e-mail to your instructor.

Roger CPA Review Questions

1. Betty, a salesperson, is an employee with $52,000 AGI who maintains a home office for the convenience of her employer, Smart Systems. The office takes up 5% of Betty's home and is used exclusively for her job. Smart Systems reimburses all of Betty's direct costs of maintaining the home office. Betty also incurs the following expenses associated with her home.

Expense	Amount
Real property taxes on residence	$3,500
Interest expense on residence	5,000
Operating expenses on residence	1,800
Depreciation on residence (based on 5% home office use)	150

Considering these facts, how much may Betty deduct from AGI on her Form 1040, assuming that she elects to itemize deductions?

a. $0

c. $9,410

b. $665

d. $10,450

2. Pinnacle Productions, Inc., holds a luxury skybox season ticket at a local sporting arena. Pinnacle uses the skybox to entertain clients while conducting business meetings. The cost of Pinnacle's luxury skybox season ticket is $25,000; the cost of the most expensive non-luxury season ticket is $15,000. How much of the luxury skybox season ticket cost may Pinnacle deduct from its corporate taxable income?

a. $7,500

c. $10,000

b. $20,000

d. $15,000

3. Claire is a self-employed individual who owns and runs Claire's Creations LLC. In 2016, she reported $225,000 in net self-employment earnings, including a deduction for 50% of the self-employment tax, prior to any Keogh deduction. Claire contributes to a defined contribution stock bonus Keogh plan. What is the highest deductible Keogh contribution Claire can make for the 2016 tax year?

a. $56,250

c. $52,000

b. $225,000

d. $45,000

Part 5 focuses on the tax effects of common legal forms with which to conduct business. The discussion includes an analysis of the life cycle of a business, from formation, to the taxation of business activities, through the termination of the entity. The specific business entities covered are the C corporation, the S corporation, the partnership, and the LLC. Rules also are reviewed as to the Federal income tax treatment of distributions from a C corporation.

Corporations: Organization, Capital Structure, and Operating Rules

LEARNING OBJECTIVES: *After completing Chapter 12, you should be able to:*

LO.1 Identify major tax and nontax considerations associated with the corporate form of business.

LO.2 Explain the tax consequences of incorporating and transferring assets to controlled corporations.

LO.3 Describe the special rules that apply when a corporation assumes a shareholder's liability.

LO.4 Identify the basis issues relevant to the shareholder and the corporation.

LO.5 Explain the tax aspects of the capital structure of a corporation.

LO.6 Characterize the tax differences between debt and equity investments.

LO.7 List and apply the tax rules unique to corporations.

LO.8 Compute the corporate income tax.

LO.9 Explain the rules unique to computing the tax of related corporations.

LO.10 Describe the reporting process for corporations.

CHAPTER OUTLINE

TAX TALK *Taxes owing to the Government ... are the price that business has to pay for protection and security.* —BENJAMIN N. CARDOZO

GROWING INTO THE CORPORATE FORM

Amber has operated her business as a sole proprietorship since it was formed 10 years ago. Now, however, she has decided to incorporate the business as Garden, Inc., because the corporate form offers several important nontax advantages, including limited liability. Also, the incorporation would enable her husband, Jimmy, to become a part owner in the business. Amber expects to transfer her business assets in exchange for Garden stock, while Jimmy will provide accounting and legal services for an equity interest. Amber's sole proprietorship assets available for transfer to the new corporation are as follows:

	Adjusted Basis	Fair Market Value
Accounts receivable	$ –0–	$ 50,000
Building	100,000	400,000
Other assets	300,000	550,000
	$400,000	$1,000,000

Aware of the problem of double taxation associated with operating as a regular corporation, Amber is considering receiving some corporate debt at the time of the incorporation. The interest expense on the debt will then provide a deduction for Garden, Inc. Amber's main concern is whether the incorporation will be a taxable transaction. Can the transaction be structured to avoid tax?

Read the chapter and formulate your response.

usiness operations may be conducted in a number of different forms. As with many business decisions, consideration must be given to the tax consequences of choosing a particular business entity. This chapter deals with the unique tax consequences of operating an entity as a regular corporation, including:

- Classification of the entity as a corporation.
- The tax consequences to the shareholders and the corporation upon the formation of the corporation.
- The capital structure of the corporation.
- Determination of the corporate income tax liability.
- Corporate tax filing requirements.

LO.1

Identify major tax and nontax considerations associated with the corporate form of business.

12-1 AN INTRODUCTION TO CORPORATE TAX

Corporations are governed by Subchapter C or Subchapter S of the Internal Revenue Code. Those governed by Subchapter C are referred to as **C corporations** or **regular corporations**. Corporations governed by Subchapter S are referred to as **S corporations**.

S corporations, which generally do not pay Federal income tax, are similar to partnerships in that ordinary business income (loss) flows through to the shareholders to be reported on their separate returns. Also like partnerships, S corporations do not aggregate all income and expense items in computing ordinary business income (loss). Certain items flow through to the shareholders and retain their separate character when reported on the shareholders' returns. The S corporation ordinary business income (loss) and the separately reported items are allocated to the shareholders according to their stock ownership interests. See Chapter 15 for detailed coverage of S corporations.

12-1a Double Taxation of Corporate Income

Unlike proprietorships, partnerships, and S corporations, C corporations are subject to an entity-level Federal income tax. This results in what is known as a *double taxation* effect. A C corporation reports its income and expenses on Form 1120. The corporation computes tax on the taxable income reported on Form 1120 using the rate schedule applicable to corporations (refer to Exhibit 12.1 later in this section). When a corporation distributes its income, the corporation's shareholders report dividend income on their own tax returns. Thus, income that has already been taxed at the corporate level is also taxed at the shareholder level. The effects of double taxation are illustrated in Examples 1 and 2.

Double Taxation Illustrated

EXAMPLE 1

Lavender Corporation has taxable income of $100,000 in 2016. It pays corporate tax of $22,250 (refer to Exhibit 12.1). This leaves $77,750, all of which is distributed as a dividend to Mike, a 43-year-old single individual and the corporation's sole shareholder. Mike has no income sources other than Lavender Corporation.

Mike has taxable income of $67,400 ($77,750 − $6,300 standard deduction − $4,050 personal exemption). He pays tax at the preferential rate applicable to qualified dividends received by individuals. His tax is $4,463 [($37,650 × 0%) + ($29,750 × 15%)].

The combined tax on the corporation's net profit is $26,713 ($22,250 paid by the corporation + $4,463 paid by the shareholder).

EXAMPLE 2

Assume the same facts as in Example 1, except that the business is organized as a sole proprietorship. Mike reports the $100,000 profit from the business on his tax return.

Mike has taxable income of $89,650 ($100,000 − $6,300 standard deduction − $4,050 personal exemption) and pays tax of $18,184. Therefore, operating the business as a sole proprietorship results in a tax *savings* of $8,529 in 2016 [$26,713 (combined tax from Example 1) − $18,184].

GLOBAL TAX ISSUES   **Choice of Organizational Form When Operating Overseas**

When the management of a corporation decides to expand its business by establishing a presence in a foreign market, the new business venture may take one of several organizational forms. As each form comes with its respective advantages and disadvantages, making the best choice can be difficult.

One common approach is to conduct the foreign activity as a *branch* operation of the U.S. corporation. The foreign branch is not a separate legal entity, but a division of the U.S. corporation established overseas. As a result, any gains and losses produced by the foreign unit are included in the corporation's overall financial results.

Another possibility is to organize the foreign operations as a *subsidiary* of the U.S. parent corporation. If this route is

chosen, the subsidiary can be either a *domestic* subsidiary (i.e., organized in the United States) or a *foreign* subsidiary (organized under the laws of a foreign country).

One fundamental tax difference between these two approaches is that the gains and losses of a domestic subsidiary may be consolidated with the operations of the U.S. parent, while the operations of a foreign subsidiary cannot. Thus, the use of a domestic subsidiary to conduct foreign operations yields generally the same final result as the use of a branch. With both approaches, the financial statements of the U.S. parent reflect the results of its worldwide operations.

Taxation of Dividends

Double taxation stems, in part, from the fact that dividend distributions are not deductible by a C corporation. Shareholders of closely held corporations frequently attempt to circumvent this disallowance by disguising a dividend distribution as some other purported transaction. One of the more common ways of disguising dividend distributions is to pay excessive compensation to shareholder-employees of a closely held corporation. The IRS scrutinizes compensation and other economic transactions (e.g., loans, leases, and sales) between shareholders and closely held corporations to ensure that payments are reasonable in amount. (See Chapter 13 for more discussion on constructive dividends.)

To alleviate some of the double taxation effect, Congress reduced the tax rate applicable to the dividend income of individuals. Qualified dividend income is currently taxed at the same preferential rate as long-term capital gains—20 percent, 15 percent, or 0 percent. Most commonly, the 15 percent rate applies. However, the 20 percent rate applies when the taxpayer's regular income tax rate is 39.6 percent and the 0 percent rate applies when the taxpayer's regular income tax rate is 15 percent or less.

In addition, a 3.8 percent additional tax applies to net investment income in excess of modified adjusted gross income of $200,000 ($250,000 if married filing jointly), thus increasing the double taxation of dividend income for high-income taxpayers.

12-1b Comparison of Corporations and Other Forms of Doing Business

Chapter 18 presents a detailed comparison of sole proprietorships, partnerships, S corporations, and C corporations as forms of doing business. However, it is appropriate at this point to consider some of the major tax and nontax factors that favor corporations over other business entities.

Consideration of tax factors requires an examination of the corporate rate structure. Exhibit 12.1 presents the income tax rate schedule applicable to corporations. The marginal tax rates for corporations range from 15 percent to 39 percent. Once a corporation has taxable income of $18,333,333 or more, a flat 35 percent tax rate is applied to its taxable income.

EXHIBIT 12.1	Corporate Income Tax Rates		

Taxable Income		Tax Is:	
Over—	**But Not Over—**		**Of the Amount Over—**
$ 0	$ 50,000	15%	$ 0
50,000	75,000	$ 7,500 + 25%	50,000
75,000	100,000	13,750 + 34%	75,000
100,000	335,000	22,250 + 39%	100,000
335,000	10,000,000	113,900 + 34%	335,000
10,000,000	15,000,000	3,400,000 + 35%	10,000,000
15,000,000	18,333,333	5,150,000 + 38%	15,000,000
18,333,333	—	35%	0

EXAMPLE 3

Beige Corporation has taxable income of $20 million in the current year. Beige's corporate income tax is $7 million, computed as follows:

	$50,000 × 15%	$ 7,500
+	$25,000 × 25%	6,250
+	$25,000 × 34%	8,500
+	$235,000 × 39%	91,650
+	$9,665,000 × 34%	3,286,100
+	$5,000,000 × 35%	1,750,000
+	$3,333,333 × 38%	1,266,667
+	$1,666,667 × 35%	583,333
		$7,000,000

OR

$20,000,000 × 35%	$7,000,000

In comparison to the corporate tax rates, the marginal tax rates for individuals range from 10 percent to 39.6 percent. In many cases, the tax burden will be greater if a business is operated as a corporation (as in Example 1). However, the corporate form of doing business presents tax savings opportunities when the applicable corporate marginal rate is lower than the applicable individual marginal rate.

TAX FACT   Corporations' Reporting Responsibilities

Like individuals, corporations are required to report their taxable income and other financial information to the IRS on an annual basis. The forms used depend on the type and size of the corporation. Based on projections, the IRS expects to receive approximately 6.9 million corporate income tax returns during the 2017 filing season.

Interestingly, nearly 79 percent of C and S corporations are expected to submit their returns electronically.

Type of Corporation	Form	Percentage
C Corporation	1120	25.1%
C Corporation	Others	5.1
S Corporation	1120S	69.8
		100.0%

Source: Fiscal Year Return Projections for the United States: 2015–2022, IRS, Publication 6292, Spring 2015 Update, Table 1.

BRIDGE DISCIPLINE **Bridge to Finance**

Investment brokers and promoters often try to entice individuals to invest their disposable income in ventures designed to produce handsome returns. In most situations, the type of business entity in which the funds are invested takes the form of a "flow-through" entity, such as a limited partnership. Such investment ventures rarely operate as regular corporations.

A limited partnership is the favored investment vehicle for several reasons. One of the most significant reasons is that the investors who become limited partners are protected from ex-posure to unlimited liability. In addition, any operating losses of the entity (which may be expected in the venture's early years) flow through to the partners and, as a result, may provide an immediate tax benefit on the partners' returns. Another major advantage of the partnership form, in contrast to the corporate form, is that the business earnings are subject to only one level of tax—at the partner or investor level. If the investments were housed in a corporation, a tax would be levied first on the corporate earnings and then at the investor level when the corporation makes distributions to the shareholders.

Susanna, an individual taxpayer in the 39.6% marginal tax rate bracket, can generate $100,000 of additional taxable income in the current year. If the income is taxed to Susanna, the associated tax is $39,600 ($100,000 × 39.6%).

If, however, Susanna is able to shift the income to a newly created corporation, the corporate tax is $22,250 (see Exhibit 12.1). Thus, by taking advantage of the lower corporate marginal tax rates, a tax *savings* of $17,350 ($39,600 − $22,250) is achieved.

EXAMPLE
4

Any attempt to take advantage of the difference between the corporate and individual marginal tax rates also must consider the double taxation effect. When the preferential rate for dividend income is considered, however, tax savings opportunities still exist.

Assume in Example 4 that the corporation distributes all of its after-tax earnings to Susanna as a dividend. The dividend results in income tax of $15,550 [($100,000 − $22,250) × 20%] to Susanna.

Thus, even when the double taxation effect is considered, the combined tax burden of $37,800 ($22,250 paid by the corporation + $15,550 paid by the shareholder) represents an income tax *savings* of $1,800 when compared to the $39,600 of tax that results when the $100,000 of income is subject to Susanna's 39.6% marginal rate.

EXAMPLE
5

Examples 4 and 5 ignore other tax issues that also must be considered in selecting the proper form of doing business, but they illustrate the tax savings that can be achieved by taking advantage of tax rate differentials. In addition to the 3.8 percent additional tax on net investment income (mentioned above), some of the other tax considerations that could affect the selection of a business form include the character of business income, the expectation of business losses, employment taxes, and state taxes.

Unlike other forms of business, the tax attributes of income and expense items of a C corporation do not pass through the corporate entity to the shareholders. As a result, if the business is expected to generate tax-favored income (e.g., tax-exempt income or long-term capital gains), one of the other (non-C corporation) forms of business may be desirable.

Losses of a C corporation are treated differently than losses of a proprietorship, a partnership, or an S corporation. A loss incurred by a proprietorship may be deductible by the owner, because all income and expense items are reported by the proprietor. Partnership and S corporation losses are passed through the entity and may be deductible by the partners or shareholders. C corporation losses, however, have no effect on the taxable income of the shareholders. Therefore, one of the non-C corporation forms of business may be desirable if business losses are anticipated.

Franco plans to start a business this year. He expects that the business will incur operating losses for the first three years and then become highly profitable. Franco decides to operate as an S corporation during the loss period because the losses will flow through and be deductible on his personal return. When the business becomes profitable, he intends to switch to C corporation status.

EXAMPLE
6

The net income of a proprietorship is subject to the self-employment tax (15.3 percent), as are some partnership allocations of income to partners. In the alternative, wages paid to a shareholder-employee of a corporation (C or S) are subject to payroll taxes. The combined corporation-employee payroll tax burden should be compared with the self-employment tax associated with the proprietorship and partnership forms of business. This analysis should include the benefit of the deduction available to a corporation for payroll taxes paid, as well as the deduction available to an individual for one-half of the self-employment taxes paid.

At the entity level, state corporate income taxes and/or franchise taxes are applicable for businesses formed as corporations. Although no entity-level Federal income tax is typically assessed on S corporations, limited liability companies (LLCs), or partnerships, a few states impose a corporate income tax or franchise tax on such business forms. Consideration of state taxation when selecting a business form is particularly relevant for businesses that operate in more than one state. (See Chapter 16 for a discussion of the taxation of multistate corporations.) At the owner level, the income of sole proprietorships, S corporations, and partnerships (including most LLCs) is subject to state individual income taxation. Similarly, dividend income from corporate distributions is subject to state income taxation without any rate preference for such income.

The tax attributes of the various forms of business entities are compared in Concept Summary 12.1.

 ## Concept Summary 12.1

Tax Treatment of Business Forms Compared

	Sole Proprietorships	Partnerships	S Corporations	Regular (C) Corporations
Entity tax return	None	Form 1065	Form 1120S	Form 1120
Taxation of entity income	No separate entity-level income tax. Proprietorship's income and expenses are reported on owner's Form 1040 (Schedule C). Character of entity income and expenses retained at owner level.	No separate entity-level income tax. Partnership's income and expenses are allocated and reported (Schedule K–1) to partners who report these items on their returns (e.g., Form 1040 for individual partners). Character of entity income and expenses retained at partner level.	Generally, no separate entity-level income tax. S corporation's income and expenses are allocated and reported (Schedule K–1) to shareholders who report these items on their returns (e.g., Form 1040 for individual shareholders). Character of entity income and expenses retained at shareholder level.	Corporate income tax applies. Marginal tax rates range from 15% to 39%.
Taxation of withdrawals/ distributions from entity	Withdrawals by owner are not subject to separate tax.	Distributions to partners are generally not subject to separate tax.	Distributions to shareholders are generally not subject to separate tax.	Character of entity income and expenses not retained at shareholder level. Instead, distributions to shareholders are generally taxed as dividend income. Preferential tax rates (0%/15%/20%) apply to qualified dividends.
Employment taxes	Schedule C income subject to self-employment tax.	Some partnership allocations subject to self-employment tax.	Compensation paid to shareholder/employees subject to payroll taxes. Shareholder's allocated portion of entity income not subject to self-employment tax.	Compensation paid to shareholder/employees subject to payroll taxes.

12-1c Nontax Considerations

Nontax considerations may override tax considerations and lead to the conclusion that a business should be operated as a corporation. The following are some of the more important *nontax considerations*:

- Sole proprietors and general partners in partnerships face the danger of *unlimited liability*. That is, creditors of the business may file claims not only against the assets of the business but also against the *personal* assets of proprietors or general partners. State corporate law protects shareholders from claims against their personal assets for corporate debts.

- The corporate form of business can provide a vehicle for *raising capital* through widespread stock ownership. Most major businesses in the United States are operated as corporations.

- Shares of stock in a corporation are *freely transferable*, whereas a partner's sale of his or her partnership interest is subject to approval by the other partners.

- Shareholders may come and go, but a corporation can continue to exist. Death or withdrawal of a partner, on the other hand, may terminate the existing partnership and cause financial difficulties that result in dissolution of the entity. Thus, *continuity of life* is a distinct advantage of the corporate form of doing business.

- Corporations have *centralized management*. All management responsibility is assigned to a board of directors, which appoints officers to carry out the corporation's business. Partnerships, by contrast, may have decentralized management, in which every partner has a right to participate in the organization's business decisions. Limited partnerships, though, may have centralized management. Centralized management is essential for the smooth operation of a widely held business.

12-1d Limited Liability Companies

The limited liability company (LLC) has proliferated greatly in recent years, particularly since 1988 when the IRS first ruled that it would treat qualifying LLCs as partnerships for tax purposes. All 50 states and the District of Columbia have passed laws that allow LLCs, and thousands of companies have chosen LLC status. As with a corporation, operating as an LLC allows its owners (called "members") to avoid unlimited liability, which is a primary *nontax* consideration in choosing this form of business organization. The tax advantage of LLCs is that qualifying businesses may be treated as proprietorships or partnerships for tax purposes, thereby avoiding the problem of double taxation associated with regular corporations.

Some states allow an LLC to have centralized management, but not continuity of life or free transferability of interests. Other states allow LLCs to adopt any or all of the corporate characteristics of centralized management, continuity of life, and free transferability of interests. The comparison of business entities in Chapter 18 includes a discussion of LLCs.

12-1e Entity Classification

To ease the entity classification problem, the check-the-box Regulations were issued by the Treasury Department.[1] The Regulations enable taxpayers to choose the tax status of a business entity without regard to its corporate (or noncorporate) characteristics. These rules simplified tax administration considerably and eliminated much of the litigation that arose under prior law.

Under the check-the-box Regulations, an unincorporated entity with *more than one* owner is, by default, classified as a partnership. An unincorporated entity with *only one* owner is, by default, classified as a disregarded entity (or DRE). A DRE is treated as a sole proprietorship if it is owned by an individual taxpayer or as a branch or a division of a corporate owner. If the entity wants to use its default status, it simply files the appropriate tax return. If it wants to use a different status or change its status, it does so by "checking a box" on Form 8832. Thus, an LLC (single or multi-member) can choose to be taxed as a C corporation and, if otherwise qualifies, even elect S corporation status. See Chapter 15 for more on S corporations.

---

[1]Reg. §§ 301.7701–1 through –4, and –7.

The status election is not available to entities that are incorporated under state law or to entities that are required to be taxed as corporations under Federal law (e.g., certain publicly traded partnerships). LLCs are not treated as being incorporated under state law, so they default to either partnership or DRE status. Although an LLC does not typically pay Federal income taxes, LLCs are obligated to report and pay employment and excise taxes.

 DIGGING DEEPER 1 | **In-depth coverage can be found on this book's companion website: www.cengagebrain.com**

LO.2

Explain the tax consequences of incorporating and transferring assets to controlled corporations.

12-2 ORGANIZATION OF AND TRANSFERS TO CONTROLLED CORPORATIONS

Property transactions normally produce tax consequences if a gain or loss is realized. As a result, unless special provisions in the Code apply, a transfer of property to a corporation in exchange for stock is a taxable transaction. The amount of gain or loss is measured by the difference between the fair market value of the stock received and the tax basis of the property transferred.

12-2a General Rules

In contrast to the typical result of full gain or loss recognition, the Code permits nonrecognition of gain or loss in limited circumstances. For example, with both § 1031 (like-kind exchanges—see Chapter 7) and § 351 (transfers of property to controlled corporations), gain or loss is postponed until a substantive change in the taxpayer's investment occurs (e.g., a sale of property or ownership shares to outsiders). When a taxpayer exchanges some of his or her property for other property of a like kind, § 1031 provides that gain (or loss) realized on the exchange is not recognized because a substantive change in the taxpayer's investment has not occurred. The deferral of gain or loss is accomplished by calculating a substituted basis for the like-kind property received. With this substituted basis, the realized gain or loss associated with the property given up is ultimately recognized when the property received in the exchange is sold.

In a similar fashion, § 351, which deals with transfers to *controlled corporations* (defined later in the chapter), provides that gain or loss is not recognized upon the transfer of property to a corporation in exchange for stock. For example, when a business is incorporated, the owner's economic status remains the same; only the *form* of the investment has changed. The investment in the business assets carries over to an investment in corporate stock. When only stock in the corporation is received, the shareholder is hardly in a position to pay a tax on any realized gain. Thus, this approach is justified under the *wherewithal to pay concept* discussed in Chapter 1. As noted later, however, when the taxpayer receives property other than stock (i.e., cash or other "boot") from the corporation, some or all of the realized gain is recognized.

A further justification for the nonrecognition of gain or loss provisions under § 351 is that Congress believes tax rules should not impede the exercise of sound business judgment (e.g., choice of the corporate form of doing business).

 EXAMPLE 7

Ron is considering incorporating his sole proprietorship. He is concerned about his personal liability for the obligations of the business. Ron realizes that if he incorporates, depending on state law, he will be liable only for the debts of the business that he has personally guaranteed. If Ron incorporates his business, the following assets will be transferred to the corporation:

	Tax Basis	Fair Market Value
Cash	$ 10,000	$ 10,000
Furniture and fixtures	20,000	60,000
Land and building	240,000	300,000
	$270,000	$370,000

continued

In exchange, Ron will receive stock in the newly formed corporation worth $370,000. Without the non-recognition provisions of § 351, Ron would recognize a taxable gain of $100,000 ($370,000 − $270,000) on the transfer. Under § 351, however, Ron does not recognize any gain because his economic status has not changed. Ron's investment in the assets of his sole proprietorship ($270,000) carries over to his investment in the incorporated business, which is now represented by his ownership of stock in the corporation. Thus, § 351 provides for tax neutrality on the initial incorporation of Ron's sole proprietorship.

In a manner similar to a like-kind exchange, if a taxpayer transfers property to a corporation and receives "boot" (money or property other than stock), § 351(b) provides that gain is recognized to the extent of the lesser of the gain realized or the boot received (the amount of money and the fair market value of other property received). Gain is characterized (e.g., ordinary, capital) according to the type of asset transferred.[2] Loss on a § 351 transaction is never recognized. The nonrecognition of gain or loss is accompanied by a substituted basis in the shareholder's stock.[3] The major shareholder consequences of a taxable property transaction versus one that is tax deferred are identified in Concept Summary 12.2.

EXAMPLE 8

Abby and Bill form White Corporation. Abby transfers property with an adjusted basis of $30,000 and a fair market value of $60,000 for 50% of White's stock. Bill transfers property with an adjusted basis of $70,000 and a fair market value of $60,000 for the remaining 50% of the stock. The transfers qualify under § 351.

Abby has a deferred gain of $30,000, and Bill has a deferred loss of $10,000. Both have a substituted basis in the stock of White Corporation. Abby has a basis of $30,000 in her stock, and Bill has a basis of $70,000 in his stock. Therefore, if either Abby or Bill later disposes of the White stock in a taxable transaction (e.g., a sale), this deferred gain/loss will then be fully recognized—a $30,000 gain to Abby and a $10,000 loss to Bill.

Alternatively, if Abby and Bill each had received White stock worth $50,000 and cash of $10,000, a gain would be recognized by Abby, but a loss would not be recognized by Bill. Specifically, Abby would recognize $10,000 of the $30,000 realized gain because she receives boot of $10,000, while Bill's receipt of boot would not trigger the recognition of a loss (i.e., recognition of loss never occurs in a § 351 transaction on the receipt of boot). Additional discussion of gain/loss recognition and the basis of stock received appears later in the chapter.

Section 351 is *mandatory* if a transaction satisfies the provision's requirements. There are three requirements for nonrecognition of gain or loss: (1) *property* is transferred (2) in exchange for *stock* and (3) the transferors must be in *control* of the transferee corporation immediately after the transfer. These three requirements are discussed next.

12-2b Transfer of Property

Questions have arisen concerning what constitutes **property** for purposes of § 351. The Code specifically excludes services rendered from the definition of property. With this exception, the definition of property is comprehensive. For example, along with plant and equipment, unrealized receivables held by a cash basis taxpayer and installment notes are considered property.[4] The transfer of an installment note in a transaction qualifying under § 351 is not a disposition of the installment note. Thus, gain is not recognized to the transferor. Proprietary processes and formulas as well as proprietary information in the general nature of a patentable invention also qualify as property under § 351.[5]

As demonstrated below, a taxpayer must report as income the fair market value of any consideration received as compensation for services because § 351 specifically excludes services from the definition of property.[6] Thus, if a taxpayer receives stock as consideration for rendering services to the corporation, the taxpayer recognizes ordinary income. In this case, the amount of income recognized by the taxpayer is equal to the fair market value of the stock received. As a consequence, the taxpayer's basis in the stock received is its fair market value.

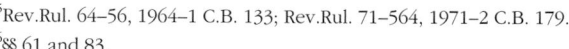

[2]Rev.Rul. 68–55, 1968–1 C.B. 140.

[3]§ 358(a). See the discussion preceding Example 29.

[4]*Hempt Brothers, Inc. v. U.S.*, 74–1 USTC ¶9188, 33 AFTR 2d 74–570, 490 F.2d 1172 (CA–3, 1974), and Reg. § 1.453–9(c)(2).

[5]Rev.Rul. 64–56, 1964–1 C.B. 133; Rev.Rul. 71–564, 1971–2 C.B. 179.

[6]§§ 61 and 83.

Concept Summary 12.2

Shareholder Consequences: Taxable Corporate Formation versus Tax-Deferred § 351 Transaction

Ann and Bob form Brown Corporation and transfer the following consideration:

	Consideration Transferred		
	Basis to Transferor	**Fair Market Value**	**Number of Shares Issued**
From Ann:			
Personal services rendered to Brown Corporation	$ –0–	$20,000	200
From Bob:			
Installment note receivable	5,000	40,000	
Inventory	10,000	30,000	800
Proprietary process	–0–	10,000	

The value of each share in Brown Corporation is $100.[7] Ann has ordinary income of $20,000 on the transfer because services do not qualify as "property." She has a basis of $20,000 in her 200 shares of stock in Brown (i.e., Ann is treated as having bought some of the Brown stock by rendering services). Bob recognizes no gain on the transfer because all of the consideration he transferred to Brown qualifies as "property" and he has "control" of Brown after the transfer. (See the discussion concerning control on the next page.) Bob has a substituted basis of $15,000 in the Brown stock.

As mentioned earlier, if property is transferred to a corporation in exchange for any property other than stock, the property received constitutes boot. The boot is taxable to the transferor-shareholder to the extent of any realized gain.[8]

---

[7]The value of closely held stock normally is presumed to be equal to the value of the property transferred.

[8]§ 351(b).

12-2c **Stock**

Generally, the term *stock* needs no clarification. It includes common stock and most preferred stock. However, the Regulations state that the term *stock* does not include stock rights and stock warrants.[9] In addition, it does not include "nonqualified preferred stock," which possesses many of the attributes of debt.[10]

Thus, any corporate debt or securities (i.e., long-term debt such as bonds) are treated as boot because they do not qualify as stock. Therefore, the receipt of debt in exchange for the transfer of appreciated property to a controlled corporation causes recognition of gain.

The Big Picture

Return to the facts of *The Big Picture* on p. 12-1. Assume that the proposed transaction qualifies under § 351, but Amber decides to receive some corporate debt along with the stock.

If Amber receives Garden stock worth $900,000 and Garden debt of $100,000 in exchange for the property transferred, Amber realizes a gain of $600,000 [$1,000,000 (value of consideration received) − $400,000 (basis in the transferred property)]. However, because the transaction qualifies under § 351, only $100,000 of the gain is recognized (this is because the $100,000 of Garden debt is treated as boot). The remaining realized gain of $500,000 is deferred.

12-2d **Control of the Corporation**

For a transaction to qualify as nontaxable under § 351, the transferor(s) of the property must be in control of the corporation immediately after the exchange. That is, the person or persons transferring *property* must have at least an 80 percent stock ownership in the corporation, resulting in the entity being a controlled corporation. The property transferors must own stock possessing at least 80 percent of the total combined voting power of all classes of stock entitled to vote *and* at least 80 percent of the total *number* of shares of all other classes of stock.[11]

Control Immediately after the Transfer

Control after the exchange can apply to a single person or to several taxpayers if they are all parties to an integrated transaction. To satisfy the timing requirement, the Regulations provide that when more than one person is involved, the exchange does not necessarily require simultaneous exchanges by two or more persons. The Regulations do, however, require that the rights of the parties (i.e., those transferring property to the corporation) be previously set out and determined. Also, the agreement to transfer property should be executed "with an expedition consistent with orderly procedure," and the transfers should occur close together in time.[12]

The Point at Which Control Is Determined

Jack exchanges property with a basis of $60,000 and a fair market value of $100,000 for 70% of the stock of Gray Corporation. The other 30% is owned by Jane, who acquired it several years ago. The fair market value of Jack's stock is $100,000.

Jack recognizes a taxable gain of $40,000 on the transfer because he does not have control immediately after the exchange and his transaction cannot be integrated with Jane's for purposes of the control requirement.

---

[9]Reg. § 1.351–1(a)(1)(ii).

[10]§ 351(g). Examples of nonqualified preferred stock include preferred stock that is redeemable within 20 years of issuance and whose dividend rate is based on factors other than corporate performance. See also Reg. § 1.351–1(a)(1)(ii).

[11]§ 368(c). Nonqualified preferred stock is treated as stock, not boot, for purposes of this control test.

[12]Reg. § 1.351–1(a)(1).

The Point at Which Control Is Determined

EXAMPLE 12

Lana, Leo, and Lori incorporate their respective businesses by forming Green Corporation. Lana exchanges her property for 300 shares in Green on January 7, 2016. Leo exchanges his property for 400 shares in Green on January 14, 2016, and Lori exchanges her property for 300 shares in Green on March 5, 2016.

The three exchanges are part of a prearranged plan, so the control requirement is met. The nonrecognition provisions of § 351 apply to all of the exchanges.

Stock need not be issued to the property transferors in the same proportion as the relative value of the property transferred by each. However, when stock received is not proportionate to the value of the property transferred, the actual effect of the transaction must be properly characterized. For example, in such situations, one transferor may actually be making a gift to another transferor.

EXAMPLE 13

Ron and Shelia, father and daughter, form Oak Corporation. Ron transfers property worth $50,000 in exchange for 100 shares of stock, while Shelia transfers property worth $50,000 for 400 shares of stock.

The transfers qualify under § 351 because Ron and Shelia have control of the Oak stock immediately after the transfers of property. However, the implicit gift of 150 shares by Ron to Shelia must be recognized and appropriately characterized. As such, the value of the gift might be subject to the gift tax.

Once control has been achieved, it is not necessarily lost if, shortly after the transaction, stock received by shareholders in a § 351 exchange is sold or given to persons who are not parties to the exchange.[13]

EXAMPLE 14

Mark and Carl form Black Corporation. They transfer appreciated property to the corporation with each receiving 50 shares of Black stock. Shortly after the formation, Mark gives 25 shares to his son.

Because Mark was not committed to making the gift, he is considered to own his original shares of Black Corporation stock and, along with Carl, to control Black Corporation "immediately after the exchange." The requirements of § 351 are met, and neither Mark nor Carl is taxed on the exchange.

A different result might materialize if a plan for the ultimate disposition of the stock existed *before* the exchange.

EXAMPLE 15

Assume the same facts as in Example 14, except that Mark immediately gives 25 shares to a business associate pursuant to a plan to satisfy an outstanding obligation.

In this case, the formation of Black would be taxable to Mark and Carl because of their lack of control (i.e., Mark and Carl, the property transferors, would have owned only 75% of the stock).

---

[13] *Wilgard Realty Co. v. Comm.*, 42–1 USTC ¶9452, 29 AFTR 325, 127 F.2d 514 (CA–2, 1942).

TAX PLANNING STRATEGIES Utilizing § 351

FRAMEWORK FOCUS: INCOME AND EXCLUSIONS

Strategy: Avoid Income Recognition.

When using § 351, ensure that all parties transferring property (including cash) receive control of the corporation. Simultaneous transfers are not necessary, but a long period of time between transfers makes the transaction vulnerable to taxation if the transfers are not properly documented as part of a single plan. To do this, the parties should document and preserve evidence of their intentions. Also, it is helpful to have some reasonable explanation for any delay in the transfers.

To meet the requirements of § 351, mere momentary control on the part of the transferor may not suffice if loss of control is compelled by a prearranged agreement.[14]

EXAMPLE 16

For many years, Todd operated a business as a sole proprietor employing Linda as manager. To dissuade Linda from quitting and going out on her own, Todd promised her a 30% interest in the business. To fulfill this promise, Todd transferred the business to newly formed Green Corporation in return for all of its stock. Immediately thereafter, Todd transfers 30% of the stock to Linda. As a consequence, he no longer meets the 80% control requirement. Section 351 probably does not apply to Todd's transfer to Green Corporation. It appears that Todd was under an obligation to relinquish control. If this preexisting obligation exists, § 351 will not be available to Todd because, as the sole property transferor, he does not have 80% control of Green Corporation. If there is no obligation and the loss of control was voluntary on Todd's part, momentary control would suffice.[15]

Make sure that later transfers of property to an existing corporation satisfy the 80 percent control requirement if recognition of gain is to be avoided. Also with respect to later transfers, a transferor's interest cannot be counted if the value of stock received is relatively small compared with the value of stock already owned. Further, the primary purpose of the transfer may not be to qualify other transferors for § 351 treatment.[16] (For a complete discussion of this issue, see "Transfers to Existing Corporations" on p. 12-15).

For contributions of property by a partner to a partnership, at formation or subsequent to formation, § 721 is available to provide nonrecognition treatment. This partnership provision generally resembles § 351. However, in such situations, any partner can make a tax-deferred contribution without regard to a control test. Thus, the 80 percent control requirement, which serves as a high threshold to be met if tax-deferred treatment is desired in a corporate setting, contrasts to the treatment given in partnership taxation where no such control test applies. See Chapters 14 and 18 for additional discussion.

Transfers for Property and Services

Section 351 treatment is lost if stock is transferred to persons who did not contribute property, causing those who did to lack control immediately after the exchange.

The Big Picture

EXAMPLE 17

Return to the facts of *The Big Picture* on p. 12-1. Assume that Amber transfers her $1,000,000 of property to Garden, Inc., and receives 50% of its stock. Jimmy receives the other 50% of the stock for services rendered (worth $1,000,000).

Both Amber and Jimmy have tax consequences from the transfers. Jimmy has ordinary income of $1,000,000 because he does not exchange property for stock. Amber has a taxable gain of $600,000 [$1,000,000 (fair market value of the stock in Garden) − $400,000 (basis in the transferred property)]. As the sole transferor of property, she receives only 50% of Garden's stock.

---

[14]Rev.Rul. 54–96, 1954–1 C.B. 111.

[15]Compare *Fahs v. Florida Machine and Foundry Co.*, 48–2 USTC ¶9329, 36 AFTR 1161, 168 F.2d 957 (CA–5, 1948), with *John C. O'Connor*, 16 TCM

213, T.C.Memo. 1957–50, *aff'd* in 58–2 USTC ¶9913, 2 AFTR 2d 6011, 260 F.2d 358 (CA–6, 1958).

[16]Reg. § 1.351–1(a)(1)(ii).

As noted earlier, a person receiving stock in exchange for services and for property transferred is taxed on the stock value related to those services but not on the stock issued for property. In addition, such a person can still be treated as a "property transferor" and in such a case, all stock received by the person transferring both property and services is counted in determining whether the transferors acquired control of the corporation.[17]

The Big Picture

EXAMPLE 18

Assume the same facts as in Example 17, except that Jimmy transfers property worth $800,000 (basis of $260,000) in addition to services rendered to Garden, Inc. (valued at $200,000).

Now Jimmy becomes a part of the control group. Amber and Jimmy, as property transferors, together receive 100% of the corporation's stock. Consequently, § 351 is applicable to the exchanges. Amber has no recognized gain. Jimmy does not recognize gain on the transfer of the property, but he recognizes ordinary income to the extent of the value of the shares issued for services rendered. Thus, Jimmy recognizes $200,000 of ordinary income currently.

Transfers for Services and Nominal Property

Note that to be part of the group meeting the 80 percent control test, the person contributing services must transfer property having more than a "relatively small value" compared with the value of services performed. Section 351 will not apply when a small amount of property is transferred and the primary purpose of the transfer is to qualify the transaction under § 351 for concurrent transferors.[18]

The IRS generally requires that before a transferor who receives stock for both property and services can be included in the control group, the value of the property transferred must be at least 10 percent of the value of the services provided.[19] If the value of the property transferred is less than this amount, the IRS will not issue an advance ruling that the exchange meets the requirements of § 351.

Determining Control Group Membership When Services Are Rendered

EXAMPLE 19

Sara and Rick form Grouse Corporation. Sara transfers land (worth $100,000, basis of $20,000) for 50% of the stock in Grouse. Rick transfers equipment (worth $50,000, adjusted basis of $10,000) and provides services worth $50,000 for 50% of the stock.

Because the value of the property Rick transfers is not small relative to the value of the services he renders, his stock in Grouse Corporation is counted in determining control for purposes of § 351; thus, the transferors own 100% of the stock in Grouse. In addition, all of Rick's stock, not just the shares received for the equipment, is counted in determining control.

As a result, Sara does not recognize gain on the transfer of the land. Rick, however, must recognize income of $50,000 on the transfer of services. Even though the transfer of the equipment qualifies under § 351, his transfer of services for stock does not.

EXAMPLE 20

Assume the same facts as in Example 19, except that the value of Rick's property is $2,000 and the value of his services is $98,000.

In this situation, the value of the property is small relative to the value of the services (and well below the 10% threshold provided by the IRS); therefore, Rick will not be considered a property transferor. Consequently, the control requirement is not met and the transaction is fully taxable to both Sara and Rick. None of Rick's stock is counted in determining control because the property he transfers has a nominal value in comparison to the value of the services he renders.

As a result, Sara recognizes $80,000 of gain on the transfer of the land. She has a basis of $100,000 in her Grouse stock. Rick must recognize income of $98,000 on the transfer for services rendered, and any realized gain or loss is recognized on the property transferred. Rick also has a $100,000 basis in his Grouse stock.

---

[17]Reg. § 1.351–1(a)(2), Ex. 3.

[18]Reg. § 1.351–1(a)(1)(ii).

[19]Rev.Proc. 77–37, 1977–2 C.B. 568.

Transfers to Existing Corporations

Once a corporation is in operation, § 351 also applies to any later transfers of property for stock by either new or existing shareholders.

> **EXAMPLE**
> **21**
>
> Sam and Beth formed Blue Corporation three years ago. Both Sam and Beth transferred appreciated property to Blue in exchange for 500 shares each in the corporation. The original transfers qualified under § 351, and neither Sam nor Beth was taxed on the exchange. In the current year, Sam transfers property (worth $100,000, adjusted basis of $5,000) for 500 additional Blue shares.
>
> Sam has a taxable gain of $95,000 on the transfer. The exchange does not qualify under § 351 because Sam does not have 80% control of Blue Corporation immediately after the transfer; he owns 1,000 shares of the 1,500 shares outstanding, or a 66²/₃% interest.

If current shareholders transfer property with a small value relative to the value of stock already owned, a special rule applies (similar to the nominal property rule noted previously). In particular, if the purpose of the transfer is to qualify a transaction under § 351, the ownership of the current shareholders is not counted when determining control. Thus, in the preceding example, if Beth had contributed $200 for one share of stock at the time of Sam's contribution, Beth's ownership would not have counted toward the 80 percent control requirement and Sam would still have had a taxable exchange.

12-2e Assumption of Liabilities—§ 357

LO.3

Describe the special rules that apply when a corporation assumes a shareholder's liability.

Without a provision to the contrary, the transfer of mortgaged property to a controlled corporation could require recognition of gain by the transferor if the corporation took over the mortgage. This would be consistent with the treatment given in like-kind exchanges under § 1031. Liabilities assumed by the other party are considered the equivalent of cash and treated as boot received. Section 357(a) provides, however, that when the acquiring corporation assumes a liability in a § 351 transaction, the liability is not treated as boot received for gain recognition purposes. Nevertheless, liabilities assumed by the transferee corporation are treated as boot in determining the basis of the stock received. As a result, the basis of the stock received is reduced by the amount of the liabilities assumed by the corporation.

> **The Big Picture**
>
> **EXAMPLE**
> **22**
>
> Return to the facts of *The Big Picture* on p. 12-1. Assume that you learn that Amber's husband, Jimmy, becomes disinterested in becoming a stockholder in Garden, Inc., and that Amber's building is subject to a liability of $70,000 that Garden assumes. Consequently, Amber receives 100% of the Garden stock and is relieved of the $70,000 liability in exchange for property with an adjusted basis of $400,000 and fair market value of $1,000,000.
>
> The exchange is tax-free under § 351 because the release of a liability is not treated as boot under § 357(a). However, the basis to Amber of the Garden stock is $330,000 [$400,000 (basis of property transferred) − $70,000 (amount of the liability assumed by Garden)].

The general rule of § 357(a) has two exceptions: (1) § 357(b) provides that if the principal purpose of the assumption of the liabilities is to avoid tax *or* if there is no bona fide business purpose behind the exchange, the liabilities are treated as boot; (2) § 357(c) provides that if the sum of the liabilities exceeds the adjusted basis of the properties transferred, the excess is taxable gain.

Exception (1): Tax Avoidance or No Bona Fide Business Purpose

Satisfying the bona fide business purpose under § 357(b) is not difficult if the liabilities are incurred in connection with the transferor's normal course of conducting a trade or business. But the bona fide business purpose requirement can cause difficulty if the

GLOBAL TAX ISSUES   Does § 351 Cover the Incorporation of a Foreign Business?

When a taxpayer wants to incorporate a business overseas by moving assets across U.S. borders, the deferral mechanism of § 351 applies in certain situations, but not in others. In general, § 351 is available to defer gain recognition when starting up a new corporation outside the United States unless so-called tainted assets are involved. Under § 367, tainted assets, which include assets such as inventory and accounts receivable, are treated as having been sold by the taxpayer prior to the corporate formation; therefore, their transfer results in the current recognition of gain. The presence of tainted assets triggers gain because Congress does not want taxpayers to be able to shift the gain outside U.S. jurisdiction. The gain recognized is ordinary or capital depending on the nature of the asset involved.

liability is taken out shortly before the property is transferred and the proceeds are utilized for personal purposes.[20] This type of situation is analogous to a cash distribution by the corporation, which is taxed as boot.

EXAMPLE 23

Dan transfers real estate (basis of $140,000 and fair market value of $190,000) to a controlled corporation in return for stock in the corporation. Shortly before the transfer, Dan mortgages the real estate and uses the $20,000 of proceeds to meet personal obligations. Thus, along with the real estate, the mortgage is transferred to the corporation. In this case, the assumption of the mortgage lacks a bona fide business purpose. Consequently, the release of the liability is treated as boot received, and Dan has a taxable gain on the transfer of $20,000, computed as follows:[21]

Stock	$ 170,000
Release of liability—treated as boot	20,000
Total amount realized	$ 190,000
Less: Basis of real estate	(140,000)
Realized gain	$ 50,000
Recognized gain	$ 20,000

The effect of the application of § 357(b) is to taint *all* liabilities transferred, even if *some* are supported by a bona fide business purpose.

EXAMPLE 24

Tim, an accrual basis taxpayer, incorporates his sole proprietorship. Among the liabilities transferred to the new corporation are trade accounts payable of $100,000 and a credit card bill of $5,000. Tim had used the credit card to purchase an anniversary gift for his wife. Under these circumstances, the *entire* $105,000 of liabilities is boot and triggers the recognition of gain to the extent gain is realized.

Exception (2): Liabilities in Excess of Basis

Section 357(c) states that if the amount of a shareholder's liabilities assumed *exceeds* the total of the adjusted bases of the properties transferred by that shareholder, the excess is taxable gain. Without this provision, if liabilities exceed the basis in the property exchanged, a taxpayer would have a negative basis in the stock received in the controlled corporation.[22] Section 357(c) precludes the negative basis possibility by treating the excess over basis as gain to the transferor.

---

[20]See, for example, *Campbell, Jr. v. Wheeler*, 65–1 USTC ¶9294, 15 AFTR 2d 578, 342 F.2d 837 (CA–5, 1965).

[21]§ 351(b).

[22]*Jack L. Easson*, 33 T.C. 963 (1960), *rev'd* in 61–2 USTC ¶9654, 8 AFTR 2d 5448, 294 F.2d 653 (CA–9, 1961).

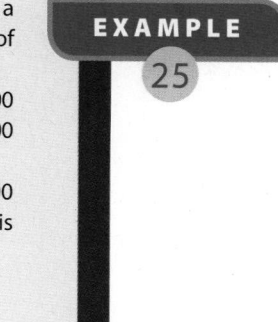

Andre transfers land and equipment with adjusted bases of $350,000 and $50,000, respectively, to a newly formed corporation in exchange for 100% of the stock. The corporation assumes $500,000 of liabilities on the transferred land.

Without § 357(c), Andre's basis in the stock of the new corporation would be negative $100,000 [$400,000 (bases of properties transferred) + $0 (gain recognized) − $0 (boot received) − $500,000 (liabilities assumed)].

Section 357(c), however, causes Andre to recognize gain of $100,000 ($500,000 liabilities assumed − $400,000 bases of assets transferred). As a result, the stock has a zero basis in Andre's hands, determined as follows:

Bases in the properties transferred ($350,000 + $50,000)	$ 400,000
Plus: Gain recognized	100,000
Less: Boot received	(–0–)
Less: Liabilities assumed	(500,000)
Basis in the stock received	$ –0–

Thus, Andre recognizes $100,000 of gain, and a negative stock basis is avoided.

The definition of liabilities under § 357(c) excludes obligations that would have been deductible to the transferor had those obligations been paid before the transfer. Thus, accounts payable of a cash basis taxpayer that give rise to a deduction are not considered liabilities for purposes of § 357(c). In addition, they are not considered in the computation of the shareholder's stock basis.

Tina, a cash basis taxpayer, incorporates her sole proprietorship. In return for all of the stock of the new corporation, she transfers the following items:

	Adjusted Basis	Fair Market Value
Cash	$10,000	$10,000
Unrealized accounts receivable (amounts due to Tina but not yet received by her)	–0–	40,000
Trade accounts payable	–0–	30,000
Note payable	5,000	5,000

Unrealized accounts receivable and trade accounts payable have a zero basis. Under the cash method of accounting, no income is recognized until the receivables are collected and no deduction materializes until the payables are satisfied. The note payable has a basis because it was issued for consideration received.

In this situation, the trade accounts payable are disregarded for gain recognition purposes and for the determination of Tina's stock basis. Thus, because the balance of the note payable does not exceed the basis of the assets transferred, Tina does not have a problem of liabilities in excess of basis (i.e., the note payable of $5,000 does not exceed the aggregate basis in the cash and accounts receivable of $10,000).

If §§ 357(b) and (c) both apply to the same transfer, § 357(b) dominates.[23] This could be significant because § 357(b) does not create gain on the transfer, as does § 357(c), but merely converts the liability to boot. Thus, the realized gain limitation continues to apply to § 357(b) transactions.

Chris owns land with a basis of $100,000 and a fair market value of $1 million. The land is subject to a mortgage of $300,000. One month prior to transferring the land to Robin Corporation, Chris borrows an additional $200,000 for personal purposes and gives the lender a second mortgage on the land. Therefore, upon the incorporation, Robin Corporation issues stock worth $500,000 to Chris and assumes the mortgages on the land.

continued

---

[23]§ 357(c)(2)(A).

Both § 357(b) and § 357(c) apply to the transfer. The mortgages on the property exceed the basis of the property. Thus, Chris has a gain of $400,000 under § 357(c). Chris borrowed $200,000 just prior to the transfer and used the loan proceeds for personal purposes. Under § 357(b), Chris has boot of $500,000 in the amount of the liabilities, which triggers $500,000 of recognized gain. Note that *all* of the liabilities are treated as boot, not just the "tainted" $200,000 liability.

	§ 357(b) Result	§ 357(c) Result
Amount realized:		
Robin Corporation stock	$ 500,000	$ 500,000
Release of mortgage on land	300,000	300,000
Release of second mortgage—personal purposes	200,000	200,000
Total amount realized	$1,000,000	$1,000,000
Basis of land	(100,000)	(100,000)
Realized gain	$ 900,000	$ 900,000
Gain recognized under § 357(b) ($300,000 + $200,000)	$ 500,000	
Gain recognized under § 357(c) [($300,000 + $200,000) − $100,000]		$ 400,000

Unfortunately for Chris, the relatively more onerous rule of § 357(b) dominates over § 357(c), requiring Chris to recognize a $500,000 gain.

Concept Summary 12.3 summarizes the tax rules that apply when liabilities are transferred in property transactions, including the special rules that apply in § 351 transactions.

Concept Summary 12.3

Tax Consequences of Liability Assumption

Property
FMV $100,000, basis $40,000

Taxpayer

Debt Relief

Red Corporation Stock

Red Corporation

General rule: (§ 1001)	If Red Corporation takes property subject to Taxpayer's liability or assumes Taxpayer's liability, Taxpayer is treated as having received cash due to the debt relief. Therefore, if the liability is $20,000, Taxpayer is treated as receiving Red stock of $80,000 and cash of $20,000 in a fully taxable transaction. Gain realized and recognized is $60,000.
Special rule in a § 351 transaction: [§ 357(a)]	Assume the same facts as above, except that the transfer is a § 351 transaction. Taxpayer is not treated as receiving cash of $20,000 for gain recognition purposes (the debt relief is *not* treated as boot). Therefore, gain recognition is avoided. The debt relief will, however, reduce the Taxpayer's basis in Red Corporation stock.
Exception to § 351 transaction rule—Tax avoidance or no bona fide business purpose: [§ 357(b)]	Assume the same facts as above, except that the transfer is a § 351 transaction and the liability does *not* have a business purpose. Taxpayer is treated as receiving cash of $20,000 for gain recognition purposes (the debt relief *is* treated as boot). Therefore, $20,000 of the realized gain is recognized.
Exception to § 351 transaction rule—Liabilities in excess of basis: [§ 357(c)]	Assume the same facts as above, except that the transfer is a § 351 transaction, the liability is $45,000, the Red stock is worth $55,000, and § 357(b) does not apply. Taxpayer recognizes a $5,000 gain (excess of $45,000 liability over $40,000 property basis).

TAX PLANNING STRATEGIES Avoiding § 351

FRAMEWORK FOCUS: TAX RATE

Strategy: Shift Net Income from High-Bracket Years to Low-Bracket Years.
Control the Character of Income and Deductions.

Section 351(a) provides for the nonrecognition of gain on transfers to controlled corporations. As such, it is often regarded as a relief provision favoring taxpayers. In some situations, however, avoiding § 351(a) may produce a more advantageous tax result. The transferors might prefer to recognize gain on the transfer of property if the tax cost is low. For example, they may be in low tax brackets, or the gain may be a capital gain that could be neutralized by available capital losses. Also, recognition of gain will lead to a stepped-up basis in the transferred property in the corporation.

Another reason a particular transferor might want to avoid § 351 concerns possible loss recognition. Recall that § 351 refers to the nonrecognition of both gains and losses. Section 351(b)(2) specifically states: "No loss to such recipient shall be recognized." A transferor who wants to recognize loss has several alternatives:

- Sell the property to the corporation for its stock. The IRS could attempt to collapse the "sale," however, by taking the approach that the transfer really falls under § 351(a).[24]

- Sell the property to the corporation for other property or boot. Because the transferor receives no stock, § 351 is inapplicable.

- Transfer the property to the corporation in return for securities or nonqualified preferred stock. Recall that § 351 does not apply to a transferor who receives securities or nonqualified preferred stock. In both this and the previous alternatives, watch for the possible disallowance of the loss under the related-party rules.

Suppose loss property is to be transferred to the corporation and no loss is recognized by the transferor due to § 351(a). This could present an interesting problem in terms of assessing the economic realities involved.

EXAMPLE 28

Iris and Ivan form Wren Corporation with the following investments: property by Iris (basis of $40,000 and fair market value of $50,000) and property by Ivan (basis of $60,000 and fair market value of $50,000). Each receives 50% of the Wren stock. Has Ivan acted wisely in settling for only 50% of the stock? At first, it would appear so because Iris and Ivan each invested property of the same value ($50,000). But what about tax considerations? By applying the general carryover basis rules, the corporation now has a basis of $40,000 in Iris's property and $60,000 in Ivan's property. In essence, Iris has shifted a possible $10,000 gain to the corporation while Ivan has transferred a $10,000 potential loss. Thus, an equitable allocation of the Wren stock would call for Ivan to receive a greater percentage interest than Iris would receive.

This issue is further complicated by the special basis adjustment required when a shareholder such as Ivan contributes property with a built-in loss to a corporation. (See the discussion of this basis adjustment for loss property in the next section.) In this situation, if Wren is to take a carryover basis in Ivan's property, Ivan must reduce his stock basis by the $10,000 built-in loss. This reduced stock basis, of course, could lead to a greater tax burden on Ivan when he sells the Wren stock. This may suggest additional support for Ivan having a greater percentage interest than Iris has.

12-2f **Basis Determination and Other Issues**

Recall that § 351(a) postpones gain or loss recognition until the taxpayer's investment changes substantively. By virtue of the basis rules described next, the postponed gain or loss is recognized when the stock is disposed of in a taxable transaction.

LO.4

Identify the basis issues relevant to the shareholder and the corporation.

---

[24]*U.S. v. Hertwig,* 68–2 USTC ¶9495, 22 AFTR 2d 5249, 398 F.2d 452 (CA–5, 1968).

EXHIBIT 12.2	Shareholder's Basis of Stock Received in Exchange for Property

Adjusted basis of property transferred	$xx,xxx
Plus: Gain recognized	xxx
Minus: Boot received (including any liabilities transferred)	(xxx)
Minus: Adjustment for loss property (if elected)	(xxx)
Equals: Basis of stock received	$xx,xxx

Basis of Stock to Shareholder

For a taxpayer transferring property to a corporation in a § 351 transaction, the basis of *stock* received in the transaction is the same as the basis the taxpayer had in the property transferred, increased by any gain recognized on the exchange of property and decreased by boot received. For basis purposes, boot received includes liabilities transferred by the shareholder to the corporation. Also note that if the shareholder receives *other property* (i.e., boot) along with the stock, that property takes a basis equal to its fair market value.[25] In Exhibit 12.2, the reference to gain recognized does not consider any income resulting from the performance of personal services. See the discussion that follows relating to an elective stock basis reduction that may be taken when a shareholder contributes property with a net built-in loss.

Basis of Property to Corporation

The basis of property received by the corporation generally is the basis of the exchanged property in the hands of the transferor increased by the amount of any gain recognized on the transfer by the transferor-shareholder.[26]

These basis rules are illustrated in Examples 29 and 30.

Calculating Basis: Shareholder Stock and Corporate Property

EXAMPLE 29

Maria and Ned form Brown Corporation. Maria transfers land (basis of $30,000 and fair market value of $70,000); Ned invests cash ($60,000). They each receive 50 shares in Brown Corporation, worth $1,200 per share, but Maria also receives $10,000 of cash from Brown. The transfers of property, the realized and recognized gain on the transfers, and the basis of the stock in Brown Corporation to Maria and Ned are as follows:

	A	B	C	D	E	F
	Basis of Property Transferred	FMV of Stock Received	Boot Received	Realized Gain (B + C − A)	Recognized Gain (Lesser of C or D)	Basis of Stock in Brown (A − C + E)
From Maria:						
Land	$30,000	$60,000	$10,000	$40,000	$10,000	$30,000
From Ned:						
Cash	60,000	60,000	–0–	–0–	–0–	60,000

Brown Corporation has a basis of $40,000 in the land (Maria's basis of $30,000 plus her recognized gain of $10,000).

---

[25]§ 358(a). Recall from earlier discussions that the basis of stock received for services equals its fair market value.

[26]§ 362(a).

Calculating Basis: Shareholder Stock and Corporate Property

Assume the same facts as in Example 29, except that Maria's basis in the land is $68,000 (instead of $30,000). Because recognized gain cannot exceed realized gain, the transfer generates only $2,000 of gain to Maria. The realized and recognized gain and the basis of the stock in Brown Corporation to Maria are as follows:

EXAMPLE 30

	A	B	C	D	E	F
	Basis of Property Transferred	FMV of Stock Received	Boot Received	Realized Gain (B + C − A)	Recognized Gain (Lesser of C or D)	Basis of Stock in Brown (A − C + E)
Land	$68,000	$60,000	$10,000	$2,000	$2,000	$60,000

Brown's basis in the land is $70,000 ($68,000 basis to Maria + $2,000 gain recognized by Maria).

Exhibit 12.3 summarizes the basis calculation for property received by a corporation. Concept Summary 12.4 shows the shareholder and corporate consequences of a transfer of property to a corporation for stock, with and without the application of § 351. The facts applicable to shareholder Maria's transfer in Example 29 are used to illustrate the differences between the transaction being tax-deferred and taxable.

EXHIBIT 12.3	Corporation's Basis in Property Received
Adjusted basis of property transferred	$xx,xxx
Plus: Gain recognized by transferor-shareholder	xxx
Minus: Adjustment for loss property (if required)	(xxx)
Equals: Basis of property to corporation	$xx,xxx

Concept Summary 12.4

Tax Consequences to the Shareholders and Corporation: With and Without the Application of § 351 (Based on the Facts of Example 29)

	With § 351			Without § 351		
Shareholder	Gain/Loss Recognized	Stock Basis	Other Property Basis	Gain/Loss Recognized	Stock Basis	Other Property Basis
Maria	Realized gain recognized to extent of boot received; loss not recognized.	Substituted (see Exhibit 12.2).	FMV	All realized gain or loss recognized.	FMV	FMV
	$10,000	$30,000	$10,000	$40,000	$60,000	$10,000

	With § 351		Without § 351	
Corporation	Gain/Loss Recognized	Property Basis	Gain/Loss Recognized	Property Basis
Brown	No gain or loss recognized on the transfer of corporate stock for property.	Carryover (see Exhibit 12.3).	No gain or loss recognized on the transfer of corporate stock for property.	FMV
	$0	$40,000	$0	$70,000

Note that the benefit to Maria of deferring $30,000 of gain under § 351 comes with a cost: her stock basis is $30,000 (rather than $60,000), and the corporation's basis in the property received is $40,000 (rather than $70,000).

Basis Adjustment for Loss Property

A corporation's basis for property received in a § 351 transaction is carried over from the shareholder. As a result, the corporation's basis has no correlation to the property's fair market value. However, in certain situations when **built-in loss property** is contributed to a corporation, the aggregate basis of the assets transferred by a shareholder exceeds their fair market value. When this built-in loss situation exists, an anti-loss duplication rule requires the basis in the loss properties to be stepped down by allocating the built-in loss propor-tionately among the assets.[27] This basis adjustment is necessary to prevent the parties from obtaining a double benefit from the losses involved.

EXAMPLE

31

In a transaction qualifying under § 351, Charles transfers the following assets to Gold Corporation in exchange for all of its stock:

	Tax Basis	Fair Market Value	Built-In Gain/(Loss)
Equipment	$100,000	$ 90,000	($10,000)
Land	200,000	230,000	30,000
Building	150,000	100,000	(50,000)
	$450,000	$420,000	($30,000)

Charles's stock basis is $450,000 [$450,000 (basis of the property transferred) + $0 (gain recognized) − $0 (boot received)]. However, Gold's basis for the loss assets transferred must be reduced by the amount of the net built-in loss ($30,000) in proportion to each asset's share of the loss.

	Unadjusted Tax Basis	Adjustment	Adjusted Tax Basis
Equipment	$100,000	($ 5,000)*	$ 95,000
Land	200,000		200,000
Building	150,000	(25,000)**	125,000
	$450,000	($30,000)	$420,000

* $\dfrac{\$10,000 \text{ (loss attributable to equipment)}}{\$60,000 \text{ (total built-in loss)}} \times \$30,000 \text{ (net built-in loss)} = \$5,000 \text{ (adjustment to basis in equipment)}.$

** $\dfrac{\$50,000 \text{ (loss attributable to building)}}{\$60,000 \text{ (total built-in loss)}} \times \$30,000 \text{ (net built-in loss)} = \$25,000 \text{ (adjustment to basis in building)}.$

Note the end result of Example 31:

- Charles still has a built-in loss in his stock basis. Thus, if he sells the Gold Corpora-tion stock, he will recognize a loss of $30,000 [$420,000 (selling price based on presumed value of the stock) − $450,000 (basis in the stock)].

- Gold Corporation can no longer recognize a loss on the sale of *all* of its assets [$420,000 (selling price based on value of assets) − $420,000 (adjusted basis in assets) = $0 (gain or loss)].

In the event a corporation is subject to the built-in loss adjustment, an alternative approach is available. If both the shareholder and the corporation elect, the basis reduction can be made to the shareholder's stock rather than to the corporation's property.

---

[27]§ 362(e)(2). This adjustment is determined separately with respect to each property transferor. This adjustment also is required in the case of a contribu-tion to capital by a shareholder.

Assume the same facts as in the previous example. If Charles and Gold elect, Charles can reduce his stock basis to $420,000 ($450,000 − $30,000). As a result, Gold's aggregate basis in the assets it receives is $450,000. If Charles has no intention of selling his stock, this election could be desirable as it benefits Gold by giving the corporation a higher depreciable basis in the equipment and building.

EXAMPLE 32

Note the end result of Example 32:

- Charles has no built-in loss. Thus, if he sells the Gold Corporation stock, he will recognize no gain or loss [$420,000 (presumed value of the stock) − $420,000 (basis in the stock)].

- Gold Corporation has a built-in loss. Thus, if it sells *all* of its assets [$420,000 (selling price based on value of assets) − $450,000 (basis in assets)], it recognizes a loss of $30,000.

Consequently, as shown in the two previous examples, the built-in loss adjustment places the loss with either the shareholder or the corporation but not both.

Stock Issued for Services Rendered

A corporation's transfer of its stock for property is not a taxable exchange.[28] A transfer of shares for services is also not a taxable transaction to a corporation.[29] But another issue arises: Can a corporation deduct as a business expense the fair market value of the stock it issues in consideration of services? Yes, unless the services are such that the payment is characterized as a capital expenditure.[30]

The Big Picture

EXAMPLE 33

Return to the facts of *The Big Picture* on p. 12-1. Amber transfers her $1,000,000 of property to Garden, Inc., and receives 50% of the stock. In addition, assume that Jimmy transfers property worth $800,000 (basis of $260,000) and agrees to serve as manager of the corporation for one year (services worth $200,000) for 50% of the stock.

Amber's and Jimmy's transfers qualify under § 351. Neither Amber nor Jimmy is taxed on the transfer of his or her property. However, Jimmy has income of $200,000, the value of the services he will render to Garden, Inc. Garden has a basis of $260,000 in the property it acquired from Jimmy, and it may claim a compensation expense deduction under § 162 for $200,000. Jimmy's stock basis is $460,000 [$260,000 (basis of property transferred) + $200,000 (income recognized for services rendered)].

The Big Picture

EXAMPLE 34

Assume in the preceding example that Jimmy receives the Garden stock as consideration for the appreciated property and for providing legal services in organizing the corporation. The value of Jimmy's legal services is $200,000.

Jimmy has no gain on the transfer of the property but has income of $200,000 for the value of the services rendered. Garden, Inc., has a basis of $260,000 in the property it acquired from Jimmy and must capitalize the $200,000 as an organizational expenditure. Jimmy's stock basis is $460,000 [$260,000 (basis of property transferred) + $200,000 (income recognized for services rendered)].

Holding Period for Shareholder and Transferee Corporation

The shareholder's holding period for stock received for a capital asset or for § 1231 property includes the holding period of the property transferred to the corporation. The holding period of the property is *tacked on* to the holding period of the stock. The holding period for stock received for any other property (e.g., inventory) begins on the day after the exchange. The transferee corporation's holding period for property acquired in a § 351 transfer is the holding period of the transferor-shareholder regardless of the character of the property to the transferor. For instance, whether the

---

[28]§ 1032.

[29]Reg. § 1.1032–1(a).

[30]Rev.Rul. 62–217, 1962–2 C.B. 59, modified by Rev.Rul. 74–503, 1974–2 C.B. 117.

property transferred is an ordinary asset (e.g., inventory), a § 1231 asset, or a capital asset, the corporation's holding period is the same as the transferor's.[31]

12-2g Recapture Considerations

In a § 351 nontaxable transfer (no boot involved) to a controlled corporation, the depreciation recapture rules do not apply.[32] Instead, any recapture potential of the property carries over to the corporation as it steps into the shoes of the transferor-shareholder for purposes of basis determination. However, to the extent gain is recognized, the recapture rules are applied.

EXAMPLE 35

Paul transfers equipment (adjusted basis of $30,000, original cost of $120,000, and fair market value of $100,000) to a controlled corporation in return for stock. If Paul had sold the equipment, it would have yielded a gain of $70,000, all of which would have been treated as ordinary income under the § 1245 depreciation recapture rules.

If the transfer comes within § 351, Paul has no recognized gain and no depreciation to recapture. If the corporation later disposes of the equipment in a taxable transaction, it must take into account the § 1245 recapture potential originating with Paul. So, for example, if the corporation were to sell the asset shortly after incorporation for $100,000, all of the $70,000 gain recognized would be given ordinary treatment because of the depreciation recapture rules.

Alternatively, if Paul had received boot of $60,000 on the transfer, all of the recognized gain would have been recaptured as ordinary income. The remaining $30,000 ($90,000 − $60,000) of recapture potential would have carried over to the corporation.

TAX PLANNING STRATEGIES Other Considerations When Incorporating a Business

FRAMEWORK FOCUS: TAX RATE

Strategy: Control the Character of Income and Deductions.
Shift Net Income from High-Bracket Taxpayers to Low-Bracket Taxpayers.

FRAMEWORK FOCUS: DEDUCTIONS

Strategy: Maximize Deductible Amounts.

FRAMEWORK FOCUS: INCOME AND EXCLUSIONS

Strategy: Avoid Income Recognition.

When a business is incorporated, the organizers must determine which assets and liabilities should be transferred to the corporation. A transfer of assets that produce passive income (rents, royalties, dividends, and interest) can cause the corporation to be a personal holding company in a tax year when operating income is low. Thus, the corporation could be subject to the personal holding company penalty tax (see the discussion in Chapter 13).

A transfer of the accounts payable of a cash basis taxpayer may prevent the organizer from taking a tax deduction if the accounts are paid by the corporation. Therefore, the parties should decide who will receive the greatest benefit from the deduction and then plan accordingly.

Leasing property to the corporation may be a more attractive alternative than transferring ownership. Leasing provides the taxpayer with the opportunity of withdrawing money from the corporation in a deductible form without the payment being characterized as a nondeductible dividend. If the property is donated to a family member in a lower tax bracket, the lease income can be shifted as well. If the depreciation and other deductions available in connection with the property are larger than the lease income, a high-tax-rate taxpayer could retain the property until the income exceeds the deductions.

continued

[31]§§ 1223(1) and (2).

[32]§§ 1245(b)(3) and 1250(d)(3).

The Big Picture

EXAMPLE
36

Return to the facts of *The Big Picture* on p. 12-1. If Amber decides to retain the $50,000 of cash basis accounts receivable rather than transfer them to the newly formed Garden, Inc., she will recognize $50,000 of ordinary income upon their collection.

Alternatively, if the receivables are transferred to Garden as the facts suggest, the corporation will recognize the ordinary income. However, a subsequent corporate distribution to Amber of the cash collected could be subject to double taxation as a dividend (see Chapter 13 for further discussion). Given the alternatives available, Amber needs to evaluate which approach is better for the parties involved.

Another way to shift income to other taxpayers is by the use of corporate debt. Shareholder debt in a corporation can be given to family members with low marginal tax rates. This technique also shifts income without a loss of control of the corporation.

12-3 CAPITAL STRUCTURE OF A CORPORATION

LO.5

Explain the tax aspects of the capital structure of a corporation.

When forming or expanding a corporation, the transaction can be financed with capital contributions or debt proceeds or a combination of the two. Evaluating the relative advantages and disadvantages of these two basic elements in the capital structure of a corporation can involve various considerations, including the tax aspects of each.

12-3a Capital Contributions

When money or property is received in exchange for capital stock (including treasury stock), the corporation does not recognize any gain or loss.[33] Also, it does not include in gross income any shareholders' contributions of money or property to the capital of the corporation or through voluntary pro rata transfers. This is the case even though there is no increase in the number of outstanding shares of stock of the corporation. The payments represent an additional price paid for the shares held by the shareholders (increasing their basis) and are treated as additions to the operating capital of the corporation.[34]

Contributions by nonshareholders, such as land contributed to a corporation by a civic group or a governmental group to induce the corporation to locate in a particular community, are also excluded from the gross income of a corporation.[35] However, property that is transferred to a corporation by a nonshareholder in exchange for goods or services rendered is taxable income to the corporation.[36]

EXAMPLE
37

A cable company charges its customers an initial fee to hook up to a new cable system installed in the area. These payments are used to finance the total cost of constructing the cable company's infrastructure. The customers will make monthly payments for the cable service. The initial payments are used for capital expenditures, but they represent payments for services to be rendered by the cable company. As such, they are taxable income and not contributions to capital by nonshareholders.

The basis of property received by a corporation from a shareholder as a **capital contribution** is equal to the basis of the property in the hands of the shareholder, although the basis may be subject to a downward adjustment when loss property is

---

[33]§ 1032.

[34]§ 118 and Reg. § 1.118–1.

[35]See *Edwards v. Cuba Railroad Co.*, 1 USTC ¶139, 5 AFTR 5398, 45 S.Ct. 614 (USSC, 1925).

[36]Reg. § 1.118–1. See also *Teleservice Co. of Wyoming Valley*, 27 T.C. 722 (1957), *aff'd* in 58–1 USTC ¶9383, 1 AFTR 2d 1249, 254 F.2d 105 (CA–3, 1958), *cert. den.* 78 S.Ct. 1360 (USSC, 1958).

contributed. The basis of property transferred to a corporation by a nonshareholder as a contribution to capital is zero.

If a corporation receives *money* as a contribution to capital from a nonshareholder, a special rule applies. The basis of any property acquired with the money during a 12-month period beginning on the day the contribution was received is reduced by the amount of the cash contribution. The excess of money received over the cost of new property is used to reduce the basis of other property held by the corporation and is applied in the following order:

1. Depreciable property.
2. Property subject to amortization.
3. Property subject to depletion.
4. All other remaining properties.

The basis of property within each category is reduced in proportion to the relative bases of the properties.[37]

EXAMPLE 38

A city donates land worth $400,000 to Cardinal Corporation as an inducement for Cardinal to locate in the city. The receipt of the land produces no taxable income to Cardinal, and the land's basis to the corporation is zero. If, in addition, the city gives the corporation $100,000 in cash, the money is not taxable income to the corporation. However, if the corporation purchases property with the $100,000 in cash within the next 12 months, the basis of the property is reduced by $100,000. Any excess cash that is retained and not used by Cardinal is handled according to the ordering rules noted previously. So, for example, if Cardinal purchases only $70,000 of property during the following year, the basis of Cardinal's other depreciable property is reduced by $30,000.

LO.6

Characterize the tax differences between debt and equity investments.

12-3b **Debt in the Capital Structure**

Various tax and nontax considerations are relevant when developing the capital structure of a corporation. The relative amounts of debt and equity and their characteristics are of primary importance.

Advantages of Debt

Significant tax differences exist between debt and equity in the capital structure, and shareholders must be aware of these differences. The advantages of issuing long-term

---

[37]§ 362(c); Reg. §§ 1.362–2(b) and 1.118–1.

debt are numerous. Interest on debt is deductible by the corporation, while dividend payments are not. Further, the shareholders are not taxed on debt repayments unless the repayments exceed basis. An investment in stock usually cannot be withdrawn tax-free as long as a corporation has earnings and profits. Withdrawals will be deemed to be taxable dividends to the extent of earnings and profits of the distributing corporation. (The concept of earnings and profits is discussed in Chapter 13.)

Another distinction between debt and equity relates to the taxation of dividend and interest income. Dividend income on equity holdings is taxed to individual investors at the low capital gains rates, while interest income on debt is taxed at the higher ordinary income rates.

EXAMPLE 39

Wade transfers cash of $100,000 to a newly formed corporation for 100% of the stock. In the first year of operations, the corporation has net income of $40,000. If the corporation distributes $7,500 to Wade, the distribution is a taxable dividend with no corresponding deduction to the corporation.

Assume, instead, that Wade transfers to the corporation cash of $50,000 for stock. In addition, he lends the corporation $50,000. The note is payable in equal annual installments of $5,000 and bears interest at the rate of 5%. At the end of the year, the corporation pays Wade interest of $2,500 ($50,000 × 5%) and a note repayment of $5,000. The interest payment is taxable to Wade and a deductible expense to the corporation. The $5,000 principal repayment on the loan is neither taxed to Wade nor deductible by the corporation. Based on the tax rates as noted, the after-tax impact to Wade and the corporation under each alternative is illustrated below.

	If the Distribution Is	
	$7,500 Dividend	$5,000 Note Repayment and $2,500 Interest
After-tax benefit to Wade*		
[$7,500 × (1 − 15%)]	$6,375	
{$5,000 + [$2,500 × (1 − 35%)]}		$6,625
After-tax cost to corporation**		
No deduction to corporation	$7,500	
{$5,000 + [$2,500 × (1 − 35%)]}		$6,625

* Assumes that Wade's dividend income is taxed at the 15% capital gains rate and that his interest income is taxed at the 35% ordinary income rate.

** Assumes that the corporation is in the 35% marginal tax bracket.

Reclassification of Debt as Equity (Thin Capitalization Problem)

In situations where the corporation is said to be thinly capitalized, the IRS contends that debt is an equity interest and denies the corporation the tax advantages of debt financing. Thin capitalization occurs when shareholder debt is high relative to shareholder equity. If a debt instrument has too many features of stock, it may be treated as a form of stock by the IRS. As a result, the principal and interest payments are considered dividends. Under § 385, the IRS has the authority to characterize corporate debt wholly as equity or as part debt and part equity. In the current environment, however, the IRS may be less inclined to raise the thin capitalization issue because the conversion of interest income to dividend income would produce a tax benefit to individual investors.

For the most part, the principles used to classify debt as equity developed in connection with closely held corporations where the holders of the debt are often shareholders. The rules have often proved inadequate for dealing with large, publicly traded corporations.

Section 385 lists several factors that *may* be used to determine whether a debtor-creditor relationship or a shareholder-corporation relationship exists. The thrust of § 385 is to authorize the Treasury to prescribe Regulations that provide more definite guidelines for determining when debt should be reclassified as equity. To date, the Treasury Department has not drafted final Regulations. Consequently, taxpayers must rely on judicial decisions to determine whether a true debtor-creditor relationship exists.

TAX IN THE NEWS A Careful Evaluation May Be Required to Distinguish Debt from Equity

While the tax advantages of debt over equity may be clear (i.e., interest payments on debt are deductible but dividend payments on capital contributions are not), being able to distinguish debt from equity may not be as obvious. In arm's-length, market-based transactions between unrelated parties, the debt versus equity question most likely would never arise. However, the difficulty of distinguishing debt and equity is particularly acute in situations where the parties involved are closely connected or related. To assist taxpayers in distinguishing debt financing and equity financing, the courts have developed a number of factors (noted below) to be considered in such an analysis.

In *NA General Partnership & Subsidiaries* (103 TCM 1916, T.C.Memo. 2012–172), the Tax Court evaluated the nature of

advances made by a parent entity to NA General Partnership & Subsidiaries (treated as a corporation for Federal tax purposes) in light of the court-developed factors. The court noted that the substance of a transaction is controlling, and not merely its form, and that none of the factors is decisive but they should be considered in light of the facts and circumstances of the case.

Based on an exhaustive evaluation of 11 factors in the taxpayer's situation, the court concluded that the advances were debt. Happily for the taxpayer, the court's decision paved the way for $932 million of payments to be treated as deductible interest rather than nondeductible dividend payments.

The courts have identified the following factors to be considered when classifying a security as debt or equity:

- Whether the debt instrument is in proper form. An open account advance is more easily characterized as a contribution to capital than a loan evidenced by a properly written note executed by the shareholder.[38]

- Whether the debt instrument bears a reasonable rate of interest and has a definite maturity date. When a shareholder advance does not provide for interest, the return expected is that inherent in an equity interest (e.g., a share of the profits or an increase in the value of the shares).[39] Likewise, a lender unrelated to the corporation will usually be unwilling to commit funds to the corporation for an indefinite period of time (i.e., no definite due date).

- Whether the debt is paid on a timely basis. A lender's failure to insist upon timely repayment (or satisfactory renegotiation) indicates that the return sought does not depend upon interest income and the repayment of principal.

- Whether payment is contingent upon earnings. A lender ordinarily will not advance funds that are likely to be repaid only if the venture is successful.

- Whether the debt is subordinated to other liabilities. Subordination tends to eliminate a significant characteristic of the creditor-debtor relationship. Creditors should have the right to share with other general creditors in the event of the corporation's dissolution or liquidation. Subordination also destroys another basic attribute of creditor status—the power to demand payment at a fixed maturity date.[40]

- Whether holdings of debt and stock are proportionate (e.g., each shareholder owns the same percentages of debt and stock). When debt and equity obligations are held in the same proportion, shareholders are, apart from tax considerations, indifferent as to whether corporate distributions are in the form of interest or dividends.

- Whether funds loaned to the corporation are used to finance initial operations or capital asset acquisitions. Funds used to finance initial operations or to acquire capital assets the corporation needs to operate are generally obtained through equity investments.

[38]*Estate of Mixon, Jr. v. U.S.*, 72–2 USTC ¶9537, 30 AFTR 2d 72–5094, 464 F.2d 394 (CA–5, 1972).

[39]*Slappey Drive Industrial Park v. U.S.*, 77–2 USTC ¶9696, 40 AFTR 2d 77–5940, 561 F.2d 572 (CA–5, 1977).

[40]*Fin Hay Realty Co. v. U.S.*, 68–2 USTC ¶9438, 22 AFTR 2d 5004, 398 F.2d 694 (CA–3, 1968).

- Whether the corporation has a high ratio of shareholder debt to shareholder equity. Thin capitalization indicates that the corporation lacks reserves to pay interest and principal on debt when corporate income is insufficient to meet current needs.[41] In determining a corporation's debt-equity ratio, courts look at the relation of the debt both to the book value of the corporation's assets and to their actual fair market value.[42]

Section 385 also authorizes the Treasury to issue Regulations classifying an instrument as *wholly* debt or equity or as *part* debt and *part* equity. This flexible approach is important because some instruments cannot readily be classified either wholly as stock or wholly as debt. It may also provide an avenue for the IRS to address problems in publicly traded corporations.

12-4 CORPORATE OPERATIONS

LO.7

List and apply the tax rules unique to corporations.

The rules related to gross income, deductions, and losses discussed in previous chapters of this text generally apply to corporations. In a few instances, it was noted that corporations face unique limitations such as the 10 percent of taxable income limitation for charitable contributions and the limitation allowing corporate capital losses to be deductible only against capital gains. Corporations also are permitted some deductions not generally available to other entities. These special deductions and other special rules regarding the determination of the corporate income tax liability are discussed in the following pages.

12-4a Deductions Available Only to Corporations

Certain deductions are specific to corporate taxpayers. These provisions include the dividends received deduction and the organizational expenditures deduction.

Dividends Received Deduction

The purpose of the **dividends received deduction** is to mitigate multiple taxation of corporate income. Without the deduction, dividends paid between corporations could be subject to several levels of tax. For example, if Corporation A pays Corporation B a dividend and B passes the dividend on to its shareholders, the dividend is taxed at three levels: Corporation A, Corporation B, and Corporation B's shareholders. The dividends received deduction alleviates this inequity by limiting or eliminating the amount of dividend income taxable to corporations.

As Exhibit 12.4 illustrates, the amount of the dividends received deduction depends on the percentage of ownership (voting power and value) the recipient corporate shareholder holds in a *domestic corporation* making the dividend distribution.[43]

The dividends received deduction cannot exceed the taxable income limitation. This limitation is equal to the corporation's taxable income multiplied by the percentage that corresponds with the deduction percentage. Thus, if a corporate shareholder owns less

EXHIBIT 12.4	Dividends Received Deduction

Percentage of Ownership by Corporate Shareholder	Deduction Percentage
Less than 20%	70%
20% or more (but less than 80%)	80%
80% or more*	100%

* The payor corporation must be a member of an affiliated group with the recipient corporation.

---

[41]A court held that a debt-equity ratio of approximately 14.6:1 was not excessive. See *Tomlinson v. 1661 Corp.*, 67–1 USTC ¶9438, 19 AFTR 2d 1413, 377 F.2d 291 (CA–5, 1967). A 26:1 ratio was found acceptable in *Delta Plastics, Inc.*, 85 TCM 940, T.C.Memo. 2003–54.

[42]In *Bauer v. Comm.*, 84–2 USTC ¶9996, 55 AFTR 2d 85–433, 748 F.2d 1365 (CA–9, 1984), a debt-equity ratio of 92:1 resulted when book value was

used. But the ratio ranged from 2:1 to 8:1 when equity included both paid-in capital and accumulated earnings.

[43]§ 243(a). Dividends from foreign corporations generally do not qualify for a dividends received deduction. But see § 245.

than 20 percent of the stock in the distributing corporation, the dividends received deduction is limited to 70 percent of taxable income. For this purpose, taxable income is computed without regard to the net operating loss (NOL) deduction, the domestic production activities deduction, the dividends received deduction, and any capital loss carryback. However, the taxable income limitation does not apply if the corporation has an NOL for the current taxable year.[44]

The following steps are useful in the computation of the deduction:

1. Multiply the dividends received by the deduction percentage.
2. Multiply the taxable income by the deduction percentage.
3. The deduction is limited to the lesser of Step 1 or Step 2, unless deducting the amount derived in Step 1 results in an NOL. If it does, the amount derived in Step 1 is used. This is referred to as the *NOL rule*.

EXAMPLE 40

Red, White, and Blue Corporations, three unrelated calendar year corporations, report the following information for the year:

	Red Corporation	White Corporation	Blue Corporation
Gross income from operations	$ 400,000	$ 320,000	$ 260,000
Expenses from operations	(340,000)	(340,000)	(340,000)
Dividends received from domestic corporations (less than 20% ownership)	200,000	200,000	200,000
Taxable income before the dividends received deduction	$ 260,000	$ 180,000	$ 120,000

In determining the dividends received deduction, use the three-step procedure described above.

Step 1 (70% × $200,000)	$140,000	$140,000	$140,000
Step 2			
70% × $260,000 (taxable income)	$182,000		
70% × $180,000 (taxable income)		$126,000	
70% × $120,000 (taxable income)			$ 84,000
Step 3			
Lesser of Step 1 or Step 2	$140,000	$126,000	
Step 1 amount results in an NOL			$140,000

White Corporation is subject to the 70% of taxable income limitation (Step 2). The NOL rule does not apply because subtracting $140,000 (Step 1) from $180,000 (taxable income before the dividends received deduction) does not yield a negative figure. Blue Corporation qualifies under the NOL rule because subtracting $140,000 (Step 1) from $120,000 (taxable income before the dividends received deduction) yields a negative figure.

In summary, each corporation has a dividends received deduction for the year as follows: $140,000 for Red Corporation, $126,000 for White Corporation, and $140,000 for Blue Corporation.

No dividends received deduction is allowed unless the corporation has held the stock for more than 45 days.[45] This restriction was enacted to close a tax loophole involving dividends on stock that is held only briefly. When stock is purchased shortly before a dividend record date and soon thereafter sold ex-dividend, a capital loss corresponding to the amount of the dividend often results (ignoring other market valuation changes). If the dividends received deduction was allowed in such cases, the capital loss resulting from the stock sale would exceed the taxable portion of the related dividend income.

---

[44]Further, the limitation does not apply in the case of the 100% deduction available to members of an affiliated group. § 246(b)(2).

[45]The stock must be held more than 45 days during the 91-day period beginning on the date that is 45 days before the ex-dividend date (or in the case of preferred stock, more than 90 days during the 181-day period beginning on the date that is 90 days before the ex-dividend date). § 246(c).

EXAMPLE 41

On October 1, 2016, Pink Corporation declares a $1 per share dividend for shareholders of record as of November 1, 2016, and payable on December 1, 2016. Black Corporation purchases 10,000 shares of Pink stock on October 28, 2016, for $25,000 and sells those 10,000 shares ex-dividend on November 4, 2016, for $15,000. (It is assumed that there is no fluctuation in the market price of the Pink stock other than the dividend element.) The sale results in a short-term capital loss of $10,000 ($15,000 amount realized − $25,000 basis). On December 1, Black receives a $10,000 dividend from Pink.

Without the holding period restriction, Black Corporation would recognize a $10,000 deduction (subject to the capital loss limitation) but only $3,000 of income [$10,000 dividend − $7,000 dividends received deduction ($10,000 × 70%)], or a $7,000 net loss. However, because Black did not hold the Pink stock for more than 45 days, no dividends received deduction is allowed.

In-depth coverage can be found on this book's companion website: www.cengagebrain.com

2 DIGGING DEEPER

Organizational Expenditures Deduction

Expenses incurred in connection with the organization of a corporation normally are chargeable to a capital account. That they benefit the corporation during its existence seems clear. But over what period should organizational expenses be amortized? The lack of a determinable and limited estimated useful life makes such a determination difficult. Section 248 was enacted to solve this problem.

Under § 248, a corporation may *elect* to amortize **organizational expenditures** over the 180-month period beginning with the month in which the corporation begins business.[46] Organizational expenditures include:

- Legal services incident to organization (e.g., drafting the corporate charter and bylaws, minutes of organizational meetings, and terms of original stock certificates).

- Necessary accounting services.

- Expenses of temporary directors and of organizational meetings of directors or shareholders.

- Fees paid to the state of incorporation.

Expenditures that *do not qualify* as organizational expenditures include those connected with issuing or selling shares of stock or other securities (e.g., commissions, professional fees, and printing costs) or with transferring assets to a corporation. These expenditures reduce the amount of capital raised and are not deductible.

The first $5,000 of organizational costs is immediately expensed, with any remaining amount of organizational costs amortized over a 180-month period. However, the $5,000 expensing amount is phased out on a dollar-for-dollar basis when these costs exceed $50,000.

EXAMPLE 42

Stork Corporation (a calendar year C corporation) began business on July 1 of the current year and incurred $52,000 of organizational expenditures. Stork wants to expense as much of these expenditures as possible, electing to amortize any amount it cannot expense. Stork's current year deduction is $4,633, determined as follows:

Immediate expense [$5,000 − ($52,000 − $50,000)]	$3,000
Amortization [($52,000 − $3,000) ÷ 180] × 6 months in tax year	1,633
Total	$4,633

To qualify for the election, the expenditure must be *incurred* before the end of the tax year in which the corporation begins business. In this regard, the corporation's method of

---

[46]The month in which a corporation begins business may not be immediately apparent. Ordinarily, a corporation begins business when it starts the business operations for which it was organized. Reg. § 1.248–1(d). For a similar problem in the Subchapter S area, see Chapter 15.

accounting is of no consequence. Thus, an expense incurred by a cash basis corporation in its first tax year qualifies even though the expense is not paid until a subsequent year.

A corporation is deemed to have made the election to amortize organizational expenditures for the taxable year in which it begins business. No separate statement or specific identification of the deducted amount as organizational expenditures is required. A corporation can elect to forgo the deemed election by clearly electing to capitalize organizational expenditures on a timely filed return for its first taxable year. In that case, the capitalized amount will be deductible by the corporation at such time as it ceases to do business and liquidates.

EXAMPLE 43

Black Corporation, an accrual basis, calendar year taxpayer, was formed and began operations on April 1, 2016. The following expenses were incurred during its first year of operations (April 1–December 31, 2016):

Expenses of temporary directors and of organizational meetings	$15,500
Fee paid to the state of incorporation	2,000
Accounting services incident to organization	18,000
Legal services for drafting the corporate charter and bylaws	32,000
Expenses incident to the printing and sale of stock certificates	48,000

Black Corporation elects to amortize the $67,500 of organizational costs under § 248. Because of the dollar cap (i.e., dollar-for-dollar reduction for amounts in excess of $50,000), none of the $5,000 expensing allowance is available. The monthly amortization is $375 [($15,500 + $2,000 + $18,000 + $32,000) ÷ 180 months], and $3,375 ($375 × 9 months) is deductible for tax year 2016.

Note that the $48,000 of expenses incident to the printing and sale of stock certificates does not qualify for the election. These expenses cannot be deducted. Instead, they reduce the amount of the capital realized from the sale of stock.

Organizational expenditures are distinguished from *startup expenditures*.[47] Startup expenditures include various investigation expenses involved in entering a new business (e.g., travel, market surveys, financial audits, and legal fees) and operating expenses such as rent and payroll that are incurred by a corporation before it actually begins to produce any gross income. At the election of the taxpayer, such expenditures are deductible in the same manner as organizational expenditures. Thus, up to $5,000 can be immediately expensed (subject to the phaseout) and any remaining amounts amortized over a period of 180 months. The same rules that apply to the deemed election (and election to forgo the deemed election) for organizational expenditures also apply to startup expenditures.

TAX PLANNING STRATEGIES   **Organizational Expenditures**

FRAMEWORK FOCUS: DEDUCTIONS

Strategy: Maximize Deductible Amounts.

To qualify for the 180-month amortization procedure of § 248, only organizational expenditures incurred in the first taxable year of the corporation can be considered. This rule could prove to be an unfortunate trap for corporations formed late in the year.

EXAMPLE 44

Thrush Corporation is formed in December 2016. Qualified organizational expenditures are incurred as follows: $62,000 in December 2016 and $30,000 in January 2017. If Thrush uses the calendar year for tax purposes, only $62,000 of the organizational expenditures qualify for amortization.

One solution to the problem posed by this example may be for Thrush Corporation to adopt a fiscal year that ends on or beyond January 31. All organizational expenditures will then have been incurred before the close of the first tax year. Alternatively, the corporation could wait until January 2017 to be formed.

---

[47]§ 195.

12-4b **Determining the Corporate Income Tax Liability**

Corporate income tax rates have fluctuated over the years. The current top statutory corporate income tax rate was reduced from 46 percent to 35 percent in 1986. Current U.S. corporate income tax rates are presented in Exhibit 12.1. Unlike the individual income tax rate brackets, the corporate income tax brackets are *not* indexed for inflation.

LO.8

Compute the corporate income tax.

The Big Picture

Return to the facts of *The Big Picture* on p. 12-1. Assume that Amber incorporates her business as a calendar year C corporation, and that it has taxable income of $51,500. The corporation's income tax liability is $7,875, determined as follows:

Tax on $50,000 at 15%	$7,500
Tax on $1,500 at 25%	375
Tax liability	$7,875

EXAMPLE

45

For taxable income in excess of $100,000, the amount of the tax is increased by the lesser of (1) 5 percent of the excess or (2) $11,750. In effect, the additional tax means a 39 percent rate for every dollar of taxable income from $100,000 to $335,000.

Silver Corporation, a calendar year taxpayer, has taxable income of $335,000 for the current year. Its income tax liability is $113,900, determined as follows:

Tax on $100,000	$ 22,250
Tax on $235,000 × 39%	91,650
Tax liability	$113,900

Note that the tax liability of $113,900 is 34% of $335,000. Thus, due to the 39% rate (34% normal rate + 5% additional tax on taxable income between $100,000 and $335,000), the benefit of the lower rates on the first $75,000 of taxable income completely phases out at $335,000. The tax rate drops back to 34% on taxable income between $335,000 and $10 million.

EXAMPLE

46

Section 11(b)(2) provides that qualified **personal service corporations (PSCs)** are taxed at a flat 35 percent rate on all taxable income. Thus, PSCs do not enjoy the tax savings of the 15 percent to 34 percent brackets applicable to other corporations. For this purpose, a PSC is a corporation that is substantially employee-owned. Also, it must engage in one of the following activities: health, law, engineering, architecture, accounting, actuarial science, performing arts, or consulting.

12-4c **Tax Liability of Related Corporations**

Members of a **controlled group** of corporations (related corporations) are subject to special rules for computing the income tax, the AMT exemption, and the § 179 election to expense certain depreciable assets.[48] If these restrictions did not exist, the shareholders of a corporation could gain significant tax advantages by splitting a single corporation into *multiple* corporations. The next two examples illustrate the potential *income tax* advantage of multiple corporations.

LO.9

Explain the rules unique to computing the tax of related corporations.

---

[48]§§ 1561(a) and 179(d)(6).

Tax Savings from Multiple Corporations

EXAMPLE 47

Gray Corporation annually yields taxable income of $300,000. The corporate tax on $300,000 is $100,250, computed as follows:

Tax on $100,000	$ 22,250
Tax on $200,000 × 39%	78,000
Tax liability	$100,250

EXAMPLE 48

Assume that Gray Corporation in the previous example is divided equally into four corporations. Each corporation would have taxable income of $75,000, and the tax for each (absent the special provisions for related corporations) would be computed as follows:

Tax on $50,000	$ 7,500
Tax on $25,000 × 25%	6,250
Tax liability	$13,750

The total liability for the four corporations would be $55,000 ($13,750 × 4). Consequently, the savings would be $45,250 ($100,250 − $55,000).

To preclude the advantages that could be gained by using multiple corporations, the tax law requires special treatment for *controlled groups* of corporations. A comparison of Examples 47 and 48 reveals that the income tax savings that could be achieved by using multiple corporations result from having more of the total taxable income taxed at lower marginal rates. To close this potential loophole, the law limits a controlled group's taxable income in the tax brackets below 35 percent to the amount the corporations in the group would have if they were one corporation. Thus, in Example 48, under the controlled corporation rules, only $12,500 (one-fourth of the first $50,000 of taxable income) for each of the four related corporations would be taxed at the 15 percent rate. The 25 percent rate would apply to the next $6,250 (one-fourth of the next $25,000) of taxable income of each corporation. This equal allocation of the $50,000 and $25,000 amounts is required unless all members of the controlled group consent to an apportionment plan providing for an unequal allocation.

Similar limitations apply to controlled groups with respect to the § 179 expense election (see Chapter 5) and to the $40,000 AMT exemption amount (see Chapter 17).

12-4d **Controlled Groups**

A controlled group of corporations includes parent-subsidiary groups, brother-sister groups, combined groups, and certain insurance companies. Parent-subsidiary controlled groups are discussed in the following section.

Parent-Subsidiary Controlled Group

A **parent-subsidiary controlled group** consists of one or more *chains* of corporations connected through stock ownership with a common parent corporation. The ownership connection can be established through either a *voting power test* or a *value test*. The voting power test requires ownership of stock possessing at least 80 percent of the total voting power of all classes of stock entitled to vote. The value test requires ownership of at least 80 percent of the total value of all shares of all classes of stock of each of the corporations, except the parent corporation, by one or more of the other corporations.[49]

---

[49]§ 1563(a)(1).

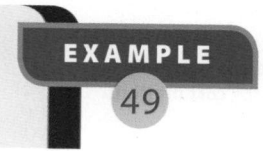

Aqua Corporation owns 80% of White Corporation. Aqua and White Corporations are members of a parent-subsidiary controlled group. Aqua is the parent corporation, and White is the subsidiary.

EXAMPLE 49

The parent-subsidiary relationship described in Example 49 is easy to recognize because Aqua Corporation is the direct owner of White Corporation. Real-world business organizations are often more complex, sometimes including numerous corporations with chains of ownership connecting them. In these complex corporate structures, determining whether the controlled group classification is appropriate becomes more difficult. The ownership requirements can be met through direct ownership (refer to Example 49) or through indirect ownership, as illustrated in the following example.

Red Corporation owns 80% of the voting stock of White Corporation, and White Corporation owns 80% of the voting stock of Blue Corporation.

Red, White, and Blue Corporations constitute a controlled group in which Red is the common parent and White and Blue are subsidiaries. This parent-subsidiary relationship is diagrammed in Exhibit 12.5. The same result would occur if Red Corporation, rather than White Corporation, owned the Blue Corporation stock.

EXAMPLE 50

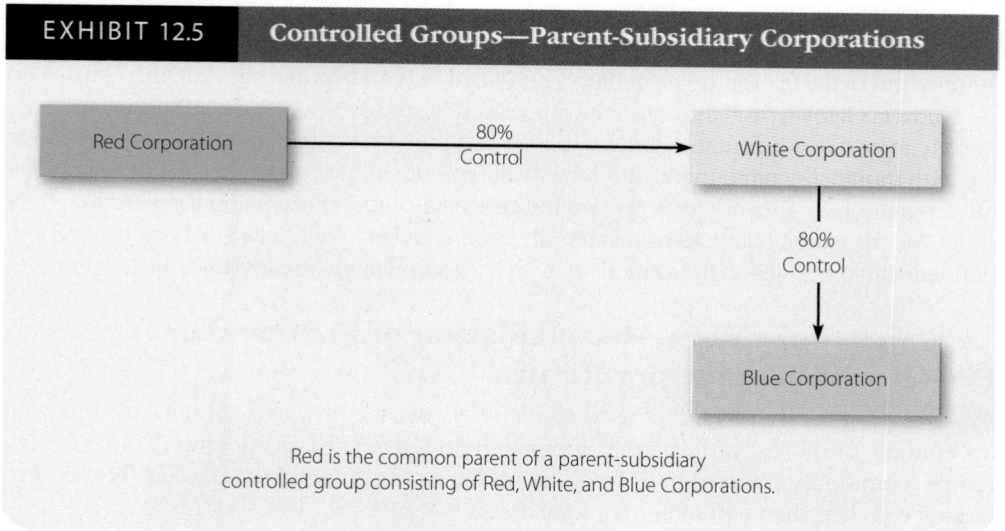

EXHIBIT 12.5   Controlled Groups—Parent-Subsidiary Corporations

Red is the common parent of a parent-subsidiary
controlled group consisting of Red, White, and Blue Corporations.

In-depth coverage can be found on this book's companion website: **www.cengagebrain.com**   **3 DIGGING DEEPER**

Application of § 482

Congress has recognized that a parent corporation has the power to shift income among its subsidiaries. Likewise, shareholders who control other related groups of corporations can shift income and deductions among the related corporations.

When the true taxable income of a subsidiary or other related corporation has been understated or overstated, the IRS can reallocate the income and deductions of the related corporations under § 482. Section 482 permits the IRS to allocate gross income, deductions, and credits between any two or more organizations, trades, or businesses that are owned or controlled by the same interests. This is appropriate when the allocation is necessary to prevent avoidance of taxes or to reflect income correctly. Controlled groups of corporations, especially multinational corporations, are particularly vulnerable to § 482.

LO.10

Describe the reporting process for corporations.

12-5 PROCEDURAL MATTERS

This section covers various aspects of the corporate income tax return, including filing requirements, estimated tax payments, and special disclosure schedules on the return.

12-5a Filing Requirements for Corporations

A corporation must file a Federal income tax return (Form 1120) whether or not it has taxable income. A corporation that was not in existence throughout an entire annual accounting period is required to file a return for the portion of the year during which it was in existence. In addition, a corporation must file a return even though it has ceased to do business if it has valuable claims for which it will bring suit. A corporation is relieved of filing income tax returns only when it ceases to do business and retains no assets.[50]

A Form 1120 must be filed on or before the fifteenth day of the fourth month following the close of a corporation's tax year.[51] Corporations with assets of $10 million or more generally are required to file electronically. A C corporation, other than a PSC, can use either a calendar year or a fiscal year to report its taxable income. The tax year of the shareholders has no effect on the corporation's tax year.

12-5b Estimated Tax Payments

A corporation must make payments of estimated tax unless its tax liability can reasonably be expected to be less than $500. The required annual payment (which includes any estimated AMT liability) is the *lesser* of (1) 100 percent of the corporation's tax for the current year or (2) 100 percent of the tax for the preceding year (if that was a 12-month tax year, the return filed showed a tax liability, and the corporation involved is not a *large corporation*). Estimated payments can be made in four installments due on or before the fifteenth day of the fourth month, the sixth month, the ninth month, and the twelfth month of the corporate taxable year.[52] The full amount of the unpaid tax is due on the due date of the return without regard to extensions. A corporation failing to pay its required estimated tax payments will be subjected to a nondeductible penalty on the amount by which the installments are less than the tax due.

12-5c Schedule M–1—Reconciliation of Income (Loss) per Books with Income per Return

Schedule M–1 of Form 1120 is used to *reconcile* net income as computed for financial accounting purposes with taxable income reported on the corporation's income tax return (commonly referred to as book-tax differences). Schedule M–1 is used by corporations with less than $10 million of total assets.

The starting point on Schedule M–1 is net income (loss) per books. Additions and subtractions are entered for items that affect financial accounting net income and taxable income differently. The following items are entered as additions (see lines 2 through 5 of Schedule M–1):

- Federal income tax expense per books (deducted in computing net income per books but not deductible in computing taxable income).

- The excess of capital losses over capital gains (deducted for financial accounting purposes but not deductible by corporations for income tax purposes).

- Income that is reported in the current year for tax purposes but is not reported in computing net income per books (e.g., prepaid income).

- Various expenses that are deducted in computing net income per books but are not deducted in computing taxable income (e.g., charitable contributions in excess of the 10 percent ceiling applicable to corporations).

[50]§ 6012(a)(2) and Reg. § 1.6012–2(a).

[51]§ 6072(a). Previously, the due date was the fifteenth day of the third month following the close of the corporation's tax year. In general, the new due date is effective for tax years beginning after 2015.

[52]§ 6655. If the due date falls on a Saturday, Sunday, or legal holiday, the due date is the next business day. See § 6655(g)(2) for the definition of a *large corporation*.

The following subtractions are entered on lines 7 and 8 of Schedule M–1:

- Income reported for financial accounting purposes but not included in taxable income (e.g., tax-exempt interest).
- Deductions taken on the tax return but not expensed in computing net income per books (e.g., domestic production activities deduction).

The result is taxable income (before the NOL deduction and the dividends received deduction). Concept Summary 12.5 provides a conceptual diagram of Schedule M–1.

Concept Summary 12.5

Conceptual Diagram of Schedule M–1 (Form 1120)

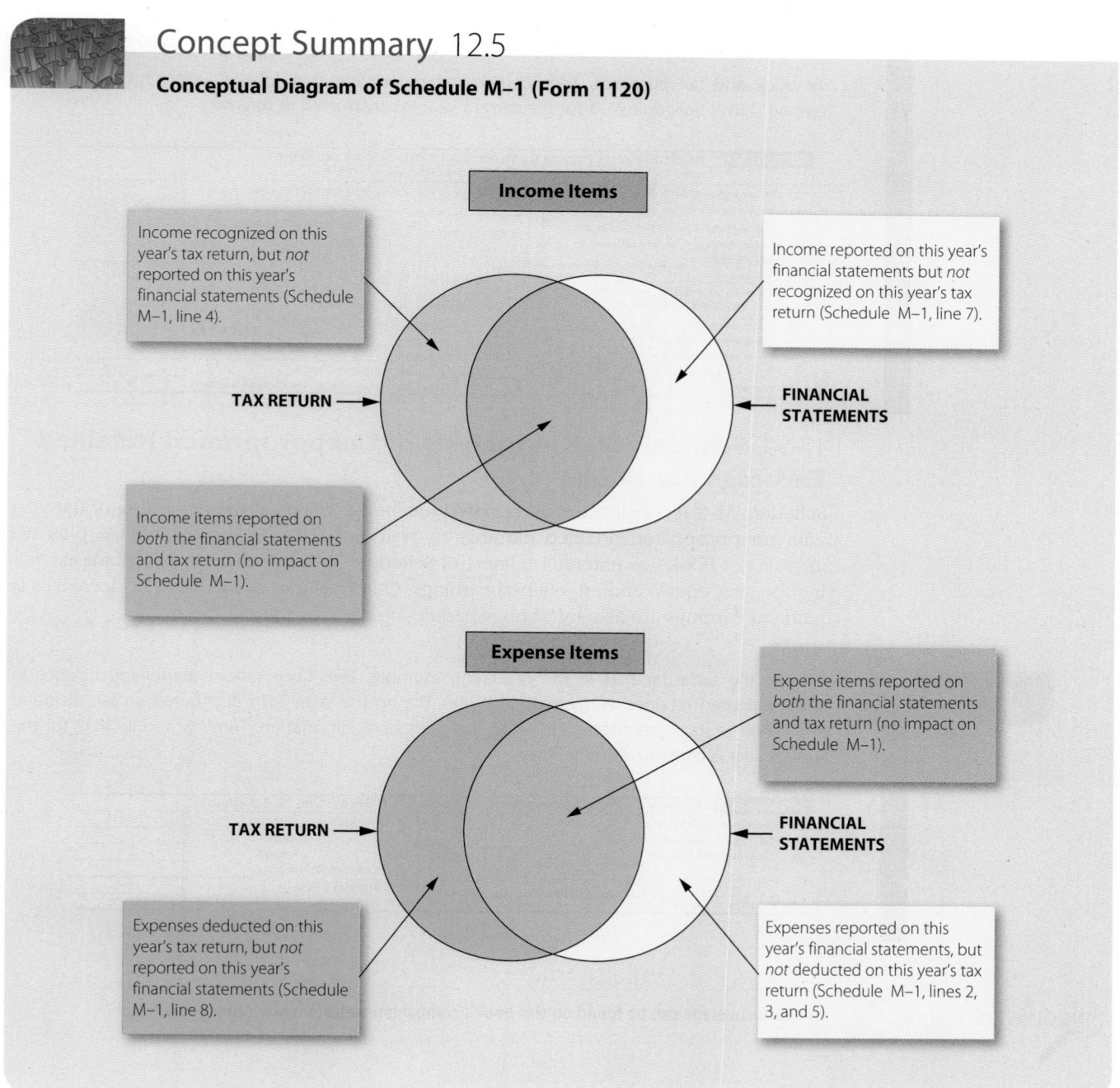

Income Items

Income recognized on this year's tax return, but *not* reported on this year's financial statements (Schedule M–1, line 4).

Income reported on this year's financial statements but *not* recognized on this year's tax return (Schedule M–1, line 7).

TAX RETURN

FINANCIAL STATEMENTS

Income items reported on *both* the financial statements and tax return (no impact on Schedule M–1).

Expense Items

Expense items reported on *both* the financial statements and tax return (no impact on Schedule M–1).

TAX RETURN

FINANCIAL STATEMENTS

Expenses deducted on this year's tax return, but *not* reported on this year's financial statements (Schedule M–1, line 8).

Expenses reported on this year's financial statements, but *not* deducted on this year's tax return (Schedule M–1, lines 2, 3, and 5).

EXAMPLE 51

During the current year, Tern Corporation had the following transactions:

Net income per books (after tax)	$ 92,400
Taxable income	50,000
Federal income tax expense per books	7,500
Interest income from tax-exempt bonds	5,000
Interest paid on loan, the proceeds of which were used to purchase the tax-exempt bonds	500
Life insurance proceeds received as a result of the death of a key employee	50,000
Premiums paid on key employee life insurance policy	2,600
Excess of capital losses over capital gains	2,000

For book and tax purposes, Tern Corporation determines depreciation under the straight-line method. Tern's Schedule M–1 for the current year is constructed as follows:

Schedule M-1	**Reconciliation of Income (Loss) per Books With Income per Return**				
	Note: The corporation may be required to file Schedule M-3 (see instructions).				
1	Net income (loss) per books	92,400	7	Income recorded on books this year not included on this return (itemize):	
2	Federal income tax per books	7,500		Tax-exempt interest $5,000	
3	Excess of capital losses over capital gains	2,000		*Life insurance proceeds on key*	
4	Income subject to tax not recorded on books this year (itemize): _____			*employee $50,000*	55,000
	_____		8	Deductions on this return not charged against book income this year (itemize):	
5	Expenses recorded on books this year not deducted on this return (itemize):		a	Depreciation . . $ _____	
a	Depreciation . . . . $ _____		b	Charitable contributions $ _____	
b	Charitable contributions . $ _____			_____	
c	Travel and entertainment . $ _____			_____	
	Prem.–life ins. $2,600; Int.–exempt bonds $500	3,100	9	Add lines 7 and 8	55,000
6	Add lines 1 through 5	105,000	10	Income (page 1, line 28)—line 6 less line 9	50,000

12-5d Schedule M–2—Analysis of Unappropriated Retained Earnings per Books

Schedule M–2 reconciles unappropriated retained earnings at the beginning of the year with unappropriated retained earnings at year-end. The beginning balance plus net income per books, as entered on line 1 of Schedule M–1, less dividend distributions during the year equals ending retained earnings. Other sources of increases or decreases in retained earnings are also listed on Schedule M–2.

EXAMPLE 52

Assume the same facts as in the preceding example. Tern Corporation's beginning balance in unappropriated retained earnings is $125,000. During the year, Tern distributed a cash dividend of $30,000 to its shareholders. Based on this additional information, Tern's Schedule M–2 for the current year is constructed as follows:

Schedule M-2	**Analysis of Unappropriated Retained Earnings per Books (Line 25, Schedule L)**				
1	Balance at beginning of year	125,000	5	Distributions: a Cash	30,000
2	Net income (loss) per books	92,400		b Stock	
3	Other increases (itemize): _____			c Property . . .	
	_____		6	Other decreases (itemize): _____	
	_____		7	Add lines 5 and 6	30,000
4	Add lines 1, 2, and 3	217,400	8	Balance at end of year (line 4 less line 7)	187,400

DIGGING DEEPER 4   In-depth coverage can be found on this book's companion website: www.cengagebrain.com

BRIDGE DISCIPLINE **Bridge to Financial Accounting**

Measures of corporate income for financial reporting and income tax purposes differ because the objectives of these measures differ. Income measures for financial reporting purposes are intended to help various stakeholders have a clear view of the corporation's financial position and operational results. Income measures for Federal income tax purposes, on the other hand, must comply with the relevant provisions of the Internal Revenue Code. The tax law is intended not only to raise revenues to fund government operations but also to reflect the objectives of government fiscal policy.

As a consequence of these differing objectives, revenue and expense measurements used to determine taxable income may differ from those used in financial reporting. In most cases, differences between book and tax measurements are temporary in nature. Two such temporary differences relate to the different methods of calculating depreciation expense and the limits placed on the deductibility of net capital losses for tax purposes. Permanent differences between book and tax income, such as the dividends received deduction and the domestic production activities deduction, also may exist.

Accounting standards for reporting income tax expenses and liabilities require that the tax impact of *temporary* differences be recognized currently in the financial statements. Because many temporary differences allow a firm to postpone its tax payments to later years, the financial statements must show the amount of the expense that is paid currently and that portion that is to be paid in a later period. The portion of the taxes to be paid in a later period is shown as a liability for such future income taxes. The liability for future income taxes is referred to as a deferred income tax liability.

See Chapter 3 for a complete discussion of this topic.

12-5e Schedule M–3—Net Income (Loss) Reconciliation for Corporations with Total Assets of $10 Million or More

Corporate taxpayers with total assets of $10 million or more are required to report much greater detail relative to differences between income (loss) reported for financial accounting purposes and income (loss) reported for tax purposes. This expanded reconciliation of book and taxable income (loss) is reported on Schedule M–3 . Corporations that are not required to file Schedule M–3 may do so voluntarily. Any corporation that files Schedule M–3 is not allowed to file Schedule M–1. Corporations (and partnerships) with $10 million to $50 million of total assets may elect to file Schedule M–1 in lieu of Schedule M–3, Parts II and III. Electing entities must still file Schedule M–3, Part I (lines 1–12). Entities with less than $10 million of assets that voluntarily file Schedule M–3 also may elect the reduced Schedule M–3 filing requirements.

Schedule M–3 is a response, at least in part, to financial reporting scandals such as Enron and WorldCom. One objective of Schedule M–3 is to create greater transparency between corporate financial statements and tax returns. Another objective is to identify corporations that engage in aggressive tax practices by requiring that transactions that create book-tax differences be disclosed on corporate tax returns. The increase in transparency and disclosure comes at a cost, however, as the IRS estimates that, on average, almost 89 hours are needed to comply with the requirements of Schedule M–3.

Total assets for purposes of the $10 million test and the income and expense amounts required by Schedule M–3 are determined from the taxpayer's financial reports. If the taxpayer files Form 10–K with the Securities and Exchange Commission (SEC), that statement is used. If no 10–K is filed, information from another financial source is used, in the following order: certified financial statements, prepared financial statements, or the taxpayer's books and records.

In-depth coverage can be found on this book's companion website: www.cengagebrain.com

5, 6 DIGGING DEEPER

12-5f Effect of Taxes on Financial Statements

Given the differences between taxable income and net income per books, what effect do these differences have on an entity's financial statements? How are income tax accruals arrived at and reported for accounting purposes? What other types of disclosures regarding present and potential tax liabilities are required to satisfy the accounting standards? Recall that these and other questions were answered and discussed at length in Chapter 3.

A corporation with total assets of $10 million or more must file Schedule UTP (Uncertain Tax Position Statement) with its Form 1120. In general, a corporation is required to report tax positions taken on a current or prior year's Federal income tax return and for which the corporation recorded a reserve for Federal income tax in its audited financial statements (or for which no reserve was recorded because of an expectation to litigate). Financial reporting of tax positions is discussed in Chapter 3.

REFOCUS ON THE BIG PICTURE

GROWING INTO THE CORPORATE FORM

Amber, the sole property transferor, must acquire at least 80 percent of the stock issued by Garden, Inc., for the transaction to qualify for tax-deferred treatment under § 351. Otherwise, she will recognize $600,000 of taxable gain as a result of the transfer. As a corollary, Jimmy must not receive more than 20 percent of Garden's stock in exchange for services (see Example 17). Even if the requirements of § 351 are met, any debt issued by the corporation will be treated as boot and will result in at least some gain recognition to Amber (see Example 10). Therefore, Amber must evaluate the cost of recognizing gain now versus the benefit of Garden obtaining an interest deduction later.

What If?

Can the § 351 transaction be modified to further reduce personal and business tax costs, both at the time of formation and in the future? Several strategies may be worth considering.

- Have Jimmy transfer some property along with the services rendered to Garden, Inc. As long as Jimmy transfers property with more than a relatively small value compared to the value of services performed, Jimmy will be considered part of the control group. This would allow Amber to own less than 80 percent of the new corporation and still have the transaction qualify under § 351.

- Instead of having Garden issue debt on formation, Amber might withhold certain assets. For example, if the building is not transferred, it can be leased to the corporation. The resulting rent payment would mitigate the double taxation problem by reducing Garden's taxable income via a rent deduction.

- An additional benefit results if Amber does not transfer the cash basis receivables to Garden. This approach avoids an income tax at the corporate level when they are collected by the corporation and another income tax on Amber when the receipts are distributed as a dividend (see Example 36).

- If Amber's sole proprietorship has any accounts payable outstanding at the time of the corporate formation, it might be wise to transfer those to Garden. The subsequent corporate payment of the liability produces a deduction that will reduce any corporate income tax.

Suggested Readings

Wei-Chih Chiang and Jianjn Du, "The Debt-Equity Debate in the *Castle Harbour* Case," *Practical Tax Strategies*, March 2013.

Ed Decker, "Why Am I Here?—Changing Times Necessitate Revisiting Prior Entity Choice Decisions," *Business Entities*, September/October 2015.

David B. Friedel and Yaw O. Awuah, "Sec. 351 Control Requirement: Opportunities and Pitfalls," *The Tax Adviser*, July 2014.

Janel Greiman and Thomas J. Nash, "Did Averting Fiscal Cliff Allow C Corporations to Overtake Passthroughs?," *Practical Tax Strategies*, August 2013.

Jeffrey L. Rubinger and Nadia E. Kruler, "Service Applies Substance Over Form Doctrine to Disallow Dividends-Received Deduction," *Journal of Taxation*, July 2013.

Edward J. Schnee and W. Eugene Seago, "Taxing the Transfer of Debts Between Debtors and Creditors," *The Tax Adviser*, July 2012.

Key Terms

Built-in loss property, 12-22	Dividends received deduction, 12-29	Regular corporations, 12-2
C corporations, 12-2	Limited liability company (LLC), 12-7	S corporations, 12-2
Capital contribution, 12-25	Limited partnerships, 12-7	Schedule M–1, 12-36
Check-the-box Regulations, 12-7	Organizational expenditures, 12-31	Schedule M–3, 12-39
Control, 12-11	Parent-subsidiary controlled group, 12-34	Securities, 12-11
Controlled group, 12-33	Personal service corporations (PSCs), 12-33	Thin capitalization, 12-27
Disregarded entity, 12-7	Property, 12-9	

Computational Exercises

1. **LO.2** Marie and Ethan form Roundtree Corporation with the transfer of the following. Marie performs personal services for the corporation with a fair market value of $80,000 in exchange for 400 shares of stock. Ethan contributes an installment note receivable (basis $25,000; fair market value $30,000), land (basis $50,000; fair market value $170,000), and inventory (basis $100,000; fair market value $120,000) in exchange for 1,600 shares. Determine Marie and Ethan's current income, gain, or loss; calculate the basis that each takes in the Roundtree stock.

2. **LO.2** Grady exchanges qualified property, basis of $12,000 and fair market value of $18,000, for 60% of the stock of Eadie Corporation. The other 40% of the stock is owned by Pedro, who acquired it five years ago. Calculate Grady 's current income, gain, or loss and the basis he takes in his shares of Eadie stock as a result of this transaction.

3. **LO.3** Jocelyn contributes land with a basis of $60,000 and fair market value of $90,000 and inventory with a basis of $5,000 and fair market value of $8,000 in exchange for 100% of Zion Corporation stock. The land is subject to a $15,000 mortgage. Determine Jocelyn's recognized gain or loss and the basis in the Zion stock received.

4. **LO.3** Martin transfers real estate with an adjusted basis of $260,000 and fair market value of $350,000 to a newly formed corporation in exchange for 100% of the stock. The corporation assumes the liability on the transferred real estate in the amount of $300,000. Determine Martin's recognized gain on the transfer and the basis for his stock.

5. **LO.4** Yvonne and Simon form Ion Corporation. Yvonne transfers equipment (basis of $110,000 and fair market value of $165,000). Simon invests $130,000 of cash. They each receive 100 shares in Ion Corporation, worth $130,000, but Yvonne also receives $35,000 of cash from Ion. Calculate Ion Corporation's basis in the equipment. In addition, determine Yvonne and Simon's basis in the Ion stock.

6. **LO.6** Chaz transfers cash of $60,000 to a newly formed corporation for 100% of the stock. In its initial year, the corporation has net income of $15,000. The income is credited to the earnings and profits account of the corporation. The corporation distributes $5,000 to Chaz.

   a. How do Chaz and the corporation treat the $5,000 distribution?

   b. Assume, instead, that Chaz transfers to the corporation cash of $30,000 for stock and cash of $30,000 for a note of the same amount. The note is payable in equal annual installments of $3,000 each (beginning at the end of the corporation's initial year of operations) and bears interest at the rate of 6%. At the end of the year, the corporation pays an amount to meet this obligation. Determine the total amount of the payment and its tax treatment to Chaz and the corporation.

7. **LO.7** Crane and Loon Corporations, two unrelated C corporations, have the following transactions for the current year:

	Crane	Loon
Gross income from operations	$180,000	$300,000
Expenses from operations	255,000	310,000
Dividends received from domestic corporations (15% ownership)	100,000	230,000

   a. Compute the dividends received deduction for Crane Corporation.

   b. Compute the dividends received deduction for Loon Corporation.

8. **LO.7** Cherry Corporation, a calendar year C corporation, is formed and begins business on April 1, 2016. In connection with its formation, Cherry incurs organizational expenditures of $54,000. Determine Cherry Corporation's deduction for organizational expenditures for 2016.

9. **LO.8** Compute the income tax liability for each of the following unrelated C corporations.

   a. Darter Corporation has taxable income of $68,000.

   b. Owl Corporation has taxable income of $10,800,000.

   c. Toucan Corporation, a personal service corporation, has taxable income of $170,000.

Problems

10. **LO.1** Janice is the sole owner of Catbird Company. In the current year, Catbird had operating income of $100,000, a long-term capital gain of $15,000, and a charitable contribution of $5,000. Janice withdrew $70,000 of profit from Catbird. How should Janice report this information on her individual tax return if Catbird Company is:

    a. An LLC?

    b. An S corporation?

    c. A C corporation?

11. **LO.1** Can a sole proprietor form as a single-member limited liability company (LLC)? If so, how would such an LLC be taxed?

12. **LO.1** In the current year, Riflebird Company had operating income of $220,000, operating expenses of $175,000, and a long-term capital loss of $10,000. How do Riflebird Company and Roger, the sole owner of Riflebird, report this information on their respective Federal income tax returns for the current year under the following assumptions?

a. Riflebird Company is a proprietorship (Roger did not make any withdrawals from the business).

b. Riflebird Company is a C corporation (no dividends were paid during the year).

13. **LO.1** Ellie and Linda are equal owners in Otter Enterprises, a calendar year business. During the current year, Otter Enterprises has $320,000 of gross income and $210,000 of operating expenses. In addition, Otter has a long-term capital gain of $15,000 and makes distributions to Ellie and Linda of $25,000 each. Discuss the impact of this information on the taxable income of Otter, Ellie, and Linda if Otter is:

a. A partnership.

b. An S corporation.

c. A C corporation.

14. **LO.1** In the current year, Azure Company has $350,000 of net operating income before deducting any compensation or other payments to its sole owner, Sasha. In addition, Azure has interest on municipal bonds of $25,000. Sasha has significant income from other sources and is in the 39.6% marginal tax bracket. Based on this information, determine the income tax consequences to Azure Company and to Sasha during the year for each of the following independent situations.

a. Azure is a C corporation and pays no dividends or salary to Sasha.

b. Azure is a C corporation and distributes $75,000 of dividends to Sasha.

c. Azure is a C corporation and pays $75,000 of salary to Sasha.

d. Azure is a sole proprietorship, and Sasha withdraws $0.

e. Azure is a sole proprietorship, and Sasha withdraws $75,000.

15. **LO.2** Sarah incorporates her small business but does not transfer the machinery   Issue ID
and equipment used by the business to the corporation. Instead, the machinery and equipment are leased to the corporation for an annual rent. What tax reasons might Sarah have for not transferring the machinery and equipment to the corporation when the business was incorporated?

16. **LO.2, 4** Seth, Pete, Cara, and Jen form Kingfisher Corporation with the following consideration:

| | Consideration Transferred | | |
	Basis to Transferor	Fair Market Value	Number of Shares Issued
From Seth—			
Inventory	$30,000	$96,000	30*
From Pete—			
Equipment ($30,000 of depreciation taken by Pete in prior years)	45,000	99,000	30**
From Cara—			
Proprietary process	15,000	90,000	30
From Jen—			
Cash	30,000	30,000	10

*Seth receives $6,000 in cash in addition to the 30 shares.
**Pete receives $9,000 in cash in addition to the 30 shares.

Assume that the value of each share of Kingfisher stock is $3,000. As to these transactions, provide the following information:

a. Seth's recognized gain or loss. Identify the nature of any such gain or loss.

b. Seth's basis in the Kingfisher Corporation stock.

c. Kingfisher Corporation's basis in the inventory.

d. Pete's recognized gain or loss. Identify the nature of any such gain or loss.

e. Pete's basis in the Kingfisher Corporation stock.

f. Kingfisher Corporation's basis in the equipment.

g. Cara's recognized gain or loss.

h. Cara's basis in the Kingfisher Corporation stock.

i. Kingfisher Corporation's basis in the proprietary process.

j. Jen's recognized gain or loss.

k. Jen's basis in the Kingfisher stock.

l. During discussions relating to the formation of Kingfisher, Seth mentions that he may be interested in either (1) just selling all of his inventory in the current year for its fair market value of $96,000 or (2) proceeding with his involvement in Kingfisher's formation as shown above but followed by a sale of his stock five years later for $90,000. What would be the tax cost of these alternative plans, stated in present value terms? Referring to Appendix F, assume a discount rate of 6%. Further, assume that Seth's marginal income tax rate is 35% and his capital gains rate is 15%.

17. **LO.2, 4** Tom and Gail form Owl Corporation with the following consideration:

	Consideration Transferred		
	Basis to Transferor	Fair Market Value	Number of Shares Issued
From Tom—			
Cash	$ 50,000	$ 50,000	
Installment note	240,000	350,000	40
From Gail—			
Inventory	$ 60,000	$ 50,000	
Equipment	125,000	250,000	
Patentable invention	15,000	300,000	60

The installment note has a face amount of $350,000 and was acquired last year from the sale of land held for investment purposes (adjusted basis of $240,000). As to these transactions, provide the following information:

a. Tom's recognized gain or loss.

b. Tom's basis in the Owl Corporation stock.

c. Owl Corporation's basis in the installment note.

d. Gail's recognized gain or loss.

e. Gail's basis in the Owl Corporation stock.

f. Owl Corporation's basis in the inventory, equipment, and patentable invention.

g. How would your answers to the preceding questions change if Tom received common stock and Gail received preferred stock?

h. How would your answers change if Gail was a partnership?

Decision Making   18. **LO.2** Jane, Jon, and Clyde incorporate their respective businesses and form Starling Corporation. On March 1 of the current year, Jane exchanges her property (basis of $50,000 and value of $150,000) for 150 shares in Starling Corporation. On April 15, Jon exchanges his property (basis of $70,000 and value of $500,000) for 500 shares in Starling. On May 10, Clyde transfers his property (basis of $90,000 and value of $350,000) for 350 shares in Starling.

a. If the three exchanges are part of a prearranged plan, what gain will each of the parties recognize on the exchanges?

b. Assume that Jane and Jon exchanged their property for stock four years ago, while Clyde transfers his property for 350 shares in the current year. Clyde's transfer is not part of a prearranged plan with Jane and Jon to incorporate their businesses. What gain will Clyde recognize on the transfer?

c. Returning to the original facts, if the property that Clyde contributes has a basis of $490,000 (instead of $90,000), how might the parties otherwise structure the transaction?

19. **LO.2** Dan and Patricia form Crane Corporation. Dan transfers land (worth $200,000, basis of $60,000) for 50% of the stock in Crane. Patricia transfers machinery (worth $150,000, adjusted basis of $30,000) and provides services worth ($50,000) for 50% of the stock.

    Issue ID

a. Will the transfers qualify under § 351? Explain.

b. What are the tax consequences to Dan and Patricia?

c. What is Crane Corporation's basis in the land and the machinery?

20. **LO.2** John organized Toucan Corporation 10 years ago. He contributed property worth $1 million (basis of $200,000) for 2,000 shares of stock in Toucan (representing 100% ownership). John later gave each of his children, Julie and Rachel, 500 shares of the stock. In the current year, John transfers property worth $350,000 (basis of $170,000) to Toucan for 1,000 more of its shares. What gain, if any, will John recognize on the transfer?

21. **LO.2** Rhonda owns 50% of the stock of Peach Corporation. She and the other 50% shareholder, Rachel, have decided that additional contributions of capital are needed if Peach is to remain successful in its competitive industry. The two shareholders have agreed that Rhonda will contribute assets having a value of $200,000 (adjusted basis of $15,000) in exchange for additional shares of stock. After the transaction, Rhonda will hold 75% of Peach Corporation and Rachel's interest will fall to 25%.

    Decision Making

a. What gain is realized on the transaction? How much of the gain will be recognized?

b. Rhonda is not satisfied with the transaction as proposed. How will the consequences change if Rachel agrees to transfer $1,000 of cash in exchange for additional stock? In this case, Rhonda would own slightly less than 75% of Peach, and Rachel's interest would be slightly more than 25%.

c. If Rhonda still is not satisfied with the result, what should be done to avoid any gain recognition?

22. **LO.2, 3, 4** Adam transfers property with an adjusted basis of $50,000 (fair market value of $400,000) to Swift Corporation for 90% of the stock. The property is subject to a liability of $60,000, which Swift assumes.

a. What is the basis of the Swift stock to Adam?

b. What is the basis of the property to Swift Corporation?

23. **LO.2, 3, 4** Allie forms Broadbill Corporation by transferring land (basis of $125,000, fair market value of $775,000), which is subject to a mortgage of $375,000. One month prior to incorporating Broadbill, Allie borrows $100,000 for personal reasons and gives the lender a second mortgage on the land. Broadbill Corporation issues stock worth $300,000 to Allie and assumes the mortgages on the land.

a. What are the tax consequences to Allie and to Broadbill Corporation?

b. How would the tax consequences to Allie differ if she had not borrowed the $100,000?

24. **LO.2, 4** Rafael transfers the following assets to Crane Corporation in exchange for all of its stock. (Assume that neither Rafael nor Crane plans to make any special tax elections at the time of incorporation.)

    Decision Making

Assets	Rafael's Adjusted Basis	Fair Market Value
Inventory	$ 60,000	$100,000
Equipment	150,000	105,000
Shelving	80,000	65,000

a.   What is Rafael's recognized gain or loss?

b.   What is Rafael's basis in the stock?

c.   What is Crane's basis in the inventory, equipment, and shelving?

d.   If Rafael has no intentions of selling his Crane stock for at least 15 years, what action would you recommend that Rafael and Crane Corporation consider? How does this change the previous answers?

25. **LO.2, 3, 4** Kesha, a sole proprietor, is engaged in a cash basis service business. In the current year, she incorporates the business to form Kiwi Corporation. She transfers assets with a basis of $500,000 (fair market value of $1.2 million), a bank loan of $450,000 (which Kiwi assumes), and $80,000 in trade payables in return for all of Kiwi's stock. What are the tax consequences of the incorporation of the business?

Issue ID   26. **LO.2** Nancy and her daughter, Kathleen, have been working together in a cattery called "The Perfect Cat." Nancy formed the business in 2001 as a sole proprietorship, and it has been very successful. Assets have a fair market value of $450,000 and a basis of $180,000. On the advice of their tax accountant, Nancy decides to incorporate "The Perfect Cat." Because of Kathleen's participation, Nancy would like her to receive shares in the corporation. What are the relevant tax issues?

Ethics and Equity   27. **LO.2** Early in the year, Charles, Lane, and Tami form the Harrier Corporation for the express purpose of developing a shopping center. All parties are experienced contractors, and they transfer various business assets (e.g., building materials, land) to Harrier in exchange for all of its stock. Three months after it is formed, Harrier purchases two cranes from Lane for their fair market value of $400,000 by issuing four annual installment notes of $100,000 each. Because the adjusted basis of the cranes is $550,000, Lane plans to recognize a § 1231 loss of $150,000 in the year of the sale. Does Lane have any potential income tax problem with this plan? Explain.

28. **LO.2, 4** Alice and Jane form Osprey Corporation. Alice transfers property, basis of $25,000 and fair market value of $200,000, for 50 shares in Osprey Corporation. Jane transfers property, basis of $50,000 and fair market value of $165,000, and agrees to serve as manager of Osprey for one year; in return, Jane receives 50 shares in Osprey. The value of Jane's services to Osprey is $35,000.

a.   What gain or income will Alice and Jane recognize on the exchange?

b.   What basis will Osprey Corporation have in the property transferred by Alice and Jane? How should Osprey treat the value of the services that Jane renders?

29. **LO.2, 4** Assume in Problem 28 that Jane receives the 50 shares of Osprey Corporation stock in consideration for the appreciated property and for the provision of accounting services in organizing the corporation. The value of Jane's services is $35,000.

a.   What gain or income does Jane recognize?

b.   What is Osprey Corporation's basis in the property transferred by Jane? How should Osprey treat the value of the services that Jane renders?

30. **LO.2, 4** In January 2016, Wanda transferred machinery worth $200,000 (adjusted basis of $30,000) to a controlled corporation, Oriole, Inc. The transfer qualified under § 351. Wanda had deducted $165,000 of depreciation on the machinery while it was used in her proprietorship. Later in 2016, Oriole sells the machinery for $190,000. What are the tax consequences to Wanda and to Oriole on the sale of the machinery?

31. **LO.5** Red Corporation wants to set up a manufacturing facility in a midwestern state. After considerable negotiations with a small town in Ohio, Red accepts the following offer: land (fair market value of $3 million) and cash of $1 million.

a.   How much gain or income, if any, must Red Corporation recognize?

b.   What basis will Red Corporation have in the land?

c.   Within one year of the contribution, Red constructs a building for $800,000 and purchases inventory for $200,000. What basis will Red Corporation have in each of those assets?

32. **LO.6** Emily Patrick (36 Paradise Road, Northampton, MA 01060) formed Teal Corporation a number of years ago with an investment of $200,000 of cash, for which she received $20,000 in stock and $180,000 in bonds bearing interest of 8% and maturing in nine years. Several years later, Emily lent the corporation an additional $50,000 on open account. In the current year, Teal Corporation becomes insolvent and is declared bankrupt. During the corporation's existence, Emily was paid an annual salary of $60,000. Write a letter to Emily in which you explain how she should treat her losses for tax purposes.

Critical Thinking
Communications

33. **LO.7** In each of the following independent situations, determine the dividends received deduction. Assume that none of the corporate shareholders owns 20% or more of the stock in the corporations paying the dividends.

	Almond Corporation	Blond Corporation	Cherry Corporation
Income from operations	$ 700,000	$ 800,000	$ 900,000
Expenses from operations	(600,000)	(850,000)	(910,000)
Qualifying dividends	100,000	100,000	100,000

34. **LO.7** Gull Corporation, a cash method, calendar year C corporation, was formed and began business on November 1, 2016. Gull incurred the following expenses during its first year of operations (November 1, 2016–December 31, 2016):

Expenses of temporary directors and organizational meetings	$21,000
Fee paid to state of incorporation	3,000
Expenses for printing and sale of stock certificates	11,000
Legal services for drafting the corporate charter and bylaws (not paid until January 2017)	19,000

  a. Assuming that Gull Corporation elects under § 248 to expense and amortize organizational expenditures, what amount may be deducted in 2016?

  b. Assume the same facts as above, except that the amount paid for the legal services was $28,000 (instead of $19,000). What amount may be deducted as organizational expenditures in 2016?

35. **LO.7** Egret Corporation, a calendar year C corporation, was formed on March 6, 2016, and opened for business on July 1, 2016. After its formation but prior to opening for business, Egret incurred the following expenditures:

Accounting	$ 7,000
Advertising	14,500
Employee payroll	11,000
Rent	8,000
Utilities	1,000

What is the maximum amount of these expenditures that Egret can deduct in 2016?

36. **LO.8** In each of the following *independent* situations, determine the corporation's income tax liability. Assume that all corporations use a calendar year for tax purposes and that the tax year involved is 2016.

	Taxable Income
Purple Corporation	$ 65,000
Azul Corporation	290,000
Pink Corporation	12,350,000
Turquoise Corporation	19,000,000
Teal Corporation (a personal service corporation)	130,000

Critical Thinking 37. **LO.9** The outstanding stock in Red, Blue, and Green Corporations, each of which has only one class of stock, is owned by the following unrelated individuals:

	Corporations		
Shareholders	**Red**	**Blue**	**Green**
Marrin	20%	10%	30%
Murray	10%	50%	20%
Moses	50%	30%	35%

a. Determine whether Red, Blue, and Green Corporations constitute a brother-sister controlled group.

b. Assume that Murray does not own stock in any of the corporations. Would a brother-sister controlled group exist? Explain.

38. **LO.10** Emerald Corporation, a calendar year and accrual method taxpayer, provides the following information and asks you to prepare Schedule M–1 for 2016:

Net income per books (after-tax)	$257,950
Federal income tax per books	41,750
Tax-exempt interest income	15,000
Life insurance proceeds received as a result of death of corporate president	150,000
Interest on loan to purchase tax-exempt bonds	1,500
Excess of capital losses over capital gains	6,000
Premiums paid on life insurance policy on life of Emerald's president	7,800

39. **LO.10** The following information for 2016 relates to Sparrow Corporation, a calendar year, accrual method taxpayer.

Net income per books (after-tax)	$174,100
Federal income tax per books	86,600
Tax-exempt interest income	4,500
MACRS depreciation in excess of straight-line depreciation used for financial accounting purposes	7,200
Excess of capital loss over capital gains	9,400
Nondeductible meals and entertainment	5,500
Interest on loan to purchase tax-exempt bonds	1,100

Based on the above information, use Schedule M–1 of Form 1120, which is available on the IRS website, to determine Sparrow's taxable income for 2016.

Critical Thinking 40. **LO.10** In the current year, Woodpecker, Inc., a C corporation with $8.5 million in assets, deducted amortization of $40,000 on its financial statements and $55,000 on its Federal tax return. Is Woodpecker required to file Schedule M–3? If a Schedule M–3 is filed by Woodpecker, how is the difference in amortization amounts treated on that schedule?

Critical Thinking 41. **LO.10** Dove Corporation, a calendar year C corporation, had the following information for 2016:

Net income per books (after-tax)	$386,250
Taxable income	120,000
Federal income tax per books	30,050
Cash dividend distributions	150,000
Unappropriated retained earnings as of January 1, 2016	796,010

Based on the above information, use Schedule M–2 of Form 1120 (see Example 52 in the text) to determine Dove's unappropriated retained earnings balance as of December 31, 2016.

42. **LO.10** In the current year, Pelican, Inc., incurs $50,000 of nondeductible fines and penalties. Its depreciation expense is $245,000 for financial statement purposes and $310,000 for tax purposes. How is this information reported on Schedule M–3? Critical Thinking

43. **LO.10** In January 2016, Pelican, Inc., established an allowance for uncollectible accounts (bad debt reserve) of $70,000 on its books and increased the allowance by $120,000 during the year. As a result of a client's bankruptcy, Pelican, Inc., decreased the allowance by $60,000 in November 2016. Pelican, Inc., deducted the $190,000 of increases to the allowance on its 2016 income statement, but was not allowed to deduct that amount on its tax return. On its 2016 tax return, the corporation was allowed to deduct the $60,000 actual loss sustained because of its client's bankruptcy. On its financial statements, Pelican, Inc., treated the $190,000 increase in the bad debt reserve as an expense that gave rise to a temporary difference. On its 2016 tax return, Pelican, Inc., took a $60,000 deduction for bad debt expense. How is this information reported on Schedule M–3? Critical Thinking

Comprehensive Tax Return Problem

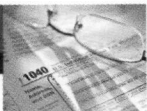

1. On November 1, 2006, Janet Morton and Kim Wong formed Pet Kingdom, Inc., to sell pets and pet supplies. Pertinent information regarding Pet Kingdom is summarized as follows:

    Tax Return Problem

    TAX SOFTWARE

    - Pet Kingdom's business address is 1010 Northwest Parkway, Dallas, TX 75225; its telephone number is (214) 555-2211; and its e-mail address is petkingdom@pki.com.
    - The employer identification number is 11-1111111, and the principal business activity code is 453910.
    - Janet and Kim each own 50% of the common stock; Janet is president and Kim is vice president of the company. No other class of stock is authorized.
    - Both Janet and Kim are full-time employees of Pet Kingdom. Janet's Social Security number is 123-45-6789, and Kim's Social Security number is 987-65-4321.
    - Pet Kingdom is an accrual method, calendar year taxpayer. Inventories are determined using FIFO and the lower of cost or market method. Pet Kingdom uses the straight-line method of depreciation for book purposes and accelerated depreciation (MACRS) for tax purposes.
    - During 2015, the corporation distributed cash dividends of $250,000.

    Pet Kingdom's financial statements for 2015 follow.

Income Statement

Income		
Gross sales		$5,750,000
Sales returns and allowances		(200,000)
Net sales		$5,550,000
Cost of goods sold		(2,300,000)
Gross profit		$3,250,000
Dividends received from stock investments in less-than-20%-owned U.S. corporations		43,750
Interest income:		
State bonds	$15,000	
Certificates of deposit	20,000	35,000
Total income		$3,328,750

(continued)

Expenses

Salaries—officers:		
Janet Morton	$262,500	
Kim Wong	262,500	$525,000
Salaries—clerical and sales		725,000
Taxes (state, local, and payroll)		238,000
Repairs and maintenance		140,000
Interest expense:		
Loan to purchase state bonds	$ 9,000	
Other business loans	207,000	216,000
Advertising		58,000
Rental expense		109,000
Depreciation*		106,000
Charitable contributions		38,000
Employee benefit programs		60,000
Premiums on term life insurance policies on lives of Janet Morton and Kim Wong; Pet Kingdom is the designated beneficiary		40,000
Total expenses		(2,255,000)
Net income before taxes		$1,073,750
Federal income tax		(356,023)
Net income per books		$ 717,727

*Depreciation for tax purposes is $136,000. You are not provided enough detailed data to complete a Form 4562 (depreciation). If you solve this problem using H&R BLOCK Tax Software, enter the amount of depreciation on line 20 of Form 1120.

Balance Sheet

Assets	January 1, 2015	December 31, 2015
Cash	$ 1,200,000	$ 1,037,750
Trade notes and accounts receivable	2,062,500	2,147,000
Inventories	2,750,000	3,030,000
Stock investment	1,125,000	1,125,000
State bonds	375,000	375,000
Certificates of deposit	400,000	400,000
Prepaid Federal tax	–0–	3,977
Buildings and other depreciable assets	5,455,000	5,455,000
Accumulated depreciation	(606,000)	(712,000)
Land	812,500	812,500
Other assets	140,000	128,500
Total assets	$13,714,000	$13,802,727

Liabilities and Equity	January 1, 2015	December 31, 2015
Accounts payable	$ 2,284,000	$ 1,975,000
Other current liabilities	175,000	155,000
Mortgages	4,625,000	4,575,000
Capital stock	2,500,000	2,500,000
Retained earnings	4,130,000	4,597,727
Total liabilities and equity	$13,714,000	$13,802,727

During 2015, Pet Kingdom made estimated tax payments of $90,000 each quarter to the IRS. Prepare a Form 1120 for Pet Kingdom for tax year 2015. Suggested software: H&R BLOCK Tax Software.

1. Charles is planning to invest $10,000 in a venture whose management is undecided as to whether it should be structured as a regular corporation or as a partnership. Charles will hold a 10% interest in the entity. Determine the treatment to Charles if the entity is a corporation and if it is a partnership. In the analysis, assume that Charles is in the 35% marginal tax bracket and that the entity, if operating as a corporation, is in the 34% marginal tax bracket. Also assume that the passive activity rules do not apply to Charles.
    a. If the entity incurs an $80,000 operating loss in year 1, what is Charles's cash outflow if the entity is a corporation? A partnership? Do not consider the 3.8% additional tax on net investment income in the analysis.
    b. In year 2, the entity earns operating income of $200,000 and makes no distributions to any of the owners. What is the Federal income tax burden on Charles if the investment is a corporation? A partnership?
    c. In year 3, the entity earns operating income of $200,000 and distributes all of that year's after-tax proceeds to the owners. What amount of cash is available to Charles if the entity operates as a corporation (assume that any distribution is a qualified dividend)? A partnership?

2. On your review of the books and records of Ridge Corporation, you note the following information pertaining to its tax provision:

Net income per books	$525,400
Book income tax expense	234,600
Dividends received deduction	70,000
Capital gains	50,000
Capital losses	(60,000)
MACRS depreciation	80,000
Book depreciation	65,000

   a. Calculate Ridge's taxable income and Federal income tax liability for the year.
   b. Calculate Ridge's deferred income tax liability.

Research Problems

Note: Solutions to Research Problems can be prepared by using the Checkpoint® Student Edition online research product, which is available to accompany this text. It is also possible to prepare solutions to the Research Problems by using tax research materials found in a standard tax library.

Research Problem 1. Tim is a real estate broker who specializes in commercial real estate. Although he usually buys and sells on behalf of others, he also maintains a portfolio of property of his own. He holds this property, mainly unimproved land, either as an investment or for sale to others.

In early 2014, Irene and Al contact Tim regarding a tract of land located just outside the city limits. Tim bought the property, which is known as the Moore farm, several years ago for $600,000. At that time, no one knew that it was located on a geological fault line. Irene, a well-known architect, and Al, a building contractor, want Tim to join them in developing the property for residential use. They are aware of the fault line but believe that they can circumvent the problem by using newly developed design and construction technology. Because of the geological flaw, however, they regard the Moore farm as being worth only $450,000. Their intent is to organize a corporation to build the housing project, and each party will receive stock commensurate to the property or services contributed.

After consulting his tax adviser, Tim agrees to join the venture if certain modifications to the proposed arrangement are made. The transfer of the land would be structured as a sale to the corporation. Instead of receiving stock, Tim would receive a note from the corporation. The note would be interest-bearing and be due in five years. The maturity value of the note would be $450,000—the amount that even Tim concedes is the fair market value of the Moore farm.

What income tax consequences ensue from Tim's suggested approach? Compare this result with what would happen if Tim merely transferred the Moore farm in return for stock in the new corporation.

Communications

Research Problem 2. A new client, John Dobson, recently formed John's Premium Steakhouse, Inc., to operate a new restaurant. The restaurant will be a first-time business venture for John, who recently retired after 30 years of military service. John transferred cash to the corporation in exchange for 100% of its stock, and the corporation is considering leasing a building and restaurant equipment. John has asked you for guidance on the tax treatment of various expenses (e.g., licensing, training, advertising) he expects the corporation to incur during the restaurant's pre-opening period. Research the tax treatment of startup expenditures, including the point at which a business begins for purposes of determining what expenses are included. Prepare a memo for the client files, describing the results of your research.

Partial list of research aids:
§ 195.
Reg. § 1.195–1.

Decision Making

Communications

Research Problem 3. Lynn Jones, Shawn, Walt, and Donna are trying to decide whether they should organize a corporation and transfer their shares of stock in several corporations to this new corporation. All of their shares are listed on the New York Stock Exchange and are readily marketable. Lynn would transfer shares in Brown Corporation, Shawn would transfer stock in Rust Corporation, Walt would transfer stock in White Corporation, and Donna would transfer stock in several corporations. The stock would be held by the newly formed corporation for investment purposes. Lynn asks you, her tax adviser, whether she would have gain on the transfer of her substantially appreciated shares in Brown Corporation if she transferred the shares to a newly formed corporation. Your input will be critical as they make their decision. Prepare a letter to your client, Lynn Jones, and a memo for the firm's files. Lynn's address is 1540 Maxwell Avenue, Highland, KY 41099.

Internet Activity

Use the tax resources of the Internet to address the following questions. Do not restrict your search to the Web, but include a review of newsgroups and general reference materials, practitioner sites and resources, primary sources of the tax law, chat rooms and discussion groups, and other opportunities.

Communications

Research Problem 4. On November 21, 2013, Max Baucus, Chairman of the Senate Finance Committee, released a proposal to change several provisions related to the taxation of business income including, but not limited to, that earned by corporations. The proposal deals primarily with cost recovery and tax accounting methods. Many of the proposed changes are similar to ones contained in House Ways and Means Committee Chairman Dave Camp's small business tax reform discussion draft released earlier in the year. Locate the staff discussion draft of Chairman Baucus's proposal, and prepare a PowerPoint presentation of no more than five slides highlighting the major reforms contained in the proposal.

Research Problem 5. Limited liability company (LLC) status has become a popular form of operating a business in the United States. Investigate how the growth of LLC status has affected the relative number of new businesses that have chosen to operate as corporations.

Roger CPA Review Questions

ROGER
CPA Review

1. In general, what is the filing deadline for a C corporation in 2016?
   a. March 15
   b. April 15
   c. The 15th day of the 3rd month after year-end
   d. The 15th day of the 4th month after year-end

2. Crimson Corp. was organized as a calendar year corporation in January 2016, incurring $51,000 in qualified organizational expenses, and began business in March 2016. What is the maximum amount Crimson may deduct for organizational expenditures on its 2016 corporate tax return?
   a. $4,000   c. $6,350
   b. $6,611   d. $7,133

3. Kellye and Becky formed Whoop! Shotz Corporation by contributing property with a fair market value of $50,000 and $70,000 cash, respectively, each for a 50% ownership in the newly formed company. What is Kellye's taxable gain in this situation if the adjusted basis in the property is $25,000 and the company is valued at $120,000?
   a. $0   c. $25,000
   b. $10,000   d. $35,000

4. Kellye, Becky, and Emily formed Whoop! Shotz Corporation with the following contributions:

Kellye	$50,000 cash
Becky	$50,000 cash
Emily	Legal services

   Each was given a one-third ownership in Whoop! Shotz. What amount of income will Emily recognize if the company is valued at $150,000 after formation?
   a. $50,000   c. $0
   b. $33,333   d. $40,000

5. Kellye and Becky create Whoop! Shotz Corporation by contributing property with a fair market value of $50,000 and cash of $70,000, respectively. Each receives a 50% share in the company, which is valued at $150,000 immediately after the formation. The property has an adjusted basis of $25,000 and is subject to a $10,000 mortgage, which is assumed by the company. What gain will Kellye recognize in this situation?
   a. $0   c. $15,000
   b. $10,000   d. $25,000

Corporations: Earnings & Profits and Distributions

LEARNING OBJECTIVES: *After completing Chapter 13, you should be able to:*

LO.1 Explain the role that earnings and profits play in determining the tax treatment of distributions.

LO.2 Compute a corporation's earnings and profits (E & P).

LO.3 Apply the rules for assigning earnings and profits to distributions.

LO.4 Evaluate the tax effects of noncash dividends on the recipient shareholder and the corporation making the distribution.

LO.5 Identify the nature and treatment of constructive dividends.

LO.6 Distinguish between taxable and nontaxable stock dividends.

LO.7 Discuss the tax treatment of stock redemptions and corporate liquidations.

TAX TALK *The relative stability of profits after taxes is evidence that the corporation profits tax is, in effect, almost entirely shifted; the government simply uses the corporation as a tax collector.* —K. E. BOULDING

THE BIG PICTURE

TAXING CORPORATE DISTRIBUTIONS

Lime Corporation, an ice cream manufacturer, has had a very profitable year. To share its profits with its two shareholders, Orange Corporation and Gustavo, it distributes cash of $200,000 to Orange and real estate worth $300,000 (adjusted basis of $20,000) to Gustavo. The real estate is subject to a mortgage of $100,000, which Gustavo assumes. The distribution is made on December 31, Lime's year-end.

Lime Corporation has had both good and bad years in the past. More often than not, however, it has lost money. Despite this year's banner profits, the GAAP-based balance sheet for Lime indicates a year-end deficit in retained earnings. Consequently, for financial reporting purposes, the distribution of cash and land is treated as a liquidating distribution, resulting in a reduction of Lime's paid-in capital account.

The tax consequences of the distributions to Lime Corporation and its shareholders depend on a variety of factors that are not directly related to the financial reporting treatment. Identify these factors, and explain the tax effects of the distributions to both Lime Corporation and its two shareholders.

Read the chapter and formulate your response.

Generally, a corporation cannot deduct distributions made to its shareholders. In contrast, shareholders may be required to treat distributions as fully subject to tax, a nontaxable recovery of capital, or capital gain.

Because distributions provide no deduction to the paying corporation and often require income recognition by the shareholders, a double tax seemingly results (i.e., at both the corporate and shareholder levels). Because of the possibility of a double tax when dealing with corporations, the tax treatment of distributions often raises issues such as the following.

- The availability of earnings to be distributed.
- The basis of the shareholder's stock.
- The character of the property being distributed.
- Whether the shareholder gives up ownership in return for the distribution.
- Whether the distribution is liquidating or nonliquidating.

LO.1

Explain the role that earnings and profits play in determining the tax treatment of distributions.

13-1 CORPORATE DISTRIBUTIONS—OVERVIEW

To the extent a distribution is made from corporate earnings and profits (E & P), the shareholder is deemed to receive a **dividend**, usually taxed in a preferential manner.[1] Generally, corporate distributions are presumed to be paid out of E & P (defined later in this chapter) and are treated as dividends, *unless* the parties to the transaction can show otherwise.

The portion of a corporate distribution that is not taxed as a dividend (because of insufficient E & P) is nontaxable to the extent of the shareholder's basis in the stock. The stock basis is reduced accordingly. The excess of the distribution over the shareholder's basis is treated as a gain from the sale or exchange of the stock.[2]

EXAMPLE 1

At the beginning of the year, Amber Corporation (a calendar year taxpayer) holds accumulated E & P of $30,000. The corporation reports no current E & P. During the year, the corporation distributes $40,000 to its *equal* shareholders, Bob and Bonnie (i.e., each receives $20,000). Only $30,000 of the $40,000 distribution is a taxable dividend.

Suppose Bob's basis in his stock is $8,000, while Bonnie's basis is $4,000. Under these conditions, Bob recognizes a taxable dividend of $15,000 and reduces the basis of his stock from $8,000 to $3,000. The $20,000 Bonnie receives from Amber Corporation is accounted for as follows.

- Taxable dividend of $15,000.
- Reduction in stock basis from $4,000 to zero.
- Taxable gain of $1,000.

13-2 EARNINGS AND PROFITS (E & P)

The notion of **earnings and profits** is similar in many respects to the financial accounting concept of retained earnings. Both are measures of the firm's accumulated capital. However, these two concepts differ in a fundamental way. The computation of retained earnings is based on financial accounting rules, while E & P is determined using rules specified in the tax law.

E & P fixes the upper limit on the amount of dividend income shareholders must recognize as a result of a distribution by the corporation. In this sense, E & P represents the corporation's economic ability to pay a dividend without impairing its capital. As a result, the effect of a specific transaction on the E & P account often can be determined by considering whether the transaction increases or decreases the corporation's capacity to pay a dividend.

---

[1] §§ 301(c)(1) and 316(a). Corporate shareholders claim a dividends received deduction. Others typically pay a tax on dividends at a maximum 15% or 20% rate.

[2] § 301(c).

TAX FACT Who Pays Dividends?

The vast majority of dividends paid by C corporations come from the very largest enterprises (measured by size of total assets) as reported on Forms 1120 for the latest tax year for which data are available.

Cash and stock dividends for the year totaled about $836 billion. Only about 13 percent of all dividend payments during a tax year are made by C corporations with less than $500 million in total assets.

Percentage of Dividends Paid, by Size of Corporate Assets

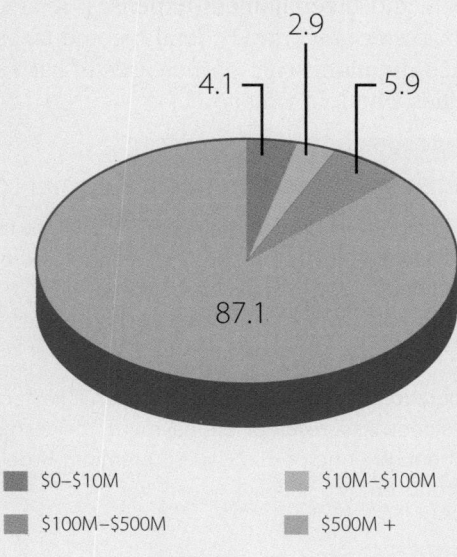

■ $0–$10M	■ $10M–$100M
■ $100M–$500M	■ $500M +

13-2a Computation of E & P

LO.2

Compute a corporation's earnings and profits (E & P).

The Code does not explicitly define the term *earnings and profits*. Instead, a series of adjustments to taxable income are identified to provide a measure of the corporation's economic income.[3] In general, E & P determinations are applied in the same manner for cash and accrual basis taxpayers.

Accumulated E & P is fixed as of the beginning of the tax year; it is the sum of the undistributed earnings of the entity since the later of its incorporation date or February 28, 1913. Current E & P is that portion of E & P attributable to the current tax year's operations. It is computed by using the corporation's Federal taxable income and then applying a series of adjustments to more closely approximate the cash flow of the entity.[4]

Additions to Taxable Income

To determine current E & P, one must add certain previously excluded income items back to taxable income. Included among these positive adjustments are interest income on municipal bonds, excluded life insurance proceeds (in excess of cash surrender value), and Federal income tax refunds from taxes paid in prior years.

In addition to excluded income items, the dividends received deduction and the domestic production activities deduction (DPAD) are added back to taxable income to determine E & P. Neither of these deductions decreases the corporation's assets. They are added back because they do not impair the corporation's ability to pay dividends: they do not reduce E & P.

---

[3]Reg. § 1.312–6(a).

[4]Section 312 describes many of the adjustments to taxable income necessary to determine E & P. Regulation § 1.312–6 addresses the effect of accounting methods on E & P.

Eagle Corporation collects $100,000 on a key employee life insurance policy (Eagle is the owner and beneficiary of the policy). At the time the policy matured on the death of the insured employee, it possessed a cash surrender value of $30,000. None of the $100,000 is included in Eagle's taxable income, but $70,000 is added to its taxable income when computing current E & P.

Subtractions from Taxable Income

Some of the corporation's nondeductible expenditures are subtracted from taxable income to arrive at E & P. These negative adjustments include the nondeductible portion of meals and entertainment expenses; related-party losses; expenses incurred to produce tax-exempt income; Federal income taxes paid; nondeductible key employee life insurance premiums (net of increases in cash surrender value); and nondeductible fines, penalties, and lobbying costs.

E & P Subtraction Modifications

Joseph Corporation sells property (basis of $10,000) to its sole shareholder for $8,000. Because of § 267 (disallowance of losses on sales between related parties), Joseph cannot deduct the $2,000 loss in computing its taxable income. But because the overall economic effect of the transaction is a decrease in Joseph's assets by $2,000, the loss reduces current E & P for the year of the sale.

Jacquie Corporation pays a $10,000 premium on a key employee life insurance policy covering the life of its president. As a result of the payment, the cash surrender value of the policy is increased by $7,000. Although none of the $10,000 premium is deductible by Jacquie for tax purposes, current E & P is reduced by $3,000.

Timing Adjustments

Some E & P adjustments shift the effect of a transaction from the year of its inclusion in or deduction from taxable income to the year in which it has an economic effect on the corporation. Charitable contribution carryovers, net operating loss carryovers, and capital loss carryovers all give rise to this kind of adjustment.

During 2016, Raven Corporation makes charitable contributions, $12,000 of which cannot be deducted in arriving at its taxable income for the year because of the 10% taxable income limitation. Consequently, the $12,000 is carried forward to 2017 and available for deduction in that year.

The excess charitable contribution reduces Raven's 2016 current E & P by $12,000 and increases its current E & P for 2017, when the deduction is allowed, by a like amount. The increase in 2017 E & P is necessary because the charitable contribution carryover reduces the taxable income for that year (the starting point for computing E & P) but already has been taken into account in determining 2016 current E & P.

Gains and losses from property transactions generally affect the determination of E & P only to the extent they are recognized for tax purposes. As a result, gains and losses deferred under the like-kind exchange provision and deferred involuntary conversion gains do not affect E & P until recognized. Accordingly, no timing adjustment is required for these items.

Accounting Method Adjustments

In addition to the above adjustments, accounting methods used for determining E & P generally are more conservative than those allowed for calculating taxable income. For example, the installment method is not permitted for E & P purposes even though, in some cases, it is allowed when computing taxable income. Accordingly, an adjustment is required for the deferred gain attributable to sales of property made during the year under the installment method. Specifically, all principal payments are treated as having been received in the year of sale.[5]

---

[5]§ 312(n)(5).

In 2016, Cardinal Corporation, a calendar year taxpayer, sells unimproved real estate (basis of $20,000) for $100,000. Under the terms of the sale, Cardinal will receive two annual payments of $50,000 beginning in 2017, each with interest of 9%. Cardinal does not elect out of the installment method.

Because Cardinal's 2016 taxable income will not reflect any of the gain from the sale, the corporation must make an $80,000 positive adjustment for that year (the deferred gain from the sale) in computing current E & P. Then $40,000 negative adjustments are required in 2017 and 2018 (i.e., when the deferred gain is recognized under the installment method).

Treatment of the gain for regular tax and E & P purposes can be summarized as follows. A similar analysis can be used for most of the timing and accounting method adjustments.

Tax Year	Regular Tax	E & P Treatment	E & P Adjustment
2016	$ –0–	$80,000	+$80,000
2017	40,000	–0–	–40,000
2018	40,000	–0–	–40,000

The alternative depreciation system (ADS) is used in computing E & P.[6] This method requires straight-line depreciation with a half-year convention, over a recovery period equal to the Asset Depreciation Range (ADR) midpoint life.[7] If MACRS cost recovery is used for income tax purposes, a positive or negative adjustment equal to the difference between MACRS and ADS must be made each year. Finally, no additional first-year depreciation is allowed under the ADS.[8]

Likewise, when assets are disposed of, an additional adjustment to taxable income is required to allow for the difference in gain or loss resulting from the difference in income tax basis and E & P basis.[9] The adjustments arising from depreciation are illustrated in the following example.

On January 2, 2016, White Corporation purchased equipment with an ADR midpoint life of 10 years for $30,000. The equipment was then depreciated over its 7-year MACRS class life. No § 179 or additional first-year depreciation was claimed. The asset was sold on July 2, 2018, for $27,000. For purposes of determining taxable income and E & P, cost recovery claimed on the equipment is summarized below.

Year	Cost Recovery Computation	MACRS	ADS	E & P Adjustment
2016	$30,000 × 14.29%	$ 4,287		
	$30,000 ÷ 10-year ADR recovery period × ½ (half-year for first year of service)		$1,500	$2,787
2017	$30,000 × 24.49%	7,347		
	$30,000 ÷ 10-year ADR recovery period		3,000	4,347
2018	$30,000 × 17.49% × ½ (half-year for year of disposal)	2,624		
	$30,000 ÷ 10-year ADR recovery period × ½ (half-year for year of disposal)		1,500	1,124
Total cost recovery		$14,258	$6,000	$8,258

Each year, White Corporation increases its taxable income by the adjustment amount indicated above to determine E & P. In addition, when computing 2018 E & P, White reduces taxable income by $8,258 to account for the excess gain recognized for income tax purposes.

continued

---

[6]§ 312(k)(3)(A).

[7]See § 168(g)(2). The ADR midpoint life for most assets is set out in Rev.Proc. 87–56, 1987–2 C.B. 674. The recovery period is 5 years for automobiles and light-duty trucks and 40 years for real property. For assets with no class life, the recovery period is 12 years.

[8]§ 168(k)(2). Under the MACRS provisions, additional first-year cost recovery is available for certain assets placed in service from 2008 through 2019. See Chapter 5.

[9]§ 312(f)(1).

	Income Tax	E & P
Amount realized	$ 27,000	$ 27,000
Adjusted basis for income tax ($30,000 cost − $14,258 MACRS)	(15,742)	
Adjusted basis for E & P ($30,000 cost − $6,000 ADS)		(24,000)
Gain on sale	$ 11,258	$ 3,000
Adjustment amount ($3,000 − $11,258)	($ 8,258)	

In addition to more conservative depreciation methods, the E & P rules impose limitations on the deductibility of § 179 expense.[10] In particular, this expense is deducted over a period of five years for E & P purposes. Therefore, in any year that § 179 is elected, 80 percent of the resulting expense is added back to taxable income to determine current E & P. In each of the following four years, a subtraction from taxable income equal to 20 percent of the § 179 expense is made.

EXAMPLE 8

On January 2, 2014, LarsonCo placed in service a five-year depreciable asset. The acquisition price of the asset was $50,000, and LarsonCo claimed a § 179 deduction for the full amount. Treatment of the § 179 amounts for regular tax and E & P purposes can be summarized as follows.

Tax Year	Regular Tax	E & P Treatment	E & P Adjustment
2014	$50,000	$10,000	+$40,000
2015	–0–	10,000	−10,000
2016	–0–	10,000	−10,000
2017	–0–	10,000	−10,000
2018	–0–	10,000	−10,000

The E & P rules also require specific accounting methods in various situations, making adjustments necessary when certain methods are used for income tax purposes. For example, E & P requires cost depletion rather than percentage depletion. When accounting for long-term contracts, E & P rules specify the percentage of completion method rather than the completed contract method. As the E & P determination does not allow for the amortization of organizational expenses, any such expense deducted when computing taxable income must be added back.

To account for income deferral under the LIFO inventory method, the E & P computation requires an adjustment for changes in the LIFO recapture amount (the excess of FIFO over LIFO inventory value) during the year. Increases in the LIFO recapture amount are added to taxable income and decreases are subtracted, to the extent of prior-year increases.

E & P rules also specify that intangible drilling costs and mine exploration and development costs be amortized over a period of 60 months and 120 months, respectively.[11] For income tax purposes, however, these costs can be deducted currently.

13-2b Summary of E & P Adjustments

E & P serves as a measure of the earnings of the corporation that are available for distribution as taxable dividends to the shareholders. Current E & P is determined by making a series of adjustments to the corporation's taxable income. These adjustments are reviewed in Concept Summary 13.1.

---

[10]§ 312(k)(3)(B).   [11]§ 312(n).

Concept Summary 13.1

Computing E & P

Transaction	Adjustment to Taxable Income to Determine Current E & P	
	Addition	**Subtraction**
Tax-exempt income	X	
Dividends received deduction	X	
Collection of proceeds from insurance policy on life of corporate employee (in excess of cash surrender value)	X	
Deferred gain on installment sale (all of the gain is added to E & P in year of sale)	X	
Future recognition of installment sale gross profit		X
Excess capital loss		X
Excess charitable contribution (over 10% limitation) in year incurred		X
Deduction of charitable contribution, NOL, or capital loss carryovers in succeeding taxable years (increase E & P because deduction reduces taxable income while E & P was reduced in a prior year)	X	
Federal income taxes paid		X
Federal income tax refund	X	
Loss on sale between related parties		X
Nondeductible fines, penalties, lobbying costs, meals, and entertainment		X
Payment of premiums on insurance policy on life of corporate employee (in excess of increase in cash surrender value of policy)		X
Realized gain (not recognized) on an involuntary conversion	No effect	
Realized gain or loss (not recognized) on a like-kind exchange	No effect	
Excess percentage depletion (only cost depletion can reduce E & P)	X	
Accelerated depreciation (E & P is reduced only by straight-line, units-of-production, or machine hours depreciation)	X	X
Additional first-year depreciation	X	
§ 179 expense in year elected (80%)	X	
§ 179 expense in four years following election (20% each year)		X
Increase (decrease) in LIFO recapture amount	X	X
Domestic production activities deduction	X	
Intangible drilling costs deducted currently (reduce E & P in future years by amortizing costs over 60 months)	X	
Mine exploration and development costs (reduce E & P in future years by amortizing costs over 120 months)	X	

13-2c Allocating E & P to Distributions

When a positive balance exists in both the current and accumulated E & P accounts, corporate distributions are deemed to be made first from current E & P and then from accumulated E & P. When distributions exceed the amount of current E & P, it becomes necessary to allocate current and accumulated E & P to each distribution made during the year. First, dollars of current E & P are applied on a pro rata basis to each distribution. Then accumulated E & P is applied in chronological order, beginning with the earliest distribution. This allocation is important if any shareholder sells stock during the year.

LO.3

Apply the rules for assigning earnings and profits to distributions.

EXAMPLE

9

On January 1 of the current year, Black Corporation holds accumulated E & P of $10,000. Current E & P for the year amounts to $30,000, earned evenly throughout the year. Megan and Matt are the sole *equal* shareholders of Black from January 1 to July 31.

On August 1, Megan sells all of her stock to Helen. Black makes two distributions to shareholders during the year: $40,000 to Megan and Matt ($20,000 to each) on July 1 and $40,000 to Matt and Helen ($20,000 to each) on December 1. Current and accumulated E & P are applied to the two distributions as follows.

	Source of Distribution		
	Current E & P	**Accumulated E & P**	**Return of Capital**
July 1 distribution ($40,000)	$15,000	$10,000	$15,000
December 1 distribution ($40,000)	15,000	–0–	25,000

Because 50% of the total distributions are made on July 1 and December 1, respectively, one-half of current E & P is assigned to each of the two distributions. Accumulated E & P is applied in chronological order, so the entire amount attaches to the July 1 distribution. The tax consequences to the shareholders follow.

	Shareholder		
	Megan	**Matt**	**Helen**
July distribution ($40,000)			
Dividend income—			
From current E & P ($15,000)	$ 7,500	$ 7,500	$ –0–
From accumulated E & P ($10,000)	5,000	5,000	–0–
Return of capital ($15,000)	7,500	7,500	–0–
December distribution ($40,000)			
Dividend income—			
From current E & P ($15,000)	–0–	7,500	7,500
From accumulated E & P ($0)	–0–	–0–	–0–
Return of capital ($25,000)	–0–	12,500	12,500
Total distribution	$20,000	$40,000	$20,000
Total dividend income	$12,500	$20,000	$ 7,500
Nontaxable return of capital (assuming sufficient basis in the stock investment)	$ 7,500	$20,000	$12,500

Because the balance in the accumulated E & P account is exhausted when it is applied to the July 1 distribution, Megan has more dividend income than Helen does, even though both receive equal distributions during the year. In addition, each shareholder's basis is reduced by the nontaxable return of capital; any excess over basis results in taxable gain.

When the tax years of the corporation and its shareholders are not the same, it may be impossible to determine the amount of current E & P on a timely basis. For example, if shareholders use a calendar year and the corporation uses a fiscal year, current E & P may not be ascertainable until after the shareholders' tax returns have been filed. To address this timing issue, the allocation rules presume that current E & P is sufficient to cover every distribution made during the year until the parties can show otherwise.

Green Corporation uses a June 30 fiscal year for tax purposes. Carol, Green's only shareholder, uses a calendar year. On July 1, 2016, Green has a zero balance in its accumulated E & P account. For fiscal year 2016–2017, the corporation incurs a $5,000 deficit in current E & P. On August 1, 2016, Green distributed $10,000 to Carol. The distribution is dividend income to Carol and is reported when she files her income tax return for the 2016 calendar year, on or before April 15, 2017.

Because Carol cannot prove until June 30, 2017, at the earliest, that the corporation has generated a deficit for the fiscal year, she must assume that the $10,000 distribution is fully drawn from a positive current E & P. When Carol learns of the deficit, she can file an amended return for 2016 showing the $10,000 as a return of capital. Alternatively, Carol can file for an extension for her 2016 return while she awaits Green Corporation's fiscal year-end.

EXAMPLE 10

Additional difficulties arise when either the current or the accumulated E & P account has a deficit balance. In particular, when current E & P is positive and accumulated E & P has a deficit balance, accumulated E & P is *not* netted against current E & P. Instead, the distribution is deemed to be a taxable dividend to the extent of the positive current E & P balance.

The Big Picture

Return to the facts of *The Big Picture* on p. 13-1. Recall that Lime Corporation had a deficit in GAAP-based retained earnings at the start of the year and banner profits during the year. Assume that these financial results translate into an $800,000 deficit in accumulated E & P at the start of the year and current E & P of $600,000. In addition, for purposes of this example, assume that there is no mortgage on the real estate.

In this case, current E & P would exceed the total cash and property distributed to the shareholders. The distributions are treated as taxable dividends; they are deemed to be paid from current E & P even though Lime still has a deficit in accumulated E & P at the end of the year.

EXAMPLE 11

In contrast to the previous rule, when a deficit exists in current E & P and a positive balance exists in accumulated E & P, the accounts are netted at the date of distribution. If the resulting balance is zero or negative, the distribution is a return of capital. If a positive balance results, the distribution is a dividend to the extent of the balance. Any loss in current E & P is deemed to accrue ratably throughout the year unless the parties can show otherwise. Various E & P rules are indicated in Concept Summary 13.2.

At the beginning of the current year, Gray Corporation (a calendar year taxpayer) holds accumulated E & P of $10,000. During the year, the corporation incurs a $15,000 deficit in current E & P that accrues ratably. On July 1, Gray distributes $6,000 in cash to Hal, its sole shareholder.

To determine how much of the $6,000 cash distribution represents dividend income to Hal, the balances of both accumulated and current E & P as of July 1 are determined and netted. This occurs because of the deficit in current E & P.

EXAMPLE 12

	Source of Distribution	
	Current E & P	Accumulated E & P
January 1		$10,000
July 1 (¹⁄₂ of $15,000 deficit in current E & P)	($7,500)	2,500

The balance in E & P just before the July 1 distribution is $2,500. Thus, of the $6,000 distribution, $2,500 is taxed as a dividend, and $3,500 represents a return of capital.

BRIDGE DISCIPLINE   **Bridge to Finance**

Investors often have tried to read the dividend policies of a corporation as indicators of the strength of the entity: constant dividend payments indicated a stable financial structure for the corporation, while dividend increases were a predictor of good times and triggered stock price increases. Reductions in historic dividend payment patterns foreshadowed financial difficulties and often caused a quick and sizable drop in share price.

Nobel Prize winners Merton Miller, University of Chicago, and Franco Modigliani, MIT, saw things differently. They viewed dividends as a remnant of various financing sources available to the corporation: if it was cheaper to finance future growth by retaining profits and decreasing or eliminating dividend payments, so be it. The entity must reduce its cost of capital wherever possible, and under this interpretation, a dividend decrease might indicate the internal financial strength of the corporation. Conversely, the payment of a dividend reduces the capital available to the entity, thereby forcing the entity to finance its operations and growth from some third-party source and risking future weakness if the cost of that capital increases.

Miller and Modigliani found that stock price and dividend policy were unrelated, and that changes in dividend patterns should not affect the capitalized value of the business. Even with lower tax rates on dividends, few shareholders complain that the typical growth stock rarely pays dividends. Nevertheless, shares of companies that pay dividends outperform those that don't pay dividends.

TAX PLANNING STRATEGIES   **Corporate Distributions**

FRAMEWORK FOCUS: INCOME AND EXCLUSIONS

Strategy: Avoid Income Recognition.

Concerning the discussion of corporate distributions, the following points are pertinent.

- Because E & P is the measure of dividend income, its periodic determination is essential to corporate planning. Thus, an E & P account should be established and maintained, particularly if the possibility exists that a corporate distribution might be a return of capital.

- Accumulated E & P is the sum of all past years' current E & P. Because there is no statute of limitations on the computation of E & P, the IRS can redetermine a corporation's current E & P for a tax year long ago. Such a change affects accumulated E & P and has a direct effect on the taxability of current distributions to shareholders.

- Distributions can be planned to avoid or minimize dividend exposure.

EXAMPLE

13

Flicker Corporation holds accumulated E & P of $100,000 as of January 1 of the current year. During the year, it expects to generate earnings from operations of $80,000 and to sell an asset for a loss of $100,000. Thus, it anticipates a current E & P deficit of $20,000. Flicker also expects to make a cash distribution of $60,000 during the year.

A tax-effective approach by Flicker would be to recognize the loss as soon as possible and immediately thereafter make the cash distribution to the shareholders. Suppose these two steps take place on January 1. Because the current E & P now shows a deficit, the accumulated E & P account must be brought up to date (refer to Example 12). Thus, at the time of the distribution, the combined E & P balance is zero [$100,000 (beginning balance in accumulated E & P) − $100,000 (existing deficit in current E & P)], and the $60,000 distribution to the shareholders constitutes a return of capital. Current deficits are deemed to accrue pro rata throughout the year unless the parties can prove otherwise. Here they can.

continued

After several unprofitable years, Darter Corporation has a deficit in accumulated E & P of $100,000 as of January 1, 2014. Starting in 2014, Darter expects to generate annual E & P of $50,000 for the next four years and would like to distribute this amount to its shareholders. The corporation's cash position (for dividend purposes) will correspond to the current E & P generated. Compare the following possibilities; Darter shareholders are indifferent between the two alternatives.

EXAMPLE 14

1. On December 31 of 2014, 2015, 2016, and 2017, Darter Corporation distributes cash of $50,000.
2. On December 31 of 2015 and 2017, Darter Corporation distributes cash of $100,000.

The two alternatives are illustrated as follows.

Year	Accumulated E & P (First of Year)	Current E & P	Distribution	Amount of Dividend
		Alternative 1		
2014	($100,000)	$50,000	$ 50,000	$50,000
2015	(100,000)	50,000	50,000	50,000
2016	(100,000)	50,000	50,000	50,000
2017	(100,000)	50,000	50,000	50,000
		Alternative 2		
2014	($100,000)	$50,000	$ –0–	$ –0–
2015	(50,000)	50,000	100,000	50,000
2016	(50,000)	50,000	–0–	–0–
2017	–0–	50,000	100,000	50,000

Alternative 1 produces $200,000 of dividend income because each $50,000 distribution is fully paid from current E & P. Alternative 2, however, produces only $100,000 of dividend income to the shareholders. The remaining $100,000 is a return of capital. Why?

When Darter made its first distribution of $100,000 on December 31, 2015, it had a deficit of $50,000 in accumulated E & P (the original deficit of $100,000 is reduced by the $50,000 of current E & P from 2014). Consequently, the $100,000 distribution yields a $50,000 dividend (the current E & P for 2015), and $50,000 is treated as a return of capital. As of January 1, 2016, Darter's accumulated E & P now has a deficit balance of $50,000, because a distribution cannot increase a deficit in E & P. Adding the remaining $50,000 of current E & P from 2016, the balance as of January 1, 2017, is zero. Thus, the second distribution of $100,000 made on December 31, 2017, also yields $50,000 of dividends (the current E & P for 2017) and a $50,000 return of capital.

By adjusting the distribution schedule only slightly, Darter shareholders cut in half their gross income from the payments.

Concept Summary 13.2

Allocating E & P to Distributions

1. Current E & P is applied first to distributions on a pro rata basis; then accumulated E & P is applied (as necessary) in chronological order beginning with the earliest distribution. See Example 9.

2. Until the parties can show otherwise, it is presumed that current E & P covers all distributions. See Example 10.

3. When a deficit exists in accumulated E & P and a positive balance exists in current E & P, distributions are regarded as dividends to the extent of current E & P. See Example 11.

4. When a deficit exists in current E & P and a positive balance exists in accumulated E & P, the two accounts are netted at the date of distribution. If the resulting balance is zero or a deficit, the distribution is treated as a return of capital, first reducing the basis of the stock to zero, then generating taxable gain. If a positive balance results, the distribution is a dividend to the extent of the balance. Any loss in current E & P is deemed to accrue ratably throughout the year unless the corporation can show otherwise. See Example 12.

Most investors look to the stocks of utilities, real estate investment trusts, and tobacco companies as the source of steady dividend payments. Alternatively, an investor could put together an effective portfolio using only stocks and mutual funds that regularly produce higher dividend yields.

Dividends can be important to the investor because:

- They may be attractive in a tax-sheltered account, like a § 401(k) plan, such that the tax inefficiency ("double taxation") of the dividends is not recognized immediately by the investor.

- Generally, a dividend-paying company is a profitable company, and corporate profits often are hard to come by.

- Earning and reinvesting dividends is an easy way to put into place an investment policy of dollar-cost averaging, a technique that forces the investor to buy more shares when prices are low and fewer shares when prices are high. Dollar-cost averaging often implements a contrarian investment strategy.

Evaluate the tax effects of noncash dividends on the recipient shareholder and the corporation making the distribution.

13-3 NONCASH DIVIDENDS

The previous discussion assumed that all distributions by a corporation to its shareholders are in the form of cash. Although most corporate distributions are paid in cash, a corporation may distribute a noncash, or property dividend for various reasons. For example, the shareholders may want a particular asset that is held by the corporation. Or a corporation that is strapped for cash may want to distribute a dividend to its shareholders.

Distributions of noncash assets are treated for tax purposes the same as distributions of cash, except for effects attributable to any difference between the basis and the fair market value of the distributed property. Distributions of property with a basis that differs from fair market value raise several tax questions.

- For the shareholder:
  - What is the amount of the distribution?
  - What is the basis of the property in the shareholder's hands?

- For the corporation:
  - Is a gain or loss recognized as a result of the distribution?
  - What is the effect of the distribution on E & P?

13-3a Noncash Dividends—Effect on the Shareholder

When a corporation distributes property rather than cash to a shareholder, the amount distributed is measured by the fair market value of the property on the date of distribution.[12] As with a cash distribution, the portion of a property distribution covered by existing E & P is a dividend, and any excess is treated as a return of capital. If the fair market value of the property distributed exceeds the corporation's E & P and the shareholder's basis in the stock investment, a capital gain usually results.

The amount distributed is reduced by any liabilities to which the distributed property is subject immediately before and after the distribution, and by any liabilities of the corporation assumed by the shareholder. The basis in the distributed property to the shareholder is the fair market value of the property on the date of the distribution.

---

[12]§ 301.

Return to the facts of *The Big Picture* on p. 13-1. Lime Corporation distributed property with a $300,000 fair market value and $20,000 adjusted basis to Gustavo, one of its shareholders. The property was subject to a $100,000 mortgage, which Gustavo assumed. As a result, Gustavo reports a distribution of $200,000 [$300,000 (fair market value) − $100,000 (liability)], which is taxed as a dividend. The basis of the property to Gustavo is $300,000, its fair market value.

Red Corporation owns 10% of Tan Corporation. Tan holds ample E & P to cover any distributions made during the year. One distribution made to Red consists of a vacant lot with a basis of $50,000 and a fair market value of $30,000. Red recognizes dividend income of $30,000 (before the dividends received deduction), and its basis in the lot becomes $30,000.

Distributing property that has depreciated in value as a property dividend may reflect poor income tax planning. Note what happens in Example 16. Basis of $20,000 disappears due to the loss (Tan's basis $50,000, fair market value $30,000). As an alternative, if Tan Corporation sells the lot, it can use the $20,000 loss to reduce its taxes. Then Tan can distribute the $30,000 cash proceeds to its shareholders.

13-3b Noncash Dividends—Effect on the Corporation

As noted earlier, the distribution of a property dividend raises two questions related to the corporation's tax position: Is a gain or loss recognized? What is the effect on E & P?

Recognition of Gain or Loss

All distributions of appreciated property trigger a recognized gain to the distributing corporation.[13] In effect, a corporation that distributes appreciated property is treated as if it had sold the property to the shareholder for its fair market value. However, the distributing corporation does *not* recognize any realized loss on the distributed property.

Return to the facts of *The Big Picture* on p. 13-1. Lime Corporation distributed property with a fair market value of $300,000 and an adjusted basis of $20,000 to Gustavo, one of its shareholders. As a result, Lime recognizes a $280,000 gain on the distribution.

A corporation distributes land with a basis of $30,000 and a fair market value of $10,000. The corporation does not recognize a loss on the distribution.

If the distributed property is subject to a liability in excess of basis or the shareholder assumes such a liability, a special rule applies. For purposes of determining gain on the distribution, the fair market value of the property is treated as being at least the amount of the liability.[14]

Assume that the land in Example 18 is subject to a liability of $35,000, which is assumed by the shareholder who receives the land. The corporation recognizes gain of $5,000 on the distribution ($35,000 liability − $30,000 basis in the land).

Effect of Corporate Distributions on E & P

Corporate distributions reduce E & P by the amount of money distributed and by the greater of the fair market value or the adjusted basis of property distributed, less the amount of any liability on the property.[15] E & P is increased by gain recognized when appreciated property is distributed as a property dividend.

---

[13]§ 311.

[14]§ 311(b)(2).

[15]§§ 312(a), (b), and (c).

Effects of Noncash Distributions

Crimson Corporation distributes property (basis $10,000 and fair market value $20,000) to Brenda, its shareholder. Crimson recognizes a $10,000 gain, which is added to its E & P. E & P then is reduced by $20,000, the fair market value of the distributed property. Brenda reports dividend income of $20,000 (presuming sufficient E & P).

Assume the same facts as in Example 20, except that the property's adjusted basis to Crimson is $25,000. Crimson's E & P is reduced by $25,000, the property's adjusted basis, which is greater than the property's fair market value. Brenda reports dividend income of $20,000 (the fair market value of the property received).

Assume the same facts as in Example 21, except that the property is subject to a liability of $6,000, which Brenda assumes. E & P now is reduced by $19,000 [$25,000 (adjusted basis) − $6,000 (liability)]. Brenda records a dividend of $14,000 [$20,000 (amount of the distribution) − $6,000 (liability)], and her basis in the property is $20,000, its fair market value.

Under no circumstances can a distribution, whether cash or property, either generate a deficit in E & P or add to a deficit in E & P. Deficits can arise only through recognized corporate losses.

EXAMPLE 23

Teal Corporation holds accumulated E & P of $10,000 at the beginning of the current tax year. During the year, it records current E & P of $15,000. At the end of the year, it distributes cash of $30,000 to its sole shareholder, Walter.

Teal's E & P at the end of the year is reduced to zero by the dividend distribution. The remaining $5,000 of the distribution to Walter cannot generate a deficit in E & P.

Source of Distribution	Effects
Current E & P	($15,000)
Accumulated E & P	(10,000)
Return of Capital	5,000

BRIDGE DISCIPLINE   **Bridge to Finance**

The double taxation of corporate income always has been controversial. Arguably, taxing dividends twice creates several undesirable economic distortions, including:

- An incentive to invest in noncorporate rather than corporate entities.

- An incentive for corporations to finance operations with debt rather than with equity because interest payments are deductible. Notably, this behavior increases the vulnerability of corporations in economic downturns.

- An incentive for corporations to retain earnings and structure distributions of profits to avoid the double tax.

Collectively, these distortions raise the cost of capital for corporate investments. In addition, elimination of the double tax would make the United States more competitive globally, as a majority of U.S. trading partners assess only one tax on corporate income.

While many support a reduced or zero tax rate on dividends, others contend that the double tax should remain in place, to rein in the concentration of economic power held by publicly traded corporations. Those favoring retention of the double tax also note that the benefits of reduced tax rates on dividends flow disproportionately to the wealthy.

DIGGING DEEPER 1   **In-depth coverage can be found on this book's companion website:** www.cengagebrain.com

13-4 CONSTRUCTIVE DIVIDENDS

LO.5

Identify the nature and treatment of constructive dividends.

Any measurable economic benefit conveyed by a corporation to its shareholders can be treated as a dividend for Federal income tax purposes even though it is not declared or designated as a dividend. A so-called constructive dividend typically is not issued pro rata to all shareholders.[16] Nor must the distribution satisfy the requirements of a dividend as set forth by applicable state law. Instead, a constructive dividend is strictly a creation of the Federal income tax law.

Constructive dividends usually arise in the context of closely held corporations. Here the dealings between the parties are less structured, and frequently, formalities are not preserved.

The constructive dividend might be seen as a substitute for actual distributions. Usually, it is intended to accomplish some tax objective not available through the direct payment of dividends. The shareholders may be attempting to distribute corporate profits in a form, such as compensation, that is deductible to the corporation. Alternatively, the shareholders may be seeking benefits for themselves while avoiding the recognition of income.

Some constructive dividends are, in reality, disguised dividends. But not all constructive dividends are deliberate attempts to avoid formal dividends; many are entered into inadvertently. An awareness of the various constructive dividend situations is essential to protect the parties from unanticipated, undesirable tax consequences.

13-4a Types of Constructive Dividends

The most frequently encountered types of constructive dividends are summarized below and on the following pages.

Shareholder Use of Corporate-Owned Property

A constructive dividend can occur when a shareholder uses the corporation's property for personal purposes at no cost. Personal use of corporate-owned automobiles, airplanes, yachts, fishing camps, hunting lodges, and other entertainment facilities is commonplace in some closely held corporations. The shareholder recognizes dividend income to the extent of the fair rental value of the property for the period of its personal use.[17]

Bargain Sale of Corporate Property to a Shareholder

Shareholders often purchase property from a corporation at a cost below the fair market value of the property. These bargain sales produce dividend income to the extent that the property's fair market value on the date of sale differs from the amount the shareholder paid for the property.[18] These situations might be avoided by appraising the property on or about the date of the sale. The appraised value should become the price to be paid by the shareholder.

Bargain Rental of Corporate Property

A bargain rental of corporate property by a shareholder also produces dividend income. Here the measure of the constructive dividend is the excess of the property's fair rental value over the rent actually paid. Again, appraisal data should be used to avoid any questionable situations.

---

[16]See *Lengsfield v. Comm.*, 57–1 USTC ¶9437, 50 AFTR 1683, 241 F.2d 508 (CA–5, 1957).

[17]*Daniel L. Reeves*, 94 TCM 287, T.C.Memo. 2007–273.

[18]Reg. § 1.301–1(j).

GLOBAL TAX ISSUES   **A Worldwide View of Dividends**

From an international perspective, U.S. double taxation of dividends is unusual. Most developed countries have adopted a policy of *corporate integration*, which imposes a single tax on corporate profits.

Corporate integration takes several forms. One popular approach is to impose a tax at the corporate level, but allow shareholders to claim a credit for corporate-level taxes paid when dividends are received. A second alternative is to allow a corporate-level deduction for dividends paid to shareholders. A third approach is to allow shareholders to exclude corporate dividends from income. A fourth alternative is the adoption of a "comprehensive business income tax," which excludes both dividend and interest income while disallowing deductions for interest expense.

Facing trade-offs between equity and the economic distortions introduced by double taxation and the prevalence of corporate integration throughout the world, U.S. tax law continues to struggle with the issue of how corporate distributions should be taxed.

Payments for the Benefit of a Shareholder

If a corporation satisfies an obligation of a shareholder, the payment is treated as a constructive dividend. The obligation involved need not be legally binding on the shareholder; it may, in fact, be a moral obligation.[19] Forgiveness of shareholder indebtedness by the corporation creates an identical problem.[20] Excessive rentals paid by a corporation for the use of shareholder property also are treated as constructive dividends.

Unreasonable Compensation

A salary payment to a shareholder-employee that is deemed to be **unreasonable compensation** frequently is treated as a constructive dividend. As a consequence, it is not deductible by the corporation. In determining the reasonableness of salary payments, the following factors are considered.

- The employee's qualifications.
- A comparison of salaries with dividend distributions.
- The prevailing rates of compensation for comparable positions in comparable business concerns.
- The nature and scope of the employee's work.
- The size and complexity of the business.
- A comparison of salaries paid with both gross and net income.
- The taxpayer's salary policy toward all employees.
- For small corporations with a limited number of officers, the amount of compensation paid to the employee in question in previous years.
- For large corporations, whether a "reasonable investor" would have agreed to the level of compensation paid.[21]

Loans to Shareholders

Advances to shareholders that are not bona fide loans usually are reclassified as constructive dividends. Whether an advance qualifies as a bona fide loan is a question of

---

[19]*Montgomery Engineering Co. v. U.S.*, 64–2 USTC ¶9618, 13 AFTR 2d 1747, 230 F.Supp. 838 (D.Ct. N.J., 1964), *aff'd* in 65–1 USTC ¶9368, 15 AFTR 2d 746, 344 F.2d 996 (CA–3, 1965).

[20]Reg. § 1.301–1(m).

[21]*Mayson Manufacturing Co. v. Comm.*, 49–2 USTC ¶9467, 38 AFTR 1028, 178 F.2d 115 (CA–6, 1949) and *Alpha Medical v. Comm.*, 99–1 USTC ¶50,461, 83 AFTR 2d 99–697, 172 F.3d 942 (CA–6, 1999).

TAX IN THE NEWS Hard Work Pays Off!

By 1985, William Rogers, a pharmacist with 25 years of experience in health care, had successfully developed and sold two businesses—a pharmacy chain and a medical supply company. In 1986, after turning down a $1 million offer to manage the home health care division of a large corporation, Rogers founded Alpha Medical, Inc., with a $1,000 contribution. Over the next four years, Rogers built Alpha Medical into a business with 60 employees, a taxable income of almost $7 million, and a 1990 return on equity of almost 100 percent. The business provided both financial management and medical consulting services to hospitals and home health care companies.

Rogers was the company's sole shareholder and president. He regularly worked 12 hours a day and was on call 24 hours a day. Rogers made all major decisions for Alpha Medical, acquired all of the company's clients, and personally negotiated all of the company's contracts. In addition, he personally developed many of the company's products and collaborated with programmers to develop proprietary software used by the company.

In 1986, Rogers received only $67,000 in compensation. The amount increased to $431,000 in 1988 and $928,000 in 1989. In 1990, Rogers was paid over $4.4 million, 64 percent of the company's taxable income, while the company paid only a $1,500 dividend.

During an audit of Alpha Medical, the IRS argued that only $400,000 of Rogers' compensation in 1990 was reasonable and that the remaining $4 million was not deductible. The IRS assessed a $1.3 million tax deficiency plus penalties.

The Tax Court split the difference between the IRS and the taxpayer, holding that $2.3 million of Rogers' pay was reasonable. On appeal, however, the Sixth Circuit Court of Appeals ruled that all $4.4 million of the compensation paid to Rogers was reasonable. In its decision, the Court of Appeals said that "in light of Rogers' record of accomplishment, risks he assumed, and amazing growth, reasonable shareholders would have gladly agreed to Rogers' level of compensation."

The Court of Appeals also explicitly noted that Rogers had been undercompensated in prior years and that he had incurred a substantial opportunity cost when he refused the $1 million job offer so that he could start Alpha Medical.

fact to be determined in light of the particular circumstances. Factors considered in determining whether the advance is a bona fide loan include the following.[22]

- Whether the advance is on open account or is evidenced by a written instrument.
- Whether the shareholder furnished collateral or other security for the advance.
- How long the advance has been outstanding.
- Whether any repayments have been made.
- The shareholder's ability to repay the advance.
- The shareholder's use of the funds (e.g., payment of routine bills versus nonrecurring, extraordinary expenses).
- The regularity of the advances.
- The dividend-paying history of the corporation.

13-4b Tax Treatment of Constructive Dividends

For tax purposes, constructive distributions are treated like actual distributions.[23] Thus, a corporate shareholder is entitled to the dividends received deduction (refer to Chapter 12). The constructive distribution constitutes dividend income only to the extent of the corporation's current and accumulated E & P.[24]

In-depth coverage can be found on this book's companion website: www.cengagebrain.com   **2 DIGGING DEEPER**

---

[22]*Fin Hay Realty Co. v. U.S.*, 68–2 USTC ¶9438, 22 AFTR 2d 5004, 398 F.2d 694 (CA–3, 1968).

[23]*Simon v. Comm.*, 57–2 USTC ¶9989, 52 AFTR 698, 248 F.2d 869 (CA–8, 1957).

[24]*DiZenzo v. Comm.*, 65–2 USTC ¶9518, 16 AFTR 2d 5107, 348 F.2d 122 (CA–2, 1965).

TAX PLANNING STRATEGIES **Constructive Dividends**

FRAMEWORK FOCUS: INCOME AND EXCLUSIONS

Strategy: Avoid Income Recognition.

Tax planning can be particularly effective in avoiding constructive dividend situations. Shareholders should try to structure their dealings with the corporation on an arm's length basis. For example, reasonable rent should be paid for the use of corporate property, and a fair price should be paid for its purchase. The parties should make every effort to support the amount involved with appraisal data or market information obtained from reliable sources at or near the time of the transaction.

Dealings between shareholders and a closely held corporation should be as formal as possible. In the case of loans to shareholders, for example, the parties should provide for an adequate rate of interest and written evidence of the debt. Shareholders also should establish and follow a realistic repayment schedule.

If shareholders want to distribute corporate profits in a form deductible to the corporation, a balanced mix of the possible alternatives lessens the risk of constructive dividend treatment. Rent for the use of shareholder property, interest on amounts borrowed from shareholders, or salaries for services rendered by shareholders are all feasible substitutes for dividend distributions. But overdoing any one approach may attract the attention of the IRS. Too much interest, for example, may mean that the corporation is thinly capitalized, and some of the debt may be reclassified as equity.

Much can be done to protect against the disallowance of unreasonable compensation. Example 24 is an illustration, all too common in a family corporation, of what *not* to do.

EXAMPLE
24

Bob Cole wholly owns Eagle Corporation. Corporate employees and annual salaries include Rebecca, Bob's wife ($120,000); Sam, Bob's son ($80,000); Bob ($640,000); and Ed, an unrelated longtime friend ($320,000). The operation of Eagle is shared about equally between Bob and Ed. Rebecca performed significant services for Eagle during its formative years but now merely attends the annual meeting of the board of directors. Sam is a full-time student and occasionally signs papers for the corporation in his capacity as treasurer.

Eagle has not made a cash distribution for 10 years, although it holds substantial accumulated E & P. Rebecca, Sam, and Bob run the risk of a finding of unreasonable compensation, based on the following factors.

- Rebecca's salary is vulnerable unless proof is available that some or all of her $120,000 annual salary is payment for services rendered to the corporation in prior years and that she was underpaid for those years.[25]

- Sam's salary also is vulnerable; he does not appear to earn the $80,000 paid to him by the corporation. Although neither Sam nor Rebecca is a shareholder, each one's relationship to Bob is enough of a tie-in to raise the unreasonable compensation issue.

- Bob's salary appears susceptible to challenge. Why is he receiving $320,000 more than Ed, when it appears that they share equally in the operation of the corporation?

- The fact that Eagle has not distributed any cash over the past 10 years, even though it is capable of doing so, increases the likelihood of a constructive dividend.

What could have been done to improve the tax position of the parties in Example 24? Rebecca and Sam are not entitled to a significant salary, as neither seems to be performing any services for the corporation. Bob probably should reduce his compensation to correspond to that paid to Ed. He then can attempt to distribute corporate earnings to himself in some other form.

continued

---

[25]See, for example, *R. J. Nicoll Co.*, 59 T.C. 37 (1972).

Paying some dividends to Bob also would help alleviate the problems raised in Example 24. The IRS has been successful in denying a deduction for salary paid to a shareholder-employee, even when the payment was reasonable, in a situation where the corporation had not distributed any dividends.[26] Most courts, however, have not denied deductions for compensation solely because a dividend was not paid. A better approach is to compare an employee's compensation with the level of compensation prevalent in the particular industry.

The corporation can substitute *indirect* compensation for Bob by paying expenses that benefit him personally but are nevertheless deductible to the corporation. For example, premiums paid by the corporation for sickness, accident, and hospitalization insurance for Bob are deductible to the corporation and generally nontaxable to him.[27] Any payments under the policy are not taxable to Bob unless they exceed his medical expenses.[28]

The corporation also can pay for travel and entertainment expenses incurred by Bob on behalf of the corporation. If these expenditures are primarily for the benefit of the corporation, Bob recognizes no taxable income, and the corporation claims a deduction.[29] The tax treatment of these benefits is discussed in more detail in Chapter 11.

When testing for reasonableness, the IRS looks at the total compensation package, including indirect compensation payments to a shareholder-employee. Thus, indirect payments must not be overlooked.

What Is the Employee's Compensation?

EXAMPLE 25

Cora, the president and sole shareholder of Willet Corporation, is paid an annual salary of $400,000 by the corporation. She would like to draw funds from the corporation but is concerned that additional salary payments might cause the IRS to contend that her salary is unreasonable.

Cora does not want Willet to pay any dividends. She also wants to donate $50,000 to her alma mater to establish scholarships for needy students. Willet Corporation could make the contribution on its president's behalf. The payment clearly benefits Cora, but the amount of the contribution is not taxed to her.[30] Willet claims a charitable contribution deduction for the payment.

EXAMPLE 26

Assume in Example 25 that Cora has made an individual pledge to the university to provide $50,000 for scholarships for needy students. Willet Corporation satisfies Cora's pledge by paying the $50,000 to the university. The $50,000 will be taxed to Cora. In this context, the $50,000 payment to the university may be treated as *indirect* compensation to Cora.[31]

In determining whether Cora's salary is unreasonable, both the *direct* payment of her $400,000 salary and the *indirect* $50,000 payment are considered. Cora's total compensation package is $450,000. Cora may be eligible for a charitable contribution deduction of up to 50% of her adjusted gross income (see Chapter 10).

Certain activities can combine both business and personal dimensions (e.g., a business trip to Hawaii). A country club membership can generate both business and personal use. Such items can be attractive as forms of indirect compensation, but disentangling the business and personal use of business assets can be a challenge.

---

[26]*McCandless Tile Service v. U.S.*, 70–1 USTC ¶9284, 25 AFTR 2d 70–870, 422 F.2d 1336 (Ct.Cls., 1970). The court in *McCandless* concluded that a return on equity of 15% of net profits was reasonable.

[27]Reg. § 1.162–10.

[28]The medical reimbursement plan must meet certain nondiscrimination requirements. § 105(h)(2).

[29]Reg. § 1.62–2(c)(4).

[30]*Henry J. Knott*, 67 T.C. 681 (1977).

[31]*Schalk Chemical Co. v. Comm.*, 62–1 USTC ¶9496, 9 AFTR 2d 1579, 304 F.2d 48 (CA–9, 1962).

Ultimately, whether a constructive dividend exists when indirect compensation is used often depends on the employer's policies and related documentation substantiating some business justification for the usage. Many companies have policies that allow for the "limited personal use" of certain corporate assets (such as computers, telephones, mobile devices, copy machines, conference rooms, and vehicles). This "limited personal use" exception is normally provided as long as the use is occasional, is not for outside employment, does not result in excessive costs, and does not interfere with work responsibilities.

LO.6

Distinguish between taxable and nontaxable stock dividends.

13-5 STOCK DIVIDENDS

On occasion, a C corporation issues a dividend in the form of its own stock (i.e., instead of using cash or other property). This may occur because the entity is short of cash or because it wants to dispose of some treasury stock that it holds. A **stock dividend** is triggered by a board directive. Stock dividends are rare events; about 2 percent of all C corporation distributions during a typical tax year involve the corporation's own shares.

As a general rule, stock dividends are excluded from income if they are pro rata distributions of stock or stock rights paid on common stock.[32] However, there are exceptions to this general rule.

DIGGING DEEPER 3 | **In-depth coverage can be found on this book's companion website: www.cengagebrain.com**

If a stock dividend is not taxable, the corporation's E & P is not reduced.[33] If a stock dividend is taxable, the distributing corporation treats the distribution in the same manner as any other taxable distribution.

If a stock dividend is taxable, the shareholder's basis of the newly received shares is fair market value and the holding period starts on the date of receipt. If a stock dividend is not taxable, the basis of the stock on which the dividend is distributed is reallocated.[34]

If the dividend shares are identical to these formerly held shares, basis in the old stock is reallocated by dividing the taxpayer's cost in the old stock by the total number of shares. If the dividend stock is not identical to the underlying shares (e.g., a stock dividend of preferred on common), basis is determined by allocating the basis of the formerly held shares between the old and new stock according to the fair market value of each. The holding period includes the holding period of the previously held stock.[35]

Stock Dividends

EXAMPLE 27

Gail bought 1,000 shares of common stock two years ago for $10,000. In the current tax year, Gail receives 10 shares of common stock as a nontaxable stock dividend. To determine Gail's basis in the new shares, the existing basis of $10,000 is divided by 1,010 (the number of shares outstanding after the distribution). Consequently, each share of stock now has a basis of $9.90 instead of the pre-dividend $10 basis.

EXAMPLE 28

Assume instead that Gail received a nontaxable preferred stock dividend of 100 shares. The preferred stock has a fair market value of $1,000, and the common stock, on which the preferred is distributed, has a fair market value of $19,000. After the receipt of the stock dividend, the basis of the common stock is $9,500, and the basis of the preferred is $500, computed as follows.

continued

---

[32]Companies often issue stock dividends or authorize stock splits to keep the stock price in an affordable range. Stock splits do not change the total value of an investment. For example, 100 shares at $100 will become 200 shares at $50 after the split. However, some studies show that a stock split often leads to an upward price trend over the year following the split.

[33]§ 312(d)(1).

[34]§ 307(a).

[35]§ 1223(5).

Fair market value of common	$19,000
Fair market value of preferred	1,000
	$20,000
Basis of common: $^{19}/_{20} \times \$10,000$	$ 9,500
Basis of preferred: $^{1}/_{20} \times \$10,000$	$ 500

In-depth coverage can be found on this book's companion website: www.cengagebrain.com   **4 DIGGING DEEPER**

13-6 STOCK REDEMPTIONS

LO.7

Discuss the tax treatment of stock redemptions and corporate liquidations.

Many investors are tempted to use a "no dividends" strategy in working with a healthy corporation whose accumulated profits and market value continue to rise over time.

EXAMPLE

29

Sally invests $100,000 in the new Cream Corporation. Cream is successful in generating operating profits, and it reinvests its accumulated profits in the business rather than paying dividends. Fifteen years later, Sally's shares are worth $300,000, and her share of Cream's E & P exceeds $1 million. Sally sells the shares for a $200,000 long-term capital gain, taxed at a rate of only 20%. By selling her stock to a third party, Sally can reduce the sales proceeds by her stock basis, resulting in a significant tax savings to her, at no detriment to Cream.

A similar strategy would seem to work where several shareholders can act in concert. Using a **stock redemption** to carry out this strategy, the corporation buys back shares from its shareholders in a market transaction. Stock redemptions occur for numerous reasons, including the following.

- To acquire the holdings of a retiring or deceased shareholder.
- To carry out a property settlement related to a divorce.
- To increase the per-share price of the stock as it trades in a market.
- To implement a business succession plan (e.g., using a buy-sell agreement to transfer shares from one generation of shareholders to a younger one).

BRIDGE DISCIPLINE Bridge to Finance

Stock buybacks are popular among U.S. corporations as a means to manipulate share prices. If a buyback is executed properly, all shareholders retain their respective levels of control over the entity, but because fewer shares now are available on the market, an artificial increase in share price occurs. Often, the market temporarily "overcorrects" for the buyback, probably because of the publicity the transaction attracts in the press, and the corporation's total capitalized value actually increases.

Most stock buybacks result in dividend income to the shareholders. Stock redemptions of this type generally do not qualify for capital gain/loss treatment under the tax law. Thus, parties must measure the costs associated with an effective distribution of retained earnings in this way. If dividend income is subject to a favorable tax rate or if the corporate owner of the redeemed shares qualifies for the dividends received deduction, there are few impediments to the plans for the buyback.

Some analysts see an increase in stock buyback activity as a sign of an increasingly healthy economy. A combination of large corporate cash balances and low market interest rates also can accelerate the buyback market.

GLOBAL TAX ISSUES   Non-U.S. Shareholders Prefer Capital Gain Treatment in Stock Redemptions

As a general rule, non-U.S. shareholders of U.S. corporations are subject to U.S. income tax on dividend income but not on capital gains. In some situations, a nonresident alien or business entity is taxed on a capital gain from the disposition of stock in a U.S. corporation, but only if the stock was effectively connected with the conduct of a U.S. trade or business of the individual. See Chapter 16.

Whether a stock redemption qualifies for capital gain treatment therefore takes on added significance for non-U.S. shareholders. If one of the qualifying stock redemption rules can be satisfied, the foreign shareholder typically will avoid U.S. income tax on the transaction. If, instead, dividend income is the result, a 30 percent withholding tax typically applies.

Stock redemptions generally result in dividend income for the shareholder whose stock is redeemed, rather than a capital gain or loss, unless the shareholder surrenders significant control in the entity as a result of the redemption. Capital gain/loss treatment largely is restricted to stock buybacks where either:

- All of the shareholder's stock is redeemed.[36]
- After the redemption, the investor is a minority shareholder and owns less than 80 percent of the interest owned in the corporation before the redemption.[37]

DIGGING DEEPER 5   In-depth coverage can be found on this book's companion website: www.cengagebrain.com

In measuring the investor's stock holdings before and after the redemption, shares owned by related taxpayers also are counted.[38]

DIGGING DEEPER 6   In-depth coverage can be found on this book's companion website: www.cengagebrain.com

EXAMPLE 30

Mike and Cheryl are husband and wife, and each owns 100 shares in Mauve Corporation, the total of all of Mauve's outstanding stock. Mauve's operations have produced a sizable aggregated operating profit over the years, such that its E & P exceeds $5 million. Mike and Cheryl have realized appreciation of $600,000 on their original investment of $100,000 each, and they would like to enjoy some of the cash that Mauve has accumulated during their holding period.

At Mike's request, instead of paying a dividend, Mauve buys back one-half of Mike's shares for $350,000. This seems to produce a $300,000 long-term capital gain [$350,000 (sales proceeds) − $50,000 (basis in 50 shares of Mauve stock)], but it results in a $350,000 dividend for Mike, as the redemption did not reduce the control of Mauve that Mike and Cheryl can exercise.

When the transaction is treated as a dividend, the investor's basis in the redeemed shares *does not disappear*; rather, it attaches to any remaining shares that he or she owns. Corporate E & P is reduced by the amount of any recognized dividend.

Stock redemptions also can result in capital gain/loss treatment when the shareholder dies or when the corporation downsizes.[39] Other tax consequences for the redeeming corporation are summarized as follows.

- If noncash property is used to acquire the redeemed shares, the corporation recognizes any realized gain (but not loss) on the distributed assets.[40]
- When the shareholder is taxed as having received a capital gain, E & P of the redeeming corporation *disappears* to the extent of the percentage of shares redeemed relative to the shares outstanding before the buyback.[41]

---

[36]§ 302(b)(3).

[37]§ 302(b)(2).

[38]Section 318 is used for this purpose.

[39]For example, see §§ 302(b)(4) and 303.

[40]§ 311.

[41]The E & P reduction cannot exceed the amount of the redemption proceeds. § 312(n)(7).

Strategy: Control the Character of Income and Deductions.

Stock redemptions offer several possibilities for tax planning.

- Usually a stock redemption triggers dividend treatment. A preferential tax rate on dividend income reduces some of the adverse consequences of a nonqualified stock redemption for noncorporate shareholders.

- Dividend treatment for a stock redemption may be preferable to a redemption that produces a capital gain if the distributing corporation has little or no E & P or where the distributee-shareholder is another C corporation. In the latter situation, dividend treatment may be preferred due to the availability of the dividends received deduction.

- Stock redemptions are particularly well suited for purchasing the interest of a retiring or deceased shareholder. Rather than the remaining shareholders buying the stock of the retiring or deceased shareholder, corporate funds are used to redeem the stock from the retiring shareholder or from the decedent shareholder's estate. The ability to use the corporation's funds to buy out a shareholder's interest also can be advantageous in property settlements between divorcing taxpayers.

13-7 CORPORATE LIQUIDATIONS

When a corporation makes a nonliquidating distribution (e.g., a cash dividend or a stock redemption), the entity typically continues as a going concern. With a complete liquidation, however, corporate existence terminates, as does the shareholder's ownership interest. A complete liquidation, like a qualifying stock redemption, produces capital gain/loss treatment to the *shareholder*. However, the tax effects of a liquidation to the *corporation* vary somewhat from those of a redemption. Gain/loss treatment is the general rule for the liquidating corporation, although some losses are disallowed.

13-7a The Liquidation Process

Shareholders may decide to liquidate a corporation for one or more reasons, including the following.

- The corporate business has been unsuccessful.
- The shareholders want to acquire the corporation's assets.
- Another person or entity wants to purchase the corporation's assets. The purchaser may buy the shareholders' stock and then liquidate the corporation to acquire the assets. Alternatively, the purchaser may buy the assets directly from the corporation. After the assets are sold, the corporation distributes the sales proceeds to its shareholders and liquidates.

A **corporate liquidation** exists when a corporation ceases to be a going concern. The corporation continues solely to wind up its affairs, pay debts, and distribute any remaining assets to its shareholders. Legal dissolution under state law is not required for a liquidation to be complete for tax purposes. A liquidation can exist even if the corporation retains a nominal amount of assets to pay remaining debts and preserve legal status.[42]

13-7b Liquidating and Nonliquidating Distributions Compared

As noted previously, a *nonliquidating* property distribution, whether in the form of a dividend or a stock redemption, triggers gain (but not loss) to the distributing corporation. For the shareholder, the receipt of cash or property produces dividend income to the extent of the corporation's E & P or, in the case of a qualifying stock redemption, results in a capital gain or loss.

---

[42]Reg. § 1.332–2(c).

However, a complete liquidation produces different tax consequences to the liquidating corporation.[43] With certain exceptions, a liquidating corporation recognizes gain *and* loss upon the distribution of its assets. Thus, a liquidation usually results in income tax for both the corporation and the shareholders; this can be seen as a form of double taxation.

EXAMPLE 31

Goose Corporation, with an E & P balance of $40,000, makes a cash distribution of $50,000 to one of its shareholders. The shareholder's basis in the Goose stock is $24,000. If the distribution is not a qualifying stock redemption or in complete liquidation, the shareholder recognizes dividend income of $40,000 (the amount of Goose's E & P) and treats the remaining $10,000 of the distribution as a return of capital (i.e., stock basis is reduced to $14,000).

If the distribution is a qualifying stock redemption or is pursuant to a complete liquidation, the shareholder recognizes a capital gain of $26,000 ($50,000 distribution − $24,000 stock basis).

DIGGING DEEPER 7   **In-depth coverage can be found on this book's companion website: www.cengagebrain.com**

TAX PLANNING STRATEGIES **Corporate Liquidations**

FRAMEWORK FOCUS: TAX RATES

Strategy: Avoid Double Taxation.

Usually, distributions in liquidation are taxed at both the corporate level and the shareholder level. When a corporation liquidates, it can, as a general rule, deduct losses on assets that have depreciated in value. These assets should not be distributed in the form of a property dividend or stock redemption, because losses are not recognized on nonliquidating distributions.

Shareholders faced with large prospective gains in a liquidation may consider shifting part or all of that gain to other taxpayers. One approach is to donate the liquidating corporation's stock to charity, producing a deduction equal to the stock's fair market value.

Alternatively, the stock may be transferred by gift to family members. Some or all of the later capital gain on liquidation could be taxed at a lower tax rate on long-term capital gains. However, possible gift tax issues on the stock transfer must be considered (see Chapter 1). Effective planning for stock transfers in the context of a liquidation therefore is crucial in arriving at the desired tax result.

13-8 RESTRICTIONS ON CORPORATE ACCUMULATIONS

Two provisions of the Code are designed to prevent corporations and their shareholders from avoiding the double tax on dividend distributions. Both provisions impose a penalty tax on undistributed income retained by the corporation. The rules underlying these provisions are complex and beyond the scope of this text. However, a brief description is provided as an introduction.

The *accumulated earnings tax*[44] imposes a 20 percent tax on the current year's corporate earnings that have been accumulated without a reasonable business need. The burden of proving what constitutes a reasonable need is borne by the taxpayer. In determining the excessive accumulated income, most businesses are allowed a $250,000 minimum exemption. Thus, most corporations can accumulate $250,000 in earnings over a series of years without fear of an accumulated earnings tax. Beyond the exemption amount, a C corporation's earnings can be accumulated, without incurring the penalty tax, for:

[43]§ 331.   [44]§§ 531–537.

- Working capital needs (e.g., to purchase inventory or pay salaries and taxes),

- Retirement of debt incurred in connection with the business,

- Investment or loans to suppliers or customers (if necessary to maintain the corporation's business), or

- Realistic business contingencies, including lawsuits or self-insurance.

The *personal holding company (PHC) tax*[45] acts to discourage the sheltering of gross income in corporations owned by individuals who are subject to high marginal income tax rates. The PHC tax is applied at a 20 percent rate; in any tax year, the IRS cannot impose both the PHC tax and the accumulated earnings tax on the same corporation. Generally, an entity is considered a PHC and may be subject to the tax if:

- More than 50 percent of the value of the outstanding stock was owned by five or fewer individuals at any time during the last half of the year, and

- A substantial portion (60 percent or more) of the corporation's income is comprised of dividends, interest, rents, royalties, or certain personal service income.

REFOCUS ON THE BIG PICTURE

TAXING CORPORATE DISTRIBUTIONS

A number of factors affect the tax treatment of Lime Corporation's distributions. The amount of current and accumulated E & P (which differs from the financial reporting concept of retained earnings) partially determines the tax effect on the shareholders. Given that Lime had a highly profitable year, it is possible that current E & P equals or exceeds the amount of the distributions. If so, they are dividends to the shareholders rather than a return of capital.

Orange Corporation receives $200,000 of dividend income that is mostly offset by the dividends received deduction. The amount of the offsetting deduction depends on the ownership percentage that Orange holds in Lime. In this situation, Orange likely would qualify for a dividends received deduction of $160,000 ($200,000 × 80%). Gustavo has $200,000 of dividend income (i.e., $300,000 value of the real estate less the $100,000 mortgage). Assuming that Lime is a domestic corporation and that Gustavo has held his stock for the entire year, the distribution is a qualified dividend. As a result, the dividend is subject to reduced income tax rates. Gustavo's basis in the real estate is its fair market value at distribution, or $300,000.

From Lime's perspective, the distribution of the appreciated property triggers a recognized gain, equal to $280,000 ($300,000 fair market value less $20,000 adjusted basis). While the gain increases Lime's E & P, the distributions to the shareholders reduce it by $200,000 for the cash and $200,000 for the real estate ($300,000 fair market value reduced by the $100,000 mortgage).

What If?

What if the balance of current E & P is less than the combined value of the cash and real estate distributed to the shareholders? Current E & P is applied pro rata to the cash and the real estate. Because the amounts received by the two shareholders are equal ($200,000 each), the current E & P applied is taxed as a dividend and is treated as described above.

To the extent the distributions are not paid from current E & P, accumulated E & P is applied in a pro rata fashion (both distributions were made on December 31). However, if Lime reports a deficit in accumulated E & P, the remaining amounts distributed to the two shareholders are first a tax-free recovery of stock basis, and any excess is taxed as a sale of the stock (probably classified as capital gain).

[45]§§ 541–547.

Suggested Readings

Julie Allen, et al., "The Forgotten Impact of Accounting Methods When Computing E & P," *Corporate Taxation*, September/October 2010.

Nick Hanauer, "Stock Buybacks Are Killing the American Economy," **www.theatlantic.com**, February 8, 2015.

John C. Ramirez, "Reasonable Compensation for Corporate Owner/Employees," *Valuation Strategies*, July/August 2012.

Edward J. Schnee and W. Eugene Seago, "Constructive Dividends from Related Entities: The Distributing Corporation's Issues," *Journal of Taxation*, March 2010.

John Waggoner, "Stock Buybacks Surge: Is That a Good Thing?," **www.usatoday.com**, May 29, 2014.

Key Terms

Accumulated E & P, 13-3

Constructive dividend, 13-15

Corporate liquidation, 13-23

Current E & P, 13-3

Dividend, 13-2

Earnings and profits, 13-2

Property dividend, 13-12

Stock dividend, 13-20

Stock redemption, 13-21

Unreasonable compensation, 13-16

Computational Exercises

1. **LO.1** At the beginning of the year, Myrna Corporation (a calendar year taxpayer) holds E & P of $32,000. The corporation generates no additional E & P during the year. On December 31, the corporation distributes $50,000 to its sole shareholder, Abby, whose stock basis is $10,000. How does the Federal income tax law treat this distribution?

2. **LO.3** On January 1 of the current year, Rhondell Corporation holds accumulated E & P of $13,000. Current E & P for the year is $84,000, earned evenly throughout the year. Elizabeth and Jonathan are the sole equal shareholders of Rhondell from January 1 to April 30. On May 1, Elizabeth sells all of her stock to Marshall.

   Rhondell makes two distributions to shareholders during the year, as indicated below. Analyze the distributions by completing the table that follows. Assume that the shareholders have sufficient basis in their stock for any amount that is treated as return of capital.

Total Distribution	From Current E & P	From Accumulated E & P	Return of Capital
April 30, 42,000 cash	_____	_____	_____
December 31, $58,000 cash	_____	_____	_____

3. **LO.5** Global Corporation distributed property with an $850,000 fair market value and a $415,000 adjusted basis to Kang, one of its shareholders. The property was subject to a $230,000 mortgage, which Kang assumed. Global's accumulated E & P totals $3 million.

   What is the amount of Kang's dividend income on the distribution? What is Kang's basis in the property received?

4. **LO.5** Fargo Corporation holds $5 million in accumulated E & P. It distributes to Leilei, one of its shareholders, land worth $310,000; basis of the land to Fargo is $260,000. Determine the Federal income tax consequences of the distribution to Fargo.

5. **LO.7** During the current year, Gnatcatcher, Inc. (E & P of $1 million), distributed $200,000 each to Brandi and Yuen in redemption of some of their Gnatcatcher stock. The two shareholders are not related; they acquired their shares five years ago. Brandi and Yuen are in the 33% income tax bracket, and each had a $45,000 basis in her redeemed stock.

   a. Assume that the distribution to Brandi is a qualifying stock redemption. Determine Brandi's tax liability on the distribution.

   b. Assume that the distribution to Yuen is a nonqualified stock redemption. Determine Yuen's tax liability on the distribution.

6. **LO.7** Rosalie owns 50% of the outstanding stock of Salmon Corporation. In a qualifying stock redemption, Salmon distributes $80,000 to Rosalie in exchange for one-half of her shares, which have a basis of $100,000. Compute Rosalie's recognized loss, if any, on the redemption.

7. **LO.7** Derk owns 250 shares of stock in Rose Corporation. The remaining 750 shares of Rose are owned as follows: 150 by Derk's daughter Rosalie, 200 by Derk's aunt Penelope, and 400 by a partnership in which Derk holds an 80% interest. Determine the number of shares that Derk owns (directly and indirectly) in Rose Corporation.

   Critical Thinking

8. **LO.7** Caramel Corporation has 5,000 shares of stock outstanding. In a qualifying stock redemption, Caramel distributes $145,000 in exchange for 1,000 of its shares. At the time of the redemption, Caramel has recorded paid-in capital of $800,000 and E & P of $300,000. Calculate the reduction to Caramel's E & P as a result of the distribution.

Problems

---

9. **LO.1, 3** At the start of the current year, Blue Corporation (a calendar year taxpayer) holds accumulated E & P of $100,000. Blue's current E & P is $60,000. At the end of the year, it distributes $200,000 ($100,000 each) to its equal shareholders, Pam and Jon. Their basis in the stock is $11,000 for Pam and $26,000 for Jon. How is the distribution treated for tax purposes?

10. **LO.2** Cardinal Corporation, a calendar year taxpayer, receives dividend income of $250,000 from a corporation in which it holds a 10% interest. Cardinal also receives interest income of $35,000 from municipal bonds. (The municipality used the proceeds from the bond issue to construct a public library.) Cardinal borrowed funds to purchase the municipal bonds and pays $20,000 of interest on the loan. Excluding these three items, Cardinal's taxable income is $500,000, on which it paid Federal income tax of $200,000 during the year.

   a. What is Cardinal's taxable income after these items are taken into account?

   b. What is Cardinal's accumulated E & P at the end of the tax year if its beginning E & P balance was $150,000?

11. **LO.2** Compute current E & P for Sparrow Corporation (a calendar year, accrual basis taxpayer). Sparrow reported the following transactions during 2016, its second year of operation.

Taxable income	$330,000
Federal income tax liability paid	112,000
Tax-exempt interest income	5,000
Meals and entertainment expenses (total)	3,000
Premiums paid on key employee life insurance	3,500
Increase in cash surrender value attributable to life insurance premiums	700
Proceeds from key employee life insurance policy	130,000

Cash surrender value of life insurance policy at distribution	$ 20,000
Excess of capital losses over capital gains	13,000
MACRS deduction	26,000
Straight-line depreciation using ADS lives	16,000
Section 179 expense elected during 2015	25,000
Dividends received from domestic corporations (less than 20% owned)	25,000

- Sparrow uses the LIFO inventory method, and its LIFO recapture amount increased by $10,000 during 2016.
- Sparrow sold some property on installments during 2015. The property was sold for $40,000 and had an adjusted basis then of $32,000. During 2016, Sparrow received a $15,000 payment on the installment sale.

12. **LO.1, 2, 3** On September 30, Silver Corporation, a calendar year taxpayer, sold a parcel of land (basis of $400,000) for a $1 million note. The note is payable in five installments, with the first payment due next year. Because Silver did not elect out of the installment method, none of the $600,000 gain is taxed this year.

    Silver Corporation had a $300,000 deficit in accumulated E & P at the beginning of the year. Before considering the effect of the land sale, Silver had a deficit in current E & P of $50,000.

    Sam, the sole shareholder of Silver, has a basis of $200,000 in his stock. If Silver distributes $900,000 to Sam on December 31, how much gross income must he report for Federal income tax purposes?

13. **LO.2** In determining Blue Corporation's current E & P for this tax year, how should taxable income be adjusted as a result of the following transactions?

    a. A capital loss carryover from two years ago, fully used this year.
    b. Nondeductible meal expenses.
    c. Interest income on municipal bonds.
    d. Nondeductible lobbying expenses.
    e. Loss on a sale between related parties.
    f. Federal income tax refund from last year's return, received this year.

14. **LO.1, 3** Chang Corporation is a calendar year taxpayer. At the beginning of the current year, Chang holds accumulated E & P of $33,000. The corporation incurs a deficit in current E & P of $46,000 that accrues ratably throughout the year. On June 30, Chang distributes $20,000 to its sole shareholder, Libby. If Libby's stock has a basis of $4,000, how is she taxed on the distribution?

15. **LO.1, 3** Complete the following schedule for each case. Unless otherwise indicated, assume that the shareholders have ample basis in the stock investment. All taxpayers use a calendar tax year.

	Accumulated E & P Beginning of Year	Current E & P	Cash Distributions (All on Last Day of Year)	Dividend Income	Return of Capital
a.	($200,000)	$ 70,000	$130,000	_____	_____
b.	150,000	(120,000)	210,000	_____	_____
c.	90,000	70,000	150,000	_____	_____
d.	120,000	(60,000)	130,000	_____	_____
e.	Same as (d), except that the distribution of $130,000 is made on June 30.			_____	_____

16. **LO.1, 3** Larry, the sole shareholder of Brown Corporation, sold his stock to Ed on July 30 for $270,000. Larry's basis in the stock was $200,000 at the beginning of the year. Brown had accumulated E & P of $120,000 on January 1 and

current E & P of $240,000. During the year, Brown made the following distributions: $450,000 cash to Larry on July 1 and $150,000 cash to Ed on December 30. How will Larry and Ed be taxed on the distributions? How much gain will Larry recognize on the sale of his stock to Ed?

17. **LO.1, 2** In each of the following independent situations, indicate the effect on taxable income and E & P, stating the amount of any increase (or decrease) in each as a result of the transaction. Assume that E & P has already been increased by taxable income.

Transaction	Taxable Income Increase (Decrease)	E & P Increase (Decrease)
a. Realized gain of $80,000 on involuntary conversion of building ($10,000 of gain is recognized).	_____	_____
b. Mining exploration costs incurred on May 1 of current year; $24,000 is deductible from current-year taxable income.	_____	_____
c. Sale of equipment to unrelated third party for $240,000; basis is $120,000 (no election out of installment method; no payments are received in current year).	_____	_____
d. Dividends of $20,000 received from 5% owned corporation, together with dividends received deduction (assume that the taxable income limit does not apply).	_____	_____
e. Domestic production activities deduction of $45,000 claimed in current year.	_____	_____
f. Section 179 expense deduction of $25,000 in current year.	_____	_____
g. Continue with the facts of (f) for the next tax year.	_____	_____
h. MACRS depreciation of $80,000. ADS depreciation would have been $90,000.	_____	_____
i. Federal income taxes of $80,000 paid in current year.	_____	_____

18. **LO.2** Penguin Corporation (a cash basis, calendar year taxpayer) recorded the following income and expenses in the current year.

Income from services	$400,000
Salaries paid to employees	70,000
Tax-exempt interest income	24,000
Dividends from a corporation in which Penguin holds a 12% interest	40,000
Short-term capital loss on the sale of stock	17,000
Estimated Federal income taxes paid	110,000

Penguin purchased seven-year MACRS property in the current year for $80,000; it did not claim any § 179 or additional first-year depreciation. The property has a 10-year ADR midpoint life. Determine Penguin's taxable income and current E & P.

19. **LO.1, 3** At the beginning of the year, Teal Corporation held accumulated E & P of $225,000. On March 30, Teal sold an asset at a loss of $225,000. For the calendar year, Teal incurred a deficit in current E & P of $305,000, which includes the $225,000 loss on the sale of the asset. If Teal made a distribution of $50,000 to its sole shareholder on April 1, how is the shareholder taxed?

20. **LO.1, 3** Green Corporation (a calendar year taxpayer) had a deficit in accumulated E & P of $250,000 at the beginning of the current year. Its net profit for the

period January 1 through July 30 was $300,000, but its E & P for the entire taxable year was only $40,000. If Green made a distribution of $60,000 to its sole shareholder on August 1, how will the shareholder be taxed?

21. **LO.1, 3** Black Corporation and Tom each own 50% of Tan Corporation's common stock. On January 1, Tan holds a deficit in accumulated E & P of $200,000. Its current E & P is $90,000. During the year, Tan makes cash distributions of $40,000 each to Black and Tom.

   a. How are the two shareholders taxed on the distribution?
   b. What is Tan's accumulated E & P at the end of the year?

22. **LO.1, 4** Heather, an individual, owns all of the outstanding stock in Silver Corporation. Heather purchased her stock in Silver nine years ago, and her basis is $56,000. At the beginning of this year, the corporation has $76,000 of accumulated E & P and no current E & P (before considering the effect of the distributions as noted below). What are the tax consequences to Heather (amount and type of income and basis in property received) and Silver Corporation (gain or loss and effect on E & P) in each of the following situations?

   a. Silver distributes land to Heather. The land was held as an investment and has a fair market value of $54,000 and an adjusted basis of $42,000.
   b. Assume that Silver has no current or accumulated E & P prior to the distribution. How would your answer to part (a) change?
   c. Assume that the land distributed in part (a) is subject to a $46,000 mortgage (which Heather assumes). How would your answer change?
   d. Assume that the land has a fair market value of $54,000 and an adjusted basis of $62,000 on the date of the distribution. How would your answer to part (a) change?

23. **LO.1, 4** Lime Corporation, with E & P of $500,000, distributes land (worth $300,000, adjusted basis of $350,000) to Harry, its sole shareholder. The land is subject to a liability of $120,000, which Harry assumes. What are the tax consequences to Lime and to Harry?

Decision Making   24. **LO.4** Raven Corporation owns three machines that it uses in its business. It no longer needs two of these machines and is considering distributing them to its two shareholders as a property dividend. The machines have a fair market value of $20,000 each. The basis of each machine is as follows: A, $27,000; B, $20,000; and C, $12,000. Raven has asked you for advice. What do you recommend?

Issue ID   25. **LO.1, 2, 3, 4** Cerulean Corporation has two equal shareholders, Eloise and Olivia. Eloise acquired her Cerulean stock three years ago by transferring property worth $700,000, basis of $300,000, for 70 shares of the stock. Olivia acquired 70 shares in Cerulean Corporation two years ago by transferring property worth $660,000, basis of $110,000. Cerulean Corporation's accumulated E & P as of January 1 of the current year is $350,000.

   On March 1 of the current year, the corporation distributed to Eloise property worth $120,000, basis to Cerulean of $50,000. It distributed cash of $220,000 to Olivia. On July 1 of the current year, Olivia sold her stock to Magnus for $820,000. On December 1 of the current year, Cerulean distributed cash of $90,000 each to Magnus and Eloise. What are the tax issues?

Decision Making   26. **LO.1, 2, 4** Petrel Corporation has accumulated E & P of $85,000 at the beginning of the year. Its current-year taxable income is $320,000. On December 31, Petrel distributed business property (land, fair market value $140,000, adjusted basis $290,000) to Juan, its sole shareholder. Juan assumes a $70,000 liability on the property.

   Included in the determination of Petrel's current taxable income is $16,000 of income recognized from an installment sale in a previous year. In addition, the corporation incurred a Federal income tax liability of $112,000, paid life insurance premiums of $4,500, and received term life insurance proceeds of $150,000 on the death of an officer.

a. What is Juan's gross income from the distribution?

b. What is Petrel's E & P after the property distribution?

c. What is Juan's tax basis in the property received?

d. How would your answers to parts (a) and (b) change if Petrel had sold the property at its fair market value, used $70,000 of the proceeds to pay off the liability, and distributed the remaining cash and any tax savings to Juan?

27. **LO.5** Parrot Corporation is a closely held company with accumulated E & P of $300,000 and current E & P of $350,000. Tom and Jerry are brothers; each owns a 50% share in Parrot, and they share management responsibilities equally. What are the tax consequences of each of the following independent transactions involving Parrot, Tom, and Jerry? How does each transaction affect Parrot's E & P?

a. Parrot sells an office building (adjusted basis of $350,000; fair market value of $300,000) to Tom for $275,000.

b. Parrot lends Jerry $250,000 on March 31 of this year. The loan is evidenced by a note that is payable on demand. No interest is charged on the loan (the current applicable Federal interest rate is 7%).

c. Parrot owns an airplane that it leases to others for a specified rental rate. Tom and Jerry also use the airplane for personal use and pay no rent. During the year, Tom used the airplane for 120 hours, and Jerry used it for 160 hours. The rental value of the airplane is $350 per hour, and its maintenance costs average $80 per hour.

d. Tom leases equipment to Parrot for $20,000 per year. The same equipment can be leased from another company for $9,000 per year.

28. **LO.5** Robin Corporation would like to transfer excess cash to its sole shareholder, Adam, who is also an employee. Adam is in the 28% tax bracket, and Robin is in the 34% bracket.

    Because Adam's contribution to Robin's profit is substantial, Robin believes that a $25,000 bonus in the current year is reasonable compensation and should be deductible in full. However, Robin is considering paying Adam a $25,000 dividend because Adam's tax rate on dividends is lower than his tax rate on compensation. Is Robin correct in believing that a dividend is the better choice? Why or why not?

Decision Making

29. **LO.6** Your client, Raptor Corporation, declares a dividend permitting its common shareholders to elect to receive 9 shares of cumulative preferred stock or 3 additional shares of Raptor common stock for every 10 shares of common stock held. Raptor has only common stock outstanding (fair market value of $45 per share). One shareholder elects to receive preferred stock, while the remaining shareholders choose the common stock.

    Raptor asks you whether the shareholders recognize any gross income on the receipt of the stock. Prepare a letter to Raptor or a memo for the tax research file regarding this matter. Raptor's address is 1812 S. Camino Seco, Tucson, AZ 85710.

Critical Thinking

Communications

30. **LO.6** Ken purchased 10,000 shares of Gold Corporation common stock six years ago for $160,000. In the current year, Ken received a preferred stock dividend of 800 shares, while the other holders of common stock received a common stock dividend. The preferred stock that Ken received is worth $80,000, and his common stock has a fair market value of $240,000.

    Gold holds ample E & P to cover any distributions made during the year. What is Ken's basis in the preferred and common stock after the dividend is received? When does his holding period commence for the preferred stock?

Critical Thinking

Critical Thinking

31. **LO.6** Denim Corporation declares a nontaxable dividend payable in rights to subscribe to common stock. One right and $60 entitle the holder to subscribe to one share of stock. One right is issued for every two shares of stock owned. At the date of distribution of the rights, the market value of the stock is $110 per share, and the market value of the rights is $55 each. Lauren owns 300 shares of stock that she purchased two years ago for $9,000. Lauren receives 150 rights, of which she exercises 105 to purchase 105 additional shares. She sells the remaining 45 rights for $2,475. What are the tax consequences of this transaction to Lauren?

Critical Thinking
Communications

32. **LO.6** Jacob Corcoran bought 10,000 shares of Grebe Corporation stock two years ago for $24,000. Last year, Jacob received a nontaxable stock dividend of 2,000 shares in Grebe. In the current tax year, Jacob sold all of the stock received as a dividend for $18,000. Prepare a letter to Jacob or a memo for the tax research file describing the tax consequences of the stock sale. Jacob's address is 925 Arapahoe Street, Boulder, CO 80304.

Issue ID

33. **LO.7** Joseph and Erica, husband and wife, jointly own all of the stock in Velvet Corporation. The two are currently involved in divorce proceedings, and pursuant to those negotiations, they have agreed that only one of them will remain a shareholder in Velvet after the divorce. Because Erica has been more involved in Velvet's management and operations over the years, the parties have agreed that Joseph's ownership should be acquired by either Erica or Velvet. What issues should be considered in determining whether Erica or Velvet should acquire Joseph's shares in the corporation?

34. **LO.1, 7** Julio is in the 33% tax bracket. He acquired 2,000 shares of stock in Gray Corporation seven years ago at a cost of $50 per share. In the current year, Julio received a payment of $150,000 from Gray Corporation in exchange for 1,000 of his shares in Gray. Gray has E & P of $1 million. What tax liability would Julio incur on the payment in each of the following situations? Assume that Julio has no capital losses.

   a.   The stock redemption qualifies for sale or exchange treatment.

   b.   The stock redemption does not qualify for sale or exchange treatment.

35. **LO.1, 7** How would your answer to Problem 34 differ if Julio were a corporate shareholder (in the 34% tax bracket) rather than an individual shareholder and the stock ownership in Gray Corporation represented a 25% interest?

Decision Making

36. **LO.1, 7** Assume in Problem 34 that Julio has a capital loss carryover of $50,000 in the current tax year. Julio has no other capital gain transactions during the year. What amount of the capital loss may Julio deduct in the current year in the following situations?

   a.   The payment from Gray Corporation is a qualifying stock redemption for tax purposes.

   b.   The payment from Gray is a nonqualified stock redemption for tax purposes.

   c.   If Julio had the flexibility to structure the transaction as described in either part (a) or (b), which form would he choose?

37. **LO.1, 7** How would your answer to parts (a) and (b) of Problem 36 differ if Julio were a corporate shareholder (in the 34% tax bracket) rather than an individual shareholder and the stock ownership in Gray Corporation represented a 25% interest?

Critical Thinking

38. **LO.7** Silver Corporation has 2,000 shares of common stock outstanding. Howard owns 600 shares, Howard's grandfather owns 300 shares, Howard's mother owns 300 shares, and Howard's son owns 100 shares. In addition, Maroon Corporation owns 500 shares. Howard owns 70% of the stock of Maroon.

   a.   Applying the stock attribution rules, how many shares does Howard own in Silver?

   b.   Assume that Howard owns only 40% of the stock in Maroon. How many shares does Howard own, directly and indirectly, in Silver?

c. Assume the same facts as in part (a) above, but in addition, Howard owns a 25% interest in the Yellow Partnership. Yellow owns 200 shares in Silver. How many shares does Howard own, directly and indirectly, in Silver?

39. **LO.7** Shonda owns 1,000 of the 1,500 shares outstanding in Rook Corporation (E & P of $1 million). Shonda paid $50 per share for the stock seven years ago. The remaining stock in Rook is owned by unrelated individuals. What are the tax consequences to Shonda in the following independent situations?

    a. Rook redeems 450 shares of Shonda's stock for $225,000.
    b. Rook redeems 600 shares of Shonda's stock for $300,000.

Critical Thinking

40. **LO.7** Broadbill Corporation (E & P $650,000) has 1,000 shares of common stock outstanding. The shares are owned by the following individuals: Tammy, 300 shares; Yvette, 400 shares; and Jeremy, 300 shares. Each of the shareholders paid $50 per share for the Broadbill stock four years ago.

    In the current year, Broadbill distributes $75,000 to Tammy in redemption of 150 of her shares. Determine the tax consequences of the redemption to Tammy and to Broadbill under the following independent circumstances.

    a. Tammy and Jeremy are grandmother and grandson.
    b. The three shareholders are siblings.

Critical Thinking

41. **LO.7** For the last 11 years, Lime Corporation has owned and operated four different trades or businesses. Lime also owns stock in several corporations that it purchased for investment purposes.

    The stock of Lime is held equally by Sultan, an individual, and by Turquoise Corporation. Sultan and Turquoise each own 1,000 shares in Lime, purchased 9 years ago at a cost of $200 per share.

    Determine whether either of the following independent transactions qualify as partial liquidations under § 302(b)(4). In each transaction, determine the tax consequences to Lime, to Turquoise, and to Sultan. Lime holds E & P of $2.1 million on the date of the distribution. Lime redeems 250 shares from each shareholder.

    a. Lime sells one of its business lines (basis $500,000, fair market value $700,000) and distributes the proceeds equally to Sultan and Turquoise.
    b. Lime equally distributes stock (basis $425,000, fair market value $700,000) that it holds in other corporations to Sultan and Turquoise.

Critical Thinking

42. **LO.7** Compare the tax treatment of liquidating and redemption distributions in terms of the following.

    a. Recognition of gain or loss by the shareholder.
    b. Basis of property received by the shareholder.

Critical Thinking

43. **LO.7** Dove Corporation (E & P of $800,000) has 1,000 shares of stock outstanding. The shares are owned as follows: Julia, 600 shares; Maxine (Julia's sister), 300 shares; and Janine (Julia's daughter), 100 shares. Dove owns land (basis $300,000, fair market value $260,000) that it purchased as an investment seven years ago.

    Dove distributes the land to Julia in exchange for all of her shares in the corporation. Julia had a basis of $275,000 in the shares. What are the tax consequences for both Dove and Julia if the distribution is:

    a. A qualifying stock redemption?
    b. A liquidating distribution?

Critical Thinking

44. **LO.5** Pink Corporation has several employees. Their names and salaries are listed below.

Judy	$470,000
Holly (Judy's daughter)	100,000
Terry (Judy's son)	100,000
John (an unrelated third party)	320,000

Issue ID

Holly and Terry are the only shareholders of Pink. Judy and John share equally in the management of the company's operations. Holly and Terry are both full-time college students at a university 200 miles away. Pink has substantial E & P and never has distributed a dividend. Discuss any income tax issues related to Pink's salary arrangement.

BRIDGE DISCIPLINE

1. Find the audited financial statements of five major U.S. corporations, each in a different operating industry (e.g., manufacturing, energy, financial services, health care).
   a. Compute the total return on each corporation's stock for the past two years.
   b. Compute the dividend yield of the stock for the past two years.

Communications   2. Find a report involving the buyback of common stock by a publicly traded U.S. corporation. In no more than four PowerPoint slides, summarize the transaction, and discuss the tax and finance motivations for the redemption presented in the article.

Communications   3. A dividend is declared by the corporation's board of directors, and it is paid to each shareholder in an equal fashion. Evaluate this statement from an accounting and Federal income tax standpoint. Summarize your position in no more than four PowerPoint slides in preparation for a presentation to your classmates in Business Law I.

Research Problems

THOMSON REUTERS
CHECKPOINT
Student Edition

Note: Solutions to Research Problems can be prepared by using the Checkpoint® Student Edition online research product, which is available to accompany this text. It is also possible to prepare solutions to the Research Problems by using tax research materials found in a standard tax library.

Communications

Research Problem 1. Kenny Merinoff and his son, John, own all of the outstanding stock of Flamingo Corporation. John and Kenny are officers in the corporation and, together with their uncle, Ira, comprise the entire board of directors. Flamingo uses the cash method of accounting and adopted a calendar year-end.

In late 2009, the board of directors adopted the following legally enforceable resolution (agreed to in writing by each of the officers).

> Salary payments made to an officer of the corporation that are disallowed in whole or in part as a deductible expense for Federal income tax purposes shall be reimbursed by such officer to the corporation to the full extent of the disallowance. It shall be the duty of the board of directors to enforce the collection of each such amount.

In 2014, Flamingo paid Kenny $800,000 in compensation. John received $650,000. As part of an audit in late 2015, the IRS found the compensation of both officers to be excessive. It disallowed deductions for $400,000 of the payment to Kenny and $350,000 of the payment to John. The IRS recharacterized the disallowed payments as constructive dividends. Complying with the resolution by the board of directors, both Kenny and John repaid the disallowed compensation to Flamingo Corporation in 2016.

John and Kenny have asked you to determine how their repayments are treated for Federal income tax purposes. John still is working as a highly compensated executive for Flamingo, while Kenny is retired and living off of his savings. Prepare a memo for your firm's tax research files describing the results of your review.

Partial list of research aids:
§ 1341.
Vincent E. Oswald, 49 T.C. 645 (1968).

Research Problem 2. Your client, White Corporation, has done well since its formation 20 years ago. This year, it recognized a $50 million capital gain from the sale of a subsidiary. White's CEO has contacted you to discuss a proposed transaction to reduce the tax on the capital gain. Under the proposal, White will purchase all of the common stock in Purple Corporation for $200 million. Purple is a profitable corporation that has $63 million in cash and marketable securities, $137 million in operating assets, and approximately $280 million in E & P.

After its acquisition, Purple will distribute $50 million in cash and marketable securities to White. Due to the 100% dividends received deduction, no taxable income results to White from the dividend. White then will resell Purple for $150 million.

The subsequent sale of Purple generates a $50 million capital loss [$150 million (sale price) − $200 million (stock basis)]. The loss from the stock sale can then be used to offset the preexisting $50 million capital gain. Will the proposed plan work? Why or why not?

Partial list of research aids:
§ 1059.

Research Problem 3. Emerald Corporation must change its method of accounting for Federal income tax purposes. The change will require that an adjustment to income be made over three tax periods. Jonas, the sole shareholder of Emerald, wants to better understand the implications of this adjustment for E & P purposes, as he anticipates a distribution from Emerald in the current year. Prepare a memo for your firm's files describing the results of your research.

Communications

Partial list of research aids:
§ 481(a).
Rev.Proc. 97–27, 1997–1 C.B. 680.

Use the tax resources of the Internet to address the following questions. Do not restrict your search to the Web, but include a review of newsgroups and general reference materials, practitioner sites and resources, primary sources of the tax law, chat rooms and discussion groups, and other opportunities.

 Internet Activity

Research Problem 4. In July 2013, Windstream Corp. (Nasdaq: WIN), a Fortune 500 and S&P 500 company, made an announcement regarding the taxation of a recent distribution. It also made a projection regarding the anticipated tax consequences of future distributions.

Locate articles or press releases regarding Windstream's announcement and related distribution. What might have led Windstream to make the announcement? What implications might the information contained in the announcement have had for investors' expectations regarding the company's future earnings? On what might the predictions regarding the taxation of future distributions have been based?

Research Problem 5. Write an e-mail query to two tax consultants who practice in your state. Ask each for an example or two of a constructive dividend that a client recently paid. Give your instructor copies of your query and the responses you receive.

Communications

Research Problem 6. Publicly traded corporations reacquire their own shares for various reasons. Through the use of a tender offer, a corporation can purchase a substantial percentage of the company's stock. Prepare an outline discussing (1) why publicly traded corporations reacquire their own shares and (2) how the tender offer process works for both corporations and shareholders. E-mail your outline to your tax professor.

Communications

Roger CPA Review Questions

1. Candy Corp. is a C corporation that began operations in year 1. Candy Corp.'s year 1 through year 3 taxable earnings and profits (E & P) are computed as follows.

Year	E & P
1	($25,000)
2	5,000
3	10,000

On the last day of year 3, Candy Corp. makes a $12,500 cash shareholder distribution, distributed equally between its two shareholders, Goode and Plenteau. How much of Goode's distribution is a nontaxable return of capital? Assume sufficient basis in Goode's stock investment.

a. $5,000   c. $1,250

b. $0   d. $6,250

2. As of December 31, Eliot Corp. reports net income per books of $100,000, which includes municipal bond interest of $4,000, a deduction for business meals of $5,000, a deduction for a net capital loss of $5,000, and a deduction for Federal income taxes of $22,000. What is Eliot Corp.'s current earnings and profits (E & P) for the tax year?

a. $98,500   c. $125,500

b. $107,500   d. $100,000

3. As of December 31, Hardy Corp. reports net income per books of $120,000, which includes straight-line depreciation expense of $5,000. Hardy Corp. claimed accelerated depreciation of $15,000 for tax purposes. Also included in book income were lobbying expenses of $4,000 and a Federal income tax refund of $5,000. What is Hardy Corp.'s current earnings and profits (E & P) for the tax year?

a. $119,000   c. $120,000

b. $109,000   d. $114,000

4. As of December 31, Caledonia Corp. reports taxable income of $150,000, which includes a $20,000 accelerated depreciation deduction; had straight-line depreciation been used, the deduction would have been $6,000. Also included in taxable income is an operating loss carryforward from a prior year of $3,000. Additionally, Caledonia earned $4,000 in municipal bond interest during the year. What is Caledonia Corp.'s current earnings and profits (E & P) for the tax year?

a. $164,000   c. $157,000

b. $171,000   d. $168,000

5. At the beginning of the year, Crispin, a C corporation, held a deficit of $35,000 in accumulated earnings and profits (E & P). For the current year, Crispin reported E & P of $12,000. Crispin distributed $10,000 during the year. What was the amount of Crispin's accumulated E & P deficit at year-end?

a. $23,000   c. $27,000

b. $33,000   d. $37,000

6. On January 1 of the current year, Quail Corp., an accrual-basis, calendar-year C corporation, held accumulated earnings and profits (E & P) of $20,000. On December 31 of the current year, Quail Corp.'s current E & P was $24,000, earned evenly throughout

the year. Ray and Devi were sole equal shareholders of Quail throughout the year. Quail made two distributions to the shareholders during the year: $30,000 on July 1 and $30,000 on December 31. How much of the December 31 distribution is taxable dividend income for Devi?

a. $7,000
b. $11,000

c. $6,000
d. $1,000

7. Compendium Corp. distributed cash and personal property to its sole shareholder. Considering the following facts, what is the amount of gain that would be recognized by Compendium as the result of making this distribution to its shareholder?

Item	Amount
Cash	$25,000
Personal property	
Fair market value	10,000
Adjusted basis	4,000
Liability on property assumed by shareholder	12,000

a. $4,000
b. $6,000

c. $8,000
d. $29,000

8. Calvin owns 40% of the outstanding shares of Copernicus Corp., which holds accumulated earnings and profits of $100,000 as of December 31, year 1. The outstanding shares not owned by Calvin are owned by parties unrelated to Calvin. On January 1 of year 2, Calvin, wishing to pursue another business opportunity, sells his stock back to Copernicus Corp. Copernicus distributes cash of $250,000 in redemption of all of Calvin's stock. If Calvin's adjusted basis for the stock on the date of redemption is $125,000, what will be the tax effect of the redemption to Calvin?

a. $125,000 capital gain
b. $25,000 dividend

c. $125,000 dividend
d. $150,000 dividend

9. Katsu Corp. distributes property to its shareholders as part of a complete liquidation. The fair market value of the property is $500,000, Katsu's adjusted basis in the property is $150,000, and the property is subject to a liability of $200,000. What amount of gain will Katsu recognize as a result of the transaction?

a. $150,000
b. $550,000

c. $300,000
d. $350,000

10. Close Corp. distributed cash and a parcel of land in a nonliquidating distribution to its sole shareholder. The following facts apply to this distribution.

Item	Amount
Cash	$50,000
Land	
Fair market value	30,000
Adjusted basis	40,000

Based on these facts, what amount of gain or loss should be recognized by Close Corp. as a result of this distribution?

a. $60,000 loss
b. No gain or loss should be recognized
c. $10,000 loss
d. $40,000 gain

CHAPTER

14

Partnerships and Limited Liability Entities

LEARNING OBJECTIVES: *After completing Chapter 14, you should be able to:*

LO.1 Identify governing principles and theories of partnership taxation.

LO.2 Apply the tax rules regarding the formation of a partnership with cash and property contributions.

LO.3 Determine the tax treatment of expenditures of a newly formed partnership and identify elections available to the partnership.

LO.4 Calculate partnership taxable income and describe how partnership items affect a partner's income tax liability.

LO.5 Determine a partner's basis in the partnership interest.

LO.6 Apply the limitations on deducting partnership losses.

LO.7 Apply the tax laws regarding transactions between a partner and the partnership.

LO.8 Explain how LLPs and LLCs differ, and list the tax advantages and disadvantages of using an LLC.

CHAPTER OUTLINE

TAX TALK *If you are truly serious about preparing your child for the future, don't teach him to subtract—teach him to deduct.* —FRAN LEBOWITZ

THE TAX CONSEQUENCES OF PARTNERSHIP FORMATION AND OPERATIONS

For 15 years, Maria has owned and operated a seaside bakery and café called The Beachsider. Each morning, customers line up on the boardwalk in front of the building and enjoy fresh coffee and croissants while waiting for a table. "The building is too small," Maria commented to her landlord, Kyle. "Is there any way we can expand?" The Beachsider is one of several older buildings on 3 acres of a 10-acre parcel that Kyle inherited 30 years ago. The remaining 7 acres are undeveloped.

Kyle and Maria talked to Josh, a real estate developer, and he proposed an expansion to The Beachsider and upgrades to the other buildings. The improvements would preserve the character of the original retail center, and the remaining acreage would be available for future expansion. Kyle and Maria were impressed with Josh's vision and excited about the plans to upgrade the property and expand Maria's business.

The parties agreed to form a partnership to own and operate The Beachsider and to improve and lease the other buildings. Josh summarized the plan as follows: "Kyle and Maria will each contribute one-half of the capital we need. Kyle's real estate is valued at about $2 million. Maria's bakery equipment and the café furnishings are valued at about $500,000. The improvements will cost about $1.5 million, which Maria has agreed to contribute to the partnership."

Josh continued, "You have agreed that I do not need to contribute any capital to the partnership. I will oversee the construction, and when it is complete, I will vest in a 5 percent interest in the partnership's capital. On an ongoing basis, I will oversee the partnership's operations in exchange for a fixed salary and 20 percent of the partnership's ongoing profits. The construction is estimated to be completed in June of this year, and my capital interest is estimated to be valued at $200,000 at that time."

What are the tax consequences if the trio forms Beachside Properties as a limited liability company (LLC) to own and operate the retail center? What issues might arise later in the life of the entity?

Read the chapter and formulate your response.

Much of the new business in today's world of commerce is conducted through what the Internal Revenue Code would classify as *partnerships*. As evidence of their popularity, more than 3 million partnership tax returns are filed with the IRS annually.

Whether termed a *joint venture* or some other designation, a partnership is formed when individuals or separate business entities get together for the specific purpose of earning profits by jointly operating a trade or business. For example, a group can limit its goals to a specific list of agreed-to projects or to a given time period, or businesses can work together without altering any of their underlying capital structures. In many service professions, such as law, medicine, and accounting, state laws prohibit the owners from using a corporation to limit their liability to clients or patients; there, the partnership form prevails.

LO.1

Identify governing principles and theories of partnership taxation.

14-1 OVERVIEW OF PARTNERSHIP TAXATION

There are several types of partnership entities, each suited for different situations. Partnerships are used in almost every imaginable industry, and their popularity among business owners continues to rise.

The tax law addressing the transactions of partners and partnerships is found in Subchapter K of the Internal Revenue Code. These provisions comprise only a few short pages in the Code, however. Most of the details of partnership tax law have evolved through extensive Regulations and a healthy number of court cases.

14-1a Forms of Doing Business—Federal Tax Consequences

This chapter and the next chapter analyze business forms that offer certain advantages over C corporations. These entities are partnerships and S corporations, which are called *flow-through* or *pass-through* entities because the owners of the trade or business elect to avoid treating the enterprise as a separate taxable entity. Instead, the owners are taxed on a proportionate share of the firm's taxable income at the end of each of its taxable years, regardless of the amount of cash or property distributions the owners receive during the year. The entity serves as an information provider to the IRS and its owners with respect to the proportionate income shares, and the tax falls directly upon the owners of those shares.

A partnership may be especially advantageous in many cases. A partnership's income is subject to only a single level of taxation, whereas C corporation income can be subject to *double taxation*. Corporate income is taxed at the entity level at rates up to 35 percent. Any after-tax corporate income that is distributed to the entity's owners may be taxed again as a dividend at the owner level.

In addition, the entity offers certain planning opportunities not available to other entities. Both C and S corporations are subject to rigorous allocation and distribution requirements (generally, each allocation or distribution is proportionate to the ownership interest of the shareholder). A partnership, though, may adjust its allocations of income and cash flow among the partners each year according to their needs, as long as certain standards are met. Any previously unrealized income (such as appreciation of corporate assets) of a C corporation is recognized at the entity level when the corporation liquidates, but a partnership generally may liquidate tax-free. Finally, many states impose reporting and licensing requirements on corporate entities, including S corporations. These include franchise or capital stock tax returns that may require annual assessments and costly professional preparation assistance. Partnerships, on the other hand, often have no reporting requirements beyond Federal and state informational tax returns.

Although partnerships may avoid many of the income tax and reporting burdens faced by other entities, they are subject to all other taxes in the same manner as any other business. Thus, the partnership files returns and pays the outstanding amount of pertinent sales taxes, property taxes, and payroll taxes.

In summary, partnerships offer advantages to both large and small businesses. For smaller business operations, a partnership enables several owners to combine their resources at low cost. For larger business operations, a partnership offers a unique ability to raise capital with low filing and reporting costs (compared to corporate bond issuances, for example). Additional discussion as to the choice of legal form in which to conduct a business is included in Chapter 18.

14-1b Definition of a Partnership

A partnership is an association of two or more persons formed to carry on a trade or business, with each contributing money, property, labor, or skill, and with all expecting to share in profits and losses. A "person" can be an individual, a corporation, or another partnership. For Federal income tax purposes, a partnership includes a syndicate, a group, a pool, a joint venture, or another unincorporated organization through which any business, financial operation, or venture is carried on. The entity must not otherwise be classified as a corporation, trust, or estate.[1]

An eligible noncorporate entity can "check the box" on the partnership tax return, indicating that the entity wants to be taxed as a partnership.[2] A partnership must have at least two owners, so a sole proprietor or one-owner limited liability entity cannot "check the box" and be taxed as a partnership.[3]

Businesses operating in several forms are taxed as partnerships. Provisions controlling these legal forms of doing business typically are dictated by the laws of the states in which the businesses operate.

- In a **general partnership**, the partners share profits and losses in some specified manner, as dictated by the partnership agreement. Creditors can reach the assets of the business and the personal assets of the general partners to satisfy any outstanding debts. A general partner can be bankrupted by a judgment against the entity, even though the partner did not cause the violation triggering the damages.

- In a **limited partnership**, profits and losses are shared as the partners agree, but ownership interests are either general (creditors can reach the personal assets of the partner) or limited (a partner's exposure to entity liabilities is limited to the partner's own capital investment). Usually, the general partners conduct most of the partnership business, and they have a greater say in making decisions that affect the entity operations.

---

[1] § 7701(a)(2).
[2] Reg. §§ 301.7701–1 to –3, as discussed in Chapter 12.
[3] § 761(a).

As movies have become more expensive to produce, many production studios have turned to limited partnerships or LLCs as a lucrative source of investment capital. For example, several well-known studios have sold limited partnership or LLC interests in entities formed to produce specific movies.

The sponsoring studio usually injects capital for a small (1–5 percent) general partnership interest, and the limited partners contribute the remaining capital—millions of dollars in most cases.

These film-financing partnerships are not necessarily private operations. A layperson with a well-connected tax or investment adviser can become a partner in the next Channing Tatum project, perhaps financed by Silver Screen Partners. Partnership shares sell for multiples of $100,000 or more, and in return, the investor can become part-owner in an entity that is certain to throw off operating losses for many years to come.

Especially interested in movie financing of this type can be non-U.S. investors. The use of partnerships and limited liability entities is a common way to attract cross-border investment, as many developed countries treat such joint ventures favorably under their tax laws, allowing deferral of income recognition and lower tax withholding on the income of these entities.

U.S. investors are attracted to joint venture financing of film projects in several countries, including Germany and Canada, and U.S. states, including Illinois and Louisiana, that offer generous tax credits for projects that are filmed and processed chiefly within their borders. The partnership tax regime can offer an immediate flow-through of these tax benefits.

The next time you go to a movie, watch the credits and think about the large number of people who invested cash in the movie, all benefiting from the partnership tax laws!

- The **limited liability partnership (LLP)** is used chiefly in the service professions, such as accounting, medicine, law, and consulting. The primary difference between an LLP and a general partnership is that an LLP partner is not personally liable for acts of negligence, fraud, or malpractice committed by other partners.

- The **limited liability company (LLC)** is discussed in more detail later in this chapter. This entity is taxed as a partnership, but its capital structure resembles that of a corporation, with shares for sale and an owner's liability limited almost strictly to the extent of his or her equity investment. Most states allow LLCs to be owned solely by one person. In that case, the entity is treated for Federal income tax purposes as an individual or C corporation, following the tax filing status of the single LLC member.

14-1c Partnership Taxation and Reporting

A partnership is not itself a taxable entity.[4] Rather, the taxable income or loss of the partnership flows through to the partners at the end of the entity's tax year.[5] Partners report their allocable share of the partnership's income or loss for the year on their tax returns. As a result, the partnership itself pays no Federal income tax on its income; instead, the partners' individual tax liabilities are affected by the activities of the entity.

Partnership Flow-Throughs

EXAMPLE 1

Adam is a 40% partner in the ABC Partnership. Both Adam's and the partnership's tax years end on December 31. This year, the partnership generates $200,000 of ordinary taxable income. However, because the partnership needs capital for expansion and debt reduction, Adam makes no cash withdrawals during the year. He meets his living expenses by reducing his investment portfolio. Adam is taxed on his $80,000 allocable share of the partnership's income ($200,000 × 40%), even though he received no distributions from the entity during the year. This allocated income is included in Adam's gross income.

---

[4]§ 701.   [5]§ 702.

Partnership Flow-Throughs

Assume the same facts as in Example 1, except that the partnership realizes a taxable loss of $100,000. Adam's $40,000 proportionate share of the loss flows through to him from the partnership, and he can deduct the loss. (Note: Loss limitation rules discussed later in the chapter may result in some or all of this loss being deducted by Adam in a later year.)

EXAMPLE

2

Separately Stated Items

Many items of partnership income, expense, gain, or loss retain their tax identity as they flow through to the partners. These separately stated items include those items that may affect any two partners' tax liability computations differently.[6] For example, the § 179 expense of a partnership is separately stated because one partner might be able to deduct his or her share of the expense completely, while another's deduction might be limited.

Separately stated items include recognized gains and losses from property transactions, dividend income, preferences and adjustments for the alternative minimum tax (see Chapter 17), foreign tax payments, and expenditures that individual partners would treat as itemized deductions (e.g., charitable contributions).

Items that are not separately stated, because all partners treat them the same on their income tax returns, are aggregated and form the *ordinary income* of the partnership. Thus, profits from product sales, advertising expenses, and depreciation recapture amounts are combined to form the entity's ordinary income. This amount then is allocated among the partners and flows through to their tax returns. The ordinary income that flows through to a general partner, as well as any salary-like guaranteed payments (discussed in text Section 14-4a) received, usually is subject to self-employment tax, as well as Federal income tax.[7]

Beth is a 25% partner in the BR Partnership, a manufacturer of solar energy panels. The cash basis entity collected sales income of $60,000 and incurred $15,000 in business expenses. In addition, it sold a corporate bond for a $9,000 long-term capital gain. Finally, the partnership made a $1,000 contribution to the local Performing Arts Fund. The fund is a qualifying charity. BR and all of its partners use a calendar tax year.

Beth is allocated ordinary taxable income of $11,250 [($60,000 − $15,000) × 25%] from the partnership. She also reports her allocated share of the entity's long-term capital gain ($2,250) and charitable contributions ($250).

The partnership ordinary income increases Beth's gross income, and is subject to both income and self-employment taxes. Beth's share of BR's capital gain and charitable contribution are combined with her other similar activities for the year as though she had incurred them herself. These items could be treated differently on the tax returns of the various partners (e.g., because a partner may be subject to a percentage limitation on charitable contribution deductions), so they are not included in the computation of ordinary partnership income. Instead, the items flow through to the partners separately.

EXAMPLE

3

Tax Reporting Rules

Even though it is not a taxpaying entity, the partnership files an information tax return, Form 1065. This return is due by the fifteenth day of the third month following the end of the tax year. For a calendar year partnership, this deadline is March 15. An automatic six-month extension is available (to September 15 for a calendar year partnership) for filing the Form 1065. Different due dates applied prior to 2016.

As part of the Form 1065, the partnership prepares a Schedule K–1 for each partner that shows that partner's share of partnership items.

---

[6]§ 703(a)(1).　　　　　　　　　　　　　　　　[7]§ 1402(a).

The partnership incurs a penalty if it fails to file a timely (by the extended due date) Form 1065. The penalty is $195 per month times the numbers of partners, up to a maximum of 12 months.

Look at Form 1065 in Appendix B, and refer to it during the following discussion. The ordinary income and expense items generated by the partnership's trade or business activities are netted to produce a single income or loss amount. The partnership reports this ordinary income or loss from its trade or business activities on Form 1065, page 1. Schedule K (page 4 of Form 1065) accumulates all items that must be separately reported to the partners, including net trade or business income or loss (from page 1). The amounts on Schedule K are allocated among and reported by the partners on each owner's Schedule K–1; in Appendix B, the Schedule K–1 immediately follows Form 1065.

EXAMPLE

4

The BR Partnership in Example 3 reports its $60,000 of sales income on Form 1065, page 1, line 1. The $15,000 of business expenses are reported in the appropriate amounts on page 1, line 2 or lines 9–20. Partnership ordinary income of $45,000 is shown on page 1, line 22, and on Schedule K, line 1. The $9,000 capital gain and the $1,000 charitable contribution are reported only on Schedule K, on lines 9a and 13a, respectively.

Beth receives a Schedule K–1 from the partnership that shows her shares of partnership ordinary income of $11,250, long-term capital gain of $2,250, and charitable contributions of $250 on lines 1, 9a, and 13 (Code A), respectively.

She combines these amounts with similar items from other sources on her personal tax return. For example, if she has a $5,000 long-term capital loss from a stock transaction during the year, her overall net capital loss is $2,750. She then evaluates this net amount to determine the amount she may deduct on her Form 1040.

The partnership reconciles book income with its tax return data on Schedule M–1 or Schedule M–3. This reconciliation is similar to the book-tax reconciliation prepared by a C corporation, as discussed in Chapter 12 (see text Section 12-5).

Schedule M–3 generally is required in lieu of Schedule M–1 if the partnership owns $10 million or more in assets at the end of the year or it reports gross receipts of at least $35 million. The net taxable income calculated on the Analysis of Net Income (Loss) schedule should agree with the reconciled taxable income on Schedule M–1 or Schedule M–3. Schedule L shows an accounting-basis balance sheet, and Schedule M–2 reconciles partners' beginning and ending capital accounts.

14-1d **Partner's Ownership Interest in a Partnership**

Each partner typically owns both a capital interest and a profits (loss) interest in the partnership. A capital interest is measured by a partner's capital sharing ratio, which is the partner's percentage ownership of the capital of the partnership. A partner's capital interest can be determined in several ways. The most widely accepted method measures the capital interest as the percentage of net asset value (asset value remaining after payment of all partnership liabilities) a partner would receive upon immediate liquidation of the partnership.

A profits (loss) interest relates to the partner's percentage allocation of current partnership operating results. Profit and loss sharing ratios usually are specified in the partnership agreement. They are used to determine each partner's allocation of partnership ordinary taxable income (loss) and separately stated items.[8] The partnership can change its profit and loss allocations at any time by amending the partnership agreement.

---

[8]§ 704(a).

Although a written partnership agreement is not required by most U.S. states, many rules governing the tax consequences to partners and their partnerships refer to such an agreement. Remember that a partner's distributive share of income, gain, loss, deduction, or credit is determined in accordance with the partnership agreement. Consequently, if taxpayers operating a business in partnership form want a measure of certainty as to the tax consequences of their activities, a carefully drafted partnership agreement is crucial.

An agreement that sets forth the obligations, rights, and powers of the partners should prove invaluable in settling controversies among them and provide some degree of certainty as to the tax consequences of the partners' actions.

The partnership agreement may provide for a **special allocation** of certain items to specified partners, or it may allocate items in a different proportion from the general profit and loss sharing ratios. These items are reported separately to the partner receiving the allocation. For a special allocation to be recognized for tax purposes, it also must produce nontax economic consequences to the partners receiving the allocation.[9]

Partnership Special Allocations

EXAMPLE
5

When the George-Helen Partnership was formed, George contributed cash and Helen contributed some City of Boise bonds that she had held for investment purposes. The partnership agreement allocates all of the tax-exempt interest income from the bonds ($15,000 this year) to Helen as an inducement for her to remain a partner.

This is an acceptable special allocation for income tax purposes; it reflects the differing economic circumstances that underlie the partners' contributions to the capital of the entity. Because Helen would have received the tax-exempt income if she had not joined the partnership, she can retain the tax-favored treatment via the special allocation.

EXAMPLE
6

Assume the same facts as in Example 5. Three years after it was formed, the George-Helen Partnership purchased some City of Butte bonds. The municipal bond interest income of $15,000 flows through to the partners as a separately stated item, so it retains its tax-exempt status.

The partnership agreement allocates all of this income to George because he is subject to a higher marginal income tax rate than is Helen. The partnership then allocates $15,000 more of the partnership's ordinary income to Helen than to George. These allocations are not effective for income tax purposes because they have no purpose other than a reduction of the partners' combined income tax liability.

A partner has a **basis in the partnership interest**, just as he or she would have a tax basis in any asset owned. When income flows through to a partner from the partnership, the partner's basis in the partnership interest increases accordingly. When a loss flows through to a partner, the interest basis is reduced.[10] A partner's basis is important when determining the treatment of distributions from the partnership to the partner, establishing the deductibility of partnership losses, and calculating gain or loss on the disposition of the partnership interest.

EXAMPLE
7

The Philly Clinic contributes $20,000 of cash to acquire a 30% capital and profits interest in the Red Robin LLC. In its first year of operations, the LLC earns ordinary income of $40,000 and makes no distributions to its members. The Clinic's initial basis is the $20,000 it paid for the interest. Philly recognizes ordinary income of $12,000 (30% interest × $40,000 ordinary income). Philly increases its basis in Red Robin by the same amount, to $32,000.

[9]§ 704(b).

[10]§§ 705, 722, and 723.

The Code provides for increases and decreases in a partner's basis so that the income or loss from partnership operations is taxed only once. In Example 7, if the Philly Clinic sold its interest at the end of the first year for $32,000, it would recognize no gain or loss. If the Code did not provide for an adjustment to the owner's basis for flow-through amounts, Philly's basis still would be $20,000. In that case, Philly would recognize a gain of $12,000 in addition to being taxed on its $12,000 share of the flow-through income from Red Robin.

 DIGGING DEEPER 1 | **In-depth coverage can be found on this book's companion website: www.cengagebrain.com**

LO.2

Apply the tax rules regarding the formation of a partnership with cash and property contributions.

14-2 FORMATION OF A PARTNERSHIP: TAX EFFECTS

14-2a Gain or Loss on Contributions to the Partnership

When a taxpayer transfers property to an entity in exchange for valuable consideration, a taxable exchange usually results. Typically, both the taxpayer and the entity realize and recognize gain or loss on the exchange.[11] The gain or loss recognized by the transferor is the difference between the fair market value of the consideration received and the adjusted basis of the property transferred.[12]

In most situations, however, neither the partner nor the partnership recognizes the gain or loss that is realized when a partner contributes property to a partnership in exchange for a partnership interest. Instead, recognition of any realized gain or loss is deferred under § 721.[13] These rules apply whenever an owner makes a contribution to the capital of the partnership or LLC, not just when the entity is formed.

There are two reasons for this nonrecognition treatment. First, forming a partnership allows investors to combine their assets toward greater economic goals than could be achieved separately. Only the form of ownership, rather than the amount owned by each investor, has changed. Requiring that gain be recognized on such transfers would make the formation of some partnerships economically unfeasible. Second, because the partnership interest received is typically not a liquid asset, the partner may not be able to generate the cash with which to pay the tax. Thus, deferral of the gain recognizes the economic realities of the business world and follows the wherewithal to pay principle. This treatment is similar to the treatment of assets transferred to a controlled corporation and the treatment of like-kind exchanges.[14]

Creating a Partnership

EXAMPLE

8

In exchange for a 60% profits and loss interest worth $60,000, Alicia transfers two assets to the Wren LLC on the day the entity is created. She contributes cash of $40,000 and retail display equipment (basis to her as a sole proprietor, $8,000; fair market value, $20,000). Because an exchange has occurred between two parties, Alicia *realizes* a $12,000 gain on this transaction. The gain realized is the fair market value of the LLC interest of $60,000 less the basis of the assets that Alicia surrendered to the entity [$40,000 (cash) + $8,000 (equipment)].

Under § 721, Alicia *does not recognize* the $12,000 realized gain in the year of contribution. Alicia might not have had sufficient cash if she had been required to pay tax on the $12,000 gain. All that she received from the entity was an illiquid LLC interest; she received no cash with which to pay any resulting tax liability.

---

[11]§ 1001(c).

[12]§ 1001(a).

[13]§ 721.

[14]§§ 351 and 1031.

Creating a Partnership

EXAMPLE 9

Assume the same facts as in Example 8, except that the equipment Alicia contributes to the LLC has an adjusted basis of $25,000. She has incurred a $5,000 *realized* loss [$60,000– ($40,000 + $25,000)], but she cannot deduct the loss. Realized losses, as well as realized gains, are deferred by § 721.

Unless it was essential that the entity receive Alicia's display equipment rather than similar equipment purchased from an outside supplier, Alicia should have considered selling the equipment to a third party. This would have allowed her to deduct a $5,000 loss in the year of the sale. Alicia then could have contributed $60,000 of cash (including the proceeds from the sale) for her interest in the entity, and Wren would have had funds to purchase similar equipment.

EXAMPLE 10

Five years after Wren (Examples 8 and 9) was created, Alicia contributes another piece of equipment to the entity. This property has a basis of $35,000 and a fair market value of $50,000. Alicia defers the recognition of the $15,000 realized gain. Section 721 is effective *whenever* an owner makes a contribution to the capital of the partnership or LLC, not just when the entity is formed.

Concept Summary 14.1

Partnership/LLC Taxation

1. Compared with a C corporation, a partnership may offer some advantages, including a single level of taxation, the availability of certain planning opportunities, and simplified administration and reporting.

2. Entities treated as a partnership for tax purposes include general partnerships, limited partnerships, limited liability companies (LLCs), and limited liability partnerships (LLPs).

3. Partnership income and losses flow through to the partners and are reported on the partners' tax returns. The partnership reports ordinary income or loss as well as *separately stated items* to the partners. Under certain conditions, items may be *specially allocated* to specified partners.

4. The partnership files Form 1065 as an information return and prepares a Schedule K–1 to report each partner's share of income and deductions.

14-2b Exceptions to Nonrecognition

Contributions to the capital of a partnership or limited liability entity sometimes trigger recognized gain or loss. Realized gain or loss may be recognized when:

- The transaction is essentially a taxable exchange of properties,
- The transaction is the equivalent of a taxable sale of properties, or
- The partnership interest is received in exchange for services rendered to the partnership by the partner.[15]

Disguised Exchange

If a transaction is essentially a taxable exchange of properties, tax on the gain is not deferred under the nonrecognition provisions of § 721.[16]

---

[15]§ 721(b). A few other exceptions to § 721 treatment also exist.

[16]Reg. § 1.731–1(c)(3).

EXAMPLE 11

Sara owns land, and Bob owns stock. Sara would like to have Bob's stock, and Bob wants Sara's land. If Sara and Bob both contribute their property to newly formed SB Partnership in exchange for interests in the partnership, the tax on the transaction appears to be deferred under § 721. The tax on a subsequent distribution by the partnership of the land to Bob and the stock to Sara also appears to be deferred under partnership distribution rules.

Not so! Tax law disregards the passage of the properties through the partnership and holds, instead, that Sara and Bob exchanged the land and stock directly. Thus, the transaction is treated as any other taxable exchange.

Disguised Sale

Immediate gain recognition also occurs in the context of a **disguised sale** of property or of a partnership interest. A disguised sale occurs when a partner contributes property to a partnership and soon thereafter receives a distribution from the partnership. This distribution could be viewed as a payment by the partnership for purchase of the property.[17]

EXAMPLE 12

Kim transfers property to the existing KLM Partnership. The property has an adjusted basis of $10,000 and a fair market value of $30,000. Two weeks later, the partnership distributes $30,000 of cash to Kim. Lacking an exception under the distribution rules, the $30,000 of cash received would not be taxable to Kim if the basis for her partnership interest prior to the distribution was greater than the amount distributed.

However, the transaction appears to be a disguised purchase-sale transaction, rather than an asset contribution and distribution. Therefore, Kim recognizes gain of $20,000 on transfer of the property, and the partnership is deemed to have purchased the property for $30,000.

A disguised sale is presumed to exist when a contribution by one partner is followed within two years by a specified distribution to him or her from the partnership.

Services

Another exception to the nonrecognition provision of § 721 occurs when a partner receives a capital interest in the partnership as compensation for services rendered to the partnership. This is not a tax-deferred transaction because services are not treated as "property" that can be transferred to a partnership on a tax-free basis. Instead, the partner performing the services recognizes ordinary compensation income equal to the fair market value of the partnership interest received.[18]

The partnership may deduct the amount included in the *service partner's* income if the services are of a deductible nature. If the services are not deductible by the partnership, they are capitalized. For example, architectural plans created by a partner are capitalized into the basis of a structure built with those plans. Alternatively, day-to-day management services performed by a partner for the partnership usually are deductible by the partnership.

EXAMPLE 13

Bill, Carol, and Dave form the BCD Partnership, with each receiving a one-third capital and profits interest in the entity. Dave receives his one-third interest as compensation for the accounting and tax planning services he rendered to the partnership. The value of a one-third capital interest in the partnership (for each of the parties) is $20,000.

The partnership deducts $20,000 for Dave's services in computing ordinary income. Dave recognizes $20,000 of compensation income, and he takes a $20,000 basis in his partnership interest. The same result would occur if the partnership had paid Dave $20,000 for his services and he immediately contributed that amount to the entity for a one-third ownership interest.

---

[17]§ 707(a)(2)(B).   [18]§ 83(a).

In-depth coverage can be found on this book's companion website: www.cengagebrain.com

2 DIGGING DEEPER

14-2c **Tax Issues Related to Contributed Property**

When a partner makes a tax-deferred contribution of an asset to the capital of a partnership, the entity assigns a *carryover basis* to the property.[19] The partnership's basis in the asset (the asset's "inside basis") is equal to the basis the partner held in the property prior to its transfer to the partnership. The partner's basis in the new partnership interest (the owner's "outside basis") equals the prior basis in the contributed asset. The tax term for this basis concept is *substituted basis*. Thus, two assets are created out of one when a partnership is formed, namely, the property in the hands of the new entity and the new asset (the partnership interest) in the hands of the partner. Both assets are assigned a basis that is derived from the partner's basis in the contributed property.

The holding period of a partner's interest includes that of the contributed property when the property was a § 1231 asset or capital asset in the partner's hands. When other assets, including cash, are contributed, the holding period starts on the day the interest is acquired.

> **EXAMPLE**
>
> **14**
>
> On June 1, José transfers property to the JKL LLC in exchange for a one-third interest in the entity. The property has an adjusted basis to José of $10,000 and a fair market value of $30,000. José incurs a $20,000 realized gain on the exchange ($30,000 − $10,000), but he does not recognize any of the gain. Jose's basis for his interest in JKL is the amount necessary to recognize the $20,000 deferred gain if his interest later is sold for its $30,000 fair market value. This amount, $10,000, is the substituted basis.
>
> The basis of the property contributed to JKL is the amount necessary to allow for the recognition of the $20,000 deferred gain if the property later is sold for its $30,000 fair market value. This amount, also $10,000, is the carryover basis.
>
> The holding period for the contributed asset also carries over to the entity. Thus, JKL's holding period for the asset includes the period during which José owned the asset individually.

Depreciation Method and Period

If depreciable property is contributed to the partnership, the partnership usually is required to use the same cost recovery method and life as had been used by the partner. The partnership merely "steps into the shoes" of the partner and continues the same cost recovery calculations.

Intangible Assets

If a partner contributes an existing "§ 197" intangible asset to the partnership, the partnership generally will "step into the shoes" of the partner in determining future amortization deductions. Section 197 intangible assets include purchased goodwill, going-concern value, information systems, customer- or supplier-related intangible assets, patents, licenses obtained from a governmental unit, franchises, trademarks, covenants not to compete, and other items.

---

[19]§ 723.

Receivables, Inventory, and Built-In Losses

To prevent ordinary income from being converted into capital gain, gain or loss is treated as ordinary when the partnership disposes of either of the following.[20]

- Contributed receivables that were unrealized in the contributing partner's hands at the contribution date. Such receivables include the right to receive payment for goods or services.

- Contributed property that was inventory in the contributor's hands on the contribution date, if the partnership disposes of the property within *five years of the contribution*. For this purpose, inventory includes all tangible property except capital and real or depreciable business assets.

A similar rule is designed to prevent a capital loss from being converted into an ordinary loss. Under the rule, if contributed property is disposed of at a loss and the property had a "built-in" capital loss on the contribution date, the loss is treated as a capital loss if the partnership disposes of the property *within five years of the contribution*. The capital loss is limited to the "built-in" loss on the date of contribution.[21]

The Big Picture

EXAMPLE 15

Return to the facts of *The Big Picture* on p. 14-1. Recall that Kyle, Maria, and Josh decide to structure their venture as an LLC. Assume that Kyle has a basis of $600,000 in the $2 million of real estate he contributed, and that Maria has a $0 basis in the bakery equipment and the café furnishings.

When Beachside Properties LLC is formed, no tax results for the LLC or for Kyle or Maria. Kyle does not recognize his $1.4 million realized gain, nor does Maria recognize her $500,000 realized gain.

Kyle takes a substituted basis of $600,000 for his interest, and Maria takes a substituted basis of $1.5 million ($1.5 million for contributed cash + $0 for contributed property). Beachside Properties assumes a carryover basis of $600,000 for the real estate contributed by Kyle and $0 for the property contributed by Maria. To the extent that the buildings and other land improvements are depreciable, the LLC "steps into Kyle's shoes" in calculating depreciation deductions.

When Josh vests in his 5% capital interest in the LLC, the $200,000 value of the interest is taxable to him, because it is a capital interest received in exchange for services. Beachside Properties probably will capitalize this amount because it relates to construction activities. Josh's 20% share of the future profits of the LLC are taxed to him as they flow through from the LLC.

14-2d Inside and Outside Bases

Reference has been made previously to the partnership's inside basis and the partners' outside basis. **Inside basis** refers to the adjusted basis of each partnership asset, as determined from the partnership's tax accounts. **Outside basis** represents each partner's basis in the partnership interest. Each partner "owns" a share of the partnership's inside basis for all of its assets, and all partners should maintain a record of their respective outside bases.

LO.3

Determine the tax treatment of expenditures of a newly formed partnership and identify elections available to the partnership.

14-2e Tax Accounting Elections

Numerous tax accounting elections must be made when a new partnership is formed. These elections are formal decisions on how a particular transaction or tax attribute should be handled. Most of these elections must be made by the partnership rather than

---

[20]§ 724. For this purpose, § 724(d)(2) waives the holding period requirement in defining § 1231 property.

[21]§ 724(c).

Concept Summary 14.2

Partnership Formation and Basis Computation

1. Generally, partners or partnerships do not recognize gain or loss when property is contributed in exchange for capital interests.

2. Partners contributing property in exchange for partnership interests take the contributed property's adjusted basis for their *outside basis* in their partnership interest. The partners are said to take a substituted basis in their partnership interest.

3. The partnership keeps the contributing partner's basis as the *inside basis* in property it receives. The contributed property is said to take a carryover basis.

4. The partnership's holding period for contributed property may include the contributing partner's holding period.

5. Income or gain is recognized by a contributing partner when services are contributed or when the capital contribution is a disguised sale or exchange.

6. Special rules may apply when the partnership disposes of contributed receivables, inventory, or loss assets.

by the partners individually.[22] For example, the *partnership* makes the elections involving the following tax accounting items.

- Inventory methods.
- Tax year and accounting method (cash, accrual, or hybrid).
- Cost recovery methods and assumptions.
- First-year cost recovery deductions for certain tangible personal property.
- Treatment (i.e., deduction or credit) of research and experimentation costs.
- Amortization of organizational costs and amortization period.
- Cost allocation methods to compute the domestic production activities deduction.

Each partner is bound by the decisions made by the partnership relative to these elections. If the partnership fails to make an election, a partner cannot make the election individually.

Although most elections are made by the partnership, each *partner* separately makes a specific election for the following relatively narrow tax accounting issues.

- Whether to take a deduction or a credit for taxes paid to foreign countries.
- Whether to claim the cost or percentage depletion method for oil and gas wells.
- Whether to reduce the basis of depreciable property first when excluding income from discharge of indebtedness.

14-2f **Initial Costs of a Partnership**

In its initial stages, a partnership incurs expenses relating to some or all of the following: forming the partnership (organizational costs), admitting partners to the partnership, marketing and selling partnership units to prospective partners (**syndication costs**), acquiring assets, starting business operations (startup costs), negotiating contracts, and dealing with other items.

Many of these expenditures are not currently deductible. However, the Code permits a deduction or ratable (straight-line) amortization of "organizational" and "startup" costs. Costs incurred to acquire tangible assets are included in the initial basis of the acquired assets, leading to depreciation deductions. "Syndication costs" may be neither amortized nor deducted.[23]

---

[22]§ 703(b).   [23]§ 709(a).

Organizational Costs

Organizational costs are incurred incident to the creation of the partnership and are capital in nature. Such costs include accounting and legal fees associated with the partnership formation.[24] Costs incurred for the following purposes are *not* organizational costs.

- Acquiring assets for the partnership.
- Transferring assets to the partnership.
- Admitting partners, other than at formation.
- Removing partners, other than at formation.
- Negotiating operating contracts.

A partnership may deduct up to $5,000 of organizational costs in the year in which it begins business. This amount is reduced, however, by these organizational costs that exceed $50,000. Any organizational costs that cannot be deducted under this provision are amortizable over 180 months beginning with the month in which the partnership begins business.

The election to deduct organizational costs is made by entering the proper amounts on the first partnership return. Lacking such a computation, no deduction or amortization of the organizational costs is allowed until the entity is liquidated.

EXAMPLE

16

The Bluejay LLC, which was formed on March 1, incurs $52,000 in organizational costs. Bluejay uses a calendar tax year. On its first tax return for the period March–December, Bluejay can deduct $5,722 for these items. This deduction is the sum of:

- $5,000 reduced by the $2,000 ($52,000 − $50,000) amount by which the organizational costs exceed $50,000 = $3,000.
- $2,722 ($49,000 × 10/180) amortization of the remaining $49,000 ($52,000 − $3,000) of organizational costs for 10 months.

If Bluejay had failed to make a proper election to deduct or amortize the organizational costs, none of these costs would have been deductible until the entity liquidated.

Startup Costs

Operating costs that are incurred after the entity is formed but before it begins business are known as startup costs. Like organizational costs, startup costs are capitalized and may be immediately expensed and/or amortized.[25] Such costs include marketing surveys prior to conducting business, pre-operating advertising expenses, costs of establishing an accounting system, and salaries paid to executives and employees before the start of business.

A partnership may deduct up to $5,000 of startup costs in the year in which it begins business. This amount is reduced, however, by the startup costs that exceed $50,000.

Costs that are not deductible under this provision are amortizable over 180 months beginning with the month in which the partnership begins business. If the deduction for startup costs is not claimed, no deduction or amortization of the startup costs is allowed until the partnership is liquidated.

DIGGING DEEPER 3

In-depth coverage can be found on this book's companion website: www.cengagebrain.com

---

[24]§ 709(b)(2).

[25]§ 195.

14-3 OPERATIONS OF THE PARTNERSHIP

A key consideration in the taxation of partnerships is that a variety of entities can be partners and each may be affected differently by the partnership's operations. In particular, any combination of individuals, corporations, trusts, estates, or other partnerships may be partners. Furthermore, at the end of each year, every partner receives a share of the partnership's income, deductions, credits, and alternative minimum tax (AMT) preferences and adjustments.[26]

These flow-through items ultimately may be reported and taxed on a wide variety of income tax returns [e.g., Forms 1040 (Individuals), 1041 (Fiduciaries), 1120 (C corporations), and 1120S (S corporations)], each facing different limitations and rules. Thus, the ultimate tax treatment of partnership operations is directly affected by how the partnership reports its operating results.

14-3a Schedules K and K–1

A partnership measures and reports two kinds of income: separately stated items and nonseparately stated ordinary (operating) income. A separately stated item is any item with tax attributes that could affect partners differently. Separately stated items are segregated and reported separately on the partnership's Schedule K and each partner's Schedule K–1. All other (nonseparately stated) income and expenses are reported as income from operations on page 1 of the partnership's Form 1065; the net amount then is allocated to the partners on Schedules K and K–1. Items passed through separately include the following.[27]

- Net short-term and net long-term capital gains or losses.
- Section 1231 gains and losses.
- Charitable contributions.
- Portfolio income items (qualified and ordinary dividends, interest, and royalties).
- Expenses related to portfolio income.
- Immediately expensed tangible personal property (§ 179).
- Data used by partners to compute their deduction for domestic production activities.[28]
- AMT preference and adjustment items.
- Self-employment income.
- Passive activity items (e.g., rental real estate income or loss).
- Intangible drilling and development costs.
- Taxes paid to other countries.

A partnership is not allowed to claim the following deductions.

- Net operating loss (NOL).
- Dividends received deduction.
- Items that are allowed only to individuals, such as standard deductions or personal exemptions.

---

[26]§ 702(a).
[27]§ 702(b).
[28]§ 199.

The Big Picture

EXAMPLE

17

Return to the facts of *The Big Picture* on p. 14-1. In its second year of operations, Beachside Properties LLC reports income and expenses from operating the café as well as rent income and expenses from leasing the other buildings. Beachside's activities are summarized as follows.

Sales revenue	$2,000,000
Cost of sales	800,000
Salaries to employees	500,000
Cost recovery deductions	91,984
Utilities, supplies, and other expenses	128,016
Taxes and licenses (including payroll taxes)	60,000
Contribution to charity	6,000
Short-term capital gain	12,000
Net income from rental real estate	300,000
Qualified dividends received	4,000
Tax-exempt income (bond interest)	2,100
AMT adjustment (cost recovery)	18,224
Payment of medical expenses on behalf of Kyle	4,000
Net operating loss (NOL) from last year's operations	250,000
Cash distribution to Maria	20,000

Refer to Form 1065 in Appendix B. Beachside's ordinary income is determined and reported on the partnership return as follows.

Nonseparately Stated Items (Ordinary Income)	
Sales revenue	$2,000,000
Cost of sales	(800,000)
Salaries to employees	(500,000)
Cost recovery deductions	(91,984)
Utilities, supplies, and other expenses	(128,016)
Taxes and licenses (including payroll taxes)	(60,000)
Ordinary income [Form 1065, page 1, line 22, and Form 1065, page 4 (Schedule K), line 1]	$ 420,000

Beachside's separately stated income and deduction items are:

Separately Stated Income and Deductions (Schedule K)	
Net income from rental real estate (line 2)	$300,000
Qualified dividends received (line 6b)	4,000
Short-term capital gain (line 8)	12,000
Contribution to charity (line 13a)	(6,000)

Beachside is not allowed a deduction for payment of Kyle's medical expenses. This payment probably is handled as a distribution to Kyle, who may report it as a medical expense on his Form 1040, Schedule A in determining itemized deductions.

Maria's distribution is not deducted by Beachside. That amount instead reduces Maria's basis in her LLC interest.

The AMT adjustment is not a separate component of Beachside's ordinary income. It is reported to Beachside's members so that they can properly calculate any AMT liability of their own.

Beachside reports the following additional information the members may utilize in preparing their own income tax returns.

continued

Additional Information (Schedule K)	
AMT adjustment—cost recovery (line 17a)	$18,224
Tax-exempt income—bond interest (line 18a)	2,100
Distributions (line 19a)	24,000
Investment income (line 20a)	4,000

The LLC members' pass-through income represents net earnings (loss) from self-employment and is reported on line 14a.

The Big Picture

EXAMPLE 18

Continue with the facts in Example 17, but now consider the entity's book-tax reconciliation. Beachside Properties LLC must prepare the Analysis of Net Income (Loss) and Schedule M–1 on Form 1065, page 5. In preparing these schedules, the LLC combines the ordinary income of $420,000 and the four separately stated income and deduction amounts in Example 17 to arrive at "net income" of $730,000. This amount is shown on line 1 of the Analysis of Net Income (Loss) and is the amount to which book income is reconciled on Schedule M–1, line 9.

The Big Picture

EXAMPLE 19

Assume the same facts as in Example 17, but now consider the effect of the LLC's operations on one of its members. Maria, a 40% owner, will receive a Schedule K–1 from Beachside Properties, on which she is allocated a 40% share of ordinary income and separately stated items. Thus, on her Form 1040, Maria includes $168,000 of ordinary income, a $2,400 charitable contribution, a $4,800 short-term capital gain, $120,000 of passive activity rent income, and $1,600 of qualified dividend income. Maria's Schedule K–1 also reports the $20,000 cash distribution received.

Maria discloses her $840 share of tax-exempt interest on the first page of Form 1040. In determining her AMT liability (if any), Maria will take into account a $7,290 positive adjustment ($18,224 × 40%).

Domestic Production Activities Deduction (§ 199)

As noted in Chapter 5, the conduct of certain businesses, usually manufacturing activities, can yield a domestic production activities deduction (DPAD). To determine the base for the deduction, domestic production gross receipts (DPGR) is computed. Then related cost of goods sold and direct and indirect expenses are subtracted to arrive at qualified production activities income (QPAI). The deduction (or DPAD) generally is 9 percent of the lesser of QPAI or taxable income.[29] When the taxpayer is not a corporation, modified AGI is substituted for taxable income. In no event, however, may the DPAD exceed 50 percent of the W–2 wages paid that are attributable to domestic production activities.[30]

When pass-through entities are involved (i.e., partnerships, S corporations, estates, and trusts), special rules apply.[31] Specifically, in the case of partnerships and limited liability entities, the following rules govern the DPAD computation and allowance.

- Whether an activity qualifies for the DPAD is determined at the entity level.

- Each partner is allocated its share of QPAI and W–2 wages related to domestic production activities. The appropriate amounts are listed on Schedule K–1 of Form 1065.

---

[29]§ 199(a).
[30]§ 199(b).

[31]The rules applicable to pass-through entities are contained in § 199(d)(1) and Reg. § 1.199–5.

A U.S. partnership may have non-U.S. partners, and these owners are taxed on their share of the entity's U.S. income. Because it might be difficult for the IRS to collect the Federal income tax that is owed by such partners, several Code sections require the partnership to withhold and pay to the U.S. Treasury an amount relating to the non-U.S. partners.

If the partnership reports U.S. business income, withholding is required using the highest applicable Federal income tax rate. For instance, the withholding amount for a partner who is a non-U.S. individual is 39.6 percent of the owner's applicable share of the year's U.S. business income. The rate is 35 percent for a non-U.S. corporate partner.

Gross income that relates to dividends, interest, rents, and the like generally is subject to withholding at a 30 percent rate. If a partnership sells U.S. real estate, the entity typically withholds 20 percent of the gain allocated to any non-U.S. partner.

Tax treaties can reduce these withholding tax rates or provide exceptions as to whether withholding is required at all. Additional material on these topics is found in Chapter 16.

- The partner combines the partnership pass-through items with those from other sources (e.g., if the partner operates a separate factory).
- The deduction then is computed at the partner level.
- Guaranteed payments, discussed in detail in text Section 14-4a, are not W–2 wages for DPAD purposes.[32]

DIGGING DEEPER 4   In-depth coverage can be found on this book's companion website: www.cengagebrain.com

Distributions, Withdrawals

Asset distributions and withdrawals by partners during the year do not affect the partnership's income determination.[33] These items usually are treated as made on the last day of the partnership's tax year. Such distributions reduce the partner's outside basis in the entity by the amount of the cash received, or by the inside basis of the asset to the entity, but not below zero. The entity's inside basis in assets is similarly reduced. The partner usually assigns to the received property a basis equal to the entity's inside basis in the distributed asset.

EXAMPLE
20

Bueno Company is a partner in the BB Partnership. The basis in Bueno's partnership interest is $10,000. The partnership distributes $3,000 cash to Bueno at the end of the year. Bueno does not recognize any gain on the distribution. It reduces its basis in BB by $3,000 (the amount of the distribution) to $7,000. Bueno's basis in the cash received is $3,000, and the partnership's inside basis for its assets is reduced by the $3,000 of cash distributed.

BB also distributes to Bueno a plot of land worth $5,000, with a $2,000 basis to BB. Neither BB nor Bueno recognizes a gain from this distribution. Bueno assigns the land a $2,000 basis, and it reduces its basis in BB by the same amount.

The result in Example 20 arises whether or not a similar distribution is made to other partners. In a partnership, all partners need not receive a pro rata distribution at the same time, as long as capital account balances are maintained appropriately.

DIGGING DEEPER 5   In-depth coverage can be found on this book's companion website: www.cengagebrain.com

---

[32]Reg. § 1.199–5(b)(1)(i).   [33]§ 731(a).

Concept Summary 14.3

Tax Reporting of Partnership Activities

Item	Partnership Level (Form 1065)	Partner Level (Schedule K–1)
1. Compute partnership ordinary income.	Page 1, line 22. Schedule K, line 1.	Line 1. Each partner's share is passed through for separate reporting. Each partner's basis is increased.
2. Compute partnership ordinary loss.	Page 1, line 22. Schedule K, line 1.	Line 1. Each partner's share is passed through for separate reporting. Each partner's basis is decreased. The amount of a partner's loss deduction may be limited. Losses that may not be deducted are carried forward for use in future years.
3. Separately reported income and deduction items such as portfolio income, capital gain and loss, AMT and foreign tax items, and § 179 deductions.	Schedule K, various lines.	Various lines. Each partner's share of each item is passed through for separate reporting.
4. Net earnings from self-employment.	Schedule K, line 14a, Code A.	Line 14, Code A.

14-3b Partnership Allocations

After ordinary income, separately stated items, and other related information are determined at the partnership level, those amounts are allocated among the partners and reported on their tax returns. Allocations are made as required by the partnership agreement, using the profit and loss sharing ratios agreed to by the owners.

Alternatively, two key special allocation rules also can affect a partner's Schedule K–1 results.[34]

Economic Effect

The partnership agreement can provide that any partner may share capital, profits, and losses in ratios that are tailored to their needs.[35] For example, a partner could have a 25 percent capital sharing ratio, yet be allocated 30 percent of the profits and 20 percent of the losses of the partnership, or, as in Examples 5 and 6, a partner could be allocated a specific amount or items of income, deduction, gain, or loss. Such special allocations are permissible if they meet the economic effect test.[36] The rules prevent partners from shifting income and loss items merely to reduce current taxes.

In-depth coverage can be found on this book's companion website: www.cengagebrain.com **6 DIGGING DEEPER**

Precontribution Gain or Loss

Certain income, gain, loss, and deductions relative to contributed property may not be allocated under the economic effect rules.[37] Instead, precontribution gain or loss is allocated among the partners to take into account the variation between the basis of the

---

[34]The Code requires or allows certain other allocations not discussed here.
[35]§ 704(a).
[36]Reg. § 1.704–1(b).
[37]§ 704(b).

property and its fair market value on the date of contribution.[38] For nondepreciable property, this means that *built-in* gain or loss on the date of contribution is allocated to the contributing partner when the property eventually is disposed of by the partnership in a taxable transaction.

The Big Picture

EXAMPLE

21

Return to the facts of *The Big Picture* on p. 14-1. When Beachside Properties LLC was formed, among other items, Kyle contributed land (value of $800,000 and basis of $600,000) and buildings (value of $1,200,000 and basis of $0). Maria contributed equipment and furnishings (value of $500,000 and basis of $0).

For book purposes, Beachside records the land and other properties at their fair market values. For tax purposes, the LLC takes carryover bases in the properties. The LLC must keep track of the differences between the basis in each property and the value at the contribution date. If any of this property is sold, the gain is allocated to the contributing partner to the extent of any previously unrecognized built-in gain.

For example, if Beachside sells the land contributed by Kyle for $1.1 million, the gain is calculated and allocated as follows.

	Book	Tax
Amount realized	$1,100,000	$1,100,000
Less: Adjusted basis	(800,000)	(600,000)
Gain realized	$ 300,000	$ 500,000
Built-in gain allocated solely to Kyle	(—0—)	(200,000)
Remaining gain (allocated among members)	$ 300,000	$ 300,000

For Federal income tax purposes, Kyle recognizes $320,000 of the gain [($300,000 × 40%) + $200,000], Maria recognizes $120,000 ($300,000 × 40%), and Josh recognizes $60,000 ($300,000 × 20%).

LO.5

Determine a partner's basis in the partnership interest.

14-3c Basis of a Partnership Interest

A partner's basis in the partnership interest is important for determining the treatment of distributions from the partnership to the partner, establishing the deductibility of partnership losses, and calculating gain or loss on the partner's disposition of the partnership interest.

A partner's basis is not reflected anywhere on the Schedule K–1. Instead, each partner maintains a personal record of the basis in the partnership interest.

Initial Basis in the Partnership Interest

A partner's basis in a newly formed partnership usually equals (1) the adjusted basis in any cash or other property contributed to the partnership plus (2) the fair market value of any services the partner performed for the partnership (i.e., the amount of ordinary income reported by the partner for services rendered to the partnership).

A partnership interest also can be acquired after the partnership has been formed. The method of acquisition controls how the partner's initial basis is computed. If the partnership interest is purchased from another partner, the purchasing partner's basis is the amount paid (cost basis) for the partnership interest. The basis of a partnership interest acquired by gift is the donor's basis for the interest plus, in certain cases, some or all of the transfer (gift) tax paid by the donor. The basis of a partnership interest acquired through inheritance generally is the fair market value of the interest on the date the partner dies.

---

[38]§ 704(c)(1)(A).

The equivalent in financial accounting to the partner's income tax basis in his or her partnership interest is the capital account. A partner's ending balance in the capital account is not required to be the same as his or her basis in the partnership interest. Just as the tax and accounting bases of a specific asset may differ, a partner's capital account and basis in the partnership interest usually are not equal.

Whereas contributions and most distributions from the partnership do not create financial accounting income, the capital account is "written up or down" to aggregate fair market value when the entity is formed. For most partnerships with simple financial transactions, *changes* to the capital account parallel closely the annual changes to the partner's basis in the partnership. Basis in one's partnership interest cannot be a negative number, but the capital account can become negative.

Oddly, the Schedules K–1 for the partners require an accounting for their capital accounts, but there is no required reconciliation for the partner's tax basis on the Schedule K–1. As a result, the tax adviser may find that a new partnership client has poor records with respect to the basis amounts of the partners, and a reconstruction must take place so that future computations will be correct. Sometimes, lacking adequate information with which to make this computation, the capital account is used because it is "close enough" and forms a good surrogate for the partner's basis in the partnership.

Basis Adjustments Due to Entity Operations

After the partnership begins its activities, or after a new partner is admitted to the partnership, the partner's basis is adjusted for numerous items. The following operating results *increase* a partner's basis.

- The partner's proportionate share of partnership income (including capital gains and tax-exempt income).
- The partner's proportionate share of any increase in partnership liabilities.

The following operating results *decrease* the partner's basis in the partnership. A partner's basis in the partnership interest cannot be reduced below zero.

- The partner's proportionate share of partnership deductions and losses (including capital losses).
- The partner's proportionate share of nondeductible expenses.
- The partner's proportionate share of any reduction in partnership liabilities.[39]

Increasing the basis for the partner's share of partnership taxable income is logical, because the partner already has been taxed on the income. By increasing the partner's basis, the partner is not taxed again on the income when he or she sells the interest or receives a distribution from the partnership.

It also is logical that tax-exempt income should increase the partner's basis. If the income is tax-exempt in the current period, it should not contribute to the recognition of gain when the partner either sells the interest or receives a distribution from the partnership. Decreasing the basis for the partner's share of deductible losses, deductions, and noncapitalizable, nondeductible expenditures is done for the same reasons.

Yuri is a one-third member in the XYZ LLC. His proportionate share of operations during the current year consists of $20,000 of ordinary taxable income and $10,000 of tax-exempt income. None of the income is distributed to Yuri.

The basis of Yuri's LLC interest before adjusting for his share of income is $35,000, and the fair market value of the interest before considering the income items is $50,000.

The unrealized gain inherent in Yuri's investment in XYZ is $15,000 ($50,000 − $35,000). Yuri's proportionate share of the income items should increase the fair market value of the interest to

EXAMPLE
22

continued

---
[39]§§ 705 and 752.

$80,000 ($50,000 + $20,000 + $10,000). When the basis of Yuri's interest is increased to $65,000 ($35,000 + $20,000 + $10,000), the unrealized gain inherent in Yuri's investment remains at $15,000.

Thus, $20,000 of ordinary taxable income is taxed to Yuri this year and should not be taxed again when Yuri either sells his interest or receives a distribution. Similarly, the tax-exempt income is exempt this year and should not increase Yuri's gain when he either sells his interest or receives a distribution from XYZ.

TAX FACT   **What Do Partnerships Do?**

Partnerships report over $24 trillion in assets on their Form 1065 balance sheets. The partnership form seems to be especially popular for businesses operating in the financial services and real estate industries. Manufacturing assets tend not to be found as frequently in these entities.

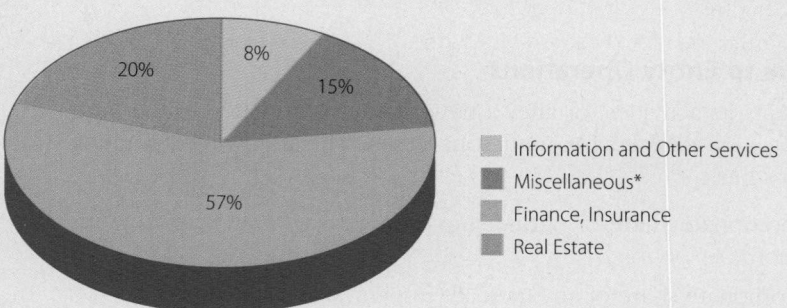

Assets of Partnerships, by Industry

- Information and Other Services
- Miscellaneous*
- Finance, Insurance
- Real Estate

*Includes aggregated amounts from the agriculture, health care, construction, manufacturing, wholesale and retail trade, education, and arts and entertainment sectors.

Partnership Liabilities

A partner's basis includes the partner's share of partnership debt.[40] Partnership debt includes most debt that is considered a liability under financial accounting rules. However, partnership debt for this purpose does *not* include the accounts payable of a cash basis partnership and certain contingent liabilities.

Partnership debt is classified as either recourse or nonrecourse.[41] For **recourse debt**, the partnership or at least one of the partners is personally liable. This liability can exist, for example, through the operation of state law or through personal guarantees that a partner makes to the creditor. If the entity defaults on the loan, the lender can pursue the other assets of the borrower, including personal-use property.

For **nonrecourse debt**, no partner is personally liable. Lenders of nonrecourse debt generally require that collateral be pledged against the loan. Upon default, the lender can claim only the collateral, not the partners' personal assets.

Liabilities and Partnership Interest Basis

EXAMPLE 23

The Bay Partnership financed its asset acquisitions with debt. If the partnership defaults on the debt, the lender can place a lien on the partners' salaries and personal assets. This constitutes recourse debt.

---

[40]§ 752.

[41]Reg. § 1.752–1(a). All of the debts of an LLC generally are treated as nonrecourse debt for its members, because it is the entity, and not the members, that is ultimately liable for repayment.

Liabilities and Partnership Interest Basis

The Tray LLC financed its asset acquisitions with debt. If the entity defaults on the debt, the lender can repossess the equipment purchased with the loan proceeds. This constitutes nonrecourse debt.

EXAMPLE
24

When Ray bought into the Sleigh LLC, the entity was in the midst of settling litigation as to its liability to those who had purchased its products and were making warranty claims against the entity. Ray's basis in his Sleigh interest does not include his share of these contingent liabilities.

EXAMPLE
25

A partner's share of entity-level debt usually increases as a result of increases in outstanding partnership debt. This creates additional basis in the partnership for the partner, against which flow-through losses can be deducted.

Jim and Becky contribute property to form the JB Partnership. Jim contributes cash of $30,000. Becky contributes land with a basis and fair market value of $45,000, subject to a liability of $15,000. The partnership borrows $50,000 to finance construction of a building on the contributed land. At the end of the first year, the accrual basis partnership owes $3,500 in trade accounts payable to various vendors. No other operating activities occurred. If Jim and Becky share equally in liabilities, the partners' bases in their partnership interests are determined as follows.

EXAMPLE
26

Jim's Basis		Becky's Basis	
Contributed cash	$30,000	Basis in contributed land	$ 45,000
		Less: Debt assumed by partnership	(15,000)
Share of debt on land (assumed by partnership)	7,500	Share of debt on land (assumed by partnership)	7,500
Share of construction loan	25,000	Share of construction loan	25,000
Share of trade accounts payable	1,750	Share of trade accounts payable	1,750
Basis, end of year 1	$64,250	Basis, end of year 1	$ 64,250

A decrease in a partner's share of partnership debt is treated as a cash distribution and decreases the partner's basis. This limits the partner's ability to deduct current-year flow-through losses.

In-depth coverage can be found on this book's companion website: www.cengagebrain.com

7 DIGGING DEEPER

14-3d Partner's Basis, Gain, and Loss

The partner's interest basis in the entity also is affected by (1) postacquisition contributions of cash or property to the partnership and (2) postacquisition distributions of cash or property from the partnership.

Ed is a one-third member in ERM LLC. On January 1, Ed's basis in his interest was $50,000. The calendar year, accrual basis entity generated ordinary taxable income of $210,000. It also received $60,000 of tax-exempt interest income from City of Buffalo bonds. It paid $3,000 in nondeductible fines and penalties.

On July 1, Ed contributed $20,000 cash and a computer (zero basis to him) to ERM. Ed's monthly cash draw from the LLC is $3,000; this is not a guaranteed payment. The only entity liabilities are trade accounts payable. On January 1, the trade accounts payable totaled $45,000; this account balance was $21,000 on December 31. Ed shares in one-third of the entity's liabilities for basis purposes.

EXAMPLE
27

continued

Ed's basis in the LLC on December 31 is $115,000, computed as follows.

Beginning basis in the LLC interest	$ 50,000
Share of ordinary income	70,000
Share of tax-exempt income	20,000
Share of nondeductible fines and penalties	(1,000)
Ed's basis in noncash capital contribution (computer)	–0–
Additional cash contributions	20,000
Capital withdrawal ($3,000 per month)	(36,000)
Share of net decrease in ERM liabilities [$1/3 \times$ ($45,000 − $21,000)]	(8,000)
Ending basis in the LLC interest	$115,000

If Ed withdraws cash of $115,000 from ERM the next year, the withdrawal is tax-free to him and reduces his basis to zero. The distribution is tax-free because Ed has recognized his share of net income throughout his association with the entity via the annual flow-through of his share of the ERM income and expense items to his personal tax return.

If Ed receives a $20,000 cash withdrawal of his share of the municipal bond interest income, that amount retains its nontaxable character; his basis was increased when ERM received the interest income.

Noncash Distributions

When a distribution involves something other than cash, the recipient partner (1) reduces the basis in the partnership interest and (2) assigns a basis to the asset received, both by the amount of the inside basis of the distributed asset. When cash and another asset are distributed at the same time, the partner first accounts for the cash received.

Loss never is recognized when a partnership makes a distribution other than possibly in its own liquidation. A partner recognizes gain only when receiving *cash* in an amount in excess of the basis in the partnership.

Distributions of Noncash Assets

EXAMPLE 28

Pert Corporation has a $100,000 basis in the PQR Partnership. Pert receives a distribution from PQR in the form of a plot of land (basis to PQR of $40,000, fair market value of $50,000). Pert does not recognize gain from the distribution. Pert's basis in the land is $40,000 (i.e., a carryover basis), and its basis in PQR now is $60,000 ($100,000 − $40,000).

EXAMPLE 29

Pert Corporation has a $100,000 basis in the PQR Partnership. Pert receives a distribution from PQR in the form of a plot of land (basis to PQR of $40,000, fair market value of $50,000) and $75,000 of cash.

Pert does not recognize any gain from the distribution because the cash received ($75,000) does not exceed Pert's partnership basis ($100,000). Pert's basis in the land is $25,000, the basis in PQR remaining after accounting for the cash ($100,000 partnership basis − $75,000 cash = $25,000 basis assigned to land). Pert's basis in the partnership now is zero ($25,000 basis after accounting for the cash − $25,000 assigned to the land).

EXAMPLE 30

Pert Corporation has a $100,000 basis in the PQR Partnership. Pert receives a distribution from PQR in the form of a plot of land (basis to PQR of $40,000, fair market value of $50,000) and $125,000 of cash. Pert recognizes $25,000 of gain from the distribution ($125,000 cash received − $100,000 basis in PQR). Pert's basis in the land is $0, as there is no basis in PQR remaining after accounting for the cash. Pert's basis in the partnership also is zero.

Capital Changes

When a partnership interest is sold, exchanged, or retired, the partner must compute the basis as of the date the transaction occurs. The partner recognizes gain or loss on the disposition of the partnership interest, and this usually is a capital gain or loss. Income "bunching" may occur if the partner recognizes the pass-through of operating income in the same tax year during which the sale of the interest occurs. To the extent the partner is allocated a share of ordinary income items (i.e., "hot assets") that have yet to be recognized by the partnership, some of the capital gain is converted to ordinary income.[42]

Hot Assets

EXAMPLE 31

When its basis in the TUV Partnership is $100,000, taking into account all earnings to date and the sale-date liabilities of the partnership, Kurt Corporation sells its interest in the entity to Gloria for $120,000. Kurt recognizes a $20,000 capital gain [$120,000 (amount realized) − $100,000 (basis in partnership interest)].

EXAMPLE 32

When its basis in the TUV Partnership is $100,000, taking into account all earnings to date and the sale-date liabilities of the partnership, Kurt Corporation sells its interest in the entity to Gloria for $120,000. At the time of the sale, Kurt's share of the TUV hot assets is $8,000. Kurt recognizes $8,000 of ordinary income and $12,000 of capital gain (i.e., the total gain of $20,000 is comprised of $8,000 of ordinary income and $12,000 of capital gain).

EXAMPLE 33

When its basis in the TUV Partnership is $100,000, taking into account all earnings to date and the sale-date liabilities of the partnership, Kurt Corporation sells its interest in the entity to Gloria for $120,000. At the time of the sale, Kurt's share of the TUV hot assets is $28,000. Kurt recognizes $28,000 of ordinary income and $8,000 of capital loss (i.e., the total gain of $20,000 is comprised of $28,000 of ordinary income and $8,000 of capital loss).

14-3e Loss Limitations

LO.6

Apply the limitations on deducting partnership losses.

Partnership losses flow through to the partners for use on their tax returns. However, the amount and nature of the partner's deductible losses may be limited. When limitations apply, all or some of the losses are suspended and carried forward until the rules allow them to be used. Only then can the losses decrease the partner's tax liability.

Three different limitations may apply to partnership losses that are passed through to a partner. The first allows the deduction of *losses* only to the extent the partner has a positive basis in the partnership interest. The tax basis in the entity cannot be reduced below zero.

Losses that are deductible under this basis limitation may then be subject to the *at-risk* limitations. Losses are deductible under this provision only to the extent the partner is at risk for the partnership interest. Any losses that survive this second limitation may be subject to a third limitation, the *passive activity loss* rules. Only losses that make it through all three of these applicable limitations are eligible to be deducted on the partner's tax return.

---

[42]Partnership items that hold unrecognized ordinary income are known as *hot assets*. Hot assets include the unrealized receivables of a cash basis partnership and a broadly defined concept of inventory. §§ 751(a) and (d).

EXAMPLE 34

Meg is a 50% member in MQ Telecomm Services LLC. On January 1, Meg's basis in her LLC interest is $50,000, and her at-risk amount is $35,000. Her share of losses from MQ for the year is $60,000, all of which is a passive activity loss. Meg owns another investment that generated $25,000 of passive activity income during the year. Meg can deduct $25,000 of the MQ losses on her Form 1040.

Applicable Provision	Deductible Loss	Suspended Loss
Basis limitation	$50,000	$10,000
At-risk limitation	35,000	15,000
Passive activity loss limitation	25,000	10,000

Meg can deduct only $50,000 under the basis limitation rule. Of this $50,000, only $35,000 is deductible under the at-risk limitation. Under the passive activity loss limitation, passive activity losses can only be deducted against passive activity income. Thus, Meg can deduct only $25,000 on her return. The remaining $35,000 of losses is suspended.

Basis Limitation

A partner may deduct losses and deductions flowing through from the partnership only to the extent of the partner's basis in the partnership.[43] Items that cannot be deducted because of this rule are suspended and carried forward (never back) for use against future increases in the partner's basis. Such increases might result from additional capital contributions, from sharing in additional partnership debts, or from future partnership income.

EXAMPLE 35

Carol and Dan do business as the CD Partnership, sharing profits and losses equally. All parties use the calendar year. At the start of the current year, the basis of Carol's partnership interest is $25,000. The partnership sustains an operating loss of $80,000 in the current year. Only $25,000 of Carol's $40,000 allocable share of the partnership loss can be deducted under the basis limitation. As a result, the basis of Carol's partnership interest is zero as of January 1 of the following year, and Carol must carry forward the remaining $15,000 of partnership losses.

Now assume that CD earns a profit of $70,000 for the next calendar year. Carol reports net partnership income of $20,000 ($35,000 share of income − $15,000 carryforward loss). The basis of Carol's partnership interest becomes $20,000.

Concept Summary 14.4 later in the chapter shows that contributions to capital, partnership income items, and distributions from the partnership are taken into account before loss items. This *losses last* rule can produce some unusual results in taxation of partnership distributions and deductibility of losses.

TAX PLANNING STRATEGIES   **Make Your Own Tax Shelter**

FRAMEWORK FOCUS: DEDUCTIONS

Strategy: Maximize Deductible Amounts.

In Example 35, Carol's entire $40,000 share of the current-year partnership loss could have been deducted under the basis limitation in the current year if she had contributed an additional $15,000 or more to the entity's capital by December 31 of the first tax year. Alternatively, if the partnership had incurred additional debt by the end of the first tax year, Carol's basis might have been increased to permit some or all of the loss to be deducted in that year.

Thus, if partnership losses are projected for a given year, careful tax planning can ensure their deductibility under the basis limitation. Note, however, that the effects of the at-risk and passive activity limitations as discussed on the next page also must be considered.

---

[43]§ 704(d).

The Basis Limitation on Losses

The Ellen-Glenn Partnership is owned equally by two partners: Ellen and the Glenn Hospital. At the beginning of the year, Ellen's basis in her partnership interest is $0. Her share of partnership income is $12,000 for the year, and she receives a $10,000 distribution from the partnership.

Under the basis adjustment ordering rules of Concept Summary 14.4, as shown on the next page, Ellen's basis first is increased by the $12,000 of partnership income; then it is decreased by her $10,000 distribution. She reports her $12,000 share of partnership taxable income on her personal tax return. Her basis in the partnership at the end of the year is $2,000 ($0 beginning basis + $12,000 income − $10,000 distribution).

EXAMPLE 36

Assume the same facts as in Example 36, except that Ellen's share of partnership operating results is a $12,000 loss instead of $12,000 of income. She again receives a $10,000 distribution.

A distribution of cash in excess of basis in the partnership interest results in a gain to the distributee partner to the extent of the excess. Ellen's distribution is considered before the deductibility of the loss is evaluated under the basis limitation.

Therefore, Ellen recognizes gain on the $10,000 distribution because she has a $0 basis in her partnership interest. Unfortunately for Ellen, the operating loss cannot be deducted under the basis limitation rule because Ellen still holds a $0 basis in her partnership interest. The loss is suspended, and Ellen carries it forward to a future tax year.

EXAMPLE 37

At-Risk Limitation

Under the at-risk rules (see Chapter 6), a partner's deductions for certain pass-through losses are limited to amounts that are economically invested in the partnership. Invested amounts include the cash and the adjusted basis of property contributed by the partner and the partner's share of partnership earnings that has not been distributed.[44]

Losses that are not deductible under the at-risk rules are suspended. When a positive at-risk amount arises in a future tax year, the suspended loss is allowed.

When some or all of the partners are personally liable for partnership recourse debt, that debt is included in the basis of the partnership for those partners. Usually, those partners also include the debt in their amount at risk.

No partner, however, carries any financial risk on nonrecourse debt. Therefore, as a general rule, partners cannot include nonrecourse debt in their amount at risk even though that debt is included in the basis of their partnership interest. This rule has an important exception, however. Real estate nonrecourse financing provided by a bank, retirement plan, or similar party or by a Federal, state, or local government generally is deemed to be at risk.[45] Such debt is termed **qualified nonrecourse debt**.

Losses and At-Risk Amounts

Kelly invests $5,000 in the Kelly Green Limited Partnership as a 5% general partner. Shortly thereafter, the partnership acquires the master recording of a well-known vocalist for $250,000 ($50,000 from the partnership and $200,000 secured from a local bank via *recourse* debt). Kelly's share of the recourse debt is $10,000, and her basis in the interest is $15,000 ($5,000 cash investment + $10,000 debt share).

Because the debt is recourse, Kelly's at-risk amount also is $15,000. Kelly's share of partnership losses in the first year of operations is $11,000. Kelly can deduct the full $11,000 of partnership losses under both the basis and the at-risk limitations because this amount is less than both her outside basis and at-risk amount.

EXAMPLE 38

---

[44]§ 465(a).   [45]§ 465(b)(6).

Losses and At-Risk Amounts

EXAMPLE 39

Assume the same facts as in Example 38, except that the bank loan is nonrecourse. Kelly's basis in the partnership interest still is $15,000, but she can deduct only $5,000 of the flow-through loss. The amount she has at risk in the partnership does not include the nonrecourse debt. (The debt does not relate to real estate, so it cannot be qualified nonrecourse debt.)

The $6,000 suspended loss ($11,000 loss pass-through − $5,000 deduction) is deducted in a future tax year when a positive at-risk amount exists. This might occur because the entity has generated an undistributed net profit, or due to a capital contribution by Kelly.

Passive Activity Rules

A partnership loss pass-through also may be disallowed under the passive activity rules. Recall from Chapter 6 that an activity is considered passive if the taxpayer (in this case, a partner) does not materially participate or if the activity is considered a rental activity.

Losses from passive partnership activities are aggregated by each partner with his or her other passive activity income and losses. Any net passive activity loss is suspended and carried forward to future years, unless the partner also has generated net passive income for the tax year. The passive activity limitation applies after the owner's basis and at-risk limitations.

Concept Summary 14.4

Partner's Basis in Partnership Interest

Basis generally is adjusted in the following order.

Initial basis: Amount paid for partnership interest, or gift or inherited basis (including share of partnership debt).

+ Partner's subsequent asset contributions and allocable debt increases.
+ Since interest acquired, partner's share of the partnership's:
  • Income items.
  • Tax-exempt income items.
  • Excess of depletion deductions over adjusted basis of property subject to depletion.
− Partner's distributions and withdrawals and allocable debt decreases.

− Since interest acquired, partner's share of the partnership's:
  • Separately stated deductions.
  • Nondeductible items not chargeable to a capital account.
  • Special depletion deduction for oil and gas wells.
  • Loss items.

The basis of a partner's interest never can be negative.

Entity-level liabilities, and thus a partner's basis in the partnership, may change from day to day, but the partner's basis generally needs to be computed only once or twice a year.

LO.7

Apply the tax laws regarding transactions between a partner and the partnership.

14-4 TRANSACTIONS BETWEEN PARTNER AND PARTNERSHIP

Many types of transactions occur between a partnership and its partners. A partner may contribute property to the partnership, perform services for the partnership, or receive distributions from the partnership. A partner may borrow money from or lend money to the partnership. Property may be bought and sold between a partner and the partnership. Several of these transactions were discussed earlier in the chapter. The remaining types of partner-partnership transactions are the focus of this section.

14-4a Guaranteed Payments

A **guaranteed payment** is a payment for services performed by the partner or for the use of the partner's capital. The payment is not determined by reference to partnership income. Guaranteed payments usually are expressed as a fixed-dollar amount or as a percentage of capital the partner has invested in the partnership. Whether the partnership deducts or capitalizes the guaranteed payment depends on the nature of the payment.

EXAMPLE 40

Donna, Deepak, and Dale formed the accrual basis DDD Partnership. DDD and each of the partners are calendar year taxpayers. According to the partnership agreement, Donna is to manage the partnership and receive a $21,000 distribution from the entity every year, payable in 12 monthly installments. Deepak is to receive an amount that is equal to 8% of his capital account, as it is computed by the firm's accountant at the beginning of the year, payable in 12 monthly installments. Dale is DDD's advertising specialist. She withdraws 4% of the partnership's net income for personal use. Donna and Deepak receive guaranteed payments from the partnership, but Dale does not.

Guaranteed payments resemble the salary or interest payments of other businesses and receive somewhat similar income tax treatment.[46] In contrast to the provision that usually applies to withdrawals of assets by partners from their partnerships, guaranteed payments are deductible (or capitalized) by the entity. Deductible guaranteed payments, like any other deductible expenses of a partnership, can create an ordinary loss for the entity.

The partner's guaranteed payment is reported as a separately stated item on Schedules K and K–1. The partner uses this information (in lieu of a Form W–2 or 1099) to report the income on the partner's tax return. Partners receiving a guaranteed payment report ordinary income and treat it as paid on the last day of the entity's tax year.

Guaranteed Payments: Income and Deductions

EXAMPLE 41

Continue with the situation introduced in Example 40. For calendar year 2016, Donna receives the $21,000 as provided by the partnership agreement, Deepak's guaranteed payment is $17,000, and Dale withdraws $20,000 under the personal expenditures clause. Before considering these amounts, the partnership's ordinary income for the year is $650,000.

DDD can deduct its payments to Donna and Deepak, so the final amount of its ordinary income is $612,000 ($650,000 − $21,000 − $17,000). Thus, each of the equal partners is allocated $204,000 of ordinary partnership income ($612,000 ÷ 3). In addition, Donna reports the $21,000 guaranteed payment as gross income, and Deepak includes the $17,000 guaranteed payment in his gross income.

Dale's partnership draw is a distribution from her interest basis and is not taxed separately to her.

EXAMPLE 42

Assume the same facts as in Example 41, except that the partnership uses a "natural business" tax year that ends on March 31, 2017. Thus, even though Donna received 9 of her 12 payments for fiscal 2017 in the 2016 calendar year, all of Donna's guaranteed payments are taxable to her in 2017. Similarly, all of Deepak's guaranteed payments are taxable to him in 2017, rather than when they are received.

The deduction for, and the gross income from, guaranteed payments is allowed on the same date that all of the other income and expense items relative to the partnership are allocated to the partners (i.e., on the last day of the entity's tax year).

14-4b Other Transactions between a Partner and a Partnership

Many common transactions between a partner and the partnership are treated as if the partner were an outsider, dealing with the partnership at arm's length.[47] Loan transactions, rental payments, and sales of property between the partner and the partnership generally are treated in this manner.

---

[46]§ 707(c).   [47]§ 707(a).

EXAMPLE 43

The Eastside Co-op, a one-third partner in the ABC Partnership, owns a tract of land the partnership wants to purchase. The land has a fair market value of $30,000 and a basis to Eastside of $17,000. If Eastside sells the land to ABC, Eastside recognizes a $13,000 gain on the sale, and ABC takes a $30,000 cost basis in the land. If the land has a fair market value of $10,000 on the sale date, Eastside recognizes a $7,000 loss.

DIGGING DEEPER 8   In-depth coverage can be found on this book's companion website: www.cengagebrain.com

Sales of Property

No loss is recognized on a sale of property between a person and a partnership when the person owns, directly or indirectly, more than 50 percent of partnership capital or profits.[48] The disallowed loss may not vanish entirely, however. If the person later sells the property at a gain, the disallowed loss reduces the gain that would otherwise be recognized.[49]

EXAMPLE 44

Barry sells land (basis, $30,000; fair market value, $45,000) to the BCD LLC, of which he controls a 60% capital interest. BCD pays him only $20,000 for the land. Barry cannot deduct his $10,000 realized loss. Barry and the LLC are related parties, and the loss is disallowed.

When BCD sells the land to an outsider at a later date, it receives a sales price of $44,000. The entity can offset the recognition of its $24,000 realized gain on the subsequent sale ($44,000 sales proceeds − $20,000 basis) by the amount of the $10,000 prior disallowed loss ($20,000 − $30,000). Thus, BCD recognizes a $14,000 gain on its sale of the land.

Using a similar rationale, any gain that is realized on a sale or exchange between a partner and a partnership in which the partner controls a capital or profits interest of more than 50 percent is recognized as ordinary income, unless the asset is a capital asset to both the seller and the purchaser.[50]

EXAMPLE 45

The Kent School purchases some land (basis, $30,000; fair market value, $45,000) for $45,000 from the JJ Realty LLC, in which Kent controls a 90% profits interest. The land was a capital asset to JJ. If Kent holds the land as a capital asset, the LLC recognizes a $15,000 capital gain. However, if the school also is a land developer and the property is not a capital asset to it, JJ recognizes $15,000 of ordinary income from the sale, even though it held the property as a capital asset.

14-4c **Partners as Employees**

A partner usually does not qualify as an employee under Federal tax law, specifically for purposes of payroll taxes (e.g., FICA or FUTA). Moreover, because a partner is not an employee, the partnership cannot deduct its payments for the partner's fringe benefits, and the partner reports as gross income the value of the fringe benefits received. Nonetheless, a general partner's share of ordinary partnership income and guaranteed payments for services generally are classified as Federal self-employment (SE) income.[51]

The partner pays an SE tax in addition to the Federal income tax on pass-through items, and the additional Medicare taxes also may apply. The combination of these tax obligations can become expensive. Tax liabilities on SE income of a partner include:

- A 12.4 percent tax on the first $118,500 (for 2015 and 2016) of SE income, for the individual's account in the FICA retirement system.

- A 2.9 percent tax on all SE income, to support the Medicare system.

---

[48]§ 707(b).

[49]This is similar to treatment under § 267.

[50]§ 707(b)(2).

[51]§ 1402(a).

TAX PLANNING STRATEGIES Transactions between Partners and Partnerships

FRAMEWORK FOCUS: DEDUCTIONS

Strategy: Maximize Deductible Amounts.

To ensure that no negative tax results occur, partners should be careful when engaging in transactions with the partnership. A partner who owns a majority of the partnership generally should not sell property at a loss to the partnership because the loss is disallowed. Similarly, a majority partner should not sell a capital asset to the partnership at a gain if the asset is to be used by the partnership as other than a capital asset. The gain on this transaction is taxed as

ordinary income to the selling partner rather than as capital gain.

As an alternative to selling property to a partnership, a partner may lease it to the partnership. The partner recognizes rent income, and the partnership has a rent deduction. A partner who needs more cash immediately can sell the property to an outside third party; then the third party can lease the property to the partnership for a fair rental.

A partner who is an individual may be subject to additional taxes that support the Federal Medicare system, on flow-through items from the entity. Certain upper-income taxpayers must pay:

- A .9 percent tax on SE income,[52] and

- A 3.8 percent tax on flow-through net investment income (NII), including interest and dividend income, passive/portfolio income, and capital gains. NII does not include tax-exempt interest income, but it does include the share of pass-through operating income for a passive or limited partner.[53]

In-depth coverage can be found on this book's companion website: **www.cengagebrain.com**   **9** DIGGING DEEPER

Concept Summary 14.5

Partner-Partnership Transactions

1. Partners can transact business with their partnerships in a non-partner capacity. These transactions include the sale and exchange of property, rentals, and loans of funds.

2. A payment to a partner may be classified as a guaranteed payment if it is for services or use of the partner's capital and is not based on partnership income. A guaranteed payment usually is deductible by the partnership and is included in the partner's income on the last day of the partnership's tax year.

3. Losses are disallowed between a partner or related party and a partnership when the partner or related party owns more than a 50% interest in the partnership's capital or profits.

4. Income from a related-party sale is treated as ordinary income if the property is not a capital asset to both the transferor and the transferee.

5. Partners are not employees of their partnership, so the entity cannot deduct payments for partner fringe benefits, nor need it withhold or pay any payroll tax for payments to partners.

6. A partner may be subject to self-employment and the additional Medicare taxes on guaranteed payments received, and on a distributive share of flow-through income.

14-5 LIMITED LIABILITY COMPANIES

The *limited liability company (LLC)* combines partnership taxation with limited personal liability for all owners of the entity. All states and the District of Columbia have passed legislation permitting the establishment of LLCs. The following sections explain the taxation, advantages, and disadvantages of using LLCs.

14-5a Taxation of LLCs

A properly structured LLC is taxed as a partnership. Because LLC members are not personally liable for the debts of the entity, the LLC effectively is treated as a limited partnership with no general partners. This may result in an unusual application of partnership taxation rules. The IRS has not specifically ruled on most aspects of LLC taxation, so several of the following comments apply rules as to how a limited partner would be taxed.

- Formation of a new LLC is treated in the same manner as formation of a partnership. Generally, no gain or loss is recognized by the LLC member or the LLC, the member takes a substituted basis in the LLC interest, and the LLC takes a carryover basis in the assets it receives.

- An LLC's income and losses are allocated proportionately. Special allocations are permitted, as long as they are supported by a nontax economic effect.

- An LLC member contributing property with built-in gains can be subject to tax on certain distributions within seven years of the contribution.

- A loss must meet the basis, at-risk, and passive activity loss requirements to be currently deductible. Because debt of an LLC is considered nonrecourse to each of the members, it is not included in the at-risk limitation unless it is "qualified nonrecourse financing."

- The initial accounting period and accounting method elections are available to an LLC.

- Property takes a carryover or substituted basis when distributed from an LLC.

14-5b Advantages of an LLC

An LLC offers certain advantages over a limited partnership.

- Generally, none of the members of an LLC is personally liable for the entity's debts. In contrast, general partners in a limited partnership have personal liability for partnership recourse debts.

- Limited partners cannot participate in the management of a partnership. All owners of an LLC have the legal right to participate in the entity's management.

An LLC also offers certain advantages over an S corporation (see Chapter 15), including the following.

- An LLC can have an unlimited number of owners, while an S corporation is limited to 100 shareholders.

- Any taxpayers, including corporations, nonresident aliens, other partnerships, and trusts, can be owners of an LLC. S corporation shares can be held only by specified parties.

- The transfer of property to an LLC in exchange for an ownership interest in the entity is governed by partnership tax provisions rather than corporate tax provisions. Thus, the transfers need not satisfy the 80 percent control requirement needed for tax-free treatment under the corporate tax statutes (see Chapter 12).

- The S corporation taxes on built-in gains and investment income do not apply to LLCs.

- An owner's basis in an LLC includes the owner's share of almost all LLC liabilities under the law. Only certain entity liabilities are included in the S corporation shareholder's basis.

- An LLC may make special allocations, whereas S corporations must allocate income, loss, etc., only on a per-share/per-day basis.

14-5c **Disadvantages of an LLC**

Only a limited body of case law interprets the various state statutes, so the application of specific provisions in a specific state may be uncertain. An additional uncertainty for LLCs that operate in more than one jurisdiction pertains to which state's law will prevail and how it will be applied.

Among other factors, statutes differ from state to state as to the type of business an LLC can conduct—primarily the extent to which a service-providing firm can operate as an LLC. Special rules also may apply where the LLC has only one member.

Despite these uncertainties and limitations, LLCs are being formed at increasing rates, and the ranks of multistate LLCs also are rising quickly.

Concept Summary 14.6

Advantages and Disadvantages of the Partnership Form

The partnership form may be attractive when one or more of the following factors is present.

- The entity is generating net taxable losses and/or valuable tax credits, which will be of use to the owners.

- The owners want to avoid complex corporate administrative and filing requirements.

- The owners want to make special allocations of certain income or deduction items that are not possible under the C or S corporation forms.

- Other means of reducing the effects of the double taxation of corporate business income (e.g., compensation to owners, interest, and rental payments) have been exhausted.

- The entity does not generate material amounts of tax preference and adjustment items, which increase the AMT liabilities of its owners.

- The entity is generating net passive activity income, which its owners can use to claim immediate deductions for net passive activity losses they have generated from other sources.

- The owners hold adequate bases in their ownership interests to facilitate the deduction of flow-through losses and the assignment of an adequate basis to assets distributed in kind to the owners.

The partnership form may be less attractive when one or more of the following factors is present.

- The tax paid by the owners on the entity's income is greater than that payable by the entity as a C corporation, and the income is not expected to be distributed soon. (If distributed by a C corporation, double taxation would likely occur.)

- The entity is generating net taxable income without distributing any cash to the owners. The owners may not have sufficient cash with which to pay the tax on the entity's earnings.

- The type of income the entity is generating (e.g., business and portfolio income) is not as attractive to its owners as net passive activity income would be, because the owners could offset net passive activity income by the net passive activity losses they have generated on their own.

- The entity is in a high-exposure business, and the owners want protection from personal liability. An LLC or LLP structure may be available, however, to limit personal liability.

- The owners want to reduce exposure to Federal self-employment and additional Medicare taxes.

14-6 **SUMMARY**

Partnerships and LLCs are popular among business owners; there are roughly twice as many partnerships and limited liability entities as there are C corporations subject to Federal income tax law. This may be partly because formation of the entity is relatively simple and tax-free. The Code places very few restrictions on who can be a partner. Partnerships are especially attractive when operating losses are anticipated or when marginal rates that would apply to partnership income are less than those that would be paid by a C corporation. Partnerships do not offer the limited liability of a corporate entity, but the use of limited partnerships, LLCs, and LLPs can offer some protection to the owners.

Partnerships are tax-reporting, not taxpaying, entities. Distributive shares of ordinary income and separately stated items are taxed to the partners on the last day of the tax year. Special allocations and guaranteed payments are allowed and offer partners the ability to tailor the cash-flow and taxable amounts that are distributed by the entity to its owners. Deductions for flow-through losses may be limited by the related-party, passive activity, and at-risk rules, as well as by the partner's basis in the partnership. The flexibility of the partnership rules makes this form continually attractive to new businesses, especially in a global setting.

REFOCUS ON THE BIG PICTURE

THE TAX CONSEQUENCES OF PARTNERSHIP FORMATION AND OPERATIONS

After considering the various types of partnerships, Kyle, Maria, and Josh decided to form Beachside Properties as an LLC. Upon formation of the entity, there was no gain or loss recognized by the LLC or any of its members (see Example 15). Beachside Properties computes its income as shown in Example 17 and allocates the income as illustrated in Example 19. The LLC's income affects the members' bases and capital accounts. An important consideration for the LLC members is whether their distributive shares and guaranteed payments will be treated as self-employment income.

What If?

What happens in the future when the LLC members decide to expand or renovate Beachside's facilities? At that time, the existing members can contribute additional funds, the entity can receive capital from new members, or the entity can borrow money. A partnership or limited liability entity is not subject to the 80 percent control requirement applicable to the formation of a corporation and subsequent transfers to it. Therefore, new investors can contribute cash or other property in exchange for interests in the entity—and the transaction will qualify for tax-deferred treatment.

Suggested Readings

J. Everett, W. Raabe, and C. Hennig, "Planning Considerations When Converting a C Corporation to an LLC," *The Tax Adviser*, February 2011.

Howard Gleckman, "Pass-Through Firms Report $800 Billion in Net Income, Can't Be Ignored in Business Tax Reform," *taxpolicycenter.org*, October 2, 2014.

Susan L. Megaard and Michael M. Megaard, "Reducing Self-Employment Taxes on Owners of LLPs and LLCs," *Business Entities*, March/April 2012.

Edward Schnee and W. Eugene Seago, "Taxation of Worthless and Abandoned Partnership Interests," *The Tax Adviser*, February 2016.

Patrick H. Smith, "Taxation by States of Single-Member LLCs," *Business Entities*, September/October 2007.

Key Terms

Basis in the partnership interest, 14-7

Capital account, 14-21

Capital interest, 14-6

Capital sharing ratio, 14-6

Disguised sale, 14-10

Economic effect test, 14-19

General partnership, 14-3

Guaranteed payment, 14-28

Inside basis, 14-12

Limited liability company (LLC), 14-4

Limited liability partnership (LLP), 14-4

Limited partnership, 14-3

Nonrecourse debt, 14-22

Organizational costs, 14-14

Outside basis, 14-12

Precontribution gain or loss, 14-19

Profit and loss sharing ratios, 14-6

Profits (loss) interest, 14-6

Qualified nonrecourse debt, 14-27

Recourse debt, 14-22

Separately stated items, 14-5

Special allocation, 14-7

Syndication costs, 14-13

Computational Exercises

1. **LO.4** Enerico contributes $100,000 cash in exchange for a 40% interest in the calendar year ABC LLC. This year, ABC generates $80,000 of ordinary taxable income. Enerico withdraws $10,000 cash from the partnership at the end of the tax year.

   a. Compute Enerico's gross income from ABC's ordinary income for the tax year.

   b. Compute Enerico's gross income from the LLC's cash distribution.

2. **LO.2** Henrietta transfers cash of $75,000 and equipment with a fair market value of $25,000 (basis to her as a sole proprietor, $10,000) in exchange for a 40% profit and loss interest worth $100,000 in the XYZ Partnership.

   a. Compute Henrietta's realized and recognized gains from the asset transfers.

   b. Compute Henrietta's basis in her interest in XYZ.

   c. What is XYZ's basis in the equipment that it now holds?

3. **LO.2** Wozniacki and Wilcox form Jewel LLC, with each investor receiving a one-half interest in the capital and profits of the LLC. Wozniacki receives his one-half interest as compensation for tax planning services that he rendered prior to the formation of the LLC. Wilcox contributes $50,000 cash. The value of a one-half capital interest in the LLC (for each of the parties) is $50,000.

   a. Compute Wozniacki's realized and recognized gain from joining Jewel.

   b. Compute Wozniacki's basis in his interest in Jewel.

   c. How does Jewel treat the services that Wozniacki has rendered?

4. **LO.5** At the beginning of the tax year, Barnaby's basis in the BBB Partnership was $50,000, including his $5,000 share of partnership debt. At the end of the tax year, his share of the entity's debt was $8,000.

   Barnaby's share of BBB's ordinary income for the year was $20,000, and he received cash distributions totaling $12,000. In addition, his share of the partnership's tax-exempt income was $1,000. Determine Barnaby's basis at the end of the tax year.

5. **LO.3** Candlewood LLC began its business on September 1; it uses a calendar tax and accounting year. Candlewood incurred $6,500 in legal fees for drafting the LLC's operating agreement and $3,000 in accounting fees for tax advice of an organizational nature, for a total of $9,500 of organizational costs.

   Candlewood also incurred $30,000 of preopening advertising expenses and $24,500 of salaries and training costs for new employees before opening for business, for a total of $54,500 of startup costs. The LLC desires to take the largest deduction available for these costs. Compute Candlewood's deductions for the first year of its operations for:

a.   Organizational expenses.

b.   Startup expenses.

6.   **LO.4** Franco owns a 60% interest in the Dulera LLC. On December 31 of the current tax year, his basis in the LLC interest is $128,000. The fair market value of the interest is $140,000. Dulera then distributes to Franco $30,000 cash and equipment with an adjusted basis of $5,000 and a fair market value of $8,000.

a.   Compute Franco's basis in Dulera after the distribution.

b.   Compute Franco's basis in the equipment that he received from Dulera.

Critical Thinking   7.   **LO.4** When Bruno's basis in his interest in the MNO LLC is $150,000, he receives cash of $55,000, a proportionate share of inventory, and land in a distribution that liquidates MNO and his interest in the LLC. The inventory has a basis to the entity of $45,000 and a fair market value of $48,000. The land's basis is $70,000, and its fair market value is $60,000. Compute Bruno's recognized gain or loss from the liquidating distribution.

Problems

Issue ID   8.   **LO.2** Janda and Kelsey contributed $1 million each to the JKL LLC in exchange for 45% capital and profits interests in the entity. Lilli will contribute no cash, but has agreed to manage the LLC's business operations in exchange for an $80,000 annual salary and a 10% interest in the LLC's capital and profits (valued at $200,000). What are the consequences of the entity formation and Lilli's compensation arrangement to the LLC members? To the LLC itself?

9.   **LO.2** Emma and Laine form the equal EL Partnership. Emma contributes cash of $100,000. Laine contributes property with an adjusted basis of $40,000 and a fair market value of $100,000.

a.   How much gain, if any, must Emma recognize on the transfer? Must Laine recognize any gain? If so, how much?

b.   What is Emma's basis in her partnership interest?

c.   What is Laine's basis in her partnership interest?

d.   What basis does the partnership take in the property transferred by Laine?

Decision Making   10.   **LO.2** Kenisha and Shawna form the equal KS LLC with a cash contribution of $360,000 from Kenisha and a property contribution (adjusted basis of $380,000, fair market value of $360,000) from Shawna.

a.   How much gain or loss, if any, does Shawna realize on the transfer? Does Shawna recognize any gain or loss? If so, how much?

b.   What is Kenisha's basis in her LLC interest?

c.   What is Shawna's basis in her LLC interest?

d.   What basis does the LLC take in the property transferred by Shawna?

e.   Are there more effective ways to structure the formation? Explain.

11.   **LO.2** Liz and John formed the equal LJ Partnership on January 1 of the current year. Liz contributed $80,000 of cash and land with a fair market value of $90,000 and an adjusted basis of $75,000. John contributed equipment with a fair market value of $170,000 and an adjusted basis of $20,000. John previously used the equipment in his sole proprietorship.

a.   How much gain or loss will Liz, John, and LJ realize?

b.   How much gain or loss will Liz, John, and LJ recognize?

   c.   What bases will Liz and John take in their partnership interests?

   d.   What bases will LJ take in the assets it receives?

   e.   How will LJ depreciate any assets it receives from the partners?

12. **LO.2, 5** Sam and Drew are equal members of the SD LLC, formed on June 1 of the current year. Sam contributed land that he inherited from his uncle in 2008. Sam's uncle purchased the land in 1983 for $30,000. The land was worth $100,000 when Sam's uncle died. The fair market value of the land was $200,000 at the date it was contributed to SD.

     Drew has significant experience developing real estate. After SD is formed, he will prepare a plan for developing the property and secure zoning approvals for the LLC. Drew normally would bill a third party $50,000 for these efforts. Drew will also contribute $150,000 of cash in exchange for his 50% interest in SD. The value of Drew's 50% interest is $200,000.

   a.   How much gain or income does Sam recognize on his contribution of the land to SD? What is the character of any gain or income recognized?

   b.   What basis does Sam take in his LLC interest?

   c.   How much gain or income will Drew recognize on the formation of SD? What is the character of any gain or income recognized?

   d.   What basis will Drew take in his LLC interest?

13. **LO.2** Continue with the facts presented in Problem 12. At the end of the first year, SD distributes $100,000 cash to Sam. No distribution is made to Drew.

   a.   How does Sam treat the payment?

   b.   How much income or gain would Sam recognize as a result of the contribution and distribution?

   c.   Under general tax rules, what basis would SD take in the land Sam contributed?

14. **LO.3** On July 1 of the current year, the R&R Partnership was formed to operate a bed-and-breakfast inn. The partnership paid $3,000 in legal fees for drafting the partnership agreement and $5,000 for accounting fees related to organizing the entity. It also paid $10,000 in syndication costs to locate and secure investments from limited partners.

     In addition, before opening the inn for business, the entity paid $15,500 for advertising and $36,000 in costs related to an open house just before the grand opening of the property. The partnership opened the inn for business on October 1.

   a.   How are these expenses classified?

   b.   How much may the partnership deduct in its initial year of operations?

   c.   How are costs treated that are not deducted currently?

15. **LO.2, 4** Phoebe and Parker are equal members of Phoenix Investors LLC. They are real estate investors who formed the entity several years ago with equal cash contributions. Phoenix then purchased a parcel of land.

     On January 1 of the current year, to acquire a one-third interest in the entity, Reece contributed to Phoenix some land she had held for investment. Reece purchased the land five years ago for $75,000; its fair market value at the contribution date was $90,000. No special allocation agreements were in effect before or after Reece was admitted to the LLC. Phoenix holds all land for investment.

     Immediately before Reece's property contribution, the Phoenix balance sheet was as follows.

	Basis	FMV		Basis	FMV
Land	$30,000	$180,000	Phoebe, capital	$15,000	$ 90,000
			Parker, capital	15,000	90,000
	$30,000	$180,000		$30,000	$180,000

    a.   At the contribution date, what is Reece's basis in her interest in Phoenix?

    b.   When does the LLC's holding period begin for the contributed land?

    c.   On June 30 of the current year, the LLC sold the land contributed by Reece for $90,000. How much is the recognized gain or loss? How is it allocated among the LLC members?

    d.   Prepare a balance sheet reflecting basis and fair market value for the entity immediately after the land sale.

16. **LO.4, 5** Amy and Mitchell are equal partners in the accrual basis AM Partnership. At the beginning of the current tax year, Amy's capital account has a balance of $300,000, and the partnership has recourse debts of $200,000 payable to unrelated parties. All partnership recourse debt is shared equally between the partners.

    The following information about AM's operations for the current year is obtained from the partnership's records.

Ordinary income	$400,000
Interest income from P&G bond	4,000
Long-term capital loss	6,000
Short-term capital gain	12,000
Charitable contribution	4,000
Cash distribution to Amy	20,000

    Year-end partnership debt payable to unrelated parties is $140,000. If all transactions are reflected in her beginning capital and basis in the same manner:

    a.   What is Amy's basis in the partnership interest at the beginning of the year?

    b.   What is Amy's basis in the partnership interest at the end of the current year?

17. **LO.4, 5** Assume the same facts as in Problem 16. What income, gains, losses, and deductions does Amy report on her income tax return? Based on the information provided, what other calculations is she required to make?

18. **LO.4, 5** Continue with the same facts of Problem 16. Consider Amy's tax-basis capital account.

    a.   What is Amy's capital account at the beginning of the year?

    b.   What is Amy's capital account at the end of the year?

    c.   How do the capital account balances differ from her basis amounts in Problem 16?

Critical Thinking   19. **LO.3** Cerulean, Inc., Coral, Inc., and Crimson, Inc., form the Three Cs Partnership on January 1 of the current year. Cerulean is a 50% partner, and Crimson and Coral are 25% partners. For reporting purposes, Crimson uses a fiscal year with an October 31 year-end, Coral uses the calendar year, and Cerulean uses a fiscal year with a February 28/29 year-end. What is the required tax year for Three Cs under the least aggregate deferral method?

20. **LO.2, 4, 5** The JM Partnership was formed to acquire land and subdivide it as residential housing lots. On March 1, 2016, Jessica contributed land valued at $600,000 to the partnership in exchange for a 50% interest. She had purchased the land in 2008 for $420,000 and held it for investment purposes (capital asset). The partnership holds the land as inventory.

    On the same date, Matt contributed land valued at $600,000 that he had purchased in 2006 for $720,000. He became a 50% owner. Matt is a real estate developer, but he held this land personally for investment purposes. The partnership holds this land as inventory.

In 2017, the partnership sells the land contributed by Jessica for $620,000. In 2018, the partnership sells the real estate contributed by Matt for $580,000.

a. What is each partner's initial basis in his or her partnership interest?

b. What is the amount of gain or loss recognized on the sale of the land contributed by Jessica? What is the character of this gain or loss?

c. What is the amount of gain or loss recognized on the sale of the land contributed by Matt? What is the character of this gain or loss?

d. How would your answer in part (c) change if the property were sold in 2023?

21. **LO.2, 5** Lee, Brad, and Rick form the LBR Partnership on January 1 of the current year. In return for a 25% interest, Lee transfers property (basis of $15,000, fair market value of $17,500) subject to a nonrecourse liability of $10,000. The liability is assumed by the partnership. Brad transfers property (basis of $16,000, fair market value of $7,500) for a 25% interest, and Rick transfers cash of $15,000 for the remaining 50% interest.

a. How much gain must Lee recognize on the transfer?

b. What is Lee's basis in his interest in the partnership?

c. How much loss may Brad recognize on the transfer?

d. What is Brad's basis in his interest in the partnership?

e. What is Rick's basis in his interest in the partnership?

f. What basis does the LBR Partnership take in the property transferred by Lee?

g. What is the partnership's basis in the property transferred by Brad?

22. **LO.2, 5** Assume the same facts as in Problem 21, except that the property contributed by Lee has a fair market value of $27,500 and is subject to a nonrecourse mortgage of $20,000.

Critical Thinking

a. What is Lee's basis in his partnership interest?

b. How much gain must Lee recognize on the transfer?

c. What is Brad's basis in his partnership interest?

d. What is Rick's basis in his partnership interest?

e. What basis does the LBR Partnership take in the property transferred by Lee?

23. **LO.5, 6** The BCD Partnership plans to distribute cash of $20,000 to partner Barb at the end of the tax year. The partnership reported a loss for the year, and Barb's share of the loss is $10,000. Barb holds a basis of $15,000 in the partnership interest, including her share of partnership liabilities. The partnership expects to report substantial income in future years.

Issue ID

Decision Making

a. How does Barb calculate the ending basis in the BCD partnership interest?

b. How much income or loss must Barb report for the tax year?

c. Will the deduction for any of the $10,000 loss be suspended? Why or why not?

d. Could any planning opportunities be used to minimize the tax ramifications of the distribution? Explain.

24. **LO.2, 3** The Pelican Partnership was formed on August 1 of the current year and admitted Morlan and Merriman as equal partners on that date. The partners both contributed $300,000 of cash to establish a children's clothing store in the local mall. The partners spent August and September buying inventory, equipment, supplies, and advertising for their "Grand Opening" on October 1. The partnership will use the accrual method of accounting. The following are some of the costs incurred during Pelican's first year of operations.

Legal fees to form partnership	$ 8,000
Advertising for "Grand Opening"	18,000
Advertising after opening	30,000
Consulting fees for establishing accounting system	20,000
Rent, at $2,000 per month	10,000
Utilities, at $1,000 per month	5,000
Salaries to salesclerks (beginning in October)	50,000
Payments to Morlan and Merriman for services ($6,000 per month each for three months)	36,000
Tax return preparation expense	12,000

In addition, on October 1, Pelican purchased all of the assets of Granny Newcombs, Inc. Of the total purchase price for these assets, $200,000 was allocated to the Granny Newcombs trade name and logo.

Determine how each of the listed costs is treated by Pelican, and identify the period over which the costs can be deducted, if any.

25. **LO.7** Four GRRLs Partnership is owned by four unrelated friends. Lacy holds a 40% interest; each of the others owns 20%. Lacy sells investment property to the partnership for its fair market value of $200,000. Her tax basis in the property was $250,000.

   a. How much loss, if any, may Lacy recognize?

   b. If Four GRRLs later sells the property for $260,000, how much gain must it recognize?

   c. How would your answers in parts (a) and (b) change if Lacy owned a 60% interest in the partnership?

   d. If Lacy's basis in the investment property was $120,000 (instead of $250,000) and she was a 60% partner, how much, if any, gain would she recognize on the sale of the property to Four GRRLs? How is it characterized?

26. **LO.7** Burgundy, Inc., and Violet Gomez are equal partners in the calendar year BV LLC. Burgundy uses a fiscal year ending April 30, and Violet uses a calendar year. Burgundy receives an annual guaranteed payment of $100,000 for use of capital contributed by Burgundy. BV's taxable income (after deducting the payment to Burgundy) is $80,000 for 2016 and $90,000 for 2017.

   a. How much income from BV must Burgundy report for its tax year ending April 30, 2017?

   b. How much income from BV must Violet report for her tax year ending December 31, 2017?

Critical Thinking   27. **LO.4, 7** Mona and Denise, mother and daughter, operate a local restaurant as an LLC. The MD LLC earned a profit of $200,000 in the current year. Denise's equal LLC interest was acquired by gift from Mona. Assume that capital is a material income-producing factor and that Mona manages the day-to-day operations of the restaurant without any help from Denise. Reasonable compensation for Mona's services is $50,000.

   a. How much of the MD income is allocated to Mona?

   b. What is the maximum amount of LLC income that can be allocated to Denise?

   c. Assuming that Denise is 15 years old, has no other income, and is claimed as a dependent by Mona, how is Denise's income from the restaurant taxed?

Critical Thinking   28. **LO.5** In each of the following independent cases in which the partnership owns no hot assets, indicate the following. All of the partners received proportionate distributions.

- Whether the partner recognizes gain or loss.
- Whether the partnership recognizes gain or loss.
- The partner's adjusted basis for the property distributed.
- The partner's outside basis in the partnership after the distribution.

a. Kim receives $20,000 of cash in partial liquidation of her interest in the partnership. Kim's outside basis for her partnership interest immediately before the distribution is $3,000.

b. Kourtni receives $40,000 of cash and land with a $30,000 inside basis to the partnership (value $50,000) in partial liquidation of her interest. Kourtni's outside basis for her partnership interest immediately before the distribution is $80,000.

c. Assume the same facts as in part (b), except that Kourtni's outside basis for her partnership interest immediately before the distribution is $60,000.

d. Klois receives $50,000 of cash and inventory with a basis of $30,000 and a fair market value of $50,000 in partial liquidation of her partnership interest. Her basis was $90,000 before the distribution.

29. **LO.4, 5, 7** At the beginning of the tax year, Melodie's basis in the MIP LLC was $60,000, including Melodie's $40,000 share of the LLC's liabilities. At the end of the year, MIP distributed to Melodie cash of $10,000 and inventory (basis of $6,000, fair market value of $10,000). MIP repaid all of its liabilities by the end of the year.   Critical Thinking

a. If this is a proportionate nonliquidating distribution, what is the tax effect of the distribution to Melodie and MIP? After the distribution, what is Melodie's basis in the inventory and in her MIP interest?

b. Would your answers to part (a) change if this had been a proportionate liquidating distribution? Explain.

30. **LO.2, 4, 5** Suzy contributed assets valued at $360,000 (basis of $200,000) in exchange for her 40% interest in Suz-Anna GP (a general partnership). Anna contributed land and a building valued at $640,000 (basis of $380,000) in exchange for the remaining interest. Anna's property was encumbered by a qualified nonrecourse debt of $100,000, which was assumed by the partnership. The partnership reports the following income and expenses for the current tax year.   Critical Thinking

Sales	$560,000
Utilities, salaries, and other operating expenses	360,000
Short-term capital gain	10,000
Tax-exempt interest income	4,000
Charitable contributions	8,000
Distribution to Suzy	10,000
Distribution to Anna	20,000

At the end of the year, Suz-Anna held recourse debt of $100,000 for partnership accounts payable and qualified nonrecourse debt of $200,000.

a. What is Suzy's basis after formation of the partnership? Anna's basis?

b. What income and separately stated items does Suz-Anna report on Suzy's Schedule K–1? What items does Suzy report on her tax return?

c. All partnership debts are shared proportionately. At the end of the tax year, what are Suzy's basis and amount at risk in her partnership interest?

31. **LO.2, 4, 5, 8** Continue with the facts presented in Problem 30, except that Suz-Anna was formed as an LLC instead of a general partnership.

   a. How would Suz-Anna's ending liabilities be treated?

   b. How would Suzy's basis and amount at risk be different? Explain.

32. **LO.4** The Sparrow Partnership plans to distribute $200,000 cash to its partners at the end of the year. Marjorie is a 40% partner and would receive $80,000. Her basis in the partnership is only $10,000, however, so she would recognize a $70,000 gain if she receives the proposed cash distribution.

   Marjorie has asked Sparrow instead to purchase a parcel of land that she has found, on which she will build her retirement residence. The partnership then will distribute that land to her. Under the partnership distribution rules, Marjorie would take a $10,000 basis in the land worth $80,000. Her basis in the partnership would be reduced to $0, but recognition of the $70,000 gain is deferred.

   Do you think this is an appropriate transaction? Explain your conclusion in an e-mail to your instructor.

Comprehensive Tax Return Problem

Tax Return Problem

TAX SOFTWARE

1. Ryan Ross (111-11-1112), Oscar Omega (222-22-2222), Clark Carey (333-33-3333), and Kim Kardigan (444-44-4444) are equal active members in ROCK the Ages LLC. ROCK serves as agent and manager for prominent musicians in the Los Angeles area. The LLC's Federal ID number is 55-5555555. It uses the cash basis and a calendar tax year, and it began operations on January 1, 2004. Its current address is 6102 Wilshire Boulevard, Suite 2100, Los Angeles, CA 90036.

   ROCK was the force behind such music icons as Rhiannon, Burgundy Six, Elena Gomez, Tyler Quick, the Moonwalkers, and Conjuring Dragons, and it has had a very profitable year. The following information was taken from the LLC's income statement for the current year.

Revenues	
Fees and commissions	$4,800,000
Taxable interest income from bank deposits	1,600
Tax-exempt interest	3,200
Net gains on stock sales	4,000
Total revenues	$4,808,800
Expenses	
Advertising and public relations	$ 380,000
Charitable contributions	28,000
Section 179 expense	20,000
Employee salaries and wages	1,000,000
Guaranteed payment (services), Ryan Ross, office manager	800,000
Guaranteed payment (services), other members	600,000
Entertainment, subject to 50% disallowance	200,000
Travel	320,000
Legal and accounting fees	132,000
Office rentals paid	80,000
Interest expense on line of credit for operations	10,000
Insurance premiums	52,000
Office expense	200,000
Payroll taxes	92,000
Utilities	54,800
Total expenses	$3,968,800

During the past few years, ROCK has taken advantage of bonus depreciation and §179 deductions and fully remodeled the premises and upgraded its leasehold improvements. This year, ROCK wrapped up its remodeling with the purchase of $20,000 of office furniture, for which it will claim a §179 deduction. ROCK uses the same cost recovery methods for both tax and financial purposes. There is no depreciation adjustment for alternative minimum tax purposes.

ROCK invests much of its excess cash in non-dividend-paying growth stocks and tax-exempt securities. During the year, the LLC sold two securities. On June 15, 2015, ROCK purchased 1,000 shares of Tech, Inc., stock for $100,000; it sold those shares on December 15, 2015, for $80,000. On March 15, 2014, ROCK purchased 2,000 shares of BioLabs, Inc., stock for $136,000; it sold those shares for $160,000 on December 15, 2015. These transactions were reported to the IRS on Forms 1099–B; ROCK's basis in these shares was reported on the form.

Net income per books for 2015 is $840,000. The firm's activities do not constitute "qualified production activities" for purposes of the § 199 deduction. On January 1, the members' capital accounts equaled $200,000 each. No additional capital contributions were made. In addition to their guaranteed payments, each member withdrew $250,000 cash during the year.

ROCK's book balance sheet as of December 31, 2015, is as follows.

	Beginning	Ending
Cash	$ 444,000	$??
Tax-exempt securities	120,000	120,000
Marketable securities	436,000	300,000
Leasehold improvements, furniture, and equipment	960,000	980,000
Accumulated depreciation	(960,000)	(980,000)
Total assets	$1,000,000	$??
Line of credit for operations	$ 200,000	$ 160,000
Capital, Ross	200,000	??
Capital, Omega	200,000	??
Capital, Carey	200,000	??
Capital, Kardigan	200,000	??
Total liabilities and capital	$1,000,000	$??

All debt is shared equally by the members. Each member has personally guaranteed the debt of the LLC.

The business code for "Agents and Managers for Artists, Athletes, Entertainers, and Other Public Figures" is 711410. The LLC's Form 1065 was prepared by Ryan Ross and sent to the Ogden, UT, IRS Service Center. All of the owners are active in ROCK's operations.

a. Prepare pages 1, 4, and 5 of the Form 1065 for ROCK the Ages LLC. Use tax basis data in completing Schedules L and M–2.

b. If you are using tax return preparation software, prepare Form 4562 and Schedule D.

c. Prepare Schedule K–1 for Ryan Ross, 15520 W. Earlson Street, Pacific Palisades, CA 90272.

BRIDGE DISCIPLINE

1. What is the function of a partner's capital account under the rules of generally accepted accounting principles (GAAP)? What is the partner's initial balance in the capital account? How and when does the capital account increase and decrease? What is the GAAP treatment of distributions to a partner?

2. Jim Dunn, Amy Lauersen, and Tony Packard have agreed to form a partnership. In return for a 30% capital interest, Dunn transferred machinery (basis $268,000, fair market value $400,000) subject to a liability of $100,000. The liability was assumed by the partnership. Lauersen transferred land (basis $450,000, fair market value $300,000) for a 30% capital interest. Packard transferred cash of $400,000 for the remaining 40% interest. Compute the initial values of Dunn's:
   a. Basis in his partnership interest for tax purposes.
   b. Capital account for financial reporting purposes.

3. To what extent are the personal assets of a general partner, limited partner, or member of an LLC subject to (a) contractual liability claims, such as trade accounts payable, and (b) malpractice claims against the entity? Answer the question for partners or members in a general partnership, an LLP, a nonprofessional LLC, and a limited partnership.

Research Problems

THOMSON REUTERS
CHECKPOINT
Student Edition

Note: Solutions to Research Problems can be prepared by using the Checkpoint® Student Edition online research product, which is available to accompany this text. It is also possible to prepare solutions to the Research Problems by using tax research materials found in a standard tax library.

Research Problem 1. Fredstone Consolidated, Inc., and Gradison Enterprises, Inc., are both real estate developers. Each entity owns a 50% general partner interest in Realty Partners, GP, a general partnership.

Fredstone and Gradison each contributed $15,000 to form the partnership. The partnership uses the $30,000 contributed by the partners and a recourse loan of $100,000 obtained from an unrelated third-party lender to acquire $130,000 of rental properties. (All amounts are in thousands.)

The partners believe that they will generate extensive tax losses in the first year due to depreciation expense and initial cash-flow requirements. Fredstone and Gradison agreed to share losses equally. To make sure that the losses can be allocated as intended, they included a provision in the partnership agreement requiring each partner to restore any deficit balance in their partnership capital account upon liquidation of the partnership.

Fredstone also was willing to include a provision that requires it to make up any deficit balance within 90 days of liquidation of the partnership. This provision does not apply to Gradison; instead, it must restore any deficit balance in its capital account within two years of liquidation of the partnership. No interest accrues on the deferred restoration payment.

Can Realty allocate the $100,000 recourse debt equally to the two partners, so that they can deduct their respective shares of partnership losses? Explain.

Critical Thinking   **Research Problem 2.** Barney Chang and Aldrin, Inc., a domestic C corporation, have decided to form BA LLC. The new entity will produce a product that Barney recently developed and patented. Barney and Aldrin each will own a 50% capital and profits interest in the LLC. Barney is a calendar year taxpayer, while Aldrin is taxed using a June 30 fiscal year end. BA does not have a "natural business year" and elects to be taxed as a partnership.

a. Determine the taxable year of the LLC under the Code and Regulations.

b. Two years after formation of BA, Barney sells half of his interest (25%) to Aldrin. Can BA retain the taxable year determined in part (a)? Why or why not?

Use the tax resources of the Internet to address the following questions. Do not restrict your search to the Web, but include a review of newsgroups and general reference materials, practitioner sites and resources, primary sources of the tax law, chat rooms and discussion groups, and other opportunities.

Internet Activity

Research Problem 3. Find an article posted by a law firm that comments on pitfalls to avoid in drafting partnership agreements. Ideally, use the home page of a firm that has offices in your state. Summarize the posting in no more than four PowerPoint slides, and send your file to your instructor.

Communications

Research Problem 4. Find a blog that concentrates on the taxation of partners and partnerships. Post a message defining the terms *inside basis* and *outside basis* and illustrating why the distinction between them is important. Respond to any replies you receive. Print your message and one or two of the replies.

Communications

Research Problem 5. Determine the statutory tax treatment in your state of a one-member LLC. Write an e-mail to your professor comparing this rule with Federal tax law.

Communications

Research Problem 6. Graph the increases in the numbers of LLCs and LLPs filing Federal tax returns for five-year periods beginning with 1970. Explain any trends in the data that you identify. Send your report as an e-mail to your instructor.

Communications

Roger CPA Review Questions

ROGER CPA Review

1. Which of the following is (are) correct about the holding period of the property acquired by a partnership as a contribution to the contributing partner's capital account?

   I. The holding period begins on the date the partner's holding period of the contributed asset began
   II. The holding period depends on the character of the property transferred
   III. The holding period excludes the period during which the property was held by the contributing partner

   a. I and II   c. I only
   b. II and III   d. None of the above

2. Guaranteed payments made by a partnership to partners for services rendered to the partnership include which of the following?

   a. Sales of partners' assets to the partnership at guaranteed amounts regardless of market values
   b. A salary of $170,000 annually without regard to partnership income
   c. Payments of principal on secured notes honored at maturity
   d. Net long-term capital gains earned by the partnership

3. Properly reported guaranteed payments have the following effect(s):

   I. The guaranteed payment increases the receiving partner's ordinary income by the entire amount paid during the entity's tax year

II. The guaranteed payment decreases every partner's tax basis in the partnership by the entire amount paid during the tax year

III. The guaranteed payment is either capitalized or deducted by the partnership in computing its ordinary income or loss for the tax year, depending on the nature of the services provided by the partner

a. All of the above
b. I and III, but not II

c. I and II, but not III
d. None of the above

4. On March 17, Packer became a partner in Cats & Dogs Co., an already formed partnership. Packer does not have property to contribute and thus contributes services in exchange for his 5% interest in Cats & Dogs. Cats & Dogs's net assets are as follows (including the value of Packer's services received by the partnership).

	Basis	Fair Market Value
January 1	$150,000	$150,000
March 17	150,000	170,000
December 31	150,000	175,000

On Packer's tax return for the year, what amount must Packer include as ordinary income from the receipt of the partnership interest?

a. $0
b. $7,500

c. $8,500
d. $8,750

5. On a partnership tax return, all of the following are subject to special limitations and must be separately passed through to the partners, except:

a. Charitable contributions
b. Salaries to non-partners

c. Long-term capital gains
d. Dividend income

6. Prairee partnership has four equal partners, Dodd, Crank, Pick, and Mack. Each of the partners had a tax basis of $320,000 as of January 1. Prairee's net business income for the year totaled $152,000. During the year, Prairee paid Mack guaranteed payments of $4,000 for deductible services rendered, which were not included in determining Prairee's net business income. In addition, each of the four partners took a cash distribution of $50,000. What amount from Prairee should be included as income on Dodd's tax return for the year?

a. $152,000
b. $42,000

c. $38,000
d. $37,000

7. Prairee partnership has four equal partners, Dodd, Crank, Pick, and Mack. Each of the partners had a tax basis of $320,000 as of January 1. Prairee's net business income for the year totaled $152,000. During the year, Prairee paid Mack guaranteed payments of $4,000 for deductible services rendered. In addition, each of the four partners took a cash distribution of $50,000. What is Mack's tax basis in Prairee on December 31?

a. $307,000
b. $358,000

c. $422,000
d. $472,000

8. Osha, a cash basis calendar year partnership, began business on April 1. Osha incurred and paid the following during the tax year.

Legal work associated with formation of the partnership	$15,260
Accounting work associated with raising additional capital	10,000

What is the maximum amount of deductible organizational costs on Osha's partnership return for the year?

a. $5,000
b. $5,513

c. $5,684
d. $6,013

9. Catherine holds a $100,000 basis in her partnership interest. On April 28 of the current tax year, the partnership distributes to her cash of $32,000, cash basis receivables with an inside basis of $0 and a fair market value of $12,000, and a parcel of land with a fair market value of $75,000 and a basis to the partnership of $65,000. After accounting for this distribution, what is Catherine's basis in the land?

   a. $65,000   c. $63,000

   b. $53,000   d. $56,000

S Corporations

LEARNING OBJECTIVES: *After completing Chapter 15, you should be able to:*

LO.1 Explain the tax effects associated with S corporation status.

LO.2 Identify corporations that qualify for the S election.

LO.3 Explain how to make and terminate an S election.

LO.4 Compute nonseparately stated income and allocate income, deductions, and credits to shareholders.

LO.5 Determine how distributions to S corporation shareholders are taxed.

LO.6 Calculate a shareholder's basis in S corporation stock.

LO.7 Explain the tax effects of losses on S shareholders.

LO.8 Compute the entity-level taxes on S corporations.

CHAPTER OUTLINE

TAX TALK *In levying taxes and in shearing sheep it is well to stop when you get down to the skin.* —AUSTIN O'MALLEY

CONVERTING A C CORPORATION TO AN S CORPORATION

Fowle, Inc., has been operating as a C corporation for a number of years, consistently earning taxable income of less than $100,000 per year. The company has accumulated its earnings for a variety of business needs and has not paid dividends to date. Thus, the corporation has been able to take advantage of lower C corporation tax rates and has avoided double taxation problems so far.

Fowle receives some tax-exempt income, generates a small domestic production activities deduction (DPAD), and holds about $200,000 of C corporation earnings and profits. The company's sole owner, David, currently draws a salary of $92,000. Fowle has issued two classes of stock, voting common and non-voting preferred.

The company now is facing increased competition as a result of cheaper imports from China. David expects very large operating losses for the next few years. David would like to know if there is a way that he can deduct the anticipated losses.

Read the chapter and formulate your response.

A n individual establishing a business has a number of choices as to the form of business entity under which to operate. Chapters 12 and 13 outline many of the rules, advantages, and disadvantages of operating as a regular C corporation. Chapter 14 discusses the partnership entity, as well as the limited liability company (LLC) and limited liability partnership (LLP) forms.

Another alternative, the **S corporation**, provides many of the benefits of partnership taxation and at the same time gives the owners limited liability protection from creditors. The S corporation rules, which are contained in **Subchapter S** of the Internal Revenue Code (§§ 1361–1379), were enacted to allow flexibility in the entity choice that businesspeople face. Thus, S status combines the legal environment of C corporations with taxation similar to that applying to partnerships.

15-1 AN OVERVIEW OF S CORPORATIONS

S corporations (like C corporations) are organized as corporations under state law. Other than for income tax purposes, they are recognized as separate legal entities and generally provide shareholders with the same liability protection afforded by C corporations. As a rule, where the S corporation provisions are silent, C corporation rules apply.

The S corporation rules should be seen as supplementary to the Federal income tax rules for all C corporations (see Chapters 12 and 13) and to those for partnerships and limited liability entities (contained in Code Subchapter K; see Chapter 14). Some provisions apply only to electing S corporations (addressed throughout this chapter), but S corporations also must apply certain tax rules of Code Subchapters C and K.

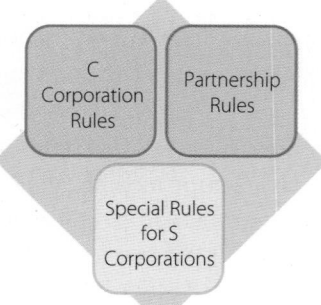

Today, the choice of a flow-through entity for a closely held business often is between an S corporation (a Federal tax entity) and an LLC (a state tax entity). Both are flow-through entities for Federal income tax purposes and provide limited liability for the owners under nontax state law. In the typical year, over 4 million S corporations file Federal income tax returns, and filings are received from over 2 million LLCs.

S Corporation Advantages

EXAMPLE 1

An S corporation earns $300,000, and all after-tax income is distributed currently. The marginal individual tax rate applicable to the entity's shareholders is 39.6% for ordinary income and 20% for dividend income. Assume that the corporate tax rate is 34%. The entity's available after-tax earnings, compared with those of a similar C corporation, are computed below.

	C Corporation	S Corporation
Earnings	$ 300,000	$ 300,000
Less: Corporate income tax	(102,000)	(–0–)
Amount available for distribution	$ 198,000	$ 300,000
Less: Income tax at owner level	(39,600)*	(118,800)**
Available after-tax earnings	$ 158,400	$ 181,200

* $198,000 × 20% dividend income tax rate.
** $300,000 × 39.6% ordinary income tax rate.

continued

The S corporation generates an extra $22,800 of after-tax earnings ($181,200 − $158,400) when compared with a similar C corporation. The C corporation might be able to reduce this disadvantage, however, by paying out its earnings as compensation, rents, or interest to its owners. In addition, tax at the owner level is deferred or avoided by not distributing after-tax earnings.

S Corporation Advantages

A new corporation elects S status and incurs a net operating loss (NOL) of $300,000. The shareholders may use their proportionate shares of the NOL to offset other taxable income in the current year, providing an immediate tax savings. In contrast, a newly formed C corporation is required to carry the NOL forward for up to 20 years and receives no tax benefit in the current year. Hence, an S corporation can accelerate the use of NOL deductions and thereby provide a greater present value for the tax savings generated by the loss.

EXAMPLE 2

15-2 QUALIFYING FOR S CORPORATION STATUS

LO.2

Identify corporations that qualify for the S election.

There are certain conditions that a corporation must meet before S corporation status is available.

15-2a Definition of a Small Business Corporation

To achieve S corporation status, a corporation *first* must qualify as a small business corporation. A small business corporation:

- Is a domestic corporation (incorporated and organized in the United States).
- Is eligible to elect S corporation status.
- Issues only one class of stock.
- Is limited to a maximum of 100 shareholders.
- Has only individuals, estates, and certain trusts and exempt organizations as shareholders.
- Has no nonresident alien shareholders.

BRIDGE DISCIPLINE   Bridge to Business Law

An S corporation is a corporation for all purposes other than its Federal and state income tax law treatment. The entity registers as a corporation with the secretary of state of the state of its incorporation. It issues shares and may hold some treasury stock. Dealings in its own stock are not taxable to the S corporation.

The corporation itself is attractive as a form of business ownership because it offers limited liability to all shareholders from the claims of customers, employees, and others. This is not the case for any type of partnership, where there always is at least one general partner bearing the ultimate personal liability for the operations of the entity. Forming an entity as an S corporation facilitates the raising of capital for the business, as an infinite number of shares can be divided in any way imaginable, so as to pass income and deductions, gains, losses, and credits through to the owners, assuming that the fairly generous "type of shareholder" requirements continue to be met.

An S corporation must comply with all licensing and registration requirements of its home state under the rules applicable to corporate entities. Some states levy privilege taxes on the right to do business in the corporate form, and the S corporation typically is not exempted from this tax.

Because an S corporation is a separate legal entity from its owners, shareholders can be treated as employees and receive qualified retirement and fringe benefits under the Code, as well as unemployment and worker's compensation protection through the corporation. Some limitations apply to the deductibility of the shareholders' fringe benefits, though.

The tax fiction of the S corporation is attractive to investors, as demonstrated by the fact that about two-thirds of all U.S. corporations have an S election in effect.

Thus, non-U.S. corporations do not qualify. S status is also not permitted for certain banks or insurance companies. S corporations are permitted to have wholly owned C and S corporation subsidiaries.[1] No maximum or minimum dollar sales or capitalization restrictions apply to S corporations.

TAX PLANNING STRATEGIES   When to Elect S Corporation Status

FRAMEWORK FOCUS: DEDUCTIONS

Strategy: Maximize Deductible Amounts.

FRAMEWORK FOCUS: TAX RATE

Strategy: Shift Net Income from High-Bracket Taxpayers to Low-Bracket Taxpayers.
Shift Net Income from High-Tax Jurisdictions to Low-Tax Jurisdictions.

A number of considerations will affect a decision to make an S election.

- Avoid the S election if shareholders have high marginal income tax rates relative to C corporation rates.

- If corporate losses are anticipated and there is unlikely to be corporate taxable income soon, S corporation status is advisable.

- If a C corporation holds an NOL carryover from prior years, the losses cannot be used in an S corporation year.

- There may be tax advantages to the S shareholder who receives a flow-through of passive activity income or the domestic production activities deduction.

- Some states treat S corporations as C corporations and apply a corporate income tax to them.

- Tax-exempt income at the S level does not lose its special tax treatment for shareholders.

- An S corporation avoids the corporate ACE adjustment, personal holding company tax, and accumulated earnings tax.

One Class of Stock

A small business corporation may have only one class of stock issued and outstanding.[2] This restriction permits differences in voting rights, but not differences in distribution or liquidation rights.[3] Thus, two classes of common stock that are identical except that one class is voting and the other is nonvoting are treated as a single class of stock for S corporation purposes.

In contrast, voting common stock and voting preferred stock (with a preference on dividends) are treated as two classes of stock. Authorized and unissued stock or treasury stock of another class does not disqualify the corporation. Likewise, unexercised stock options, phantom stock, stock appreciation rights, warrants, and convertible debentures usually do not constitute a second class of stock.[4]

DIGGING DEEPER 1   In-depth coverage can be found on this book's companion website: www.cengagebrain.com

Although the one-class-of-stock requirement seems straightforward, it is possible for debt to be reclassified as stock, resulting in an unexpected loss of S corporation status.[5] To mitigate concern over possible reclassification of debt as a second class of stock, the law provides a set of *safe harbor* provisions. Neither straight debt[6] nor short-term advances[7] constitute a second class of stock.

---

[1] Other eligibility rules exist. § 1361(b).
[2] § 1361(b)(1)(D).
[3] § 1361(c)(4).
[4] Reg. § 1.1361–1(l)(1).

[5] Refer to the discussion of debt-versus-equity classification in Chapter 12.
[6] § 1361(c)(5)(A).
[7] Reg. § 1.1361–1(l)(1).

TAX FACT The Business of S Corporations

S corporations file more than 4 million tax returns every year, concentrated in the services and financial industries.

S Corporation Returns Filed (%), 2012 Tax Year

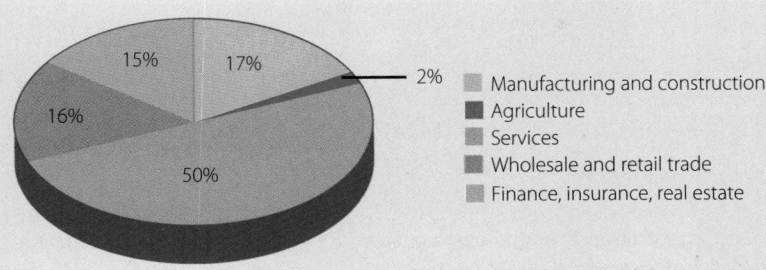

- Manufacturing and construction
- Agriculture
- Services
- Wholesale and retail trade
- Finance, insurance, real estate

The Big Picture

EXAMPLE 3

Return to the facts of *The Big Picture* on p. 15-1. Fowle, Inc., could elect to be an S corporation, except that one class of stock is voting common and the other class is nonvoting preferred. If S status is desired, a recapitalization of the Fowle stock is required, perhaps issuing nonvoting common in place of the preferred stock, which would satisfy the one-class-of-stock requirement.

In-depth coverage can be found on this book's companion website: www.cengagebrain.com   **2 DIGGING DEEPER**

Shareholder Limitations

An S corporation is limited to 100 shareholders. If shares of stock are owned jointly by two individuals, they generally are treated as separate shareholders. However, family members (e.g., ancestors, descendants, spouses, and former spouses) of the investor can be counted as one shareholder for purposes of determining the number of shareholders.[8]

EXAMPLE 4

Fred and Wilma (husband and wife) jointly own 10 shares in Oriole, Inc., an S corporation, with the remaining 90 shares outstanding owned by 99 other shareholders. Fred and Wilma are divorced. Both before and after the divorce, the 100-shareholder limit is met, and Oriole can qualify as a small business corporation.

S corporation shareholders may be individuals, estates, or certain trusts and exempt organizations.[9] This limitation prevents partnerships, corporations, most LLCs, LLPs, and most IRAs from owning S corporation stock. Without this rule, partnerships and corporate shareholders could easily circumvent the 100-shareholder limitation.

EXAMPLE 5

Paul and 200 other individuals want to form an S corporation. Paul reasons that if the group forms a partnership, the partnership can then form an S corporation and act as a single shareholder, thereby avoiding the 100-shareholder rule. Paul's plan will not work, because partnerships cannot own stock in an S corporation.

---

[8]§§ 1361(c)(1)(A)(ii) and (B)(i). TD 9422, 2008–42 I.R.B. 898.

[9]§ 1361(b)(1)(B). A one-member LLC typically is an eligible S shareholder.

Nonresident aliens cannot own stock in an S corporation.[10] Thus, individuals who are not U.S. citizens *must live in the United States* to own S corporation stock. Shareholders who live in community property states and are married to a nonresident alien[11] cannot own S corporation stock, because the nonresident alien spouse is treated as owning half of the stock.[12] Similarly, if a resident alien shareholder permanently moves outside the United States, the S election is terminated.

TAX PLANNING STRATEGIES   Beating the 100-Shareholder Limit

FRAMEWORK FOCUS: TAX RATE

Strategy: Avoid Double Taxation.

Although partnerships and corporations cannot own small business corporation stock, S corporations themselves can be partners in a partnership or shareholders in a corporation. In this way, the 100-shareholder requirement can be bypassed in a limited sense. For example, if two S corporations, each with 80 shareholders, form a partnership, the shareholders of both corporations can enjoy the limited liability conferred by S corporation status and a single level of tax on the resulting profits, even though there are 160 shareholders involved.

LO.3

Explain how to make and terminate an S election.

15-2b **Making the Election**

To become an S corporation, the entity must file a valid election with the IRS. The election is made on Form 2553, and all shareholders must consent. For S corporation status to apply in the current tax year, the election must be filed either in the previous year or on or before the fifteenth day of the third month of the current year.[13]

The Big Picture

EXAMPLE 6

Return to the facts of *The Big Picture* on p. 15-1. Suppose that in 2016, David decides to elect that Fowle, Inc., become an S corporation beginning January 1, 2017. Fowle's S election can be made at any time in 2016 or by March 15, 2017. An election after March 15, 2017, will not be effective until the 2018 calendar tax year.

Even if the 2½-month deadline is met, an S election is not valid unless the corporation qualifies as a small business corporation for the *entire* tax year. Otherwise, the election is effective for the following tax year.

A corporation that does not yet exist cannot make an S corporation election.[14] A new corporation's 2½-month election period begins at the earliest of any of the following events.

- When the corporation has shareholders.
- When it acquires assets.
- When it begins doing business.[15]

---

[10]§ 1362(b)(1)(C).

[11]Assets acquired by a married couple are generally considered community property in these states: Alaska (by election), Arizona, California, Idaho, Louisiana, Nevada, New Mexico, Texas, Washington, and Wisconsin.

[12]See *Ward v. U.S.*, 81–2 USTC ¶9674, 48 AFTR 2d 81–5942, 661 F.2d 226 (Ct.Cls., 1981), where the court found that the stock was owned as community property. Because the taxpayer-shareholder (a U.S. citizen) was married to a citizen and resident of Mexico, the nonresident alien prohibi-

tion was violated. If the taxpayer-shareholder had held the stock as separate property, the S election would have been valid.

[13]§ 1362(b). Extensions of time to file Form 2553 may be possible in certain situations; see Rev.Proc. 2007–62, 2007–41 I.R.B. 786.

[14]See, for example, *T.H. Campbell & Bros., Inc.*, 34 TCM 695, T.C.Memo. 1975–149; Ltr.Rul. 8807070.

[15]Reg. § 1.1372–2(b)(1). Also see, for example, *Nick A. Artukovich*, 61 T.C. 100 (1973).

15-2c **Shareholder Consent**

A qualifying election requires the consent of all of the corporation's shareholders.[16] Consent must be in writing, and it generally must be filed by the election deadline. Both husband and wife must consent if they own their stock jointly (as joint tenants, tenants in common, tenants by the entirety, or community property).[17] In certain circumstances (e.g., a shareholder is out of the country when the consent form is due), one may receive an extension of time to file a consent.

TAX PLANNING STRATEGIES **Making a Proper Election**

FRAMEWORK FOCUS: TAX RATE

Strategy: Avoid Double Taxation.

- Because S corporation status is *elected*, strict compliance with the requirements is demanded by both the IRS and the courts. Any failure to meet a condition in the law may lead to loss of the S election and raise the specter of double tax.

- Make sure that all shareholders timely file a proper consent. If any doubt exists concerning the shareholder status of an individual, it would be wise to request that he

or she sign a consent anyway.[18] Missing consents are fatal to the election, whereas there is no problem with submitting too many consents.

- Make sure the election is timely and properly filed. Either deliver the election to an IRS office in person or send it by certified or registered mail or via a major overnight delivery service. The date used to determine timeliness is the postmark date, not the date the IRS receives the election.

In-depth coverage can be found on this book's companion website: www.cengagebrain.com   **3   DIGGING DEEPER**

15-2d **Loss of the Election**

An S election remains in force until it is revoked or lost. Election or consent forms are not required for future years. However, an S election can terminate if any of the following occurs.[19]

- Shareholders owning a majority of shares (voting and nonvoting) voluntarily revoke the election.

- A new shareholder owning more than one-half of the stock affirmatively refuses to consent to the election.

- The corporation no longer qualifies as a small business corporation.

- The corporation does not meet the passive investment income limitation.

Voluntary Revocation

A **voluntary revocation** of the S election requires the consent of shareholders owning a majority of shares on the day the revocation is to be made.[20] A revocation filed up to and including the fifteenth day of the third month of the tax year is effective for the entire tax year, unless a later date is specified. Similarly, unless an effective date is specified, a revocation made after the first $2^1/_2$ months of the current tax year is effective for the following tax year.

---

[16]§ 1362(a)(2).

[17]Rev.Rul. 60–183, 1960–1 C.B. 625; *William Pestcoe*, 40 T.C. 195 (1963); Reg. § 1.1362–6(b)(3)(iii). This rule likely also applies to all family members who are being treated as one shareholder.

[18]See *William B. Wilson*, 34 TCM 463, T.C.Memo. 1975–92.

[19]§ 1362(d).

[20]§ 1362(d)(1)(B).

The shareholders of Petunia Corporation, a calendar year S corporation, voluntarily revoke the S election on January 5, 2016. They do not specify a future effective date in the revocation. If the revocation is properly executed and timely filed, Petunia will be a C corporation for the entire 2016 tax year. If the revocation is not made until June 2016, Petunia remains an S corporation in 2016 and becomes a C corporation at the beginning of 2017.

A corporation can revoke its S status *prospectively* by specifying a future date when the revocation is to be effective. A revocation that designates a future effective date splits the corporation's tax year into a short S corporation year and a short C corporation year. The day on which the revocation occurs is treated as the first day of the C corporation year. The corporation allocates income or loss for the entire year on a pro rata basis using the number of days in each short year.

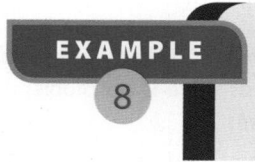

Assume the same facts as in the preceding example, except that Petunia designates July 1, 2016, as the revocation date. Accordingly, June 30 is the last day of the S corporation's tax year. The C corporation's tax year runs from July 1, 2016, to December 31, 2016. Income or loss for the 12-month period is allocated between the two short years (i.e., 184/366 to the C corporation year).

Rather than allocating on a pro rata basis, the corporation can elect to compute the actual income or loss attributable to the two short years. This election requires the consent of everyone who was a shareholder at any time during the S corporation's short year and everyone who owns stock on the first day of the C corporation's year.[21]

Loss of S Corporation Status

If an S corporation fails to qualify as a small business corporation at any time after the election has become effective, its status as an S corporation ends. The termination occurs on the day the corporation ceases to be a small business corporation.[22] Thus, if the corporation ever has more than 100 shareholders, a second class of stock, or a nonqualifying shareholder, or it otherwise fails to meet the definition of a small business corporation, the S election is terminated immediately.

Peony Corporation has been a calendar year S corporation for three years. On August 13, one of its 100 shareholders sells *some* of her stock to an outsider. Peony now has 101 shareholders, and it ceases to be a small business corporation. Peony is an S corporation through August 12 and a C corporation from August 13 to December 31.

Passive Investment Income Limitation

The Code provides a **passive investment income (PII)** limitation for some S corporations that previously were C corporations, or for S corporations that have merged with C corporations. If an S corporation holds C corporation earnings and profits (E & P) and it generates passive investment income in excess of 25 percent of its gross receipts for three consecutive tax years, the S election is terminated as of the beginning of the fourth year.[23]

---

[21]§ 1362(e)(3).
[22]§ 1362(d)(2)(B).

[23]§ 1362(d)(3)(A)(ii).

For 2015, 2016, and 2017, Chrysanthemum Corporation, a calendar year S corporation, derived passive investment income in excess of 25% of its gross receipts. If Chrysanthemum holds accumulated E & P from years in which it was a C corporation, its S election is terminated as of January 1, 2018.

PII includes dividends, interest, rents, gains and losses from sales of capital assets, and royalties net of investment deductions. Rents are not considered PII if the corporation renders significant personal services to the occupant.

Violet Corporation owns and operates an apartment building. The corporation provides utilities for the building, maintains the lobby, and furnishes trash collection for tenants. These activities are not considered significant personal services, so any rent income earned by the corporation will be considered PII.

Alternatively, if Violet also provides maid services to its tenants (personal services beyond what normally would be expected from a landlord in an apartment building), the rent income would no longer be PII.

Reelection after Termination

After an S election has been terminated, the corporation must wait five years before reelecting S corporation status. The five-year waiting period is waived if:

- There is a more-than-50% change in ownership of the corporation after the first year for which the termination is applicable, or
- The event causing the termination was not reasonably within the control of the S corporation or its majority shareholders.

TAX PLANNING STRATEGIES **Preserving the S Election**

FRAMEWORK FOCUS: TAX RATE

Strategy: Avoid Double Taxation.

Unexpected loss of S corporation status can be costly to a corporation and its shareholders. Given the complexity of the rules facing these entities, constant vigilance is necessary to preserve the S election.

- As a starting point, the corporation's management and shareholders should be made aware of the various transactions that can lead to the loss of an election.
- Prevent violations of the small business corporation limitations. Because most such violations result from transfers

of stock, the corporation and its shareholders should consider adopting a set of stock transfer restrictions.

A carefully designed set of restrictions could prevent sale of stock to nonqualifying entities or violation of the 100-shareholder rule. Similarly, stock could be repurchased by the corporation under a buy-sell agreement upon the death of a shareholder, thereby preventing nonqualifying trusts from becoming shareholders.[24]

---

[24]Most such agreements do not create a second class of stock. Rev.Rul. 85–161, 1985–2 C.B. 191; *Portage Plastics Co. v. U.S.*, 72–2 USTC ¶9567, 30 AFTR 2d 72–5229, 470 F.2d 308 (CA–7, 1973).

LO.4

Compute nonseparately stated income and allocate income, deductions, and credits to shareholders.

15-3 OPERATIONAL RULES

S corporations are treated much like partnerships for tax purposes. Each year, the S corporation determines nonseparately stated income or loss and separately stated income, deductions, and credits. These items are taxed only once, as they pass through to shareholders without incurring a corporate-level income tax. All items are allocated to each shareholder based on average ownership of stock throughout the year.[25] The flow-through of each item of income, deduction, and credit from the corporation to the shareholder is illustrated in Exhibit 15.1.

15-3a Computation of Taxable Income

An S corporation's taxable income or loss is determined in a manner similar to the tax rules that apply to partnerships, except that S corporations recognize gains (but not losses) on distributions of appreciated property to shareholders.[26] With a few exceptions, S corporations generally make tax accounting and other elections at the corporate level.[27] Other special provisions affecting only the computation of C corporation income, such as the dividends received deduction, do not extend to S corporations.[28]

In general, S corporation items are divided into (1) nonseparately stated income or loss and (2) separately stated income, losses, deductions, and credits that could uniquely affect the tax liability of any shareholder. In essence, nonseparate items are aggregated into an undifferentiated amount that constitutes S corporation ordinary income or loss.

| EXHIBIT 15.1 | Flow-Through of Items of Income and Loss to S Corporation Shareholders |

Corporate Level

Shareholder Level

S Corporation

Ordinary Income · Trade or Business Expenses · Depreciation Recapture

Passive Activity Gain/Loss · Nonseparately Computed Amount · Tax-Exempt Income

Domestic Production Activities Deduction · Short-Term Capital Gain/Loss

AMT Preferences and Adjustments · Portfolio Income

Charitable Contributions · Long-Term Capital Gain/Loss

---

[25]§§ 1366(a), (b), and (c).
[26]§ 1363(b).

[27]Certain elections are made at the shareholder level (e.g., the choice between a foreign tax deduction or credit; see Chapter 16).
[28]§ 703(a)(2).

The following is the income statement for Larkspur, Inc., an S corporation.

Sales		$ 40,000
Less: Cost of goods sold		(23,000)
Gross profit on sales		$ 17,000
Less: Interest expense	$1,200	
Charitable contributions	400	
Advertising expenses	1,500	
Other operating expenses	2,000	(5,100)
Book income from operations		$ 11,900
Add: Tax-exempt interest income	$ 300	
Dividend income	200	
Long-term capital gain	500	1,000
Less: Short-term capital loss		(150)
Net income per books		$ 12,750

Larkspur's ordinary income (i.e., S corporation nonseparately stated income) is calculated as follows, using net income for book purposes as the starting point.

Net income per books		$12,750
Separately stated items		
Remove: Tax-exempt interest income	$300	
Dividend income	200	
Long-term capital gain	500	(1,000)
Add Back: Charitable contributions	$400	
Short-term capital loss	150	550
Ordinary income (nonseparately stated income)		$12,300

Larkspur's $12,300 nonseparately stated income, as well as each of the five separately stated items, is divided among the shareholders based upon their stock ownership.

An S corporation reports details as to the differences between book income and pass-through items on its Form 1120S, Schedule M–1 or M–3.

In-depth coverage can be found on this book's companion website: www.cengagebrain.com

4 DIGGING DEEPER

15-3b **Allocation of Income and Loss**

Each shareholder is allocated a pro rata portion of nonseparately stated income or loss and all separately stated items. The pro rata allocation method assigns an equal amount of each of the S items to each day of the year.[29] If a shareholder's stock holding changes during the year, this allocation assigns the shareholder a pro rata share of each item for each day the stock is owned. On the date of transfer, the transferor is considered to own the stock.[30]

---

[29]§§ 1366(a)(1) and 1377(a)(1).

[30]Reg. § 1.1377–1(a)(2)(ii).

About 90 percent of S corporations have only one or two shareholders.

Returns Filed by Number of S Corporation Shareholders, 2012 Tax Year

1%
5% 4%
27%
63%

Shareholders: ■ One ■ Two ■ Three ■ Four to Ten ■ More than Ten

EXAMPLE 13

Pat, a shareholder, owned 10% of Larkspur's stock (from Example 12) for 100 days and 12% for the remaining 265 days. Using the required per-day allocation method, Pat's share of the S corporation ordinary income is $1,409, the total of $12,300 × [10% × (100/365)] plus $12,300 × [12% × (265/365)]. All of Pat's Schedule K–1 totals flow through to the corresponding lines on his individual income tax return (Form 1040).

The Short-Year Election

If a shareholder's interest is completely terminated during the tax year by a sale or by a disposition following death, all shareholders owning stock during the year and the corporation may elect to treat the S taxable year as two taxable years. The first year ends on the date of the termination. Under this election, there is an interim closing of the books, and the shareholders report their shares of the S corporation items as they occurred during the short tax year.[31]

The short-year election provides an opportunity to shift income, losses, and credits among shareholders (e.g., items that have a clearly identifiable date of occurrence). The election is desirable in circumstances where more loss can be allocated to taxpayers with higher marginal tax rates.

EXAMPLE 14

Alicia, the owner of all of the shares of an S corporation, transfers her stock to Cindy halfway through the tax year. There is a $100,000 NOL for the entire tax year, but $30,000 of the loss occurs during the first half of the year. Without a short-year election, $50,000 of the loss is allocated to Alicia and $50,000 is allocated to Cindy.

If the corporation makes the short-year election, Cindy is allocated $70,000 of the loss. In this case, the sales price of the stock probably would be increased to recognize the tax benefits being transferred from Alicia to Cindy.

⊙ DIGGING DEEPER **5**   In-depth coverage can be found on this book's companion website: www.cengagebrain.com

---

[31]§ 1377(a)(2).

TAX PLANNING STRATEGIES **Salary Structure**

FRAMEWORK FOCUS: TAX RATE

Strategy: Shift Net Income from High-Bracket Taxpayers to Low-Bracket Taxpayers.
Avoid Double Taxation.

The amount of any salary paid to a shareholder-employee of an S corporation can have varying tax consequences and should be considered carefully. Larger amounts might be advantageous if the maximum contribution allowed under the employee's retirement plan has not been reached. Smaller amounts may be beneficial if the parties are trying to shift taxable income to lower-bracket shareholders, reduce payroll taxes, curtail a reduction of Social Security benefits, or restrict losses that do not pass through because of the basis limitation.

A strategy of decreasing compensation and correspondingly increasing distributions to shareholder-employees often results in substantial savings in employment taxes. However, a shareholder of an S corporation cannot always perform substantial services and arrange to receive distributions rather than compensation so that the corporation may avoid paying employment taxes. The shareholder may be deemed an employee, and any distributions will be recharacterized as wages subject to FICA and FUTA taxes.[32] For planning purposes, some level of compensation should be paid to all shareholder-employees to avoid any recharacterization of distributions as deductible salaries—especially in personal service corporations.

15-3c **Tax Treatment of Distributions to Shareholders**

S corporations do not generate E & P while the S election is in effect. Indeed, all profits are taxed in the year earned, as though they were distributed on a pro rata basis to the shareholders. Thus, distributions from S corporations do not constitute dividends in the traditional sense—there is no corporate E & P to distribute.

It is possible, however, for S corporations to have an accumulated E & P (AEP) account. This can occur when:

- The S corporation was previously a C corporation, or
- A C corporation with its own AEP merged into the S corporation.

Distributions from S corporations are measured as the cash received plus the fair market value of any other distributed property. The tax treatment of distributions differs, depending upon whether the S corporation holds AEP.

LO.5

Determine how distributions to S corporation shareholders are taxed.

S Corporation with No AEP

If the S corporation holds no AEP, the distribution is a tax-free recovery of capital to the extent it does not exceed the basis of the shareholder's stock. When the amount of the distribution exceeds the stock basis, the excess is treated as a gain from the sale or exchange of property (capital gain in most cases). The vast majority of S corporations fall into this favorable category.

Hyacinth, Inc., a calendar year S corporation, holds no AEP. During the year, Juan, an individual shareholder of the corporation, receives a cash distribution of $12,200 from Hyacinth. Juan's basis in his stock is $9,700. Juan recognizes a capital gain of $2,500, the excess of the distribution over the stock basis ($12,200 − $9,700). The remaining $9,700 is tax-free, but it reduces Juan's basis in his stock to zero.

EXAMPLE 15

---

[32]Rev.Rul. 74–44, 1974–1 C.B. 287; *Spicer Accounting, Inc. v. U.S.*, 91–1 USTC ¶50,103, 66 AFTR 2d 90–5806, 918 F.2d 90 (CA-9, 1990); *Radtke v. U.S.*, 90–1 USTC ¶50,113, 65 AFTR 2d 90–1155, 895 F.2d 1196 (CA-7, 1990); *Joseph M. Grey Public Accountant, P.C.*, 119 T.C. 121 (2002); *David E. Watson, P.C. v. U.S.*, 2010–1 USTC ¶50,444, 105 AFTR 2d 2010–2624, 714 F. Supp.2d 954 (D.C. S.IA). The IRS uses salary surveys and other statistical methods to determine the appropriate compensation level. *McAlary Ltd.*, T.C. Summary Opinion 2013–62.

TAX IN THE NEWS   **Some Guidelines for S Corporation Shareholder-Employee Compensation**

Shareholder compensation issues differ between C and S corporations. Usually, a C corporation guards against shareholder salaries being "too high," so as to avoid IRS charges of unreasonable compensation and the conversion of a salary into a nondeductible dividend distribution. An S corporation must make certain that its shareholder salaries are not "too low," to counter potential IRS assertions that the compensation structure was designed to avoid payroll tax liabilities.

An IRS fact sheet provides taxpayers with these factors to determine reasonable compensation for an S shareholder.[33]

- Training, education, and experience.
- Duties and responsibilities.

- Time and effort devoted to business.
- Dividend history.
- Payments to nonshareholders-employees.
- Timing and manner of paying bonuses to key employees.
- What comparable businesses pay for similar services.
- Compensation agreements.
- Use of a formula to determine compensation.

S Corporation with AEP

A more complex set of rules applies to S corporations that hold AEP. These rules treat distributions of pre-election (C corporation) and post-election (S corporation) earnings differently. Distributions of AEP are taxed as dividends, while distributions of previously taxed S corporation earnings are tax-free to the extent of the shareholder's basis in the stock.

Distributions are deemed to be first from previously taxed, undistributed earnings of the S corporation. These distributions are tax-free and are determined by reference to a special account, the **accumulated adjustments account (AAA)** .[34] Next, AEP is distributed as taxable dividends (i.e., as payments from AEP). After AEP is depleted, tax-free distributions are made from the **other adjustments account (OAA)**, as discussed below. Remaining amounts of the distribution are received tax free until the shareholder's stock basis reaches zero,[35] with any excess being treated typically as capital gain.

Ordering Rules for Distributions

EXAMPLE 16

Short, a calendar year S corporation, distributes $1,300 of cash to its only shareholder, Otis, on December 31. Otis's basis in his stock is $1,400, AAA is $500, and Short holds $750 of AEP before the distribution.

The first $500 of the distribution is a tax-free recovery of basis from the AAA. The next $750 is a taxable dividend distribution from AEP. The remaining $50 of cash is a tax-free recovery of basis. Immediately after the distribution, Short records a zero balance in AAA and AEP. Otis's stock basis now is $850.

	Corporate AAA	Corporate AEP	Otis's Stock Basis
Beginning balance	$ 500	$ 750	$1,400
Distribution from AAA	(500)		(500)
Distribution from AEP		(750)	
Distribution from stock basis			(50)
Ending balance	$ –0–	$ –0–	$ 850

---

[33]FS-2008-25, Wage Compensation for S Corporation Officers, August 2008.

[34]For S corporations in existence prior to 1983, an account similar to the AAA was used. This account, called *previously taxed income* (PTI), can be

distributed in cash tax free to shareholders after AAA has been distributed. See §§ 1368(c)(1) and (e)(1).

[35]§ 1368(c).

Ordering Rules for Distributions

Assume the same facts as in the preceding example. The next year, Short's income totals zero. It distributes $1,000 to Otis. Of the distribution, $850 is a tax-free recovery of the stock basis, and $150 is taxed to Otis as a capital gain.

EXAMPLE 17

With the consent of all of its shareholders, an S corporation can elect to have a distribution treated as if it first were made from AEP rather than from the AAA. This mechanism is known as an **AAA bypass election**. This election may be desirable when making distributions to move the entity to the no-AEP system of accounting for distributions, at a maximum tax cost of 20 percent of the AEP (i.e., the maximum income tax rate applied to dividends for most shareholders).

Rotor, an S corporation, has $50 of AEP. An AAA bypass election for Rotor's next shareholder distribution would eliminate the need to track the AAA and would greatly simplify the accounting for future distributions. The cost for this simplification is the tax on $50 of dividend income.

EXAMPLE 18

Accumulated Adjustments Account

The AAA is the cumulative total of undistributed nonseparately and separately stated income and deduction items for the S corporation. The AAA provides a mechanism to ensure that earnings of an S corporation are taxed only once. Changes to the AAA are reported annually in Schedule M–2 on page 4 of the Form 1120S.

The initial AAA balance is zero when an S election is made. AAA then is computed at the end of each tax year rather than at the time of a distribution. First, add to the year's beginning balance any current nonseparately computed income and positive separately stated items (except tax-exempt income). Next, account for distributions *prior* to subtracting the negative items.

AAA is applied to the distributions made during the year on a pro rata basis (in a fashion similar to the application of current E & P, discussed in Chapter 13). The determination of AAA is summarized in Exhibit 15.2.

Although adjustments to AAA and stock basis adjustments are similar, there are some important differences between the two amounts. In particular,

- The AAA is not affected by tax-exempt income and related expenses.
- The AAA can have a negative balance. All losses decrease the AAA balance, even those in excess of the shareholder's basis. However, distributions may not make the AAA negative or increase a negative balance in the account.

EXHIBIT 15.2	Adjustments to the Corporate AAA

Increase by:

1. Schedule K income items other than tax-exempt income.
2. Nonseparately computed income.

Decrease by:

3. Distribution(s) from AAA (but not below zero).
4. Negative Schedule K items other than distributions (e.g., losses, deductions).

• Every shareholder has a proportionate interest in the AAA, regardless of the amount of his or her stock basis.[36] In fact, AAA is a corporate account, so there is no connection between the amount and any specific shareholder.[37] Thus, the benefits of AAA can be shifted from one shareholder to another. For example, when an S corporation shareholder sells stock to another party, any AAA balance on the purchase date can be distributed tax free to the purchaser.

Other Adjustments Account

The OAA tracks the entity's net items that affect basis but not the AAA, such as tax-exempt income and any related nondeductible expenses. Distributions from this account are tax-free.

Schedule M–2

Page 4 of the Form 1120S includes Schedule M–2, a reconciliation of beginning and ending balances in the AAA and OAA accounts. Most tax professionals recommend that the Schedule M–2 be kept current even if the entity has retained no AEP, so that if future events require the use of these amounts, they need not be reconstructed after the fact.

EXAMPLE 19

Poinsettia, an S corporation, records the following items.

AAA, beginning of year	$ 8,500
OAA, beginning of year	–0–
Ordinary income	25,000
Tax-exempt interest income	4,000
Key employee life insurance proceeds received	5,000
Payroll penalty expense	2,000
Charitable contributions	3,000
Unreasonable compensation	5,000
Premiums on key employee life insurance	2,100
Distributions to shareholders	16,000

Poinsettia's Schedule M–2 appears as follows.

Schedule M-2	**Analysis of Accumulated Adjustments Account, Other Adjustments Account, and Shareholders' Undistributed Taxable Income Previously Taxed** (see instructions)		
		(a) Accumulated adjustments account	**(b)** Other adjustments account	**(c)** Shareholders' undistributed taxable income previously taxed
1	Balance at beginning of tax year	8,500	0	
2	Ordinary income from page 1, line 21 . . .	25,000		
3	Other additions		9,000**	
4	Loss from page 1, line 21	( )		
5	Other reductions	(10,000*)	(2,100)	
6	Combine lines 1 through 5	23,500	6,900	
7	Distributions other than dividend distributions	16,000		
8	Balance at end of tax year. Subtract line 7 from line 6	7,500	6,900	

$2,000 (payroll penalty) + $3,000 (charitable contributions) + $5,000 (unreasonable compensation).
**$4,000 (tax-exempt interest income) + $5,000 (life insurance proceeds).*

Effect of Terminating the S Election

Normally, distributions to shareholders from a C corporation are taxed as dividends to the extent of E & P. However, any distribution of *cash* by a C corporation to shareholders during a one-year period[38] following an S election termination receives special treatment. Such a distribution is treated as a tax-free recovery of stock basis to the extent

---

[36]§ 1368(c).
[37]§ 1368(e)(1)(A).

[38]§ 1377(b).

that it does not exceed the AAA.[39] Because *only* cash distributions reduce the AAA during this *post-election termination period*, a corporation should not make property distributions during this time. Instead, the entity should sell property and distribute the proceeds to shareholders.

The Big Picture

EXAMPLE

20

Return to the facts of *The Big Picture* on p. 15-1. Assume that Fowle has operated as an S corporation for many years and that the entity turned profitable once it mastered the pricing methods of its import markets. Then David decides to terminate the S election as of the end of the year. On December 31 of that year, Fowle's AAA balance totals $1.3 million.

David can receive a nontaxable distribution of cash during the next year, to the full extent of the entity's AAA balance. Any cash distributions so received reduce the basis of David's Fowle stock, but not below zero.

TAX PLANNING STRATEGIES The Accumulated Adjustments Account

FRAMEWORK FOCUS: TAX RATE

Strategy: Avoid Double Taxation.

The AAA is needed to determine the tax treatment of distributions from S corporations with AEP *and* distributions made during the post-termination election period. Therefore, it is important for all S corporations (even those with no AEP) to maintain a current AAA (and OAA) balance. Without an accurate AAA balance, distributions could needlessly be classified as taxable dividends. Alternatively, it will be costly to reconstruct the AAA after the S election terminates.

Distributions should be made when AAA is positive. If future years bring operating losses, AAA is reduced and shareholder exposure to AEP and taxable dividends increases.

Concept Summary 15.1

Distributions from an S Corporation

Where Earnings and Profits Exist	Where No Earnings and Profits Exist
1. Distributions are tax-free to the extent of the accumulated adjustments account (AAA).*	
2. Next, the distribution constitutes dividend income to the extent of accumulated E & P (AEP).†	
3. Distributions are tax-free to the extent of the other adjustments account (OAA).*	
4. Any residual distribution is nontaxable to the extent of the shareholder's basis in stock.*	1. Distributions are nontaxable to the extent of shareholder's basis in stock.*
5. Excess is treated as gain from a sale or exchange of stock (capital gain in virtually all cases).	2. Excess is treated as gain from a sale or exchange of stock (capital gain in virtually all cases).

*The distribution reduces the shareholder's stock basis. A shareholder's stock basis serves as the upper limit on the amount that may be received tax free.
†The AAA bypass election is available to pay out AEP before reducing the AAA [§ 1368 (e) (3)].

---

[39]§ 1371(e).

15-3d Tax Treatment of Noncash Distributions by the Corporation

An S corporation recognizes a gain on any distribution of appreciated property as if the asset were sold to the shareholder at its fair market value.[40] The corporate gain is passed through to the shareholders, and the asset's basis to the receiving shareholder is stepped up to fair market value. The character of the gain—capital gain or ordinary income—depends upon the type of asset being distributed.

The S corporation does not recognize a loss when distributing assets that are worth less than their basis. As with gain property, the shareholder's basis is equal to the asset's fair market value. Thus, the potential loss is postponed until the shareholder sells the stock of the S corporation. Because loss property receives a step-down in basis without any loss recognition by the S corporation, distributions of loss property should be avoided. See Concept Summary 15.2.

Noncash Distributions by an S Corporation

EXAMPLE 21

Yarrow, Inc., an S corporation for 12 years, distributes to Xiang, one of its shareholders, a tract of land held as an investment. The land was purchased for $22,000 many years ago and currently is worth $82,000. Yarrow recognizes a capital gain of $60,000, which increases the AAA by $60,000. The gain flows through proportionately to all of Yarrow's shareholders and is taxed to them.

This tax-free noncash distribution reduces AAA and Xiang's S stock basis by $82,000 (fair market value). The tax consequences are the same for appreciated property whether (a) it is distributed to shareholders and they dispose of it, or (b) the corporation sells the property and distributes the proceeds to its shareholders.

EXAMPLE 22

Continue with the facts of Example 21. If the land had been purchased for $82,000 and was currently worth $22,000, Xiang would take a $22,000 basis in the land. The $60,000 realized loss is not recognized at the corporate level. The loss does not reduce Yarrow's AAA. However, if the S corporation sells the asset to an unrelated party, it does recognize the loss and reduces AAA.

EXAMPLE 23

Assume the same facts as in Examples 21 and 22, except that Yarrow is a C corporation (E & P balance of $1 million) or a partnership. Assume that Xiang's basis before the distribution in her corporate stock or partnership interest is $100,000, and ignore any corporate-level taxes. Compare the results.

	Appreciated Property		
	S Corporation	C Corporation	Partnership
Entity gain/loss	$60,000	$60,000	$ –0–
Owner's gain/loss/dividend	60,000	82,000	–0–
Owner's basis in land	82,000	82,000	22,000

	Property That Has Declined in Value		
	S Corporation	C Corporation	Partnership
Entity gain/loss	$ –0–	$ –0–	$ –0–
Owner's gain/loss/dividend	–0–	22,000	–0–
Owner's basis in land	22,000	22,000	82,000

---

[40]§ 311(b).

Concept Summary 15.2

Consequences of Noncash Distributions

	Appreciated Property	Depreciated Property
S corporation	Realized gain is recognized by the corporation, which passes it through to the shareholders. This gain increases a shareholder's stock basis, generating a basis in the property equal to FMV. On the distribution, the shareholder's stock basis is reduced by the FMV of the property (but not below zero).	Realized loss is not recognized. The shareholder takes an FMV basis in the property, and stock basis is reduced by the same amount. AAA is reduced by the amount of the unrecognized loss.
C corporation	Realized gain is recognized under § 311(b) and increases E & P (net of tax). The shareholder reports a taxable dividend to the extent of corporate E & P, equal to the property's FMV (reduced by any liabilities assumed). The shareholder takes a basis in the asset equal to its FMV.	Realized loss is not recognized. The shareholder takes an FMV basis in the property.
Partnership	No gain is recognized by the partnership or partner. The partner takes a carryover basis in the asset, but the asset basis is limited to the partner's basis in the partnership.	Realized loss is not recognized. The partner takes a carryover basis in the asset, but the asset basis is limited to the partner's basis in the partnership.

15-3e **Shareholder's Basis in S Stock**

The calculation of the initial tax basis of stock in an S corporation is similar to that for the basis of stock in a C corporation and depends upon the manner in which the shares are acquired (e.g., gift, inheritance, purchase, exchange under § 351). Once the initial tax basis is determined, various transactions during the life of the corporation affect the shareholder's basis in the stock. Although each shareholder is required to compute his or her own basis in the S shares, neither Form 1120S nor Schedule K–1 provides a place for tracking this amount.

A shareholder's basis is increased by stock purchases and capital contributions. Operations during the year cause the following additional upward adjustments to basis.[41]

- Nonseparately computed income.
- Separately stated income items (e.g., tax-exempt income).

Basis then is reduced by distributions not reported as income by the shareholder (e.g., an AAA distribution). Next, the following items reduce basis (but not below zero).

- Nondeductible expenses of the corporation (e.g., fines, penalties, and illegal kick-backs).
- Nonseparately computed loss.
- Separately stated loss and deduction items.

As under the partnership rules, basis first is increased by income items; then it is decreased by distributions and finally by losses.[42] In most cases, this *losses last* rule is advantageous to the S shareholder.

LO.6

Calculate a shareholder's basis in S corporation stock.

EXAMPLE

24

In its first year of operation, Iris, Inc., a calendar year S corporation, earns income of $2,000. Before accounting for the entity's operating results, assume the stock basis of Iris's sole shareholder, Marty, is zero. Therefore, Marty's stock basis is increased to $2,000. On February 2 in its second year of operation, Iris distributes $2,000 to Marty. During the remainder of the second year, the corporation incurs a $2,000 loss.

Under the S corporation ordering rules, the $2,000 distribution is tax-free AAA to Marty. The distribution is accounted for before the loss. The $2,000 loss is suspended until Marty generates additional stock basis (e.g., from capital contributions or future entity profits).

---

[41]§ 1367(a).   [42]Reg. § 1.1367–1(f).

A shareholder's basis in S corporation stock never is reduced below zero. Once stock basis reaches zero, any additional basis reductions (losses or deductions, but *not* distributions) decrease the shareholder's basis in loans made to the S corporation (but not below zero). Any excess of losses or deductions over both stock and loan bases is not deductible in the current year. Thus, until additional basis is created due to capital contributions or flow-through income, the loss deductions are suspended.

When there is a capital contribution or an item of flow-through income after stock basis has been reduced to zero, basis first is restored to the shareholder loans, up to the original principal amount.[43] Then, basis in the stock is restored.

EXAMPLE 25

Stacey, a sole shareholder, holds a $7,000 stock basis and a $2,000 basis in a loan that she made to Romulus, a calendar year S corporation with zero AEP. At the beginning of the year, the corporation's AAA and OAA balances are zero. Ordinary income for the year is $8,200. During the year, the corporation also received $2,000 of tax-exempt interest income.

Cash of $17,300 is distributed to Stacey on November 15. As a result, Stacey recognizes only a $100 capital gain.

	Corporate AAA	Corporate OAA	Stacey's Stock Basis	Stacey's Loan Basis
Beginning balance	$ –0–	$ –0–	$ 7,000	$2,000
Ordinary income	8,200		8,200	
Tax-exempt income		2,000	2,000	
Subtotal	$ 8,200	$ 2,000	$17,200	$2,000
Distribution ($17,300)				
From AAA	(8,200)		(8,200)	
From OAA		(2,000)	(2,000)	
From stock basis			(7,000)	
Ending balance	$ –0–	$ –0–	$ –0–	$2,000
Distribution in excess of stock basis (capital gain)			$ 100	

Pass-through losses can reduce loan basis, but distributions do not. Stock basis cannot be reduced below zero, so the $100 excess distribution does not reduce Stacey's loan basis.

The basis rules for S corporation stock are similar to the rules for determining a partner's basis in a partnership interest. However, a partner's basis in the partnership interest includes the partner's direct investment plus a *ratable share* of partnership liabilities.[44] If a partnership borrows from a partner, the partner receives a basis increase as if the partnership had borrowed from an unrelated third party.[45] In contrast, corporate borrowing has no effect on the stock basis of an S corporation shareholder. Loans from a shareholder to the S corporation have a tax basis only for the shareholder making the loan.

If a loan's basis has been reduced and is not restored, income is recognized when the corporation repays the loan. If the corporation issued a note as evidence of the debt, repayment constitutes an amount received in exchange for a capital asset and the amount that exceeds the shareholder's basis is capital gain.[46] However, if the loan is

[43]§ 1367(b)(2); Reg. § 1.1367–2(e).
[44]§ 752(a).
[45]Reg. § 1.752–1(e).
[46]*Joe M. Smith*, 48 T.C. 872 (1967), *aff'd* and *rev'd* in 70–1 USTC ¶9327, 25 AFTR 2d 70–936, 424 F.2d 219 (CA–9, 1970); Rev.Rul. 64–162, 1964–1 C.B.

304. An open account loan is treated as evidenced by a note if the shareholder's net payable at the end of the tax year exceeds $25,000. Reg. § 1.1367–2.

made on open account, the repayment constitutes ordinary income to the extent it exceeds the shareholder's basis in the loan. Thus, a written note should be provided to avoid the ordinary income implications of an open account.

The Big Picture

EXAMPLE 26

Return to the facts of *The Big Picture* on p. 15-1. Assume that Fowle has made an S election. At the beginning of 2016, David's basis in his Fowle stock was $90,000. During the year, he made a $40,000 loan to the corporation, using a written debt instrument and market interest rates.

Fowle generated a $93,000 taxable loss for 2016. Thus, at the beginning of 2017, David's stock basis was zero, and the basis in his loan to Fowle was $37,000.

Fowle repaid the loan in full on March 1, 2017. David recognizes a $3,000 capital gain as a result of the repayment.

In-depth coverage can be found on this book's companion website: www.cengagebrain.com

6 DIGGING DEEPER

TAX PLANNING STRATEGIES Working with Suspended Losses

FRAMEWORK FOCUS: INCOME AND EXCLUSION

Strategy: Avoid Income Recognition.

Distributions made to shareholders with suspended losses usually create capital gain income because there is no stock basis to offset. Typically, distributions should be deferred until the shareholder creates stock basis in some form. In this way, no gross income is recognized until the suspended losses are fully used.

The Big Picture

EXAMPLE 27

Continue with the facts of Example 26, except that Fowle's loss cannot be deducted by David because he has a zero basis in both the stock and debt of the entity. David purchases $5,000 of additional stock in Fowle. David gets an immediate deduction for his investment, due to his $93,000 in suspended losses. Alternatively, if Fowle shows a $5,000 profit for the year, David pays no tax on the flow-through income, as it is offset by the suspended losses.

However, if Fowle distributes $5,000 to David in 2017 without earning any profit for the year, and prior to any capital contribution by him, David recognizes a $5,000 capital gain, because the distribution exceeds the zero stock basis.

15-3f Treatment of Losses

Net Operating Loss

LO.7

Explain the tax effects of losses on S shareholders.

One major advantage of an S election is the ability to pass through net operating losses (NOLs) of the corporation directly to the shareholders. A shareholder can deduct an NOL for the year in which the S corporation's tax year ends. The corporation does not deduct the NOL. A shareholder's basis in the stock is reduced by any NOL pass-through, but not below zero. The entity's AAA is reduced by the same deductible amount.[47]

---

[47]§§ 1368(a)(1)(A) and (e)(1)(A).

Deductions for an S corporation's pass-throughs (e.g., NOL, capital loss, and charitable contributions) cannot exceed a shareholder's stock basis *plus* the basis of any loans made by the shareholder to the corporation.[48] A shareholder is entitled to carry forward a loss pass-through to the extent the loss for the year exceeds basis. Any pass-through carried forward may be deducted *only* by the *same* shareholder if and when the basis in the stock of or loans to the corporation is restored.[49]

EXAMPLE 28

Ginny owns 10% of the stock of Pilot, a calendar year S corporation. Her basis in the shares is $10,000 at the beginning of year 1. The indicated events are accounted for under the S corporation rules as follows.

Tax Year	Event	Tax Consequences
1	Ginny's share of Pilot's operating loss is $15,000.	Ginny deducts $10,000. Her stock basis is reduced to zero. She holds a $5,000 suspended loss.
2	Ginny's share of Pilot's operating loss is $4,000.	No current deduction allowed for the loss, as Ginny has no stock basis to offset. Her suspended loss is now $9,000.
3	Ginny's share of Pilot's operating loss is $7,000. She purchases an additional $10,000 of stock from Pilot.	The purchase creates $10,000 of stock basis. Ginny deducts $10,000—the current $7,000 loss and $3,000 of the suspended loss. Stock basis again is zero, and the new suspended loss is $6,000.
4	Ginny sells all of her Pilot shares to Christina on January 1.	The $6,000 suspended loss disappears— it cannot be transferred to Christina.

TAX PLANNING STRATEGIES **Loss Considerations**

FRAMEWORK FOCUS: DEDUCTIONS

Strategy: Maximize Deductible Amounts.

A net loss in excess of tax basis may be carried forward and deducted only by the same shareholder in succeeding years. Thus, before disposing of the stock, a shareholder should increase stock/loan basis to flow through the loss. The next shareholder cannot acquire the loss carryover.

The NOL provisions create a need for sound tax planning during the last election year and the post-termination transition period. If it appears that the S corporation is going to sustain an NOL or use up any loss carryover, each shareholder's basis should be analyzed to determine whether it can absorb the owner's share of the loss. If basis is insufficient to absorb the loss, further investments should be considered before the end of the post-termination period. Such investments can be accomplished through additional stock purchases from the corporation or from other shareholders to increase basis.

EXAMPLE 29

A calendar year C corporation records a $20,000 NOL in 2016. The corporation makes a valid S election in 2017 and incurs another $20,000 NOL in that year. At all times during 2017, the stock of the corporation was owned by the same 10 shareholders, each of whom owned 10% of the stock.

Tim, one of the shareholders, holds a stock basis of $1,800 at the beginning of 2017. None of the 2016 NOL may be carried forward into the S year. Although Tim's share of the 2017 NOL is $2,000, his deduction for the loss is limited to $1,800 in 2017 with a $200 carryover to 2018.

---

[48]See *Donald J. Sauvigne*, 30 TCM 123, T.C.Memo. 1971–30.   [49]§ 1366(d).

Concept Summary 15.3

Treatment of S Corporation Losses

Step 1. Allocate total loss to the shareholder on a daily basis, based upon stock ownership.

Step 2. If the shareholder's loss exceeds his or her stock basis, apply any excess to the basis of corporate indebtedness to the shareholder. Loss allocations do not reduce stock or loan basis below zero.

Step 3. Where a flow-through loss exceeds the stock and loan basis, any excess is suspended and carried over to succeeding tax years.

Step 4. In succeeding tax years, any net increase in basis restores the debt basis first, up to its original amount.

Step 5. Once debt basis is restored, any remaining net increase restores stock basis.

If the S election terminates, any suspended loss carryover may be deducted during the post-termination period to the extent of the stock basis at the end of this period. Any loss remaining at the end of this period is lost forever.

At-Risk Rules

As discussed in Chapters 6 and 14, S corporation shareholders, like partners, are limited in the amount of loss they may deduct by their "at-risk" amounts.

An at-risk amount is determined separately for each shareholder. The amount of the corporate losses that are passed through and deductible by the shareholders is not affected by the amount the corporation has at risk. A shareholder usually is considered at risk with respect to an activity to the extent of cash and the adjusted basis of other property contributed to the electing corporation, any amount borrowed for use in the activity for which the taxpayer has personal liability for payment from personal assets, and the net fair market value of personal assets that secure nonrecourse borrowing.

Any losses that are suspended under the at-risk rules are carried forward to future tax years. The S stock basis limitations and at-risk limitations are applied before the passive activity limitations (see below).

Carl has a basis of $35,000 in his S corporation stock. He takes a $15,000 nonrecourse loan from a relative and lends the proceeds to the S corporation. Carl now has a stock basis of $35,000 and a loan basis of $15,000. However, due to the at-risk limitation, he can deduct only $35,000 of losses from the S corporation.

EXAMPLE 30

Passive Activity Losses and Credits

S corporations are not directly subject to the passive activity limits, but corporate rental activities are inherently passive, and other activities of an S corporation may be passive unless the shareholder(s) materially participate(s) in operating the business.

If the corporate activity involves rentals or the shareholders do not materially participate, the shareholders can apply these losses or credits only against income from other passive activities. An S shareholder's stock basis is reduced by passive activity losses that flow through to the shareholder, even though the shareholder may not be entitled to a current deduction due to the passive activity loss limitations.

Passive activity gains and income flow through to the shareholder as investment income, and this income is subject to the additional Medicare tax (see Chapter 10).

15-3g Other Operational Rules

Several other points may be made about the possible effects of various Code provisions on S corporations.

- An S corporation must make estimated tax payments with respect to any recognized built-in gain and excess passive investment income tax (discussed next).

- Any family member who renders services or furnishes capital to an S corporation must be paid reasonable compensation. Otherwise, the IRS can make adjustments to reflect the value of the services or capital. This rule may make it more difficult for related parties to shift S corporation taxable income to children or other family members.

- The flow-through of S items to a shareholder is not self-employment income and is not subject to the self-employment tax.[50] Compensation for services rendered to an S corporation is, however, subject to FICA taxes for the employee-shareholder. This treatment of earned income of S corporations is attractive compared to the treatment of a proprietorship or a partnership, whose income is taxed as self-employment income to the owners.

- A number of qualified fringe benefits, which typically are received by employees on a tax-free basis, are subject to Federal income tax when received by a more-than-2% shareholder-employee of an S corporation. These benefits include the value of group term life insurance, medical insurance, and meals and lodging furnished for the convenience of the employer. These items are treated as wages and are subject to most payroll taxes. The employee can deduct medical insurance premiums on his or her Form 1040.

- An S corporation is liable for a penalty if it does not file its Form 1120S on a timely basis. The penalty is $195 per month times the number of S shareholders, for up to 12 months.[51]

- An accrual basis S corporation uses the cash method of accounting for purposes of deducting business expenses and interest owed to a cash basis related party.[52] Thus, the timing of the shareholder's income and the corporate deduction must match.

- The various amounts needed to compute the domestic production activities deduction (DPAD; see Chapter 5) are passed through to the S corporation shareholders, and the deduction is computed at the shareholder level. For instance, domestic production gross receipts (DPGR), the corresponding cost of goods sold, and attributable W–2 wages, among other items, are separately stated items reported to the shareholders on a pro rata basis.

- The S election is not recognized by the District of Columbia and several states, including Connecticut, Michigan, and Tennessee. Thus, some or all of the entity's income may be subject to a state-level income tax.

- An S corporation may issue § 1244 stock to its shareholders to obtain ordinary loss treatment (see Chapter 8).

- Loss deductions may be disallowed due to a lack of a profit motive. If the activities at the corporate level are not profit-motivated, the losses may be disallowed under the hobby loss rules (see Chapter 11).[53]

BRIDGE DISCIPLINE   **Bridge to Public Finance**

Proceeds from the Federal self-employment tax are used by the Federal government to fund retirement and health care entitlements. Any shortfalls in these funds mean that the following may occur.

- Citizens needing retirement annuities and/or health care services will receive less than is needed. This may not be a desirable result in a moral or ethical sense, as life will be more difficult than it otherwise might be for those of modest means.

- Retirement income and health care services must be funded from general revenues, meaning almost exclusively funds from the Federal income tax. This represents a mismatch of payor and payee, an income redistribution result that would not be attractive to some. In a zero-sum sense, benefits of this sort reduce funding for other budgetary needs of the Federal government (e.g., for defense, transportation, or research).

---

[50]Rev.Rul. 59–221, 1959–1 C.B. 225.

[51]§ 6699. The penalty is waived if the entity can show reasonable cause for the failure to file.

[52]§ 267(b).

[53]§ 183; *Michael J. Houston,* 69 TCM 2360, T.C.Memo. 1995–159; *Mario G. De Mendoza, III,* 68 TCM 42, T.C.Memo. 1994–314.

15-4 ENTITY-LEVEL TAXES

LO.8

Compute the entity-level taxes on S corporations.

Normally, an S corporation does *not* pay any Federal income tax, because all items flow through to the shareholders. But an S corporation that previously was a C corporation may be required to pay a built-in gains tax, a LIFO recapture tax, a general business credit recapture, or a passive investment income tax.

15-4a Tax on Pre-Election Built-In Gain

Without the built-in gains tax , it would be possible to avoid the corporate double tax on a disposition of appreciated property by electing S corporation status.

> **EXAMPLE 31**
>
> Zinnia, Inc., a C corporation, owns a single asset with a basis of $100,000 and a fair market value of $500,000. If Zinnia sells this asset and distributes the cash to its shareholders, there are two levels of tax, one at the corporate level and one at the shareholder level. Alternatively, if Zinnia distributes the asset to its shareholders as a dividend, a double tax still results.
>
> In an attempt to avoid the double tax, Zinnia elects S corporation status. It then sells the asset and distributes the proceeds to shareholders. Without the built-in gains tax, the gain would be taxed only once, at the shareholder level. The distribution of the sales proceeds would be a tax-free reduction of the stock basis and the AAA. However, the built-in gains tax assures that Zinnia would not avoid the double tax. (See Example 32.)

The built-in gains tax generally applies to C corporations that convert to S status. It is a *corporate-level* tax on any built-in gain recognized when the S corporation disposes of an asset in a taxable disposition within 10 calendar years after the date on which the S election took effect. The 10-year holding period is reduced to 7 years for tax years beginning in 2009 and 2010, and to 5 years for tax years after 2010.[54]

General Rules

The base for the built-in gains tax includes any unrealized gain on appreciated assets (e.g., real estate, cash basis receivables, goodwill) held by a corporation on the day it elects S status. The highest corporate tax rate (currently 35 percent) is applied to the unrealized gain when any of the assets are sold. Any gain from the sale (net of the built-in gains tax)[55] also passes through as a taxable gain to shareholders.

> **EXAMPLE 32**
>
> Assume the same facts as in the preceding example. A corporate-level built-in gains tax must be paid by Zinnia if it sells the asset after electing S status. Upon sale of the asset, Zinnia owes a tax of $140,000 ($400,000 × 35%). In addition, Zinnia's shareholders report a $260,000 taxable flow-through gain ($400,000 − $140,000). The built-in gains tax effectively imposes a double tax on Zinnia and its shareholders, as would have been the case had Zinnia remained a C corporation.

In-depth coverage can be found on this book's companion website: www.cengagebrain.com   **7 DIGGING DEEPER**

The amount of built-in gain recognized in any year is limited to an *as if* taxable income for the year, computed as if the corporation were a C corporation. Any built-in gain that escapes taxation due to the taxable income limitation is carried forward and recognized in future tax years. Thus, a corporation can defer a built-in gain tax liability if it has a low or negative taxable income.

---

[54]§ 1374(d)(7)(B).   [55]§ 1366(f)(2).

EXAMPLE 33

Vinca, an S corporation, recognizes $400,000 of built-in gains during 2017. Had Vinca been a C corporation, its 2017 taxable income would have been $300,000. Thus, the amount of built-in gain subject to tax in 2017 is $300,000. The excess built-in gain of $100,000 is carried forward and taxed in 2018 (assuming adequate C corporation taxable income in that year).

There is no statutory limit on the carryforward period, but the gain would effectively expire at the end of the built-in gain recognition period.[56]

An S corporation can offset built-in gains with unexpired NOLs or capital losses from C corporation years.

EXAMPLE 34

Yowler, an S corporation, reports a built-in gain of $100,000 and taxable income of $90,000. Yowler holds a $12,000 NOL carryforward and an $8,000 capital loss carryforward from C corporation years prior to its S election. Yowler's built-in gains tax liability is calculated as follows.

Lesser of taxable income or built-in gain	$ 90,000
Less: NOL carryforward from C year	(12,000)
Capital loss carryforward from C year	(8,000)
Tax base	$ 70,000
Highest corporate income tax rate	× .35
Tentative tax	$ 24,500
Less: Business credit carryforward from C year	(4,000)
Built-in gains tax liability	$ 20,500

The $10,000 realized (but not taxed) built-in gain in excess of taxable income is carried forward to the next year, as long as the next year is within the built-in gain recognition period.

TAX PLANNING STRATEGIES **Managing the Built-In Gains Tax**

FRAMEWORK FOCUS: INCOME AND EXCLUSION

Strategy: Avoid Income Recognition.
    Postpone Recognition of Income to Achieve Tax Deferral.

Although limitations exist on contributions of loss property to the corporation before S status is elected, it still is possible for a corporation to minimize built-in gains and maximize built-in losses prior to the S election. A cash basis S corporation can accomplish this by reducing receivables, accelerating payables, and accruing compensation costs.

To further reduce or defer the tax, the corporation may take advantage of the taxable income limitation by shifting income and deductions to minimize taxable income in years when built-in gain is recognized. Although the postponed built-in gain is carried forward to future years, the time value of money makes the postponement beneficial. For example, paying compensation to shareholder-employees in place of a distribution creates a deduction that reduces taxable income and postpones the built-in gains tax.

Built-in *loss* property may be sold in the same year built-in gain property is sold to reduce or eliminate the built-in gains tax. Generally, the taxpayer should sell built-in loss property in a year when an equivalent amount of built-in gain property is sold. Otherwise, the built-in loss could be wasted.

EXAMPLE 35

Tulip, Inc., an S corporation, holds a built-in gain of $110,000 and reports current taxable income of $120,000 before payment of salaries to its shareholders. If Tulip pays at least $120,000 in salaries to the shareholders (rather than making a distribution), its taxable income drops to zero and the built-in gains tax is postponed. Thus, Tulip may want to keep its salaries higher, to postpone the built-in gains tax in future years and reap a benefit from the time value of money. Of course, paying the salaries may increase the associated payroll tax liabilities.

---

[56]§ 1374(d)(7); Notice 90–27, 1990–1 C.B. 336.

LIFO Recapture Tax

When a C corporation uses the FIFO method for its last year before making the S election, any built-in gain is recognized and taxed as the inventory is sold. A LIFO-basis corporation would not recognize this gain unless the corporation invaded the LIFO layer during the built-in gains tax period. To preclude a deferral of gain recognition by a C corporation that elects S status, any LIFO recapture amount at the time of the S election is subject to a corporate-level tax.

The taxable LIFO recapture amount equals the excess of the inventory's value under FIFO over the LIFO value. The resulting tax, determined by including the LIFO recapture amount in the last C corporation tax return, is payable in four equal installments, with the first payment due on or before the due date for the corporate return for the last C corporation year (without regard to any extensions). The remaining three installments are paid on or before the due dates of the succeeding corporate returns. No interest is due if payments are made by the due dates, and no estimated taxes are due on the four tax installments. No refund is allowed if the LIFO value is higher than the FIFO value.

EXAMPLE 36

Daffodil Corporation converts from a C corporation to an S corporation at the beginning of 2017. Daffodil used the LIFO inventory method in 2016 and held an ending LIFO inventory of $110,000 (FIFO value of $190,000). Daffodil's marginal tax rate on its final C corporation tax return is 35%.

Daffodil adds the $80,000 LIFO recapture amount to its 2016 taxable income, resulting in an increased tax liability of $28,000 ($80,000 × 35%). Daffodil pays one-fourth of the tax ($7,000) with its 2016 (final) C corporation tax return. The three succeeding installments of $7,000 each are paid with Daffodil's 2017–2019 S corporation tax returns.

15-4b **Passive Investment Income Penalty Tax**

A tax is imposed on the excess passive income of S corporations that possess AEP from C corporation years. The tax rate is the highest corporate income tax rate for the year (currently 35 percent). The rate is applied to excess net passive income (ENPI), which is determined using the following formula.

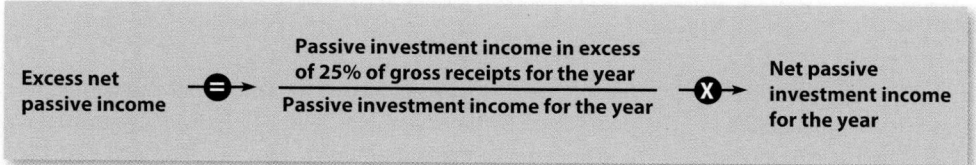

$$\text{Excess net passive income} = \frac{\text{Passive investment income in excess of 25\% of gross receipts for the year}}{\text{Passive investment income for the year}} \times \text{Net passive investment income for the year}$$

Passive investment income (PII) includes gross receipts derived from royalties, rents, dividends, interest, and annuities. Only the net gain from the disposition of capital assets is taken into account in computing PII gross receipts.[57] Net passive income is PII reduced by any deductions directly connected with the production of that income. Any PII tax reduces the gross income that flows through to the shareholders.

---

[57]§§ 1362(d)(3)(B) and (C).

TAX IN THE NEWS   The Self-Employment Income Advantage

A significant advantage of an S corporation involves the current definition of self-employment income. Although compensation for services rendered to an S corporation is subject to FICA taxes, a shareholder-employee's share of income from an S corporation is not self-employment income. The rationale for this discrepancy is that the S shareholder does not personally carry on the entity's trade or business. In contrast, the earned income of a partnership or proprietorship is treated as self-employment income to the partner or proprietor.

The choice between a salary and pass-through income is not clear-cut, however.

- Although a salary is subject to payroll tax and pass-through income is not [*P.B. Ding v. Comm.*, 2000–1 USTC

¶50137, 84 AFTR 2d 99–7517, 200 F.3d 587 (CA–9, 1999)], this income does not accrue Social Security benefits for its recipient.

- S corporation income distributions do not count as compensation for computing an employee's contribution formula for a qualified retirement plan.

- The IRS and the courts require an S shareholder to take a reasonable salary.

- If a partner or proprietor reports salary income from other sources and the aggregate salaries exceed the annual FICA ceiling, the partnership or proprietorship may provide tax savings compared to those of an S corporation.

The excess net passive income (ENPI) cannot exceed a hypothetical C corporate taxable income for the year, before considering special C corporation deductions (e.g., the dividends received deduction) or an NOL carryover.[58]

EXAMPLE 37

Lilac Corporation, an electing S corporation, records gross receipts totaling $264,000 (of which $110,000 is PII). Expenditures directly connected to the production of the PII total $30,000. Therefore, Lilac reports net PII of $80,000 ($110,000 − $30,000), and its PII exceeds 25% of its gross receipts by $44,000 [$110,000 PII − (25% × $264,000)]. Excess net passive income (ENPI) is $32,000, calculated as follows.

$$\text{ENPI} = \frac{\$44,000}{\$110,000} \times \$80,000 = \$32,000$$

Lilac's PII tax is $11,200 ($32,000 × 35%).

TAX PLANNING STRATEGIES   Avoid PII Pitfalls

FRAMEWORK FOCUS: TAX RATE

Strategy: Avoid Double Taxation.

Watch for a possible violation of the PII limitation. Avoid a consecutive third year with excess passive income when the corporation has accumulated E & P from C corporation years. In this connection, assets that produce passive income (e.g., stocks and bonds, certain rental assets) might be retained by the shareholders in their individual capacities and kept out of the corporation.

DIGGING DEEPER 8   **In-depth coverage can be found on this book's companion website:** www.cengagebrain.com

[58]§§ 1374(d)(4) and 1375(a) and (b).

TAX FACT The S Corporation Economy

Total assets controlled by S corporations make up a significant part of the economy. The 4.2 million S corporations that file Federal tax returns, representing over 9 million shareholders, employ $3.6 trillion in assets in their investments and operations.

Here are some more data about the S corporation sector.

- Trade or business income accounts for over 95 percent of all S corporation net income.
- About 70 percent of all S corporations report a positive amount of gross income.
- About 60 percent of all S corporations report business gross receipts of $250,000 or less.

15-5 SUMMARY

The S corporation rules are elective and can be used to benefit a number of owners of small businesses.

- When the business is profitable, the S corporation election removes the threat of double taxation on corporate profits.
- When the business is generating losses, deductions for allocable losses are immediately available to the shareholders.

About 70 percent of all U.S. corporations operate under the S rules. Flow-through income is taxed to the shareholders, who increase basis in their corporate stock accordingly. In this manner, subsequent distributions to shareholders can be made tax free. Flow-through losses reduce stock and debt basis, but loss deductions are suspended when basis reaches zero. Flow-through items that could be treated differently by various shareholders are separately stated on Schedule K–1 of the Form 1120S.

The S rules are designed for the closely held business with a simple capital structure. Eligibility rules are not oppressive, and they do not include any limitations on the corporation's capitalization value, sales, number or distribution of employees, or other operating measures. Accounting for an S corporation's shareholder distributions can be complex, though, and maintenance of S status must be monitored on an ongoing basis.

Corporate-level taxes seldom are assessed on S corporations, but they guard against abuses of the S rules, such as shifting appreciated assets from higher C corporation rates to lower individual rates (the built-in gains tax) or doing the same with investment assets (the tax on excessive PII).

REFOCUS ON THE BIG PICTURE

CONVERTING A C CORPORATION TO AN S CORPORATION

As long as Fowle, Inc., is a C corporation, David cannot deduct on his individual tax return the losses the business incurs. However, the corporation can carry any net operating losses (NOLs) back and claim refunds for prior taxes paid and carry any remaining NOLs forward to reduce taxes paid if the company becomes profitable again.

If David wants to deduct the losses on his individual return, the corporation should make an S election or possibly become an LLC. Assuming that Fowle meets the one class of stock requirement, an S election may be appropriate. The election should be made before any losses are incurred because any regular corporate NOLs do not flow through to an S shareholder.

Fowle should make a timely election on Form 2553, and David must consent to the election in writing. For the S election to be effective this year, it should be made on or before the fifteenth day of the third month of the current year.

continued

The S corporation's DPAD computations flow through to David, as does Fowle's tax-exempt interest income. The entity may want to reconsider its salary and fringe benefits levels for David, so as to minimize the creation of a payroll tax burden, and to manage the restrictions on deductions for fringe benefits provided to an S shareholder. Fowle's tax-exempt interest can be distributed to David tax free only after all of the entity's AEP has been accounted for.

What If?

What if David expects the loss years to be followed by increased profitability as the company shifts some of its manufacturing to other countries with cheaper labor and material costs? In this case, David expects that the corporation will make significant distributions to him. How might this affect David's decision about whether the corporation should make an S election?

David should be aware of several rules that may result in income tax being paid by the S corporation or by him as the shareholder. First, distributions from an S corporation may be treated as taxable dividends to a shareholder to the extent the S corporation has earnings and profits dating to its years as a C corporation. While distributions are deemed to be made first from accumulated net S corporation earnings (i.e., the balance in AAA), distributions in excess of that amount may be treated as a taxable dividend, being paid from AEP (accumulated E & P).

In addition, David should be aware that an S corporation that has been a C corporation in the past may be required to pay a built-in gains tax or LIFO recapture tax. The base for the built-in gains tax includes any unrealized gain on appreciated assets held by Fowle, Inc., on the day the company becomes an S corporation. The highest Federal corporate income tax rate is applied to the unrealized gains when any of the assets are sold within a specified number of years. If Fowle uses the LIFO inventory method, any LIFO recapture amount at the time of the S election also is subject to a corporate-level tax.

Suggested Readings

"Benefits of Using an S Corporation for Trading," **forbes.com**, May 13, 2014.

"Forming an S Corporation to Reduce Self-Employment Taxes," **www.mymoneyblog.com**.

John R. Cooper, "Appraisal Considerations in C to S Conversions," *Practical Tax Strategies*, November 2015.

Tony Nitti, "S Corporation Shareholder Compensation: How Much Is Enough?" *The Tax Adviser*, August 2011.

Ryan H. Pace, "Debunking the Notion That S Corporations Are Taxed 'Just Like' Partnerships," *Business Entities*, July/August 2007.

Key Terms

Computational Exercises

1. **LO.4** Dion, a shareholder, owned 20% of MeadowBrook's stock for 292 days and 25% for the remaining 73 days in the year. Using the per-day allocation method, compute Dion's share of the following S corporation items.

	Schedule K Totals	Dion's Schedule K–1 Totals
Ordinary income	$60,000	_____
Tax-exempt interest	1,000	_____
Charitable contributions	3,400	_____

2. **LO.4, 6** Greiner, Inc., a calendar year S corporation, holds no AEP. During the year, Chad, an individual shareholder, receives a $30,000 cash distribution from Greiner. Prior to the distribution, Chad's basis in his Greiner stock is $25,000.
   a. Determine Chad's ordinary income and capital gain, if any, from the distribution.
   b. What is the basis of Chad's Greiner stock after accounting for the distribution?

3. **LO.5, 6** Holbrook, a calendar year S corporation, distributes $15,000 cash to its only shareholder, Cody, on December 31. Cody's basis in his stock is $20,000, Holbrook's AAA balance is $8,000, and Holbrook holds $2,500 AEP before the distribution. Complete the chart below.

	Distribution from Account	Effect on Stock Basis	Balance after Distribution
From AAA Account	_____	_____	_____
From AEP Account	_____	_____	_____
From Cody's stock basis	_____	_____	_____

4. **LO.5** Ten years ago, Vogel, Inc., an S corporation, purchased a plot of investment land for $45,000. This year, Vogel distributed the land, now worth $120,000, to Jamari, its majority shareholder.
   a. Determine the effects of the distribution on the gross income of Vogel and Jamari, and on Vogel's AAA balance.
   b. How would your responses change if the land had been purchased for $120,000 and now was worth $45,000?

5. **LO.7** Kaiwan, Inc., a calendar year S corporation, is partly owned by Sharrod, whose beginning stock basis is $32,000. During the year, Sharrod's share of a Kaiwan long-term capital gain (LTCG) is $5,000, and his share of an ordinary loss is $18,000. Sharrod then receives a $20,000 cash distribution. Compute the following.
   a. Sharrod's deductible loss.
   b. Sharrod's suspended loss.
   c. Sharrod's new basis in the Kaiwan stock.

Problems

6. **LO.2** Which of the following can be a shareholder of an S corporation?
   a. Resident alien.
   b. Partnership.
   c. IRA.
   d. C corporation.

7. **LO.2** Isaac and 121 of his close friends want to form an S corporation. Isaac reasons that if he and his friends form a partnership, the partnership then can

establish an S corporation and act as a single shareholder, thereby avoiding the 100 shareholder rule. Will Isaac's plan work? Why or why not?

8. **LO.2** Joey lives in North Carolina, a common law state. He is a shareholder in an S corporation. If he marries a nonresident alien, will the S election terminate? Would your answer change if he lived in Louisiana? Explain.

Issue ID 9. **LO.3** On March 2, the two 50% shareholders of a calendar year corporation decide to elect S status. One of the shareholders, Terry, purchased her stock from a previous shareholder (a nonresident alien) on January 18 of the same year. Identify any potential problems for Terry or the corporation.

Communications 10. **LO.5, 6** Scott Tierney owns 21% of an S corporation. He is confused with respect to the amounts of the corporate AAA and his stock basis. Write a memo to the tax research file, identifying the key differences between AAA and an S shareholder's stock basis.

11. **LO.6** For each of the following independent statements, indicate whether the transaction will increase (+), decrease (−), or have no effect (*NE*) on the basis of a shareholder's stock in an S corporation.
   a. Expenses related to tax-exempt income.
   b. Short-term capital gain.
   c. Nonseparately computed loss.
   d. Section 1231 gain.
   e. Depletion *not* in excess of basis.
   f. Separately computed income.
   g. Nontaxable return-of-capital distribution by the corporation.
   h. Advertising expenses.
   i. Business gifts in excess of $25.
   j. Depreciation recapture income.
   k. Dividends received by the S corporation from an investment in ExxonMobil stock.
   l. LIFO recapture tax paid.
   m. Long-term capital loss.
   n. Cash distribution to shareholder out of AAA.

Issue ID 12. **LO.6, 7** Junie's share of her S corporation's net operating loss is $50,000, but her stock basis is only $30,000. Point out the Federal income tax consequences that Junie must face.

13. **LO.5, 6** Mary is a shareholder in CarrollCo, a calendar year S corporation. At the beginning of the year, her stock basis is $10,000, her share of the AAA is $2,000, and her share of corporate AEP is $6,000. At the end of the year, Mary receives a $6,000 cash distribution from CarrollCo.

   Mary's share of S corporation items includes a $2,000 long-term capital gain and a $10,000 ordinary loss. Determine the effects of these events on Mary's share of CarrollCo's AAA, on CarrollCo's AEP, and on Mary's stock basis.

14. **LO.4** The profit and loss statement of Kitsch Ltd., an S corporation, shows $100,000 book income. Kitsch is owned equally by four shareholders. From supplemental data, you obtain the following information about items that are included in book income.

Selling expenses	($21,200)
Tax-exempt interest income	3,000
Dividends received	9,000
§ 1231 gain	7,000
Depreciation recapture income	11,000
Collected bad debts previously deducted	5,000
Long-term capital loss	(6,000)
Salary paid to owners (each)	(12,000)
Cost of goods sold	(91,000)

a. Compute Kitsch's nonseparately stated income or loss for the tax year.

b. What would be the share of this year's nonseparately stated income or loss items for James Billings, one of the Kitsch shareholders?

15. **LO.4** Maul, Inc., a calendar year S corporation, incurred the following items.

Tax-exempt interest income	$ 7,000
Sales	140,000
Depreciation recapture income	12,000
Long-term capital gain	20,000
§ 1231 gain	7,000
Cost of goods sold	(42,000)
Administrative expenses	(15,000)
Depreciation expense (MACRS)	(17,000)
Charitable contributions	(7,000)

a. Calculate Maul's nonseparately computed income or loss.

b. If Carl is a 40% shareholder of Maul, what is Carl's share of Maul's long-term capital gain?

16. **LO.4** Zebra, Inc., a calendar year S corporation, incurred the following items this year. Sammy is a 40% Zebra shareholder throughout the year.

Operating income	$100,000
Cost of goods sold	(40,000)
Depreciation expense (MACRS)	(10,000)
Administrative expenses	(5,000)
§ 1231 gain	21,000
Depreciation recapture income	25,000
Short-term capital loss from stock sale	(6,000)
Long-term capital loss from stock sale	(4,000)
Long-term capital gain from stock sale	15,000
Charitable contributions	(4,500)

a. Calculate Sammy's share of Zebra's nonseparately computed income or loss.

b. Calculate Sammy's share of any Zebra long-term capital gain.

17. **LO.4** On January 1, Bobby and Alicia own equally all of the stock of an electing S corporation called Prairie Dirt Delight. The company has a $60,000 loss for the year (not a leap year). On the 219th day of the year, Bobby sells his half of the stock to his son, Bubba. How much of the $60,000 loss, if any, is allocated to Bubba?

18. **LO.4, 5** McLin, Inc., a calendar year S corporation, holds $90,000 of AEP. Tobias, the sole McLin shareholder, has an $80,000 basis in his stock with a zero balance in the AAA.

Decision Making

a. Determine the tax aspects if a $90,000 salary is paid to Tobias.

b. Same as part (a), except that Tobias receives a cash distribution of $90,000 from AEP.

19. **LO.4, 5** Tiger, Inc., a calendar year S corporation, is owned equally by four shareholders: Ann, Becky, Chris, and David. Tiger owns investment land that was purchased for $160,000 four years ago. On September 14, when the land is worth $240,000, it is distributed to David. Assuming that David's basis in his S corporation stock is $270,000 on the distribution date, discuss any Federal income tax ramifications.

20. **LO.4, 5, 6** Spence, Inc., a calendar year S corporation, generates an ordinary loss of $110,000 and makes a distribution of $140,000 to its sole shareholder, Storm Nelson. Nelson's stock basis and AAA at the beginning of the year both total $200,000. Write a memo to your senior manager, Aaron McMullin, discussing the tax treatment of Spence's activities.

Communications

21. **LO.5** Polly has been the sole shareholder of a calendar year S corporation since its inception. Polly's stock basis is $15,500, and she receives a distribution of $19,000. Corporate-level accounts indicate a $6,000 balance in AAA and a $500 balance in AEP. How is Polly taxed on the distribution? What is her stock basis after the distribution?

Communications 22. **LO.4, 7** Sweetie, a calendar year S corporation, reports an ordinary loss of $80,000 and a capital loss of $20,000. Mei Freiberg owns 30% of the corporate stock and holds a $24,000 basis in the stock. Determine the amounts of the ordinary loss and capital loss, if any, that flow through to Freiberg. Prepare a memo for the tax research files explaining your computations.

23. **LO.4, 5, 6** Valence Corporation's Form 1120S shows ordinary income of $88,000 for the year. Daniel owns 40% of the Valence stock throughout the year. The following information is obtained from the corporate records.

Salary paid to Daniel	($40,000)
Tax-exempt interest income	5,000
Charitable contributions	(6,000)
Dividends received from a non-U.S. corporation	5,000
Long-term capital loss	(6,000)
Depreciation recapture income	11,000
Refund of prior-year state income taxes	5,000
Cost of goods sold	(80,000)
Short-term capital loss	(7,000)
Administrative expenses	(18,000)
Short-term capital gain	14,000
Selling expenses	(11,000)
Daniel's beginning stock basis	32,000
Daniel's additional stock purchases	9,000
Beginning AAA	45,000
Daniel's loan to corporation	20,000

a. Compute Valence's book income or loss.

b. Compute Daniel's ending stock basis.

c. Calculate ending corporate AAA.

24. **LO.5** If the beginning balance in Swan, Inc.'s OAA is $6,700 and the following transactions occur, what is Swan's ending OAA balance?

Depreciation recapture income	$ 21,600
Payroll tax penalty	(4,200)
Tax-exempt interest income	4,012
Nontaxable life insurance proceeds	100,000
Life insurance premiums paid (nondeductible)	(3,007)

25. **LO.5, 6** Cougar, Inc., is a calendar year S corporation. Cougar's Form 1120S shows nonseparately stated ordinary income of $80,000 for the year. Johnny owns 40% of the Cougar stock throughout the year. The following information is obtained from Cougar's corporate records.

Tax-exempt interest income	$ 3,000
Salary paid to Johnny	(52,000)
Charitable contributions	(6,000)
Dividends received from a non-U.S. corporation	5,000
Short-term capital loss	(6,000)
Depreciation recapture income	11,000
Refund of prior state income taxes	5,000
Cost of goods sold	(72,000)

Long-term capital loss	($ 7,000)
Administrative expenses	(18,000)
Long-term capital gain	14,000
Selling expenses	(11,000)
Johnny's beginning stock basis	32,000
Johnny's additional stock purchases	9,000
Beginning AAA	31,000
Johnny's loan to corporation	20,000

a. Compute Cougar's book income or loss.

b. Compute Johnny's ending stock basis.

c. Calculate Cougar's ending AAA balance.

26. **LO.6** Maple, Inc., is an S corporation with a single shareholder, Bob Maple. Bob believes that his stock basis in the entity is $50,000, but he has lost some of the records to substantiate this amount. Maple reports an ordinary loss for the year of $80,000. What are the Federal income tax aspects to consider?   Issue ID

27. **LO.6, 7** Orange, Inc., a calendar year corporation in Clemson, South Carolina, elects S corporation status for 2016. The company generated a $74,000 NOL in 2015 and another NOL of $43,000 in 2016.   Issue ID

Orange stock always is owned by the same four shareholders, each owning 25% of the stock. Pete, one of the shareholders, holds a $6,020 basis in this Orange stock at the beginning of 2016. Identify the Federal income tax issues that Pete faces.

28. **LO.7** Samuel Reese sold 1,000 shares of his stock in Maroon, Inc., an S corporation. He sold the stock for $15,700 after he had owned it for six years. Samuel had paid $141,250 for the stock, which was issued under § 1244. Samuel is married and separately owns the 1,000 shares. Determine the appropriate Federal income tax treatment of any gain or loss on the stock sale.   Critical Thinking

29. **LO.7** Blue is the owner of all of the shares of Blue Bell, an S corporation. Blue is considering receiving a salary of $110,000 from the business. She will pay the 7.65% FICA taxes on the salary, and the S corporation will pay the same amount of FICA tax. If Blue reduces her salary to $50,000 and takes an additional $60,000 as a cash distribution from AAA, how would her Federal income tax liabilities change?   Critical Thinking / Decision Making

30. **LO.1** One of your clients, Texas, Inc., is considering electing S status. Both of Texas's equal shareholders paid $30,000 for their stock. As of the beginning of 2016, Texas's Subchapter C NOL carryforward is $110,000. Its taxable income projections for the next few years are as follows. Will you counsel Texas to make the S election? Explain.   Critical Thinking / Decision Making

2016	$40,000
2017	25,000
2018	25,000
2019	25,000

31. **LO.6, 7** C&C Properties is an S corporation that owns two rental real estate undertakings: Carrot Plaza and Cantaloupe Place. Both properties produce an annual $10,000 operating loss. C&C's Schedule K aggregates the results of the two locations into one number.   Critical Thinking

Dan and Marta, C&C's two equal shareholders, both hold a $7,000 stock basis in C&C as of the beginning of the year. Marta actively participates in the Cantaloupe location, but not at Carrot. Dan actively participates at neither location. Determine the amount of the available loss pass-throughs for both shareholders.

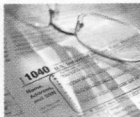

Comprehensive Tax Return Problem

Tax Return Problem

TAX SOFTWARE

1. John Parsons (123-45-6781) and George Smith (123-45-6782) are 70% and 30% owners, respectively, of Premium, Inc. (11-1111111), a candy company located at 1005 16th Street, Cut and Shoot, TX 77303. Premium's S election was made on January 15, 2009, its date of incorporation. The following information was taken from the company's 2015 income statement. Premium's book income for the year was $704,574.

Interest income	$ 100,000
Gross sales receipts	2,410,000
Beginning inventory	9,607
Direct labor	(203,102)
Direct materials purchased	(278,143)
Direct other costs	(249,356)
Ending inventory	3,467
Salaries and wages	(442,103)
Officers' salaries ($75,000 each to Parsons and Smith)	(150,000)
Repairs	(206,106)
Depreciation expense, tax and book	(15,254)
Interest expense	(35,222)
Rent expense (operating)	(40,000)
Taxes	(65,101)
Charitable contributions (cash)	(20,000)
Advertising expenses	(20,000)
Payroll penalties	(15,000)
Other deductions	(59,899)

A 2015 comparative balance sheet appears below.

	January 1	December 31
Cash	$ 47,840	$?
Accounts receivable	93,100	123,104
Inventories	9,607	3,467
Prepaid expenses	8,333	17,582
Building and equipment	138,203	185,348
Accumulated depreciation	(84,235)	(?)
Land	2,000	2,000
Total assets	$214,848	$844,422
Accounts payable	$ 42,500	$ 72,300
Notes payable (less than 1 year)	4,500	2,100
Notes payable (more than 1 year)	26,700	24,300
Capital stock	30,000	30,000
Retained earnings	111,148	?
Total liabilities and capital	$214,848	$844,422

Premium's accounting firm provides the following additional information.

Cash distributions to shareholders	$100,000
Beginning balance, accumulated adjustments account	$111,148

Using the preceding information, prepare a complete Form 1120S and Schedule K–1s for John Parsons and George Smith, both of whom live at 5607 20th Street, Cut and Shoot, TX 77303. Do not complete the Form 4562. If any information is missing, make realistic assumptions.

BRIDGE DISCIPLINE

1. Using an online research service, determine whether your state:
   a. Allows flow-through treatment for Federal S corporations.
   b. Requires any state-specific form to elect or elect out of S treatment at the state level.
   c. Places any additional withholding tax burdens on out-of-state U.S. shareholders or on non-U.S. shareholders of an S corporation.
   d. Requires any additional information disclosures or compliance deadlines for S corporations operating in the state *other than* to the revenue department (e.g., a report that must be filed with the secretary of state).
   e. Accepts "composite" or "block" income tax returns.

2. Using no more than five slides, at least two of which include a chart or graphic to illustrate your observations, prepare a presentation for your fellow students at the annual Pay It Forward conference at the university student union. In your talk, discuss the societal implications of the rule that excludes from the self-employment tax any flow-through income (other than salary and wages) that is assigned to a shareholder in an S corporation, while taxing that of the owners of a partnership or an LLC.

Communications

Research Problems

Note: Solutions to Research Problems can be prepared by using the Checkpoint® Student Edition online research product, which is available to accompany this text. It is also possible to prepare solutions to the Research Problems by using tax research materials found in a standard tax library.

THOMSON REUTERS
CHECKPOINT®
Student Edition

Research Problem 1. Alice owns 100% of Medical Data, a C corporation, and 100% of Your Realtors, an S corporation. She worked full time for Medical Data (i.e., she materially participated in the entity), but Alice did not materially participate in Your Realtors. During the tax years 2014 through 2016, Your Realtors leased real estate to Medical Data.

Decision Making

Alice reported these rental amounts as passive activity income on her Schedule E, and she offset that income against passive activity losses from other entities. The IRS reclassified this rental income as nonpassive income under Reg. § 1.469–2(f)(6). Who is right? Does § 469 apply to S corporations? Elaborate.

Research Problem 2. Sean Moon is president, secretary, treasurer, sole director, and sole shareholder of Streetz, an S corporation real estate company. He manages all aspects of the company's operations, and he is the only person working at the company that holds a real estate broker's license. Sean works 12-hour days and takes few days off. Corporate records indicate the following.

Year	Gross Receipts	Net Income
2015	$376,453	$122,605
2016	405,244	161,660
2017	518,189	231,454

Moon and his wife, Kim, filed joint Federal income tax returns, but they did not report any wages or salaries on their returns. During 2017, Moon transferred $240,000 from Streetz to his personal account.

You are an expert witness for the IRS. Identify the items that you would present to the U.S. Tax Court with respect to the amount of Moon's compensation that is subject to employment taxes and any other taxes due for 2017 (especially the additional Medicare net investment income tax). *Hint:* This is a reasonable compensation issue.

Internet Activity

Use the tax resources of the Internet to address the following questions. Do not restrict your search to the Web, but include a review of newsgroups and general reference materials, practitioner sites and resources, primary sources of the tax law, chat rooms and discussion groups, and other opportunities.

Communications   **Research Problem 3.** Use spreadsheet software to graph the growth in the number of S corporation returns filed. Obtain data for these years: 1980, 1985, 1990, 1995, 2000, 2005, and 2010. In a note to your instructor, explain the trends that you found in S returns filed.

Communications   **Research Problem 4.** Summarize the trends in court decisions concerning salaries paid to shareholders of small S corporations. Title your essay "S Corporation Salaries: Too Much or Too Little?" Send your essay in an e-mail to your instructor.

Communications   **Research Problem 5.** Summarize in no more than five slides the purpose and provisions of the S Corporation Modernization Act of 2009.

Roger CPA Review Questions

1. Mindy, an individual, owns 100% of Markee, an S corporation, and she has an initial stock basis of $10,000. This is the first year of Markee's operations. Additional items reported by Markee during the current year are:

Municipal bond interest	$10,000
Ordinary income	3,400
Shareholder distributions	5,000

    What was Mindy's basis in Markee at the end of the tax year?

    a. $5,000   c. $15,000
    b. $8,400   d. $18,400

2. Mindy, an individual, owns 100% of Markee, an S corporation, and she has an initial stock basis of $10,000. This is the first year of Markee's operations. Additional items reported by Markee during the current year are:

Municipal bond interest	$10,000
Ordinary income	3,400
Shareholder distributions	5,000

    What amount of the $5,000 distribution is taxable to Mindy?

    a. $0   c. $3,400
    b. $1,600   d. $5,000

3. Monie, an individual taxpayer, owns 50% of Monie & Co, an S corporation. At the beginning of the tax year, Monie's basis in Monie & Co stock was $55,000. During the year, Monie & Co realized ordinary loss in the amount of $45,000 and a short-term capital loss of $15,000. Monie & Co made total distributions of $70,000 to its shareholders during this taxable year. What amount of the $70,000 distribution is taxable to Monie?

    a. $70,000   c. $25,000
    b. $35,000   d. $10,000

4. Which of the following would cause a revocation of S status for an existing S corporation?

   I. A partnership becomes a shareholder of an S corporation
   II. An S corporation becomes a partner in a partnership
   III. An S corporation becomes a shareholder in a C corporation
   IV. A nonresident alien becomes a shareholder of an S corporation

   a. None of the above
   b. II and III

   c. I and IV
   d. All of the above

5. Rocket Co, an S corporation, pays single-coverage health insurance premiums of $17,000 per year. Philip is a 1% shareholder-employee in Rocket. On Philip's behalf, Rocket pays Philip's family coverage under the health insurance plan. What amount of insurance premiums is includible in Philip's gross income?

   a. $17,000
   b. $170

   c. $17
   d. $0

6. Shareholders of Rayle Co, a calendar year corporation whose S status was terminated during 2016, are looking to reapply for the S status as soon as possible. What is the earliest year a new S election can be made, in the absence of IRS consent to an earlier election?

   a. 2021
   b. 2020

   c. 2019
   d. 2016

7. Pankee, Inc., was formed as a C corporation and made an S election five years ago. Which of the following statements correctly describes the taxability of Pankee's distributions to its shareholders?

   a. A distribution to the shareholders will be taxable to the shareholders, if it is treated as coming from the S corporation's accumulated adjusted account and represents an amount already taxed to the shareholders

   b. A distribution to the shareholders will be nontaxable to the shareholders, if it is treated as coming from the S corporation's accumulated adjusted account and represents an amount already taxed to the shareholders

   c. A distribution to the shareholders will be nontaxable to the shareholders, if it is treated as coming from the S corporation's accumulated earnings and profits, earned during its years as a C corporation

   d. A distribution to the shareholders will be nontaxable to the shareholders regardless of whether it is treated as coming from the S corporation's accumulated adjusted account or its accumulated earnings and profits

8. As of January 1, 2015, Kirk owned all 300 shares of Cork, Inc., a calendar year S corporation. On September 1, 2015 (243 days after January 1), Kirk sold 50 shares each to Steve and Moe and kept the remaining 200 shares for himself. For the year ended December 31, 2015, Cork reported nonseparately computed income of $109,500 and made no distributions to its shareholders. What amount of nonseparately stated income from Cork should Kirk report on his 2015 tax return?

   a. $97,300
   b. $109,500

   c. $73,000
   d. $36,500

Part 6 covers several topics that are relevant to all types of business entities. Business entities operate in both the international and state arenas. Therefore, multijurisdictional taxation is addressed from both a multinational business and a multistate business perspective. A review then follows of tax credits allowed to reduce the Federal income tax liability on business income and the application of the AMT to C corporations. Part 6 concludes with a comparative analysis of the different types of business entities previously discussed.

Multijurisdictional Taxation

LEARNING OBJECTIVES: *After completing Chapter 16, you should be able to:*

LO.1 Discuss the computational and compliance issues that arise when a taxpayer operates in more than one taxing jurisdiction.

LO.2 Identify the sources of tax law applicable to a taxpayer operating in more than one country.

LO.3 Outline the U.S. tax effects related to the offshore operations of a U.S. taxpayer.

LO.4 Describe the tax effects related to the U.S. operations of a non-U.S. taxpayer.

LO.5 Identify the sources of tax law applicable to a taxpayer operating in more than one U.S. state.

LO.6 Apply principles designed to compute state taxable income for a taxpayer operating in more than one U.S. state.

LO.7 Synthesize key aspects of international and multistate tax systems to identify common rules and issues taxpayers face in both systems.

CHAPTER OUTLINE

TAX TALK *Don't tax you, don't tax me; tax the fellow behind the tree.* —RUSSELL B. LONG
Don't tax you, don't tax me; tax the companies across the sea. —DAN ROSTENKOWSKI

THE BIG PICTURE

GOING INTERNATIONAL

VoiceCo, a domestic corporation, designs, manufactures, and sells specialty microphones for use in theaters. All of its activities take place in Florida, although it ships products to customers all over the United States. When it received inquiries about its products from foreign customers, VoiceCo decided to test the foreign market and placed ads in foreign trade journals. Soon it was taking orders from foreign customers.

VoiceCo is concerned about its potential foreign income tax exposure. Although it has no assets or employees in the foreign jurisdictions, it now is involved in international commerce. Is VoiceCo subject to income taxes in foreign countries? Must it pay U.S. income taxes on the profits from its foreign sales? What if VoiceCo pays taxes to other countries? Does it receive any benefit from these payments on its U.S. tax return?

VoiceCo has established a manufacturing plant in Ireland to meet the European demand for its products. VoiceCo incorporated the Irish operation as a controlled foreign corporation (CFC) named VoiceCo-Ireland. So long as VoiceCo-Ireland does not distribute profits to VoiceCo, will the profits escape U.S. taxation? What are the consequences to VoiceCo of being the owner of the CFC?

Read the chapter and formulate your response.

One of the tax planning principles that has been discussed throughout this text relates to the use of favorable tax jurisdictions—moving income into lower-taxed districts and deductions into higher-taxed ones. Many individuals dream of moving all of their income and wealth to a tax-friendly state or a proverbial island in the tropics, never to be taxed again. This chapter examines the temptations that attract taxpayers to this idea and various ways in which this goal can and cannot be accomplished.

16-1 THE MULTIJURISDICTIONAL TAXPAYER

Discuss the computational and compliance issues that arise when a taxpayer operates in more than one taxing jurisdiction.

Companies large and small must deal with the consequences of earning income through activities in different jurisdictions. A small business may have its center of operations in a single city but have customers in many states and countries. Consider the typical U.S. multinational corporation. Its assets, employees, customers, suppliers, lenders, and owners are located in numerous locations, crossing city, county, state, national, and even "virtual" borders.

EXAMPLE 1

RobotCo, a corporation created and organized in Delaware, produces and sells robotic manufacturing equipment. It holds its valuable patents and intangible property in Delaware and Bermuda. The company has manufacturing operations in Ireland, Singapore, Germany, Texas, and New Jersey. It operates distribution centers in Canada, the United Kingdom, Germany, Hong Kong, Texas, New Jersey, Georgia, California, Illinois, and Arizona. RobotCo's sales force spends time in Europe, Asia, Mexico, Canada, and almost every state in the union. RobotCo's engineers likewise provide technical service to customers wherever they may be located. And in recent years, RobotCo has developed a substantial Web presence.

RobotCo must determine its potential exposure to tax in each of these jurisdictions. Such exposure usually is based on RobotCo's nexus (or economic connection) to the various locations. Unfortunately for all concerned, each of these taxing jurisdictions uses a different taxing system and methods, imposes taxes under differing structures, and even defines the tax base differently. How does RobotCo divide its income among the various jurisdictions that want a piece of the tax pie, determine its tax costs, mitigate any potential double taxation, and file the appropriate returns with this diverse set of taxing authorities? Such questions and more must be addressed by modern-day businesses.

Thousands of state and local jurisdictions are involved in the taxation of interstate transactions through income, property, sales, or other taxes. State and local taxes make up over one-third of all taxes collected in the United States. Global trade also represents a major portion of the U.S. economy. In a recent year, U.S. exports of goods and services amounted to $2.35 trillion, with imports reaching $2.85 trillion. U.S. companies hold direct investments abroad exceeding $5 trillion, and foreign companies had invested over $3 trillion in U.S. businesses. Hundreds of countries and many more political subdivisions participated in the taxation of these transactions. These interstate and international trade flows, along with cross-state and cross-country investments, create significant Federal, state, and local tax consequences for both U.S. and foreign entities.

16-2 U.S. TAXATION OF MULTINATIONAL TRANSACTIONS

Cross-border transactions create the need for special tax considerations for both the United States and its trading partners. From a U.S. perspective, international tax laws should promote the global competitiveness of U.S. enterprises and at the same time

BRIDGE·DISCIPLINE **Bridge to International Law**

Many of the provisions of the U.S. tax law relating to international transactions are thinly disguised extensions of a principle of international law—the ability of sovereign countries to protect the safety and privacy of their citizens abroad.

For instance, U.S. tax auditors often have difficulty obtaining or reviewing the documentation supporting deductions claimed by U.S. taxpayers operating overseas. Banking, credit card, and other records that are available (in the course of business or forcibly by summons) for strictly U.S. transactions are not available once those same transactions cross national borders.

How could the U.S. tax base include rental and royalty income of a U.S. investor operating through a corporation in another country when property ownership and taxation records are not available for substantiation or audit outside the country of the investment? Perhaps this explains why the U.S. tax base typically excludes such items.

Conversely, when the taxing agencies of multiple countries are allowed by law to trade among themselves information about business operations and taxpayers, the fairness and completeness of the taxing process may improve. But such lengthening of the reach of the taxing authorities results from diplomatic negotiations among the countries, not from the passage of legislation.

protect the tax revenue base of the United States. These two objectives sometimes conflict, however. The need to deal with both objectives contributes to the complexity of the rules governing the U.S. taxation of cross-border transactions.

U.S. persons engage in activities outside the United States for many different reasons. Consider two U.S. corporations that have established sales subsidiaries in foreign countries. Dedalus, Inc., operates in Germany, a high-tax country, because customers demand local attention from sales agents. Mulligan, Inc., operates in the Cayman Islands, a tax haven country, simply to shift income outside the United States. U.S. tax law must fairly address both situations with the same law.

EXAMPLE 2

U.S. international tax provisions are concerned primarily with two types of potential taxpayers: U.S. persons earning income from outside the United States and non-U.S. persons earning income from inside the United States.[1] U.S. persons earning income only from inside the United States do not create any international tax issues and are taxed under the purely domestic provisions of the Internal Revenue Code. Non-U.S. persons earning income from outside the United States are not within the taxing jurisdiction of the United States (unless this income is somehow directly connected to U.S. operations).

The U.S. taxation of international transactions can be organized in terms of "outbound" and "inbound" taxation. **Outbound taxation** refers to the U.S. taxation of foreign-source income earned by U.S. taxpayers. **Inbound taxation** refers to the U.S. taxation of U.S.-source income earned by foreign taxpayers. Exhibit 16.1 summarizes these concepts.

U.S. taxpayers often "internationalize" gradually over time. A U.S. business may operate on a strictly domestic basis for several years, then explore offshore markets by exporting its products abroad, and later license its products to a foreign manufacturer or enter into a joint venture with a foreign partner. If its forays into non-U.S. markets are successful, the U.S. business may create a foreign subsidiary and move a portion of its operations abroad by establishing a sales or manufacturing facility.

---

[1]The term *person* includes an individual, corporation, partnership, trust, estate, or association. § 7701(a)(1). The terms *domestic* and *foreign* are defined in §§ 7701(a)(4) and (5).

EXHIBIT 16.1   **U.S. Taxation of Cross-Border Transactions**

```
                          Taxpayer

              U.S.                      Non-U.S.

U.S.-source      Foreign-source    U.S.-source      Foreign-source
income           income            income           income

Taxed in         Taxed in both     Potentially      Generally taxed
United States*   U.S. and          taxed in         only in
                 non-U.S.          United States*   non-U.S.
                 jurisdictions*                     jurisdiction*

                 Foreign tax
                 credit
                 allowed
```

            "Outbound"   **"Inbound"**

*Income may or may not be subject to tax in the non-U.S. jurisdiction, depending on local country tax law.
Some U.S.-source income is exempt from tax in the United States for both U.S. and non-U.S. persons.

For the U.S. owners, a domestically controlled foreign corporation can have significant U.S. tax consequences, including potential deferrals of income recognition from offshore activities. Non-U.S. businesses likewise enter the U.S. market in stages. In either case, each step generates increasingly significant international tax consequences. Exhibit 16.2 shows a typical timeline for "going global."

DIGGING DEEPER 1   In-depth coverage can be found on this book's companion website: **www.cengagebrain.com**

EXHIBIT 16.2   **Global Activities Timeline**

TIME

| Domestic operations only | Export | License to foreign person | Foreign branch | Separate foreign entity |

                 Current U.S. Taxation   **Potential Deferral**

16-2a **Sources of Law**

U.S. individuals and companies operating across national borders are subject to the laws of every jurisdiction in which they operate or invest. Accordingly, the source of law depends on the nature of a taxpayer's connection with a particular country.

LO.2

Identify the sources of tax law applicable to a taxpayer operating in more than one country.

For U.S. persons, the Internal Revenue Code addresses the tax consequences of earning income anywhere in the world. However, U.S. persons also must comply with the local tax law of the other nations in which they operate.

For non-U.S. persons, U.S. statutory law is relevant to income they earn that is connected to U.S. income-producing activities, whether those activities involve a passive investment or an active trade or business. Whether non-U.S. persons also are subject to potential tax in their home countries on their U.S. income depends on their own local tax law.

It is difficult for the United States (or any country) to craft local tax laws that equitably address all of the potential issues that arise when two countries attempt to tax the same income. Furthermore, any uncertainty as to tax consequences can be an impediment to global business investment. Consequently, countries enter into income tax treaties with each other to provide more certainty to taxpayers.

Tax treaties are the result of specific negotiations with a treaty partner, so each treaty is unique. Nevertheless, all tax treaties are organized in the same way and address similar issues. For example, all treaties include provisions regarding the taxation of investment income, business profits from a permanent establishment (PE), personal service income, and exceptions for certain persons (e.g., athletes, entertainers, students, and teachers).

Permanent establishment (PE) is an important concept that is defined in all income tax treaties. A person has a PE within a country when its activities within that country rise beyond a minimal level. Tax treaties outline the activities that create a PE, including an office, plant, or other fixed place of business. Treaties also specify certain activities that do not create a PE (e.g., a temporary construction project). Once a person has a PE within a country, the business profits associated with the PE become subject to tax in that country.

Amelia, Inc., a U.S. corporation, sells boating supplies to customers in the United States and Canada. Amelia has no assets in Canada. All Canadian sales transactions are conducted via the Internet or telephone from Amelia's Florida office. Because Amelia does not have any assets in Canada or conduct any activities within Canada, it does not have a Canadian PE. Consequently, Canada does not impose an income tax on the profit associated with Amelia's Canadian sales. However, if Amelia opens a sales office in Canada, a PE will exist, and Canada will tax the profits associated with the PE.

EXAMPLE 3

Although the United States has entered into almost 70 income tax treaties, many jurisdictions where U.S. taxpayers operate are not covered by a treaty. Where there is no tax treaty, the more subjective test of whether a person is "engaged in a trade or business" within a country replaces the PE determination. Both the PE concept and the engaged in a trade or business concept are closely related to the determination of whether a person has nexus within a jurisdiction for state and local tax purposes (discussed later in this chapter).

16-2b **Tax Issues**

Authority to Tax

LO.3

Outline the U.S. tax effects related to the offshore operations of a U.S. taxpayer.

The United States taxes the *worldwide* income of U.S. taxpayers.[2] The United States claims the right to tax all of a U.S. person's income because of the protection of

---

[2]Gross income for a U.S. person includes all income from whatever source derived. "Source" in this context means not only type of income (e.g., wages or interest) but also geographic source (e.g., the United States or Belgium). § 61.

TAX FACT U.S. Income Tax Treaties in Force

The United States has entered into income tax treaties with the following nations.

Armenia	France	Lithuania	South Africa
Australia	Georgia	Luxembourg	Spain
Austria	Germany	Malta	Sri Lanka
Azerbaijan	Greece	Mexico	Sweden
Bangladesh	Hungary	Moldova	Switzerland
Barbados	Iceland	Morocco	Tajikistan
Belarus	India	Netherlands	Thailand
Belgium	Indonesia	New Zealand	Trinidad
Bulgaria	Ireland	Norway	Tunisia
Canada	Israel	Pakistan	Turkey
China	Italy	Philippines	Turkmenistan
Cyprus	Jamaica	Poland	Ukraine
Czech Republic	Japan	Portugal	United Kingdom
Denmark	Kazakhstan	Romania	Uzbekistan
Egypt	Korea	Russia	Venezuela
Estonia	Kyrgyzstan	Slovak Republic	
Finland	Latvia	Slovenia	

U.S. law provided to a person connected to the United States through citizenship, residency, or place of organization.

Because non-U.S. governments also may tax some of the U.S. person's income when it is earned within the other country's borders, U.S. taxpayers may be subjected to double taxation. There are two broad methods of mitigating this double taxation problem. Under the *territorial* approach, a country simply exempts from tax the income derived from sources outside its borders. Most European and Asian countries have adopted this approach.[3] The second approach, and the one adopted by the United States, is to tax the *worldwide* income of all domestic persons and then provide a **foreign tax credit** (FTC) against home country taxes for taxes paid to other countries on the same income. The United States allows its taxpayers to reduce their U.S. tax liability by some or all of the foreign income taxes paid on income earned outside the United States.

EXAMPLE 4

Gator Enterprises, Inc., a U.S. corporation, operates a manufacturing branch in Italy because of customer demand there, local availability of raw materials, and the high cost of shipping finished goods. This branch income is taxed in the United States as part of Gator's worldwide income, but it also is taxed in Italy. Without the availability of a foreign tax credit to mitigate this double taxation, Gator Enterprises would suffer an excessive tax burden and could not compete with local Italian companies.

The United States does adopt the territorial approach in taxing non-U.S. persons. Such inbound taxpayers generally are subject to tax only on income earned within U.S. borders.

EXAMPLE 5

Purdie, Ltd., a corporation based in the United Kingdom, operates in the United States. Although it is not a U.S. person, Purdie is taxed in the United States on its U.S.-source business income. If Purdie, Ltd., could operate free of U.S. tax, its U.S.-based competitors would face a serious disadvantage.

---

[3]In some cases, countries allow the territorial exemption from home country taxation only if the income has been subject to tax in another country. Other countries, however, exempt such income even if no source country tax is imposed.

FINANCIAL DISCLOSURE INSIGHTS **Effective Tax Strategies Using Overseas Operations**

In a global economy, publicly traded business entities can operate in many taxing jurisdictions. For instance, General Electric reports that it files current-year tax returns with more than 250 countries, amounting to over 7,000 income tax returns at the Federal and local levels worldwide. Note that this tax activity does not take into account the sales, value added, property, and other tax returns that are required by the U.S. states and localities.

The financial reports of profitable U.S. companies indicate that overseas operations can produce tax benefits of their own, not taking into account the effects of increased market share and financial stability. For instance, the trucking firm Ryder Systems recently reported current tax refunds of about $235,000 and deferred tax savings of about $500,000 on non-U.S. profits of about $11.5 million.

In a recent period, Eli Lilly reduced its effective tax rate by about one-third due to overseas operations. And General Electric recently reduced its effective tax rate to a negative amount because of various income deferrals related to overseas earnings. These deferral techniques are discussed later in the chapter.

Income Sourcing

Determining the source of net income is a critical component in calculating the U.S. tax consequences to both U.S. and foreign persons. A number of specific provisions contained in §§ 861 through 865 address the income-sourcing rules for all types of income, including interest, dividends, rents, royalties, services, and sales of assets. Although sometimes complex and subject to various special exceptions, these sourcing rules generally assign income to a geographic source based on the location where the economic activity producing the income took place. In some cases, this relationship is clear, and in others, the connection is more obscure.

Sourcing Rules

EXAMPLE 6

Wickless, Inc., a U.S. corporation, provides scuba diving lessons to customers in Florida and in the Bahamas. These services are sourced based on the place where the activity is performed. The services performed in Florida are U.S.-source income, and those performed in the Bahamas are foreign-source income. Because Wickless, Inc., is a U.S. person, all the income, U.S. and foreign, is subject to U.S. taxation. But the foreign-source portion is important in determining any available foreign tax credits for Wickless.

EXAMPLE 7

Brown, Inc., a U.S. corporation, receives dividend income from Takeda Corporation, a Japanese corporation, based on its ownership of Takeda common stock. Brown purchased the stock in the United States and receives all payments in the United States. At first glance, it appears that all of the activities related to earning the dividend income take place in the United States. Nevertheless, the dividend income is treated as foreign source because it is paid by a foreign corporation.[4]

In addition to sourcing income, the U.S. rules require taxpayers to assign deductions to U.S.- or foreign-source categories. Deductions that are directly related to an activity or property are first allocated to classes of income to which they directly relate (e.g., sales, services, rentals). This is followed by an apportionment between the U.S. and foreign groupings using some reasonable basis (e.g., revenue, gross profit, assets, units sold, time spent). If a deduction is not definitely related to any class of gross income, the deduction is first assigned to all classes of gross income and then apportioned between U.S.- and foreign-source income.

---

[4]Section 861(a)(2) establishes that only dividends from domestic corporations are U.S.-source income.

TAX FACT **Where Do We Stand?**

The drastic reductions in marginal tax rates brought about in the United States in 1981 and 1986, and the ongoing effort by Congress to make the Federal corporate income tax neutral as to the business decisions of U.S. entities operating in the global economy, have rippled through the rest of the world. Even perpetually high-tax countries such as Sweden and the United Kingdom were forced to cut back marginal tax rate structures to remain competitive and often had to change the tax base to match the revisions of the U.S. tax law.

As a result of this dramatic evolution in international tax rates, the average marginal business income tax rate in developed countries now lies between 25 and 30 percent, down from perhaps 50 percent in the 1960s. This description does not take into account, though, the dependence of many U.S. trading partners on transaction taxes, such as the value added tax and wealth-based taxes, which make difficult an apples-to-apples comparison of rates alone. Further, each country treats payroll taxes and entitlements differently, and these are increasingly expensive components of the tax structure. After taking these other taxes into account, the United States may be closer to the worldwide average.

But U.S. corporate income tax law has not changed much since the 1980s, and the rest of the world appears to be continuing the rate-cutting the United States started. The United States may need another round of rate cuts to stay in the game. By one measure, at least, after significant rate cuts by Japan and the United Kingdom, the United States applies the highest corporate income tax rate in the developed world.

Top Statutory Corporate Income Tax Rates for Selected Countries	
Bermuda	0.0%
France	34.4%
Germany	30.2%
Ireland	12.5%
Japan	32.1%
Mexico	30.0%
Sweden	22.0%
United Kingdom	20.0%
United States	39.0%

Note: Includes additional taxes on corporate taxable income levied by states, cities, provinces, cantons, and other smaller jurisdictions.

The Big Picture

EXAMPLE 8

Return to the facts of *The Big Picture* on p. 16-1. Assume that VoiceCo makes an overseas investment and generates $2 million of gross income and a $50,000 expense, all related to its microphone manufacturing and sales. The expense is allocated and apportioned on the basis of gross income.

	Gross Income			Apportionment	
	Foreign	U.S.	Allocation	Foreign	U.S.
Sales	$1,000,000	$500,000	$37,500*	$25,000	$12,500**
Manufacturing	400,000	100,000	12,500	10,000	2,500***
Totals			$50,000	$35,000	$15,000

* $50,000 × ($1,500,000/$2,000,000) = $37,500.
** $37,500 × ($500,000/$1,500,000) = $12,500.
*** $12,500 × ($100,000/$500,000) = $2,500.

If VoiceCo could show that $45,000 of the expense was directly related to its sales income, the $45,000 would be allocated directly to that class of gross income, with the remainder allocated and apportioned between U.S. and foreign source ratably.

		Apportionment	
	Allocation	Foreign	U.S.
Sales	$45,000	$30,000	$15,000
Manufacturing	5,000	4,000	1,000
Totals	$50,000	$34,000	$16,000

GLOBAL TAX ISSUES   Deferral and Repatriation

U.S. taxpayers with offshore operations have a choice as to how they structure such operations for U.S. tax purposes. If the U.S. taxpayer operates through an unincorporated foreign branch, the net profits from the branch are subject to current taxation in the U.S. tax return of the U.S. taxpayer.

If instead the U.S. taxpayer operates abroad through a separate wholly owned foreign corporation, the income from the operation is deferred from U.S. taxation until the profits are repatriated back to the United States (via a dividend or similar distribution), or when they are treated as repatriated through the operation of the Subpart F deemed dividend provisions (as discussed later). This option can have a significant effect on a U.S. taxpayer's current-period tax burden, particularly if the foreign operations are in a lower-tax jurisdiction.

As discussed in Chapter 3, under ASC 740 (APB 23), this deferral of taxes also can reduce the financial statement tax expense if the offshore profits are reinvested indefinitely outside the United States.

Many deductions may be allocated and apportioned based on any reasonable method the taxpayer chooses.[5] However, the U.S. tax rules impose a specific method for certain types of deductions, including interest and research and experimentation expenses. Interest expense is allocated and apportioned based on the theory that money is fungible. For example, if a taxpayer borrows to support its manufacturing activity, this frees up other funds for use to support its investment activities. Accordingly, the tax rules require that interest expense be allocated and apportioned to all activities and property of the taxpayer, regardless of the specific purpose for incurring the debt on which interest is paid. Taxpayers must allocate and apportion interest expense on the basis of asset location, using either the fair market value or the tax book value of the assets.

TAX IN THE NEWS   The IRS Watches from Abroad

Taxpayers long have tried to shield information from the IRS about assets and income (e.g., in the proverbial Swiss bank account). Computing resources and cooperation among government taxing authorities make it more difficult to do so than ever before.

The IRS stations agents in Beijing, Hong Kong, Sydney, the British Virgin Islands (BVI), and other jurisdictions where it perceives that taxpayers are shifting financial resources with tax evasion motives. For instance, the Treasury pays attention when it learns that the profits of U.S. corporations entail over 1,000 percent of the GDP of the Cayman Islands and of the BVI. When U.S. profits constitute 38 percent of Ireland's GDP, and 15 percent of that of the Netherlands, something more than just business decisions likely are involved.

It often takes many years for the U.S. government to put together a case to show the tax evasion activities of a U.S. person. Typical IRS tools include information-sharing agreements among governments and/or taxing agencies, whistleblower programs, and litigation.

The U.S. Foreign Account Tax Compliance Act (FATCA) requires that a bank (even one organized outside the United States) provide the IRS with certain identifying information about all U.S. persons with an account at the bank. FATCA, along with other efforts to disclose holdings in non-U.S. banks, can be an effective revenue-raiser for the United States.

---

[5]Reg. § 1.861–8.

The Big Picture

EXAMPLE 9

Return to the facts of *The Big Picture* on p. 16-1. Assume that VoiceCo makes an overseas investment and generates both U.S.-source and foreign-source gross income for the current year. VoiceCo's assets (measured at tax book value) are as follows.

Assets generating U.S.-source income	$18,000,000
Assets generating foreign-source income	5,000,000
	$23,000,000

VoiceCo incurs interest expense of $800,000 for the current year. Using the tax book value method, interest expense is apportioned to foreign-source income as follows.

$$\frac{\$5,000,000 \text{ (foreign assets)}}{\$23,000,000 \text{ (total assets)}} \times \$800,000 \text{ (interest expense)} = \$173,913$$

TAX PLANNING STRATEGIES   Sourcing Income from Sales of Inventory

FRAMEWORK FOCUS: TAX RATE

Strategy: Control the Character of Income and Deductions.

Generally, income from the sale of personal property is sourced according to the residence of the seller under § 865. Several important exceptions exist for inventory. Income from the sale of purchased inventory is sourced in the country in which the sale takes place under the "title passage" rule. This rule provides the taxpayer with flexibility regarding the sourcing of income and deductions, and it allows for the creation of zero-taxed foreign-source income.

USCo, a domestic corporation, purchases inventory for resale from unrelated parties and sells the inventory to customers in the United States and Brazil. If title on the Brazilian sales passes in the United States (i.e., risks of loss shift to the Brazilian customers at the shipping point), the inventory income is U.S. source. If title passes outside the United States (e.g., at the customer's warehouse in Brazil), the inventory income is foreign source.

Although the Code identifies the income item as foreign source, this income likely is not subject to any Brazilian tax because USCo has no employees, assets, or

activities in Brazil. Although the income is subject to U.S. tax in either case (as it represents taxable income to a U.S. person), in the latter case, USCo has generated foreign-source income with no corresponding foreign income tax. This will prove useful in managing USCo's ability to use foreign tax credits, as discussed later in this chapter.

When a taxpayer both produces and sells inventory, the income is apportioned between the country of production and the country of sale. Taxpayers often elect a 50–50 allocation method as allowed by § 863(b), where 50 percent of the profits from the sale are automatically assigned to the location of the production assets and 50 percent of the profits are assigned to the location where title passes.

Assume that USCo manufactures inventory in its Texas plant and sells the inventory to customers in Mexico. Regardless of the actual economic profit relationship between the manufacturing and selling activities, 50 percent of the profit on the Mexican sales can be assigned to foreign-source income by simply passing title outside the United States.

Foreign Tax Credit

As discussed earlier, the United States retains the right to tax its citizens and residents on their worldwide taxable income. To reduce the possibility of double taxation, Congress created the foreign tax credit (FTC).

A qualified taxpayer is allowed a tax credit for foreign income taxes paid or accrued. All of the taxes paid by the taxpayer to various countries on its operations are combined to compute the FTC. The credit is a dollar-for-dollar reduction of U.S. income tax liability.

TAX FACT **Corporate Use of the Foreign Tax Credit**

Information from recent Forms 1120 indicates that the foreign tax credit is used by a small number of corporate taxpayers, but that the credit spans a very large portion of the global economy.

Of foreign tax payments reported on Forms 1118 and 1120, more than 45 percent were paid to European countries, with the most going to the United Kingdom, Luxembourg, Norway, and the Netherlands. Tax payments to Canada accounted for 5 percent of the total. Pacific Rim countries received over 8 percent of total foreign tax payments, and all of Africa totaled only about 7 percent.

Tax returns claiming a foreign tax credit	7,200
Total assets of corporations claiming the credit	$32.2 trillion
Taxable income of corporations claiming the credit	$833 billion
U.S. income tax liability of corporations claiming the credit	$292 billion
Foreign tax credit claimed	$110 billion
Foreign income taxes available for the credit	$210 billion

Applying the FTC

EXAMPLE 10

Caulkin Tools, Inc., a U.S. corporation, operates a branch operation in Mexico from which it earns taxable income of $750,000 for the current year. Caulkin pays income tax of $150,000 on these earnings to the Mexican tax authorities. Caulkin also includes the $750,000 in gross income for U.S. tax purposes.

Before considering the FTC, Caulkin owes $255,000 in U.S. income taxes on this foreign-source income. Thus, total taxes on the $750,000 could equal $405,000 ($150,000 + $255,000), a 54% effective rate.

But Caulkin takes an FTC of $150,000 against its U.S. tax liability on the foreign-source income. Caulkin's total taxes on the $750,000 now are $255,000 ($150,000 + $105,000), a 34% effective rate.

EXAMPLE 11

MettCo, Inc., a domestic corporation, receives a $5,000 dividend from DeanCo, Ltd., a foreign corporation owned less than 5% by MettCo. The foreign country imposes a 20% withholding tax on dividend payments to nonresidents. Accordingly, DeanCo withholds $1,000 ($5,000 × 20%) from the dividend and remits this tax to the local country tax authorities. DeanCo pays the remaining $4,000 to MettCo.

Although MettCo did not directly pay the $1,000 in foreign tax, the entire amount is allowed as a direct tax to MettCo for FTC purposes. MettCo reports $5,000 in dividend income on its U.S. tax return (the gross amount of the dividend), but it receives an FTC against any U.S. tax for the $1,000 in foreign withholding tax.

The FTC is elective for the tax year. Lacking an election to take the FTC, a deduction is claimed for foreign taxes paid or incurred. One cannot take a credit and a deduction for the same foreign income taxes, and in most situations, the FTC is more valuable to the taxpayer.

FTC Limits The United States does not grant an FTC for all foreign taxes paid, and there are limits on the amount of foreign taxes that can be taken as a credit. First, only foreign *income* taxes are potentially creditable. Second, the FTC allowed in any tax year is limited to the U.S. tax imposed on the foreign-source income included on the U.S. tax return.[6] Thus, taxpayers are allowed a credit for the lesser of the foreign income taxes paid or accrued or the following limitation.

$$\text{FTC limit} = \frac{\text{Foreign-source taxable income}}{\text{Worldwide taxable income}} \times \text{U.S. tax liability before FTC}$$

---

[6]Sections 901, 902, and 903 provide definitions of creditable foreign taxes. Section 904 contains the FTC limitation rules.

Worldwide taxable income is the total taxable income reported on the taxpayer's U.S. tax return, not the total worldwide income of a group of related domestic and foreign entities. Any potential FTCs disallowed because of the FTC limitation may be carried back 1 year or forward 10 years, subject to the FTC limits in those tax years.

EXAMPLE 12

Lassaline, Inc., a domestic corporation, invests in the bonds of non-U.S. corporations. Lassaline's worldwide taxable income for the tax year is $1.2 million, consisting of $1 million of profits from U.S. sales and $200,000 of interest income from foreign sources. Foreign taxes of $90,000 were withheld on these interest payments.

Lassaline's U.S. tax before the FTC is $408,000. Its FTC is limited to $68,000 [($200,000/$1,200,000) × $408,000]. Thus, Lassaline's net U.S. tax liability is $340,000 after allowing the $68,000 FTC. The remaining $22,000 of FTCs ($90,000 − $68,000) may be carried back or forward.

TAX PLANNING STRATEGIES Utilizing the Foreign Tax Credit

FRAMEWORK FOCUS: TAX CREDITS

Strategy: Maximize Tax Credits.

The FTC limitation can prevent the total amount of foreign taxes paid in high-tax jurisdictions from being credited. Taxpayers can overcome this problem by generating additional foreign-source income that is subject to no or low foreign taxation.

A U.S. taxpayer's ability to use FTCs is directly related to its level of foreign-source income relative to its total taxable income. To the extent a U.S. taxpayer can keep the average tax rate on its foreign-source income at or below the U.S. tax rate on such income, the foreign taxes will be fully creditable. Consequently, combining high- and low-tax foreign-source income is an important planning objective.

EXAMPLE 13

Compare the following scenarios where Genius, a U.S. corporation, incurs FTC situations that differ depending on its ability to mix high- and low-taxed income. In the first scenario, Genius earns only $500,000 of highly taxed foreign-source income. In the second scenario, it also generates $100,000 of low-taxed foreign-source income.

	Only Highly Taxed Income	With Low-Taxed Income
Foreign-source income	$500,000	$600,000
Foreign taxes	275,000	280,000
U.S.-source income	700,000	700,000
U.S. taxes (34%)	408,000	442,000
FTC limitation	170,000*	204,000**

* ($500,000/$1,200,000) × $408,000 = $170,000.
** ($600,000/$1,300,000) × $442,000 = $204,000.

When the low-taxed income is added, Genius's actual foreign taxes increase by only $5,000 ($280,000 versus $275,000), but its FTC limitation increases by $34,000 (from $170,000 to $204,000). The ability to "cross-credit" high- and low-taxed foreign income is available, though, only when all of the foreign-source income is classified in the same income basket.

To limit the ability of U.S. taxpayers to cross-credit foreign taxes, the FTC rules provide for two separate foreign tax credit income categories (or baskets): passive and general. In any tax year, taxpayers are allowed to credit the lesser of foreign income taxes paid or accrued or the FTC limit only *within each separate basket*. The separate FTC limitation categories for different types of income each use this same basic FTC limitation formula. The separate limitation categories affect the amount of FTC that can be taken by generally segregating income subject to a high level of foreign tax from lower-taxed foreign income.

EXAMPLE 14

BenCo, Inc., a U.S. corporation, operates a foreign branch in Adagio that earns taxable income of $1.5 million from manufacturing operations and $600,000 from passive activities. BenCo pays Adagio income taxes of $600,000 (40%) and $100,000 ($16\frac{2}{3}\%$), respectively, on this foreign-source income.

The corporation earns $4 million of U.S.-source taxable income, resulting in worldwide taxable income of $6.1 million. BenCo's U.S. taxes before the FTC are $2,074,000 (at 34%). The following table illustrates the effect of the separate limitation baskets on cross-crediting.

Separate Foreign Income Category	Net Taxable Amount	Foreign Taxes	U.S. Tax before FTC at 34%	FTC Allowed with Separate Limits
General	$1,500,000	$600,000	$510,000	$510,000
Passive	600,000	100,000	204,000	100,000
Total	$2,100,000	$700,000	$714,000	$610,000

Without the separate limitation provisions, the FTC would be the lesser of (1) $700,000 foreign taxes or (2) $714,000 share of U.S. tax [($2,100,000/$6,100,000) × $2,074,000]. The "basket" provisions reduce the FTC by $90,000 ($700,000 versus $610,000). In this way, the foreign-source income taxed at the foreign tax rate of 40% cannot be aggregated with foreign-source income taxed at only $16\frac{2}{3}\%$.

Direct and Indirect FTCs U.S. taxpayers may claim FTCs for foreign taxes they pay directly or through withholding as so-called direct credits. In addition, U.S. corporate taxpayers may claim FTCs for foreign taxes paid indirectly. If a U.S. corporation operates in a foreign country through a branch, the direct credit is available to the U.S. parent for foreign taxes paid.

If, however, a U.S. corporation operates in a country through a foreign subsidiary, the direct credit is not available for foreign taxes paid by the foreign corporation. An indirect or **deemed-paid credit** is available to U.S. corporate taxpayers that receive actual or constructive dividends from foreign corporations that have paid foreign income taxes.[7] These foreign taxes are deemed paid by the corporate shareholders in the same proportion as the dividends actually or constructively received bear to the foreign corporation's undistributed E & P.

$$\text{Deemed-paid credit} = \frac{\text{Actual or constructive dividend}}{\text{Undistributed E \& P}} \times \text{Foreign taxes paid}$$

If a U.S. taxpayer claims a deemed-paid credit, § 78 requires the corporation to *gross up* (add to income) the dividend income by the amount of the deemed-paid credit. If the FTC is not claimed, the income gross-up is not required.

EXAMPLE 15

Wren, Inc., a domestic corporation, owns 50% of Finch, Inc., a foreign corporation. Wren receives a dividend of $120,000 from Finch. Finch paid foreign taxes of $500,000 on its E & P, which totals $1.2 million. Wren's deemed-paid foreign taxes for FTC purposes are $50,000.

Cash dividend from Finch	$120,000
Deemed-paid foreign taxes [($120,000/$1,200,000) × $500,000]	50,000
Gross income to Wren	$170,000

Wren includes $170,000 in gross income for the year. As a result of the dividend received, Wren can claim a credit for the $50,000 in deemed-paid foreign taxes.

---

[7]U.S. corporations must meet certain minimum ownership requirements under § 902 to claim a deemed-paid credit. In the formula for the indirect credit, only foreign taxes paid and E & P generated after 1986 are used.

FINANCIAL DISCLOSURE INSIGHTS **Overseas Operations and Book-Tax Differences**

Non-U.S. operations account for a large portion of the permanent book-tax differences of U.S. business entities. These differences may relate to different tax bases, different tax rate structures, or special provisions concerning tax-based financing with the other country. For instance, lower tax rates applied by Ireland, Bermuda, and the Netherlands recently reduced Cisco's current-year tax liabilities by about $1 billion per year.

Tax planning strategies using non-U.S. operations also are found in the deferred tax asset and liability accounts. Tax deferrals allowed under current U.S. tax rules and carryforwards of the foreign tax credit can be substantial for some businesses. For example, IBM recently reported a deferred tax asset relating to delays in using its FTCs amounting to about $500 million. For the operating arm of General Electric, that amount was about $2 billion.

DIGGING DEEPER 2   In-depth coverage can be found on this book's companion website: www.cengagebrain.com

Controlled Foreign Corporations

Foreign corporations—even those controlled by U.S. shareholders—generally are not included in a U.S. consolidated income tax return. Consequently, in the absence of some other provision, the income of a foreign corporation is included on the U.S. shareholder's U.S. income tax return only when dividend income is received. To minimize current U.S. tax liability, taxpayers often attempt to defer the recognition of taxable income. One way to do this is to shift the income-generating activity to a foreign entity; then the income earned will not be subject to U.S. tax until it is repatriated.

For example, a U.S. person can create a foreign holding company to own the stock of foreign operating affiliates or intangible assets, such as patents and trademarks. Thus, the income generated by these offshore holdings would escape current U.S. taxation. A non-U.S. corporation also can be used to accumulate income from sales or service activities by acting as an intermediary between the U.S. corporation and an offshore customer. The subsidiary would be used to purchase goods from the U.S. parent or domestic affiliates and then resell the goods to overseas customers or provide services on behalf of the U.S. parent or affiliates.

In some cases, the use of intermediate overseas subsidiaries is based on a substantive business purpose. In other cases, they are employed only to reduce tax costs. Because of this potential for abuse, Congress has enacted various provisions to limit the availability of deferral.

The most important of these antideferral provisions are those affecting **controlled foreign corporations (CFCs)**. Subpart F of the Code provides that certain types of "tainted" income generated by CFCs are included in current-year gross income by the U.S. shareholders, without regard to actual distributions. U.S. shareholders must include in gross income their pro rata share of **Subpart F income**. This rule applies to U.S. shareholders who own stock in the corporation on the last day of the tax year or on the last day the foreign corporation is a CFC.

EXAMPLE 16

Jordan, Ltd., a calendar year foreign corporation, is a CFC for the entire tax year. Taylor, Inc., a U.S. corporation, owns 60% of Jordan's one class of stock for the entire year. Jordan earned $100,000 of Subpart F income for the year and makes no actual distributions during the year. Taylor, a calendar year taxpayer, includes $60,000 in gross income as a constructive dividend for the tax year.

To the extent Jordan has paid any foreign income taxes, Taylor may claim an indirect foreign tax credit for the portion of the foreign taxes related to the $60,000 constructive dividend.

What Is a CFC? A CFC is any non-U.S. corporation in which more than 50 percent of the total combined voting power of all classes of voting stock, or the total value of the stock of the corporation, is owned by U.S. shareholders on any day during the taxable year of the foreign corporation. The offshore subsidiaries of most multinational U.S. parent corporations are CFCs.

For the purposes of determining whether a foreign corporation is a CFC, a **U.S. shareholder** is a U.S. person who owns, or is considered to own, 10 percent or more of the total combined voting power of all classes of voting stock of the foreign corporation. Stock owned directly, indirectly, and constructively is counted. Indirect ownership involves stock held through a foreign entity, such as a foreign corporation, foreign partnership, or foreign trust. This stock is considered to be actually owned proportionately by the shareholders, partners, or beneficiaries.

Constructive ownership rules, with certain modifications, apply in determining whether a U.S. person is a U.S. shareholder, in determining whether a foreign corporation is a CFC, and for certain related-party provisions of Subpart F.

Subpart F Income A U.S. shareholder of a CFC does not necessarily lose the ability to defer U.S. taxation of income earned by the CFC. Only certain income earned by the CFC triggers immediate U.S. taxation as a constructive dividend. This tainted income, often referred to as Subpart F income, can be characterized as income that is easily shifted or has little or no economic connection with the CFC's country of incorporation. Examples include:

- Passive/portfolio income such as interest, dividends, rents, and royalties.
- Sales income where neither the manufacturing activity nor the customer base is in the CFC's country and either the property supplier or the customer is related to the CFC.
- Service income where the CFC is providing services on behalf of its U.S. owners outside the CFC's country.

Subpart F Income

EXAMPLE 17

Collins, Inc., a domestic corporation, sells $1 million of its products to customers in Europe. All manufacturing and sales activities take place in the United States. Collins has no employees, assets, or operations in Europe and thus is not subject to income tax in any European jurisdiction.

Collins reported the following tax consequences from these inventory sales.

Sales revenue	$1,000,000
Cost of goods sold	(600,000)
Net income	$ 400,000
U.S. tax at 35%	$ 140,000

Assume that Collins instead creates a wholly owned foreign subsidiary in the Cayman Islands, where no income taxes are imposed on corporate income. Collins then sells the inventory to the subsidiary at an intercompany transfer price of $700,000, and the subsidiary sells the inventory to the ultimate European customers for $1 million. The subsidiary does not further process the inventory and is only minimally involved in the sales function, as Collins's employees arrange the transactions with the ultimate customers. In essence, the sale to the subsidiary can be seen as a "paper" transaction.

continued

If there were no tax law restrictions, this structure would create the following tax consequences.

	Collins, Inc.	Foreign Subsidiary
Sales revenue	$ 700,000	$1,000,000
Cost of goods sold	(600,000)	(700,000)
Net income	$ 100,000	$ 300,000
U.S. tax at 35%	$ 35,000	
Foreign tax at 0%		$ –0–

Because the Cayman subsidiary is not engaged in a U.S. trade or business, it is not subject to any U.S. tax on its income. So long as the subsidiary's profits are kept outside the United States, Collins believes it can avoid any U.S. income tax on these profits (i.e., the deferral privilege). Thus, at first glance, it appears that using the foreign subsidiary significantly reduces Collins's current tax cost from $140,000 to $35,000.

However, Collins will find this strategy attacked by the U.S. taxing authorities on two fronts, either of which results in the loss of all or most of the tax savings.

First, the IRS may use the transfer pricing rules of § 482 to claim that the $700,000 intercompany transfer price between Collins and its subsidiary is not a correct **arm's length price**. The IRS may claim that the transfer price should be $1 million because the subsidiary does not add any value to the inventory through further processing or sales activities and all of the risks of the transaction are borne by Collins. With this transfer pricing adjustment, Collins will record a $400,000 profit from the sales and the same $140,000 tax cost as if it had not used the foreign subsidiary as an intermediary.

Under the Subpart F rules, the subsidiary's $300,000 income creates a constructive dividend for Collins, thus producing a $105,000 tax cost ($300,000 × 35%). Combined with its original $35,000 tax, Collins's total tax cost for the sales is $140,000 ($35,000 + $105,000), and the use of the foreign subsidiary does not achieve any tax savings.

EXAMPLE 18

Assume that, in Example 17, Collins's foreign subsidiary instead was incorporated in Ireland, where the tax rate on such sales income is 12.5%. The subsidiary purchases raw materials from Collins and performs substantial manufacturing activity in Ireland before selling the inventory to customers in Hong Kong.

In this case, the sales income is not Subpart F income. Because of the substantial activity provided by the Ireland subsidiary, there is economic substance to the non-U.S. entity that generates the income.

The fact that the Irish subsidiary pays a substantially lower tax rate than the U.S. parent does not by itself trigger a constructive dividend. However, Collins must still document the appropriateness of its intercompany transfer price on raw material sales to its Irish subsidiary.

TAX PLANNING STRATEGIES Avoiding Constructive Dividends

FRAMEWORK FOCUS: TAX CREDITS

Strategy: Maximize Deductible Amounts.

To defer U.S. taxes on foreign income, U.S. taxpayers often create separate foreign subsidiaries to hold their offshore operations. This approach is successful so long as the foreign subsidiaries do not pay dividends to the U.S. owners and do not earn Subpart F income that creates constructive dividends. U.S. companies often set up foreign holding companies in tax-favorable jurisdictions to hold the foreign operating subsidiaries.

For example, a U.S. parent might create a CFC holding company with two operating subsidiaries. The subsidiaries both pay interest to the holding company on intercompany loans. The interest is deductible by the operating subsidiaries at a high tax rate (providing tax savings in those countries) and is taxed to the holding company at a relatively low tax rate. This approach provides a net tax savings to the foreign group. However, the interest payments to the holding company may constitute Subpart F income and trigger a constructive dividend back to the U.S. parent. If so, the tax savings related to the intercompany loans are offset by the U.S. taxes on the Subpart F income.

A mechanism exists that allows the holding company to avoid Subpart F treatment for the interest income. The **check-the-box Regulations** provide a great deal of flexibility for U.S.-based multinational corporations. For example, corporations are allowed to elect (i.e., check the box on a form) to treat certain foreign subsidiaries as unincorporated branches for U.S. purposes rather than separate legal entities. This election does not change the treatment of the entities under local tax law.

Using the check-the-box rules, the U.S. parent can elect to treat the foreign subsidiaries as branches for U.S. purposes. In this case, the two subsidiaries are treated as mere divisions of the holding company. Accordingly, the intercompany loans do not exist from a U.S. perspective, and there is no interest income because the interest payments are treated as simply fund transfers within a single corporation. Without the interest income, there is no Subpart F income and thus no constructive dividends. However, the foreign tax savings still exist because the interest payments do exist from a non-U.S. tax perspective, and they continue to provide interest deductions at the subsidiary level.

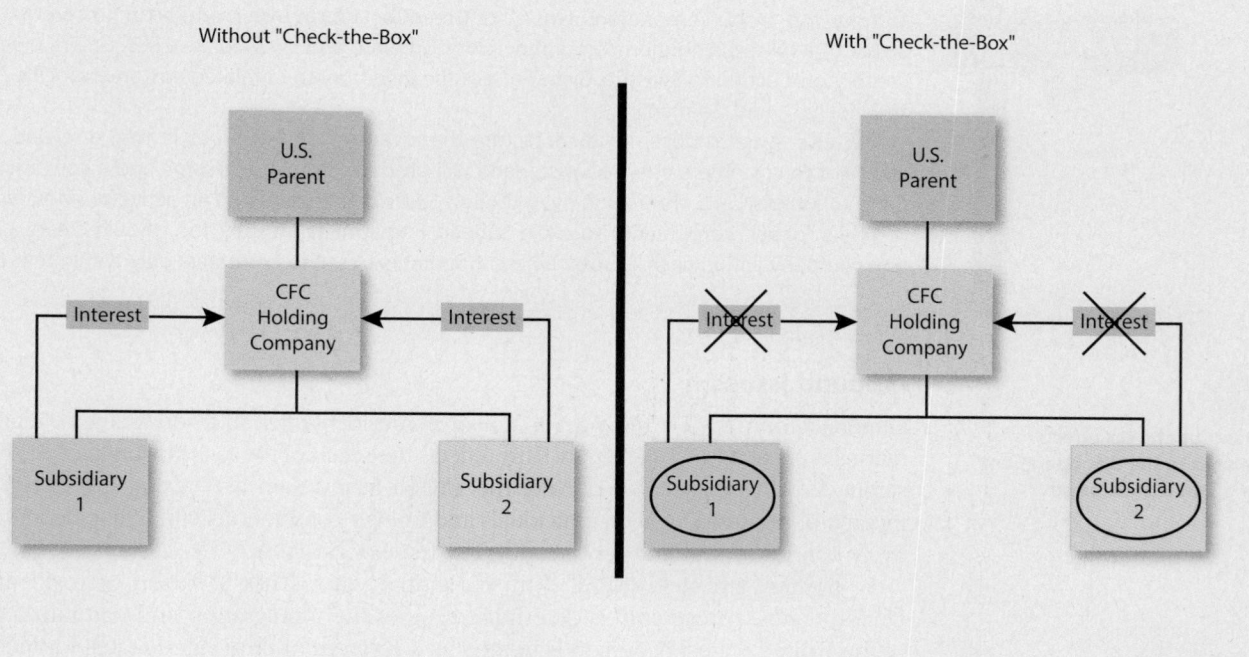

Subpart F Income—Summary The Subpart F provisions are quite complex and subject to numerous exceptions. Still, in general, any time a CFC earns income that has little economic connection to its local country, the income potentially can create a constructive dividend to the CFC's U.S. shareholders. Alternatively, if the CFC is actively generating the income, it likely is not Subpart F income.

TAX IN THE NEWS   Taxes Take a Smaller Bite Out of Apple

Apple, Inc., is a good case study for how effective tax planning can make a successful tech company even more profitable after taxes are considered. The company's business model produces plenty of free cash flow, but it operates in an industry that is based as much on intellectual property as physical plant and employee productivity. As the current tax laws largely were drafted to operate in a manufacturing and merchandising economy, Apple and other similar companies can exploit to their tax advantage a number of items that a more current tax code might address.

Apple's tax planning appears to follow the letter and the spirit of current tax law. Even though most of Apple's executives, engineers, and designers work in the United States, much of the company's profit is taxed elsewhere. Here are some highlights of how Apple uses current tax laws effectively.

- Over time, the company moves its physical plant to low-tax jurisdictions such as Nevada, Ireland, and the Netherlands.

- The company lobbies for and then uses tax incentives (e.g., for research and experimentation activities) that are offered by the Federal, state, and local governments.

- Apple uses tax planning arrangements that create subsidiaries in low-tax countries (e.g., in the British Virgin Islands). Using proper transfer pricing techniques, sales transactions are routed through the low-tax jurisdictions, and more profits are left after tax for corporate growth and development.

- Another tax-shifting strategy employs so-called commissionaires, who arrange sales of the company's goods but never take possession of any inventory. Thus, Apple's profit derived from the work distributors in high-tax countries is taxed in a low-tax country such as Singapore.

In response to criticism surrounding its tax planning, Apple counters that the company and its employees still pay billions of dollars in payroll, sales, property, and individual income taxes. And Apple's retail stores certainly draw customer traffic that benefits other tenants in shopping malls.

One downside of these tax-shifting strategies is that Apple can defer the Federal income tax on such profits only as long as the related cash remains overseas; a repatriation would trigger high-rate U.S. taxes. The U.S. Treasury might have a good argument if Apple's offshore cash was "idle," but surely most of it is used to grow the business as it operates in a global environment.

EXAMPLE 19

Murphy, Inc., a U.S. corporation owns all of GreenCo, Ltd., an Irish manufacturing corporation, and SwissCo, a Swiss distribution corporation. Both GreenCo and SwissCo are CFCs. GreenCo sells its inventory production to SwissCo. SwissCo sells the inventory to unrelated customers located in Switzerland, Italy, and Germany.

Because SwissCo does not manufacture the inventory and acquires it from a related supplier, any sales to customers outside Switzerland will produce Subpart F income and a constructive dividend to Murphy, Inc. This is true even though SwissCo is engaged in an active business and is not merely a "paper" corporation. To avoid Subpart F treatment, Murphy, Inc., should create a distribution company within each country where it operates to sell to customers only within that country.

LO.4

Describe the tax effects related to the U.S. operations of a non-U.S. taxpayer.

Inbound Issues

Generally, only the U.S.-source income of nonresident alien individuals and foreign corporations is subject to U.S. taxation. This reflects the reach of the U.S. tax jurisdiction. This constraint, however, does not prevent the United States from also taxing the foreign-source income of nonresident alien individuals and foreign corporations when that income is effectively connected with the conduct of a U.S. trade or business.

A **nonresident alien (NRA)** is an individual who is not a citizen or resident of the United States. *Citizenship* is determined under the immigration and naturalization laws of the United States. A person is treated as a *resident* of the United States for income tax purposes if he or she meets either the green card test or the substantial presence test. If either of these tests is met for the calendar year, the individual is deemed a U.S. resident for the year.

TAX FACT The Inbound Sector

Inbound corporate operations produce a small but significant portion of U.S. income tax collections.

With an average U.S. income tax rate of about 37 percent on inbound commerce, perhaps some of the other countries in the world look at the United States as a high-tax jurisdiction.

Number of Forms 1120-F filed	20,000
Taxable income reported	$9.1 billion
Net tax liability	$3.4 billion

Two important definitions determine the U.S. tax consequences to non-U.S. persons with U.S.-source income: "the conduct of a U.S. trade or business" and "**effectively connected income**." Specifically, for a foreign person's noninvestment income to be subject to U.S. taxation, the non-U.S. person must be considered engaged in a U.S. trade or business and must earn income effectively connected with that business.

General criteria for determining whether a U.S. trade or business exists include the location of production activities, management, distribution activities, and other business functions. The Code does not explicitly define a U.S. trade or business, but case law has described the concept as activities carried on in the United States that are regular, substantial, and continuous.

Once a non-U.S. person is considered engaged in a U.S. trade or business, all U.S.-source income other than investment and capital gain income is considered effectively connected to that trade or business and is therefore subject to U.S. taxation. Effectively connected income is taxed at the same rates that apply to U.S. persons, and deductions for expenses attributable to that income are allowed.

Certain U.S.-source income that is *not* effectively connected with the conduct of a U.S. trade or business is subject to a flat 30 percent tax. This income includes dividends; certain interest; rents; royalties; certain compensation; premiums; annuities; and other income of this type from fixed, determinable, annual or periodic (**FDAP**) sources. This tax generally is levied by a withholding mechanism that requires the payors of the income to withhold 30 percent of gross amounts (or a lower rate as established by a treaty). This method improves the collectability of Federal taxes from nonresidents and non-U.S. corporations.

> **EXAMPLE**
> **20**
>
> Robert, a citizen and resident of New Zealand, produces wine for export. During the current year, Robert earns $500,000 from exporting wine to unrelated wholesalers in the United States. The title to the wine passes to the U.S. wholesalers in New York. Robert has no offices or employees in the United States. The income from the wine sales is U.S.-source income, but because Robert is not engaged in a U.S. trade or business, the income is not subject to taxation in the United States.
>
> Robert begins operating a hot dog cart in New York City. This activity constitutes a U.S. trade or business. Consequently, all U.S.-source income other than FDAP or capital gain income is taxed in the United States as income effectively connected with a U.S. trade or business. Thus, both the hot dog cart profits and the $500,000 in wine income are taxed in the United States.

Several exceptions exempt non-U.S. persons from U.S. taxation on their U.S. investment income that is not connected with a U.S. business. For example, certain U.S.-sourced portfolio debt investments and capital gains (other than gains on U.S. real property investments) are exempt from U.S. tax for most non-U.S. investors. Gains from investments in U.S. real property usually are subject to U.S. income taxation. Concept Summary 16.1 summarizes the U.S. income taxation of non-U.S. persons.

In-depth coverage can be found on this book's companion website: www.cengagebrain.com

3 DIGGING DEEPER

When Congress changes the U.S. tax law, it seldom applies tax rate changes retroactively or prospectively—the rate changes usually are applicable on the date the tax bill is effective. Other countries do not always enact tax law changes in this way. Sometimes a country will adopt a schedule of tax rate increases or decreases to go into effect over a period of years.

Tax legislation of this sort can have an important effect on the U.S. taxpayer's effective tax rate as computed in the footnotes to the financial statements. When another country adopts prospective tax rate changes, an increase or decrease in the effective tax rate is reported with respect to the deferred tax accounts for GAAP purposes. Specifically, the effective tax rate decreases when a tax rate cut is scheduled in a country that does business with the U.S. party, and the rate increases when a tax rate increase is adopted for future tax years. In the last three decades, most developed countries have been cutting business income tax rates.

A recent effective tax rate computation for Berkshire Hathaway showed a decrease of about 1 percentage point due to scheduled tax rate cuts in Germany and the United Kingdom. Allied Healthcare Products showed a similar adjustment of about 2 percentage points. In contrast, the effective tax rate increased by about 1 percentage point for American Travellers Life Insurance Company.

Concept Summary 16.1

U.S. Income Tax Treatment of a Non-U.S. Person's Income*

Type of Income	Tax Rate
U.S.-source fixed, determinable, annual, or periodic (FDAP) income (not effectively connected to a U.S. business)	Generally 30% withholding on gross amount (or lower treaty rate) with certain limited exceptions.
U.S.-source income effectively connected with a U.S. trade or business	Regular individual or corporate rates applied against net income (after deductions).
Gain on U.S. real property (direct or indirect interest)	Taxed as if effectively connected to a U.S. trade or business.
Capital gains (other than on U.S. real property) not effectively connected to a U.S. trade or business	Foreign corporation: Not subject to U.S. tax. Individual: Generally not taxed but may be subject to a 30% U.S. tax if taxpayer is physically present in the United States for 183 days or more in a taxable year.
Foreign-source business income	Generally not subject to U.S. taxation unless attributable to a U.S. office or fixed place of business.

*Subject to change under treaty provisions.

16-3 CROSSING STATE LINES: STATE AND LOCAL INCOME TAXATION IN THE UNITED STATES

Very few taxpayers sell goods and services solely in the U.S. state in which they are based. Sales in other states are attractive for a variety of business reasons, including the expansion of market share and the achievement of economies of scale. By extending its operations into other states, a firm may be able to lower its labor and distribution costs, obtain additional sources of long-term debt and equity, and perhaps find a more favorable tax climate.

Many of the same issues discussed earlier in the chapter concerning international operations are encountered when a multistate operation is in place. Both international and multistate operations raise basic questions such as where did the transaction occur and who is liable for the collection of the tax.

TAX FACT **State Tax Revenue Sources**

The corporate income tax accounts for only a small portion of total tax revenues of the states. For 2013, over $850 billion in taxes was collected by the states (i.e., more than $2,700 per U.S. individual).

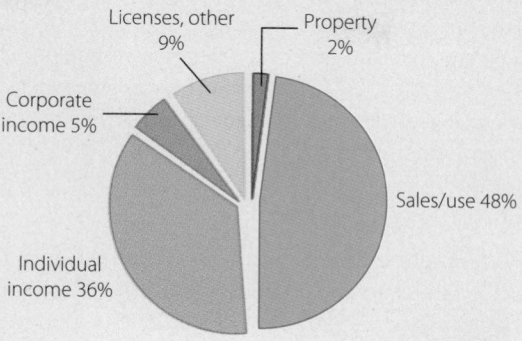

- Licenses, other 9%
- Property 2%
- Corporate income 5%
- Sales/use 48%
- Individual income 36%

However, as state and local income taxation has evolved in the United States, differences in terminology, definitions, and scope of the tax have arisen. Although prior knowledge of the U.S. international tax regime can be helpful in studying the state and local income tax structure, there still is much to learn. In addition, the sheer number of income taxing districts at the state and local level make an encounter with the state and local income tax laws of the United States a challenging experience.

16-3a **Sources of Law**

Think of how complicated a tax professional's work would be if there were several hundred different Internal Revenue Codes, each with its own Regulations, rulings, and court decisions. That description is hardly an exaggeration of the state and local income tax law faced by a taxpayer operating in more than one jurisdiction. Unless a firm's salable goods or services are designed, made, and sold strictly within one taxing jurisdiction, the multistate regime comes into effect.

Almost every U.S. state taxes the recognized income of proprietors, corporations, and other entities that have a presence in the state.[8] All of those states have constitutional provisions allowing an income tax and aggregated legislation defining the tax base, specifying when the tax is due and from whom, and otherwise administering the tax. A separate revenue department interprets the law and administers the annual taxing process.

Every one of these systems is distinct and different in multiple ways—the name and location of the chief tax official, the definitions of what is taxable and deductible and what is not, the due dates and filing requirements applicable to the tax, and the taxpayer-friendliness of the audit and appeals system.

Income taxes are levied by states, cities, counties, villages, commuter districts, school districts, stadium boards, and numerous other bodies that have been granted such taxing authority by their states. By one estimate, a business taxpayer might possibly be exposed to over 1,000 different income taxing jurisdictions in the United States at the state and local levels. Politicians often think they can gain economic development advantages over neighboring states by granting special tax breaks—"Locate your assembly plant here, and we'll exempt one-half of your employees' wages from the state income tax." Economic development goals, as well as fluctuating needs to either increase or decrease tax revenues, mean that state and local tax laws are constantly changing.

> **LO.5**
>
> **Identify the sources of tax law applicable to a taxpayer operating in more than one U.S. state.**

---

[8]Some states tax the investment income of individuals, but those taxes are not addressed in this chapter. Nevada, South Dakota, Washington, and Wyoming do not have a corporate income tax. Washington uses a business and occupation tax; several states impose a tax on the gross receipts (not on the net income) of a business.

TAX IN THE NEWS   So Where Did You Work Today?

The dream of many technology employees is to work at home with the employer's computer and communications equipment. Not only is the dress code there targeted to the worker's comfort, but the employee can avoid the time and cost of commuting. The employer saves by not having to provide office space.

But what are the tax effects when the employee or independent contractor submits work to an employer located in a different state? The general rule has been that state income taxes fall in full in the state where the work is done. Is this still the rule, or must the employee apportion the hours of the day among the various states that receive the work product? If so, on what basis should such apportionment be made? Furthermore, how will the worker reduce any potential taxation of the same income by more than one state?

The Federal government has mostly stayed out of the fray and not attempted to force states and localities to use a single common tax formula and administrative organization. Only in **Public Law 86–272** (P.L. 86–272) has Congress attempted to bring order to the multistate income tax process. This 1959 pro-interstate commerce provision exempts from state and local taxation a sale of tangible personal property where the only contact with the state is the **solicitation** activity of the taxpayer.

In the past 20 or 30 years, the states have taken some steps to coordinate their activities. Several groups of states exchange information as to the seller and purchase price for cross-border sales so that income and sales/use tax obligations can be computed and collected properly. A few states have reciprocity arrangements with their neighbors to straighten out the complications that can arise when an employee lives in one jurisdiction but works in another.

EXAMPLE

21

Harry works at the Illinois plant of Big Corporation, but he lives in Iowa. His wages are subject to Iowa tax. If Illinois and Iowa had a reciprocity agreement in place, either (1) Big would collect and remit income tax at Iowa's rates and remit the tax to the Iowa revenue department or (2) Big would collect Illinois tax, and that state would keep the withholdings paid, in full satisfaction of Harry's Iowa tax obligations for the year.

About half of the states are members of the **Multistate Tax Commission (MTC)**, a body that proposes legislation to the states and localities and issues its own regulations and informational materials. A majority of the non-MTC members follow the agency's rules virtually without exception. The Uniform Division of Income for Tax Purposes Act (UDITPA) is made available to states and localities interested in a coherent set of income assignment rules, and it forms the basis for the income tax statutes in most of the MTC member states.

The MTC, which provides very specific formulas and definitions to be used in computing state taxable income, is as close as the states have come so far to a multilateral tax treaty process. If all states and localities followed all of the MTC rules, taxpayers would be unable to gain any "border advantages" or disadvantages. But political concerns likely will keep this coordinated result from ever happening.

16-3b Tax Issues

The key issues facing a state or locality in drafting and implementing an income tax model are the same as those facing the international tax community. The results of the deliberative process, though, have produced somewhat different sets of rules and terminology.

Authority to Tax

A business is taxable in the state in which it is resident, organized, or incorporated. Tax liabilities also arise in other jurisdictions where **nexus** exists; that is, a sufficient presence in the other state has been established on an ongoing basis. Such presence might come about because the corporation was organized there, the proprietor lives there, an in-state customer made a purchase, or the business employed people or equipment within the borders of the state. The precise activities that create nexus vary from jurisdiction to jurisdiction, although most of the taxing states follow the broad rules of P.L. 86–272 and the regulations of the MTC.[9]

When a taxpayer operates in more than one state, total taxable income for the year is split among the jurisdictions in which the operations take place. Portions of the total income amount are assigned to each of the business locations, so several tax returns and payments will be due. For a taxpayer considering an expansion of operations, the tax adviser can make an important contribution in helping to decide with which state(s) nexus will be created.

The nexus rules of state/local taxation serve much the same function as do the permanent establishment provisions of international taxation. The PE standards are based in the language of the applicable tax treaty and interpretive court decisions. They look for real estate holdings and manufacturing equipment. Permanent establishment is found when an office in the host country participates significantly in the making of a sales or service contract.

In-depth coverage can be found on this book's companion website: www.cengagebrain.com   **4 DIGGING DEEPER**

Income Sourcing

LO.6

Apply principles designed to compute state taxable income for a taxpayer operating in more than one U.S. state.

The multistate business, like its international counterpart, must divide the taxable income generated for the year among the states in which it operates. Then tax liability is computed for the states in which nexus has been established. The computational template illustrated in Exhibit 16.3 indicates how most states derive their shares of the entity's aggregate taxable income. Usually, the starting point for this computation is Federal taxable income.

State modification items come about because each state creates its own tax base in the legislative process, and some of the rules adopted may differ from those used in the Internal Revenue Code. The modification items reflect such differences in the tax base. For example, modifications might be created to reflect the following differences between state and Federal taxable income.

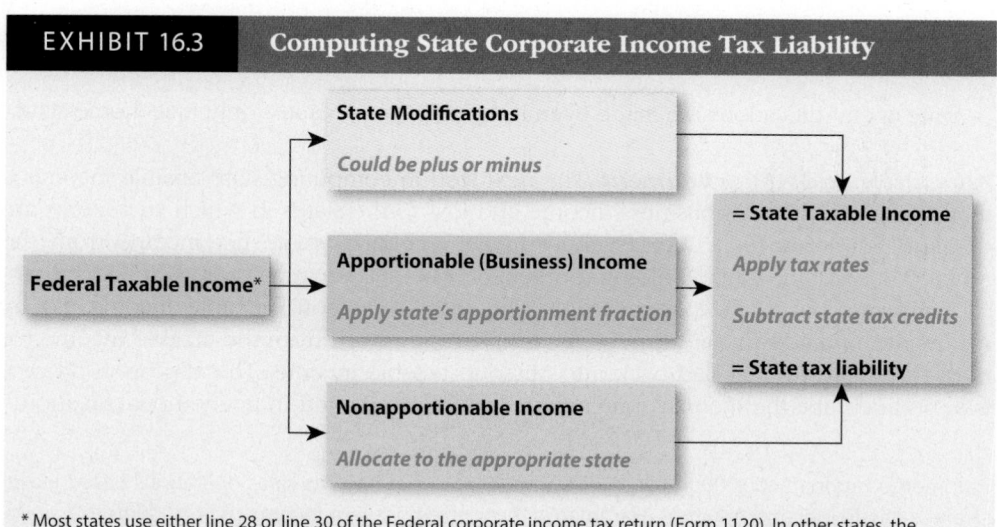

EXHIBIT 16.3   Computing State Corporate Income Tax Liability

* Most states use either line 28 or line 30 of the Federal corporate income tax return (Form 1120). In other states, the corporation is required to identify and report each element of income and deduction on the state return.

---

[9]Income and sales/use tax regimes use different nexus standards. Generally, it has been "easier" to establish nexus for sales/use tax purposes; most states have a separate set of rules to determine the taxability of income or a transaction. But recent U.S. Supreme Court cases apply a "physical presence" test for the sales/use tax, a somewhat stricter test than the income tax nexus rules of the MTC. This chapter concentrates on income tax nexus provisions.

TAX PLANNING STRATEGIES Nexus: To Have or Have Not

FRAMEWORK FOCUS: TAX RATE

Strategy: Shift Net Income from High-Tax Jurisdictions to Low-Tax Jurisdictions.

Most taxpayers try to avoid establishing nexus in a new state, for example, by providing a sales representative with a cash auto allowance rather than a company car, by restricting the location of inventory to only a few states, or by limiting a salesperson's activities to those that are protected by the solicitation standard of P.L. 86–272. This effort to avoid nexus stems in part from the additional compliance burden that falls upon the taxpayer when a new set of income tax returns, information forms, and deadlines must be dealt with in the new state.

Another concern is that the marginal tax rate that applies to the net taxable income generated by the taxpayer may increase. Such a tax increase occurs, of course, only when the applicable tax rate in the new state is higher than the rate that would apply in the home state. If a business already is based in a tax-friendly state such as Florida or Texas or in a no-tax state such as Nevada, its aggregate tax liability is sure to increase.

Still, nexus is not necessarily a bad thing. Consider what happens if a business based in California, Maryland, Wisconsin, or another high-tax jurisdiction purposely creates nexus in a low- or no-tax state. If the new state applies a lower marginal rate than is available in the home state or offers special exemptions or exclusions that match the taxpayer's operations, the aggregate tax bill can decrease. Then the planning efforts include determining which activities will *create* nexus in the new jurisdiction and meeting or maintaining that standard.

For instance, an entertainer based in Manhattan is subject to the high income taxes of New York City and New York State. By establishing a permanent office in Tennessee, nexus will be created, and some portion of the taxpayer's income will be subject to taxation there, instead of New York. These are permanent savings, accruing immediately to after-tax income and the share price of the stock of the taxpayer.

- The state might allow a different cost recovery schedule.
- The state might tax interest income from its own bonds or from those of other states.
- The state might allow a deduction for Federal income taxes paid.
- The state might disallow a deduction for payment of its own income taxes.
- The state might allow a net operating loss (NOL) deduction only for losses generated in the state.
- The state's NOL deduction might reflect different carryover periods than Federal law allows.

State tax modifications are made even if the taxpayer operates only in its home state.

Allocation and Apportionment The next step in computing state taxable income is to allocate items of nonbusiness income and loss to the states in which such items are derived. For instance, a Kansas entity might recognize some net income from the rental of a Missouri office building to a tenant. The net rental amount is in Federal taxable income, but it must appear only and fully in Missouri taxable income. So by means of the modification process, the rents are removed from the taxable income for both states and then added back into Missouri taxable income. The allocation process is very much like the income-sourcing procedures employed in international taxation.

EXAMPLE 22

HammerCo reports $400,000 in taxable income for the year from its sales operations based exclusively in Mississippi and Arkansas. HammerCo recognized net rent income of $60,000 from a building it owns in Mississippi. It earned $20,000 in interest income from Arkansas bonds. This amount is excluded from Federal taxable income, and it is taxed under Mississippi law, but not by Arkansas. HammerCo also claimed a Federal NOL carryforward of $75,000 from a prior period. Mississippi follows Federal law for NOLs, but Arkansas does not allow such carryovers. Thus, Federal taxable income totals $385,000 ($400,000 + $60,000 − $75,000).

continued

HammerCo's modifications to determine the state tax base, after starting with Federal taxable income, are as follows.

Mississippi		Arkansas	
Amount	**Modification**	**Amount**	**Modification**
− $60,000	Total nonbusiness income	− $60,000	Total nonbusiness income
+ $20,000	Municipal bond interest income	+ $75,000	Remove Federal NOL deduction
+ $60,000	Net rent income from Mississippi rentals		

The business income of the taxpayer is **apportioned** among the states in which it operates. The apportionment percentage for the state is multiplied times the apportionable income of the taxpayer to measure the extent of the taxpayer's exposure to the state's income tax. The application of the apportionment percentage is illustrated in Exhibit 16.3.

Most states apply an apportionment procedure involving three factors, each meant to estimate the taxpayer's relative activities in the state.

- The **sales factor** = In-state sales/total sales.
- The **payroll factor** = In-state payroll/total payroll.
- The **property factor** = In-state property/total property.

The state's apportionment percentage is the average of these three factors. This three-factor apportionment can be traced to the earliest days of state income taxation. Today, most states add additional weight to the sales factor, believing it to be the most accurate and measurable reflection of the taxpayer's in-state activities. It is common to "double-weight" the sales factor. Many states use a sales-factor-only apportionment procedure.

EXAMPLE 23

LinkCo, Inc., operates in two states. It reports the following results for the year. LinkCo's apportionment percentages for both states are computed as shown. Amounts are stated in millions of dollars.

	State A	State B	Totals
Sales	$30	$20	$50
Payroll	40	20	60
Property	45	5	50
Sales factor	$30/$50 = .6	$20/$50 = .4	
Payroll factor	$40/$60 = .67	$20/$60 = .33	
Property factor	$45/$50 = .9	$5/$50 = .1	
Apportionment percentage	(.6 + .67 + .9) ÷ 3 = .72	(.4 + .33 + .1) ÷ 3 = .28	

Note that 100% of LinkCo's income is apportioned between the two states: 72% to State A and 28% to State B.

Now assume that State A double-weights the sales factor. LinkCo's apportionment percentages are computed as follows.

	State A	State B	Totals
Sales	$30	$20	$50
Payroll	40	20	60
Property	45	5	50
Sales factor	$30/$50 = .6	$20/$50 = .4	
Payroll factor	$40/$60 = .67	$20/$60 = .33	
Property factor	$45/$50 = .9	$5/$50 = .1	
Apportionment percentage	(.6 + .6 + .67 + .9) ÷ 4 = .69	(.4 + .33 + .1) ÷ 3 = .28	

continued

State B's apportionment computations are not affected by A's double-weighting of the sales factor. The percentages now do not total 100%. The effect of the special weighting is to reduce LinkCo's tax liability in A. This is likely LinkCo's "home state" given the location of its personnel and plant and equipment.

Finally, assume that State B uses a "sales-factor-only" weighting. The A apportionment percentage is .69, and the B percentage is .4. Now the apportionment percentages *exceed* 100%.

Most states follow the regulations of the MTC and the outline of the UDITPA in defining and applying the apportionment factors. But because the states do not follow identical rules in the makeup of the factors, the apportionment percentages seldom total precisely to 100 percent. Some other aspects of the three-factor approach include the following.

- Sales are assigned using the tax accounting methods of the taxpayer. Sales are assigned using the "ultimate destination" concept; that is, a sale is usually assigned to the state of the purchaser.

- If a sale is made into a state with no income tax or a state with which the taxpayer has not established nexus, tax is likely escaped. But over a third of the states apply a **throwback rule** that causes the sale to be sourced to the state of the seller (i.e., by overriding the "ultimate destination" rule).

- Payroll is assigned to the state in which the employee's services primarily are performed. Payroll includes wages, bonuses, commissions, and taxable fringe benefits. Some states exclude officer compensation because it can distort the computations. Some states exclude contributions to a § 401(k) plan.

- The property factor uses an average historical cost basis, net of accumulated depreciation. Idle property is ignored, but construction in progress is included. Property in transit is assigned to the state of its presumed destination.

- Property leased but not owned by the taxpayer is included in the property factor at eight times the annual rentals paid.

Many states use specialized apportionment percentages for industries whose sales and asset profile is not properly reflected in the traditional three-factor formula. For instance, the airline industry might divide its income based on passenger-miles beginning and ending in the state. Truckers might be able to divide taxable income among the states based on in-state vehicle-trips or tons-per-day. Communications companies might use the in-state miles of cable or number of wireless devices to make up an apportionment formula.

DIGGING DEEPER 5 | **In-depth coverage can be found on this book's companion website:** www.cengagebrain.com

The Unitary Theory   About 30 states use a **unitary approach** in computing the apportionment factors. Conglomerates are required, or can elect, to base their computations on the data for all of their affiliated corporations, not just the legal entities that do business with the state. Affiliates included under the unitary theory share a majority ownership with a parent or group of shareholders. They also often share data processing, sales force, and marketing resources.

The *combined return* that the unitary business files includes much more data than might be expected on a separate-entity basis, but the taxing jurisdictions often believe that the unitary figures offer a more accurate reflection of the taxpayer's activity within the state and that, therefore, a more accurate tax liability can be derived.

FINANCIAL DISCLOSURE INSIGHTS **State/Local Taxes and the Tax Expense**

In applying GAAP principles for a business entity, state and local tax expenses are found in several places in the taxpayer's financial reports. In the tax footnote, the state/local tax costs often are reported in dollar and/or percentage terms, in both current and deferred components. The following are examples of state/local tax expenses that were reported in a recent year.

Corporations also report permanent book-tax differences in determining the effective tax rate for the reporting period. In a recent year, Berkshire Hathaway reported that state/local permanent book-tax differences reduced its effective income tax rate by about 1.5 percentage points. Ford Motor reported a similar rate reduction, but Ryder Systems's effective tax rate increased by about 6 percentage points for the year due to such permanent book-tax differences.

	Current State/Local Tax Expense ($ million)	Deferred State/Local Tax Expense ($ million)
Eli Lilly	$ 49	($ 1)
ExxonMobil	340	221
Ryder Systems	6	3
Ford Motor	7	(59)

Kipp Industries is a holding company for three subsidiaries: GrapeCo operating in California, PotatoCo operating in Idaho, and BratCo operating in Germany. Only GrapeCo has nexus with California. But because California is a unitary state, the California apportionment percentage is computed also using PotatoCo and BratCo data.

EXAMPLE

24

In-depth coverage can be found on this book's companion website: www.cengagebrain.com

6 DIGGING DEEPER

Concept Summary 16.2 sets out some of the key issues in corporate multistate income taxation.

Concept Summary 16.2

Corporate Multistate Income Taxation

1. A taxpayer is subject to income tax in the state in which it resides or is organized.

2. A taxpayer is subject to income tax in states where it has a business presence and enjoys the resources of the host state in conducting its operations.

3. A multistate taxpayer must divide its aggregate taxable income for the year among the states in which it conducts business.

4. Nonbusiness income is allocated to the state in which it is generated.

5. Business income is apportioned among the states in which the taxpayer has nexus.

6. Apportionment usually is conducted using a formula based on the relative sales, employment, and asset holdings in the various states.

7. The sales factor uses a destination test, while the payroll and property factors use a source test.

8. Most states weight the sales factor higher than the other apportionment factors.

9. Some states apply a special apportionment formula for certain industries when the traditional three-factor formula could distort the income division procedure in some way.

10. About 30 states employ the unitary theory in deriving the apportionment factors, using the data from a group of corporations to compute the apportionment formula. Other states allow or require a consolidated return from a conglomerate.

TAX PLANNING STRATEGIES   **Where Should My Income Go?**

FRAMEWORK FOCUS: TAX RATE

Strategy: Shift Net Income from High-Tax Jurisdictions to Low-Tax Jurisdictions.

Every state defines its apportionment factors in a slightly different manner. The multistate taxpayer needs to keep track of these differences and place activities in the state that will serve them best.

Planning with the sales factor includes a detailed analysis of the destination point of the product shipments for the year, especially when the firm has customers in low- and no-tax states. The property factor should include only assets that are used in the taxpayer's trade or business, not the investment, leasing, or research functions. Permanently idle property is excluded from the property factor as well. The payroll factor can be manipulated by hiring independent contractors to carry out certain sales and distribution work or by relocating highly paid managers to low-tax states.

By setting up an investment holding company in a no- or low-tax state such as Delaware or Nevada and transferring income-producing securities and intangible assets to that entity, significant tax reductions can be obtained. When the net investment income is paid back to the parent corporation, the dividends received deduction eliminates the tax liability there.

The unitary system does not always result in a tax increase, although the additional record-keeping burden of operating in a unitary state cannot be understated. If the affiliates make available less profitable operations or a presence in low- or no-tax states or countries, the current tax liability may be reduced. The record-keeping burden can be reduced if the taxpayer makes a **waters'-edge election**, which allows it to include only affiliate data from within the boundaries of the United States.

Return to the facts of Example 24. If Kipp Industries files a waters'-edge election, the unitary group that files a California income tax return can be limited to GrapeCo and PotatoCo since BratCo operates outside the United States.

LO.7

Synthesize key aspects of international and multistate tax systems to identify common rules and issues taxpayers face in both systems.

16-4   COMMON CHALLENGES

Practical and policy issues facing the U.S. states, developed countries, and the taxpayers operating in all of them show a great degree of similarity between the multistate and international tax regimes. Terminology may differ, and the evolution of tax solutions may take radically different paths, but the key issues that face the multijurisdictional community are at once challenging and rewarding.

16-4a   **Authority to Tax**

The old-economy orientation of the nexus and permanent establishment rules presents great difficulty in today's economy, as jurisdictions attempt to describe the income and sales/use tax base fairly. An electronic presence also exploits the resources of the host country and should trigger a tax in the visited jurisdiction. Mathematically, the apportionment and sourcing rules should result in only a modest tax liability in the host jurisdiction, but it is improper to maintain that no presence exists and no tax should be paid in the context of a toll-free telephone number or Internet sale.

But perhaps the notion of *presence* is becoming less important over time, and the level of resource usage in the host jurisdiction also is declining. For example, just-in-time

Multijurisdictional companies operate across state and country borders. The transfer price used by a company can have a significant effect on the amount of profits subject to taxation within a particular taxing jurisdiction. Companies face other concerns when establishing transfer pricing policies. For example, the internal determination of how a division of the company is performing may be based on transfer pricing between related entities within the global group. Furthermore, the compensation of the managers within those divisions may be tied directly to divisional performance.

If an intercompany price is set in a manner that optimizes the global tax position, a separate cost accounting policy may be required to determine an entity's profitability for purposes of compensating employees. Tax advisers often face resistance from operations managers when suggesting improved transfer pricing methods, because such improvements often change the traditional division of profits among different parts of the business.

manufacturing and purchasing strategies reduce the need for warehousing by some taxpayers. Human capital can be dispersed through telecommuting, video conferencing, and project rotation using work-group software that provides acceptable levels of data security. If the future is to a great degree wireless, perhaps the standard of presence will diminish, as the buyer and the seller are both "everywhere."

16-4b Division of Income

The multistate apportionment procedure could use an overhaul. The fact that a majority of states change the weighting of the sales factor indicates that some other income division method might better serve taxpayers and governments. Three-factor apportionment was designed for an age of traveling sales representatives and sales of built, grown, and manufactured goods. Sales reps were assigned territories they could drive through on short notice, so they usually lived close to their customer base. In that case, the sales and payroll factors could be highly redundant.

Today, with communication and distribution systems more highly developed, the sales factor appears incrementally to be the preferred income-sourcing device. Sales of goods and services should be assigned based on a destination test so that the transaction is assigned to the state of the purchaser.

The three-factor formula further breaks down for income derived from specialized industries, as evidenced by the special computational methods allowed by many states. Perhaps the economy is so specialized today that income simply cannot be assigned by the use of one simple formula. Nonetheless, more uniformity among the states as to definitions and computational rules for the factors would be welcome.

The U.S. Treasury has held hearings in the last decade concerning the adoption of an apportionment approach to the sourcing of international taxable income. Although a formulary apportionment would represent a more reliable and predictable method of dividing multinational income and deduction amounts, the data collection burden that such a system would create may be too much to expect from most of the trading partners in the short term. Moreover, the model treaties developed by the United States and the Organization for Economic Cooperation and Development (OECD) include language relating to the income-sourcing rules and transfer pricing at arm's length, not an apportionment approach.

16-4c Transfer Pricing

The transfer pricing system used in international trade requires the taxpayer to keep a database of comparable prices and transactions, even though often no such comparability exists. Especially when dealing with proprietary goods and design, it may be

BRIDGE DISCIPLINE Bridge to Economic Development and Political Science

The tax professional occasionally is in a position to negotiate with a state or city taxing jurisdiction to garner tax relief for a client as an incentive to locate a plant or distribution center in that geographic area. In times when construction budgets are high and interstate competition is fierce to attract or retain businesses that are making location decisions, such tax concessions can be significant.

For instance, to encourage a business to build a large distribution center in the area, community leaders might be agreeable to:

- Paying for roads, sewer, water, and other improvements through taxpayer bonds;

- Reducing property taxes by 50 percent for the first 10 years of the center's operations; and

- Permanently excluding any distribution-related vehicles and equipment from the personal property tax.

An incentive-granting community provides the concessions even though the influx of new workers will place a great strain on public school facilities and likely necessitate improvements in traffic patterns and other infrastructure.

Consider the position of a large employer that has been located in the area for more than 50 years. By how much should it be willing to absorb the tax increases that result when economic development concessions are used to attract new, perhaps temporary, businesses to the area? Should the employer challenge the constitutionality of the grant of such sizable tax breaks to some, but not all, business taxpayers in the jurisdiction? Should higher "impact fees" be assessed on new developments?

Does your analysis change if the new business competes with the longtime resident for sales? For employees? For political power?

impossible to find comparable goods and, therefore, an acceptable transfer price for them. One solution to this situation would be to allow additional definitions of comparable goods, or of ranges of acceptable transfer prices, perhaps subjected to audit on a rotating five-year basis. The use of advance pricing agreements further allows a greater degree of control by the governments in data collection and analysis, ideally prior to the undertaking of the sales or manufacturing transactions.

DIGGING DEEPER 7   In-depth coverage can be found on this book's companion website: www.cengagebrain.com

16-4d Tax Havens

When taxpayers perceive effective tax rates as too high, planning usually includes seeking out a tax haven . If income-producing securities or profitable service operations can be moved to another jurisdiction, ideally one with significantly lower marginal tax rates on that type of income, permanent tax savings can be achieved. A tax haven usually applies minimal rules for a taxpayer to establish residency, and it adopts little or no cooperation in international exchanges of tax and financial information. The Bahamas, Monaco, and Panama, among other countries, often are seen as tax havens.

When a government witnesses a loss of its tax base due to the transfer of assets and income out of the jurisdiction, anti-tax-haven legislation is discussed, but it seldom is effective. The U.S. international tax regime shows several distinct attempts to find and tax income moved offshore, but those taxes collect only nominal revenues in the typical tax year. Income-shifting devices currently used by multistate taxpayers have been attacked by the states in various ways, but legislators hesitate to be too aggressive, probably out of fear of the state being branded "anti-business."

Perhaps a separate set of nexus rules could be created to address the most portable types of income, such as that from interest and dividends. But this difficult problem likely needs a multilateral solution, which is unlikely to be found in the short term among states and countries, each with unique revenue shortfalls and political profiles.

16-4e **Interjurisdictional Agreements**

Treaties are documents that address many issues other than the taxable income computation. They involve several players within the governmental structure, and they take several years to draft and adopt. Treaties involving the United States tend to be only bilateral, meaning that it is difficult to anticipate and coordinate the interaction of several treaties as they apply to a single taxpayer.

At the multistate level, the Federal government has been slow to take up issues involving a synchronization of the income tax systems used by the states. Although this reluctance may be partly for strictly constitutional reasons, it is largely because of the difficulties presented by the lack of uniformity among the states' tax laws and enforcement efforts.

But the future must hold a greater degree of cooperation among various taxing jurisdictions, at least in the trading of information and the coordination of enforcement efforts. The United States must create additional treaties or information-sharing agreements with countries in South America and Africa. And the future of the European Union probably holds a series of revised agreements addressing tax issues with U.S. entities that relocate intangible assets overseas and that move administrative operations offshore to avoid the U.S. concept of worldwide taxation.

Procedural developments may accomplish the same result. For instance, block filing by S corporations and their shareholders with various states accomplishes a number of income division and information-sharing goals. In this context and others, sharing data, while still respecting the confidentiality needs of the taxpayer and requirements of the governments, represents a technologically sound method of collecting taxes in today's multijurisdictional economy.

In-depth coverage can be found on this book's companion website: www.cengagebrain.com   **8   DIGGING DEEPER**

REFOCUS ON THE BIG PICTURE

GOING INTERNATIONAL

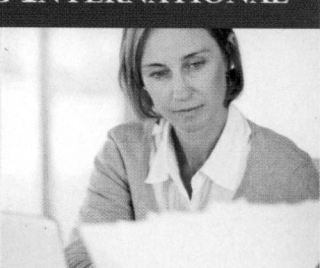

Simply selling into a foreign jurisdiction probably will not trigger any overseas income tax consequences. However, income earned from foreign sales is taxed currently to VoiceCo in the United States. By establishing a CFC in Ireland, VoiceCo benefits from income tax deferral. As long as the income is not distributed to VoiceCo and as long as the income is not Subpart F income, VoiceCo can avoid current Federal income taxes on the profits of VoiceCo-Ireland. If VoiceCo receives dividends from its foreign subsidiary, it can claim foreign tax credits, which help alleviate the double taxation that would otherwise result.

What If?

VoiceCo is considering building a new manufacturing facility in another state in the United States. How will VoiceCo's expansion decision be affected by state tax considerations? In making the decision to expand, VoiceCo should consider a variety of state tax issues, including whether the state imposes a corporate income tax at all and, if so, whether the state requires unitary reporting. Other relevant issues affecting the tax calculation in the state include what apportionment formula is used by the state and whether the state has a throwback rule.

© YURI ARCURS/SHUTTERSTOCK.COM

Suggested Readings

Jason W. Klimek, "A Big Data Approach to Formulary Apportionment," *Corporate Taxation*, May/June 2014.

Albena Peters, "Controlled Foreign Corporation Rules in the United States, Canada, and Germany," *Corporate Taxation*, March/April 2012.

Michael S. Schadewald and William A. Raabe, "Present and Future Directions in Federal and State Taxation of Income from Cross Border Trade," *TAXES*, April 1997.

Brett R. Wilkinson and Katherine Wilkinson, "The Creditability of Foreign Taxes," *The Tax Adviser*, January 2014.

Key Terms

Allocate, 16-24

Apportioned, 16-25

Arm's length price, 16-16

Check-the-box Regulations, 16-17

Controlled foreign corporations (CFCs), 16-14

Deemed-paid credit, 16-13

Effectively connected income, 16-19

FDAP, 16-19

Foreign tax credit, 16-6

Inbound taxation, 16-3

Income tax treaties, 16-5

Multistate Tax Commission (MTC), 16-22

Nexus, 16-22

Nonresident alien (NRA), 16-18

Outbound taxation, 16-3

Payroll factor, 16-25

Permanent establishment (PE), 16-5

Property factor, 16-25

Public Law 86–272, 16-22

Sales factor, 16-25

Separate foreign tax credit income categories, 16-12

Solicitation, 16-22

Subpart F income, 16-14

Tax haven, 16-30

Throwback rule, 16-26

Unitary approach, 16-26

U.S. shareholder, 16-15

Waters'-edge election, 16-28

Computational Exercises

1. **LO.3** Cordero, Inc., is a calendar-year taxpayer and a CFC for the entire tax year. Vance Company, a U.S. corporation, owns 75% of Cordero's one class of stock for the entire year. Cordero's Subpart F income for the year is $450,000, and no distributions were made to the parent. Determine Vance's gross income from the Subpart F constructive dividend from Cordero.

2. **LO.3** Enders, Inc., a domestic corporation, reports $290,000 total taxable income for the year, consisting of $208,800 in U.S.-source business profits and $81,200 of income from foreign investment securities. Overseas tax authorities withheld $24,000 in income taxes on the investment income. Enders's U.S. tax before the FTC is $78,000. Compute Enders's foreign tax credit for the year.

3. **LO.6** Castle Corporation conducts business and has nexus in States A, B, and C. All of the states use a three-equal-factors apportionment formula, with the factors evenly weighted. Castle generates $555,000 apportionable income and $75,000 allocable income related to State C activities. Castle's sales, payroll, and property are divided evenly among the three states. Compute taxable income for:

   a. State A.

   b. State B.

   c. State C.

4. **LO.6** Fillon operates manufacturing facilities in States A and B. Fillon has nexus with both states; apportionment factors are .70 for A and .30 for B. Taxable income for the year totaled $150,000, with a $200,000 A profit and a $50,000 B loss. Calculate taxable income for the year for:

   a. State A.

   b. State B.

5. **LO.6** Beckett Corporation has nexus with States A and B. Apportionable income for the year totals $800,000. Beckett's apportionment factors for the year use the following data. Compute Beckett's B taxable income for the year; B uses a three-factor apportionment formula, with a double-weighted sales factor.

	State A	State B	Totals
Sales	$960,000	$640,000	$1,600,000
Property	180,000	–0–	180,000
Payroll	220,000	–0–	220,000

6. **LO.6** Chirp Corporation owns two subsidiaries. Song, located in State A, generated $500,000 taxable income this year. Bird, located in State B, generated a $100,000 loss for the period.

   a. Determine Song's taxable income in States A and B, assuming that the subsidiaries constitute independent corporations under the tax law.

   b. How does your answer change if the companies constitute a unitary business?

Problems

7. **LO.3** BlueCo, a domestic corporation, incorporates GreenCo, a new wholly owned entity in Germany. Under both German and U.S. legal principles, this entity is a corporation. BlueCo faces a 35% U.S. tax rate.

   GreenCo earns $1,500,000 in net profits from its German activities, and GreenCo makes no dividend distributions to BlueCo. How much Federal income tax will BlueCo pay for the current year as a result of GreenCo's earnings, assuming that there is no deemed dividend under Subpart F? Ignore any foreign tax credit (FTC) implications.

8. **LO.3** Evaluate this statement: It is unfair that the United States taxes its citizens and residents on their worldwide income.

9. **LO.3** Describe the different approaches used by countries to tax the earnings of their citizens and residents generated outside the borders of the country.

10. **LO.3** Create, Inc., produces inventory in its foreign manufacturing plants for sale in the United States. Its foreign manufacturing assets have a tax book value of $5 million and a fair market value of $15 million. Its assets related to the sales activity have a tax book value of $2 million and a fair market value of $5 million. Create's interest expense totaled $400,000 for the current year.

   Decision Making

   a. What amount of interest expense is allocated and apportioned to foreign-source income using the tax book value method? What amount of Create's interest expense is allocated and apportioned to foreign-source income using the fair market value method?

   b. If Create wants to maximize its FTC, which method should it use?

11. **LO.3** Chock, a U.S. corporation, purchases inventory for resale from distributors within the United States and resells this inventory at a $1 million profit to customers outside the United States. Title to the goods passes outside the United States. What is the source of Chock's inventory sales income?

12. **LO.3** Willa, a U.S. corporation, owns the rights to a patent related to a medical device. Willa licenses the rights to use the patent to IrishCo, which uses the patent in its manufacturing facility located in Ireland. What is the source of the $1 million royalty income received by Willa from IrishCo for the use of the patent?

13. **LO.3** USCo incurred $100,000 in interest expense for the current year. The tax book value of USCo's assets generating foreign-source income is $5 million. The tax book value of USCo's assets generating U.S.-source income is $45 million. How much of the interest expense is allocated and apportioned to foreign-source income?

14. **LO.3** QuinnCo could not claim all of the income taxes it paid to Japan as a foreign tax credit (FTC) this year. What computational limit probably kept QuinnCo from taking its full FTC? Explain.

15. **LO.3** FoldIt, a U.S. business, paid income taxes to Mexico relative to profitable sales of shipping boxes it made in that country. Can it claim a deduction for these taxes in computing U.S. taxable income? A tax credit? Both? Explain.

16. **LO.3** Klein, a domestic corporation, receives a $10,000 dividend from ForCo, a wholly owned foreign corporation. The deemed-paid (indirect) foreign tax credit associated with this dividend is $3,000. What is the total gross income included in Klein's tax return as a result of this dividend?

17. **LO.3** ABC, Inc., a domestic corporation, reports $50 million of taxable income, including $15 million of general limitation foreign-source taxable income, on which ABC paid $5 million in foreign income taxes. The U.S. tax rate is 35%. What is ABC's foreign tax credit?

18. **LO.3** Mary, a U.S. citizen, is the sole shareholder of CanCo, a Canadian corporation. During its first year of operations, CanCo earns $14 million of foreign-source taxable income, pays $6 million of Canadian income taxes, and distributes a $2 million dividend to Mary. Can Mary claim a deemed-paid (indirect) foreign tax credit on her Form 1040 with respect to receipt of a dividend distribution from CanCo? Why or why not?

19. **LO.3** ABC, Inc., a domestic corporation, owns 100% of HighTax, a foreign corporation. HighTax has $50 million of undistributed E & P, all of which is attributable to general limitation income, and $30 million of foreign income taxes paid. HighTax distributes a $5 million dividend to ABC. The dividend, which is subject to a 5% foreign withholding tax, is ABC's only item of income during the year. ABC's marginal U.S. tax rate is 35%. How much foreign tax credit and carryover is produced by the dividend?

20. **LO.3** USCo, a domestic corporation, reports worldwide taxable income of $1.5 million, including a $400,000 dividend from ForCo, a wholly owned foreign corporation. ForCo's undistributed E & P totals $16 million, and it has paid $10 million of foreign income taxes attributable to these earnings. All foreign income is in the general limitation basket. What is USCo's deemed-paid (indirect) foreign tax credit related to the dividend received (before consideration of any limitation)?

21. **LO.3** USCo, a domestic corporation, reports worldwide taxable income of $500,000, including a $300,000 dividend from ForCo, a wholly owned foreign corporation. ForCo's undistributed E & P totals $1 million, and it has paid $200,000 of foreign income taxes attributable to these earnings. All foreign income is in the general limitation basket. What is USCo's deemed-paid (indirect) foreign tax credit related to the dividend received (before consideration of any limitation)?

22. **LO.3** Fleming, Inc., a domestic corporation, operates in both Canada and the United States. This year, the business generated taxable income of $400,000 from foreign sources and $300,000 from U.S. sources. All of Fleming's foreign-source income is in the general limitation basket. Fleming's total worldwide taxable income is $700,000. Fleming pays Canadian taxes of $152,000. What is Fleming's allowed FTC for the tax year? Assume a 35% U.S. income tax rate.

23. **LO.3** Drake, Inc., a U.S. corporation, operates a branch sales office in Turkey. During the current year, Drake earned $500,000 in taxable income from U.S. sources and $100,000 in taxable income from sources in Turkey. Drake paid $40,000 in income taxes to Turkey. All of the income is characterized as general

limitation income. Compute Drake's U.S. income tax liability after consideration of any foreign tax credit. Drake's U.S. tax rate is 35%.

24. **LO.3** Crank, Inc., a U.S. corporation, operates a branch sales office in Ghana. During the current year, Crank earned $200,000 in taxable income from U.S. sources and $50,000 in taxable income from sources in Ghana. Crank paid $5,000 in income taxes to Ghana. All of the income is characterized as general limitation income. Compute Crank's U.S. income tax liability after consideration of any foreign tax credit. Crank's U.S. tax rate is 35%.

25. **LO.3** Harold, Inc., a domestic corporation, earned $500,000 from foreign manufacturing activities on which it paid $150,000 of foreign income taxes. Harold's foreign sales income is taxed at a 45% foreign tax rate. Both sales and manufacturing income are assigned to the general limitation basket. What amount of foreign sales income can Harold earn without generating any excess FTCs for the current year? Assume a 35% U.S. rate.

Decision Making

26. **LO.3** Food, Inc., a domestic corporation, owns 70% of the stock of Drink, Inc., a foreign corporation. For the current year, Food receives a dividend of $20,000 from Drink. Drink's E & P (after taxes) and foreign taxes are $6 million and $800,000, respectively. What is Food's total gross income from receipt of this dividend if it elects to claim the FTC for deemed-paid foreign taxes?

27. **LO.3** Orion, Inc., a U.S. corporation, reports foreign-source income and pays foreign taxes for the tax year as follows.

	Income	Taxes
Passive basket	$150,000	$ 13,000
General basket	300,000	150,000

Orion's worldwide taxable income is $600,000, and U.S. taxes before the FTC are $210,000 (assume a 35% rate). What is Orion's U.S. tax liability after the FTC?

28. **LO.3** Discuss the policy reasons for the existence of the Subpart F rules. Give two examples of Subpart F income.

Issue ID

29. **LO.3** USCo owns 65% of the voting stock of LandCo, a Country X corporation. Terra, an unrelated Country Y corporation, owns the other 35% of LandCo. LandCo owns 100% of the voting stock of OceanCo, a Country Z corporation. Assuming that USCo is a U.S. shareholder, do LandCo and OceanCo meet the definition of a CFC? Explain.

30. **LO.3** Is a foreign corporation owned equally by 100 unrelated U.S. citizens considered to be a controlled foreign corporation (CFC)? Explain.

31. **LO.3** Hart Enterprises, a domestic corporation, owns 100% of OK, Ltd., an Irish corporation. OK's gross income for the year is $10 million. Determine whether any of the following transactions produce Subpart F gross income for the current year.

a. OK earned $600,000 from sales of products purchased from Hart and sold to customers outside Ireland.

b. OK earned $1 million from sales of products purchased from Hart and sold to customers in Ireland.

c. OK earned $400,000 from sales of products purchased from unrelated suppliers and sold to customers in Germany.

d. OK purchased raw materials from Hart, used these materials to manufacture finished goods, and sold these goods to customers in Italy. OK earned $300,000 from these sales.

e. OK earned $50,000 in dividend income from Canada and Mexico passive investments.

32. **LO.3** HiramCo, a U.S. entity, operates a manufacturing business in both Mexico and Costa Rica, and it holds its investment portfolio in Sweden. How many foreign tax credit computations must HiramCo make? Be specific, and use the term *basket* in your answer.

33. **LO.4** Give a simple answer to Andre's question: "If I move to the United States, how will the Federal government tax my widget sales and capital gains?" Andre will be living in New York City, where state and local taxes are very high. Ignore the effects of tax treaties in your answer.

34. **LO.3** Skills, Inc., a U.S. corporation, reports current foreign-source income classified in two different FTC income baskets. It earns $50,000 in passive foreign-source income, and it suffers a net loss of $30,000 in the general limitation basket. What is the numerator of Skills's FTC limitation formula for the passive basket in the current year? Explain.

Decision Making   35. **LO.3** Night, Inc., a domestic corporation, earned $300,000 from foreign manufacturing activities, on which it paid $90,000 of foreign income taxes. Night's foreign sales income is taxed at a 50% foreign tax rate. What amount of foreign sales income can Night earn without generating any excess FTCs for the current year? Assume a 34% U.S. tax rate.

36. **LO.4** Evaluate the following statement: Non-U.S. persons never are subject to U.S. taxation on U.S.-source investment income, so long as they are not engaged in a U.S. trade or business.

Critical Thinking   37. **LO.3** Lili, Inc., a domestic corporation, operates a branch in France. The earnings record of the branch is as follows.

Year	Taxable Income (Loss)	Foreign Taxes Paid
1	($ 25,000)	$ –0–
2	(40,000)	–0–
3	(10,000)	–0–
4	120,000	40,000

Lili, Inc., reports U.S.-source taxable income of $500,000 each year. What is the allowed FTC for year 4? Assume a 35% U.S. tax rate.

Communications   38. **LO.3, 4** Write a memo for the tax research file on the difference between "inbound" and "outbound" activities in the context of U.S. taxation of international income.

39. **LO.3** Warwick, Inc., a U.S. corporation, owns 100% of NewGrass, Ltd., a foreign corporation. NewGrass earns only general limitation income. During the current year, NewGrass paid Warwick a $10,000 dividend. The deemed-paid foreign tax credit associated with this dividend is $3,000. The foreign jurisdiction requires a withholding tax of 10%, so Warwick received only $9,000 in cash as a result of the dividend. What is Warwick's total U.S. gross income reported as a result of the cash dividend?

40. **LO.5** Evaluate this statement: A state can tax only its resident individuals and the corporations and partnerships that are organized in-state.

Issue ID   41. **LO.5** You are working with the top management of one of your clients in selecting
Communications   the U.S. location for a new manufacturing operation. Craft a plan for the CEO to use in discussions with the economic development representatives of each of the top candidate states. In no more than two PowerPoint slides, list some of the tax incentives the CEO should request from a particular state during the bilateral negotiations between the parties. Your list should be both creative and aggressive in its requests.

42. **LO.5** Considering only the aggregate state income tax liability, how should Norris, who sells widgets from its domicile State A, deploy its sales force? The states that entail the taxpayer's entire customer base use the following flat income tax rates. — Decision Making

State A	5%
State B	3
State C	6
State D	0

43. **LO.5** Continue to consider the case of the taxpayer in Problem 42. Is it acceptable to you if Norris purposely shifts its sales force among the states to reduce its tax liabilities? In your response, first explain the tax-related motivations of the taxpayer in this regard. — Ethics and Equity

44. **LO.6** Compute state taxable income for HippCo, Inc. Its Federal taxable income for the year is $1 million. Its operations are confined to Oregon and Montana. HippCo generates only business and interest income for the year.

- Federal cost recovery deductions totaled $200,000. Montana used this amount, but Oregon allowed only $120,000.
- Interest income of $25,000 from Oregon bonds was excluded from Federal taxable income. Oregon taxes all municipal bond income, while Montana taxes all such interest except that from its own bonds.
- Interest income from Treasury bonds that was recognized on the Federal return came to $11,000. Neither state taxes such income.

45. **LO.6** Continue with the facts of Problem 44. Using the format of Exhibit 16.3, compute state taxable income for HippCo, assuming also that the taxpayer recognized $225,000 of net rent income during the year from a warehouse building in Montana. Federal taxable income still is $1 million.

46. **LO.6** PinkCo, Inc., operates in two states. It reports the following results for the year. Compute the apportionment percentage for both states. Amounts are stated in millions of dollars.

	State A	State B	Totals
Sales	$25	$ 75	$100
Payroll	20	30	50
Property	0	100	100

47. **LO.6** Repeat the computations of Problem 46, but now assume that State B uses a double-weighted sales factor in its apportionment formula.

48. **LO.6** Repeat the computations of Problem 46, but now assume that State A is a sales-factor-only state and that State B uses the following weights: sales .70, payroll .15, and property .15.

49. **LO.6** State A enjoys a prosperous economy, with high real estate values and compensation levels. State B's economy has seen better days—property values are depressed, and unemployment is higher than in other states. Most consumer goods are priced at about 10% less in B as compared with prices in A. Both A and B apply unitary income taxation on businesses that operate in-state. Does unitary taxation distort the assignment of taxable income between A and B? Explain. — Issue ID

50. **LO.6** Hernandez, which has been an S corporation since inception, is subject to tax in States Y and Z. On Schedule K of its Federal Form 1120S, Hernandez reported ordinary income of $500,000 from its business, taxable interest income of $10,000, capital loss of $30,000, and $40,000 of dividend income from a corporation in which it owns 30%. — Critical Thinking Communications

Both states apportion income by use of a three-factor formula that equally weights sales, payroll, and the average cost of property; both states treat interest and dividends as business income. In addition, both Y and Z follow Federal provisions with respect to the determination of corporate taxable income. Y recognizes S status, but Z does not.

Based on the following information, write a memo to the shareholders of Hernandez, detailing the amount of taxable income on which Hernandez will pay tax in Y and Z. Hernandez corporate offices are located at 5678 Alabaster Circle, Bowling Green, KY 42103.

	State Y	State Z
Sales	$1,000,000	$800,000
Property (average cost)	500,000	100,000
Payroll	800,000	200,000

Issue ID

Communications

51. **LO.6** Prepare a PowerPoint presentation (maximum of six slides) entitled "Planning Principles for Our Multistate Clients." The slides will be used to lead a 20-minute discussion with colleagues in the corporate tax department. Keep the outline general, but assume that your colleagues already work with clients operating in at least 15 states. Address only income tax issues.

Issue ID

Communications

52. **LO.3, 7** Miha Ohua is the CFO of a U.S. company that has operations in Europe and Asia. The company has several manufacturing subsidiaries in low-tax foreign countries where the tax rate averages 6%. These subsidiaries purchase raw materials used in the production process from related subsidiaries located in countries where the tax rate averages 33%.

Miha is considering establishing a transfer price for the raw materials so that the higher-tax subsidiaries charge a low price for the raw materials. In this way, little of the profit is left in these subsidiaries, and most of the profits end up in the low-tax subsidiaries. This approach might reduce the U.S. company's overall global tax rate. Write a memo to Miha, outlining the issues with this plan.

BRIDGE DISCIPLINE

1. What type of information-sharing agreements does the IRS have with the revenue agency of the Bahamas? Canada? Germany? Israel? Argentina?

Communications

2. Write a paper of no more than two pages discussing the treatment of state and local taxes that is found in the text of U.S. income tax treaties with two other countries.

Communications

3. Several U.S. states finance their operations without the benefit of a corporate income tax. Prepare five to seven PowerPoint slides, and make a presentation to your school's Accounting Club. In your presentation, discuss the public economic and policy effects of using nontraditional revenue sources to fund state operating and infrastructure projects. Compare the taxing and expenditure process used in your state with at least two of these jurisdictions: Alaska; Hawaii; Michigan; Texas; Washington, D.C.; and Washington State.

4. The trend in state income taxation is to move to an apportionment formula that places extra weight on the sales factor. Several states now use sales-factor-only apportionment. Explain why this development is attractive to the taxing states.

Note: Solutions to Research Problems can be prepared by using the Checkpoint® Student Edition online research product, which is available to accompany this text. It is also possible to prepare solutions to the Research Problems by using tax research materials found in a standard tax library.

Communications

Research Problem 1. Jerry Jeff Keen, the CFO of Boots Unlimited, a Texas corporation, has come to you regarding a potential restructuring of business operations. Boots long has manufactured its western boots in plants in Texas and Oklahoma.

Recently, Boots has explored the possibility of setting up a manufacturing subsidiary in Ireland, where manufacturing profits are taxed at 10%. Jerry Jeff sees this as a great idea, given that the alternative is to continue all manufacturing in the United States, where profits are taxed at 34%. Boots plans to continue all of the cutting, sizing, and hand tooling of leather in its U.S. plants. This material will be shipped to Ireland for final assembly, with the finished product shipped to retail outlets all over Europe and Asia. Your initial concern is whether the income generated by the Irish subsidiary is Subpart F income. Address this issue in a research memo, along with any planning suggestions.

Partial list of research aids:
§ 954(d).
Reg. § 1.954–3(a).
Bausch & Lomb, 71 TCM 2031, T.C.Memo. 1996–57.

Research Problem 2. Polly Ling is a successful professional golfer. She is a resident of a country that does not have a tax treaty with the United States. Ling plays matches around the world, about one-half of which are in the United States. Ling's reputation is without blemish; in fact, she is known as being exceedingly honest and upright, and many articles discuss how she is a role model for young golfers due to her tenacious and successful playing style and her favorable character traits. Every year, she reports the most penalty strokes on herself among the participants in women's matches, and this is seen as reinforcing her image as an honest and respectful competitor.

This combination of quality play and laudable reputation has brought many riches to Ling. She comes to you with several Federal income tax questions. She knows that as a non-U.S. resident, any of her winnings from tournament play that occurs in the United States are subject to U.S. income taxation. But what about each of the following items? How does U.S. tax law affect Ling? Apply the sourcing rules in this regard, and determine whether the graduated U.S. Federal income tax rate schedules apply.

- Endorsement income from YourGolf, for wearing clothing during matches with its logo prominently displayed. Ling must play in at least 10 tournaments per year that are televised around the world. She also must participate in photo sessions and in blogs and tweets associated with the tournaments. Payment to Ling is structured as a flat fee, with bonuses paid if she finishes in the top five competitors for each match. This is known as an *on-court endorsement*.

- Endorsement income from GolfZone, for letting the company use her likeness in a video game that simulates golf tournaments among known golfers and other players that the (usually middle-aged men and women) gamers identify. In this way, the gamer seems to be playing against Ling on famous golf courses. Two-thirds of all dollar sales of the game licenses are to U.S. customers.

- Endorsement income from Eliteness, for appearing in print and Internet ads that feature Ling wearing the company's high-end watches. One-fifth of all dollar sales of the watches are to U.S. customers. The latter two items are known as *off-court endorsements*.

Internet Activity

Use the tax resources of the Internet to address the following questions. Do not restrict your search to the Web, but include a review of newsgroups and general reference materials, practitioner sites and resources, primary sources of the tax law, chat rooms and discussion groups, and other opportunities.

Research Problem 3. Supervise and Wager Company produces consumer goods that are distributed and sold primarily in North America, Europe, and Asia. The business includes a U.S. parent company, S&W, Inc., and separate operating subsidiaries in each region in which the company conducts significant business.

The company's board is considering a structural reorganization to reduce the global tax costs. Options include reorganizing the parent company in either Bermuda or Ireland. Under any option, current shareholders will contribute their stock in the U.S. parent company in return for an equivalent amount of stock in the new parent. The U.S. parent will be liquidated, and the new corporation then will be the sole shareholder of the operating subsidiaries.

    a.   What might S&W be trying to achieve with the proposed organizational restructuring?

    b.   What insight can you provide regarding the immediate and longer-term tax consequences of the reorganization? *Hint:* Use the word *inversion* in your search term.

Research Problem 4. Make a list of five countries with which the United States does *not* have in force a bilateral income tax treaty.

Communications   **Research Problem 5.** For your analysis, choose 10 countries, one of which is the United States. Create a table showing whether each country applies a worldwide or territorial approach to international income taxation. Then list the country's top income tax rate on business profits. Send a copy of this table to your instructor.

Communications   **Research Problem 6.** Locate data on the size of the international economy, including data on international trade, foreign direct investment of U.S. firms, and investments in the United States by foreign firms. Useful Web locations include **www.census.gov** and **www.bea.gov**. Prepare an analysis of these data for a three-year period, using spreadsheet and graphing software, and e-mail your findings to your instructor.

Communications   **Research Problem 7.** Read the "tax footnote" of five publicly traded U.S. corporations. Find the effective state/local income tax rates of each. Create a PowerPoint presentation (maximum of five slides) for your instructor, summarizing the search and reporting your findings.

Research Problem 8. Identify three states considered to be in the same economic region as your own.

    a.   For each of the three states and your own state, answer the following questions, creating a table with your answers. Answers to most can be found at **www.taxadmin.org**.

        i.   What is the overall tax burden per capita, and where does it rank among all states?

        ii.   What is the overall tax burden as a percentage of personal income, and where does it rank among all states?

        iii.   From what source(s) does it raise most of its revenues (e.g., sales/use tax, highway tolls)?

        iv.   What is the highest marginal tax rate on corporate income?

        v.   What is its apportionment formula, including factors and weights?

    b.   What advice or insight might you provide to your state legislature regarding your state's tax system, based on your findings for part (a)?

Business Tax Credits and Corporate Alternative Minimum Tax

LEARNING OBJECTIVES: *After completing Chapter 17, you should be able to:*

LO.1 Explain the difference in the use of credits and deductions as a Federal tax policy tool.

LO.2 Apply various business-related tax credits.

LO.3 Explain the reason for the alternative minimum tax.

LO.4 Identify and calculate AMT adjustments.

LO.5 Identify and calculate the tax preferences that are included in determining the AMT.

LO.6 State and explain the function of adjusted current earnings (ACE).

LO.7 Compute the AMT liability for corporations and individuals.

CHAPTER OUTLINE

TAX TALK *A government which robs Peter to pay Paul can always count on the support of Paul.* —GEORGE BERNARD SHAW

DEALING WITH TAX CREDITS AND THE AMT

Mike, the CEO of Progress Corporation, is committed to helping revitalize the crumbling downtown area in his hometown. The area has experienced high unemployment as companies have left for the suburbs, and Mike is considering expanding his business and purchasing an old office building in a historic section of downtown. The building will require substantial renovations, and Mike has heard that there are tax credits that might help reduce his costs. He would also like to hire inner-city workers and help working families by providing on-site child care. He is interested in learning whether his company might take advantage of any other tax credits offered by the Federal government that might reduce his costs.

Read the chapter and formulate your response.

LO.1

Explain the difference in the use of credits and deductions as a Federal tax policy tool.

Federal tax law often serves other purposes besides merely raising revenue for the government. Evidence of equity, social, and economic considerations, among others, is found throughout the tax law. These considerations also have considerable import in the area of tax credits. Congress has generally used tax credits to promote social or economic objectives or to work toward greater tax equity among different types of taxpayers. For example, the disabled access credit was enacted to accomplish a social objective: to encourage taxpayers to renovate older buildings so that they would be accessible to the disabled and be in compliance with the Americans with Disabilities Act. As another example, the foreign tax credit, which has been a part of the law for decades, has as its chief purpose the economic and equity objectives of mitigating the burden of multiple taxation on a single stream of income.

A tax credit should not be confused with an income tax deduction. Certain expenditures (e.g., business expenses) are permitted as deductions from gross income in arriving at taxable income. While the tax benefit received from a tax deduction depends on the tax rate, a tax credit is not affected by the tax rate of the taxpayer. All taxpayers can benefit equally when a tax credit is used.

EXAMPLE 1

Assume that Congress wants to encourage a certain type of expenditure. One way to accomplish this objective is to allow a tax credit of 25% for such expenditures. Another way is to allow a deduction for the expenditures. Assume that Red Corporation's tax rate is 15%, while Blue Corporation's tax rate is 34%. The following tax benefits are available to each corporation for a $1,000 expenditure.

	Red	Blue
Tax benefit if a 25% credit is allowed	$250	$250
Tax benefit if a deduction is allowed	150	340

As these results indicate, tax credits can provide benefits on a more equitable basis than tax deductions often do.

In order to prevent taxpayers with high income from completely avoiding a Federal income tax liability, the alternative minimum tax (AMT) was introduced in 1969 and has since been amended on multiple occasions. Many of the adjustments and tax preference items necessary to arrive at alternative minimum taxable income (AMTI) are the same for individuals and corporations. Other items such as the tax rates and exemptions are different between individuals and corporations, but the objective is identical—to force taxpayers that are more profitable than their regular taxable income reflects to pay additional income taxes.

LO.2

Apply various business-related tax credits.

17-1 BUSINESS-RELATED TAX CREDIT PROVISIONS

Congress has generally used tax credits to achieve social or economic objectives or to promote equity among different types of taxpayers. This section of the chapter describes the operation of the general business credit along with the most common types of credits that affect a business.

17-1a General Business Credit

The general business credit is comprised of a number of other credits, each of which is computed separately under its own set of rules. The general business credit combines these credits into one amount to limit the annual credit that can be used to offset a taxpayer's income tax liability.

The number of individual income tax returns claiming tax credits has fluctuated over the years, usually due to tax law changes, revenue needs, and political requirements.

Year	Returns Claiming Credits (in Millions)
1975	65.9
1985	21.0
1995	15.2
2000	37.7
2008	55.2
2011	49.6
2013	32.6

Source: IRS Tax Statistics.

Two special rules apply to the general business credit. First, any unused credit is carried back 1 year, then forward 20 years. Second, for any tax year, the general business credit is limited to the taxpayer's *net income tax* reduced by the greater of:[1]

- The *tentative minimum tax* [see the discussion of the alternative minimum tax (AMT) later in this chapter].
- 25 percent of *net regular tax liability* that exceeds $25,000.[2]

Net regular tax liability is the regular tax liability reduced by certain nonrefundable credits (e.g., foreign tax credit).

EXAMPLE 2

Tanager Corporation's general business credit for the current year is $70,000. Tanager's net income tax is $150,000, tentative minimum tax is $130,000, and net regular tax liability is $150,000. Tanager has no other tax credits. The general business credit allowed for the tax year is computed as follows.

Net income tax	$ 150,000
Less: The greater of—	
• $130,000 (tentative minimum tax)	
• $31,250 [25% × ($150,000 − $25,000)]	(130,000)
Amount of general business credit allowed for tax year	$ 20,000

Tanager then has $50,000 ($70,000 − $20,000) of unused general business credits that may be carried back or forward.

Treatment of Unused General Business Credits

Unused general business credits are initially carried back one year and reduce the tax liability of that year. Thus, the taxpayer may receive a tax refund as a result of the carryback. Any remaining unused credits are then carried forward 20 years.[3]

A FIFO method is applied to the carryback, carryovers, and utilization of credits earned during a particular year. The oldest credits are used first in determining the amount of the general business credit. The FIFO method minimizes the potential for loss of a general business credit benefit due to the expiration of credit carryovers and generally works to the taxpayer's benefit.

[1] § 38(c). This rule works to keep the general business credit from completely eliminating the tax liability for many taxpayers.

[2] § 38(c)(3)(B). The $25,000 amount is apportioned among the members of a controlled group.

[3] § 39(a)(1).

TAX IN THE NEWS   **Many Taxpayers Become "Nonpayers" Because of Tax Credits**

One of the key domestic policy initiatives in recent years has been to reduce marginal tax rates and then retain a lower marginal rate structure than was used under prior law. Many opponents of this policy have argued that the main beneficiaries of the lower tax rates are upper-income taxpayers who are the most affluent individuals in our country. However, economists have estimated that these policies also have led to more Americans than ever before being relieved of any Federal income tax liability.

Since 2000, the number of "nonpayers" has grown by about 59 percent. In 2013, almost 60 million Americans filed a tax return and did not owe any taxes because of deductions and credits available to them. Thus, more than 40 percent of all filers were "nonpayers."

Sources: Based on "Record Number of Tax Filers Paid No Federal Income Taxes in 2008," *Tax Foundation*, March 10, 2010; "How Much Do Nonpayers Earn?," *Tax Foundation*, September 18, 2012; and 2014 IRS Data Book.

EXAMPLE

3

This example illustrates the use of general business credit carryovers for the taxpayer's 2016 tax year.

General business credit carryovers (unused in prior tax years)		
2013	$ 4,000	
2014	6,000	
2015	2,000	
Total carryovers	$12,000	
2016 general business credit		$ 40,000
Total credit allowed in 2016 (based on tax liability)	$50,000	
Less: Carryovers used		
2013	(4,000)	
2014	(6,000)	
2015	(2,000)	
Remaining credit allowed in 2016	$38,000	
2016 general business credit used		(38,000)
2016 unused amount carried forward to 2017		$ 2,000

Each component of the general business credit is determined separately under its own set of rules. Some of the more important credits that make up the general business credit are explained here in the order listed in Exhibit 17.1.

EXHIBIT 17.1	**Principal Components of the General Business Credit**

The general business credit combines (but is not limited to) the following.

- Tax credit for rehabilitation expenditures
- Work opportunity tax credit
- Research activities credit
- Various energy credits
- Low-income housing credit
- Disabled access credit
- Credit for small employer pension plan startup costs
- Credit for employer-provided child care

BRIDGE DISCIPLINE **Bridge to Finance**

When calculating the cash-flow benefit of particular tax attributes and making a decision based on this analysis, an inappropriate decision can be made unless present value analysis is incorporated into the calculation.

The general business credit and the related carryback and carryover provisions can be used to illustrate the cash-flow impact.

Blonde, Inc.'s general business credit for 2016 is $400,000. However, the amount that may be used to reduce the current-year tax liability is only $280,000. None can be used in 2015 (the carryback year), so the $120,000 is carried forward. The $120,000 of unused general business credit is expected to offset Blonde's future tax liability as follows.

2017	$20,000
2018	40,000
2019	60,000

It appears that the cash-flow benefit to Blonde is $400,000. In nominal dollars, this result is correct. However, when the present value concept is applied, the cash-flow benefit is only $376,280 (assuming that Blonde's discount rate is 4 percent).

2016	$280,000 × 1.000	=	$280,000
2017	20,000 × .9615	=	19,230
2018	40,000 × .9246	=	36,984
2019	60,000 × .8890	=	53,340
			$389,554

The carryforward period for the general business credit is 20 years. Using a 4 percent discount rate, one dollar in 20 years is worth about 46 cents ($1 × .4564) today. So taxpayers should use the general business credit to offset tax liability as rapidly as possible.

17-1b Tax Credit for Rehabilitation Expenditures

Taxpayers are allowed a tax credit for expenditures incurred to rehabilitate older industrial and commercial buildings and certified historic structures. The rehabilitation expenditures credit is intended to discourage businesses from moving from economically distressed areas (e.g., an inner city) to outlying locations and to encourage the preservation of historic structures. The current operating features of this credit follow.[4]

Rate of the Credit for Rehabilitation Expenses	Nature of the Property
10%	Nonresidential buildings and residential rental property, other than certified historic structures, originally placed in service before 1936
20%	Nonresidential and residential certified historic structures

Taxpayers who claim the rehabilitation credit must reduce the basis of the rehabilitated building by the credit allowed.[5]

The Big Picture

EXAMPLE 4

Return to the facts of *The Big Picture* on p. 17-1. Assume that Progress spends $60,000 to rehabilitate a building (adjusted basis of $40,000) that had been placed in service in 1932.

Progress is allowed a credit of $6,000 (10% × $60,000) for rehabilitation expenditures. The corporation then increases the basis of the building by $54,000 [$60,000 (rehabilitation expenditures)− $6,000 (credit allowed)].

If the building were a historic structure, the credit allowed would be $12,000 (20% × $60,000) and the building's depreciable basis would increase by $48,000 [$60,000 (rehabilitation expenditures) − $12,000 (credit allowed)].

---

[4]§ 47.

[5]§ 50(c).

To qualify for the credit, buildings must be substantially rehabilitated. A building has been *substantially rehabilitated* if qualified rehabilitation expenditures exceed the *greater of*:

- The adjusted basis of the property before the rehabilitation expenditures, or
- $5,000.

Qualified rehabilitation expenditures do not include the cost of acquiring a building, the cost of facilities related to a building (such as a parking lot), and the cost of enlarging an existing building. Stringent rules apply concerning the retention of the building's original internal and external walls.

Recapture of Tax Credit for Rehabilitation Expenditures

The rehabilitation credit taken is recaptured if the rehabilitated property is disposed of prematurely or if it ceases to be qualifying property. The **rehabilitation expenditures credit recapture** is added to the taxpayer's regular tax liability in the recapture year. The recapture amount also is *added* to the adjusted basis of the building.

The portion of the credit recaptured is a specified percentage of the credit that was taken by the taxpayer. This percentage is based on the period the property was held by the taxpayer, as shown in Exhibit 17.2. If the property is held at least five years, no recapture will result.

EXAMPLE 5

On March 15, 2013, Chickadee Corporation rehabilitated a building qualifying for the 10% credit. The company spent $30,000 in qualifying rehabilitation expenditures and claimed a $3,000 credit ($30,000 × 10%). The basis of the building was increased by $27,000 ($30,000 − $3,000).

Chickadee sold the building on December 15, 2016. Chickadee recaptures a portion of the rehabilitation credit based on the schedule in Exhibit 17.2. Because Chickadee held the rehabilitated property for more than three years but less than four, 40% of the credit, or $1,200, is added to the company's 2016 income tax liability. In addition, the adjusted basis of the building is increased by the $1,200 recapture amount.

17-1c **Work Opportunity Tax Credit**

The **work opportunity tax credit**[6] was enacted to encourage employers to hire individuals from a variety of targeted and economically disadvantaged groups. Examples of such targeted persons include long-term unemployed individuals (those unemployed for at least 27 weeks), qualified ex-felons, high-risk youths, food stamp recipients, veterans, summer youth employees, and long-term family assistance recipients.

EXHIBIT 17.2	Recapture Calculation for Rehabilitation Expenditures Credit

If the Property Is Held for	The Recapture Percentage Is
Less than 1 year	100%
One year or more but less than 2 years	80%
Two years or more but less than 3 years	60%
Three years or more but less than 4 years	40%
Four years or more but less than 5 years	20%

---

[6]§ 51. The credit is available for qualifying employees who start work before 2020.

Computation of the Work Opportunity Tax Credit: General

The credit generally is equal to 40 percent of the first $6,000 of wages (per eligible employee) for the first 12 months of employment. The credit is not available for wages paid to an employee after the *first year* of employment. If the employee's first year overlaps two of the employer's tax years, however, the employer may take the credit over two tax years. If the credit is claimed, the employer's tax deduction for wages is reduced by the amount of the credit.

To qualify an employer for the 40 percent credit, the employee must (1) be certified by a designated local agency as being a member of one of the targeted groups and (2) have completed at least 400 hours of service to the employer. If an employee meets the first condition but not the second, the credit is reduced to 25 percent, provided the employee has completed a minimum of 120 hours of service to the employer.

| In-depth coverage can be found on this book's companion website: www.cengagebrain.com | **1** DIGGING DEEPER |

The Big Picture

EXAMPLE 6

Return to the facts of *The Big Picture* on p. 17-1. In January 2016, Progress Corporation hires four individuals who are certified to be members of a qualifying targeted group. Each employee works 1,000 hours and is paid wages of $8,000 during the year.

Progress's work opportunity credit is $9,600 [($6,000 × 40%) × 4 employees]. If the tax credit is taken, Progress reduces its deduction for wages paid by $9,600. No credit is available for wages paid to these employees after their first year of employment.

EXAMPLE 7

On June 1, 2016, Maria, a calendar year taxpayer, hires Joe, a member of a certified group, and obtains the required certification to qualify Maria for the work opportunity credit. During his seven months of work in 2016, Joe is paid $3,500 for 500 hours of work. Maria is allowed a credit of $1,400 ($3,500 × 40%) for 2016.

Joe continues to work for Maria in 2017 and is paid $7,000 through May 31, 2017. Because up to $6,000 of first-year wages are eligible for the credit, Maria is also allowed a 40% credit on $2,500 [$6,000 − $3,500 (wages paid in 2016)] of 2017 wages paid. The credit is $1,000 ($2,500 × 40%). None of Joe's wages paid after May 31, 2017, the end of the first year of Joe's employment, are eligible for the credit.

Computation of the Work Opportunity Tax Credit: Long-Term Family Assistance Recipient

The credit[7] is available to employers hiring individuals who have been long-term recipients of family assistance welfare benefits. In general, *long-term recipients* are those individuals who are certified by a designated local agency as being members of a family receiving assistance under a public aid program for the 18-month period ending on the hiring date. Unlike the work opportunity credit for other targeted groups, which applies only to first-year wages paid to qualified individuals, this credit is available for qualified wages paid in the first *two years* of employment. If an employee's first and second work years overlap two or more of the employer's tax years, the employer may take the credit during the applicable tax years.

The credit is equal to 40 percent of the first $10,000 of qualified wages paid to an employee in the first year of employment plus 50 percent of the first $10,000 of quali-

---

[7]This component of the work opportunity tax credit previously was known as the welfare-to-work credit (§ 51A).

fied wages in the second year of employment, resulting in a maximum credit per qualified employee of $9,000 [$4,000 (year 1) + $5,000 (year 2)]. The credit rate is higher for second-year wages to encourage employers to retain qualified individuals, thereby promoting the overall welfare-to-work goal.

EXAMPLE 8

In April 2016, Blue Company hires three individuals who are certified as long-term family assistance recipients. Each employee is paid $12,000 during 2016. Two of the three individuals continue to work for Blue in 2017, earning $9,000 each during the year.

Blue's work opportunity tax credit is $12,000 [(40% × $10,000) × 3 employees] for 2016 and $9,000 [(50% × $9,000) × 2 employees] for 2017. In each year, Blue must reduce its deduction for wages paid by the amount of the credit for that year.

17-1d Research Activities Credit

To encourage business-related research and development (R & D) in the U.S. business community, a credit is allowed for certain qualifying expenditures paid or incurred by a taxpayer. The **research activities credit** is the *sum* of three components: (1) an incremental research activities credit, (2) a basic research credit, and (3) an energy research credit.[8]

Incremental Research Activities Credit

The incremental research activities credit applies at a 20 percent rate to the *excess* of qualified research expenses for the taxable year (the credit year) over a base amount.[9] Determining the *base amount* involves a relatively complex series of computations meant to approximate recent historical levels of research activity by the taxpayer. Thus, the credit is allowed only for increases in research expenses.

In general, *research expenditures* qualify if the research relates to discovering technological information that is intended for use in the development of a new or improved business component of the taxpayer. Such expenses qualify fully if the research is performed in-house (by the taxpayer or its employees). If the research is conducted by persons outside the taxpayer's business (e.g., under terms of a contract), only 65 percent of the amount paid qualifies for the credit.[10]

EXAMPLE 9

Bobwhite Company incurs the following research expenditures.

In-house wages, supplies, computer time	$135,000
Payment to Cutting Edge Scientific (a contractor)	100,000

Bobwhite's qualified research expenditures are $200,000 [$135,000 + ($100,000 × 65%)]. If the base amount is $100,000, the incremental research activities credit is $20,000 [($200,000 − $100,000) × 20%].

Beyond the general guidelines described above, the Code does not give specific examples of qualifying research. However, the credit is *not* allowed for:[11]

- Research conducted after the beginning of commercial production of the business component.
- Surveys and studies such as market research, testing, or routine data collection.

---

[8]§ 41. An eligible small business ($50 million or less in gross receipts) can use the credit to reduce its alternative minimum tax (AMT) liability. In addition, a qualified startup company (less than $5 million in gross receipts) can offset the credit against its payroll tax liability.

[9]In lieu of determining the incremental research credit as described here, a taxpayer may elect to calculate the credit using an alternative simplified credit procedure. See §§ 41(c)(4) and (5).

[10]§ 41(b)(3)(A). In the case of payments to a qualified research consortium, § 41(b)(3)(A) provides that 75% of the amount paid qualifies for the credit. In contrast, for amounts paid to an energy research consortium, § 41(b)(3)(D) allows the full amount to qualify for the credit.

[11]§ 41(d).

- Research conducted *outside* the United States (other than research undertaken in Puerto Rico or U.S. possessions).
- Research in the social sciences, arts, or humanities.

Qualified expenditures are not only eligible for the 20 percent credit but also can be *expensed* in the year incurred. As a result, a taxpayer must either:[12]

- Use the full credit and reduce the expense deduction for research expenses by 100 percent of the credit, or
- Retain the full expense deduction and reduce the credit by the product of the full credit times the maximum corporate tax rate (35 percent).

As an alternative to the expense deduction, the taxpayer may *capitalize* the research expenses and *amortize* them over 60 months or more. In this case, the amount capitalized and subject to amortization is reduced by the full amount of the credit *only* if the credit exceeds the amount allowable as a deduction.

EXAMPLE

10

Assume the same facts as in Example 9, which shows that the potential incremental research activities credit is $20,000. In the current year, the amounts Bobwhite can deduct and the credit amount under each of the three choices are computed as follows.

	Credit Amount	Deduction Amount
• Full credit and reduced deduction		
$20,000 − $0	$20,000	
$200,000 − $20,000		$180,000
• Reduced credit and full deduction		
$20,000 − [(100% × $20,000) × 35%]	13,000	
$200,000 − $0		200,000
• Full credit and capitalize and elect to amortize costs over 60 months		
$20,000 − $0	20,000	
($200,000/60) × 12		40,000

The value of the deduction depends on Bobwhite's marginal tax rates.

Basic Research Credit

Corporations (other than S corporations or personal service corporations) are allowed an additional 20 percent credit for basic research expenditures incurred, in *excess* of a base amount.[13] This credit is not available to individual taxpayers. *Basic research expenditures* are defined as amounts paid in cash to a qualified basic research organization, such as a college or university or a tax-exempt organization operated primarily to conduct scientific research.

Basic research is defined generally as any original investigation for the advancement of scientific knowledge not having a specific commercial objective. The definition excludes basic research conducted outside the United States and basic research in the social sciences, arts, or humanities.

Energy Research Credit

This component of the research credit is intended to stimulate additional energy research. The calculation of the credit is relatively straightforward; it is equal to

---

[12]§§ 174 and 280C(c). Recall the discussion of rules for deducting research and experimental expenditures in Chapter 5.

[13]§ 41(e).

20 percent of the amounts paid or incurred by a taxpayer to an energy research consortium for energy research.

17-1e Energy Credits

The Internal Revenue Code contains a variety of credits for businesses and individuals to encourage the conservation of natural resources and the development of energy sources other than oil and gas. The primary goals of the tax provisions are to improve energy-related infrastructure and encourage higher levels of energy conservation. Most of these credits are temporary in nature, and many of them expire in 2016.

Some of the more widely applicable provisions include credits for:

- Builders who construct energy-efficient homes.
- Individuals who make energy-saving improvements to their residences.
- Businesses that buy fuel cell and microturbine power plants.
- Taxpayers who purchase alternative power motor vehicles and refueling property.

Like many other tax credits, the **energy credits** have been designed to modify taxpayer behavior. More specifically, in this case, Congress's intention is that these credits will lead to greater conservation and more efficient use of energy.

17-1f Disabled Access Credit

The **disabled access credit** is designed to encourage small businesses to make their facilities more accessible to disabled individuals. The credit is available for any eligible access expenditures paid or incurred by an eligible small business. The credit is calculated at the rate of 50 percent of the eligible expenditures that exceed $250 but do not exceed $10,250. Thus, the maximum amount of the credit is $5,000 ($10,000 × 50%).[14]

An *eligible small business* is a business that during the previous year either had gross receipts of $1 million or less or had no more than 30 full-time employees. A sole proprietorship, a partnership, a regular corporation, or an S corporation can qualify as such an entity.

Eligible access expenditures generally include any reasonable and necessary amounts that are paid or incurred to make certain changes to older facilities. These changes must involve the removal of architectural, communication, physical, or transportation barriers that otherwise would make a business inaccessible to disabled individuals. Qualifying projects include installing ramps, widening doorways, and adding raised markings on elevator control buttons.

The facility must have been placed in service prior to November 5, 1990 for any improvements to be eligible for the credit. To the extent a disabled access credit is available, the property's depreciable basis is reduced by the amount of the credit.

EXAMPLE 11

This year, Red, Inc., an eligible business, makes $11,000 of capital improvements to business realty that had been placed in service in June 1990. The expenditures are intended to make Red's business more accessible to the disabled and are considered eligible expenditures for purposes of the disabled access credit.

The amount of the credit is $5,000 [($10,250 maximum − $250 floor) × 50%]. The depreciable basis of the capital improvement is $6,000 [$11,000 (cost) − $5,000 (amount of the credit)].

17-1g Credit for Small Employer Pension Plan Startup Costs

Small businesses are entitled to a nonrefundable credit for administrative costs associated with establishing and maintaining certain qualified retirement plans.[15] While such costs (e.g., payroll system changes, retirement-related education programs, and consulting fees) generally are deductible as ordinary and necessary business expenses, the

---

[14]§ 44.

[15]§ 45E.

credit is intended to lower the after-tax cost of establishing a qualified retirement program and thereby to encourage qualifying businesses to offer retirement plans for their employees.

The **credit for small employer pension plan startup costs** is available for eligible employers at the rate of 50 percent of qualified startup costs. An eligible employer is one with fewer than 100 employees who have earned at least $5,000 of compensation. The maximum credit is $500 (based on a maximum $1,000 of qualifying expenses), and the deduction for the startup costs incurred is reduced by the amount of the credit. The credit can be claimed for qualifying costs incurred in each of the three years beginning with the tax year in which the retirement plan becomes effective (maximum total credit of $1,500).

EXAMPLE 12

Maple Company decides to establish a qualified retirement plan for its employees. In the process, it pays consulting fees of $1,200 to a firm that will provide educational seminars to Maple's employees and will assist the payroll department in making necessary changes to the payroll system.

Maple may claim a credit for the pension plan startup costs of $500 ($1,200 of qualifying costs, limited to $1,000 × 50%), and its deduction for these expenses is reduced to $700 ($1,200 − $500).

17-1h Credit for Employer-Provided Child Care

An employer can deduct expenditures incurred to provide for the care of children of employees as ordinary and necessary business expenses. Alternatively, employers may claim a credit for qualifying expenditures incurred while providing child care facilities to their employees during normal working hours.[16]

The **credit for employer-provided child care**, limited annually to $150,000, is composed of the aggregate of two components: 25 percent of qualified child care expenses and 10 percent of qualified child care resource and referral services. *Qualified child care expenses* include the costs of acquiring, constructing, rehabilitating, expanding, and operating a child care facility. *Child care resource and referral services* include amounts paid or incurred under a contract to provide child care resource and referral services to an employee.

Any qualifying expenses otherwise deductible by the taxpayer are reduced by the amount of the credit. In addition, the taxpayer's basis for any property acquired or constructed and used for qualifying purposes is reduced by the amount of the credit. If within 10 years of being placed in service a child care facility ceases to be used for a qualified use, the taxpayer recaptures a portion of the credit previously claimed.[17]

The Big Picture

EXAMPLE 13

Return to the facts of *The Big Picture* on p. 17-1. During the year, Progress Corporation constructs a child care facility for $400,000 to be used by its employees who have preschool-aged children in need of child care services while their parents are at work. In addition, Progress incurs salary costs for child care workers and other administrative costs associated with the facility of $100,000 during the year.

As a result, Progress's credit for employer-provided child care is $125,000 [($400,000 + $100,000) × 25%]. Correspondingly, the basis of the facility is reduced to $300,000 ($400,000 − $100,000), and the deduction for salaries and administrative costs is reduced to $75,000 ($100,000 − $25,000).

In-depth coverage can be found on this book's companion website: www.cengagebrain.com   **2 DIGGING DEEPER**

---

[16] § 45F.   [17] § 45F(d).

GLOBAL TAX ISSUES **Sourcing Income in Cyberspace—Getting It Right When Calculating the Foreign Tax Credit**

The overall limitation on the foreign tax credit plays a critical role in restricting the amount of the credit available to a taxpayer. In the overall limitation formula, the taxpayer must characterize the year's taxable income as either earned (or sourced) inside or outside the United States. As a general rule, a relatively greater percentage of foreign-source income in the formula leads to a larger foreign tax credit. But classifying income as either foreign or U.S. source is not always a simple matter.

The existing income-sourcing rules were developed long before the existence of the Internet, and taxing authorities are finding it challenging to apply these rules to Internet transactions. Where does a sale take place when the web server is in Scotland, the seller is in India, and the customer is in Illinois? Where is a service performed when all activities take place over the Net? These questions and more must be answered by the United States and its trading partners as the Internet economy grows in size and importance.

17-1i Foreign Tax Credit

Individual taxpayers and corporations may claim a credit for foreign income tax paid on income earned and subject to tax in another country or a U.S. possession.[18] The **foreign tax credit (FTC)** is designed to mitigate the possibility of double taxation of foreign income.

EXAMPLE 14

Ace Tools, Inc., a U.S. corporation, has a branch operation in Mexico from which it earns taxable income of $750,000 for the current year. Ace pays income tax of $150,000 on these earnings to the Mexican tax authorities. Ace must also include the $750,000 in gross income for U.S. tax purposes.

Before considering the FTC, Ace owes $255,000 in U.S. income taxes on this foreign-source income. Thus, total taxes on the $750,000 could equal $405,000 ($150,000 + $255,000), a 54% effective rate. But Ace takes the FTC of $150,000 against its U.S. tax liability on the foreign-source income. Ace Tools' total taxes on the $750,000 now are $255,000 ($150,000 + $105,000), a 34% effective rate.

The tax year's FTC equals the *lesser* of the foreign taxes imposed or the *overall limitation* determined according to the following formula. Thus, where applicable foreign tax rates exceed those of the United States, the credit offsets no more than the marginal U.S. tax on the double-taxed income.

$$\frac{\text{Foreign-source taxable income}}{\text{Worldwide taxable income}} \times \text{U.S. tax before FTC}$$

Foreign taxes paid but not allowed as a credit due to the overall limitation are carried back 1 tax year and then forward 10 years.[19]

EXAMPLE 15

Oriole, Inc., a U.S. corporation, conducts business in a foreign country. Oriole's worldwide taxable income for the tax year is $120,000, consisting of $100,000 in income from U.S. operations and $20,000 of income from the foreign source. Foreign tax of $6,000 was paid to foreign tax authorities on the $20,000. Before the FTC, Oriole's U.S. tax on the $120,000 is $30,050.

The corporation's FTC is $5,008 {lesser of $6,000 paid or $5,008 limitation [$30,050 × ($20,000/$120,000)]}. Oriole's net U.S. tax liability is $25,042 ($30,050 − $5,008).

Thus, Oriole carries over (back 1 year and forward 10 years) a $992 FTC ($6,000 − $5,008) because of the overall limitation.

---

[18]§ 27 provides for the credit, but the qualifications and calculation procedure for the credit are contained in §§ 901–908. Alternatively, the taxpayer can *deduct* the foreign taxes paid. See Chapter 16 for more details.

[19]§ 904(c).

17-1j **Small Employer Health Insurance Credit**

Under the Affordable Care Act (ACA), a tax credit is available to a qualified small employer for nonelective contributions to purchase health insurance for its employees.[20] The insurance must be purchased through a Small Business Health Options Program (SHOP) Marketplace established as part of the ACA. The credit is available only for two consecutive tax years.

To qualify for the credit in 2016, the employer must have no more than 25 full-time equivalent employees whose annual full-time wages average no more than $51,800 ($51,600 in 2015). The employer must pay at least half the cost of the health insurance premiums.[21] The credit is 50 percent of the health insurance premiums paid. It is subject to a phaseout if the employer has more than 10 full-time equivalent employees and/or has annual full-time wages that average more than $25,900 ($25,800 in 2015).[22]

Concept Summary 17.1 provides an overview of the tax credits discussed in this chapter.

Concept Summary 17.1

Tax Credits

Credit	Computation	Comments
General business (§ 38)	May not exceed net income tax minus the greater of tentative minimum tax or 25% of net regular tax liability that exceeds $25,000.	Components include tax credit for rehabilitation expenditures, work opportunity tax credit, research activities credit, low-income housing credit, disabled access credit, credit for small employer pension plan startup costs, and credit for employer-provided child care.
		Unused credit may be carried back 1 year and forward 20 years. FIFO method applies to carrybacks, carryovers, and credits earned during current year.
Rehabilitation expenditures (§ 47)	Qualifying investment times rehabilitation percentage, depending on type of property. Regular rehabilitation rate is 10%; rate for certified historic structures is 20%.	Part of general business credit and therefore subject to same carryback, carryover, and FIFO rules. Purpose is to discourage businesses from moving from economically distressed areas to new locations.
Work opportunity (§ 51)	Credit is limited to 40% of the first $6,000 of wages paid to each eligible employee. For long-term family assistance recipients, credit is limited to 40% of first $10,000 of wages paid to each eligible employee in first year of employment, plus 50% of first $10,000 of wages paid to same employee in second year of employment.	Part of the general business credit and therefore subject to the same carryback, carryover, and FIFO rules. Purpose is to encourage employment of members of economically disadvantaged groups.
Research activities (§ 41)	Incremental credit is 20% of excess of computation-year expenditures over a base amount. Basic research credit is allowed to certain corporations for 20% of cash payments to qualified organizations that exceed a specially calculated base amount. An energy research credit is allowed for 20% of qualifying payments made to an energy research consortium.	Part of general business credit and therefore subject to same carryback, carryover, and FIFO rules. Purpose is to encourage high-tech and energy research in the United States.
Low-income housing (§ 42)	Appropriate rate times eligible basis (portion of project attributable to low-income units).	Part of general business credit and therefore subject to same carryback, carryover, and FIFO rules. Recapture may apply. Purpose is to encourage construction of housing for low-income individuals. Credit is available each year for 10 years.

continued

---

[20]§ 45R.

[21]§§ 45R(d)(1) and (4). The wage amount is indexed for inflation each year.

[22]§ 45R(c). The credit percentage for tax-exempt employers is 35%.

Tax Credits—(Continued)

Credit	Computation	Comments
Energy credits	Various items to encourage individuals and businesses to "go green."	Part of general business credit and therefore subject to same carryback, carryover, and FIFO rules.
Disabled access (§ 44)	Credit is 50% of eligible access expenditures that exceed $250 but do not exceed $10,250. Maximum credit is $5,000.	Part of general business credit and therefore subject to same carryback, carryover, and FIFO rules. Purpose is to encourage small businesses to become more accessible to disabled individuals. Available only to eligible small businesses.
Credit for small employer pension plan startup costs (§ 45E)	The credit equals 50% of qualified startup costs incurred by eligible employers. Maximum annual credit is $500. Deduction for related expenses is reduced by the amount of the credit.	Part of general business credit and therefore subject to same carryback, carryover, and FIFO rules. Purpose is to encourage small employers to establish qualified retirement plans for their employees.
Credit for employer-provided child care (§ 45F)	Credit is equal to 25% of qualified child care expenses plus 10% of qualified expenses for child care resource and referral services. Maximum credit is $150,000. Deduction for related expenses or basis must be reduced by the amount of the credit.	Part of general business credit and therefore subject to same carryback, carryover, and FIFO rules. Purpose is to encourage employers to provide child care for their employees' children during normal working hours.
Foreign tax (§ 27)	Foreign taxable income/total worldwide taxable income × U.S. tax = Overall limitation. Lesser of foreign taxes imposed or overall limitation.	Unused credits may be carried back 1 year and forward 10 years. Purpose is to reduce double taxation of foreign income.
Small Employer Health Insurance Credit (§ 45R)	The credit is 50% of the health insurance premiums paid (subject to a phaseout).	To qualify for the credit, the employer must have no more than 25 full-time equivalent employees whose annual full-time wages average no more than $51,800 (2016).

Explain the reason for the alternative minimum tax.

17-2 CORPORATE ALTERNATIVE MINIMUM TAX

A perception that many large corporations were not paying their fair share of Federal income tax was especially widespread in the early 1980s. A study released in 1986 reported that 130 of the 250 largest corporations in the United States—including Reynolds Metals, General Dynamics, and Georgia Pacific—paid no Federal taxes in at least one year between 1981 and 1985. Political pressure subsequently led to the adoption of an **alternative minimum tax (AMT)** to ensure that corporations with substantial economic income pay at least a minimum amount of Federal taxes.

The AMT limits the tax savings for some taxpayers who are seen as gaining "too much" from exclusions, deductions, and credits available under the law. A separate tax system with a proportional tax rate is applied each year to a corporation's economic income. If the tentative AMT is greater than the regular corporate income tax, then the corporation must pay the regular tax plus this excess, the AMT.

Since its inception, the AMT has been vulnerable to criticisms that it is too complex. Smaller corporations especially find that the imposition of a second tax structure unduly increases their compliance burdens. Thus, under current rules, most smaller corporations are not subject to the AMT at all. A C corporation is exempted from the AMT if it meets the following tests:

- It was treated as a small corporation exempt from the AMT for all prior years beginning after 1997.

- Its annual average gross receipts for the three-year period (or portion thereof during which the corporation was in existence) ending before its current tax year did not exceed $7.5 million ($5 million if the corporation had only one prior tax year).

This provision exempts approximately 95 percent of all C corporations from the AMT. A corporation *automatically* is classified as a small corporation in the first tax year of existence. A corporation that fails these tests for any year will be subject to the AMT rules for that year and all future years.

17-2a The AMT Formula

The AMT is imposed in addition to the regular corporate income tax, but is computed in a manner separate from it.[23] Typically for the AMT, more items are subject to tax under AMT rules, some gross income items are accelerated, and some deductions are deferred.

The formula for determining the AMT liability of corporate taxpayers appears in Exhibit 17.3 and follows the format of Form 4626 (Alternative Minimum Tax—Corporations).

The base for the AMT, **alternative minimum taxable income (AMTI)**, begins with regular taxable income before any deductions for net operating losses (NOLs). A series of additions and subtractions is then made. Most AMT adjustments relate to *timing differences* that arise because of different regular income tax and AMT treatments. Adjustments that are caused by timing differences eventually reverse; that is, positive adjustments are offset by negative adjustments in the future, and vice versa. A common AMT adjustment is depreciation; AMT depreciation is determined using longer lives than those used for regular MACRS. Preference items always increase alternative minimum taxable income (AMTI).

AMT Adjustments: Timing Differences

> **EXAMPLE 16**
>
> In 2016, Bobwhite, Inc., deducted depreciation expense of $30,000 for regular income tax purposes. For AMT purposes, assume that the depreciation is spread evenly over the next three years ($10,000 per year). The AMT adjustment for 2016 is computed as follows.
>
> | | |
> |---|---:|
> | Depreciation deducted for regular income tax purposes | $ 30,000 |
> | Depreciation deducted for AMT purposes | (10,000) |
> | AMT adjustment (positive) | $ 20,000 |

> **EXAMPLE 17**
>
> Assume the same facts as in Example 16. The timing difference that gave rise to the positive adjustment in 2016 will reverse in the future. For AMT purposes, Bobwhite will deduct $10,000 in 2017 and $10,000 in 2018. The regular income tax deduction in each of those years will be $0, because the entire $30,000 expenditure was deducted in 2016. This results in a negative AMT adjustment of $10,000 each in 2017 and 2018. The AMT adjustments over the three-year period are summarized below.
>
> | Year | Regular Income Tax Deduction | AMT Deduction | AMT Adjustment |
> |---|---|---|---|
> | 2016 | $30,000 | $10,000 | $ 20,000 |
> | 2017 | –0– | 10,000 | (10,000) |
> | 2018 | –0– | 10,000 | (10,000) |
> | Totals | $30,000 | $30,000 | $ –0– |
>
> Timing differences eventually reverse. Thus, positive AMT adjustments can be offset later by negative adjustments.

---

[23]The AMT provisions are contained in §§ 55 through 59.

EXHIBIT 17.3		AMT Formula for Corporations
		Regular taxable income before NOL deduction
Plus/minus:		AMT adjustments (except ACE adjustment)
Plus:		Tax preferences
	Equals:	AMTI before AMT NOL deduction and ACE adjustment
Plus/minus:		ACE adjustment
	Equals:	AMTI before AMT NOL deduction
Minus:		AMT NOL deduction (limited to 90%)
	Equals:	Alternative minimum taxable income (AMTI)
Minus:		Exemption
	Equals:	AMT base
Times:		20% rate
	Equals:	Tentative AMT before credits
Minus:		AMT foreign tax credit and other credits
	Equals:	Tentative minimum tax (TMT)
Minus:		Regular income tax liability before credits minus regular foreign tax credit
	Equals:	Alternative minimum tax (AMT) if positive

LO.4

Identify and calculate AMT adjustments.

17-2b AMT Adjustments

As Exhibit 17.3 indicates, the starting point for computing AMTI is the taxable income of the corporation before any NOL deduction. Certain *adjustments* must be made to this amount. Unlike tax preference items, which always increase AMTI, the adjustments may be either increases or decreases to taxable income.

Although NOLs are listed separately in Exhibit 17.3, they are actually adjustments that reduce taxable income. They are listed separately in Exhibit 17.3 and on the AMT tax form because they may not exceed more than 90 percent of AMTI. Thus, the NOL adjustment cannot be determined until all other adjustments and tax preference items are considered.

Computing Adjustments

It is necessary to determine not only the amount of an adjustment but also whether the adjustment is positive or negative. Careful study of Examples 16 and 17 reveals the following pattern with regard to *deductions*.

- If the deduction allowed for regular income tax purposes exceeds the deduction allowed for AMT purposes, the difference is a positive adjustment.
- If the deduction allowed for AMT purposes exceeds the deduction allowed for regular income tax purposes, the difference is a negative adjustment.

Conversely, the direction of an adjustment attributable to an *income* item can be determined as follows.

- If the income reported for regular income tax purposes exceeds the income reported for AMT purposes, the difference is a negative adjustment.
- If the income reported for AMT purposes exceeds the income reported for regular income tax purposes, the difference is a positive adjustment.

The principal AMT adjustments are discussed next. The adjustment for circulation expenditures was discussed previously.

Depreciation of Post-1986 Real Property

Tax legislation enacted in 1997 eliminated the AMT depreciation adjustment for real property by providing that the MACRS recovery periods (see Exhibit 5.6) used in calculating the regular income tax also apply in calculating the AMT. Note, however, that this AMT recovery period conformity provision applies only to property placed in service after 1998.[24] Thus, the AMT depreciation adjustment discussed below applies only for real property placed in service before 1999.

For real property placed in service after 1986 (MACRS property) and before 1999, AMT depreciation is computed under the alternative depreciation system (ADS), which uses the straight-line method over a 40-year life. The depreciation lives for regular income tax purposes are 27.5 years for residential rental property and 39 years for all other real property.[25] The difference between AMT depreciation and regular income tax depreciation is treated as an adjustment in computing the AMT. The differences will be positive during the asset's regular income tax life because the cost is written off over a shorter period for regular income tax purposes.

Exhibit 5.6 is used to compute regular income tax depreciation on real property placed in service after 1986. For AMT purposes, depreciation on real property placed in service after 1986 and before 1999 is computed under the ADS (refer to Exhibit 5.10).

EXAMPLE

18

In January 1998, Robin Rentals placed in service a residential building that cost $100,000. Regular income tax depreciation, AMT depreciation, and the AMT adjustment are computed as follows.

	Depreciation		
Year	Regular Income Tax	AMT	AMT Adjustment
1998	$ 3,485[1]	$ 2,396[2]	$ 1,089
1999–2015	61,812[3]	42,500[4]	19,312
2016	3,636	2,500	1,136
Total	$68,933	$47,396	$21,537

[1] $100,000 cost × 3.485% (Exhibit 5.6) = $3,485
[2] $100,000 cost × 2.396% (Exhibit 5.10) = $2,396
[3] $100,000 cost × 3.636% (Exhibit 5.6) = $3,636 for 17 years
[4] $100,000 cost × 2.500% (Exhibit 5.10) = $2,500 for 17 years

If the building had been placed in service after 1998, there would have been no AMT depreciation adjustment for the tax year it was placed in service or for subsequent years. The depreciation for the tax year the building was placed in service for both regular income tax purposes and AMT purposes would have been $3,485 ($100,000 × 3.485%).

After real property placed in service before 1999 has been held for the entire depreciation period for regular income tax purposes, the asset is fully depreciated. However, the depreciation period under the ADS is 41 years due to application of the mid-month convention, so depreciation will continue for AMT purposes. This causes negative adjustments after the property has been fully depreciated for regular income tax purposes.

EXAMPLE

19

Assume the same facts as in the previous example for the building placed in service in 1998. Regular income tax depreciation in the year 2027 (the thirtieth year of the asset's life) is zero (refer to Exhibit 5.6). AMT depreciation is $2,500 ($100,000 cost × 2.500% from Exhibit 5.10).

Therefore, Robin has a negative AMT adjustment of $2,500 ($0 regular income tax depreciation − $2,500 AMT depreciation).

---

[24]§ 56(a)(1)(A)(i).

[25]The 39-year life generally applies to nonresidential real property placed in service on or after May 13, 1993.

After real property is fully depreciated for both regular income tax and AMT purposes, the positive and negative adjustments that have been made for AMT purposes will net to zero.

Depreciation of Post-1986 Personal Property

For most personal property placed in service after 1986 (MACRS property), the MACRS deduction for regular income tax purposes is based on the 200 percent declining-balance method with a switch to straight-line when that method produces a larger depreciation deduction for the asset. Refer to Exhibit 5.4 for computing regular income tax depreciation.

For AMT purposes, the taxpayer must use the ADS for such property placed in service before 1999. This method is based on the 150 percent declining-balance method with a similar switch to straight-line for all personal property.[26] Refer to Exhibit 5.8 for percentages to be used in computing AMT depreciation.

The MACRS deduction for personal property is larger than the ADS deduction in the early years of an asset's life. However, the ADS deduction is larger in the later years. This is so because ADS lives are sometimes longer than MACRS lives and use less accelerated depreciation methods.[27] Over the ADS life of the asset, the same aggregate amount of depreciation is deducted for both regular income tax and AMT purposes. In the same manner as other timing adjustments, the AMT adjustments for depreciation will net to zero over the ADS life of the asset.

The taxpayer may elect to use the ADS for regular income tax purposes. If this election is made, no AMT adjustment is required because the depreciation deduction is the same for regular income tax and for the AMT. The election eliminates the burden of maintaining two sets of tax depreciation records at the cost of a higher regular tax liability.

For personal property placed in service after 1998, MACRS recovery periods are used in calculating AMT depreciation, but the 150 percent declining-balance method still is used. Thus, if the taxpayer elects to use the 150 percent declining-balance method for regular income tax purposes, there are no AMT adjustments. Conversely, if the taxpayer uses the 200 percent declining-balance method for regular income tax purposes, there is an AMT adjustment for depreciation.

As discussed in Chapter 5, for regular tax purposes, an additional first-year depreciation deduction equal to a specified percentage of the unadjusted depreciable basis of qualified property is available for property placed in service before 2020. For property to which this additional first-year depreciation deduction (also known as bonus depreciation) is elected, no depreciation adjustment for AMT purposes is required. This is true both in the year the asset is placed in service and in all succeeding years in which the asset is depreciated.

Pollution Control Facilities

For regular income tax purposes, the cost of certified pollution control facilities may be amortized over a period of 60 months. For AMT purposes, the cost of these facilities placed in service after 1986 and before 1999 is depreciated under the ADS over the appropriate class life, determined as explained previously for depreciation of post-1986 property.[28] The required adjustment for AMTI is the difference between the amortization deduction allowed for regular income tax purposes and the depreciation deduction computed under the ADS. The adjustment may be positive or negative.

The AMT adjustment for pollution control facilities is reduced for property placed in service after 1998. This reduction is achieved by providing conformity in

---

[26]§ 56(a)(1).

[27]Class lives and recovery periods are established for all assets in Rev.Proc. 87–56, 1987–2 C.B. 674.

[28]§ 56(a)(5).

the recovery periods used for regular income tax purposes and AMT purposes (MACRS recovery periods).

| In-depth coverage can be found on this book's companion website: www.cengagebrain.com | 3 DIGGING DEEPER |

Circulation Expenditures

Circulation expenditures are expenses incurred to establish, maintain, or increase the circulation of a newspaper, a magazine, or another periodical. For regular income tax purposes, circulation expenditures, other than those the taxpayer elects to charge to a capital account, may be expensed in the year incurred.[29] For AMT purposes, circulation expenditures are not deductible in the year incurred. In computing AMTI, these expenditures must be capitalized and amortized ratably over the three-year period beginning in the year the expenditures were made.[30]

Completed Contract Method of Accounting

For a long-term contract, taxpayers are required to use the percentage of completion method for AMT purposes.[31] However, in limited circumstances, taxpayers can use the completed contract method for regular income tax purposes.[32] The resulting AMT adjustment is equal to the difference between income reported under the percentage of completion method and the amount reported using the completed contract method.[33] The adjustment can be either positive or negative, depending on the amount of income recognized under the different methods.

A taxpayer can avoid an AMT adjustment on long-term contracts by using the percentage of completion method for regular income tax purposes rather than the completed contract method.

Adjusted Gain or Loss

When a sale or disposition of property occurs, gain or loss reported for regular income tax may differ from gain or loss determined for the AMT. This difference occurs because the adjusted basis of the property for AMT purposes must reflect any current and prior AMT adjustments for the following.[34]

- Depreciation.
- Circulation expenditures.
- Amortization of certified pollution control facilities.

A negative gain or loss adjustment is required if:

- The gain for AMT purposes is less than the gain for regular income tax purposes,
- The loss for AMT purposes is more than the loss for regular income tax purposes, or
- A loss is computed for AMT purposes and a gain is computed for regular income tax purposes.

Otherwise, the AMT gain or loss adjustment is positive.

---

[29]§ 173(a).
[30]§ 56(b)(2)(A)(i).
[31]§ 56(a)(3).

[32]See Chapter 18 of *South-Western Federal Taxation: Individual Income Taxes* for a detailed discussion of the completed contract and percentage of completion methods of accounting.
[33]§ 56(a)(3).
[34]§ 56(a)(6).

In January 1998, Cardinal Corporation paid $100,000 for a duplex acquired for rental purposes. Regular income tax depreciation, AMT depreciation, and the AMT adjustment are computed as follows.

	Depreciation		
Year	**Regular Income Tax**	**AMT**	**AMT Adjustment**
1998	$ 3,485[1]	$ 2,396[2]	$ 1,089
1999	3,636[3]	2,500[4]	1,136
2000–2014	54,540[5]	37,500[6]	17,040
2015	3,636	2,500	1,136

[1] $100,000 cost × 3.485% (Exhibit 5.6) = $3,485
[2] $100,000 cost × 2.396% (Exhibit 5.10) = $2,396
[3] $100,000 cost × 3.636% (Exhibit 5.6) = $3,636
[4] $100,000 cost × 2.500% (Exhibit 5.10) = $2,500
[5] $3,636 each year for 15 years (2000 through 2014)
[6] $2,500 each year for 15 years (2000 through 2014)

Cardinal then sold the duplex on December 20, 2016, for $105,000. Regular income tax depreciation for 2016 is $3,485 [($100,000 cost × 3.636% from Exhibit 5.6) × $(^{11.5}/_{12})$]. AMT depreciation for 2016 is $2,396 [($100,000 cost × 2.500% from Exhibit 5.10) × $(^{11.5}/_{12})$]. Cardinal's positive AMT adjustment for 2016 is $1,089 ($3,485 regular income tax depreciation − $2,396 AMT depreciation).

Because depreciation on the duplex differs for regular income tax and AMT purposes, Cardinal's adjusted basis for the property is different for regular income tax and AMT purposes. Consequently, the gain or loss on disposition of the duplex is different for regular income tax and AMT purposes.

The adjusted basis for Cardinal's duplex is $31,218 for regular income tax purposes and $52,708 for AMT purposes.

	Regular Income Tax	**AMT**
Cost	$100,000	$100,000
Depreciation:		
1998	(3,485)	(2,396)
1999	(3,636)	(2,500)
2000–2014	(54,540)	(37,500)
2015	(3,636)	(2,500)
2016	(3,485)	(2,396)
Adjusted basis	$ 31,218	$ 52,708

The regular income tax gain is $73,782, and the AMT gain is $52,292.

	Regular Income Tax	**AMT**
Amount realized	$105,000	$105,000
Adjusted basis	(31,218)	(52,708)
Recognized gain	$ 73,782	$ 52,292

Because the regular income tax and AMT gain on the sale of the duplex differ, Cardinal makes a negative AMT adjustment of $21,490 ($73,782 regular income tax gain − $52,292 AMT gain). The negative adjustment matches the $21,490 total of the 18 positive adjustments for depreciation ($1,089 in 1998 + $1,136 in 1999 + $17,040 from 2000 through 2014 + $1,136 in 2015 + $1,089 in 2016).

Passive Activity Losses

Net losses on passive activities are not deductible in computing either the regular income tax or the AMT for closely held C corporations (cannot offset portfolio income) and personal service corporations (cannot offset either active income or portfolio income).[35] This does not, however, eliminate the possibility of adjustments attributable to passive activities.

The rules for computing taxable income differ from the rules for computing AMTI. It follows, then, that the rules for computing such a loss for regular income tax purposes differ from the AMT rules for computing such a loss. Therefore, any *passive activity loss* computed for regular income tax purposes may differ from the passive activity loss computed for AMT purposes.

EXAMPLE

21

Robin, Inc., a personal service corporation, acquired two passive activities in 2016. Robin received net passive activity income of $10,000 from Activity A and had no AMT adjustments or preferences in connection with the activity. Activity B had gross income of $27,000 and operating expenses (not affected by AMT adjustments or preferences) of $19,000. Robin claimed MACRS depreciation of $20,000 for Activity B; depreciation under the ADS would have been $15,000. In addition, Robin deducted $10,000 of percentage depletion in excess of basis. The following comparison illustrates the differences in the computation of the passive activity loss for regular income tax and AMT purposes for Activity B.

	Regular Income Tax	AMT
Gross income	$27,000	$27,000
Deductions:		
Operating expenses	($19,000)	($19,000)
Depreciation	(20,000)	(15,000)
Depletion	(10,000)	–0–
Total deductions	($49,000)	($34,000)
Passive activity loss	($22,000)	($ 7,000)

Because the adjustment for depreciation ($5,000) applies and the preference for depletion ($10,000) is not taken into account in computing AMTI, the regular income tax passive activity loss of $22,000 for Activity B is reduced by these amounts, resulting in a passive activity loss of $7,000 for AMT purposes.

For regular income tax purposes, Robin would offset the $10,000 of net passive activity income from Activity A with $10,000 of the passive activity loss from Activity B. For AMT purposes, the corporation would offset the $10,000 of net passive activity income from Activity A with the $7,000 passive activity loss allowed from Activity B, resulting in passive activity income of $3,000. Thus, in computing AMTI, Robin makes a positive passive activity loss adjustment of $3,000 [$10,000 (passive activity loss allowed for regular income tax) − $7,000 (passive activity loss allowed for the AMT)].[36]

For regular income tax purposes, Robin, Inc., has a suspended passive activity loss of $12,000 [$22,000 (amount of loss) − $10,000 (used in 2016)]. This suspended passive activity loss can offset passive activity income in the future or can offset active or portfolio income when the corporation disposes of the loss activity (refer to Chapter 6). For AMT purposes, Robin's suspended passive activity loss is $0 [$7,000 (amount of loss) − $7,000 (amount used in 2016)].

17-2c Tax Preferences

LO.5

Identify and calculate the tax preferences that are included in determining the AMT.

AMTI includes designated tax preference items. Tax preferences always increase AMTI. Some of the principal tax preferences are discussed on the following pages.

Percentage Depletion

Congress enacted the percentage depletion rules to provide taxpayers with incentives to invest in the development of specified natural resources. Percentage depletion is computed by multiplying a rate specified in the Code times the gross income from the property (refer to Chapter 5). The percentage rate is based on the type of mineral involved. The basis of the property is reduced by the amount of depletion taken until

---

[35]§ 469(a).

[36]The depreciation adjustment and depletion preference are combined as part of the passive activity loss adjustment and are *not* reported separately.

the basis reaches zero. However, once the basis of the property reaches zero, taxpayers are allowed to continue taking percentage depletion deductions. Thus, over the life of the property, depletion deductions may greatly exceed the cost of the property.

For AMT purposes, percentage depletion can never exceed the basis of the property. The percentage depletion preference is equal to the excess of the regular income tax deduction for percentage depletion over the adjusted basis of the property at the end of the taxable year.[37] Basis is determined without regard to the depletion deduction for the taxable year. This preference item is figured separately for each piece of property for which the taxpayer is claiming depletion.

> **EXAMPLE 22**
>
> Finch, Inc., owns a mineral property that qualifies for a 22% depletion rate. The basis of the property at the beginning of the year is $10,000. Gross income from the property for the year is $100,000. For regular income tax purposes, Finch's percentage depletion deduction (assume that it is not limited by taxable income from the property) is $22,000. For AMT purposes, Finch has a tax preference of $12,000 ($22,000 − $10,000).

Interest on Private Activity Bonds

Income from private activity bonds is not included in taxable income, and expenses related to carrying such bonds are not deductible for regular income tax purposes. However, interest on private activity bonds usually is included as a preference in computing AMTI. Expenses incurred in carrying the bonds are offset against the interest income in computing the tax preference.[38] As a result of special legislation, interest on private activity bonds issued in 2009 or 2010 is not a tax preference.

The Code contains a lengthy, complex definition of **private activity bonds**.[39] In general, such debt is issued by states or municipalities, but more than 10 percent of the proceeds are used to benefit private business. For example, a bond issued by a city whose proceeds are used to construct a factory that is leased to a private business at a favorable rate is a private activity bond. Interest from municipal bonds that are not private activity bonds is not a tax preference item.

TAX PLANNING STRATEGIES **Avoiding Preferences and Adjustments**

FRAMEWORK FOCUS: TAX RATE

Strategy: Control the Character of Income and Deductions.

Investments in state and local bonds are attractive for income tax purposes because the interest is not included in gross income. Some of these bonds (most private activity bonds) are issued to generate funds that are not used for an essential function of the government (e.g., to provide infrastructure for shopping malls or industrial parks or to build sports facilities). The interest on such bonds is a tax preference item (except for private activity bonds issued in 2009 and 2010) and could lead to the imposition of the AMT. When the AMT applies, an investment in regular tax-exempt bonds or even fully taxed private-sector bonds might yield a higher after-tax rate of return.

If the security is a private activity bond, the interest usually is a tax preference for AMT purposes. According to the

Bond Market Association, interest from almost 8.7 percent of the $1.9 trillion municipal bond market is subject to the AMT. The association's website (**www.investinginbonds .com**) provides a primer on the AMT's effect on municipal bonds and explains how to determine whether the related interest is subject to the AMT.

For a corporation anticipating AMT problems, capitalizing rather than expensing certain costs can avoid generating preferences and adjustments. The decision should be based on the present discounted value of after-tax cash flows under the available alternatives. Costs that may be capitalized and amortized, rather than expensed, include circulation expenditures, mine exploration and development costs, and research and experimentation expenditures.

---

[37]§ 57(a)(1). Percentage depletion on oil and gas wells taken by independent producers and royalty owners does not create an AMT preference. See § 613A(c).

[38]§ 57(a)(5).
[39]§ 141.

Intangible Drilling Costs

In computing regular taxable income, taxpayers can deduct certain intangible drilling and development costs in the year incurred, although such costs are normally capital in nature. The deduction is allowed for costs incurred in connection with oil and gas wells and geothermal wells. For AMT purposes, excess intangible drilling costs (IDC) for the year are treated as a preference.[40] The excess IDC preference is computed as follows:

	IDC expensed in the year incurred
Minus:	Deduction if IDC were capitalized and amortized over 10 years
Equals:	Excess of IDC expense over amortization
Minus:	65% of net oil and gas or geothermal income
Equals:	Tax preference item

The IDC preference is computed separately for oil and gas wells and geothermal wells. A taxpayer can avoid the preference for IDC by electing to deduct the expenditures over a 10-year period for regular income tax purposes.

Ben, who incurred IDC of $50,000 during the year, elected to expense that amount. His net oil and gas income for the year was $60,000. Currently, Ben has no income from geothermal wells. Ben's preference for IDC is $6,000 [($50,000 IDC − $5,000 amortization) − (65% × $60,000 income)].

EXAMPLE
23

17-2d Adjusted Current Earnings (ACE)

LO.6

State and explain the function of adjusted current earnings (ACE).

The **adjusted current earnings (ACE)** rules make up a third measure of income, in addition to AMT income and taxable income. S corporations, real estate investment trusts, regulated investment companies, and real estate mortgage investment conduits are not subject to the ACE provisions. ACE represents another attempt by Congress to ensure that large corporations with significant financial accounting income pay a fair share of Federal corporate income tax. ACE is computed by adjusting AMT income for items that are often treated differently for taxable income versus financial accounting income.

The ACE adjustment, unique to the Federal income tax, can be negative or positive. AMTI is increased by 75 percent of the excess of ACE over unadjusted AMTI, or AMTI is reduced by 75 percent of the excess of unadjusted AMTI over ACE. Any negative ACE adjustment is limited to the aggregate of the positive adjustments under ACE for prior years reduced by the previously claimed negative adjustments (see Concept Summary 17.2).[41] Any unused negative adjustment is lost forever.

A calendar year corporation reports the following.

	2015	2016	2017
Unadjusted AMTI	$3,000,000	$3,000,000	$3,100,000
Adjusted current earnings	4,000,000	3,000,000	2,000,000

- In 2015, because ACE exceeds unadjusted AMTI by $1 million, the positive ACE adjustment is $750,000 (75% × $1,000,000).
- No adjustment is necessary for 2016.
- Unadjusted AMTI exceeds ACE by $1,100,000 in 2017, so there is a potential negative ACE adjustment of $825,000. Because the total increases to AMTI for prior years equal $750,000 (and there are no negative adjustments), only $750,000 of the potential negative ACE adjustment reduces AMTI for 2017. Further, $75,000 of the negative ACE amount is lost forever ($825,000 − $750,000).

EXAMPLE
24

---

[40]§ 57(a)(2).

[41]§§ 56(g)(1) and (2). *Unadjusted AMTI* is AMTI before the ACE adjustment and the AMT NOL deduction; the IRS refers to this item as "pre-adjustment AMTI."

Concept Summary 17.2

Determining the ACE Adjustment*

```
┌─────────────────────────────┐
│   Calculate Taxable Income  │
└─────────────────────────────┘
                │
┌─────────────────────────────┐
│        Calculate AMTI by    │
│     adjusting Taxable Income│
│       for all preferences   │
│   and adjustments           │
│   (except ACE and NOL)      │
└─────────────────────────────┘
                │
┌─────────────────────────────┐
│ Calculate Adjusted Current  │
│ Earnings by adjusting AMTI  │
│ as required (many of the    │
│ adjustments based on earnings│
│ and profits adjustments)    │
└─────────────────────────────┘
                │
            ◇ Is
        Adjusted Current
           Earnings
      greater than pre-
         adjustment
            AMTI?

   Yes ◀─────────────────▶ No

┌──────────────────────────┐   ┌──────────────────────────┐
│ Increase AMTI by 75% of  │   │ Decrease AMTI by 75% of  │
│ the excess of Adjusted   │   │ the excess of AMTI       │
│ Current Earnings over    │   │ (pre-adjustment) over    │
│ AMTI (pre-adjustment)    │   │ Adjusted Current Earnings│
│                          │   │ to extent of net         │
│                          │   │ previous increases       │
└──────────────────────────┘   └──────────────────────────┘
```

*Reprinted (with edits) from *Oil and Gas Tax Quarterly* with permission. Copyright 1989 Matthew Bender & Company, Inc., a part of LexisNexis. All rights reserved.

The starting point for computing ACE is AMTI, which is regular taxable income after AMT adjustments (other than the NOL and ACE adjustments) and tax preferences.[42] Pre-NOL AMTI is adjusted for certain items to determine ACE.

DIGGING DEEPER 4   In-depth coverage can be found on this book's companion website: www.cengagebrain.com

EXAMPLE 25

Crimson Corporation calculates its ACE adjustment as follows:

AMTI		$ 5,780,000
Plus:		
Municipal bond interest	$210,000	
Installment gain	140,000	
70% dividends received deduction	300,000	
Income element in cash surrender life insurance	60,000	
Organization expense amortization	70,000	780,000
Subtotal		$ 6,560,000

continued

[42]§ 56(g)(3).

Less:		
Life insurance premiums paid	$240,000	(240,000)
Adjusted current earnings		$ 6,320,000
AMTI		(5,780,000)
Base amount		$ 540,000
Times 75%		× .75
ACE adjustment (positive)		$ 405,000

ACE should not be confused with current Earnings & Profits (E & P). Many items are treated in the same manner, but certain items that are deductible in computing E & P (but are not deductible in calculating taxable income) generally are not deductible in computing ACE (e.g., Federal income taxes). Concept Summary 17.3 compares the effects that various transactions have on the determination of ACE and E & P.

Concept Summary 17.3

How Various Transactions Affect ACE and E & P

	Effect on Unadjusted AMTI in Arriving at ACE	Effect on Taxable Income in Arriving at Corporate E & P
Tax-exempt income (net of expenses)	Add	Add
Federal income tax	No effect	Subtract
Dividends received deduction (80% and 100% rules)	No effect	Add
Dividends received deduction (70% rule)	Add	Add
Exemption amount ($40,000)	No effect	No effect
Excess charitable contribution	No effect	Subtract
Excess capital losses	No effect	Subtract
Disallowed meals and entertainment expenses	No effect	Subtract
Penalties and fines	No effect	Subtract
Intangible drilling costs deducted currently	Add	Add
Deferred gain on installment sales	Add	Add
Realized (not recognized) gain (e.g., involuntary conversion, like-kind exchanges)	No effect	No effect
Loss on sale between related parties	No effect	Subtract
Key employee insurance proceeds	Add	Add
Premiums paid on key employee life insurance	Subtract	Subtract
Cash surrender value increase on life insurance policy	Add	Add
Organization expense amortization	Add	Add

17-2e Alternative Tax Net Operating Loss Deduction

In computing taxable income, taxpayers can deduct net operating loss (NOL) carryovers and carrybacks. While the NOL deduction is allowed for AMT purposes, the regular income tax NOL must be modified to compute AMTI correctly. The starting point in computing the alternative tax NOL deduction (ATNOLD) is the NOL computed for regular income tax purposes. The regular income tax NOL is modified for AMT adjustments and tax preferences to arrive at the ATNOLD. Preferences and adjustment items that have benefited the taxpayer in computing the regular income tax NOL (in other words, the adjustments and preferences that have increased the regular tax NOL) are added back, thereby reducing or eliminating the NOL for AMT purposes.[43]

EXAMPLE 26

In 2016, Sparrow Corporation incurred an NOL of $400,000. Sparrow owns an item of MACRS five-year property, placed in service on March 15, 2016, at a cost of $1,000,000. Regular tax depreciation is $200,000 ($1,000,000 × 20%), and AMT depreciation is $150,000 ($1,000,000 × 15%). Sparrow's deductions also include tax preferences of $80,000. Its ATNOLD carryback to 2014 is $270,000 [$400,000 regular income tax NOL − $80,000 tax preferences deducted in computing the NOL − ($200,000 regular tax depreciation − $150,000 AMT depreciation)].

In keeping with the goal of ensuring that taxpayers with economic income pay some minimum amount of tax, a ceiling exists on the amount of the ATNOLD that can be deducted in the carryback or carryforward year. The deduction is limited to 90 percent of AMTI (before the ATNOLD) for the carryback or carryforward year.[44]

EXAMPLE 27

Assume the same facts as in the previous example, except that Sparrow's AMTI (before the ATNOLD) in 2014 is $190,000. Therefore, of the $270,000 ATNOLD carried back to 2014 from 2016, only $171,000 ($190,000 × 90%) can be used in recalculating the 2014 AMT. The unused $99,000 of 2016 ATNOLD is next carried to 2015 for use in recalculating that year's AMT.

A taxpayer who has an ATNOLD that is carried back or over to another year must use the ATNOLD against AMTI in the carryback or carryforward year, even if the taxpayer is not subject to the AMT. This can result in the loss of an ATNOLD, even when the taxpayer does not have an AMT liability.

EXAMPLE 28

Swan's ATNOLD for 2016 (carried over from 2015) is $10,000. AMTI in 2016, before considering the ATNOLD, is $25,000. If Swan's regular income tax exceeds the tentative minimum tax (TMT), the AMT does not apply. Nevertheless, Swan's ATNOLD of $10,000 is "used up" in 2016 and is not available for carryover to a later year.

For regular income tax purposes, the NOL generally can be carried back 2 years and forward 20 years. However, the taxpayer may elect to forgo the 2-year carryback. These rules generally apply to the ATNOLD as well, except that the election to forgo the 2-year carryback is available for the ATNOLD only if the taxpayer elected it for the regular income tax NOL.

Compute the AMT liability for corporations and individuals.

17-2f **Computation of Alternative Minimum Taxable Income**

The following example illustrates the effect of tax preferences and adjustments in arriving at AMTI.

EXAMPLE 29

Tan Corporation (a calendar year company) recorded the following transactions:

Taxable income	$4,250,000
Income deferred by using completed contract method (versus percentage of completion method)	450,000
Percentage depletion claimed (the property has a zero adjusted basis)	1,575,000
Interest on City of Elmira (Michigan) 2012 private activity bonds	1,175,000
	continued

Tan Corporation is not a small corporation for AMT purposes. Its AMTI is determined as follows:

Taxable income		$4,250,000
Adjustments		
Income deferred by using completed contract method (versus percentage of completion method)		
Tax preferences		450,000
Excess depletion deduction	$1,575,000	
Interest on private activity municipal bonds	1,175,000	2,750,000
AMTI		$7,450,000

TAX PLANNING STRATEGIES Optimum Use of the AMT and Regular Corporate Income Tax Rate Difference

FRAMEWORK FOCUS: TAX RATE

Strategy: Shift Net Income from High-Bracket Years to Low-Bracket Years.

A corporation that cannot avoid the AMT in a particular year often can save taxes by taking advantage of the difference between the AMT and the regular income tax rates. In general, a corporation that expects to be subject to the AMT should consider accelerating income and deferring deductions for the remainder of the year. Because the difference between the regular income tax rate and the AMT rate may be as much as 15 percentage points, this strategy may result in the income being taxed at less than it would be if reported in the next year (a non-AMT year). If the same corporation expects to be subject to the AMT for the next year (or years) and is not subject to AMT this year, this technique should be reversed.

Falcon Corporation expects to be in the 34% regular income tax bracket in 2017, but is subject to the AMT in 2016. In late 2016, Falcon is contemplating selling a tract of unimproved land (basis of $200,000 and fair market value of $1 million), which is classified as inventory. Under these circumstances, it may be preferable to sell the land in 2016. The gain of $800,000 ($1,000,000 − $200,000) generates a tax of $160,000 [$800,000 (recognized gain) × 20% (AMT rate)].

> EXAMPLE
> 30

If, however, the land is sold in 2017, the resulting tax is $272,000 [$800,000 (recognized gain) × 34% (regular corporate income tax rate)]. A nominal savings of $112,000 ($272,000 − $160,000) materializes by making the sale in 2016.

Whenever one accelerates income or defers deductions, a present value analysis should be conducted. This technique to accelerate gross income is attractive only if it reduces the present value of tax liabilities.

17-2g AMT Rate and Exemption

The AMT rate is 20 percent. The rate is applied to the *AMT base*, which is AMTI reduced by the *AMT exemption*. The exemption amount for a corporation is $40,000 reduced by 25 percent of the amount by which AMTI exceeds $150,000. The exemption phases out entirely when AMTI reaches $310,000.

Beige Corporation has AMTI of $180,000. Because the exemption amount is reduced by $7,500 [25% × ($180,000 − $150,000)], the exemption amount remaining is $32,500 ($40,000 − $7,500).

> EXAMPLE
> 31

As a result, Beige Corporation's alternative minimum tax base (refer to Exhibit 17.3) is $147,500 ($180,000 − $32,500).

17-2h Minimum Tax Credit

The minimum tax credit acts to make the AMT merely a *prepayment of tax* for corporations. Essentially, the AMT paid in one tax year may be carried forward indefinitely and used as a credit against the corporation's future *regular* tax liability that exceeds its tentative minimum tax. The minimum tax credit may not be carried back and may not be offset against any future AMT liability.

EXAMPLE 32

Return to the facts of Example 29. As Tan Corporation's AMTI exceeds $310,000, there is no AMT exemption amount. The tentative minimum tax is $1,490,000 (20% of $7,450,000).

Tan's regular income tax liability is $1,445,000 ($4,250,000 × 34%). As a result, its AMT liability is $45,000 ($1,490,000 − $1,445,000). The minimum tax credit carried forward is $45,000, the current year's AMT. The credit can be used to reduce regular income tax liability in a future tax year (but not below the tentative minimum tax for that year).

17-2i Other Aspects of the AMT

Form 4626 (Alternative Minimum Tax—Corporations) is the form corporations use to report AMT amounts to the IRS. Any AMT calculated is carried over to Schedule J of Form 1120 (U.S. Corporation Income Tax Return). In addition to paying their regular income tax liability, corporations must make estimated tax payments of the AMT liability. Even corporations that prepare quarterly financial statements may find that this requirement adds to compliance costs.

In a year in which the corporation is subject to the AMT, the AMT amount creates a minimum tax credit available for carryover to future years. This credit can be used in the future to the extent the regular tax liability exceeds the tentative minimum tax for a year. This credit can be carried forward indefinitely. Certain small corporations can use specified tax credits to reduce the AMT liability.[45] For all other corporations, only the foreign tax credit can be claimed in an AMT year.

---

[45]§ 38(c)(5)(A). For tax years beginning after 2015, this now includes the research activities credit.

TAX IN THE NEWS **The Corporate AMT**

In most cases, the corporate AMT is a temporary tax. That is because a current year AMT liability can be used to offset a future year regular tax liability. Overall, the corporate AMT does not raise much revenue, as illustrated by the following table:

Year	AMT Revenues (in billions)	AMT Credits (in billions)	Net AMT Revenue (in billions)
1987–1999	$55.1	$32.6	$22.5
2000	3.9	5.2	(1.3)
2001	1.8	3.3	(1.5)
2002	2.5	2.0	0.5
2003	2.3	3.4	(1.1)

Year	AMT Revenues (in billions)	AMT Credits (in billions)	Net AMT Revenue (in billions)
2004	3.4	3.7	(0.3)
2005	3.3	7.1	(3.8)
2006	3.7	5.9	(2.2)
2007	3.2	3.2	0.0
2008	2.3	1.9	0.4
2009	3.1	1.4	1.7
2010	3.2	1.5	1.7
2011	3.4	1.6	1.8
2012	3.5	2.8	0.7

Source: Internal Revenue Service Statistics of Income Division.

17-3 INDIVIDUAL ALTERNATIVE MINIMUM TAX

The AMT applicable to individuals is similar to the corporate AMT. Most of the adjustments and preferences discussed previously apply equally to individuals and corporations. However, there are several important differences.

- The individual AMT rate is slightly progressive, with rates at 26 percent on the first $186,300 in 2016 ($93,150 for married, filing separately) of AMTI and at 28 percent on any additional AMTI.

- The alternative rate on net capital gain of 0, 15, or 20 percent applies.

- The AMT exemption and phaseout amounts are tied to the individual's filing status for the year. The exemption phases out at a rate of $1 for every $4 of AMTI.[46] The exemption amounts for 2016 are listed in the table below.

Filing Status	Exemption Amount	Phaseout Range Begins at	Phaseout Range Ends at
Married, joint	$83,800	$159,700	$494,900
Married, separate	41,900	79,850	247,450
Single or Head of household	53,900	119,700	335,300

- Individuals make no AMT adjustment for ACE.

- Some additional adjustments apply to individual taxpayers. Taxes and miscellaneous itemized deductions subject to the 2%-of-AGI floor are not allowed as deductions for AMTI. Medical expenses are allowed only to the extent they exceed 10 percent of AGI (even for taxpayers age 65 and over who face only a 7.5 percent floor for the regular income tax). Interest expense deductions are limited to qualified residence interest, interest on certain student loans, and investment interest (subject to limitations). The 3 percent phaseout of itemized deductions that applies to certain high-income taxpayers (refer to Chapter 9) does *not* apply in computing the individual AMT. Finally, the standard deduction and personal and dependency exemptions are not allowed as deductions when computing AMTI. Other individual-specific adjustments also exist, including an adjustment accelerating the taxation of incentive stock options. Personal nonrefundable credits can offset any AMT liability.

- Determination of the minimum tax credit is more complex for individual taxpayers. The credit usually applies only to AMT generated as a result of *timing* differences.

[46]AMT exemption amounts for 2015 were $83,400, $41,700, and $53,600, respectively.

In most years, the disallowance of a deduction for state and local income taxes and for personal and dependency exemptions accounts for 85 percent of the AMT revenue collected from individuals.

The individual AMT and the corporate AMT have the same objective: to force taxpayers who have more economic income than that reflected in taxable income to pay a fair share of Federal income tax.

REFOCUS ON THE BIG PICTURE

DEALING WITH TAX CREDITS AND THE AMT

ISTOCKPHOTO.COM/MONKEY BUSINESS IMAGES

Tax credits are used by the Federal government to promote certain social and economic objectives. Credits are dollar-for-dollar reductions in tax liability. While tax credits may have strict qualification requirements, taking advantage of available credits may significantly reduce a business's tax liability. Progress Corporation qualifies for a 10 percent tax credit for rehabilitating a building that was placed in service before 1936 (see Example 4). In addition, Progress hires workers from economically disadvantaged groups, so it qualifies for the work opportunity tax credit (see Example 6).

The company also qualifies for the credit for employer-provided child care, equal to 25 percent of qualified child care expenses (see Example 13). Mike and his CPA might also want to explore taking advantage of the disabled access credit, which is designed to encourage small businesses to make their facilities accessible to disabled individuals.

What If?

Mike has heard horror stories about the alternative minimum tax (AMT) and is concerned about its potential impact on his company. What if Mike's company is subject to the AMT?

If Progress Corporation is subject to the AMT, the company's general business credits (including the tax credit for rehabilitation expenditures, the work opportunity tax credit, the disabled access credit, and the credit for employer-provided child care) are limited to the taxpayer's regular income tax reduced by the greater of the company's tentative minimum tax or 25 percent of the regular income tax liability exceeding $25,000. Accordingly, much of the tax benefit may be lost or require a carryback or carryover to another tax year. However, small corporations with average gross receipts under certain thresholds may be exempt from the AMT. Before Mike proceeds with his plans, his exposure to the AMT should be determined.

Suggested Readings

Beth Henricks, "Enlist Human Resources to Screen for Employment Tax Credits," *Practical Tax Strategies*, April 2008.

Thomas Horan and Margaret Horan, "Strategies for Reducing the Alternative Minimum Tax Liability," *The CPA Journal*, March 2013.

Kreig D. Mitchell, "The R&D Tax Credit for Start-Up Companies," *Practical Tax Strategies*, February 2012.

Tom Prieto, "AMT Planning with Listed Options," *Practical Tax Strategies*, October 2010.

William R. Swindle, "Recent Cases Provide Relief for Substantiating Research Tax Credit Claims," *Practical Tax Strategies*, June 2010.

Dean Zerbe, Benjamin Yaker, and David Ji, "New Law Opens Door for Businesses to Take R&D Tax Credit," *Practical Tax Strategies*, April 2011.

Key Terms

Computational Exercises

1. **LO.2** Carlson's general business credit for the current year is $84,000 His net income tax is $190,000, tentative minimum tax is $175,000, and net regular tax liability is $185,000. He has no other tax credits. Determine the amount of Carlson's general business credit for the year.

2. **LO.2** Emily spent $135,000 to rehabilitate a building (adjusted basis of $90,000) that originally had been placed in service in 1935.
   a. What is Emily's rehabilitation expenditures tax credit?
   b. What would be your answer if the building was a historic structure?

3. **LO.2** During 2016, Lincoln Company hires seven individuals who are certified to be members of a qualifying targeted group. Each employee works in excess of 600 hours and is paid wages of $7,500 during the year. Determine the amount of Lincoln's work opportunity credit.

4. **LO.2** Dorcas incurs the following research expenditures.

In-house wages	$60,000
In-house supplies	5,000
Payment to ABC, Inc., for research	80,000

   a. Determine the amount of qualified research expenditures.
   b. Assuming that the base amount is $50,000, determine Dorcas's incremental research activities credit.

5. **LO.3** Siga, Inc., a calendar year Corporation, records the following gross receipts and taxable income for 2014 through 2016.

Year	Gross Receipts	Taxable Income
2014	$4,200,000	$ 900,000
2015	7,000,000	1,600,000
2016	7,700,000	1,900,000

   Siga's first year of operations was 2014. Is Siga exempt from AMT in 2014, 2015, or 2016?

6. **LO.4** Brennen sold a machine used in his business for $180,000. The machine was purchased eight years ago for $340,000. Depreciation up to the date of the sale for regular income tax purposes was $210,000 and $190,000 for AMT purposes.
   What, if any, AMT adjustment arises as a result of the sale of the machine?

7. **LO.4** Pineview Corporation placed an asset (three-year MACRS class life) costing $5,000 in service on June 1, 2016. Complete the table below by providing the AMT adjustment and indicate whether the adjustment increases or decreases taxable income.

Year	Tax Deduction	AMT Deduction	AMT Adjustment	Increases or Decreases
2016	$1,667	$1,250	_____	_____
2017	2,222	1,875	_____	_____
2018	740	1,250	_____	_____
2019	371	625	_____	_____

8. **LO.6** Given the following information, determine the ACE adjustment for each year.

	2016	2017	2018
Unadjusted AMTI	$ 800,000	$2,000,000	$1,500,000
Adjusted current earnings	1,200,000	2,000,000	900,000

Problems

9. **LO.2** Charles has a tentative general business credit of $42,000 for the current year. His net regular tax liability before the general business credit is $107,000, and his tentative minimum tax is $88,000. Compute Charles's allowable general business credit for the year.

10. **LO.2** Oak Corporation holds the following general business credit carryovers.

2012	$ 5,000
2013	15,000
2014	6,000
2015	19,000
Total carryovers	$45,000

If the general business credit generated by activities during 2016 equals $36,000 and the total credit allowed during the current year is $60,000 (based on tax liability), what amounts of the current general business credit and carryovers are utilized against the 2016 income tax liability? What is the amount of the unused credit carried forward to 2017?

11. **LO.2** In January 2015, Iris Corporation purchased and placed in service a 1933 building that houses retail businesses. The cost was $300,000, of which $25,000 applied to the land. In modernizing the facility, Iris Corporation incurred $312,000 of renovation costs of the type that qualify for the rehabilitation credit. These improvements were placed in service in October 2016.

   a. Compute Iris Corporation's rehabilitation tax credit for 2016.
   b. Calculate the cost recovery deductions for the building and the renovation costs for 2016.

Decision Making
Communications

12. **LO.2** In the current year, Paul Chaing (4522 Fargo Street, Geneva, IL 60134) acquires a qualifying historic structure for $350,000 (excluding the cost of the land) and plans to substantially rehabilitate the structure. He is planning to spend either $320,000 or $380,000 on rehabilitation expenditures.

   Write a letter to Paul and a memo for the tax files explaining, for the two alternative expenditures, (1) the computation that determines the rehabilitation expenditures tax credit available to Paul, (2) the effect of the credit on Paul's adjusted basis in the property, and (3) the cash-flow differences as a result of the tax consequences related to his expenditure choice.

13. **LO.2** The tax credit for rehabilitation expenditures is available to help offset the costs related to substantially rehabilitating certain buildings. The credit is calculated on the rehabilitation expenditures incurred and not on the acquisition cost of the building itself.

    Ethics and Equity

    You are a developer who buys, sells, and does construction work on real estate in the inner city of your metropolitan area. A potential customer approaches you about acquiring one of your buildings that easily could qualify for the 20% rehabilitation credit on historic structures. The stated sales price of the structure is $100,000 (based on appraisals ranging from $80,000 to $120,000), and the rehabilitation expenditures, if the job is done correctly, would be about $150,000.

    Your business has been slow recently due to the sluggish real estate market in your area, and the potential customer makes the following proposal: if you reduce the sales price of the building to $75,000, he will pay you $175,000 to perform the rehabilitation work. Although the buyer's total expenditures would be the same, he would benefit from this approach by obtaining a larger tax credit ($25,000 increased rehabilitation costs × 20% = $5,000).

    It has been a long time since you have sold any of your real estate. How will you respond?

14. **LO.2** Green Corporation hires six individuals on January 4, 2016, all of whom qualify for the work opportunity credit. Three of these individuals receive wages of $8,500 during 2016, and each individual works more than 400 hours during the year. The other three individuals each work 300 hours and receive wages of $5,000 during the year.

    a. Calculate the amount of Green's work opportunity credit for 2016.

    b. If Green pays total wages of $140,000 to its employees during the year, how much of this amount is deductible in 2016 assuming that the work opportunity credit is taken?

15. **LO.2** In March 2016, Sparrow Corporation hired three individuals—Austin, Adam, and Angela—all of whom are certified as long-term family assistance recipients. Each of these individuals earned $11,000 during 2016. Only Adam continued to work for Sparrow in 2017, and he earned $13,500 then. In March 2017, Sparrow hired Sam, who also is certified as a long-term family assistance recipient. During 2017, Sam earned $12,000.

    a. Compute Sparrow Corporation's work opportunity credit for 2016 and 2017.

    b. If Sparrow pays total wages to its employees of $325,000 in 2016 and $342,000 in 2017, what is its wage deduction in each of those years?

16. **LO.2** Tom, a calendar year taxpayer, informs you that during the year, he incurs expenditures of $40,000 that qualify for the incremental research activities credit. In addition, it is determined that his research-credit base amount for the year is $32,800.

    Decision Making

    a. Determine Tom's incremental research activities credit for the year.

    b. Tom is in the 25% tax bracket. Determine which approach to the research expenditures and the research activities credit (other than capitalization and subsequent amortization) would provide the greater tax benefit to Tom.

17. **LO.2** Ahmed Zinna (16 Southside Drive, Charlotte, NC 28204), one of your clients, owns two retail establishments in downtown Charlotte and has come to you seeking advice concerning the tax consequences of complying with the Americans with Disabilities Act. He understands that he needs to install various features at his

    Communications

stores (e.g., ramps, doorways, and restrooms that are handicapped-accessible) to make them more accessible to disabled individuals.

Ahmed asks whether any tax credits will be available to help offset the cost of the necessary changes. He estimates the cost of the planned changes to his facilities as follows.

Location	Projected Cost
Calvin Street	$22,000
Stowe Avenue	8,500

Ahmed reminds you that the Calvin Street store was constructed in 2004, while the Stowe Avenue store is in a building that was constructed in 1947. Ahmed operates his business as a sole proprietorship and has approximately eight employees at each location. Write a letter to Ahmed in which you summarize your conclusions concerning the tax consequences of the proposed capital improvements.

18. **LO.2** Blue Horizons, Inc., a U.S. corporation, is a manufacturing concern that sells most of its products in the United States. It also conducts some business in the European Union through various branches. During the current year, Blue Horizons reports taxable income of $700,000, of which $500,000 is U.S.-sourced and $200,000 is foreign-sourced. Foreign income taxes paid amounted to $45,000. Blue Horizons's U.S. income tax liability is $238,000. What is its U.S. income tax liability net of the allowable foreign tax credit?

19. **LO.3** Aqua, Inc., a calendar year corporation, has the following gross receipts and taxable income for 2013 through 2016:

Year	Gross Receipts	Taxable Income
2013	$6,000,000	$1,400,000
2014	7,000,000	1,312,000
2015	7,500,000	985,000
2016	7,200,000	1,002,000

Aqua's first year of operations was 2013.
  a. When is Aqua first exempt from the AMT as a small corporation?
  b. Is Aqua subject to the AMT for 2016? Explain.

20. **LO.4** Falcon, Inc., owns a silver mine that it purchased several years ago for $925,000. The adjusted basis at the beginning of the year is $400,000. For the year, Falcon deducts depletion of $700,000 (greater of cost depletion of $290,000 or percentage depletion of $700,000) for regular income tax purposes.
  a. Calculate Falcon's AMT preference.
  b. Calculate Falcon's adjusted basis for regular income tax purposes.
  c. Calculate Falcon's adjusted basis for AMT purposes.

Decision Making

Communications

21. **LO.5** In March 2016, Grackle, Inc., acquired used equipment for its business at a cost of $300,000. The equipment is five-year class property for regular income tax purposes and for AMT purposes. Grackle does not claim any available additional first-year depreciation.
  a. If Grackle depreciates the equipment using the method that will produce the greatest deduction for 2016 for regular income tax purposes, what is the amount of the AMT adjustment? Grackle does not elect § 179 limited expensing.
  b. How can Grackle reduce the AMT adjustment to $0? What circumstances would motivate Grackle to do so?
  c. Draft a letter to Helen Carlon, Grackle's controller, regarding the choice of depreciation methods. Helen's address is 500 Monticello Avenue, Glendale, AZ 85306.

22. **LO.5** Rust Company is a real estate construction business with average annual gross receipts of $3 million. Rust uses the completed contract method on a particular contract that requires 16 months to complete. The contract is for $500,000, with estimated costs of $300,000. At the end of 2016, $180,000 of costs had been incurred. The contract is completed in 2017, with the total cost being $295,000. Determine the amount of adjustments for AMT purposes for 2016 and 2017.

23. **LO.5** Allie, who was an accounting major in college, is the controller of a medium-   **Ethics and Equity** size construction corporation. She prepares the corporate tax return each year. Due to reporting a home construction contract using the completed contract method, the corporation is subject to the AMT in 2016. Allie files the 2016 corporate tax return in early February 2017. The total tax liability is $58,000 ($53,000 regular income tax liability + $5,000 AMT).

In early March, Allie reads an article on minimizing income taxes. Based on this article, she decides that it would be beneficial for the corporation to report the home construction contract using the percentage of completion method on its 2016 return. Although this will increase the corporation's 2016 income tax liability, it will minimize the total income tax liability over the two-year construction period. Therefore, Allie files an amended return on March 14, 2017. Evaluate Allie's actions from both a tax avoidance and an ethical perspective.

24. **LO.5** Buford sells an apartment building for $720,000. His adjusted basis is $500,000 for regular income tax purposes and $550,000 for AMT purposes. Calculate Buford's:
    a. Gain for regular income tax purposes.
    b. Gain for AMT purposes.
    c. AMT adjustment, if any.

25. **LO.5** Pheasant, Inc., is going to be subject to the AMT in 2016. The corporation   **Issue ID** owns an investment building and is considering disposing of it and investing in other realty. Based on an appraisal of the building's value, the realized gain would be $85,000.

Ed has offered to purchase the building from Pheasant with a December 29, 2016 closing date. Ed wants to close the transaction in 2016 because he will receive certain beneficial tax consequences only if the transaction is closed prior to 2017. Abby has offered to purchase the building with a January 2, 2017 closing date.

The adjusted basis of the building is $95,000 greater for AMT purposes than for the regular income tax. Pheasant expects to be in the 34% regular income tax bracket.

What are the relevant Federal income tax issues that Pheasant faces in making its decision?

26. **LO.5** Flicker, Inc., a closely held corporation, acquired a passive activity this year. Gross income from operations of the activity was $160,000. Operating expenses, not including depreciation, were $122,000. Regular income tax depreciation of $49,750 was computed under MACRS. AMT depreciation, computed using the ADS, was $41,000. Compute Flicker's passive activity loss deduction and passive activity loss suspended for regular income tax purposes. Then determine the same amounts for AMT purposes.

27. **LO.6** Janice Boyer, the controller of one of your clients, calls you to ask what impact current E & P has on ACE. She wants to know if ACE is the same as current E & P. Prepare a tax file memo indicating what you told Ms. Boyer.

28. **LO.6** Based on the following facts, calculate adjusted current earnings (ACE).

Alternative minimum taxable income (AMTI before ACE adjustment)	$5,120,000
Municipal bond interest	630,000
Expenses related to municipal bonds	50,000
Key employee life insurance proceeds in excess of cash surrender value	2,000,000
Organization expense amortization	100,000
Cost of goods sold	6,220,000
Advertising expenses	760,000
Loss between related parties	260,000
Life insurance premiums paid	300,000

29. **LO.6** Purple Corporation, a calendar year taxpayer, began operations in 2014. It reported the following amounts for its first four tax years. Calculate Purple's positive and negative ACE adjustments for each year.

	Unadjusted AMTI	ACE
2014	$85,000,000	$70,000,000
2015	70,000,000	90,000,000
2016	54,000,000	40,000,000
2017	60,000,000	20,000,000

30. **LO.4, 5, 6** Determine whether each of the following transactions is a preference (P), is an adjustment (A), or is not applicable (NA) for purposes of the corporate AMT.
    a. Depletion in excess of basis taken by Giant Oil Company.
    b. Accelerated depreciation on property.
    c. Charitable contributions of cash.
    d. Adjusted current earnings.
    e. Untaxed appreciation on property donated to charity.
    f. Dividends received deduction.

31. **LO.7** In the current year, Redland Corporation's regular tax liability was $28,000, and its AMTI was $232,000. Redland is not a small corporation, and this is not its first year of operations.
    a. Compute Redland's current year AMT.
    b. How would your answer to part (a) change if Redland's regular tax liability was $88,000 in the current year?

32. **LO.7** Peach Corporation (a calendar year company) recorded the following transactions. Assume that the corporation is not a small corporation, this is not its first year of operations, and it does not record an ACE adjustment.

Taxable income	$5,000,000
Regular tax depreciation on realty in excess of ADS (placed in service in 1991)	1,700,000
Amortization of certified pollution control facilities (in excess of ADS amortization)	200,000
Tax-exempt interest on private activity bonds issued in 2013	300,000
Percentage depletion in excess of the property's adjusted basis	700,000

    a. Determine Peach Corporation's AMTI.
    b. Determine the alternative minimum tax base (refer to Exhibit 17.3).
    c. Determine the tentative minimum tax.
    d. What is the amount of the AMT?

33. **LO.7** Included in Alice's regular taxable income and in her AMT base is a $300,000 capital gain on the sale of stock she owned for three years. Alice is in the 35%

tax bracket for regular income tax purposes. In calculating her regular income tax liability, she uses the appropriate alternative tax rate on net capital gain of 20%.

a. What rate should Alice use in calculating her tentative AMT?

b. What is Alice's AMT adjustment?

c. How would your answers in parts (a) and (b) change if the taxpayer were a C corporation in the 34% tax bracket for regular income tax purposes?

34. **LO.5** In the current year, DYL Corporation earned taxable and tax-exempt interest from the following investments.

Investment	Interest Income
10-year municipal bond (issued in 2009)	$1,300
10-year private activity bond (issued in 2010)	1,600
10-year Treasury bond (issued in 2013)	2,000
10-year private activity bond (issued in 2014)	900
Savings account	1,100

DYL Corporation purchased all of the bonds on their issuance date. In addition, DYL Corporation borrowed funds with which to purchase the 2010 private activity bond and incurred interest expense of $350 on that loan in the current year.

a. How much interest income will DYL Corporation recognize for regular tax purposes in the current year?

b. What is its current year AMT preference or adjustment for interest?

35. **LO.4, 5** Jane and Robert Brown are married and have eight children, all of whom are eligible to be claimed as the couple's dependents. Robert earns $94,000 working as an accountant, and Jane earns $35,000 as a teaching aide. Given their large family, they live in a frugal manner. The Browns maintain a large garden and some fruit trees from which they get most of their produce, and the children take family and consumer science classes so that they can help make their clothing. The couple has no other income besides their salaries (all of their investment income is earned in retirement savings), and their itemized deductions are less than the standard deduction. In addition, they have no additional adjustments or preferences for AMT purposes.

a. What is the couple's 2016 regular tax liability?

b. What is the couple's 2016 AMT?

c. Express the calculation of the couple's AMT for 2016 as an Excel formula. Place any parameter that could change annually in a separate cell, and incorporate the cell references into the formula.

36. **LO.2, 3, 4** Pat, who is age 66 and single with no dependents, received a salary of $90,000 in 2016. She earned interest income of $1,000, dividend income of $5,000, gambling winnings of $4,000, and interest income from private activity bonds (issued in 2006) of $40,000. The dividends are not qualified dividends. The following additional information is relevant.

Medical expenses (before 7.5%-of-AGI floor)	$12,000
State income taxes	4,100
Real estate taxes	2,800
Mortgage interest on residence	3,100
Investment interest expense	1,800
Gambling losses	5,100

Compute Pat's tentative minimum tax for 2016.

37. **LO.2, 5** Renee and Sanjeev Patel, who are married, reported taxable income of $273,000 for 2016. They incurred positive AMT adjustments of $38,000,

negative AMT adjustments of $14,000, and tax preference items of $67,500. The couple itemizes their deductions.

    a. Compute the Patels' AMTI for 2016.

    b. Compute their tentative minimum tax for 2016.

BRIDGE DISCIPLINE

1. Balm, Inc., has a general business credit for 2016 of $90,000. Balm's regular income tax liability before credits is $140,000, and its tentative AMT is $132,000.
   a. Calculate the amount of general business credit Balm can use in 2016, and calculate its general business credit carryback and carryforward, if any.
   b. Balm projects a $140,000 regular 2017 income tax liability. Its tentative AMT will be $132,000. Balm is considering making an investment early in 2017 that annually will produce $45,000 of tax-exempt income. Balm is trying to decide between two alternatives. The first alternative is a tax-exempt bond that is a 2014 private activity bond. The second alternative is a tax-exempt bond that is not a private activity bond. Advise Balm on the preferable investment.

2. Cooper Partnership, a calendar year partnership, made qualifying rehabilitation expenditures to a building that it has used in its business for eight years. These improvements were placed in service on January 5, 2015. The amount of the rehabilitation expenditures credit was $40,000.

   Cooper is negotiating to sell the building in either December 2016 or January 2017. The sales price will be $600,000, and the recognized gain will be $100,000. Provide support for the CFO's position that Cooper should delay the sale until 2017.

3. For many years, Saul's sole proprietorship and his related Form 1040 have had a number of AMT tax preferences and AMT adjustments. He has made the AMT calculation each year, but the calculated amount always has been $0. Saul's regular taxable income and the AMT adjustments and preferences for 2016 are the same as for last year. Yet, he must pay AMT this year. Explain how this could happen.

Research Problems

THOMSON REUTERS

Note: Solutions to Research Problems can be prepared by using the Checkpoint®️ Student Edition online research product, which is available to accompany this text. It is also possible to prepare solutions to the Research Problems by using tax research materials found in a standard tax library.

Research Problem 1. During a recent Sunday afternoon excursion, Miriam, an admirer of early twentieth-century architecture, discovers a 1920s-era house in the countryside outside Mobile, Alabama. She wants not only to purchase and renovate this particular house but also to move the structure into Mobile so that her community can enjoy its architectural features.

Being aware of the availability of the tax credit for rehabilitation expenditures, she wants to maximize her use of the provision, if it is available in this case, once the renovation work begins in Mobile. However, Miriam also informs you that she will pursue the purchase, relocation, and renovation of the house only if the tax credit is available.

Comment on Miriam's decision and on whether any renovation expenditures incurred will qualify for the tax credit for rehabilitation expenditures.

Partial list of research aids:
George S. Nalle III v. Comm., 72 AFTR 2d 93–5705, 997 F.2d 1134, 93–2 USTC ¶50,468 (CA–5, 1993).

Research Problem 2. Your ophthalmologist, Dr. Hunter Francis (55 Wheatland Drive, Hampton, CT 06247), has been very pleased with the growth of his practice in the 15 years he has been in business. This growth has resulted, at least in part, because he has aggressively marketed his services and tried to accommodate clients with various needs.

Communications

This year, Dr. Francis purchased a sophisticated piece of equipment that enables him to diagnose persons with mental handicaps, hearing impairments, and physical disabilities without having to go through a series of questions. In addition, he can treat his patients who are not disabled more accurately and efficiently by using this equipment.

Since purchasing the machine this year for $9,500, Dr. Francis has used it on many occasions. Unfortunately, he has not been able to attract any patients with disabilities, even though previously he referred such people to other ophthalmologists who owned the necessary equipment. Therefore, the primary purpose for acquiring the equipment (i.e., to attract patients with disabilities) has not been realized, but he has put it to good use in treating other patients. Write a letter to Dr. Francis explaining whether he may claim the disabled access credit for this acquisition.

Research Problem 3. Teal, Inc., owns two warehouses that were placed in service before 1987. This year, accelerated depreciation on Warehouse A is $36,000 (straight-line depreciation would have been $30,000). On Warehouse B, accelerated depreciation was $16,000 (straight-line depreciation would have been $20,000). What is the amount of Teal's AMT tax preference for excess depreciation?

Use the tax resources of the Internet to address the following questions. Do not restrict your search to the Web, but include a review of newsgroups and general reference materials, practitioner sites and resources, primary sources of the tax law, chat rooms and discussion groups, and other opportunities.

Internet Activity

Research Problem 4. The foreign tax credit is especially valuable when a U.S. business earns income in a country whose income tax rates exceed those of the United States. List five countries whose tax rates on business income exceed those of the United States and five where the corresponding U.S. rates are higher.

Research Problem 5. Ascertain whether your state's income tax has an AMT component. If your state does not levy an income tax, choose a contiguous state that does. List the AMT tax rate for corporations, and describe if or how the AMT tax base follows Federal AMTI.

Roger CPA Review Questions

1. When an entity is responsible for paying the alternative minimum tax (AMT) due to adjustments related to the timing of income, how might that excess tax be recovered?
    a.   File a claim for a refund in the year paid.
    b.   Carry forward to offset against a future AMT liability only.
    c.   Carry forward to offset against future AMT or regular tax liabilities.
    d.   Carry forward to offset against a future regular tax liability only.

2. Identify any item or items below which are added to Alternative Minimum Taxable Income (AMTI) in order to compute the Adjusted Current Earnings (ACE) adjustment.

    I.   Dividends-received deduction on dividends received from a 20%-owned corporation.

II. Municipal bond interest, excluding any municipal bond interest already included in AMTI.

III. Life insurance proceeds on the death of a key employee.

a. I and III only

b. I, II and III

c. I and II only

d. II and III only

3. Mary, age 65, reported adjusted gross income of $150,000 for the year. Mary also incurred $20,000 in medical expenses. In computing Mary's alternative minimum tax, what is the adjustment for Mary's medical expenses?

a. $3,750

b. $5,000

c. $8,750

d. $11,250

4. Which of the following will increase a taxpayer's alternative minimum taxable income (AMTI)?

	Personal Exemption	Property Taxes	Medical Expenses Over 10% of AGI
a.	Yes	Yes	Yes
b.	Yes	Yes	No
c.	No	Yes	Yes
d.	Yes	No	Yes

5. Which of the following best describes the effect of a tax credit?

a. It reduces a person's gross income.

b. It reduces a person's adjusted gross income.

c. It reduces a person's taxable income.

d. It reduces a person's tax liability.

Research Problem 2. Your ophthalmologist, Dr. Hunter Francis (55 Wheatland Drive, Hampton, CT 06247), has been very pleased with the growth of his practice in the 15 years he has been in business. This growth has resulted, at least in part, because he has aggressively marketed his services and tried to accommodate clients with various needs.

Communications

This year, Dr. Francis purchased a sophisticated piece of equipment that enables him to diagnose persons with mental handicaps, hearing impairments, and physical disabilities without having to go through a series of questions. In addition, he can treat his patients who are not disabled more accurately and efficiently by using this equipment.

Since purchasing the machine this year for $9,500, Dr. Francis has used it on many occasions. Unfortunately, he has not been able to attract any patients with disabilities, even though previously he referred such people to other ophthalmologists who owned the necessary equipment. Therefore, the primary purpose for acquiring the equipment (i.e., to attract patients with disabilities) has not been realized, but he has put it to good use in treating other patients. Write a letter to Dr. Francis explaining whether he may claim the disabled access credit for this acquisition.

Research Problem 3. Teal, Inc., owns two warehouses that were placed in service before 1987. This year, accelerated depreciation on Warehouse A is $36,000 (straight-line depreciation would have been $30,000). On Warehouse B, accelerated depreciation was $16,000 (straight-line depreciation would have been $20,000). What is the amount of Teal's AMT tax preference for excess depreciation?

Use the tax resources of the Internet to address the following questions. Do not restrict your search to the Web, but include a review of newsgroups and general reference materials, practitioner sites and resources, primary sources of the tax law, chat rooms and discussion groups, and other opportunities.

 Internet Activity

Research Problem 4. The foreign tax credit is especially valuable when a U.S. business earns income in a country whose income tax rates exceed those of the United States. List five countries whose tax rates on business income exceed those of the United States and five where the corresponding U.S. rates are higher.

Research Problem 5. Ascertain whether your state's income tax has an AMT component. If your state does not levy an income tax, choose a contiguous state that does. List the AMT tax rate for corporations, and describe if or how the AMT tax base follows Federal AMTI.

Roger CPA Review Questions

 ROGER *CPA Review*

1. When an entity is responsible for paying the alternative minimum tax (AMT) due to adjustments related to the timing of income, how might that excess tax be recovered?

   a. File a claim for a refund in the year paid.

   b. Carry forward to offset against a future AMT liability only.

   c. Carry forward to offset against future AMT or regular tax liabilities.

   d. Carry forward to offset against a future regular tax liability only.

2. Identify any item or items below which are added to Alternative Minimum Taxable Income (AMTI) in order to compute the Adjusted Current Earnings (ACE) adjustment.

   I. Dividends-received deduction on dividends received from a 20%-owned corporation.

    II. Municipal bond interest, excluding any municipal bond interest already included in AMTI.

    III. Life insurance proceeds on the death of a key employee.

    a. I and III only   c. I and II only

    b. I, II and III   d. II and III only

3. Mary, age 65, reported adjusted gross income of $150,000 for the year. Mary also incurred $20,000 in medical expenses. In computing Mary's alternative minimum tax, what is the adjustment for Mary's medical expenses?

    a. $3,750   c. $8,750

    b. $5,000   d. $11,250

4. Which of the following will increase a taxpayer's alternative minimum taxable income (AMTI)?

	Personal Exemption	Property Taxes	Medical Expenses Over 10% of AGI
a.	Yes	Yes	Yes
b.	Yes	Yes	No
c.	No	Yes	Yes
d.	Yes	No	Yes

5. Which of the following best describes the effect of a tax credit?

    a. It reduces a person's gross income.

    b. It reduces a person's adjusted gross income.

    c. It reduces a person's taxable income.

    d. It reduces a person's tax liability.

Comparative Forms of Doing Business

LEARNING OBJECTIVES: *After completing Chapter 18, you should be able to:*

LO.1 Identify the principal legal and tax forms for conducting a business.

LO.2 Apply nontax factors in the choice among alternative organizational forms.

LO.3 Contrast the conduit and entity approaches to legal organizational forms.

LO.4 Identify which organizational forms result in the double taxation of business income.

LO.5 Identify the influence of the conduit and entity perspectives on the tax treatment of an

entity's operations and the entity's relation to its owners.

LO.6 Identify techniques for avoiding double taxation.

LO.7 Analyze the effects of the disposition of a business on the owners and the entity for each of the forms for conducting a business.

LO.8 Compare the tax consequences of the choice among the most common forms of doing business.

CHAPTER OUTLINE

TAX TALK *[My firm] had a rule—at least it seemed to be a rule—that everybody that came had to spend at least a year working on taxes. The general rationale for the rule as I could understand it was that taxes were so important to everything that you do, whatever the kind of case you are handling, you have to know something about the tax consequences of things.* —Charles A. Horsky

CHOOSING A BUSINESS FORM AND OTHER INVESTMENTS

Bill and George are going to start a new business and have come to you for advice on the most appropriate organizational form for the business. They have narrowed the choice to a C corporation, an S corporation, or an LLC but would like you to advise them as to the primary advantages and disadvantages of the different forms. They have an adequate amount in savings to finance the business initially. Limited liability is a significant concern as is limiting the amount of taxes paid. Bill and George anticipate that the company will lose money in the first two years of operation. After that, however, they expect to earn $200,000 in before-tax profit and distribute any after-tax profit to the owners. Bill and George are both single, and both are subject to a 28 percent marginal tax rate.

George also is considering investing $10,000 in a limited partnership. As a way of leveraging the risks and rewards associated with his investments, Bill earlier had acquired a 30 percent interest in a boutique retail coffee franchise outlet. Bill now is considering selling this investment, which has experienced rapid appreciation. Because he is considering cashing out the gain, he needs to know the adjusted basis of his ownership interest.

Read the chapter and formulate your response.

A variety of factors, both tax and nontax, can affect the choice of the legal form in which a business is conducted. The form that is appropriate at one point in the life of a business and its owners may not be appropriate at a different time.

This chapter provides the basis for comparing and contrasting the tax consequences of several business decisions across different types of tax and legal forms. Understanding the comparative tax consequences of those decisions and being able to apply them effectively to specific fact patterns will facilitate effective tax planning, including the initial choice of an organizational form in which to conduct a business.

18-1 FORMS OF DOING BUSINESS

LO.1

Identify the principal legal and tax forms for conducting a business.

The principal legal forms in which to conduct a business are the sole proprietorship, partnership, limited liability company, and corporation. The specific legal attributes of each of these organizational forms, including their relations to their owners and non-owners, are determined by the laws of the state in which they are organized.

These same forms generally are recognized for Federal income tax purposes as well, with the tax treatment determined by the legal form. However, three major exceptions exist. First, the "check-the-box" Regulations provide for LLCs to generally be treated either as sole proprietorships (called *disregarded entities*) or partnerships for tax purposes, depending on the number of owners. An LLC with only one owner is a disregarded entity for tax purposes. A disregarded entity is treated as a sole proprietorship if the owner is an individual or as a division of a corporate owner. An LLC with more than one owner is treated as a partnership.

Second, the same Regulations allow most unincorporated entities to elect to be treated as corporations for Federal income tax purposes.[1] Therefore, an entity may be taxed as a corporation even though it is not organized as such under state law. Finally, a corporation may elect to be treated as an S corporation for tax purposes.[2] The income of an S corporation is taxed similarly to that of a partnership. However, the designation has no effect on the corporation for state law purposes.

About 7 million corporations file U.S. income tax returns every year, and about 4.4 million of these use S corporation status. About 3.4 million partnership returns are filed every year, with over 60 percent of those being filed by LLCs. More than 22 million individual returns report sole proprietorship activities in a typical tax year. The business entity forms that are growing in number the fastest are the sole proprietorship (twice as many as 15 years ago) and the partnership (perhaps due to the popularity of limited liability companies).

TAX IN THE NEWS **Should You Check That Box?**

The check-the-box rules have been evolving since their introduction into the Regulations in late 1996. They are designed to remove tax considerations from the owners' choice of the legal form in which to conduct business. These provisions act to reduce the owners' exposure to the double taxation of taxable business profits. But taxpayers considering the use of these rules have run into several complications.

• Changing tax entity classifications comes at a cost. Changing the business form from a corporation to a partnership might trigger taxes for both the entity and its owners, defeating the purpose of the entity change.

• State income tax laws do not always match those of the Federal tax code. Several states have been slow to adopt the check-the-box rules, and others have modified the rules in some way. For instance, in several states, a one-member limited liability company does not receive the expected tax treatment of a partnership; it is reclassified as a corporation or sole proprietorship. Uncertainty as to the state income tax treatment of a check-the-box selection alone may keep the owners from exercising their supposed freedom of choice of tax entity.

---

[1]Reg. §§ 301.7701–1 through –4, and –6.

[2]§§ 1361 and 1362. See Chapter 15.

18-2 NONTAX FACTORS AFFECTING THE CHOICE OF BUSINESS FORM

Taxes are only one of many factors to consider when making a business decision, including the choice of the legal form of the entity. Above all, any business decision should make economic sense.

The Big Picture

EXAMPLE 1

Return to the facts of *The Big Picture* on p. 18-1. George is considering investing $10,000 in a limited partnership. The partnership is expected to generate losses for two years before generating any profits. George projects that he will be able to deduct his share of the losses up to his $10,000 capital contribution within the next two years. Because George's marginal tax rate is 28%, the investment will produce tax savings of $2,800 ($10,000 × 28%).

However, there is a substantial risk that he will not recover any of his original investment. If this occurs, his negative cash flow from the investment in the limited partnership is $7,200 ($10,000 − $2,800). The tax savings cannot make up for the loss of the investment itself. George must decide whether the investment makes economic sense.

18-2a Limited Liability

A corporation generally offers its owners some form of limited liability under state law. This means that a shareholder cannot be held liable for the debts or actions of the corporation. Therefore, a shareholder's liability is limited to his or her investment. This absence of personal liability on the part of the owners is the most frequently cited advantage of the corporate form.

EXAMPLE 2

Ed, Fran, and Gabriella each invest $25,000 for all of the shares of stock of Brown Corporation. Brown obtains creditor financing of $100,000. Brown is the defendant in a personal injury suit resulting from an accident involving one of its delivery trucks. The court awards a judgment of $2.5 million to the plaintiff. The award exceeds Brown's insurance coverage by $1.5 million. Even though the judgment probably will result in Brown's bankruptcy, the shareholders will have no personal liability for the unpaid corporate debts.

Limited liability is not available to all corporations. For many years, state laws did not permit professional individuals (e.g., accountants, attorneys, architects, and physicians) to incorporate. Even though professionals now are allowed to incorporate, the statutes do not provide limited liability for the performance of professional services.

Even if state law provides for limited liability, the shareholders of small corporations may be forced, in effect, to forgo this benefit. For example, a corporation may be unable to obtain external financing (e.g., a bank loan) at reasonable interest rates unless the shareholders guarantee the loan.

The limited partnership form provides limited liability, but only to its limited partners. For those partners, liability is limited to the amount invested plus any additional amount they agree to invest. However, limited partnerships are generally required to have at least one general partner. A general partner has unlimited liability.

EXAMPLE 3

HIJ is a limited partnership. Hazel, the general partner, invests $250,000 in HIJ. Iris and Jane, the limited partners, each invest $50,000. While the potential loss for Iris and Jane is limited to $50,000 each, Hazel's liability exposure is unlimited.

It may be possible to provide a general partner with limited liability indirectly by establishing a corporation to serve as the general partner. When a venture is structured this way, the shareholders of the general partner have limited their liability under the corporate statutes. In Exhibit 18.1, Individual A is protected from personal liability by being merely the shareholder of Corporation A.

EXHIBIT 18.1   **Limited Partnership with a Corporate General Partner**

Like corporations, LLCs provide liability protection to all of its owners. This, coupled with the ability to be taxed as a partnership, is the most frequently cited benefit of an LLC. However, as discussed below, other corporate characteristics often are missing from LLCs. Limited liability partnerships (LLPs) also provide liability protection to all of their owners, but only for liabilities arising from the negligence or wrongdoing of the other owners. Partners in an LLP are not protected from the entity's contractual liabilities.

18-2b **Other Factors**

Other nontax factors may be significant in selecting an organization form. For example, in addition to limited liability, the corporation generally is characterized by unlimited life (i.e., the corporation's existence is unaffected by a change in its ownership), separation of ownership and management, and the free transferability of interests. One or more of these characteristics is usually absent in other business forms.

18-2c **Capital Formation**

The combination of liability exposure with other nontax factors may significantly affect an entity's ability to raise capital. A sole proprietorship is limited to the capital that can be provided, or raised, by the proprietor. A partnership has a greater opportunity to raise funds through the pooling of owner resources. However, sole proprietorships and general partners are subject to any liabilities generated by the business.

EXAMPLE 4

Adam and Beth decide to form a partnership, AB. Adam contributes cash of $200,000, and Beth contributes land with an adjusted basis of $60,000 and a fair market value of $200,000. The partnership plans to construct an apartment building at a cost of $800,000. AB borrows $700,000 to construct the apartment building. AB has acquired a total of $1.1 million of financing, more than either Adam or Beth may have been able to acquire on their own.

Many professional service firms (e.g., accountants, architects, attorneys) have chosen to become limited liability partnerships. In the accounting profession, this includes all of the Big 4 (i.e., Deloitte, EY, KPMG, and PwC) and most regional and local accounting firms.

An LLP helps to provide protection for the purely personal assets of the partners. Under the LLP organizational structure, the only partners whose personal assets are at risk to pay a judgment are those actually involved in the negligence or wrongdoing at issue. Note, however, that the entity is still responsible for the full judgment. Thus, the capital of the entity is still at risk.

A limited partnership offers greater potential to raise capital than does a general partnership because a limited partnership can secure funds from investors (i.e., limited partners) without exposing them to the liabilities related to the venture or involving them in the management of the business.

EXAMPLE 5

Carol and Dave form a limited partnership, CD. Carol contributes cash of $200,000, and Dave contributes land with an adjusted basis of $60,000 and a fair market value of $200,000. The partnership is going to construct a shopping center at a cost of $5 million. Included in this cost is the purchase price of $800,000 for land adjacent to that contributed by Dave. Thirty limited partnership interests are sold for $100,000 each to raise $3 million. CD then borrows another $2 million from a third party. Each limited partner is liable only for the $100,000 they invest, even if CD is unable to repay the loan.

Of the different business entities, the corporate form offers the greatest ease and potential for obtaining owner financing because it can offer investors a combination of liability protection and liquidity that other business forms cannot. The ultimate examples of this form are the large public companies that are listed on the stock exchanges.

18-3 THE CONDUIT AND ENTITY PERSPECTIVES OF LEGAL BUSINESS FORMS

LO.3

Contrast the conduit and entity approaches to legal organizational forms.

All business forms other than the sole proprietorship are artificial entities. Their legal rights and responsibilities, including their relations to their owners as well as other parties, are defined under state law.

State law generally uses one of two perspectives when defining the rights and responsibilities of a business entity. In its simplest form, the conduit, or aggregate, perspective treats the business as simply an aggregation of its owners joined together in an agency relationship. Under the conduit perspective, the business has no existence separate from its owners. Conversely, the entity perspective considers the business as separate and distinct from its owners, with its own rights and responsibilities.

The rights and responsibilities afforded to corporations consistently reflect the entity perspective, with the corporation able to contract with other parties and responsible for its own debts. Shareholders have neither the right to directly manage the corporation, nor are they liable for its debts.

The approach to partnerships, including LLCs, is less consistent. Partnerships more often reflect the aggregate approach to an entity. For example, general partners have the right to participate directly in the management of a partnership, as well as to bind the partnership to contracts. It follows then that general partners are liable for the debts arising from the partnership's activities and contractual obligations. Further, a significant change in ownership may result in the dissolution of the partnership. However, partnerships also reflect the entity perspective in several respects. For example, a partnership's income is determined separately from that of its owners. Limited partners and LLC members are protected from the liabilities of the entity.

As discussed below, the taxation of business entities follows from the legal approach taken to each.

GLOBAL TAX ISSUES   **Do Corporations Pay Taxes?**

A disadvantage of being a C corporation is the potential for double taxation. This potential disappears, however, if the taxable income of the corporation is zero or negative.

A Government Accountability Office (GAO) study indicates that for the period 1996–2000, more than 60 percent of U.S. corporations did not owe or pay any Federal income taxes. Neither did 70 percent of foreign-owned corporations doing business in the United States. By 2003, corporate tax receipts

had fallen to 7.4 percent of overall Federal receipts, the lowest percentage since 1983.

Another GAO study released in early 2009 found that 83 of the largest publicly traded corporations maintain subsidiaries in 50 tax havens. Senator Carl Levin (who requested the GAO study) along with Senator Byron Dorgan (now retired), concluded that "too many corporations are finagling ways to dodge paying Uncle Sam, despite the benefits they receive from doing business in this country."

LO.4

Identify which organizational forms result in the double taxation of business income.

LO.5

Identify the influence of the conduit and entity perspectives on the tax treatment of an entity's operations and the entity's relation to its owners.

18-3a **Effect on the Taxation of Business Operations**

The view of the corporation as an entity separate from its owners leads to it also being considered a separate taxable entity, with its income subject to the income tax and the alternative minimum tax (AMT). As the corporation's shareholders, taxpayers distinct from the corporation, are taxed on this income when it is distributed, the income generated by a corporation is subject to double taxation before it is available to shareholders. This potential for double taxation frequently is cited as the major disadvantage of the corporate form, although several techniques, discussed below, can mitigate or eliminate the burden of double taxation.

Conversely, the sole proprietorship and partnership, including the LLC, are not considered taxpayers separate and distinct from their owners and, therefore, are subject to neither the regular income nor the AMT. Rather, the owners of these entities are directly and immediately responsible for any tax on the income these entities generate (i.e., these entities are "flow-through" entities). Therefore, the income generated by proprietorships and partnerships is taxed only once before it is available to owners, escaping double taxation. Further, the income, gains, losses, etc., generated by sole proprietorships and partnerships retain their character when recognized by the entity's owners. This can be beneficial (e.g., capital gains recognized by the entity may continue to receive preferential treatment) or disadvantageous (e.g., preference items generated by the entity may trigger the AMT) for a partner in a partnership relative to a shareholder of a corporation. Finally, as discussed further below, the conduit perspective also eliminates the owner's ability to defer the recognition of this income.

As discussed earlier, S corporations provide a way for certain corporations and their shareholders to avoid double taxation while retaining corporate status. However, the ownership structure of an S corporation is restricted in both the number and type of shareholders it may have. Further, wherewithal to pay problems may arise, as the owners of

TAX IN THE NEWS   **Who Pays Corporate AMT?**

One of the issues often raised in debates over tax legislation is whether the corporate AMT should be repealed. Among the topics discussed are the revenue generated, the related compliance costs, and the number of corporations subject to the AMT.

According to the IRS, nearly 6 million corporate tax returns were filed for tax year 2012. Of these returns, under 12,000 included any AMT liability, totaling over $5 billion.

Proponents of the corporate AMT argue that these statistics show that the AMT is being paid by corporations

targeted by the law (i.e., large corporations). Opponents argue that the same statistics show that the compliance costs borne by the mass of corporations do not justify the continuation of this tax system.

The exemption from the AMT for small corporations may be providing the needed solution. Large corporations must make minimal Federal income tax payments when the AMT applies. Most C corporations no longer need to compute the tax.

TAX PLANNING STRATEGIES Planning for the AMT

FRAMEWORK FOCUS: TAX RATE

Strategy: Shift Net Income from High-Bracket Years to Low-Bracket Years.

If the AMT will apply in the current year, the entity should consider accelerating income and delaying deductions, so that current-year taxable income is taxed at the lower AMT rate.

For a C corporation, the potential rate differential is 15 percentage points (20 percent AMT rate versus 35 percent top regular tax rate). For an individual (i.e., as a sole proprietor, as a partner, or as an S corporation shareholder), the potential tax rate differential is 11.6 percentage points (28 percent highest AMT rate versus 39.6 percent top regular tax rate).

A present value analysis should be used to make such decisions about any income acceleration and deduction deferrals.

partnerships and S corporations are taxed on the entity's earnings regardless of whether distributions are made.[3]

Flow-through entities may provide another advantage with respect to the taxation of operating income. Recall from Chapter 17 that the ACE adjustment related to the AMT applies only to C corporations. This may cause the income of a C corporation to be subject to the AMT while the same income taxable to the owners of a flow-through entity would not be. The ACE adjustment may cause a C corporation to pay tax on more alternative minimum taxable income than would the owners of a flow-through entity. On the other hand, the owners of a business may avoid AMT on operating income if the income is earned by a small corporation that is exempt from the AMT.[4]

In-depth coverage can be found on this book's companion website: www.cengagebrain.com **1 DIGGING DEEPER**

18-3b Effect on the Ability to Specially Allocate Income among Owners

Business entities may have several reasons to attribute certain income and expenses to specific owners, including the following (refer to Chapter 14).

- A desire to share profits and losses differently from the share in capital (e.g., based on relative contributions to the generation of those profits or losses).
- A desire to share profits and losses differently from year to year.
- A desire to allocate a built-in gain or loss on contributed property to the contributing owner.

Partnerships, including LLCs, can allocate taxable income, gains, losses, etc., among their owners in any way they desire, as long as the economic consequences follow that same allocation (i.e., as long as the allocation has a *substantial economic effect*). In fact, a special allocation generally is required when a partnership sells property originally contributed by a partner, if the property had a built-in gain or loss at the time of the contribution.

The right of shareholders to corporate income is legally determined by their stock ownership. Therefore, special allocations of taxable income, gains, losses, etc., are not permitted in C corporations. Indirectly, however, shareholders may be able to achieve results similar to those produced by special allocations by making payments to owners (e.g., salary payments, lease rental payments, and interest payments) and by using different classes of stock (e.g., preferred and common). However, even in these cases, the breadth of the treatment and the related flexibility are far less than that available under the conduit perspective.

---

[3]Recall the Chapter 15 discussions of the taxes on an S corporation's built-in gains, LIFO recapture, and investment income. These taxes ensure that income earned before a corporation elects S status remains subject to double taxation.

[4]§§ 56(c)(1) and (f). Refer to the discussion of the corporate AMT (and ACE) in Chapter 17.

TAX FACT Profitability of Partnerships

Since 1980, the number of partnership income tax returns has more than doubled (i.e., from 1.4 million returns to 3.4 million returns). The beneficial tax treatment of LLCs is expected to cause this trend to continue. While the partnership provides a tax shelter opportunity by passing losses through to the partner, a majority of partnerships are profitable.

	1985	1990	1995	2000	2010	2013
% of returns with profits	53%	56%	63%	60%	50%	56%
% of returns with losses	47%	44%	37%	40%	50%	44%

Source: IRS Tax Stats.

Although the income generated by S corporations generally is treated in a manner similar to that generated by partnerships, S corporations still are corporations, with the owners' right to income determined by their stock ownership. Therefore, like C corporations, special allocations are unavailable to S corporations. This treatment is mandated by the per-share and per-day allocation rule in § 1377(a). Although S corporations are limited to one class of stock, they still can use salary, interest, and rental payments to owners to shift income to the desired recipient.

DIGGING DEEPER 2   In-depth coverage can be found on this book's companion website: **www.cengagebrain.com**

EXAMPLE

6

Khalid contributes land with an adjusted basis of $10,000 and a fair market value of $50,000 for a 50% ownership interest in Maple Company. At the same time, Tracy contributes cash of $50,000 for the remaining 50% ownership interest. Because Maple is unable to obtain the desired zoning, it subsequently sells the land for $50,000.

Khalid holds a realized gain of $40,000 ($50,000 − $10,000) and a recognized gain of $0 resulting from the contribution. His basis in his ownership interest in Maple is $10,000, and Maple takes a basis in the land of $10,000. Maple realizes and recognizes a gain of $40,000 ($50,000 − $10,000) when it sells the land.

If Maple is a corporation, the appreciation of the land attributable to the time it was owned by Khalid becomes part of the corporation's taxable income, the resulting tax is paid by the corporation, and the tax burden is indirectly shared equally by both shareholders. There is no way by which the corporation can allocate the recognized gain, and the related tax burden, directly to Khalid.

If Maple is a partnership, the entire $40,000 recognized gain on the sale is allocated to Khalid, regardless of his profits or equity interest. Note that although S corporations are taxed similarly to partnerships, the S corporation provisions do not allow special allocations. If the entity were an S corporation, Khalid and Tracy would each include $20,000 of the recognized gain in their taxable income.

18-3c Effect on the Tax Treatment of Capital Contributions

Because the conduit approach applies to partnerships, § 721 generally provides for no recognition on the contribution of property to a partnership in exchange for a partnership interest. Section 721 protects both contributions associated with the formation of the partnership and later contributions. The partnership takes a carryover basis in the contributed property, and the partners have a carryover basis in their partnership interests.[5]

Because the entity approach applies to corporations, the transfer of property to a corporation in exchange for its stock is more likely to be a taxable event. However, if the § 351 control requirement (80 percent) is satisfied, no gain or loss is recognized. In this case, both the corporate property and the shareholders' stock take a carryover basis.[6] This control requirement increases the likelihood of gain recognition for shareholders who contribute appreciated property to the corporation *after* its formation.

---

[5]Refer to the pertinent discussion in Chapter 14.   [6]Refer to the pertinent discussion in Chapter 12.

BRIDGE DISCIPLINE **Bridge to Business Law and Financial Accounting**

When a business entity is created and assets are transferred to the business entity by the owners, the tax balance sheet and the financial accounting balance sheet generally show different amounts for the assets. The balance sheet amounts reflect the extent to which the *conduit theory* or *entity perspective* is applied.

The conduit perspective assumes that the business entity is merely an extension of the owners. Therefore, the transfer of the assets by the owners to the entity is not a taxable event. The owners' basis for their ownership interests is a substituted basis, though, and not fair market value. The business entity's basis for its assets is a carryover basis.

The entity prospective views the business entity is separate and apart from the owners. Therefore, the transfer of assets by the owners to the entity is a taxable event. The owners' basis for their ownership interests is a new basis (i.e., fair market value). The business entity's basis for its assets is a new basis (i.e., fair market value).

Financial accounting generally takes the entity perspective. Thus, the critical value is the fair market value of each asset contributed by an owner to the business entity. Tax law generally applies the conduit theory. Thus, the critical value for income tax computations is the owner's adjusted basis for the contributed assets.

18-3d Effect on the Basis of an Ownership Interest

Because the contribution of property to a partnership or an LLC in exchange for an ownership interest is not a taxable event under § 721, the owner's basis for the ownership interest carries over from the contributed property. The same is true of contributions to C and S corporations if the 80 percent control requirement of § 351 is satisfied. If the control requirement is not satisfied, any realized gain or loss on a contribution of property to a corporation is recognized by the shareholder, and the investor's stock basis is equal to the fair market value of the contributed property.

In a partnership or an LLC, because the owner directly and immediately recognizes the income, gains, losses, etc., of the entity, profits and losses of the entity also affect the owner's basis in the entity interest. Likewise, the owner's basis is increased by the share of entity liability increases and is decreased by the share of liability decreases. Accordingly, ownership basis changes frequently.[7] Conversely, because a C corporation is a taxpaying entity, the shareholder's basis for the stock is not affected by corporate profits and losses or corporate liability changes.

The treatment of an S corporation shareholder falls between that of the partner and the C corporation shareholder. Because the owner directly and immediately recognizes the income, gains, losses, etc., of an S corporation, an S corporation shareholder's stock basis is increased by the share of profits and decreased by the share of losses. However, because S corporation shareholders are not liable for the corporation's liabilities, the shareholder's stock basis is not affected by the corporation's liabilities.

The Big Picture

EXAMPLE

7

Return to the facts of *The Big Picture* on p. 18-1. Bill contributed cash of $100,000 to an entity for a 30% ownership interest in the franchise. The entity borrowed $50,000 and repaid $20,000 of this amount by the end of the taxable year. The profits for the year are $90,000.

If the entity is a partnership or LLC, Bill's basis at the end of the period is $136,000 ($100,000 investment + $9,000 share of net liability increase + $27,000 share of profits). If Bill is a C corporation shareholder instead, his stock basis is $100,000 ($100,000 original investment). If the corporation is an S corporation, Bill's stock basis is $127,000 ($100,000 + $27,000).

18-3e Effect on the Application of the At-Risk and Passive Activity Loss Rules

The at-risk and passive activity loss rules prevent certain taxpayers from recognizing losses that might otherwise be available to them. The at-risk rules prevent affected taxpayers from recognizing losses for which they are not at a risk of economic loss. The

---

[7]§§ 705 and 752.

passive activity loss rules generally allow affected taxpayers to recognize losses from passive activities only to offset income from passive activities.

The at-risk and passive activity loss rules apply to individuals and closely held C corporations. The passive activity loss rules apply to personal service corporations as well. Although neither set of rules applies to flow-through entities directly, the rules are especially relevant to the individual owners of these entities who may not be at risk for all of the losses that may pass through to them from the entity, or may not actively participate in the entity's activities. See Chapter 6 for a detailed discussion.

The at-risk rules are particularly relevant to partners who may have nonrecourse debt included in the basis of their partnership interest (see discussion in Chapter 14). Note that the exclusion of the debt from a partner's amount at risk, in spite of it being included in the basis of the partnership interest, will cause a partner to be treated similarly to a shareholder in an S corporation who may not include the debt in the basis of his or her stock at all. However, as partnership recourse debt may also be included in a partner's basis in the partnership interest, taxpayers may be able to recognize more losses generated by a pass-through entity by organizing the entity as a partnership rather than an S corporation. Of course, this will expose the owners to a greater risk of economic loss.

EXAMPLE
8

Walt is the general partner and Ira and Vera are the limited partners in the WIV limited partnership. Walt contributes land with an adjusted basis of $40,000 and a fair market value of $50,000 for his partnership interest, and Ira and Vera each contribute cash of $100,000 for their partnership interests. They agree to share profits and losses equally. To finance construction of an apartment building, the partnership obtains $600,000 of nonrecourse financing (not qualified nonrecourse financing; see Chapter 14), using the land and the building as the pledged assets. Each partner's basis for the partnership interest is as follows.

	Walt	Ira	Vera
Contribution	$ 40,000	$100,000	$100,000
Share of nonrecourse debt	200,000	200,000	200,000
Basis	$240,000	$300,000	$300,000

Without the at-risk rules, Ira and Vera could recognize losses up to $300,000 each even though they invested only $100,000 and have no personal liability for the nonrecourse debt. However, the at-risk rules limit loss recognition to the at-risk basis, which is $100,000 for Ira and $100,000 for Vera.

The at-risk rules also affect the general partner. Because Walt is not at risk for the nonrecourse debt, his at-risk basis is $40,000. If the mortgage were recourse debt, his at-risk basis would be $640,000 ($40,000 + $600,000), as the general partner.

If, instead, the entity were an S corporation and Walt received 20% of the stock and Ira and Vera each received 40%, the basis for their stock is computed as follows.

	Walt	Ira	Vera
Contribution	$40,000	$100,000	$100,000
Share of nonrecourse debt	–0–	–0–	–0–
Basis	$40,000	$100,000	$100,000

Note that the at-risk rules prevent any nonrecourse debt included in basis of a partner's interest from increasing the ability to recognize losses over what would be available if the owners had organized as an S corporation. Whether WIV had organized as a partnership or an S corporation, Walt would be able only to recognize losses up to $40,000, while Ira and Vera would only be able to recognize losses up to $100,000.

If the debt were recourse debt, however, it would be included in the at-risk basis of Walt's partnership interest, allowing him to recognize losses up to $640,000. It would not, however, affect the basis of his stock if WIV had organized as an S corporation.

The passive activity loss rules generally allow individuals and personal service corporations to recognize losses from passive activities only to offset income from passive activities. The passive activity losses of a closely held corporation, however, also can be used to offset active income.

Neither the at-risk nor the passive activity loss rules apply to larger C corporations. Therefore, C corporations that are not closely held can recognize losses for which they may not be at risk or from activities in which they do not materially participate.

As discussed above, the at-risk and passive activity loss rules apply to individuals and closely held C corporations. A *closely held C corporation* exists when more than 50 percent of the value of the outstanding stock at any time during the last half of the taxable year is owned by or for not more than five individuals.

The general passive loss rules apply to personal service corporations. Therefore, passive activity losses can be offset only against passive activity income. For closely held C corporations, the application of the passive activity rules is less harsh. Passive activity losses can be offset against both active and passive income.

A corporation is classified as a *personal service corporation* if the following requirements are satisfied.[8]

- The principal activity of the corporation is the performance of personal services.
- The services are substantially performed by owner-employees.
- Owner-employees own more than 10 percent in value of the stock of the corporation.

Because the conduit concept applies to partnerships, S corporations, and limited liability entities, passive activity income and losses are separately stated at the entity level and are passed through to the owners with their passive character maintained.

18-3f Effect on the Tax Treatment of Distributions

The application of the conduit perspective to partnerships, including LLCs, results in distributions not being taxed to the owners. The application of the entity perspective produces the opposite result: distributions that would be tax-free if made to partners generally are taxable when made to shareholders of C corporations.

A combination entity/conduit approach applies to property distributions from S corporations. The entity perspective generally applicable to corporations leads to the recognition of gain by the corporation for any appreciation attributable to the distributed property.[9] However, the conduit concept leads to the gain being taxed also at the shareholder level.

Tan, an S corporation, is equally owned by Leif and Matt. Tan distributes two parcels of land to Leif and Matt. Tan has a basis of $10,000 for each parcel. Each parcel has a fair market value of $15,000. The distribution results in a $10,000 ($30,000 − $20,000) recognized gain for Tan. Leif and Matt each report $5,000 of the gain on their individual income tax returns.

EXAMPLE
9

Stock redemptions and complete liquidations receive identical treatment whether a C or S corporation is involved.[10]

18-3g State Taxation

In selecting a form for doing business, the determination of the tax consequences should not be limited to Federal income taxes. Consideration also should be given to state income taxes and, if applicable, local income taxes.

The S corporation provides a good illustration of this point. Suppose that the owners of a new venture are considering how to organize their new business. The business is

---

[8]§ 469, derived from the definition in § 269A.

[9]§ 311(b).

[10]§§ 302, 331, and 336.

expected to generate losses in its first few years of operation. The owners' main concerns are personal protection from the venture's liabilities and the ability to recognize its losses immediately against their individual taxable incomes. They narrow their choices to an LLC and S corporation.

Believing the choices equally able to meet their objectives, the investors choose the S corporation because of their relative familiarity with the corporate form. However, they later learn that the state in which they incorporate does not recognize the Federal S election. Therefore, the losses are not deductible by the owners when they calculate their state taxable incomes, leading to a greater state income tax liability than if they had chosen to operate as an LLC.

18-4 **MINIMIZING DOUBLE TAXATION**

As explained earlier, only income earned in the corporate form is potentially subject to double taxation. However, two institutional factors help mitigate the double taxation of income earned by corporations. First, corporate income is generally subject to a set of progressive tax rates separate from its owners. Therefore, some corporate income may be taxed at rates below the top statutory rate that applies to corporations (i.e., 35 percent), or even the rate that would have applied to the corporation's owners (10–39.6 percent). This will be true even if the income is subject to the AMT, as the AMT rate for corporations (20 percent) is lower than that for individuals (26–28 percent).[11] Second, the lower tax rates that apply to dividends statutorily reduces the burden of double taxation on all qualified dividends.

Several other planning techniques also are available for further reducing, or eliminating, the second layer of taxation.

- Making distributions to the shareholders that are deductible by the corporation.
- Deferring distributions to the shareholders.
- Making distributions that qualify for return of capital treatment at the shareholder level.
- Making the S corporation election.

18-4a **Making Deductible Distributions**

Corporations often make distributions to their owners in a form that results in a deduction for the corporation. Structuring their affairs such that distributions from a corporation to its shareholders are deductible represents good tax planning. Common examples of such deductible distributions include:

- Salary payments to shareholder-employees.
- Lease or rental payments to shareholder-lessors.
- Interest payments to shareholder-creditors.

Recognizing the potential for abuse, the IRS scrutinizes these types of distributions carefully. All three forms are evaluated for *reasonableness*.[12] In addition, shareholder loans that lack a sufficient number of the characteristics usually associated with debt may be reclassified as equity.[13] IRS success with either approach raises the specter of double taxation.

---

[11]If the corporation is a personal service corporation (see Chapter 12), the corporation is subject to a flat tax rate of 35%.

[12]§ 162(a)(1). *Mayson Manufacturing Co. v. Comm.*, 49–2 USTC ¶9467, 38 AFTR 1028, 178 F.2d 115 (CA–6, 1949); *Harolds Club v. Comm.*, 65–1 USTC ¶9198, 15 AFTR 2d 241, 340 F.2d 861 (CA–9, 1965).

[13]§ 385; Rev.Rul. 83–98, 1983–2 C.B. 40; *Bauer v. Comm.*, 84–2 USTC ¶9996, 55 AFTR 2d 85–433, 748 F.2d 1365 (CA–9, 1984).

TAX IN THE NEWS   **Changing the Tax Treatment of Debt**

Interest payments made by a business on entity debt are deductible. Dividend payments made by a business on entity equity are not deductible. The same tax results as to these payments could be achieved by either of the following changes.

- Make the dividend payments deductible.

- Make the interest payments nondeductible.

Although only at the embryonic stage, serious analysis is under way with respect to the latter approach. A proposal by the panel appointed by President Obama considered the change in the current tax treatment of debt among one of the main aspects of a corporate tax overhaul.

Congress and legislative advisers have requested a study on the issue by the Joint Committee on Taxation. Among the factors supporting such an analysis are the following.

- Curtailing the interest deductions would generate revenue.

- Limiting such interest deductions could help discourage another buildup of leverage by financial firms, which many people believe contributed to the 2008 U.S. financial meltdown.

- The present advantage of debt financing when compared with equity financing would disappear.

- The problems arising from thin capitalizations would be eliminated.

Of course, with any change in the tax law, there are winners and losers. Perceived losers would include Wall Street, big manufacturers, and small businesses that do not have access to equity markets.

Source: Based on John D. McKinnon, "Potential Tax Change Is Red Flag for Some Firms," *Wall Street Journal*, April 4, 2011, p. A2.

Using Deductible Distributions to Avoid Double Taxation

EXAMPLE 10

Donna owns all the stock of Green Corporation and is the chief executive officer. Green's taxable income before salary payments to Donna is as follows.

Year 1	Year 2	Year 3
$80,000	$50,000	$250,000

Donna receives a monthly salary of $3,000. In December of each year, Donna reviews the operations for the year and determines the year-end bonus she is to receive. Donna's yearly bonuses are as follows.

Year 1	Year 2	Year 3
$44,000	$14,000	$214,000

The apparent purpose of Green's bonus program is to reduce the corporate taxable income to zero and thereby avoid double taxation. An examination of Green's tax return by the IRS would likely result in a deduction disallowance for unreasonable compensation.

EXAMPLE 11

Tom and Vicki each contribute $20,000 to TV Corporation for all of its stock. In addition, they each lend $80,000 to TV. The loan is documented by formal notes, the interest rate is 8%, and the maturity date is 10 years from the date of the loan.

The notes provide the opportunity for the corporation to make payments of $6,400 each year to both Tom and Vicki, and for the payments not to be subject to double taxation. This happens because the interest payments are includible in the gross income of Tom and Vicki, but are deductible by TV in calculating its taxable income. At the time of repayment in 10 years, neither Tom nor Vicki recognizes gross income from the repayment; the $80,000 amount realized is equal to the basis for the note of $80,000.

continued

If the IRS succeeded in reclassifying the notes as equity, Tom and Vicki still would recognize gross income of $6,400, but the interest would be reclassified as dividend income (which may be taxed at the 15% rate). Because dividend payments are not deductible by TV, the corporation's taxable income would increase by $12,800 ($6,400 × 2). To make matters worse, the repayment of the notes in 10 years would not qualify as a recovery of capital, resulting in additional dividend income for Tom and Vicki.

18-4b **Deferring Distributions**

Double taxation will not occur unless the corporation makes (actual or deemed) distributions to the shareholders. A policy of deferring distributions to shareholders can postpone the second layer of taxation on corporate earnings. The retained earnings will drive the value of the shares upward, equal to the accumulated after-tax cash. Further tax savings can occur if the shares are held until the investor's death. Under the basis step-up rule, the basis of the stock for the beneficiaries will be the fair market value at the date of the decedent's death rather than the decedent's basis, and any gain realized during the decedent's lifetime will disappear.[14]

DIGGING DEEPER 3   **In-depth coverage can be found on this book's companion website: www.cengagebrain.com**

18-4c **Return-of-Capital Distributions**

The exposure to double taxation can be reduced if the corporate distributions to the shareholders can qualify for return of capital rather than dividend treatment. This can occur when the corporation's earnings and profits (E & P) are low or negative in amount (see discussion in Chapter 13). The stock redemption and liquidation provisions offer an opportunity to avoid dividend treatment altogether. Under these rules, the distribution may be treated as a sale of the shareholder's stock, resulting in a tax-free recovery of basis and then recognition of low-tax long-term capital gain.[15]

18-4d **S Corporation Status**

Electing S corporation status generally eliminates double taxation.[16] Several factors should be considered when making this election.

- Are all of the shareholders willing to consent to the election?
- Can the qualification requirements for S status be satisfied at the time of the election?
- Can the S corporation requirements continue to be satisfied?
- For what period will the conditions that make the election beneficial continue to prevail?
- Will the corporate distribution policy create wherewithal to pay problems at the shareholder level?

Another benefit of electing S corporation status is that the corporation is not subject to the accumulated earnings or personal holding company taxes.

---

[14]The absence of distributions to shareholders could create an accumulated earnings tax (AET) problem under § 531. However, as long as earnings are used to finance expansion, the "reasonable needs" provision will be satisfied, and the corporation will avoid any AET. Refer to the discussion of the AET in Chapter 13.

[15]See § 302 and Chapter 13.

[16]Recall the Chapter 15 discussions of the taxes on an S corporation's built-in gains, LIFO recapture, and investment income. These taxes ensure that income earned before a corporation elects S corporation status remains subject to double taxation.

TAX FACT Income Tax Returns Filed by Business Entities

Type of Taxpayer	Tax Returns Filed (millions)			
	1980	1990	2000	2012
Individual	93.1	112.3	126.9	146.2
Partnership	1.4	1.8	2.1	3.3
C corporation	2.1	2.3	2.2	2.3
S corporation	.5	1.5	2.8	4.1

The number of S corporation returns has increased dramatically since 1980. LLCs usually file using the Federal income tax partnership rules, and the popularity of this entity form has led to a notable increase in the number of partnership returns filed.

Source: IRS Tax Stats.

EXAMPLE 12

Hawk Corporation has been operating as an S corporation since it began its business two years ago. For both of the prior years, Hawk incurred a tax loss. Hawk has taxable income of $75,000 this year and expects that its earnings will increase each year in the foreseeable future. Part of this earnings increase results from Hawk's expansion into other communities in the state. Because most of this expansion will be financed internally, no dividend distributions will be made to Hawk's shareholders.

Assuming that all of Hawk's shareholders are in the 33% tax bracket, their tax liability on corporate earnings will be $24,750 ($75,000 × 33%). Even though Hawk will not distribute any cash to the shareholders, they still will be required to pay the tax liability. This creates a wherewithal to pay problem. In addition, the corporate tax liability would have been less if Hawk had not been an S corporation [(15% × $50,000) + (25% × $25,000) = $13,750].

The shareholders' wherewithal to pay problem could be resolved by terminating the S corporation election. The tax liability would then be imposed at the corporate level. Because Hawk does not intend to make any dividend distributions, double taxation at the present time would be avoided. Terminating the election also reduces the overall tax liability by $11,000 ($24,750 − $13,750).[17]

In making the decision about the form of business entity, Hawk's shareholders should consider more than the current taxable year. If the S election is terminated, another election might not be available for five years. Thus, the decision to revoke the election should be made using at least a five-year planning horizon. Perhaps a better solution would be to retain the election and distribute enough dividends to the S corporation shareholders to enable them to pay the shareholder tax liability.

BRIDGE DISCIPLINE Bridge to Economics

Corporations such as Coca-Cola, IBM, Microsoft, Walmart, and Exxon-Mobil are major players not only in their industries but also in the world economy. However, some people also are attracted to "mom-and-pop stores," which cumulatively play a major role in the economy.

In recognition of the important role of small businesses and their size competitive disadvantage at times, Congress has provided small businesses with beneficial tax treatment that is not available to major business entities. Included among such beneficial treatments are the following.

- § 11 – beneficial tax rates.
- § 44 – disabled access credit.
- § 55(e) – exemption from the AMT for small corporations.

- § 179 – limited expensing for tangible personal property.
- § 1045 – deferral of gain for qualified small business stock.
- § 1202 – partial exclusion of gain for certain small business stock.
- § 1244 – ordinary loss treatment.

Each of these provisions defines "small" in a different way. Sometimes, however, when beneficial tax treatment is provided for a business entity, *small* may be used inappropriately. The classic example is the small business corporation of Subchapter S. Some S corporations hold billions of dollars of assets. They are "small" chiefly in the sense that the number of shareholders cannot exceed 100 unrelated shareholders.

---

[17]The absence of distributions to shareholders could create an accumulated earnings tax (AET) problem under § 531. However, as long as earnings are used to finance expansion, the "reasonable needs" provision will be satisfied, and the corporation will avoid any AET. Refer to the discussion of the AET in Chapter 13.

EXAMPLE 13

Emerald Corporation commenced business in January 2015. The two shareholders, Diego and Jaime, are both in the 28% tax bracket. The following operating results are projected for the first five years of operations.

2015	2016	2017	2018	2019
($50,000)	$400,000	$600,000	$800,000	$1,000,000

The corporation plans to expand rapidly. Therefore, no distributions will be made to shareholders. In addition, beginning in 2016, preferred stock will be offered to a substantial number of investors to help finance the expansion.

If the S corporation election is made for 2015, the $50,000 loss can be passed through to Diego and Jaime. The loss will generate a positive cash-flow effect of $14,000 ($50,000 × 28%). Assume that the election is either revoked or involuntarily terminated at the beginning of 2016 as a result of the issuance of the preferred stock. The C corporation tax liability for 2016 is $136,000 ($400,000 × 34%).

If the S corporation election is not made for 2014, the $50,000 loss is a net operating loss. The amount can be carried forward to reduce the 2015 corporate taxable income to $350,000 ($400,000 − $50,000). The resultant tax liability is $119,000 ($350,000 × 34%).

Should the S corporation election be made for just the one-year period? The answer is unclear. With an assumed after-tax rate of return to Diego and Jaime of 10%, the value of the $14,000 one year hence is $15,400 ($14,000 × 110%). Even considering the time value of money, the combined corporation-shareholder negative cash-flow effect of $120,600 ($136,000 − $15,400) in the case of an S election is not significantly different from the $119,000 corporate tax liability that would result for a C corporation.

LO.7

Analyze the effects of the disposition of a business on the owners and the entity for each of the forms for conducting a business.

18-5 DISPOSITION OF A BUSINESS OR AN OWNERSHIP INTEREST

A key factor in evaluating the tax consequences of a business disposition is whether the disposition is viewed as the sale of an ownership interest or as a sale of assets. Generally, the tax consequences are more favorable to the seller if the transaction is treated as a sale of the ownership interest. Conversely, the purchaser will prefer that the transaction be treated as a purchase of the individual assets, as this results in a higher basis in those assets. This difference in the preferences of the parties may influence the price paid by the seller.

18-5a Sole Proprietorships

Regardless of the form of the transaction, the sale of a sole proprietorship is treated as the sale of individual assets. Thus, gains and losses must be calculated separately for each asset. Classification as capital gain or ordinary income depends on the nature and holding period of the individual assets. Ordinary income property such as inventory will result in ordinary gains and losses. Section 1231 property such as land, buildings, and machinery used in the business will produce § 1231 gains and losses (subject to depreciation recapture under §§ 1245 and 1250). Capital assets such as investment land and stocks qualify for capital gain or loss treatment.

If the amount realized exceeds the fair market value of the identifiable assets sold, the excess is treated as goodwill, which generates capital gain for the seller. If instead the excess payment is allocated to a covenant not to compete, the related gain is classified as ordinary income rather than capital gain. Both goodwill and covenants are amortized by the purchaser over a 15-year statutory period.[18]

---

[18]§ 197.

Seth, who is in the 35% tax bracket, sells his sole proprietorship to Wilma for $600,000. The identifiable assets are as follows.

	Adjusted Basis	Fair Market Value
Inventory	$ 20,000	$ 25,000
Accounts receivable	40,000	40,000
Machinery and equipment*	125,000	150,000
Buildings**	175,000	250,000
Land	40,000	100,000
	$400,000	$565,000

*Potential § 1245 recapture of $50,000.
**Potential § 1250 recapture of $20,000.

The sale produces the following results for Seth.

	Gain (Loss)	Ordinary Income	§ 1231 Gain	Capital Gain
Inventory	$ 5,000	$ 5,000		
Accounts receivable	–0–			
Machinery and equipment	25,000	25,000		
Buildings	75,000	20,000	$ 55,000	
Land	60,000		60,000	
Goodwill	35,000			$35,000
	$200,000	$50,000	$115,000	$35,000

If the sale is structured this way, Wilma can deduct the $35,000 paid for goodwill over a 15-year period. If instead Wilma paid the $35,000 to Seth for a covenant not to compete for a period of seven years, Seth's $35,000 gain would be taxed to him as ordinary income. If the covenant has no legal relevance to Wilma, in exchange for treating the payment as a goodwill payment, she should negotiate for a price reduction that reflects Seth's benefit from the lower capital gains tax.

18-5b Partnerships and Limited Liability Companies

The sale of a partnership or LLC can be structured as the sale of assets or as the sale of an ownership interest. If the transaction takes the form of an asset sale, it is treated the same as for a sole proprietorship (described previously).

The sale of an ownership interest generally is treated as the sale of a capital asset. Therefore, structuring a transaction as a sale of an ownership interest may be preferable to structuring it as a sale of the partnership assets. However, this benefit is severely curtailed by the need to recognize gain related to appreciation of many of the partnership's ordinary income-producing assets as ordinary gain, even on the sale of an ownership interest.[19]

From a buyer's perspective, tax consequences are not affected by the form of the transaction. If the transaction is an asset purchase, the basis for the assets equals the amount paid. If a buyer intends to continue to operate as an LLC or a partnership, the assets can be contributed to the entity under § 721. Therefore, the owner's basis in the entity interest is equal to the purchase price for the assets. Likewise, if ownership interests are purchased, the owner's basis is the purchase price paid. The partnership's basis for the assets is the purchase price because the original partnership was terminated.[20]

A problem may arise when a taxpayer purchases a partnership or LLC interest (rather than the entire business) from another owner. In such a case, the amount paid for the interest may not be equal to the new owner's share of the entity's basis in its assets. Put another way, the basis of the assets inside the entity may not reflect the amount paid for them by the new owner. To help prevent this problem, the entity may make an election

---

[19]§ 751. [20]§ 708(b)(1)(B).

to adjust its basis in its assets to reflect the amount paid by the new owner. This basis adjustment is allocable entirely to the new owner (see Chapter 14), ensuring the new owner can recover the (indirect) cost of the underlying assets.

Roz buys a one-third interest in the RST Partnership for $50,000 (outside basis). All of the entity's assets are depreciable, and their basis to the partnership (inside basis) is $90,000. If a § 754 election is in effect, the partnership can step up the basis of its depreciable assets by $20,000, the difference between Roz's outside and inside basis amounts [$50,000 − (1/3 × $90,000)]. All of the "new" asset basis is allocated to Roz.

Such an election, once made, is binding on the entity and applies to all subsequent exchanges of ownership interests. Therefore, while it may benefit a new owner if the entity's assets have appreciated prior to the acquisition date, creating a positive basis adjustment for the acquiring owner, it may be detrimental to a future acquirer if assets are depreciated at the time of acquisition, resulting in a negative basis adjustment for the new owner.[21]

18-5c C Corporations

The sale of a business held by a C corporation can be structured as either an asset sale or a stock sale. The stock sale has the dual advantage to the seller of being less complex both as a legal transaction and as a tax transaction. It also has the advantage of providing a way to avoid double taxation. Finally, any gain or loss on the sale of the stock is treated as a capital gain or loss to the shareholder.

Jane and Zina each own 50% of the stock of Purple Corporation. They have owned the business for 10 years. Jane's basis in her stock is $40,000, and Zina's basis in her stock is $60,000. They agree to sell the stock to Rex for $300,000. Jane recognizes a long-term capital gain of $110,000 ($150,000 − $40,000), and Zina recognizes a long-term capital gain of $90,000 ($150,000 − $60,000). Rex takes a basis in his stock of $300,000. Purple's basis in its assets does not change as a result of the stock sale.

Conversely, the purchaser will prefer that the transaction be structured as a sale of the individual assets, assuming those assets have a fair market value in excess of their basis to the corporation. This allows the purchaser to increase the basis of the assets to their fair market value.

Returning to Example 16, assume that Purple's assets have a fair market value of $300,000 but an adjusted basis to Purple of $100,000. If the transaction is structured as a stock sale, Rex will take a basis in his stock of $300,000, and Purple's basis in its assets will be unaffected. Conversely, if the transaction is structured as an asset sale, Rex will take a basis of $300,000 in his acquired assets. However, Purple will recognize a gain of $200,000 ($300,000 − $100,000) in addition to the gain recognized by Jane and Zina on the liquidation of Purple.

18-5d S Corporations

Because the S corporation is a corporation under state law, it is subject to the provisions for a C corporation discussed in the prior section. An asset sale at the corporate level or a liquidating distribution of assets produces gain or loss recognition at the corporate level. However, under the conduit concept applicable to the S corporation, the recognized gain or loss is passed through to the shareholders. Therefore, double taxation is avoided directly for a stock sale (because only the shareholder is involved) and indirectly for an asset sale (because the conduit perspective ignores the involvement of the corporation).

Double taxation might seem to be avoided by making an S corporation election prior to the liquidation of a C corporation, but the built-in gains tax eliminates this opportunity; taxation occurs at the corporate level, and double taxation results.

Concept Summary 18.1 reviews the tax consequences of business dispositions.

---

[21]§§ 743 and 754.

TAX PLANNING STRATEGIES Selling Stock or Assets

FRAMEWORK FOCUS: TAX RATE

Strategy: Avoid Double Taxation.

Structuring the transfer of the business as a stock sale may produce detrimental tax results for the purchaser. As Example 17 illustrates, the basis of the corporation's assets is not affected by the stock sale. If the fair market value of the stock exceeds the corporation's adjusted basis for its assets, the purchaser is denied the opportunity to step up the basis of the assets to reflect the amount in effect paid for them through the stock acquisition—no § 754 election is available for C corporations.

If an asset sale is used, the seller of the business can be either the corporation or its shareholders. If the seller is the corporation, the corporation sells the business (the assets), pays any debts not transferred, and makes a liquidating distribution to the shareholders. If the sellers are the shareholders, the corporation pays any debts that will not be transferred and makes a liquidating distribution to the shareholders; then the shareholders sell the business.

Regardless of the approach used for an asset sale, double taxation occurs. The corporation is taxed on the actual sale

of the assets, and it is taxed as if it had sold the assets when it makes the liquidating distribution to the shareholders. The shareholders are taxed when they receive cash or assets distributed in kind by the corporation.

An asset sale resolves the purchaser's problem of not being able to step up the basis of the assets to their fair market value. The basis for each asset is its purchase price. Then the purchaser needs to transfer the property to a corporation in a § 351 transaction.

From the perspective of the seller, the ideal form of the transaction is a stock sale. Conversely, from the purchaser's perspective, the ideal form is an asset purchase. Thus, a conflict exists between the buyer's and the seller's objectives regarding the form of the transaction. Therefore, the bargaining ability of the seller and the purchaser to structure the sale as a stock sale or an asset sale, respectively, is critical.

Concept Summary 18.1

Tax Treatment of Disposition of a Business

Form of Entity	Form of Transaction	Tax Consequences	
		Seller	**Buyer**
Sole proprietorship	Sale of individual assets.	Gain or loss is calculated separately for the individual assets. Classification as capital or ordinary depends on the nature and holding period of the individual assets. If amount realized exceeds the fair market value of the identifiable assets, the excess is allocated to goodwill (except to the extent identified with a covenant not to compete), which is a capital asset.	Basis for individual assets is the allocated cost. Prefers that any excess of purchase price over the fair market value of identifiable assets be identified with a covenant not to compete. Otherwise, the buyer is neutral, because both goodwill and covenants are amortized over a 15-year statutory period.
	Sale of the business.	Treated as a sale of the individual assets (as above).	Treated as a purchase of the individual assets (as above).
Partnership and limited liability company	Sale of individual assets.	Treatment is the same as for the sole proprietorship.	Treatment is the same as for the sole proprietorship. If the intent is to operate in partnership form, the assets can be contributed to a partnership under § 721.
	Sale of ownership interest.	Entity interest is treated as the sale of a capital asset (subject to ordinary income potential for unrealized receivables and substantially appreciated inventory).	Basis for new owner's ownership interest is the cost. The new entity's basis for the assets is also the pertinent cost (i.e., contributed to the entity under § 721) because the original entity will have terminated.

continued

Tax Treatment of Disposition of a Business—(Continued)

Form of Entity	Form of Transaction	Tax Consequences	
		Seller	**Buyer**
C corporation	Sale of corporate assets by corporation (i.e., corporation sells assets, pays debts, and makes liquidating distribution to the shareholders).	Double taxation occurs. Corporation is taxed on the sale of the assets with the gain or loss determination and the classification as capital or ordinary treated the same as for the sole proprietorship. Shareholders calculate gain or loss as the difference between the stock basis and the amount received from the corporation in the liquidating distribution. Capital gain or loss usually results, because stock typically is a capital asset.	Basis for individual assets is the allocated cost. If the intent is to operate in corporate form, the assets can be contributed to a corporation in a tax-deferred manner under § 351.
	Sale of corporate assets by the shareholders (i.e., corporation pays debts and makes liquidating distribution to the shareholders).	Double taxation occurs. At the time of the liquidating distribution to the shareholders, the corporation is taxed as if it had sold the assets. Shareholders calculate gain or loss as the difference between the stock basis and the fair market value of the assets received from the corporation in the liquidating distribution. Capital gain or loss usually results, because stock typically is a capital asset.	Same as corporate asset sale.
	Sale of corporate stock.	Enables double taxation to be avoided. Because the corporation is not a party to the transaction, there are no tax consequences at the corporate level. Shareholders calculate gain or loss as the difference between the stock basis and the amount received for the stock. Capital gain or loss usually results, because stock typically is a capital asset.	Basis for the stock is its cost. The basis for the corporate assets is not affected by the stock purchase.
S corporation	Sale of corporate assets by corporation.	Recognition occurs at the corporate level on the sale of the assets, with the gain or loss determination and the classification as capital or ordinary treated the same as for the sole proprietorship. Conduit concept applicable to the S corporation results in the recognized amount being taxed at the shareholder level. Double taxation associated with the asset sale is avoided, because the shareholder's stock basis is increased by the amount of gain recognition and decreased by the amount of loss recognition. Shareholders calculate gain or loss as the difference between the stock basis and the amount received from the corporation in the liquidating distribution. Capital gain or loss usually results, because stock typically is a capital asset.	Basis for individual assets is the allocated cost. If the intent is to operate in corporate form (i.e., as an S corporation), the assets can be contributed to a corporation in a tax-deferred manner under § 351.
	Sale of corporate assets by the shareholders.	At the time of the liquidating distribution to the shareholders, recognition occurs at the corporation level as if the corporation had sold the assets. The resulting tax consequences for the shareholders and the corporation are the same as for the sale of corporate assets by the S corporation.	Same as corporate asset sale by the S corporation.
	Sale of corporate stock.	Same as the treatment for the sale of stock of a C corporation.	Same as the treatment for the purchase of stock of a C corporation.

18-6 CONVERSION TO OTHER ENTITY TYPES

As the owners' tax and nontax goals change, they may decide to change the organizational form in which the business is conducted. This raises three primary issues.

- Does the conversion result in the recognition of gain or loss?
- What is the basis for the ownership interest in the new entity form?
- What is the basis of the assets held by the new entity?

18-6a Sole Proprietorship

The conversion of a sole proprietorship into another entity form can be achieved without any recognition of gain or loss at the entity or owner level. This result occurs regardless of the choice of the new entity form. If the proprietorship is converted into a partnership or an LLC, nonrecognition can be achieved.[22] If the business is converted into either an S corporation or a C corporation, nonrecognition is available.[23]

If the proprietorship converts into a partnership or an LLC, the owner's basis in the ownership interest carries over from the contributed property.[24] Similarly, if the proprietorship converts into a corporation, the shareholder's basis for the stock received carries over from the shareholder's basis in the contributed property.[25]

After a conversion, the partnership or LLC takes a carryover basis for its assets.[26] Similarly, a corporation takes a carryover basis for its assets.[27]

18-6b C Corporation

A C corporation can convert into any of the following entity forms.

- Sole proprietorship.
- Partnership or LLC.
- S corporation.

Converting to an S corporation merely requires the election of S status.[28] As discussed in Chapter 15, the S election can be made only if all shareholders consent to the election and if the S corporation qualification requirements are satisfied.[29] These qualification requirements become maintenance requirements that must be met to retain the S election.

The election of S status produces the following tax consequences.

- No recognition of gain or loss.
- Carryover basis for the shareholders' stock.
- Carryover basis for the assets of the corporation.

If a C corporation converts into a sole proprietorship, a partnership, or an LLC, the corporation must be liquidated. This produces the following tax consequences.

- Recognition of gain or loss at the corporate level.[30]
- Recognition of gain or loss at the shareholder level.[31]
- Fair market value basis for the assets distributed in liquidation.[32]

---

[22]§ 721(a).
[23]§ 351(a).
[24]§ 722.
[25]§ 358(a).
[26]§ 723.
[27]§ 362(a).

[28]§ 1362(a).
[29]§§ 1361(a), 1361(b), and 1362(a)(2).
[30]§ 336(a).
[31]§ 331(a).
[32]§ 334(a).

After liquidation, the C corporation's former shareholders contribute the assets to the new entity. The tax consequences to the owners and to the entity are the same as those discussed earlier.

18-6c **Partnership**

A partnership or an LLC can convert into either of the following entity forms, both of which permit having multiple owners.

- C corporation.

- S corporation.

The owners can transfer their interests to the C corporation or S corporation in exchange for the stock of the entity. Because the transfer likely satisfies the § 351 requirements, any realized gain or loss is not recognized.[33] If, however, the 80 percent control requirement is not satisfied, the realized gain or loss is recognized by the owners.[34]

Assuming that the § 351 requirements for nonrecognition are satisfied, the following tax results occur.

- The basis of the stock to the shareholders is a carryover basis.[35]
- The basis of the assets to the corporation is a carryover basis.[36]

LO.8

Compare the tax consequences of the choice among the most common forms of doing business.

18-7 OVERALL COMPARISON OF BUSINESS FORMS

Concept Summary 18.2 provides a detailed comparison of the tax consequences of the choice among the most common forms of doing business.

Concept Summary 18.2

Tax Attributes of Different Forms of Doing Business (Assume That Partners and Shareholders Are All Individuals)

	Sole Proprietorship	Partnership/Limited Liability Company	S Corporation	C Corporation
Restrictions on type or number of owners	One owner. The owner must be an individual.	Must have at least 2 owners.	Only individuals, estates, certain trusts, and certain tax-exempt entities can be owners. Maximum number of shareholders limited to 100.*	None, except some states require a minimum of two shareholders.
Incidence of tax	Sole proprietorship's income and deductions are reported on Schedule C of the individual's Form 1040. A separate Schedule C is prepared for each business.	Entity not subject to Federal income tax. Owners in their separate capacity subject to tax on their distributive share of income. Entity files Form 1065.	Except for certain built-in gains and passive investment income when earnings and profits are present from C corporation tax years, entity not subject to Federal income tax. S corporation files Form 1120S. Shareholders are subject to tax on income attributable to their stock ownership.	Income subject to double taxation. Entity subject to tax, and shareholder subject to tax on any corporate dividends received. Corporation files Form 1120.

*Spouses and family members can be treated as one shareholder.

continued

---

[33]§ 351(a).
[34]§ 368(c).

[35]§ 358(a).
[36]§ 362(a).

Tax Attributes of Different Forms of Doing Business—(Continued)

	Sole Proprietorship	Partnership/Limited Liability Company	S Corporation	C Corporation
Highest tax rate (before additional Medicare taxes)	39.6% at individual level.	39.6% at owner level.	39.6% at shareholder level.	35% at corporate level plus 20%/15%/0% on any corporate dividends at shareholder level (if qualified dividends; otherwise 39.6%).
Choice of tax year	Same tax year as owner.	Selection generally restricted to coincide with tax year of majority owners or principal owners or to tax year determined under the least aggregate deferral method.	Restricted to a calendar year unless IRS approves a different year for business purposes or other exceptions apply.	Unrestricted selection allowed at time of filing first tax return.
Timing of taxation	Based on owner's tax year.	Owners report their share of income in their tax year within which the entity's tax year ends. Owners in their separate capacities are subject to payment of estimated taxes.	Shareholders report their shares of income in their tax year within which the corporation's tax year ends. Shareholders may be subject to payment of estimated taxes.	Corporation subject to tax at close of its tax year. May be subject to payment of estimated taxes. Dividends are subject to tax at the shareholder level in the tax year received.
Basis for allocating income to owners	Not applicable (only one owner).	Profit and loss sharing agreement. Cash basis items of cash basis entities are allocated on a daily basis. Other entity items are allocated after considering varying interests of owners.	Pro rata share based on stock ownership. Shareholder's pro rata share is determined on a daily basis, according to the number of shares of stock held on each day of the corporation's tax year.	Not applicable.
Contribution of property to the entity	Not a taxable transaction.	Generally not a taxable transaction.	Is a taxable transaction unless the § 351 requirements are satisfied.	Is a taxable transaction unless the § 351 requirements are satisfied.
Character of income taxed to owners	Retains source characteristics.	Conduit—retains source characteristics.	Conduit—retains source characteristics.	All source characteristics are lost when income is distributed to owners.
Basis for allocating a net operating loss to owners	Not applicable (only one owner).	Profit and loss sharing agreement. Cash basis items of cash basis entities are allocated on a daily basis. Other entity items are allocated after considering varying interests of owners.	Prorated among shareholders on a daily basis.	Not applicable.
Limitation on losses deductible by owners	Investment in business assets.	Owner's investment plus share of liabilities.	Shareholder's investment plus loans made by shareholder to corporation.	Not applicable.
Subject to at-risk rules?	Yes, at the owner level. Indefinite carryover of excess loss.	Yes, at the owner level. Indefinite carryover of excess loss.	Yes, at the shareholder level. Indefinite carryover of excess loss.	Yes, for closely held corporations. Indefinite carryover of excess loss.
Subject to passive activity loss rules?	Yes, at the owner level. Indefinite carryover of excess loss.	Yes, at the owner level. Indefinite carryover of excess loss.	Yes, at the shareholder level. Indefinite carryover of excess loss.	Yes, for closely held corporations and personal service corporations. Indefinite carryover of excess loss.

continued

Tax Attributes of Different Forms of Doing Business—(Continued)

	Sole Proprietorship	Partnership/Limited Liability Company	S Corporation	C Corporation
Tax consequences of earnings retained by entity	Taxed to owner when earned and increases his or her investment in the sole proprietorship.	Taxed to owners when earned and increases interest bases in the entity.	Taxed to shareholders when earned and increases interest bases in stock.	Taxed to corporation when earned and may be subject to penalty tax if accumulated unreasonably.
Nonliquidating distributions to owners	Not taxable.	Not taxable unless money received exceeds recipient owner's basis in entity interest. Existence of § 751 assets may cause recognition of ordinary income.	Generally not taxable unless the distribution exceeds the shareholder's AAA or stock basis. Existence of accumulated earnings and profits could cause some distributions to be dividends.	Taxable in year of receipt to extent of earnings and profits or if exceeds basis in stock.
Capital gains (before additional Medicare taxes)	Taxed at owner level using maximum rate of 0%, 15%, 20%, 25%, or 28%.	Conduit—owners must account for their respective shares. Taxed at owner level.	Conduit, with certain exceptions (a possible penalty tax)—shareholders must account for their respective shares. Tax treatment determined at shareholder level.	Taxed at corporate level with a maximum 35% rate. No other benefits.
Capital losses	Only $3,000 of capital losses can be offset each tax year against ordinary income. Indefinite carryover.	Conduit—owners must account for their respective shares. Tax treatment determined at owner level.	Conduit—shareholders must account for their respective shares. Tax treatment determined at shareholder level.	Carried back three years and carried forward five years. Deductible only to offset other entity capital gains.
§ 1231 gains and losses	Taxable or deductible at owner level. Five-year lookback rule for § 1231 losses.	Conduit—owners must account for their respective shares. Tax treatment determined at owner level.	Conduit—shareholders must account for their respective shares. Tax treatment determined at shareholder level.	Taxable or deductible at corporate level only. Five-year lookback rule for § 1231 losses.
Foreign tax credits	Available at owner level.	Conduit—tax payments passed through to owners.	Generally conduit—tax payments passed through to shareholders.	Available at corporate level only.
§ 1244 treatment of loss on sale of interest	Not applicable.	Not applicable.	Available.	Available.
Basis treatment of entity liabilities	Not applicable.	Includible in interest basis.	Not includible in stock basis.	Not includible in stock basis.
Special tax on built-in gains	Not applicable.	Not applicable.	Possible corporate tax.	Not applicable.
Special allocations to owners	Not applicable (only one owner).	Available if supported by substantial economic effect.	Not available.	Not applicable.
Deduction for fringe benefits to owners	None.	None.	None unless a 2% or less shareholder.	Available within antidiscrimination rules.
Effect of liquidation/ redemption/ reorganization on basis of entity assets	Not applicable.	Usually carried over from entity to owner.	Taxable step-up to fair market value.	Taxable step-up to fair market value.

continued

Tax Attributes of Different Forms of Doing Business—(Continued)

	Sole Proprietorship	Partnership/Limited Liability Company	S Corporation	C Corporation
Sale of ownership interest	Treated as the sale of individual assets. Classification of recognized gain or loss depends on the nature of the individual assets.	Treated as the sale of an entity interest. Recognized gain or loss is classified as capital, although appreciated inventory and receivables are subject to ordinary income treatment.	Treated as the sale of corporate stock. Recognized gain is classified as capital gain. Recognized loss is classified as capital loss, subject to ordinary loss treatment under § 1244.	Treated as the sale of corporate stock. Recognized gain is classified as capital gain. Recognized loss is classified as capital loss, subject to ordinary loss treatment under § 1244.
Distribution of appreciated property	Not taxable.	No recognition at the entity level.	Gain or loss recognition at the corporate level to the extent of the appreciation. Conduit—amount of recognized gain is passed through to shareholders.	Taxable at the corporate level to the extent of any realized appreciation.
Splitting of income among family members	Not applicable (only one owner).	Difficult—IRS will not recognize a family member as an owner unless certain requirements are met.	Rather easy—gift of stock will transfer tax on a pro rata share of income to the donee. However, IRS can make adjustments to reflect adequate compensation for services.	Same as an S corporation, except that donees will be subject to tax only on earnings distributed to them. Other than unreasonable compensation, IRS generally cannot make adjustments to reflect adequate compensation for services and capital.
Organizational costs	Startup expenditures are eligible for $5,000 limited expensing (subject to phaseout) and amortizing balance over 180 months.	Organizational and startup expenditures each are eligible for $5,000 limited expensing (subject to phaseout) and amortizing balance over 180 months.	Same as partnership.	Same as partnership.
Charitable contributions	Various limitations apply at owner level.	Conduit—owners are subject to deduction limitations in their own capacities.	Conduit—shareholders are subject to deduction limitations in their own capacities.	Limited to 10% of taxable income before certain deductions.
Alternative minimum tax	Applies at owner level. AMT rates are 26% and 28%.	Applies at the owner level rather than at the entity level. AMT preferences and adjustments are passed through from the entity to the owners.	Applies at the shareholder level rather than at the corporate level. AMT preferences and adjustments are passed through from the S corporation to the shareholders.	Applies at the corporate level. AMT rate is 20%. Smaller C corporations are exempt.
ACE adjustment to AMTI	Does not apply.	Does not apply.	Does not apply.	The adjustment is made in calculating AMTI. The adjustment is 75% of the excess of adjusted current earnings over unadjusted AMTI. In certain cases, the adjustment may be negative.

REFOCUS ON THE BIG PICTURE

CHOOSING A BUSINESS FORM AND OTHER INVESTMENTS

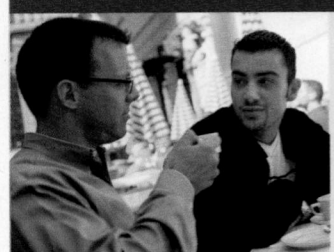

Conducting their business as a C corporation, an S corporation, or an LLC would meet Bill and George's objectives of providing limited liability. From a tax perspective, both the S corporation and the LLC would allow the early-year losses to be passed through to the owners. This cannot be achieved with a C corporation, in which the losses are trapped until future years when the company is profitable. Once the entity turns profitable, the tax consequences are as follows.

- As a C corporation, the entity would pay income tax of $61,250 on taxable earnings of $200,000. If the remaining after-tax earnings of $138,750 are distributed equally to Bill and George (each owner would receive a taxable dividend of $69,375), each shareholder pays an additional income tax of $10,406 ($69,375 × 15%). The combined entity/owner tax liability is $82,062, resulting in after-tax cash flows of $117,938.

- If the entity is operated as an S corporation or an LLC, no tax is paid at the entity level. However, the entire $200,000 is taxed as ordinary income at the owner level, resulting in each owner paying $28,000 ($100,000 × 28%) income tax. The combined entity/owner tax liability is $56,000, resulting in after-tax cash flows of $144,000.

It appears that either the S corporation or the LLC meets Bill and George's objectives of having limited liability and minimizing tax liability. The LLC form offers an additional advantage in that an LLC need not satisfy the numerous statutory qualification requirements to elect and maintain S corporation status. However, based on the facts in this situation, it is unlikely that satisfying the requirements would create any difficulty for Bill and George.

The results of George's investing in a limited partnership appear in Example 1. While beneficial tax results are expected to occur, George needs to be aware of the economic risk of losing his $10,000 investment.

For Bill, the recognized gain on the sale of his investment in the retail coffee franchise outlet is dependent on that entity's form. If the franchise were a pass-through entity, the recognized gain would be different than if the entity were a C corporation: entity profits increase the owner's interest basis in a pass-through entity, whereas entity profits have no effect on a shareholder's basis in C corporation stock.

What If?

Assume instead that Bill and George decide to expand the business and reinvest the annual $200,000 before-tax earnings instead of paying out dividends to the owners. If the business is organized as a C corporation, it can accumulate the earnings—as long as the company has reasonable business needs—and avoid the additional tax that is paid by Bill and George when the company makes taxable dividend distributions. Although the entity-level tax of $61,250 still must be paid, after-tax cash flows increase to $138,750. While the S corporation or LLC with after-tax cash flows of $144,000 still would be preferred in this situation, the double tax problem of the C corporation can be minimized with effective planning.

Suggested Readings

John O. Everett, Cherie J. Hennig, and William A. Raabe, "Converting a C Corporation into an LLC: Quantifying the Tax Costs and Benefits," *Journal of Taxation*, August 2010.

Janel Grieman and Thomas J. Nash, "Did Averting Fiscal Cliff Allow C Corporations to Overtake Passthroughs?" *Practical Tax Strategies*, August 2013.

W. Eugene Seago and Edward J. Schnee, "Double Deductions Resulting from Transfers to Controlled Corporations" *Journal of Taxation*, March 2011.

Timothy Todd, "Whose Goodwill Is It? The Taxation of Goodwill in Owner-Entity Transactions," *Journal of Taxation*, February 2015.

Michael A. Yuhas and Richard Harris, "The Retiring LLC Member: Sale Versus Liquidation," *Journal of Taxation*, January 2016.

Key Terms

Conduit perspective, 18-5   Entity perspective, 18-5

Computational Exercises

1. **LO.5** Roscoe contributes a personal-use asset, adjusted basis $15,000 and fair market value $28,000, to a new business in which he is an owner. Determine Roscoe's recognized gain on the transfer, and the basis of the asset to the business, if the new operation is a:

   a. Sole proprietorship.

   b. Partnership, where Roscoe holds a 10% interest.

   c. Corporation, where Roscoe holds a 25% interest and all shareholders contribute assets for stock in the transaction.

2. **LO.5** Mira and Lemma are equal owners of a business entity. Each contributed $25,000 cash to the business. Then the entity acquired a $100,000 loan from a bank. This year, operating profits totaled $30,000. Determine Lemma's interest basis at the end of the tax year, assuming that the entity is:

   a. A partnership.

   b. A C corporation.

   c. An S corporation.

3. **LO.5** Castle and Dorabella formed an S corporation; Castle owns 75% of the outstanding shares, and Dorabella owns the rest. When the entity's AAA balance is $1 million, it distributes an asset to each shareholder; the basis of each asset to the corporation is $45,000. Castle's asset is worth $90,000, and Dorabella's is worth $50,000. Determine the indicated amounts that result from the distribution.

   a. The corporation's recognized gain, if any.

   b. Dorabella's recognized gross income.

   c. Castle's recognized gross income.

Problems

4. **LO.2** Sea Green Enterprises reports the following assets and liabilities on its balance sheet.

	Net Book Value	Fair Market Value
Assets	$600,000	$925,000
Liabilities	200,000	200,000

Sea Green has just lost a product liability suit with damages of $10 million being awarded to the plaintiff. Although Sea Green will appeal the judgment, legal counsel indicates that the judgment is highly unlikely to be overturned by the appellate court. The product liability insurance carried by Sea Green includes a payout ceiling of $6 million. What is the amount of liability of the entity and its owners if Sea Green is:

a. A sole proprietorship?

b. A partnership or an LLC?

c. A C corporation?

d. An S corporation?

5. **LO.3** With which of the two perspectives to business forms, conduit or entity, is each of the following most consistent?

a. Limited liability for the entity's owners.

b. Unlimited life for the entity.

c. The ability of owners to participate directly in the management of the entity.

d. The ability of owners to transfer assets to the entity without recognizing gain or loss.

e. The payment of a wage from the entity to an owner who provides services to the entity.

f. The inclusion of entity debt in the basis of an owner's interest in the entity.

6. **LO.4** Red, White, Blue, and Orange report taxable income as follows.

Corporation	Taxable Income
Red	$ 99,000
White	330,000
Blue	900,000
Orange	40,000,000

a. Calculate the marginal tax rate and the effective tax rate for each of the C corporations.

b. Explain why the marginal tax rate for a C corporation can exceed 35% but the effective tax rate cannot.

Decision Making

Communications

7. **LO.2, 4** Amy and Jeff Barnes will operate their florist shop as a partnership or as an S corporation. Their mailing address is 5700 Richmond Highway, Alexandria, VA 22301. After paying salaries of $100,000 to each of the owners, the shop's annual earnings are projected to be about $150,000. The earnings are to be invested in the growth of the business. Write a letter to Amy and Jeff, advising them of which of the two entity forms they should select.

Decision Making

8. **LO.3, 4** Gerald is an entrepreneur who likes to be actively involved in his business ventures. He is going to invest $500,000 in a business that he projects will produce a tax loss of approximately $125,000 per year in the short run. However, Gerald is confident that, once consumers become aware of the new product being sold by the business and the quality of the service it provides, the business will generate a profit of at least $200,000 per year. Gerald generates substantial other

income (from both business ventures and investment activities) each year. Advise Gerald on the business form he should select for the short run. He will be the sole owner of the business.

9. **LO.2, 3, 4** Duke and Jacquie Coleman, married filing jointly, will establish a manu-   Decision Making
    facturing business. The couple anticipates that the business will be profit-
    able immediately due to a patent that Jacquie holds; profits for the first year will be
    about $300,000 and will increase at a rate of about 20% per year for the foreseeable
    future. Advise the Colemans as to the form of business entity that they should select.
    The Colemans are in the 39.6% Federal income tax bracket.

10. **LO.4** Plum Corporation will begin operations on January 1. Earnings for the next   Decision Making
     five years are projected to be relatively stable at about $80,000 per year. The
     shareholders of Plum are in the 33% tax bracket.
    a. Plum will reinvest its after-tax earnings in the growth of the company. Should
       Plum operate as a C corporation or as an S corporation?
    b. Plum will distribute its after-tax earnings each year to its shareholders. Should
       Plum operate as a C corporation or as an S corporation?

11. **LO.3, 4** Mabel and Alan, who are in the 35% tax bracket, recently acquired a fast-
     food franchise. Both of them will work in the business and receive a salary
    of $175,000. They anticipate that the annual profits of the business, after deducting
    salaries, will be approximately $450,000. The entity will distribute enough cash each
    year to Mabel and Alan to cover their Federal income taxes associated with any flow-
    through income from the franchise.
    a. What amount will the entity distribute if the franchise operates as a C corporation?
    b. What amount will the entity distribute if the franchise operates as an S corporation?
    c. What will be the amount of the combined entity/owner tax liability in parts (a)
       and (b)?

12. **LO.3, 4** Owl is a closely held corporation owned by eight shareholders (each has
     12.5% of the stock). Selected financial information provided by Owl follows.

Taxable income	$6,250,000
Positive AMT adjustments (excluding ACE adjustment)	600,000
Negative AMT adjustments	(30,000)
Tax preferences	5,000,000
Retained earnings	900,000
Accumulated E & P	2,000,000
ACE adjustment	750,000

    a. Calculate Owl's regular Federal income tax liability and AMT if it is a C corporation.
    b. Calculate Owl's regular Federal income tax liability and AMT if it is an S corporation.
    c. How would your answers in parts (a) and (b) change if Owl was not closely held
       (e.g., 5,000 shareholders with no shareholder owning more than 2% of the stock)?

13. **LO.4** Falcon Corporation, a calendar year taxpayer, is a deepwater offshore   Decision Making
     drilling company that is planning to sell drilling equipment that it no longer
    needs. The drilling equipment has an adjusted basis of $400,000 ($700,000 −
    $300,000 depreciation) and a fair market value of $500,000. The AMT adjusted
    basis of the equipment is $425,000.
       The buyer of the drilling equipment would like to close the transaction prior to
    the end of the calendar year. Falcon is considering the following options.

    · $500,000 in cash payable on December 31, 2016.
    · The sale is closed on December 31, 2016; the consideration is a $500,000 note
      issued by the buyer. The maturity date of the note is January 2, 2017, with the
      equipment pledged as security.

Falcon projects that its taxable income for 2016 and 2017 will be $400,000 (gross receipts of about $9.5 million) without the sale. Falcon has other AMT adjustments and tax preferences of $425,000 in 2016, which will not recur in 2017. Determine the tax consequences to Falcon under both options, and recommend the option that is preferable.

14. **LO.5** Using the legend provided, indicate which form of business entity each of the following characteristics describes. Some of the characteristics may apply to more than one form of business entity.

Legend
P = Applies to partnership and LLC
S = Applies to S corporation
C = Applies to C corporation

  a. Basis for an ownership interest is increased by an investment by the owner.
  b. Basis for an ownership interest is decreased by a distribution to the owner.
  c. Basis for an ownership interest is increased by entity profits.
  d. Basis for an ownership interest is decreased by entity losses.
  e. Basis for an ownership interest is increased as the entity's liabilities increase.
  f. Basis for an ownership interest is decreased as the entity's liabilities decrease.

Decision Making 15. **LO.5** Phillip and Evans form a business entity. Each contributes the following property.

	Phillip	Evans
Cash	$600,000	
Land		$600,000*

*Fair market value. Evans's adjusted basis is $200,000.

Three months later, the entity sells the land for $652,000 because of unexpected zoning problems. The proceeds are to be applied toward the purchase of another parcel of land, to be used for real estate development. Determine the Federal income tax consequences to the entity and to the owners upon both the formation and the later sale of the land. Perform your analysis assuming that the entity is:

  a. A partnership.
  b. An S corporation.
  c. A C corporation.

How could the parties structure the transaction so as to defer any recognized tax gain? Be specific.

16. **LO.5** Agnes, Becky, and Carol form a business entity with each contributing the following.

	Adjusted Basis	Fair Market Value
Agnes: Cash	$100,000	$100,000
Becky: Land	60,000	120,000
Carol: Services		50,000

Their ownership percentages will be as follows.

Agnes	40%
Becky	40%
Carol	20%

Becky's land has a $20,000 mortgage that is assumed by the entity. Carol is an attorney who receives her ownership interest in exchange for legal services. Determine the recognized gain to the owners, the basis for their ownership interests, and the entity's basis for its assets if the entity is organized as:

    a.   A partnership.

    b.   A C corporation.

    c.   An S corporation.

17. **LO.5** Eloise contributes $40,000 to MeldCo in exchange for a 30% ownership inter-
est. During the first year of operations, MeldCo earns a profit of $200,000. At
the end of that year, MeldCo holds liabilities of $75,000.

    a.   Calculate Eloise's basis for her stock if MeldCo is a C corporation.

    b.   Calculate Eloise's basis for her stock if MeldCo is an S corporation.

    c.   Calculate Eloise's basis for her partnership interest if MeldCo is a partnership.

18. **LO.5** ListCo reports the following income for the current tax year.

Operations	$92,000
Tax-exempt interest income	19,000
Long-term capital gain	60,000

ListCo holds earnings and profits (AAA for an S corporation) of $900,000 at the
beginning of the year. Then ListCo distributes $200,000 in total to the owners.

    a.   Calculate the taxable income if ListCo is (1) a C corporation and (2) an S
corporation.

    b.   Determine the effect of the distribution on the shareholders if ListCo is (1) a
C corporation and (2) an S corporation.

19. **LO.5** For many years, Sophie has owned and operated several apartment buildings.   Ethics and Equity
In 2011 and upon the advice of her attorney, Sophie transferred the apart-
ment buildings to a newly created corporation. Her main reason for incorporating
the business was to achieve the legal protection of limited liability.

    Every year since 2011, Sophie has prepared and filed a Form 1120 for the corpo-
ration. No corporate income tax has been paid because, after the deduction of various expenses (including Sophie's "management fee"), the corporation reports zero
taxable income.

    This year, Sophie decides that filing Form 1120 is a waste of time and serves no
useful purpose. Instead, she plans to report all of the financial activities of the apartment business on her own individual Form 1040.

    Comment on the propriety of what Sophie plans to do.

20. **LO.5** The Coffee Company engages in the following transactions during the taxable
year.

- Sells stock held for three years as an investment for $30,000 (adjusted basis of
$20,000).
- Sells land used in the business for $65,000. The land has been used as a parking
lot and originally cost $40,000.
- Receives tax-exempt interest on municipal bonds of $5,000.
- Receives dividends on IBM stock of $80,000.

Describe the effect of these transactions on the entity and its owners if the entity is
organized as:

    a.   A partnership.

    b.   A C corporation.

    c.   An S corporation.

21. **LO.5** Swift Corporation distributes land (basis of $55,000 and fair market value of
$120,000) to Sam and cash ($240,000) to Allison in exchange for part of their
stock. Other shareholders do not redeem any of their stock. Sam surrenders shares

of stock that have a basis of $25,000. Prior to the stock redemption, Sam owned 20% of the Swift stock, and after the redemption, he owns 15%.

At the same time, Swift distributes cash to Allison, and she surrenders shares of stock with a basis of $40,000. Prior to the stock redemption, Allison owned 70% of the Swift stock, and after the redemption, she owns 60%.

Determine the tax consequences to Swift, Sam, and Allison if Swift is:

a.   A C corporation.

b.   An S corporation.

22. **LO.5** Indigo, Inc., a personal service corporation, incurs the following income and losses.

Active income	$325,000
Portfolio income	49,000
Passive activity loss	333,000

a.   Calculate Indigo's taxable income.

b.   Assume that instead of being a personal service corporation, Indigo is a closely held C corporation. Calculate Indigo's taxable income.

c.   Would the answer in part (b) change if the passive loss was $320,000 rather than $333,000? Explain.

23. **LO.5** Rosa contributes $50,000 to FlipCo in exchange for a 10% ownership interest. Rosa materially participates in FlipCo's business.

FlipCo incurs a loss of $900,000 for the current tax year. Entity liabilities at the end of the year are $700,000. Of this amount, $150,000 is for recourse debt, and $550,000 is for nonrecourse debt.

a.   Assume that FlipCo is a partnership. How much of Rosa's share of the loss can she deduct for the year on her individual tax return? What is Rosa's basis for her partnership interest at the end of the year?

b.   Assume that FlipCo is a C corporation. How much of Rosa's share of the loss can she deduct for the year on her individual tax return? What is Rosa's basis for her stock at the end of the year?

24. **LO.5** Bishop contributes undeveloped land to a business entity in January for a 40% ownership interest. Bishop's basis for the land is $140,000, and the fair market value is $600,000. The business entity was formed three years ago by Petula and Rene, who have equal ownership. The entity is successful in getting the land rezoned from agricultural to residential use, but the owners decide to sell the land so that the entity can invest in another project.

In August, the land is sold for $650,000. Determine the tax consequences of the sale of the undeveloped land for the business entity and the three owners if the entity is organized as:

a.   A C corporation.

b.   An S corporation.

c.   A partnership.

d.   An LLC.

25. **LO.5** Jo and Velma are equal owners of the JV Partnership. Jo invests $500,000 cash in the partnership. Velma contributes land and a building (basis to her of $125,000, fair market value of $500,000). The entity then borrows $250,000 cash using recourse financing and $100,000 using nonrecourse financing.

a.   Compute the outside basis in the partnership interest for Jo and Velma.

b.   Compute the at-risk amount for Jo and Velma.

26. **LO.5** Megan owns 55% and Vern owns 45% of a business entity. The owners would like to use the entity to share profits (55% for Megan and 45% for Vern) and

to share losses (80% for Vern and 20% for Megan). Determine the tax consequences if the entity has a tax loss of $160,000 and is organized as:

a. A partnership.

b. A C corporation.

c. An S corporation.

27. **LO.5** Sanjay contributes land to a business entity in January of the current year for a 30% ownership interest. Sanjay's basis for the land is $60,000, and the fair market value is $100,000. The business entity was formed three years ago by Polly and Rita, who have equal ownership. The entity is unsuccessful in getting the land rezoned from agricultural to residential. In October of the current year, the land is sold for $110,000.

Determine the tax consequences of the sale of the land for the entity and its owners if the entity is organized as:

a. A C corporation.

b. An S corporation.

c. A partnership.

28. **LO.4, 6** Bryan operates his business as a C corporation. He is the only shareholder. The accumulated E & P is $800,000. Starting next year, Bryan will distribute $200,000 cash per year, plus all of the annual current-year earnings. Recognizing that the distribution would be taxed as dividend income, he has developed the following tax strategy.   *Ethics and Equity*

• Sell the corporate assets to himself for the fair market value.

• Have the corporation invest the sales proceeds in a mutual fund.

• Contribute the assets to an LLC and operate his business in this legal form.

Evaluate Bryan's proposal to avoid double taxation.

29. **LO.6** Heron Corporation has been in operation for 10 years. Since Heron's creation, all of its stock has been owned by Andy, who initially invested $200,000 in the corporation. Heron has been successful far beyond Andy's expectations, and the current fair market value of the stock is $10 million. While he has been paid a salary of $200,000 per year by the corporation, all of Heron's earnings have been reinvested in the growth of the corporation.   *Ethics and Equity*

Critical Thinking

Heron currently is being audited by the IRS. One of the issues raised by the IRS agent is the possibility of the assessment of the accumulated earnings tax. Andy is not concerned about this issue because he believes Heron can easily justify the accumulations based on its past rapid expansion by opening new outlets. The expansion program is fully documented in the minutes of Heron's board of directors. Andy has provided this information to the IRS agent.

Two years ago, Andy decided that he would curtail any further expansion into new markets by Heron. In his opinion, further expansion would exceed his ability to manage the corporation effectively. Because the tax year under audit is three years in the past, Andy sees no reason to provide the IRS agent with this information.

Heron will continue its policy of no dividend payments into the foreseeable future. Andy believes that if the accumulated earnings issue is satisfactorily resolved on this audit, it probably will not be raised again on any subsequent audits. Thus, double taxation in the form of the tax on dividends at the shareholder level or the accumulated earnings tax at the corporate level can be avoided.

What is Heron's responsibility to disclose to the IRS agent the expected change in its growth strategy? Are Andy's beliefs regarding future accumulated earnings tax issues realistic? Explain.

Critical Thinking   30. **LO.6** Two sisters and their brother, all unmarried, own and operate a dairy farm. They live on the farm and take their meals there for the "convenience of the employer." The fair market value of their lodging is $45,000, and the fair market value of their meals is $18,000. The meals are prepared by the farm cook, who provides their meals along with those of the eight other farm employees.

a.   Determine the tax consequences of the meals and lodging to the sisters and their brother if the farm is incorporated.

b.   Determine the tax consequences of the meals and lodging to the sisters and their brother if the farm is not incorporated.

Critical Thinking   31. **LO.6** A business entity has four equal owners. Its taxable income before the cost of certain fringe benefits paid to owners and other employees is $400,000. The amounts paid for these fringe benefits are reported as follows.

	Owners	Other Employees
Group term life insurance	$20,000	$ 40,000
Meals and lodging incurred for the convenience of the employer	50,000	75,000
Qualified retirement plan	30,000	90,000

a.   Calculate the Federal taxable income of the entity, assuming that it is a(n):

• Partnership.

• C corporation.

• S corporation.

b.   Determine the Federal income effects on the owners, assuming the use of each of the three business forms.

32. **LO.6** Turtle, a C corporation, reports taxable income of $300,000 before paying salaries to the three equal shareholder-employees, Britney, Shania, and Alan. Turtle follows a policy of distributing all after-tax earnings to the shareholders.

a.   Determine the tax consequences for Turtle, Britney, Shania, and Alan if the corporation pays salaries to Britney, Shania, and Alan as follows.

Option 1		Option 2	
Britney	$135,000	Britney	$67,500
Shania	90,000	Shania	45,000
Alan	75,000	Alan	37,500

b.   Is Turtle likely to encounter any tax problems associated with either option? Explain.

33. **LO.6** Parrott, Inc., a C corporation, is owned by Abner (60%) and Deanna (40%). Abner is the president, and Deanna is the vice president for sales. Parrott, Abner, and Deanna are cash basis taxpayers. Late in the year, Parrott encounters working capital difficulties. Therefore, Abner loans the corporation $810,000 and Deanna loans the corporation $540,000. Each loan uses a 5% note that is due in five years with interest payable annually.

a.   Determine the tax consequences to Parrott, Abner, and Deanna if the notes are classified as debt.

b.   Determine the tax consequences to Parrott, Abner, and Deanna if the notes are classified as equity.

Decision Making   34. **LO.6** Laurie Gladin owns land and a building that she has been using in her sole proprietorship. She is going to incorporate her sole proprietorship as a C corporation. Laurie must decide whether to contribute the land and building to the corporation or to lease them to the corporation. The net income of the sole proprietorship for the past five years has averaged $250,000. Advise Laurie on the tax consequences. Summarize your analysis in a memo for the tax file.

Communications

35. **LO.6** Marci and Jennifer each own 50% of the stock of Lavender, a C corporation. After each of them is paid a "reasonable" salary of $150,000, the taxable income of Lavender typically is about $800,000.

    The corporation is about to purchase a $2 million shopping mall ($1,500,000 allocated to the building and $500,000 allocated to the land). The mall will be rented to tenants at a net rental rate (including rental commissions, depreciation, etc.) of $600,000 annually. Marci and Jennifer will contribute $1 million each to the corporation to provide the cash required for the acquisition.

    Their CPA has suggested that Marci and Jennifer purchase the shopping mall as individuals and lease it to Lavender for a fair rental of $400,000. Both Marci and Jennifer are in the 35% tax bracket. The acquisition will occur on January 2 next year. Determine whether the shopping mall should be acquired by Lavender or by Marci and Jennifer in accordance with their CPA's recommendation. Depreciation on the shopping mall for the year is $37,000.

    Decision Making

36. **LO.6** Since Garnet Corporation was formed five years ago, its stock has been held as follows: 525 shares by Frank and 175 shares by Grace. Their basis in the stock is $350,000 for Frank and $150,000 for Grace. As part of a stock redemption, Garnet redeems 125 of Frank's shares for $175,000 and 125 of Grace's shares for $175,000.

    Decision Making

    a.   What are the tax consequences of the stock redemption to Frank and Grace?
    b.   How would the tax consequences to Frank and Grace be different if, instead of the redemption, they each sell 125 shares to Chuck (an unrelated party)?
    c.   What factors should influence their decision on whether to redeem or sell the 250 shares of stock?

37. **LO.6** Oscar created Lavender Corporation four years ago. The C corporation has paid Oscar as president a salary of $200,000 each year. Annual earnings after taxes approximate $700,000 each year. Lavender has not paid any dividends, nor does it intend to do so in the future. Instead, Oscar wants his heirs to receive the stock with a step-up in stock basis when he dies. Identify the relevant tax issues.

    Issue ID

38. **LO.6** Tammy and Willy own 40% of the stock of Roadrunner, an S corporation. The other 60% is owned by 99 other shareholders, all of whom are single and unrelated. Tammy and Willy have agreed to a divorce and are in the process of negotiating a property settlement. Identify the relevant tax issues for Tammy and Willy.

    Issue ID

39. **LO.6** Clay Corporation has been an S corporation since its incorporation 10 years ago. During the first three years of operations, it incurred total losses of $250,000. Since then, Clay has generated earnings of approximately $180,000 each year. None of the earnings have been distributed to the three equal shareholders, Claire, Lynn, and Todd, because the corporation has been in an expansion mode.

    Decision Making

    At the beginning of this year, Claire sells her stock to Nell for $400,000. Nell has reservations about the utility of the S election. Therefore, Lynn, Todd, and Nell are discussing whether the election should be continued. They expect the earnings to remain at approximately $180,000 each year. However, because they perceive that the company's expansion period is over and Clay has adequate working capital, they may start distributing the earnings to the shareholders. All of the shareholders are in the 33% tax bracket.

    Advise the three shareholders as to whether Clay's S election should be maintained.

40. **LO.8** Emily and Freda are negotiating with George to purchase the business he operates as Pelican, Inc. The assets of Pelican, Inc., a C corporation, are recorded as follows.

Asset	Basis	FMV
Cash	$ 20,000	$ 20,000
Accounts receivable	50,000	50,000
Inventory	100,000	110,000
Furniture and fixtures	150,000	170,000*
Building	200,000	250,000**
Land	40,000	150,000

*Potential depreciation recapture is $45,000.
**The straight-line method was used to depreciate the building. Accumulated
   depreciation is $340,000.

George's basis for the Pelican stock is $560,000. George is subject to a 35% marginal tax rate, and Pelican faces a 34% marginal tax rate.

a.   Emily and Freda purchase the *stock* of Pelican from George for $908,000. Determine the tax consequences to Emily and Freda, Pelican, and George.

b.   Emily and Freda purchase the *assets* from Pelican for $908,000. Determine the tax consequences to Emily and Freda, Pelican, and George.

c.   The purchase price is $550,000 because the fair market value of the building is $150,000 and the fair market value of the land is $50,000. No amount is assigned to goodwill. Emily and Freda purchase the *stock* of Pelican from George. Determine the tax consequences to Emily and Freda, Pelican, and George.

Decision Making   41. **LO.8** Linda is the owner of a sole proprietorship. The entity has the following assets.

Asset	Basis	FMV
Cash	$10,000	$10,000
Accounts receivable	–0–	25,000
Office furniture and fixtures*	15,000	17,000
Building**	75,000	90,000
Land	60,000	80,000

*Potential depreciation recapture is $5,000.
**The straight-line method has been used to depreciate the building.

Linda sells the business for $260,000 to Juan.

a.   Determine the tax consequences to Linda, including the classification of any recognized gain or loss.

b.   Determine the tax consequences to Juan.

c.   Advise Juan on how the purchase agreement could be modified to produce more beneficial tax consequences for him.

Decision Making   42. **LO.8** Gail and Harry own the GH Partnership. They have conducted the business as a partnership for 10 years. The bases for their partnership interests are as follows.

Gail	Harry
$100,000	$150,000

GH Partnership holds the following assets.

Asset	Basis	FMV
Cash	$ 10,000	$ 10,000
Accounts receivable	30,000	28,000
Inventory	25,000	26,000
Building*	100,000	150,000
Land	250,000	400,000

*The straight-line method has been used to depreciate the building. Accumulated
   depreciation is $70,000.

Gail and Harry sell their partnership interests to Keith and Liz for $307,000 each.

a. Determine the tax consequences of the sale to Gail, Harry, and GH Partnership.

b. From a tax perspective, should it matter to Keith and Liz whether they purchase Gail and Harry's partnership interests or the partnership assets from GH Partnership? Explain.

43. **LO.8** Hector and Walt are purchasing the Copper Partnership from Jan and Gail for $700,000; Hector and Walt will be equal partners. During the negotiations, Jan and Gail succeeded in having the transaction structured as the purchase of the partnership rather than as a purchase of the individual assets. The adjusted basis of the individual assets of Copper is $580,000.

Decision Making

a. What are Hector's and Walt's bases for their partnership interests (i.e., outside bases)?

b. What is Copper's adjusted basis for its assets after the transaction? Would an optional adjustment-to-basis election be helpful? Why or why not?

44. **LO.8** Vladimir owns all of the stock of Ruby Corporation. The fair market value of the stock (and Ruby's assets) is about four times his adjusted basis for the stock. Vladimir is negotiating with an investor group for the sale of the corporation. Identify the relevant tax issues for Vladimir.

Issue ID

45. **LO.8** Maurice Allred is going to purchase either the stock or the assets of Jewel Corporation. All of the Jewel stock is owned by Charley. Maurice and Charley agree that Jewel is worth $700,000. The tax basis for Jewel's assets is $500,000.

Decision Making
Communications

Write a letter to Maurice, advising him on whether he should negotiate to purchase the stock or the assets. Prepare a memo for the tax research file on this matter. Maurice's address is 100 Aspen Green, Chattanooga, TN 37403.

46. **LO.2, 3, 4, 5, 6, 7, 8** Using the legend provided, indicate which form of business entity each of the following characteristics describes. Some of the characteristics may apply to more than one form of business entity.

Legend	
SP	= Applies to sole proprietorship
P	= Applies to partnership and LLC
S	= Applies to S corporation
C	= Applies to C corporation
N	= Applies to none

a. Has limited liability.

b. Greatest ability to raise capital.

c. Subject to double taxation.

d. Subject to the ACE adjustment in computing AMT income.

e. Limit on types and number of shareholders.

f. Has unlimited liability.

g. Sale of the business can be subject to double taxation.

h. Contribution of property to the entity in exchange for an ownership interest can result in the nonrecognition of realized gain.

i. Profits and losses affect the basis for an ownership interest.

j. Entity liabilities affect the basis for an ownership interest.

k. Distributions of earnings are taxed as dividend income to the owners.

l. Total invested capital cannot exceed $1 million.

m. AAA is an account that relates to this entity.

BRIDGE DISCIPLINE

1. Parchment, Inc., is created with the following asset and liability contributions. Jake and Fran each receive 100 shares of Parchment common stock.

Shareholder	Assets	Basis	Fair Market Value
Jake	Cash	$100,000	$100,000
Fran	Land	40,000	120,000*

*The land is subject to a mortgage of $20,000 that Parchment assumes.

   a. Prepare a financial accounting balance sheet for Parchment. Discuss the relevance of conduit theory and entity theory in the creation of Parchment.
   b. Prepare a tax balance sheet for Parchment. Discuss the relevance of conduit theory and entity theory in the creation of Parchment.
   c. Assume that Parchment sells the land for $150,000 four months after Parchment was created. Discuss the effect of the sale on the financial accounting balance sheet and the tax balance sheet.

2. Assume that Parchment in (1) elects S corporation status at the time of its creation. Respond to parts (a), (b), and (c).

3. Assume that Parchment in (1) is a general partnership rather than a corporation. Respond to parts (a), (b), and (c). Would your answer change if Parchment were an LLC that "checked the box" to be taxed as a partnership? Explain.

4. Teal, Inc., owns total assets of $100 million, and it reports annual revenues of $700 million. Lavender, Inc., owns total assets of $12 million, and it reports annual revenues of $900,000. Both corporations have been in existence for three years.
   a. Explain why neither Teal nor Lavender computes an AMT liability for its first tax year.
   b. Explain why, in later years, Teal computes an AMT liability and Lavender is not required to do so.
   c. Do you think that this different tax treatment for Teal and Lavender is equitable? Explain your position.

Research Problems

Note: Solutions to Research Problems can be prepared by using the Checkpoint® Student Edition online research product, which is available to accompany this text. It is also possible to prepare solutions to the Research Problems by using tax research materials found in a standard tax library.

Research Problem 1. The Turnaround LLC was formed several years ago. It incurred losses for several years, reducing many of its members' bases in their interests to zero. However, the business recently obtained some new and promising contracts, and there is an expectation of profits in the coming years.

   Turnaround then admitted several new members, who each made capital contributions for their interests. The new owners anticipate that it will be necessary to reinvest any profits back into the business for some time. As there no longer will be losses to pass through, and any double taxation of profits will be delayed for some time, the owners of Turnaround are considering converting the business to a C corporation.

The business controls the following assets. There is no § 754 election in effect.

	Fair Market Value	Adjusted Basis
Cash	$ 500,000	$500,000
PP&E	500,000	500,000
Customer contracts	1,000,000	–0–

The original owners of Turnaround now hold a 50% capital and profits interest. They have come to you for advice regarding the potential tax consequences of the conversion for them, as well as for the new corporation.

Partial list of research aids:
Rev.Rul. 70–239, 1970–1 C.B. 74.
Rev.Rul. 84–111, 1984–2 C.B. 88.
Rev.Rul. 2004–59, 2004–24 I.R.B 1050.
Treas. Reg. § 301.7701–3(g)(i).

Research Problem 2. Crane is a partner in the Cardinal Partnership. A dispute arose with the partnership regarding Crane's share of current earnings. The partnership contends that the amount is $75,000, while Crane believes his share is $100,000.

Crane ceased being a partner on November 1. As a result of the dispute, the partnership distributed only $75,000 to Crane. It placed the disputed $25,000 in escrow. However, Crane's Schedule K–1 from the partnership included the full $100,000. Crane believes that the K–1 should include only the $75,000 that is not in dispute. Is Crane correct? Explain.

Internet Activity

Use the tax resources of the Internet to address the following questions. Do not restrict your search to the Web, but include a review of newsgroups and general reference materials, practitioner sites and resources, primary sources of the tax law, chat rooms and discussion groups, and other opportunities.

Research Problem 3. Find a blog posting or discussion thread with comments from tax professionals about Federal income tax consequences that occur when a business converts from an LLC to an S corporation or when a C corporation converts to a pass-through entity. Summarize the comments and suggestions that you find in these discussions in a one-page memo to your instructor.

Communications

Research Problem 4. For your state, list the forms that are required to be filed when a pass-through entity incorporates or when a corporation converts to a pass-through entity. Give statutory citations for the conversion rules, due dates for any required forms, and addresses for where the forms are to be sent. Attach a copy of one of the forms to a memo summarizing your findings, and send the documents to your instructor.

Communications

Appendix A

Tax Rate Schedules and Tables

(The 2016 Tax Tables and 2016 Sales Tax Tables can be accessed at the IRS website when released: **www.irs.gov**)

2015 Tax Rate Schedules—Individuals

Single—Schedule X

If taxable income is: Over—	But not over—	The tax is:	of the amount over—
$ 0	$ 9,225	.........10%	$ 0
9,225	37,450	$ 922.50 + 15%	9,225
37,450	90,750	5,156.25 + 25%	37,450
90,750	189,300	18,481.25 + 28%	90,750
189,300	411,500	46,075.25 + 33%	189,300
411,500	413,200	119,401.25 + 35%	411,500
413,200	....	119,996.25 + 39.6%	413,200

Head of household—Schedule Z

If taxable income is: Over—	But not over—	The tax is:	of the amount over—
$ 0	$ 13,150	.........10%	$ 0
13,150	50,200	$ 1,315.00 + 15%	13,150
50,200	129,600	6,872.50 + 25%	50,200
129,600	209,850	26,722.50 + 28%	129,600
209,850	411,500	49,192.50 + 33%	209,850
411,500	439,000	115,737.00 + 35%	411,500
439,000	....	125,362.00 + 39.6%	439,000

Married filing jointly or Qualifying widow(er)—Schedule Y–1

If taxable income is: Over—	But not over—	The tax is:	of the amount over—
$ 0	$ 18,450	.........10%	$ 0
18,450	74,900	$ 1,845.00 + 15%	18,450
74,900	151,200	10,312.50 + 25%	74,900
151,200	230,450	29,387.50 + 28%	151,200
230,450	411,500	51,577.50 + 33%	230,450
411,500	464,850	111,324.00 + 35%	411,500
464,850	....	129,996.50 + 39.6%	464,850

Married filing separately—Schedule Y–2

If taxable income is: Over—	But not over—	The tax is:	of the amount over—
$ 0	$ 9,225	.........10%	$ 0
9,225	37,450	$ 922.50 + 15%	9,225
37,450	75,600	5,156.25 + 25%	37,450
75,600	115,225	14,693.75 + 28%	75,600
115,225	205,750	25,788.75 + 33%	115,225
205,750	232,425	55,662.00 + 35%	205,750
232,425	....	64,998.25 + 39.6%	232,425

2016 Tax Rate Schedules—Individuals

Single—Schedule X

If taxable income is: Over—	But not over—	The tax is:	of the amount over—
$ 0	$ 9,275	.........10%	$ 0
9,275	37,650	$ 927.50 + 15%	9,275
37,650	91,150	5,183.75 + 25%	37,650
91,150	190,150	18,558.75 + 28%	91,150
190,150	413,350	46,278.75 + 33%	190,150
413,350	415,050	119,934.75 + 35%	413,350
415,050	....	120,529.75 + 39.6%	415,050

Head of household—Schedule Z

If taxable income is: Over—	But not over—	The tax is:	of the amount over—
$ 0	$ 13,250	.........10%	$ 0
13,250	50,400	$ 1,325.00 + 15%	13,250
50,400	130,150	6,897.50 + 25%	50,400
130,150	210,800	26,835.00 + 28%	130,150
210,800	413,350	49,417.00 + 33%	210,800
413,350	441,000	116,258.50 + 35%	413,350
441,000	....	125,936.00 + 39.6%	441,000

Married filing jointly or Qualifying widow(er)—Schedule Y–1

If taxable income is: Over—	But not over—	The tax is:	of the amount over—
$ 0	$ 18,550	.........10%	$ 0
18,550	75,300	$ 1,855.00 + 15%	18,550
75,300	151,900	10,367.50 + 25%	75,300
151,900	231,450	29,517.50 + 28%	151,900
231,450	413,350	51,791.50 + 33%	231,450
413,350	466,950	111,818.50 + 35%	413,350
466,950	....	130,578.50 + 39.6%	466,950

Married filing separately—Schedule Y–2

If taxable income is: Over—	But not over—	The tax is:	of the amount over—
$ 0	$ 9,275	.........10%	$ 0
9,275	37,650	$ 927.50 + 15%	9,275
37,650	75,950	5,183.75 + 25%	37,650
75,950	115,725	14,758.75 + 28%	75,950
115,725	206,675	25,895.75 + 33%	115,725
206,675	233,475	55,909.25 + 35%	206,675
233,475	....	65,289.25 + 39.6%	233,475

2015 Tax Table— Individuals

See the instructions for line 44 to see if you must use the Tax Table below to figure your tax.

Example. Mr. and Mrs. Brown are filing a joint return. Their taxable income on Form 1040, line 43, is $25,300. First, they find the $25,300-25,350 taxable income line. Next, they find the column for married filing jointly and read down the column. The amount shown where the taxable income line and filing status column meet is $2,876. This is the tax amount they should enter on Form 1040, line 44.

Sample Table

At Least	But Less Than	Single	Married filing jointly*	Married filing separately	Head of a household
			Your tax is—		
25,200	25,250	3,323	2,861	3,323	3,126
25,250	25,300	3,330	2,869	3,330	3,134
25,300	25,350	3,338	(2,876)	3,338	3,141
25,350	25,400	3,345	2,884	3,345	3,149

If line 43 (taxable income) is—

At least	But less than	Single	Married filing jointly *	Married filing separately	Head of a household
			Your tax is—		
0	5	0	0	0	0
5	15	1	1	1	1
15	25	2	2	2	2
25	50	4	4	4	4
50	75	6	6	6	6
75	100	9	9	9	9
100	125	11	11	11	11
125	150	14	14	14	14
150	175	16	16	16	16
175	200	19	19	19	19
200	225	21	21	21	21
225	250	24	24	24	24
250	275	26	26	26	26
275	300	29	29	29	29
300	325	31	31	31	31
325	350	34	34	34	34
350	375	36	36	36	36
375	400	39	39	39	39
400	425	41	41	41	41
425	450	44	44	44	44
450	475	46	46	46	46
475	500	49	49	49	49
500	525	51	51	51	51
525	550	54	54	54	54
550	575	56	56	56	56
575	600	59	59	59	59
600	625	61	61	61	61
625	650	64	64	64	64
650	675	66	66	66	66
675	700	69	69	69	69
700	725	71	71	71	71
725	750	74	74	74	74
750	775	76	76	76	76
775	800	79	79	79	79
800	825	81	81	81	81
825	850	84	84	84	84
850	875	86	86	86	86
875	900	89	89	89	89
900	925	91	91	91	91
925	950	94	94	94	94
950	975	96	96	96	96
975	1,000	99	99	99	99

1,000

At least	But less than	Single	Married filing jointly *	Married filing separately	Head of a household
			Your tax is—		
1,000	1,025	101	101	101	101
1,025	1,050	104	104	104	104
1,050	1,075	106	106	106	106
1,075	1,100	109	109	109	109
1,100	1,125	111	111	111	111
1,125	1,150	114	114	114	114
1,150	1,175	116	116	116	116
1,175	1,200	119	119	119	119
1,200	1,225	121	121	121	121
1,225	1,250	124	124	124	124
1,250	1,275	126	126	126	126
1,275	1,300	129	129	129	129
1,300	1,325	131	131	131	131
1,325	1,350	134	134	134	134
1,350	1,375	136	136	136	136
1,375	1,400	139	139	139	139
1,400	1,425	141	141	141	141
1,425	1,450	144	144	144	144
1,450	1,475	146	146	146	146
1,475	1,500	149	149	149	149
1,500	1,525	151	151	151	151
1,525	1,550	154	154	154	154
1,550	1,575	156	156	156	156
1,575	1,600	159	159	159	159
1,600	1,625	161	161	161	161
1,625	1,650	164	164	164	164
1,650	1,675	166	166	166	166
1,675	1,700	169	169	169	169
1,700	1,725	171	171	171	171
1,725	1,750	174	174	174	174
1,750	1,775	176	176	176	176
1,775	1,800	179	179	179	179
1,800	1,825	181	181	181	181
1,825	1,850	184	184	184	184
1,850	1,875	186	186	186	186
1,875	1,900	189	189	189	189
1,900	1,925	191	191	191	191
1,925	1,950	194	194	194	194
1,950	1,975	196	196	196	196
1,975	2,000	199	199	199	199

2,000

At least	But less than	Single	Married filing jointly *	Married filing separately	Head of a household
			Your tax is—		
2,000	2,025	201	201	201	201
2,025	2,050	204	204	204	204
2,050	2,075	206	206	206	206
2,075	2,100	209	209	209	209
2,100	2,125	211	211	211	211
2,125	2,150	214	214	214	214
2,150	2,175	216	216	216	216
2,175	2,200	219	219	219	219
2,200	2,225	221	221	221	221
2,225	2,250	224	224	224	224
2,250	2,275	226	226	226	226
2,275	2,300	229	229	229	229
2,300	2,325	231	231	231	231
2,325	2,350	234	234	234	234
2,350	2,375	236	236	236	236
2,375	2,400	239	239	239	239
2,400	2,425	241	241	241	241
2,425	2,450	244	244	244	244
2,450	2,475	246	246	246	246
2,475	2,500	249	249	249	249
2,500	2,525	251	251	251	251
2,525	2,550	254	254	254	254
2,550	2,575	256	256	256	256
2,575	2,600	259	259	259	259
2,600	2,625	261	261	261	261
2,625	2,650	264	264	264	264
2,650	2,675	266	266	266	266
2,675	2,700	269	269	269	269
2,700	2,725	271	271	271	271
2,725	2,750	274	274	274	274
2,750	2,775	276	276	276	276
2,775	2,800	279	279	279	279
2,800	2,825	281	281	281	281
2,825	2,850	284	284	284	284
2,850	2,875	286	286	286	286
2,875	2,900	289	289	289	289
2,900	2,925	291	291	291	291
2,925	2,950	294	294	294	294
2,950	2,975	296	296	296	296
2,975	3,000	299	299	299	299

* This column must also be used by a qualifying widow(er).

(Continued)

2015 Tax Table—Individuals *Continued*

If line 43 (taxable income) is—		And you are—			
At least	But less than	Single	Married filing jointly *	Married filing separately	Head of a house-hold
			Your tax is—		

3,000

At least	But less than	Single	MFJ *	MFS	HoH
3,000	3,050	303	303	303	303
3,050	3,100	308	308	308	308
3,100	3,150	313	313	313	313
3,150	3,200	318	318	318	318
3,200	3,250	323	323	323	323
3,250	3,300	328	328	328	328
3,300	3,350	333	333	333	333
3,350	3,400	338	338	338	338
3,400	3,450	343	343	343	343
3,450	3,500	348	348	348	348
3,500	3,550	353	353	353	353
3,550	3,600	358	358	358	358
3,600	3,650	363	363	363	363
3,650	3,700	368	368	368	368
3,700	3,750	373	373	373	373
3,750	3,800	378	378	378	378
3,800	3,850	383	383	383	383
3,850	3,900	388	388	388	388
3,900	3,950	393	393	393	393
3,950	4,000	398	398	398	398

4,000

At least	But less than	Single	MFJ *	MFS	HoH
4,000	4,050	403	403	403	403
4,050	4,100	408	408	408	408
4,100	4,150	413	413	413	413
4,150	4,200	418	418	418	418
4,200	4,250	423	423	423	423
4,250	4,300	428	428	428	428
4,300	4,350	433	433	433	433
4,350	4,400	438	438	438	438
4,400	4,450	443	443	443	443
4,450	4,500	448	448	448	448
4,500	4,550	453	453	453	453
4,550	4,600	458	458	458	458
4,600	4,650	463	463	463	463
4,650	4,700	468	468	468	468
4,700	4,750	473	473	473	473
4,750	4,800	478	478	478	478
4,800	4,850	483	483	483	483
4,850	4,900	488	488	488	488
4,900	4,950	493	493	493	493
4,950	5,000	498	498	498	498

5,000

At least	But less than	Single	MFJ *	MFS	HoH
5,000	5,050	503	503	503	503
5,050	5,100	508	508	508	508
5,100	5,150	513	513	513	513
5,150	5,200	518	518	518	518
5,200	5,250	523	523	523	523
5,250	5,300	528	528	528	528
5,300	5,350	533	533	533	533
5,350	5,400	538	538	538	538
5,400	5,450	543	543	543	543
5,450	5,500	548	548	548	548
5,500	5,550	553	553	553	553
5,550	5,600	558	558	558	558
5,600	5,650	563	563	563	563
5,650	5,700	568	568	568	568
5,700	5,750	573	573	573	573
5,750	5,800	578	578	578	578
5,800	5,850	583	583	583	583
5,850	5,900	588	588	588	588
5,900	5,950	593	593	593	593
5,950	6,000	598	598	598	598

6,000

At least	But less than	Single	MFJ *	MFS	HoH
6,000	6,050	603	603	603	603
6,050	6,100	608	608	608	608
6,100	6,150	613	613	613	613
6,150	6,200	618	618	618	618
6,200	6,250	623	623	623	623
6,250	6,300	628	628	628	628
6,300	6,350	633	633	633	633
6,350	6,400	638	638	638	638
6,400	6,450	643	643	643	643
6,450	6,500	648	648	648	648
6,500	6,550	653	653	653	653
6,550	6,600	658	658	658	658
6,600	6,650	663	663	663	663
6,650	6,700	668	668	668	668
6,700	6,750	673	673	673	673
6,750	6,800	678	678	678	678
6,800	6,850	683	683	683	683
6,850	6,900	688	688	688	688
6,900	6,950	693	693	693	693
6,950	7,000	698	698	698	698

7,000

At least	But less than	Single	MFJ *	MFS	HoH
7,000	7,050	703	703	703	703
7,050	7,100	708	708	708	708
7,100	7,150	713	713	713	713
7,150	7,200	718	718	718	718
7,200	7,250	723	723	723	723
7,250	7,300	728	728	728	728
7,300	7,350	733	733	733	733
7,350	7,400	738	738	738	738
7,400	7,450	743	743	743	743
7,450	7,500	748	748	748	748
7,500	7,550	753	753	753	753
7,550	7,600	758	758	758	758
7,600	7,650	763	763	763	763
7,650	7,700	768	768	768	768
7,700	7,750	773	773	773	773
7,750	7,800	778	778	778	778
7,800	7,850	783	783	783	783
7,850	7,900	788	788	788	788
7,900	7,950	793	793	793	793
7,950	8,000	798	798	798	798

8,000

At least	But less than	Single	MFJ *	MFS	HoH
8,000	8,050	803	803	803	803
8,050	8,100	808	808	808	808
8,100	8,150	813	813	813	813
8,150	8,200	818	818	818	818
8,200	8,250	823	823	823	823
8,250	8,300	828	828	828	828
8,300	8,350	833	833	833	833
8,350	8,400	838	838	838	838
8,400	8,450	843	843	843	843
8,450	8,500	848	848	848	848
8,500	8,550	853	853	853	853
8,550	8,600	858	858	858	858
8,600	8,650	863	863	863	863
8,650	8,700	868	868	868	868
8,700	8,750	873	873	873	873
8,750	8,800	878	878	878	878
8,800	8,850	883	883	883	883
8,850	8,900	888	888	888	888
8,900	8,950	893	893	893	893
8,950	9,000	898	898	898	898

9,000

At least	But less than	Single	MFJ *	MFS	HoH
9,000	9,050	903	903	903	903
9,050	9,100	908	908	908	908
9,100	9,150	913	913	913	913
9,150	9,200	918	918	918	918
9,200	9,250	923	923	923	923
9,250	9,300	930	928	930	928
9,300	9,350	938	933	938	933
9,350	9,400	945	938	945	938
9,400	9,450	953	943	953	943
9,450	9,500	960	948	960	948
9,500	9,550	968	953	968	953
9,550	9,600	975	958	975	958
9,600	9,650	983	963	983	963
9,650	9,700	990	968	990	968
9,700	9,750	998	973	998	973
9,750	9,800	1,005	978	1,005	978
9,800	9,850	1,013	983	1,013	983
9,850	9,900	1,020	988	1,020	988
9,900	9,950	1,028	993	1,028	993
9,950	10,000	1,035	998	1,035	998

10,000

At least	But less than	Single	MFJ *	MFS	HoH
10,000	10,050	1,043	1,003	1,043	1,003
10,050	10,100	1,050	1,008	1,050	1,008
10,100	10,150	1,058	1,013	1,058	1,013
10,150	10,200	1,065	1,018	1,065	1,018
10,200	10,250	1,073	1,023	1,073	1,023
10,250	10,300	1,080	1,028	1,080	1,028
10,300	10,350	1,088	1,033	1,088	1,033
10,350	10,400	1,095	1,038	1,095	1,038
10,400	10,450	1,103	1,043	1,103	1,043
10,450	10,500	1,110	1,048	1,110	1,048
10,500	10,550	1,118	1,053	1,118	1,053
10,550	10,600	1,125	1,058	1,125	1,058
10,600	10,650	1,133	1,063	1,133	1,063
10,650	10,700	1,140	1,068	1,140	1,068
10,700	10,750	1,148	1,073	1,148	1,073
10,750	10,800	1,155	1,078	1,155	1,078
10,800	10,850	1,163	1,083	1,163	1,083
10,850	10,900	1,170	1,088	1,170	1,088
10,900	10,950	1,178	1,093	1,178	1,093
10,950	11,000	1,185	1,098	1,185	1,098

11,000

At least	But less than	Single	MFJ *	MFS	HoH
11,000	11,050	1,193	1,103	1,193	1,103
11,050	11,100	1,200	1,108	1,200	1,108
11,100	11,150	1,208	1,113	1,208	1,113
11,150	11,200	1,215	1,118	1,215	1,118
11,200	11,250	1,223	1,123	1,223	1,123
11,250	11,300	1,230	1,128	1,230	1,128
11,300	11,350	1,238	1,133	1,238	1,133
11,350	11,400	1,245	1,138	1,245	1,138
11,400	11,450	1,253	1,143	1,253	1,143
11,450	11,500	1,260	1,148	1,260	1,148
11,500	11,550	1,268	1,153	1,268	1,153
11,550	11,600	1,275	1,158	1,275	1,158
11,600	11,650	1,283	1,163	1,283	1,163
11,650	11,700	1,290	1,168	1,290	1,168
11,700	11,750	1,298	1,173	1,298	1,173
11,750	11,800	1,305	1,178	1,305	1,178
11,800	11,850	1,313	1,183	1,313	1,183
11,850	11,900	1,320	1,188	1,320	1,188
11,900	11,950	1,328	1,193	1,328	1,193
11,950	12,000	1,335	1,198	1,335	1,198

* This column must also be used by a qualifying widow(er).

(Continued)

2015 Tax Table—Individuals *Continued*

If line 43 (taxable income) is— / And you are—

12,000

At least	But less than	Single	Married filing jointly *	Married filing separately	Head of a household
12,000	12,050	1,343	1,203	1,343	1,203
12,050	12,100	1,350	1,208	1,350	1,208
12,100	12,150	1,358	1,213	1,358	1,213
12,150	12,200	1,365	1,218	1,365	1,218
12,200	12,250	1,373	1,223	1,373	1,223
12,250	12,300	1,380	1,228	1,380	1,228
12,300	12,350	1,388	1,233	1,388	1,233
12,350	12,400	1,395	1,238	1,395	1,238
12,400	12,450	1,403	1,243	1,403	1,243
12,450	12,500	1,410	1,248	1,410	1,248
12,500	12,550	1,418	1,253	1,418	1,253
12,550	12,600	1,425	1,258	1,425	1,258
12,600	12,650	1,433	1,263	1,433	1,263
12,650	12,700	1,440	1,268	1,440	1,268
12,700	12,750	1,448	1,273	1,448	1,273
12,750	12,800	1,455	1,278	1,455	1,278
12,800	12,850	1,463	1,283	1,463	1,283
12,850	12,900	1,470	1,288	1,470	1,288
12,900	12,950	1,478	1,293	1,478	1,293
12,950	13,000	1,485	1,298	1,485	1,298

13,000

At least	But less than	Single	Married filing jointly *	Married filing separately	Head of a household
13,000	13,050	1,493	1,303	1,493	1,303
13,050	13,100	1,500	1,308	1,500	1,308
13,100	13,150	1,508	1,313	1,508	1,313
13,150	13,200	1,515	1,318	1,515	1,319
13,200	13,250	1,523	1,323	1,523	1,326
13,250	13,300	1,530	1,328	1,530	1,334
13,300	13,350	1,538	1,333	1,538	1,341
13,350	13,400	1,545	1,338	1,545	1,349
13,400	13,450	1,553	1,343	1,553	1,356
13,450	13,500	1,560	1,348	1,560	1,364
13,500	13,550	1,568	1,353	1,568	1,371
13,550	13,600	1,575	1,358	1,575	1,379
13,600	13,650	1,583	1,363	1,583	1,386
13,650	13,700	1,590	1,368	1,590	1,394
13,700	13,750	1,598	1,373	1,598	1,401
13,750	13,800	1,605	1,378	1,605	1,409
13,800	13,850	1,613	1,383	1,613	1,416
13,850	13,900	1,620	1,388	1,620	1,424
13,900	13,950	1,628	1,393	1,628	1,431
13,950	14,000	1,635	1,398	1,635	1,439

14,000

At least	But less than	Single	Married filing jointly *	Married filing separately	Head of a household
14,000	14,050	1,643	1,403	1,643	1,446
14,050	14,100	1,650	1,408	1,650	1,454
14,100	14,150	1,658	1,413	1,658	1,461
14,150	14,200	1,665	1,418	1,665	1,469
14,200	14,250	1,673	1,423	1,673	1,476
14,250	14,300	1,680	1,428	1,680	1,484
14,300	14,350	1,688	1,433	1,688	1,491
14,350	14,400	1,695	1,438	1,695	1,499
14,400	14,450	1,703	1,443	1,703	1,506
14,450	14,500	1,710	1,448	1,710	1,514
14,500	14,550	1,718	1,453	1,718	1,521
14,550	14,600	1,725	1,458	1,725	1,529
14,600	14,650	1,733	1,463	1,733	1,536
14,650	14,700	1,740	1,468	1,740	1,544
14,700	14,750	1,748	1,473	1,748	1,551
14,750	14,800	1,755	1,478	1,755	1,559
14,800	14,850	1,763	1,483	1,763	1,566
14,850	14,900	1,770	1,488	1,770	1,574
14,900	14,950	1,778	1,493	1,778	1,581
14,950	15,000	1,785	1,498	1,785	1,589

15,000

At least	But less than	Single	Married filing jointly *	Married filing separately	Head of a household
15,000	15,050	1,793	1,503	1,793	1,596
15,050	15,100	1,800	1,508	1,800	1,604
15,100	15,150	1,808	1,513	1,808	1,611
15,150	15,200	1,815	1,518	1,815	1,619
15,200	15,250	1,823	1,523	1,823	1,626
15,250	15,300	1,830	1,528	1,830	1,634
15,300	15,350	1,838	1,533	1,838	1,641
15,350	15,400	1,845	1,538	1,845	1,649
15,400	15,450	1,853	1,543	1,853	1,656
15,450	15,500	1,860	1,548	1,860	1,664
15,500	15,550	1,868	1,553	1,868	1,671
15,550	15,600	1,875	1,558	1,875	1,679
15,600	15,650	1,883	1,563	1,883	1,686
15,650	15,700	1,890	1,568	1,890	1,694
15,700	15,750	1,898	1,573	1,898	1,701
15,750	15,800	1,905	1,578	1,905	1,709
15,800	15,850	1,913	1,583	1,913	1,716
15,850	15,900	1,920	1,588	1,920	1,724
15,900	15,950	1,928	1,593	1,928	1,731
15,950	16,000	1,935	1,598	1,935	1,739

16,000

At least	But less than	Single	Married filing jointly *	Married filing separately	Head of a household
16,000	16,050	1,943	1,603	1,943	1,746
16,050	16,100	1,950	1,608	1,950	1,754
16,100	16,150	1,958	1,613	1,958	1,761
16,150	16,200	1,965	1,618	1,965	1,769
16,200	16,250	1,973	1,623	1,973	1,776
16,250	16,300	1,980	1,628	1,980	1,784
16,300	16,350	1,988	1,633	1,988	1,791
16,350	16,400	1,995	1,638	1,995	1,799
16,400	16,450	2,003	1,643	2,003	1,806
16,450	16,500	2,010	1,648	2,010	1,814
16,500	16,550	2,018	1,653	2,018	1,821
16,550	16,600	2,025	1,658	2,025	1,829
16,600	16,650	2,033	1,663	2,033	1,836
16,650	16,700	2,040	1,668	2,040	1,844
16,700	16,750	2,048	1,673	2,048	1,851
16,750	16,800	2,055	1,678	2,055	1,859
16,800	16,850	2,063	1,683	2,063	1,866
16,850	16,900	2,070	1,688	2,070	1,874
16,900	16,950	2,078	1,693	2,078	1,881
16,950	17,000	2,085	1,698	2,085	1,889

17,000

At least	But less than	Single	Married filing jointly *	Married filing separately	Head of a household
17,000	17,050	2,093	1,703	2,093	1,896
17,050	17,100	2,100	1,708	2,100	1,904
17,100	17,150	2,108	1,713	2,108	1,911
17,150	17,200	2,115	1,718	2,115	1,919
17,200	17,250	2,123	1,723	2,123	1,926
17,250	17,300	2,130	1,728	2,130	1,934
17,300	17,350	2,138	1,733	2,138	1,941
17,350	17,400	2,145	1,738	2,145	1,949
17,400	17,450	2,153	1,743	2,153	1,956
17,450	17,500	2,160	1,748	2,160	1,964
17,500	17,550	2,168	1,753	2,168	1,971
17,550	17,600	2,175	1,758	2,175	1,979
17,600	17,650	2,183	1,763	2,183	1,986
17,650	17,700	2,190	1,768	2,190	1,994
17,700	17,750	2,198	1,773	2,198	2,001
17,750	17,800	2,205	1,778	2,205	2,009
17,800	17,850	2,213	1,783	2,213	2,016
17,850	17,900	2,220	1,788	2,220	2,024
17,900	17,950	2,228	1,793	2,228	2,031
17,950	18,000	2,235	1,798	2,235	2,039

18,000

At least	But less than	Single	Married filing jointly *	Married filing separately	Head of a household
18,000	18,050	2,243	1,803	2,243	2,046
18,050	18,100	2,250	1,808	2,250	2,054
18,100	18,150	2,258	1,813	2,258	2,061
18,150	18,200	2,265	1,818	2,265	2,069
18,200	18,250	2,273	1,823	2,273	2,076
18,250	18,300	2,280	1,828	2,280	2,084
18,300	18,350	2,288	1,833	2,288	2,091
18,350	18,400	2,295	1,838	2,295	2,099
18,400	18,450	2,303	1,843	2,303	2,106
18,450	18,500	2,310	1,849	2,310	2,114
18,500	18,550	2,318	1,856	2,318	2,121
18,550	18,600	2,325	1,864	2,325	2,129
18,600	18,650	2,333	1,871	2,333	2,136
18,650	18,700	2,340	1,879	2,340	2,144
18,700	18,750	2,348	1,886	2,348	2,151
18,750	18,800	2,355	1,894	2,355	2,159
18,800	18,850	2,363	1,901	2,363	2,166
18,850	18,900	2,370	1,909	2,370	2,174
18,900	18,950	2,378	1,916	2,378	2,181
18,950	19,000	2,385	1,924	2,385	2,189

19,000

At least	But less than	Single	Married filing jointly *	Married filing separately	Head of a household
19,000	19,050	2,393	1,931	2,393	2,196
19,050	19,100	2,400	1,939	2,400	2,204
19,100	19,150	2,408	1,946	2,408	2,211
19,150	19,200	2,415	1,954	2,415	2,219
19,200	19,250	2,423	1,961	2,423	2,226
19,250	19,300	2,430	1,969	2,430	2,234
19,300	19,350	2,438	1,976	2,438	2,241
19,350	19,400	2,445	1,984	2,445	2,249
19,400	19,450	2,453	1,991	2,453	2,256
19,450	19,500	2,460	1,999	2,460	2,264
19,500	19,550	2,468	2,006	2,468	2,271
19,550	19,600	2,475	2,014	2,475	2,279
19,600	19,650	2,483	2,021	2,483	2,286
19,650	19,700	2,490	2,029	2,490	2,294
19,700	19,750	2,498	2,036	2,498	2,301
19,750	19,800	2,505	2,044	2,505	2,309
19,800	19,850	2,513	2,051	2,513	2,316
19,850	19,900	2,520	2,059	2,520	2,324
19,900	19,950	2,528	2,066	2,528	2,331
19,950	20,000	2,535	2,074	2,535	2,339

20,000

At least	But less than	Single	Married filing jointly *	Married filing separately	Head of a household
20,000	20,050	2,543	2,081	2,543	2,346
20,050	20,100	2,550	2,089	2,550	2,354
20,100	20,150	2,558	2,096	2,558	2,361
20,150	20,200	2,565	2,104	2,565	2,369
20,200	20,250	2,573	2,111	2,573	2,376
20,250	20,300	2,580	2,119	2,580	2,384
20,300	20,350	2,588	2,126	2,588	2,391
20,350	20,400	2,595	2,134	2,595	2,399
20,400	20,450	2,603	2,141	2,603	2,406
20,450	20,500	2,610	2,149	2,610	2,414
20,500	20,550	2,618	2,156	2,618	2,421
20,550	20,600	2,625	2,164	2,625	2,429
20,600	20,650	2,633	2,171	2,633	2,436
20,650	20,700	2,640	2,179	2,640	2,444
20,700	20,750	2,648	2,186	2,648	2,451
20,750	20,800	2,655	2,194	2,655	2,459
20,800	20,850	2,663	2,201	2,663	2,466
20,850	20,900	2,670	2,209	2,670	2,474
20,900	20,950	2,678	2,216	2,678	2,481
20,950	21,000	2,685	2,224	2,685	2,489

* This column must also be used by a qualifying widow(er).

(Continued)

2015 Tax Table—Individuals *Continued*

21,000

At least	But less than	Single	Married filing jointly *	Married filing separately	Head of a household
21,000	21,050	2,693	2,231	2,693	2,496
21,050	21,100	2,700	2,239	2,700	2,504
21,100	21,150	2,708	2,246	2,708	2,511
21,150	21,200	2,715	2,254	2,715	2,519
21,200	21,250	2,723	2,261	2,723	2,526
21,250	21,300	2,730	2,269	2,730	2,534
21,300	21,350	2,738	2,276	2,738	2,541
21,350	21,400	2,745	2,284	2,745	2,549
21,400	21,450	2,753	2,291	2,753	2,556
21,450	21,500	2,760	2,299	2,760	2,564
21,500	21,550	2,768	2,306	2,768	2,571
21,550	21,600	2,775	2,314	2,775	2,579
21,600	21,650	2,783	2,321	2,783	2,586
21,650	21,700	2,790	2,329	2,790	2,594
21,700	21,750	2,798	2,336	2,798	2,601
21,750	21,800	2,805	2,344	2,805	2,609
21,800	21,850	2,813	2,351	2,813	2,616
21,850	21,900	2,820	2,359	2,820	2,624
21,900	21,950	2,828	2,366	2,828	2,631
21,950	22,000	2,835	2,374	2,835	2,639

22,000

At least	But less than	Single	Married filing jointly *	Married filing separately	Head of a household
22,000	22,050	2,843	2,381	2,843	2,646
22,050	22,100	2,850	2,389	2,850	2,654
22,100	22,150	2,858	2,396	2,858	2,661
22,150	22,200	2,865	2,404	2,865	2,669
22,200	22,250	2,873	2,411	2,873	2,676
22,250	22,300	2,880	2,419	2,880	2,684
22,300	22,350	2,888	2,426	2,888	2,691
22,350	22,400	2,895	2,434	2,895	2,699
22,400	22,450	2,903	2,441	2,903	2,706
22,450	22,500	2,910	2,449	2,910	2,714
22,500	22,550	2,918	2,456	2,918	2,721
22,550	22,600	2,925	2,464	2,925	2,729
22,600	22,650	2,933	2,471	2,933	2,736
22,650	22,700	2,940	2,479	2,940	2,744
22,700	22,750	2,948	2,486	2,948	2,751
22,750	22,800	2,955	2,494	2,955	2,759
22,800	22,850	2,963	2,501	2,963	2,766
22,850	22,900	2,970	2,509	2,970	2,774
22,900	22,950	2,978	2,516	2,978	2,781
22,950	23,000	2,985	2,524	2,985	2,789

23,000

At least	But less than	Single	Married filing jointly *	Married filing separately	Head of a household
23,000	23,050	2,993	2,531	2,993	2,796
23,050	23,100	3,000	2,539	3,000	2,804
23,100	23,150	3,008	2,546	3,008	2,811
23,150	23,200	3,015	2,554	3,015	2,819
23,200	23,250	3,023	2,561	3,023	2,826
23,250	23,300	3,030	2,569	3,030	2,834
23,300	23,350	3,038	2,576	3,038	2,841
23,350	23,400	3,045	2,584	3,045	2,849
23,400	23,450	3,053	2,591	3,053	2,856
23,450	23,500	3,060	2,599	3,060	2,864
23,500	23,550	3,068	2,606	3,068	2,871
23,550	23,600	3,075	2,614	3,075	2,879
23,600	23,650	3,083	2,621	3,083	2,886
23,650	23,700	3,090	2,629	3,090	2,894
23,700	23,750	3,098	2,636	3,098	2,901
23,750	23,800	3,105	2,644	3,105	2,909
23,800	23,850	3,113	2,651	3,113	2,916
23,850	23,900	3,120	2,659	3,120	2,924
23,900	23,950	3,128	2,666	3,128	2,931
23,950	24,000	3,135	2,674	3,135	2,939

24,000

At least	But less than	Single	Married filing jointly *	Married filing separately	Head of a household
24,000	24,050	3,143	2,681	3,143	2,946
24,050	24,100	3,150	2,689	3,150	2,954
24,100	24,150	3,158	2,696	3,158	2,961
24,150	24,200	3,165	2,704	3,165	2,969
24,200	24,250	3,173	2,711	3,173	2,976
24,250	24,300	3,180	2,719	3,180	2,984
24,300	24,350	3,188	2,726	3,188	2,991
24,350	24,400	3,195	2,734	3,195	2,999
24,400	24,450	3,203	2,741	3,203	3,006
24,450	24,500	3,210	2,749	3,210	3,014
24,500	24,550	3,218	2,756	3,218	3,021
24,550	24,600	3,225	2,764	3,225	3,029
24,600	24,650	3,233	2,771	3,233	3,036
24,650	24,700	3,240	2,779	3,240	3,044
24,700	24,750	3,248	2,786	3,248	3,051
24,750	24,800	3,255	2,794	3,255	3,059
24,800	24,850	3,263	2,801	3,263	3,066
24,850	24,900	3,270	2,809	3,270	3,074
24,900	24,950	3,278	2,816	3,278	3,081
24,950	25,000	3,285	2,824	3,285	3,089

25,000

At least	But less than	Single	Married filing jointly *	Married filing separately	Head of a household
25,000	25,050	3,293	2,831	3,293	3,096
25,050	25,100	3,300	2,839	3,300	3,104
25,100	25,150	3,308	2,846	3,308	3,111
25,150	25,200	3,315	2,854	3,315	3,119
25,200	25,250	3,323	2,861	3,323	3,126
25,250	25,300	3,330	2,869	3,330	3,134
25,300	25,350	3,338	2,876	3,338	3,141
25,350	25,400	3,345	2,884	3,345	3,149
25,400	25,450	3,353	2,891	3,353	3,156
25,450	25,500	3,360	2,899	3,360	3,164
25,500	25,550	3,368	2,906	3,368	3,171
25,550	25,600	3,375	2,914	3,375	3,179
25,600	25,650	3,383	2,921	3,383	3,186
25,650	25,700	3,390	2,929	3,390	3,194
25,700	25,750	3,398	2,936	3,398	3,201
25,750	25,800	3,405	2,944	3,405	3,209
25,800	25,850	3,413	2,951	3,413	3,216
25,850	25,900	3,420	2,959	3,420	3,224
25,900	25,950	3,428	2,966	3,428	3,231
25,950	26,000	3,435	2,974	3,435	3,239

26,000

At least	But less than	Single	Married filing jointly *	Married filing separately	Head of a household
26,000	26,050	3,443	2,981	3,443	3,246
26,050	26,100	3,450	2,989	3,450	3,254
26,100	26,150	3,458	2,996	3,458	3,261
26,150	26,200	3,465	3,004	3,465	3,269
26,200	26,250	3,473	3,011	3,473	3,276
26,250	26,300	3,480	3,019	3,480	3,284
26,300	26,350	3,488	3,026	3,488	3,291
26,350	26,400	3,495	3,034	3,495	3,299
26,400	26,450	3,503	3,041	3,503	3,306
26,450	26,500	3,510	3,049	3,510	3,314
26,500	26,550	3,518	3,056	3,518	3,321
26,550	26,600	3,525	3,064	3,525	3,329
26,600	26,650	3,533	3,071	3,533	3,336
26,650	26,700	3,540	3,079	3,540	3,344
26,700	26,750	3,548	3,086	3,548	3,351
26,750	26,800	3,555	3,094	3,555	3,359
26,800	26,850	3,563	3,101	3,563	3,366
26,850	26,900	3,570	3,109	3,570	3,374
26,900	26,950	3,578	3,116	3,578	3,381
26,950	27,000	3,585	3,124	3,585	3,389

27,000

At least	But less than	Single	Married filing jointly *	Married filing separately	Head of a household
27,000	27,050	3,593	3,131	3,593	3,396
27,050	27,100	3,600	3,139	3,600	3,404
27,100	27,150	3,608	3,146	3,608	3,411
27,150	27,200	3,615	3,154	3,615	3,419
27,200	27,250	3,623	3,161	3,623	3,426
27,250	27,300	3,630	3,169	3,630	3,434
27,300	27,350	3,638	3,176	3,638	3,441
27,350	27,400	3,645	3,184	3,645	3,449
27,400	27,450	3,653	3,191	3,653	3,456
27,450	27,500	3,660	3,199	3,660	3,464
27,500	27,550	3,668	3,206	3,668	3,471
27,550	27,600	3,675	3,214	3,675	3,479
27,600	27,650	3,683	3,221	3,683	3,486
27,650	27,700	3,690	3,229	3,690	3,494
27,700	27,750	3,698	3,236	3,698	3,501
27,750	27,800	3,705	3,244	3,705	3,509
27,800	27,850	3,713	3,251	3,713	3,516
27,850	27,900	3,720	3,259	3,720	3,524
27,900	27,950	3,728	3,266	3,728	3,531
27,950	28,000	3,735	3,274	3,735	3,539

28,000

At least	But less than	Single	Married filing jointly *	Married filing separately	Head of a household
28,000	28,050	3,743	3,281	3,743	3,546
28,050	28,100	3,750	3,289	3,750	3,554
28,100	28,150	3,758	3,296	3,758	3,561
28,150	28,200	3,765	3,304	3,765	3,569
28,200	28,250	3,773	3,311	3,773	3,576
28,250	28,300	3,780	3,319	3,780	3,584
28,300	28,350	3,788	3,326	3,788	3,591
28,350	28,400	3,795	3,334	3,795	3,599
28,400	28,450	3,803	3,341	3,803	3,606
28,450	28,500	3,810	3,349	3,810	3,614
28,500	28,550	3,818	3,356	3,818	3,621
28,550	28,600	3,825	3,364	3,825	3,629
28,600	28,650	3,833	3,371	3,833	3,636
28,650	28,700	3,840	3,379	3,840	3,644
28,700	28,750	3,848	3,386	3,848	3,651
28,750	28,800	3,855	3,394	3,855	3,659
28,800	28,850	3,863	3,401	3,863	3,666
28,850	28,900	3,870	3,409	3,870	3,674
28,900	28,950	3,878	3,416	3,878	3,681
28,950	29,000	3,885	3,424	3,885	3,689

29,000

At least	But less than	Single	Married filing jointly *	Married filing separately	Head of a household
29,000	29,050	3,893	3,431	3,893	3,696
29,050	29,100	3,900	3,439	3,900	3,704
29,100	29,150	3,908	3,446	3,908	3,711
29,150	29,200	3,915	3,454	3,915	3,719
29,200	29,250	3,923	3,461	3,923	3,726
29,250	29,300	3,930	3,469	3,930	3,734
29,300	29,350	3,938	3,476	3,938	3,741
29,350	29,400	3,945	3,484	3,945	3,749
29,400	29,450	3,953	3,491	3,953	3,756
29,450	29,500	3,960	3,499	3,960	3,764
29,500	29,550	3,968	3,506	3,968	3,771
29,550	29,600	3,975	3,514	3,975	3,779
29,600	29,650	3,983	3,521	3,983	3,786
29,650	29,700	3,990	3,529	3,990	3,794
29,700	29,750	3,998	3,536	3,998	3,801
29,750	29,800	4,005	3,544	4,005	3,809
29,800	29,850	4,013	3,551	4,013	3,816
29,850	29,900	4,020	3,559	4,020	3,824
29,900	29,950	4,028	3,566	4,028	3,831
29,950	30,000	4,035	3,574	4,035	3,839

* This column must also be used by a qualifying widow(er).

(Continued)

2015 Tax Table—Individuals Continued

30,000

If line 43 (taxable income) is—		And you are—			
At least	But less than	Single	Married filing jointly *	Married filing separately	Head of a household
		Your tax is—			
30,000	30,050	4,043	3,581	4,043	3,846
30,050	30,100	4,050	3,589	4,050	3,854
30,100	30,150	4,058	3,596	4,058	3,861
30,150	30,200	4,065	3,604	4,065	3,869
30,200	30,250	4,073	3,611	4,073	3,876
30,250	30,300	4,080	3,619	4,080	3,884
30,300	30,350	4,088	3,626	4,088	3,891
30,350	30,400	4,095	3,634	4,095	3,899
30,400	30,450	4,103	3,641	4,103	3,906
30,450	30,500	4,110	3,649	4,110	3,914
30,500	30,550	4,118	3,656	4,118	3,921
30,550	30,600	4,125	3,664	4,125	3,929
30,600	30,650	4,133	3,671	4,133	3,936
30,650	30,700	4,140	3,679	4,140	3,944
30,700	30,750	4,148	3,686	4,148	3,951
30,750	30,800	4,155	3,694	4,155	3,959
30,800	30,850	4,163	3,701	4,163	3,966
30,850	30,900	4,170	3,709	4,170	3,974
30,900	30,950	4,178	3,716	4,178	3,981
30,950	31,000	4,185	3,724	4,185	3,989

31,000

At least	But less than	Single	Married filing jointly *	Married filing separately	Head of a household
31,000	31,050	4,193	3,731	4,193	3,996
31,050	31,100	4,200	3,739	4,200	4,004
31,100	31,150	4,208	3,746	4,208	4,011
31,150	31,200	4,215	3,754	4,215	4,019
31,200	31,250	4,223	3,761	4,223	4,026
31,250	31,300	4,230	3,769	4,230	4,034
31,300	31,350	4,238	3,776	4,238	4,041
31,350	31,400	4,245	3,784	4,245	4,049
31,400	31,450	4,253	3,791	4,253	4,056
31,450	31,500	4,260	3,799	4,260	4,064
31,500	31,550	4,268	3,806	4,268	4,071
31,550	31,600	4,275	3,814	4,275	4,079
31,600	31,650	4,283	3,821	4,283	4,086
31,650	31,700	4,290	3,829	4,290	4,094
31,700	31,750	4,298	3,836	4,298	4,101
31,750	31,800	4,305	3,844	4,305	4,109
31,800	31,850	4,313	3,851	4,313	4,116
31,850	31,900	4,320	3,859	4,320	4,124
31,900	31,950	4,328	3,866	4,328	4,131
31,950	32,000	4,335	3,874	4,335	4,139

32,000

At least	But less than	Single	Married filing jointly *	Married filing separately	Head of a household
32,000	32,050	4,343	3,881	4,343	4,146
32,050	32,100	4,350	3,889	4,350	4,154
32,100	32,150	4,358	3,896	4,358	4,161
32,150	32,200	4,365	3,904	4,365	4,169
32,200	32,250	4,373	3,911	4,373	4,176
32,250	32,300	4,380	3,919	4,380	4,184
32,300	32,350	4,388	3,926	4,388	4,191
32,350	32,400	4,395	3,934	4,395	4,199
32,400	32,450	4,403	3,941	4,403	4,206
32,450	32,500	4,410	3,949	4,410	4,214
32,500	32,550	4,418	3,956	4,418	4,221
32,550	32,600	4,425	3,964	4,425	4,229
32,600	32,650	4,433	3,971	4,433	4,236
32,650	32,700	4,440	3,979	4,440	4,244
32,700	32,750	4,448	3,986	4,448	4,251
32,750	32,800	4,455	3,994	4,455	4,259
32,800	32,850	4,463	4,001	4,463	4,266
32,850	32,900	4,470	4,009	4,470	4,274
32,900	32,950	4,478	4,016	4,478	4,281
32,950	33,000	4,485	4,024	4,485	4,289

33,000

If line 43 (taxable income) is—		And you are—			
At least	But less than	Single	Married filing jointly *	Married filing separately	Head of a household
		Your tax is—			
33,000	33,050	4,493	4,031	4,493	4,296
33,050	33,100	4,500	4,039	4,500	4,304
33,100	33,150	4,508	4,046	4,508	4,311
33,150	33,200	4,515	4,054	4,515	4,319
33,200	33,250	4,523	4,061	4,523	4,326
33,250	33,300	4,530	4,069	4,530	4,334
33,300	33,350	4,538	4,076	4,538	4,341
33,350	33,400	4,545	4,084	4,545	4,349
33,400	33,450	4,553	4,091	4,553	4,356
33,450	33,500	4,560	4,099	4,560	4,364
33,500	33,550	4,568	4,106	4,568	4,371
33,550	33,600	4,575	4,114	4,575	4,379
33,600	33,650	4,583	4,121	4,583	4,386
33,650	33,700	4,590	4,129	4,590	4,394
33,700	33,750	4,598	4,136	4,598	4,401
33,750	33,800	4,605	4,144	4,605	4,409
33,800	33,850	4,613	4,151	4,613	4,416
33,850	33,900	4,620	4,159	4,620	4,424
33,900	33,950	4,628	4,166	4,628	4,431
33,950	34,000	4,635	4,174	4,635	4,439

34,000

At least	But less than	Single	Married filing jointly *	Married filing separately	Head of a household
34,000	34,050	4,643	4,181	4,643	4,446
34,050	34,100	4,650	4,189	4,650	4,454
34,100	34,150	4,658	4,196	4,658	4,461
34,150	34,200	4,665	4,204	4,665	4,469
34,200	34,250	4,673	4,211	4,673	4,476
34,250	34,300	4,680	4,219	4,680	4,484
34,300	34,350	4,688	4,226	4,688	4,491
34,350	34,400	4,695	4,234	4,695	4,499
34,400	34,450	4,703	4,241	4,703	4,506
34,450	34,500	4,710	4,249	4,710	4,514
34,500	34,550	4,718	4,256	4,718	4,521
34,550	34,600	4,725	4,264	4,725	4,529
34,600	34,650	4,733	4,271	4,733	4,536
34,650	34,700	4,740	4,279	4,740	4,544
34,700	34,750	4,748	4,286	4,748	4,551
34,750	34,800	4,755	4,294	4,755	4,559
34,800	34,850	4,763	4,301	4,763	4,566
34,850	34,900	4,770	4,309	4,770	4,574
34,900	34,950	4,778	4,316	4,778	4,581
34,950	35,000	4,785	4,324	4,785	4,589

35,000

At least	But less than	Single	Married filing jointly *	Married filing separately	Head of a household
35,000	35,050	4,793	4,331	4,793	4,596
35,050	35,100	4,800	4,339	4,800	4,604
35,100	35,150	4,808	4,346	4,808	4,611
35,150	35,200	4,815	4,354	4,815	4,619
35,200	35,250	4,823	4,361	4,823	4,626
35,250	35,300	4,830	4,369	4,830	4,634
35,300	35,350	4,838	4,376	4,838	4,641
35,350	35,400	4,845	4,384	4,845	4,649
35,400	35,450	4,853	4,391	4,853	4,656
35,450	35,500	4,860	4,399	4,860	4,664
35,500	35,550	4,868	4,406	4,868	4,671
35,550	35,600	4,875	4,414	4,875	4,679
35,600	35,650	4,883	4,421	4,883	4,686
35,650	35,700	4,890	4,429	4,890	4,694
35,700	35,750	4,898	4,436	4,898	4,701
35,750	35,800	4,905	4,444	4,905	4,709
35,800	35,850	4,913	4,451	4,913	4,716
35,850	35,900	4,920	4,459	4,920	4,724
35,900	35,950	4,928	4,466	4,928	4,731
35,950	36,000	4,935	4,474	4,935	4,739

36,000

If line 43 (taxable income) is—		And you are—			
At least	But less than	Single	Married filing jointly *	Married filing separately	Head of a household
		Your tax is—			
36,000	36,050	4,943	4,481	4,943	4,746
36,050	36,100	4,950	4,489	4,950	4,754
36,100	36,150	4,958	4,496	4,958	4,761
36,150	36,200	4,965	4,504	4,965	4,769
36,200	36,250	4,973	4,511	4,973	4,776
36,250	36,300	4,980	4,519	4,980	4,784
36,300	36,350	4,988	4,526	4,988	4,791
36,350	36,400	4,995	4,534	4,995	4,799
36,400	36,450	5,003	4,541	5,003	4,806
36,450	36,500	5,010	4,549	5,010	4,814
36,500	36,550	5,018	4,556	5,018	4,821
36,550	36,600	5,025	4,564	5,025	4,829
36,600	36,650	5,033	4,571	5,033	4,836
36,650	36,700	5,040	4,579	5,040	4,844
36,700	36,750	5,048	4,586	5,048	4,851
36,750	36,800	5,055	4,594	5,055	4,859
36,800	36,850	5,063	4,601	5,063	4,866
36,850	36,900	5,070	4,609	5,070	4,874
36,900	36,950	5,078	4,616	5,078	4,881
36,950	37,000	5,085	4,624	5,085	4,889

37,000

At least	But less than	Single	Married filing jointly *	Married filing separately	Head of a household
37,000	37,050	5,093	4,631	5,093	4,896
37,050	37,100	5,100	4,639	5,100	4,904
37,100	37,150	5,108	4,646	5,108	4,911
37,150	37,200	5,115	4,654	5,115	4,919
37,200	37,250	5,123	4,661	5,123	4,926
37,250	37,300	5,130	4,669	5,130	4,934
37,300	37,350	5,138	4,676	5,138	4,941
37,350	37,400	5,145	4,684	5,145	4,949
37,400	37,450	5,153	4,691	5,153	4,956
37,450	37,500	5,163	4,699	5,163	4,964
37,500	37,550	5,175	4,706	5,175	4,971
37,550	37,600	5,188	4,714	5,188	4,979
37,600	37,650	5,200	4,721	5,200	4,986
37,650	37,700	5,213	4,729	5,213	4,994
37,700	37,750	5,225	4,736	5,225	5,001
37,750	37,800	5,238	4,744	5,238	5,009
37,800	37,850	5,250	4,751	5,250	5,016
37,850	37,900	5,263	4,759	5,263	5,024
37,900	37,950	5,275	4,766	5,275	5,031
37,950	38,000	5,288	4,774	5,288	5,039

38,000

At least	But less than	Single	Married filing jointly *	Married filing separately	Head of a household
38,000	38,050	5,300	4,781	5,300	5,046
38,050	38,100	5,313	4,789	5,313	5,054
38,100	38,150	5,325	4,796	5,325	5,061
38,150	38,200	5,338	4,804	5,338	5,069
38,200	38,250	5,350	4,811	5,350	5,076
38,250	38,300	5,363	4,819	5,363	5,084
38,300	38,350	5,375	4,826	5,375	5,091
38,350	38,400	5,388	4,834	5,388	5,099
38,400	38,450	5,400	4,841	5,400	5,106
38,450	38,500	5,413	4,849	5,413	5,114
38,500	38,550	5,425	4,856	5,425	5,121
38,550	38,600	5,438	4,864	5,438	5,129
38,600	38,650	5,450	4,871	5,450	5,136
38,650	38,700	5,463	4,879	5,463	5,144
38,700	38,750	5,475	4,886	5,475	5,151
38,750	38,800	5,488	4,894	5,488	5,159
38,800	38,850	5,500	4,901	5,500	5,166
38,850	38,900	5,513	4,909	5,513	5,174
38,900	38,950	5,525	4,916	5,525	5,181
38,950	39,000	5,538	4,924	5,538	5,189

* This column must also be used by a qualifying widow(er).

(Continued)

2015 Tax Table—Individuals *Continued*

39,000

If line 43 (taxable income) is— At least	But less than	Single	Married filing jointly *	Married filing separately	Head of a household
39,000	39,050	5,550	4,931	5,550	5,196
39,050	39,100	5,563	4,939	5,563	5,204
39,100	39,150	5,575	4,946	5,575	5,211
39,150	39,200	5,588	4,954	5,588	5,219
39,200	39,250	5,600	4,961	5,600	5,226
39,250	39,300	5,613	4,969	5,613	5,234
39,300	39,350	5,625	4,976	5,625	5,241
39,350	39,400	5,638	4,984	5,638	5,249
39,400	39,450	5,650	4,991	5,650	5,256
39,450	39,500	5,663	4,999	5,663	5,264
39,500	39,550	5,675	5,006	5,675	5,271
39,550	39,600	5,688	5,014	5,688	5,279
39,600	39,650	5,700	5,021	5,700	5,286
39,650	39,700	5,713	5,029	5,713	5,294
39,700	39,750	5,725	5,036	5,725	5,301
39,750	39,800	5,738	5,044	5,738	5,309
39,800	39,850	5,750	5,051	5,750	5,316
39,850	39,900	5,763	5,059	5,763	5,324
39,900	39,950	5,775	5,066	5,775	5,331
39,950	40,000	5,788	5,074	5,788	5,339

40,000

At least	But less than	Single	Married filing jointly *	Married filing separately	Head of a household
40,000	40,050	5,800	5,081	5,800	5,346
40,050	40,100	5,813	5,089	5,813	5,354
40,100	40,150	5,825	5,096	5,825	5,361
40,150	40,200	5,838	5,104	5,838	5,369
40,200	40,250	5,850	5,111	5,850	5,376
40,250	40,300	5,863	5,119	5,863	5,384
40,300	40,350	5,875	5,126	5,875	5,391
40,350	40,400	5,888	5,134	5,888	5,399
40,400	40,450	5,900	5,141	5,900	5,406
40,450	40,500	5,913	5,149	5,913	5,414
40,500	40,550	5,925	5,156	5,925	5,421
40,550	40,600	5,938	5,164	5,938	5,429
40,600	40,650	5,950	5,171	5,950	5,436
40,650	40,700	5,963	5,179	5,963	5,444
40,700	40,750	5,975	5,186	5,975	5,451
40,750	40,800	5,988	5,194	5,988	5,459
40,800	40,850	6,000	5,201	6,000	5,466
40,850	40,900	6,013	5,209	6,013	5,474
40,900	40,950	6,025	5,216	6,025	5,481
40,950	41,000	6,038	5,224	6,038	5,489

41,000

At least	But less than	Single	Married filing jointly *	Married filing separately	Head of a household
41,000	41,050	6,050	5,231	6,050	5,496
41,050	41,100	6,063	5,239	6,063	5,504
41,100	41,150	6,075	5,246	6,075	5,511
41,150	41,200	6,088	5,254	6,088	5,519
41,200	41,250	6,100	5,261	6,100	5,526
41,250	41,300	6,113	5,269	6,113	5,534
41,300	41,350	6,125	5,276	6,125	5,541
41,350	41,400	6,138	5,284	6,138	5,549
41,400	41,450	6,150	5,291	6,150	5,556
41,450	41,500	6,163	5,299	6,163	5,564
41,500	41,550	6,175	5,306	6,175	5,571
41,550	41,600	6,188	5,314	6,188	5,579
41,600	41,650	6,200	5,321	6,200	5,586
41,650	41,700	6,213	5,329	6,213	5,594
41,700	41,750	6,225	5,336	6,225	5,601
41,750	41,800	6,238	5,344	6,238	5,609
41,800	41,850	6,250	5,351	6,250	5,616
41,850	41,900	6,263	5,359	6,263	5,624
41,900	41,950	6,275	5,366	6,275	5,631
41,950	42,000	6,288	5,374	6,288	5,639

42,000

At least	But less than	Single	Married filing jointly *	Married filing separately	Head of a household
42,000	42,050	6,300	5,381	6,300	5,646
42,050	42,100	6,313	5,389	6,313	5,654
42,100	42,150	6,325	5,396	6,325	5,661
42,150	42,200	6,338	5,404	6,338	5,669
42,200	42,250	6,350	5,411	6,350	5,676
42,250	42,300	6,363	5,419	6,363	5,684
42,300	42,350	6,375	5,426	6,375	5,691
42,350	42,400	6,388	5,434	6,388	5,699
42,400	42,450	6,400	5,441	6,400	5,706
42,450	42,500	6,413	5,449	6,413	5,714
42,500	42,550	6,425	5,456	6,425	5,721
42,550	42,600	6,438	5,464	6,438	5,729
42,600	42,650	6,450	5,471	6,450	5,736
42,650	42,700	6,463	5,479	6,463	5,744
42,700	42,750	6,475	5,486	6,475	5,751
42,750	42,800	6,488	5,494	6,488	5,759
42,800	42,850	6,500	5,501	6,500	5,766
42,850	42,900	6,513	5,509	6,513	5,774
42,900	42,950	6,525	5,516	6,525	5,781
42,950	43,000	6,538	5,524	6,538	5,789

43,000

At least	But less than	Single	Married filing jointly *	Married filing separately	Head of a household
43,000	43,050	6,550	5,531	6,550	5,796
43,050	43,100	6,563	5,539	6,563	5,804
43,100	43,150	6,575	5,546	6,575	5,811
43,150	43,200	6,588	5,554	6,588	5,819
43,200	43,250	6,600	5,561	6,600	5,826
43,250	43,300	6,613	5,569	6,613	5,834
43,300	43,350	6,625	5,576	6,625	5,841
43,350	43,400	6,638	5,584	6,638	5,849
43,400	43,450	6,650	5,591	6,650	5,856
43,450	43,500	6,663	5,599	6,663	5,864
43,500	43,550	6,675	5,606	6,675	5,871
43,550	43,600	6,688	5,614	6,688	5,879
43,600	43,650	6,700	5,621	6,700	5,886
43,650	43,700	6,713	5,629	6,713	5,894
43,700	43,750	6,725	5,636	6,725	5,901
43,750	43,800	6,738	5,644	6,738	5,909
43,800	43,850	6,750	5,651	6,750	5,916
43,850	43,900	6,763	5,659	6,763	5,924
43,900	43,950	6,775	5,666	6,775	5,931
43,950	44,000	6,788	5,674	6,788	5,939

44,000

At least	But less than	Single	Married filing jointly *	Married filing separately	Head of a household
44,000	44,050	6,800	5,681	6,800	5,946
44,050	44,100	6,813	5,689	6,813	5,954
44,100	44,150	6,825	5,696	6,825	5,961
44,150	44,200	6,838	5,704	6,838	5,969
44,200	44,250	6,850	5,711	6,850	5,976
44,250	44,300	6,863	5,719	6,863	5,984
44,300	44,350	6,875	5,726	6,875	5,991
44,350	44,400	6,888	5,734	6,888	5,999
44,400	44,450	6,900	5,741	6,900	6,006
44,450	44,500	6,913	5,749	6,913	6,014
44,500	44,550	6,925	5,756	6,925	6,021
44,550	44,600	6,938	5,764	6,938	6,029
44,600	44,650	6,950	5,771	6,950	6,036
44,650	44,700	6,963	5,779	6,963	6,044
44,700	44,750	6,975	5,786	6,975	6,051
44,750	44,800	6,988	5,794	6,988	6,059
44,800	44,850	7,000	5,801	7,000	6,066
44,850	44,900	7,013	5,809	7,013	6,074
44,900	44,950	7,025	5,816	7,025	6,081
44,950	45,000	7,038	5,824	7,038	6,089

45,000

At least	But less than	Single	Married filing jointly *	Married filing separately	Head of a household
45,000	45,050	7,050	5,831	7,050	6,096
45,050	45,100	7,063	5,839	7,063	6,104
45,100	45,150	7,075	5,846	7,075	6,111
45,150	45,200	7,088	5,854	7,088	6,119
45,200	45,250	7,100	5,861	7,100	6,126
45,250	45,300	7,113	5,869	7,113	6,134
45,300	45,350	7,125	5,876	7,125	6,141
45,350	45,400	7,138	5,884	7,138	6,149
45,400	45,450	7,150	5,891	7,150	6,156
45,450	45,500	7,163	5,899	7,163	6,164
45,500	45,550	7,175	5,906	7,175	6,171
45,550	45,600	7,188	5,914	7,188	6,179
45,600	45,650	7,200	5,921	7,200	6,186
45,650	45,700	7,213	5,929	7,213	6,194
45,700	45,750	7,225	5,936	7,225	6,201
45,750	45,800	7,238	5,944	7,238	6,209
45,800	45,850	7,250	5,951	7,250	6,216
45,850	45,900	7,263	5,959	7,263	6,224
45,900	45,950	7,275	5,966	7,275	6,231
45,950	46,000	7,288	5,974	7,288	6,239

46,000

At least	But less than	Single	Married filing jointly *	Married filing separately	Head of a household
46,000	46,050	7,300	5,981	7,300	6,246
46,050	46,100	7,313	5,989	7,313	6,254
46,100	46,150	7,325	5,996	7,325	6,261
46,150	46,200	7,338	6,004	7,338	6,269
46,200	46,250	7,350	6,011	7,350	6,276
46,250	46,300	7,363	6,019	7,363	6,284
46,300	46,350	7,375	6,026	7,375	6,291
46,350	46,400	7,388	6,034	7,388	6,299
46,400	46,450	7,400	6,041	7,400	6,306
46,450	46,500	7,413	6,049	7,413	6,314
46,500	46,550	7,425	6,056	7,425	6,321
46,550	46,600	7,438	6,064	7,438	6,329
46,600	46,650	7,450	6,071	7,450	6,336
46,650	46,700	7,463	6,079	7,463	6,344
46,700	46,750	7,475	6,086	7,475	6,351
46,750	46,800	7,488	6,094	7,488	6,359
46,800	46,850	7,500	6,101	7,500	6,366
46,850	46,900	7,513	6,109	7,513	6,374
46,900	46,950	7,525	6,116	7,525	6,381
46,950	47,000	7,538	6,124	7,538	6,389

47,000

At least	But less than	Single	Married filing jointly *	Married filing separately	Head of a household
47,000	47,050	7,550	6,131	7,550	6,396
47,050	47,100	7,563	6,139	7,563	6,404
47,100	47,150	7,575	6,146	7,575	6,411
47,150	47,200	7,588	6,154	7,588	6,419
47,200	47,250	7,600	6,161	7,600	6,426
47,250	47,300	7,613	6,169	7,613	6,434
47,300	47,350	7,625	6,176	7,625	6,441
47,350	47,400	7,638	6,184	7,638	6,449
47,400	47,450	7,650	6,191	7,650	6,456
47,450	47,500	7,663	6,199	7,663	6,464
47,500	47,550	7,675	6,206	7,675	6,471
47,550	47,600	7,688	6,214	7,688	6,479
47,600	47,650	7,700	6,221	7,700	6,486
47,650	47,700	7,713	6,229	7,713	6,494
47,700	47,750	7,725	6,236	7,725	6,501
47,750	47,800	7,738	6,244	7,738	6,509
47,800	47,850	7,750	6,251	7,750	6,516
47,850	47,900	7,763	6,259	7,763	6,524
47,900	47,950	7,775	6,266	7,775	6,531
47,950	48,000	7,788	6,274	7,788	6,539

* This column must also be used by a qualifying widow(er).

(Continued)

2015 Tax Table—Individuals *Continued*

48,000 / 49,000 / 50,000

If line 43 (taxable income) is—		And you are—			
At least	But less than	Single	Married filing jointly *	Married filing separately	Head of a household
		Your tax is—			
48,000					
48,000	48,050	7,800	6,281	7,800	6,546
48,050	48,100	7,813	6,289	7,813	6,554
48,100	48,150	7,825	6,296	7,825	6,561
48,150	48,200	7,838	6,304	7,838	6,569
48,200	48,250	7,850	6,311	7,850	6,576
48,250	48,300	7,863	6,319	7,863	6,584
48,300	48,350	7,875	6,326	7,875	6,591
48,350	48,400	7,888	6,334	7,888	6,599
48,400	48,450	7,900	6,341	7,900	6,606
48,450	48,500	7,913	6,349	7,913	6,614
48,500	48,550	7,925	6,356	7,925	6,621
48,550	48,600	7,938	6,364	7,938	6,629
48,600	48,650	7,950	6,371	7,950	6,636
48,650	48,700	7,963	6,379	7,963	6,644
48,700	48,750	7,975	6,386	7,975	6,651
48,750	48,800	7,988	6,394	7,988	6,659
48,800	48,850	8,000	6,401	8,000	6,666
48,850	48,900	8,013	6,409	8,013	6,674
48,900	48,950	8,025	6,416	8,025	6,681
48,950	49,000	8,038	6,424	8,038	6,689
49,000					
49,000	49,050	8,050	6,431	8,050	6,696
49,050	49,100	8,063	6,439	8,063	6,704
49,100	49,150	8,075	6,446	8,075	6,711
49,150	49,200	8,088	6,454	8,088	6,719
49,200	49,250	8,100	6,461	8,100	6,726
49,250	49,300	8,113	6,469	8,113	6,734
49,300	49,350	8,125	6,476	8,125	6,741
49,350	49,400	8,138	6,484	8,138	6,749
49,400	49,450	8,150	6,491	8,150	6,756
49,450	49,500	8,163	6,499	8,163	6,764
49,500	49,550	8,175	6,506	8,175	6,771
49,550	49,600	8,188	6,514	8,188	6,779
49,600	49,650	8,200	6,521	8,200	6,786
49,650	49,700	8,213	6,529	8,213	6,794
49,700	49,750	8,225	6,536	8,225	6,801
49,750	49,800	8,238	6,544	8,238	6,809
49,800	49,850	8,250	6,551	8,250	6,816
49,850	49,900	8,263	6,559	8,263	6,824
49,900	49,950	8,275	6,566	8,275	6,831
49,950	50,000	8,288	6,574	8,288	6,839
50,000					
50,000	50,050	8,300	6,581	8,300	6,846
50,050	50,100	8,313	6,589	8,313	6,854
50,100	50,150	8,325	6,596	8,325	6,861
50,150	50,200	8,338	6,604	8,338	6,869
50,200	50,250	8,350	6,611	8,350	6,879
50,250	50,300	8,363	6,619	8,363	6,891
50,300	50,350	8,375	6,626	8,375	6,904
50,350	50,400	8,388	6,634	8,388	6,916
50,400	50,450	8,400	6,641	8,400	6,929
50,450	50,500	8,413	6,649	8,413	6,941
50,500	50,550	8,425	6,656	8,425	6,954
50,550	50,600	8,438	6,664	8,438	6,966
50,600	50,650	8,450	6,671	8,450	6,979
50,650	50,700	8,463	6,679	8,463	6,991
50,700	50,750	8,475	6,686	8,475	7,004
50,750	50,800	8,488	6,694	8,488	7,016
50,800	50,850	8,500	6,701	8,500	7,029
50,850	50,900	8,513	6,709	8,513	7,041
50,900	50,950	8,525	6,716	8,525	7,054
50,950	51,000	8,538	6,724	8,538	7,066

51,000 / 52,000 / 53,000

If line 43 (taxable income) is—		And you are—			
At least	But less than	Single	Married filing jointly *	Married filing separately	Head of a household
		Your tax is—			
51,000					
51,000	51,050	8,550	6,731	8,550	7,079
51,050	51,100	8,563	6,739	8,563	7,091
51,100	51,150	8,575	6,746	8,575	7,104
51,150	51,200	8,588	6,754	8,588	7,116
51,200	51,250	8,600	6,761	8,600	7,129
51,250	51,300	8,613	6,769	8,613	7,141
51,300	51,350	8,625	6,776	8,625	7,154
51,350	51,400	8,638	6,784	8,638	7,166
51,400	51,450	8,650	6,791	8,650	7,179
51,450	51,500	8,663	6,799	8,663	7,191
51,500	51,550	8,675	6,806	8,675	7,204
51,550	51,600	8,688	6,814	8,688	7,216
51,600	51,650	8,700	6,821	8,700	7,229
51,650	51,700	8,713	6,829	8,713	7,241
51,700	51,750	8,725	6,836	8,725	7,254
51,750	51,800	8,738	6,844	8,738	7,266
51,800	51,850	8,750	6,851	8,750	7,279
51,850	51,900	8,763	6,859	8,763	7,291
51,900	51,950	8,775	6,866	8,775	7,304
51,950	52,000	8,788	6,874	8,788	7,316
52,000					
52,000	52,050	8,800	6,881	8,800	7,329
52,050	52,100	8,813	6,889	8,813	7,341
52,100	52,150	8,825	6,896	8,825	7,354
52,150	52,200	8,838	6,904	8,838	7,366
52,200	52,250	8,850	6,911	8,850	7,379
52,250	52,300	8,863	6,919	8,863	7,391
52,300	52,350	8,875	6,926	8,875	7,404
52,350	52,400	8,888	6,934	8,888	7,416
52,400	52,450	8,900	6,941	8,900	7,429
52,450	52,500	8,913	6,949	8,913	7,441
52,500	52,550	8,925	6,956	8,925	7,454
52,550	52,600	8,938	6,964	8,938	7,466
52,600	52,650	8,950	6,971	8,950	7,479
52,650	52,700	8,963	6,979	8,963	7,491
52,700	52,750	8,975	6,986	8,975	7,504
52,750	52,800	8,988	6,994	8,988	7,516
52,800	52,850	9,000	7,001	9,000	7,529
52,850	52,900	9,013	7,009	9,013	7,541
52,900	52,950	9,025	7,016	9,025	7,554
52,950	53,000	9,038	7,024	9,038	7,566
53,000					
53,000	53,050	9,050	7,031	9,050	7,579
53,050	53,100	9,063	7,039	9,063	7,591
53,100	53,150	9,075	7,046	9,075	7,604
53,150	53,200	9,088	7,054	9,088	7,616
53,200	53,250	9,100	7,061	9,100	7,629
53,250	53,300	9,113	7,069	9,113	7,641
53,300	53,350	9,125	7,076	9,125	7,654
53,350	53,400	9,138	7,084	9,138	7,666
53,400	53,450	9,150	7,091	9,150	7,679
53,450	53,500	9,163	7,099	9,163	7,691
53,500	53,550	9,175	7,106	9,175	7,704
53,550	53,600	9,188	7,114	9,188	7,716
53,600	53,650	9,200	7,121	9,200	7,729
53,650	53,700	9,213	7,129	9,213	7,741
53,700	53,750	9,225	7,136	9,225	7,754
53,750	53,800	9,238	7,144	9,238	7,766
53,800	53,850	9,250	7,151	9,250	7,779
53,850	53,900	9,263	7,159	9,263	7,791
53,900	53,950	9,275	7,166	9,275	7,804
53,950	54,000	9,288	7,174	9,288	7,816

54,000 / 55,000 / 56,000

If line 43 (taxable income) is—		And you are—			
At least	But less than	Single	Married filing jointly *	Married filing separately	Head of a household
		Your tax is—			
54,000					
54,000	54,050	9,300	7,181	9,300	7,829
54,050	54,100	9,313	7,189	9,313	7,841
54,100	54,150	9,325	7,196	9,325	7,854
54,150	54,200	9,338	7,204	9,338	7,866
54,200	54,250	9,350	7,211	9,350	7,879
54,250	54,300	9,363	7,219	9,363	7,891
54,300	54,350	9,375	7,226	9,375	7,904
54,350	54,400	9,388	7,234	9,388	7,916
54,400	54,450	9,400	7,241	9,400	7,929
54,450	54,500	9,413	7,249	9,413	7,941
54,500	54,550	9,425	7,256	9,425	7,954
54,550	54,600	9,438	7,264	9,438	7,966
54,600	54,650	9,450	7,271	9,450	7,979
54,650	54,700	9,463	7,279	9,463	7,991
54,700	54,750	9,475	7,286	9,475	8,004
54,750	54,800	9,488	7,294	9,488	8,016
54,800	54,850	9,500	7,301	9,500	8,029
54,850	54,900	9,513	7,309	9,513	8,041
54,900	54,950	9,525	7,316	9,525	8,054
54,950	55,000	9,538	7,324	9,538	8,066
55,000					
55,000	55,050	9,550	7,331	9,550	8,079
55,050	55,100	9,563	7,339	9,563	8,091
55,100	55,150	9,575	7,346	9,575	8,104
55,150	55,200	9,588	7,354	9,588	8,116
55,200	55,250	9,600	7,361	9,600	8,129
55,250	55,300	9,613	7,369	9,613	8,141
55,300	55,350	9,625	7,376	9,625	8,154
55,350	55,400	9,638	7,384	9,638	8,166
55,400	55,450	9,650	7,391	9,650	8,179
55,450	55,500	9,663	7,399	9,663	8,191
55,500	55,550	9,675	7,406	9,675	8,204
55,550	55,600	9,688	7,414	9,688	8,216
55,600	55,650	9,700	7,421	9,700	8,229
55,650	55,700	9,713	7,429	9,713	8,241
55,700	55,750	9,725	7,436	9,725	8,254
55,750	55,800	9,738	7,444	9,738	8,266
55,800	55,850	9,750	7,451	9,750	8,279
55,850	55,900	9,763	7,459	9,763	8,291
55,900	55,950	9,775	7,466	9,775	8,304
55,950	56,000	9,788	7,474	9,788	8,316
56,000					
56,000	56,050	9,800	7,481	9,800	8,329
56,050	56,100	9,813	7,489	9,813	8,341
56,100	56,150	9,825	7,496	9,825	8,354
56,150	56,200	9,838	7,504	9,838	8,366
56,200	56,250	9,850	7,511	9,850	8,379
56,250	56,300	9,863	7,519	9,863	8,391
56,300	56,350	9,875	7,526	9,875	8,404
56,350	56,400	9,888	7,534	9,888	8,416
56,400	56,450	9,900	7,541	9,900	8,429
56,450	56,500	9,913	7,549	9,913	8,441
56,500	56,550	9,925	7,556	9,925	8,454
56,550	56,600	9,938	7,564	9,938	8,466
56,600	56,650	9,950	7,571	9,950	8,479
56,650	56,700	9,963	7,579	9,963	8,491
56,700	56,750	9,975	7,586	9,975	8,504
56,750	56,800	9,988	7,594	9,988	8,516
56,800	56,850	10,000	7,601	10,000	8,529
56,850	56,900	10,013	7,609	10,013	8,541
56,900	56,950	10,025	7,616	10,025	8,554
56,950	57,000	10,038	7,624	10,038	8,566

* This column must also be used by a qualifying widow(er).

(Continued)

2015 Tax Table—Individuals *Continued*

If line 43 (taxable income) is—		And you are—			
At least	But less than	Single	Married filing jointly *	Married filing separately	Head of a household
		Your tax is—			

57,000

At least	But less than	Single	Married filing jointly *	Married filing separately	Head of a household
57,000	57,050	10,050	7,631	10,050	8,579
57,050	57,100	10,063	7,639	10,063	8,591
57,100	57,150	10,075	7,646	10,075	8,604
57,150	57,200	10,088	7,654	10,088	8,616
57,200	57,250	10,100	7,661	10,100	8,629
57,250	57,300	10,113	7,669	10,113	8,641
57,300	57,350	10,125	7,676	10,125	8,654
57,350	57,400	10,138	7,684	10,138	8,666
57,400	57,450	10,150	7,691	10,150	8,679
57,450	57,500	10,163	7,699	10,163	8,691
57,500	57,550	10,175	7,706	10,175	8,704
57,550	57,600	10,188	7,714	10,188	8,716
57,600	57,650	10,200	7,721	10,200	8,729
57,650	57,700	10,213	7,729	10,213	8,741
57,700	57,750	10,225	7,736	10,225	8,754
57,750	57,800	10,238	7,744	10,238	8,766
57,800	57,850	10,250	7,751	10,250	8,779
57,850	57,900	10,263	7,759	10,263	8,791
57,900	57,950	10,275	7,766	10,275	8,804
57,950	58,000	10,288	7,774	10,288	8,816

58,000

At least	But less than	Single	Married filing jointly *	Married filing separately	Head of a household
58,000	58,050	10,300	7,781	10,300	8,829
58,050	58,100	10,313	7,789	10,313	8,841
58,100	58,150	10,325	7,796	10,325	8,854
58,150	58,200	10,338	7,804	10,338	8,866
58,200	58,250	10,350	7,811	10,350	8,879
58,250	58,300	10,363	7,819	10,363	8,891
58,300	58,350	10,375	7,826	10,375	8,904
58,350	58,400	10,388	7,834	10,388	8,916
58,400	58,450	10,400	7,841	10,400	8,929
58,450	58,500	10,413	7,849	10,413	8,941
58,500	58,550	10,425	7,856	10,425	8,954
58,550	58,600	10,438	7,864	10,438	8,966
58,600	58,650	10,450	7,871	10,450	8,979
58,650	58,700	10,463	7,879	10,463	8,991
58,700	58,750	10,475	7,886	10,475	9,004
58,750	58,800	10,488	7,894	10,488	9,016
58,800	58,850	10,500	7,901	10,500	9,029
58,850	58,900	10,513	7,909	10,513	9,041
58,900	58,950	10,525	7,916	10,525	9,054
58,950	59,000	10,538	7,924	10,538	9,066

59,000

At least	But less than	Single	Married filing jointly *	Married filing separately	Head of a household
59,000	59,050	10,550	7,931	10,550	9,079
59,050	59,100	10,563	7,939	10,563	9,091
59,100	59,150	10,575	7,946	10,575	9,104
59,150	59,200	10,588	7,954	10,588	9,116
59,200	59,250	10,600	7,961	10,600	9,129
59,250	59,300	10,613	7,969	10,613	9,141
59,300	59,350	10,625	7,976	10,625	9,154
59,350	59,400	10,638	7,984	10,638	9,166
59,400	59,450	10,650	7,991	10,650	9,179
59,450	59,500	10,663	7,999	10,663	9,191
59,500	59,550	10,675	8,006	10,675	9,204
59,550	59,600	10,688	8,014	10,688	9,216
59,600	59,650	10,700	8,021	10,700	9,229
59,650	59,700	10,713	8,029	10,713	9,241
59,700	59,750	10,725	8,036	10,725	9,254
59,750	59,800	10,738	8,044	10,738	9,266
59,800	59,850	10,750	8,051	10,750	9,279
59,850	59,900	10,763	8,059	10,763	9,291
59,900	59,950	10,775	8,066	10,775	9,304
59,950	60,000	10,788	8,074	10,788	9,316

60,000

At least	But less than	Single	Married filing jointly *	Married filing separately	Head of a household
60,000	60,050	10,800	8,081	10,800	9,329
60,050	60,100	10,813	8,089	10,813	9,341
60,100	60,150	10,825	8,096	10,825	9,354
60,150	60,200	10,838	8,104	10,838	9,366
60,200	60,250	10,850	8,111	10,850	9,379
60,250	60,300	10,863	8,119	10,863	9,391
60,300	60,350	10,875	8,126	10,875	9,404
60,350	60,400	10,888	8,134	10,888	9,416
60,400	60,450	10,900	8,141	10,900	9,429
60,450	60,500	10,913	8,149	10,913	9,441
60,500	60,550	10,925	8,156	10,925	9,454
60,550	60,600	10,938	8,164	10,938	9,466
60,600	60,650	10,950	8,171	10,950	9,479
60,650	60,700	10,963	8,179	10,963	9,491
60,700	60,750	10,975	8,186	10,975	9,504
60,750	60,800	10,988	8,194	10,988	9,516
60,800	60,850	11,000	8,201	11,000	9,529
60,850	60,900	11,013	8,209	11,013	9,541
60,900	60,950	11,025	8,216	11,025	9,554
60,950	61,000	11,038	8,224	11,038	9,566

61,000

At least	But less than	Single	Married filing jointly *	Married filing separately	Head of a household
61,000	61,050	11,050	8,231	11,050	9,579
61,050	61,100	11,063	8,239	11,063	9,591
61,100	61,150	11,075	8,246	11,075	9,604
61,150	61,200	11,088	8,254	11,088	9,616
61,200	61,250	11,100	8,261	11,100	9,629
61,250	61,300	11,113	8,269	11,113	9,641
61,300	61,350	11,125	8,276	11,125	9,654
61,350	61,400	11,138	8,284	11,138	9,666
61,400	61,450	11,150	8,291	11,150	9,679
61,450	61,500	11,163	8,299	11,163	9,691
61,500	61,550	11,175	8,306	11,175	9,704
61,550	61,600	11,188	8,314	11,188	9,716
61,600	61,650	11,200	8,321	11,200	9,729
61,650	61,700	11,213	8,329	11,213	9,741
61,700	61,750	11,225	8,336	11,225	9,754
61,750	61,800	11,238	8,344	11,238	9,766
61,800	61,850	11,250	8,351	11,250	9,779
61,850	61,900	11,263	8,359	11,263	9,791
61,900	61,950	11,275	8,366	11,275	9,804
61,950	62,000	11,288	8,374	11,288	9,816

62,000

At least	But less than	Single	Married filing jointly *	Married filing separately	Head of a household
62,000	62,050	11,300	8,381	11,300	9,829
62,050	62,100	11,313	8,389	11,313	9,841
62,100	62,150	11,325	8,396	11,325	9,854
62,150	62,200	11,338	8,404	11,338	9,866
62,200	62,250	11,350	8,411	11,350	9,879
62,250	62,300	11,363	8,419	11,363	9,891
62,300	62,350	11,375	8,426	11,375	9,904
62,350	62,400	11,388	8,434	11,388	9,916
62,400	62,450	11,400	8,441	11,400	9,929
62,450	62,500	11,413	8,449	11,413	9,941
62,500	62,550	11,425	8,456	11,425	9,954
62,550	62,600	11,438	8,464	11,438	9,966
62,600	62,650	11,450	8,471	11,450	9,979
62,650	62,700	11,463	8,479	11,463	9,991
62,700	62,750	11,475	8,486	11,475	10,004
62,750	62,800	11,488	8,494	11,488	10,016
62,800	62,850	11,500	8,501	11,500	10,029
62,850	62,900	11,513	8,509	11,513	10,041
62,900	62,950	11,525	8,516	11,525	10,054
62,950	63,000	11,538	8,524	11,538	10,066

63,000

At least	But less than	Single	Married filing jointly *	Married filing separately	Head of a household
63,000	63,050	11,550	8,531	11,550	10,079
63,050	63,100	11,563	8,539	11,563	10,091
63,100	63,150	11,575	8,546	11,575	10,104
63,150	63,200	11,588	8,554	11,588	10,116
63,200	63,250	11,600	8,561	11,600	10,129
63,250	63,300	11,613	8,569	11,613	10,141
63,300	63,350	11,625	8,576	11,625	10,154
63,350	63,400	11,638	8,584	11,638	10,166
63,400	63,450	11,650	8,591	11,650	10,179
63,450	63,500	11,663	8,599	11,663	10,191
63,500	63,550	11,675	8,606	11,675	10,204
63,550	63,600	11,688	8,614	11,688	10,216
63,600	63,650	11,700	8,621	11,700	10,229
63,650	63,700	11,713	8,629	11,713	10,241
63,700	63,750	11,725	8,636	11,725	10,254
63,750	63,800	11,738	8,644	11,738	10,266
63,800	63,850	11,750	8,651	11,750	10,279
63,850	63,900	11,763	8,659	11,763	10,291
63,900	63,950	11,775	8,666	11,775	10,304
63,950	64,000	11,788	8,674	11,788	10,316

64,000

At least	But less than	Single	Married filing jointly *	Married filing separately	Head of a household
64,000	64,050	11,800	8,681	11,800	10,329
64,050	64,100	11,813	8,689	11,813	10,341
64,100	64,150	11,825	8,696	11,825	10,354
64,150	64,200	11,838	8,704	11,838	10,366
64,200	64,250	11,850	8,711	11,850	10,379
64,250	64,300	11,863	8,719	11,863	10,391
64,300	64,350	11,875	8,726	11,875	10,404
64,350	64,400	11,888	8,734	11,888	10,416
64,400	64,450	11,900	8,741	11,900	10,429
64,450	64,500	11,913	8,749	11,913	10,441
64,500	64,550	11,925	8,756	11,925	10,454
64,550	64,600	11,938	8,764	11,938	10,466
64,600	64,650	11,950	8,771	11,950	10,479
64,650	64,700	11,963	8,779	11,963	10,491
64,700	64,750	11,975	8,786	11,975	10,504
64,750	64,800	11,988	8,794	11,988	10,516
64,800	64,850	12,000	8,801	12,000	10,529
64,850	64,900	12,013	8,809	12,013	10,541
64,900	64,950	12,025	8,816	12,025	10,554
64,950	65,000	12,038	8,824	12,038	10,566

65,000

At least	But less than	Single	Married filing jointly *	Married filing separately	Head of a household
65,000	65,050	12,050	8,831	12,050	10,579
65,050	65,100	12,063	8,839	12,063	10,591
65,100	65,150	12,075	8,846	12,075	10,604
65,150	65,200	12,088	8,854	12,088	10,616
65,200	65,250	12,100	8,861	12,100	10,629
65,250	65,300	12,113	8,869	12,113	10,641
65,300	65,350	12,125	8,876	12,125	10,654
65,350	65,400	12,138	8,884	12,138	10,666
65,400	65,450	12,150	8,891	12,150	10,679
65,450	65,500	12,163	8,899	12,163	10,691
65,500	65,550	12,175	8,906	12,175	10,704
65,550	65,600	12,188	8,914	12,188	10,716
65,600	65,650	12,200	8,921	12,200	10,729
65,650	65,700	12,213	8,929	12,213	10,741
65,700	65,750	12,225	8,936	12,225	10,754
65,750	65,800	12,238	8,944	12,238	10,766
65,800	65,850	12,250	8,951	12,250	10,779
65,850	65,900	12,263	8,959	12,263	10,791
65,900	65,950	12,275	8,966	12,275	10,804
65,950	66,000	12,288	8,974	12,288	10,816

* This column must also be used by a qualifying widow(er).

(Continued)

2015 Tax Table—Individuals *Continued*

66,000

At least	But less than	Single	Married filing jointly *	Married filing separately	Head of a household
66,000	66,050	12,300	8,981	12,300	10,829
66,050	66,100	12,313	8,989	12,313	10,841
66,100	66,150	12,325	8,996	12,325	10,854
66,150	66,200	12,338	9,004	12,338	10,866
66,200	66,250	12,350	9,011	12,350	10,879
66,250	66,300	12,363	9,019	12,363	10,891
66,300	66,350	12,375	9,026	12,375	10,904
66,350	66,400	12,388	9,034	12,388	10,916
66,400	66,450	12,400	9,041	12,400	10,929
66,450	66,500	12,413	9,049	12,413	10,941
66,500	66,550	12,425	9,056	12,425	10,954
66,550	66,600	12,438	9,064	12,438	10,966
66,600	66,650	12,450	9,071	12,450	10,979
66,650	66,700	12,463	9,079	12,463	10,991
66,700	66,750	12,475	9,086	12,475	11,004
66,750	66,800	12,488	9,094	12,488	11,016
66,800	66,850	12,500	9,101	12,500	11,029
66,850	66,900	12,513	9,109	12,513	11,041
66,900	66,950	12,525	9,116	12,525	11,054
66,950	67,000	12,538	9,124	12,538	11,066

67,000

At least	But less than	Single	Married filing jointly *	Married filing separately	Head of a household
67,000	67,050	12,550	9,131	12,550	11,079
67,050	67,100	12,563	9,139	12,563	11,091
67,100	67,150	12,575	9,146	12,575	11,104
67,150	67,200	12,588	9,154	12,588	11,116
67,200	67,250	12,600	9,161	12,600	11,129
67,250	67,300	12,613	9,169	12,613	11,141
67,300	67,350	12,625	9,176	12,625	11,154
67,350	67,400	12,638	9,184	12,638	11,166
67,400	67,450	12,650	9,191	12,650	11,179
67,450	67,500	12,663	9,199	12,663	11,191
67,500	67,550	12,675	9,206	12,675	11,204
67,550	67,600	12,688	9,214	12,688	11,216
67,600	67,650	12,700	9,221	12,700	11,229
67,650	67,700	12,713	9,229	12,713	11,241
67,700	67,750	12,725	9,236	12,725	11,254
67,750	67,800	12,738	9,244	12,738	11,266
67,800	67,850	12,750	9,251	12,750	11,279
67,850	67,900	12,763	9,259	12,763	11,291
67,900	67,950	12,775	9,266	12,775	11,304
67,950	68,000	12,788	9,274	12,788	11,316

68,000

At least	But less than	Single	Married filing jointly *	Married filing separately	Head of a household
68,000	68,050	12,800	9,281	12,800	11,329
68,050	68,100	12,813	9,289	12,813	11,341
68,100	68,150	12,825	9,296	12,825	11,354
68,150	68,200	12,838	9,304	12,838	11,366
68,200	68,250	12,850	9,311	12,850	11,379
68,250	68,300	12,863	9,319	12,863	11,391
68,300	68,350	12,875	9,326	12,875	11,404
68,350	68,400	12,888	9,334	12,888	11,416
68,400	68,450	12,900	9,341	12,900	11,429
68,450	68,500	12,913	9,349	12,913	11,441
68,500	68,550	12,925	9,356	12,925	11,454
68,550	68,600	12,938	9,364	12,938	11,466
68,600	68,650	12,950	9,371	12,950	11,479
68,650	68,700	12,963	9,379	12,963	11,491
68,700	68,750	12,975	9,386	12,975	11,504
68,750	68,800	12,988	9,394	12,988	11,516
68,800	68,850	13,000	9,401	13,000	11,529
68,850	68,900	13,013	9,409	13,013	11,541
68,900	68,950	13,025	9,416	13,025	11,554
68,950	69,000	13,038	9,424	13,038	11,566

69,000

At least	But less than	Single	Married filing jointly *	Married filing separately	Head of a household
69,000	69,050	13,050	9,431	13,050	11,579
69,050	69,100	13,063	9,439	13,063	11,591
69,100	69,150	13,075	9,446	13,075	11,604
69,150	69,200	13,088	9,454	13,088	11,616
69,200	69,250	13,100	9,461	13,100	11,629
69,250	69,300	13,113	9,469	13,113	11,641
69,300	69,350	13,125	9,476	13,125	11,654
69,350	69,400	13,138	9,484	13,138	11,666
69,400	69,450	13,150	9,491	13,150	11,679
69,450	69,500	13,163	9,499	13,163	11,691
69,500	69,550	13,175	9,506	13,175	11,704
69,550	69,600	13,188	9,514	13,188	11,716
69,600	69,650	13,200	9,521	13,200	11,729
69,650	69,700	13,213	9,529	13,213	11,741
69,700	69,750	13,225	9,536	13,225	11,754
69,750	69,800	13,238	9,544	13,238	11,766
69,800	69,850	13,250	9,551	13,250	11,779
69,850	69,900	13,263	9,559	13,263	11,791
69,900	69,950	13,275	9,566	13,275	11,804
69,950	70,000	13,288	9,574	13,288	11,816

70,000

At least	But less than	Single	Married filing jointly *	Married filing separately	Head of a household
70,000	70,050	13,300	9,581	13,300	11,829
70,050	70,100	13,313	9,589	13,313	11,841
70,100	70,150	13,325	9,596	13,325	11,854
70,150	70,200	13,338	9,604	13,338	11,866
70,200	70,250	13,350	9,611	13,350	11,879
70,250	70,300	13,363	9,619	13,363	11,891
70,300	70,350	13,375	9,626	13,375	11,904
70,350	70,400	13,388	9,634	13,388	11,916
70,400	70,450	13,400	9,641	13,400	11,929
70,450	70,500	13,413	9,649	13,413	11,941
70,500	70,550	13,425	9,656	13,425	11,954
70,550	70,600	13,438	9,664	13,438	11,966
70,600	70,650	13,450	9,671	13,450	11,979
70,650	70,700	13,463	9,679	13,463	11,991
70,700	70,750	13,475	9,686	13,475	12,004
70,750	70,800	13,488	9,694	13,488	12,016
70,800	70,850	13,500	9,701	13,500	12,029
70,850	70,900	13,513	9,709	13,513	12,041
70,900	70,950	13,525	9,716	13,525	12,054
70,950	71,000	13,538	9,724	13,538	12,066

71,000

At least	But less than	Single	Married filing jointly *	Married filing separately	Head of a household
71,000	71,050	13,550	9,731	13,550	12,079
71,050	71,100	13,563	9,739	13,563	12,091
71,100	71,150	13,575	9,746	13,575	12,104
71,150	71,200	13,588	9,754	13,588	12,116
71,200	71,250	13,600	9,761	13,600	12,129
71,250	71,300	13,613	9,769	13,613	12,141
71,300	71,350	13,625	9,776	13,625	12,154
71,350	71,400	13,638	9,784	13,638	12,166
71,400	71,450	13,650	9,791	13,650	12,179
71,450	71,500	13,663	9,799	13,663	12,191
71,500	71,550	13,675	9,806	13,675	12,204
71,550	71,600	13,688	9,814	13,688	12,216
71,600	71,650	13,700	9,821	13,700	12,229
71,650	71,700	13,713	9,829	13,713	12,241
71,700	71,750	13,725	9,836	13,725	12,254
71,750	71,800	13,738	9,844	13,738	12,266
71,800	71,850	13,750	9,851	13,750	12,279
71,850	71,900	13,763	9,859	13,763	12,291
71,900	71,950	13,775	9,866	13,775	12,304
71,950	72,000	13,788	9,874	13,788	12,316

72,000

At least	But less than	Single	Married filing jointly *	Married filing separately	Head of a household
72,000	72,050	13,800	9,881	13,800	12,329
72,050	72,100	13,813	9,889	13,813	12,341
72,100	72,150	13,825	9,896	13,825	12,354
72,150	72,200	13,838	9,904	13,838	12,366
72,200	72,250	13,850	9,911	13,850	12,379
72,250	72,300	13,863	9,919	13,863	12,391
72,300	72,350	13,875	9,926	13,875	12,404
72,350	72,400	13,888	9,934	13,888	12,416
72,400	72,450	13,900	9,941	13,900	12,429
72,450	72,500	13,913	9,949	13,913	12,441
72,500	72,550	13,925	9,956	13,925	12,454
72,550	72,600	13,938	9,964	13,938	12,466
72,600	72,650	13,950	9,971	13,950	12,479
72,650	72,700	13,963	9,979	13,963	12,491
72,700	72,750	13,975	9,986	13,975	12,504
72,750	72,800	13,988	9,994	13,988	12,516
72,800	72,850	14,000	10,001	14,000	12,529
72,850	72,900	14,013	10,009	14,013	12,541
72,900	72,950	14,025	10,016	14,025	12,554
72,950	73,000	14,038	10,024	14,038	12,566

73,000

At least	But less than	Single	Married filing jointly *	Married filing separately	Head of a household
73,000	73,050	14,050	10,031	14,050	12,579
73,050	73,100	14,063	10,039	14,063	12,591
73,100	73,150	14,075	10,046	14,075	12,604
73,150	73,200	14,088	10,054	14,088	12,616
73,200	73,250	14,100	10,061	14,100	12,629
73,250	73,300	14,113	10,069	14,113	12,641
73,300	73,350	14,125	10,076	14,125	12,654
73,350	73,400	14,138	10,084	14,138	12,666
73,400	73,450	14,150	10,091	14,150	12,679
73,450	73,500	14,163	10,099	14,163	12,691
73,500	73,550	14,175	10,106	14,175	12,704
73,550	73,600	14,188	10,114	14,188	12,716
73,600	73,650	14,200	10,121	14,200	12,729
73,650	73,700	14,213	10,129	14,213	12,741
73,700	73,750	14,225	10,136	14,225	12,754
73,750	73,800	14,238	10,144	14,238	12,766
73,800	73,850	14,250	10,151	14,250	12,779
73,850	73,900	14,263	10,159	14,263	12,791
73,900	73,950	14,275	10,166	14,275	12,804
73,950	74,000	14,288	10,174	14,288	12,816

74,000

At least	But less than	Single	Married filing jointly *	Married filing separately	Head of a household
74,000	74,050	14,300	10,181	14,300	12,829
74,050	74,100	14,313	10,189	14,313	12,841
74,100	74,150	14,325	10,196	14,325	12,854
74,150	74,200	14,338	10,204	14,338	12,866
74,200	74,250	14,350	10,211	14,350	12,879
74,250	74,300	14,363	10,219	14,363	12,891
74,300	74,350	14,375	10,226	14,375	12,904
74,350	74,400	14,388	10,234	14,388	12,916
74,400	74,450	14,400	10,241	14,400	12,929
74,450	74,500	14,413	10,249	14,413	12,941
74,500	74,550	14,425	10,256	14,425	12,954
74,550	74,600	14,438	10,264	14,438	12,966
74,600	74,650	14,450	10,271	14,450	12,979
74,650	74,700	14,463	10,279	14,463	12,991
74,700	74,750	14,475	10,286	14,475	13,004
74,750	74,800	14,488	10,294	14,488	13,016
74,800	74,850	14,500	10,301	14,500	13,029
74,850	74,900	14,513	10,309	14,513	13,041
74,900	74,950	14,525	10,319	14,525	13,054
74,950	75,000	14,538	10,331	14,538	13,066

* This column must also be used by a qualifying widow(er).

(Continued)

2015 Tax Table—Individuals *Continued*

If line 43 (taxable income) is— / And you are— / Your tax is—

75,000

At least	But less than	Single	Married filing jointly*	Married filing separately	Head of a household
75,000	75,050	14,550	10,344	14,550	13,079
75,050	75,100	14,563	10,356	14,563	13,091
75,100	75,150	14,575	10,369	14,575	13,104
75,150	75,200	14,588	10,381	14,588	13,116
75,200	75,250	14,600	10,394	14,600	13,129
75,250	75,300	14,613	10,406	14,613	13,141
75,300	75,350	14,625	10,419	14,625	13,154
75,350	75,400	14,638	10,431	14,638	13,166
75,400	75,450	14,650	10,444	14,650	13,179
75,450	75,500	14,663	10,456	14,663	13,191
75,500	75,550	14,675	10,469	14,675	13,204
75,550	75,600	14,688	10,481	14,688	13,216
75,600	75,650	14,700	10,494	14,701	13,229
75,650	75,700	14,713	10,506	14,715	13,241
75,700	75,750	14,725	10,519	14,729	13,254
75,750	75,800	14,738	10,531	14,743	13,266
75,800	75,850	14,750	10,544	14,757	13,279
75,850	75,900	14,763	10,556	14,771	13,291
75,900	75,950	14,775	10,569	14,785	13,304
75,950	76,000	14,788	10,581	14,799	13,316

76,000

At least	But less than	Single	Married filing jointly*	Married filing separately	Head of a household
76,000	76,050	14,800	10,594	14,813	13,329
76,050	76,100	14,813	10,606	14,827	13,341
76,100	76,150	14,825	10,619	14,841	13,354
76,150	76,200	14,838	10,631	14,855	13,366
76,200	76,250	14,850	10,644	14,869	13,379
76,250	76,300	14,863	10,656	14,883	13,391
76,300	76,350	14,875	10,669	14,897	13,404
76,350	76,400	14,888	10,681	14,911	13,416
76,400	76,450	14,900	10,694	14,925	13,429
76,450	76,500	14,913	10,706	14,939	13,441
76,500	76,550	14,925	10,719	14,953	13,454
76,550	76,600	14,938	10,731	14,967	13,466
76,600	76,650	14,950	10,744	14,981	13,479
76,650	76,700	14,963	10,756	14,995	13,491
76,700	76,750	14,975	10,769	15,009	13,504
76,750	76,800	14,988	10,781	15,023	13,516
76,800	76,850	15,000	10,794	15,037	13,529
76,850	76,900	15,013	10,806	15,051	13,541
76,900	76,950	15,025	10,819	15,065	13,554
76,950	77,000	15,038	10,831	15,079	13,566

77,000

At least	But less than	Single	Married filing jointly*	Married filing separately	Head of a household
77,000	77,050	15,050	10,844	15,093	13,579
77,050	77,100	15,063	10,856	15,107	13,591
77,100	77,150	15,075	10,869	15,121	13,604
77,150	77,200	15,088	10,881	15,135	13,616
77,200	77,250	15,100	10,894	15,149	13,629
77,250	77,300	15,113	10,906	15,163	13,641
77,300	77,350	15,125	10,919	15,177	13,654
77,350	77,400	15,138	10,931	15,191	13,666
77,400	77,450	15,150	10,944	15,205	13,679
77,450	77,500	15,163	10,956	15,219	13,691
77,500	77,550	15,175	10,969	15,233	13,704
77,550	77,600	15,188	10,981	15,247	13,716
77,600	77,650	15,200	10,994	15,261	13,729
77,650	77,700	15,213	11,006	15,275	13,741
77,700	77,750	15,225	11,019	15,289	13,754
77,750	77,800	15,238	11,031	15,303	13,766
77,800	77,850	15,250	11,044	15,317	13,779
77,850	77,900	15,263	11,056	15,331	13,791
77,900	77,950	15,275	11,069	15,345	13,804
77,950	78,000	15,288	11,081	15,359	13,816

78,000

At least	But less than	Single	Married filing jointly*	Married filing separately	Head of a household
78,000	78,050	15,300	11,094	15,373	13,829
78,050	78,100	15,313	11,106	15,387	13,841
78,100	78,150	15,325	11,119	15,401	13,854
78,150	78,200	15,338	11,131	15,415	13,866
78,200	78,250	15,350	11,144	15,429	13,879
78,250	78,300	15,363	11,156	15,443	13,891
78,300	78,350	15,375	11,169	15,457	13,904
78,350	78,400	15,388	11,181	15,471	13,916
78,400	78,450	15,400	11,194	15,485	13,929
78,450	78,500	15,413	11,206	15,499	13,941
78,500	78,550	15,425	11,219	15,513	13,954
78,550	78,600	15,438	11,231	15,527	13,966
78,600	78,650	15,450	11,244	15,541	13,979
78,650	78,700	15,463	11,256	15,555	13,991
78,700	78,750	15,475	11,269	15,569	14,004
78,750	78,800	15,488	11,281	15,583	14,016
78,800	78,850	15,500	11,294	15,597	14,029
78,850	78,900	15,513	11,306	15,611	14,041
78,900	78,950	15,525	11,319	15,625	14,054
78,950	79,000	15,538	11,331	15,639	14,066

79,000

At least	But less than	Single	Married filing jointly*	Married filing separately	Head of a household
79,000	79,050	15,550	11,344	15,653	14,079
79,050	79,100	15,563	11,356	15,667	14,091
79,100	79,150	15,575	11,369	15,681	14,104
79,150	79,200	15,588	11,381	15,695	14,116
79,200	79,250	15,600	11,394	15,709	14,129
79,250	79,300	15,613	11,406	15,723	14,141
79,300	79,350	15,625	11,419	15,737	14,154
79,350	79,400	15,638	11,431	15,751	14,166
79,400	79,450	15,650	11,444	15,765	14,179
79,450	79,500	15,663	11,456	15,779	14,191
79,500	79,550	15,675	11,469	15,793	14,204
79,550	79,600	15,688	11,481	15,807	14,216
79,600	79,650	15,700	11,494	15,821	14,229
79,650	79,700	15,713	11,506	15,835	14,241
79,700	79,750	15,725	11,519	15,849	14,254
79,750	79,800	15,738	11,531	15,863	14,266
79,800	79,850	15,750	11,544	15,877	14,279
79,850	79,900	15,763	11,556	15,891	14,291
79,900	79,950	15,775	11,569	15,905	14,304
79,950	80,000	15,788	11,581	15,919	14,316

80,000

At least	But less than	Single	Married filing jointly*	Married filing separately	Head of a household
80,000	80,050	15,800	11,594	15,933	14,329
80,050	80,100	15,813	11,606	15,947	14,341
80,100	80,150	15,825	11,619	15,961	14,354
80,150	80,200	15,838	11,631	15,975	14,366
80,200	80,250	15,850	11,644	15,989	14,379
80,250	80,300	15,863	11,656	16,003	14,391
80,300	80,350	15,875	11,669	16,017	14,404
80,350	80,400	15,888	11,681	16,031	14,416
80,400	80,450	15,900	11,694	16,045	14,429
80,450	80,500	15,913	11,706	16,059	14,441
80,500	80,550	15,925	11,719	16,073	14,454
80,550	80,600	15,938	11,731	16,087	14,466
80,600	80,650	15,950	11,744	16,101	14,479
80,650	80,700	15,963	11,756	16,115	14,491
80,700	80,750	15,975	11,769	16,129	14,504
80,750	80,800	15,988	11,781	16,143	14,516
80,800	80,850	16,000	11,794	16,157	14,529
80,850	80,900	16,013	11,806	16,171	14,541
80,900	80,950	16,025	11,819	16,185	14,554
80,950	81,000	16,038	11,831	16,199	14,566

81,000

At least	But less than	Single	Married filing jointly*	Married filing separately	Head of a household
81,000	81,050	16,050	11,844	16,213	14,579
81,050	81,100	16,063	11,856	16,227	14,591
81,100	81,150	16,075	11,869	16,241	14,604
81,150	81,200	16,088	11,881	16,255	14,616
81,200	81,250	16,100	11,894	16,269	14,629
81,250	81,300	16,113	11,906	16,283	14,641
81,300	81,350	16,125	11,919	16,297	14,654
81,350	81,400	16,138	11,931	16,311	14,666
81,400	81,450	16,150	11,944	16,325	14,679
81,450	81,500	16,163	11,956	16,339	14,691
81,500	81,550	16,175	11,969	16,353	14,704
81,550	81,600	16,188	11,981	16,367	14,716
81,600	81,650	16,200	11,994	16,381	14,729
81,650	81,700	16,213	12,006	16,395	14,741
81,700	81,750	16,225	12,019	16,409	14,754
81,750	81,800	16,238	12,031	16,423	14,766
81,800	81,850	16,250	12,044	16,437	14,779
81,850	81,900	16,263	12,056	16,451	14,791
81,900	81,950	16,275	12,069	16,465	14,804
81,950	82,000	16,288	12,081	16,479	14,816

82,000

At least	But less than	Single	Married filing jointly*	Married filing separately	Head of a household
82,000	82,050	16,300	12,094	16,493	14,829
82,050	82,100	16,313	12,106	16,507	14,841
82,100	82,150	16,325	12,119	16,521	14,854
82,150	82,200	16,338	12,131	16,535	14,866
82,200	82,250	16,350	12,144	16,549	14,879
82,250	82,300	16,363	12,156	16,563	14,891
82,300	82,350	16,375	12,169	16,577	14,904
82,350	82,400	16,388	12,181	16,591	14,916
82,400	82,450	16,400	12,194	16,605	14,929
82,450	82,500	16,413	12,206	16,619	14,941
82,500	82,550	16,425	12,219	16,633	14,954
82,550	82,600	16,438	12,231	16,647	14,966
82,600	82,650	16,450	12,244	16,661	14,979
82,650	82,700	16,463	12,256	16,675	14,991
82,700	82,750	16,475	12,269	16,689	15,004
82,750	82,800	16,488	12,281	16,703	15,016
82,800	82,850	16,500	12,294	16,717	15,029
82,850	82,900	16,513	12,306	16,731	15,041
82,900	82,950	16,525	12,319	16,745	15,054
82,950	83,000	16,538	12,331	16,759	15,066

83,000

At least	But less than	Single	Married filing jointly*	Married filing separately	Head of a household
83,000	83,050	16,550	12,344	16,773	15,079
83,050	83,100	16,563	12,356	16,787	15,091
83,100	83,150	16,575	12,369	16,801	15,104
83,150	83,200	16,588	12,381	16,815	15,116
83,200	83,250	16,600	12,394	16,829	15,129
83,250	83,300	16,613	12,406	16,843	15,141
83,300	83,350	16,625	12,419	16,857	15,154
83,350	83,400	16,638	12,431	16,871	15,166
83,400	83,450	16,650	12,444	16,885	15,179
83,450	83,500	16,663	12,456	16,899	15,191
83,500	83,550	16,675	12,469	16,913	15,204
83,550	83,600	16,688	12,481	16,927	15,216
83,600	83,650	16,700	12,494	16,941	15,229
83,650	83,700	16,713	12,506	16,955	15,241
83,700	83,750	16,725	12,519	16,969	15,254
83,750	83,800	16,738	12,531	16,983	15,266
83,800	83,850	16,750	12,544	16,997	15,279
83,850	83,900	16,763	12,556	17,011	15,291
83,900	83,950	16,775	12,569	17,025	15,304
83,950	84,000	16,788	12,581	17,039	15,316

* This column must also be used by a qualifying widow(er).

(Continued)

2015 Tax Table—Individuals *Continued*

84,000

At least	But less than	Single	Married filing jointly *	Married filing separately	Head of a household
84,000	84,050	16,800	12,594	17,053	15,329
84,050	84,100	16,813	12,606	17,067	15,341
84,100	84,150	16,825	12,619	17,081	15,354
84,150	84,200	16,838	12,631	17,095	15,366
84,200	84,250	16,850	12,644	17,109	15,379
84,250	84,300	16,863	12,656	17,123	15,391
84,300	84,350	16,875	12,669	17,137	15,404
84,350	84,400	16,888	12,681	17,151	15,416
84,400	84,450	16,900	12,694	17,165	15,429
84,450	84,500	16,913	12,706	17,179	15,441
84,500	84,550	16,925	12,719	17,193	15,454
84,550	84,600	16,938	12,731	17,207	15,466
84,600	84,650	16,950	12,744	17,221	15,479
84,650	84,700	16,963	12,756	17,235	15,491
84,700	84,750	16,975	12,769	17,249	15,504
84,750	84,800	16,988	12,781	17,263	15,516
84,800	84,850	17,000	12,794	17,277	15,529
84,850	84,900	17,013	12,806	17,291	15,541
84,900	84,950	17,025	12,819	17,305	15,554
84,950	85,000	17,038	12,831	17,319	15,566

85,000

At least	But less than	Single	Married filing jointly *	Married filing separately	Head of a household
85,000	85,050	17,050	12,844	17,333	15,579
85,050	85,100	17,063	12,856	17,347	15,591
85,100	85,150	17,075	12,869	17,361	15,604
85,150	85,200	17,088	12,881	17,375	15,616
85,200	85,250	17,100	12,894	17,389	15,629
85,250	85,300	17,113	12,906	17,403	15,641
85,300	85,350	17,125	12,919	17,417	15,654
85,350	85,400	17,138	12,931	17,431	15,666
85,400	85,450	17,150	12,944	17,445	15,679
85,450	85,500	17,163	12,956	17,459	15,691
85,500	85,550	17,175	12,969	17,473	15,704
85,550	85,600	17,188	12,981	17,487	15,716
85,600	85,650	17,200	12,994	17,501	15,729
85,650	85,700	17,213	13,006	17,515	15,741
85,700	85,750	17,225	13,019	17,529	15,754
85,750	85,800	17,238	13,031	17,543	15,766
85,800	85,850	17,250	13,044	17,557	15,779
85,850	85,900	17,263	13,056	17,571	15,791
85,900	85,950	17,275	13,069	17,585	15,804
85,950	86,000	17,288	13,081	17,599	15,816

86,000

At least	But less than	Single	Married filing jointly *	Married filing separately	Head of a household
86,000	86,050	17,300	13,094	17,613	15,829
86,050	86,100	17,313	13,106	17,627	15,841
86,100	86,150	17,325	13,119	17,641	15,854
86,150	86,200	17,338	13,131	17,655	15,866
86,200	86,250	17,350	13,144	17,669	15,879
86,250	86,300	17,363	13,156	17,683	15,891
86,300	86,350	17,375	13,169	17,697	15,904
86,350	86,400	17,388	13,181	17,711	15,916
86,400	86,450	17,400	13,194	17,725	15,929
86,450	86,500	17,413	13,206	17,739	15,941
86,500	86,550	17,425	13,219	17,753	15,954
86,550	86,600	17,438	13,231	17,767	15,966
86,600	86,650	17,450	13,244	17,781	15,979
86,650	86,700	17,463	13,256	17,795	15,991
86,700	86,750	17,475	13,269	17,809	16,004
86,750	86,800	17,488	13,281	17,823	16,016
86,800	86,850	17,500	13,294	17,837	16,029
86,850	86,900	17,513	13,306	17,851	16,041
86,900	86,950	17,525	13,319	17,865	16,054
86,950	87,000	17,538	13,331	17,879	16,066

87,000

At least	But less than	Single	Married filing jointly *	Married filing separately	Head of a household
87,000	87,050	17,550	13,344	17,893	16,079
87,050	87,100	17,563	13,356	17,907	16,091
87,100	87,150	17,575	13,369	17,921	16,104
87,150	87,200	17,588	13,381	17,935	16,116
87,200	87,250	17,600	13,394	17,949	16,129
87,250	87,300	17,613	13,406	17,963	16,141
87,300	87,350	17,625	13,419	17,977	16,154
87,350	87,400	17,638	13,431	17,991	16,166
87,400	87,450	17,650	13,444	18,005	16,179
87,450	87,500	17,663	13,456	18,019	16,191
87,500	87,550	17,675	13,469	18,033	16,204
87,550	87,600	17,688	13,481	18,047	16,216
87,600	87,650	17,700	13,494	18,061	16,229
87,650	87,700	17,713	13,506	18,075	16,241
87,700	87,750	17,725	13,519	18,089	16,254
87,750	87,800	17,738	13,531	18,103	16,266
87,800	87,850	17,750	13,544	18,117	16,279
87,850	87,900	17,763	13,556	18,131	16,291
87,900	87,950	17,775	13,569	18,145	16,304
87,950	88,000	17,788	13,581	18,159	16,316

88,000

At least	But less than	Single	Married filing jointly *	Married filing separately	Head of a household
88,000	88,050	17,800	13,594	18,173	16,329
88,050	88,100	17,813	13,606	18,187	16,341
88,100	88,150	17,825	13,619	18,201	16,354
88,150	88,200	17,838	13,631	18,215	16,366
88,200	88,250	17,850	13,644	18,229	16,379
88,250	88,300	17,863	13,656	18,243	16,391
88,300	88,350	17,875	13,669	18,257	16,404
88,350	88,400	17,888	13,681	18,271	16,416
88,400	88,450	17,900	13,694	18,285	16,429
88,450	88,500	17,913	13,706	18,299	16,441
88,500	88,550	17,925	13,719	18,313	16,454
88,550	88,600	17,938	13,731	18,327	16,466
88,600	88,650	17,950	13,744	18,341	16,479
88,650	88,700	17,963	13,756	18,355	16,491
88,700	88,750	17,975	13,769	18,369	16,504
88,750	88,800	17,988	13,781	18,383	16,516
88,800	88,850	18,000	13,794	18,397	16,529
88,850	88,900	18,013	13,806	18,411	16,541
88,900	88,950	18,025	13,819	18,425	16,554
88,950	89,000	18,038	13,831	18,439	16,566

89,000

At least	But less than	Single	Married filing jointly *	Married filing separately	Head of a household
89,000	89,050	18,050	13,844	18,453	16,579
89,050	89,100	18,063	13,856	18,467	16,591
89,100	89,150	18,075	13,869	18,481	16,604
89,150	89,200	18,088	13,881	18,495	16,616
89,200	89,250	18,100	13,894	18,509	16,629
89,250	89,300	18,113	13,906	18,523	16,641
89,300	89,350	18,125	13,919	18,537	16,654
89,350	89,400	18,138	13,931	18,551	16,666
89,400	89,450	18,150	13,944	18,565	16,679
89,450	89,500	18,163	13,956	18,579	16,691
89,500	89,550	18,175	13,969	18,593	16,704
89,550	89,600	18,188	13,981	18,607	16,716
89,600	89,650	18,200	13,994	18,621	16,729
89,650	89,700	18,213	14,006	18,635	16,741
89,700	89,750	18,225	14,019	18,649	16,754
89,750	89,800	18,238	14,031	18,663	16,766
89,800	89,850	18,250	14,044	18,677	16,779
89,850	89,900	18,263	14,056	18,691	16,791
89,900	89,950	18,275	14,069	18,705	16,804
89,950	90,000	18,288	14,081	18,719	16,816

90,000

At least	But less than	Single	Married filing jointly *	Married filing separately	Head of a household
90,000	90,050	18,300	14,094	18,733	16,829
90,050	90,100	18,313	14,106	18,747	16,841
90,100	90,150	18,325	14,119	18,761	16,854
90,150	90,200	18,338	14,131	18,775	16,866
90,200	90,250	18,350	14,144	18,789	16,879
90,250	90,300	18,363	14,156	18,803	16,891
90,300	90,350	18,375	14,169	18,817	16,904
90,350	90,400	18,388	14,181	18,831	16,916
90,400	90,450	18,400	14,194	18,845	16,929
90,450	90,500	18,413	14,206	18,859	16,941
90,500	90,550	18,425	14,219	18,873	16,954
90,550	90,600	18,438	14,231	18,887	16,966
90,600	90,650	18,450	14,244	18,901	16,979
90,650	90,700	18,463	14,256	18,915	16,991
90,700	90,750	18,475	14,269	18,929	17,004
90,750	90,800	18,488	14,281	18,943	17,016
90,800	90,850	18,502	14,294	18,957	17,029
90,850	90,900	18,516	14,306	18,971	17,041
90,900	90,950	18,530	14,319	18,985	17,054
90,950	91,000	18,544	14,331	18,999	17,066

91,000

At least	But less than	Single	Married filing jointly *	Married filing separately	Head of a household
91,000	91,050	18,558	14,344	19,013	17,079
91,050	91,100	18,572	14,356	19,027	17,091
91,100	91,150	18,586	14,369	19,041	17,104
91,150	91,200	18,600	14,381	19,055	17,116
91,200	91,250	18,614	14,394	19,069	17,129
91,250	91,300	18,628	14,406	19,083	17,141
91,300	91,350	18,642	14,419	19,097	17,154
91,350	91,400	18,656	14,431	19,111	17,166
91,400	91,450	18,670	14,444	19,125	17,179
91,450	91,500	18,684	14,456	19,139	17,191
91,500	91,550	18,698	14,469	19,153	17,204
91,550	91,600	18,712	14,481	19,167	17,216
91,600	91,650	18,726	14,494	19,181	17,229
91,650	91,700	18,740	14,506	19,195	17,241
91,700	91,750	18,754	14,519	19,209	17,254
91,750	91,800	18,768	14,531	19,223	17,266
91,800	91,850	18,782	14,544	19,237	17,279
91,850	91,900	18,796	14,556	19,251	17,291
91,900	91,950	18,810	14,569	19,265	17,304
91,950	92,000	18,824	14,581	19,279	17,316

92,000

At least	But less than	Single	Married filing jointly *	Married filing separately	Head of a household
92,000	92,050	18,838	14,594	19,293	17,329
92,050	92,100	18,852	14,606	19,307	17,341
92,100	92,150	18,866	14,619	19,321	17,354
92,150	92,200	18,880	14,631	19,335	17,366
92,200	92,250	18,894	14,644	19,349	17,379
92,250	92,300	18,908	14,656	19,363	17,391
92,300	92,350	18,922	14,669	19,377	17,404
92,350	92,400	18,936	14,681	19,391	17,416
92,400	92,450	18,950	14,694	19,405	17,429
92,450	92,500	18,964	14,706	19,419	17,441
92,500	92,550	18,978	14,719	19,433	17,454
92,550	92,600	18,992	14,731	19,447	17,466
92,600	92,650	19,006	14,744	19,461	17,479
92,650	92,700	19,020	14,756	19,475	17,491
92,700	92,750	19,034	14,769	19,489	17,504
92,750	92,800	19,048	14,781	19,503	17,516
92,800	92,850	19,062	14,794	19,517	17,529
92,850	92,900	19,076	14,806	19,531	17,541
92,900	92,950	19,090	14,819	19,545	17,554
92,950	93,000	19,104	14,831	19,559	17,566

* This column must also be used by a qualifying widow(er).

(Continued)

2015 Tax Table—Individuals *Continued*

93,000

| If line 43 (taxable income) is— | | And you are— | | | | |
| At least | But less than | Single | Married filing jointly * | Married filing separately | Head of a household |
		Your tax is—			
93,000	93,050	19,118	14,844	19,573	17,579
93,050	93,100	19,132	14,856	19,587	17,591
93,100	93,150	19,146	14,869	19,601	17,604
93,150	93,200	19,160	14,881	19,615	17,616
93,200	93,250	19,174	14,894	19,629	17,629
93,250	93,300	19,188	14,906	19,643	17,641
93,300	93,350	19,202	14,919	19,657	17,654
93,350	93,400	19,216	14,931	19,671	17,666
93,400	93,450	19,230	14,944	19,685	17,679
93,450	93,500	19,244	14,956	19,699	17,691
93,500	93,550	19,258	14,969	19,713	17,704
93,550	93,600	19,272	14,981	19,727	17,716
93,600	93,650	19,286	14,994	19,741	17,729
93,650	93,700	19,300	15,006	19,755	17,741
93,700	93,750	19,314	15,019	19,769	17,754
93,750	93,800	19,328	15,031	19,783	17,766
93,800	93,850	19,342	15,044	19,797	17,779
93,850	93,900	19,356	15,056	19,811	17,791
93,900	93,950	19,370	15,069	19,825	17,804
93,950	94,000	19,384	15,081	19,839	17,816

94,000

At least	But less than	Single	Married filing jointly *	Married filing separately	Head of a household
94,000	94,050	19,398	15,094	19,853	17,829
94,050	94,100	19,412	15,106	19,867	17,841
94,100	94,150	19,426	15,119	19,881	17,854
94,150	94,200	19,440	15,131	19,895	17,866
94,200	94,250	19,454	15,144	19,909	17,879
94,250	94,300	19,468	15,156	19,923	17,891
94,300	94,350	19,482	15,169	19,937	17,904
94,350	94,400	19,496	15,181	19,951	17,916
94,400	94,450	19,510	15,194	19,965	17,929
94,450	94,500	19,524	15,206	19,979	17,941
94,500	94,550	19,538	15,219	19,993	17,954
94,550	94,600	19,552	15,231	20,007	17,966
94,600	94,650	19,566	15,244	20,021	17,979
94,650	94,700	19,580	15,256	20,035	17,991
94,700	94,750	19,594	15,269	20,049	18,004
94,750	94,800	19,608	15,281	20,063	18,016
94,800	94,850	19,622	15,294	20,077	18,029
94,850	94,900	19,636	15,306	20,091	18,041
94,900	94,950	19,650	15,319	20,105	18,054
94,950	95,000	19,664	15,331	20,119	18,066

95,000

At least	But less than	Single	Married filing jointly *	Married filing separately	Head of a household
95,000	95,050	19,678	15,344	20,133	18,079
95,050	95,100	19,692	15,356	20,147	18,091
95,100	95,150	19,706	15,369	20,161	18,104
95,150	95,200	19,720	15,381	20,175	18,116
95,200	95,250	19,734	15,394	20,189	18,129
95,250	95,300	19,748	15,406	20,203	18,141
95,300	95,350	19,762	15,419	20,217	18,154
95,350	95,400	19,776	15,431	20,231	18,166
95,400	95,450	19,790	15,444	20,245	18,179
95,450	95,500	19,804	15,456	20,259	18,191
95,500	95,550	19,818	15,469	20,273	18,204
95,550	95,600	19,832	15,481	20,287	18,216
95,600	95,650	19,846	15,494	20,301	18,229
95,650	95,700	19,860	15,506	20,315	18,241
95,700	95,750	19,874	15,519	20,329	18,254
95,750	95,800	19,888	15,531	20,343	18,266
95,800	95,850	19,902	15,544	20,357	18,279
95,850	95,900	19,916	15,556	20,371	18,291
95,900	95,950	19,930	15,569	20,385	18,304
95,950	96,000	19,944	15,581	20,399	18,316

96,000

At least	But less than	Single	Married filing jointly *	Married filing separately	Head of a household
96,000	96,050	19,958	15,594	20,413	18,329
96,050	96,100	19,972	15,606	20,427	18,341
96,100	96,150	19,986	15,619	20,441	18,354
96,150	96,200	20,000	15,631	20,455	18,366
96,200	96,250	20,014	15,644	20,469	18,379
96,250	96,300	20,028	15,656	20,483	18,391
96,300	96,350	20,042	15,669	20,497	18,404
96,350	96,400	20,056	15,681	20,511	18,416
96,400	96,450	20,070	15,694	20,525	18,429
96,450	96,500	20,084	15,706	20,539	18,441
96,500	96,550	20,098	15,719	20,553	18,454
96,550	96,600	20,112	15,731	20,567	18,466
96,600	96,650	20,126	15,744	20,581	18,479
96,650	96,700	20,140	15,756	20,595	18,491
96,700	96,750	20,154	15,769	20,609	18,504
96,750	96,800	20,168	15,781	20,623	18,516
96,800	96,850	20,182	15,794	20,637	18,529
96,850	96,900	20,196	15,806	20,651	18,541
96,900	96,950	20,210	15,819	20,665	18,554
96,950	97,000	20,224	15,831	20,679	18,566

97,000

At least	But less than	Single	Married filing jointly *	Married filing separately	Head of a household
97,000	97,050	20,238	15,844	20,693	18,579
97,050	97,100	20,252	15,856	20,707	18,591
97,100	97,150	20,266	15,869	20,721	18,604
97,150	97,200	20,280	15,881	20,735	18,616
97,200	97,250	20,294	15,894	20,749	18,629
97,250	97,300	20,308	15,906	20,763	18,641
97,300	97,350	20,322	15,919	20,777	18,654
97,350	97,400	20,336	15,931	20,791	18,666
97,400	97,450	20,350	15,944	20,805	18,679
97,450	97,500	20,364	15,956	20,819	18,691
97,500	97,550	20,378	15,969	20,833	18,704
97,550	97,600	20,392	15,981	20,847	18,716
97,600	97,650	20,406	15,994	20,861	18,729
97,650	97,700	20,420	16,006	20,875	18,741
97,700	97,750	20,434	16,019	20,889	18,754
97,750	97,800	20,448	16,031	20,903	18,766
97,800	97,850	20,462	16,044	20,917	18,779
97,850	97,900	20,476	16,056	20,931	18,791
97,900	97,950	20,490	16,069	20,945	18,804
97,950	98,000	20,504	16,081	20,959	18,816

98,000

At least	But less than	Single	Married filing jointly *	Married filing separately	Head of a household
98,000	98,050	20,518	16,094	20,973	18,829
98,050	98,100	20,532	16,106	20,987	18,841
98,100	98,150	20,546	16,119	21,001	18,854
98,150	98,200	20,560	16,131	21,015	18,866
98,200	98,250	20,574	16,144	21,029	18,879
98,250	98,300	20,588	16,156	21,043	18,891
98,300	98,350	20,602	16,169	21,057	18,904
98,350	98,400	20,616	16,181	21,071	18,916
98,400	98,450	20,630	16,194	21,085	18,929
98,450	98,500	20,644	16,206	21,099	18,941
98,500	98,550	20,658	16,219	21,113	18,954
98,550	98,600	20,672	16,231	21,127	18,966
98,600	98,650	20,686	16,244	21,141	18,979
98,650	98,700	20,700	16,256	21,155	18,991
98,700	98,750	20,714	16,269	21,169	19,004
98,750	98,800	20,728	16,281	21,183	19,016
98,800	98,850	20,742	16,294	21,197	19,029
98,850	98,900	20,756	16,306	21,211	19,041
98,900	98,950	20,770	16,319	21,225	19,054
98,950	99,000	20,784	16,331	21,239	19,066

99,000

At least	But less than	Single	Married filing jointly *	Married filing separately	Head of a household
99,000	99,050	20,798	16,344	21,253	19,079
99,050	99,100	20,812	16,356	21,267	19,091
99,100	99,150	20,826	16,369	21,281	19,104
99,150	99,200	20,840	16,381	21,295	19,116
99,200	99,250	20,854	16,394	21,309	19,129
99,250	99,300	20,868	16,406	21,323	19,141
99,300	99,350	20,882	16,419	21,337	19,154
99,350	99,400	20,896	16,431	21,351	19,166
99,400	99,450	20,910	16,444	21,365	19,179
99,450	99,500	20,924	16,456	21,379	19,191
99,500	99,550	20,938	16,469	21,393	19,204
99,550	99,600	20,952	16,481	21,407	19,216
99,600	99,650	20,966	16,494	21,421	19,229
99,650	99,700	20,980	16,506	21,435	19,241
99,700	99,750	20,994	16,519	21,449	19,254
99,750	99,800	21,008	16,531	21,463	19,266
99,800	99,850	21,022	16,544	21,477	19,279
99,850	99,900	21,036	16,556	21,491	19,291
99,900	99,950	21,050	16,569	21,505	19,304
99,950	100,000	21,064	16,581	21,519	19,316

$100,000
or over
use the Tax
Computation
Worksheet

* This column must also be used by a qualifying widow(er).

Income Tax Rates—Estates and Trusts

Tax Year 2015

Taxable Income		The Tax Is:	Of the Amount
Over—	But not Over—		Over—
$ 0	$ 2,500	15%	$ 0
2,500	5,900	$ 375.00 + 25%	2,500
5,900	9,050	1,225.00 + 28%	5,900
9,050	12,300	2,107.00 + 33%	9,050
12,300	....	3,179.50 + 39.6%	12,300

Tax Year 2016

Taxable Income		The Tax Is:	Of the Amount
Over—	But not Over—		Over—
$ 0	$ 2,550	15%	$ 0
2,550	5,950	$ 382.50 + 25%	2,550
5,950	9,050	1,232.50 + 28%	5,950
9,050	12,400	2,100.50 + 33%	9,050
12,400	....	3,206.00 + 39.6%	12,400

Income Tax Rates—Corporations

Taxable Income		The Tax Is:	Of the Amount
Over—	But not Over—		Over—
$ 0	$ 50,000	15%	$ 0
50,000	75,000	$ 7,500 + 25%	50,000
75,000	100,000	13,750 + 34%	75,000
100,000	335,000	22,250 + 39%	100,000
335,000	10,000,000	113,900 + 34%	335,000
10,000,000	15,000,000	3,400,000 + 35%	10,000,000
15,000,000	18,333,333	5,150,000 + 38%	15,000,000
18,333,333	....	35%	0

Unified Transfer Tax Rates

For Gifts Made and for Deaths in 2011–2012

If the Amount with Respect to Which the Tentative Tax to Be Computed Is:	The Tentative Tax Is:
Not over $10,000	18 percent of such amount.
Over $10,000 but not over $20,000	$1,800, plus 20 percent of the excess of such amount over $10,000.
Over $20,000 but not over $40,000	$3,800, plus 22 percent of the excess of such amount over $20,000.
Over $40,000 but not over $60,000	$8,200, plus 24 percent of the excess of such amount over $40,000.
Over $60,000 but not over $80,000	$13,000, plus 26 percent of the excess of such amount over $60,000.
Over $80,000 but not over $100,000	$18,200, plus 28 percent of the excess of such amount over $80,000.
Over $100,000 but not over $150,000	$23,800, plus 30 percent of the excess of such amount over $100,000.
Over $150,000 but not over $250,000	$38,800, plus 32 percent of the excess of such amount over $150,000.
Over $250,000 but not over $500,000	$70,800, plus 34 percent of the excess of such amount over $250,000.
Over $500,000	$155,800, plus 35 percent of the excess of such amount over $500,000.

Unified Transfer Tax Rates

For Gifts Made and for Deaths after 2012

If the Amount with Respect to Which the Tentative Tax to Be Computed Is:	The Tentative Tax Is:
Not over $10,000	18 percent of such amount.
Over $10,000 but not over $20,000	$1,800, plus 20 percent of the excess of such amount over $10,000.
Over $20,000 but not over $40,000	$3,800, plus 22 percent of the excess of such amount over $20,000.
Over $40,000 but not over $60,000	$8,200, plus 24 percent of the excess of such amount over $40,000.
Over $60,000 but not over $80,000	$13,000, plus 26 percent of the excess of such amount over $60,000.
Over $80,000 but not over $100,000	$18,200, plus 28 percent of the excess of such amount over $80,000.
Over $100,000 but not over $150,000	$23,800, plus 30 percent of the excess of such amount over $100,000.
Over $150,000 but not over $250,000	$38,800, plus 32 percent of the excess of such amount over $150,000.
Over $250,000 but not over $500,000	$70,800, plus 34 percent of the excess of such amount over $250,000.
Over $500,000 but not over $750,000	$155,800, plus 37 percent of the excess of such amount over $500,000.
Over $750,000 but not over $1,000,000	$248,300, plus 39 percent of the excess of such amount over $750,000.
Over $1,000,000	$345,800, plus 40 percent of the excess of such amount over $1,000,000.

2015 OPTIONAL SALES TAX TABLES

When Used

The election to deduct state and local general sales taxes requires that the taxpayer forgo any deduction for state and local income taxes. Whether this is advisable or not depends on a comparison of the amounts involved. In making the choice, however, the outcome could be influenced by the additional sales tax incurred due to certain "big ticket" purchases that were made. For example, a taxpayer who chose to deduct state and local income taxes for 2014 might well prefer the sales tax deduction in 2015 if a new boat was purchased or home improvements were made during the year. To make the sales tax election, the taxpayer must enter the amount on Schedule A, line 5, and check box b.

If the sales tax election is made, the amount of the deduction can be determined by use of the *actual expense method* or the *optional sales tax tables* issued by the IRS. The actual expense method can be used only when the taxpayer has actual receipts to support the deduction claimed. In the absence of receipts, the usual case with most taxpayers, resorting to the optional sales tax tables is necessary. Under neither method, however, is the purchase of items used in a taxpayer's trade or business to be considered.

Adjustments Necessary

The optional sales tax tables are based on a number of assumptions that require adjustments to be made. As the starting point for the use of the tables is AGI, nontaxable receipts have not been included. Examples of receipts that should be added include: tax-exempt interest, veterans' benefits, nontaxable combat pay, public assistance payments, workers' compensation, nontaxable Social Security, and other retirement benefits. They do not include any large nontaxable items that are not likely to be spent. For example, a $100,000 inheritance should not be added if it was invested in a certificate of deposit.

The tables represent the sales tax on the average (and recurring) expenditures based on level of income by family size and do not include exceptional purchases. Therefore, add to the table amount any sales taxes on major purchases (such as motor vehicles, aircraft, boats, and home building materials, etc.).

When the optional sales tax tables are utilized, special adjustments may be needed when a taxpayer has lived in more than one taxing jurisdiction (e.g., state, county, city) during the year. The adjustments involve apportionment of taxes based on days involved and are illustrated in Instructions for Schedule A (Form 1040), pages A-3 to A-6.

Local Sales Taxes

Local sales taxes (i.e., those imposed by counties, cities, transit authorities) may or may not require a separate determination. In those states where they are not imposed, no further computations are necessary. This is also the case where the local taxes are uniform and are incorporated into the state sales tax table. In other situations, another step is necessary to arrive at the optional sales tax table deduction. Depending on where the taxpayer lives, one of two procedures needs to be used. In one procedure, the local sales tax is arrived at by using the **state table** amount—see Example 1 and the related worksheet. In the other procedure, special **local tables** issued by the IRS for specified state and local jurisdictions are modified (if necessary) and used—see Example 2 and the related worksheet.

Use Illustrated

EXAMPLE 1 The Archers file a joint return for 2015 reflecting AGI of $88,000 and claiming three exemptions. They have tax-exempt interest of $3,000, and during the year they incurred sales tax of $1,650 on the purchase of an automobile for their dependent teenage son. They live in Bellaire, Texas, where the general sales tax rates are 6.25% for state and 2% for local. Since the IRS *has not issued* optional local sales tax tables for Texas, use the Worksheet below to arrive at the Archers' general sales tax deduction of $3,025.

Sales Tax Deduction Worksheet
(To be used when *no* IRS Optional Local Sales Tax Table Available)

Adjusted Gross Income (AGI) as listed on line 38 of Form 1040		$88,000
Add nontaxable items		3,000
Table income to be used for purposes of line 1 below		$91,000
1. Use table income to determine table amount—go to state of residence and find applicable range of table income and exemption column* for *state* sales tax		$ 1,042
2a. Enter local general sales tax rate	2.00	
2b. Enter state general sales tax rate	6.25	
2c. Divide 2a by 2b	0.32	
2d. Multiply line 1 by line 2c for the local sales tax		333
3. Enter general sales tax on large purchases		1,650
4. Deduction for general sales tax (add lines 1 + 2d + 3) and report on line 5 of Schedule A of Form 1040		$ 3,025

*Use total of personal and dependency exemptions as reported in item 6d of Form 1040.

EXAMPLE 2 The Hardys file a joint return for 2015, reporting AGI of $42,000 and claiming four exemptions (two personal and two dependency). They received $30,000 in nontaxable pension benefits. Although the Hardys do not keep sales tax receipts, they can prove that they paid $4,800 in sales tax on the purchase of a new boat in 2015. The Hardys are residents of Georgia and live in a jurisdiction that imposes a 2% local sales tax. Since the IRS *has issued* optional local sales tax tables for Georgia, use the Worksheet below to arrive at the Hardys' general sales tax deduction of $5,647.

Sales Tax Deduction Worksheet
(To be used for Alaska, Arizona, Arkansas,
Colorado, Georgia, Illinois, Louisiana, Missouri, New York,
North Carolina, South Carolina, Tennessee, Utah, and Virginia)

Adjusted Gross Income (AGI) as listed on line 38 of Form 1040		$42,000
Add nontaxable income		30,000
Table income to be used for purposes of line 1 below		$72,000
1. Use the table income to determine *state* sales tax amount—go to table for state of residence and find applicable income range and exemption column*		$ 523
2a. Enter local general sales tax rate	2.0	
2b. Enter IRS *local* sales tax table amount (based on a 1% tax rate)	$162	
2c. Multiply line 2b by 2a for the local sales tax		324
3. Enter general sales tax on large purchases		4,800
4. Deduction for general sales tax (add lines 1 + 2c + 3) and report on line 5 of Schedule A of Form 1040		$ 5,647

*Use total of personal and dependency exemptions as reported in item 6d of Form 1040.

2015 Optional State Sales Tax Tables (State Sales Tax Rate Shown Next to State Name)

Alabama (1, 4.0000%) — Arizona (2, 5.6000%) — Arkansas (2, 6.5000%)

Income At least	But less than	Alabama 1	2	3	4	5	Over 5	Arizona 1	2	3	4	5	Over 5	Arkansas 1	2	3	4	5	Over 5
$0	$20,000	215	255	284	306	325	352	198	220	234	245	254	267	283	318	340	358	372	392
$20,000	$30,000	318	376	417	449	476	514	333	369	393	412	427	448	458	514	551	579	602	634
$30,000	$40,000	372	439	485	522	553	597	409	453	482	505	523	549	554	621	665	699	727	766
$40,000	$50,000	418	492	544	585	619	668	477	528	562	588	610	640	639	716	767	806	838	883
$50,000	$60,000	459	540	596	641	678	732	540	597	635	665	689	723	715	802	859	902	938	988
$60,000	$70,000	496	583	643	691	731	788	597	661	703	735	762	799	786	880	943	991	1030	1085
$70,000	$80,000	531	622	686	737	780	840	651	720	766	802	831	871	851	954	1022	1074	1116	1176
$80,000	$90,000	563	659	726	780	825	889	702	777	826	864	896	939	913	1023	1095	1151	1197	1261
$90,000	$100,000	593	694	764	820	867	934	751	831	883	924	958	1004	971	1088	1165	1225	1273	1341
$100,000	$120,000	633	739	814	873	923	994	817	903	961	1005	1041	1092	1050	1176	1260	1324	1376	1449
$120,000	$140,000	685	799	879	942	996	1072	905	1000	1063	1112	1152	1208	1153	1292	1384	1454	1512	1592
$140,000	$160,000	733	854	939	1006	1063	1144	988	1091	1160	1214	1257	1318	1251	1401	1500	1576	1639	1726
$160,000	$180,000	778	906	995	1066	1125	1210	1066	1177	1252	1309	1356	1422	1341	1502	1609	1691	1758	1851
$180,000	$200,000	820	954	1047	1121	1184	1273	1140	1259	1339	1400	1451	1521	1428	1599	1713	1800	1871	1971
$200,000	$225,000	865	1004	1102	1179	1245	1338	1219	1346	1431	1497	1550	1625	1519	1701	1822	1914	1990	2096
$225,000	$250,000	912	1058	1160	1242	1310	1407	1305	1441	1531	1601	1659	1739	1617	1811	1940	2038	2119	2231
$250,000	$275,000	957	1109	1215	1300	1371	1473	1387	1531	1627	1701	1762	1847	1711	1916	2052	2156	2241	2360
$275,000	$300,000	999	1157	1268	1356	1430	1535	1466	1618	1720	1798	1862	1952	1801	2016	2159	2269	2359	2484
$300,000	or more	1254	1445	1579	1685	1775	1903	1951	2152	2286	2390	2475	2594	2345	2625	2811	2953	3070	3233

California (3, 7.5000%) — Colorado (2, 2.9000%) — Connecticut (4, 6.3500%)

Income At least	But less than	California 1	2	3	4	5	Over 5	Colorado 1	2	3	4	5	Over 5	Connecticut 1	2	3	4	5	Over 5
$0	$20,000	271	298	316	329	340	356	104	115	122	127	132	138	247	272	289	301	311	325
$20,000	$30,000	446	489	518	540	558	583	167	184	195	204	211	220	406	447	474	494	511	533
$30,000	$40,000	543	595	630	656	678	708	202	222	235	245	253	265	493	543	576	601	621	649
$40,000	$50,000	629	689	729	760	785	819	232	255	270	281	291	304	570	628	666	695	718	751
$50,000	$60,000	707	775	820	854	882	921	259	285	301	314	325	340	641	706	749	781	808	844
$60,000	$70,000	780	854	903	940	971	1014	285	312	330	345	356	372	706	778	825	860	889	929
$70,000	$80,000	847	927	980	1021	1054	1100	308	338	358	373	385	402	766	845	896	934	966	1009
$80,000	$90,000	911	997	1054	1097	1133	1182	330	362	383	399	412	431	824	908	963	1004	1038	1085
$90,000	$100,000	972	1063	1123	1170	1208	1260	351	385	407	424	438	458	878	968	1026	1070	1107	1156
$100,000	$120,000	1054	1152	1217	1267	1308	1365	380	415	439	458	473	494	951	1048	1112	1160	1199	1253
$120,000	$140,000	1162	1270	1341	1396	1441	1504	417	456	482	502	518	541	1047	1155	1225	1278	1321	1380
$140,000	$160,000	1264	1381	1458	1518	1567	1634	452	494	522	543	561	586	1138	1255	1331	1389	1436	1501
$160,000	$180,000	1359	1485	1568	1632	1684	1756	485	529	559	582	601	627	1224	1349	1431	1493	1543	1613
$180,000	$200,000	1451	1584	1673	1740	1796	1873	516	563	595	619	639	667	1305	1439	1526	1592	1646	1721
$200,000	$225,000	1547	1689	1783	1855	1914	1996	548	599	632	658	679	708	1391	1533	1626	1697	1755	1834
$225,000	$250,000	1651	1802	1902	1979	2042	2129	584	637	672	699	722	753	1483	1636	1735	1810	1872	1956
$250,000	$275,000	1751	1910	2016	2097	2164	2256	618	673	710	739	763	796	1571	1733	1838	1918	1983	2073
$275,000	$300,000	1847	2014	2126	2211	2281	2378	650	708	747	777	802	836	1656	1827	1938	2022	2091	2185
$300,000	or more	2431	2649	2793	2904	2995	3121	846	920	970	1008	1040	1083	2173	2398	2544	2654	2744	2869

District of Columbia (4, 5.7500%) — Florida (1, 6.0000%) — Georgia (2, 4.0000%)

Income At least	But less than	District of Columbia 1	2	3	4	5	Over 5	Florida 1	2	3	4	5	Over 5	Georgia 1	2	3	4	5	Over 5
$0	$20,000	168	181	190	197	203	211	230	253	268	280	289	302	143	158	169	176	183	192
$20,000	$30,000	279	302	316	328	337	350	381	418	443	462	477	499	231	255	271	284	294	308
$30,000	$40,000	341	369	387	400	412	427	464	510	540	563	582	608	279	308	327	342	354	372
$40,000	$50,000	397	428	449	465	478	496	539	591	626	653	674	704	321	355	377	394	408	427
$50,000	$60,000	448	483	506	524	539	559	607	666	705	735	759	793	360	397	422	440	456	478
$60,000	$70,000	494	533	559	579	595	618	669	734	777	810	837	874	396	436	463	483	500	524
$70,000	$80,000	538	580	608	630	647	672	728	799	845	881	910	950	429	472	501	523	542	567
$80,000	$90,000	579	625	655	678	697	723	783	859	909	947	979	1022	460	506	537	561	580	608
$90,000	$100,000	619	667	699	724	744	772	836	917	970	1011	1044	1090	489	538	571	596	617	646
$100,000	$120,000	672	725	759	786	808	838	907	994	1052	1096	1132	1182	529	582	617	644	666	697
$120,000	$140,000	742	800	839	868	892	926	1001	1097	1160	1209	1249	1304	582	639	677	707	731	765
$140,000	$160,000	809	872	914	946	972	1008	1090	1194	1263	1316	1359	1419	631	693	734	766	793	829
$160,000	$180,000	871	939	984	1018	1046	1086	1173	1285	1359	1416	1462	1526	677	743	787	821	850	889
$180,000	$200,000	931	1003	1051	1088	1118	1160	1252	1372	1451	1511	1561	1629	721	791	838	874	904	945
$200,000	$225,000	994	1071	1122	1161	1193	1238	1336	1463	1547	1612	1664	1738	767	842	891	929	961	1005
$225,000	$250,000	1063	1145	1199	1241	1275	1322	1427	1562	1652	1721	1777	1855	817	896	949	989	1023	1069
$250,000	$275,000	1128	1215	1272	1316	1353	1403	1513	1657	1752	1825	1884	1967	865	948	1003	1046	1081	1131
$275,000	$300,000	1191	1282	1343	1390	1428	1481	1596	1748	1848	1925	1988	2075	911	998	1056	1101	1138	1189
$300,000	or more	1576	1696	1775	1837	1887	1956	2106	2304	2435	2536	2618	2732	1189	1300	1374	1432	1479	1545

Hawaii (1,6, 4.0000%) — Idaho (1, 6.0000%) — Illinois (2, 6.2500%)

Income At least	But less than	Hawaii 1	2	3	4	5	Over 5	Idaho 1	2	3	4	5	Over 5	Illinois 1	2	3	4	5	Over 5
$0	$20,000	241	280	306	327	344	367	321	381	422	454	481	520	230	257	275	290	302	319
$20,000	$30,000	373	433	473	504	530	567	482	568	627	674	713	769	364	405	433	455	473	500
$30,000	$40,000	444	514	562	599	629	672	566	665	734	788	834	898	437	485	518	544	565	596
$40,000	$50,000	505	585	638	680	715	764	639	749	826	886	937	1009	501	554	592	621	646	681
$50,000	$60,000	560	648	708	754	792	846	704	824	908	974	1029	1108	559	618	659	691	719	757
$60,000	$70,000	610	706	770	821	862	921	762	892	982	1053	1112	1197	612	675	720	755	785	827
$70,000	$80,000	656	759	828	882	927	990	816	954	1050	1125	1189	1279	661	729	777	815	846	891
$80,000	$90,000	699	808	882	940	987	1054	867	1012	1113	1193	1260	1355	708	779	830	870	904	951
$90,000	$100,000	740	855	933	994	1044	1115	914	1067	1172	1256	1326	1426	751	827	880	923	958	1008
$100,000	$120,000	794	918	1002	1067	1120	1196	978	1139	1251	1340	1415	1521	810	891	948	993	1031	1085
$120,000	$140,000	865	1000	1091	1161	1220	1302	1060	1234	1354	1450	1530	1644	887	975	1036	1085	1127	1185
$140,000	$160,000	932	1076	1174	1250	1313	1401	1137	1322	1450	1552	1637	1758	960	1053	1119	1172	1216	1279
$160,000	$180,000	994	1147	1251	1331	1398	1493	1209	1403	1539	1646	1736	1863	1028	1127	1197	1253	1299	1366
$180,000	$200,000	1052	1214	1324	1409	1480	1579	1276	1480	1622	1734	1829	1963	1092	1196	1270	1329	1379	1449
$200,000	$225,000	1113	1284	1400	1490	1565	1670	1347	1560	1709	1827	1926	2067	1160	1269	1347	1409	1461	1536
$225,000	$250,000	1179	1360	1482	1577	1656	1767	1422	1646	1802	1926	2030	2177	1233	1348	1430	1496	1551	1629
$250,000	$275,000	1241	1431	1560	1660	1743	1859	1494	1727	1890	2019	2128	2282	1302	1423	1509	1578	1635	1718
$275,000	$300,000	1300	1499	1634	1738	1825	1947	1562	1805	1974	2109	2221	2382	1369	1495	1585	1656	1717	1803
$300,000	or more	1655	1907	2076	2209	2318	2472	1969	2266	2473	2637	2775	2971	1772	1928	2040	2130	2205	2313

(Continued)

2015 Optional State Sales Tax Tables *(Continued)*

Indiana — 7.0000%

Income At least	But less than	1	2	3	4	5	Over 5
$0	$20,000	271	301	320	335	347	364
$20,000	$30,000	429	476	506	530	549	575
$30,000	$40,000	514	570	607	635	657	689
$40,000	$50,000	589	652	694	726	752	788
$50,000	$60,000	656	727	774	809	838	878
$60,000	$70,000	718	795	846	885	916	960
$70,000	$80,000	775	858	913	955	989	1036
$80,000	$90,000	828	918	976	1020	1057	1107
$90,000	$100,000	879	974	1035	1082	1121	1174
$100,000	$120,000	947	1049	1115	1166	1207	1264
$120,000	$140,000	1036	1147	1220	1275	1320	1383
$140,000	$160,000	1120	1239	1318	1377	1426	1494
$160,000	$180,000	1198	1325	1409	1472	1524	1597
$180,000	$200,000	1272	1407	1495	1563	1618	1694
$200,000	$225,000	1349	1492	1586	1658	1716	1797
$225,000	$250,000	1433	1585	1684	1760	1822	1907
$250,000	$275,000	1512	1672	1777	1857	1922	2012
$275,000	$300,000	1588	1756	1866	1949	2018	2113
$300,000	or more	2045	2260	2400	2508	2595	2716

Iowa — 6.0000%

Income At least	But less than	1	2	3	4	5	Over 5
$0	$20,000	237	263	280	294	305	320
$20,000	$30,000	392	436	465	488	506	531
$30,000	$40,000	479	533	568	596	618	649
$40,000	$50,000	556	619	660	692	717	753
$50,000	$60,000	626	697	744	779	809	849
$60,000	$70,000	691	769	821	860	893	937
$70,000	$80,000	751	837	893	936	971	1020
$80,000	$90,000	809	901	961	1008	1046	1098
$90,000	$100,000	863	962	1026	1076	1116	1172
$100,000	$120,000	936	1044	1114	1168	1212	1273
$120,000	$140,000	1034	1152	1230	1289	1338	1405
$140,000	$160,000	1126	1255	1340	1404	1457	1531
$160,000	$180,000	1212	1351	1442	1512	1569	1648
$180,000	$200,000	1294	1443	1541	1615	1676	1761
$200,000	$225,000	1381	1540	1644	1724	1789	1880
$225,000	$250,000	1475	1645	1757	1842	1912	2008
$250,000	$275,000	1565	1745	1864	1954	2028	2131
$275,000	$300,000	1651	1842	1967	2063	2141	2249
$300,000	or more	2180	2432	2598	2725	2829	2972

Kansas — 6.3264%

Income At least	But less than	1	2	3	4	5	Over 5
$0	$20,000	357	422	467	503	532	574
$20,000	$30,000	542	639	706	759	803	865
$30,000	$40,000	639	753	831	893	944	1018
$40,000	$50,000	722	850	939	1008	1066	1149
$50,000	$60,000	797	938	1035	1111	1175	1265
$60,000	$70,000	865	1017	1122	1204	1273	1371
$70,000	$80,000	927	1090	1202	1290	1364	1468
$80,000	$90,000	985	1158	1276	1370	1448	1559
$90,000	$100,000	1040	1221	1346	1445	1527	1644
$100,000	$120,000	1113	1306	1440	1545	1632	1757
$120,000	$140,000	1208	1417	1561	1675	1770	1904
$140,000	$160,000	1296	1520	1674	1796	1897	2041
$160,000	$180,000	1378	1615	1779	1907	2015	2167
$180,000	$200,000	1455	1705	1877	2013	2126	2287
$200,000	$225,000	1536	1799	1980	2123	2242	2411
$225,000	$250,000	1622	1900	2090	2241	2366	2544
$250,000	$275,000	1704	1994	2194	2352	2483	2670
$275,000	$300,000	1782	2085	2294	2458	2595	2790
$300,000	or more	2245	2622	2882	3086	3257	3500

Kentucky — 6.0000%

Income At least	But less than	1	2	3	4	5	Over 5
$0	$20,000	220	243	259	271	281	295
$20,000	$30,000	355	392	417	436	451	473
$30,000	$40,000	429	473	503	526	544	570
$40,000	$50,000	494	545	579	605	626	656
$50,000	$60,000	554	610	648	676	700	733
$60,000	$70,000	608	670	711	742	768	804
$70,000	$80,000	659	725	769	803	831	870
$80,000	$90,000	707	778	825	861	891	932
$90,000	$100,000	752	827	877	915	947	991
$100,000	$120,000	813	894	947	989	1023	1070
$120,000	$140,000	894	982	1040	1085	1123	1174
$140,000	$160,000	969	1064	1127	1176	1216	1272
$160,000	$180,000	1040	1141	1209	1261	1304	1363
$180,000	$200,000	1108	1215	1287	1342	1387	1450
$200,000	$225,000	1179	1292	1368	1427	1475	1542
$225,000	$250,000	1256	1376	1456	1518	1569	1640
$250,000	$275,000	1329	1455	1540	1605	1659	1734
$275,000	$300,000	1399	1532	1621	1689	1746	1824
$300,000	or more	1825	1995	2109	2197	2269	2369

Louisiana — 4.0000%

Income At least	But less than	1	2	3	4	5	Over 5
$0	$20,000	155	170	180	188	194	202
$20,000	$30,000	257	282	298	310	320	334
$30,000	$40,000	314	343	363	378	390	407
$40,000	$50,000	364	398	421	438	452	472
$50,000	$60,000	410	449	474	493	509	531
$60,000	$70,000	452	495	523	544	561	585
$70,000	$80,000	492	538	568	591	610	636
$80,000	$90,000	529	579	611	636	657	685
$90,000	$100,000	565	618	652	679	700	730
$100,000	$120,000	613	670	708	736	760	792
$120,000	$140,000	676	739	781	812	838	874
$140,000	$160,000	736	805	850	884	912	951
$160,000	$180,000	793	866	914	951	981	1023
$180,000	$200,000	846	925	976	1015	1047	1092
$200,000	$225,000	903	986	1041	1083	1117	1165
$225,000	$250,000	964	1053	1112	1156	1193	1243
$250,000	$275,000	1023	1117	1179	1226	1265	1318
$275,000	$300,000	1079	1178	1244	1294	1334	1391
$300,000	or more	1424	1554	1639	1705	1758	1832

Maine — 5.5000%

Income At least	But less than	1	2	3	4	5	Over 5
$0	$20,000	164	178	188	195	201	209
$20,000	$30,000	271	293	308	319	328	341
$30,000	$40,000	329	356	374	388	399	414
$40,000	$50,000	382	412	433	449	461	479
$50,000	$60,000	429	464	487	504	518	538
$60,000	$70,000	473	511	536	555	571	592
$70,000	$80,000	514	555	582	603	620	643
$80,000	$90,000	553	596	625	648	666	691
$90,000	$100,000	590	636	667	690	710	736
$100,000	$120,000	639	689	722	748	769	798
$120,000	$140,000	705	760	796	824	847	878
$140,000	$160,000	767	826	865	895	920	955
$160,000	$180,000	825	888	930	962	989	1026
$180,000	$200,000	880	948	992	1027	1055	1094
$200,000	$225,000	939	1010	1058	1094	1124	1166
$225,000	$250,000	1002	1078	1128	1167	1199	1243
$250,000	$275,000	1063	1143	1196	1237	1270	1317
$275,000	$300,000	1121	1205	1261	1304	1339	1388
$300,000	or more	1476	1584	1656	1712	1758	1821

Maryland — 6.0000%

Income At least	But less than	1	2	3	4	5	Over 5
$0	$20,000	203	226	241	254	264	279
$20,000	$30,000	333	368	393	413	429	452
$30,000	$40,000	404	447	476	500	520	547
$40,000	$50,000	467	516	550	577	599	631
$50,000	$60,000	525	579	617	647	672	708
$60,000	$70,000	578	637	679	712	739	778
$70,000	$80,000	628	691	736	772	801	843
$80,000	$90,000	675	743	790	828	860	905
$90,000	$100,000	719	791	842	882	916	964
$100,000	$120,000	779	856	911	954	991	1042
$120,000	$140,000	858	943	1002	1050	1090	1146
$140,000	$160,000	933	1024	1089	1140	1183	1244
$160,000	$180,000	1003	1100	1169	1224	1270	1335
$180,000	$200,000	1070	1173	1246	1304	1353	1422
$200,000	$225,000	1140	1249	1327	1388	1440	1514
$225,000	$250,000	1216	1332	1414	1480	1535	1613
$250,000	$275,000	1289	1411	1498	1567	1625	1707
$275,000	$300,000	1359	1487	1578	1650	1711	1797
$300,000	or more	1785	1949	2065	2158	2237	2348

Massachusetts — 6.2500%

Income At least	But less than	1	2	3	4	5	Over 5
$0	$20,000	195	210	219	227	233	241
$20,000	$30,000	312	335	350	361	371	384
$30,000	$40,000	375	402	420	434	445	460
$40,000	$50,000	431	462	482	498	510	528
$50,000	$60,000	482	516	538	556	570	589
$60,000	$70,000	528	565	590	608	624	645
$70,000	$80,000	571	611	638	658	674	697
$80,000	$90,000	611	654	682	704	721	746
$90,000	$100,000	650	695	725	747	766	792
$100,000	$120,000	701	750	782	806	826	853
$120,000	$140,000	769	822	857	883	905	935
$140,000	$160,000	833	890	927	955	979	1011
$160,000	$180,000	892	953	992	1023	1048	1082
$180,000	$200,000	949	1013	1055	1087	1113	1150
$200,000	$225,000	1008	1076	1120	1154	1182	1220
$225,000	$250,000	1072	1144	1191	1227	1256	1297
$250,000	$275,000	1133	1208	1258	1296	1327	1369
$275,000	$300,000	1192	1271	1322	1362	1394	1439
$300,000	or more	1546	1646	1711	1762	1803	1860

Michigan — 6.0000%

Income At least	But less than	1	2	3	4	5	Over 5
$0	$20,000	212	235	249	261	270	283
$20,000	$30,000	341	376	399	416	431	451
$30,000	$40,000	411	452	480	501	518	542
$40,000	$50,000	473	520	551	575	595	622
$50,000	$60,000	529	581	616	643	665	695
$60,000	$70,000	581	637	675	704	728	761
$70,000	$80,000	629	690	730	762	787	823
$80,000	$90,000	674	739	782	816	843	881
$90,000	$100,000	717	786	831	867	896	936
$100,000	$120,000	774	848	897	935	966	1010
$120,000	$140,000	850	930	984	1025	1059	1107
$140,000	$160,000	922	1008	1066	1110	1147	1198
$160,000	$180,000	988	1080	1142	1189	1228	1283
$180,000	$200,000	1052	1149	1214	1264	1306	1363
$200,000	$225,000	1118	1222	1290	1343	1387	1448
$225,000	$250,000	1191	1300	1373	1429	1475	1540
$250,000	$275,000	1259	1374	1451	1510	1559	1627
$275,000	$300,000	1325	1445	1526	1588	1639	1710
$300,000	or more	1725	1878	1980	2059	2124	2215

Minnesota — 6.8750%

Income At least	But less than	1	2	3	4	5	Over 5
$0	$20,000	243	261	272	281	288	298
$20,000	$30,000	399	429	448	463	475	491
$30,000	$40,000	485	522	546	563	578	597
$40,000	$50,000	562	605	632	653	669	692
$50,000	$60,000	632	680	711	734	753	778
$60,000	$70,000	696	749	783	809	830	858
$70,000	$80,000	756	814	851	879	901	932
$80,000	$90,000	813	875	915	945	969	1002
$90,000	$100,000	866	933	976	1008	1034	1069
$100,000	$120,000	939	1011	1057	1092	1120	1159
$120,000	$140,000	1035	1114	1166	1204	1235	1278
$140,000	$160,000	1125	1212	1268	1310	1343	1390
$160,000	$180,000	1210	1303	1363	1408	1445	1495
$180,000	$200,000	1290	1390	1455	1503	1542	1595
$200,000	$225,000	1375	1482	1551	1602	1644	1701
$225,000	$250,000	1468	1582	1655	1710	1754	1815
$250,000	$275,000	1555	1676	1754	1812	1859	1924
$275,000	$300,000	1640	1768	1850	1911	1961	2029
$300,000	or more	2155	2324	2432	2513	2579	2669

Mississippi — 7.0000%

Income At least	But less than	1	2	3	4	5	Over 5
$0	$20,000	404	472	519	556	586	629
$20,000	$30,000	618	722	792	848	893	958
$30,000	$40,000	731	853	936	1001	1055	1131
$40,000	$50,000	829	967	1061	1134	1195	1281
$50,000	$60,000	917	1069	1172	1253	1320	1415
$60,000	$70,000	997	1161	1273	1361	1433	1536
$70,000	$80,000	1071	1247	1366	1460	1538	1648
$80,000	$90,000	1139	1326	1453	1553	1636	1752
$90,000	$100,000	1204	1401	1535	1640	1727	1850
$100,000	$120,000	1290	1501	1644	1756	1849	1981
$120,000	$140,000	1403	1631	1786	1908	2009	2151
$140,000	$160,000	1508	1752	1919	2049	2157	2310
$160,000	$180,000	1605	1864	2041	2179	2295	2457
$180,000	$200,000	1697	1971	2157	2303	2424	2595
$200,000	$225,000	1793	2082	2278	2432	2560	2740
$225,000	$250,000	1896	2200	2408	2570	2705	2895
$250,000	$275,000	1993	2313	2531	2701	2842	3042
$275,000	$300,000	2086	2420	2648	2826	2974	3182
$300,000	or more	2640	3059	3344	3567	3753	4014

Missouri — 4.2250%

Income At least	But less than	1	2	3	4	5	Over 5
$0	$20,000	158	180	195	206	216	230
$20,000	$30,000	256	290	314	332	348	369
$30,000	$40,000	309	351	379	401	420	445
$40,000	$50,000	357	404	437	462	483	512
$50,000	$60,000	400	453	489	517	540	573
$60,000	$70,000	440	497	537	567	593	629
$70,000	$80,000	476	539	581	614	642	681
$80,000	$90,000	511	578	623	659	688	730
$90,000	$100,000	544	615	663	701	732	776
$100,000	$120,000	589	665	716	757	791	838
$120,000	$140,000	647	730	787	831	868	920
$140,000	$160,000	702	792	853	901	941	997
$160,000	$180,000	754	850	915	966	1009	1069
$180,000	$200,000	803	905	974	1028	1074	1137
$200,000	$225,000	855	963	1036	1094	1142	1209
$225,000	$250,000	911	1025	1103	1164	1215	1287
$250,000	$275,000	964	1085	1167	1231	1285	1360
$275,000	$300,000	1015	1142	1228	1296	1352	1431
$300,000	or more	1327	1489	1600	1687	1759	1861

2015 Optional State Sales Tax Tables

Nebraska — 5.5000%

Income At least	But less than	1	2	3	4	5	Over 5
$0	$20,000	217	240	256	267	276	289
$20,000	$30,000	360	398	423	443	458	480
$30,000	$40,000	439	486	517	540	559	586
$40,000	$50,000	509	564	600	627	649	680
$50,000	$60,000	573	635	675	706	731	766
$60,000	$70,000	632	701	745	779	807	845
$70,000	$80,000	688	762	810	847	878	919
$80,000	$90,000	740	820	872	912	944	989
$90,000	$100,000	790	875	931	973	1008	1056
$100,000	$120,000	857	949	1010	1056	1094	1146
$120,000	$140,000	945	1048	1115	1166	1207	1265
$140,000	$160,000	1029	1141	1214	1269	1315	1378
$160,000	$180,000	1107	1228	1307	1366	1415	1483
$180,000	$200,000	1182	1311	1395	1459	1512	1584
$200,000	$225,000	1261	1399	1489	1557	1613	1690
$225,000	$250,000	1347	1494	1590	1663	1723	1805
$250,000	$275,000	1429	1585	1687	1764	1828	1915
$275,000	$300,000	1507	1672	1780	1862	1929	2021
$300,000	or more	1988	2206	2349	2457	2545	2668

Nevada — 6.8500%

Income At least	But less than	1	2	3	4	5	Over 5
$0	$20,000	248	274	292	305	316	332
$20,000	$30,000	395	435	462	483	500	523
$30,000	$40,000	475	523	554	579	599	627
$40,000	$50,000	545	599	635	663	686	717
$50,000	$60,000	608	668	708	739	764	799
$60,000	$70,000	666	732	775	808	836	874
$70,000	$80,000	721	790	837	873	902	943
$80,000	$90,000	771	846	895	933	965	1008
$90,000	$100,000	819	898	950	990	1024	1070
$100,000	$120,000	884	968	1024	1067	1103	1152
$120,000	$140,000	969	1060	1121	1168	1207	1261
$140,000	$160,000	1049	1147	1213	1263	1304	1362
$160,000	$180,000	1124	1228	1297	1351	1395	1457
$180,000	$200,000	1195	1305	1378	1435	1482	1547
$200,000	$225,000	1269	1385	1463	1523	1572	1641
$225,000	$250,000	1350	1472	1555	1618	1670	1743
$250,000	$275,000	1426	1555	1641	1708	1763	1839
$275,000	$300,000	1500	1634	1725	1794	1852	1932
$300,000	or more	1944	2114	2228	2316	2388	2490

New Jersey — 7.0000%

Income At least	But less than	1	2	3	4	5	Over 5
$0	$20,000	245	262	273	281	288	298
$20,000	$30,000	405	433	451	465	476	492
$30,000	$40,000	493	528	550	567	581	600
$40,000	$50,000	572	612	638	657	673	695
$50,000	$60,000	644	689	718	740	758	782
$60,000	$70,000	711	760	792	816	836	863
$70,000	$80,000	773	826	861	887	908	938
$80,000	$90,000	831	889	926	954	977	1009
$90,000	$100,000	887	948	988	1018	1043	1076
$100,000	$120,000	962	1028	1071	1104	1131	1167
$120,000	$140,000	1062	1134	1182	1218	1247	1288
$140,000	$160,000	1156	1235	1286	1325	1357	1401
$160,000	$180,000	1244	1329	1384	1426	1460	1508
$180,000	$200,000	1328	1418	1478	1522	1559	1609
$200,000	$225,000	1416	1513	1576	1624	1663	1716
$225,000	$250,000	1512	1615	1683	1734	1775	1832
$250,000	$275,000	1604	1713	1784	1838	1882	1943
$275,000	$300,000	1692	1807	1882	1939	1986	2050
$300,000	or more	2231	2382	2480	2555	2616	2700

New Mexico — 5.1250%

Income At least	But less than	1	2	3	4	5	Over 5
$0	$20,000	236	256	268	277	284	295
$20,000	$30,000	383	415	434	449	461	478
$30,000	$40,000	464	502	526	544	558	578
$40,000	$50,000	535	579	606	627	644	667
$50,000	$60,000	600	649	680	703	722	747
$60,000	$70,000	659	713	747	772	793	821
$70,000	$80,000	714	772	809	837	859	890
$80,000	$90,000	766	829	868	898	922	954
$90,000	$100,000	816	882	924	956	981	1016
$100,000	$120,000	882	954	999	1033	1061	1098
$120,000	$140,000	970	1048	1098	1136	1166	1207
$140,000	$160,000	1052	1137	1192	1232	1265	1310
$160,000	$180,000	1129	1220	1279	1322	1357	1405
$180,000	$200,000	1202	1300	1362	1408	1445	1496
$200,000	$225,000	1279	1383	1449	1498	1538	1592
$225,000	$250,000	1363	1473	1543	1596	1638	1696
$250,000	$275,000	1442	1558	1633	1688	1733	1794
$275,000	$300,000	1518	1641	1719	1777	1825	1889
$300,000	or more	1980	2140	2242	2318	2379	2463

New York — 4.0000%

Income At least	But less than	1	2	3	4	5	Over 5
$0	$20,000	143	153	160	166	170	176
$20,000	$30,000	235	252	264	272	279	289
$30,000	$40,000	286	307	321	331	340	351
$40,000	$50,000	331	355	371	383	393	407
$50,000	$60,000	372	400	417	431	442	457
$60,000	$70,000	410	440	460	475	487	503
$70,000	$80,000	446	478	499	515	529	547
$80,000	$90,000	479	514	537	554	568	588
$90,000	$100,000	511	548	572	591	606	626
$100,000	$120,000	554	594	620	640	656	679
$120,000	$140,000	610	655	683	705	723	748
$140,000	$160,000	664	712	743	767	786	813
$160,000	$180,000	714	765	799	824	845	874
$180,000	$200,000	762	816	852	879	902	932
$200,000	$225,000	812	870	908	937	961	994
$225,000	$250,000	867	929	969	1000	1025	1060
$250,000	$275,000	918	984	1027	1060	1086	1123
$275,000	$300,000	969	1038	1083	1117	1145	1184
$300,000	or more	1273	1363	1423	1467	1504	1555

North Carolina — 4.7500%

Income At least	But less than	1	2	3	4	5	Over 5
$0	$20,000	216	248	269	286	299	318
$20,000	$30,000	342	391	424	450	471	501
$30,000	$40,000	409	468	508	538	564	599
$40,000	$50,000	468	535	580	615	644	685
$50,000	$60,000	521	596	646	685	717	762
$60,000	$70,000	570	651	706	748	783	833
$70,000	$80,000	615	703	762	807	845	898
$80,000	$90,000	657	751	814	863	903	959
$90,000	$100,000	697	796	863	915	957	1017
$100,000	$120,000	751	857	929	984	1030	1094
$120,000	$140,000	821	937	1015	1076	1126	1196
$140,000	$160,000	887	1012	1096	1162	1216	1291
$160,000	$180,000	948	1082	1172	1241	1299	1379
$180,000	$200,000	1006	1148	1243	1317	1378	1463
$200,000	$225,000	1067	1217	1318	1396	1461	1551
$225,000	$250,000	1132	1292	1399	1482	1550	1646
$250,000	$275,000	1195	1362	1475	1562	1635	1736
$275,000	$300,000	1254	1430	1548	1640	1716	1822
$300,000	or more	1613	1838	1989	2106	2202	2338

North Dakota — 5.0000%

Income At least	But less than	1	2	3	4	5	Over 5
$0	$20,000	178	199	213	224	234	247
$20,000	$30,000	283	314	336	353	367	388
$30,000	$40,000	340	377	402	423	439	463
$40,000	$50,000	390	431	460	483	502	529
$50,000	$60,000	435	481	513	538	559	589
$60,000	$70,000	476	526	561	588	611	643
$70,000	$80,000	514	568	605	634	659	694
$80,000	$90,000	550	607	647	678	704	741
$90,000	$100,000	585	644	686	719	746	785
$100,000	$120,000	630	694	739	774	803	845
$120,000	$140,000	690	760	808	846	878	924
$140,000	$160,000	747	821	873	914	948	997
$160,000	$180,000	800	878	933	977	1014	1065
$180,000	$200,000	850	933	991	1037	1075	1130
$200,000	$225,000	902	990	1051	1100	1140	1198
$225,000	$250,000	959	1051	1116	1167	1210	1271
$250,000	$275,000	1013	1110	1178	1231	1277	1341
$275,000	$300,000	1065	1166	1237	1293	1340	1407
$300,000	or more	1378	1504	1593	1664	1723	1808

Ohio — 5.7500%

Income At least	But less than	1	2	3	4	5	Over 5
$0	$20,000	223	244	258	268	277	289
$20,000	$30,000	367	400	423	440	454	473
$30,000	$40,000	446	487	514	534	551	574
$40,000	$50,000	516	563	594	618	637	664
$50,000	$60,000	581	633	668	694	716	746
$60,000	$70,000	640	697	735	765	788	821
$70,000	$80,000	695	757	799	830	856	892
$80,000	$90,000	747	814	858	892	920	958
$90,000	$100,000	796	868	915	951	980	1021
$100,000	$120,000	863	940	991	1030	1062	1106
$120,000	$140,000	951	1036	1092	1134	1169	1218
$140,000	$160,000	1035	1126	1187	1233	1271	1324
$160,000	$180,000	1113	1211	1276	1325	1366	1422
$180,000	$200,000	1187	1292	1361	1413	1457	1517
$200,000	$225,000	1265	1377	1450	1506	1552	1616
$225,000	$250,000	1350	1469	1547	1606	1655	1723
$250,000	$275,000	1431	1556	1639	1702	1754	1826
$275,000	$300,000	1509	1641	1728	1794	1849	1924
$300,000	or more	1984	2155	2268	2355	2425	2524

Oklahoma — 4.5000%

Income At least	But less than	1	2	3	4	5	Over 5
$0	$20,000	239	279	308	330	348	375
$20,000	$30,000	368	428	471	504	532	572
$30,000	$40,000	436	507	557	596	629	675
$40,000	$50,000	496	576	631	675	712	765
$50,000	$60,000	550	637	698	747	787	845
$60,000	$70,000	598	693	759	811	855	918
$70,000	$80,000	643	744	815	871	918	985
$80,000	$90,000	686	792	867	926	976	1047
$90,000	$100,000	725	838	916	979	1031	1106
$100,000	$120,000	778	898	982	1049	1105	1185
$120,000	$140,000	848	977	1068	1140	1201	1287
$140,000	$160,000	913	1051	1148	1225	1290	1383
$160,000	$180,000	973	1119	1222	1304	1373	1471
$180,000	$200,000	1030	1184	1293	1379	1451	1554
$200,000	$225,000	1090	1252	1366	1457	1533	1642
$225,000	$250,000	1154	1325	1445	1541	1621	1735
$250,000	$275,000	1215	1394	1520	1620	1704	1824
$275,000	$300,000	1273	1460	1591	1695	1783	1908
$300,000	or more	1622	1853	2016	2146	2256	2412

Pennsylvania — 6.0000%

Income At least	But less than	1	2	3	4	5	Over 5
$0	$20,000	197	214	225	234	241	251
$20,000	$30,000	318	345	363	377	388	404
$30,000	$40,000	385	417	439	455	468	487
$40,000	$50,000	443	480	505	524	539	560
$50,000	$60,000	496	538	565	586	603	627
$60,000	$70,000	545	590	620	643	662	688
$70,000	$80,000	590	639	671	696	716	744
$80,000	$90,000	633	685	720	746	768	798
$90,000	$100,000	673	729	765	793	816	848
$100,000	$120,000	728	787	827	857	882	916
$120,000	$140,000	799	865	908	941	968	1005
$140,000	$160,000	867	937	984	1020	1049	1089
$160,000	$180,000	929	1005	1055	1093	1124	1168
$180,000	$200,000	989	1069	1122	1163	1196	1242
$200,000	$225,000	1052	1137	1194	1237	1272	1321
$225,000	$250,000	1120	1211	1270	1316	1353	1405
$250,000	$275,000	1185	1280	1343	1391	1431	1486
$275,000	$300,000	1247	1347	1413	1464	1506	1563
$300,000	or more	1624	1752	1838	1903	1956	2031

Rhode Island — 7.0000%

Income At least	But less than	1	2	3	4	5	Over 5
$0	$20,000	252	272	285	295	303	314
$20,000	$30,000	406	439	460	476	488	506
$30,000	$40,000	490	529	555	574	589	611
$40,000	$50,000	564	609	638	660	678	703
$50,000	$60,000	631	682	714	739	759	787
$60,000	$70,000	692	748	784	811	833	863
$70,000	$80,000	749	810	849	878	902	935
$80,000	$90,000	803	868	910	941	967	1002
$90,000	$100,000	854	923	967	1001	1028	1065
$100,000	$120,000	922	997	1045	1081	1110	1150
$120,000	$140,000	1013	1094	1147	1187	1219	1263
$140,000	$160,000	1097	1186	1243	1286	1321	1369
$160,000	$180,000	1176	1271	1332	1378	1416	1467
$180,000	$200,000	1251	1352	1418	1467	1506	1561
$200,000	$225,000	1330	1438	1507	1559	1602	1660
$225,000	$250,000	1416	1530	1604	1659	1704	1766
$250,000	$275,000	1497	1618	1696	1754	1802	1867
$275,000	$300,000	1575	1702	1784	1846	1896	1964
$300,000	or more	2046	2211	2318	2398	2463	2552

South Carolina — 6.0000%

Income At least	But less than	1	2	3	4	5	Over 5
$0	$20,000	234	258	274	285	295	308
$20,000	$30,000	381	420	445	464	480	501
$30,000	$40,000	462	509	539	562	581	607
$40,000	$50,000	533	587	622	649	670	700
$50,000	$60,000	598	658	698	728	752	785
$60,000	$70,000	657	724	767	800	827	863
$70,000	$80,000	713	785	832	867	896	936
$80,000	$90,000	765	843	893	931	962	1005
$90,000	$100,000	815	897	951	991	1024	1070
$100,000	$120,000	881	970	1028	1072	1108	1157
$120,000	$140,000	969	1067	1131	1179	1218	1272
$140,000	$160,000	1052	1158	1227	1280	1322	1381
$160,000	$180,000	1129	1243	1318	1374	1419	1482
$180,000	$200,000	1203	1325	1404	1463	1512	1579
$200,000	$225,000	1280	1410	1494	1558	1610	1681
$225,000	$250,000	1364	1502	1592	1660	1715	1791
$250,000	$275,000	1444	1590	1685	1757	1815	1896
$275,000	$300,000	1521	1674	1774	1850	1911	1996
$300,000	or more	1986	2187	2317	2416	2496	2607

South Dakota — 4.0000%

Income At least	But less than	1	2	3	4	5	Over 5
$0	$20,000	227	266	293	315	332	357
$20,000	$30,000	351	412	453	485	512	550
$30,000	$40,000	417	489	537	576	608	653
$40,000	$50,000	475	556	611	654	690	741
$50,000	$60,000	527	616	677	724	764	821
$60,000	$70,000	573	670	736	788	832	893
$70,000	$80,000	617	721	792	847	894	960
$80,000	$90,000	657	768	843	903	952	1022
$90,000	$100,000	696	812	892	955	1007	1080
$100,000	$120,000	747	871	957	1024	1080	1159
$120,000	$140,000	813	949	1042	1115	1175	1261
$140,000	$160,000	876	1021	1121	1199	1264	1356
$160,000	$180,000	934	1088	1194	1278	1347	1445
$180,000	$200,000	988	1152	1264	1352	1425	1529
$200,000	$225,000	1046	1218	1337	1429	1507	1616
$225,000	$250,000	1107	1290	1415	1513	1594	1710
$250,000	$275,000	1166	1357	1489	1591	1677	1799
$275,000	$300,000	1221	1422	1559	1667	1757	1884
$300,000	or more	1555	1807	1981	2116	2230	2390

Tennessee — 7.0000%

Income At least	But less than	1	2	3	4	5	Over 5
$0	$20,000	350	404	441	469	493	527
$20,000	$30,000	551	634	690	735	771	823
$30,000	$40,000	659	757	824	877	920	981
$40,000	$50,000	753	865	941	1000	1050	1119
$50,000	$60,000	839	962	1046	1112	1167	1244
$60,000	$70,000	917	1051	1142	1214	1273	1357
$70,000	$80,000	989	1133	1231	1308	1372	1462
$80,000	$90,000	1057	1210	1315	1396	1464	1560
$90,000	$100,000	1121	1283	1393	1480	1552	1653
$100,000	$120,000	1206	1380	1499	1591	1668	1777
$120,000	$140,000	1319	1508	1637	1738	1821	1939
$140,000	$160,000	1424	1628	1766	1875	1965	2092
$160,000	$180,000	1522	1739	1886	2002	2098	2233
$180,000	$200,000	1616	1845	2001	2123	2224	2367
$200,000	$225,000	1713	1955	2120	2249	2356	2507
$225,000	$250,000	1819	2074	2249	2385	2499	2658
$250,000	$275,000	1919	2187	2371	2514	2633	2802
$275,000	$300,000	2014	2296	2488	2638	2763	2939
$300,000	or more	2591	2947	3190	3380	3538	3761

Texas — 6.2500%

Income At least	But less than	1	2	3	4	5	Over 5
$0	$20,000	243	272	291	306	318	335
$20,000	$30,000	399	447	479	503	523	551
$30,000	$40,000	486	544	583	613	637	671
$40,000	$50,000	562	630	675	710	738	777
$50,000	$60,000	632	709	759	798	830	874
$60,000	$70,000	697	781	837	879	914	963
$70,000	$80,000	757	848	909	955	994	1047
$80,000	$90,000	813	912	977	1027	1068	1125
$90,000	$100,000	867	972	1042	1095	1139	1200
$100,000	$120,000	940	1054	1129	1187	1235	1301
$120,000	$140,000	1036	1161	1245	1309	1361	1434
$140,000	$160,000	1126	1263	1354	1423	1480	1560
$160,000	$180,000	1211	1358	1456	1530	1592	1677
$180,000	$200,000	1292	1449	1553	1633	1698	1790
$200,000	$225,000	1377	1545	1656	1741	1811	1908
$225,000	$250,000	1469	1648	1767	1858	1932	2036
$250,000	$275,000	1557	1747	1872	1969	2048	2158
$275,000	$300,000	1641	1842	1974	2076	2160	2276
$300,000	or more	2157	2420	2595	2729	2839	2992

Utah — 4.7000%

Income At least	But less than	1	2	3	4	5	Over 5
$0	$20,000	230	265	288	306	321	342
$20,000	$30,000	363	416	451	479	502	535
$30,000	$40,000	434	497	539	572	599	638
$40,000	$50,000	497	568	616	653	684	728
$50,000	$60,000	553	632	685	726	761	809
$60,000	$70,000	604	690	748	793	830	883
$70,000	$80,000	652	744	806	855	895	951
$80,000	$90,000	697	795	861	912	955	1016
$90,000	$100,000	739	842	912	967	1012	1076
$100,000	$120,000	796	907	982	1040	1089	1157
$120,000	$140,000	870	991	1072	1136	1189	1263
$140,000	$160,000	940	1070	1157	1226	1283	1363
$160,000	$180,000	1005	1143	1236	1309	1370	1455
$180,000	$200,000	1067	1212	1311	1389	1453	1543
$200,000	$225,000	1132	1285	1390	1471	1539	1634
$225,000	$250,000	1201	1364	1475	1561	1632	1733
$250,000	$275,000	1268	1438	1555	1645	1721	1827
$275,000	$300,000	1331	1510	1632	1727	1806	1916
$300,000	or more	1713	1939	2094	2214	2314	2454

Vermont — 6.0000%

Income At least	But less than	1	2	3	4	5	Over 5
$0	$20,000	160	168	173	176	179	183
$20,000	$30,000	249	261	268	273	277	283
$30,000	$40,000	297	310	318	325	330	337
$40,000	$50,000	338	353	363	370	375	383
$50,000	$60,000	375	392	402	410	416	425
$60,000	$70,000	409	427	438	447	454	463
$70,000	$80,000	440	459	472	481	488	498
$80,000	$90,000	469	490	503	513	520	531
$90,000	$100,000	497	519	532	542	551	562
$100,000	$120,000	534	557	572	582	591	603
$120,000	$140,000	582	607	623	635	644	657
$140,000	$160,000	627	654	671	684	694	708
$160,000	$180,000	669	698	716	729	740	755
$180,000	$200,000	709	739	758	772	784	799
$200,000	$225,000	750	782	802	817	829	846
$225,000	$250,000	795	828	850	865	878	895
$250,000	$275,000	837	872	895	911	925	943
$275,000	$300,000	878	914	938	955	969	988
$300,000	or more	1120	1166	1195	1217	1234	1258

Virginia — 4.3000%

Income At least	But less than	1	2	3	4	5	Over 5
$0	$20,000	168	192	208	220	230	245
$20,000	$30,000	266	301	325	344	359	381
$30,000	$40,000	318	359	388	410	428	454
$40,000	$50,000	364	411	443	468	489	518
$50,000	$60,000	405	457	492	520	543	575
$60,000	$70,000	443	499	538	568	593	628
$70,000	$80,000	479	539	580	612	639	676
$80,000	$90,000	512	576	619	653	682	722
$90,000	$100,000	543	610	656	692	722	764
$100,000	$120,000	585	657	706	745	777	822
$120,000	$140,000	640	718	772	813	848	897
$140,000	$160,000	692	776	833	878	915	967
$160,000	$180,000	740	829	890	937	977	1033
$180,000	$200,000	786	880	944	994	1036	1095
$200,000	$225,000	835	933	1001	1054	1098	1160
$225,000	$250,000	887	991	1062	1118	1164	1230
$250,000	$275,000	936	1045	1120	1179	1228	1296
$275,000	$300,000	984	1098	1176	1237	1288	1360
$300,000	or more	1271	1413	1511	1588	1652	1742

Washington — 6.5000%

Income At least	But less than	1	2	3	4	5	Over 5
$0	$20,000	247	273	290	304	315	330
$20,000	$30,000	413	456	484	506	525	550
$30,000	$40,000	505	558	593	620	642	672
$40,000	$50,000	588	649	689	720	746	782
$50,000	$60,000	664	732	778	813	842	882
$60,000	$70,000	733	809	859	898	930	974
$70,000	$80,000	799	881	936	978	1012	1060
$80,000	$90,000	861	949	1008	1053	1090	1142
$90,000	$100,000	920	1014	1077	1125	1165	1220
$100,000	$120,000	999	1101	1170	1222	1265	1325
$120,000	$140,000	1105	1217	1293	1350	1398	1464
$140,000	$160,000	1204	1327	1409	1472	1524	1596
$160,000	$180,000	1298	1430	1518	1586	1642	1719
$180,000	$200,000	1388	1529	1623	1695	1754	1837
$200,000	$225,000	1482	1633	1733	1810	1873	1962
$225,000	$250,000	1585	1746	1853	1935	2003	2097
$250,000	$275,000	1683	1853	1967	2054	2126	2226
$275,000	$300,000	1778	1957	2077	2169	2245	2350
$300,000	or more	2357	2593	2751	2872	2972	3111

West Virginia — 6.0000%

Income At least	But less than	1	2	3	4	5	Over 5
$0	$20,000	239	265	282	295	306	321
$20,000	$30,000	395	438	467	488	506	531
$30,000	$40,000	481	534	569	596	617	647
$40,000	$50,000	558	620	660	691	716	751
$50,000	$60,000	628	698	743	778	806	846
$60,000	$70,000	693	770	820	858	889	933
$70,000	$80,000	754	837	891	933	967	1015
$80,000	$90,000	811	900	959	1004	1041	1092
$90,000	$100,000	865	961	1023	1071	1111	1165
$100,000	$120,000	938	1042	1110	1162	1205	1264
$120,000	$140,000	1035	1150	1225	1282	1329	1395
$140,000	$160,000	1127	1251	1333	1396	1447	1518
$160,000	$180,000	1212	1347	1435	1502	1558	1634
$180,000	$200,000	1294	1438	1532	1604	1663	1745
$200,000	$225,000	1380	1534	1634	1711	1774	1861
$225,000	$250,000	1474	1638	1745	1827	1895	1988
$250,000	$275,000	1563	1737	1851	1938	2009	2108
$275,000	$300,000	1649	1832	1953	2045	2120	2224
$300,000	or more	2173	2415	2574	2696	2795	2933

Wisconsin — 5.0000%

Income At least	But less than	1	2	3	4	5	Over 5
$0	$20,000	203	224	238	248	257	268
$20,000	$30,000	333	368	390	407	421	440
$30,000	$40,000	405	447	474	495	512	535
$40,000	$50,000	469	517	549	573	592	619
$50,000	$60,000	527	581	617	644	666	696
$60,000	$70,000	580	640	679	709	733	766
$70,000	$80,000	630	695	737	770	796	832
$80,000	$90,000	677	747	792	827	855	894
$90,000	$100,000	721	796	844	881	912	953
$100,000	$120,000	781	862	915	955	987	1033
$120,000	$140,000	860	949	1007	1052	1088	1137
$140,000	$160,000	935	1032	1095	1143	1182	1236
$160,000	$180,000	1005	1109	1177	1228	1271	1329
$180,000	$200,000	1072	1183	1255	1310	1355	1417
$200,000	$225,000	1142	1260	1337	1396	1444	1510
$225,000	$250,000	1218	1344	1426	1489	1540	1611
$250,000	$275,000	1290	1424	1511	1577	1632	1706
$275,000	$300,000	1360	1501	1593	1663	1720	1799
$300,000	or more	1784	1969	2090	2181	2256	2360

Wyoming — 4.0000%

Income At least	But less than	1	2	3	4	5	Over 5
$0	$20,000	156	171	181	189	195	203
$20,000	$30,000	257	281	298	310	320	334
$30,000	$40,000	312	342	362	377	389	407
$40,000	$50,000	362	397	419	437	451	471
$50,000	$60,000	407	446	472	491	507	529
$60,000	$70,000	449	492	520	541	558	583
$70,000	$80,000	488	534	564	588	607	633
$80,000	$90,000	525	574	607	632	652	680
$90,000	$100,000	560	612	647	674	695	725
$100,000	$120,000	607	664	701	730	753	786
$120,000	$140,000	669	732	773	805	830	866
$140,000	$160,000	728	796	841	875	903	942
$160,000	$180,000	783	856	904	941	971	1012
$180,000	$200,000	835	913	964	1004	1036	1080
$200,000	$225,000	891	974	1028	1070	1104	1151
$225,000	$250,000	951	1039	1097	1142	1178	1228
$250,000	$275,000	1008	1101	1163	1210	1248	1302
$275,000	$300,000	1063	1161	1226	1276	1316	1372
$300,000	or more	1399	1527	1612	1677	1730	1803

Note: Residents of **Alaska** do not have a state sales tax, but should follow the instructions on the next page to determine their local sales tax amount.

1 Use the Ratio Method to determine your local sales tax deduction, then add that to the appropriate amount in the state table. Your state sales tax rate is provided next to the state name.

2 Follow the instructions on the next page to determine your local sales tax deduction, then add that to the appropriate amount in the state table.

3 The California table includes the 1.25% uniform local sales tax rate in addition to the 6.25% state sales tax rate for a total of 7.50%. Some California localities impose a larger local sales tax. Taxpayers who reside in those jurisdictions should use the Ratio Method to determine their local sales tax deduction, then add that to the appropriate amount in the state table. The denominator of the correct ratio is 7.50%, and the numerator is the total sales tax rate minus 7.50%.

4 This state does not have a local general sales tax, so the amount in the state table is the only amount to be deducted.

5 The Nevada table includes the 2.25% uniform local sales tax rate in addition to the 4.6000% state sales tax rate for a total of 6.85%. Some Nevada localities impose a larger local sales tax. Taxpayers who reside in those jurisdictions should use the Ratio Method to determine their local sales tax deduction, then add that to the appropriate amount in the state table. The denominator of the correct ratio is 6.85%, and the numerator is the total sales tax rate minus 6.85%.

6 The 4.0% rate for Hawaii is actually an excise tax but is treated as a sales tax for purpose of this deduction.

Which Optional Local Sales Tax Table Should I Use?

IF you live in the state of...	AND you live in...	THEN use Local Table...
Alaska	Any locality	C
Arizona	Chandler, Glendale, Gilbert, Mesa, Peoria, Phoenix, Scottsdale, Tempe, Tucson, Yuma, or any other locality	B
Arkansas	Any Locality	B
Colorado	Adams County, Arapahoe County, Boulder County, Centennial, Colorado Springs, Denver City/Denver County, El Paso County, Larimer County, Pueblo County, or any other locality	A
	Aurora, Boulder, Fort Collins, Greeley, Jefferson County, Lakewood, Longmont or Pueblo City.	B
	Arvada, Thornton or Westminster	C
Georgia	Any locality	B
Illinois	Any locality	A
Louisiana	Ascension Parish, Bossier Parish, Caddo Parish, Calcasieu Parish, East Baton Rouge Parish, Iberia Parish, Jefferson Parish, Lafayette Parish, Lafourche Parish, Livingston Parish, Orleans Parish, Ouachita Parish, Rapides Parish, St. Bernard Parish, St. Landry Parish, St. Tammany Parish, Tangipahoa Parish or Terrebonne Parish	C
	Any other locality	B
Mississippi	Cities of Jackson and Tupelo only	B
Missouri	Any locality	B
New York	Counties: Albany, Allegany, Broome, Cattaraugus, Cayuga, Chemung, Clinton, Cortland, Dutchess, Erie, Essex, Franklin, Fulton, Genesee, Herkimer, Jefferson, Lewis, Livingston, Madison, Monroe, Montgomery, Nassau, Niagara, Oneida, Onondaga, Ontario, Orange, Orleans, Oswego, Otsego, Putnam, Rensselaer, Rockland, St. Lawrence, Saratoga, Schenectady, Schoharie, Schuyler, Seneca, Steuben, Suffolk, Sullivan, Tompkins, Ulster, Warren, Washington, Westchester, Wyoming or Yates	B
	Counties: Chautauqua, Chenango, Columbia, Delaware, Greene, Hamilton, Tioga, Wayne, New York City or Norwich City	A
	Any other locality	D*
North Carolina	Any locality	A
South Carolina	Aiken County, Anderson County, Georgetown County, Horry County, Lexington County, Newberry County, Orangeburg County, York County or Myrtle Beach	A
	Bamberg County, Charleston County, Cherokee County, Chesterfield County, Darlington County, Dillon County, Florence County, Hampton County, Jasper County, Lee County, Marion County, Marlboro County or Any other locality	B
Tennessee	Any locality	B
Utah	Any locality	A
Virginia	Any locality	B

* Note: Local Table D is just 25% of the NY State table.

2015 Optional Local Sales Tax Tables

Income		Local Table A						Local Table B						Local Table C						Local Table D					
At least	But less than	1	2	3	4	5	Over 5	1	2	3	4	5	Over 5	1	2	3	4	5	Over 5	1	2	3	4	5	Over 5
$0	$20,000	35	39	42	43	45	47	44	52	56	60	63	68	55	64	70	75	79	85	36	38	40	42	43	44
20,000	30,000	56	62	66	69	71	75	69	80	87	93	98	104	86	99	108	116	121	130	59	63	66	68	70	72
30,000	40,000	68	74	79	82	85	89	82	95	103	110	116	124	102	118	128	137	144	154	72	77	80	83	85	88
40,000	50,000	78	85	90	94	98	102	93	108	117	125	131	140	116	134	146	155	163	174	83	89	93	96	98	102
50,000	60,000	87	95	101	105	109	114	104	119	130	139	146	155	128	148	162	172	181	193	93	100	104	108	111	114
60,000	70,000	95	104	110	115	119	125	113	130	142	151	158	169	140	161	176	187	197	210	103	110	115	119	122	126
70,000	80,000	103	113	119	124	129	135	122	140	152	162	170	182	150	173	189	201	211	225	112	120	125	129	132	137
80,000	90,000	110	120	128	133	137	144	130	149	162	173	181	194	160	185	201	214	225	240	120	129	134	139	142	147
90,000	100,000	117	128	135	141	146	153	137	158	172	183	192	205	169	195	213	226	238	254	128	137	143	148	152	157
100,000	120,000	126	138	146	152	157	164	148	169	184	196	206	219	182	209	228	243	255	272	139	149	155	160	164	170
120,000	140,000	139	151	160	166	172	180	161	185	201	213	224	239	198	228	248	264	277	296	153	164	171	176	181	187
140,000	160,000	150	163	173	180	186	194	174	199	216	230	241	257	213	245	267	284	298	318	166	178	186	192	197	203
160,000	180,000	161	175	185	193	199	208	185	212	230	245	257	274	228	261	285	303	318	339	179	191	200	206	211	219
180,000	200,000	171	186	196	204	211	221	196	224	244	259	272	290	241	277	301	320	336	358	191	204	213	220	226	233
200,000	225,000	181	197	208	217	224	234	208	238	258	274	287	306	255	293	318	338	355	379	203	218	227	234	240	249
225,000	250,000	193	210	221	231	238	249	220	252	273	290	304	324	270	310	337	358	376	400	217	232	242	250	256	265
250,000	275,000	204	222	234	243	251	262	232	265	288	305	320	341	284	326	354	377	395	421	230	246	257	265	272	281
275,000	300,000	214	233	246	256	264	276	243	278	301	320	335	357	298	342	371	394	414	441	242	260	271	279	286	296
300,000	or more	278	301	317	330	340	355	311	354	384	407	426	454	380	434	471	501	525	559	318	341	356	367	376	389

Appendix B

Tax Forms

(Tax forms can be obtained from the IRS website: **www.irs.gov**)

Form **1040** Department of the Treasury—Internal Revenue Service (99)
U.S. Individual Income Tax Return **2015** OMB No. 1545-0074 IRS Use Only—Do not write or staple in this space.

For the year Jan. 1–Dec. 31, 2015, or other tax year beginning	, 2015, ending	, 20	See separate instructions.

Your first name and initial | Last name | Your social security number

If a joint return, spouse's first name and initial | Last name | Spouse's social security number

Home address (number and street). If you have a P.O. box, see instructions. | Apt. no. | ▲ Make sure the SSN(s) above and on line 6c are correct.

City, town or post office, state, and ZIP code. If you have a foreign address, also complete spaces below (see instructions).

Presidential Election Campaign
Check here if you, or your spouse if filing jointly, want $3 to go to this fund. Checking a box below will not change your tax or refund. ☐ You ☐ Spouse

Foreign country name | Foreign province/state/county | Foreign postal code

Filing Status

Check only one box.

1 ☐ Single
2 ☐ Married filing jointly (even if only one had income)
3 ☐ Married filing separately. Enter spouse's SSN above and full name here. ▶
4 ☐ Head of household (with qualifying person). (See instructions.) If the qualifying person is a child but not your dependent, enter this child's name here. ▶
5 ☐ Qualifying widow(er) with dependent child

Exemptions

6a ☐ **Yourself.** If someone can claim you as a dependent, **do not** check box 6a . . . . . .
b ☐ **Spouse** . . . .

c **Dependents:**

If more than four dependents, see instructions and check here ▶ ☐

(1) First name Last name	(2) Dependent's social security number	(3) Dependent's relationship to you	(4) ✓ if child under age 17 qualifying for child tax credit (see instructions)
			☐
			☐
			☐
			☐

d Total number of exemptions claimed . . . .

Boxes checked on 6a and 6b
No. of children on 6c who:
• lived with you
• did not live with you due to divorce or separation (see instructions)
Dependents on 6c not entered above
Add numbers on lines above ▶

Income

Attach Form(s) W-2 here. Also attach Forms W-2G and 1099-R if tax was withheld.

If you did not get a W-2, see instructions.

7	Wages, salaries, tips, etc. Attach Form(s) W-2	7	
8a	**Taxable** interest. Attach Schedule B if required	8a	
b	**Tax-exempt** interest. **Do not** include on line 8a . . .	8b		
9a	Ordinary dividends. Attach Schedule B if required	9a	
b	Qualified dividends	9b		
10	Taxable refunds, credits, or offsets of state and local income taxes	10	
11	Alimony received	11	
12	Business income or (loss). Attach Schedule C or C-EZ	12	
13	Capital gain or (loss). Attach Schedule D if required. If not required, check here ▶ ☐	13	
14	Other gains or (losses). Attach Form 4797	14	
15a	IRA distributions .	15a		b Taxable amount . . .	15b	
16a	Pensions and annuities	16a		b Taxable amount . . .	16b	
17	Rental real estate, royalties, partnerships, S corporations, trusts, etc. Attach Schedule E	17	
18	Farm income or (loss). Attach Schedule F	18	
19	Unemployment compensation	19	
20a	Social security benefits	20a		b Taxable amount . . .	20b	
21	Other income. List type and amount	21	
22	Combine the amounts in the far right column for lines 7 through 21. This is your **total income** ▶	22	

Adjusted Gross Income

23	Educator expenses	23		
24	Certain business expenses of reservists, performing artists, and fee-basis government officials. Attach Form 2106 or 2106-EZ	24		
25	Health savings account deduction. Attach Form 8889 .	25		
26	Moving expenses. Attach Form 3903	26		
27	Deductible part of self-employment tax. Attach Schedule SE .	27		
28	Self-employed SEP, SIMPLE, and qualified plans . .	28		
29	Self-employed health insurance deduction . .	29		
30	Penalty on early withdrawal of savings	30		
31a	Alimony paid b Recipient's SSN ▶	31a		
32	IRA deduction	32		
33	Student loan interest deduction	33		
34	Tuition and fees. Attach Form 8917	34		
35	Domestic production activities deduction. Attach Form 8903	35		
36	Add lines 23 through 35	36	
37	Subtract line 36 from line 22. This is your **adjusted gross income** . . . . . ▶	37	

For Disclosure, Privacy Act, and Paperwork Reduction Act Notice, see separate instructions.   Cat. No. 11320B   Form **1040** (2015)

Form 1040 (2015)   Page **2**

Tax and Credits	**38**	Amount from line 37 (adjusted gross income)	**38**
	39a	Check if: ☐ **You** were born before January 2, 1951, ☐ Blind. ☐ **Spouse** was born before January 2, 1951, ☐ Blind. } Total boxes checked ► 39a	
	b	If your spouse itemizes on a separate return or you were a dual-status alien, check here ► 39b ☐	

Standard Deduction for—
• People who check any box on line 39a or 39b **or** who can be claimed as a dependent, see instructions.
• All others:
Single or Married filing separately, $6,300
Married filing jointly or Qualifying widow(er), $12,600
Head of household, $9,250

40	**Itemized deductions** (from Schedule A) **or** your **standard deduction** (see left margin) . .	**40**
41	Subtract line 40 from line 38	**41**
42	**Exemptions.** If line 38 is $154,950 or less, multiply $4,000 by the number on line 6d. Otherwise, see instructions	**42**
43	**Taxable income.** Subtract line 42 from line 41. If line 42 is more than line 41, enter -0- . .	**43**
44	**Tax** (see instructions). Check if any from: **a** ☐ Form(s) 8814 **b** ☐ Form 4972 **c** ☐ _____	**44**
45	**Alternative minimum tax** (see instructions). Attach Form 6251	**45**
46	Excess advance premium tax credit repayment. Attach Form 8962	**46**
47	Add lines 44, 45, and 46 . . . . ►	**47**
48	Foreign tax credit. Attach Form 1116 if required	48 _____
49	Credit for child and dependent care expenses. Attach Form 2441	49 _____
50	Education credits from Form 8863, line 19	50 _____
51	Retirement savings contributions credit. Attach Form 8880	51 _____
52	Child tax credit. Attach Schedule 8812, if required . . .	52 _____
53	Residential energy credits. Attach Form 5695	53 _____
54	Other credits from Form: **a** ☐ 3800 **b** ☐ 8801 **c** ☐	54 _____
55	Add lines 48 through 54. These are your **total credits**	**55**
56	Subtract line 55 from line 47. If line 55 is more than line 47, enter -0- . . . . . ►	**56**

Other Taxes		
	57	Self-employment tax. Attach Schedule SE	**57**
	58	Unreported social security and Medicare tax from Form: **a** ☐ 4137 **b** ☐ 8919	**58**
	59	Additional tax on IRAs, other qualified retirement plans, etc. Attach Form 5329 if required . .	**59**
	60a	Household employment taxes from Schedule H	**60a**
	b	First-time homebuyer credit repayment. Attach Form 5405 if required	**60b**
	61	Health care: individual responsibility (see instructions) Full-year coverage ☐ . .	**61**
	62	Taxes from: **a** ☐ Form 8959 **b** ☐ Form 8960 **c** ☐ Instructions; enter code(s) _____	**62**
	63	Add lines 56 through 62. This is your **total tax** . . . . ►	**63**

Payments		
	64	Federal income tax withheld from Forms W-2 and 1099 . .	64 _____
	65	2015 estimated tax payments and amount applied from 2014 return	65 _____
If you have a qualifying child, attach Schedule EIC.	**66a**	**Earned income credit (EIC)**	66a _____
	b	Nontaxable combat pay election 66b _____	
	67	Additional child tax credit. Attach Schedule 8812 . . .	67 _____
	68	American opportunity credit from Form 8863, line 8 . . .	68 _____
	69	Net premium tax credit. Attach Form 8962	69 _____
	70	Amount paid with request for extension to file	70 _____
	71	Excess social security and tier 1 RRTA tax withheld . . .	71 _____
	72	Credit for federal tax on fuels. Attach Form 4136 . . .	72 _____
	73	Credits from Form: **a** ☐ 2439 **b** ☐ Reserved **c** ☐ 8885 **d** ☐	73 _____
	74	Add lines 64, 65, 66a, and 67 through 73. These are your **total payments** . . . . . ►	**74**

Refund		
	75	If line 74 is more than line 63, subtract line 63 from line 74. This is the amount you **overpaid**	**75**
	76a	Amount of line 75 you want **refunded to you**. If Form 8888 is attached, check here . ► ☐	**76a**
Direct deposit? See instructions.	**b**	Routing number _____ ► **c** Type: ☐ Checking ☐ Savings	
	d	Account number _____	
	77	Amount of line 75 you want **applied to your 2016 estimated tax** ►	77 _____

Amount You Owe		
	78	**Amount you owe.** Subtract line 74 from line 63. For details on how to pay, see instructions ►	**78**
	79	Estimated tax penalty (see instructions)	79 _____

Third Party Designee	Do you want to allow another person to discuss this return with the IRS (see instructions)? ☐ **Yes.** Complete below. ☐ **No**
	Designee's name _____ Phone no. ►_____ Personal identification number (PIN) ►_____

Sign Here
Joint return? See instructions.
Keep a copy for your records.

Under penalties of perjury, I declare that I have examined this return and accompanying schedules and statements, and to the best of my knowledge and belief, they are true, correct, and complete. Declaration of preparer (other than taxpayer) is based on all information of which preparer has any knowledge.

Your signature	Date	Your occupation	Daytime phone number
Spouse's signature. If a joint return, **both** must sign.	Date	Spouse's occupation	If the IRS sent you an Identity Protection PIN, enter it here (see inst.)

Paid Preparer Use Only

Print/Type preparer's name	Preparer's signature	Date	Check ☐ if self-employed	PTIN
Firm's name ►			Firm's EIN ►	
Firm's address ►			Phone no.	

SCHEDULE A
(Form 1040)

Department of the Treasury
Internal Revenue Service (99)

Itemized Deductions

► **Information about Schedule A and its separate instructions is at** *www.irs.gov/schedulea.*
► **Attach to Form 1040.**

OMB No. 1545-0074

20**15**

Attachment
Sequence No. **07**

Name(s) shown on Form 1040

Your social security number

Medical and Dental Expenses

Caution: Do not include expenses reimbursed or paid by others.

1   Medical and dental expenses (see instructions) . . . . . | **1** |
2   Enter amount from Form 1040, line 38 | **2** |
3   Multiply line 2 by 10% (.10). But if either you or your spouse was born before January 2, 1951, multiply line 2 by 7.5% (.075) instead | **3** |
4   Subtract line 3 from line 1. If line 3 is more than line 1, enter -0- . . . . | **4** |

Taxes You Paid

5   State and local **(check only one box):**
   a ☐ Income taxes, **or**
   b ☐ General sales taxes | **5** |
6   Real estate taxes (see instructions) . . . . | **6** |
7   Personal property taxes . . . . | **7** |
8   Other taxes. List type and amount ► _____
   _____ | **8** |
9   Add lines 5 through 8 . . . . | **9** |

Interest You Paid

Note:
Your mortgage interest deduction may be limited (see instructions).

10   Home mortgage interest and points reported to you on Form 1098 | **10** |
11   Home mortgage interest not reported to you on Form 1098. If paid to the person from whom you bought the home, see instructions and show that person's name, identifying no., and address ►
   _____
   _____ | **11** |
12   Points not reported to you on Form 1098. See instructions for special rules . . . . | **12** |
13   Mortgage insurance premiums (see instructions) . . . . | **13** |
14   Investment interest. Attach Form 4952 if required. (See instructions.) | **14** |
15   Add lines 10 through 14 . . . . | **15** |

Gifts to Charity

If you made a gift and got a benefit for it, see instructions.

16   Gifts by cash or check. If you made any gift of $250 or more, see instructions . . . . . . | **16** |
17   Other than by cash or check. If any gift of $250 or more, see instructions. You **must** attach Form 8283 if over $500 . . . | **17** |
18   Carryover from prior year . . . . | **18** |
19   Add lines 16 through 18 . . . . | **19** |

Casualty and Theft Losses

20   Casualty or theft loss(es). Attach Form 4684. (See instructions.) . . . . | **20** |

Job Expenses and Certain Miscellaneous Deductions

21   Unreimbursed employee expenses—job travel, union dues, job education, etc. Attach Form 2106 or 2106-EZ if required. (See instructions.) ► _____ | **21** |
22   Tax preparation fees . . . . | **22** |
23   Other expenses—investment, safe deposit box, etc. List type and amount ► _____
   _____ | **23** |
24   Add lines 21 through 23 . . . . | **24** |
25   Enter amount from Form 1040, line 38 | **25** |
26   Multiply line 25 by 2% (.02) . . . . | **26** |
27   Subtract line 26 from line 24. If line 26 is more than line 24, enter -0- . . . . | **27** |

Other Miscellaneous Deductions

28   Other—from list in instructions. List type and amount ► _____
   _____ | **28** |

Total Itemized Deductions

29   Is Form 1040, line 38, over $154,950?
   ☐ **No.** Your deduction is not limited. Add the amounts in the far right column for lines 4 through 28. Also, enter this amount on Form 1040, line 40.
   ☐ **Yes.** Your deduction may be limited. See the Itemized Deductions Worksheet in the instructions to figure the amount to enter. | **29** |

30   If you elect to itemize deductions even though they are less than your standard deduction, check here . . . . ► ☐

For Paperwork Reduction Act Notice, see Form 1040 instructions.

Cat. No. 17145C

Schedule A (Form 1040) 2015

SCHEDULE C
(Form 1040)

Department of the Treasury
Internal Revenue Service (99)

Profit or Loss From Business
(Sole Proprietorship)

▶ Information about Schedule C and its separate instructions is at *www.irs.gov/schedulec*.
▶ **Attach to Form 1040, 1040NR, or 1041; partnerships generally must file Form 1065.**

OMB No. 1545-0074

20**15**

Attachment
Sequence No. **09**

Name of proprietor

Social security number (SSN)

A	Principal business or profession, including product or service (see instructions)	**B** Enter code from instructions ▶
C	Business name. If no separate business name, leave blank.	**D** Employer ID number (EIN), (see instr.)

E Business address (including suite or room no.) ▶
City, town or post office, state, and ZIP code

F Accounting method: **(1)** ☐ Cash **(2)** ☐ Accrual **(3)** ☐ Other (specify) ▶

G Did you "materially participate" in the operation of this business during 2015? If "No," see instructions for limit on losses . ☐ Yes ☐ No

H If you started or acquired this business during 2015, check here . . . . ▶ ☐

I Did you make any payments in 2015 that would require you to file Form(s) 1099? (see instructions) . . . . . ☐ Yes ☐ No

J If "Yes," did you or will you file required Forms 1099? . . . . ☐ Yes ☐ No

Part I Income

1	Gross receipts or sales. See instructions for line 1 and check the box if this income was reported to you on Form W-2 and the "Statutory employee" box on that form was checked . . . . ▶ ☐	**1**	
2	Returns and allowances	**2**	
3	Subtract line 2 from line 1	**3**	
4	Cost of goods sold (from line 42)	**4**	
5	**Gross profit.** Subtract line 4 from line 3	**5**	
6	Other income, including federal and state gasoline or fuel tax credit or refund (see instructions)	**6**	
7	**Gross income.** Add lines 5 and 6 . . . . ▶	**7**	

Part II Expenses. Enter expenses for business use of your home **only** on line 30.

8	Advertising	**8**		18	Office expense (see instructions)	**18**
9	Car and truck expenses (see instructions)	**9**		19	Pension and profit-sharing plans .	**19**
10	Commissions and fees .	**10**		20	Rent or lease (see instructions):	
11	Contract labor (see instructions)	**11**		a	Vehicles, machinery, and equipment	**20a**
12	Depletion	**12**		b	Other business property . . .	**20b**
13	Depreciation and section 179 expense deduction (not included in Part III) (see instructions)	**13**		21	Repairs and maintenance . . .	**21**
				22	Supplies (not included in Part III) .	**22**
				23	Taxes and licenses	**23**
				24	Travel, meals, and entertainment:	
14	Employee benefit programs (other than on line 19) . .	**14**		a	Travel	**24a**
15	Insurance (other than health)	**15**		b	Deductible meals and entertainment (see instructions) .	**24b**
16	Interest:			25	Utilities	**25**
a	Mortgage (paid to banks, etc.)	**16a**		26	Wages (less employment credits).	**26**
b	Other	**16b**		27a	Other expenses (from line 48) . .	**27a**
17	Legal and professional services	**17**		b	**Reserved for future use** . . .	**27b**

28	**Total expenses** before expenses for business use of home. Add lines 8 through 27a . . . . . . ▶	**28**	
29	Tentative profit or (loss). Subtract line 28 from line 7	**29**	
30	Expenses for business use of your home. Do not report these expenses elsewhere. Attach Form 8829 unless using the simplified method (see instructions). **Simplified method filers only:** enter the total square footage of: (a) your home: _____ and (b) the part of your home used for business: _____ . Use the Simplified Method Worksheet in the instructions to figure the amount to enter on line 30	**30**	
31	**Net profit or (loss).** Subtract line 30 from line 29. • If a profit, enter on both **Form 1040, line 12** (or **Form 1040NR, line 13**) and on **Schedule SE, line 2.** (If you checked the box on line 1, see instructions). Estates and trusts, enter on **Form 1041, line 3.** • If a loss, you **must** go to line 32.	**31**	
32	If you have a loss, check the box that describes your investment in this activity (see instructions). • If you checked 32a, enter the loss on both **Form 1040, line 12,** (or **Form 1040NR, line 13**) and on **Schedule SE, line 2.** (If you checked the box on line 1, see the line 31 instructions). Estates and trusts, enter on **Form 1041, line 3.** • If you checked 32b, you **must** attach **Form 6198.** Your loss may be limited.	**32a** ☐ All investment is at risk. **32b** ☐ Some investment is not at risk.	

For Paperwork Reduction Act Notice, see the separate instructions.   Cat. No. 11334P   Schedule C (Form 1040) 2015

Schedule C (Form 1040) 2015   Page **2**

Part III	**Cost of Goods Sold** (see instructions)

33   Method(s) used to
     value closing inventory: **a** ☐ Cost   **b** ☐ Lower of cost or market   **c** ☐ Other (attach explanation)

34   Was there any change in determining quantities, costs, or valuations between opening and closing inventory?
     If "Yes," attach explanation . . . .   ☐ **Yes**   ☐ **No**

35	Inventory at beginning of year. If different from last year's closing inventory, attach explanation . . .	35
36	Purchases less cost of items withdrawn for personal use	36
37	Cost of labor. Do not include any amounts paid to yourself	37
38	Materials and supplies	38
39	Other costs	39
40	Add lines 35 through 39	40
41	Inventory at end of year	41
42	**Cost of goods sold.** Subtract line 41 from line 40. Enter the result here and on line 4	42

Part IV	**Information on Your Vehicle.** Complete this part **only** if you are claiming car or truck expenses on line 9 and are not required to file Form 4562 for this business. See the instructions for line 13 to find out if you must file Form 4562.

43   When did you place your vehicle in service for business purposes? (month, day, year) ▶ _____ / _____ / _____

44   Of the total number of miles you drove your vehicle during 2015, enter the number of miles you used your vehicle for:

 a Business _____   **b** Commuting (see instructions) _____   **c** Other _____

45   Was your vehicle available for personal use during off-duty hours? . . . .   ☐ **Yes**   ☐ **No**

46   Do you (or your spouse) have another vehicle available for personal use?. . . . .   ☐ **Yes**   ☐ **No**

47a Do you have evidence to support your deduction? . . . .   ☐ **Yes**   ☐ **No**

 b If "Yes," is the evidence written? . . . .   ☐ **Yes**   ☐ **No**

Part V	**Other Expenses.** List below business expenses not included on lines 8–26 or line 30.

48	**Total other expenses.** Enter here and on line 27a	48

Schedule C (Form 1040) 2015

SCHEDULE D
(Form 1040)

Department of the Treasury
Internal Revenue Service (99)

Capital Gains and Losses

▶ Attach to Form 1040 or Form 1040NR.
▶ **Information about Schedule D and its separate instructions is at** *www.irs.gov/scheduled.*
▶ **Use Form 8949 to list your transactions for lines 1b, 2, 3, 8b, 9, and 10.**

OMB No. 1545-0074

2015

Attachment
Sequence No. **12**

Name(s) shown on return

Your social security number

Part I   Short-Term Capital Gains and Losses—Assets Held One Year or Less

See instructions for how to figure the amounts to enter on the lines below. This form may be easier to complete if you round off cents to whole dollars.	(d) Proceeds (sales price)	(e) Cost (or other basis)	(g) Adjustments to gain or loss from Form(s) 8949, Part I, line 2, column (g)	(h) Gain or (loss) Subtract column (e) from column (d) and combine the result with column (g)
1a Totals for all short-term transactions reported on Form 1099-B for which basis was reported to the IRS and for which you have no adjustments (see instructions). However, if you choose to report all these transactions on Form 8949, leave this line blank and go to line 1b .				
1b Totals for all transactions reported on Form(s) 8949 with **Box A** checked				
2 Totals for all transactions reported on Form(s) 8949 with **Box B** checked				
3 Totals for all transactions reported on Form(s) 8949 with **Box C** checked				

4 Short-term gain from Form 6252 and short-term gain or (loss) from Forms 4684, 6781, and 8824 .	**4**	
5 Net short-term gain or (loss) from partnerships, S corporations, estates, and trusts from Schedule(s) K-1	**5**	
6 Short-term capital loss carryover. Enter the amount, if any, from line 8 of your **Capital Loss Carryover Worksheet** in the instructions	**6**	( )
7 **Net short-term capital gain or (loss).** Combine lines 1a through 6 in column (h). If you have any long-term capital gains or losses, go to Part II below. Otherwise, go to Part III on the back	**7**	

Part II   Long-Term Capital Gains and Losses—Assets Held More Than One Year

See instructions for how to figure the amounts to enter on the lines below. This form may be easier to complete if you round off cents to whole dollars.	(d) Proceeds (sales price)	(e) Cost (or other basis)	(g) Adjustments to gain or loss from Form(s) 8949, Part II, line 2, column (g)	(h) Gain or (loss) Subtract column (e) from column (d) and combine the result with column (g)
8a Totals for all long-term transactions reported on Form 1099-B for which basis was reported to the IRS and for which you have no adjustments (see instructions). However, if you choose to report all these transactions on Form 8949, leave this line blank and go to line 8b .				
8b Totals for all transactions reported on Form(s) 8949 with **Box D** checked				
9 Totals for all transactions reported on Form(s) 8949 with **Box E** checked				
10 Totals for all transactions reported on Form(s) 8949 with **Box F** checked.				

11 Gain from Form 4797, Part I; long-term gain from Forms 2439 and 6252; and long-term gain or (loss) from Forms 4684, 6781, and 8824	**11**	
12 Net long-term gain or (loss) from partnerships, S corporations, estates, and trusts from Schedule(s) K-1	**12**	
13 Capital gain distributions. See the instructions	**13**	
14 Long-term capital loss carryover. Enter the amount, if any, from line 13 of your **Capital Loss Carryover Worksheet** in the instructions	**14**	( )
15 **Net long-term capital gain or (loss).** Combine lines 8a through 14 in column (h). Then go to Part III on the back	**15**	

For Paperwork Reduction Act Notice, see your tax return instructions.   Cat. No. 11338H   Schedule D (Form 1040) 2015

Part III	**Summary**

16 Combine lines 7 and 15 and enter the result **16**

- If line 16 is a **gain,** enter the amount from line 16 on Form 1040, line 13, or Form 1040NR, line 14. Then go to line 17 below.
- If line 16 is a **loss,** skip lines 17 through 20 below. Then go to line 21. Also be sure to complete line 22.
- If line 16 is **zero,** skip lines 17 through 21 below and enter -0- on Form 1040, line 13, or Form 1040NR, line 14. Then go to line 22.

17 Are lines 15 and 16 **both** gains?
☐ **Yes.** Go to line 18.
☐ **No.** Skip lines 18 through 21, and go to line 22.

18 Enter the amount, if any, from line 7 of the **28% Rate Gain Worksheet** in the instructions . . ▶ **18**

19 Enter the amount, if any, from line 18 of the **Unrecaptured Section 1250 Gain Worksheet** in the instructions . . . . ▶ **19**

20 Are lines 18 and 19 **both** zero or blank?
☐ **Yes.** Complete the **Qualified Dividends and Capital Gain Tax Worksheet** in the instructions for Form 1040, line 44 (or in the instructions for Form 1040NR, line 42). **Do not** complete lines 21 and 22 below.

☐ **No.** Complete the **Schedule D Tax Worksheet** in the instructions. **Do not** complete lines 21 and 22 below.

21 If line 16 is a loss, enter here and on Form 1040, line 13, or Form 1040NR, line 14, the **smaller** of:

- The loss on line 16 or
- ($3,000), or if married filing separately, ($1,500)   } . . . . **21** ( )

Note: When figuring which amount is smaller, treat both amounts as positive numbers.

22 Do you have qualified dividends on Form 1040, line 9b, or Form 1040NR, line 10b?

☐ **Yes.** Complete the **Qualified Dividends and Capital Gain Tax Worksheet** in the instructions for Form 1040, line 44 (or in the instructions for Form 1040NR, line 42).

☐ **No.** Complete the rest of Form 1040 or Form 1040NR.

Form **1065**
Department of the Treasury
Internal Revenue Service

U.S. Return of Partnership Income

For calendar year 2015, or tax year beginning _____ , 2015, ending _____ , 20 _____ .

▶ Information about Form 1065 and its separate instructions is at *www.irs.gov/form1065*.

OMB No. 1545-0123

2015

A Principal business activity	Name of partnership
B Principal product or service	Number, street, and room or suite no. If a P.O. box, see the instructions.
C Business code number	City or town, state or province, country, and ZIP or foreign postal code

Type or Print

D Employer identification number

E Date business started

F Total assets (see the instructions)

$ _____

G Check applicable boxes: **(1)** ☐ Initial return **(2)** ☐ Final return **(3)** ☐ Name change **(4)** ☐ Address change **(5)** ☐ Amended return
(6) ☐ Technical termination - also check (1) or (2)

H Check accounting method: **(1)** ☐ Cash **(2)** ☐ Accrual **(3)** ☐ Other (specify) ▶ _____

I Number of Schedules K-1. Attach one for each person who was a partner at any time during the tax year ▶ _____

J Check if Schedules C and M-3 are attached . . . . ☐

Caution. Include **only** trade or business income and expenses on lines 1a through 22 below. See the instructions for more information.

Income

1a	Gross receipts or sales	**1a**
b	Returns and allowances	**1b**
c	Balance. Subtract line 1b from line 1a	**1c**
2	Cost of goods sold (attach Form 1125-A)	**2**
3	Gross profit. Subtract line 2 from line 1c	**3**
4	Ordinary income (loss) from other partnerships, estates, and trusts (attach statement) . .	**4**
5	Net farm profit (loss) (attach Schedule F (Form 1040))	**5**
6	Net gain (loss) from Form 4797, Part II, line 17 (attach Form 4797)	**6**
7	Other income (loss) (attach statement)	**7**
8	**Total income (loss).** Combine lines 3 through 7	**8**

Deductions (see the instructions for limitations)

9	Salaries and wages (other than to partners) (less employment credits)	**9**
10	Guaranteed payments to partners	**10**
11	Repairs and maintenance	**11**
12	Bad debts	**12**
13	Rent	**13**
14	Taxes and licenses	**14**
15	Interest	**15**
16a	Depreciation (if required, attach Form 4562)	**16a**
b	Less depreciation reported on Form 1125-A and elsewhere on return	**16b**	**16c**
17	Depletion **(Do not deduct oil and gas depletion.)**	**17**
18	Retirement plans, etc.	**18**
19	Employee benefit programs	**19**
20	Other deductions (attach statement)	**20**
21	**Total deductions.** Add the amounts shown in the far right column for lines 9 through 20 .	**21**
22	**Ordinary business income (loss).** Subtract line 21 from line 8	**22**

Sign Here

Under penalties of perjury, I declare that I have examined this return, including accompanying schedules and statements, and to the best of my knowledge and belief, it is true, correct, and complete. Declaration of preparer (other than general partner or limited liability company member manager) is based on all information of which preparer has any knowledge.

▶ _____
Signature of general partner or limited liability company member manager

▶ _____
Date

May the IRS discuss this return with the preparer shown below (see instructions)? ☐ **Yes** ☐ **No**

Paid Preparer Use Only

Print/Type preparer's name	Preparer's signature	Date	Check ☐ if self-employed	PTIN
Firm's name ▶			Firm's EIN ▶	
Firm's address ▶			Phone no.	

For Paperwork Reduction Act Notice, see separate instructions.   Cat. No. 11390Z   Form **1065** (2015)

Form 1065 (2015)   Page **2**

Schedule B	Other Information		

		Yes	No
1	What type of entity is filing this return? Check the applicable box:		

a	☐ Domestic general partnership	**b**	☐ Domestic limited partnership
c	☐ Domestic limited liability company	**d**	☐ Domestic limited liability partnership
e	☐ Foreign partnership	**f**	☐ Other ▶

		Yes	No
2	At any time during the tax year, was any partner in the partnership a disregarded entity, a partnership (including an entity treated as a partnership), a trust, an S corporation, an estate (other than an estate of a deceased partner), or a nominee or similar person?		
3	At the end of the tax year:		
a	Did any foreign or domestic corporation, partnership (including any entity treated as a partnership), trust, or tax-exempt organization, or any foreign government own, directly or indirectly, an interest of 50% or more in the profit, loss, or capital of the partnership? For rules of constructive ownership, see instructions. If "Yes," attach Schedule B-1, Information on Partners Owning 50% or More of the Partnership		
b	Did any individual or estate own, directly or indirectly, an interest of 50% or more in the profit, loss, or capital of the partnership? For rules of constructive ownership, see instructions. If "Yes," attach Schedule B-1, Information on Partners Owning 50% or More of the Partnership		
4	At the end of the tax year, did the partnership:		
a	Own directly 20% or more, or own, directly or indirectly, 50% or more of the total voting power of all classes of stock entitled to vote of any foreign or domestic corporation? For rules of constructive ownership, see instructions. If "Yes," complete (i) through (iv) below		

(i) Name of Corporation	(ii) Employer Identification Number (if any)	(iii) Country of Incorporation	(iv) Percentage Owned in Voting Stock

		Yes	No
b	Own directly an interest of 20% or more, or own, directly or indirectly, an interest of 50% or more in the profit, loss, or capital in any foreign or domestic partnership (including an entity treated as a partnership) or in the beneficial interest of a trust? For rules of constructive ownership, see instructions. If "Yes," complete (i) through (v) below . .		

(i) Name of Entity	(ii) Employer Identification Number (if any)	(iii) Type of Entity	(iv) Country of Organization	(v) Maximum Percentage Owned in Profit, Loss, or Capital

		Yes	No
5	Did the partnership file Form 8893, Election of Partnership Level Tax Treatment, or an election statement under section 6231(a)(1)(B)(ii) for partnership-level tax treatment, that is in effect for this tax year? See Form 8893 for more details		
6	Does the partnership satisfy **all four** of the following conditions?		
a	The partnership's total receipts for the tax year were less than $250,000.		
b	The partnership's total assets at the end of the tax year were less than $1 million.		
c	Schedules K-1 are filed with the return and furnished to the partners on or before the due date (including extensions) for the partnership return.		
d	The partnership is not filing and is not required to file Schedule M-3		
	If "Yes," the partnership is not required to complete Schedules L, M-1, and M-2; Item F on page 1 of Form 1065; or Item L on Schedule K-1.		
7	Is this partnership a publicly traded partnership as defined in section 469(k)(2)?		
8	During the tax year, did the partnership have any debt that was cancelled, was forgiven, or had the terms modified so as to reduce the principal amount of the debt?		
9	Has this partnership filed, or is it required to file, Form 8918, Material Advisor Disclosure Statement, to provide information on any reportable transaction?		
10	At any time during calendar year 2015, did the partnership have an interest in or a signature or other authority over a financial account in a foreign country (such as a bank account, securities account, or other financial account)? See the instructions for exceptions and filing requirements for FinCEN Form 114, Report of Foreign Bank and Financial Accounts (FBAR). If "Yes," enter the name of the foreign country. ▶		

Form **1065** (2015)

Form 1065 (2015)   Page **3**

Schedule B	Other Information *(continued)*		

		Yes	No
11	At any time during the tax year, did the partnership receive a distribution from, or was it the grantor of, or transferor to, a foreign trust? If "Yes," the partnership may have to file Form 3520, Annual Return To Report Transactions With Foreign Trusts and Receipt of Certain Foreign Gifts. See instructions		
12a	Is the partnership making, or had it previously made (and not revoked), a section 754 election? . . . . . . See instructions for details regarding a section 754 election.		
b	Did the partnership make for this tax year an optional basis adjustment under section 743(b) or 734(b)? If "Yes," attach a statement showing the computation and allocation of the basis adjustment. See instructions		
c	Is the partnership required to adjust the basis of partnership assets under section 743(b) or 734(b) because of a substantial built-in loss (as defined under section 743(d)) or substantial basis reduction (as defined under section 734(d))? If "Yes," attach a statement showing the computation and allocation of the basis adjustment. See instructions		
13	Check this box if, during the current or prior tax year, the partnership distributed any property received in a like-kind exchange or contributed such property to another entity (other than disregarded entities wholly owned by the partnership throughout the tax year) . . . . ▶ ☐		
14	At any time during the tax year, did the partnership distribute to any partner a tenancy-in-common or other undivided interest in partnership property?		
15	If the partnership is required to file Form 8858, Information Return of U.S. Persons With Respect To Foreign Disregarded Entities, enter the number of Forms 8858 attached. See instructions ▶		
16	Does the partnership have any foreign partners? If "Yes," enter the number of Forms 8805, Foreign Partner's Information Statement of Section 1446 Withholding Tax, filed for this partnership. ▶		
17	Enter the number of Forms 8865, Return of U.S. Persons With Respect to Certain Foreign Partnerships, attached to this return. ▶		
18a	Did you make any payments in 2015 that would require you to file Form(s) 1099? See instructions		
b	If "Yes," did you or will you file required Form(s) 1099?		
19	Enter the number of Form(s) 5471, Information Return of U.S. Persons With Respect To Certain Foreign Corporations, attached to this return. ▶		
20	Enter the number of partners that are foreign governments under section 892. ▶		

Designation of Tax Matters Partner (see instructions)

Enter below the general partner or member-manager designated as the tax matters partner (TMP) for the tax year of this return:

Name of designated TMP ▶		Identifying number of TMP ▶	
If the TMP is an entity, name of TMP representative ▶		Phone number of TMP ▶	
Address of designated TMP ▶			

Form **1065** (2015)

Form 1065 (2015)   Page **4**

Schedule K		Partners' Distributive Share Items		Total amount	

Income (Loss)

	1	Ordinary business income (loss) (page 1, line 22)	**1**		
	2	Net rental real estate income (loss) (attach Form 8825)	**2**		
	3a	Other gross rental income (loss)	3a		
	b	Expenses from other rental activities (attach statement)	3b		
	c	Other net rental income (loss). Subtract line 3b from line 3a	**3c**		
	4	Guaranteed payments	**4**		
	5	Interest income	**5**		
	6	Dividends: **a** Ordinary dividends	**6a**		
	b	Qualified dividends	6b		
	7	Royalties	**7**		
	8	Net short-term capital gain (loss) (attach Schedule D (Form 1065))	**8**		
	9a	Net long-term capital gain (loss) (attach Schedule D (Form 1065))	**9a**		
	b	Collectibles (28%) gain (loss)	9b		
	c	Unrecaptured section 1250 gain (attach statement) . .	9c		
	10	Net section 1231 gain (loss) (attach Form 4797)	**10**		
	11	Other income (loss) (see instructions) Type ▶	**11**		

Deductions

	12	Section 179 deduction (attach Form 4562)	**12**		
	13a	Contributions	**13a**		
	b	Investment interest expense	**13b**		
	c	Section 59(e)(2) expenditures: **(1)** Type ▶ _____ **(2)** Amount ▶	13c(2)		
	d	Other deductions (see instructions) Type ▶	**13d**		

Self-Employment

	14a	Net earnings (loss) from self-employment	**14a**		
	b	Gross farming or fishing income	**14b**		
	c	Gross nonfarm income	**14c**		

Credits

	15a	Low-income housing credit (section 42(j)(5))	**15a**		
	b	Low-income housing credit (other)	**15b**		
	c	Qualified rehabilitation expenditures (rental real estate) (attach Form 3468, if applicable)	**15c**		
	d	Other rental real estate credits (see instructions) Type ▶ _____	**15d**		
	e	Other rental credits (see instructions) Type ▶ _____	**15e**		
	f	Other credits (see instructions) Type ▶	**15f**		

Foreign Transactions

	16a	Name of country or U.S. possession ▶ _____			
	b	Gross income from all sources	**16b**		
	c	Gross income sourced at partner level	**16c**		
		Foreign gross income sourced at partnership level			
	d	Passive category ▶ _____ **e** General category ▶ _____ **f** Other ▶	**16f**		
		Deductions allocated and apportioned at partner level			
	g	Interest expense ▶ _____ **h** Other . . . . ▶	**16h**		
		Deductions allocated and apportioned at partnership level to foreign source income			
	i	Passive category ▶ _____ **j** General category ▶ _____ **k** Other ▶	**16k**		
	l	Total foreign taxes (check one): ▶ Paid ☐ Accrued ☐	**16l**		
	m	Reduction in taxes available for credit (attach statement)	**16m**		
	n	Other foreign tax information (attach statement)			

Alternative Minimum Tax (AMT) Items

	17a	Post-1986 depreciation adjustment	**17a**		
	b	Adjusted gain or loss	**17b**		
	c	Depletion (other than oil and gas)	**17c**		
	d	Oil, gas, and geothermal properties—gross income	**17d**		
	e	Oil, gas, and geothermal properties—deductions	**17e**		
	f	Other AMT items (attach statement)	**17f**		

Other Information

	18a	Tax-exempt interest income	**18a**		
	b	Other tax-exempt income	**18b**		
	c	Nondeductible expenses	**18c**		
	19a	Distributions of cash and marketable securities	**19a**		
	b	Distributions of other property	**19b**		
	20a	Investment income	**20a**		
	b	Investment expenses	**20b**		
	c	Other items and amounts (attach statement)			

Form **1065** (2015)

Form 1065 (2015)   Page **5**

Analysis of Net Income (Loss)

1   Net income (loss). Combine Schedule K, lines 1 through 11. From the result, subtract the sum of Schedule K, lines 12 through 13d, and 16l **1**

2 Analysis by partner type:	**(i)** Corporate	**(ii)** Individual (active)	**(iii)** Individual (passive)	**(iv)** Partnership	**(v)** Exempt Organization	**(vi)** Nominee/Other
a General partners						
b Limited partners						

Schedule L	**Balance Sheets per Books**	Beginning of tax year		End of tax year	
	Assets	**(a)**	**(b)**	**(c)**	**(d)**
1	Cash				
2a	Trade notes and accounts receivable . . .				
b	Less allowance for bad debts				
3	Inventories				
4	U.S. government obligations				
5	Tax-exempt securities				
6	Other current assets (attach statement) . .				
7a	Loans to partners (or persons related to partners)				
b	Mortgage and real estate loans				
8	Other investments (attach statement) . . .				
9a	Buildings and other depreciable assets . .				
b	Less accumulated depreciation				
10a	Depletable assets				
b	Less accumulated depletion				
11	Land (net of any amortization)				
12a	Intangible assets (amortizable only) . . .				
b	Less accumulated amortization				
13	Other assets (attach statement)				
14	Total assets				
	Liabilities and Capital				
15	Accounts payable				
16	Mortgages, notes, bonds payable in less than 1 year				
17	Other current liabilities (attach statement) .				
18	All nonrecourse loans				
19a	Loans from partners (or persons related to partners)				
b	Mortgages, notes, bonds payable in 1 year or more				
20	Other liabilities (attach statement)				
21	Partners' capital accounts				
22	Total liabilities and capital				

Schedule M-1	**Reconciliation of Income (Loss) per Books With Income (Loss) per Return**

Note. The partnership may be required to file Schedule M-3 (see instructions).

1 Net income (loss) per books		**6** Income recorded on books this year not included on Schedule K, lines 1 through 11 (itemize):	
2 Income included on Schedule K, lines 1, 2, 3c, 5, 6a, 7, 8, 9a, 10, and 11, not recorded on books this year (itemize): _____		**a** Tax-exempt interest $ _____	
3 Guaranteed payments (other than health insurance)		**7** Deductions included on Schedule K, lines 1 through 13d, and 16l, not charged against book income this year (itemize):	
4 Expenses recorded on books this year not included on Schedule K, lines 1 through 13d, and 16l (itemize):		**a** Depreciation $ _____	
a Depreciation $ _____		**8** Add lines 6 and 7	
b Travel and entertainment $ _____		**9** Income (loss) (Analysis of Net Income (Loss), line 1). Subtract line 8 from line 5 .	
5 Add lines 1 through 4			

Schedule M-2	**Analysis of Partners' Capital Accounts**

1 Balance at beginning of year . . .		**6** Distributions: **a** Cash	
2 Capital contributed: **a** Cash . . .		**b** Property	
b Property . .		**7** Other decreases (itemize): _____	
3 Net income (loss) per books			
4 Other increases (itemize): _____		**8** Add lines 6 and 7	
5 Add lines 1 through 4		**9** Balance at end of year. Subtract line 8 from line 5	

651113

☐ Final K-1   ☐ Amended K-1   OMB No. 1545-0123

Schedule K-1
(Form 1065)

20**15**

Department of the Treasury
Internal Revenue Service

For calendar year 2015, or tax
year beginning _____ , 2015
ending _____ , 20 _____

Partner's Share of Income, Deductions,
Credits, etc.   ▶ See back of form and separate instructions.

Part I	**Information About the Partnership**

A   Partnership's employer identification number

B   Partnership's name, address, city, state, and ZIP code

C   IRS Center where partnership filed return

D   ☐ Check if this is a publicly traded partnership (PTP)

Part II	**Information About the Partner**

E   Partner's identifying number

F   Partner's name, address, city, state, and ZIP code

G   ☐ General partner or LLC   ☐ Limited partner or other LLC
          member-manager   member

H   ☐ Domestic partner   ☐ Foreign partner

I1   What type of entity is this partner? _____

I2   If this partner is a retirement plan (IRA/SEP/Keogh/etc.), check here
· ☐

J   Partner's share of profit, loss, and capital (see instructions):

	Beginning	**Ending**
Profit	%	%
Loss	%	%
Capital	%	%

K   Partner's share of liabilities at year end:
Nonrecourse . . . . $ _____
Qualified nonrecourse financing . $ _____
Recourse . . . . $ _____

L   Partner's capital account analysis:
Beginning capital account . . . $ _____
Capital contributed during the year $ _____
Current year increase (decrease) . $ _____
Withdrawals & distributions . $ (_____)
Ending capital account . . . . $ _____

☐ Tax basis   ☐ GAAP   ☐ Section 704(b) book
☐ Other (explain)

M   Did the partner contribute property with a built-in gain or loss?
☐ Yes   ☐ No
If "Yes," attach statement (see instructions)

Part III	**Partner's Share of Current Year Income,**
	Deductions, Credits, and Other Items

1 Ordinary business income (loss)	**15** Credits	
2 Net rental real estate income (loss)		
3 Other net rental income (loss)	**16** Foreign transactions	
4 Guaranteed payments		
5 Interest income		
6a Ordinary dividends		
6b Qualified dividends		
7 Royalties		
8 Net short-term capital gain (loss)		
9a Net long-term capital gain (loss)	**17** Alternative minimum tax (AMT) items	
9b Collectibles (28%) gain (loss)		
9c Unrecaptured section 1250 gain		
10 Net section 1231 gain (loss)	**18** Tax-exempt income and nondeductible expenses	
11 Other income (loss)		
	19 Distributions	
12 Section 179 deduction		
13 Other deductions	**20** Other information	
14 Self-employment earnings (loss)		

*See attached statement for additional information.

For IRS Use Only

Form **1120**
Department of the Treasury
Internal Revenue Service

U.S. Corporation Income Tax Return

For calendar year 2015 or tax year beginning _____ , 2015, ending _____ , 20 _____

▶ Information about Form 1120 and its separate instructions is at www.irs.gov/form1120.

OMB No. 1545-0123

2015

A Check if:

1a Consolidated return (attach Form 851) . ☐
  b Life/nonlife consoli-dated return . . . ☐
2 Personal holding co. (attach Sch. PH) . ☐
3 Personal service corp. (see instructions) . ☐
4 Schedule M-3 attached ☐

TYPE OR PRINT

Name

Number, street, and room or suite no. If a P.O. box, see instructions.

City or town, state, or province, country, and ZIP or foreign postal code

B Employer identification number

C Date incorporated

D Total assets (see instructions)
$

E Check if: (1) ☐ Initial return (2) ☐ Final return (3) ☐ Name change (4) ☐ Address change

Income	1a	Gross receipts or sales	1a	
	b	Returns and allowances	1b	
	c	Balance. Subtract line 1b from line 1a	1c	
	2	Cost of goods sold (attach Form 1125-A)	2	
	3	Gross profit. Subtract line 2 from line 1c	3	
	4	Dividends (Schedule C, line 19)	4	
	5	Interest	5	
	6	Gross rents	6	
	7	Gross royalties	7	
	8	Capital gain net income (attach Schedule D (Form 1120))	8	
	9	Net gain or (loss) from Form 4797, Part II, line 17 (attach Form 4797)	9	
	10	Other income (see instructions—attach statement)	10	
	11	**Total income.** Add lines 3 through 10 . . . . ▶	11	

Deductions (See instructions for limitations on deductions.)	12	Compensation of officers (see instructions—attach Form 1125-E) . . . . . ▶	12	
	13	Salaries and wages (less employment credits)	13	
	14	Repairs and maintenance	14	
	15	Bad debts	15	
	16	Rents	16	
	17	Taxes and licenses	17	
	18	Interest	18	
	19	Charitable contributions	19	
	20	Depreciation from Form 4562 not claimed on Form 1125-A or elsewhere on return (attach Form 4562) . .	20	
	21	Depletion	21	
	22	Advertising	22	
	23	Pension, profit-sharing, etc., plans	23	
	24	Employee benefit programs	24	
	25	Domestic production activities deduction (attach Form 8903)	25	
	26	Other deductions (attach statement)	26	
	27	**Total deductions.** Add lines 12 through 26 . . . . ▶	27	
	28	Taxable income before net operating loss deduction and special deductions. Subtract line 27 from line 11.	28	
	29a	Net operating loss deduction (see instructions)	29a	
	b	Special deductions (Schedule C, line 20)	29b	
	c	Add lines 29a and 29b	29c	

Tax, Refundable Credits, and Payments	30	**Taxable income.** Subtract line 29c from line 28 (see instructions)	30	
	31	Total tax (Schedule J, Part I, line 11)	31	
	32	Total payments and refundable credits (Schedule J, Part II, line 21)	32	
	33	Estimated tax penalty (see instructions). Check if Form 2220 is attached . . . . ▶ ☐	33	
	34	**Amount owed.** If line 32 is smaller than the total of lines 31 and 33, enter amount owed	34	
	35	**Overpayment.** If line 32 is larger than the total of lines 31 and 33, enter amount overpaid	35	
	36	Enter amount from line 35 you want: **Credited to 2016 estimated tax** ▶ **Refunded** ▶	36	

Sign Here

Under penalties of perjury, I declare that I have examined this return, including accompanying schedules and statements, and to the best of my knowledge and belief, it is true, correct, and complete. Declaration of preparer (other than taxpayer) is based on all information of which preparer has any knowledge.

▶ _____   _____   ▶ _____
Signature of officer   Date   Title

May the IRS discuss this return with the preparer shown below (see instructions)? ☐ Yes ☐ No

Paid Preparer Use Only

Print/Type preparer's name	Preparer's signature	Date	Check ☐ if self-employed	PTIN

Firm's name ▶   Firm's EIN ▶

Firm's address ▶   Phone no.

For Paperwork Reduction Act Notice, see separate instructions.   Cat. No. 11450Q   Form **1120** (2015)

Form 1120 (2015)   Page **2**

Schedule C	Dividends and Special Deductions (see instructions)	(a) Dividends received	(b) %	(c) Special deductions (a) × (b)
1	Dividends from less-than-20%-owned domestic corporations (other than debt-financed stock)		70	
2	Dividends from 20%-or-more-owned domestic corporations (other than debt-financed stock)		80	
3	Dividends on debt-financed stock of domestic and foreign corporations		see instructions	
4	Dividends on certain preferred stock of less-than-20%-owned public utilities . . .		42	
5	Dividends on certain preferred stock of 20%-or-more-owned public utilities		48	
6	Dividends from less-than-20%-owned foreign corporations and certain FSCs . . .		70	
7	Dividends from 20%-or-more-owned foreign corporations and certain FSCs . . .		80	
8	Dividends from wholly owned foreign subsidiaries		100	
9	**Total.** Add lines 1 through 8. See instructions for limitation			
10	Dividends from domestic corporations received by a small business investment company operating under the Small Business Investment Act of 1958		100	
11	Dividends from affiliated group members		100	
12	Dividends from certain FSCs		100	
13	Dividends from foreign corporations not included on lines 3, 6, 7, 8, 11, or 12 . . .			
14	Income from controlled foreign corporations under subpart F (attach Form(s) 5471) .			
15	Foreign dividend gross-up			
16	IC-DISC and former DISC dividends not included on lines 1, 2, or 3			
17	Other dividends			
18	Deduction for dividends paid on certain preferred stock of public utilities			
19	**Total dividends.** Add lines 1 through 17. Enter here and on page 1, line 4 . . . ▶			
20	**Total special deductions.** Add lines 9, 10, 11, 12, and 18. Enter here and on page 1, line 29b . . . . ▶			

Form **1120** (2015)

Form 1120 (2015)   Page **3**

Schedule J   Tax Computation and Payment (see instructions)

Part I—Tax Computation

1	Check if the corporation is a member of a controlled group (attach Schedule O (Form 1120)) ▶ ☐		
2	Income tax. Check if a qualified personal service corporation (see instructions) ▶ ☐	**2**	
3	Alternative minimum tax (attach Form 4626)	**3**	
4	Add lines 2 and 3	**4**	
5a	Foreign tax credit (attach Form 1118)	**5a**	
b	Credit from Form 8834 (see instructions)	**5b**	
c	General business credit (attach Form 3800)	**5c**	
d	Credit for prior year minimum tax (attach Form 8827)	**5d**	
e	Bond credits from Form 8912	**5e**	
6	**Total credits.** Add lines 5a through 5e	**6**	
7	Subtract line 6 from line 4	**7**	
8	Personal holding company tax (attach Schedule PH (Form 1120))	**8**	
9a	Recapture of investment credit (attach Form 4255)	**9a**	
b	Recapture of low-income housing credit (attach Form 8611)	**9b**	
c	Interest due under the look-back method—completed long-term contracts (attach Form 8697)	**9c**	
d	Interest due under the look-back method—income forecast method (attach Form 8866)	**9d**	
e	Alternative tax on qualifying shipping activities (attach Form 8902)	**9e**	
f	Other (see instructions—attach statement)	**9f**	
10	**Total.** Add lines 9a through 9f	**10**	
11	**Total tax.** Add lines 7, 8, and 10. Enter here and on page 1, line 31	**11**	

Part II—Payments and Refundable Credits

12	2014 overpayment credited to 2015	**12**	
13	2015 estimated tax payments	**13**	
14	2015 refund applied for on Form 4466	**14** ( )	
15	Combine lines 12, 13, and 14	**15**	
16	Tax deposited with Form 7004	**16**	
17	Withholding (see instructions)	**17**	
18	**Total payments.** Add lines 15, 16, and 17	**18**	
19	Refundable credits from:		
a	Form 2439	**19a**	
b	Form 4136	**19b**	
c	Form 8827, line 8c	**19c**	
d	Other (attach statement—see instructions)	**19d**	
20	**Total credits.** Add lines 19a through 19d	**20**	
21	**Total payments and credits.** Add lines 18 and 20. Enter here and on page 1, line 32	**21**	

Schedule K   Other Information (see instructions)

		Yes	No
1	Check accounting method: **a** ☐ Cash **b** ☐ Accrual **c** ☐ Other (specify) ▶ _____		
2	See the instructions and enter the:		
a	Business activity code no. ▶ _____		
b	Business activity ▶ _____		
c	Product or service ▶ _____		
3	Is the corporation a subsidiary in an affiliated group or a parent-subsidiary controlled group? If "Yes," enter name and EIN of the parent corporation ▶ _____		
4	At the end of the tax year:		
a	Did any foreign or domestic corporation, partnership (including any entity treated as a partnership), trust, or tax-exempt organization own directly 20% or more, or own, directly or indirectly, 50% or more of the total voting power of all classes of the corporation's stock entitled to vote? If "Yes," complete Part I of Schedule G (Form 1120) (attach Schedule G)		
b	Did any individual or estate own directly 20% or more, or own, directly or indirectly, 50% or more of the total voting power of all classes of the corporation's stock entitled to vote? If "Yes," complete Part II of Schedule G (Form 1120) (attach Schedule G)		

Form **1120** (2015)

Form 1120 (2015)   Page **4**

Schedule K	**Other Information** *continued* (see instructions)			Yes	No

5 At the end of the tax year, did the corporation:

a Own directly 20% or more, or own, directly or indirectly, 50% or more of the total voting power of all classes of stock entitled to vote of any foreign or domestic corporation not included on **Form 851,** Affiliations Schedule? For rules of constructive ownership, see instructions. If "Yes," complete (i) through (iv) below.

(i) Name of Corporation	**(ii)** Employer Identification Number (if any)	**(iii)** Country of Incorporation	**(iv)** Percentage Owned in Voting Stock

b Own directly an interest of 20% or more, or own, directly or indirectly, an interest of 50% or more in any foreign or domestic partnership (including an entity treated as a partnership) or in the beneficial interest of a trust? For rules of constructive ownership, see instructions. If "Yes," complete (i) through (iv) below.

(i) Name of Entity	**(ii)** Employer Identification Number (if any)	**(iii)** Country of Organization	**(iv)** Maximum Percentage Owned in Profit, Loss, or Capital

6 During this tax year, did the corporation pay dividends (other than stock dividends and distributions in exchange for stock) in excess of the corporation's current and accumulated earnings and profits? (See sections 301 and 316.) . . . .

If "Yes," file **Form 5452,** Corporate Report of Nondividend Distributions.

If this is a consolidated return, answer here for the parent corporation and on Form 851 for each subsidiary.

7 At any time during the tax year, did one foreign person own, directly or indirectly, at least 25% of **(a)** the total voting power of all classes of the corporation's stock entitled to vote or **(b)** the total value of all classes of the corporation's stock? . . . .

For rules of attribution, see section 318. If "Yes," enter:

(i) Percentage owned ▶ _____ and **(ii)** Owner's country ▶ _____

(c) The corporation may have to file **Form 5472,** Information Return of a 25% Foreign-Owned U.S. Corporation or a Foreign Corporation Engaged in a U.S. Trade or Business. Enter the number of Forms 5472 attached ▶ _____

8 Check this box if the corporation issued publicly offered debt instruments with original issue discount . . . . . . ▶ ☐

If checked, the corporation may have to file **Form 8281,** Information Return for Publicly Offered Original Issue Discount Instruments.

9 Enter the amount of tax-exempt interest received or accrued during the tax year ▶ $ _____

10 Enter the number of shareholders at the end of the tax year (if 100 or fewer) ▶ _____

11 If the corporation has an NOL for the tax year and is electing to forego the carryback period, check here . . . . . ▶ ☐

If the corporation is filing a consolidated return, the statement required by Regulations section 1.1502-21(b)(3) must be attached or the election will not be valid.

12 Enter the available NOL carryover from prior tax years (do not reduce it by any deduction on line 29a.) ▶ $ _____

13 Are the corporation's total receipts (page 1, line 1a, plus lines 4 through 10) for the tax year **and** its total assets at the end of the tax year less than $250,000? . . . .

If "Yes," the corporation is not required to complete Schedules L, M-1, and M-2. Instead, enter the total amount of cash distributions and the book value of property distributions (other than cash) made during the tax year ▶ $ _____

14 Is the corporation required to file Schedule UTP (Form 1120), Uncertain Tax Position Statement (see instructions)? . . . .

If "Yes," complete and attach Schedule UTP.

15a Did the corporation make any payments in 2015 that would require it to file Form(s) 1099? . . . .

b If "Yes," did or will the corporation file required Forms 1099? . . . .

16 During this tax year, did the corporation have an 80% or more change in ownership, including a change due to redemption of its own stock? . . . .

17 During or subsequent to this tax year, but before the filing of this return, did the corporation dispose of more than 65% (by value) of its assets in a taxable, non-taxable, or tax deferred transaction? . . . .

18 Did the corporation receive assets in a section 351 transfer in which any of the transferred assets had a fair market basis or fair market value of more than $1 million? . . . .

Form **1120** (2015)

Form 1120 (2015)

Page **5**

Schedule L	Balance Sheets per Books	Beginning of tax year		End of tax year	
	Assets	**(a)**	**(b)**	**(c)**	**(d)**
1	Cash				
2a	Trade notes and accounts receivable . . .				
b	Less allowance for bad debts	(	)	(	)
3	Inventories				
4	U.S. government obligations				
5	Tax-exempt securities (see instructions) . .				
6	Other current assets (attach statement) . .				
7	Loans to shareholders				
8	Mortgage and real estate loans				
9	Other investments (attach statement) . . .				
10a	Buildings and other depreciable assets . .				
b	Less accumulated depreciation	(	)	(	)
11a	Depletable assets				
b	Less accumulated depletion	(	)	(	)
12	Land (net of any amortization)				
13a	Intangible assets (amortizable only) . . .				
b	Less accumulated amortization	(	)	(	)
14	Other assets (attach statement)				
15	Total assets				
	Liabilities and Shareholders' Equity				
16	Accounts payable				
17	Mortgages, notes, bonds payable in less than 1 year				
18	Other current liabilities (attach statement) . .				
19	Loans from shareholders				
20	Mortgages, notes, bonds payable in 1 year or more				
21	Other liabilities (attach statement)				
22	Capital stock: **a** Preferred stock				
	b Common stock				
23	Additional paid-in capital				
24	Retained earnings—Appropriated (attach statement)				
25	Retained earnings—Unappropriated . . .				
26	Adjustments to shareholders' equity (attach statement)				
27	Less cost of treasury stock		(	)	(	)
28	Total liabilities and shareholders' equity . .				

Schedule M-1	Reconciliation of Income (Loss) per Books With Income per Return

Note: The corporation may be required to file Schedule M-3 (see instructions).

1	Net income (loss) per books		7	Income recorded on books this year not included on this return (itemize):	
2	Federal income tax per books				
3	Excess of capital losses over capital gains .			Tax-exempt interest $ _____	
4	Income subject to tax not recorded on books this year (itemize):_____				
	_____		8	Deductions on this return not charged against book income this year (itemize):	
5	Expenses recorded on books this year not deducted on this return (itemize):		**a**	Depreciation . . $ _____	
a	Depreciation . . . . $ _____		**b**	Charitable contributions $ _____	
b	Charitable contributions . $ _____			_____	
c	Travel and entertainment . $ _____				
	_____		9	Add lines 7 and 8	
6	Add lines 1 through 5		10	Income (page 1, line 28)—line 6 less line 9	

Schedule M-2	Analysis of Unappropriated Retained Earnings per Books (Line 25, Schedule L)

1	Balance at beginning of year		5	Distributions: **a** Cash	
2	Net income (loss) per books			**b** Stock	
3	Other increases (itemize):_____			**c** Property . . .	
	_____		6	Other decreases (itemize):_____	
	_____		7	Add lines 5 and 6	
4	Add lines 1, 2, and 3		8	Balance at end of year (line 4 less line 7)	

Form **1120** (2015)

Form **1120S**

Department of the Treasury
Internal Revenue Service

U.S. Income Tax Return for an S Corporation

► **Do not file this form unless the corporation has filed or is attaching Form 2553 to elect to be an S corporation.**
► **Information about Form 1120S and its separate instructions is at** *www.irs.gov/form1120s.*

OMB No. 1545-0123

2015

For calendar year 2015 or tax year beginning _____ **, 2015, ending** _____ **, 20** ____

A S election effective date		**D** Employer identification number
B Business activity code number (see instructions)	**TYPE OR PRINT** Name / Number, street, and room or suite no. If a P.O. box, see instructions. / City or town, state or province, country, and ZIP or foreign postal code	**E** Date incorporated
C Check if Sch. M-3 attached ☐		**F** Total assets (see instructions) $

G Is the corporation electing to be an S corporation beginning with this tax year? ☐ Yes ☐ No   If "Yes," attach Form 2553 if not already filed

H Check if: **(1)** ☐ Final return **(2)** ☐ Name change **(3)** ☐ Address change **(4)** ☐ Amended return **(5)** ☐ S election termination or revocation

I Enter the number of shareholders who were shareholders during any part of the tax year . . . . ►

Caution: Include **only** trade or business income and expenses on lines 1a through 21. See the instructions for more information.

Income

1a	Gross receipts or sales	**1a**	
b	Returns and allowances	**1b**	
c	Balance. Subtract line 1b from line 1a	**1c**	
2	Cost of goods sold (attach Form 1125-A)	**2**	
3	Gross profit. Subtract line 2 from line 1c	**3**	
4	Net gain (loss) from Form 4797, line 17 (attach Form 4797)	**4**	
5	Other income (loss) (see instructions—attach statement)	**5**	
6	**Total income (loss).** Add lines 3 through 5 . . . . ►	**6**	

Deductions (see instructions for limitations)

7	Compensation of officers (see instructions—attach Form 1125-E) . . .	**7**	
8	Salaries and wages (less employment credits)	**8**	
9	Repairs and maintenance	**9**	
10	Bad debts	**10**	
11	Rents	**11**	
12	Taxes and licenses	**12**	
13	Interest	**13**	
14	Depreciation not claimed on Form 1125-A or elsewhere on return (attach Form 4562) . . .	**14**	
15	Depletion (**Do not deduct oil and gas depletion.**)	**15**	
16	Advertising	**16**	
17	Pension, profit-sharing, etc., plans	**17**	
18	Employee benefit programs	**18**	
19	Other deductions (attach statement)	**19**	
20	**Total deductions.** Add lines 7 through 19 . . . . ►	**20**	
21	**Ordinary business income (loss).** Subtract line 20 from line 6	**21**	

Tax and Payments

22a	Excess net passive income or LIFO recapture tax (see instructions) . .	**22a**	
b	Tax from Schedule D (Form 1120S)	**22b**	
c	Add lines 22a and 22b (see instructions for additional taxes) . . .	**22c**	
23a	2015 estimated tax payments and 2014 overpayment credited to 2015	**23a**	
b	Tax deposited with Form 7004	**23b**	
c	Credit for federal tax paid on fuels (attach Form 4136)	**23c**	
d	Add lines 23a through 23c	**23d**	
24	Estimated tax penalty (see instructions). Check if Form 2220 is attached . . . . . ► ☐	**24**	
25	**Amount owed.** If line 23d is smaller than the total of lines 22c and 24, enter amount owed . .	**25**	
26	**Overpayment.** If line 23d is larger than the total of lines 22c and 24, enter amount overpaid . .	**26**	
27	Enter amount from line 26 **Credited to 2016 estimated tax** ► _____ **Refunded** ►	**27**	

Sign Here

Under penalties of perjury, I declare that I have examined this return, including accompanying schedules and statements, and to the best of my knowledge and belief, it is true, correct, and complete. Declaration of preparer (other than taxpayer) is based on all information of which preparer has any knowledge.

► _____
Signature of officer   Date   ⊠   Title

May the IRS discuss this return with the preparer shown below (see instructions)? ☐ Yes ☐ No

Paid Preparer Use Only

Print/Type preparer's name	Preparer's signature	Date	Check ☐ if self-employed	PTIN
Firm's name ►			Firm's EIN ►	
Firm's address ►			Phone no.	

For Paperwork Reduction Act Notice, see separate instructions.   Cat. No. 11510H   Form **1120S** (2015)

Form 1120S (2015)

Page **2**

Schedule B   Other Information (see instructions)

			Yes	No
1	Check accounting method: **a** ☐ Cash **b** ☐ Accrual **c** ☐ Other (specify) ▶ _____			
2	See the instructions and enter the: **a** Business activity ▶ _____ **b** Product or service ▶ _____			
3	At any time during the tax year, was any shareholder of the corporation a disregarded entity, a trust, an estate, or a nominee or similar person? If "Yes," attach Schedule B-1, Information on Certain Shareholders of an S Corporation . .			
4	At the end of the tax year, did the corporation:			
a	Own directly 20% or more, or own, directly or indirectly, 50% or more of the total stock issued and outstanding of any foreign or domestic corporation? For rules of constructive ownership, see instructions. If "Yes," complete (i) through (v) below			

(i) Name of Corporation	(ii) Employer Identification Number (if any)	(iii) Country of Incorporation	(iv) Percentage of Stock Owned	(v) If Percentage in (iv) is 100%, Enter the Date (if any) a Qualified Subchapter S Subsidiary Election Was Made

			Yes	No
b	Own directly an interest of 20% or more, or own, directly or indirectly, an interest of 50% or more in the profit, loss, or capital in any foreign or domestic partnership (including an entity treated as a partnership) or in the beneficial interest of a trust? For rules of constructive ownership, see instructions. If "Yes," complete (i) through (v) below			

(i) Name of Entity	(ii) Employer Identification Number (if any)	(iii) Type of Entity	(iv) Country of Organization	(v) Maximum Percentage Owned in Profit, Loss, or Capital

			Yes	No
5 a	At the end of the tax year, did the corporation have any outstanding shares of restricted stock?			
	If "Yes," complete lines (i) and (ii) below.			
	(i) Total shares of restricted stock. . . . . ▶ _____			
	(ii) Total shares of non-restricted stock . . . . ▶ _____			
b	At the end of the tax year, did the corporation have any outstanding stock options, warrants, or similar instruments? .			
	If "Yes," complete lines (i) and (ii) below.			
	(i) Total shares of stock outstanding at the end of the tax year ▶ _____			
	(ii) Total shares of stock outstanding if all instruments were executed ▶ _____			
6	Has this corporation filed, or is it required to file, **Form 8918**, Material Advisor Disclosure Statement, to provide information on any reportable transaction?			
7	Check this box if the corporation issued publicly offered debt instruments with original issue discount . . . . ▶ ☐			
	If checked, the corporation may have to file **Form 8281**, Information Return for Publicly Offered Original Issue Discount Instruments.			
8	If the corporation: **(a)** was a C corporation before it elected to be an S corporation **or** the corporation acquired an asset with a basis determined by reference to the basis of the asset (or the basis of any other property) in the hands of a C corporation **and (b)** has net unrealized built-in gain in excess of the net recognized built-in gain from prior years, enter the net unrealized built-in gain reduced by net recognized built-in gain from prior years (see instructions) . . . . ▶ $ _____			
9	Enter the accumulated earnings and profits of the corporation at the end of the tax year. $ _____			
10	Does the corporation satisfy **both** of the following conditions?			
a	The corporation's total receipts (see instructions) for the tax year were less than $250,000			
b	The corporation's total assets at the end of the tax year were less than $250,000			
	If "Yes," the corporation is not required to complete Schedules L and M-1.			
11	During the tax year, did the corporation have any non-shareholder debt that was canceled, was forgiven, or had the terms modified so as to reduce the principal amount of the debt?			
	If "Yes," enter the amount of principal reduction $ _____			
12	During the tax year, was a qualified subchapter S subsidiary election terminated or revoked? If "Yes," see instructions .			
13a	Did the corporation make any payments in 2015 that would require it to file Form(s) 1099?			
b	If "Yes," did the corporation file or will it file required Forms 1099?			

Form **1120S** (2015)

Form 1120S (2015)   Page **3**

Schedule K	Shareholders' Pro Rata Share Items		Total amount	
Income (Loss)	**1** Ordinary business income (loss) (page 1, line 21)	**1**		
	2 Net rental real estate income (loss) (attach Form 8825)	**2**		
	3a Other gross rental income (loss) **3a**			
	b Expenses from other rental activities (attach statement) . . **3b**			
	c Other net rental income (loss). Subtract line 3b from line 3a .	**3c**		
	4 Interest income	**4**		
	5 Dividends: **a** Ordinary dividends	**5a**		
	b Qualified dividends **5b**			
	6 Royalties	**6**		
	7 Net short-term capital gain (loss) (attach Schedule D (Form 1120S))	**7**		
	8a Net long-term capital gain (loss) (attach Schedule D (Form 1120S))	**8a**		
	b Collectibles (28%) gain (loss) **8b**			
	c Unrecaptured section 1250 gain (attach statement) **8c**			
	9 Net section 1231 gain (loss) (attach Form 4797)	**9**		
	10 Other income (loss) (see instructions) . . Type ▶	**10**		
Deductions	**11** Section 179 deduction (attach Form 4562)	**11**		
	12a Charitable contributions	**12a**		
	b Investment interest expense	**12b**		
	c Section 59(e)(2) expenditures **(1)** Type ▶ _____ **(2)** Amount ▶	**12c(2)**		
	d Other deductions (see instructions) . . . Type ▶	**12d**		
Credits	**13a** Low-income housing credit (section 42(j)(5))	**13a**		
	b Low-income housing credit (other)	**13b**		
	c Qualified rehabilitation expenditures (rental real estate) (attach Form 3468, if applicable) . .	**13c**		
	d Other rental real estate credits (see instructions) Type ▶	**13d**		
	e Other rental credits (see instructions) . . . Type ▶	**13e**		
	f Biofuel producer credit (attach Form 6478)	**13f**		
	g Other credits (see instructions) . . . . . Type ▶	**13g**		
Foreign Transactions	**14a** Name of country or U.S. possession ▶			
	b Gross income from all sources	**14b**		
	c Gross income sourced at shareholder level	**14c**		
	Foreign gross income sourced at corporate level			
	d Passive category	**14d**		
	e General category	**14e**		
	f Other (attach statement)	**14f**		
	Deductions allocated and apportioned at shareholder level			
	g Interest expense	**14g**		
	h Other	**14h**		
	Deductions allocated and apportioned at corporate level to foreign source income			
	i Passive category	**14i**		
	j General category	**14j**		
	k Other (attach statement)	**14k**		
	Other information			
	l Total foreign taxes (check one): ▶ ☐ Paid ☐ Accrued	**14l**		
	m Reduction in taxes available for credit (attach statement)	**14m**		
	n Other foreign tax information (attach statement)			
Alternative Minimum Tax (AMT) Items	**15a** Post-1986 depreciation adjustment	**15a**		
	b Adjusted gain or loss	**15b**		
	c Depletion (other than oil and gas)	**15c**		
	d Oil, gas, and geothermal properties—gross income	**15d**		
	e Oil, gas, and geothermal properties—deductions	**15e**		
	f Other AMT items (attach statement)	**15f**		
Items Affecting Shareholder Basis	**16a** Tax-exempt interest income	**16a**		
	b Other tax-exempt income	**16b**		
	c Nondeductible expenses	**16c**		
	d Distributions (attach statement if required) (see instructions)	**16d**		
	e Repayment of loans from shareholders	**16e**		

Form **1120S** (2015)

Form 1120S (2015)   Page **4**

Schedule K		Shareholders' Pro Rata Share Items (continued)			Total amount	

	17a	Investment income	**17a**		
Other Information	**b**	Investment expenses	**17b**		
	c	Dividend distributions paid from accumulated earnings and profits	**17c**		
	d	Other items and amounts (attach statement)			
Recon-ciliation	**18**	**Income/loss reconciliation.** Combine the amounts on lines 1 through 10 in the far right column. From the result, subtract the sum of the amounts on lines 11 through 12d and 14l	**18**		

Schedule L	Balance Sheets per Books	Beginning of tax year		End of tax year	
	Assets	(a)	(b)	(c)	(d)
1	Cash				
2a	Trade notes and accounts receivable . . .				
b	Less allowance for bad debts	( )		( )	
3	Inventories				
4	U.S. government obligations				
5	Tax-exempt securities (see instructions) . .				
6	Other current assets (attach statement) . . .				
7	Loans to shareholders				
8	Mortgage and real estate loans				
9	Other investments (attach statement)				
10a	Buildings and other depreciable assets . . .				
b	Less accumulated depreciation	( )		( )	
11a	Depletable assets				
b	Less accumulated depletion	( )		( )	
12	Land (net of any amortization)				
13a	Intangible assets (amortizable only)				
b	Less accumulated amortization	( )		( )	
14	Other assets (attach statement)				
15	Total assets				
	Liabilities and Shareholders' Equity				
16	Accounts payable				
17	Mortgages, notes, bonds payable in less than 1 year				
18	Other current liabilities (attach statement) . .				
19	Loans from shareholders				
20	Mortgages, notes, bonds payable in 1 year or more				
21	Other liabilities (attach statement)				
22	Capital stock				
23	Additional paid-in capital				
24	Retained earnings				
25	Adjustments to shareholders' equity (attach statement)				
26	Less cost of treasury stock		( )		( )
27	Total liabilities and shareholders' equity . .				

Form **1120S** (2015)

Schedule M-1	**Reconciliation of Income (Loss) per Books With Income (Loss) per Return**

Note: The corporation may be required to file Schedule M-3 (see instructions)

1	Net income (loss) per books		**5**	Income recorded on books this year not included on Schedule K, lines 1 through 10 (itemize):	
2	Income included on Schedule K, lines 1, 2, 3c, 4, 5a, 6, 7, 8a, 9, and 10, not recorded on books this year (itemize)_____		**a**	Tax-exempt interest $ _____	
3	Expenses recorded on books this year not included on Schedule K, lines 1 through 12 and 14l (itemize):		**6**	Deductions included on Schedule K, lines 1 through 12 and 14l, not charged against book income this year (itemize):	
a	Depreciation $ _____		**a**	Depreciation $ _____	
b	Travel and entertainment $ _____		**7**	Add lines 5 and 6	
4	Add lines 1 through 3		**8**	Income (loss) (Schedule K, line 18). Line 4 less line 7	

Schedule M-2	**Analysis of Accumulated Adjustments Account, Other Adjustments Account, and Shareholders' Undistributed Taxable Income Previously Taxed** (see instructions)

		(a) Accumulated adjustments account	**(b)** Other adjustments account	**(c)** Shareholders' undistributed taxable income previously taxed
1	Balance at beginning of tax year			
2	Ordinary income from page 1, line 21 . . .			
3	Other additions			
4	Loss from page 1, line 21	( )		
5	Other reductions	( )	( )	
6	Combine lines 1 through 5			
7	Distributions other than dividend distributions			
8	Balance at end of tax year. Subtract line 7 from line 6			

671113

**Schedule K-1
(Form 1120S)**
Department of the Treasury
Internal Revenue Service

2015

For calendar year 2015, or tax
year beginning _____ , 2015
ending _____ , 20 _____

☐ Final K-1   ☐ Amended K-1   OMB No. 1545-0123

Part III	**Shareholder's Share of Current Year Income, Deductions, Credits, and Other Items**		
1 Ordinary business income (loss)		**13** Credits	
2 Net rental real estate income (loss)			
3 Other net rental income (loss)			
4 Interest income			
5a Ordinary dividends			
5b Qualified dividends		**14** Foreign transactions	
6 Royalties			
7 Net short-term capital gain (loss)			
8a Net long-term capital gain (loss)			
8b Collectibles (28%) gain (loss)			
8c Unrecaptured section 1250 gain			
9 Net section 1231 gain (loss)			
10 Other income (loss)		**15** Alternative minimum tax (AMT) items	
11 Section 179 deduction		**16** Items affecting shareholder basis	
12 Other deductions			
		17 Other information	

Shareholder's Share of Income, Deductions, Credits, etc.   ► See back of form and separate instructions.

Part I	**Information About the Corporation**

A   Corporation's employer identification number

B   Corporation's name, address, city, state, and ZIP code

C   IRS Center where corporation filed return

Part II	**Information About the Shareholder**

D   Shareholder's identifying number

E   Shareholder's name, address, city, state, and ZIP code

F   Shareholder's percentage of stock
ownership for tax year . . . . _____ %

For IRS Use Only

* See attached statement for additional information.

For Paperwork Reduction Act Notice, see Instructions for Form 1120S.   IRS.gov/form1120s   Cat. No. 11520D   **Schedule K-1 (Form 1120S) 2015**

Form **2553**

(Rev. December 2013)

Department of the Treasury
Internal Revenue Service

Election by a Small Business Corporation
(Under section 1362 of the Internal Revenue Code)

▶ See Parts II and III on page 3.
▶ You can fax this form to the IRS (see separate instructions).
▶ Information about Form 2553 and its separate instructions is at *www.irs.gov/form2553.*

OMB No. 1545-0123

Note. This election to be an S corporation can be accepted only if all the tests are met under *Who May Elect* in the instructions, all shareholders have signed the consent statement, an officer has signed below, and the exact name and address of the corporation (entity) and other required form information have been provided.

Part I	Election Information

Type or Print

Name (see instructions)	**A** Employer identification number
Number, street, and room or suite no. (If a P.O. box, see instructions.)	**B** Date incorporated
City or town, state, and ZIP code	**C** State of incorporation

D Check the applicable box(es) if the corporation (entity), after applying for the EIN shown in **A** above, changed its ☐ name or ☐ address

E Election is to be effective for tax year beginning (month, day, year) (see instructions) . . . . . ▶ _____

Caution. A corporation (entity) making the election for its first tax year in existence will usually enter the beginning date of a short tax year that begins on a date other than January 1.

F Selected tax year:
(1) ☐ Calendar year
(2) ☐ Fiscal year ending (month and day) ▶ _____
(3) ☐ 52-53-week year ending with reference to the month of December
(4) ☐ 52-53-week year ending with reference to the month of ▶ _____
If box (2) or (4) is checked, complete Part II.

G If more than 100 shareholders are listed for item J (see page 2), check this box if treating members of a family as one shareholder results in no more than 100 shareholders (see test 2 under *Who May Elect* in the instructions) ▶ ☐

H Name and title of officer or legal representative who the IRS may call for more information | **I** Telephone number of officer or legal representative

If this S corporation election is being filed late, I declare that I had reasonable cause for not filing Form 2553 timely, and if this late election is being made by an entity eligible to elect to be treated as a corporation, I declare that I also had reasonable cause for not filing an entity classification election timely and that the representations listed in Part IV are true. See below for my explanation of the reasons the election or elections were not made on time and a description of my diligent actions to correct the mistake upon its discovery (see instructions).

Sign Here

Under penalties of perjury, I declare that I have examined this election, including accompanying documents, and, to the best of my knowledge and belief, the election contains all the relevant facts relating to the election, and such facts are true, correct, and complete.

▶ _____   _____   _____
   Signature of officer   Title   Date

For Paperwork Reduction Act Notice, see separate instructions.   Cat. No. 18629R   Form **2553** (Rev. 12-2013)

Form 2553 (Rev. 12-2013)   Page **2**

Part I	**Election Information** (continued) **Note.** If you need more rows, use additional copies of page 2.						
J Name and address of each shareholder or former shareholder required to consent to the election. (see instructions)	**K** **Shareholder's Consent Statement** Under penalties of perjury, I declare that I consent to the election of the above-named corporation (entity) to be an S corporation under section 1362(a) and that I have examined this consent statement, including accompanying documents, and, to the best of my knowledge and belief, the election contains all the relevant facts relating to the election, and such facts are true, correct, and complete. I understand my consent is binding and may not be withdrawn after the corporation (entity) has made a valid election. If seeking relief for a late filed election, I also declare under penalties of perjury that I have reported my income on all affected returns consistent with the S corporation election for the year for which the election should have been filed (see beginning date entered on line E) and for all subsequent years.		**L** Stock owned or percentage of ownership (see instructions)		**M** Social security number or employer identification number (see instructions)	**N** Shareholder's tax year ends (month and day)
	Signature	Date	Number of shares or percentage of ownership	Date(s) acquired		

Form **4562**

Department of the Treasury
Internal Revenue Service   (99)

Depreciation and Amortization
(Including Information on Listed Property)
▶ Attach to your tax return.
▶ **Information about Form 4562 and its separate instructions is at** *www.irs.gov/form4562.*

OMB No. 1545-0172

2015

Attachment
Sequence No. **179**

Name(s) shown on return	Business or activity to which this form relates	Identifying number

Part I **Election To Expense Certain Property Under Section 179**
Note: If you have any listed property, complete Part V before you complete Part I.

1	Maximum amount (see instructions)	**1**	
2	Total cost of section 179 property placed in service (see instructions)	**2**	
3	Threshold cost of section 179 property before reduction in limitation (see instructions)	**3**	
4	Reduction in limitation. Subtract line 3 from line 2. If zero or less, enter -0-	**4**	
5	Dollar limitation for tax year. Subtract line 4 from line 1. If zero or less, enter -0-. If married filing separately, see instructions	**5**	

6	(a) Description of property	(b) Cost (business use only)	(c) Elected cost

7	Listed property. Enter the amount from line 29	**7**		
8	Total elected cost of section 179 property. Add amounts in column (c), lines 6 and 7	**8**	
9	Tentative deduction. Enter the **smaller** of line 5 or line 8	**9**	
10	Carryover of disallowed deduction from line 13 of your 2014 Form 4562	**10**	
11	Business income limitation. Enter the smaller of business income (not less than zero) or line 5 (see instructions)	**11**	
12	Section 179 expense deduction. Add lines 9 and 10, but do not enter more than line 11	**12**	
13	Carryover of disallowed deduction to 2016. Add lines 9 and 10, less line 12 ▶	**13**	

Note: Do not use Part II or Part III below for listed property. Instead, use Part V.

Part II **Special Depreciation Allowance and Other Depreciation (Do not** include listed property.) (See instructions.)

14	Special depreciation allowance for qualified property (other than listed property) placed in service during the tax year (see instructions)	**14**	
15	Property subject to section 168(f)(1) election	**15**	
16	Other depreciation (including ACRS)	**16**	

Part III **MACRS Depreciation (Do not** include listed property.) (See instructions.)

Section A

17	MACRS deductions for assets placed in service in tax years beginning before 2015	**17**	
18	If you are electing to group any assets placed in service during the tax year into one or more general asset accounts, check here . . . . ▶ ☐		

Section B—Assets Placed in Service During 2015 Tax Year Using the General Depreciation System

(a) Classification of property	(b) Month and year placed in service	(c) Basis for depreciation (business/investment use only—see instructions)	(d) Recovery period	(e) Convention	(f) Method	(g) Depreciation deduction
19a 3-year property						
b 5-year property						
c 7-year property						
d 10-year property						
e 15-year property						
f 20-year property						
g 25-year property			25 yrs.		S/L	
h Residential rental property			27.5 yrs.	MM	S/L	
			27.5 yrs.	MM	S/L	
i Nonresidential real property			39 yrs.	MM	S/L	
				MM	S/L	

Section C—Assets Placed in Service During 2015 Tax Year Using the Alternative Depreciation System

20a Class life					S/L	
b 12-year			12 yrs.		S/L	
c 40-year			40 yrs.	MM	S/L	

Part IV **Summary** (See instructions.)

21	Listed property. Enter amount from line 28	**21**	
22	**Total.** Add amounts from line 12, lines 14 through 17, lines 19 and 20 in column (g), and line 21. Enter here and on the appropriate lines of your return. Partnerships and S corporations—see instructions .	**22**	
23	For assets shown above and placed in service during the current year, enter the portion of the basis attributable to section 263A costs	**23**		

For Paperwork Reduction Act Notice, see separate instructions.   Cat. No. 12906N   Form **4562** (2015)

Form 4562 (2015)   Page **2**

Part V Listed Property (Include automobiles, certain other vehicles, certain aircraft, certain computers, and property used for entertainment, recreation, or amusement.)

Note: For any vehicle for which you are using the standard mileage rate or deducting lease expense, complete **only** 24a, 24b, columns (a) through (c) of Section A, all of Section B, and Section C if applicable.

Section A—Depreciation and Other Information (Caution: See the instructions for limits for passenger automobiles.)

24a Do you have evidence to support the business/investment use claimed? ☐ Yes ☐ No   **24b** If "Yes," is the evidence written? ☐ Yes ☐ No

(a) Type of property (list vehicles first)	(b) Date placed in service	(c) Business/investment use percentage	(d) Cost or other basis	(e) Basis for depreciation (business/investment use only)	(f) Recovery period	(g) Method/Convention	(h) Depreciation deduction	(i) Elected section 179 cost
25 Special depreciation allowance for qualified listed property placed in service during the tax year and used more than 50% in a qualified business use (see instructions) . **25**								
26 Property used more than 50% in a qualified business use:								
		%						
		%						
		%						
27 Property used 50% or less in a qualified business use:								
		%				S/L –		
		%				S/L –		
		%				S/L –		
28 Add amounts in column (h), lines 25 through 27. Enter here and on line 21, page 1 . **28**								
29 Add amounts in column (i), line 26. Enter here and on line 7, page 1 . . . . **29**								

Section B—Information on Use of Vehicles

Complete this section for vehicles used by a sole proprietor, partner, or other "more than 5% owner," or related person. If you provided vehicles to your employees, first answer the questions in Section C to see if you meet an exception to completing this section for those vehicles.

	(a) Vehicle 1		(b) Vehicle 2		(c) Vehicle 3		(d) Vehicle 4		(e) Vehicle 5		(f) Vehicle 6	
30 Total business/investment miles driven during the year (**do not** include commuting miles) .												
31 Total commuting miles driven during the year .												
32 Total other personal (noncommuting) miles driven												
33 Total miles driven during the year. Add lines 30 through 32												
34 Was the vehicle available for personal use during off-duty hours?	Yes	No	Yes	No	Yes	No	Yes	No	Yes	No	Yes	No
35 Was the vehicle used primarily by a more than 5% owner or related person? . .												
36 Is another vehicle available for personal use?												

Section C—Questions for Employers Who Provide Vehicles for Use by Their Employees

Answer these questions to determine if you meet an exception to completing Section B for vehicles used by employees who **are not** more than 5% owners or related persons (see instructions).

		Yes	No
37	Do you maintain a written policy statement that prohibits all personal use of vehicles, including commuting, by your employees?		
38	Do you maintain a written policy statement that prohibits personal use of vehicles, except commuting, by your employees? See the instructions for vehicles used by corporate officers, directors, or 1% or more owners . .		
39	Do you treat all use of vehicles by employees as personal use?		
40	Do you provide more than five vehicles to your employees, obtain information from your employees about the use of the vehicles, and retain the information received?		
41	Do you meet the requirements concerning qualified automobile demonstration use? (See instructions.) . . .		

Note: If your answer to 37, 38, 39, 40, or 41 is "Yes," do not complete Section B for the covered vehicles.

Part VI Amortization

(a) Description of costs	(b) Date amortization begins	(c) Amortizable amount	(d) Code section	(e) Amortization period or percentage	(f) Amortization for this year
42 Amortization of costs that begins during your 2015 tax year (see instructions):					
43 Amortization of costs that began before your 2015 tax year **43**					
44 **Total.** Add amounts in column (f). See the instructions for where to report **44**					

Form **4562** (2015)

Form **4626**

Department of the Treasury
Internal Revenue Service

Alternative Minimum Tax—Corporations

► **Attach to the corporation's tax return.**

► **Information about Form 4626 and its separate instructions is at** *www.irs.gov/form4626.*

OMB No. 1545-0123

20**15**

Name | Employer identification number

Note: *See the instructions to find out if the corporation is a small corporation exempt from the alternative minimum tax (AMT) under section 55(e).*

1	Taxable income or (loss) before net operating loss deduction	**1**
2	**Adjustments and preferences:**	
a	Depreciation of post-1986 property	**2a**
b	Amortization of certified pollution control facilities.	**2b**
c	Amortization of mining exploration and development costs	**2c**
d	Amortization of circulation expenditures (personal holding companies only)	**2d**
e	Adjusted gain or loss	**2e**
f	Long-term contracts	**2f**
g	Merchant marine capital construction funds.	**2g**
h	Section 833(b) deduction (Blue Cross, Blue Shield, and similar type organizations only)	**2h**
i	Tax shelter farm activities (personal service corporations only)	**2i**
j	Passive activities (closely held corporations and personal service corporations only)	**2j**
k	Loss limitations	**2k**
l	Depletion	**2l**
m	Tax-exempt interest income from specified private activity bonds	**2m**
n	Intangible drilling costs	**2n**
o	Other adjustments and preferences	**2o**
3	Pre-adjustment alternative minimum taxable income (AMTI). Combine lines 1 through 2o.	**3**
4	**Adjusted current earnings (ACE) adjustment:**	
a	ACE from line 10 of the ACE worksheet in the instructions	**4a**
b	Subtract line 3 from line 4a. If line 3 exceeds line 4a, enter the difference as a negative amount (see instructions).	**4b**
c	Multiply line 4b by 75% (.75). Enter the result as a positive amount	**4c**
d	Enter the excess, if any, of the corporation's total increases in AMTI from prior year ACE adjustments over its total reductions in AMTI from prior year ACE adjustments (see instructions). **Note:** *You* **must** *enter an amount on line 4d (even if line 4b is positive).*	**4d**
e	ACE adjustment.	
	• If line 4b is zero or more, enter the amount from line 4c	**4e**
	• If line 4b is less than zero, enter the **smaller** of line 4c or line 4d as a negative amount	
5	Combine lines 3 and 4e. If zero or less, stop here; the corporation does not owe any AMT	**5**
6	Alternative tax net operating loss deduction (see instructions).	**6**
7	**Alternative minimum taxable income.** Subtract line 6 from line 5. If the corporation held a residual interest in a REMIC, see instructions	**7**
8	**Exemption phase-out** (if line 7 is $310,000 or more, skip lines 8a and 8b and enter -0- on line 8c):	
a	Subtract $150,000 from line 7 (if completing this line for a member of a controlled group, see instructions). If zero or less, enter -0-	**8a**
b	Multiply line 8a by 25% (.25).	**8b**
c	Exemption. Subtract line 8b from $40,000 (if completing this line for a member of a controlled group, see instructions). If zero or less, enter -0-	**8c**
9	Subtract line 8c from line 7. If zero or less, enter -0-	**9**
10	Multiply line 9 by 20% (.20)	**10**
11	Alternative minimum tax foreign tax credit (AMTFTC) (see instructions)	**11**
12	Tentative minimum tax. Subtract line 11 from line 10	**12**
13	Regular tax liability before applying all credits except the foreign tax credit	**13**
14	**Alternative minimum tax.** Subtract line 13 from line 12. If zero or less, enter -0-. Enter here and on Form 1120, Schedule J, line 3, or the appropriate line of the corporation's income tax return . . .	**14**

For Paperwork Reduction Act Notice, see separate instructions.   Cat. No. 12955I   Form **4626** (2015)

Form **4797**	**Sales of Business Property**	OMB No. 1545-0184

Form **4797**

Department of the Treasury
Internal Revenue Service

Sales of Business Property

**(Also Involuntary Conversions and Recapture Amounts
Under Sections 179 and 280F(b)(2))**

▶ **Attach to your tax return.**

▶ **Information about Form 4797 and its separate instructions is at** *www.irs.gov/form4797.*

2015

Attachment
Sequence No. **27**

Name(s) shown on return | Identifying number

1 Enter the gross proceeds from sales or exchanges reported to you for 2015 on Form(s) 1099-B or 1099-S (or substitute statement) that you are including on line 2, 10, or 20 (see instructions) . . . . | **1** |

Part I **Sales or Exchanges of Property Used in a Trade or Business and Involuntary Conversions From Other Than Casualty or Theft—Most Property Held More Than 1 Year** (see instructions)

2	**(a)** Description of property	**(b)** Date acquired (mo., day, yr.)	**(c)** Date sold (mo., day, yr.)	**(d)** Gross sales price	**(e)** Depreciation allowed or allowable since acquisition	**(f)** Cost or other basis, plus improvements and expense of sale	**(g)** Gain or (loss) Subtract (f) from the sum of (d) and (e)

3 Gain, if any, from Form 4684, line 39	**3**	
4 Section 1231 gain from installment sales from Form 6252, line 26 or 37	**4**	
5 Section 1231 gain or (loss) from like-kind exchanges from Form 8824	**5**	
6 Gain, if any, from line 32, from other than casualty or theft	**6**	
7 Combine lines 2 through 6. Enter the gain or (loss) here and on the appropriate line as follows:	**7**	

Partnerships (except electing large partnerships) and S corporations. Report the gain or (loss) following the instructions for Form 1065, Schedule K, line 10, or Form 1120S, Schedule K, line 9. Skip lines 8, 9, 11, and 12 below.

Individuals, partners, S corporation shareholders, and all others. If line 7 is zero or a loss, enter the amount from line 7 on line 11 below and skip lines 8 and 9. If line 7 is a gain and you did not have any prior year section 1231 losses, or they were recaptured in an earlier year, enter the gain from line 7 as a long-term capital gain on the Schedule D filed with your return and skip lines 8, 9, 11, and 12 below.

8 Nonrecaptured net section 1231 losses from prior years (see instructions)	**8**	
9 Subtract line 8 from line 7. If zero or less, enter -0-. If line 9 is zero, enter the gain from line 7 on line 12 below. If line 9 is more than zero, enter the amount from line 8 on line 12 below and enter the gain from line 9 as a long-term capital gain on the Schedule D filed with your return (see instructions)	**9**	

Part II **Ordinary Gains and Losses** (see instructions)

10 Ordinary gains and losses not included on lines 11 through 16 (include property held 1 year or less):

11 Loss, if any, from line 7	**11** ( )
12 Gain, if any, from line 7 or amount from line 8, if applicable	**12**	
13 Gain, if any, from line 31	**13**	
14 Net gain or (loss) from Form 4684, lines 31 and 38a	**14**	
15 Ordinary gain from installment sales from Form 6252, line 25 or 36	**15**	
16 Ordinary gain or (loss) from like-kind exchanges from Form 8824	**16**	
17 Combine lines 10 through 16	**17**	

18 For all except individual returns, enter the amount from line 17 on the appropriate line of your return and skip lines a and b below. For individual returns, complete lines a and b below:

a If the loss on line 11 includes a loss from Form 4684, line 35, column (b)(ii), enter that part of the loss here. Enter the part of the loss from income-producing property on Schedule A (Form 1040), line 28, and the part of the loss from property used as an employee on Schedule A (Form 1040), line 23. Identify as from "Form 4797, line 18a." See instructions . . | **18a** |

b Redetermine the gain or (loss) on line 17 excluding the loss, if any, on line 18a. Enter here and on Form 1040, line 14 | **18b** |

For Paperwork Reduction Act Notice, see separate instructions. | Cat. No. 13086I | Form **4797** (2015)

Form 4797 (2015)   Page **2**

Part III	Gain From Disposition of Property Under Sections 1245, 1250, 1252, 1254, and 1255 (see instructions)

19	(a) Description of section 1245, 1250, 1252, 1254, or 1255 property:	**(b)** Date acquired (mo., day, yr.)	**(c)** Date sold (mo., day, yr.)
A			
B			
C			
D			

	These columns relate to the properties on lines 19A through 19D. ▶		**Property A**	**Property B**	**Property C**	**Property D**
20	Gross sales price (**Note:** *See line 1 before completing.*) .	20				
21	Cost or other basis plus expense of sale	21				
22	Depreciation (or depletion) allowed or allowable. . .	22				
23	Adjusted basis. Subtract line 22 from line 21. . . .	23				
24	Total gain. Subtract line 23 from line 20	24				
25	**If section 1245 property:**					
a	Depreciation allowed or allowable from line 22 . . .	25a				
b	Enter the **smaller** of line 24 or 25a	25b				
26	**If section 1250 property:** If straight line depreciation was used, enter -0- on line 26g, except for a corporation subject to section 291.					
a	Additional depreciation after 1975 (see instructions) .	26a				
b	Applicable percentage multiplied by the **smaller** of line 24 or line 26a (see instructions)	26b				
c	Subtract line 26a from line 24. If residential rental property or line 24 is not more than line 26a, skip lines 26d and 26e	26c				
d	Additional depreciation after 1969 and before 1976. .	26d				
e	Enter the **smaller** of line 26c or 26d	26e				
f	Section 291 amount (corporations only)	26f				
g	Add lines 26b, 26e, and 26f.	26g				
27	**If section 1252 property:** Skip this section if you did not dispose of farmland or if this form is being completed for a partnership (other than an electing large partnership).					
a	Soil, water, and land clearing expenses	27a				
b	Line 27a multiplied by applicable percentage (see instructions)	27b				
c	Enter the **smaller** of line 24 or 27b	27c				
28	**If section 1254 property:**					
a	Intangible drilling and development costs, expenditures for development of mines and other natural deposits, mining exploration costs, and depletion (see instructions)	28a				
b	Enter the **smaller** of line 24 or 28a	28b				
29	**If section 1255 property:**					
a	Applicable percentage of payments excluded from income under section 126 (see instructions)	29a				
b	Enter the **smaller** of line 24 or 29a (see instructions) .	29b				

Summary of Part III Gains. Complete property columns A through D through line 29b before going to line 30.

30	Total gains for all properties. Add property columns A through D, line 24	30	
31	Add property columns A through D, lines 25b, 26g, 27c, 28b, and 29b. Enter here and on line 13	31	
32	Subtract line 31 from line 30. Enter the portion from casualty or theft on Form 4684, line 33. Enter the portion from other than casualty or theft on Form 4797, line 6	32	

Part IV	Recapture Amounts Under Sections 179 and 280F(b)(2) When Business Use Drops to 50% or Less (see instructions)

			(a) Section 179	**(b)** Section 280F(b)(2)
33	Section 179 expense deduction or depreciation allowable in prior years.	33		
34	Recomputed depreciation (see instructions)	34		
35	Recapture amount. Subtract line 34 from line 33. See the instructions for where to report . .	35		

Form **4797** (2015)

Form **6251**

Department of the Treasury
Internal Revenue Service (99)

Alternative Minimum Tax—Individuals

▶ Information about Form 6251 and its separate instructions is at *www.irs.gov/form6251.*
▶ **Attach to Form 1040 or Form 1040NR.**

OMB No. 1545-0074

20**15**

Attachment
Sequence No. **32**

Name(s) shown on Form 1040 or Form 1040NR

Your social security number

Part I **Alternative Minimum Taxable Income** (See instructions for how to complete each line.)

1	If filing Schedule A (Form 1040), enter the amount from Form 1040, line 41, and go to line 2. Otherwise, enter the amount from Form 1040, line 38, and go to line 7. (If less than zero, enter as a negative amount.)	**1**	
2	Medical and dental. If you or your spouse was 65 or older, enter the **smaller** of Schedule A (Form 1040), line 4, **or** 2.5% (.025) of Form 1040, line 38. If zero or less, enter -0-	**2**	
3	Taxes from Schedule A (Form 1040), line 9	**3**	
4	Enter the home mortgage interest adjustment, if any, from line 6 of the worksheet in the instructions for this line	**4**	
5	Miscellaneous deductions from Schedule A (Form 1040), line 27.	**5**	
6	If Form 1040, line 38, is $154,950 or less, enter -0-. Otherwise, see instructions	**6**	( )
7	Tax refund from Form 1040, line 10 or line 21	**7**	( )
8	Investment interest expense (difference between regular tax and AMT).	**8**	
9	Depletion (difference between regular tax and AMT)	**9**	
10	Net operating loss deduction from Form 1040, line 21. Enter as a positive amount	**10**	
11	Alternative tax net operating loss deduction	**11**	( )
12	Interest from specified private activity bonds exempt from the regular tax	**12**	
13	Qualified small business stock, see instructions	**13**	
14	Exercise of incentive stock options (excess of AMT income over regular tax income)	**14**	
15	Estates and trusts (amount from Schedule K-1 (Form 1041), box 12, code A)	**15**	
16	Electing large partnerships (amount from Schedule K-1 (Form 1065-B), box 6)	**16**	
17	Disposition of property (difference between AMT and regular tax gain or loss)	**17**	
18	Depreciation on assets placed in service after 1986 (difference between regular tax and AMT)	**18**	
19	Passive activities (difference between AMT and regular tax income or loss)	**19**	
20	Loss limitations (difference between AMT and regular tax income or loss)	**20**	
21	Circulation costs (difference between regular tax and AMT)	**21**	
22	Long-term contracts (difference between AMT and regular tax income)	**22**	
23	Mining costs (difference between regular tax and AMT)	**23**	
24	Research and experimental costs (difference between regular tax and AMT)	**24**	
25	Income from certain installment sales before January 1, 1987	**25**	( )
26	Intangible drilling costs preference	**26**	
27	Other adjustments, including income-based related adjustments	**27**	
28	**Alternative minimum taxable income.** Combine lines 1 through 27. (If married filing separately and line 28 is more than $246,250, see instructions.)	**28**	

Part II **Alternative Minimum Tax (AMT)**

29 Exemption. (If you were under age 24 at the end of 2015, see instructions.)

IF your filing status is . . .	AND line 28 is not over . . .	THEN enter on line 29 . . .		
Single or head of household	$119,200	$53,600		
Married filing jointly or qualifying widow(er)	158,900	83,400	} . .	**29**
Married filing separately.	79,450	41,700		

If line 28 is **over** the amount shown above for your filing status, see instructions.

30 Subtract line 29 from line 28. If more than zero, go to line 31. If zero or less, enter -0- here and on lines 31, 33, and 35, and go to line 34 . . . . | **30** |

31
• If you are filing Form 2555 or 2555-EZ, see instructions for the amount to enter.
• If you reported capital gain distributions directly on Form 1040, line 13; you reported qualified dividends on Form 1040, line 9b; **or** you had a gain on both lines 15 and 16 of Schedule D (Form 1040) (as refigured for the AMT, if necessary), complete Part III on the back and enter the amount from line 64 here. . . .
• **All others:** If line 30 is $185,400 or less ($92,700 or less if married filing separately), multiply line 30 by 26% (.26). Otherwise, multiply line 30 by 28% (.28) and subtract $3,708 ($1,854 if married filing separately) from the result. | **31** |

32 Alternative minimum tax foreign tax credit (see instructions) . . . . | **32** |

33 Tentative minimum tax. Subtract line 32 from line 31 . . . . | **33** |

34 Add Form 1040, line 44 (minus any tax from Form 4972), and Form 1040, line 46. Subtract from the result any foreign tax credit from Form 1040, line 48. If you used Schedule J to figure your tax on Form 1040, line 44, refigure that tax without using Schedule J before completing this line (see instructions) . . . . . | **34** |

35 **AMT.** Subtract line 34 from line 33. If zero or less, enter -0-. Enter here and on Form 1040, line 45 . . . . . | **35** |

For Paperwork Reduction Act Notice, see your tax return instructions.   Cat. No. 13600G   Form **6251** (2015)

Form 6251 (2015)   Page **2**

Part III   Tax Computation Using Maximum Capital Gains Rates

Complete Part III only if you are required to do so by line 31 or by the Foreign Earned Income Tax Worksheet in the instructions.

36 Enter the amount from Form 6251, line 30. If you are filing Form 2555 or 2555-EZ, enter the amount from line 3 of the worksheet in the instructions for line 31	**36**	
37 Enter the amount from line 6 of the Qualified Dividends and Capital Gain Tax Worksheet in the instructions for Form 1040, line 44, or the amount from line 13 of the Schedule D Tax Worksheet in the instructions for Schedule D (Form 1040), whichever applies (as refigured for the AMT, if necessary) (see instructions). If you are filing Form 2555 or 2555-EZ, see instructions for the amount to enter	**37**	
38 Enter the amount from Schedule D (Form 1040), line 19 (as refigured for the AMT, if necessary) (see instructions). If you are filing Form 2555 or 2555-EZ, see instructions for the amount to enter	**38**	
39 If you did not complete a Schedule D Tax Worksheet for the regular tax or the AMT, enter the amount from line 37. Otherwise, add lines 37 and 38, and enter the **smaller** of that result or the amount from line 10 of the Schedule D Tax Worksheet (as refigured for the AMT, if necessary). If you are filing Form 2555 or 2555-EZ, see instructions for the amount to enter	**39**	
40 Enter the **smaller** of line 36 or line 39	**40**	
41 Subtract line 40 from line 36	**41**	
42 If line 41 is $185,400 or less ($92,700 or less if married filing separately), multiply line 41 by 26% (.26). Otherwise, multiply line 41 by 28% (.28) and subtract $3,708 ($1,854 if married filing separately) from the result . . . ▶	**42**	
43 Enter: • $74,900 if married filing jointly or qualifying widow(er), • $37,450 if single or married filing separately, or • $50,200 if head of household. }	**43**	
44 Enter the amount from line 7 of the Qualified Dividends and Capital Gain Tax Worksheet in the instructions for Form 1040, line 44, or the amount from line 14 of the Schedule D Tax Worksheet in the instructions for Schedule D (Form 1040), whichever applies (as figured for the regular tax). If you did not complete either worksheet for the regular tax, enter the amount from Form 1040, line 43; if zero or less, enter -0-. If you are filing Form 2555 or 2555-EZ, see instructions for the amount to enter	**44**	
45 Subtract line 44 from line 43. If zero or less, enter -0-	**45**	
46 Enter the **smaller** of line 36 or line 37	**46**	
47 Enter the **smaller** of line 45 or line 46. This amount is taxed at 0%	**47**	
48 Subtract line 47 from line 46	**48**	
49 Enter: • $413,200 if single • $232,425 if married filing separately • $464,850 if married filing jointly or qualifying widow(er) • $439,000 if head of household } . . .	**49**	
50 Enter the amount from line 45	**50**	
51 Enter the amount from line 7 of the Qualified Dividends and Capital Gain Tax Worksheet in the instructions for Form 1040, line 44, or the amount from line 19 of the Schedule D Tax Worksheet, whichever applies (as figured for the regular tax). If you did not complete either worksheet for the regular tax, enter the amount from Form 1040, line 43; if zero or less, enter -0-. If you are filing Form 2555 or Form 2555-EZ, see instructions for the amount to enter	**51**	
52 Add line 50 and line 51	**52**	
53 Subtract line 52 from line 49. If zero or less, enter -0-	**53**	
54 Enter the smaller of line 48 or line 53	**54**	
55 Multiply line 54 by 15% (.15) . . . . ▶	**55**	
56 Add lines 47 and 54	**56**	
If lines 56 and 36 are the same, skip lines 57 through 61 and go to line 62. Otherwise, go to line 57.		
57 Subtract line 56 from line 46	**57**	
58 Multiply line 57 by 20% (.20) . . . . ▶	**58**	
If line 38 is zero or blank, skip lines 59 through 61 and go to line 62. Otherwise, go to line 59.		
59 Add lines 41, 56, and 57	**59**	
60 Subtract line 59 from line 36	**60**	
61 Multiply line 60 by 25% (.25) . . . . ▶	**61**	
62 Add lines 42, 55, 58, and 61	**62**	
63 If line 36 is $185,400 or less ($92,700 or less if married filing separately), multiply line 36 by 26% (.26). Otherwise, multiply line 36 by 28% (.28) and subtract $3,708 ($1,854 if married filing separately) from the result	**63**	
64 Enter the **smaller** of line 62 or line 63 here and on line 31. If you are filing Form 2555 or 2555-EZ, do not enter this amount on line 31. Instead, enter it on line 4 of the worksheet in the instructions for line 31 . .	**64**	

Form **6251** (2015)

Form **8949**

Department of the Treasury
Internal Revenue Service

Sales and Other Dispositions of Capital Assets

▶ Information about Form 8949 and its separate instructions is at *www.irs.gov/form8949*.
▶ File with your Schedule D to list your transactions for lines 1b, 2, 3, 8b, 9, and 10 of Schedule D.

OMB No. 1545-0074

20**15**

Attachment
Sequence No. **12A**

Name(s) shown on return | Social security number or taxpayer identification number

Before you check Box A, B, or C below, see whether you received any Form(s) 1099-B or substitute statement(s) from your broker. A substitute statement will have the same information as Form 1099-B. Either will show whether your basis (usually your cost) was reported to the IRS by your broker and may even tell you which box to check.

Part I   **Short-Term.** Transactions involving capital assets you held 1 year or less are short term. For long-term transactions, see page 2.

Note: You may aggregate all short-term transactions reported on Form(s) 1099-B showing basis was reported to the IRS and for which no adjustments or codes are required. Enter the totals directly on Schedule D, line 1a; you aren't required to report these transactions on Form 8949 (see instructions).

You *must* check Box A, B, *or* C below. Check only one box. If more than one box applies for your short-term transactions, complete a separate Form 8949, page 1, for each applicable box. If you have more short-term transactions than will fit on this page for one or more of the boxes, complete as many forms with the same box checked as you need.

☐ **(A)** Short-term transactions reported on Form(s) 1099-B showing basis was reported to the IRS (see **Note** above)
☐ **(B)** Short-term transactions reported on Form(s) 1099-B showing basis was **not** reported to the IRS
☐ **(C)** Short-term transactions not reported to you on Form 1099-B

1

(a) Description of property (Example: 100 sh. XYZ Co.)	(b) Date acquired (Mo., day, yr.)	(c) Date sold or disposed of (Mo., day, yr.)	(d) Proceeds (sales price) (see instructions)	(e) Cost or other basis. See the **Note** below and see *Column (e)* in the separate instructions	(f) Code(s) from instructions	(g) Amount of adjustment	(h) Gain or (loss). Subtract column (e) from column (d) and combine the result with column (g)

Above the adjustment columns: **Adjustment, if any, to gain or loss.** If you enter an amount in column (g), enter a code in column (f). **See the separate instructions.**

2 Totals. Add the amounts in columns (d), (e), (g), and (h) (subtract negative amounts). Enter each total here and include on your Schedule D, **line 1b** (if **Box A** above is checked), **line 2** (if **Box B** above is checked), or **line 3** (if **Box C** above is checked) ▶

Note: If you checked Box A above but the basis reported to the IRS was incorrect, enter in column (e) the basis as reported to the IRS, and enter an adjustment in column (g) to correct the basis. See *Column (g)* in the separate instructions for how to figure the amount of the adjustment.

For Paperwork Reduction Act Notice, see your tax return instructions.   Cat. No. 37768Z   Form **8949** (2015)

Form 8949 (2015)   Attachment Sequence No. **12A**   Page **2**

Name(s) shown on return. Name and SSN or taxpayer identification no. not required if shown on other side	Social security number or taxpayer identification number

Before you check Box D, E, or F below, see whether you received any Form(s) 1099-B or substitute statement(s) from your broker. A substitute statement will have the same information as Form 1099-B. Either will show whether your basis (usually your cost) was reported to the IRS by your broker and may even tell you which box to check.

Part II   **Long-Term.** Transactions involving capital assets you held more than 1 year are long term. For short-term transactions, see page 1.

Note: You may aggregate all long-term transactions reported on Form(s) 1099-B showing basis was reported to the IRS and for which no adjustments or codes are required. Enter the totals directly on Schedule D, line 8a; you aren't required to report these transactions on Form 8949 (see instructions).

You *must* **check Box D, E,** *or* **F below. Check only one box.** If more than one box applies for your long-term transactions, complete a separate Form 8949, page 2, for each applicable box. If you have more long-term transactions than will fit on this page for one or more of the boxes, complete as many forms with the same box checked as you need.

☐ **(D)** Long-term transactions reported on Form(s) 1099-B showing basis was reported to the IRS (see **Note** above)

☐ **(E)** Long-term transactions reported on Form(s) 1099-B showing basis was **not** reported to the IRS

☐ **(F)** Long-term transactions not reported to you on Form 1099-B

1 (a) Description of property (Example: 100 sh. XYZ Co.)	(b) Date acquired (Mo., day, yr.)	(c) Date sold or disposed of (Mo., day, yr.)	(d) Proceeds (sales price) (see instructions)	(e) Cost or other basis. See the **Note** below and see *Column (e)* in the separate instructions	Adjustment, if any, to gain or loss. If you enter an amount in column (g), enter a code in column (f). See the separate instructions.		(h) Gain or (loss). Subtract column (e) from column (d) and combine the result with column (g)
					(f) Code(s) from instructions	(g) Amount of adjustment	
2 Totals. Add the amounts in columns (d), (e), (g), and (h) (subtract negative amounts). Enter each total here and include on your Schedule D, **line 8b** (if **Box D** above is checked), **line 9** (if **Box E** above is checked), or **line 10** (if **Box F** above is checked) ▶							

Note: If you checked Box D above but the basis reported to the IRS was incorrect, enter in column (e) the basis as reported to the IRS, and enter an adjustment in column (g) to correct the basis. See *Column (g)* in the separate instructions for how to figure the amount of the adjustment.

Form **8949** (2015)

Form **8959**

Department of the Treasury
Internal Revenue Service

Additional Medicare Tax

▶ If any line does not apply to you, leave it blank. See separate instructions.
▶ Attach to Form 1040, 1040NR, 1040-PR, or 1040-SS.
▶ Information about Form 8959 and its instructions is at *www.irs.gov/form8959.*

OMB No. 1545-0074

2015

Attachment
Sequence No. **71**

Name(s) shown on return

Your social security number

Part I Additional Medicare Tax on Medicare Wages

1	Medicare wages and tips from Form W-2, box 5. If you have more than one Form W-2, enter the total of the amounts from box 5	**1**
2	Unreported tips from Form 4137, line 6	**2**
3	Wages from Form 8919, line 6	**3**
4	Add lines 1 through 3	**4**
5	Enter the following amount for your filing status: Married filing jointly. . . . . $250,000 Married filing separately . . . . $125,000 Single, Head of household, or Qualifying widow(er) $200,000	**5**
6	Subtract line 5 from line 4. If zero or less, enter -0-	**6**
7	Additional Medicare Tax on Medicare wages. Multiply line 6 by 0.9% (.009). Enter here and go to Part II	**7**

Part II Additional Medicare Tax on Self-Employment Income

8	Self-employment income from Schedule SE (Form 1040), Section A, line 4, or Section B, line 6. If you had a loss, enter -0- (Form 1040-PR and Form 1040-SS filers, see instructions.)	**8**
9	Enter the following amount for your filing status: Married filing jointly. . . . . $250,000 Married filing separately . . . . $125,000 Single, Head of household, or Qualifying widow(er) $200,000	**9**
10	Enter the amount from line 4	**10**
11	Subtract line 10 from line 9. If zero or less, enter -0-	**11**
12	Subtract line 11 from line 8. If zero or less, enter -0-	**12**
13	Additional Medicare Tax on self-employment income. Multiply line 12 by 0.9% (.009). Enter here and go to Part III	**13**

Part III Additional Medicare Tax on Railroad Retirement Tax Act (RRTA) Compensation

14	Railroad retirement (RRTA) compensation and tips from Form(s) W-2, box 14 (see instructions)	**14**
15	Enter the following amount for your filing status: Married filing jointly. . . . . $250,000 Married filing separately . . . . $125,000 Single, Head of household, or Qualifying widow(er) $200,000	**15**
16	Subtract line 15 from line 14. If zero or less, enter -0-	**16**
17	Additional Medicare Tax on railroad retirement (RRTA) compensation. Multiply line 16 by 0.9% (.009). Enter here and go to Part IV	**17**

Part IV Total Additional Medicare Tax

18	Add lines 7, 13, and 17. Also include this amount on Form 1040, line 62, (Form 1040NR, 1040-PR, and 1040-SS filers, see instructions) and go to Part V	**18**

Part V Withholding Reconciliation

19	Medicare tax withheld from Form W-2, box 6. If you have more than one Form W-2, enter the total of the amounts from box 6	**19**
20	Enter the amount from line 1	**20**
21	Multiply line 20 by 1.45% (.0145). This is your regular Medicare tax withholding on Medicare wages	**21**
22	Subtract line 21 from line 19. If zero or less, enter -0-. This is your Additional Medicare Tax withholding on Medicare wages	**22**
23	Additional Medicare Tax withholding on railroad retirement (RRTA) compensation from Form W-2, box 14 (see instructions)	**23**
24	**Total Additional Medicare Tax withholding.** Add lines 22 and 23. Also include this amount with federal income tax withholding on Form 1040, line 64 (Form 1040NR, 1040-PR, and 1040-SS filers, see instructions)	**24**

For Paperwork Reduction Act Notice, see your tax return instructions. Cat. No. 59475X Form **8959** (2015)

Form **8960**	**Net Investment Income Tax—**	OMB No. 1545-2227
Department of the Treasury Internal Revenue Service (99)	**Individuals, Estates, and Trusts** ▶ **Attach to your tax return.** ▶ **Information about Form 8960 and its separate instructions is at** *www.irs.gov/form8960.*	**20**15 Attachment Sequence No. **72**

Name(s) shown on your tax return | Your social security number or EIN

Part I   Investment Income   ☐ Section 6013(g) election (see instructions)
☐ Section 6013(h) election (see instructions)
☐ Regulations section 1.1411-10(g) election (see instructions)

1	Taxable interest (see instructions)	**1**	
2	Ordinary dividends (see instructions)	**2**	
3	Annuities (see instructions)	**3**	
4a	Rental real estate, royalties, partnerships, S corporations, trusts, etc. (see instructions)	**4a**	
b	Adjustment for net income or loss derived in the ordinary course of a non-section 1411 trade or business (see instructions)	**4b**	
c	Combine lines 4a and 4b	**4c**	
5a	Net gain or loss from disposition of property (see instructions) .	**5a**	
b	Net gain or loss from disposition of property that is not subject to net investment income tax (see instructions)	**5b**	
c	Adjustment from disposition of partnership interest or S corporation stock (see instructions)	**5c**	
d	Combine lines 5a through 5c	**5d**	
6	Adjustments to investment income for certain CFCs and PFICs (see instructions)	**6**	
7	Other modifications to investment income (see instructions)	**7**	
8	Total investment income. Combine lines 1, 2, 3, 4c, 5d, 6, and 7	**8**	

Part II   Investment Expenses Allocable to Investment Income and Modifications

9a	Investment interest expenses (see instructions)	**9a**	
b	State, local, and foreign income tax (see instructions)	**9b**	
c	Miscellaneous investment expenses (see instructions)	**9c**	
d	Add lines 9a, 9b, and 9c	**9d**	
10	Additional modifications (see instructions)	**10**	
11	Total deductions and modifications. Add lines 9d and 10	**11**	

Part III   Tax Computation

12	Net investment income. Subtract Part II, line 11 from Part I, line 8. Individuals complete lines 13–17. Estates and trusts complete lines 18a–21. If zero or less, enter -0-	**12**	
	Individuals:		
13	Modified adjusted gross income (see instructions)	**13**	
14	Threshold based on filing status (see instructions)	**14**	
15	Subtract line 14 from line 13. If zero or less, enter -0-	**15**	
16	Enter the smaller of line 12 or line 15	**16**	
17	Net investment income tax for individuals. Multiply line 16 by 3.8% (.038). **Enter here and include on your tax return** (see instructions)	**17**	
	Estates and Trusts:		
18a	Net investment income (line 12 above)	**18a**	
b	Deductions for distributions of net investment income and deductions under section 642(c) (see instructions)	**18b**	
c	Undistributed net investment income. Subtract line 18b from 18a (see instructions). If zero or less, enter -0-	**18c**	
19a	Adjusted gross income (see instructions)	**19a**	
b	Highest tax bracket for estates and trusts for the year (see instructions)	**19b**	
c	Subtract line 19b from line 19a. If zero or less, enter -0- . . .	**19c**	
20	Enter the smaller of line 18c or line 19c	**20**	
21	Net investment income tax for estates and trusts. Multiply line 20 by 3.8% (.038). **Enter here and include on your tax return** (see instructions)	**21**	

For Paperwork Reduction Act Notice, see your tax return instructions.   Cat. No. 59474M   Form **8960** (2015)

Appendix C

Glossary

The key terms in this glossary have been defined to reflect their conventional use in the field of taxation. The definitions may therefore be incomplete for other purposes.

A

AAA bypass election. In the context of a distribution by an S corporation, an election made by the entity to designate that the distribution is first from accumulated earnings and profits (AEP) and only then from the accumulated adjustments account (AAA).

Abandoned spouse. The abandoned spouse provision enables a married taxpayer with a dependent child whose spouse did not live in the taxpayer's home during the last six months of the tax year to file as a head of household rather than as married filing separately.

Accelerated cost recovery system (ACRS). A method in which the cost of tangible property is recovered (depreciated) over a prescribed period of time. This depreciation approach disregards salvage value, imposes a period of cost recovery that depends upon the classification of the asset into one of various recovery periods, and prescribes the applicable percentage of cost that can be deducted each year. A modified system is currently the default cost recovery method; it is referred to as MACRS. § 168.

Accelerated death benefits. The amount received from a life insurance policy by the insured who is terminally ill or chronically ill. Any realized gain may be excluded from the gross income of the insured if the policy is surrendered to the insurer or is sold to a licensed viatical settlement provider. § 101(g).

Acceleration rule. Treatment of an intercompany transaction on a consolidated return, when a sold asset leaves the group.

Accident and health benefits. Employee fringe benefits provided by employers through the payment of health and accident insurance premiums or the establishment of employer-funded medical reimbursement plans. Employers generally are entitled to a deduction for such payments, whereas employees generally exclude such fringe benefits from gross income. §§ 105 and 106.

Accident and health insurance benefits. See *accident and health benefits*.

Accountable plan. A type of expense reimbursement plan that requires an employee to render an adequate accounting to the employer and return any excess reimbursement or allowance. If the expense qualifies, it will be treated as a deduction *for* AGI.

Accounting income. The accountant's concept of income is generally based upon the realization principle. Financial accounting income may differ from taxable income (e.g., accelerated depreciation might be used for Federal income tax and straight-line depreciation for financial accounting purposes). Differences are included in a reconciliation of taxable and accounting income on Schedule M–1 or Schedule M–3 of Form 1120 for corporations.

Accounting method. The method under which income and expenses are determined for tax purposes. Important accounting methods include the cash basis and the accrual basis. Special methods are available for the reporting of gain on installment sales, recognition of income on construction projects (the completed contract and percentage of completion methods), and the valuation of inventories (last-in, first-out and first-in, first-out). §§ 446–474.

Accounting period. The period of time, usually a year, used by a taxpayer for the determination of tax liability. Unless a fiscal year is chosen, taxpayers must determine and pay their income tax liability by using the calendar year (January 1 through December 31) as the period of measurement. An example of a fiscal year is July 1 through June 30. A change in accounting period (e.g., from a calendar year to a fiscal year) generally requires the consent of the IRS. Usually, taxpayers are free to select either an initial calendar or a fiscal year without the consent of the IRS. §§ 441–444.

Accrual method. A method of accounting that reflects expenses incurred and income earned for any one tax year. In contrast to the cash basis of accounting, expenses need not be paid to be deductible, nor need income be received to be taxable. Unearned income (e.g., prepaid interest and rent) generally is taxed in the year of receipt regardless of the method of accounting used by the taxpayer. § 446(c)(2).

Accumulated adjustments account (AAA). An account that aggregates an S corporation's post-1982 income, loss, and deductions for the tax year (including nontaxable income and nondeductible losses and expenses). After the year-end income and expense adjustments are made, the account is reduced by distributions made during the tax year.

Accumulated E & P. See *accumulated earnings and profits (AEP)*.

Accumulated earnings and profits (AEP). Net undistributed tax-basis earnings of a corporation aggregated from March 1, 1913, to the end of the prior tax year. Used to determine the amount of dividend income associated with a distribution to shareholders. § 316 and Reg. § 1.316–2.

Accumulated earnings credit. A reduction allowed in arriving at accumulated taxable income, in determining the accumulated earnings tax.

Accumulated earnings tax. A special tax imposed on C corporations that accumulate (rather than distribute) their earnings beyond the reasonable needs of the business. The accumulated earnings tax and related interest are imposed on accumulated taxable income in addition to the corporate income tax. §§ 531–537.

Accumulated taxable income (ATI). The base upon which the accumulated earnings tax is imposed. Generally, it is the taxable income of the corporation as adjusted for certain items (e.g., the Federal income tax, excess charitable contributions, the dividends received deduction) less the dividends paid deduction and the accumulated earnings credit. § 535.

Accuracy-related penalties. Major civil taxpayer penalties relating to the accuracy of tax return data, including misstatements stemming from taxpayer negligence and improper valuation of income and deductions, are coordinated under this umbrella term. The penalty usually equals 20 percent of the understated tax liability.

ACE adjustment. An adjustment in computing corporate alternative minimum taxable income (AMTI), computed at 75 percent of the excess of adjusted current earnings (ACE) over unadjusted AMTI. ACE computations reflect longer and slower cost recovery deductions and other restrictions on the timing of certain recognition events. Exempt interest, life insurance proceeds, and other receipts that are included in earnings and profits but not in taxable income also increase the ACE adjustment. If unadjusted AMTI exceeds ACE, the ACE adjustment is negative. The negative adjustment is limited to the aggregate of the positive adjustments under ACE for prior years, reduced by any previously claimed negative adjustments.

Acquiescence. Agreement by the IRS on the results reached in certain judicial decisions; sometimes abbreviated *Acq.* or *A.*

Acquisition indebtedness. Debt incurred in acquiring, constructing, or substantially improving a qualified residence of the taxpayer. The interest on such loans is deductible as qualified residence interest. However, interest on such debt is deductible only on the portion of the indebtedness that does not exceed $1,000,000 ($500,000 for married persons filing separate returns). § 163(h)(3).

Active income. Wages, salary, commissions, bonuses, profits from a trade or business in which the taxpayer is a material participant, gain on the sale or other disposition of assets used in an active trade or business, and income from intangible property if the taxpayer's personal efforts significantly contributed to the creation of the property. The passive activity loss rules require classification of income and losses into three categories with active income being one of them.

Ad valorem taxes. A tax imposed on the value of property. The most common ad valorem tax is that imposed by states, counties, and cities on real estate. Ad valorem taxes can be imposed on personal property as well.

Additional first-year depreciation. This provision, effective for property acquired after December 31, 2011, and placed in service before January 1, 2020, provides for an additional cost recovery deduction of 50 percent in the tax year the qualified property is placed in service. (The bonus depreciation percentage is reduced to 40 percent in 2018 and 30 percent in 2019.) Qualified property includes most types of new property other than buildings. The taxpayer can elect to forgo this bonus depreciation. Different rules applied between 2008 and 2011.

Adjusted basis. The cost or other basis of property reduced by depreciation allowed or allowable and increased by capital improvements. Other special adjustments are provided in § 1016 and the related Regulations.

Adjusted current earnings (ACE). Used to determine an adjustment in computing corporate alternative minimum taxable income (AMTI). ACE reflects restrictions on the timing of certain recognition events. Exempt interest, life insurance proceeds, and other receipts that are included in earnings and profits but not in taxable income also increase ACE.

Adjustments. See *AMT adjustments*.

Adoption expenses credit. A provision intended to assist taxpayers who incur nonrecurring costs directly associated with the adoption process, such as legal costs, social service review costs, and transportation costs. Up to $13,460 of costs incurred to adopt an eligible child qualify for the credit (unique rules apply when adopting a special needs child). A taxpayer may claim the credit in the year qualifying expenses are paid or incurred if the expenses are paid during or after the year in which the adoption is finalized. For qualifying expenses paid or incurred in a tax year prior to the year the adoption is finalized, the credit must be claimed in the tax year following the tax year during which the expenses are paid or incurred. § 23.

Affiliated group. A parent-subsidiary group of corporations that is eligible to elect to file on a consolidated basis. Eighty percent ownership of the voting power and value of all of the corporations must be achieved every day of the tax year, and an identifiable parent corporation must exist (i.e., it must own at least 80 percent of another group member without applying attribution rules).

Aggregate (or conduit) concept. The theory of partnership taxation under which, in certain cases, a partnership is treated as a mere collection of the activities of each partner. See also *entity concept*.

Alimony and separate maintenance payments. Alimony deductions result from the payment of a legal obligation arising from the termination of a marital relationship.

Payments designated as alimony generally are included in the gross income of the recipient and are deductible *for* AGI by the payor.

Alimony recapture. The amount of alimony that previously has been included in the gross income of the recipient and deducted by the payor that now is deducted by the recipient and included in the gross income of the payor as the result of front-loading. § 71(f).

All events test. For accrual method taxpayers, income is earned when (1) all of the events have occurred that fix the right to receive the income and (2) the amount can be determined with reasonable accuracy. Accrual of income cannot be postponed simply because a portion of the income may have to be returned in a subsequent period. The all events test also is utilized to determine when expenses can be deducted by an accrual basis taxpayer. The application of the test could cause a variation between the treatment of an item for accounting and for tax purposes. For example, a reserve for warranty expense may be properly accruable under Generally Accepted Accounting Principles but not be deductible under the Federal income tax law. Because of the application of the all events test, the deduction becomes available in the year the warranty obligation becomes fixed and the amount is determinable with reasonable certainty. Reg. §§ 1.446–1(c)(1)(ii) and 1.461–1(a)(2).

Allocate. The assignment of income for various tax purposes. A multistate corporation's nonbusiness income usually is allocated to the state where the nonbusiness assets are located; it is not apportioned with the rest of the entity's income. The income and expense items of an estate or a trust are allocated between income and corpus components. Specific items of income, expense, gain, loss, and credit can be allocated to specific partners if a substantial economic nontax purpose for the allocation is established.

Alternate valuation date. Property passing from a decedent by death may be valued for estate tax purposes as of the date of death or the alternate valuation date. The alternate valuation date is six months after the date of death or the date the property is disposed of by the estate, whichever comes first. To use the alternate valuation date, the executor or administrator of the estate must make an affirmative election. Election of the alternate valuation date is not available unless it decreases the amount of the gross estate and reduces the estate tax liability.

Alternative depreciation system (ADS). A cost recovery system that produces a smaller deduction than would be calculated under ACRS or MACRS. The alternative system must be used in certain instances and can be elected in other instances. § 168(g).

Alternative minimum tax (AMT). The AMT is a fixed percentage of alternative minimum taxable income (AMTI). AMTI generally starts with the taxpayer's adjusted gross income (for individuals) or taxable income (for other taxpayers). To this amount, the taxpayer (1) adds designated preference items (e.g., tax-exempt interest income on private activity bonds), (2) makes other specified adjustments (e.g., to reflect a longer, straight-line cost recovery deduction), (3) adjusts certain AMT itemized deductions for individuals (e.g., interest incurred on housing but not taxes paid), and (4) subtracts an exemption amount. The taxpayer must pay the greater of the resulting AMT (reduced for larger corporations by only the foreign tax credit) or the regular income tax (reduced by all allowable tax credits). The AMT does not apply at all to certain small C corporations. AMT preferences and adjustments are assigned to partners, LLC members, and S corporation shareholders.

Alternative minimum tax credit. The AMT can result from timing differences that give rise to positive adjustments in calculating the AMT base. To provide equity for the taxpayer when these timing differences reverse, the regular tax liability may be reduced by a tax credit for a prior year's minimum tax liability attributable to timing differences. § 53.

Alternative minimum taxable income (AMTI). The base (prior to deducting the exemption amount) for computing a taxpayer's alternative minimum tax. This consists of the taxable income for the year modified for AMT adjustments and AMT preferences. § 55(b)(2).

Alternative tax. An option that is allowed in computing the tax on net capital gain. For the corporate taxpayer, the rate is 35 percent (the same as the highest regular corporate tax rate). Thus, for corporate taxpayers, the alternative tax does not produce a beneficial result. For noncorporate taxpayers, the rate is usually 15 percent (but is 25 percent for unrecaptured § 1250 gain and 28 percent for collectibles and § 1202 gain). However, if the noncorporate taxpayer is in either the 10 percent or the 15 percent tax bracket, the alternative tax rate is 0 percent (rather than 15 percent). Certain high-income taxpayers (i.e., in the 39.6 percent tax bracket) have an alternative tax rate of 20 percent. §§ 1(h) and 1201.

Alternative tax NOL deduction (ATNOLD). In calculating the AMT, the taxpayer is allowed to deduct NOL carryovers and carrybacks. However, for this purpose, a special calculation is required that is referred to as the ATNOLD. The regular income tax is modified for AMT adjustments and preferences to produce the ATNOLD. § 56(d).

American Opportunity credit. This credit replaces the HOPE scholarship credit for years after 2008 and applies for qualifying expenses for the first four years of postsecondary education. Qualified expenses include tuition and related expenses and books and other course materials. Room and board are ineligible for the credit. The maximum credit available per student is $2,500 (100 percent of the first $2,000 of qualified expenses and 25 percent of the next $2,000 of qualified expenses). Eligible students include the taxpayer, taxpayer's spouse, and taxpayer's dependents. To qualify for the credit, a student must take at least one-half of the full-time course load for at least one academic term at a qualifying educational institution. The credit is phased out for higher-income taxpayers. § 25A.

Amortization. The tax deduction for the cost or other basis of an intangible asset over the asset's estimated useful life. Examples of amortizable intangibles include patents, copyrights, and leasehold interests. Most purchased intangible assets (e.g., goodwill) can be amortized for income tax purposes over a 15-year period.

Amount realized. The amount received by a taxpayer upon the sale or exchange of property. Amount realized is the sum of the cash and the fair market value of any property or services received by the taxpayer plus any related debt assumed by the buyer. Determining the amount realized is the starting point for arriving at realized gain or loss. § 1001(b).

AMT adjustments. In calculating AMTI, certain adjustments are added to or deducted from taxable income. These adjustments generally reflect timing differences. § 56.

AMT exemption. An amount deducted from alternative minimum taxable income in deriving alternative minimum tax base. The exemption amount is phased out when AMTI exceeds specified threshold amounts.

AMT preferences. In calculating alternative minimum taxable income (AMTI), certain preference items are added to taxable income. AMT preferences generally reflect differences between the regular tax and the alternative minimum tax (AMT) computational bases. For instance, interest income from certain state and local bonds may be an AMT preference item.

Annual exclusion. In computing the taxable gifts for the year, each donor excludes the first $14,000 (for 2016) of a gift to each donee. Usually, the annual exclusion is not available for gifts of future interests. § 2503(b).

Annuity. A fixed sum of money payable to a person at specified times for a specified period of time or for life. If the party making the payment (i.e., the obligor) is regularly engaged in this type of business (e.g., an insurance company), the arrangement is classified as a commercial annuity. A so-called private annuity involves an obligor that is not regularly engaged in selling annuities (e.g., a charity or family member).

Apportion. The assignment of the business income of a multistate corporation to specific states for income taxation. Usually, the apportionment procedure accounts for the property, payroll, and sales activity levels of the various states, and a proportionate assignment of the entity's total income is made using a three-factor apportionment formula. These activities indicate the commercial domicile of the corporation relative to that income. Some states exclude nonbusiness income from the apportionment procedure; they allocate nonbusiness income to the states where the nonbusiness assets are located.

Appreciated inventory. In partnership taxation, appreciated inventory is a hot asset, and a partner's share of its ordinary income potential must be allocated. If a partner sells an interest in the partnership, ordinary income is recognized to the extent of the partner's share in the partnership's inventory and unrealized receivables. The definition of "inventory" here is broad enough to include any accounts receivable, including unrealized receivables.

Arm's length. See *arm's length price.*

Arm's length price. The standard under which unrelated parties would determine an exchange price for a transaction. Suppose, for example, Cardinal Corporation sells property to its sole shareholder for $10,000. In testing whether the $10,000 is an "arm's length" price, one would ascertain the price that would have been negotiated between the corporation and an unrelated party in a bargained exchange.

ASC 740 (SFAS 109). Under Generally Accepted Accounting Principles, the rules for the financial reporting of the tax expense of an enterprise. Permanent differences affect the enterprise's effective tax rate. Temporary differences create a deferred tax asset or a deferred tax liability on the balance sheet.

ASC 740-10 (FIN 48). An interpretation by the Financial Accounting Standards Board. When an uncertain tax return position exists, this interpretation is used to determine the financial reporting treatment, if any, for the taxpayer. If it is more likely than not (i.e., a greater than 50 percent probability) that the uncertain return position will be sustained (e.g., by the courts) on its technical merits, it must be reported on the financial statements. The amount to be reported then is computed based on the probabilities of the outcome of the technical review, and the amounts at which the dispute would be resolved. If the more-likely-than-not test is failed, no current financial disclosure of the results of the return position is required.

ASC 740-30 (APB 23). Under Generally Accepted Accounting Principles, the rules for the financial reporting of the tax expense relative to a U.S. corporation's non-U.S. subsidiary. If the parent documents that it is permanently reinvesting the non-U.S. earnings of a non-U.S. subsidiary, the parent does not record as an expense any U.S. income tax the parent might pay on such earnings (i.e., the book tax expense is deferred until such earnings are, if ever, repatriated to the United States).

Asset use test. In the context of a corporate reorganization, a means by which to determine if the continuity of business enterprise requirement is met. The acquiring corporation must continue to use the target entity's assets in the acquiror's business going forward; if this is not the case, the requirement is failed.

Assignment of income. A taxpayer attempts to avoid the recognition of income by assigning to another the property that generates the income. Such a procedure will not avoid income recognition by the taxpayer making the assignment if the income was earned at the point of the transfer. In this case, the income is taxed to the person who earns it.

At-risk limitation. Generally, a taxpayer can deduct losses related to a trade or business, S corporation, partnership, or investment asset only to the extent of the at-risk amount. The taxpayer has an amount at risk in a business or investment venture to the extent that personal assets have been subjected to the risks of the business. Typically, the taxpayer's at-risk amount includes (1) the amount of money or other property that the investor contributed to the venture for the investment, (2) the amount of any of the entity's liabilities for which the taxpayer personally is liable and that relate to the investment, and (3) an allocable share of nonrecourse debts incurred by the venture from third parties in arm's length transactions for real estate investments.

Attribution. Under certain circumstances, the tax law applies attribution (constructive ownership) rules to assign to one taxpayer the ownership interest of another taxpayer. If, for example, the stock of Gold Corporation is held 60 percent by Marsha and 40 percent by Sidney, Marsha may be deemed to own 100 percent of Gold Corporation if Marsha and Sidney are mother and child. In that case, the stock owned by Sidney is attributed to Marsha. Stated differently, Marsha has a 60 percent direct and a 40 percent indirect interest in Gold Corporation. It can also be said that Marsha is the constructive owner of Sidney's interest.

Automatic mileage method. Automobile expenses are generally deductible only to the extent the automobile is used in business or for the production of income. Personal commuting expenses are not deductible. The taxpayer may deduct actual expenses (including depreciation and insurance), or the standard (automatic) mileage rate may be used (54 cents per mile for 2016 and 57.5 cents per mile for 2015). Automobile expenses incurred for medical purposes or in connection with job-related moving expenses are deductible to the extent of actual out-of-pocket expenses or at the rate of 19 cents per mile for 2016 and 23 cents per mile for 2015. For charitable activities, the rate is 14 cents per mile.

B

Bad debt. A deduction is permitted if a business account receivable subsequently becomes partially or completely worthless, providing the income arising from the debt previously was included in income. Available methods are the specific charge-off method and the reserve method. However, except for certain financial institutions, TRA of 1986 repealed the use of the reserve method for 1987 and thereafter. If the reserve method is used, partially or totally worthless accounts are charged to the reserve. A nonbusiness bad debt deduction is allowed as a short-term capital loss if the loan did not arise in connection with the creditor's trade or business activities. Loans between related parties (family members) generally are classified as nonbusiness. § 166.

Balance sheet approach. The process under ASC 740 (SFAS 109) by which an entity's deferred tax expense or deferred tax benefit is determined as a result of the reporting period's changes in the balance sheet's deferred tax asset and deferred tax liability accounts.

Basis in partnership interest. The acquisition cost of the partner's ownership interest in the partnership. Includes purchase price and associated debt acquired from other partners and in the course of the entity's trade or business.

Benchmarking. The tax professional's use of two or more entities' effective tax rates and deferred tax balance sheet accounts. Used chiefly to compare the effectiveness of the entities' tax planning techniques, and to suggest future tax-motivated courses of action.

Blockage rule. A factor to be considered in valuing a large block of corporate stock. Application of this rule generally justifies a discount in the asset's fair market value, because the disposition of a large amount of stock at any one time may depress the value of the shares in the marketplace.

Boot. Cash or property of a type not included in the definition of a tax-deferred exchange. The receipt of boot causes an otherwise tax-deferred transfer to become immediately taxable to the extent of the lesser of the fair market value of the boot or the realized gain on the transfer. For example, see transfers to controlled corporations under § 351(b), reorganizations under § 368, and like-kind exchanges under § 1031(b).

Branch profits tax. A tax on the effectively connected earnings and profits of the U.S. branch of a foreign corporation. The tax is levied in addition to the usual § 11 tax in an amount equal to 30 percent of the dividend equivalent amount. Treaties can override the tax or reduce the withholding percent-age. Earnings reinvested in the U.S. operations of the entity are not subject to the tax until repatriation.

Built-in gains tax. A penalty tax designed to discourage a shift of the incidence of taxation on unrealized gains from a C corporation to its shareholders, via an S election. Under this provision, any recognized gain during the first 10 (or seven or five) years of S status generates a corporate-level tax on a base not to exceed the aggregate untaxed built-in gains brought into the S corporation upon its election from C corporation taxable years.

Built-in loss property. Property contributed to a corporation under § 351 or as a contribution to capital that has a basis in excess of its fair market value. An adjustment is necessary to step down the basis of the property to its fair market value. The adjustment prevents the corporation and the contributing shareholder from obtaining a double tax benefit. The corporation allocates the adjustment proportionately among the assets with the built-in loss. As an alternative to the corporate adjustment, the shareholder may elect to reduce the basis in the stock.

Business bad debt. A tax deduction allowed for obligations obtained in connection with a trade or business that have become either partially or completely worthless. In contrast to nonbusiness bad debts, business bad debts are deductible as business expenses. § 166.

Business purpose. A justifiable business reason for carrying out a transaction. Mere tax avoidance is not an acceptable business purpose. The presence of a business purpose is crucial in the area of corporate reorganizations and certain liquidations.

Buy-sell agreement. An arrangement, particularly appropriate in the case of a closely held corporation or a partnership, whereby the surviving owners (shareholders or partners) or the entity agrees to purchase the interest of a withdrawing owner. The buy-sell agreement provides for an orderly disposition of an interest in a business and may aid in setting the value of the interest for estate tax purposes.

Bypass amount. The amount that can be transferred by gift or at death free of any unified transfer tax. For 2016, the bypass amount is $5.45 million for estate tax and $5.45 million for gift tax.

Bypass election. In the context of a distribution by an S corporation, an election made by the entity to designate that the distribution is first from accumulated earnings and profits and only then from the accumulated adjustments account (AAA).

C

C corporation. A separate taxable entity subject to the rules of Subchapter C of the Code. This business form may create a double taxation effect relative to its shareholders. The entity is subject to the regular corporate tax and a number of penalty taxes at the Federal level.

Cafeteria benefit plans. See *cafeteria plan*.

Cafeteria plan. An employee benefit plan under which an employee is allowed to select from among a variety of employer-provided fringe benefits. Some of the benefits may be taxable, and some may be statutory nontaxable benefits (e.g., health and accident insurance and group term life insurance). The employee is taxed only on the taxable benefits selected. A cafeteria benefit plan is also referred to as a flexible benefit plan. § 125.

Capital account. The financial accounting analog of a partner's tax basis in the entity.

Capital asset. Broadly speaking, all assets are capital except those specifically excluded from that definition by the Code. Major categories of noncapital assets include property held for resale in the normal course of business (inventory), trade accounts and notes receivable, and depreciable property and real estate used in a trade or business (§ 1231 assets). § 1221.

Capital contribution. Various means by which a shareholder makes additional funds available to the corporation (placed at the risk of the business), sometimes without the receipt of additional stock. If no stock is received, the contributions are added to the basis of the shareholder's existing stock investment and do not generate gross income to the corporation. § 118.

Capital gains. The gain from the sale or exchange of a capital asset.

Capital gain property. Property contributed to a charitable organization that if sold rather than contributed, would have resulted in long-term capital gain to the donor.

Capital interest. Usually, the percentage of the entity's net assets that a partner would receive on liquidation. Typically determined by the partner's capital sharing ratio.

Capital losses. The loss from the sale or exchange of a capital asset.

Capital sharing ratio. A partner's percentage ownership of the entity's capital.

Cash balance plan. A hybrid form of pension plan similar in some aspects to a defined benefit plan. Such a plan is funded by the employer, and the employer bears the investment risks and rewards. But like defined contribution plans, a cash balance plan establishes allocations to individual employee accounts, and the payout for an employee depends on investment performance.

Cash method. See *cash receipts method.*

Cash receipts method. A method of accounting that reflects deductions as paid and income as received in any one tax year. However, deductions for prepaid expenses that benefit more than one tax year (e.g., prepaid rent and prepaid interest) usually are spread over the period benefited rather than deducted in the year paid. § 446(c)(1).

Casualty loss. A casualty is defined as "the complete or partial destruction of property resulting from an identifiable event of a sudden, unexpected or unusual nature" (e.g., floods, storms, fires, auto accidents). Individuals may deduct a casualty loss only if the loss is incurred in a trade or business or in a transaction entered into for profit or arises from fire, storm, shipwreck, or other casualty or from theft. Individuals usually deduct personal casualty losses as itemized deductions subject to a $100 nondeductible amount and to an annual floor equal to 10 percent of adjusted gross income that applies after the $100 per casualty floor has been applied. Special rules are provided for the netting of certain casualty gains and losses.

Certiorari. Appeal from a U.S. Court of Appeals to the U.S. Supreme Court is by Writ of Certiorari. The Supreme Court

does not have to accept the appeal and usually does not (*cert. den.*) unless there is a conflict among the lower courts that needs to be resolved or a constitutional issue is involved.

Charitable contribution. Contributions are deductible (subject to various restrictions and ceiling limitations) if made to qualified nonprofit charitable organizations. A cash basis taxpayer is entitled to a deduction solely in the year of payment. Accrual basis corporations may accrue contributions at year-end if payment is properly authorized before the end of the year and payment is made within two and one-half months after the end of the year. § 170.

Check-the-box Regulations. By using the check-the-box rules prudently, an entity can select the most attractive tax results offered by the Code, without being bound by legal forms. By default, an unincorporated entity with more than one owner is taxed as a partnership; an unincorporated entity with one owner is a disregarded entity, taxed as a sole proprietorship or corporate division. No action is necessary by the taxpayer if the legal form or default status is desired. Form 8832 is used to "check a box" and change the tax status. Not available if the entity is incorporated under state law.

Child tax credit. A tax credit based solely on the number of qualifying children under age 17. The maximum credit available is $1,000 per child. A qualifying child must be claimed as a dependent on a parent's tax return to qualify for the credit. Taxpayers who qualify for the child tax credit may also qualify for a supplemental credit. The supplemental credit is treated as a component of the earned income credit and is therefore refundable. The credit is phased out for higher-income taxpayers. § 24.

Circuit Court of Appeals. Any of 13 Federal courts that consider tax matters appealed from the U.S. Tax Court, a U.S. District Court, or the U.S. Court of Federal Claims. Appeal from a U.S. Court of Appeals is to the U.S. Supreme Court by Certiorari.

Circular 230. A portion of the Federal tax Regulations that describes the levels of conduct at which a tax preparer must operate. Circular 230 dictates, for instance, that a tax preparer may not charge an unconscionable fee or delay the execution of a tax audit with inappropriate delays. Circular 230 requires that there be a reasonable basis for a tax return position and that no frivolous returns be filed.

Citator. A tax research resource that presents the judicial history of a court case and traces the subsequent references to the case. When these references include the citating cases' evaluations of the cited case's precedents, the research can obtain some measure of the efficacy and reliability of the original holding.

Claim of right doctrine. A judicially imposed doctrine applicable to both cash and accrual basis taxpayers that holds that an amount is includible in income upon actual or constructive receipt if the taxpayer has an unrestricted claim to the payment. For the tax treatment of amounts repaid when previously included in income under the claim of right doctrine, see § 1341.

Closely held C corporation. A regular corporation (i.e., the S election is not in effect) for which more than 50 percent of the value of its outstanding stock is owned, directly or indirectly, by five or fewer individuals at any time during the tax year. The term is relevant in identifying C corporations that are subject to the passive activity loss provisions. § 469.

Closely held corporation. A corporation where stock ownership is not widely dispersed. Rather, a few shareholders are in control of corporate policy and are in a position to benefit personally from that policy.

Closing agreement. In a tax dispute, the parties sign a closing agreement to spell out the terms under which the matters are settled. The agreement is binding on both the Service and the taxpayer.

Collectibles. A special type of capital asset, the gain from which is taxed at a maximum rate of 28 percent if the holding period is more than one year. Examples include art, rugs, antiques, gems, metals, stamps, some coins and bullion, and alcoholic beverages held for investment.

Combined return. In multistate taxation, a group of unitary corporations may elect or be required to file an income tax return that includes operating results for all of the affiliates, not just those with nexus in the state. Thus, apportionment data is reported for the group's worldwide or water's-edge operations.

Community property. Louisiana, Texas, New Mexico, Arizona, California, Washington, Idaho, Nevada, and Wisconsin have community property systems. Alaska residents can elect community property status for assets. The rest of the states are common law property jurisdictions. The difference between common law and community property systems centers around the property rights possessed by married persons. In a common law system, each spouse owns whatever he or she earns. Under a community property system, one-half of the earnings of each spouse is considered owned by the other spouse. Assume, for example, that Jeff and Alice are husband and wife and that their only income is the $50,000 annual salary Jeff receives. If they live in New York (a common law state), the $50,000 salary belongs to Jeff. If, however, they live in Texas (a community property state), the $50,000 salary is owned one-half each by Jeff and Alice.

Compensatory damages. Damages received or paid by the taxpayer can be classified as compensatory damages or as punitive damages. Compensatory damages are paid to compensate one for harm caused by another. Compensatory damages are excludible from the recipient's gross income.

Complete termination redemption. Sale or exchange treatment is available relative to this type of redemption. The shareholder must retire all of his or her outstanding shares in the corporation (ignoring family attribution rules) and cannot hold an interest, other than that of a creditor, for the 10 years following the redemption. § 302(b)(3).

Completed contract method. A method of reporting gain or loss on certain long-term contracts. Under this method of accounting, all gross income and expenses are recognized in the tax year in which the contract is completed. Reg. § 1.451–3.

Complex trust. Not a simple trust. Such trusts may have charitable beneficiaries, accumulate income, and distribute corpus. §§ 661–663.

Composite return. In multistate taxation, an S corporation may be allowed to file a single income tax return that

assigns pass-through items to resident and nonresident shareholders. The composite or "block" return allows the entity to remit any tax that is attributable to the nonresident shareholders.

Conduit concept. An approach assumed by the tax law in the treatment of certain entities and their owners. Specific tax characteristics pass through the entity without losing their identity. For example, items of income and expense, capital gains and losses, tax credits, etc., realized by a partnership pass through the partnership (a conduit) and are subject to taxation at the partner level. Also, in an S corporation, certain items pass through and are reported on the returns of the shareholders.

Conservation easements. An interest in real property that maintains its natural or pristine condition. Most often it restricts the development of the property. Properly structured, the grant of such an easement can generate an income tax deduction for the donor. If the grant takes place after the owner's death, a § 2055 charitable contribution deduction results, and a portion of the property's value is excluded from the gross estate. § 2031(c).

Conservatism principle. The theory behind much of Generally Accepted Accounting Principles, under which assurance is provided that an entity's balance sheet assets are not overstated, nor liabilities understated. For instance, under ASC 740 (SFAS 109), a deferred tax asset is not recorded until it is more likely than not that the future tax benefit will be realized.

Consolidated returns. A procedure whereby certain affiliated corporations may file a single return, combine the tax transactions of each corporation, and arrive at a single income tax liability for the group. The election to file a consolidated return usually is binding on future years. §§ 1501–1505 and related Regulations.

Consolidation. The combination of two or more corporations into a newly created corporation. Thus, Black Corporation and White Corporation combine to form Gray Corporation. A consolidation may qualify as a nontaxable reorganization if certain conditions are satisfied. §§ 354 and 368(a)(1)(A).

Constructive dividend. A taxable benefit derived by a shareholder from his or her corporation that is not actually initiated by the board of directors as a dividend. Examples include unreasonable compensation, excessive rent payments, bargain purchases of corporate property, and shareholder use of corporate property. Constructive dividends generally are found in closely held corporations.

Constructive liquidation scenario. The means by which recourse debt is shared among partners in basis determination.

Constructive receipt. If income is unqualifiedly available although not physically in the taxpayer's possession, it still is subject to the income tax. An example is accrued interest on a savings account. Under the constructive receipt concept, the interest is taxed to a depositor in the year available, rather than the year actually withdrawn. The fact that the depositor uses the cash basis of accounting for tax purposes is irrelevant. See Reg. § 1.451–2.

Continuity of business enterprise. In a tax-favored reorganization, the acquiring corporation must continue the historic business of the target or use a significant portion of the target's assets in the new business.

Continuity of interest. In a tax-favored reorganization, a shareholder or corporation that has substantially the same investment after an exchange as before should not be taxed on the transaction. Specifically, the seller must acquire an equity interest in the acquiring corporation equal in value to at least 40 percent of all the outstanding stock of the target entity.

Control. Holding a specified level of stock ownership in a corporation. For § 351, the new shareholder(s) must hold at least 80 percent of the total combined voting power of all voting classes of stock and at least 80 percent of the shares of all nonvoting classes. Other tax provisions require different levels of control to bring about desired effects, such as 50 or 100 percent.

Controlled foreign corporation (CFC). A non-U.S. corporation in which more than 50 percent of the total combined voting power of all classes of stock entitled to vote or the total value of the stock of the corporation is owned by U.S. shareholders on any day during the taxable year of the foreign corporation. For purposes of this definition, a U.S. shareholder is any U.S. person who owns, or is considered to own, 10 percent or more of the total combined voting power of all classes of voting stock of the foreign corporation. Stock owned directly, indirectly, and constructively is used in this measure. See *U.S. shareholder.*

Controlled group. A controlled group of corporations is required to share the lower corporate tax rates and various other tax benefits among the members of the group. A controlled group may be either a brother-sister or a parent-subsidiary group.

Corporate liquidation. Occurs when a corporation distributes its net assets to its shareholders and ceases to be a going concern. Generally, a shareholder recognizes capital gain or loss upon the liquidation of the entity, regardless of the corporation's balance in its earnings and profits account. The liquidating corporation recognizes gain and loss on assets that it sells during the liquidation period and on assets that it distributes to shareholders in kind.

Corpus. The body or principal of a trust. Suppose, for example, Grant transfers an apartment building into a trust, income payable to Ruth for life, remainder to Shawn upon Ruth's death. Corpus of the trust is the apartment building.

Correspondence audit. An audit conducted by the IRS by the U.S. mail. Typically, the IRS writes to the taxpayer requesting the verification of a particular deduction or exemption. The remittance of copies of records or other support is requested of the taxpayer.

Cost depletion. Depletion that is calculated based on the adjusted basis of the asset. The adjusted basis is divided by the expected recoverable units to determine the depletion per unit. The depletion per unit is multiplied by the units sold during the tax year to calculate cost depletion.

Cost recovery. The system established in the Internal Revenue Code used to recover the cost of an asset using specific lives, methods, and conventions. Cost recovery methods include MACRS (generally, assets placed in service after 1986) and ACRS (generally, assets placed in service after 1980 and before 1987). § 168.

Court of Federal Claims. A trial court (court of original jurisdiction) that decides litigation involving Federal tax matters. Appeal from this court is to the Court of Appeals for the Federal Circuit.

Court of original jurisdiction. The Federal courts are divided into courts of original jurisdiction and appellate courts. A dispute between a taxpayer and the IRS is first considered by a court of original jurisdiction (i.e., a trial court). The four Federal courts of original jurisdiction are the U.S. Tax Court, the U.S. District Court, the Court of Federal Claims, and the Small Cases Division of the U.S. Tax Court.

Coverdell education savings account (§ 530 plan). Coverdell education savings account exempts from tax the earnings on amounts placed in a qualified account for the education expenses of a named beneficiary. Contributions are limited to $2,000 per year per beneficiary and the proceeds can be withdrawn without tax provided the funds are used to pay qualified educational expenses for primary, secondary, or higher education. The account is named for the late Senator Paul Coverdell (R-GA), who sponsored the legislation in Congress. § 530.

Credit for certain retirement plan contributions. A nonrefundable credit is available based on eligible contributions of up to $2,000 to certain qualified retirement plans, such as traditional and Roth IRAs and § 401(k) plans. The benefit provided by this credit is in addition to any deduction or exclusion that otherwise is available resulting from the qualifying contribution. The amount of the credit depends on the taxpayer's AGI and filing status. § 25B.

Credit for child and dependent care expenses. A tax credit ranging from 20 percent to 35 percent of employment-related expenses (child and dependent care expenses) for amounts of up to $6,000 is available to individuals who are employed (or deemed to be employed) and maintain a household for a dependent child under age 13, disabled spouse, or disabled dependent. § 21.

Credit for employer-provided child care. A nonrefundable credit is available to employers who provide child care facilities to their employees during normal working hours. The credit, limited to $150,000, is comprised of two components. The portion of the credit for qualified child care expenses is equal to 25 percent of these expenses, while the portion of the credit for qualified child care resource and referral services is equal to 10 percent of these expenses. Any qualifying expenses otherwise deductible by the taxpayer must be reduced by the amount of the credit. In addition, the taxpayer's basis for any property used for qualifying purposes is reduced by the amount of the credit. § 45F.

Credit for small employer pension plan startup costs. A nonrefundable credit available to small businesses based on administrative costs associated with establishing and maintaining certain qualified plans. While such qualifying costs generally are deductible as ordinary and necessary business expenses, the availability of the credit is intended to lower the costs of starting a qualified retirement program and therefore encourage qualifying businesses to establish retirement plans for their employees. The credit is available for eligible employers at the rate of 50 percent of qualified startup costs. The maximum credit is $500 (based on a maximum $1,000 of qualifying expenses). § 45E.

Crop insurance proceeds. The proceeds received when an insured crop is destroyed. Section 451(d) permits the farmer to defer reporting the income from the insurance proceeds until the tax year following the taxable year of the destruction.

Crop method. A method of accounting for agricultural crops that are planted in one year but harvested in a subsequent year. Under this method, the costs of raising the crop are accumulated as inventory and are deducted when the income from the crop is realized.

Cross-purchase buy-sell agreement. Under this arrangement, the surviving owners of the business agree to buy out the withdrawing owner. Assume, for example, Ron and Sara are equal shareholders in Tip Corporation. Under a cross-purchase buy-sell agreement, Ron and Sara would contract to purchase the other's interest, should that person decide to withdraw from the business.

Current E & P. Net tax-basis earnings of a corporation aggregated during the current tax year. A corporate distribution is deemed to be first from the entity's current earnings and profits and then from accumulated earnings and profits. Shareholders recognize dividend income to the extent of the earnings and profits of the corporation. A dividend results to the extent of current earnings and profits, even if there is a larger negative balance in accumulated earnings and profits.

Current tax expense. Under ASC 740 (SFAS 109), the book tax expense that relates to the current reporting period's net income and is actually payable (or creditable) to the appropriate governmental agencies for the current period. Also known as "cash tax" or "tax payable."

D

De minimis fringe. Benefits provided to employees that are too insignificant to warrant the time and effort required to account for the benefits received by each employee and the value of those benefits. Such amounts are excludible from the employee's gross income. § 132.

De minimis fringe benefits. See *de minimis fringe*.

Death benefits. A payment made by an employer to the beneficiary or beneficiaries of a deceased employee on account of the death of the employee.

Debt-financed income. Included in computations of the unrelated business income of an exempt organization, the gross income generated from debt-financed property.

Deceased spouse's unused exclusion (DSUE). In computing the Federal estate tax, the decedent uses the exclusion amount to shelter an amount of the gross estate from taxation. When the first spouse to die fails to use a portion of his/her exclusion amount, the unused portion is "portable," and becomes available to the surviving spouse. The surviving spouse can use the DSUE only of his/her last spouse to predecease.

Deduction for qualified tuition and related expenses. Taxpayers are allowed a deduction of up to $4,000 for higher education expenses. Certain taxpayers are not eligible for the deduction: those whose gross AGI exceeds a specified amount and those who can be claimed as a dependent by another taxpayer. These expenses are classified as a deduction *for* AGI, and they need not be employment-related. § 222.

Deductions *for* adjusted gross income. The Federal income tax is not imposed upon gross income. Rather, it is imposed upon taxable income. Congressionally identified deductions for individual taxpayers are subtracted either from gross income to arrive at adjusted gross income or from adjusted gross income to arrive at the tax base, taxable income.

Deductions *from* adjusted gross income. See *deductions for adjusted gross income.*

Deductions in respect of a decedent. Deductions accrued at the moment of death but not recognizable on the final income tax return of a decedent because of the method of accounting used. Such items are allowed as deductions on the estate tax return and on the income tax return of the estate (Form 1041) or the heir (Form 1040). An example of a deduction in respect of a decedent is interest expense accrued to the date of death by a cash basis debtor.

Deemed-paid credit. A foreign tax credit allowed to a U.S. taxpayer that has received an actual or constructive dividend from a non-U.S. corporation that has paid foreign income taxes. The credit is computed using the proportion of foreign income taxes paid by the payor corporation to its post-1986 undistributed earnings. Under § 78, the U.S. taxpayer claiming a deemed-paid credit includes the same amount in gross income for the tax year.

Deferred compensation. Compensation that will be taxed when received or upon the removal of certain restrictions on receipt and not when earned. Contributions by an employer to a qualified pension or profit sharing plan on behalf of an employee are an example. The contributions will not be taxed to the employee until the funds are made available or distributed to the employee (e.g., upon retirement).

Deferred tax asset. Under ASC 740 (SFAS 109), an item created on an enterprise's balance sheet by a temporary book-tax difference, such that a tax benefit is not recognized until a later date, although it already has been reported in the financial statements (e.g., the carryforward of a disallowed deduction).

Deferred tax benefit. Under ASC 740 (SFAS 109), a reduction in the book tax expense that relates to the current reporting period's net income but will not be realized until a future reporting period. Creates or adds to the entity's deferred tax asset balance sheet account. For instance, the carryforward of a net operating loss is a deferred tax benefit.

Deferred tax expense. Under ASC 740 (SFAS 109), a book tax expense that relates to the current reporting period's net income but will not be realized until a future reporting period. Creates or adds to the entity's deferred tax liability balance sheet account. For instance, a deferred tax expense is created when tax depreciation deductions for the period are "accelerated" and exceed the corresponding book depreciation expense.

Deferred tax liability. As determined under the rules of ASC 740 (SFAS 109), an item created on an enterprise's balance sheet by a temporary book-tax difference, such that a tax benefit is recognized earlier for tax purposes than it is in the financial accounting records (e.g., the use of an accelerated cost recovery deduction).

Defined benefit plan. Qualified plans can be dichotomized into defined benefit plans and defined contribution plans. Under a defined benefit plan, a formula defines the benefits employees are to receive. The formula usually includes years of service, employee compensation, and some stated percentage. The employer must make annual contributions based on actuarial computations that will be sufficient to pay the vested retirement benefits.

Defined contribution pension plan. Qualified plans can be dichotomized into defined benefit plans and defined contribution plans. Under a defined contribution plan, a separate account is maintained for each covered employee. The employee's benefits under the plan are based solely on (1) the amount contributed and (2) income from the fund that accrues to the employee's account. The plan defines the amount the employer is required to contribute (e.g., a flat dollar amount, an amount based on a special formula, or an amount equal to a certain percentage of compensation).

Dependency exemption. See *personal and dependency exemptions*.

Depletion. The process by which the cost or other basis of a natural resource (e.g., an oil or gas interest) is recovered upon extraction and sale of the resource. The two ways to determine the depletion allowance are the cost and percentage (or statutory) methods. Under cost depletion, each unit of production sold is assigned a portion of the cost or other basis of the interest. This is determined by dividing the cost or other basis by the total units expected to be recovered. Under percentage (or statutory) depletion, the tax law provides a special percentage factor for different types of minerals and other natural resources. This percentage is multiplied by the gross income from the interest to arrive at the depletion allowance. §§ 613 and 613A.

Depreciation. The deduction for the cost or other basis of a tangible asset over the asset's estimated useful life. Typically used for financial reporting purposes and for tax purposes if assets were placed in service prior to 1981 (for assets placed in service after 1980, cost recovery is used for tax purposes).

Determination letter. Upon the request of a taxpayer, the IRS will comment on the tax status of a completed transaction. Determination letters frequently are used to determine whether a retirement or profit sharing plan qualifies under the Code, and to determine the tax-exempt status of certain nonprofit organizations.

Disabled access credit. A tax credit designed to encourage small businesses to make their facilities more accessible to disabled individuals. The credit is equal to 50 percent of the eligible expenditures that exceed $250 but do not exceed $10,250. Thus, the maximum amount for the credit is $5,000. The adjusted basis for depreciation is reduced by the amount of the credit. To qualify, the facility must have been placed in service before November 6, 1990. § 44.

Disaster area losses. A casualty sustained in an area designated as a disaster area by the president of the United States. In such an event, the disaster loss may be treated as having occurred in the taxable year immediately preceding the year in which the disaster actually occurred. Thus, immediate tax benefits are provided to victims of a disaster. § 165(i).

Disclaimer. Rejections, refusals, or renunciations of claims, powers, or property. Section 2518 sets forth the conditions required to avoid gift tax consequences as the result of a disclaimer.

Disguised sale. When a partner contributes property to the entity and soon thereafter receives a distribution from

the partnership, the transactions are collapsed and the distribution is seen as a purchase of the asset by the partnership. § 707(a)(2)(B).

Disproportionate distribution. A distribution from a partnership to one or more of its partners in which at least one partner's interest in partnership hot assets is increased or decreased. For example, a distribution of cash to one partner and hot assets to another changes both partners' interest in hot assets and is disproportionate. The intent of rules for taxation of disproportionate distributions is to ensure that each partner eventually recognizes his or her proportionate share of partnership ordinary income.

Disproportionate redemption. Sale or exchange treatment is available relative to this type of redemption. After the exchange, the shareholder owns less than 80 percent of his or her pre-redemption interest in the corporation and only a minority interest in the entity. § 302(b)(2).

Disregarded entity. The Federal income tax treatment of business income usually follows the legal form of the taxpayer (i.e., an individual's sole proprietorship is reported on the Form 1040; a C corporation's taxable income is computed on Form 1120. The check-the-box Regulations are used if the unincorporated taxpayer wants to use a different tax regime. Under these rules, a disregarded entity is taxed as an individual or a corporate division; other tax regimes are not available. For instance, a one-member limited liability company is a disregarded entity.

Distributable net income (DNI). The measure that determines the nature and amount of the distributions from estates and trusts that the beneficiaries must include in income. DNI also limits the amount that estates and trusts can claim as a deduction for such distributions. § 643(a).

District Court. See *Federal District Court*.

Dividend. A nondeductible distribution to the shareholders of a corporation. A dividend constitutes gross income to the recipient if it is paid from the current or accumulated earnings and profits of the corporation.

Dividend equivalent amount (DEA). The amount subject to the branch profits tax, it is equal to the effectively connected E & P of the U.S. branch of a foreign corporation, reduced/(increased) by an increase/(reduction) in U.S. net equity.

Dividends received deduction. A deduction allowed a shareholder that is a corporation for dividends received from a domestic corporation. The deduction usually is 70 percent of the dividends received, but it could be 80 or 100 percent depending upon the ownership percentage held by the recipient corporation. §§ 243–246.

Divisive reorganization. A "Type D" spin-off, split-off, or split-up, reorganization in which the original corporation divides its active business (in existence for at least five years) assets among two or more corporations. The stock received by the original corporation shareholders must be at least 80 percent of the other corporations.

Dock sales. A purchaser uses its owned or rented vehicles to take possession of the product at the seller's shipping dock. In most states, the sale is apportioned to the operating state of the purchaser, rather than the seller. See also *apportion* and *sales factor*.

Dollar-value LIFO. An inventory technique that focuses on the dollars invested in the inventory rather than the particular items on hand each period. Each inventory item is assigned to a pool. A pool is a collection of similar items and is treated as a separate inventory. At the end of the period, each pool is valued in terms of prices at the time LIFO was adopted (base period prices), whether or not the particular items were actually on hand in the year LIFO was adopted, to compare with current prices to determine if there has been an increase or decrease in inventories.

Domestic production activities deduction (DPAD). A deduction based on 9 percent of the lesser of qualified production activities income (QPAI) or taxable income (for a corporate taxpayer). The deduction is further limited to 50 percent of the W–2 production wages paid. In the case of an individual taxpayer, modified adjusted gross income is substituted for taxable income. § 199.

Domestic production gross receipts (DPGR). A key component in computing the domestic production activities deduction (DPAD). Includes receipts from the sale and other disposition of qualified production property produced in significant part within the United States. DPGR is defined in § 199(c)(4).

E

Earned income credit. A tax credit designed to provide assistance to certain low-income individuals who generally have a qualifying child. This is a refundable credit. To receive the most beneficial treatment, the taxpayer must have qualifying children. However, it is possible to qualify for the credit without having a child. See the text chapter on credits for the computation procedure required in order to determine the amount of the credit allowed.

Earnings and profits (E & P). Measures the economic capacity of a corporation to make a distribution to shareholders that is not a return of capital. Such a distribution results in dividend income to the shareholders to the extent of the corporation's current and accumulated earnings and profits.

Economic effect test. Requirements that must be met before a special allocation may be used by a partnership. The premise behind the test is that each partner who receives an allocation of income or loss from a partnership bears the economic benefit or burden of the allocation.

Economic income. The change in the taxpayer's net worth, as measured in terms of market values, plus the value of the assets the taxpayer consumed during the year. Because of the impracticality of this income model, it is not used for tax purposes.

Economic performance test. One of the requirements that must be satisfied for an accrual basis taxpayer to deduct an expense. The accrual basis taxpayer first must satisfy the all events test. That test is not deemed satisfied until economic performance occurs. This occurs when property or services are provided to the taxpayer, or in the case in which the taxpayer is required to provide property or services, whenever the property or services are actually provided by the taxpayer.

Education expenses. Employees may deduct education expenses that are incurred either (1) to maintain or improve existing job-related skills or (2) to meet the express requirements of the employer or the requirements imposed by law to retain employment status. The expenses are not deductible if the education is required to meet the minimum educational standards for the taxpayer's job or if the education qualifies the individual for a new trade or business. Reg. § 1.162–5.

Educational savings bonds. U.S. Series EE bonds whose proceeds are used for qualified higher educational expenses for the taxpayer, the taxpayer's spouse, or a dependent. The interest may be excluded from gross income, provided the taxpayer's adjusted gross income does not exceed certain amounts. § 135.

Effective tax rate. The financial statements for an entity include several footnotes, one of which reconciles the expected (statutory) income tax rate (e.g., 35 percent for a C corporation) with the effective tax rate (i.e., total tax expense as a percentage of book income). The reconciliation often is done in dollar and/or percentage terms.

Effectively connected income. Income of a nonresident alien or foreign corporation that is attributable to the operation of a U.S. trade or business under either the asset-use or the business-activities test.

E-file. The electronic filing of a tax return. The filing is either direct or indirect. As to direct, the taxpayer goes online using a computer and tax return preparation software. Indirect filing occurs when a taxpayer utilizes an authorized IRS e-file provider. The provider often is the tax return preparer.

E-filing. See *e-file.*

Employment taxes. Taxes that an employer must pay on account of its employees. Employment taxes include FICA (Federal Insurance Contributions Act) and FUTA (Federal Unemployment Tax Act) taxes. Employment taxes are paid to the IRS in addition to income tax withholdings at specified intervals. Such taxes can be levied on the employees, the employer, or both.

Energy credits. See *energy tax credits.*

Energy tax credits. Various tax credits are available to those who invest in certain energy property. The purpose of the credit is to create incentives for conservation and to develop alternative energy sources.

Enrolled agents (EAs). A tax practitioner who has gained admission to practice before the IRS by passing an IRS examination and maintaining a required level of continuing professional education.

Entertainment expenses. Expenses that are deductible only if they are directly related to or associated with a trade or business. Various restrictions and documentation requirements have been imposed upon the deductibility of entertainment expenses to prevent abuses by taxpayers. See, for example, the provision contained in § 274(n) that disallows 50 percent (20 percent prior to 1994) of entertainment expenses. § 274.

Entity accounting income. Entity accounting income is not identical to the taxable income of a trust or estate, nor is it determined in the same manner as the entity's financial accounting income would be. The trust document or will determines whether certain income, expenses, gains, or losses are allocated to the corpus of the entity or to the entity's income beneficiaries. Only the items that are allocated to the income beneficiaries are included in entity accounting income.

Entity buy-sell agreement. An arrangement whereby the entity is to purchase a withdrawing owner's interest. When the entity is a corporation, the agreement generally involves a stock redemption on the part of the withdrawing shareholder. See also *buy-sell agreement* and *cross-purchase buy-sell agreement.*

Entity concept. The theory of partnership taxation under which a partnership is treated as a separate and distinct entity from the partners and has its own tax attributes.

Equity method. Under Generally Accepted Accounting Principles, the method of financial reporting for the operations of a subsidiary when the parent corporation owns between 20 and 50 percent of the subsidiary's stock. Creates a book-tax difference, as the two entities' operating results are combined for book purposes, but a Federal income tax consolidated return cannot be filed.

Estate freeze. Procedures directed toward fixing and stabilizing the value of an interest retained in a business, while transferring the growth portion to family members. In the case of a closely held corporation, the estate freeze usually involves keeping the preferred stock and giving away the common stock. The ultimate objective is to reduce estate value when the original owner-donor dies.

Estate tax. A tax imposed on the right to transfer property by death. Thus, an estate tax is levied on the decedent's estate and not on the heir receiving the property.

Estimated tax. The amount of tax (including alternative minimum tax and self-employment tax) a taxpayer expects to owe for the year after subtracting tax credits and income tax withheld. The estimated tax must be paid in installments at designated intervals (e.g., for the individual taxpayer, by April 15, June 15, September 15, and January 15 of the following year).

Excess lobbying expenditures. An excise tax is applied on otherwise tax-exempt organizations with respect to the excess of total lobbying expenditures over grass roots lobbying expenditures for the year.

Excess loss account. When a subsidiary has generated more historical losses than its parent has invested in the entity, the parent's basis in the subsidiary is zero, and the parent records additional losses in an excess loss account. This treatment allows the parent to continue to deduct losses of the subsidiary, even where no basis reduction is possible, while avoiding the need to show a negative stock basis on various financial records. If the subsidiary stock is sold while an excess loss account exists, capital gain income usually is recognized to the extent of the balance in the account.

Excise taxes. A tax on the manufacture, sale, or use of goods; on the carrying on of an occupation or activity; or on the transfer of property. Thus, the Federal estate and gift taxes are, theoretically, excise taxes.

Exclusion amount. The value of assets that is exempt from transfer tax due to the credit allowed for gifts or transfers by death. For gifts and deaths in 2016, the exclusion amount is $5.45 million. An exclusion amount unused by a deceased spouse may be used by the surviving spouse. See also *exemption equivalent amount.*

Exempt organizations. An organization that is either partially or completely exempt from Federal income taxation. § 501.

Exemption amount. See *AMT exemption.*

Exemption equivalent. The maximum value of assets that can be transferred to another party without incurring any Federal gift or estate tax because of the application of the unified tax credit. See also *exemption equivalent amount.*

Exemption equivalent amount. The nontaxable amount (in 2016, $5.45 million for gift tax and estate tax) that is the equivalent of the unified transfer tax credit allowed.

Expanded affiliated group (EAG). For purposes of the domestic production activities deduction (DPAD), all members of an expanded affiliated group (EAG) are treated as a single corporation. Thus, the activities of any member of the group are attributed to the other members. An EAG must meet the requirements for filing a consolidated return with ownership levels lowered to 50 percent. § 199(d)(4)(B).

F

Fair market value. The amount at which property would change hands between a willing buyer and a willing seller, neither being under any compulsion to buy or to sell and both having reasonable knowledge of the relevant facts. Reg. §§ 1.1001–1(a) and 20.2031–1(b).

Farm price method. A method of accounting for agricultural crops. The inventory of crops is valued at its market price less the estimated cost of disposition (e.g., freight and selling expense).

FDAP. Income of a nonresident alien or non-U.S. corporation that is received in the form of dividends, interest, rents, royalties, certain compensation, premiums, annuities, and other "fixed, determinable, annual, or periodic" forms. FDAP income usually is subject to U.S. income taxation at a flat 30 percent tax rate.

Federal District Court. A trial court for purposes of litigating Federal tax matters. It is the only trial court in which a jury trial can be obtained.

Feeder organization. An entity that carries on a trade or business for the benefit of an exempt organization. However, such a relationship does not result in the feeder organization itself being tax-exempt. § 502.

FICA tax. An abbreviation that stands for Federal Insurance Contributions Act, commonly referred to as the Social Security tax. The FICA tax is comprised of the Social Security tax (old age, survivors, and disability insurance) and the Medicare tax (hospital insurance) and is imposed on both employers and employees. The employer is responsible for withholding from the employee's wages the Social Security tax at a rate of 6.2 percent on a maximum wage base and the Medicare tax at a rate of 1.45 percent (no maximum wage base). The maximum Social Security wage base for 2016 is $118,500 and for 2015 is $118,500.

Field audit. An audit conducted by the IRS on the business premises of the taxpayer or in the office of the tax practitioner representing the taxpayer.

Filing status. Individual taxpayers are placed in one of five filing statuses each year (single, married filing jointly, married filing separately, surviving spouse, or head of household). Marital status and household support are key determinants. Filing status is used to determine the taxpayer's filing requirements, standard deduction, eligibility for certain deductions and credits, and tax liability.

Final Regulations. See *finalized Regulations.*

Finalized Regulations. The U.S. Treasury Department Regulations (abbreviated Reg.) represent the position of the IRS as to how the Internal Revenue Code is to be interpreted. Their purpose is to provide taxpayers and IRS personnel with rules of general and specific application to the various provisions of the tax law. Regulations are published in the *Federal Register* and in all tax services.

Financial Accounting Standards Board (FASB). See *Generally Accepted Accounting Principles (GAAP).*

Fiscal year. A 12-month period ending on the last day of a month other than December. In certain circumstances, a taxpayer is permitted to elect a fiscal year instead of being required to use a calendar year.

Flat tax. In its pure form, a flat tax would eliminate all exclusions, deductions, and credits and impose a one-rate tax on gross income.

Flexible spending plans. An employee benefit plan that allows the employee to take a reduction in salary in exchange for the employer paying benefits that can be provided by the employer without the employee being required to recognize income (e.g., medical and child care benefits).

Flow-through entity. The entity is a tax reporter rather than a taxpayer. The owners are subject to tax. Examples are partnerships, S corporations, and limited liability companies.

Foreign earned income exclusion. The Code allows exclusions for earned income generated outside the United States to alleviate any tax base and rate disparities among countries. In addition, the exclusion is allowed for housing expenditures incurred by the taxpayer's employer with respect to the non-U.S. assignment, and self-employed individuals can deduct foreign housing expenses incurred in a trade or business. The exclusion is limited to $101,300 per year for 2016 ($100,800 in 2015). § 911.

Foreign Investment in Real Property Tax Act (FIRPTA). Under the Foreign Investment in Real Property Tax Act, gains or losses realized by nonresident aliens and non-U.S. corporations on the disposition of U.S. real estate creates U.S. source income and are subject to U.S. income tax.

Foreign tax credit (FTC). A U.S. citizen or resident who incurs or pays income taxes to a foreign country on income subject to U.S. tax may be able to claim some of these taxes as a credit against the U.S. income tax. §§ 27 and 901–905.

Franchise. An agreement that gives the transferee the right to distribute, sell, or provide goods, services, or facilities within a specified area. The cost of obtaining a franchise may be amortized over a statutory period of 15 years. In general, the franchisor's gain on the sale of franchise rights is an ordinary gain because the franchisor retains a significant power, right, or continuing interest in the subject of the franchise. §§ 197 and 1253.

Franchise tax. A tax levied on the right to do business in a state as a corporation. Although income considerations may come into play, the tax usually is based on the capitalization of the corporation.

Fraud. Tax fraud falls into two categories: civil and criminal. Under civil fraud, the IRS may impose as a penalty an amount equal to as much as 75 percent of the underpayment [§ 6651(f)]. Fines and/or imprisonment are prescribed for conviction of various types of criminal tax fraud (§§ 7201–7207). Both civil and criminal fraud involve a specific intent on the part of the taxpayer to evade the tax; mere negligence is not enough. Criminal fraud requires the additional element of willfulness (i.e., done deliberately and with evil purpose). In practice, it becomes difficult to distinguish between the degree of intent necessary to support criminal, rather than civil, fraud. In either situation, the IRS has the burden of proof to show the taxpayer committed fraud.

Fringe benefits. Compensation or other benefit received by an employee that is not in the form of cash. Some fringe benefits (e.g., accident and health plans, group term life insurance) may be excluded from the employee's gross income and therefore are not subject to the Federal income tax.

Frivolous return. A tax return that included a position that has no more than a 5 percent chance of being sustained upon review. Taxpayer and tax preparer penalties are assessed if a frivolous position is included in a filed tax return.

Fruit and tree metaphor. The courts have held that an individual who earns income from property or services cannot assign that income to another. For example, a father cannot assign his earnings from commissions to his child and escape income tax on those amounts.

Functional currency. The currency of the economic environment in which the taxpayer carries on most of its activities and in which the taxpayer transacts most of its business.

FUTA tax. An employment tax levied on employers. Jointly administered by the Federal and state governments, the tax provides funding for unemployment benefits. FUTA applies at a rate of 6.0 percent on the first $7,000 of covered wages paid during the year for each employee in 2016. The Federal government allows a credit for FUTA paid (or allowed under a merit rating system) to the state. The credit cannot exceed 5.4 percent of the covered wages.

Future interest. An interest that will come into being at some future time. It is distinguished from a present interest, which already exists. Assume that Dan transfers securities to a newly created trust. Under the terms of the trust instrument, income from the securities is to be paid each year to Wilma for her life, with the securities passing to Sam upon Wilma's death. Wilma has a present interest in the trust because she is entitled to current income distributions. Sam has a future interest because he must wait for Wilma's death to benefit from the trust. The annual exclusion of $14,000 (in 2016) is not allowed for a gift of a future interest. § 2503(b).

G

General business credit. The summation of various nonrefundable business credits, including the tax credit for rehabilitation expenditures, business energy credit, work opportunity credit, research activities credit, low-income housing credit, and disabled access credit. The amount of general business credit that can be used to reduce the tax liability is limited to the taxpayer's net income tax reduced by the greater of (1) the tentative minimum tax or (2) 25 percent of the net regular tax liability that exceeds $25,000. Unused general business credits can be carried back one year and forward 20 years. § 38.

General partners. A partner who is fully liable in an individual capacity for the debts of the partnership to third parties. A general partner's liability is not limited to the investment in the partnership. See also *limited partner*.

General partnership (GP). A partnership that is owned by one or more general partners. Creditors of a general partnership can collect amounts owed them from both the partnership assets and the assets of the partners individually.

Generally Accepted Accounting Principles (GAAP). Guidelines relating to how to construct the financial statements of enterprises doing business in the United States. Promulgated chiefly by the Financial Accounting Standards Board (FASB).

Gift tax. A tax imposed on the transfer of property by gift. The tax is imposed upon the donor of a gift and is based on the fair market value of the property on the date of the gift.

Golden parachute payments. A severance payment to employees that meets the following requirements: (1) the payment is contingent on a change of ownership of a corporation through a stock or asset acquisition and (2) the aggregate present value of the payment equals or exceeds three times the employee's average annual compensation. To the extent the severance payment meets these conditions, a deduction is disallowed to the employer for the excess of the payment over a statutory base amount (a five-year average of compensation if the taxpayer was an employee for the entire five-year period). In addition, a 20 percent excise tax is imposed on the employee who receives the excess severance pay. §§ 280G and 4999.

Goodwill. The reputation and built-up business of a company. For accounting purposes, goodwill has no basis unless it is purchased. In the purchase of a business, goodwill generally is the difference between the purchase price and the fair market value of the assets acquired. The intangible asset goodwill can be amortized for tax purposes over a 15-year period. Reg. § 1.167(a)–3.

Grantor. A transferor of property. The creator of a trust is usually referred to as the grantor of the entity.

Grantor trust. A trust under which the grantor retains control over the income or corpus (or both) to such an extent that he or she is treated as the owner of the property and its income for income tax purposes. Income from a grantor trust is taxable to the grantor and not to the beneficiary who receives it. §§ 671–679.

Grass roots expenditures. Exempt organizations are prohibited from engaging in political activities, but spending incurred to influence the opinions of the general public relative to specific legislation is permitted by the law.

Gross estate. The property owned or previously transferred by a decedent that is subject to the Federal estate tax. The gross estate can be distinguished from the probate estate, which is property actually subject to administration by the administrator or executor of an estate. §§ 2031–2046.

Gross income. Income subject to the Federal income tax. Gross income does not include all economic income. That is, certain exclusions are allowed (e.g., interest on municipal bonds).

For a manufacturing or merchandising business, gross income usually means gross profit (gross sales or gross receipts less cost of goods sold). § 61 and Reg. § 1.61–3(a).

Group term life insurance. Life insurance coverage provided by an employer for a group of employees. Such insurance is renewable on a year-to-year basis, and typically no cash surrender value is built up. The premiums paid by the employer on the insurance are not taxed to the employees on coverage of up to $50,000 per person. § 79 and Reg. § 1.79–1(b).

Guaranteed payments. Payments made by a partnership to a partner for services rendered or for the use of capital to the extent the payments are determined without regard to the income of the partnership. The payments are treated as though they were made to a nonpartner and thus are deducted by the entity.

H

H.R. 10 plans. See *Keogh plans*.

Half-year convention. A cost recovery convention that assumes that all property is placed in service at mid-year and thus provides for a half-year's cost recovery for that year.

Head of household. An unmarried individual who maintains a household for another and satisfies certain conditions set forth in § 2(b). This status enables the taxpayer to use a set of income tax rates that are lower than those applicable to other unmarried individuals but higher than those applicable to surviving spouses and married persons filing a joint return.

Health Savings Account (HSA). A medical savings account created in legislation enacted in December 2003 that is designed to replace and expand Archer Medical Savings Accounts.

Highly compensated employee. The employee group is generally divided into two categories for fringe benefit (including pension and profit sharing plans) purposes. These are (1) highly compensated employees and (2) non-highly compensated employees. For most fringe benefits, if the fringe benefit plan discriminates in favor of highly compensated employees, it will not be a qualified plan with respect, at a minimum, to the highly compensated employees.

Historic business test. In a corporate reorganization, a means by which to determine if the continuity of business enterprise requirement is met. The acquiring corporation must continue to operate the target entity's existing business(es) going forward; if this is not the case, the requirement is failed.

Hobby losses. Losses from an activity not engaged in for profit. The Code restricts the amount of losses that an individual can deduct for hobby activities so that these transactions cannot be used to offset income from other sources. § 183.

Holding period. The period of time during which property has been held for income tax purposes. The holding period is significant in determining whether gain or loss from the sale or exchange of a capital asset is long or short term. § 1223.

Home equity loans. Loans that utilize the personal residence of the taxpayer as security. The interest on such loans is deductible as qualified residence interest. However, interest is deductible only on the portion of the loan that does not exceed the lesser of (1) the fair market value of the residence, reduced by the acquisition indebtedness, or (2) $100,000 ($50,000 for married persons filing separate returns). A major benefit of a home equity loan is that there are no tracing rules regarding the use of the loan proceeds. § 163(h)(3).

Hot assets. Unrealized receivables and substantially appreciated inventory under § 751. When hot assets are present, the sale of a partnership interest or the disproportionate distribution of the assets can cause ordinary income to be recognized.

Hybrid method. A combination of the accrual and cash methods of accounting. That is, the taxpayer may account for some items of income on the accrual method (e.g., sales and cost of goods sold) and other items (e.g., interest income) on the cash method.

I

Imputed interest. For certain long-term sales of property, the IRS can convert some of the gain from the sale into interest income if the contract does not provide for a minimum rate of interest to be paid by the purchaser. The seller recognizes less long-term capital gain and more ordinary income (interest income). § 483 and the related Regulations.

Inbound taxation. U.S. tax effects when a non-U.S. person begins an investment or business activity in the United States.

Incentive stock options (ISOs). A type of stock option that receives favorable tax treatment. If various qualification requirements can be satisfied, there are no recognition tax consequences when the stock option is granted. However, the spread (the excess of the fair market value at the date of exercise over the option price) is a tax preference item for purposes of the alternative minimum tax. The gain on disposition of the stock resulting from the exercise of the stock option will be classified as long-term capital gain if certain holding period requirements are met (the employee must not dispose of the stock within two years after the option is granted or within one year after acquiring the stock). § 422.

Income. For tax purposes, an increase in wealth that has been realized.

Income in respect of a decedent (IRD). Income earned by a decedent at the time of death but not reportable on the final income tax return because of the method of accounting that appropriately is utilized. Such income is included in the gross estate and is taxed to the eventual recipient (either the estate or heirs). The recipient is, however, allowed an income tax deduction for the estate tax attributable to the income. § 691.

Income tax provision. Under ASC 740 (SFAS 109), a synonym for the book tax expense of an entity for the financial reporting period. Following the "matching principle," all book tax expense that relates to the net income for the reporting period is reported on that period's financial statements, including not only the current tax expense, but also any deferred tax expense and deferred tax benefit.

Income tax treaties. See *tax treaty.*

Independent contractor. A self-employed person as distinguished from one who is employed as an employee.

Indexation. A procedure whereby adjustments are made by the IRS to key tax components (e.g., standard deduction, tax brackets, personal and dependency exemptions) to reflect inflation. The adjustments usually are made annually and are based on the change in the consumer price index.

Individual Retirement Account (IRA). A type of retirement plan to which an individual with earned income can contribute a statutory maximum of $5,500 in 2016. IRAs can be classified as traditional IRAs or Roth IRAs. With a traditional IRA, an individual can contribute and deduct a maximum of $5,500 per tax year in 2016. The deduction is a deduction *for* AGI. However, if the individual is an active participant in another qualified retirement plan, the deduction is phased out proportionally between certain AGI ranges (note that the phaseout limits the amount of the deduction and not the amount of the contribution). With a Roth IRA, an individual can contribute a maximum of $5,500 per tax year in 2016. No deduction is permitted. However, if a five-year holding period requirement is satisfied and if the distribution is a qualified distribution, the taxpayer can make tax-free withdrawals from a Roth IRA. The maximum annual contribution is phased out proportionally between certain AGI ranges. §§ 219 and 408A.

Individual Shared Responsibility Payment (ISRP). A mandate or penalty tax that individuals owe starting in 2014 for any month in which they do not have health coverage and do not qualify for an exemption. This mandate was created as part of the Affordable Care Act to encourage individuals to obtain health care coverage. If owed, the penalty is the greater of a "flat dollar amount" or a percentage of household income less the filing threshold. When fully in effect in 2016, the flat dollar amount is $695 and the percent applied to household income is 2.5 percent. For a family, the flat dollar amount cannot exceed three times the flat dollar amount. After 2016, the $695 amount is adjusted annually. The overall cap on the penalty is the national average cost of a bronze level plan (this amount is published by the IRS). Worksheets for computing the penalty are included in the instructions to Form 8965 (Health Coverage Exemptions). § 5000A.

Inheritance tax. A tax imposed on the right to receive property from a decedent. Thus, theoretically, an inheritance tax is imposed on the heir. The Federal estate tax is imposed on the estate.

Inside basis. A partnership's basis in the assets it owns.

Installment method. A method of accounting enabling certain taxpayers to spread the recognition of gain on the sale of property over the collection period. Under this procedure, the seller arrives at the gain to be recognized by computing the gross profit percentage from the sale (the gain divided by the contract price) and applying it to each payment received. § 453.

Intangible drilling and development costs (IDCs). Taxpayers may elect to expense or capitalize (subject to amortization) intangible drilling and development costs. However, ordinary income recapture provisions apply to oil and gas properties on a sale or other disposition if the expense method is elected. §§ 263(c) and 1254(a).

Intermediate sanctions. The IRS can assess excise taxes on disqualified persons and organization management associated with so-called public charities engaging in excess benefit transactions. An excess benefit transaction is one in which a disqualified person engages in a non-fair market value transaction with the exempt organization or receives unreasonable compensation. Prior to the idea of intermediate sanctions, the only option available to the IRS was to revoke the organization's exempt status.

International Accounting Standards Board (IASB). The body that promulgates International Financial Reporting Standards (IFRS). Based in London, representing accounting standard setting bodies in over 100 countries, the IASB develops accounting standards that can serve as the basis for harmonizing conflicting reporting standards among nations.

International Financial Reporting Standards (IFRS). Produced by the International Accounting Standards Board (IASB), guidelines developed since 2001 as to revenue recognition, accounting for business combinations, and a conceptual framework for financial reporting. IFRS provisions are designed so that they can be used by all entities, regardless of where they are based or conduct business. IFRS have gained widespread acceptance throughout the world, and the SEC is considering how to require U.S. entities to use IFRS in addition to, or in lieu of, the accounting rules of the Financial Accounting Standards Board.

Interpretive Regulations. A Regulation issued by the Treasury Department that purports to explain the meaning of a particular Code Section. An interpretive Regulation is given less deference than a legislative Regulation.

Investment income. Consisting of virtually the same elements as portfolio income, a measure by which to justify a deduction for interest on investment indebtedness.

Investment interest. Payment for the use of funds used to acquire assets that produce investment income. The deduction for investment interest is limited to net investment income for the tax year.

Investor loss. Losses on stock and securities. If stocks and bonds are capital assets in the hands of the holder, a capital loss materializes as of the last day of the taxable year in which the stocks or bonds become worthless. Under certain circumstances involving stocks and bonds of affiliated corporations, an ordinary loss is permitted upon worthlessness.

Involuntary conversion. The loss or destruction of property through theft, casualty, or condemnation. Gain realized on an involuntary conversion can, at the taxpayer's election, be deferred for Federal income tax purposes if the owner reinvests the proceeds within a prescribed period of time in property that is similar or related in service or use. § 1033.

Itemized deductions. Personal and employee expenditures allowed by the Code as deductions from adjusted gross income. Examples include certain medical expenses, interest on home mortgages, state income taxes, and charitable contributions. Itemized deductions are reported on Schedule A of Form 1040. Certain miscellaneous itemized deductions are reduced by 2 percent of the taxpayer's adjusted gross income. In addition, a taxpayer whose adjusted gross income exceeds a certain level (indexed annually) must reduce the itemized deductions by 3 percent of the excess of adjusted gross income over that level. Medical, casualty and theft, and investment interest deductions are not subject to the 3 percent reduction. The 3 percent reduction may not reduce itemized deductions that are subject to the reduction to below 20 percent of their initial amount.

J

Joint tenants. Two or more persons having undivided ownership of property with the right of survivorship. Right of survivorship gives the surviving owner full ownership of the property. Suppose Bob and Tami are joint tenants of a tract of land. Upon Bob's death, Tami becomes the sole owner of the property. For the estate tax consequences upon the death of a joint tenant, see § 2040.

K

Keogh plans. Retirement plans available to self-employed taxpayers. They are also referred to as H.R. 10 plans. Under such plans, a taxpayer may deduct each year up to 100 percent of net earnings from self-employment or $53,000 for 2016, whichever is less. If the plan is a profit sharing plan, the percentage is 25 percent.

Kiddie tax. Passive income, such as interest and dividends, that is recognized by a child under age 19 (or under age 24 if a full-time student) is taxed to him or her at the rates that would have applied had the income been incurred by the child's parents, generally to the extent the income exceeds $2,100 for 2016. The additional tax is assessed regardless of the source of the income or the income's underlying property. If the child's parents are divorced, the custodial parent's rates are used. The parents' rates reflect any applicable alternative minimum tax and the phaseouts of lower tax brackets and other deductions. § 1(g).

L

Least aggregate deferral method. An algorithm set forth in the Regulations to determine the tax year for a partnership or an S corporation with owners whose tax years differ. The tax year selected is the one that produces the least aggregate deferral of income for the owners.

Least aggregate deferral rule. See *least aggregate deferral method.*

Legislative Regulations. Some Code Sections give the Secretary of the Treasury or his delegate the authority to prescribe Regulations to carry out the details of administration or to otherwise complete the operating rules. Regulations issued pursuant to this type of authority truly possess the force and effect of law. In effect, Congress is almost delegating its legislative powers to the Treasury Department.

Lessee. One who rents property from another. In the case of real estate, the lessee is also known as the tenant.

Lessor. One who rents property to another. In the case of real estate, the lessor is also known as the landlord.

Letter ruling. The written response of the IRS to a taxpayer's request for interpretation of the revenue laws with respect to a proposed transaction (e.g., concerning the tax-free status of a reorganization). Not to be relied on as precedent by other than the party who requested the ruling.

Liabilities in excess of basis. On the contribution of capital to a corporation, an investor recognizes gain on the exchange to the extent contributed assets carry liabilities with a face amount in excess of the tax basis of the contributed assets.

This rule keeps the investor from holding the investment asset received with a negative basis. § 357(c).

Life insurance proceeds. A specified sum (the face value or maturity value of the policy) paid to the designated beneficiary of the policy by the life insurance company upon the death of the insured.

Lifetime learning credit. A tax credit for qualifying expenses for taxpayers pursuing education beyond the first two years of postsecondary education. Individuals who are completing their last two years of undergraduate studies, pursuing graduate or professional degrees, or otherwise seeking new job skills or maintaining existing job skills are all eligible for the credit. Eligible individuals include the taxpayer, taxpayer's spouse, and taxpayer's dependents. The maximum credit is 20 percent of the first $10,000 of qualifying expenses and is computed per taxpayer. The credit is phased out for higher-income taxpayers. § 25A.

Like-kind exchanges. An exchange of property held for productive use in a trade or business or for investment (except inventory and stocks and bonds) for other investment or trade or business property. Unless non-like-kind property (boot) is received, the exchange is fully tax-deferred. § 1031.

Limited liability company (LLC). A legal entity allowed by all of the states. The entity is subject to Federal income tax treatment as though it were a partnership in which all members or owners of the LLC are treated much like limited partners. There are no restrictions on ownership, all members may participate in management, and none has personal liability for the entity's debts.

Limited liability limited partnership (LLLP). A limited partnership for which the general partners are also protected from entity liabilities. An LLLP—or "triple LP"—can be formed in about 20 states. In those states, a limited partnership files with the state to adopt LLLP status.

Limited liability partnership (LLP). A legal entity allowed by many of the states, where a general partnership registers with the state as an LLP. Owners are general partners, but a partner is not liable for any malpractice committed by other partners. The personal assets of the partners are at risk for the entity's contractual liabilities, such as accounts payable. The personal assets of a specific partner are at risk for his or her own professional malpractice and tort liability and for malpractice and torts committed by those whom he or she supervises.

Limited partners. A partner whose liability to third-party creditors of the partnership is limited to the amounts invested in the partnership. See also *general partner* and *limited partnership*.

Limited partnership (LP). A partnership in which some of the partners are limited partners. At least one of the partners in a limited partnership must be a general partner.

Liquidating distribution. A distribution by a partnership or corporation that is in complete liquidation of the entity's trade or business activities. Typically, such distributions generate capital gain or loss to the investors without regard, for instance, to the earnings and profits of the corporation or to the partnership's basis in the distributed property. They can, however, lead to recognized gain or loss at the corporate level.

Listed property. Property that includes (1) any passenger automobile; (2) any other property used as a means of transportation; (3) any property of a type generally used for purposes of entertainment, recreation, or amusement; (4) any computer or peripheral equipment (with an exception for exclusive business use); (5) any cellular telephone (or other similar telecommunications equipment); and (6) any other property of a type specified in the Regulations. If listed property is predominantly used for business, the taxpayer is allowed to use the statutory percentage method of cost recovery. Otherwise, the straight-line cost recovery method must be used. § 280F.

Living trust. A revocable trust. Often touted as a means of avoiding some probate costs.

Lobbying expenditures. An expenditure made for the purpose of influencing legislation. Such payments can result in the loss of the exempt status of, and the imposition of Federal income tax on, an exempt organization.

Long-term care insurance. Insurance that helps pay the cost of care when the insured is unable to care for himself or herself. Such insurance is generally thought of as insurance against the cost of an aged person entering a nursing home. The employer can provide the insurance, and the premiums may be excluded from the employee's gross income. § 7702B.

Long-term contract. A building, installation, construction, or manufacturing contract that is entered into but not completed within the same tax year. A manufacturing contract is a long-term contract only if the contract is to manufacture (1) a unique item not normally carried in finished goods inventory or (2) items that normally require more than 12 calendar months to complete. The two available methods to account for long-term contracts are the percentage of completion method and the completed contract method. The completed contract method can be used only in limited circumstances. § 460.

Long-term nonpersonal use capital assets. Includes investment property with a long-term holding period. Such property disposed of by casualty or theft may receive § 1231 treatment.

Long-term tax-exempt rate. Used in deriving the yearly limitation on net operating loss and other tax benefits that carry over from the target to the acquiring when there is an equity structure shift. The highest of the Federal long-term interest rates in effect for any of the last three months. § 382.

Lower of cost or market (replacement cost). An elective inventory method, whereby the taxpayer may value inventories at the lower of the taxpayer's actual cost or the current replacement cost of the goods. This method cannot be used in conjunction with the LIFO inventory method.

Low-income housing credit. Beneficial treatment to owners of low-income housing is provided in the form of a tax credit. The calculated credit is claimed in the year the building is placed in service and in the following nine years. § 42.

Lump-sum distribution. Payment of the entire amount due at one time rather than in installments. Such distributions often occur from qualified pension or profit sharing plans upon the retirement or death of a covered employee. The recipient of a lump-sum distribution may recognize both long-term capital gain and ordinary income upon the receipt of the distribution. The ordinary income portion may be subject to a special 10-year income averaging provision. § 402(e).

M

Majority interest partners. Partners who have more than a 50 percent interest in partnership profits and capital, counting only those partners who have the same taxable year. The term is of significance in determining the appropriate taxable year of a partnership. § 706(b).

Marital deduction. A deduction allowed against the taxable estate or taxable gifts upon the transfer of property from one spouse to another.

Marriage penalty. The additional tax liability that results for a married couple when compared with what their tax liability would be if they were not married and filed separate returns.

Matching rule. Treatment of an intercompany transaction on a consolidated return, when a sold asset remains within the group.

Material participation. If an individual taxpayer materially participates in a nonrental trade or business activity, any loss from that activity is treated as an active loss that can be offset against active income. Material participation is achieved by meeting any one of seven tests provided in the Regulations. § 469(h).

Meaningful reduction test. A decrease in the shareholder's voting control. Used to determine whether a stock redemption qualifies for sale or exchange treatment.

Medical expenses. Medical expenses of an individual, a spouse, and dependents are allowed as an itemized deduction to the extent such amounts (less insurance reimbursements) exceed 10 percent (or 7.5 percent if at least age 65) of adjusted gross income. § 213.

Merger. The absorption of one corporation by another with the corporation being absorbed losing its legal identity. Flow Corporation is merged into Jobs Corporation, and the shareholders of Flow receive stock in Jobs in exchange for their stock in Flow. After the merger, Flow ceases to exist as a separate legal entity. If a merger meets certain conditions, it is not currently taxable to the parties involved. § 368(a)(1).

Mid-month convention. A cost recovery convention that assumes that property is placed in service in the middle of the month that it is actually placed in service.

Mid-quarter convention. A cost recovery convention that assumes that property placed in service during the year is placed in service at the middle of the quarter in which it is actually placed in service. The mid-quarter convention applies if more than 40 percent of the value of property (other than eligible real estate) is placed in service during the last quarter of the year.

Minimum tax credit. See *alternative minimum tax credit.*

Miscellaneous itemized deductions. A special category of itemized deductions that includes expenses such as professional dues, tax return preparation fees, job-hunting costs, unreimbursed employee business expenses, and certain investment expenses. Such expenses are deductible only to the extent they exceed 2 percent of adjusted gross income. § 67.

Modified accelerated cost recovery system (MACRS). A method in which the cost of tangible property is recovered over a prescribed period of time. Enacted by the Economic Recovery Tax Act (ERTA) of 1981 and substantially modified by the Tax Reform Act (TRA) of 1986 (the modified system is referred to as MACRS), the approach disregards salvage value, imposes a period of cost recovery that depends upon the classification of the asset into one of various recovery periods, and prescribes the applicable percentage of cost that can be deducted each year. § 168.

Modified adjusted gross income. A key determinant in computing the domestic production activities deduction (DPAD) and certain other tax provisions (e.g., deduction for higher education tuition, exclusion of interest on education savings bonds). §§ 135, 144, and 199.

Moving expenses. A deduction *for* AGI is permitted to employees and self-employed individuals provided certain tests are met. The taxpayer's new job must be at least 50 miles farther from the old residence than the old residence was from the former place of work. In addition, an employee must be employed on a full-time basis at the new location for 39 weeks in the 12-month period following the move. Deductible moving expenses include the cost of moving the household and personal effects, transportation, and lodging expenses during the move. The cost of meals during the move is not deductible. Qualified moving expenses that are paid (or reimbursed) by the employer can be excluded from the employee's gross income. In this case, the related deduction by the employee is not permitted. §§ 62(a)(15), 132(a)(6), and 217.

Multiple support agreement. To qualify for a dependency exemption, the support test must be satisfied. This requires that over 50 percent of the support of the potential dependent be provided by the taxpayer. Where no one person provides more than 50 percent of the support, a multiple support agreement enables a taxpayer to still qualify for the dependency exemption. Any person who contributed more than 10 percent of the support is entitled to claim the exemption if each person in the group who contributed more than 10 percent files a written consent (Form 2120). Each person who is a party to the multiple support agreement must meet all of the other requirements for claiming the dependency exemption. § 152(c).

Multistate Tax Commission (MTC). A regulatory body of the states that develops operating rules and regulations for the implementation of the UDITPA and other provisions that assign the total taxable income of a multistate corporation to specific states.

N

National sales tax. Intended as a replacement for the current Federal income tax. Unlike a value added tax (VAT), which is levied on the manufacturer, it would be imposed on the consumer upon the final sale of goods and services. To keep the tax from being regressive, low-income taxpayers would be granted some kind of credit or exemption.

Negligence. Failure to exercise the reasonable or ordinary degree of care of a prudent person in a situation that results in harm or damage to another. A penalty is assessed on taxpayers who exhibit negligence or intentional disregard of rules and Regulations with respect to the underpayment of certain taxes.

Net capital gain (NCG). The excess of the net long-term capital gain for the tax year over the net short-term capital loss.

The net capital gain of an individual taxpayer is eligible for the alternative tax. § 1222(11).

Net capital loss (NCL). The excess of the losses from sales or exchanges of capital assets over the gains from sales or exchanges of such assets. Up to $3,000 per year of the net capital loss may be deductible by noncorporate taxpayers against ordinary income. The excess net capital loss carries over to future tax years. For corporate taxpayers, the net capital loss cannot be offset against ordinary income, but it can be carried back three years and forward five years to offset net capital gains. §§ 1211, 1212, and 1221(10).

Net investment income. The excess of investment income over investment expenses. Investment expenses are those deductible expenses directly connected with the production of investment income. Investment expenses do not include investment interest. The deduction for investment interest for the tax year is limited to net investment income. § 163(d).

Net operating loss (NOL). To mitigate the effect of the annual accounting period concept, § 172 allows taxpayers to use an excess loss of one year as a deduction for certain past or future years. In this regard, a carryback period of two (or more) years and a carryforward period of 20 years currently are allowed.

Nexus. The degree of activity that must be present before a taxing jurisdiction has the right to impose a tax on an out-of-state entity. The rules for income tax nexus are not the same as for sales tax nexus.

Ninety-day letter. This notice is sent to a taxpayer upon request, upon the expiration of the 30-day letter, or upon exhaustion by the taxpayer of his or her administrative remedies before the IRS. The notice gives the taxpayer 90 days in which to file a petition with the U.S. Tax Court. If a petition is not filed, the IRS will demand payment of the assessed deficiency. §§ 6211–6216.

No-additional-cost service. Services the employer may provide the employee at no additional cost to the employer. Generally, the benefit is the ability to utilize the employer's excess capacity (e.g., vacant seats on an airliner). Such amounts are excludible from the recipient's gross income.

Nonaccountable plan. An expense reimbursement plan that does not have an accountability feature. The result is that employee expenses must be claimed as deductions *from* AGI. An exception is moving expenses that are deductions *for* AGI.

Nonacquiescence. Disagreement by the IRS on the result reached in certain judicial decisions. *Nonacq.* or *NA.*

Nonbusiness bad debt. A bad debt loss that is not incurred in connection with a creditor's trade or business. The loss is classified as a short-term capital loss and is allowed only in the year the debt becomes entirely worthless. In addition to family loans, many investor losses are nonbusiness bad debts. § 166(d).

Nonliquidating distribution. A payment made by a partnership or corporation to the entity's owner when the entity's legal existence does not cease thereafter. If the payor is a corporation, such a distribution can result in dividend income to the shareholders. If the payor is a partnership, the partner usually assigns a basis in the distributed property that is equal to the lesser of the partner's basis in the partnership interest or the basis of the distributed asset to the partnership. In this regard, the partner first assigns basis to any cash that he or she receives in the distribution. The partner's remaining basis, if any, is assigned to the noncash assets according to their relative bases to the partnership.

Nonqualified deferred compensation (NQDC). Compensation arrangements that are frequently offered to executives. Such plans may include stock options, restricted stock, etc. Often, an executive may defer the recognition of taxable income. The employer, however, does not receive a tax deduction until the employee is required to include the compensation in income.

Nonqualified stock option (NQSO). A type of stock option that does not satisfy the statutory requirements of an incentive stock option. If the NQSO has a readily ascertainable fair market value (e.g., the option is traded on an established exchange), the value of the option must be included in the employee's gross income at the date of the grant. Otherwise, the employee does not recognize income at the grant date. Instead, ordinary income is recognized in the year of exercise of the option.

Nonrecourse debt. Debt secured by the property that it is used to purchase. The purchaser of the property is not personally liable for the debt upon default. Rather, the creditor's recourse is to repossess the related property. Nonrecourse debt generally does not increase the purchaser's at-risk amount.

Nonrefundable credits. A credit that is not paid if it exceeds the taxpayer's tax liability. Some nonrefundable credits qualify for carryback and carryover treatment.

Nonresident alien (NRA). An individual who is neither a citizen nor a resident of the United States. Citizenship is determined under the immigration and naturalization laws of the United States. Residency is determined under § 7701(b) of the Internal Revenue Code.

Nontaxable exchange. A transaction in which realized gains or losses are not recognized. The recognition of gain or loss is postponed (deferred) until the property received in the nontaxable exchange is subsequently disposed of in a taxable transaction. Examples are § 1031 like-kind exchanges and § 1033 involuntary conversions.

Not essentially equivalent redemption. Sale or exchange treatment is given to this type of redemption. Although various safe-harbor tests are failed, the nature of the redemption is such that dividend treatment is avoided, because it represents a meaningful reduction in the shareholder's interest in the corporation. § 302(b)(1).

O

Occupational fee. A tax imposed on various trades or businesses. A license fee that enables a taxpayer to engage in a particular occupation.

Occupational taxes. See *occupational fee.*

Offer in compromise. A settlement agreement offered by the IRS in a tax dispute, especially where there is doubt as to the collectibility of the full deficiency. Offers in compromise can include installment payment schedules, as well as reductions in the tax and penalties owed by the taxpayer.

Office audit. An audit conducted by the IRS in the agent's office.

Office in the home expenses. Employment and business-related expenses attributable to the use of a residence (e.g., den or office) are allowed only if the portion of the residence is exclusively used on a regular basis as a principal place of business of the taxpayer or as a place of business that is used by patients, clients, or customers. If the expenses are incurred by an employee, the use must be for the convenience of the employer as opposed to being merely appropriate and helpful. In computing the office in the home expenses, a taxpayer can use either the regular method or simplified method. As a general rule, the regular method requires more effort and recordkeeping but results in a larger deduction. § 280A.

One-year rule for prepaid expenses. Taxpayers who use the cash method are required to use the accrual method for deducting certain prepaid expenses (i.e., must capitalize the item and can deduct only when used). If a prepayment will not be consumed or expire by the end of the tax year following the year of payment, the prepayment must be capitalized and prorated over the benefit period. Conversely, if the prepayment will be consumed by the end of the tax year following the year of payment, it can be expensed when paid. To obtain the current deduction under the one-year rule, the payment must be a required payment rather than a voluntary payment.

Operating agreement. The governing document of a limited liability company. This document is similar in structure, function, and purpose to a partnership agreement.

Optional adjustment election. See *Section 754 election*.

Options. The sale or exchange of an option to buy or sell property results in capital gain or loss if the property is a capital asset. Generally, the closing of an option transaction results in short-term capital gain or loss to the writer of the call and the purchaser of the call option. § 1234.

Ordinary and necessary. An ordinary expense is common and accepted in the general industry or type of activity in which the taxpayer is engaged. It comprises one of the tests for the deductibility of expenses incurred or paid in connection with a trade or business; for the production or collection of income; for the management, conservation, or maintenance of property held for the production of income; or in connection with the determination, collection, or refund of any tax. §§ 162(a) and 212. A necessary expense is appropriate and helpful in furthering the taxpayer's business or income-producing activity. §§ 162(a) and 212.

Ordinary income property. Property contributed to a charitable organization that, if sold rather than contributed, would have resulted in other than long-term capital gain to the donor (i.e., ordinary income property and short-term capital gain property). Examples are inventory and capital assets held for less than the long-term holding period.

Organizational costs. See *organizational expenditures*.

Organizational expenditures. Items incurred early in the life of a corporation or partnership that are eligible for a $5,000 limited expensing (subject to phaseout) and an amortization of the balance over 180 months. Organizational expenditures exclude those incurred to obtain capital (underwriting fees) or assets (subject to cost recovery).

Typically, eligible expenditures include legal and accounting fees and state incorporation payments. Such items must be incurred by the end of the entity's first tax year. §§ 248 and 709(b).

Original issue discount (OID). The difference between the issue price of a debt obligation (e.g., a corporate bond) and the maturity value of the obligation when the issue price is less than the maturity value. OID represents interest and must be amortized over the life of the debt obligation using the effective interest method. The difference is not considered to be original issue discount for tax purposes when it is less than one-fourth of 1 percent of the redemption price at maturity multiplied by the number of years to maturity. §§ 1272 and 1273(a)(3).

Other adjustments account (OAA). Used in the context of a distribution from an S corporation. The net accumulation of the entity's exempt income (e.g., municipal bond interest).

Other property. In a corporate reorganization, any property in the exchange that is not stock or securities, such as cash or land. This amount constitutes boot. This result is similar to that in a like-kind exchange.

Outbound taxation. U.S. tax effects when a U.S. person begins an investment or business activity outside the United States.

Outside basis. A partner's basis in his or her partnership interest.

Ownership change. An event that triggers a § 382 limitation for the acquiring corporation.

P

Parent-subsidiary controlled group. A controlled or affiliated group of corporations where at least one corporation is at least 80 percent owned by one or more of the others. The affiliated group definition is more difficult to meet.

Partial liquidation. A stock redemption where noncorporate shareholders are permitted sale or exchange treatment. In certain cases, an active business must have existed for at least five years. Only a portion of the outstanding stock in the entity is retired.

Partnership. For income tax purposes, a partnership includes a syndicate, group, pool, or joint venture, as well as ordinary partnerships. In an ordinary partnership, two or more parties combine capital and/or services to carry on a business for profit as co-owners. § 7701(a)(2).

Partnership agreement. The governing document of a partnership. A partnership agreement should describe the rights and obligations of the partners; the allocation of entity income, deductions, and cash flows; initial and future capital contribution requirements; conditions for terminating the partnership; and other matters.

Passive activity loss. Any loss from (1) activities in which the taxpayer does not materially participate or (2) rental activities (subject to certain exceptions). Net passive losses cannot be used to offset income from nonpassive sources. Rather, they are suspended until the taxpayer either generates net passive income (and a deduction of such losses is allowed) or disposes of the underlying property (at which time the loss deductions are allowed in full). One relief provision allows landlords who actively participate in the rental activities to deduct up to $25,000 of passive losses annually. However, a phaseout of the $25,000 amount commences when the landlord's AGI exceeds $100,000. Another relief provision applies for material participation in a real estate trade or business.

Passive investment company. A means by which a multistate corporation can reduce the overall effective tax rate by isolating investment income in a low- or no-tax state.

Passive investment income (PII). Gross receipts from royalties, certain rents, dividends, interest, annuities, and gains from the sale or exchange of stock and securities. When earnings and profits (E & P) also exists, if the passive investment income of an S corporation exceeds 25 percent of the corporation's gross receipts for three consecutive years, S status is lost.

Patent. An intangible asset that may be amortized over a statutory 15-year period as a § 197 intangible. The sale of a patent usually results in favorable long-term capital gain treatment. §§ 197 and 1235.

Payroll factor. The proportion of a multistate corporation's total payroll that is traceable to a specific state. Used in determining the taxable income that is to be apportioned to that state.

Pension plan. A type of deferred compensation arrangement that provides for systematic payments of definitely determinable retirement benefits to employees who meet the requirements set forth in the plan.

Percentage depletion. Depletion based on a statutory percentage applied to the gross income from the property. The taxpayer deducts the greater of cost depletion or percentage depletion. § 613.

Percentage of completion method. A method of reporting gain or loss on certain long-term contracts. Under this method of accounting, the gross contract price is included in income as the contract is completed. Reg. § 1.451–3.

Permanent and total disability. A person is considered permanently and totally disabled if he or she is unable to engage in any substantial gainful activity due to a physical or mental impairment. In addition, this impairment must be one that can be expected to result in death or that has lasted or can be expected to last for a continuous period of not less than 12 months. The taxpayer generally must provide the IRS a physician's statement documenting this condition.

Permanent differences. Under ASC 740 (SFAS 109), tax-related items that appear in the entity's financial statements or its tax return but not both. For instance, interest income from a municipal bond is a permanent book-tax difference.

Permanent establishment (PE). A level of business activity, as defined under an income tax treaty, that subjects the taxpayer to taxation in a country other than that in which the taxpayer is based. Often evidenced by the presence of a plant, an office, or other fixed place of business. Inventory storage and temporary activities do not rise to the level of a PE. PE is the treaty's equivalent to nexus.

Permanently reinvesting. Under ASC 740-30 (APB 23) of Generally Accepted Accounting Principles, a special rule that relates to the book tax expense of non-U.S. subsidiaries. If a parent corporation documents that it is permanently reinvesting the non-U.S. earning of a non-U.S.

subsidiary, the parent does not record as an expense any U.S. income tax that the parent might pay on such earnings, i.e., the book tax expense is deferred until such earnings are (if ever) repatriated to the United States.

Personal and dependency exemptions. The tax law provides an exemption for each individual taxpayer and an additional exemption for the taxpayer's spouse if a joint return is filed. An individual may also claim a dependency exemption for each dependent, provided certain tests are met. The amount of the personal and dependency exemptions is $4,050 in 2016 ($4,000 in 2015). The exemption is subject to phaseout once adjusted gross income exceeds certain statutory threshold amounts.

Personal casualty gain. The recognized gain from any involuntary conversion of personal use property arising from fire, storm, shipwreck, or other casualty, or from theft.

Personal casualty loss. The recognized loss from any involuntary conversion of personal use property arising from fire, storm, shipwreck, or other casualty, or from theft.

Personal exemptions. See *personal and dependency exemptions.*

Personal holding company tax. A penalty tax imposed on certain closely held corporations with excessive investment income. Assessed at the top individual tax rate on personal holding company income, reduced by dividends paid and other adjustments. § 541.

Personal residence. If a residence has been owned and used by the taxpayer as the principal residence for at least two years during the five-year period ending on the date of sale, up to $250,000 of realized gain is excluded from gross income. For a married couple filing a joint return, the $250,000 is increased to $500,000 if either spouse satisfies the ownership requirement and both spouses satisfy the use requirement. § 121.

Personal service corporation (PSC). A corporation whose principal activity is the performance of personal services (e.g., health, law, engineering, architecture, accounting, actuarial science, performing arts, or consulting) and where such services are substantially performed by the employee-owners. The 35 percent statutory income tax rate applies to PSCs.

Personalty. All property that is not attached to real estate (realty) and is movable. Examples of personalty are machinery, automobiles, clothing, household furnishings, and personal effects.

Points. Loan origination fees that may be deductible as interest by a buyer of property. A seller of property who pays points reduces the selling price by the amount of the points paid for the buyer. While the seller is not permitted to deduct this amount as interest, the buyer may do so.

Portfolio income. Income from interest, dividends, rentals, royalties, capital gains, or other investment sources. Net passive losses cannot be used to offset net portfolio income.

Power of appointment. A legal right granted to someone by a will or other document that gives the holder the power to dispose of property or the income from property. When the holder may appoint the property to his or her own benefit, the power usually is called a general power of appointment. If the holder cannot benefit himself or herself but may only appoint to certain other persons, the power is a special power of appointment. Assume Gary places

$500,000 worth of securities in trust granting Donna the right to determine each year how the trustee is to divide the income between Ann and Babs. Under these circumstances, Donna has a special power of appointment. If Donna had the further right to appoint the income to herself, she probably possesses a general power of appointment. For the estate tax and gift tax effects of powers of appointment, see §§ 2041 and 2514.

Precedents. A previously decided court decision that is recognized as authority for the disposition of future decisions.

Precontribution gain or loss. Partnerships allow for a variety of special allocations of gain or loss among the partners, but gain or loss that is "built in" on an asset contributed to the partnership is assigned specifically to the contributing partner. § 704(c)(1)(A).

Preferences. See *AMT preferences*.

Preferred stock bailout. A process where a shareholder used the issuance and sale, or later redemption, of a preferred stock dividend to obtain long-term capital gains, without any loss of voting control over the corporation. In effect, the shareholder received corporate profits without suffering the consequences of dividend income treatment. This procedure led Congress to enact § 306, which, if applicable, converts the prior long-term capital gain on the sale or redemption of the tainted stock to dividend income.

Premium Tax Credit (PTC). A tax credit that is refundable and available in advance of filing a return for the year. The PTC serves to reduce the cost of health coverage obtained on the Marketplace (Exchange). A PTC is available to individuals who purchase coverage on the Exchange and have household income equal to or greater than 100 percent of the Federal poverty line (FPL) and no greater than 400 percent of the FPL. Also, an individual must not have been able to obtain affordable coverage from his or her employer. If obtained in advance, the PTC is given to the insurance provider to lower the monthly premium cost to the individual. The PTC is reconciled on Form 8962 (Premium Tax Credit) filed with Form 1040 or 1040-A (not Form 1040-EZ). Individuals who obtain insurance through the Marketplace receive Form 1095-A (Health Insurance Marketplace Statement) by January 31 of the following year. This form provides information necessary to claim or reconcile the PTC, including the monthly cost of premiums and the amount of PTC received in advance each month. § 36B.

Previously taxed income (PTI). Under prior law, the undistributed taxable income of an S corporation was taxed to the shareholders as of the last day of the corporation's tax year and usually could be withdrawn by the shareholders without tax consequences at some later point in time. The role of PTI has been taken over by the accumulated adjustments account. See also *accumulated adjustments account (AAA)*.

Principal partner. A partner with a 5 percent or greater interest in partnership capital or profits. § 706(b)(3).

Private activity bonds. Interest on state and local bonds is excludible from gross income. § 103. Certain such bonds are labeled private activity bonds. Although the interest on such bonds is excludible for regular income tax purposes, it is treated as a tax preference in calculating the AMT.

Private foundations. An exempt organization that is subject to additional statutory restrictions on its activities and on contributions made to it. Excise taxes may be levied on certain prohibited transactions, and the Code places more stringent restrictions on the deductibility of contributions to private foundations. § 509.

Probate costs. The costs incurred in administering a decedent's estate.

Probate estate. The property of a decedent that is subject to administration by the executor or administrator of an estate.

Procedural Regulations. A Regulation issued by the Treasury Department that is a housekeeping-type instruction indicating information that taxpayers should provide the IRS as well as information about the internal management and conduct of the IRS itself.

Profit and loss sharing ratios. Specified in the partnership agreement and used to determine each partner's allocation of ordinary taxable income and separately stated items. Profits and losses can be shared in different ratios. The ratios can be changed by amending the partnership agreement or by using a special allocation. § 704(a).

Profit sharing plan. A deferred compensation plan established and maintained by an employer to provide for employee participation in the company's profits. Contributions are paid from the employer's current or accumulated profits to a trustee. Separate accounts are maintained for each participant employee. The plan must provide a definite, predetermined formula for allocating the contributions among the participants. It also must include a definite, predetermined formula for distributing the accumulated funds after a fixed number of years, on the attainment of a stated age, or on the occurrence of certain events such as illness, layoff, or retirement.

Profits (loss) interest. The extent of a partner's entitlement to an allocation of the partnership's operating results. This interest is measured by the profit and loss sharing ratios.

Property. Assets defined in the broadest legal sense. Property includes the unrealized receivables of a cash basis taxpayer, but not services rendered. § 351.

Property dividend. Generally treated in the same manner as a cash distribution, measured by the fair market value of the property on the date of distribution. Distribution of appreciated property causes the distributing C or S corporation to recognize gain. The distributing corporation does not recognize loss on property that has depreciated in value.

Property factor. The proportion of a multistate corporation's total property that is traceable to a specific state. Used in determining the taxable income that is to be apportioned to that state.

Proportionate distribution. A distribution in which each partner in a partnership receives a pro rata share of hot assets being distributed. For example, a distribution of $10,000 of hot assets equally to two 50 percent partners is a proportionate distribution.

Proposed Regulations. A Regulation issued by the Treasury Department in proposed, rather than final, form. The interval between the proposal of a Regulation and its finalization permits taxpayers and other interested parties to comment on the propriety of the proposal.

Proprietorship. A business entity for which there is a single owner. The net profit of the entity is reported on the owner's Federal income tax return (Schedule C of Form 1040).

Public Law 86–272. A congressional limit on the ability of the state to force a multistate corporation to assign taxable income to that state. Under P.L. 86–272, where orders for tangible personal property are both filled and delivered outside the state, the entity must establish more than the mere solicitation of such orders before any income can be apportioned to the state.

Punitive damages. Damages received or paid by the taxpayer can be classified as compensatory damages or as punitive damages. Punitive damages are those awarded to punish the defendant for gross negligence or the intentional infliction of harm. Such damages are includible in gross income. § 104.

Q

Qualified ABLE program. A state program that allows funds to be set aside for the benefit of an individual who became disabled or blind before age 26. Cash may be put into the fund annually up to the annual gift tax exclusion amount. Distributions to the designated beneficiary are not taxable provided they do not exceed qualified disability expenses for the year. § 529A.

Qualified business unit (QBU). A subsidiary, branch, or other business entity that conducts business using a currency other than the U.S. dollar.

Qualified dividend income (QDI). See *qualified dividends*.

Qualified dividends. Distributions made by domestic (and certain non-U.S.) corporations to noncorporate shareholders that are subject to tax at the same rates as those applicable to net long-term capital gains (i.e., 0 percent, 15 percent, or 20 percent). The 20 percent rate applies to certain high-income taxpayers (i.e., whose tax bracket is 39.6 percent). The dividend must be paid out of earnings and profits, and the shareholders must meet certain holding period requirements as to the stock. §§ 1(h)(1) and (11).

Qualified employee discount. Discounts offered employees on merchandise or services that the employer ordinarily sells or provides to customers. The discounts must be generally available to all employees. In the case of property, the discount cannot exceed the employer's gross profit (the sales price cannot be less than the employer's cost). In the case of services, the discounts cannot exceed 20 percent of the normal sales price. § 132.

Qualified joint venture. At the election of the taxpayers, certain joint ventures between spouses can avoid partnership classification. Known as a qualified joint venture, the spouses generally report their share of the business activities from the venture as sole proprietors (using two Schedule C forms). This would be reported on Schedule E if the venture relates to a rental property. § 761(f).

Qualified nonrecourse debt. Debt issued on realty by a bank, retirement plan, or governmental agency. Included in the at-risk amount by the investor. § 465(b)(6).

Qualified production activities income (QPAI). A key determinant in computing the domestic production activities deduction (DPAD). It consists of domestic production gross receipts (DPGR) reduced by cost of goods sold and other assignable expenses. Thus, QPAI represents the profit derived from domestic production activities. § 199.

Qualified real property business indebtedness. Indebtedness that was incurred or assumed by the taxpayer in connection with real property used in a trade or business and is secured by such real property. The taxpayer must not be a C corporation. For qualified real property business indebtedness, the taxpayer may elect to exclude some or all of the income realized from cancellation of debt on qualified real property. If the election is made, the basis of the property must be reduced by the amount excluded. The amount excluded cannot be greater than the excess of the principal amount of the outstanding debt over the fair market value (net of any other debt outstanding on the property) of the property securing the debt. § 108(c).

Qualified residence interest. A term relevant in determining the amount of interest expense the individual taxpayer may deduct as an itemized deduction for what otherwise would be disallowed as a component of personal interest (consumer interest). Qualified residence interest consists of interest paid on qualified residences (principal residence and one other residence) of the taxpayer. Debt that qualifies as qualified residence interest is limited to $1 million of debt to acquire, construct, or substantially improve qualified residences (acquisition indebtedness) plus $100,000 of other debt secured by qualified residences (home equity indebtedness). The home equity indebtedness may not exceed the fair market value of a qualified residence reduced by the acquisition indebtedness for that residence. § 163(h)(3).

Qualified small business corporation. For purposes of computing an exclusion upon the sale of qualified small business stock, a C corporation that has aggregate gross assets not exceeding $50 million and that is conducting an active trade or business. § 1202.

Qualified small business stock. Stock in a qualified small business corporation, purchased as part of an original issue after August 10, 1993. The shareholder may exclude from gross income 50 (or 75 or 100) percent of the realized gain on the sale of the stock if he or she held the stock for more than five years. § 1202.

Qualified terminable interest property (QTIP). Generally, the marital deduction (for gift and estate tax purposes) is not available if the interest transferred will terminate upon the death of the transferee spouse and pass to someone else. Thus, if Jim (the husband) places property in trust, life estate to Mary (the wife), and remainder to their children upon Mary's death, this is a terminable interest that will not provide Jim (or Jim's estate) with a marital deduction. If, however, the transfer in trust is treated as qualified terminable interest property (the QTIP election is made), the terminable interest restriction is waived and the marital deduction becomes available. In exchange for this deduction, the surviving spouse's gross estate must include the value of the QTIP election assets, even though he or she has no control over the ultimate disposition of the asset. Terminable interest property qualifies for this election if the donee (or heir) is the only beneficiary of the asset during his or her lifetime and receives income distributions relative to the property at least annually. For gifts, the donor spouse is the one who makes the QTIP election. For property transferred by death, the executor of the estate of the deceased spouse makes the election. §§ 2056(b)(7) and 2523(f).

Qualified transportation fringes. Transportation benefits provided by the employer to the employee. Such benefits include (1) transportation in a commuter highway vehicle between the employee's residence and the place of employment, (2) a transit pass, and (3) qualified parking. Qualified transportation fringes are excludible from the employee's gross income to the extent categories (1) and (2) above do not exceed $255 per month in 2016 and category (3) does not exceed $255 per month in 2016. These amounts are indexed annually for inflation. § 132.

Qualified tuition program. A program that allows college tuition to be prepaid for a beneficiary. When amounts in the plan are used, nothing is included in gross income provided they are used for qualified higher education expenses. § 529.

Qualifying child. An individual who, as to the taxpayer, satisfies the relationship, abode, and age tests. To be claimed as a dependent, such individual must also meet the citizenship and joint return tests and not be self-supporting. §§ 152(a)(1) and (c).

Qualifying relative. An individual who, as to the taxpayer, satisfies the relationship, gross income, support, citizenship, and joint return tests. Such an individual can be claimed as a dependent of the taxpayer. §§ 152(a)(2) and (d).

R

Rate reconciliation. Under Generally Accepted Accounting Principles, a footnote to the financial statements often includes a table that accounts for differences in the statutory income tax rate that applies to the entity (say, 35 percent) and the higher or lower effective tax rate that the entity realized for the reporting period. The rate reconciliation includes only permanent differences between the book tax expense and the entity's income tax provision. The rate reconciliation table often is expressed in dollar and/or percentage terms.

Realized gain. See *realized gain or loss.*

Realized gain or loss. The difference between the amount realized upon the sale or other disposition of property and the adjusted basis of the property. § 1001.

Realized loss. See *realized gain or loss.*

Realty. Real estate.

Reasonable cause. Relief from taxpayer and preparer penalties often is allowed where reasonable cause is found for the taxpayer's actions. For example, reasonable cause for the late filing of a tax return might be a flood that damaged the taxpayer's record-keeping systems and made a timely completion of the return difficult.

Reasonable needs of the business. A means of avoiding the penalty tax on an unreasonable accumulation of earnings. In determining the base for this tax (accumulated taxable income), § 535 allows a deduction for "such part of earnings and profits for the taxable year as are retained for the reasonable needs of the business." § 537.

Reasonableness. See *reasonableness requirement.*

Reasonableness requirement. The Code includes a reasonableness requirement with respect to the deduction of salaries and other compensation for services. What constitutes reasonableness is a question of fact. If an expense is unreasonable, the amount that is classified as unreasonable is not allowed as a deduction. The question of reasonableness generally arises with respect to closely held corporations where there is no separation of ownership and management. § 162(a)(1).

Recapitalization. A "Type E" reorganization, constituting a major change in the character and amount of outstanding equity of a corporation. Tax-free are stock for stock, bonds for bonds, and bonds for stock. For example, common stock exchanged for preferred stock can qualify as a tax-free "Type E" reorganization.

Recognized gain. See *recognized gain or loss.*

Recognized gain or loss. The portion of realized gain or loss subject to income taxation.

Recognized loss. See *recognized gain or loss.*

Recourse debt. Debt for which the lender may both foreclose on the property and assess a guarantor for any payments due under the loan. A lender also may make a claim against the assets of any general partner in a partnership to which debt is issued, without regard to whether the partner has guaranteed the debt.

Recovery of capital doctrine. When a taxable sale or exchange occurs, the seller may be permitted to recover his or her investment (or other adjusted basis) in the property before gain or loss is recognized.

Redemption to pay death taxes. Sale or exchange treatment is available relative to this type of stock redemption, to the extent of the proceeds up to the total amount paid by the estate or heir for estate/inheritance taxes and administration expenses. The stock value must exceed 35 percent of the value of the decedent's adjusted gross estate. In meeting this test, shareholdings in corporations where the decedent held at least 20 percent of the outstanding shares are combined.

Refundable credits. A credit that is paid to the taxpayer even if the amount of the credit (or credits) exceeds the taxpayer's tax liability.

Regular corporations. See *C corporation.*

Rehabilitation expenditures credit. A credit that is based on expenditures incurred to rehabilitate industrial and commercial buildings and certified historic structures. The credit is intended to discourage businesses from moving from older, economically distressed areas to newer locations and to encourage the preservation of historic structures. § 47.

Rehabilitation expenditures credit recapture. When property that qualifies for the rehabilitation expenditures credit is disposed of or ceases to be used in the trade or business of the taxpayer, some or all of the tax credit claimed on the property may be recaptured as additional tax liability. The amount of the recapture is the difference between the amount of the credit claimed originally and what should have been claimed in light of the length of time the property was actually held or used for qualifying purposes. § 50.

Related party. Various Code Sections define related parties and often include a variety of persons within this (usually detrimental) category. Generally, related parties are accorded different tax treatment from that applicable to other taxpayers who enter into similar transactions. For instance, realized losses that are generated between related parties are not recognized in the year of the loss. However, these deferred losses can be used to offset recognized gains that occur upon the subsequent sale of the asset to a nonrelated party. Other uses of a related-party definition include the conversion of gain upon the sale of a depreciable asset into all ordinary income (§ 1239) and the identification of constructive ownership of stock relative to corporate distributions, redemptions, liquidations, reorganizations, and compensation.

Related-party transactions. The tax law places restrictions upon the recognition of gains and losses between related parties because of the potential for abuse. For example, restrictions are placed on the deduction of losses from the sale or exchange of property between related parties. In addition, under certain circumstances, related-party gains that would otherwise be classified as capital gain are classified as ordinary income. §§ 267, 707(b), and 1239.

Rental activity. Any activity where payments are received principally for the use of tangible property is a rental activity. Temporary Regulations provide that in certain circumstances, activities involving rentals of real and personal property are not to be treated as rental activities. The Temporary Regulations list six exceptions.

Reorganization. Occurs, among other instances, when one corporation acquires another, a single corporation divides into two or more entities, a corporation makes a substantial change in its capital structure, a corporation undertakes a change in its legal name or domicile, or a corporation goes through a bankruptcy proceeding and continues to exist. The exchange of stock and other securities in a corporate reorganization can be effected favorably for tax purposes if certain statutory requirements are followed strictly. Tax consequences include the nonrecognition of any gain that is realized by the shareholders except to the extent of boot received. § 368.

Required taxable year. A partnership or limited liability company must use a required tax year as its tax accounting period, or one of three allowable alternative tax year-ends. The required tax year is determined using the least aggregate deferral rule. But if there is a common tax year used by owners holding a majority of the entity's capital or profits interests, or used by all of the owners who hold 5 percent or more of the capital or profits interests, then that tax year-end is used by the entity.

Research activities credit. A tax credit whose purpose is to encourage research and development. It consists of three components: the incremental research activities credit, the basic research credit, and the energy credit. The incremental research activities credit is equal to 20 percent of the excess qualified research expenditures over the base amount. The basic research credit is equal to 20 percent of the excess of basic research payments over the base amount. § 41.

Research and experimental expenditures. The Code provides three alternatives for the tax treatment of research and experimentation expenditures. They may be expensed in the year paid or incurred, deferred subject to amortization, or capitalized. If the taxpayer does not elect to expense such costs or to defer them subject to amortization (over 60 months), the expenditures must be capitalized. § 174. Three types of research activities credits are available: the basic research credit, the incremental research activities credit, and the energy credit. The rate for each type is 20 percent. § 41.

Reserve method. A method of accounting whereby an allowance is permitted for estimated uncollectible accounts. Actual write-offs are charged to the reserve, and recoveries of amounts previously written off are credited to the reserve. The Code permits only certain financial institutions to use the reserve method. § 166.

Residential rental real estate. Buildings for which at least 80 percent of the gross rents are from dwelling units (e.g., an apartment building). This type of building is distinguished from nonresidential (commercial or industrial) buildings in applying the recapture of depreciation provisions. The term also is relevant in distinguishing between buildings that are eligible for a 27.5-year life versus a 39-year life for MACRS purposes. Generally, residential buildings receive preferential treatment.

Restricted property plan. An arrangement whereby an employer transfers property (usually stock) to an employee at a bargain price (for less than the fair market value). If the transfer is accompanied by a substantial risk of forfeiture and the property is not transferable, no compensation results to the employee until the restrictions disappear. An example of a substantial risk of forfeiture would be a requirement that the employee return the property if his or her employment is terminated within a specified period of time. § 83.

Revenue Agent's Report (RAR). A Revenue Agent's Report (RAR) reflects any adjustments made by the agent as a result of an audit of the taxpayer. The RAR is mailed to the taxpayer along with the 30-day letter, which outlines the appellate procedures available to the taxpayer.

Revenue neutrality. A description that characterizes tax legislation when it neither increases nor decreases the total revenue collected by the taxing jurisdiction. Thus, any tax revenue losses are offset by tax revenue gains.

Revenue Procedures. A matter of procedural importance to both taxpayers and the IRS concerning the administration of the tax laws is issued as a Revenue Procedure (abbreviated Rev.Proc.). A Revenue Procedure is published in an *Internal Revenue Bulletin* (I.R.B.).

Revenue Rulings. A Revenue Ruling (abbreviated Rev.Rul.) is issued by the National Office of the IRS to express an official interpretation of the tax law as applied to specific transactions. It is more limited in application than a Regulation. A Revenue Ruling is published in an *Internal Revenue Bulletin* (I.R.B.).

Reversionary interest. The trust property that reverts to the grantor after the expiration of an intervening income interest. Assume that Phil places real estate in trust with income to Junior for 11 years, and upon the expiration of this term, the property returns to Phil. Under these circumstances, Phil holds a reversionary interest in the property. A reversionary interest is the same as a remainder interest, except that, in the latter case, the property passes to someone other than the original owner (e.g., the grantor of a trust) upon the expiration of the intervening interest.

Roth IRA. See *Individual Retirement Account (IRA)*.

S

S corporation. The designation for a small business corporation. See also *Subchapter S.*

Sale or exchange. A requirement for the recognition of capital gain or loss. Generally, the seller of property must receive money or relief from debt to have sold the property. An exchange involves the transfer of property for other property. Thus, collection of a debt is neither a sale nor an exchange. The term *sale or exchange* is not defined by the Code.

Sales factor. The proportion of a multistate corporation's total sales that is traceable to a specific state. Used in determining the taxable income that is to be apportioned to that state.

Sales tax. A state- or local-level tax on the retail sale of specified property. Generally, the purchaser pays the tax, but the seller collects it, as an agent for the government. Various taxing jurisdictions allow exemptions for purchases of specific items, including certain food, services, and manufacturing equipment. If the purchaser and seller are in different states, a use tax usually applies.

Schedule K–1. A tax information form prepared for each partner in a partnership, each shareholder of an S corporation, and some beneficiaries of certain trusts. The Schedule K–1 reports the owner's share of the entity's ordinary income or loss from operations, as well as the owner's share of separately stated items.

Schedule M–1. On the Form 1120, a reconciliation of book net income with Federal taxable income. Accounts for temporary and permanent differences in the two computations, such as depreciation differences, exempt income, and nondeductible items. On Forms 1120S and 1065, the Schedule M–1 reconciles book income with the owners' aggregate ordinary taxable income.

Schedule M–3. An *expanded* reconciliation of book net income with Federal taxable income (see *Schedule M–1*). Required of C and S corporations and partnerships/LLCs with total assets of $10 million or more.

Scholarship. Scholarships are generally excluded from the gross income of the recipient unless the payments are a disguised form of compensation for services rendered. However, the Code imposes restrictions on the exclusion. The recipient must be a degree candidate. The excluded amount is limited to amounts used for tuition, fees, books, supplies, and equipment required for courses of instruction. Amounts received for room and board are not eligible for the exclusion. § 117.

Section 121 exclusion. If a residence has been owned and used by the taxpayer as the principal residence for at least two years during the five-year period ending on the date of sale, up to $250,000 of realized gain is excluded from gross income. For a married couple filing a joint return, the $250,000 is increased to $500,000 if either spouse satisfies the ownership requirement and both spouses satisfy the use requirement.

Section 179 expensing. The ability to deduct a capital expenditure in the year an asset is placed in service rather than over the asset's useful life or cost recovery period. The annual ceiling on the deduction is $500,000 in 2015 and 2016. However, the deduction is reduced dollar for dollar when § 179 property placed in service during the taxable year exceeds $2,010,000 ($2 million in 2015). In addition, the amount expensed under § 179 cannot exceed the aggregate amount of taxable income derived from the conduct of any trade or business by the taxpayer.

Section 179 expensing election. See *Section 179 expensing.*

Section 338 election. When a corporation acquires at least 80 percent of a subsidiary within a 12-month period, it can elect to treat the acquisition of such stock as an asset purchase. The acquiring corporation's basis in the subsidiary's assets then is the cost of the stock. The subsidiary is deemed to have sold its assets for an amount equal to the grossed-up basis in its stock.

Section 382 limitation. When one corporation acquires another, the acquiring corporation's ability to use the loss and credit carryovers of the target may be limited, in an anti-abuse provision specified in the Code. Generally, for instance, the maximum NOL deduction available to the acquiring is the value of the target when acquired times the long-term tax-exempt interest rate on that date.

Section 401(k) plan. A cash or deferred arrangement plan that allows participants to elect to receive up to $18,000 in 2016 in cash (taxed currently) or to have a contribution made on their behalf to a profit sharing or stock bonus plan (excludible from gross income). The plan may also be in the form of a salary reduction agreement between the participant and the employer.

Section 754 election. An election that may be made by a partnership to adjust the basis of partnership assets to reflect a purchasing partner's outside basis in interest or to reflect a gain, loss, or basis adjustment of a partner receiving a distribution from a partnership. The intent of the election is to maintain the equivalence between outside and inside basis for that partner. Once the election is made, the partnership must make basis adjustments for all future transactions, unless the IRS consents to revoke the election.

Section 1231 gains and losses. If the combined gains and losses from the taxable dispositions of § 1231 assets plus the net gain from business involuntary conversions (of both § 1231 assets and long-term capital assets) is a gain, the gains and losses are treated as long-term capital gains and losses. In arriving at § 1231 gains, however, the depreciation recapture provisions (e.g., § 1245) are applied first to produce ordinary income. If the net result of the combination is a loss, the gains and losses from § 1231 assets are treated as ordinary gains and losses. § 1231(a).

Section 1231 lookback. For gain to be classified as § 1231 gain, the gain must survive the § 1231 lookback. To the extent of nonrecaptured § 1231 losses for the five prior tax years, the gain is classified as ordinary income. § 1231(c).

Section 1231 property. Depreciable assets and real estate used in trade or business and held for the required long-term holding period. § 1231(b).

Section 1244 stock. Stock issued under § 1244 by qualifying small business corporations. If § 1244 stock becomes worthless, the shareholders may claim an ordinary loss rather than the usual capital loss, within statutory limitations.

Section 1245 property. Property that is subject to the recapture of depreciation under § 1245. For a definition of § 1245 property, see § 1245(a)(3).

Section 1245 recapture. Upon a taxable disposition of § 1245 property, all depreciation claimed on the property is recaptured as ordinary income (but not to exceed any recognized gain from the disposition).

Section 1250 property. Real estate that is subject to the recapture of depreciation under § 1250. For a definition of § 1250 property, see § 1250(c).

Section 1250 recapture. Upon a taxable disposition of § 1250 property, accelerated depreciation or cost recovery claimed on the property may be recaptured as ordinary income.

Securities. Generally, stock, debt, and other financial assets. To the extent securities other than the stock of the transferee corporation are received in a § 351 exchange, the new shareholder recognizes a gain. For purposes of corporate reorganizations, generally, debt with terms longer than 10 years. To the extent stock and securities are transferred in a corporate reorganization under § 368, no gain or loss is recognized.

Self-employment tax. A tax of 12.4 percent is levied on individuals with net earnings from self-employment (up to $118,500 in 2016) to provide Social Security benefits (i.e., the old age, survivors, and disability insurance portion) for such individuals. In addition, a tax of 2.9 percent is levied on individuals with net earnings from self-employment (with no statutory ceiling) to provide Medicare benefits (i.e., the hospital insurance portion) for such individuals. If a self-employed individual also receives wages from an employer that are subject to FICA, the self-employment tax will be reduced. A partial deduction is allowed in calculating the self-employment tax. Individuals with net earnings of $400 or more from self-employment are subject to this tax. §§ 1401 and 1402.

Separate foreign tax credit income categories. The foreign tax credit of a taxpayer is computed for each of several types of income sources, as specified by the Code to limit the results of tax planning. FTC income "baskets" include general and passive. The FTC for the year is the sum of the credits as computed within all of the taxpayer's separate FTC baskets used for the tax year.

Separate return limitation year (SRLY). A series of rules limits the amount of an acquired corporation's net operating loss carryforwards that can be used by the acquiror. Generally, a consolidated return can include the acquiree's net operating loss carryforward only to the extent of the lesser of the subsidiary's (1) current-year or (2) cumulative positive contribution to consolidated taxable income.

Separately stated items. Any item of a partnership or an S corporation that might be taxed differently to any two owners of the entity. These amounts are not included in the ordinary income of the entity, but are instead reported separately to the owners; tax consequences are determined at the owner level.

Severance taxes. A tax imposed upon the extraction of natural resources.

Short period. See *short taxable year.*

Short sale. A sale that occurs when a taxpayer sells borrowed property (usually stock) and repays the lender with substantially identical property either held on the date of the short sale or purchased after the sale. No gain or loss is rec-

ognized until the short sale is closed, and such gain or loss is generally short-term. § 1233.

Short taxable year. A tax year that is less than 12 months. A short taxable year may occur in the initial reporting period, in the final tax year, or when the taxpayer changes tax years.

Significant participation activity. Seven tests determine whether an individual has achieved material participation in an activity, one of which is based on more than 500 hours of participation in significant participation activities. A significant participation activity is one in which the individual's participation exceeds 100 hours during the year. Temp.Reg. § 1.469–5T.

Simple trust. Trusts that are not complex trusts. Such trusts may not have a charitable beneficiary, accumulate income, or distribute corpus.

Simplified employee pension (SEP) plans. An employer may make contributions to an employee's IRA in amounts not exceeding the lesser of 15 percent of compensation or $53,000 per individual in 2016. These employer-sponsored simplified employee pensions are permitted only if the contributions are nondiscriminatory and are made on behalf of all employees who have attained age 21 and have worked for the employer during at least three of the five preceding calendar years. § 219(b).

Small business corporation. A corporation that satisfies the definition of § 1361(b), § 1244(c), or both. Satisfaction of § 1361(b) permits an S election, and satisfaction of § 1244 enables the shareholders of the corporation to claim an ordinary loss on the worthlessness of stock.

Small business stock (§ 1244 stock). See *Section 1244 stock.*

Small Cases Division. A division within the U.S. Tax Court where jurisdiction is limited to claims of $50,000 or less. There is no appeal from this court.

Solicitation. A level of activity brought about by the taxpayer within a specific state. Under Public Law 86-272, certain types of solicitation activities do not create nexus with the state. Exceeding mere solicitation, though, creates nexus.

Special allocation. Any amount for which an agreement exists among the partners of a partnership outlining the method used for spreading the item among the partners.

Special use value. Permits the executor of an estate to value, for estate tax purposes, real estate used in a farming activity or in connection with a closely held business at its current use value rather than at its most suitable or optimal use value. Under this option, a farm is valued for farming purposes even though, for example, the property might have a higher potential value as a shopping center. For the executor of an estate to elect special use valuation, the conditions of § 2032A must be satisfied.

Specific charge-off method. A method of accounting for bad debts in which a deduction is permitted only when an account becomes partially or completely worthless.

Spin-off. A type of reorganization where, for example, Apple Corporation transfers some assets to Core Corporation in exchange for Core stock representing control. Apple then distributes the Core stock to its shareholders.

Split-off. A type of reorganization where, for example, Apple Corporation transfers some assets to Core Corporation in exchange for Core stock representing control. Apple then distributes the Core stock to its shareholders in exchange for some of their Apple stock. Not all shareholders need to exchange stock.

Split-up. A type of reorganization where, for example, Firefly Corporation transfers some assets to Fire Corporation and the remainder to Fly Corporation. In return, Firefly receives enough Fire and Fly stock representing control of each corporation. Firefly then distributes the Fire and Fly stock to its shareholders in return for all of their Firefly stock. Firefly then liquidates, and its shareholders now have control of Fire and Fly.

Sprinkling trust. When a trustee has the discretion to either distribute or accumulate the entity accounting income of the trust and to distribute it among the trust's income beneficiaries in varying magnitudes. The trustee can "sprinkle" the income of the trust.

Standard deduction. The individual taxpayer can either itemize deductions or take the standard deduction. The amount of the standard deduction depends on the taxpayer's filing status (single, head of household, married filing jointly, surviving spouse, or married filing separately). For 2016, the amount of the standard deduction ranges from $6,300 (for single) to $12,600 (for married, filing jointly). Additional standard deductions of either $1,250 (for married taxpayers) or $1,550 (for single taxpayers) are available if the taxpayer is blind or age 65 or over. Limitations exist on the amount of the standard deduction of a taxpayer who is another taxpayer's dependent. The standard deduction amounts are adjusted for inflation each year. § 63(c).

Startup expenditures. Expenditures paid or incurred prior to the beginning of the business that would have been deductible as an ordinary and necessary business expense if business operations had begun. Examples of such expenditures include advertising; salaries and wages; travel and other expenses incurred in lining up prospective distributors, suppliers, or customers; and salaries and fees to executives, consultants, and professional service providers. A taxpayer will immediately expense the first $5,000 (subject to phaseout) of startup expenditures and amortize the balance over a period of 180 months, unless the taxpayer elects to not do so.

Statute of limitations. Provisions of the law that specify the maximum period of time in which action may be taken concerning a past event. Code §§ 6501–6504 contain the limitation periods applicable to the IRS for additional assessments, and §§ 6511–6515 relate to refund claims by taxpayers.

Statutory employees. Statutory employees are considered self-employed independent contractors for purposes of reporting income and expenses on their tax returns. Generally, a statutory employee must meet three tests:

* It is understood from a service contract that the services will be performed by the person.

* The person does not have a substantial investment in facilities (other than transportation used to perform the services).

* The services involve a continuing relationship with the person for whom they are performed.

For further information on statutory employees, see Circular E, *Employer's Tax Guide* (IRS Publication 15).

Step transaction. Disregarding one or more transactions to arrive at the final result. Assume, for example, Beta Corporation creates Alpha Corporation by transferring assets desired by Beta's sole shareholder, Carl. Carl then causes Alpha to liquidate to obtain the assets. Under these circumstances, the IRS may contend that the creation and liquidation of Alpha be disregarded. What really happened was a dividend distribution from Beta to Carl.

Step-down in basis. A reduction in the tax basis of property.

Step-up in basis. An increase in the income tax basis of property. A step-up in basis occurs when a decedent dies owning appreciated property. Since the estate or heir acquires a basis in the property equal to the property's fair market value on the date of death (or alternate valuation date if available and elected), any appreciation is not subject to the income tax. Thus, a step-up in basis is the result, with no immediate income tax consequences.

Stock bonus plan. A type of deferred compensation plan in which the employer establishes and maintains the plan and contributes employer stock to the plan for the benefit of employees. The contributions need not be dependent on the employer's profits. Any benefits of the plan are distributable in the form of employer stock, except that distributable fractional shares may be paid in cash.

Stock dividend. Not taxable if pro rata distributions of stock or stock rights on common stock. Section 305 governs the taxability of stock dividends and sets out five exceptions to the general rule that stock dividends are nontaxable.

Stock option. The right to purchase a stated number of shares of stock from a corporation at a certain price within a specified period of time. §§ 421 and 422.

Stock redemption. A corporation buys back its own stock from a specified shareholder. Typically, the corporation recognizes any realized gain on the noncash assets that it uses to effect a redemption, and the shareholder obtains a capital gain or loss upon receipt of the purchase price.

Stock rights. Assets that convey to the holder the power to purchase corporate stock at a specified price, often for a limited period of time. Stock rights received may be taxed as a distribution of earnings and profits. After the right is exercised, the basis of the acquired share includes the investor's purchase price or gross income, if any, to obtain the right. Disposition of the right also can be taxable.

Subchapter S. Sections 1361–1379 of the Internal Revenue Code. An elective provision permitting certain small business corporations (§ 1361) and their shareholders (§ 1362) to elect to be treated for income tax purposes in accordance with the operating rules of §§ 1363–1379. However, some S corporations usually avoid the corporate income tax, and corporate losses can be claimed by the shareholders.

Subpart F. Identifies the current tax treatment of income earned by a controlled foreign corporation. Certain types of income are included in U.S. gross income by U.S. shareholders of such an entity as they are generated, not when they are repatriated.

Subpart F income. See *Subpart F*.

Substance over form. A standard used when one must ascertain the true reality of what has occurred. Suppose, for example, a father sells stock to his daughter for $1,000. If the stock is really worth $50,000 at the time of the transfer, the substance of the transaction is probably a gift to her of $49,000.

Substantial authority. Taxpayer and tax preparer understatement penalties are waived where substantial authority existed for the disputed position taken on the return.

Substantial risk of forfeiture (SRF). A term that is associated with a restricted property plan. Generally, an employee who receives property (e.g., stock of the employer-corporation) from the employer at a bargain price or at no cost must include the bargain element in gross income. However, the employee currently does not have to do so if there is a substantial risk of forfeiture. A substantial risk of forfeiture exists if a person's rights to full enjoyment of property are conditioned upon the future performance, or the refraining from the performance, of substantial services by the individual. § 83.

Sunset provision. A provision attached to new tax legislation that will cause such legislation to expire at a specified date. Sunset provisions are attached to tax cut bills for long-term budgetary reasons to make their effect temporary. Once the sunset provision comes into play, the tax cut is rescinded and former law is reinstated. An example of a sunset provision is contained in the Tax Relief Reconciliation Act of 2001 that related to the estate tax. After the estate tax was phased out in 2010, a sunset provision called for the reinstatement of the estate tax as of January 1, 2011.

Supreme Court. See *U.S. Supreme Court.*

Surviving spouse. When a husband or wife predeceases the other spouse, the survivor is known as a surviving spouse. Under certain conditions, a surviving spouse may be entitled to use the income tax rates in § 1(a) (those applicable to married persons filing a joint return) for the two years after the year of death of his or her spouse. § 2. With respect to the Federal estate tax, this term describes the second spouse to die of a married couple, for the period between the two dates of death.

Syndication costs. Incurred in promoting and marketing partnership interests for sale to investors. Examples include legal and accounting fees, printing costs for prospectus and placement documents, and state registration fees. These items are capitalized by the partnership as incurred, with no amortization thereof allowed.

T

Tax avoidance. The minimization of one's tax liability by taking advantage of legally available tax planning opportunities. Tax avoidance can be contrasted with tax evasion, which entails the reduction of tax liability by illegal means.

Tax benefit rule. A provision that limits the recognition of income from the recovery of an expense or a loss properly deducted in a prior tax year to the amount of the deduction that generated a tax saving. Assume that last year Gary had medical expenses of $4,000 and adjusted gross income of $30,000. Because of the AGI limitation, Gary could deduct only $1,000 of these expenses [$4,000 − (10% × $30,000)]. If this year Gary is reimbursed in full by his insurance company for the $4,000 of expenses, the tax benefit rule limits the amount of income from the reimbursement to $1,000 (the amount previously deducted with a tax saving).

Tax Court. See *U.S. Tax Court.*

Tax credit for the elderly or disabled. An elderly (age 65 and over) or disabled taxpayer may receive a tax credit amounting to 15 percent of $5,000 ($7,500 for qualified married individuals filing jointly). This amount is reduced by Social Security benefits, excluded pension benefits, and one-half of the taxpayer's adjusted gross income in excess of $7,500 ($10,000 for married taxpayers filing jointly). § 22.

Tax credits. Amounts that directly reduce a taxpayer's tax liability. The tax benefit received from a tax credit is not dependent on the taxpayer's marginal tax rate, whereas the benefit of a tax deduction or exclusion is dependent on the taxpayer's tax bracket.

Tax evasion. The reduction of taxes by the use of subterfuge or fraud or other nonlegal means. For example, a cash basis taxpayer tries to increase his or her charitable contribution deduction by prepaying next year's church pledge with a pre-dated check issued in the following year.

Tax haven. A country in which either locally sourced income or residents of the country are subject to a low rate of taxation.

Tax preferences items. See *AMT preferences.*

Tax preparer. One who prepares tax returns for compensation. A tax preparer must register with the IRS and receive a special ID number to practice before the IRS and represent taxpayers before the agency in tax audit actions. The conduct of a tax preparer is regulated under Circular 230. Tax preparers also are subject to penalties for inappropriate conduct when working in the tax profession.

Tax Rate Schedules. Rate schedules that are used by upper-income taxpayers and those not permitted to use the tax table. Separate rate schedules are provided for married individuals filing jointly, heads of households, single taxpayers, estates and trusts, and married individuals filing separate returns. § 1.

Tax research. The method used to determine the best available solution to a situation that possesses tax consequences. Both tax and nontax factors are considered.

Tax shelters. The typical tax shelter generated large losses in the early years of the activity. Investors would offset these losses against other types of income and therefore avoid paying income taxes on this income. These tax shelter investments could then be sold after a few years and produce capital gain income, which is taxed at a lower rate compared to ordinary income. The passive activity loss rules and the at-risk rules now limit tax shelter deductions.

Tax Table. A table that is provided for taxpayers with less than $100,000 of taxable income. Separate columns are provided for single taxpayers, married taxpayers filing jointly, heads of households, and married taxpayers filing separately. § 3.

Tax treaties. An agreement between the U.S. Department of State and another country designed to alleviate double taxation of income and asset transfers and to share administrative information useful to tax agencies in both countries. The United States has income tax treaties with almost 70 countries and transfer tax treaties with about 20.

Taxable estate. The taxable estate is the gross estate of a decedent reduced by the deductions allowed by §§ 2053–2057 (e.g., administration expenses, marital and charitable deductions). The taxable estate is subject to the unified transfer tax at death. § 2051.

Taxable gift. The amount of a gift that is subject to the unified transfer tax. Thus, a taxable gift has been adjusted by the annual exclusion and other appropriate deductions (e.g., marital and charitable). § 2053.

Taxable year. The annual period over which income is measured for income tax purposes. Most individuals use a calendar year, but many businesses use a fiscal year based on the natural business year.

Technical Advice Memoranda (TAM). TAMs are issued by the IRS in response to questions raised by IRS field personnel during audits. They deal with completed rather than proposed transactions and are often requested for questions related to exempt organizations and employee plans.

Technical termination of a partnership. The entity is treated for tax purposes as though it has terminated, even though it continues its activities. When there has been a sale or exchange of more than 50 percent of the capital interests of the partnership within 12 months, the partnership is deemed to have terminated when the 50 percent threshold is crossed. A new partnership immediately is formed through asset contributions by the partners. These activities can affect the entity's tax year and its bases in the assets it holds.

Temporary differences. Under ASC 740 (SFAS 109), tax-related items that appear in the entity's financial statements and its tax return, but in different time periods. For instance, doubtful accounts receivable often create a temporary book-tax difference, as a bad debt reserve is used to compute an expense for financial reporting purposes, but a bad debt often is deductible only under the specific write-off rule for tax purposes, and the difference observed for the current period creates a temporary difference.

Temporary Regulations. A Regulation issued by the Treasury Department in temporary form. When speed is critical, the Treasury Department issues Temporary Regulations that take effect immediately. These Regulations have the same authoritative value as Final Regulations and may be cited as precedent for three years. Temporary Regulations are also issued as proposed Regulations.

Tenants by the entirety. Essentially, a joint tenancy between husband and wife.

Tenants in common. A form of ownership where each tenant (owner) holds an undivided interest in property. Unlike a joint tenancy or a tenancy by the entirety, the interest of a tenant in common does not terminate upon that individual's death (there is no right of survivorship). Assume that Tim and Cindy acquire real estate as equal tenants in common. Upon Tim's death, his one-half interest in the property passes to his estate or heirs, not automatically to Cindy.

Terminable interests. An interest in property that terminates upon the death of the holder or upon the occurrence of some other specified event. The transfer of a terminable in-

terest by one spouse to the other may not qualify for the marital deduction. §§ 2056(b) and 2523(b).

Theft losses. A loss from larceny, embezzlement, or robbery. It does not include misplacement of items.

Thin capitalization. When debt owed by a corporation to the shareholders becomes too large in relation to the corporation's capital structure (i.e., stock and shareholder equity), the IRS may contend that the corporation is thinly capitalized. In effect, some or all of the debt is reclassified as equity. The immediate result is to disallow any interest deduction to the corporation on the reclassified debt. To the extent of the corporation's earnings and profits, interest payments and loan repayments on the reclassified debt are treated as dividends to the shareholders.

Thirty-day letter. A letter that accompanies an RAR (Revenue Agent's Report) issued as a result of an IRS audit of a taxpayer (or the rejection of a taxpayer's claim for refund). The letter outlines the taxpayer's appeal procedure before the IRS. If the taxpayer does not request any such procedures within the 30-day period, the IRS issues a statutory notice of deficiency (the 90-day letter).

Throwback rule. If there is no income tax in the state to which a sale otherwise would be apportioned, the sale essentially is exempt from state income tax, even though the seller is domiciled in a state that levies an income tax. Nonetheless, if the seller's state has adopted a throwback rule, the sale is attributed to the seller's state and the transaction is subjected to a state-level tax.

Traditional IRA. See *Individual Retirement Account (IRA).*

Transfer pricing. The process of setting internal prices for transfers of goods and services among related taxpayers. For example, what price should be used when Subsidiary purchases management services from Parent? The IRS can adjust transfer prices when it can show that the taxpayers were attempting to avoid tax by, say, shifting losses, deductions, or credits from low-tax to high-tax entities or jurisdictions.

Transportation expenses. Transportation expenses for an employee include only the cost of transportation (e.g., taxi fares and automobile expenses) in the course of employment when the employee is not away from home in travel status. Commuting expenses are not deductible.

Travel expenses. Expenses that include meals (generally subject to a 50 percent disallowance) and lodging and transportation expenses while away from home in the pursuit of a trade or business (including that of an employee).

Treaty shopping. An international investor attempts to use the favorable aspects of a tax treaty to his or her advantage, often elevating the form of the transaction over its substance (e.g., by establishing only a nominal presence in the country offering the favorable treaty terms).

U

UDITPA. The Uniform Division of Income for Tax Purposes Act has been adopted in some form by many of the states. The Act develops criteria by which the total taxable income of a multistate corporation can be assigned to specific states.

Unclaimed property. A U.S. state may have the right to acquire property that has been made available to an individual or legal entity for a fixed period of time, where the claimant has not taken possession of the property after a notice period. Examples of such property that a state could acquire are an uncashed payroll check, or an unused gift card.

Undistributed PHCI. The tax base for the personal holding company tax. § 545.

Unearned income. Income received but not yet earned. Normally, such income is taxed when received, even for accrual basis taxpayers.

Unified transfer tax. Rates applicable to transfers by gift and death made after 1976. § 2001(c).

Unified transfer tax credit. A credit allowed against any unified transfer tax. §§ 2010 and 2505.

Uniform capitalization (UNICAP) rules. Under § 263A, the Regulations provide a set of rules that all taxpayers (regardless of the particular industry) can use to determine the items of cost (and means of allocating those costs) that must be capitalized with respect to the production of tangible property.

Unitary approach. See *unitary theory.*

Unitary theory. Sales, property, and payroll of related corporations are combined for nexus and apportionment purposes, and the worldwide income of the unitary entity is apportioned to the state. Subsidiaries and other affiliated corporations found to be part of the corporation's unitary business (because they are subject to overlapping ownership, operation, or management) are included in the apportionment procedure. This approach can be limited if a water's-edge election is in effect.

Unit-livestock-price method. A method of accounting for the cost of livestock. The livestock are valued using a standard cost of raising an animal with the characteristics of the animals on hand to the same age as those animals.

Unrealized receivables. Amounts earned by a cash basis taxpayer but not yet received. Because of the method of accounting used by the taxpayer, these amounts have a zero income tax basis. When unrealized receivables are distributed to a partner, they generally convert a transaction from nontaxable to taxable or an otherwise capital gain to ordinary income (i.e., as a "hot asset").

Unreasonable compensation. A deduction is allowed for "reasonable" salaries or other compensation for personal services actually rendered. To the extent compensation is "excessive" ("unreasonable"), the distribution could be treated as a dividend, such that no deduction is allowed. The problem of unreasonable compensation usually is limited to closely held corporations, where the motivation is to pay out profits in some form that is deductible to the corporation.

Unreasonable position. A tax preparer penalty is assessed regarding the understatement of a client's tax liability due to a tax return position that is found to be too aggressive. The penalty is avoided if there is substantial authority for the position or if the position is disclosed adequately on the tax return. The penalty equals the greater of $1,000 or one-half of the tax preparer's fee that is traceable to the aggressive position.

Unrecaptured § 1250 gain. Gain from the sale of depreciable real estate held more than one year. The gain is equal to or less than the depreciation taken on such property and is reduced by § 1245 and § 1250 gain.

Unrelated business income (UBI). Income recognized by an exempt organization that is generated from activities not related to the exempt purpose of the entity. For instance, the gift shop located in a hospital may generate unrelated business income. § 511.

Unrelated business income tax (UBIT). Levied on the unrelated business income of an exempt organization.

U.S. Court of Federal Claims. A trial court (court of original jurisdiction) that decides litigation involving Federal tax matters. Appeal from this court is to the Court of Appeals for the Federal Circuit.

U.S. shareholder. For purposes of classification of an entity as a controlled foreign corporation, a U.S. person who owns, or is considered to own, 10 percent or more of the total combined voting power of all classes of voting stock of a foreign corporation. Stock owned directly, indirectly, and constructively is counted for this purpose.

U.S. Supreme Court. The highest appellate court or the court of last resort in the Federal court system and in most states. Only a small number of tax decisions of the U.S. Courts of Appeal are reviewed by the U.S. Supreme Court under its certiorari procedure. The Supreme Court usually grants certiorari to resolve a conflict among the Courts of Appeal (e.g., two or more appellate courts have assumed opposing positions on a particular issue) or when the tax issue is extremely important (e.g., size of the revenue loss to the Federal government).

U.S. Tax Court. One of four trial courts of original jurisdiction that decides litigation involving Federal income, death, or gift taxes. It is the only trial court where the taxpayer must not first pay the deficiency assessed by the IRS. The Tax Court will not have jurisdiction over a case unless a statutory notice of deficiency (90-day letter) has been issued by the IRS and the taxpayer files the petition for hearing within the time prescribed.

U.S. trade or business. A set of activities that is carried on in a regular, continuous, and substantial manner. A non-U.S. taxpayer is subject to U.S. tax on the taxable income that is effectively connected with a U.S. trade or business.

Use tax. A sales tax that is collectible by the seller where the purchaser is domiciled in a different state.

V

Vacation homes. The Code places restrictions upon taxpayers who rent their residences or vacation homes for part of the tax year. The restrictions may result in a scaling down of expense deductions for the taxpayers. § 280A.

Valuation allowance. Under ASC 740 (SFAS 109), a tax-related item is reported for book purposes only when it is more likely than not that the item actually will be realized. When the "more likely than not" test is failed, a contra-asset account is created to offset some or all of the related deferred tax asset. For instance, if the entity projects that it will not be able to use all of its net operating loss carryforward due to a lack of future taxable income, a valuation allowance is created to reduce the net deferred tax asset that corresponds to the carryforward. If income projections later change and it appears that the carryforward will be used, the valuation allowance is reversed or "released." Creation of a valuation allowance usually increases the current tax expense and thereby reduces current book income, and its release often increases book income in the later reporting period.

Value added tax (VAT). A national sales tax that taxes the increment in value as goods move through the production process. A VAT is much used in other countries but has not yet been incorporated as part of the U.S. Federal tax structure.

Vesting requirements. A qualified deferred compensation arrangement must satisfy a vesting requirement. Under this provision, an employee's right to accrued plan benefits derived from employer contributions must be nonforfeitable in accordance with one of two vesting time period schedules (or two required alternate vesting schedules for certain employer matching contributions).

Voluntary revocation. The owners of a majority of shares in an S corporation elect to terminate the S status of the entity as of a specified date. The day on which the revocation is effective is the first day of the corporation's C tax year.

W

W–2 wages. The domestic production activities deduction (DPAD) cannot exceed 50 percent of the W–2 wages paid for any particular year. Prop.Reg. § 199–2(f)(2) provides several methods for calculating the W–2 wages, but the payments must involve common law employees. To qualify, employees need to be involved in the production process. § 199.

Wash sale. A loss from the sale of stock or securities that is disallowed because the taxpayer, within 30 days before or after the sale, has acquired stock or securities substantially identical to those sold. § 1091.

Water's edge. A limitation on the worldwide scope of the unitary theory. If a corporate water's-edge election is in effect, the state can consider in the apportionment procedure only the activities that occur within the boundaries of the United States.

Water's-edge election. See *water's edge.*

Wherewithal to pay. This concept recognizes the inequity of taxing a transaction when the taxpayer lacks the means with which to pay the tax. Under it, there is a correlation between the imposition of the tax and the ability to pay the tax. It is particularly suited to situations in which the taxpayer's economic position has not changed significantly as a result of the transaction.

Whistleblower Program. An IRS initiative that offers special rewards to informants who provide evidence regarding tax evasion activities of businesses or high-income individuals. More than $2 million of tax, interest, and penalty must be at stake. The reward can reach 30 percent of the tax recovery that is attributable to the whistleblower's information.

Withholding allowances. The number of withholding allowances serves as the basis for determining the amount of income taxes withheld from an employee's salary or wages. The more withholding allowances claimed, the less income tax withheld by an employer. An employee may claim withholding allowances for personal exemptions for self and spouse (unless claimed as a dependent of another person), dependency exemptions, and special withholding allowances.

Work opportunity tax credit. Employers are allowed a tax credit equal to 40 percent of the first $6,000 of wages (per eligible employee) for the first year of employment. Eligible employees include certain hard-to-employ individuals (e.g., qualified ex-felons, high-risk youth, food stamp recipients, and veterans). The employer's deduction for wages is reduced by the amount of the credit taken. For qualified summer youth employees, the 40 percent rate is applied to the first $3,000 of qualified wages.

Working condition fringes. A type of fringe benefit received by the employee that is excludible from the employee's gross income. It consists of property or services provided (paid or reimbursed) by the employer for which the employee could take a tax deduction if the employee had paid for them. § 132.

Worthless securities. A loss (usually capital) is allowed for a security that becomes worthless during the year. The loss is deemed to have occurred on the last day of the year. Special rules apply to securities of affiliated companies and small business stock. § 165.

Writ of Certiorari. Appeal from a U.S. Court of Appeals to the U.S. Supreme Court is by Writ of Certiorari. The Supreme Court need not accept the appeal, and it usually does not (*cert. den.*) unless a conflict exists among the lower courts that must be resolved or a constitutional issue is involved.

Appendix D-1

Table of Code Sections Cited

Appendix D-2

Table of Regulations Cited

Treasury Regulations

Reg. Sec.	This Work Page
1.183–1(b)(1)	11-43
1.183–2(b)(1) through (9)	11-42
1.195–1	12-52
1.199–5	14-17
1.199–5(b)(1)(i)	14-18
1.212–1(f)	11-24
1.213–1(e)(1)(iii)	10-13
1.248–1(d)	12-31
1.267(b)–1(b)(1)	2-24
1.274–4	11-20
1.280F–7(a)	5-33
1.301–1(j)	7-8, 13-15
1.301–1(m)	13-16
1.307–1(a)	7-10
1.312–6	13-3
1.312–6(a)	13-3
1.332–2(c)	13-23
1.351–1(a)(1)	12-11
1.351–1(a)(1)(ii)	12-11, 12-13, 12-14
1.351–1(a)(2)	2-7, 12-14
1.362–2(b)	12-26
1.408–10(b)	8-17
1.441–1	4-6
1.446–1(a)(2)	5-4
1.446–1(a)(3)	4-7
1.446–1(c)(1)(i)	4-7
1.446–1(c)(2)(i)	4-7
1.451–1(a)	4-9
1.451–2	4-7
1.451–2(a)	4-10
1.451–2(b)	4-10, 4-11
1.451–5(b)	4-12
1.451–5(c)	4-12
1.453–9(c)(2)	12-9
1.461–1(a)	5-5
1.461–4(g)(6)	5-21
1.469–2(f)(6)	15-37
1.469–4	6-21
1.469–4(c)(3)	6-21
1.469–4(d)	6-21
1.469–4(f)	6-22
1.469–9	6-28
1.672(b)–1	2-36
1.704–1(b)	14-19
1.731–1(c)(3)	14-9
1.752–1(a)	14-22
1.752–1(e)	15-20
1.861–8	16-9
1.954–3(a)	16-39
1.1001–1(a)	7-2
1.1001–1(b)	7-3
1.1001–1(b)(2)	7-4

Treasury Regulations

Reg. Sec.	This Work Page
1.1001–1(c)(1)	7-2
1.1002–1(a)	7-6
1.1002–1(c)	7-19
1.1011–1	7-3, 7-12
1.1012–1(a)	7-8
1.1012–1(b)	7-4
1.1012–1(c)(1)	7-8
1.1015–1(a)(1)	7-10
1.1015–1(a)(3)	7-10
1.1015–5(c)(2)	7-11
1.1015–5(c)(5)	7-11
1.1016–1	7-3
1.1016–3(a)(1)(i)	7-4
1.1016–5(a)	7-5
1.1016–5(b)	7-5
1.1016–6(a)	7-4
1.1031(a)–1(a)	7-19
1.1031(a)–1(b)	7-20
1.1031(d)–2	7-24
1.1032–1(a)	12-23
1.1033(a)–1	7-26
1.1033(a)–1(a)	7-25
1.1033(a)–2(a)	7-25
1.1033(a)–2(c)(1)	7-28
1.1033(a)–2(c)(3)	7-27
1.1091–1(a)	7-15
1.1091–1(c)	7-16
1.1091–1(f)	7-15
1.1091–2(a)	7-16
1.1221–1(b)	8-12
1.1223–1(a)	7-24
1.1223–1(b)	7-12
1.1223–1(d)	7-16
1.1223–1(e)	7-9
1.1234–1(a)(1)	8-7
1.1235–2(b)(1)	8-9
1.1241–1(a)	8-12
1.1245–2(a)(4)	7-24, 8-35
1.1245–2(c)(2)	8-35
1.1245–4(a)(1)	8-34
1.1245–4(c)	8-35
1.1250–2(d)(1)	7-24, 8-35
1.1250–2(d)(3)	8-35
1.1250–3(a)(1)	8-34
1.1250–3(c)	8-35
1.1361–1(l)(1)	15-4
1.1362–6(b)(3)(iii)	15-7
1.1367–1(f)	15-19
1.1367–2	15-20
1.1367–2(e)	15-20
1.1372–2(b)(1)	15-6
1.1377–1(a)(2)(ii)	15-11

Appendix D-3

Table of Revenue Procedures and Revenue Rulings Cited

Appendix E

Table of Cases Cited

Appendix F

Present Value and Future Value Tables

Present Value of $1

N/R	1%	2%	3%	4%	5%	6%	7%	8%	9%	10%	11%	12%
1	0.9901	0.9804	0.9709	0.9615	0.9524	0.9434	0.9346	0.9259	0.9174	0.9091	0.9009	0.8929
2	0.9803	0.9612	0.9426	0.9246	0.9070	0.8900	0.8734	0.8573	0.8417	0.8264	0.8116	0.7972
3	0.9706	0.9423	0.9151	0.8890	0.8638	0.8396	0.8163	0.7938	0.7722	0.7513	0.7312	0.7118
4	0.9610	0.9238	0.8885	0.8548	0.8227	0.7921	0.7629	0.7350	0.7084	0.6830	0.6587	0.6355
5	0.9515	0.9057	0.8626	0.8219	0.7835	0.7473	0.7130	0.6806	0.6499	0.6209	0.5935	0.5674
6	0.9420	0.8880	0.8375	0.7903	0.7462	0.7050	0.6663	0.6302	0.5963	0.5645	0.5346	0.5066
7	0.9327	0.8706	0.8131	0.7599	0.7107	0.6651	0.6227	0.5835	0.5470	0.5132	0.4817	0.4523
8	0.9235	0.8535	0.7894	0.7307	0.6768	0.6274	0.5820	0.5403	0.5019	0.4665	0.4339	0.4039
9	0.9143	0.8368	0.7664	0.7026	0.6446	0.5919	0.5439	0.5002	0.4604	0.4241	0.3909	0.3606
10	0.9053	0.8203	0.7441	0.6756	0.6139	0.5584	0.5083	0.4632	0.4224	0.3855	0.3522	0.3220
11	0.8963	0.8043	0.7224	0.6496	0.5847	0.5268	0.4751	0.4289	0.3875	0.3505	0.3173	0.2875
12	0.8874	0.7885	0.7014	0.6246	0.5568	0.4970	0.4440	0.3971	0.3555	0.3186	0.2858	0.2567
13	0.8787	0.7730	0.6810	0.6006	0.5303	0.4688	0.4150	0.3677	0.3262	0.2897	0.2575	0.2292
14	0.8700	0.7579	0.6611	0.5775	0.5051	0.4423	0.3878	0.3405	0.2992	0.2633	0.2320	0.2046
15	0.8613	0.7430	0.6419	0.5553	0.4810	0.4173	0.3624	0.3152	0.2745	0.2394	0.2090	0.1827
16	0.8528	0.7284	0.6232	0.5339	0.4581	0.3936	0.3387	0.2919	0.2519	0.2176	0.1883	0.1631
17	0.8444	0.7142	0.6050	0.5134	0.4363	0.3714	0.3166	0.2703	0.2311	0.1978	0.1696	0.1456
18	0.8360	0.7002	0.5874	0.4936	0.4155	0.3503	0.2959	0.2502	0.2120	0.1799	0.1528	0.1300
19	0.8277	0.6864	0.5703	0.4746	0.3957	0.3305	0.2765	0.2317	0.1945	0.1635	0.1377	0.1161
20	0.8195	0.6730	0.5537	0.4564	0.3769	0.3118	0.2584	0.2145	0.1784	0.1486	0.1240	0.1037

Present Value of an Ordinary Annuity of $1

N/R	1%	2%	3%	4%	5%	6%	7%	8%	9%	10%	11%	12%
1	0.9901	0.9804	0.9709	0.9615	0.9524	0.9434	0.9346	0.9259	0.9174	0.9091	0.9009	0.8929
2	1.9704	1.9416	1.9135	1.8861	1.8594	1.8334	1.8080	1.7833	1.7591	1.7355	1.7125	1.6901
3	2.9410	2.8839	2.8286	2.7751	2.7232	2.6730	2.6243	2.5771	2.5313	2.4869	2.4437	2.4018
4	3.9020	3.8077	3.7171	3.6299	3.5460	3.4651	3.3872	3.3121	3.2397	3.1699	3.1024	3.0373
5	4.8534	4.7135	4.5797	4.4518	4.3295	4.2124	4.1002	3.9927	3.8897	3.7908	3.6959	3.6048
6	5.7955	5.6014	5.4172	5.2421	5.0757	4.9173	4.7665	4.6229	4.4859	4.3553	4.2305	4.1114
7	6.7282	6.4720	6.2303	6.0021	5.7864	5.5824	5.3893	5.2064	5.0330	4.8684	4.7122	4.5638
8	7.6517	7.3255	7.0197	6.7327	6.4632	6.2098	5.9713	5.7466	5.5348	5.3349	5.1461	4.9676
9	8.5660	8.1622	7.7861	7.4353	7.1078	6.8017	6.5152	6.2469	5.9952	5.7590	5.5370	5.3282
10	9.4713	8.9826	8.5302	8.1109	7.7217	7.3601	7.0236	6.7101	6.4177	6.1446	5.8892	5.6502
11	10.3676	9.7868	9.2526	8.7605	8.3064	7.8869	7.4987	7.1390	6.8052	6.4951	6.2065	5.9377
12	11.2551	10.5753	9.9540	9.3851	8.8633	8.3838	7.9427	7.5361	7.1607	6.8137	6.4924	6.1944
13	12.1337	11.3484	10.6350	9.9856	9.3936	8.8527	8.3577	7.9038	7.4869	7.1034	6.7499	6.4235
14	13.0037	12.1062	11.2961	10.5631	9.8986	9.2950	8.7455	8.2442	7.7862	7.3667	6.9819	6.6282
15	13.8651	12.8493	11.9379	11.1184	10.3797	9.7122	9.1079	8.5595	8.0607	7.6061	7.1909	6.8109
16	14.7179	13.5777	12.5611	11.6523	10.8378	10.1059	9.4466	8.8514	8.3126	7.8237	7.3792	6.9740
17	15.5623	14.2919	13.1661	12.1657	11.2741	10.4773	9.7632	9.1216	8.5436	8.0216	7.5488	7.1196
18	16.3983	14.9920	13.7535	12.6593	11.6896	10.8276	10.0591	9.3719	8.7556	8.2014	7.7016	7.2497
19	17.2260	15.6785	14.3238	13.1339	12.0853	11.1581	10.3356	9.6036	8.9501	8.3649	7.8393	7.3658
20	18.0456	16.3514	14.8775	13.5903	12.4622	11.4699	10.5940	9.8181	9.1285	8.5136	7.9633	7.4694

Future Value of $1

N/R	1%	2%	3%	4%	5%	6%	7%	8%	9%	10%	11%	12%
1	1.0100	1.0200	1.0300	1.0400	1.0500	1.0600	1.0700	1.0800	1.0900	1.1000	1.1100	1.1200
2	1.0201	1.0404	1.0609	1.0816	1.1025	1.1236	1.1449	1.1664	1.1881	1.2100	1.2321	1.2544
3	1.0303	1.0612	1.0927	1.1249	1.1576	1.1910	1.2250	1.2597	1.2950	1.3310	1.3676	1.4049
4	1.0406	1.0824	1.1255	1.1699	1.2155	1.2625	1.3108	1.3605	1.4116	1.4641	1.5181	1.5735
5	1.0510	1.1041	1.1593	1.2167	1.2763	1.3382	1.4026	1.4693	1.5386	1.6105	1.6851	1.7623
6	1.0615	1.1262	1.1941	1.2653	1.3401	1.4185	1.5007	1.5869	1.6771	1.7716	1.8704	1.9738
7	1.0721	1.1487	1.2299	1.3159	1.4071	1.5036	1.6058	1.7138	1.8280	1.9487	2.0762	2.2107
8	1.0829	1.1717	1.2668	1.3686	1.4775	1.5938	1.7182	1.8509	1.9926	2.1436	2.3045	2.4760
9	1.0937	1.1951	1.3048	1.4233	1.5513	1.6895	1.8385	1.9990	2.1719	2.3579	2.5580	2.7731
10	1.1046	1.2190	1.3439	1.4802	1.6289	1.7908	1.9672	2.1589	2.3674	2.5937	2.8394	3.1058
11	1.1157	1.2434	1.3842	1.5395	1.7103	1.8983	2.1049	2.3316	2.5804	2.8531	3.1518	3.4785
12	1.1268	1.2682	1.4258	1.6010	1.7959	2.0122	2.2522	2.5182	2.8127	3.1384	3.4985	3.8960
13	1.1381	1.2936	1.4685	1.6651	1.8856	2.1329	2.4098	2.7196	3.0658	3.4523	3.8833	4.3635
14	1.1495	1.3195	1.5126	1.7317	1.9799	2.2609	2.5785	2.9372	3.3417	3.7975	4.3104	4.8871
15	1.1610	1.3459	1.5580	1.8009	2.0789	2.3966	2.7590	3.1722	3.6425	4.1772	4.7846	5.4736
16	1.1726	1.3728	1.6047	1.8730	2.1829	2.5404	2.9522	3.4259	3.9703	4.5950	5.3109	6.1304
17	1.1843	1.4002	1.6528	1.9479	2.2920	2.6928	3.1588	3.7000	4.3276	5.0545	5.8951	6.8660
18	1.1961	1.4282	1.7024	2.0258	2.4066	2.8543	3.3799	3.9960	4.7171	5.5599	6.5436	7.6900
19	1.2081	1.4568	1.7535	2.1068	2.5270	3.0256	3.6165	4.3157	5.1417	6.1159	7.2633	8.6128
20	1.2202	1.4859	1.8061	2.1911	2.6533	3.2071	3.8697	4.6610	5.6044	6.7275	8.0623	9.6463

Future Value of an Ordinary Annuity of $1

N/R	1%	2%	3%	4%	5%	6%	7%	8%	9%	10%	11%	12%
1	1.0000	1.0000	1.0000	1.0000	1.0000	1.0000	1.0000	1.0000	1.0000	1.0000	1.0000	1.0000
2	2.0100	2.0200	2.0300	2.0400	2.0500	2.0600	2.0700	2.0800	2.0900	2.1000	2.1100	2.1200
3	3.0301	3.0604	3.0909	3.1216	3.1525	3.1836	3.2149	3.2464	3.2781	3.3100	3.3421	3.3744
4	4.0604	4.1216	4.1836	4.2465	4.3101	4.3746	4.4399	4.5061	4.5731	4.6410	4.7097	4.7793
5	5.1010	5.2040	5.3091	5.4163	5.5256	5.6371	5.7507	5.8666	5.9847	6.1051	6.2278	6.3528
6	6.1520	6.3081	6.4684	6.6330	6.8019	6.9753	7.1533	7.3359	7.5233	7.7156	7.9129	8.1152
7	7.2135	7.4343	7.6625	7.8983	8.1420	8.3938	8.6540	8.9228	9.2004	9.4872	9.7833	10.0890
8	8.2857	8.5830	8.8923	9.2142	9.5491	9.8975	10.2598	10.6366	11.0285	11.4359	11.8594	12.2997
9	9.3685	9.7546	10.1591	10.5828	11.0266	11.4913	11.9780	12.4876	13.0210	13.5795	14.1640	14.7757
10	10.4622	10.9497	11.4639	12.0061	12.5779	13.1808	13.8164	14.4866	15.1929	15.9374	16.7220	17.5487
11	11.5668	12.1687	12.8078	13.4864	14.2068	14.9716	15.7836	16.6455	17.5603	18.5312	19.5614	20.6546
12	12.6825	13.4121	14.1920	15.0258	15.9171	16.8699	17.8885	18.9771	20.1407	21.3843	22.7132	24.1331
13	13.8093	14.6803	15.6178	16.6268	17.7130	18.8821	20.1406	21.4953	22.9534	24.5227	26.2116	28.0291
14	14.9474	15.9739	17.0863	18.2919	19.5986	21.0151	22.5505	24.2149	26.0192	27.9750	30.0949	32.3926
15	16.0969	17.2934	18.5989	20.0236	21.5786	23.2760	25.1290	27.1521	29.3609	31.7725	34.4054	37.2797
16	17.2579	18.6393	20.1569	21.8245	23.6575	25.6725	27.8881	30.3243	33.0034	35.9497	39.1899	42.7533
17	18.4304	20.0121	21.7616	23.6975	25.8404	28.2129	30.8402	33.7502	36.9737	40.5447	44.5008	48.8837
18	19.6147	21.4123	23.4144	25.6454	28.1324	30.9057	33.9990	37.4502	41.3013	45.5992	50.3959	55.7497
19	20.8109	22.8406	25.1169	27.6712	30.5390	33.7600	37.3790	41.4463	46.0185	51.1591	56.9395	63.4397
20	22.0190	24.2974	26.8704	29.7781	33.0660	36.7856	40.9955	45.7620	51.1601	57.2750	64.2028	72.0524

Appendix G

Tax Formulas

2015 Tax Rate Schedules

Single—Schedule X

If taxable income is: Over—	But not over—	The tax is:	of the amount over—
$ 0	$ 9,225	........10%	$ 0
9,225	37,450	$ 922.50 + 15%	9,225
37,450	90,750	5,156.25 + 25%	37,450
90,750	189,300	18,481.25 + 28%	90,750
189,300	411,500	46,075.25 + 33%	189,300
411,500	413,200	119,401.25 + 35%	411,500
413,200	....	119,996.25 + 39.6%	413,200

Head of household—Schedule Z

If taxable income is: Over—	But not over—	The tax is:	of the amount over—
$ 0	$ 13,150	........10%	$ 0
13,150	50,200	$ 1,315.00 + 15%	13,150
50,200	129,600	6,872.50 + 25%	50,200
129,600	209,850	26,722.50 + 28%	129,600
209,850	411,500	49,192.50 + 33%	209,850
411,500	439,000	115,737.00 + 35%	411,500
439,000	....	125,362.00 + 39.6%	439,000

Married filing jointly or Qualifying widow(er)—Schedule Y–1

If taxable income is: Over—	But not over—	The tax is:	of the amount over—
$ 0	$ 18,450	........10%	$ 0
18,450	74,900	$ 1,845.00 + 15%	18,450
74,900	151,200	10,312.50 + 25%	74,900
151,200	230,450	29,387.50 + 28%	151,200
230,450	411,500	51,577.50 + 33%	230,450
411,500	464,850	111,324.00 + 35%	411,500
464,850	....	129,996.50 + 39.6%	464,850

Married filing separately—Schedule Y–2

If taxable income is: Over—	But not over—	The tax is:	of the amount over—
$ 0	$ 9,225	........10%	$ 0
9,225	37,450	$ 922.50 + 15%	9,225
37,450	75,600	5,156.25 + 25%	37,450
75,600	115,225	14,693.75 + 28%	75,600
115,225	205,750	25,788.75 + 33%	115,225
205,750	232,425	55,662.00 + 35%	205,750
232,425	....	64,998.25 + 39.6%	232,425

2016 Tax Rate Schedules

Single—Schedule X

If taxable income is: Over—	But not over—	The tax is:	of the amount over—
$ 0	$ 9,275	........10%	$ 0
9,275	37,650	$ 927.50 + 15%	9,275
37,650	91,150	5,183.75 + 25%	37,650
91,150	190,150	18,558.75 + 28%	91,150
190,150	413,350	46,278.75 + 33%	190,150
413,350	415,050	119,934.75 + 35%	413,350
415,050	....	120,529.75 + 39.6%	415,050

Head of household—Schedule Z

If taxable income is: Over—	But not over—	The tax is:	of the amount over—
$ 0	$ 13,250	........10%	$ 0
13,250	50,400	$ 1,325.00 + 15%	13,250
50,400	130,150	6,897.50 + 25%	50,400
130,150	210,800	26,835.00 + 28%	130,150
210,800	413,350	49,417.00 + 33%	210,800
413,350	441,000	116,258.50 + 35%	413,350
441,000	....	125,936.00 + 39.6%	441,000

Married filing jointly or Qualifying widow(er)—Schedule Y–1

If taxable income is: Over—	But not over—	The tax is:	of the amount over—
$ 0	$ 18,550	........10%	$ 0
18,550	75,300	$ 1,855.00 + 15%	18,550
75,300	151,900	10,367.50 + 25%	75,300
151,900	231,450	29,517.50 + 28%	151,900
231,450	413,350	51,791.50 + 33%	231,450
413,350	466,950	111,818.50 + 35%	413,350
466,950	....	130,578.50 + 39.6%	466,950

Married filing separately—Schedule Y–2

If taxable income is: Over—	But not over—	The tax is:	of the amount over—
$ 0	$ 9,275	........10%	$ 0
9,275	37,650	$ 927.50 + 15%	9,275
37,650	75,950	5,183.75 + 25%	37,650
75,950	115,725	14,758.75 + 28%	75,950
115,725	206,675	25,895.75 + 33%	115,725
206,675	233,475	55,909.25 + 35%	206,675
233,475	....	65,289.25 + 39.6%	233,475

Basic Standard Deduction Amounts

Filing Status	2015	2016
Single	$ 6,300	$ 6,300
Married, filing jointly	12,600	12,600
Surviving spouse	12,600	12,600
Head of household	9,250	9,300
Married, filing separately	6,300	6,300

Amount of Each Additional Standard Deduction

Filing Status	2015	2016
Single	$1,550	$1,550
Married, filing jointly	1,250	1,250
Surviving spouse	1,250	1,250
Head of household	1,550	1,550
Married, filing separately	1,250	1,250

Personal and Dependency Exemption

2015	2016
$4,000	$4,050

Income Tax Rates—Corporations

Taxable Income		The Tax Is:	Of the Amount
Over	But not Over		Over
$ 0	$ 50,000	15%	$ 0
50,000	75,000	$ 7,500 + 25%	50,000
75,000	100,000	13,750 + 34%	75,000
100,000	335,000	22,250 + 39%*	100,000
335,000	10,000,000	113,900 + 34%	335,000
10,000,000	15,000,000	3,400,000 + 35%	10,000,000
15,000,000	18,333,333	5,150,000 + 38%**	15,000,000
18,333,333	....	35%	0

* Five percentage points of this rate represents a phaseout of the benefits of the lower
tax rates on the first $75,000 of taxable income.

**Three percentage points of this rate represents a phaseout of the benefits of the lower
tax rate (34% rather than 35%) on the first $10 million of taxable income.

AMT Formula for Individuals

Regular Taxable Income (before standard deduction and exemptions)	
Plus or minus:	AMT Adjustments
Plus:	AMT Preferences
Equals:	Alternative minimum taxable income (AMTI)
Minus:	AMT Exemption
Equals:	Tentative minimum tax (TMT) base
Times:	26% and 28% AMT rates
Equals:	Tentative minimum tax before foreign tax credit
Minus:	AMT foreign tax credit
Equals:	Tentative minimum tax
Minus:	Regular income tax liability (after foreign tax credit)
Equals:	Alternative minimum tax (if TMT > Regular tax liability)

AMT Exemption Phaseout for Individuals for 2016

Filing Status	Exemption	Phaseout Begins at	Ends at
Married, filing jointly	$83,800	$159,700	$494,900
Single or head of household	53,900	119,700	335,300
Married, filing separately	41,900	79,850	247,450

AMT Formula for Corporations

Regular Taxable Income before NOL Deduction	
Plus or minus:	AMT Adjustments (except ACE adjustment)
Plus:	AMT Preferences
Equals:	AMTI before AMT NOL deduction and ACE adjustment
Plus or minus:	ACE adjustment
Equals:	AMTI before AMT NOL deduction
Minus:	AMT NOL deduction (limited to 90% of amount from prior line)
Equals:	Alternative minimum taxable income (AMTI)
Minus:	AMT Exemption
Equals:	Tentative minimum tax base
Times:	20% AMT rate
Equals:	Tentative minimum tax before AMT foreign tax credit
Minus:	AMT foreign tax credit
Equals:	Tentative minimum tax (TMT)
Minus:	Regular income tax liability (after foreign tax credit)
Equals:	Alternative minimum tax (if TMT > Regular tax liability)

Tax Formula for Corporate Taxpayers

Income (broadly defined)	$xxx,xxx
Less: Exclusions (income that is not subject to tax)	(xx,xxx)
Gross income	$xxx,xxx
Less: Certain business deductions	(xx,xxx)
Taxable income	$xxx,xxx
Federal income tax (see Tax Rate Schedule inside front cover of text)	$ xx,xxx
Less: Tax credits (including prepayments of Federal income taxes)	(x,xxx)
Tax due (or refund)	$ xx,xxx

Tax Formula for Individuals

Income (broadly defined)	$xx,xxx
Less: Exclusions (income that is not subject to tax)	(x,xxx)
Gross income	$xx,xxx
Less: Deductions *for* adjusted gross income	(x,xxx)
Adjusted gross income	$xx,xxx
Less: The greater of—	
Total itemized deductions	
or standard deduction	(x,xxx)
Less: Personal and dependency exemptions	(x,xxx)
Taxable income	$xx,xxx
Tax on taxable income	$ x,xxx
Less: Tax credits (including Federal income tax withheld and	
other prepayments of Federal income taxes)	(xxx)
Tax due (or refund)	$ xxx

Index